The Dictionary of Painting and Sculpture

ART
AND ARTISTS

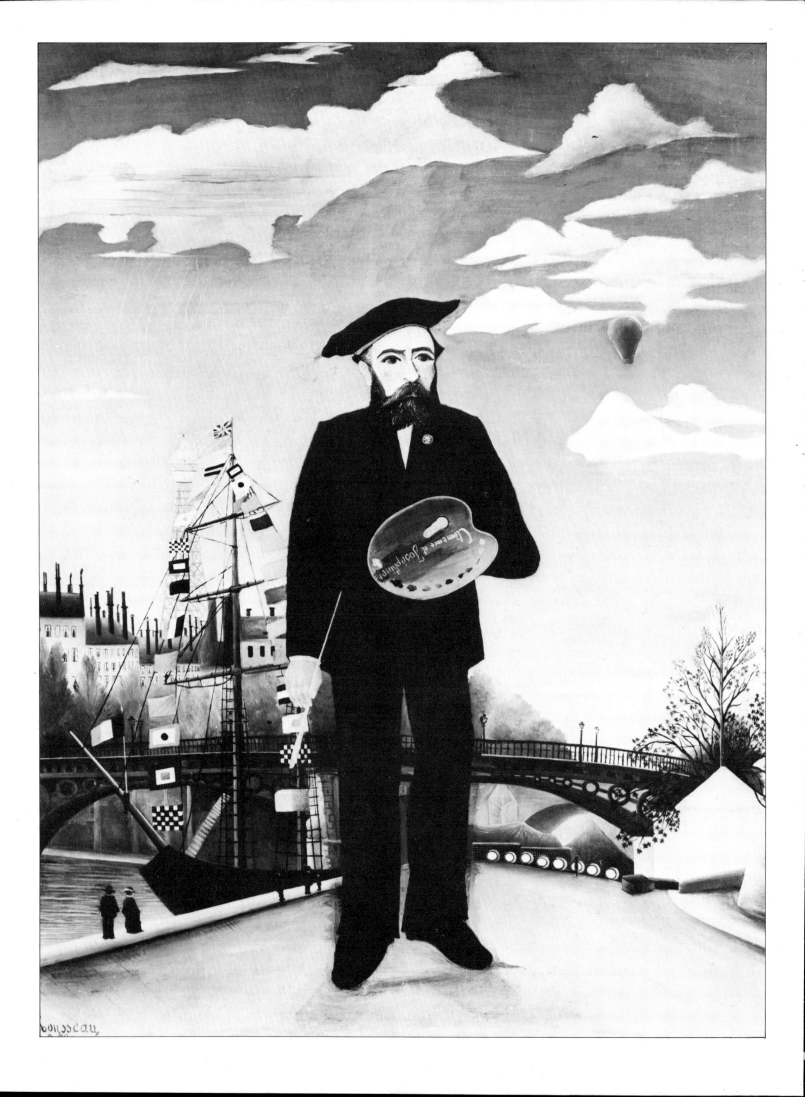

The Dictionary of Painting and Sculpture

ART
AND ARTISTS

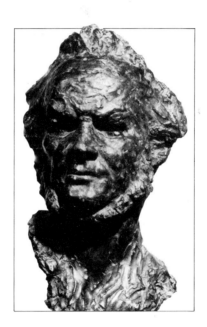

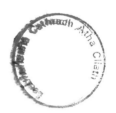

MITCHELL BEAZLEY

The Mitchell Beazley Library of Art

Editor-in-Chief and Editor of Volume 1
Jack Tresidder
Senior Executive Art Editor
Michael McGuinness
Senior Editor and Editor of Volumes 2 and 3
Paul Holberton
Editor of Volume 4
Jane Crawley
Editors
Ian Chilvers
Jane Cochrane
Katharine Kemp
Jean McNamee
Roslin Mair
Judy Martin
Susan Meehan
Senior Designer
Marnie Searchwell
Designers
Paul Bickerstaff
Alan Brown
Peter Courtley
Gerry Douglas
Jane Owen
Chief Picture Researcher
Flavia Howard
Picture Researchers
Celestine Dars
Tessa Politzer
Sandy Shepherd
Researchers
Julian George
Andrew Heritage
Tony Livesey
Julian Mannering
Kate Miller
Robert Stewart
Editorial Assistants
Barbara Gish
Amber Newell
Proof Reader
Gillian Beaumont
Indexers
Hilary and Richard Bird
Production Controller
Suzanne Semmes

THE MITCHELL BEAZLEY LIBRARY OF ART
was edited and designed by
Mitchell Beazley Publishers, Mill House,
87–89 Shaftesbury Avenue, London W1V 7AD

ISBN 0 85533 177 1 Slipcased set

ISBN 0 85533 358 8 Volume 4

Composed by Filmtype Services Limited, Scarborough, England
and Tradespools Ltd, Frome, England

Origination by Gilchrist Bros, Leeds, England
and Scala Istituto Fotografico Editorale, Florence

Printed in the Netherlands
by Koninklijke Smeets Offset b.v., Weert

Chief Contributor and General Editor

DAVID PIPER

Major Contributors to the Library

Christopher Cornford
Peter Owen
Philip Rawson
L. R. Rogers

Consultants in America

Bernard S. Myers (coordinator)
Robert S. Bianchi
Hirschel B. Chipp
George A. Corbin
Creighton E. Gilbert
Charles T. Little
Susan B. Matheson
Linda Nochlin
Jerome J. Pollitt
Marylin M. Rhie
David E. Rust
Margaretta M. Salinger
Maurice Tuchman

Contributors and Consultants

Clare Abbott
Francis Ames-Lewis
David A. Anfam
Penny Bateman
Jane Beckett
Sandra Berresford
Peter Bird
Laurel Bradley
Barbara Brend
Ben Burt
Colin Campbell
Shigeo Chiba
A. H. Christie
Alexandrina Le Clézio
Craig Clunas
Susan Compton
Richard Demarco
Peter Draper
K. A. Edwards
Angela Emanuel
Susan Foister
John Glaves-Smith
Jennifer Godsell
Patricia Godsell
Christopher Green
Antony Griffiths
James Hamilton
Martin Hammer
Roberta L. Harris
Anne Harrison
Larissa Haskell
James Hickey
Brian Hickman
Joke Hofkamp
Richard Humphreys
Paul Ioannides
Michael Jacobs
Anne Clark James
Ingrid Jenkner
Marc Jordan
Anne Kirker
Alastair Laing
Nigel Llewellyn
J. P. Losty
Jules Lubbock

B. J. Mack
Melissa McQuillan
Peter Mitchell
Stefan Muthesius
Jill Nicklin
Keith Nicklin
Sarah O'Brien Twohig
Young-sook Pak
Sir Cecil Parrott
Stevan K. Pavlowitch
Richard Pestell
Geraldine Prince
Birgitta Rapp
Michael Ridley
Professor Sixten Ringbom
Malcolm Rogers
Irit Rogoff
Sara Selwood
Richard Shone
Evelyn Silber
Sam Smiles
Frances Spalding
Lindsay Stainton
Mary Anne Stevens
Roy Strong
Glenn Sujo Volsky
John Sunderland
Kay Sutton
Margaret Tatton-Brown
Julie Thomas
Rosemary Treble
Philip Troutman
Adriana Turpin
Peter Vergo
Gray Watson
Claudine Webster
Roderick Whitfield
Cecilia Whitford
Frank Whitford
Gillian Wilson
Rosalind Wood
Christopher Wright
Alison Yarrington
Iain Zaczek

USING THE DICTIONARY

This volume is primarily a biographical dictionary of painters and sculptors. It also contains entries on art movements, groups, techniques and critical terms, and on prominent patrons and writers on art. Where an important field of painting or sculpture cannot be treated in biographical terms – Egyptian art, for instance – entries on sites are included. Subjects associated with architecture and the decorative arts are covered only where the connections with painting and sculpture are very close. Ranging as it does world-wide from prehistoric times to the present day, the Dictionary must necessarily be selective, but with more than 3,000 entries it should cover most of the names and terms likely to be encountered by the general reader. Contemporary artists are well represented, in spite of the difficulty of assessing their eventual significance or stature.

In assembling the biographical and technical information in a succinct form, the intention has been not simply to catalogue facts but to characterize the subject of the entry so as to give the reader a clear impression of the work discussed and of its place in the history of art. Entry lengths generally reflect the relative importance of the artist or topic, but take account of information already contained in the Understanding and History volumes in the Library, to which this book is a companion and supplement. They reflect also the fact that some artists' work is less easily summarized than others', and that the lives of many early masters are very obscure.

An important feature of the Dictionary is the number of specific works cited. These are usually in public galleries and museums and are chosen as pointers to the artist's individual style or development. In the Dictionary itself, the illustrations are confined to portraits (or photographs) of artists, the majority of them self-portraits. Essentially their interest is biographical – complementing the account of the artist's life. They also, however, illustrate the artist's style as a portraitist or self-portraitist, and collectively show how astonishingly varied the self-image of the artist has been.

INDEXING AND CROSS-REFERENCING
In the alphabetical sequence of entries, which starts opposite, artists will be found under the most commonly used form of their name, which may be a nickname or pseudonym (thus Guercino). Alternative names are bracketed. Italian Old Masters whose full names include da, del or di are listed usually under the first element of their names (Leonardo da Vinci) unless more commonly known by the last element (Caravaggio). With the exception of La or Le (La Tour, Georges de), prefixes are generally ignored for the purpose of indexing (thus Gogh, Vincent van). There are a few cases where usage dictates otherwise: Peter De Wint, for instance, is found under De Wint, Peter. Some alternative names are cross-referenced, notably all Chinese names, where the older Wade-Giles spellings may be more familiar to readers than the modern pinyin system adopted here.

Within entries, words in SMALL CAPITALS refer the reader to useful information in another entry. These are used sparingly since almost all movements or technical terms referred to in the Dictionary can be looked up under their own entries, as can nearly all the artists mentioned. The names of those few artists who do not have separate entries are followed by bracketed birth and death dates, or are given in **bold** type where they are discussed in the body of another entry – the usual method of dealing with families of artists. Occasionally, the same convention is used with art terms; thus iconology is discussed within the entry on iconography.

Cross-references to other volumes in the Library are given at the end of many entries; page numbers in **bold** type refer to full and illustrated discussion, those in *italic* type refer to illustrated works, and those in ordinary type indicate other references.

ABBREVIATIONS
In describing the locations of cited works of art, the names of some well-known institutions have been abbreviated or words such as "Gallery" or "Museum" have been omitted; thus "New York, Metropolitan" stands for "New York, Metropolitan Museum of Art". The following abbreviations are used:

BL	British Library
BM	British Museum
BN	Bibliothèque Nationale
coll.	collection
MFA	Museum of Fine Arts
MOMA	Museum of Modern Art
NG	National Gallery
NPG	National Portrait Gallery
V&A	Victoria and Albert Museum

(Frontispiece) HENRI ROUSSEAU: *Self-portrait*, 1890; (Title page) DAUMIER: *Self-portrait*, 1855

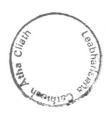

Aachen, Hans von 1552–1615
German MANNERIST painter. He was born in Cologne and had a cosmopolitan career, training in the Netherlands and working in Italy before settling in Prague as court painter to Rudolf II in 1597. He mainly painted religious, mythological and allegorical scenes in which smoothly modelled, elongated figures are arranged in elegant poses (*The victory of truth*, 1598, Munich, Alte Pinakothek). His work is similar to Spranger's, but gentler in feeling, and like Spranger his influence was widespread because of the many engravings after his designs.

Aalto, Alvar 1898–1976
Finnish artist. One of the greatest architects of the 20th century, Aalto was also an important furniture designer and an abstract sculptor and painter of some distinction. Most of his career was spent in Finland, but the first major exhibition of his work was held in the Museum of Modern Art, New York, in 1938, and he taught for several years in the USA, notably at the Massachusetts Institute of Technology, for which he designed a hall of residence (1947–49). The relationship between Aalto's work in the various fields in which he worked is very complex, but he saw his sculpture partially as a means of research into questions of form, and his architectural and sculptural interests come together in his war memorial at Suomussalmi (1960). The soft shapes, irregular curvature and trumpet-like forms of his sculpture challenged Constructivist angularity and contributed to post-1945 "romanticism".

Aaltonen, Wäinö 1894–1966
Finnish sculptor. After Finland's declaration of independence (1917) he soon became a sculptor of near-official status. His style combines classicist traits and heavy monumentality, and always shows close attention to material, as in the five allegorical figures in the Plenary Assembly Hall of the Parliamentary Building in Helsinki (1930–32). His more informal work includes intimate portraits, figural paintings and experiments with collage.

Abakanowicz, Magdalena
born 1930
Polish sculptor, a pioneer of large-scale woven structures. Made from sisal, jute and rope and woven with tapestry techniques, they are designed, in her own words, to "extend the possibilities of man's contact with a work of art through touch and by being surrounded by it". She came to prominence in the early 1960s, and her lead was widely followed in western Europe and the USA, breaking down the barriers between "art" and "craft" and extending the range of sculptural materials and methods. Her work is best represented in Polish museums, but can be seen elsewhere, for instance in the Museum of Modern Art, New York.

Abbate, Niccolò dell' c.1512–71
Italian painter. He worked in his native Modena and in Bologna, mainly on frescos in palaces, until 1552, when he joined Primaticcio at FONTAINEBLEAU. He is most important for his landscapes peopled with elegant figures from mythological stories, which look forward to Claude and Poussin (*Orpheus and Eurydice*, c.1560, London, NG).

Abbey, Edwin Austin 1852–1911
American painter and illustrator, chiefly of historical scenes. He had a very successful career, both in America and in England, where he lived for many years, his greatest triumph being his appointment as official painter at Edward VII's coronation in 1902. His work varied from murals in the Boston Public Library to illustrations in popular journals such as *Harper's Magazine*, which delighted a vast public. He was undoubtedly at his best in the latter field and in book illustration, for his large historical tableaux tend to sink into bathos. The best collection of his paintings is in the Yale University Art Gallery at New Haven, Connecticut, and includes the well-known *Richard Duke of Gloucester and the Lady Anne*, the sensation of the 1896 Royal Academy exhibition. Abbey's passion for historical accuracy was so great that he repainted an area of Lady Anne's dress when he discovered a detail of the heraldry was incorrect.

Abd as-Samad active c.1535–95
Indian Mughal painter, first recorded at the court of Shah Tahmasp Safavi at Tabriz, where he contributed to the later stages of the Houghton *Shahnameh* (New York, Metropolitan). He joined the court of the exiled Grecian Mughal Emperor Humayun at Kabul in 1549, and went with him to India in 1555. Given control of Emperor Akbar's atelier of painters, Abd as-Samad trained these Indian artists in Safavid techniques. Very few pages from imperial manuscripts of the Akbar period (1556–1605) can be attributed to Abd as-Samad himself, but certain dated pages from *The Gulshan Album of Jehangir* are by him (1588, Washington, Freer; 1591, Los Angeles, County Museum), and he is known to have contributed to the *Darabnameh* (c.1580, London, BL) and the Dyson-Perrins *Nizami* (completed 1596, BL). Even in these late paintings he is still basically an Iranian painter, interested more in surface decoration than in volume.

Abildgaard, Nicolai Abraham
1743–1809
Danish painter, sculptor, architect, designer and writer on art, successively a representative of ROMANTIC CLASSICISM and pure NEOCLASSICISM. The former phase was due to friendships formed while studying in Rome (1772–77) with Sergel and Fuseli; the latter phase accompanied his conversion into an establishment figure, decorating palaces in Copenhagen and directing the Academy of Fine Arts. In his last decade he designed some pure Grecian furniture for himself, and painted two cycles of pictures illustrating the Roman authors Apuleius and Terence, which are prob-

ably his finest works (Copenhagen, Statens Museum for Kunst). Thorvaldsen was his pupil and assistant.

Aboriginal art see AUSTRALIAN ABORIGINAL ART

Abstract art
Art which does not attempt to represent the appearance of objects, real or imaginary. Abstract art, then, is not a style, but a description of any art which eschews representation. In the decorative arts abstraction has been present for millennia, but it appeared in European painting and sculpture only in the second decade of the 20th century when it emerged, in different forms, in several places, in the work of artists such as Delaunay, Kandinsky, Kupka, Malevich and Mondrian. Modern non-representational painting or sculpture arises from either (1) the reduction of natural forms to their essentials or (2) the combination of shapes, lines and colours divorced from representational intent and created for their own sake. In its first meaning the concept of abstract art can be seen to develop from CUBISM and the attempt to penetrate beneath the surface of reality—the sculpture of Brancusi perfectly represents this process of abstracting from nature. The second meaning entails the belief that shapes, lines and colours have aesthetic values in their own right, the basic inspiration for most movements of abstract art. The concept, stimulated to some extent by photography, which relieved the artist of his obligations as a recorder of appearances, was current by the late 19th century, when Maurice Denis proclaimed that "A picture . . . is essentially a flat surface covered in colours arranged in a certain order." Although many works do not fit neatly into either category, two broad trends are discernible in modern abstraction: the hard-edged, carefully-finished, often geometric style of CONSTRUCTIVISM, DE STIJL or SUPREMATISM; and the freer, more intuitive and expressionistic style of ABSTRACT EXPRESSIONISM, ORPHISM or TACHISME. Together they have dominated 20th-century painting and sculpture. See vol. 1 p. 132; vol. 3 pp. 126ff

Abstract Expressionism
Term originally used in connection with Kandinsky's early abstract work but more usually applied to a movement which developed in New York in the 1940s. The term does not denote one particular style, as the work of the artists involved varied considerably, but rather an attitude which called for freedom from traditional social and aesthetic values, and which, in contrast to the documentary realism which had dominated American painting in the 20th century, placed emphasis on spontaneous personal expression. SURREALISM, with its stress on the role of the Unconscious in the act of creation, was a fundamental source of inspiration. ACTION PAINTING, as practised by Pollock and others, is the kind of work most

usually associated with the movement, but artists as diverse as Gorky and Tobey are included, and some Abstract Expressionists, notably De Kooning, retained figurative images in their work. A feature common to these four artists, however, and to others associated with the movement, was a preference for very large canvases. During the 1950s Abstract Expressionism became an international phenomenon. It was the first movement in the USA to develop independently of European examples, and the first to influence art in Europe. See vol. 3 pp. 210ff

Abstraction–Création
Association of abstract artists based in Paris. It was formed in 1931, by both painters and sculptors, Frenchmen and foreigners, partly in reaction to the rise of Surrealism, and under the inspiration of the geometric art of the De Stijl and Constructivist movements. Each year between 1932 and 1936 the members held a group exhibition and published an illustrated annual called *Abstraction–Création, Art non-figuratif*, thus providing a focus for new developments. Under the leadership of Herbin and Vantongerloo, there were at one point over 400 members, including Arp, Gabo, Hélion, Kandinsky, Kupka, Lissitzky, Mondrian, Ben Nicholson and Pevsner.

Abu'l Hasan 1588–c.1630
Indian Mughal painter. He joined Shah Salim's studio in Allahabad, 1599–1604, where he contributed a stunning painting to the *Salim Anvar-I Suhayli* manuscript (c.1604–10, London, BL). He was given the title of Nadir al-Zaman (Wonder of the Age) by Jehangir, who regarded him as the greatest of his court painters. His most famous work is the *Squirrels in a plane tree* (c.1610, New Delhi, India Office Library), but he also painted various formal portraits of the Emperor and representations of his dreams, for example the *Emperor Jehangir contemplating a portrait of Akbar* (c.1600, Paris, Musée Guimet). In this he reveals an acute psychological penetration, as well as a technical mastery of painting in depth that marks an advance over artists of the Akbar period.

Abu Simbel
Site in lower Nubia, NEW KINGDOM Egypt, of two vast temples hewn from the living rock for Ramesses II (1304–1237 BC). They were reconstructed at a higher level to save them from the rising waters of the Nile after the New High Dam was built in 1967. The façades of both temples, cut from the rock face, simulate the pylon entrances of free-standing temples such as KARNAK. At the entrance to the larger temple of Ramesses are four seated statues of the King, nearly 20 metres (65 ft) high. Such colossal statues of Ramesses, also found at Karnak, Luxor and MEMPHIS, are potent symbols made to rigid formulae, without personality. The smaller temple at Abu Simbel has six standing statues of the King and Queen at the entrance. In both

temples scenes in sunken relief, once brightly painted, show the King at war and the King and Queen performing sacred rites. Ramesses II's successors never surpassed the scale on which he built his temples. See vol. 2 p. 27

Academy
Name applied to an association of artists or scholars organized in a professional institution. The word and concept had its origins in Greek culture, specifically in Plato's Academy, a school of philosophy founded near Athens in about 387 BC. The first official art academy, the **Accademia del Disegno**, was founded in 1563 in Florence by Vasari with Duke Cosimo I de' Medici and Michelangelo as its directors. A continuing concern of this and succeeding academies was to supersede the guild system and raise the status of the artist above that of mere craftsman by insisting on theoretical as well as practical study. The **Accademia di S. Luca**, founded in Rome in 1593, ran a teaching programme devoted to church doctrine as well as art theory. Led by Federico Zuccari, and reorganized in 1627 and 1633 by Pope Urban VIII, it gained an important place in the art world of Rome, and numbered foreign artists among its members. The Carracci founded a private academy in Bologna in the 1580s, laying particular stress on drawing from the life, which was to become an important feature in most subsequent academies. However, the pattern for European academies up to the late 18th century was set by the French **Académie Royale de Peinture et de Sculpture**, founded in 1648 with the support of Louis XIV. It became a successful teaching institution in the 1660s when the King's minister Colbert and its director Lebrun reorganized it so as to control the teaching and commissioning of art throughout France. Thus for the first time "**academic art**" acquired a precise meaning, describing an art conforming to rigid standards of taste officially imposed upon the artists, who were arranged in a hierarchy of categories corresponding to the genre they practised, with HISTORY PAINTING at the top. The annual SALON and the prestigious PRIX DE ROME were features of the Academy, which was disbanded in 1793 but reconstituted in 1816 under the name of the Académie des Beaux-Arts. A spate of academies, often to some extent controlled or subsidized by royal authority, appeared in Europe in the 18th century. The ROYAL ACADEMY in London was exceptional in being free of state control and having a relatively open annual exhibition. The American Academy of Fine Arts was founded in New York in 1802, but under John Trumbull's tyrannical and conservative directorship the younger members resigned and formed the NATIONAL ACADEMY OF DESIGN in 1826. Although in the 19th century academies were increasingly criticized for stifling creative impulses by the strict application of rules and standards, they were still influential. Several in Germany were highly regarded; the Munich Academy, for example, became under the directorship of Cornelius the European centre for the revival of fresco painting. In France a few independent academies of the type known as the "ATELIER LIBRE" made more individual contributions, but the term "academic" became increasingly pejorative in the 19th century and in the 20th century has come to describe mediocre representational painting.

Academy figure
Careful painting or drawing of a nude figure executed, usually by a student, as a technical exercise. They are generally a little under half life-size and show the figure in an heroic posture. The tradition goes back to the Carracci, and continued into the 20th century. Two early 19th-century French examples are in the National Gallery, London, one of them ascribed to Géricault.

Accademia del Disegno
see ACADEMY

Accademia di S. Luca see ACADEMY

Acconci, Vito born 1940
American BODY artist. His work explores his own body as a work of art. Many of his performances are deliberately tasteless and masochistic. In *Rubbing piece* (1970, New York) he rubbed his arm until a sore was produced. See vol. 3 p. **243**

Achaemenian art
Art of the nomadic Achaemenian tribes of the Zagros mountains and the Persian plateau. They produced few interesting artefacts before the 6th century BC, although the Luristan bronzes, some of which date from the 2nd millennium BC, are notable (a fine horse bit is in the Walters Art Gallery, Baltimore). Cyrus the Great, the first Achaemenid ruler of Persia, created an empire in the late 6th century BC which took in most of the Near East, and then began to establish an art which befitted such an empire. The design and decoration of Persian palaces such as Pasagardae, Susa and Persepolis owed something to Egyptian and much to MESOPOTAMIAN traditions, as, for example, in the glazed and moulded tiles of Susa showing royal guards and monsters (mainly Paris, Louvre), and the *lamassu* (composite man/beast demons) and stone carved reliefs of the palace platforms and buildings at Persepolis, the Persian capital. These reliefs show peaceful processions, unlike the ASSYRIAN prototypes, and may have been carved by enslaved Ionian sculptors working to a specifically Persian master plan. Details of dress and drapery are undeniably Greek, as are the fluted columns of, for example, the 100-column Hall of Darius the Great. Yet the huge bull, griffin and lion sculptures adorning gateways are characteristically Persian and show the development of an indigenous style. This may be seen, too, in the rock cut reliefs of the royal tombs at Naqsh-i-Rustam, and also in gold and silver work (for example the superb Oxus Treasure, 7th–4th centuries BC, mainly BM, London) where a controlled richness prevails. See vol. 2 p. 29

Achilles Painter
active mid-5th century BC
Greek vase-painter from Athens, who is named after a fine RED-FIGURE amphora in the Vatican which bears a noble figure of Achilles. He worked mainly on white-ground *lekythoi* for use in funeral rites. Limiting his scheme to one or two gracefully disposed figures, he is regarded as perhaps the finest exponent of the so-called free style of vase-painting (450–420 BC). Almost 200 of his paintings have been recognized, mainly elegiac domestic scenes. See vol. 2 p. *44*

Acrylic paint
Quick-drying synthetic paint which was first exploited by artists in the late 1940s. A most versatile medium, it can be used on almost any painting surface, in thin washes or heavy IMPASTO, and a variety of finishes can be achieved with the use of additives—from matt to high gloss. It now rivals oil-paint. See vol. 1 p. **152**

Action painting
Term first used by the art critic Harold Rosenberg in 1952 to describe both a process and a style of painting which appeared in the USA during the 1940s. He proposed that in this type of painting the canvas becomes an arena in which the artist acts. The paint, dripped and splashed over the canvas, records a moment from the artist's biography, breaking down the distinction between art and life. The canvas is thus seen as the record of an event, and the more extreme manifestations of Action Painting, with which the concept is most closely associated in the public imagination, involve such feats as riding a bicycle over the canvas. The term is occasionally used interchangeably with ABSTRACT EXPRESSIONISM, but this usage is inexact, for while all Action Paintings are Abstract Expressionist, not all Abstract Expressionist works are Action Paintings. Rosenberg was not specific, but Pollock and De Kooning are presumably his models for Action Painting. In Europe this form of painting is often called TACHISME. See vol. 3 pp. 212ff

Adam, Henri-Georges 1904–67
French artist, best known for his sculpture, although he also worked in graphics and tapestry design. Under the inspiration of Brancusi he turned to sculpture around 1940, creating works which evidently impressed Picasso. His later sculptures, organic abstractions sometimes set in groups, are often decorated with geometric designs.

Adam family
Family of French sculptors from Nancy. The first was **Jacob-Sigisbert** (1670–1747), but much better known are his three sons, **Lambert-Sigisbert** (1700–59), **Nicolas-Sébastien** (1705–78) and **François-Gérard** (1710–61). The three brothers trained under their father and in Rome, where Bernini proved a decisive influence on the vigorous sense of movement which characterized their work. The driving force was Lambert-Sigisbert, whose success began in Rome, where he won the competition for the Trevi Fountain (1731), though his designs were not executed. His decorative BAROQUE style found ideal expression in the lead group of *Neptune and Amphitrite* (1740) in the Bassin de Neptune at Versailles, where his work can be seen beside that of his rivals Bouchardon and Jean-Baptiste Lemoyne the Younger. Nicolas-Sébastien practised a more reflective version of the same idiom, producing his masterpiece in the tomb of Catharina Opalinska (1749, Nancy, Nôtre Dame de Bon Secours). François-Gérard was the least talented of the three, but he produced some fine garden statues for Frederick the Great at Potsdam. Clodion was their nephew.

Adami, Valerio born 1935
Italian painter and graphic artist, one of the leading POP artists. He studied in Milan, where he has mainly worked, but he was in London, 1961–62, and in Paris, 1962–64. During the 1960s his style gradually changed from abstraction towards very formal types of figuration. His most characteristic pictures resemble frames from comic strips, but are distinguished by subtle colouring and a wry sense of humour. In style, though not in subject matter, his work is close to Caulfield's, and his images are often fragmented, requiring the viewer to reconstruct them. See vol. 3 p. *255*

Adams, Robert born 1917
British sculptor. At first mainly a carver, during the 1950s he pioneered the use of welded iron in abstract sculpture. Later he worked in highly polished bronze. His work often approaches the geometric austerity of the CONSTRUCTIVISTS but is essentially within the more organic tradition of Hepworth.

Adler, Jankel 1895–1949
Polish painter. From 1922 to 1933 he worked in Düsseldorf, and in 1933 emigrated to Paris, finally settling in Britain in 1939. Klee and Picasso were among the most important influences on his work, which was very eclectic. His most original paintings are probably those of Jewish life in Poland (*Two rabbis*, 1942, New York, MOMA).

Adrian-Nilsson, Gösta 1884–1965
Swedish painter. Around 1914 in Berlin, he developed a decorative, semi-abstract style, often with dark glowing colours (*The horsetamer*, 1915, Sweden, Norrköping Museum). These witness the influence of FUTURISM and CUBISM, and some of his paintings of about 1919 were the first purely non-figurative art to be produced in Sweden. He published his theoretical views on art in *The Divine Geometry* in 1922, at a time when he was in close contact with Léger. During the 1930s he took up SURREALISM and was the inspirer of the Swedish Surrealist group in Halmstad.

Aelst, Willem van 1625–*c.*1683
Dutch still-life and flower painter. He trained at Delft with his uncle **Evert** van Aelst (1602–57) before working in Paris, Florence and Rome, 1645–56. In Italy, he was court painter to the Grand Duke of Tuscany, Ferdinando II de' Medici. *Still life with dead game* (1652, Florence, Pitti) is an example of the work he painted for him. After his return to Amsterdam in 1657, van Aelst settled to a richly abundant production of elegant flower-pieces, still lifes, and "spoils of the hunt" subjects, his palette dominated by cool blues and greys. Rachel Ruysch was one of his pupils.

Aerial perspective see PERSPECTIVE

Aertsen, Pieter 1508–75
Netherlandish painter, born in Amsterdam. He worked both there and in Antwerp, pioneering the development of still-life and genre painting as independent art forms. In *Christ with Martha and Mary* (1559, Brussels, Musées Royaux des Beaux-Arts), for example, the ostensibly religious subject matter is completely overshadowed by the large-scale depiction of peasants and market scenes in the foreground, and in *Butcher's shop with the Flight into Egypt* (1551, Uppsala, University) the distant figures are dwarfed by the animal carcasses. His superbly textured still lifes anticipated the work of Snyders, while moralizing genre scenes, such as *The egg dance* (1557, Amsterdam, Rijksmuseum), made him the forerunner of Steen. His nephew Beuckelaer was his most important pupil. See vol. 2 p. *162*

Aestheticism
Tenet which holds that the beauty of an art object is its own justification, that there is no need for a social or moral purpose. The phrase "*l'art pour l'art*" (art for art's sake) is supposed to have been first used by the philosopher Victor Cousin in a lecture at the Sorbonne in Paris in 1818. In the late 19th century the doctrine was much discussed, and among those who challenged it were Ruskin, who had a famous controversy with Whistler on the subject, Morris and

the novelist Tolstoy. The excesses of aestheticism, brilliantly parodied by Gilbert and Sullivan in *Patience* (1881), hardly survived into the 20th century, when most critics would suggest that the creation and appreciation of art can be rewarding in themselves but that social, religious, political and other factors should not be ignored.

Aesthetics

Branch of philosophy dealing with concepts such as beauty and taste, on which the criticism of the arts is based. The term was first used by the German philosopher Alexander Gottlieb Baumgarten (1714–62).

African art

Term usually applied to the wood, bronze and ivory sculpture, the pots, decorated gourds and baskets, the beadwork, musical instruments and textiles of the black peoples of the sub-Saharan part of the African continent. Many other objects or phenomena which cannot be put on a plinth or hung on a wall—designs painted on the body and styles of coiffure for instance, as well as dance and song—have only recently come to be recognized as just as worthy of the description "African art". While the carved wooden mask, for example, has been collected from many parts of Africa and subjected to scholarly scrutiny, rarely have the costumes, insignia, drums, rattles and horns which are often an integral part of the same ritual performance—the masquerade—been dealt with in the same ways. One of the consequences of the dearth of data from thorough field research has been an inaccurate, excessively ethnocentric view of African art on the part of scholars and creative artists in Europe and America. Because the abstract, stylized forms of art from the Congo and West Africa had a great impact on European art in the early part of the 20th century, African art is often thought to be predominantly non-naturalistic. Much African art, however, is highly naturalistic, notably representations in bronze and terracotta from IFE and those in wood covered with animal skin from the forest region of south-east Nigeria and west Cameroon. Another misconception is that African art is primarily a village art, but much of it was produced in the towns and cities of mighty kingdoms, or by small groups of hunters and gatherers, by pastoralists or itinerant craftsmen. The status of the artist also varied greatly. In some communities woodcarving might be practised by a chief, in others by subject or hired artists, and, while in some areas the potter or blacksmith was revered, in others he was despised. We know that highly organized guilds of craftsmen supplied the palace art of BENIN, but are much less certain about the status or socio-economic organization of the stone-mason among the builders of Great Zimbabwe. For many decades art historians have viewed African art as being in drastic decline through the influence of Christianity and Islam, colonial government and commerce. While it is true that some traditional forms of art are dying out or being transformed, Africa could be said to be undergoing a period of artistic renaissance. A great variety of new materials, from cement to tinplate, has been exploited in recent years, and innovative artwork is vigorously produced and enthusiastically employed by the rapidly expanding urban sector. Drinking-parlour murals and painted signboards are just two of the flourishing genres. In the modern Africa, dances and masquerades are sponsored in the market place by purveyors of blood-tonic, worm medicine and "vapour rubs", while at the same time African art historians analyse their forbears' contributions to humanity in learned journals. See vol. 2 pp. 14–17

Afro (Afro Basaldella) born 1912
Italian abstract painter, the brother of the sculptors Mirko and Dino Basaldella. His early work was influenced by Cubism but a strong decorative element was present in his art from the beginning. He reached maturity as an artist in the late 1940s, and his distinctive style is due to a unity of decorative, expressive and structural elements. During the 1950s he associated with the FRONTE NUOVO DELLE ARTI. In 1958 he painted a mural, *The garden of hope*, for the UNESCO building in Paris. He has taught in the USA and in Rome.

Agam, Yaacov born 1928
Israeli artist who has worked mainly in Paris. His output, which has included films and writing, is very varied and complex, but he is best known as a KINETIC artist. The viewer is often able to rearrange the components of his works and is thus invited to contribute to the creative process. Agam often makes use of strong patterns with light and sound effects. He has travelled widely in Europe and lectured in the USA.

Agasandros see ALEXANDROS

Agasse, Jacques Laurent
1767–1849
Anglo-Swiss painter, primarily of animal subjects. He was born in Geneva and studied in Paris with Jacques-Louis David and at the veterinary school. He first briefly visited England in 1790 and settled there permanently in 1800. *The stud farm* (1808, Winterthur, Oskar Reinhart Foundation) shows the clarity and elegance of line and gift for individual characterization which raises his paintings above the realms of anatomical study. His career was at first successful, and included royal commissions, but his work eventually lost its appeal for patrons and he died penniless in London. The best collection of his works is in the Museum of Art and History, Geneva.

Agatharchos active 5th century BC
Greek painter. Vitruvius says he painted the scenery for a tragedy of Aeschylus in Athens and that his written comments led to the first formulations of the principles of perspective. See vol. 2 p. 44

Agorakritos active 5th century BC
Greek sculptor, a native of the island of Paros and a pupil of Phidias. His best-known work was a colossal statue of Nemesis for the people of Rhamnous, where excavation has revealed a massive head corresponding to descriptions of the work. This is now in the British Museum, London, and displays a simple, idealizing style.

Agostino di Duccio 1418–81
Florentine sculptor and architect. His master is unknown, but he clearly knew well the work of Donatello, Michelozzo and Luca della Robbia. His first dated works are the four signed reliefs (1442) showing *Scenes from the life of St Gimignanus* on the façade of Modena Cathedral. Banished from Florence for theft in 1446, he went to Venice and then Rimini, where he produced allegorical reliefs (c.1450–57) for the Tempio Malatestiano, one of Alberti's most famous buildings. They display a graceful, very linear style, and extensive mythological imagery. Agostino's reliefs for the façade of S. Bernardino, Perugia (1457–62), his principal work as an architect, are even more mannered, with distinctive swirling draperies and histrionic expressions. Returning to Florence in the mid-1460s, he worked on giant figures for the Cathedral, which are now lost; he last worked in Perugia. Apart from the major works mentioned, Agostino's lively, fresh and highly personal style can best be seen in his reliefs of *The Virgin and Child* (generally of problematic dating), of which the Louvre, Paris, the National Gallery, Washington, and the V&A Museum, London, have examples. See vol. 2 p. 115

Ahmad Musa, Ustad active c.1330
Persian or Eastern Turkish painter who flourished in the reign of Abu Sa'id (1316–35), presumably in Tabriz. No certain works by him survive, but he is said to have instituted the mode of Persian painting which obtained until the 16th century and beyond. Pages of *Kalilal wa Dimnah* (Istanbul, University Library) and of the *Mi'rahnameh* (Istanbul, Topkapi Sarayi Library) are among the likeliest of the attributions made to him; they reveal an infusion of strong earthy colours into the recently acquired lightly tinted Chinese style, robust compositions, and the impression of tragic grandeur typical of the period.

Air-brush

Instrument powered by compressed air used to spray paint. In appearance it is rather like a large fountain pen and is held in a similar manner, with the forefinger controlling the supply of air. It can be used to cover a surface smoothly and quickly and with its fine mist makes it possible to produce delicate mixtures and gradations of colours and tones. Its use is chiefly associated with commercial artists, but it is also employed by hard-edge abstractionists, Op artists, Superrealists and any other painters requiring a very smooth, impersonal surface.

Aizenberg, Roberto born 1928
Argentine SURREALIST painter. A pupil of Juan Batlle-Planas, 1950–53, he inherited the tradition of metaphysical painting which had dominated modern art in the Argentine during the 1940s and 1950s. His works depict entirely imaginary figures floating or placed in a landscape. More recent works show the influence of Magritte and Delvaux. His realistic drawings are executed with the utmost precision (*Monument*, 1966, Caracas, Private coll.).

Ajanta

Series of Indian Buddhist caves in the north-western Deccan (Maharashtra state), dating from the 2nd century BC to the 8th century AD. They are in two basic formats: the *vihara* or monastery, a rectangular cave with pillars, and cells round the walls; and the *chaitya* or prayer-hall, a long hall at right angles to the cliff surface, with colonnades and an apsidal end with a *stupa*, a hemispherical reliquary which was circumambulated in worship. The majority of the caves were carved in two distinct periods; the earliest, up to the 2nd century AD, are Hinayana in inspiration, then, after an interval of several centuries, comes a group of Mahayana caves from the 5th century onwards. These latter are decorated with important sculptures, in what can loosely be called a Gupta idiom. However, it is the fresco-paintings which make Ajanta so important, for they constitute the only large-scale series of paintings surviving from ancient India.

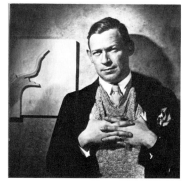

Aalto: Photograph, 1930. Helsinki, Museum of Finnish Architecture

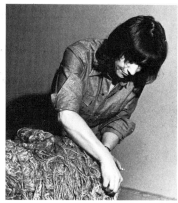

Abakanowicz: Photograph, 1977. Lausanne, Galerie Pauli

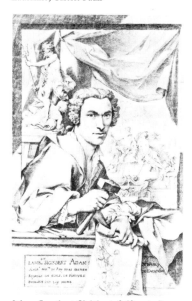

Adam, Lambert-Sigisbert: Self-portrait drawing, c.1740. Oxford, Ashmolean

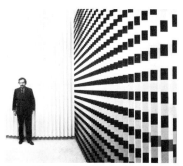

Agam: Photograph by his mural in the Elysée Palace, Paris, 1974 (Camera Press)

A small number date from the 1st century BC to the 2nd century AD, but most are from the Gupta era, some from the 4th and 5th centuries, but a greater number from the 6th and 7th centuries. The early mural paintings are characterized by cool, poised forms and friezelike compositions; the later, more agitated ones by languorous female beauties and hot colours. See vol. 3 pp. 14, 16

Albani, Francesco 1578–1660
Italian painter. He trained in his native Bologna under Calvaert and the Carracci, and worked in Rome, *c.*1600–17, assisting Annibale Carracci and Domenichino as well as executing his own commissions (frescos in Palazzo Verospi, now the Credito Italiano, *c.*1616). Returning to Bologna, he set up a successful studio, producing altarpieces as well as the mythological scenes and allegories set in landscapes for which he is best known. These charming, lighthearted works, of which the best-known examples are the series *The Four Elements* (1626–28) in the Pinacoteca, Turin, were particularly popular in 18th-century England.

Albers, Josef 1888–1976
German painter and designer, who became an American citizen in 1939. He studied and taught at the BAUHAUS, his work there reflecting a preoccupation with basic design principles, particularly for furniture. In 1933 he emigrated to the USA and taught at Black Mountain College until moving to Yale University in 1950. There he worked on his series of wholly abstract canvases, collectively called *Homage to the Square*, in which he reduced the composition to a simple arrangement of three or four squares set inside one another, painted in flat colours. He was acknowledged as an expert on colour relationships, and developed his theories on the subject in *The Interaction of Colour*, 1963. Ideas which he brought from the Bauhaus and his own disciplined techniques had much influence on OP art. See vol. 3 pp. **220–221**

Alberti, Leon Battista 1404–72
Italian humanist writer, architect, sculptor and painter, born in Genoa and educated at Padua and Bologna, but active chiefly in Florence and Rome. He is principally famous as an architect and art theorist, but he wrote on a wide variety of subjects, was considered a fine athlete and musician, and in the sum of all his interests and achievements epitomizes the humanist ideal of the "universal man". His theoretical writings were the most important of the 15th century, and he can be seen as the intellectual spokesman of the early RENAISSANCE. His most famous book, modelled on Vitruvius, is *On Architecture* (*De Re Aedificatoria*), begun in about 1450, the first treatise on architecture since antiquity and the first to be printed (1485). He also wrote treatises on painting and sculpture: *On Painting* (written in Latin as *De Pictura* in 1435 and translated by Alberti into Italian for the benefit of Brunelleschi as *Della Pittura* the following year) and *On Sculpture* (*De Statua*), probably written slightly earlier, although some authorities date it as late as the 1460s. *On Painting*, which mentions Donatello, Ghiberti, Luca della Robbia and Masaccio, as well as Brunelleschi, deals with the principles of painting and contains the first systematic guide to perspective. *On Sculpture* also shows an awareness of contemporary practice and knowledge of classical precept, besides providing the sculptor with a canon of human proportions. Alberti saw art in human, not religious, terms, and in all his writings displayed a rational and idealist approach typical of Renaissance humanism. His buildings, among them the churches of S. Sebastiano (1460) and S. Andrea (1470) at Mantua and the Tempio Malatestiano (1450) at Rimini, for which Agostino di Duccio provided the sculptural decoration, are among the most important of the early Renaissance, but very little of his painting and sculpture survives. None of his recorded paintings and perspectival scenes has been firmly identified, but two *Self-portrait* relief plaques are generally accepted as his (Paris, Louvre and Washington, NG). See vol. 2 p. 100

Albrecht D. (Dieter Albrecht)
born 1944
West German artist (he emigrated from East Germany in 1958), who has used several different media and attempted to forge links between them. During the 1960s he worked much with collage and performance; during the 1970s two major concerns were his publishing press and his "endless music", influenced especially by music from Bali. He has also made creative use of newspaper cuttings and photocopies. The economic situation of the Third World countries and the connection between private and public violence are two areas he has explored.

Albright, Ivan Le Lorraine
born 1897
American painter of minutely detailed canvases sometimes described as examples of MAGIC REALISM. His mature work is remarkably consistent: he focuses upon decay, especially in his many portraits, and an hallucinatory intensity is achieved through accentuated tonal contrasts and proliferation of detail. His compositions, often worked on over long periods, explore a world of feverishly symbolic desolation, typified in *That which I should have done I did not do* (1931–41, Chicago, Art Institute), in which an age-encrusted unopened door suggests a tomb.

Aldegrever, Heinrich 1502–55/61
German painter and engraver. His output consisted mainly of small engravings on religious subjects, strongly influenced by Dürer, but he was also a fine portraitist. Little is known for certain of his work as a painter.

Alechinsky, Pierre born 1927
Belgian abstract painter. He was a member of the JEUNE PEINTURE BELGE group in 1947, and in 1949 joined COBRA. In the 1940s he also worked in Paris with Hayter. In 1955 he travelled in Japan, and made a film called *Calligraphie Japonaise* in 1956 which won him an award that year at the Bergamo Festival. Like the other members of CoBrA he uses brilliant colour, fantastic imagery and expressive brushwork.

Aleš, Mikuláš 1852–1913
Czech painter and graphic artist. Following the example of Mánes he devoted himself to sketches and paintings of romantic heroes from Czech history and legend. His numerous works are chiefly in the Museum of the Star Hunting Lodge near Prague and the South Bohemian Gallery at Hluboká, both of which have been named after him, and there are decorations in the National Theatre and the municipal Hall of Prague.

Alexandros
active late 2nd or 1st century BC
Greek sculptor, the creator of "*The Venus de Milo*", the most famous of all classical statues, now in the Louvre, Paris. Nothing is known of the sculptor, whose work was found on the island of Melos in 1820. The name on the plinth has also been read as **Agasandros**. See vol. 2 p. *43*

Algardi, Alessandro 1598–1654
Italian sculptor. With Duquesnoy he was the leading sculptor in 17th-century Rome apart from Bernini, whom he replaced in papal favour during the pontificate of Innocent X (1644–55). He trained in the Carracci Academy in Bologna and his style, much more subdued than Bernini's, can be seen as a sculptural parallel to Sacchi's classicism in painting. His three most important works are the Tomb of Leo XI (1634–44) and the relief, *The meeting of Pope Leo I and Attila* (1646–53), both in St Peter's Rome; and the free-standing group *The decapitation of St Paul* (1641–47) in S. Paolo, Bologna. These are all large works—the relief is 7.5 metres (25 ft) high—but Algardi is seen at his best in his portrait busts, which are much more sober than Bernini's, but show a firm grasp of character and a fine feeling for texture (*Cardinal Laudivio Zacchia*, 1626?, West Berlin, Staatliche Museen). See vol. 1 p. *196*

Algarotti, Francesco 1712–64
The leading Italian art critic of the 18th century. He was born in and chiefly associated with Venice, although he travelled widely and was a friend of some of the great European figures of his day, notably Voltaire, as well as of artists such as Canaletto and Giambattista Tiepolo. None of his writings, which are marked by a strange mixture of pedantic erudition and acute responsiveness to the idiosyncrasies of an artist's style, was of lasting importance, but he helped to introduce Venice to the latest ideas of the Enlightenment as well as to spread Venetian culture. An important collector himself, Algarotti's most original idea was a plan for an art gallery reflecting the history of European painting, which he drew up while working for Augustus, Elector of Saxony, in Dresden.

Alkamenes active late 5th century BC
Greek sculptor, a pupil and later rival of Phidias. His work is described by a number of classical authors, but no undoubted original works survive. Copies, however, reveal that he worked in a solemn archaizing style.

Alken, Henry Senior 1785–1851
The best-known member of a family of British sporting artists. He was a prolific painter in oils and watercolours of hunting and coaching scenes, but is best known for his prints of these subjects which he originally produced anonymously under the name "Ben Tally Ho". The finest of these are exceedingly lively and colourful, but the quality of his work declined after about 1820.

Allan, David 1744–96
Scottish history, portrait and genre painter, sometimes (not very accurately) called "the Scottish Hogarth". From 1767 to 1777 he was in Rome, where he trained under Gavin Hamilton. On returning to Britain, he worked as a portraitist in London for about two years, then settled in Edinburgh. Genre subjects such as *The penny wedding* (1795, Edinburgh, NG) became his chief interest and a significant influence on Wilkie.

Alla prima
Method of painting, primarily in oils, in which the finished paint surface is achieved in one operation by working directly on to the ground, without any UNDERPAINTING. The technique was used in the 17th century, but did not become the normal method of procedure in oil-painting until the mid-19th century. "*Alla prima*" is Italian for "at first"; the French term "*au premier coup*" (at first stroke) is used in the same way, and English equivalents are "wet-on-wet" and "direct painting".

Allebé, Augustus 1838–1927
Dutch painter. Admiration for Delacroix and Dechamps is reflected in his Romantic early style, but he developed to a moderate realism. He painted still lifes and made animal drawings, but is best known for his genre scenes (*The well protected child*, 1867, Amsterdam, Rijksmuseum). From 1870 he was an influential teacher at the Amsterdam Academy and he was its Director from 1880 to 1906.

Allegory
An imaginative device, in literature as well as the visual arts, whereby a work contains a secondary meaning, conveyed by symbols and allusions, in addition to and compatible with its literal content. The allegory may be commonly known (for instance allegorical figures of virtues and vices frequently represented by medieval sculptors) or abstruse, requiring specialized knowledge to interpret it. A notable example of the latter is Giorgione's apparently allegorical painting *The tempest* (first decade of the 16th century, Venice, Accademia), a work which has still not been definitively interpreted. The device was used by Greek painters (the most famous example is the lost *Calumny* by Apelles) and was widely exploited in the Renaissance, Mannerist and Baroque periods. In the 16th and 17th centuries a favourite outlet for allegory was the emblem book, in which symbolic pictures were accompanied by texts explaining their meaning. One of these, Cesare Ripa's *Iconologia*, first published in Italian in 1593, became a favourite handbook for artists. See vol. 1 pp. 86 ff

Allied Artists Association
Group of British artists formed on the initiative of the art critic Frank Rutter in reaction to the increasingly conservative NEW ENGLISH ART CLUB. Sickert was the leader of the group. The first London exhibition, held at the Albert Hall in 1908, contained over 3,000 entries on account of its jury-free system based on the Paris Salon des Indépendants. It aimed to include craftsmen as well as painters and sculptors and to be international. Gaudier-Brzeska exhibited with the Association in 1913 and Kandinsky, Brancusi and Zadkine were all shown in Britain for the first time at these events.

Allori, Alessandro 1535–1607
Florentine painter, brought up and trained by Bronzino. At the age of 19 he went to Rome but returned to Florence in 1560, where he executed portraits, religious works, highly decorative frescos and tapestry designs for the Medici. *The pearl fishers* in the Studiolo of Francesco I (*c.*1570, Florence, Palazzo Vecchio), with its graceful, slender nudes depicted in exaggerated movement, is typical of his delightful style.

Allori, Cristofano 1577–1621
Florentine painter, the son of Alessandro. He was one of the most attractive painters working in Florence in the 17th century and was particularly skilled at

depicting rich materials. His master-piece, *Judith with the head of Holofernes* (*c.*1615, versions Florence, Pitti; British Royal Collection, and elsewhere), depicts his beautiful mistress as Judith, and the severed head of Holofernes is a self-portrait. During the 18th and 19th centuries the Pitti version was one of the most celebrated paintings in Italy.

All-over painting
Term at first associated with Pollock's "drip" paintings, in which the traditional ideas of composition—of the painting having a centre, top or bottom—are completely abandoned. The surface is continuous and indivisible, every part of it having the same value as every other part, the paint frequently being splattered or dripped on to the flat canvas from all directions. The term is also used to describe any painting with a repetitive motif or a single large colour field.

Allston, Washington 1779–1843
American painter, the pioneer of ROMANTIC landscape in his country. Apart from two periods in Europe (1801–08, 1811–18), during the first of which he studied under West at the Royal Academy, he worked in and around Boston. He concentrated on the most grandiose and spectacular aspects of nature, often incorporating religious subjects (Claude, John Martin and Turner were among his sources), and was a forerunner of the HUDSON RIVER school. His *Moonlit landscape* (1819, Boston, MFA), a work of deep lyrical feeling, shows the heights Allston reached at his best, but his later years were mainly dissipated on his very pedestrian *Belshazzar's feast*, begun in 1817 and still unfinished at his death (Detroit Institute of Arts). Allston also wrote poetry and was a friend of Samuel Taylor Coleridge, whose portrait he painted (1814, London, NPG). His most important pupil was Morse. See vol. 3 p. **69**

Alma-Tadema, Sir Lawrence 1836–1912
Dutch-born painter, most of whose career was spent in England, where he became one of the most successful artists of his day. He began by specializing in Merovingian and Egyptian scenes, but after visiting Pompeii in 1863 turned to archaeologically exact paintings of classical Greece and Rome, which helped to fashion the vision of the ancient world later associated with Hollywood films. He moved to England in 1870, and became a naturalized British subject three years later. His paintings usually include beautiful women, and are often sentimental or titillating, although *In the tepidarium* (1881, Port Sunlight, Lady Lever Art Gallery), shows how erotic he could be. It also displays his skill in painting marble: *Punch* called him a "marbellous artist". He had several imitators, including his wife Lady **Laura** (1852–1909) and his daughter **Anna** (died 1943), but his reputation sank on his death and has only recently revived. Almost all his paintings include an opus number in Roman numerals, the last being CCCCVIII. See vol. 3 p. **87**

Alsloot, Denys van *c.*1570–*c.*1628
Flemish painter, born and trained in Brussels. He specialized in landscapes, his earlier works owing much to the cosmic panoramas of Valkenborch, and the luxuriously wooded scenes of his later period to the influence of "Velvet" Brueghel and the Coninxloos. After 1599, he accepted commissions from Archduchess Isabella for a number of paintings of processions (examples London, V&A).

Alt, Rudolf von 1812–1905
Austrian watercolourist. After studying history painting at the Vienna Academy he travelled throughout the Austrian Empire, recording its peoples and cultures in an attractive BIEDERMEIER style characterized by fine detail and jewel-like colour. A much-loved figure in the Viennese art world, he became the first honorary president of the newly founded Vienna SEZESSION in 1897.

Altamira
Site, in northern Spain, of the first prehistoric cave-paintings to be discovered (1879). They were at first dismissed as forgeries and accepted as genuine only in the first decade of the 20th century, their date now being put at about 13000 BC. Various animals are depicted, but most famous are the bison, painted in an astonishingly vivid naturalistic manner. Only Lascaux has cave-paintings of comparable quality. See vol. 2 p. 13

Altarpiece
Picture, screen or decorated wall standing behind an altar in a Christian church. Altarpieces first appeared in the 11th century, following the liturgical change in which the clergy celebrating the mass moved from behind the altar to in front of it, but they did not become an essential part of church furnishings until the 14th century. A **reredos** is an altarpiece which rises from ground level, and a **retable** is one which stands on the back of the altar or on a pedestal behind it; sometimes a single altar has both. Reredoses take many different forms, varying with time and place, and can be of great size, splendour and complexity. Two widely differing examples in England are the magnificently pinnacled "Neville Screen" (1372–80) in Durham Cathedral, probably designed by the architect Henry Yeveley, and Graham Sutherland's tapestry of *Christ in Majesty* (finished 1962) which occupies the whole east wall of Coventry Cathedral. Although retables can also be very large and elaborate, they are usually smaller than reredoses, often take the form of paintings, and are sometimes easily portable. The exquisite late 14th-century Wilton Diptych in the National Gallery, London, was probably once a retable, and a good example of a modern retable is Sutherland's painting *Noli me tangere* (1961) in the Chapel of St Mary Magdalen in Chichester Cathedral, completely different in scale and feeling from his huge Coventry tapestry.

Altdorfer, Albrecht *c.*1480–1538
German painter and printmaker, the leading practitioner of the so-called DANUBE school. One of the most original German artists of the 16th century, his style was marked by fantasy of invention, expressively distorted figures, brilliant colours and dazzling effects of light. He mainly painted religious works, but his most important contribution to the history of art perhaps lies in his development of landscape as an independent genre; in *St George and the dragon* (1510, Munich, Alte Pinakothek) the figures are almost lost in the background of dense foliage, and in *Landscape with a footbridge* (*c.*1520, London, NG) there are no figures at all. In 1526 he was appointed town architect of Regensburg, where he spent most of his life, and although he is not known to have designed any buildings, an interest in architecture is evidenced in the elaborate and fanciful buildings which are such striking features in some of his late works (*Susannah and the Elders*, 1526, Munich, Alte Pinakothek). His extraordinarily vivid imagination was given even freer rein in his masterpiece, *The Battle of Alexander and Darius on the Issus* (1529, Munich, Alte Pinakothek), commissioned by Duke William IV of Bavaria as one of a series of classical battle scenes. In this he achieves a sense of truly cosmic drama as the two minutely depicted armies clash in a vast panorama of land, sea and sky. See vol. 1 pp. **52–53**, *53*; vol. 2 p. **156**

Altichiero da Zevio
documented 1369–84
Italian painter. He was born in Verona, but almost all his surviving work was executed in Padua, where in 1379 he completed the frescos in the chapel of S. Felice in the Basilica of S. Antonio. At about the same time he began work on the cycles of *The lives of SS Catherine, Lucy and George* in the Oratory of S. Giorgio in collaboration with an otherwise unknown artist called **Avanzo**, the extent of whose participation is uncertain. Altichiero's work is distinguished by impressively grave and weighty figures and he was the finest of Giotto's Paduan followers, although he worked much later than Giotto himself.

Alvarez y Cubero, José 1768–1827
Spain's leading NEOCLASSICAL sculptor, who was sometimes called "the Spanish Canova". Much of his career was spent in Rome, where he met Canova, who became his friend and the most important influence on his work. He was appointed director of the Madrid Academy in 1826, and his style was influential on Spanish sculpture for many subsequent years. There are examples in the Museum of Modern Art, Madrid, including *Nestor and Antilochus*, 1818.

Aman-Jean, Edmond 1860–1936
French painter, etcher and lithographer. Although he met Seurat while a student and shared a studio with him for several years, he was essentially a SYMBOLIST artist. He exhibited at the first two Salons de la Rose + Croix (1892 and 1893) and also designed the posters for them. His most characteristic works are studies of mysterious, withdrawn women, which reflect his admiration for Burne-Jones and Rossetti (*Mademoiselle Thadée C. Jacquet*, 1892, Paris, Musée d'Orsay). After about 1912 he worked in an INTIMISTE style influenced by Bonnard.

Amaravati
The greatest Buddhist site in the Andhra region—central and southern India—before its complete destruction in the 19th century. Important groups of sculpture from the site are now in the British Museum in London and the Government Museum, Madras, and together with the related sculptural survivals from the neighbouring Buddhist site of **Nagarjunakonda** provide evidence of the flourishing Andhra school of sculpture from the 1st to 3rd centuries AD. The limestone *stupa* was more highly decorated than others we know of, while both the surrounding railing and the gateways were elaborately carved. The Andhra sculptors had advanced beyond the standard stocky type of earlier Buddhist sculpture and were producing a human figure of elegant proportions and tapering limbs. They also demonstrated a sure sense of narrative, particularly in the highly organized reliefs of crowd scenes, which are the first in Indian sculpture. See vol. 3 p. 13

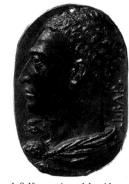

Alberti: Self-portrait medal, mid-1430s. Washington, NG, Samuel H. Kress coll.

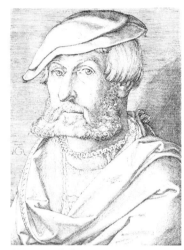

Aldegrever: Self-portrait engraving, 1537. (Mansell)

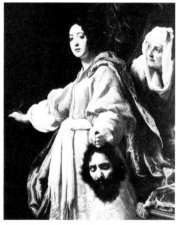

Allori, Cristofano: Self-portrait as Holofernes in *Judith with the head of Holofernes*, *c.*1615. Florence, Pitti (Scala)

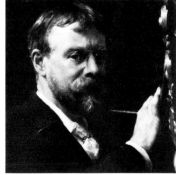

Alma-Tadema: Self-portrait (detail), *c.*1897. Florence, Uffizi (Alinari)

Amarna art
Art of the NEW KINGDOM city of El Amarna (ancient Akhen-Aten—Horizon of the Aten) founded by the Pharaoh Akhenaten (1379–1361 BC) for the cult of his personal deity, the sun god (Aten). The Pharaoh's features are well known from numerous portrait statues, for instance the 30 colossal figures made for the new temple at KARNAK (examples in Cairo, Egyptian Museum). At Amarna the traditional arrangement of scenes in registers and the canon of proportion were abandoned, and human figures in free-standing sculpture, reliefs and painting are far more naturalistic than those governed by the old rules, and are often relaxed in pose. Sunken reliefs in the tombs and temples portray a carefree courtly life with no hint of the afterworld, and the paintings in palaces and temples are invested with great freedom of movement. Though figures are distinctive (for example *Two princesses* in the Ashmolean Museum, Oxford), the country scenes are not dissimilar to those in the painted palace of King Amenhotep III at THEBES. After Akhenaten's death his buildings were destroyed by traditionalists, Amarna was abandoned and the pharaohs returned to the cult of Amun, the principal state god of the New Kingdom. Some of the finest examples of Amarna art come from the tomb of one of Akhenaten's successors, TUTANKHAMUN, having been made before the reaction had taken place. See vol. 2 p. 26

Amateur
An artist who creates works for his own pleasure as opposed to a professional, for whom making art is a livelihood. The distinction arose in Western art during the Renaissance, before which time artists were generally considered craftsmen. In Europe, amateurs have rarely been more than footnotes to the history of art, but in Chinese painting the part played by the LITERATI or amateurs has been of great importance. Painting was recognized in China as not only worthy of a scholar and gentleman, but as desirable for the cultivation and expression of his personality. Amateur artists, who painted only when they felt inspired to do so, were accorded a higher status than the professional, and some of the greatest Chinese painters were amateurs.

Amberger, Christoph *c.*1500–61/2
German painter, principally of portraits. He worked in Augsburg, a city which had strong commercial links with Italy, and Venetian influence—especially that of Titian, who met Amberger when he visited Augsburg in 1548—is apparent in much of his work. His portraits are sharp and lucid with careful attention paid to details of dress and jewellery as well as to the sitter's physiognomy (*Charles V*, *c.*1532, West Berlin, Staatliche Museen). His few religious paintings, of which the most important was the altarpiece which he painted for Augsburg Cathedral in 1554, are much less successful.

American Abstract Artists' Group
Association of artists founded in New York City in 1936 to support the cause of abstract art in America. The original nucleus consisted of Bolotowsky, Diller, Greene and G.L.K. Morris, and over 200 artists have been involved in the group, whose continuing existence is marked by sporadic exhibitions and catalogues. While most early members worked in precise styles related to NEO-PLASTICISM, more painterly elements and influences from SURREALISM and OP art have subsequently been assimilated.

Amigoni, Jacopo 1682–1752
Italian decorative painter, who worked principally outside Italy. He was born in Naples and studied in Venice, where he fell markedly under the influence of Sebastiano Ricci. He moved to Rome in about 1725, then went to Flanders and Bavaria, where he executed a spectacular series of decorations (1730) in the castle of Schleissheim. Apart from a visit to Paris in 1736, he was in England from 1730 to 1739, his best surviving works from this period being the series of paintings representing *The story of Jupiter and Io* at Moor Park, Hertfordshire. In 1739 he returned for eight years to Venice, before finally becoming court painter to Ferdinand VI at Madrid. Although his art represents the lighter and more colourful side of Venetian painting in the early 18th century, it differs from that of Ricci and Pellegrini in its careful modelling. See vol. 2 p. **235**

Amman, Jost 1539–91
Swiss printmaker. He was born in Zurich and worked briefly in Basel before settling for life in Nuremberg in 1561. His output of prints, which are more important for the historical information they convey than for their artistic quality, was huge, and he was the most prolific book illustrator of his time; one of his pupils said that the drawings he made during a period of four years would have filled a hay wagon. One painting by him is known; "*Portrait of a Wise Man*" in the Kunstmuseum, Basel.

Ammanati, Bartolommeo 1511–92
Florentine MANNERIST sculptor, famous for his huge Neptune fountain (1560–75) in the Piazza della Signoria. He beat Cellini and Giambologna, among other sculptors, in a competition for the commission. The colossal white marble statue of Neptune seems grotesquely oversized in contrast with the suave bronze figures which decorate the basin, but the work is undoubtedly impressive. As an old man he was so affected by the strictures of the Counter-Reformation that he is said to have destroyed some of his nude sculpture. He was more distinguished as an architect than as a sculptor; the graceful Ponte S. Trinita and the garden façade of the Pitti Palace are both his work.

Anamorphosis
Painting or drawing of an object distorted in such a way that the image becomes lifelike only when seen from a particular angle or by means of a special lens or mirror. It is first mentioned in the notes of Leonardo. Well-known examples are the skull in the foreground of Holbein's "*The Ambassadors*" (1533, London, NG) and a portrait of Edward VI of England of uncertain attribution (1546, London, NPG). Anamorphosis is, however, mainly a technical exercise and does not appear in many major works.

Ancients, The
Group of English Romantic artists, inspired by Blake, who were active together from about 1824 until the early 1830s. Palmer was the central figure of the group, and other leading members such as Calvert and Richmond were frequent visitors to him during his Shoreham period. They painted mainly pastoral subjects, and were particularly indebted to Blake's woodcuts to Virgil's *Eclogues* (1821), which Palmer described as "visions of little dells, and nooks, and corners of Paradise; models of the exquisitest pitch of intense poetry". Only Palmer at his best, however, matched Blake's intensity.

Andre, Carl born 1935
American sculptor. Like other MINIMAL sculptors, he conceives of art works as real rather than symbolic or metaphorical objects. In contrast to traditional free-standing sculpture, which has a vertical emphasis and is displayed on a pedestal, Andre's works are emphatically horizontal, using interchangeable units of one material—lead, copper, aluminium, steel, bricks, rocks—which are arranged on the floor or ground. In his own words his sculptures are "more like roads than buildings". His method draws attention to the material, to the site and to forces relating the two such as gravity. In 1976 there was a public outcry in England over the Tate Gallery's purchase (four years earlier) of Andre's *Equivalent VIII* (1966), which consists of 120 firebricks arranged in a rectangle two bricks deep. See vol. 3 p. **247**

Andrea da Firenze (Andrea Bonaiuti) active *c.*1343–77
Florentine painter, famous for the frescos of Dominican subject matter (begun 1365) in the chapter-house (the so-called Spanish Chapel) of S. Maria Novella. This is the most impressive cycle of its time, executed in a dignified hieratic style similar to that of Orcagna. The most famous scene is that commonly known as *The triumph of the Church*, which contains a splendid pack of dogs—*domini canes* (dogs of the Lord), a pun on Dominicans—and an imaginative view of Florence Cathedral, then uncompleted, which shows it with a dome surprisingly similar to that erected by Brunelleschi more than 50 years later.

Andrea del Castagno (Andrea di Bartolo di Bargilla) *c.*1421–57
Florentine painter, one of the leading artists of the generation following Masaccio. In 1440 he is said to have painted frescos on the façade of the Palazzo del Podestà of Florentine traitors hanged by their heels after the Battle of Anghiari, from which he earned the nickname Andreino degli Impiccati (of the hanged men). These are destroyed and his earliest extant works are frescos (1441–42) in the apse of S. Terasio presso S. Zaccaria in Venice. His greatest works are in Florence, notably the frescos on the Passion of Christ (*c.*1445–50) in the refectory of the convent of S. Apollonia, now the Castagno Museum. These combine something of the monumentality of Masaccio with the sinewy realism of Donatello, for whose style Castagno found a convincing pictorial equivalent. Later works in Florence include the equestrian fresco of *Niccolò da Tolentino* (1456), in the Cathedral, a pendant to Uccello's *Sir John Hawkwood*, and altar frescos (*c.*1445) of *St Julian* and *The vision of St Jerome* for SS. Annunziata; the *St Jerome* shows a raw emotion which stands comparison with Donatello's *Mary Magdalen*. The best of his paintings apart from frescos is probably the *David* (*c.*1448, Washington, NG), which is painted on a leather shield. Castagno's death from the plague cut short an outstanding career. According to Vasari, he murdered his friend Domenico Veneziano, and although the discovery in the 19th century that Domenico outlived him shows that this cannot be true, Castagno probably did have an irascible temperament, which comes out in the harsh vigour and intense feeling of his work. See vol. 1 p. *143*; vol. 2 p. **110**

Andrea del Sarto (Andrea d'Agnolo) 1486–1530
Florentine painter. His nickname "del Sarto" (of the tailor) derives from his father's profession. In 1518–19 he worked in France for Francis I, but apart from that was based in Florence, where by the second decade of the 16th century he was established with Fra Bartolommeo as the leading painter—Leonardo, Michelangelo and Raphael all having left the city by 1509. He was a pupil of Piero di Cosimo and Raffaellino del Garbo, but his elegantly poised classical style owed most to the example of Raphael and Fra Bartolommeo. His output consisted mainly of religious works, and included major cycles of frescos, painted at intervals throughout his career, in the cloisters of the church of SS. Annunziata and of the confraternity of the Scalzi, the latter in *grisaille*. The most famous of his altarpieces, worthy of Raphael in its grandeur and grace, is "*The Madonna of the Harpies*" (1517, Florence, Uffizi), and almost as popular is the portrait of *A young man* (*c.*1520, London, NG), which best illustrates the dreamily romantic quality of his portraits, among the most distinctive and attractive of the High Renaissance. The ease and fluency of these paintings were constant factors in Andrea's art, and although there are features in his work which can be called Mannerist, he never showed any of the neurotic tension of his pupils Pontormo and Rosso. His marvellous gifts as a draughtsman and colourist have always been admired, but his critics throughout the centuries have complained that he lacked the vigour and inventiveness that would have carried him to the highest ranks as a painter. Vasari thought that this was due to Andrea's domineering wife—Robert Browning took up the idea in a poem (1855), as did Freud's disciple Ernest Jones in his psychoanalytic study of the painter (1913). See vol. 2 p. **164**

Andrea di Bartolo *c.*1370–1428
Sienese painter, the son and pupil of Bartolo di Fredi. With his father he painted an altarpiece (lost), commissioned by the Shoemakers' Guild for Siena Cathedral in 1389. Only three signed altarpieces are extant and none is dated. In one of these, *The Madonna and Child with saints* (Siena, Pinacoteca), the figures have a plasticity derived from Taddeo di Bartolo, but the effect remains somewhat stiff and lifeless.

Andrews, Michael born 1928
British painter, best known for ambitious multifigure compositions such as *All night long* (1963–64, Melbourne, NG of Victoria). Based, like much of his work, on photographs culled from various sources, it depicts, on a large scale, an expensive and decadent night-club. Later paintings have concentrated less on the figure, dealing with themes such as a city at night or fish under water.

Angelico, Fra (Guido di Pietro) died 1455
Florentine painter, one of the most celebrated artists of the early Renaissance. He was a Dominican monk, and all his art was religious. Nothing is known of his training. He began working in an International Gothic style, but even in the gorgeously decorative *Annunciation* (Cortona, Diocesan Museum), probably dating from the late 1420s and one of his earliest known paintings, Masaccio's influence is evident in the architecture of the loggia, which has a single vanishing point. Angelico indeed, far from being the "inspired saint" of popular legend, was a very progressive artist who understood Masaccio's naturalism and his conquest of perspective better than almost any of his contemporaries. This is

particularly evident in his *Descent from the Cross* (c.1440?, Florence, S. Marco Museum), in which the solid figures are placed convincingly in a landscape setting more complex than any by Masaccio. The altarpiece had been begun by Lorenzo Monaco, and the three scenes by him in the pinnacles of the frame, although only about a decade earlier, look primitive compared to the main panel. In 1438 Angelico and his assistants began his greatest work, the decoration of his monastery of S. Marco, now a museum devoted to his work, with an extensive series of frescos. In scenes intended for meditation (many are in the monks' cells) he achieved a sense of blissful, radiant simplicity and great emotional directness. In 1445 he was summoned to Rome, where he spent most of the rest of his career working on papal commissions in the Vatican and Old St Peter's, but it is essentially on his S. Marco frescos that his great reputation and popularity rest. The name Angelico was being used of him soon after his death, but it is not known when "the blessed Angelico" was beatified, or even if the title was ever official. See vol. 1 p. 93; vol. 2 pp. 108–109

Anglo-Saxon art
General term for art produced in England from the time of the Teutonic invasions in the 5th and 6th centuries until the Norman Conquest of 1066. The largest single group of Anglo-Saxon artefacts comes from the 7th-century pagan ship-burial at Sutton Hoo. The richly-decorated jewellery found there (now in the British Museum, London) displays the love of abstract and animal ornament derived from CELTIC art, which was typical of Anglo-Saxon craftsmen. Subsequent Anglo-Saxon art is Christian. The artistic quality of the period can best be judged from illuminated manuscripts (comparatively little architecture or sculpture survives in its original condition). No single centre was of paramount importance throughout the Anglo-Saxon period, but in the late 7th and early 8th century the finest work was produced in the northern kingdom of Northumbria. The masterpiece from the time is the Lindisfarne Gospels (c.690, London, BL), famous for its extraordinary interlace ornament, stemming from the tradition of Irish illumination (see Celtic art). Later an important area for the production of manuscripts was south-east England, and there was a distinctive school, developed in the 10th century, called the Winchester school, most obviously recognizable by its bold leafy borders. See vol. 2 pp. 67, 68, 74

Anguier brothers
French sculptors, **François**, c.1604–69, and **Michel**, c.1613–86. The details of their careers before they went to Rome in about 1641 are fairly obscure. In Rome they studied with Algardi, and took a version of his moderate Baroque style back to France, François returning in 1643 and Michel in 1651, when he joined his brother in work on the Montmorency tomb (1649–52) in the Chapel of the Lycée at Moulins. Thereafter their paths largely diverged, and Michel had the more distinguished career. His two best-known works (both in Paris) are the decoration of the interior of the church of Val-de-Grâce (1662–67) and the group of *The Nativity* (1665) in St Roch.

Anguisciola, Sofonisba 1527–1625
Italian painter, born in Cremona. She attracted considerable attention during her lifetime as a portraitist (Philip II of Spain invited her to Madrid in 1559 and

van Dyck visited her in Genoa in 1623), but more on account of her curiosity value as a woman artist than for the quality of her work, which is rather stiff. Her best paintings are those of herself and her family; she had five sisters who were also painters, but they are all very obscure figures.

Angus, Rita 1908–70
New Zealand painter. Her portraits and regional landscapes, in oil and watercolour, are tightly organized and boldly painted in bright, clear colours. With Woollaston, she was the dominant figure in New Zealand art of the 1940s, and forthright works such as *Mrs Betty Curnow* (1942, Auckland City Art Gallery) helped to establish a local style.

Anker, Albert 1831–1910
Swiss Realist painter of peasant village life. He frequently exhibited at the Paris Salon, and received a gold medal in 1866. His peasant scenes are notable for their high local colour and realistic feeling for rough textures, but his sentimental notions of beauty and the ideal of country life have caused them to fall out of favour; his late still lifes are now generally considered to be his most successful works. There are examples of his work in the Kunstmuseum, Basel.

An Kyon 1418–94
Korean landscape painter of the Yi Dynasty. His life is little known but as a court painter he was a close friend of the Prince An Pyong (1418–53), his patron, and painted for him the famous *Dream of the peach-blossom garden* (now in Japan, Nara, University Library) in a complex and fantastic Northern Song style. Clearly he had studied the Chinese masterpieces in the Prince's collection. Most of his work is now in the National Museum of Korea in Seoul. See vol. 3 p. 43

Annigoni, Pietro born 1910
Italian painter. He has executed frescos in Italian churches and has had ambitions as a painter of grand allegorical scenes, but since about 1950 it is as a portraitist that he has gained an international reputation. His many sitters including President John F. Kennedy and several members of the British royal family. His painting, modelled in style and technique on the masters of the Italian Renaissance, has probably aroused as much ridicule as praise, but he is undoubtedly one of the few living artists who is well known to, and liked by, the general public. In 1970 the National Portrait Gallery in London, which now owns the painting, exhibited one of his portraits of Queen Elizabeth II, painted in 1969, to huge crowds.

Anquetin, Louis 1861–1932
French painter, a friend of van Gogh and Toulouse-Lautrec. When Seurat's *Grande Jatte* was exhibited in 1886, he began to experiment with Pointillism and in the following year he was involved with Bernard in the development of CLOISONNISME (*The street, five o'clock in the evening*, 1887, Hartford, Wadsworth Atheneum). He was seen by some contemporaries as the major pioneer of the style, but Gauguin strongly denied that he had been influenced by him.

Anselmi, Michelangelo c.1492–1556
Italian painter, born in Tuscany, perhaps in Siena, of a Parmesan family. He settled permanently in Parma in about 1520 and his early style was based on Correggio and refined by contact with the Sienese Mannerists, Sodoma and

Beccafumi. His mature works reveal the influence of Parmigianino (*The baptism of Christ*, c.1530, Reggio Emilio, S. Prospero), and it was he who was chosen to execute the frescos in the apse of the church of the Steccata, a commission on which Parmigianino had defaulted.

Antelami, Benedetto
active late 12th century
Italian sculptor of the late Romanesque period. His earliest known work is the low-relief *Deposition from the Cross* (1178) in Parma Cathedral, which he signed. The largest ensemble of his sculpture (executed with assistance) adorns the baptistery at Parma (begun around 1196), an octagonal arcaded structure, of which he may also have been the architect. Solemn figures showing the influence of classical sculpture inhabit the friezes and tympana, and southern French features also appear. Antelami was the most notable Italian sculptor before Nicola Pisano and had wide influence in Italy. See vol. 1 p. 42

Antenor active c.540–500 BC
Greek sculptor from Athens, famed for his bronze group of the tyrannicides Harmodios and Aristogeiton (lost), which was carried off to Persia by Xerxes in 480 BC. A massive marble *Kore* found on the Acropolis has been identified as his work by its inscription, and the solid monumental style of the female figures of the east pediment of the temple of Apollo at Delphi suggests it may be by him.

Antes, Horst born 1936
West German figurative painter, with roots in the EXPRESSIONIST tradition. He is most famous for his large close-up profile views of "gnome" people, which depict semi-human archetypes, reminiscent of African or Oceanic sculpture. Nearly all his work, in fact, has a sculptural quality, but this is combined with the use of bright, non-naturalistic colours, often in rainbow-like stripes (*Figure with animal mask*, 1962, Rotterdam, Boymans-van Beuningen).

Anthonisz., Cornelis c.1499–1556
Netherlandish painter and engraver. He is best known for his formal group portraits, notably *The civic guard* (1533, Amsterdam, Historical Museum), one of the earliest examples of the type later made famous by Hals. He was also a cartographer, and in 1544 made a large map of Amsterdam, his native city.

Antico, L' (Pier Jacopo Alari Bonacolsi) c.1460–1528
North Italian sculptor, medallist and restorer of classical bronze sculpture, chiefly patronized by the Dukes of Mantua and Isabella d'Este. His name derived from his antique-style statuettes, produced in response to a growing taste for antique sculpture. The best-known example of his work, the bronze *Apollo* with gilt hair and cloak (1497–98, Venice, Ca d'Oro) was based on "*The Apollo Belvedere*", which he studied in Rome in 1497.

Antique, the
The physical remains of the ancient world, or, as the expression is usually more particularly understood in art historical usage, of Greek and Roman sculpture. The veneration of classical statuary as the standard by which the representation of the human figure should be judged is chiefly associated with the RENAISSANCE and NEOCLASSICAL periods, but its influence has been a recurring feature throughout the entire history of Western art.

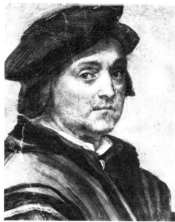

Andrea del Sarto: Self-portrait, 1528–30. Florence, Uffizi (Mansell)

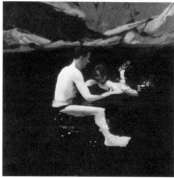

Andrews: *Melanie and me swimming*, 1978–79. London, Tate

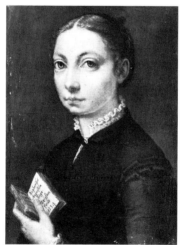

Anguisciola: Self-portrait, 1554. Vienna, Kunsthistorisches Museum

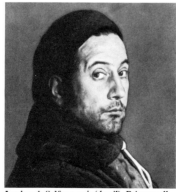

Annigoni: Self-portrait (detail). Private coll. (Alinari)

Antolínez, José 1635–75
Spanish painter, active in Madrid. He worked in a rather agitated style distinguished by bright but delicate colouring, and specialized in paintings of the Immaculate Conception, which account for about a third of his known output. The ecstasy of Mary Magdalen was another favourite theme with him, and there are examples of both subjects in the Prado, Madrid.

Antonello da Messina *c.*1430–79
Italian painter, the only major artist of the 15th century to come from Sicily. Vasari said he was trained by Jan van Eyck and brought the latter's technique to Italy. This is untrue, but he was an accomplished master of oil-painting and helped to popularize the medium in Italy. There is no evidence to suggest he ever visited Flanders, but a reliable 16th-century source says he trained in Naples, and there he could have seen paintings by Jan van Eyck and Rogier van der Weyden. He is first recorded, in Messina, in 1456, and the earliest date on any of his paintings is 1465 on the *Salvador mundi* (London, NG), which is based on Flemish models. In 1475–76 he visited Venice and painted a large altarpiece for S. Cassiano, of which two fragments survive (Vienna, Kunsthistorisches). Vasari's tale of Giovanni Bellini's clandestine visit to Antonello's studio to learn the "secret" of oil-painting is as apocryphal as the story of his training in Flanders, but Antonello certainly influenced Giovanni's technique. His striking combination of Italian amplitude of form and Flemish precision of detail is perhaps best seen in his bust-length portraits, of which there are particularly fine examples in the Louvre, Paris, and the National Gallery, London. The latter has been considered a self-portrait. See vol. 1 p. *145*; vol. 2 pp. **122–123**

Antunez, Nemisio born 1918
Chilean painter, who works in a style recalling Surrealism and Metaphysical Painting. He has worked in the USA and France as well as Chile, and his best-known painting is probably the large mural *The heart of the Andes* (completed 1966) in the United Nations building in New York. He was exiled from Chile after the military coup of 1973.

Antwerp Mannerists
Term applied to a group of mainly anonymous artists working in Antwerp in the early 16th century. During this period, when Antwerp superseded Bruges as the principal centre of artistic activity in the Low Countries, Flemish art was dominated by the influx of Italianate motifs, brought back by painters from their travels in the south. The trend was initiated by Gossaert's trip to Rome in 1508 and was marked by a number of distinctive features: tall, slender figures and a new interest in the nude; a tendency to violent movement and exaggerated gestures; a profusion of half-understood Renaissance motifs, such as friezes, fragments of classical architecture, statuary and *putti*; a preference for obscure subjects or, more frequently, for familiar themes shown from an unusual viewpoint—in particular with religious paintings where the nominal subject was overshadowed by genre scenes, still lifes or landscapes. The work of the Antwerp Mannerists had little in common with Italian Mannerism.

Apelles active 4th century BC
Greek painter, from Colophon in Asia Minor. He was esteemed the greatest painter of the ancient world, and although no work survives, detailed and enthusiastic accounts by classical authors have aroused the curiosity of later ages. Descriptions of his allegorical painting of *Calumny*, for example, inspired the emulation of Renaissance artists, including Botticelli (painting in the Uffizi, Florence) and Mantegna (drawing in the British Museum, London), and accounts of his most famous painting, "*Aphrodite Anadyomene*", which showed the goddess wringing from her hair the water of the sea from which she has just risen, lie behind Titian's painting of the subject (Edinburgh, NG, on loan from the Earl of Ellesmere). As court painter to Philip of Macedon and his son, Alexander the Great, Apelles executed a series of portraits of Alexander and is reputed to have been the only painter for whom the latter would consent to sit. He was famed above all for his grace, and has been thought of as the Raphael of the ancient world. See vol. 2 pp. **44–45**

Apollinaire, Guillaume 1880–1918
French writer and critic, who exercised an important influence on avantgarde poets and painters in the early 20th century. Born in Rome of Polish and Italian parentage (his real name was Wilhelm Apollinaris de Kostrowitsky), he had settled in Paris by 1902. One of his initial friendships there was with Picasso, whose early Symbolist work provoked Apollinaire's first important art criticism. By 1913, when he published *The Cubist Painters*, he was at the forefront of the Parisian avantgarde and an influential champion of Cubism, Futurism and Orphism. He coined the term SURREALISM in the preface to his play *The Breasts of Tiresias* (1917), and his writings were also a profound influence upon this movement, especially in their emphasis on fantasy and eroticism.

Apollodoros see ZEUXIS

Apollonios active 2nd century BC
Greek sculptor from Athens, whose signature appears on the broken marble torso of a male nude known as "*The Belvedere Torso*" (Vatican Museum). Opinion is divided as to whether this powerful Hellenistic work is an original or a Roman copy, but until the early 19th century it was admired as one of the greatest works of antique art, and influenced Michelangelo and many other artists. The date of its discovery is unrecorded, but it was well known by the end of the 15th century. It has been claimed that the bronze statue of a *Boxer* in the Terme Museum, Rome, which has stylistic similarities to the torso, also bears Apollonios' signature. See vol. 2 p. *46*

Appel, Karel born 1921
Dutch abstract painter. In 1948 he was a co-founder of the Reflex group, which opposed geometric abstraction and in Paris became COBRA. He moved to Paris in 1950, but more recently has lived in New York where he has continued his career as a painter, sculptor and graphic artist. His work is known for its strident colour and violent drawing in which human and animal forms may be discerned (*Cry of liberty*, 1948, Amsterdam, Stedelijk). His series of nudes of 1962–63 show the influence of De Kooning. Appel's coloured sculptures in metal are three-dimensional transformations of his paintings. See vol. 3 p. **225**

Apt, Ulrich the Elder died 1532
German painter, recorded in Augsburg from 1481, the most notable of a family of painters. In 1516 he executed a series of wall-paintings in the Augsburg Town Hall with Breu, but otherwise is best known as a painter of altarpieces, of which the *Adoration of the Magi* (1510, Paris, Louvre) is a good example.

Aqa Mirak, Sayyid Jalal al Din, al-Hasani of Isfahan active 1530–50
Persian painter, working in Tabriz, an intimate of Shah Tahmasp. He was one of several artists who signed miniatures in the magnificent *Khamseh* of 1539–43 in the British Library, London. A pupil of Bihzad, or possibly Shaykh Zadeh, Aqa Mirak shows Bihzadian influence in the clarity of his compositions. His figures, sometimes square-jawed and bearded, have a stately grace, and his background rocks are especially limpid. See vol. 3 p. *27*

Aqa Riza ibn Ali Azgnar al Kashani see RIZA ABBASI

Aquarelle
The French term for watercolour, also used in English to describe the purest form of the technique, chiefly associated with 18th-century British painters, in which no ink or body colour is used.

Aquatint
Process of INTAGLIO printing which gives finely granulated tonal areas in monochrome or colour. A metal plate is powdered with acid-resisting resin, fused by heating, and is then placed in a bath of acid which bites between the resin particles to produce an evenly pitted surface. The longer the acid works on the plate, the darker the grey on printing. The design is drawn, and tones are varied, by brushing the plate with varnish, a process known as stopping out. The aquatint, frequently combined with linear etching, was perfected by the second half of the 18th century and has been used notably by Goya, Degas and Camille Pissarro. See vol. 1 p. 167

Arabesque
Linear decoration based on scrolling plant forms. It dates back at least to Hellenistic art, and in a more stylized form was a common feature in Islamic art. In Renaissance arabesque ornament, figures were often interwoven with the plant forms. See vol. 3 p. 23

Arakawa, Shusaku born 1936
Japanese artist, who has lived in New York since 1961. His output has been very varied, and has included Happenings and films, but he is probably best known for his series of paintings known as *Diagram*, begun in 1963. This explored the relationship between pictorial images and verbal signs by juxtaposing silhouettes of objects such as tennis rackets and combs with words corresponding to them.

Arcangelo di Cola da Camerino
*c.*1390–1429
Italian INTERNATIONAL GOTHIC painter from the Marches. He visited Florence in 1420 and in 1422 went to Rome to paint for Pope Martin V. The diptych in the Frick Collection, New York, is a fine example of his unemotional religious images, his decorative colour and pattern and delicately-painted faces. He probably assisted Gentile da Fabriano, who markedly influenced his style.

Archaic art
Term applied to the artistic products of Greek civilization from the second half the 7th century until the first quarter of the 5th century BC. In sculpture this period marks the evolution of life-size stone figures (which were not produced before the mid-7th century) from the hieratic poses borrowed from Egyptian and Mesopotamian art through many formal developments of great beauty to the fluent naturalism of the early classical period (see KOUROS). In vase-painting the human figure replaced animal subjects as the principal means of expression and the RED-FIGURE technique took over from BLACK-FIGURE. Corinth, an important early centre of Archaic art, declined in the 6th century and during most of the period the most significant developments were taking place in Athens. See vol. 2 pp. 34–35

Archipenko, Alexander 1887–1964
Russian-born sculptor, who became an American citizen in 1928. He was one of the most independent and original of modern sculptors, working in a variety of styles and techniques. He moved to Paris in 1908 and was involved in the Cubist movement, developing a kind of sculpture in which he greatly simplified the forms of the human body and pared parts of it away completely to create contrasts of void and solid (*Walking woman*, 1912, Denver Art Museum). At about the same time he invented "sculpto-painting" in which wooden and metal elements project from the background as continuations of the forms painted on it, as in *The bather* (1915, Philadelphia Museum of Art). He also used colour in his sculptures in a novel way (*Medrano II*, New York, Guggenheim). His later work, which included some realistic portraits (*Wilhelm Furtwängler*, 1927, Darmstadt, Landesmuseum), was less influential, but constantly inventive. See vol. 3 p. **178**

Arcimboldo, Giuseppe 1527–93
Italian painter. He was born in Milan and was active there as a designer of tapestries and stained glass until 1562, when he went to Prague to be court painter to the Emperor Ferdinand I and later Rudolf II until 1587. He is famous for his bizarre compositions of flowers, fruits, vegetables (and sometimes inorganic objects) arranged to resemble human forms, as for example in the series of heads representing *The Seasons* (1563, Vienna, Kunsthistorisches), in which *Summer* is composed largely of ripe fruits, *Winter* of a gnarled old tree stump, and so on.

Ardizzone, Edward 1900–79
British artist, born in China. He is best known for children's books which he wrote and illustrated, though he illustrated works by many other authors. He was happiest when portraying rural or domestic scenes evoking a cosy, English way of life. During World War II, however, he worked as a war artist, and *On a fortified island, the night watch* (1941, London, Tate) shows his treatment of a very different kind of subject.

Arman (Armand Fernandez)
born 1928
French-born artist, who gained American nationality in 1972. Between 1947 and 1953 he studied Zen Buddhism and astrology, and was a judo instructor in 1951. In 1967 he worked as a designer for the Renault car company. He is a highly inventive assemblage artist in the tradition of Schwitters, using junk and parts of dismantled objects to give the familiar a shock effect.

Armature
Skeletal framework, usually of metal, which serves as an interior support for a sculpture in plaster, clay, wax or any

other soft material incapable of supporting itself. The term is also used for the iron framework of windows to which panels of stained glass are attached. See vol. 1 p. 184

Armitage, Kenneth born 1916
British sculptor. His initial interest in carving was replaced by modelling—a more appropriate technique for the spindly shapes of his human figures in works such as *People in the wind* (1950, London, Tate). His drawing exploits strong contrasts between the blackness of charcoal and the whiteness of paper, and since the late 1960s these graphic effects have often been incorporated in his sculpture.

Armory Show
Art exhibition, more correctly known as the International Exhibition of Modern Art, shown at the Armory of the 69th Regiment, New York, from 17 February to 15 March, 1913. It was organized by a group of artists calling themselves the Association of American Painters and Sculptors, who intended to rival the National Academy of Design and wished to promote new developments in American art. Smaller versions of the exhibition were shown at the Art Institute of Chicago and Copley Hall, Boston. In all it was seen by about 30,000 people. About one third of the works shown were foreign, and this European section was intended to demonstrate the evolution of modern art. It included works by Goya, Ingres, Delacroix, Corot, Courbet, the Symbolists, Impressionists, Post-Impressionists and Neo-Impressionists. Although Kirchner and Kandinsky were included, the French dominated the selection of contemporary art. The modern works shown, particularly Duchamp's *Nude descending a staircase* (1912, Philadelphia, Museum of Art), aroused hostile criticism, but the exhibition stimulated American painters to revise their attitudes to art and challenged the tradition of representational painting in the USA. See vol. 3 p. 204

Arnolfo di Cambio c. 1245–1302?
Pisan sculptor and architect, first documented in 1265 in Siena as the assistant of Nicola Pisano, whose heroic style he continued. By 1277 he was in Rome, where he was employed on tombs for cardinals and popes, and designed the splendid *ciboria* (altar canopies) for S. Paolo fuori le Mura (1285) and S. Cecilia in Trastevere (1293), which are GOTHIC in form, showing an awareness of French architectural detail. His most important tomb to survive in anything like its original condition is that of Cardinal de Braye (died 1282) in S. Domenico, Orvieto, which set the style for wall tombs for over a century. The lower part is mainly intact, and even retains traces of its original colour. In a document of 1300 he is named as the architect of Florence Cathedral, which had been begun in 1294, and he also worked on sculpture for a now destroyed façade. Most of the surviving figures are in the Cathedral museum, but there are others elsewhere, including an *Annunciatory angel* in the Fogg Art Museum, Cambridge, Mass. The famous bronze statue of *St Peter* in St Peter's, Rome, is attributed to Arnolfo, and a work certainly by him, the antique-inspired *Charles of Anjou* (Rome, Capitoline) is remarkable as one of the earliest modern portrait statues. Both as sculptor and architect (Vasari connects him with the design of other Florentine buildings, including S. Croce and the Palazzo

Vecchio) he is one of the most important Italian Gothic artists. See vol. 2 p. 81

Arosenius, Ivar 1878–1909
Swedish painter and draughtsman. He is best known for his small watercolours, influenced by English *fin-de-siècle* art and full of delicate, wistful feeling. Oriental fantasies, fairy-tales and indoor scenes of his daughter and wife were among his favourite subjects. He also executed imaginative and delightfully decorative book illustrations.

Arp, Jean or **Hans** 1887–1966
French artist, active in several fields but principally famous as one of the greatest of abstract sculptors. In 1915, in collaboration with his future wife Sophie Taeuber, he experimented with collages and cut-paper reliefs, as in *Square arranged according to the laws of chance* (1916–17, New York, MOMA). He was involved in 1916 in the formation of the original Dada group in Zurich, and turned in the following year from geometric abstract painting to a more formal language which he used in drawings, woodcuts and wooden relief constructions painted in bright colours, such as *Navel, shirt and head* (1926, Basel, Kunstmuseum). In 1920 he settled in Paris, where he was associated both with Surrealism and with the Abstraction-Création group. He began to make sculptures in 1930, extending the possibilities of Brancusi's reductive simplifications to create sensual forms, ambiguously evoking human anatomy, stones and fruit, which for him distilled the organic essence of life (*Hybrid fruit called pagoda*, 1934, London, Tate). See vol. 1 p. 112; vol. 3 pp. 166, 181

Arpino, Il Cavaliere d' (Giuseppe Cesari) 1568–1640
Italian MANNERIST painter. Most of his life was spent in Rome, where he was highly favoured by successive popes with decorative commissions, notably the designing of the mosaics in the dome of St Peter's (1603–12). His early style was bold and richly coloured (fresco cycle in Cappella Olgiati, S. Prassede, 1592–95) but he became increasingly hollow and facile. He ignored the innovations of the Carracci and Caravaggio (his one-time assistant), and his style was outdated by the time of his death.

Arriccio or **Arricciato** see FRESCO

Art Autre see INFORMAL ART

Art Brut see DUBUFFET

Arte Povera
Term coined by the Italian art critic Germano Celant to unite the diverse forms of Conceptual art and Land art which began to appear in Europe and the USA in the 1960s. He tried to promote the notion that the use of materials such as soil would undermine the commercialism of the art world.

Arthois, Jacques d' 1613–86
Flemish landscape painter. He was active in Brussels and specialized in woodland scenes, often large in scale. His style is similar to Coninxloo's, but freer and more naturalistic, and the figures in his paintings are often the work of other artists, notably Teniers the Younger. Arthois was prolific and successful, but he had an unstable character and died in poverty. His brother **Nicolas** and his son **Jean-Baptiste**, the dates of both of whom are uncertain, painted in a style indistinguishable from that of Jacques.

Art-Language
Loosely-knit British group who, from the late 1960s onwards, have operated in an area between art theory and art practice. Their work has taken the form of verbal discussion, principally in their journal *Art-Language*, first published in 1969, and collective exhibitions. The scope of their enquiries is deliberately open-ended and defies any brief summary, but they have made use of the disciplines of linguistic philosophy and sociology in an attempt to define art, recognizing that the number of activities which have been described as such is bewilderingly varied. Although much of their work is Marxist in orientation, they have rejected the argument made by some left-wing critics and artists that art should take the form of an immediately accessible political statement. Indeed, the most frequent charge made against their work is its incomprehensibility.

Art Nouveau
Decorative style which influenced all areas of design in the 1890s and was popular until World War I, during which period many architects and designers were concerned to create a "new style" appropriate to their era. Art Nouveau is a term with international currency, but the style is also known as *Jugendstil* in Germany, *Modernista* in Spain, *Sezessionstil* in Austria, *Stile Liberty* in Italy and sometimes as *Style Moderne* in France. The style comprised two main currents, each deriving some inspiration from the English ARTS AND CRAFTS movement. On the one hand, a preference for asymmetry, linearity and flowing organic structure characterized the work of furniture makers, of jewellery and glass designers, such as the American Louis C. Tiffany, and of graphic artists such as Beardsley and Mucha. The architectural style of, for example, the Belgian Victor Horta and the Spaniard Antonio Gaudí also belonged to this tendency. Others meanwhile developed a more austere style, whose geometric simplicity foreshadowed progressive developments in the 20th century, as in the buildings, furniture and decorative designs of the Scottish architect Charles Rennie Mackintosh. Art Nouveau was principally manifested in architecture and the applied arts, but its influence can be seen in the work of many painters and sculptors. See vol. 3 p. 121

Arts and crafts movement
Decorative arts movement in England in the second half of the 19th century, the name deriving from the Arts and Crafts Exhibition Society founded in 1888. The intention was to reassert the worth of the handmade individual object in the face of increasing industrialization and mass-production. The ideas of John Ruskin and the architect Augustus Welby Pugin formed a basis for the movement, but it was left chiefly to William Morris, who like them wished to revive the medieval guild system, to transform their ideas into artistic activity. Arts and crafts designers worked in various styles but in general they tried to produce objects which were both functional and decorative. The movement had links with ART NOUVEAU and had some influence on the BAUHAUS.

Arundel, Thomas Howard 2nd Earl of 1586–1646
English collector and patron. A leading figure at the court of Charles I, he was the first Englishman who combined a passionate interest in the arts with a knowledge of European and antique

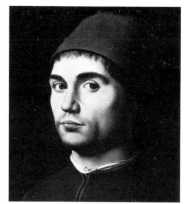

Antonello da Messina: Self-portrait? (detail), c.1475. London, NG

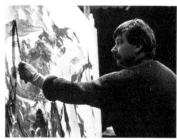

Appel: Photograph (courtesy of the Royal Netherlands Embassy)

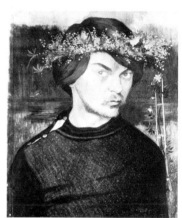

Arosenius: Self-portrait watercolour, 1906. Stockholm, Nationalmuseum

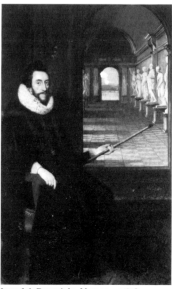

Arundel: Portrait by Mytens, c.1618. London, NPG

civilization. He travelled abroad several times, most notably to Italy in 1613–15 with Inigo Jones, with whom he carried out archaeological investigations in Rome. In 1636 he met Hollar in Cologne and was responsible for bringing him to England. Rubens and van Dyck were among the artists he patronized (both did portraits of him, as did Hollar) and he brought together an art collection second in England only to Charles I's. Much of his classical sculpture is in the Ashmolean Museum, Oxford.

Asam brothers
Bavarian artist-architects and decorators, who introduced a highly individual form of the Roman Baroque to south Germany. **Cosmas Damian** (1686–1739) was chiefly a fresco painter, whilst **Egid Quirin** (1692–1750) specialized in sculpture and stucco. Both practised as architects. They studied in Rome from 1711 to 1714, and were profoundly influenced by Bernini and Pozzo. Cosmas Damian painted vivid semi-illusionistic frescos in churches and palaces from Baden to Bohemia, and Egid Quirin sculpted the remarkable *Assumption* in the monastery church at Rohr (1722), but their greatest achievements were collaborative—the spectacular and dramatically-lit churches of Weltenburg (1716–21) and St John Nepomuk, Munich (1733–46). The latter is attached to their own house, and is known as the "Asamkirche" as they themselves paid for it. See vol. 2 p. **241**

Ascription see ATTRIBUTION

Ashcan school
Group of American urban realist painters active from about 1908 until World War I. It included five members of The EIGHT— Glackens, Henri, Luks, Shinn and Sloan—who were united by their rejection of officially approved styles and subject matter, and felt a desire to paint American life and to be recognized as specifically American painters. Other artists associated with the Ashcan school include Bellows, Coleman, Davies, Du Bois, Hopper and Maurer. Inspired by their leader, Henri, they followed the socially orientated tradition of Goya and Daumier and were influenced by the technique of Manet, painting in a subdued palette with broad, rapid brushstrokes. Their paintings, such as Bellows' *City dwellers* (1913, Los Angeles County Museum of Art), were concerned with the life of slum dwellers, ethnic groups and outcasts. Although identified as reformers and radicals, they usually avoided serious issues in their work, concentrating on the picturesqueness of their subject. See vol. 3 p. **204**

Aspertini, Amico *c.*1475–1552
Italian painter. He was born in Bologna and studied under Francia. His output included frescos (cycle in the Church of S. Frediano, Lucca, 1507–09), façade decorations and altarpieces, painted in a complex and eclectic Mannerist style, sometimes enlivened by bizarre touches of invention. His sketchbooks (London, BM) of drawings after classical remains (he was in Rome 1500–03) record contemporary knowledge of the Antique.

Asselyn, Jan *c.*1615–52
Dutch painter of landscapes and animals, nicknamed "Crabbetje" (little crab) because of his deformed hand. He spent about a decade in Italy in the 1630s and 1640s and was one of the most distinguished members of the second generation of Italianate landscape painters. His style was based on Claude, and is particularly marked by warm glowing effects of light. The best-known painting by Asselyn is not a landscape, however, but the celebrated *Threatened swan* (Amsterdam, Rijksmuseum), which has been interpreted as an allegory in defence of Dutch nationalism. Rembrandt was Asselyn's friend.

Assemblage
Term coined by Dubuffet in the 1950s to describe works of art constructed from everyday objects. The term may refer to both three-dimensional and planar constructions and thus includes COLLAGE. See vol. 1 pp. 154–155, 192–193

Assisi
Town in Umbria, the birthplace of St Francis (*c.*1181–1226), the church dedicated to whom contains some of the most important and problematic paintings in the history of Italian art. S. Francesco (begun 1228, consecrated 1253) has a crypt-like lower structure as well as an upper building. In the Lower Church are frescos by Pietro Lorenzetti, Simone Martini and others. The Upper Church contains various series of disputed attribution. Those in the apse and transepts are usually given to Cimabue, and may date from about 1280. There are two outstanding cycles in the nave, probably dating from the 1290s and usually given to two artists named from the subject matter, "the Isaac Master" and "the Master of St Francis". The latter of these is often (but controversially) identified with Giotto, on the grounds that the frescos are too good and too innovative to be by anyone else. The questions relating to the dating and attribution of the nave frescos in the Upper Church—"the Assisi problem"—are among the most discussed in the history of art. See vol. 2 pp. 78, 82

Assyrian art
Art of the upper Tigris valley region, from its emergence as an independent state (early 2nd millennium BC) to its zenith in the Neo-Assyrian period (*c.*883–612 BC). The major artistic expression of the Neo-Assyrians and their great invention was the narrative relief. Sculpted on limestone slabs forming a dado 2–3 m (6–10 ft) high, these are found around state rooms and courtyards in the palaces at Nimrud, Khorsabad and Nineveh. The subject matter centres on the king, shown many times on military campaign or hunting lions, bulls and other game in royal parks. Generally the reliefs have a static and repetitive quality not overcome until the great series of *Lion Hunt* reliefs from Assurbanipal's palace at Nineveh (London, BM) which date to the mid-7th century BC. *Lamassu* (composite man/beast demons) were carved in high relief and set in pairs to guard the great arched doors of the palaces. In the provincial capitals wall-paintings replaced reliefs, but with the same designs and purpose, namely to impress the viewer with the relentless power of the Assyrian Empire. Victory stelae, such as the well-known Black Obelisk of Shalmaneser III (BM) have the same aim. The famous Nimrud Ivories (Baghdad Museum and BM), used as decorative panels, were largely the product of Levantine craftsmen, of whom some were possibly Assyrian slaves, but an indigenous "school" of Assyrian ivory working technique is also recognized (see PHOENICIAN art). See vol. 2 pp. 30–31

Ast, Balthasar van der
1593/94–1657
Dutch still-life painter, brother-in-law to Ambrosius Bosschaert the Elder, and second only to him in the Bosschaert dynasty of flower and fruit painters. He was born at Middelburg and trained there under Bosschaert after his parents' death in 1609. He joined the Utrecht Guild of Painters in 1619 and settled in Delft in 1632. Van der Ast widened the Bosschaert range of compositions and was especially skilled in combining flowers, fruits, shells, and attendant creatures in one work (*Fruit and flowers*, Pasadena, Norton Simon Foundation). Some of his paintings are composed exclusively of shells. At Utrecht, he had as a young pupil Jan Davidz. de Heem, the great master of the next generation of still-life painters.

Atelier
French term for an artist's studio or workshop. The "**ateliers libres**" were informal academies which developed in the 19th century at which a model was provided but no teaching. They were much frequented by avantgarde artists. Gleyre's atelier was used as a meeting-place by the young Monet, Renoir and Sisley, and there is a vivid description of its casual mode of operation in George Du Maurier's novel *Trilby* (1894).

Athenodoros see PERGAMENE SCHOOL

Atlan, Jean 1913–60
French painter and poet born in Algeria, a Berber and an Orthodox Jew. He studied philosophy in Paris, 1930–1934. In 1944 he gave his first exhibition in Paris, and every painting was bought by Gertrude Stein. After World War II he was involved with the COBRA group of painters, and in 1950 settled in Paris. He was a painter of highly expressive symbolic and abstract canvases.

Atlas see CARYATID

Attribution
The assigning to an artist of a work whose authorship cannot be positively established. Attributions are made on various grounds (documentary evidence is often suggestive rather than conclusive), but usually depend on stylistic comparison with works whose authorship is beyond doubt or at least generally accepted. **Ascription** is often used interchangeably with "attribution", but it has been reasonably suggested that it should be employed to imply a greater degree of doubt or to designate an old attribution which is not firmly accepted but to which no one has provided a better alternative. An autograph work is not one which is signed, but one which is considered to be entirely in the artist's own hand. "Studio" or "workshop of", "school of" and "circle of" generally suggest progressively less involvement from the artist named (he may himself have physically contributed in the first case), but they all imply a degree of direct contact with him. "Follower of" and "imitator of" may be of any date. The word "after" is used to designate a copy, of any date, of a known work of the artist named.

Aubertin, Bernard born 1934
French painter. He began as a painter of realist canvases in the 1940s, but in 1957 met Yves Klein, and under his influence produced a series of abstract monochromes with heavily impastoed surfaces, made with instruments such as spoons and combs. Later he inserted nails, screws and matches into the support. Following the example of Klein, he also began to set fire to his works, hoping thereby to free the onlooker from too heavy a reliance on the materiality of art.

Audran, Claude III 1658–1734
French draughtsman and decorative painter, the outstanding member of a family of several generations of artists. Like Gillot, he transformed the arabesque style of Bérain into an elegant Rococo idiom. His decorations are mainly destroyed, but they are known through his drawings, a large collection of which is in the National Museum at Stockholm. He was made Keeper of the Luxembourg in 1704 and introduced his pupil Watteau to Rubens' *Marie de Médicis* cycle, which was housed there.

Audubon, John James 1784–1851
American naturalist and artist, famous for his book *The Birds of America*. He was born in the West Indies and brought up in France, where he briefly studied drawing in the studio of J.-L. David. In 1803 he went to America, where he worked as a naturalist and taxidermist and also painted portraits and gave drawing lessons. His interest in ornithology dominated his life, however, and by 1820 he had begun to make a comprehensive record of all the bird species of North America. Unable to find a publisher in America, he came to England in 1826, and between 1827 and 1838 the London firm of Havell & Son issued his great work in large folio volumes of hand-coloured aquatints. When this huge venture was completed, Audubon embarked on *The Viviparous Quadrupeds of North America*, which was completed after his death by his sons. Audubon's drawings, many of which are in the New York Historical Society, combine superb draughtsmanship, pure colour and lively observation with scientific accuracy, and his *The Birds of America* is today rightly considered one of the most beautiful and valuable of all illustrated books.

Auerbach, Frank born 1931
British painter, born in Berlin. He was in England by 1939 and trained under Bomberg, a major influence. His painting has always been figurative but is characterized by the use of very thick oil-paint which sometimes obscures the legibility of the subject. Early paintings such as *E.O.W. Nude* (1953–54, London, Tate), tend to be in restricted, earthy colours and the build-up of paint is almost sculptural. From the early 1960s the colour has become brighter, although still anti-naturalistic, and the subject defined through bold linear strokes. As well as figures and portraits, a frequent theme has been the building site. He has also made powerful drawings in charcoal and chalk, usually of the head, the result of an obsessive process of addition and erasure. See vol. 3 p. **251**

Ault, George Copeland 1891–1948
American painter, best known for his paintings of nocturnal scenes. He was one of the most individual painters of the PRECISIONIST movement, adding mystery and poetry to the geometric sharpness of the style in his melancholy paintings of New York at night.

Australian Aboriginal art
The art of the original inhabitants of Australia, whose artistic tradition now survives only in a few areas. The Aboriginals were a nomadic hunting and gathering people of simple material culture. Their most elaborate artistic works were usually for religious ceremonies, to symbolize mythical characters and events which related their communities to the land and its natural species. Regional styles varied from naturalistic to highly stylized or abstract representa-

tions of these themes, employing painting on rocks, on the ground, on bark or wood, and on the human body, and engraving and sculpture in some areas. See vol. 2 p. 23

Automatism
Method of producing works without conscious intention regarding the appearance of the end product. The resulting arbitrary and uncontrolled effects have been exploited most notably by the SURREALISTS and by some ABSTRACT EXPRESSIONISTS.

Automatistes, Les
Radical circle of Canadian abstract painters who first exhibited in New York, Paris and Montreal in 1946. Led by Borduas and Riopelle, they practised the SURREALIST technique of AUTOMATIC painting and conclusively freed Canadian painting from its reliance on objective subject matter. The tone and content of Borduas' manifesto, *Universal Refusal* (1948), reveal his understanding of the Surrealist Manifesto of 1924.

Automne, Salon d' see SALON

Avantgarde
French word meaning "vanguard", used to describe art or artists departing from accepted tradition or the ACADEMIC norm to explore techniques or concepts of art in an original way.

Avanzo see ALTICHIERO

Aved, Jacques-André-Joseph
1702–66
French portrait painter, trained at Amsterdam and then in Paris. He was a favourite painter of middle-class sitters and his interest in the details of domestic life brings him closer to his friend Chardin than to fashionable portrait painters such as Nattier. *Madame Crozat* (1741, Montpellier, Musée Fabre) is one of his best-known works.

Avercamp, Hendrick 1585–1634
Dutch painter, the pioneer and leading exponent in his country of the winter landscape. He was known as the mute of Kampen because he was deaf and dumb, and he was the only artist of real distinction to work in this town, which was relatively far from any major artistic centre. His isolation may have contributed to his originality, for he seems to have found his distinctive style early in his career and changed little thereafter. He was influenced by Flemish tradition (Bruegel created memorable winter scenes), but Avercamp's paintings are much more colourful and lively than any possible models. Frozen waterways abound with brightly painted figures skating, tobogganing, golfing and promenading, silhouetted against the white background, and depicted with fine detail (*Winter scene with skaters near a castle*, c.1610, London, NG). Unusually, Avercamp also sold his drawings and watercolours to his patrons (a good collection is in Windsor Castle). His nephew **Barent** Avercamp (1612–79) was an excellent follower. Their works are among the most unfailingly popular of all Dutch paintings of the 17th century, not least with manufacturers of Christmas cards. See vol. 2 p. 220

Avery, Milton 1893–1965
American painter. He was largely self-taught and his early work was particularly influenced by Matisse and the Fauves—although he did not travel abroad until 1952. His preferred subjects—landscapes, beaches with bath-

ers, friends and family—are painted in flat areas of thin, yet richly-pigmented paint. He was a close friend of Rothko and his later work, though always remaining figurative, formed a bridge between Matisse's use of colour and the experimentation of the colour field and hard-edge painters of the 1950s (*Sea grasses and blue sea*, 1958, New York, MOMA). See vol. 3 p. **251**; vol. 4 p. *157*

Avignon, School of
School of painting which flourished at Avignon when the papal court settled there between 1309 and 1376 because of anarchic conditions in Rome. During this period many Italian writers and artists sought patronage there; the most famous was Simone Martini, who died in Avignon in 1344. The most important surviving relics are the anonymous frescos of hunting and fishing scenes in the Papal Palace, which show a surprising and delightful naturalism. The 15th-century school of Avignon was a regional French school and had different origins and characteristics. The most famous work associated with it is "The Avignon Pietà" (Paris, Louvre). See vol. 2 p. 97

Ay-o (Takao Iijima) born 1931
Japanese painter. His early work was in a Japanese version of POP art, but later he became obsessed with optical effects and in particular the theme of the rainbow. *Rainbow tactile room*, for example (exhibited at the 1966 Venice Biennale), was a complete multicoloured environment in which walls, furniture and utensils all contributed to the effect. Much of his career has been spent outside Japan, particularly in the USA.

Ayres, Gillian born 1930
British painter. She was one of the first British artists to be affected by American ABSTRACT EXPRESSIONISM. Early paintings such as *Mushroom* (1958, Manchester City Art Gallery) were influenced by Pollock's "drip" techniques, but her work became less random in the 1960s when she employed hard-edged organic forms. Later works are looser in handling and their intense colour makes them among the most richly sensuous of recent British painting (*Bellona*, 1976–78, Arts Council of Great Britain).

Ayrton, Michael 1921–75
British painter, sculptor, book illustrator and art critic. His early paintings, such as *Entrance to a wood* (1945, Arts Council of Great Britain), have a strong affinity to the Neo-Romanticism of Sutherland or Minton in their evocation of the visionary and disturbing qualities of landscape. He took up sculpture in 1954, and much of his later work is rooted in classical mythology, in particular the legend of Daedalus and Icarus, which he used as an analogy for his own endeavours as an artist (*Icarus transformed I*, 1961, London, Tate). His obsession with the myth went so far that he designed and built a large maze of stone and brick in the Catskill Mountains, New York State, in imitation of the labyrinth Daedalus built for King Minos.

Aztec art
Art of the Aztec people of Mexico, particularly in the period from the founding of their capital city Tenochtitlán (on the site of the present Mexico City) in 1325 until its destruction by the Spanish conquistador Cortés in 1521. During this period the Aztecs gained control of a large part of Mexico and apart from Tenochtitlán, there were major settlements at Tenayuca, Tepozteco and Malinalco, where there are

remains of mural paintings (a rare survival) representing warriors or hunting deities. Sculpture, in low relief and in the round, was the art at which the Aztecs chiefly excelled, and their religious beliefs, which placed particular emphasis on human sacrifice, were frequently given expression in the great pyramids and temples dedicated to members of their rich pantheon of gods. The best collection of Aztec sculpture is in the Museo Nacional de Antropología in Mexico City. The products and craftsmanship of other peoples were also prized by the Aztecs, who imported fine lapidary work, woodcarving, turquoise mosaic work and pictorial books and then copied many of the techniques. In general the Aztecs were great organizers rather than great artists, but their artistic wealth is indicated by Dürer's comment when, in 1520, he saw the gifts which Montezuma, the Aztec emperor, had sent to the Holy Roman Emperor Charles V: "I too have seen the things brought to the Emperor from the new land of Gold . . . and in all my life I have never seen anything which so stirred my heart as those objects." See vol. 2 p. 19

Baburen, Dirck van
before 1595–1624
Dutch painter, after Honthorst and Terbrugghen Holland's leading CARAVAGGESQUE artist. He trained in Utrecht with Moreelse, and in about 1612 went to Rome, where his work in the Pietà Chapel of S. Pietro in Montorio, notably the sombre and powerful *Entombment* (1617), shows a deep debt to Caravaggio. Especially in his later works, however, his brushwork was broader and more personal and his light less murky than in the work of most Caravaggesque artists. After his return to Utrecht in about 1620 he painted mainly genre subjects, of which one of the finest is *The procuress* (1622, Boston, MFA). This was evidently well known in the 17th century, for it appears in the background of two Vermeer paintings.

Baciccia see GAULLI

Backer, Jacob Adriaenz. 1608–51
Dutch painter, chiefly of portraits. He studied in Leeuwarden, but by 1633 was in Amsterdam, where he came heavily under the influence of Rembrandt. Backer had a successful career with formal portraits such as *The Regentesses of the Amsterdam Orphan Home* (1633, still *in situ*), but he is perhaps seen at his best in more personal works such as the quietly restrained portrait of a boy (1634, The Hague, Mauritshuis), which is painted in delicate shades of grey.

Baço, Jaime c.1413–61
Spanish painter, called Master Jacomart, the leading Valencian painter of his day. He was summoned to Naples by Alfonso V before 1442, but returned to Valencia in 1451. Only one extant work is known, an altarpiece depicting *SS. Lawrence and Peter* (1460) in the church of Cati near Valencia, but this is sometimes attributed rather to his assistant **Juan Reixach** (died after 1484). In style it follows Netherlandish models rather than Italian ones.

Bacon, Francis born 1909
British painter, born in Dublin. He

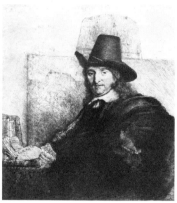
Asselyn: Portrait etching by Rembrandt, c.1647. Amsterdam, Rijksmuseum

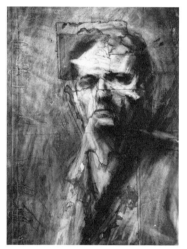
Auerbach: Self-portrait drawing. R. B. Kitaj coll.

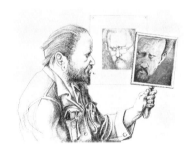
Ayrton: Self-portrait drawing for *Fabrications*, 1973. Mrs Ayrton coll.

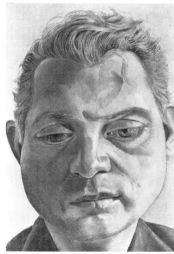
Bacon, Francis: Portrait by Freud, 1952. London, Tate

came to London in 1925. As an artist he was largely self-taught. He destroyed much of his early work and what little survives of his paintings of the 1930s shows the influence of Picasso combined with a more personal streak of horrific fantasy that was to become characteristic. This can be seen in his first major work, *Three studies at the base of a Crucifixion* (1944, London, Tate), which depicts twisted and distorted grey figures against a pungent orange background. The disturbing quality of Bacon's strongest paintings comes less from the imagery than from his handling of paint, the figure and features twisted to reveal the blood beneath the skin. This is particularly so in portraits of his friends such as *Henrietta Moraes* (1966, Manchester City Art Gallery). Even in such cases he prefers to work from photographs rather than from life and the smeared paint textures with which he evokes the face are reminiscent of the blurring created by movement during photography. Favourite images have included Velazquez's portrait of Pope Innocent X, sometimes depicted screaming or accompanied by hunks of meat, and Muybridge's photographs of figures in motion. In spite of his formidable international reputation Bacon is a somewhat isolated figure, as it has been hard for other artists to absorb his influence without producing a mere pastiche. See vol. 1 p. 91; vol. 3 pp. **234–235**.

Bacon, Sir Nathaniel 1585–1627
The outstanding English amateur painter of the 17th century, a Suffolk country gentleman by birth. He is recorded as painting mythological scenes, but none of these is extant, and most of his few surviving paintings (best represented at Gorhambury House, Hertfordshire) are either self-portraits or large-scale still lifes, both influenced by Netherlandish painting. A miniature on copper by him in the Ashmolean Museum, Oxford, has been described as the first British landscape.

Badalocchio, Sisto 1585–after 1620
Italian painter and engraver, one of the most interesting but also most obscure artists of his period. He may have studied with Agostino Carracci in his native Parma before becoming an assistant of Annibale Carracci, in whose house in Rome he and Lanfranco lodged. Following Annibale's death in 1609, he returned to Parma and is assumed to have died young. If so a brilliant career was probably cut short, for his dome fresco in S. Giovanni Evangelista, Reggio Emilia, is a more successful development of Correggio's illusionism than Lanfranco's famous and influential painting in S. Andrea della Valle in Rome, and it may even be earlier. His easel-paintings are also striking and original, showing a sonorous beauty of colouring and rich poetry which are hard to parallel among his contemporaries.

Badger, Joseph 1708–65
American portrait painter. He was born in Boston and became the principal successor there to Smibert, whose style he imitated in a somewhat naive and stilted way (*Jonathan Edwards*, New Haven, Yale University Art Gallery).

Baertling, Olle born 1911
Swedish abstract painter, trained by Lhôte and Léger. He was influenced by Mondrian and his art is dominated by variations of triangles, sometimes in dissonant colours, reflecting his interest in the interaction of form and colour (*Terga*, 1962, Stockholm University).

Baglione, Giovanni c.1573–1644
Italian painter and writer. He is most important for his *Lives of the Painters, Sculptors and Architects* (1642), a fundamental source for the period covered, 1572–1642. He had a successful career as a painter, receiving commissions from the papacy, and from the Duke of Mantua, but his paintings are now virtually forgotten, apart from a few early Caravaggesque works.

Baillairgé, François 1759–1830
French-Canadian wood sculptor and painter, active in Quebec city, the leading member of a family of artists. He studied in Paris, 1778–81, and absorbed the elegant classicism of the Louis XVI style, which later permeated his sculptural decoration for church interiors in Quebec. His ensembles, such as that in St Joachim (1817), consist of garlands, ornamented pilasters and brackets, and medallions containing restrained figural compositions in low relief.

Baily, Edward Hodges 1788–1867
British sculptor, born in Bristol and active mainly in London. He was Flaxman's pupil and a student at the Royal Academy, where he won a gold medal in 1811. He is now chiefly remembered for his public sculpture such as the statue of *Nelson* (1843) in Trafalgar Square, London. *Eve at the fountain* (1822, Bristol, City Art Gallery) is, however, more typical of the allegorical works on which his contemporary British and European reputation was based.

Baitei, Ki 1744–1810
Japanese painter, a native of Kyoto. Baitei was a servant of a nobleman who, discovering his artistic talent, put him under the tutelage of Buson. In the 1780s Baitei retired to Otsu, where he lived on the banks of Lake Biwa. He loved the scenery there and produced an album of prints called *Keisai saga*, based on his sketches. Most of his paintings are landscapes, but he also made some notable pictures of beautiful women.

Baj, Enrico born 1924
Italian painter, sculptor and graphic artist. During the 1960s he associated with Duchamp in New York and with Breton in Paris, and his work is influenced by Surrealism. He incorporates elements that already command certain associations, such as old pieces of card, lace and yellowed flowers, often with satirical intent, as in *The General* (1962, Milan, Galleria Studio Marconi).

Bakhuysen, Ludolf 1631–1708
Dutch marine painter. He trained as a calligrapher before moving to Amsterdam. He was the last of the major marine painters of the 17th century, and when the van de Veldes left for England in 1672 he was regarded as the leading painter of seascapes in Amsterdam. Peter the Great was a patron. *Stormy sea* (1697, Amsterdam, Rijksmuseum) displays his preference for dramatic seascapes. He painted a few portraits.

Bakhuyzen, Hendrikus van de Sande 1795–1860
Dutch painter of landscapes with cattle. Together with Koekkoek and Schelfhout he was one of the foremost Dutch landscape painters of the first part of the 19th century and is counted among the precursors of the HAGUE school.

Bakst, Léon 1866–1924
Russian artist, a member of the WORLD OF ART group. He is best known for his designs for the Ballets Russes, the company of the great ballet impresario Diaghilev. His exotic, colourful designs for *Schéhérazade* (1910) started a new fashion in Paris in interior décor. The sensuality of his female costume designs with richly-patterned, semi-transparent drapery have made his wash drawings enduringly popular. His designs for *The Sleeping Princess* (1921, London, V&A) are more conventional. See vol. 3 p. **156**

Baldovinetti, Alesso 1425–99
Florentine painter, mosaicist and stained-glass designer, exceptionally well documented since his diary survives. His master is unknown, but his work reflects the influence of Domenico Veneziano, with whom he worked on the choir of S. Egidio, Florence (1441–51), and of Fra Angelico. His style is rather archaic, but he has a graceful meditative quality and a distinctive sensitivity to shapes and patterns of vegetation which place him among the most attractive artists of his age. His best-known work is probably the fresco of *The Nativity* (1460–62, Florence, SS. Annunziata), and there is also an outstanding fresco in the mortuary chapel of Cardinal James, Prince of Portugal (1465–73, Florence, S. Miniato al Monte). A fine profile portrait of a lady (c.1465) in the National Gallery, London, is attributed to him. Ghirlandaio was his pupil.

Balduccio, Giovanni di
documented 1315–49
Pisan sculptor, first recorded working under Tino di Camaino. During the 1320s he was in Lombardy, Pisa and Florence, but settled in Milan in about 1334, making the shrines to St Peter Martyr in S. Eustorgio, and perhaps that to St Augustine in S. Pietro in Ciel d'Oro, Pavia. These were the first major works in the Pisan style in North Italy.

Baldung Grien, Hans
1484/5–1545
One of the outstanding German painters and engravers of the 16th century, born in Gmund, Swabia. He is assumed to have worked from about 1503 in Dürer's workshop in Nuremberg, and his earliest work shows this master's influence (*The knight, death and the maiden*, 1503–05, Paris, Louvre). After 1508 he was active principally in Strasbourg. From 1512–17 he worked on his masterpiece, the altarpiece for the Cathedral of Freiburg-im-Bresgau, which in its brilliant, rich colours and expressive distortions shows the influence of Grünewald. He also painted portraits and in the latter part of his career small mythologies and allegories sometimes macabre or erotic in feeling. *Death and the maiden* was a favourite subject (example 1517, Basel, Offentlich Kunstsammlung) and his taste for the gruesome again brings him close to Grünewald. His woodcuts often treat similar subjects, the best-known being *The bewitched stable boy* (1544). His figures, particularly nudes, are generally realistic and betray his knowledge of contemporary Italian art but they are often in mysterious northern settings. See vol. 2 p. **155**

Balen, Hendrick van 1575?–1632
Flemish MANNERIST painter, active in Brussels. He studied in Italy early in his career and became van Dyck's first teacher in 1609. As well as religious works, he painted mythological scenes in the manner of "Velvet" Brueghel (*The marriage of Peleus and Thetis*, 1609, Dresden, Gemäldegalerie), and sometimes painted the figures in the landscapes of Brueghel and other artists.

Balestra, Antonio 1666–1740
Italian painter, born in Verona, where he was the leading fresco-painter in the late 17th and early 18th centuries. He studied in Venice and with Maratta in Rome. In contrast to Venetian artists, those in Verona were always susceptible to central Italian influences and Balestra's classical and academic manner owed more to Maratta than to contemporary Venetians (*The Nativity*, 1704–05, Venice, S. Zaccaria).

Balla, Giacomo 1871–1958
Italian painter and sculptor, one of the leading FUTURIST artists. His early work was influenced by DIVISIONISM encountered on a visit to Paris in 1900. He taught Boccioni and Severini in Rome, introducing them to Divisionist theory, and in return was invited to join the Futurists in 1910. His famous *Dynamism of a dog on a leash* (1912, New York, MOMA) attempted to include motion in a picture in the manner of time-lapse photography. By 1913, however, his investigations of speed and movement had become increasingly more sophisticated, as in his *Swifts: paths of movement and dynamic sequences* (New York, MOMA), and were to result in the almost abstract *Mercury passing in front of the sun* (1914, Milan, Gianni Mattioli coll.). His series of pictures dealing with movement can be seen as fulfilling the Futurist demand for art that directly involved the spectator in works that probed the essence of speed, light and human reactions to them. After the War, with Prampolini, he was involved with Futurism once more, but by 1930 he was painting in an objective manner that he maintained until some later experiments in the 1950s. See vol. 3 pp. **152–153**

Balthus (Count Balthasar Klossowski de Rola) born 1908
French painter, born in Paris into a Polish artistic family. He received encouragement from the poet Rilke, and from Bonnard and Derain. His commanding portrait of Derain (1936) is in the Museum of Modern Art, New York. A realist painter, he has lived in seclusion outside Paris producing interior scenes which focus on the mysterious sexual obsessions of adolescence. The dreamlike eroticism of *The living room* (1941–43, Minneapolis, Institute of Arts) suggests affinities with Surrealism. His style has been constant, apart from a lightened palette. See vol. 3 p. **185**; vol. 4 p. 55

Bamboccianti
Group of artists, working in Rome in the second and third quarters of the 17th century, who painted small scenes of street life, peasants, brigands and other picturesque subjects. The painters were mainly from northern Europe, and the leader of the group was the Dutchman van Laer, called "Bamboccio" ("clumsy baby" or "simpleton") on account of his deformed body. Cerquozzi and Miel were among the other leading Bamboccianti, whose work was very popular both in Italy and Northern Europe, although it was disapproved of by academic theorists such as Bellori.

Bandinelli, Baccio 1493–1560
Florentine sculptor, a pupil of Rustici. He was much favoured by the Medici family, producing decorations for Leo X's triumphal entry into Florence in 1515, and taking over the project for a pendant sculpture to Michelangelo's *David*, outside the main door of the Palazzo della Signoria. Michelangelo's replacement by Bandinelli, who produced the highly political *Hercules and*

Cacus, caused much ill-feeling amongst the citizens. He also made the Memorial for Leo X in S. Maria sopra Minerva in Rome, and the statue of Duke Cosimo's father, *Giovanni delle Bande Nere*, outside S. Lorenzo in Florence. His style can be described as ponderously Michelangelesque, and it is easy to understand why Cellini levelled so many insults against him in his *Autobiography*. See vol. 2 p. 168

Banks, Thomas 1735–1805
British NEOCLASSICAL sculptor. From 1772 to 1779 he studied in Rome where he became closely associated with Fuseli and Sergel. In 1781 he spent a year in Russia, working for Catherine the Great. On his return to England he executed many funeral monuments, including *Sir Eyre Coote* (1784–89, London, Westminster Abbey) and, much admired by his contemporaries, the effigy of *Penelope Boothby* (1793, Ashbourne, Derbyshire).

Baranov-Rossiné, Vladimir Davidovich 1888–1942
Russian artist. He worked in Paris, 1910–14, and achieved fame with a proto-Dadaist assemblage of various unlikely materials entitled *Symphony no. 2* (1914). In post-Revolutionary Moscow he made a successful Opto-Phonic Piano (1923, Paris, Musée d'Art Moderne), with which he gave a number of "colour-concerts" in Paris and Moscow, demonstrating a synthesis of the visual arts and music. From 1925 he painted in Paris, and settled there permanently in 1930.

Barbari, Jacopo de' active 1500–16
Venetian painter and engraver, much of whose working life was spent in Germany and the Netherlands. His engravings helped to spread Italian ideas to these countries and his work was particularly admired by Dürer. His best-known painting, *The dead bird* (1504, Munich, Alte Pinakothek), is an early example of still life in northern Europe. As an engraver he is particularly remembered for his very large *View of Venice* (1497–1500), an important record of the city's appearance. See vol. 2 p. 159

Barberini family
Aristocratic Italian family, the leading patrons of BAROQUE art in 17th-century Rome. The most important member was Maffeo (1568–1644), who, on becoming Pope Urban VIII in 1623, is said to have told Bernini: "Your luck is great to see Cardinal Maffeo Barberini Pope, but ours is much greater to have Cavalier Bernini alive in our pontificate." Their relationship was one of the most successful in the history of patronage, Bernini's work for him including two masterpieces in St Peter's—the marble statue of St Longinus and the enormous Baldacchino over the site of St Peter's grave. The amount of bronze required for this was so great that some was even stripped from the Pantheon, giving rise to the adage: *Quod non fecerunt barbari, fecerunt Barberini* (What the barbarians did not do, the Barberini did). Bernini also helped to design the Palazzo Barberini, which contains important ceiling frescos by Pietro da Cortona and Andrea Sacchi.

Barbizon school
Group of French landscape painters who settled in Barbizon, a village on the outskirts of the forest of Fontainebleau, in the 1840s. English landscapists such as Constable and Bonington and 17th-century Dutch landscape painters provided their initial inspiration, but the basis of Barbizon art was direct study

from nature. This naturalistic depiction of landscape divested of academic conventions helped prepare the way for the IMPRESSIONISTS. The exhibited works were often studio compositions, but the studies from nature showed the more advanced ideas of the age in bold use of pigment and interest in PLEIN-AIR effects. Daubigny, Diaz de la Peña, Dupré, Théodore Rousseau and Troyon were the most notable artists of the colony, but Millet and Corot also had close links with it. See vol. 3 pp. 92–93

Barlach, Ernst 1870–1938
German EXPRESSIONIST sculptor, graphic artist and writer. His early drawings and ceramic sculptures were inspired by Art Nouveau, but the expressive anonymity of the peasants he saw in Russia (1906) led him to create simplified figures, in which man's spiritual being is manifested through the whole gamut of emotions, from despair to ecstasy. He attempted to re-create the emotional intensity of German medieval carving, and his famous war memorial in the form of a hovering bronze angel in Güstrow Cathedral (1927) and his figures in St Catherine's, Lübeck (1930–32) seem completely at home in their Gothic settings. His preferred medium was wood, and even when he worked in bronze he retained the broad simplifications of his carvings. He published an autobiography in 1928, and made important contributions to Expressionist drama. There are museums devoted to his work in Güstrow (his former studio) and Hamburg. See vol. 3 p. **131**

Barlow, Francis 1626–1704
English decorative painter, etcher and illustrator, the first British sporting artist. He was trained as a portrait painter, but soon specialized in faithfully observed yet naively composed scenes of bird and animal life and of country sports. Apart from two overdoors at Ham House, London, none of his decorative schemes survives in its original location, but a group of large paintings from such a scheme is at Clandon Park, Surrey. A prolific and vigorous draughtsman, he illustrated a number of popular books, notably John Ogilby's edition of *Aesop's Fables* (1666) and Richard Blome's *The Gentleman's Recreation* (1686). A large group of his drawings is in the British Museum, London. See vol. 2 p. **207**

Barna da Siena active 3rd quarter of the 14th century
Probably the most important Sienese painter of his time, although little is known of his life. Reconstruction of his output depends on accepting Ghiberti's attribution to him of the frescos on *The life of Christ* in the Collegiata at San Gimignano (*c.*1350). These show an extreme conservatism and dependence on Duccio and Simone Martini, but are of high quality. Several other fine works are reasonably attributed to Barna, including a *Crucifixion* in the Episcopal Palace at Arezzo (1369), the small and exquisite *Christ carrying the Cross* in the Frick Collection, New York, and the large *Mystic marriage of St Catherine* in the Museum of Fine Arts, Boston.

Barocci, Federico *c.*1535–1612
Italian painter, one of the most original artists in Italy in the late 16th century. He was born and trained in Urbino and, apart from two periods in Rome early in his career, seems rarely to have left his native town, where he mainly painted altarpieces. The neurotic temperament which caused him to abandon frescos

in the Vatican (1563) because he thought jealous rivals were attempting to poison him is reflected in the nervous sensitivity of his work, which is marked by great delicacy of feeling and vivid but extremely subtle pastel colours. With these qualities, however, went a vigour and freshness of design and handling which place Barocci apart from the main currents of Mannerism and make him a forerunner of the Baroque (*The Circumcision*, 1590, Paris, Louvre).

Baroque
Critical and historical term which in connection with the visual arts is used in several distinct ways. Most commonly it signifies the dominant style of art in Europe between the Mannerist and Rococo eras, a style characterized by dynamic movement, overt emotion and self-confident rhetoric. The style was roughly coterminous with the 17th century, but flourished well into the 18th in various areas, notably Central Europe and South America. The term is also used as a period label for the 17th century in general, so it is possible to talk of "the Baroque age", "Baroque music" or "Baroque science". Used in this way the term can be confusing as artists as diverse as Poussin and Pozzo would both be labelled "Baroque painters". In a third sense, the term (usually with a small "b") is used to describe visual art from any period which shows the characteristics associated with the Baroque art of the 17th century. For example the violent movement and exaggerated expressions of Hellenistic sculpture can be described as "baroque". The word may derive from the Portuguese for a misshapen pearl, and was first used as a term of abuse—an adjective meaning grotesque or capricious—and this definition, sometimes expanded to include heaviness and over-ornateness, is still current. Its usage in this sense, however, depends on the outdated notion that Baroque art was merely a decadent coda to the Renaissance. Baroque art did build on the achievements of the High Renaissance in reaction against the vapid Mannerism of much late 16th-century art, but it was also a dynamic response to the call of Counter-Reformation churchmen to portray religious scenes with solid realism and emotional directness. It began in Rome, Caravaggio and the Carracci being the first great figures of the movement. The fully developed style known as High Baroque came into being in the 1620s. Bernini was the presiding genius, and his Cornaro Chapel is the most celebrated example of the Baroque desire to achieve an overpowering emotional impact through architecture, painting and sculpture working in unison. From Italy the style spread in various forms—in Flanders, Rubens, the greatest Baroque painter, dominated the scene—but took root only in Catholic countries, Protestants preferring less ostentatious art. See vol. 2 p. 176 ff

Barry, James 1741–1806
Irish painter. Barry attracted the patronage of the statesman and aesthetician Edmund Burke, who financed his journey, via Paris, to Rome in 1765. In 1773 he became a member of the Royal Academy, and in 1782 Professor of Painting. Barry's ideals formed in Rome never left him, and so intent was he on raising the standard of HISTORY painting in England that he offered to paint, without fee, *The progress of human culture* (1777–83) for the Society of Arts in London, perhaps the finest single decorative achievement in the GRAND MANNER by a British artist, though

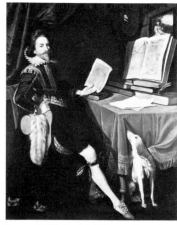
Bacon, Sir Nathaniel: Self-portrait, *c.*1625. The Gorhambury Collection (by permission of the Earl of Verulam)

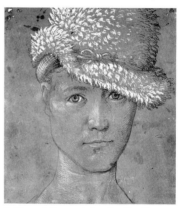
Baldung: Self-portrait drawing (detail), 1502. Basel, Kupferstichkabinett

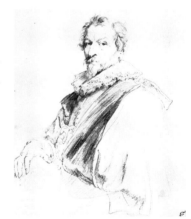
Balen: Drawing by van Dyck. Trustees of the Chatsworth Settlement

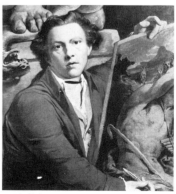
Barry: Self-portrait (detail), *c.*1780. Dublin, NG of Ireland

it was not well received. Barry had a strong belief in his own genius and his uncompromising, quarrelsome character led to his expulsion from the Academy in 1799.

Bartolini, Luigi 1892–1963
Italian graphic artist. He began to etch in 1914 and established himself as one of Italy's foremost EXPRESSIONISTS. Simplicity of form, delicacy and strength of draughtsmanship, and skilful tonal manipulation give his graphic work a restrained power and dignity.

Bartolo di Fredi
documented 1353–97
The foremost Sienese painter of the second half of the 14th century after Barna, who seems to have strongly influenced him. His major surviving work, the fresco cycle of scenes from the Old Testament in the Collegiata at San Gimignano (1367) shows, however, an overlay of interest in the descriptive realism of the Lorenzetti.

Bartolommeo, Fra (Baccio della Porta) 1472/75–1517
Florentine painter, one of the leading artists of the High Renaissance. He trained with Rosselli and in 1500 became a monk in the convent of S. Marco, where Fra Angelico had worked. His earliest surviving work, *The Last Judgment* (1499, Museo di S. Marco), is badly damaged, and he gave up painting after he became a monk until 1504, when he began his *Vision of St Bernard* (Florence, Accademia). This is a reworking in High Renaissance style of a painting by Filippino Lippi on the same subject. All the exquisite particularization of the Lippi has gone in favour of noble, idealized types clothed in voluminous draperies. The painting has affinities with Perugino in its gracefulness and sweetness, but the figures are much more solid and classical. Subsequently his work became even broader, his figures remote and quietly poised (*The mystic marriage of St Catherine*, 1511, Paris, Louvre). Often his paintings seem rather academic, but his drawings (he was a prolific draughtsman) are very lively. Many artists found Bartolommeo's version of High Renaissance style easier to assimilate than the much more personal work of Leonardo or Michelangelo, and his work had extensive influence, notably on Andrea del Sarto. See vol. 2 p. **129**

Bartolommeo Veneto
active 1st half of the 16th century
Italian painter who signed himself as "half-Venetian and half-Cremonese". The signed works, dating from 1502 to 1506, are of religious subjects, and are essentially pastiches of Giovanni Bellini. Thereafter he seems to have produced fashionable portraits such as *Martinengo* (1542) in the National Gallery, London.

Barye, Antoine-Louis 1796–1875
French sculptor and painter of animal subjects. He was closely linked with the Romantics in his choice of violent and exotic subject matter, although his interpretations of animal life were naturalistic. He studied sculpture before training as a painter under Gros, but was most influenced by his scientific observations made at the Paris zoo. His masterful bronze sculpture of a *Tiger devouring a gavial* (Baltimore, Walters Art Gallery) won him a medal in the Salon of 1831, enabling him to set up independently. Although only widely recognized after his death, Barye pioneered the way for other realist animal sculptors. See vol. 3 p. **79**

Basaiti, Marco active 1496–1530
Venetian painter. His style is close to Bellini's but his figures are slenderer (somewhat like Carpaccio's) with strange gesticulating hands and fine elongated fingers. *The calling of the children of Zebedee* (1510, Venice, Accademia) is one of his finest works.

Basaldella, Dino born 1909
Italian sculptor. He has concentrated on sculptures constructed of numbers of rugged forms, usually made in iron, joined in a seemingly illogical manner. The weight of each unit seems to defy balance and gravity. His brother **Mirko** (1910–69) was also a sculptor, and the work of both men is popular in the USA. Better known than either, however, is their younger brother, simply known by his Christian name, Afro.

Basawan active 1580?–1600
Mughal painter, one of the greatest of the Akbar period, though a Hindu of unknown origin. He contributed to the *Darabnameh* (c.1580–85, London, BL), the *Razmnameh* (1580s, Jaipur, City Palace) and also the *Baharistan* of Jami (1595, Oxford, Bodleian). His work in the *Darabnameh* is perhaps the earliest Mughal painting to show the fully developed realism in figures, architecture and background towards which the school was working in this early period.

Baschenis, Evaristo 1617–77
Italian still-life painter. Most of his work depicts musical instruments, and in this field he has no equal. His noble and severe paintings, showing the influence of Caravaggio's early work, are totally different in effect from the much homelier and less intellectual still lifes of contemporary Dutch and Flemish artists. The Accademia Carrara in Bergamo, his home town, has the best collection of his work.

Baskin, Leonard born 1922
American sculptor and graphic artist. He has described himself as a "moral realist" and his figures, despite their fullness, have a desolate, tragic air which may indicate an awareness of Barlach's Expressionist style. His monstrous hybrids such as *Seated birdman* (1961, New York, MOMA), suggest a ritual fall from the grace of nature.

Bassa, Ferrer c.1285/90–1348
Spanish artist, the outstanding Gothic painter and miniaturist in Catalonia. Records of his employment date from 1324, and Alfonso IV of Aragon is known to have ordered his miniatures, but few of his paintings survive. His only securely assigned work is the fresco decoration (1345) of the Chapel of S. Miguel in Pedralbes monastery near Barcelona, which strongly reflects contemporary Italian influence.

Bassano, Jacopo (Jacopo da Ponte) 1517/8?–92
Italian painter, the most important of a family of artists. He trained with his father **Francesco the Elder** (c.1475–1539) and, apart from a period as a pupil of Bonifazio Veronese in Venice in the 1530s, worked in Bassano, the town from which he took his name. His early style is illustrated in his robust bucolic versions of Bible stories (examples in the Museo Civico at Bassano), and although his art was later refined by the influence of prints after Raphael and Parmigianino, he always retained a certain earthiness. In his mature works, he tempered Mannerist tendencies and evolved an extremely original chiaroscuro in which smoky coloured shapes emerge from the grey darkness of the background (*The Adoration of the shepherds*, 1568, Bassano, Museo Civico). His best paintings are full of vividly observed life. As Vasari and other contemporaries noted he was a superb painter of animals, and he helped to popularize the taste for paintings in which the genre content takes over from the ostensible religious subject. He had four painter sons, **Francesco the Younger** (1549–92), **Gerolamo** (1566–1621), **Giovanni Battista** (1553–1613) and **Leandro** (1557–1622), who continued his style. See vol. 2 p. **171**

Bastien-Lepage, Jules 1848–84
French painter, mainly of portraits and scenes of rural life. A pupil of the successful academic artist Cabanel, Bastien-Lepage was influenced in subject matter by Millet and the Barbizon painters but had an Impressionistic palette. Zola described his work as "Impressionism corrected, sweetened and adapted to the taste of the crowd", and sentimentality now seems the overriding characteristic of works such as *Haymakers* (1877, Paris, Louvre) and *Joan of Arc* (1879, New York, Metropolitan), which won him a large contemporary reputation and were widely influential.

Batlle-Planas, Juan 1911–66
Argentine SURREALIST painter, one of the pioneers of modern art in his country. The series of works entitled *Paranoiac Radiographs*, begun in 1937, initiated his Surrealist phase which was followed by his "red globes", counted among his most accomplished work. The so-called "Tibetan" period which followed showed his interest in European developments, in particular the work of Tanguy and the Surrealist landscapes of Miró. He left many followers in the Argentine, including Aizenberg.

Batoni, Pompeo 1708–87
Italian painter, the most successful in 18th-century Rome. He was born in Lucca, and studied with Conca in Rome, where he formed his style mainly on the model of Raphael and the Antique. His first important commission was the high altarpiece of S. Gregorio Magno (1735), but he is best known as a portraitist; after Mengs left Rome in 1761, he had no serious rival. It was almost obligatory for distinguished visitors to sit for him, often against a background of ancient ruins (*General Gordon wearing a kilt outside the Colosseum*, 1766, Aberdeenshire, Fyvie Castle). His portraits are sometimes cold or pompous but they are never less than extremely polished technically—as are his mythological paintings—and at their best have great dignity and élan. Batoni was patronized by three popes, became curator of the papal collections, and his home was a meeting place for Rome's intellectual and social élite.

Bauchant, André 1873–1958
French painter, and market gardener. He first exhibited his NAIVE paintings in 1921, and in 1928 the German critic Wilhelm Uhde exhibited his work with that of the other Naive painters, Bombois, Rousseau, Séraphine and Vivin. He is best known for his minutely-detailed biblical, mythological and historical scenes (*Greek dance in a landscape*, 1937, London, Tate). See vol. 3 p. **141**

Baudelaire, Charles 1821–67
French writer, one of the most influential art critics of the 19th century. His maxim, "The beautiful is always bizarre", is reflected in his poetry (*Les Fleurs du Mal*, 1857) and in his brilliant art criticism, much of which praises the imaginative powers of Delacroix, the artist against whom he measured the painters of his own generation. However, in championing his ideal of modern life as the proper subject of art, only Guys won his full approval; Courbet, Daumier, Manet and Millet he admired but found wanting in this respect. His last critical essay *The Painter of Modern Life* (1863), advocating the cult of the artificial and urban and the amorality of true art, had enormous influence on Manet and later on the SYMBOLIST painters. See vol. 3 pp. 88, 94, 122

Baugin, Lubin c.1610–63
French painter, known as "*Le petit Guide*" (little Guido) because the small pictures of the Holy Family for which he is best known owed much to the influence of Guido Reni. It is now thought that he also painted still lifes, the best being the *Still life with a chequerboard* or *The five senses* (Paris, Louvre) signed "Baugin". See vol. 1 p. **73**

Bauhaus
German school of architecture, design and craftsmanship founded at Weimar in 1919 by the architect Walter Gropius. Its declared aim was to reunite all forms of artistic activity—sculpture, painting and the decorative and applied arts—and to reintegrate them into the discipline of architecture. The building was the focus of art: painting and sculpture were part of its furniture. In removing the conventional distinctions that had existed between the fine and applied arts, the Bauhaus introduced a new concept of art based on craftwork—inspired by the memory of craftsmen's guilds. Thus all students underwent a six-month preliminary course introducing them to the study of materials, forms and techniques: the academic studio was replaced by a series of workshops (such as those for mural-painting, weaving, stage design, glass-painting, metalwork) led by a *Formmeister* (master of form) working beside the students. Paradoxically, despite the declared emphasis on design and architecture, the first masters appointed were mostly painters, notably Feininger, Itten, Klee, Schlemmer and Kandinsky. When the Bauhaus moved to Dessau in 1925–26 the major influence shifted from the expressionist abstraction of Kandinsky and Itten to the Constructivism and functionalism of Moholy-Nagy and Albers. Craftwork gave way to a concentration on industrialized production. Gropius resigned in 1928 and was succeeded by the architect Hannes Meyer, who in turn was replaced in 1930 by the architect Mies van der Rohe. In 1932 the Bauhaus moved to Berlin and in 1933 was closed by the Nazis. Its ideas continued to be influential, especially in the USA, where many of the original teachers, including Moholy-Nagy and Albers, settled. See vol. 3 pp. 190–191

Baumeister, Willi 1889–1955
German painter. After 1919, influenced by Léger, he developed a mechanistic imagery, often incorporating the human figure. He taught typography, commercial art and fabric design in Frankfurt from 1928 to 1933, and in his own work experimented with various contrasting materials and textures, adding sand or cement to an oil-painting, for example, to give the surface a relief quality. In the late 1930s the figurative tendency in his work was replaced by a vocabulary of organic forms and hieroglyphs, partly linear and

partly planar, inspired by prehistoric cave-paintings (*Homage to Jerome Bosch*, 1953, Stuttgart, Felicitas-Karg Baumeister coll.). He was forbidden to exhibit by the Nazis, but in 1946 became professor at the Stuttgart Academy.

Bayer, Herbert born 1900
Austrian artist. He studied and taught at the Bauhaus until 1928 when he established a graphics studio in Berlin. During the 1930s he absorbed the techniques of photomontage into his oil-paintings, heightening the surreal effect which had already been a feature of his work. In 1938 he moved to the USA and worked in advertising and as an exhibition architect in New York, designing, for example, the Museum of Modern Art's Bauhaus exhibition (1938). His painting has been accused of slickness and insincerity as it seems to lend a spurious "good taste" to the formulae of modernist abstraction, but his work in design has had a great influence, particularly in typography.

Bayeu, Francisco 1734–95
Spanish painter, principally remembered today as the brother-in-law of Goya, who painted a famous portrait of him (1795, Madrid, Prado). Bayeu was born in Saragossa and was attached to the court in Madrid from 1763. He painted frescos, in a style owing something both to Mengs and to Giambattista Tiepolo, in Saragossa and Toledo, and in the royal palaces of Madrid, Aranjuez, El Pardo and La Granja, and also executed numerous cartoons for tapestries. The latter are similar to some of Goya's early works, but only Bayeu's portraits of himself and of his family display a power remotely comparable to that of his brother-in-law.

Bazaine, Jean born 1904
French artist. He trained as a sculptor but began painting in 1924 and held his first exhibition in Paris in 1932. He has denied that he is a truly abstract painter, but since 1945 he has produced largely non-figurative paintings, mosaics and stained glass. His work can be seen in churches at Assy and Audincourt and at the UNESCO building in Paris. He published *Notes on Today's Painting* in 1948.

Bazille, Frédéric 1841–70
French painter. He arrived in Paris in 1862 to study at Gleyre's studio and there met Monet, Renoir and Sisley. His major contribution to the formation of the IMPRESSIONIST movement lies in his paintings of figures out of doors, either in strong sunlight or, as in *The artist's family* (1867, Paris, Jeu de Paume), dappled shade. He gave much-needed financial support to Monet and Renoir. His death in the Franco-Prussian War cut short a promising career. See vol. 3 pp. **98–99**

Baziotes, William 1912–63
American painter, a leading member of the NEW YORK school. From 1936 to 1941 he worked for the FEDERAL ARTS PROJECT, first as a teacher and then as a painter. During the 1940s he shared ideas and techniques with the artists who came to be labelled Abstract Expressionists, but his paintings retained a clearer imagery and a more delicate handling of paint. An interest in the Surrealist concept of automatism and the biomorphism of artists such as Miró is evident in, for example, *Dwarf* (1947, New York, MOMA). See vol. 3 p. **219**

Beale, Mary 1633–99
British portrait painter. She trained with Robert Walker, but her friend and mentor Lely was the dominant influence

on her pedestrian style. Her output was prolific, and she specialized in clerical sitters, frequently using a mock carved stone oval as a surround (examples, London, NPG). Her career is recorded in the notebooks of her husband, Charles Beale, an artist's colourman.

Beardsley, Aubrey 1872–98
English illustrator, whose work seems to epitomize the *fin-de-siècle* decadence of the 1890s. He had little formal training, and his style was very distinctive, conveying a menacing sense of evil and decay with its extremely sophisticated Art Nouveau line, finely-controlled contrasts of black and white, and concentration on grotesqueness and morbid eroticism. Burne-Jones and Japanese prints were among his sources. He first came to public notice with his illustrations for Malory's *Morte d'Arthur* (1893) and gained notoriety with his work for a quarterly periodical, *The Yellow Book*, of which he became art editor in 1894, and with illustrations to Oscar Wilde's *Salome* (1894). With Wilde he ranks as the outstanding figure of AESTHETICISM in England. Despite his early death from tuberculosis, his output was large. His reputation sank after his death, but he is now very popular. See vol. 3 p. **121**

Beaumont, Claudio Francesco 1694–1766
Italian painter. He was the leading decorative painter in Piedmont in the 18th century, and spent most of his life in his native Turin, working for the Piedmontese royal family. However, before his appointment to the court in 1731, he had been in Rome, where he came into contact with Trevisani, and, through him, with many of the French artists who were visiting Italy. Beaumont's decorations, for instance those in the Palazzo Reale, Turin, with their preference for elegance of effect over dramatic illusionism, are closer in spirit to contemporary French than to Italian painting.

Beaumont, Sir George Howland 1753–1827
British art patron and amateur landscape painter. He had a wide circle of acquaintances among both writers and artists, and his collection included works by Reynolds, Wilson, J.R. Cozens and Girtin as well as by Old Masters such as Rubens and Claude. A lover and painter of the Lake District and the Roman Campagna, he was a man of refined but conservative tastes. He left much of his collection to the National Gallery, London, which he helped to found.

Beauneveu, André
active 1360–before 1403
French sculptor and painter. He worked for Charles V, the Count of Flanders and for Duc Jean de Berri. His work survives in the figures on the royal tombs in St Denis outside Paris and in some of the illuminations of the Psalter of the Duc de Berri (Paris, BN). His style, both in sculpture and painting, is monumental, and heralds the general movement in 15th-century northern Europe towards naturalism.

Beccafumi, Domenico
c.1486–1551
Italian painter, the most inventive of the Sienese MANNERISTS. His style was based on the work of contemporary Florentines, but also drew on the tradition of Sienese devotional painting going back to Duccio. He delighted in creating rich effects of light playing on the elaborately intertwined limbs of his wraith-like figures. *The birth of the Virgin*

(c.1543, Siena, Pinacoteca) is a typical example in which the candlelight, casting a glare on some of the figures and leaving others in darkness, creates a dreamlike effect. See vol. 2 p. **165**

Becerra, Gaspar c.1520–70
Spanish painter and sculptor. His essential training was in Rome, in the circle of Michelangelo, where he assisted Vasari and provided the drawings for Valverde's *Anatomia* (published 1556). He returned to Spain in 1557, and became court painter to Philip II in 1563, when he began the mythological paintings on the ceiling of the palace of El Pardo, near Madrid. His high reputation in his time and for some decades after his death depended on his having imported to Spain an authentic and competent Roman MANNERIST painting when respect for Michelangelo was at its highest. The sculptures of the high altar of Astorga Cathedral are important works.

Becher, Bernhard born 1931 and **Hilla** born 1936
German artists, husband and wife, who have worked as a team since 1959 and whose main medium is architectural photography. Their particular interest is in early industrial structures. Photographs of these, arranged sequentially, as in books, or in absolutely straightforward vertical/horizontal grids (for example, *Pitheads*, 1972–73, London, Nigel Greenwood Inc.) evoke an aesthetic response typical of much avantgarde art, especially Minimal and Conceptual, of the 1960s and 1970s.

Beckmann, Max 1884–1950
German painter and draughtsman, one of the greatest of EXPRESSIONIST artists. He trained at Weimar (1900–03) and after visiting Paris and Italy moved in 1904 to Berlin, where he became a successful member of the Sezession and painted large-scale dramatic works. The appalling suffering he witnessed as a field hospital orderly during World War I led him to a highly personal, expressionistically distorted style, influenced by German Gothic art, in which he reflected the disillusionment and misery around him. *The night* (1918–19, Düsseldorf, Kunstsammlung Nordrhein-Westfalen) is a scene of anonymous nocturnal torture and murder taking place in a cramped attic, rendered in sickly greens reminiscent of decaying flesh. From this time Beckmann's sole concern was to reveal the ambiguity and uncertainty of existence. He assumed the responsibility of the artist-seer, using his own face as a seismograph to record the anguish of contemporary events in Germany and often adopting the role of clown or king, thus linking his art with the concept of life as a theatrical pageant. This theme was further developed in the series of nine triptychs painted between 1932 and his death, which constitute moral statements about aggression of any kind, and about the responsibility of the individual to react to it (*Departure*, 1932–35, New York, MOMA). On hearing that works by him were to be included in the Nazi Degenerate Art exhibition in 1937 he emigrated to Holland, where he lived until he moved to the USA in 1947. He taught at Washington University, St Louis, 1947–49, then moved to New York, where he died. See vol. 1 p. 98; vol. 3 pp. **196–197**

Bedoli, Girolamo c.1500?–1569
Italian painter, born in Parma. He probably knew Parmigianino from youth, and became his cousin by marriage in 1529, when he adopted the name

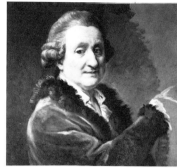
Batoni: Self-portrait (detail), 1773–87. Florence, Uffizi (Alinari)

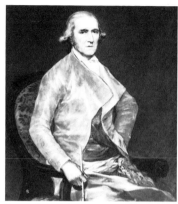
Bayeu: Portrait by Goya, 1795. Madrid, Prado (Alinari)

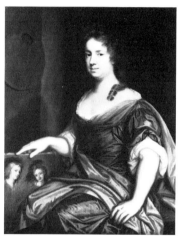
Beale: Self-portrait, c.1665. London, NPG

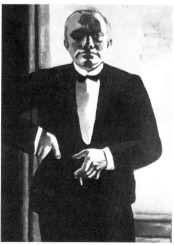
Beckmann: *Self-portrait in tuxedo*, 1927. Harvard, Busch-Reisinger Museum

Mazzola-Bedoli. His most important work is *The Immaculate Conception* (c.1533, Parma, Pinacoteca), which closely resembles Parmigianino, but outdoes him in excessive ornament and artificiality. He was frequently employed as a fresco-painter, most successfully in the Cathedral at Parma where he painted *Christ as the Judge on the Last Day* in the apse, a fine exposition of MANNERIST decorative principles.

Beechey, Sir William 1753–1839
British portraitist, possibly a pupil of Zoffany. He worked in Norwich from 1782 until 1787, when he began a very successful career in London. In 1793 he was appointed portrait painter to Queen Charlotte and in 1798 was knighted. His works are elegant but uninventive.

Beert, Osias c.1580–1624
Flemish painter of flowers and still lifes, active in Antwerp. His straightforwardly, almost naively, arranged compositions and virtuosity in the rendering of detail and surface texture have much in common with the work of Flegel in Germany and Floris van Dyck in Holland. He is particularly known for his skill in painting oysters (*Still life with oysters*, Madrid, Prado).

Beham, Barthel 1502–40
German painter and graphic artist, a native of Nuremberg and follower of Dürer. In 1525 he was expelled from the town for his extreme Protestantism, along with his brother Hans and Georg Pencz. He went to work at the court of Duke William IV of Bavaria and died on a visit to Italy. Italian influence is clear in the classical detail and subject matter of many of his woodcuts and engravings and in the smooth finish of his paintings, which were mainly portraits (*Leonhard Eck*, 1527, New York, Metropolitan).

Beham, Hans Sebald 1500–50
German engraver. With his brother and Georg Pencz he was expelled from his native Nuremberg in 1525 for extreme Protestantism. He soon returned, but later settled in Frankfurt, where, in 1533, he designed important biblical woodcuts. His numerous small, clearly drawn engravings of religious, mythological and genre scenes owe much to the example of Dürer but have a rhythm and liveliness of their own.

Bell, Clive 1881–1964
British art critic. A close associate of Fry, he collaborated with him in introducing advanced French art to the British public in the years before World War I. He selected the British section of the Second Post-Impressionist exhibition (1912), which included Grant, Gore and Bell's wife, Vanessa. His most influential book, *Art* (1914), advanced the theory of SIGNIFICANT FORM. See vol. 3 p. 198

Bell, Graham 1910–43
British painter. Born in South Africa, he came to Britain in 1931. From 1934 to 1937 he worked as a journalist and was subsequently a polemicist, in word and art, for an objective realism depicting contemporary society. After a brief period as an abstractionist in the early 1930s he became a teacher at the EUSTON ROAD school in 1938. *The café* (c.1937, Manchester, City Art Gallery) is characteristic of his sober and closely observed views of working-class life.

Bell, Vanessa 1879–1961
British painter and designer. A central figure in the BLOOMSBURY group, she was the wife of Clive Bell and the sister of the writer Virginia Woolf. Her paintings were influenced by Post-Impressionism, in particular the work of Gauguin and Matisse. *Studland Beach* (c.1912, London, Tate) is characteristic of her move away from realism towards an art determined by the requirements of form and design. By 1914 she was painting totally abstract works, reminiscent of Kupka, but she had no lasting commitment to abstraction and her later work was more traditional.

Bella, Stefano della 1610–74
One of the greatest Italian engravers. He was born in Florence and trained as a goldsmith, but under the influence of Callot turned to etching. He worked mainly for the Grand Duke of Tuscany, but in 1639–49 was based in Paris, where Richelieu was among his patrons. He visited Holland in 1647 and was deeply impressed by Rembrandt's etchings. He was prolific (more than 1,000 prints are known), illustrating many aspects of contemporary life in his delicate, detailed style. A large collection of his drawings is at Windsor Castle.

Bellange, Jacques active c.1600–17
French MANNERIST painter, engraver and decorator, who worked in the Duchy of Lorraine for the court at Nancy. All his decorative work has disappeared and only two pictures are certainly by him—a pair representing *The Annunciation* in the Staatliche Kunsthalle, Karlsruhe. His reputation rests on his etchings and a few drawings, which in their attenuated Mannerism derive from Rosso Fiorentino and Parmigianino. Most of them are of religious subjects and have a sophisticated courtly elegance, but also a mystic intensity which is extremely personal. A few genre subjects bring him close to his great contemporary, Callot, who also worked in Nancy.

Bellano, Bartolommeo died before 1496/97
Paduan bronze sculptor, almost certainly trained in Donatello's workshop in Padua in the 1440s. He was strongly influenced by the master's naturalistic style, as the statuette *David* (Philadelphia, Museum of Art) reveals. He is known to have worked in Venice (he competed unsuccessfully for the Colleoni monument commission) and was sent with Gentile Bellini to visit Sultan Mehmet II in 1479–80. In Padua he executed the dramatic, naturalistic relief of *Samson destroying the Temple* for S. Antonio (1483–84).

Bellechose, Henri active 1415–1440/4
Netherlandish painter, born in Brabant. He succeeded Jean Malouel as painter to the Duke of Burgundy at Dijon in 1415, and in 1416 is recorded as completing an unfinished altarpiece by Malouel, now identified as *The martyrdom of St Denis* (Paris, Louvre). The rounded naturalism of the parts he did, for example the figures of God and the executioner, contrasts with the general effect of gentle refinement and elegance.

Bellegambe, Jean c.1470/80–c.1535
Netherlandish painter and designer active in Douai, then under Spanish rule, where he was the leading artist of his day. The elongated figures and rich colouring of *The adoration of the Trinity* (c.1515, Douai Museum) are typical of his style. His elaborate Renaissance architectural settings, perhaps inspired by those of the Antwerp Mannerists, often exceed the bounds of credibility.

Belling, Rudolf born 1886
German sculptor. After studying in Berlin (1911–12) he became a member of the NOVEMBERGRUPPE in 1918. From 1920 he was closely associated with Archipenko, from whom he derived a figurative style based on a fusion of Cubist and Futurist principles (*Head*, 1923, New York, MOMA). From 1937 to 1966 he taught at the Academy in Istanbul. His sculpture became increasingly decorative and stylized, but after settling in Munich in 1966 he returned to more experimental forms.

Bellini, Gentile c.1429/30?–1507
Venetian painter, the son of Jacopo and elder brother of Giovanni. Initially more famous than his brother, he was knighted by the Holy Roman Emperor in 1469, and became official painter to the Doge in 1474. Many of the works on which his contemporary reputation was based have, however, perished. These included decorations in the Hall of the Grand Council in the Doge's Palace and erotic scenes for the private apartments of Sultan Mehmet II, executed when Gentile was court envoy in Istanbul, 1479–81. A portrait of the Sultan painted during this period is in the National Gallery, London. His most important surviving works are large and highly detailed views of religious events in Venice, full of rich anecdotal detail. Two are in the Accademia: *A procession of relics in the Piazza San Marco* (1496) and *The miracle at Ponte di Lorenzo* (1500). See vol. 2 p. **122**

Bellini, Giovanni c.1430?–1516
Venetian painter, the son of Jacopo and brother of Gentile. He was the greatest artist of the family, and during his long, varied and highly successful career was largely responsible for making Venice an artistic centre to rival Florence. There are relatively few securely dated works, especially from the earlier part of his career, but the main outlines of his development are clear as he moved from a sharp, precise, Gothic style learned from his father to one of classical dignity and great painterly subtlety, in which form is suggested by contrasts of tone and colour rather than by lines. His strength of design was influenced by his brother-in-law, Mantegna, and his fluid oil technique by Antonello da Messina, who worked in Venice in 1475–76. Bellini's vision, however, was very personal, and essentially calm and contemplative. One of his great achievements was the integration of figures and landscapes, so that the latter does not merely act as a pleasing backdrop but actively helps to establish the mood of the painting. Usually this is one of serenity, but in *The Agony in the Garden* (1460s, London, NG) it is one of tension, and in *St Francis in ecstasy* (1470s, New York, Frick) one of joy. *The Madonna and Child* was his most common subject, and the felicity and poignancy of his variations on this theme are rivalled only by Raphael's. They range from the wistful playfulness of "*The Barberini Madonna*" (c.1490, Glasgow, Art Gallery, Burrell coll.) to the monumental grandeur of the S. Zaccaria altarpiece (1505, Venice, S. Zaccaria). Bellini attracted to his studio most of the best up-and-coming Venetian painters as students, including Giorgione and Titian, and his influence was enormous. He himself benefited from the contact, for his art continued to develop until the end: *Venus with a mirror* (1515, Vienna, Kunsthistorisches), for example, was influenced by Giorgione, whom Bellini outlived. See vol. 1 pp. *48*, **82–83**; vol. 2 pp. **123**, **138–139**

Bellini, Jacopo c.1400–70/71
Venetian painter, the father of Gentile and Giovanni and the father-in-law of Mantegna. He probably visited Florence with his master Gentile da Fabriano in 1425. In Venice he ran a flourishing workshop with his sons, but only a handful of paintings by him have survived—simple half-length *Madonnas* of which there are signed examples in the Accademia, Venice, and the Brera, Milan. *The Madonna and Child with Lionello d'Este* (1441?, Paris, Louvre) has a radiantly lit landscape. More important are his two sketchbooks (London, BM, and Paris, Louvre), which together contain more than 200 lead-point drawings. Some of these are remarkable in showing elaborate figure groups in complex spatial settings which display a complete understanding of perspective. His son Gentile inherited the books, and he, Giovanni and Mantegna used the drawings as compositional sources. The celebrated paintings of *The Agony in the Garden* by Giovanni and Mantegna (both London, NG), for example, clearly derive from a drawing in the British Museum sketchbook. See vol. 2 p. **122**

Bellmer, Hans born 1902
Polish-French painter, graphic artist and sculptor. Born in Silesia, he studied and worked in Germany before settling in Paris in 1938, where he had friends among the Surrealists. Fascinated by the erotic, he is best known for his versions of *Doll* (example, 1936, London, Tate), whose dislocated anatomy and bulbous forms are very disturbing.

Bellori, Giovanni Pietro 1615–96
Italian antiquarian, biographer and writer on artistic theory, a friend of Poussin and Duquesnoy. In 1664 Bellori read his *Idea of the Painter, of the Sculptor and of the Architect* to the Academy of St Luke in Rome, and it was published in 1672 as a preface to his *Lives of Modern Painters, Sculptors and Architects*, an important source book. The *Idea* was the most characteristic and influential statement of idealist art theory in the 17th century, and was the forerunner of Winckelmann's Neoclassical ideas.

Bellotto, Bernardo 1720–80
Venetian view-painter whose meticulously detailed works are sometimes indistinguishable from those of his master and uncle, Canaletto. He spent most of his life outside Venice. From 1747 to 1758 and from 1761 to 1767 he was in Dresden, where he became court painter to Augustus II, Elector of Saxony; his *Ruins of the old Kreuzkirche, Dresden* (1765, Dresden, Staatliche Kunstsammlungen), is a moving portrayal of the consequences of the Prussian bombardment of 1760. He later worked in Vienna, Munich, St Petersburg and Warsaw, where he spent the last 12 years of his life as court painter to Stanislaus II.

Bellows, George Wesley 1882–1925
American artist. He achieved considerable recognition as an academic painter, being elected the youngest Academician of his time in 1913. He was an extremely hearty, vivacious man (originally trained as a baseball player) and his work shows his bold, dashing approach to life. It was admired by the ASHCAN school, with whom he was associated, having been taught by Henri. His *Cliff dwellers* (1913, Los Angeles, County Museum of Art) reflects the school's concern with the life of the poor in New York. His famous paintings of boxers, such as *Stag at Sharky's* (1909, Cleve-

land Museum of Art), are vigorous and realistic. Bellows increasingly identified himself with progressive artistic programmes; he exhibited with Henri's group of Independent Artists in 1910, and helped organize the Armory Show. See vol. 3 p. 204

Belyutin, Eliy born 1924
Russian painter. He began as a socialist-realist painter, but in the 1940s began to experiment with abstract art. In 1954 he founded a studio called "New Reality", where, using the requirements of modern design as his pretext, he was able to teach the principles of abstract art. The studio was closed under pressure from Khrushchev in 1962.

Bencovich, Federico 1677–1756
Italian painter of Dalmatian origin. He was probably born in Venice, and was trained in Bologna under Carlo Cignani. Although much of his later life was spent in Venice, he seems to have been best appreciated in central Europe, and in 1735 he became court painter to the Prince-Bishop of Bamberg and Würzburg; his last years were spent in Gorizia. His work has a dark, mannered and melodramatic quality which derives ultimately from Tintoretto; few Venetian painters interpreted his art with such violence and distortion as Bencovich.

Benedetto da Maiano 1442–97
Florentine sculptor, who frequently worked with his architect brother, Giuliano. He was assistant to Antonio Rossellino before receiving his first major commission, an altar in a chapel designed by Giuliano and frescoed by Ghirlandaio in the Collegiata of San Gimignano (c. 1468–75). His use of low relief landscape and architectural settings, and expressive but robust figures, shows the influence of both Donatello and Ghiberti. His masterpiece—much praised by Vasari—is the marble pulpit with reliefs of the life of St Francis, c. 1472–75, in S. Croce in Florence. Its patron, Pietro Mellini, was the subject of Benedetto's grave but naturalistic portrait bust (1474, Florence, Bargello). During the 1480s and early 1490s he was at work on reliefs and monuments for the Pope at the Holy House, Loreto, and for the Neapolitan court.

Benin art
Art of the ancient kingdom of the Edo-speaking people generally known as the Bini, who still inhabit the area to the north-east of the Niger delta. The kingdom of Benin flourished from the 13th to the 19th century and its magnificent bronzes and ivories have been prized in the West ever since a hoard was carried to London by the British expedition of 1897 as loot (now preserved in the British Museum). Benin art is essentially a court art in which the *Oba* (King) of the Edo celebrates his hereditary right to rule. Court patronage sustained a large network of craft guilds—smiths, potters and carvers of ivory and wood. According to legend, towards the end of the 14th century the Oba of Benin sent to Ife for a smith to teach his people how to cast commemorative copper alloy (essentially bronze) heads using a CIRE-PERDUE process, and amongst the earliest Benin sculptures are various extremely thin, hollow cast bronze heads of a realistic style similar to those of classical IFE. However, even at this early stage the stylization which was to become increasingly predominant in Benin portrait heads was already present. Dating from the mid-16th century are the numerous bronze plaques decorated with kings,

warriors and servants in high relief. As the kingdom grew in complexity, its art became correspondingly extravagant and the term "baroque" has been applied to its closing phases. However, the vitality of indigenous African art is attested by the busy workshops of today's Benin artists. See vol. 2 p. 15

Bening, Alexander before 1455–1519 and **Simon** 1483/4–1561
Netherlandish miniaturists, father and son, from Ghent. Alexander entered the guild there in 1469, and was registered in Bruges in 1486, but subsequently returned to Ghent. Simon spent most of his working life in Bruges and ran the last great workshop to illuminate prayerbooks. His miniatures echo the panels of Memlinc and van der Goes. His daughter **Lievine Teerlinck** (died after 1570) painted portrait miniatures at Henry VIII's court in England.

Benner, Gerrit born 1897
Dutch painter. He is self-taught and began painting late, but became one of Holland's leading and most influential artists. His works are expressionist with large violent forms painted in a thick impasto, evoking the elemental aspects of his native landscape in Friesland. He has produced many series of drawings on themes such as dunes, birds and children, which have a childlike simplicity.

Benois, Alexandre 1870–1960
Russian painter, critic and theatre designer. He was one of the founder members of the WORLD OF ART movement and is best known for his designs for Diaghilev's Ballets Russes, in which he treated sets and costumes as an integral whole. The decorative nature of his paintings is analogous to the romantic effects he achieved with muted tones and pastel shades for ballet productions such as *Les Sylphides* (1909). On the other hand his designs for *Petroushka* (1911) derive inspiration from the bright colours and simplified, abstract patterns of folk art. See vol. 3 p. 156

Benson, Ambrosius died 1550
Netherlandish painter and portraitist, born in Milan but working in Bruges from 1519. He absorbed the devotional tradition of Jan van Eyck and Gerard David, and his oeuvre is dominated by reflective, holy women—even in such obviously secular scenes as *The after-dinner concert* (Basel, Kunstmuseum). Equally, his most graceful work, *The Virgin with prophets and sibyls* (Antwerp, Musées Royaux des Beaux-Arts) harks back directly to van der Goes. He combined a warm palette with smooth modelling and firm contours, but his compositions were rarely well integrated, the landscapes being copied from David and tacked on by assistants. Nevertheless, he adapted well to French and Italian markets with a thriving export business.

Benton, Thomas Hart 1889–1975
American painter. He experimented with Synchromism after the 1914 exhibition in New York, producing abstractions such as *Bubbles* (c. 1914–17, Baltimore, Museum of Art). By 1919, however, he had turned to REGIONALIST themes manifest in such stylized works as *The Lord is My Shepherd* (c. 1926, New York, Whitney). He is best remembered for his mural commissions such as *American life* (1930–31, New York, New School for Social Research), painted as a satire of American society. His works have a restless energy caused by a use of pervasive rhythmic lines which affects not only the people he

paints but also their environments. This dynamism influenced Benton's most famous pupil, Pollock. See vol. 3 p. 206

Bérain, Jean 1640–1711
French decorator and designer. From 1682 until his death Bérain was chief designer at the court of Louis XIV, where he worked on many stage settings, costumes and ceremonies. His work was much lighter in vein than many of his contemporaries and he anticipated the Rococo taste of the 18th century. There are many engravings after his designs.

Bérard, Christian 1902–49
French painter and stage designer, associated with NEO-ROMANTICISM. His fantastic landscapes have affinities with the work of Dali though they are less disturbing in their imagery. He also painted portraits of hypnotic intensity (*Jean Cocteau*, 1928, New York, MOMA).

Berchem, Nicolaes 1620–83
Dutch landscape painter born in Haarlem, the son of Pieter Claesz. He painted many subjects during his prolific career, but apparently not still life, his father's speciality. The works for which he is best known are Italianate landscapes, and he ranks with Jan Both as the most popular exponent of this genre. He was in Italy in the 1640s (with J.B. Weenix, who may have been his cousin) and possibly again in the 1650s; he moved from Haarlem to Amsterdam in 1677. His style absorbed many influences, but he had no interest in the scientific recording of appearances or heroic idealization. His easy, informal art was especially popular in the 18th century, and artists as diverse as Watteau and Gainsborough responded to his appeal. His popularity with English collectors is indicated by the many paintings in London galleries. Dujardin and de Hoogh were among his pupils. See vol. 2 p. 221

Berckheyde, Gerrit 1638–98
Dutch landscape painter, principally famed for his architectural views. He travelled as a young man with his teacher and brother **Job** (1630–93) to Germany in the service of the Elector Palatine. Like those of Saenredam, his paintings are often accurate studies of views in Haarlem, The Hague and Amsterdam, interiors and exteriors, sometimes repeated with little variation. Three views of his native Haarlem are in the National Gallery, London.

Berczy, William von Moll 1748–1813
Canadian portrait and history painter. He worked in Europe as an itinerant miniaturist in the 1770s, and in 1790 went to England, where he studied the works of Zoffany. By 1805 he was installed in Montreal as a fashionable portrait painter. *The Woolsey family* (1808–09, Ottawa, NG), an exceptionally fine conversation piece, is executed with Neoclassical precision and a romantic appreciation for landscape.

Berenson, Bernard 1865–1959
American art critic and connoisseur, born in Lithuania. He lived in Italy for most of his life, and was accepted as a leading authority on Italian Renaissance paintings, his certificates of authenticity being eagerly sought by dealers. He was associated with several prominent collectors, most notably Isabella Stewart Gardner, who bought on his advice many of the paintings, including Titian's *Rape of Europa*, which are now in the museum she founded in Boston. Although many of his attributions are no

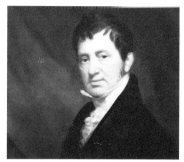
Beechey: Self-portrait (detail), c. 1836. London, NPG

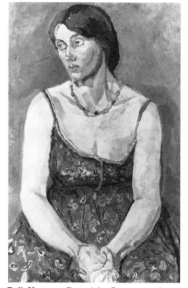
Bell, Vanessa: Portrait by Grant, c. 1918. London, NPG

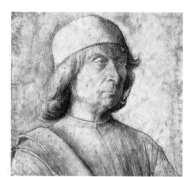
Bellini, Gentile: Drawing by Giovanni Bellini? (detail), undated. West Berlin, Staatliche Museen

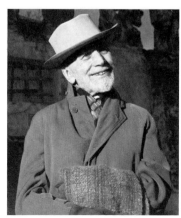
Berenson: Photograph taken at the Villa Palagonia, Sicily, 1957 (Popperfoto)

longer accepted and his impartiality has been questioned, several of Berenson's books are still widely read and used. He left his villa I Tatti at Settignano near Florence, with its fine art collection and superb library of books and photographs, to Harvard University, where he had been a student.

Bergh, Richard 1858–1919
Swedish painter and writer, one of the leading members of the Swedish Artists' Union (*Konstnärsförbundet*). He studied in Stockholm and in Paris where he was interested in French open-air painting, and admired Bastien-Lepage. Landscapes and imaginary scenes were among his varied output, but he is best known for his penetrating portraits of himself, his family, close artist friends and authors such as August Strindberg.

Berghe, Fritz van den 1883–1939
Belgian painter. His early paintings, principally portraits, interiors and landscapes, are Impressionist in style. He was in Holland, 1914–20, with de Smet, where he was strongly influenced by Expressionism and inspired by Polynesian art. Around 1926 he began to introduce fantastic and Surrealist elements in the Flemish tradition of Bosch and Ensor (*Genealogy*, 1929, Basel, Kunstmuseum).

Bergmüller, Johann Georg 1688–1762
South German painter, founder of the 18th-century Augsburg school of fresco-painting. Accepted as a master-painter in Augsburg in 1713, he became one of the directors of the Academy in 1730. He revived the tradition of façade-painting in Augsburg, and painted altarpieces and frescos (notably at Diessen, 1736) in churches in Bavaria and Swabia. Holzer was among his pupils.

Berlin Painter active c.500–460 BC
Athenian RED-FIGURE vase-painter, of the school of Euthymides. About 300 vases by him have been recognized, generally decorated with one gracefully moving figure on either side, drawn in a fine flowing line against a black ground. On the amphora in West Berlin (Staatliche Museen), however, from which he is named, there is an exquisite group of Hermes, a satyr and a faun drawn one behind the other.

Berlinghieri family
Family of Italian painters living in Lucca, north-east of Pisa, in the 13th century. A Crucifix in the Lucca Gallery signed *Berlingeri* is usually given to **Berlinghiero** Berlinghieri, the founder of the family, and a Crucifix in the Accademia, Florence, has also been attributed to him. His three sons— **Bonaventura**, **Barone** and **Marco**— were also painters; a *St Francis* (Pescia, S. Francesco) by Bonaventura, the most talented of the three, is dated 1235 and is probably one of the earliest paintings to represent Franciscan ideas. The Berlinghieri family are among the earliest Italian painters identified by name.

Berman, Eugene 1898–1972
Russian painter. He fled to Paris during the Russian Revolution, and became associated with NEO-ROMANTICISM, specializing in architectural views of landscapes which made evocative use of distant perspectives in a manner reminiscent of Chirico. In 1937 he moved to the USA, where his paintings took on a more overt air of Surrealist fantasy. As well as painting, he did much work for the theatre as a set and costume designer.

Bermejo, Bartolomé active 1474– after 1498
Spanish painter and stained-glass designer, active in Aragon and later Barcelona. His early works, in which the influence of Netherlandish or French art is prominent, are characterized by a jewel-like brilliancy of colour and attention to detailed ornament. In later works, a new breadth of vision appears: his famous *Pietà* (1490, Barcelona Cathedral) is powerfully dramatic and realistic, and tempered by a sombre poetry and real feeling of anguish.

Bernard, Emile 1868–1941
French painter, writer and critic. He entered Cormon's studio in 1884 and there met Anquetin, Toulouse-Lautrec and van Gogh. During the winter of 1886–87 he evolved with Anquetin the style known as CLOISONNISME, which emulated the technique of the enamellist in its use of strong contour and flat areas of colours. The Symbolist mood and hieratic anti-naturalism of his *Breton women at a pardon* (1888, Paris, Private coll.) acted as a stimulus for Gauguin and the two worked closely together between 1888 and 1891. Thereafter, following a brief association with the Nabis, he increasingly looked to Cézanne and the tradition of monumental classicism. See vol. 3 p. 120

Berni, Antonio born 1904
Argentinian painter. He studied in Paris under Lhôte and Friesz before returning in 1931 to Buenos Aires, where he founded the movement New Realism, which aimed to set up painting collectives. In 1932, in collaboration with Siqueiros, he executed a number of murals in Buenos Aires. His early work shows the influence of Metaphysical Painting, but more recently he has worked mainly as a graphic artist.

Bernini, Gianlorenzo 1598–1680
Italian sculptor, architect, painter, playwright and theatre designer, the dominant figure of the BAROQUE in Rome. He trained under his father, **Pietro** (1562–1629), a highly accomplished Mannerist sculptor (*St John the Baptist*, 1616, Rome, S. Andrea della Valle) and developed a style marked by profound emotional insight, dynamic energy and astonishing technical virtuosity. He was remarkably precocious and his early career flourished under the patronage of Cardinal Scipione Borghese, for whom he executed a series of life-size statues between 1618 and 1625 (Rome, Borghese Gallery), which established his reputation as the leading artist of the day. On the election of Maffeo Barberini as Pope Urban VIII (1623), Bernini became virtually the artistic dictator of Rome. For St Peter's he designed the Baldacchino (1624–33) and carved the twice life-size *St Longinus* (1629–38), which clearly demonstrated his superiority to the other leading sculptors of the day—Bolgi, Duquesnoy and Mochi—who made the companion figures for the other three crossing piers. The next Pope, however, Innocent X (1644–55), had little sympathy with the artist who had done so much for his hated predecessor, and Algardi became his favoured sculptor, leaving Bernini freer to execute private commissions, including his most celebrated work, the Cornaro Chapel with *The ecstasy of St Theresa*, 1645–52, in S. Maria della Vittoria, a triumph of the Baroque fusion of the arts. In 1655 he returned to work on St Peter's, and designed two of his most ambitious works, the *Cathedra Petri* in the apse (1656–66) and the huge

Piazza (1656–67). He travelled to Paris in 1665 to design the east front of the Louvre for Louis XIV, but his plans were never executed and he returned to Rome having completed only a portrait bust (1665, Paris, Louvre) of the King. As a portrait sculptor he was (and is) unrivalled, equally at home with the grandest official commissions and intimate works such as the portrait of his mistress *Costanza Buonarelli* (c.1635, Florence, Bargello). In his last years he evolved a very personal, intensely spiritual style (*Blessed Lodovica Albertoni*, 1671–74, Rome, S. Francesco a Ripa). With his buildings, fountains and other statuary, Bernini left a deeper impression on the face of Rome (almost all his work is there) than any artist has on any other city. He painted mainly as a private diversion (there are several self-portraits), but the few paintings certainly by him are of high quality (*SS. Andrew and Thomas*, 1627, London, NG). He also employed painters to carry out his designs, as in the Cornaro Chapel, and his ideas were influential on other painters, notably Gaulli. In his energy, virtuosity and spiritual conviction, Bernini is the archetypal Baroque artist. See vol. 1 pp. 92, 173, 180; vol. 2 pp. **188–191**

Bernward of Hildesheim died 1022
German churchman, Abbot of the Benedictine monastery of Hildesheim, Saxony, from 993 until his death, and a considerable patron of art during the OTTONIAN period. Bernward is said to have been an artist himself, but nothing is known from his hand. For St Michael's, Hildesheim (begun 1001) he commissioned the celebrated bronze doors (finished 1015), now in Hildesheim Cathedral, which marked the reappearance of CIRE-PERDUE casting, all but lost since Charlemagne's time. Also in the Cathedral is his other great surviving commission, a bronze column made for the Paschal candle. The lively figure style of both owes much to Carolingian tradition, and the Column especially, with its scenes arranged in a continuous band as on the Columns of Trajan or Marcus Aurelius in Rome, shows a strong awareness of classical precedent. There are several works from his period in the Cathedral Treasury at Hildesheim. See vol. 2 p. 69

Berri, Jean, Duc de 1340–1416
The youngest brother of Charles V of France and one of the most lavish and influential patrons of his time. His insatiable desire for beautiful things extended from jewellery to castles, but he is best known for his manuscript collection, the most famous of which is *Les Très Riches Heures du Duc de Berri* (Chantilly, Musée Condé), illuminated by the Limbourg brothers. See vol. 2 p. 89

Berrocal, Miguel-Ortiz born 1933
Spanish sculptor. Most of his work is in bronze, which he polishes to a high finish, and is invariably based on the human torso (*Torso of Benjamin*, 1961, Rotterdam, Boymans Museum). Often his sculptures are made of separate elements which can be taken apart and reassembled, thus allowing the spectator to handle the work piece by piece. The main influence on his style are Spanish Baroque, Picasso and Surrealism. He has taught sculpture in Germany and lives mainly in Paris and Italy—he has a foundry in a castle near Verona.

Berruguete, Alonso c.1480/90–1561
Spanish sculptor and painter, son of Pedro. He was the leading sculptor in the

reign of the Emperor Charles V, for whom he was court sculptor and painter. Like his father, he went to Italy, and is recorded soon after 1504 in Florence. By 1517, he was back in Spain and among the first to introduce a style based on Italian High Renaissance art. He developed an individual, highly emotive style, employing some of the early Italian Mannerist distortions of form and expressive of the growing atmosphere of mysticism in his country. Perhaps his most splendid single display is in Toledo Cathedral: the carved reliefs of the choir-stalls (from 1541; shared with the comparatively traditional Bigarny), and the large *Transfiguration*, in which El Greco must have recognized a kindred spirit.

Berruguete, Pedro active 1477–1503
Spanish painter at the court of Ferdinand and Isabella. He is identified with "Pietro Spagnuolo", who worked at Urbino in the 1470s, and the famous portrait of *Federigo da Montefeltro and his son* (c.1477, Urbino, Galleria Nazionale delle Marche) is almost certainly by him. In 1482 Berruguete returned to Spain and his late paintings, for example the altarpiece of *St Thomas Aquinas* (Avila, Santo Tomás) combine monumentality with a gift for narrative detail. He was the first Spanish painter successfully to fuse the Hispano-Netherlandish tradition of realistic representation with the Renaissance style. See vol. 2 pp. 97, 112

Bertholle, Jean 1909–70
French painter. Under the impact of Bissière's teaching at the Académie Ranson in Paris he abandoned his early interest in Surrealism in favour of a more abstract style. *Composition* (1955, Paris, Musée d'Art Moderne) shows his typical use of blues and blacks and of a grid-like compositional structure.

Berthon, George Théodore 1806–92
Canadian portrait painter, born in Vienna. He taught and studied briefly in England, emigrating to Toronto in 1837. Conservative official portraits of public dignitaries (many in the Ontario Government Collection, Toronto) form the bulk of his output, although he is better known for his family portraits, particularly *The three Robinson sisters* (1846, Toronto, Art Gallery of Ontario), which exudes a sophisticated refinement reminiscent of Reynolds.

Bertoia, Jacopo (Jacopo Zanguidi) 1544–74
Italian painter, born in Parma. He assimilated the style of Parmigianino, whom he excelled in inventive fantasy in the frescos he painted in the Sala del Bacio of the Palazzo del Giardino, Parma (1566–73). From 1568 he began to divide his time between Parma and Rome, painting, in a more sober style, the *Passion* cycle in the Oratorio del Gonfalone, Rome. It was completed by other Mannerists, since Cardinal Farnese insisted that Bertoia should decorate the Farnese palace at Caprarola, work which occupied the painter's last years (1569 and 1572–74).

Bertoldo di Giovanni c.1420–91
Florentine sculptor, a pupil of Donatello, teacher of Michelangelo, and curator of Lorenzo de'Medici's collections. He rose to prominence when he finished Donatello's bronze reliefs on the pulpits in S. Lorenzo, Florence, but he is best known for his bronze *Battle* relief (c.1480–90, Florence, Bargello). Its interlocked figures of men and horses are

based on an ancient sarcophagus in the Campo Santo at Pisa, and Bertoldo's work in turn inspired Michelangelo's *Battle of Lapiths and Centaurs* (c.1492, Florence, Casa Buonarroti).

Besnard, Albert 1849–1934
French painter. He spent four years in Italy after winning the Prix de Rome in 1874, and later visited London, where he moved within the Pre-Raphaelite circle of painters, but more decisive for his art were the Impressionists. Blending their colour with correct academic drawing he created a style which proved very popular and gained him many official honours. His work varied from portraits (*Mme Roger Jourdain*, 1886, Nice, Musée des Beaux-Arts) to large decorative schemes such as the ceiling at the Comédie Française, Paris, 1905–13.

Bettes the Elder, John active 1531–before 1576
British painter and wood-engraver, first recorded in 1531. He is perhaps the "IB" who signed the border of the title-page of William Cunningham's book *Cosmographical Glasse* (1559). Around the *Portrait of a man* (signed and dated 1545, London, Tate) a handful of works may be grouped. They are strongly influenced by Holbein, with whom Bettes may have worked.

Beuckelaer, Joachim
c.1530–1573/4
Netherlandish painter born in Antwerp, where he became a member of the painters' guild in 1560. He was a pupil of his uncle, Aertsen, and shared his preference for depicting cameos of religious events in panels dominated by genre scenes and still lifes (*Christ in the house of Mary and Martha*, 1565, Brussels, Musées Royaux des Beaux-Arts). His style, however, was more linear. Mor employed him as a drapery artist.

Beuys, Joseph born 1921
West German artist, the single most important influence on the West German (and arguably European) avantgarde of the 1970s. He disseminated his ideas partly through his teaching post at the Düsseldorf Academy, from which he was dismissed in 1972, and also through a wide variety of other means: his reputation itself must be counted one of his major artistic achievements. In 1943, when a Luftwaffe pilot, he was shot down in the Crimea, and the local Tatars who rescued him used fat and felt to keep him warm. These two materials came to play important parts in his personal mythology, as did iron and copper, used, for example, in *Fond IV/4* (2nd version, 1970–74, Krefeld, Kaiser Wilhelm Museum). His "*Fonds*" or "Foundations" acted, literally and metaphorically, as batteries and the central concern of Beuys' art is perhaps the generation and understanding of energy. Among his more famous "Actions" were *How to explain pictures to a dead hare* (1965), in which his face was covered in honey and gold leaf, and *Coyote* (1974), a week-long "dialogue" with a live coyote in New York. Alchemical and mystical references abound in Beuys' work, since he believes scientific positivism is unable to cope with the present human predicament and environment. His career is remarkable for the idealistic seriousness with which he has pursued his main aim—a complete revolution, and regeneration, of human consciousness, with art as the catalyst. See vol. 3 p. **243**

Bevan, Robert 1865–1925
British painter. He studied in Paris and

worked at Pont-Aven in the 1890s. Paintings of this period reflect the influence of Bernard and Gauguin, and after he settled in London in 1900 his work continued to show the impact of Divisionism and the Nabis. A founder member of the CAMDEN TOWN group, he was in fact less interested in the city as a subject than in rural life. He particularly liked scenes with horses, painted in creamy yellows and purple. There are several examples of his work in the Tate Gallery, London.

Bewick, Thomas 1753–1828
British wood-engraver. He spent most of his life in Newcastle upon Tyne, where he had a flourishing business. His first independent work dates from the late 1760s, but he made his name with *A General History of Quadrupeds* (1790), and followed this with *A History of British Birds* (2 volumes, 1797 and 1804). Bewick revived the art of wood engraving, transforming it into an economical process for fine book illustration. He had considerable technical skill, but his success lay partly in making use of simple, bold contrasts of tone and not trying to transcend the limits of the medium. Coupled with his keen observation of rural life and sure decorative sense, this has ensured the lasting popularity of his work. See vol. 1 p. **166**

Beyeren, Abraham van 1620/21–90
Dutch still-life painter. He was born in The Hague, and lived in various towns in the Netherlands, finally settling in Overschie in 1678. At first he specialized in fish subjects, but, like his contemporary Kalf, later devoted himself primarily to the sumptuous banquet theme, although he also painted *vanitas* subjects, flower-pieces, still lifes with dead game and occasionally seascapes. The majestic *Still life with a lobster and turkey* (Oxford, Ashmolean) is a late work, representative of his use of rich colours glowing against sombre backgrounds. His reputation in his lifetime was small, but he is now considered one of the greatest Dutch still-life painters, and his very painterly touch distinguishes him from most of his contemporaries. See vol. 1 p. *72*; vol. 2 p. **233**

Bhuvaneshvara
Temple city in the province of Orissa in eastern India, sacred to the god Shiva. It once had some 700 temples, built round a sacred lake between the 7th and 12th centuries. The surviving temples range from tiny one-hall chapels to the mighty temple of the Lingaraja (first half of the 11th century) which dominates the entire city. The typical Orissan temple consists of the shrine, surmounted by a tower, usually square in plan with rounded corners, with an assembly hall in front rising to a pyramidal roof composed of horizontal courses. The sculpture which decorates the temple walls at Bhuvaneshvara changed its character over the five centuries from a vigorous post-Gupta sculptural style to the refined and sensuous idiom of the 12th century, superbly calculated to blend with the architectural details and decorations. See vol. 3 p. 18

Bianchi, Mosé 1840–1904
Italian painter from Lombardy, associated with the SCAPIGLIATI. Extremely versatile, he tried various genres and media, including fresco. His works depicting choirboys, such as *Return from the festival* (1887, Milan, Galleria d'Arte Moderna), were very popular, but he is at his best in sea studies executed at Chioggia in the late 1870s and in scenes

of Milan and Monza (*Snow in Milan*, c.1895, Milan, Galleria d'Arte Moderna). Painted from life, these represent immediate impressions of light and atmosphere. Although famous in the 1870s and 1880s, he died in poverty.

Bibiena family
Italian family of Bolognese QUADRATURISTI and stage designers. Notable were the brothers **Ferdinando** (1657–1743) and **Francesco** (1659–1739), and Ferdinando's sons, **Giuseppe** (1696–1757) and **Antonio** (1700–74). Their elaborate and pompous style, which was challenged by the lighter one of Colonna, found support in central Europe, and they worked in Vienna, Dresden, Bayreuth and elsewhere.

Bicci di Lorenzo 1373–1452
Florentine painter, the father of Neri di Bicci. The firm modelling and observant narrative of his early work were influenced by Agnolo Gaddi. Later a more fluid, linear INTERNATIONAL GOTHIC style with dainty figures, picturesque detail and luscious colour emerges in small predella panels, such as the delightful *Scenes from the life of St Nicholas* (1433, Oxford, Ashmolean, and New York, Metropolitan). His larger altarpieces, however, tend to follow outworn 14th-century formulae.

Biddle, George 1885–1973
American painter of strong social-realist bias. He studied in Munich and Paris and was influenced by Velazquez, Degas and Cassatt. His frescos for the Justice Department in Washington DC, which aroused political controversy at the time (1935), display a solid realism possibly influenced by the Mexican muralists Rivera and Orozco. Biddle helped persuade President Roosevelt of the need for government sponsorship in the arts early in 1933.

Biederman, Charles born 1906
American artist. From the late 1930s he made coloured geometric reliefs, and argued in his book *Art as the Evolution of Visual Knowledge* (1948) that such work represented the necessary step forward from the painting of Mondrian. Although he was little recognized in America his thinking had a strong influence on British Constructivists such as Victor Pasmore and Mary Martin.

Biedermeier
Style in painting, furnishing and decorative crafts predominant in Austria and Germany in the period from the end of the Napoleonic Wars (1815) to the "Year of Revolutions" (1848). The name is taken from the comic figure Gottlieb Biedermeier, featured in the satirical review "*Fliegende Blätter*" (Flying Leaves), who represents the small, honest, bourgeois man, self-satisfied and complacent but also plain and unpretentious. The kind of paintings which appealed to the social class he represented were interiors, portraits and landscapes, treated with meticulous attention to detail and a total lack of heroic action and sentiment. Waldmüller was the quintessential Biedermeier artist, and other leading exponents were Daffinger and Spitzweg. Although strictly applicable only to Austria and Germany, the term is often extended to the art of other areas, notably Denmark, where Købke was the finest exponent.

Bierstadt, Alfred 1830–1902
American landscape painter. German-born, he was brought up in America, and returned to Germany in 1853 to study at

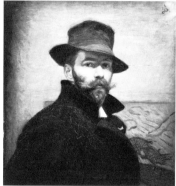
Bergh: Self-portrait (detail), 1895. Private coll. (Stockholm, Nationalmuseum)

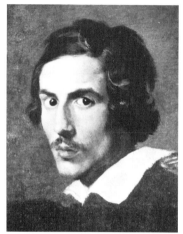
Bernini: Self-portrait, c.1625. Rome, Galleria Borghese (Scala)

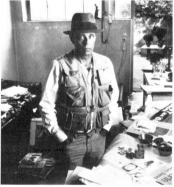
Beuys: Photograph by David Montgomery/ *The Sunday Times*

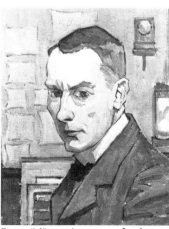
Bevan: Self-portrait, 1913–14. London, NPG (Anthony d'Offay Gallery)

the Düsseldorf Academy. He travelled in Germany and Switzerland and spent a winter in Rome before returning in 1857 to America. Bierstadt is best known for his grandiose interpretations of the American landscape, which are among the finest paintings of the ROCKY MOUNTAIN school (*Thunderstorm in the Rocky Mountains*, 1859, Boston, MFA).

Bigarny, Felipe 1470s?–1543
Burgundian sculptor and architect, also called Felipe de Borgoña. He was active in Spain from 1498, when his three stone reliefs for the enclosure of the high altar of Burgos Cathedral were commissioned. The carving reflects Italianate influence, particularly in the naturalistic treatment of the human figure, but the style is basically Gothic. Bigarny worked with Alonso Berruguete in Toledo and with Diego de Siloë in the cathedrals of Granada and Burgos; his fine tomb of Canon Lerma (1524, Burgos Cathedral) shows Siloë's influence.

Bigot, Trophîme active *c.*1620–40
French CARAVAGGESQUE painter. A hypothetical oeuvre has been established on stylistic criteria, but controversy still surrounds this painter. He concentrated on candle-light pictures rather in the manner of Honthorst, and, before Bigot was proposed as the author of the paintings now given to him, they were referred to as the work of "the Candle-light Master". His subjects are often unusual (*Doctor weighing urine*, Oxford, Ashmolean). After an early career in Rome he seems to have settled near Aix-en-Provence, but there has been confusion with another painter of the same name (probably his father, born 1579) who worked in the same area in the 1630s, but in a non-Caravaggesque style.

Bihzad Ustad Kamal al-Din
*c.*1455–1533/5
Persian or Eastern Turkish painter, working chiefly in Herat. As an orphan he was brought up by Mirak Naqqash, and his early patrons were Mir Ali Shir Navai and Sultan Husayn Bayqara. After the fall of Herat, Bihzad moved to Tabriz to join the court of Shah Tahmasp, perhaps in 1514, and in 1522 he was appointed head of the library. Qasim Ali, Shaykh Zaden, Aqa Mirak and Muzaffir Ali are mentioned as his pupils, and a considerable number of manuscript illustrations and separate drawings are attributed to this great master, some obviously falsely. Indisputable signatures are found in the *Bustan* of 1488 (Cairo, National Library), and a late picture may be *Pir and youth* (1524, Washington, Freer). Bihzad's work is felt to represent the acme of Persian miniature-painting; the harmonious compositions matching simplicity with richness, tranquillity with dynamism, and precision of outline with purity of colour. See vol. 3 p. 27

Bill, Max born 1908
Swiss painter, designer, sculptor and writer, born in Winterthur. He taught design and architecture at the Bauhaus, 1927–29, and during the early 1930s was a prominent member of the ABSTRACTION-CRÉATION group. The main influences on his work were those of the Bauhaus and De Stijl aesthetics. His painting and sculpture is non-figurative and is concerned with the relationship between aesthetic and mathematical theories (*Endless surface*, bronze, 1953–56, Antwerp, Middelheim Museum).

Bingham, George Caleb 1811–79
American painter, brought up in Missouri, where the river life later provided his favourite subject matter. He studied law and theology, was apprenticed to a cabinet-maker and painted signs before attending the Pennsylvania Academy of Fine Arts in 1838. Later he exhibited genre scenes in New York, painted portraits in Washington and returned to Missouri, where he was elected a member of the legislature. His most successful period was 1845–55, when he executed those precisely painted, dreamlike scenes of river life in the days of the fur trade with which his name is most often associated (*Fur traders descending the Missouri*, 1845, New York, Metropolitan). He studied in Düsseldorf, 1856–58, but thereafter never recovered the freshness of his genre scenes or the distilled romantic quality of his river landscapes. See vol. 3 p. **69**

Biomorphic form
Abstract form deriving from organic rather than geometric shapes, curvaceous rather than linear. As developed by Arp and Moore, biomorphic forms were generally suggestive of nature and organic processes. Brancusi's simplifications, for instance of heads or birds, were more specific in inspiration.

Birolli, Renato 1906–59
Italian painter. In 1938, with Guttuso and others, he founded the anti-Fascist group Corrente in Milan. His interest in the artist's role in society had a profound influence on other modern Italian artists, particularly those associated with the FRONTE NUOVO DELLE ARTI, which he founded in 1947. His work ranged from Post-Impressionism in the 1930s via the School of Paris to his late style in which figurative elements are subjected to Expressionist transformations verging on abstraction.

Bishn Das active *c.*1590–1640
Indian Mughal artist. As a youth he and a painter uncle contributed a painting to the dispersed *Baburnameh* (*c.*1590, London, V&A). His first major work is in the *Salim Anvar-i Suhayli* (1604–10, London, BL). On the accession of the Emperor Jehangir in 1605 Bishn Das rose rapidly in the imperial studio. Valued chiefly as a portraitist, he was sent on the embassy to Shah Abbas at Isfahan (1613–20) to make portraits of the Shah and his nobles, now known mostly from copies. He seems to have lost favour under Shah Jahan (1627–58) and worked outside the imperial atelier.

Bishop, Isabel born 1902
American social-realist painter. Her main subject matter is the urban landscape and its shifting figures, usually focusing on the transient life around Union Square, New York (*Waiting*, 1938, New Jersey, Newark Museum).

Bissier, Julius 1893–1965
German painter. Largely self-taught, he began painting only after World War I. Until about 1927 he painted in a realist style owing much to Neue Sachlichkeit, but in that year he met the Freiburg sinologist Ernst Grosser, through whom he discovered Chinese hieroglyphs and calligraphy. This led him to develop his own calligraphic language of symbolic shapes and natural forms verging on the abstract, translated into symbols of the bitter experiences of his life (*Nest in the thorn bush*, 1938, Düsseldorf, Kunstsammlung Nordrhein-Westfalen).

Bissière, Roger 1888–1964
French painter, who worked briefly in a Cubist idiom after his meeting with Braque around 1922. From 1925 to 1938 he taught at the Académie Ranson in Paris, strongly influencing pupils such as Le Moal, Bertholle and Manessier. In 1939 he contracted an eye complaint and moved to Boissierette, where he made wooden carvings and patchwork tapestries. He started painting again in 1945 and in 1948 had a successful eye operation. *Grey and violet* (1957, Museum of Luxembourg) typifies his late style, strongly influenced by Klee, in which references to reality are submerged within a grid-like compositional structure, interspersed with patches of rich colour.

Bitumen
Rich brown pigment, similar to tar, which never completely dries. Its use in 18th- and 19th-century painting has caused much damage from cracking, notably in some of Reynolds' paintings.

Blackburn, Joseph
*c.*1700–after 1778
American portrait painter of English origin. He worked in Bermuda in 1752, and in New England—mainly Boston and Portsmouth, New Hampshire—from 1754 to 1763. He then went to England and probably settled there permanently, although the latter part of his career, like his early life, is obscure. His elegant portraits of fashionable sitters, similar in style to those of his English contemporaries Highmore and Hudson, introduced a new Rococo charm to the Colonies, and are particularly notable for their accomplished painting of fine materials. Two excellent examples of his work, still in their original frames, are the portraits of the sisters *Mrs David Chesebrough* and *Mary Sylvester* (both 1754, New York, Metropolitan).

Black-figure vase-painting
Technique of Greek vase-painting, developed at Corinth in the 7th century BC, in which the details of black silhouette figures painted on pots were picked out in incised lines which revealed the red clay underneath. Further features such as hair and beards came to be added in dark red and white accessory colours. The technique reached its highest development at Athens in the next century. See vol. 2 p. 35

Blake, Peter born 1932
British painter, with Richard Hamilton a major pioneer of POP art in England. *On the balcony* (1955–57, London, Tate) is an early example of his distinctive style. He uses media imagery, pictures from comics, pin-ups and adverts, but there is a restrained and sometimes gently sentimental feeling in his work.

Blake, William 1757–1827
English painter, engraver and poet, one of the greatest figures of the Romantic period. In 1772 he was apprenticed to an antiquarian engraver, and during this seven-year period made engravings of Gothic art for the Society of Antiquaries. In 1779 he became a student at the Royal Academy, where he befriended Flaxman and Stothard. Throughout the 1780s he worked as a commercial engraver while publishing his own poems with hand-coloured illustrations integrated with the engraved text, a technique he claimed was revealed to him in 1787 by the spirit of his brother Robert. He also worked in watercolour and a kind of tempera, but rejected oil-painting. His first illuminated poems, *Songs of Innocence*, were published in 1789, the sequel, *Songs of Experience*, in 1794. As well as his own writings he illustrated the Bible, Milton and Shakespeare, expressing his esoteric symbolism in an intensely visionary manner. His work was admired by the circle of the poet William Hayley, which included Flaxman, and in 1800 he moved to Felpham in Sussex to have closer contact with this group. Under Linnell's patronage he was able to work without fear of poverty from 1820 until his death on what are perhaps his masterpieces, illustrations to *The Book of Job* and Dante's *Divine Comedy*. Although a less isolated figure than was once thought (his sources can be traced in other great masters of line such as Dürer, and he had considerable influence on Palmer and the ANCIENTS), Blake's work is among the most personal in the history of art. His output was prolific—there are major collections in Cambridge (Fitzwilliam), Cambridge, Mass. (Fogg Art Museum), London (BM and Tate) and elsewhere. See vol. 1 pp. *84*, *87*, *98*, *164*; vol. 3 pp. **62–63**

Blakelock, Ralph Albert
1847–1919
American painter of romantic landscapes. He was self-taught and his use of unstable layers of pigment which have damaged most of his works may be due to lack of technical knowledge. He travelled in the Far West (1869–72), sketching Indians, and returned to little success in his native New York. In 1899, impoverished and insane, he was confined to an asylum, where he remained oblivious of the growing influence of his works and their critical and popular acclaim. *Moonlight sonata* (1892, Boston, MFA) is typical of his mature work, an emotional and symbolic rather than realistic view of nature painted in heavy impasto.

Blanchard, Jacques 1600–38
French painter. He was born and trained in Paris but nothing survives from the period before 1624, when he went to Rome. There he rapidly became the most BAROQUE French painter of his generation and a stay in Venice, 1625–27, introduced further richness into his art (*Angelica and Medor*, *c.*1628, New York, Metropolitan). From 1629 he was in Paris establishing his reputation as a decorator, although he is now chiefly associated with fairly small works marked by delicate sentiment and cool, silvery effects of light (*Charity*, 1637, London, Courtauld Institute Galleries).

Blanchard, Maria 1881–1932
Spanish/French painter of Spanish, French and Polish parentage. She was born in Santander, Spain, but came to Paris in 1906 and settled there permanently in 1916. Her paintings reflect an early involvement with Cubism but she became concerned also to explore mysterious, melancholy moods, the result perhaps of her being crippled from childhood. *Boy with ice-cream* (1925, Paris, Musée d'Art Moderne) is a typical example of her muted palette and sensitive observation of children.

Blaue Reiter, Der (The Blue Rider)
Group of EXPRESSIONIST painters formed in Munich in 1911–12. The name "Blue Rider", taken from a painting by Kandinsky, was the title of the almanac conceived by Kandinsky and Marc in 1911 (and published in 1912) and also of the exhibition organized by them in December 1911 at the Gallery Thannhäuser in Munich. The most important artists involved were Kandinsky, Marc, Macke, Jawlensky, Münter, Klee, Kubin and Campendonck. They did not constitute a movement or coherent group but were drawn together by a mutual belief that "the creative spirit is

concealed within matter" (Kandinsky) and that forms and colours were the external expression of this spirit. They also believed that the characteristics of a great spiritual epoch could be discerned in contemporary art throughout Europe. Thus they included in the almanac and in their exhibitions work by the major avantgarde artists in Germany, France, Italy and Russia, with particular emphasis on the naive realism of Henri Rousseau and on Delaunay's Orphic Cubism. They also included examples of children's art, Asiatic art, tribal art and folk art alongside European art from medieval times to the present. The almanac (intended as the first in a series) was inspired by the idea of the total work of art to be created out of a synthesis of music, literature and the visual arts. It ensured that the novel approach of the Blaue Reiter artists was widely known, while two touring exhibitions in 1911 and 1912 brought their work to all the major German cities. The group disbanded in 1914. See vol. 3 pp. 136–137

Blaue Vier (Blue Four)
Group of four painters, Feininger, Jawlensky, Kandinsky and Klee, formed, at the suggestion of their patroness Galka Scheyer, in March 1924. She also proposed the name to be given to the group, deriving essentially from the BLAUE REITER, with which all four artists had been associated before World War I. Its aim was to publicize their work and ideas abroad with Galka Scheyer acting as their agent. She organized an exhibition in San Francisco in May 1924, which, in conjunction with a series of lectures on the artists, later toured the Western States. Her large collection of *Blaue Vier* paintings was given to the Norton Simon Museum in Pasadena.

Blechen, Karl 1798–1840
German painter of landscapes and interiors, largely self-taught. In 1823 he became acquainted with Friedrich and Dahl, and their work exercised a strong influence on his early landscapes, which included highly wrought Gothic ruinscapes. A visit to Italy in 1828, however, turned him from Romanticism to a naturalism akin to Corot's. His casual choice of subject matter and airy brushwork anticipated the later school of German naturalist painters (*View of houses and gardens in Berlin*, c.1838, West Berlin, Staatliche Museen).

Bles, Herri met de c.1510–60
Flemish landscapist. He came from Dinant and was perhaps the nephew of Joachim Patenier—he qualified as the master "Herry de Patenir" in Antwerp in 1535. Unlike Joachim, he constructed his paintings in oblique, curving planes rather than in horizontal layers. He studded his pictures with numerous minute figures, birds and animals, producing the cluttered effect that characterizes such works as *Landscape with Diana* (Strasbourg, Musée de la Ville).

Bloemaert, Abraham 1564–1651
Dutch painter of landscapes and historical subjects. The doyen of the Utrecht school, Bloemaert changed his style with the times. His early works are in a Mannerist style acquired during a period in France in the 1580s. In 1593 he settled in Utrecht and numbered the best painters who worked there among his pupils, including Honthorst and Terbrugghen. When these younger men returned from Rome, they influenced Bloemaert towards a Caravaggesque style, as can be seen in his *Supper at Emmaus* (1622, Brussels, Musées

Royaux des Beaux-Arts). His landscape paintings remained rooted in the Mannerist tradition, but his landscape drawings were largely naturalistic. Many engravings were made after his work, and he was widely influential.

Blondeel, Lancelot 1496–1561
Flemish painter, sculptor and architect born in Poperinghe, west Flanders. In 1519, he joined the painters' guild of Bruges, where he produced distinctive altarpieces with elaborate, Italianate decoration—caryatids, grotesques, *putti* and swags of fruit invade his panels, often overwhelming the solemn religious tone of the scene depicted (*The legend of SS. Cosmas and Damian*, 1523, Bruges, St James). He was a versatile artist, and among his other accomplishments was the creation of decorations for feast days and the restoration of the van Eycks' Ghent altarpiece with Scorel, c.1550.

Bloomsbury group
Group of writers, thinkers and artists who were highly influential in British cultural and intellectual life from 1910 onwards. Of those attached to the art world, the most significant were the painters Vanessa Bell and Duncan Grant and the critics Roger Fry and Clive Bell. They were responsible for the introduction of Post-Impressionism to the British and their views had a powerful impact on advanced taste until the early 1930s.

Bluemner, Oscar 1867–1938
American painter, principally of landscapes. Born in Germany and trained as an architect, he moved to the USA in 1892. He revisited Europe in 1912 and was much influenced by Matisse's bold drawing and harmonious compositions. While always remaining independent of current artistic movements, he was attracted by the colour theories of Delaunay and the Synchromists. In *Old canal port* (1914, New York, Whitney) the cubic forms are painted with an Expressionist use of colour.

Blume, Peter born 1906
American painter brought to New York from Russia in 1911. Blume's early paintings, such as *South of Scranton* (1931, New York, Metropolitan), are Surrealistic, combining neat Precisionist surfaces with ironic and fantastic imagery. His best-known work is probably *The eternal city* (1937, New York, MOMA), a Bosch-like allegory of Mussolini's Italy.

Blythe, David Gilmore 1815–65
American painter. He was first apprenticed to a woodcarver, then to a ship's carpenter until he settled in Pittsburgh. There he observed and painted the ridiculous aspects of society in works such as *The Pittsburgh horse-market* (1858, Pittsburgh, Carnegie Institute).

Boccaccino, Boccaccio active 1493–c.1525
Italian painter. He trained in Ferrara, but worked largely in Cremona. His most important works are the frescos he painted in the Cathedral there in 1518. They are highly dramatic with billowing draperies, forceful gestures and splendid perspectival panoramas and interiors.

Boccioni, Umberto 1882–1916
Italian painter and sculptor, one of the leading FUTURIST artists. He joined the Futurists in 1909, writing *The Technical Manifesto of Futurist Painting* (1910) and *The Manifesto of Futurist Sculpture* (1912). His early work was DIVISIONIST and he used this method for his first

Futurist paintings, such as *The city rises* (1910, New York, MOMA). After exposure to Cubism in Paris in 1912 his formal vocabulary was enriched and he evolved a style that depicted forms in semi-abstraction with lines and planes defining simultaneously the subject and its potential or actual movement. These "force lines" can be seen in such works as *Dynamism of a cyclist* (1913, Milan, Gianni Mattioli coll.). As a sculptor his innovations range from combinations of objects and their surroundings (*Fusion of head and window*, 1912; destroyed 1916) to recommendations for the introduction of motorized sculpture. His investigation of bodily movement culminated in his *Unique forms of continuity in space* (1913, casts in London, Tate; New York, MOMA, and elsewhere), one of the masterpieces of 20th-century sculpture. He was killed during World War I. See vol. 1 p. 27; vol. 3 pp. **152–153**

Bocion, François-Louis-David 1828–90
Swiss landscape painter. He studied in Gleyre's Paris studio, returning to Switzerland on the outbreak of the 1848 Revolution. After a year of travels in Italy he returned to Lausanne and remained there until his death, working mainly as a teacher. His subject matter was chiefly the lakes and mountains around Lausanne and scenes from the history of the canton of Vaud executed in a Romantic style. Much of his work is in the Vaud Museum, Lausanne.

Böcklin, Arnold 1827–1901
With Hodler, the leading Swiss painter of the 19th century. He began his studies in 1845 in Düsseldorf, and many of his early landscapes show the influence of Friedrich. In 1847 he studied in Geneva with Calame, another strong influence on the formation of his Romantic style. The large mural *Pan in the reeds* (1857, Munich, Neue Pinakothek) made his reputation and marked the beginning of the development of his private mythology of nymphs, fauns, satyrs and other beings who express man's primitive emotions and fears. From 1850 to 1857 he had lived in Rome and from the late 1860s onwards he spent most of his time in Italy, finding inspiration in its light, landscape and ancient myths. On his visits to Switzerland and Germany most of his time was taken up with experiments with flying machines, but he was nevertheless the most popular and influential artist in the German-speaking world in the 1880s and 1890s. By this time his style had developed to an emotionally charged Symbolism, and the mystical yearning for the unknown which characterizes most of his mature work is best exemplified in *The island of the dead*, of which he produced five versions from 1880 onwards (examples in Basel, Kunstmuseum, and New York, Metropolitan). This became one of the best-known and most reproduced images of its time. Böcklin's work was one of the most important manifestations of Symbolism outside France and was seen by the Surrealists to anticipate their own ideas and imagery. The Kunstmuseum in his native Basel has the best collection of his work, including a staircase fresco which was commissioned by the museum in 1868. See vol. 3 p. **123**

Bodegón
Spanish term (literally "tavern") for domestic scenes in which a still life is a prominent feature.

Bodmer, Walter born 1903
Swiss artist. His earliest work was real-

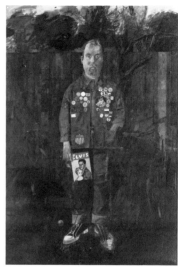
Blake, Peter: *Self-portrait with badges*, 1961. London, Tate

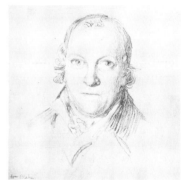
Blake, William: Drawing by Flaxman?, 1804. Cambridge, Fitzwilliam (Mansell)

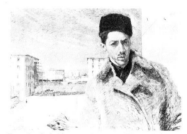
Boccioni: Self-portrait, 1908. Fiorentini coll. (Alinari)

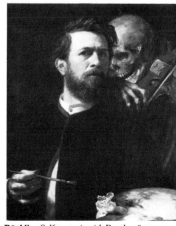
Böcklin: *Self-portrait with Death*, 1872. West Berlin, Staatliche Museen

ist, but in the 1930s he turned to a Cubist style indebted to Picasso. He has also made complex wire sculptures which have the intricacy and visual wit of the work of Klee and Miró.

Body art
A recent art form, deriving in part from HAPPENINGS, in part from CONCEPTUAL art, in which the artist's body is used to demonstrate or realize its owner's artistic ideas. Those associated with Body art include Acconci and Nauman.

Body colour
Colour which is opaque rather than transparent. The term is applied specifically to watercolour pigments mixed with a white filler to make them opaque, and is sometimes used interchangeably with GOUACHE.

Boeckl, Herbert 1894–1960
Austrian painter. After studying architecture he began to paint (1912) and his first works show the influence of Cézanne and then of Schiele and Kokoschka. Later he was influenced by Cubism and began to paint religious pictures such as the series of *The life of St Joseph of Copertino* (1950–54) and the frescos for the Engelskapelle in Seckau (1952).

Bohemian art
Art of a period of renaissance in Bohemia (approximately present-day Czechoslovakia) in the late 14th and early 15th centuries. In the reign of Emperor Charles IV, King of Bohemia (1346–78), Prague underwent an artistic revival initially stimulated by the Emperior's lavish patronage and cultivated taste. A new university was founded and a huge new Gothic cathedral built by a French architect, Matthias of Arras, and his successor, the sculptor Peter Parler. The Emperor ordered numerous reliquaries, Italianate murals and mosaics for the Cathedral. The royal tombs there were presumably inspired by those of St Denis, France, which Charles had visited. In his castle at Karlstein an extraordinary number of panels and murals have survived, including work by Master Theoderic. The Emperor's counsellors were also energetic in patronage, fostering a court art which was second to none in Europe. French and Sienese influence is apparent in many manuscript and panel paintings, notably in the work of the Master of Vyšši Brod. In the late 14th century the Bohemian **soft style** emerged in painting (in the work of the Master of Třeboň, for instance) and in sculpture: the *Schöne Madonnen* statues (the Krumau Madonna in the Kunsthistorisches Museum, Vienna, is a fine example) are graceful in line and softly modelled. This Bohemian art was important to the formation of INTERNATIONAL GOTHIC, but the Hussite wars in the early 15th century severely disrupted artistic activity.

Boilly, Louis-Léopold 1761–1845
French genre and portrait painter, active mainly in Paris. Some of his more intimate genre scenes, reminiscent of the 18th century, were unsuited to Jacobin taste but his *Triumph of Marat* (1794, Lille, Musée) vindicated him with the Revolutionary Tribunal. During the Restoration, Boilly received little recognition, and although his best-known work, *The arrival of the stage-coach* (1803, Paris, Louvre) won a gold medal in the Salon, it remained unsold. From 1823, he took up lithography, popularizing his scenes from contemporary life. He is said to have painted more than 5,000 portraits.

Boizot, Simon-Louis 1743–1809
French ROCOCO sculptor. A pupil of Michel-Ange Slodtz, he had a career of exemplary academic success. In 1774 he was appointed director at the Sèvres porcelain factory. Although he worked on statues at St Sulpice, Paris, and made competent portrait busts, his typical work is on a small scale and rather flaccid (*Cupid*, 1772, Paris, Louvre).

Bol, Ferdinand 1616–80
Dutch painter. He was born in Dordrecht, and was a pupil of Rembrandt in Amsterdam in the late 1630s. His works of the 1640s, particularly portraits, are very close in style to Rembrandt's, and attributions have been disputed between them. Bol enjoyed success as an efficient painter of historical subjects, notably for the new Town Hall in Amsterdam, and of portraits, and after marrying a wealthy widow in 1669 evidently gave up painting. *Admiral de Ruyter* (1667, versions in Amsterdam, Rijksmuseum; The Hague, Mauritshuis; London, National Maritime Museum) shows the influence of the fashionable van der Helst which characterized his later portraits.

Bol, Hans 1534–93
Flemish painter, born in Malines. He began his career with large-scale panels, but after 1567 devoted himself to smaller works in gouache and watercolour. He followed in the tradition of the 15th-century miniaturists but added a new dimension in his realistic landscapes, the spirit of which pervades the work of his pupil, Hoefnagel.

Boldini, Giovanni 1842–1931
Italian painter who achieved an international reputation as a portraitist. He studied in Florence, where he met the Macchiaoli, and in 1867 met Manet and Degas in Paris. He also studied Romney, Gainsborough and Reynolds in London, Hals in Holland and Velazquez in Spain. Their influence is reflected in his rapid brushwork and range of blacks, whites and silvery greys, as in the full-length portrait of *Mme Max* (1896, Paris, Musée d'Orsay). His city scenes, still lifes and graphic work are equally vivacious. See vol. 3 p. 152

Bolgi, Andrea 1605–56
Italian sculptor. He worked in Florence with Pietro Tacca, then settled in Rome, where during the 1630s he became one of Bernini's principal assistants. His best-known work, *St Helena* (1629–39), one of the four huge statues for the crossing piers in St Peter's, is typical of his dry, static style. In 1653 he moved to Naples, where he tried unsuccessfully to infuse his work with Baroque dynamism.

Bolotowsky, Ilya born 1907
Russian-born American painter. He was a founder member of the American Abstract Artists' Association in 1936, and evolved a style using brilliant colouring in asymmetrical rectilinear compositions which reflect his admiration for Mondrian (*Scarlet diamond*, 1969, Buffalo, Albright-Knox). He is also a teacher, playwright and film-maker.

Bolswert, Schelte à *c.*1586–1659
Flemish engraver. He joined Rubens in about 1633 and probably produced more prints after Rubens than any other engraver, carrying on long after the master's death. One of his most impressive prints is after Rubens' *Moses and the brazen serpent*, the rich tones capturing well the drama of the original. His brother, **Boetius** (*c.*1580–1633), also engraved Rubens' work.

Boltraffio, Giovanni Antonio *c.*1466–1516
Italian painter, best known as the pupil and assistant of Leonardo in Milan. He painted portraits and devotional pictures in a style close to his master's, and the attribution of the portrait of a woman known as "*La Belle Ferronnière*" (Paris, Louvre) is still disputed between them. Although his work is solidly constructed and often heavily modelled, at his best he has a lightness of touch and a certain appealing fantasy of invention. His work is well represented in museums in Milan.

Bomberg, David 1890–1957
British painter. In 1913 he went to Paris with Epstein and his early work shows the influence of Léger. Before World War I he was considered one of the most avantgarde British painters. The huge work, *In the hold* (1913–14, London, Tate), anticipates later artists' use of a rigid grid pattern; here he fragments the subject into multicoloured splinters while retaining a lucid design. His later painting, landscapes and portraits, were so boldly coloured and executed that the intense observation behind them was largely ignored. He exerted a strong influence on painters such as Auerbach. See vol. 3 p. **155**

Bombois, Camille (1883–1970)
French NAIVE painter, who, amongst other jobs, worked for some time as a circus wrestler before taking up painting. The critic Wilhelm Uhde exhibited his work in 1928 alongside that of Rousseau, Bauchant, Vivin and Séraphine. His imaginative pictures of circus life, such as *Country fair athlete* (*c.*1930, Paris, Musée d'Art Moderne), are distinguished by the simplicity of their clear outlines and bright colours and by the tragic heroism of their protagonists.

Bonazza, Antonio 1698–1763
Italian sculptor of genre subjects. Most of his life was spent in and around Padua, and his best-known works are to be found in the garden of the Villa Widman at Bagnoli di Sopra, about 20 miles south of the city. These are of comic figures dressed in contemporary costume, and are notable for their vivid lifelike quality. Carlo Goldoni, the playwright whose name is invariably coupled with that of the other great Venetian master of genre subjects, Pietro Longhi, was significantly a frequent guest at the villa.

Bondol, Jean de active 1368–81
Flemish miniaturist, also called Jean de Bruges and Jan Hennequin. All his recorded activity took place in Paris, where he was head of a large workshop and official painter to Charles V. A Bible dedicated to Charles which Bondol illustrated (The Hague, Rijksmuseum Meermanno-Westreenianum) contains an unusually realistic portrait of the king. His only other certain work was the design of the celebrated *Apocalypse* tapestries (Angers, Museum of Tapestries), in which French courtly elegance is tempered with Netherlandish realism.

Bone, Sir Muirhead 1876–1953
British painter and graphic artist. From 1890 to 1894 he was trained as an architect and buildings remained his principal subject matter. His work often combined a meticulous attention to detail and perspective with a sense of drama close to Piranesi (*British Museum Reading Room*, 1907, London, Tate).

Bonevardi, Marcelo born 1929
Argentine painter and sculptor. He trained as an architect and taught Plastic Arts at Cordoba University in 1956. In 1958 he settled in New York among a large group of Latin American painters including Fernandez-Muro. He is best known for his series of relief constructions inset with small geometric or organically shaped figures.

Bonfigli, Benedetto active 1445–96
Umbrian painter. He spent most of his life in Perugia, executing altarpieces, processional banners and a series of fine historical frescos for the Palazzo Pubblico (1455 onwards), but is also recorded painting the Vatican decorations for the Jubilee in 1450. His style was based on Tuscan modes, particularly the decorative manner of Gozzoli and Domenico di Bartolo.

Bonheur, Rosa 1822–99
French painter, trained by her father **Raymond** Bonheur (died 1849). She began to exhibit in the Salon in 1841 and achieved popular success with her detailed, realistic portrayals of animals. *The horse fair* (1853, New York, Metropolitan), reproduced in engraving internationally, made her reputation as a successful academic painter.

Bonifazio Veronese (Bonifazio de' Pitati) *c.*1487–1553
Italian painter, born in Verona, but usually considered a member of the Venetian school. He is first recorded in 1528, in Venice, and on stylistic evidence it seems likely that he trained with Palma Vecchio. His work is in the grandiose style of the Venetian High Renaissance, with sumptuously attired figures in magnificent architectural settings opening out upon a rich landscape (*The Judgment of Solomon*, 1533, Venice, Accademia).

Bonington, Richard Parkes 1802–28
English painter in oil and watercolour, most of whose working life was spent in France. His family moved to Calais in about 1817, and soon after Bonington went to Paris, where he became a pupil of Gros. A marvellous colourist, his watercolours of romantic, medieval and oriental subjects, genre scenes and landscapes were executed with a fluid and brilliant technique. His first works to be exhibited at the Paris Salon (two scenes of Normandy shown in 1822) were much praised. In the "English" Salon of 1824 his work—shown alongside Constable's—was perhaps just as influential on French painters, not least on his friend Delacroix. In 1826 he travelled in Italy, notably to Venice, of which he left many memorable paintings. He died in London of consumption in 1828. The best collection of his work is in the Wallace Collection, London. See vol. 3 p. **92**

Bonnard, Pierre 1867–1947
French painter, one of the most important late exemplars of the IMPRESSIONIST tradition. In the later 1880s he attended the Académie Julian in Paris where he met Sérusier, Denis, Vuillard and Ranson. Together they founded the NABIS, inspired by a common stylistic debt to Gauguin and the Japanese print and a strong commitment to the decorative arts. In the 1890s Bonnard executed designs not only for posters, prints and book illustrations but also for decorative panels, stained glass and furniture. *Women with a dog* (1891, Williamstown, Clark Art Institute) shows how in his easel-painting, too, he stressed pattern and design at the expense of definition of form in space. After 1900 he reverted to a

more naturalistic style, rooted in Impressionism. *Nude in the bath* (1937, Paris, Petit Palais) is typical of his later INTIMISTE works both in its use of bright colours and fluid brush-strokes, and its intimate domestic imagery. See vol. 1 p. *125*; vol. 3 p. **120**

Bonnat, Joseph-Florentin-Léon
1833–1922
French painter, one of the most successful portraitists of the Third Republic. Bonnat's early work reflects his realist Spanish training, but he achieved fame with society portraits, painted with photographic verisimilitude. The money he made from these enabled him to form a magnificent collection, notably of Old Master drawings, which he donated to his native city of Bayonne.

Bontecou, Lee born 1931
American sculptor. Her reliefs are constructed from canvas stretched over a wire framework and often incorporate found objects, evoking aggression and savagery. *Untitled* (1962, Stockholm, Moderna Museet), with its steel forms and apertures like inhuman orifices, is characteristic.

Bontemps, Pierre *c.*1505/10–68
French sculptor, first recorded in 1536, working under Primaticcio on decorative sculpture at Fontainebleau. He was in Paris by 1550 when his two most famous works were begun, both of them in the abbey church of St Denis near Paris—the effigies and sculptural decoration of the tomb of Francis I, designed by the architect Philibert de L'Orme, and the monument for the heart of Francis I. Both show his elegant, sophisticated style and technical skill.

Bonvin, François 1817–87
French painter. A minor realist in the circle of Courbet, Bonvin was clearly influenced by the 17th-century Dutch genre tradition and by Chardin. He was awarded a gold medal in the Salon of 1850–51 for the *Orphanage school* (Langres, Musée), a fine example of his gentle treatment of traditional genre subjects. His realism was more popular and less provocative than Courbet's.

Bordone, Paris 1500–71
Italian painter. He was born in Treviso, and had settled in Venice by 1518 although he also made visits to Augsburg and France. He became a pupil of Titian, whom he found very disagreeable. Generally his handling is harder than Titian's and more linear. He is best known for his Giorgionesque scenes, but his finest work is perhaps the unusual *Fisherman giving the ring to the Doge* (*c.*1535, Venice, Accademia), with its figures linked rhythmically within a deep architectural setting. His portrait of a young lady (*c.*1550, London, NG) is typical of the lustre and rigidity of his style. Among his later works are some mildly prurient allegories.

Borduas, Paul Emile 1905–60
Canadian abstract painter who worked in and around Montreal. He was apprenticed as a church decorator and then went to study with Denis in Paris. There he acquired a poetically charged style with Fauve overtones (*Woman with a mandoline*, 1941, Montreal, Musée d'Art Contemporaine). In 1941–42, inspired by the work of Paris Surrealists seen in New York, he began to produce "automatic" paintings in gouache. With Riopelle he formed Les AUTOMATISTES, and in 1948 he published the manifesto *Universal Refusal*, in which he reviled

the parochialism constraining many other Canadian painters. In his later work he experimented with all-over surface animation inspired by Pollock and Riopelle. He had a resounding influence on young Canadian artists.

Borès, Francisco born 1898
Spanish painter. He was trained in Madrid, and left for Paris in 1923. Contact with the avantgarde there, in particular with Gris and Miró, produced Cubist-inspired work and, later, contributions to Surrealism. However, he soon developed his characteristic style in which the original Cubist analysis of a motif is maintained as a linear two-dimensional construct placed against a uniform pastel-coloured background.

Borges, Jacobo born 1931
Venezuelan painter. He has contributed to a resurgence of declamatory social themes in figurative painting, independent of Mexican influences. He studied in Caracas and Europe, remaining in Paris until 1956. In the 1960s he was heavily involved in politics, but returned to painting in 1970 and exploited a wealth of techniques (filmmaking, printing and drawing) earning himself a place among the most outstanding creators of his generation in Latin America. A representative painting is *The show has begun* (1964, Caracas, Galleria de Arte Nacional).

Borghese, Camillo 1552–1621 and **Scipione** 1576–1633
Italian churchmen, amongst the leading patrons and collectors in 17th-century Rome. Camillo (Scipio's uncle) became Pope Paul V in 1605, and the most important artistic event during his pontificate was the building of the façade of St Peter's by the architect Carlo Maderno. The greatest monument to his taste, however, is his large and sumptuous memorial chapel in S. Maria Maggiore, begun in 1605: over the next decade many of the leading artists in Rome worked in it—the sculptors Pietro Bernini, Stefano Maderno and Francesco Mochi; the painters Il Cavaliere d'Arpino and Guido Reni. Scipione Borghese was, with Pope Urban VIII, the most important of Gianlorenzo Bernini's patrons, commissioning from him the early figure groups which established him as the greatest sculptor of his age. These, together with busts by Bernini of Camillo and Scipione and the rest of their splendid collections, are housed in the superb Villa Borghese, in Rome.

Borglum, Gutzon 1867–1941
American sculptor of Danish descent. He is famous for his spectacular portraits of Presidents Washington, Jefferson, Lincoln and Theodore Roosevelt, which he drilled and dynamited out of Mount Rushmore in the Black Hills of South Dakota. This enormous project, begun in 1930 and finished only after Borglum's death, is a great work of engineering rather than of art. Another huge monument, commemorating the Confederate Army, was begun on Stone Mountain, Georgia, in 1916 but never completed. Borglum's brother **Solon Hannibal** Borglum (1868–1922) was also a sculptor, noted for his horses, cowboys and Indians. See vol. 1 p. *203*

Borisov-Musatov, Viktor
1870–1905
Russian painter. He studied in Moscow, St Petersburg and Paris, returning to Russia in 1895 after the death of Gustave Moreau, in whose studio he had worked for the previous five years.

Pictures such as *The reservoir* (1902, Moscow, Tretyakov Gallery) possess a Chekhovian charm, and his style of painting in a muted range of pastel blues and greens, leaving areas of canvas bare, was adopted by a number of younger painters, including Kuznetsov, Goncharova and Larionov. This group exhibited together in March 1907, adopting a blue rose as an emblem and including a retrospective of Borisov-Musatov.

Borrassá, Luís active 1388–1424
Spanish painter active in Catalonia. Little is known of his life, but four documented altarpieces survive (example, 1411, in Tarrasa, S. Maria). He was a pupil of Serra and his work is typical of the INTERNATIONAL GOTHIC.

Bortnyik, Sándor 1893–1977
Hungarian artist. From 1925 he ran a graphics school in Budapest called Workshop and a theatre group called The Green Donkey. After World War I he was Director of the Budapest School of Fine Arts until 1956. A typical example of his early Cubist-inspired work is *Red locomotive* (1918, Budapest, Museum of Working Class Movement). Its large, simple forms contain symbolic references to the movement towards a new socialist society.

Bortoloni, Mattia 1696–1750
Italian decorative painter, trained in Venice and active mainly in Lombardy and Piedmont. His first major works (1716) in the Villa Cornaro at Piombino Dese display a bizarrely elongated figurative style that might owe something to Francesco Maffei. Later in life he fell under the influence of Tiepolo but still retained a highly idiosyncratic and expressive manner. His greatest work is the dome decoration of the sanctuary of Vicoforte at Mondovi, one of the most dynamic frescos in northern Italy, and also reputedly the largest in the world.

Bosboom, Johannes 1817–91
Dutch painter in oils and watercolour, a member of the HAGUE school. He is best known for paintings of church interiors in the manner of 17th-century Dutch artists such as de Witte (*Church interior*, 1848, Amsterdam, Rijksmuseum).

Bosch, Jerome active *c.*1470–1516
Netherlandish painter named after the town of s'Hertogenbosch (Bois-le-Duc) in northern Brabant, where he seems to have spent all his life. His real name was Jerome van Aken. None of his paintings, of which about 40 survive, is dated, and it is very difficult to trace his development. Some of his works are fairly conventional (*The Crucifixion*, Brussels, Musées Royaux des Beaux-Arts); others exhibit that bizarre and colourful imagery, drawing on a medley of religious symbolism and folk legends, that is the basis of his fame. Elements in his imagery can be traced to contemporary woodcuts and devotional prints, and stylisitically—for his stiff, gangly figures—he can be compared to local Dutch painters such as the Master of the Virgo inter Virgines, but there is much about his work that continues to baffle—its purpose and appeal and the interpretation of its imagery. He worked mainly for local churches, but also received courtly commissions, and after his death Philip II of Spain avidly collected his paintings. The finest collection of his work is now in the Prado, Madrid, including his most famous allegory and his masterpiece, *The Garden of Earthly Delights*, where his fantastic and horrific imagery was given its fullest expression, and his painterly

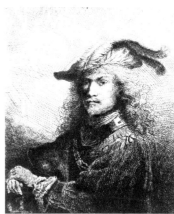
Bol, Ferdinand: Self-portrait etching, 1660. Vienna, Albertina

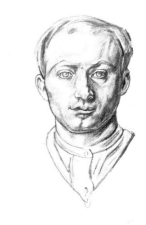
Bomberg: Self-portrait, 1913–14. London, NPG

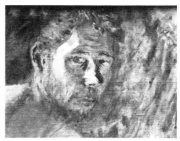
Bonnard: Self-portrait, *c.*1920. Private coll. (Giraudon)

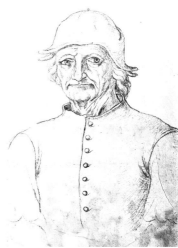
Bosch: Self-portrait drawing. Arras, Bibliothèque Municipale (Giraudon)

brilliance, especially in landscape (a factor often ignored), reached its height. He inspired imitators even in his lifetime and his influence was rapidly spread through prints, so that weird Bosch-like creatures appear, for example, in Domenico Campagnola's engravings. Only Bruegel, however, had the genius to incorporate Bosch's imagery into his own vision. Bosch's work took on a second life in the early 20th century, when it was seen as a precursor of Surrealism and suitable for psychoanalysis. See vol. 1 p. *90*; vol. 2 pp. **98–99**

Bosschaert, Ambrosius 1573–1621
Flemish painter of flower-pieces and still lifes, who spent most of his working life in Holland. He developed the painting of flower-pieces as an independent genre at about the same time as "Velvet" Brueghel, and his works, usually on a small scale and on copper, are, like Brueghel's, exquisitely detailed and delicately coloured, though generally more simple and classical in design. His *Vase of flowers* (*c.*1620, The Hague, Mauritshuis) is justly celebrated as one of the most beautiful of all flower paintings. Bosschaert's output was small but his role was crucial. Among those who carried on his tradition were his three sons, **Ambrosius** the Younger (1609–45), **Johannes** (1610/11–?) and **Abraham** (1612/13–43), and his brother-in-law, van der Ast. See vol. 2 p. **232**

Bosse, Abraham 1602–76
French engraver. He made engravings after his own designs, usually scenes from everyday life, in particular that of the bourgeoisie, which form a valuable record of life in the middle years of the 17th century. Even his biblical scenes are in contemporary dress. The value of his work as an historical record has tended to obscure his quality as an artist, but he had a sure sense of characterization and classical composition and was a very fine technician.

Botero, Fernando born 1932
Colombian painter and draughtsman. In 1952 he studied in Madrid and frequented the Prado. His close observation of detail and almost Mannerist treatment of figures, inflated or deformed to emphasize sensual and expressive qualities, are elements which recall Spanish painting (*Santa Rosa de Lima*, Texas University Art Museum). The combination of local subjects and European manner is often humorous and sardonic. Botero currently lives and works in Paris and New York.

Both, Jan *c.*1618–52
Dutch painter, with Berchem the most popular of the Italianate landscape painters. He was born in Utrecht where he was the pupil of Bloemaert, and he travelled in Italy about 1637–41. None of his many paintings may be securely ascribed to these years, but the works produced after his return to Utrecht echo Claude's use of warm golden light and misty atmospheres, as in the well-known *Italian landscape with artists sketching* (Amsterdam, Rijksmuseum). This is a large painting, and Both was one of the few Dutch landscape painters who worked convincingly on such a scale. He also painted much smaller scenes, showing simple country people going about their daily tasks. The figures in his paintings were sometimes added by other artists. In *Landscape with the judgment of Paris* (London, NG) they are by Poelenburgh. Like Berchem, Both was very popular in the 18th century. His brother **Andries** (*c.*1608–41) was also a painter and lived with Jan for some time in Rome. He was accidentally drowned in Venice. See vol. 2 p. **221**

Botticelli, Sandro *c.*1445–1510
Florentine painter, one of the most distinctive and popular of Renaissance artists. He trained with Filippo Lippi, whose linear style he developed to new heights of gracefulness, adding to it a rich language of sometimes highly personal gesture. His first documented commission, in 1470, was for one of a series of *Virtues* (the others painted by Piero Pollaiuolo) for the Mercanzia, the merchants' meeting-house. The *Fortitude* panel (Florence, Uffizi) reveals the mature artist in its compositional strength, linear precision and grace. By 1480 he had his own workshop and at least three assistants, and his frescos for the *Moses* and *Christ* cycles in the Sistine Chapel, Rome (*c.*1482), established his reputation. His most characteristic works are on panel and he produced many altarpieces, among them the celebrated tondo "*The Madonna of the Magnificat*" (1480s, Uffizi), one of numerous memorable representations of the Virgin and Child. His ideal of feminine beauty is shown also in his mythological paintings for the Medici—most notably in his most famous painting, *The birth of Venus* (*c.*1482–84, Uffizi). During the 1490s his style became more severe and charged with emotion, as in paintings such as the deeply moving *Pietà* (Munich, Alte Pinakothek), and the strange *Calumny of Apelles* (Uffizi), based on a description of the famous painting of antiquity. Equally dramatic, but in a joyful mood, is the enigmatic "*Mystic Nativity*" (1500, London, NG). Botticelli also painted superb portraits (examples in Uffizi and London, NG) and created a series of pen drawings of unrivalled delicacy as illustrations for Dante's *Divine Comedy* (*c.*1490–97, Berlin, Staatsbibliothek, and Vatican, Library). His linear style was out of date by the time he died, and his reputation was revived only in the second half of the 19th century, when his wan female figures were a major influence on the Pre-Raphaelites and his flowing line was an inspiration for Art Nouveau. See vol. 1 pp. *86*; *110*; vol. 2 pp. **116–119**

Botticini, Francesco 1445–97
Florentine painter, a pupil of Neri di Bicci. He was heavily indebted to Filippino Lippi, Botticelli and Verrocchio, and, although his work had little originality, at its best it had considerable charm. He painted many religious subjects; *Madonna and angels adoring Child* (Florence, Pitti) is a good example.

Bouchardon, Edmé 1698–1762
French sculptor. He studied with his father **Jean-Baptiste** (1667–1742), a sculptor and architect, and with Guillaume I Coustou. His stay at the French Academy in Rome, 1723–32, gave him first-hand experience of antique sculpture, which decisively influenced his style. The bust of *Philippe Stosch* (1727, West Berlin, Staatliche Museen) is a remarkable work for its date in the severity of its classicism, but his style softened and became more naturalistic in the 1730s. The famous *Cupid making a bow from Hercules' club* (*c.*1750, Paris, Louvre) is comparatively sensuous, but even so it did not please court taste, and although Bouchardon was considered by many contemporaries to be the greatest French sculptor of the century, he lost ground to less classical sculptors. When he died he was working on the Louis XV monument for Paris (destroyed), a classicizing reply to Lemoyne's Baroque statue of the King at Bordeaux.

Boucher, François 1703–70
French painter of mythology, gallantry, landscape and portraits, one of the greatest of ROCOCO artists. He was trained by Lemoyne and as an engraver—one of his early tasks being the engraving of Watteau's works. In 1723 he won first prize at the Academy and from 1727 to 1730/31 was in Italy. He was received into the Academy in 1734 with *Rinaldo and Armida* (Paris, Louvre), and was soon busy with stage designs, decorative work and tapestry cartoons (from 1755 he was Director of the famous Gobelins tapestry factory). *The Triumph of Venus* (1740, Stockholm, National Museum), glowing, artificial and erotic, is characteristic of his subject matter and style. Madame de Pompadour, Louis XV's most famous mistress, was among his patrons, sitting for her portrait several times (examples London, V&A and Wallace Coll.), and it was she who bought *The rising* and *The setting of the sun* (1753, Wallace Coll.), the peak of Boucher's achievement. More intimate in scale and feeling are such works as the exquisite *Evening landscape* (1743, Barnard Castle, Bowes Museum), the charmingly informal portrait of *Madame Boucher* (1743, New York, Frick) and the *Reclining girl* (1751, Munich, Alte Pinakothek), which is thought to represent Louisa O'Murphy, one of Louis XV's mistresses, and is one of the most celebrated female nudes in the history of art. By the time he became Premier Peintre du Roi in 1765 his style was under attack by Diderot, but he now seems, with his pupil Fragonard, to represent his age better than any other French artist. See vol. 1 p. *26*; vol. 2 pp. **240, 243**, *246*; vol. 4 p. *187*

Boucicaut Master active *c.*1405
French painter, named after his major work, the Hours of Marshal Boucicaut (*c.*1405, Paris, Musée Jacquemart-André). This manuscript, with its magnificent, delicately painted figures and superb colours, is an outstanding example of the INTERNATIONAL GOTHIC style. The Boucicaut Master has been identified with Jacques Coene, a native of Bruges who is recorded in Paris in 1398 and in Milan in 1399: for this there is no direct evidence, but Coene's contemporary reputation accords well with the large number of manuscripts illuminated by the Boucicaut Master's shop in Paris or by his followers. The Boucicaut Master heralds the innovations of the van Eycks in his use of aerial perspective, and his *Funeral service* (fol. 142v) is a prototype of the stately interior of what is perhaps Jan van Eyck's earliest surviving painting, *The Virgin in a church* (*c.*1425, West Berlin, Staatliche Museen). See vol. 2 p. **91**

Boudin, Eugène 1824–98
French painter of seascapes and beach scenes. Encouraged by Millet to take up painting, he first displayed his pictures in his framing shop in Le Havre. Briefly a pupil of Isabey, Boudin recorded the changing skies and seas of Honfleur and Le Havre, and the fashionable beaches of Trouville, in numerous small paintings which greatly influenced the Impressionists, especially Monet (*Women on the beach at Trouville*, 1872, Honfleur, Musée Boudin). His originality lay in his spontaneous, delicate brushwork, which concentrated on the essential. He exhibited at the first Impressionist exhibition of 1874. See vol. 3 p. **98**

Bouguereau, Adolphe William 1825–1905
French painter. He won the Prix de Rome in 1850 and with Cabanel became the most influential upholder of the conservative values of academic art. His characteristic works are coyly erotic history and mythological paintings finished with photographic realism (*Nymphs and a satyr*, 1873, Williamstown, Clark Institute). See vol. 3 p. 87

Boulenger, Hippolyte 1837–74
Belgian painter of landscapes. A pupil of Navez, he settled in Tervuren (1863), where, with the arrival of other painters, a school of Tervuren was established, based on the example of the BARBIZON school. They broke away from the academic style of landscape painting and painted *en plein air*. Boulenger's free technique, subtle colour and accent on atmosphere, seen in his *View of Dinant* (1870, Brussels, Musées Royaux des Beaux-Arts), made him a precursor of Impressionism and Belgian Luminism.

Bourdelle, Antoine 1861–1929
French sculptor, painter and designer. He worked as Rodin's chief assistant from 1893 to 1908 and while still under his influence produced the dramatic bronze *Beethoven, large tragic mask* (1901, Paris, Musée Bourdelle), one of 21 versions of the subject. However by 1910 he abandoned his Rodinesque expressive realism for a smoother style which reflected the influence of ancient Greek sculpture. His high relief for the Champs-Elysées Theatre, 1912, inspired by Isadora Duncan's dancing, was conceived in terms of strong linear rhythms, making use of drapery lines and distorting the human body for the expression of movement. Bourdelle also created smaller more intimate figures, and classically majestic monuments which won him widespread popularity.

Bourdichon, Jean *c.*1457–1521
French painter, active at Tours, who was much patronized by the French court. He is known to have painted portraits and religious scenes, but apart from a recently identified triptych in the Museo di Capodimonte in Naples none of his large-scale work is known to survive, and his reputation now rests on his manuscript illuminations. The most important example is the Hours of Anne of Brittany (finished 1508, Paris, BN), which contains more than 50 paintings and borders of exquisitely naturalistic flowers, fruit and insects. This manuscript shows that Bourdichon worked largely in the local tradition, but the unmistakable influence of Perugino (compare the *St Sebastian* with Perugino's version in the Louvre, Paris) suggests that he had visited Italy.

Bourdon, Sébastien 1616–71
French painter. In 1634 he went to Rome where he spent three years mastering the styles of a number of painters especially Claude, Gaspard Dughet and Pieter van Laer (Bamboccio). He then returned to Paris where his imitative works deceived collectors, and to this day his oeuvre is difficult to reconstruct. In the years 1652–54 he became court painter to Queen Christina of Sweden and concentrated on portraits (a portrait of the Queen is in the Prado, Madrid). Most of the rest of his career was spent in Paris, painting portraits which are characterized by soft edges and brownish tonalities. See vol. 2 p. **199**

Bourgeois, Louise born 1911
American sculptor, born in Paris,

where she trained with Léger. In 1938 she moved to New York. Until the late 1940s, when she turned seriously to sculpture, she was primarily a painter and printmaker. She was recognized as a major artist in the 1950s for her abstract constructions in painted wood. *Quarantania I* (1948–53, New York, MOMA) is characteristic with its slender, vertical posts suggestive of human figures. In the 1960s she began to work in stone, metal, plaster and latex, and many of her pieces seem descriptive of sexual conditions.

Bouts, Dirk or **Dieric** died 1475
Netherlandish painter. He was probably born in Haarlem in the 1420s, but spent most of his working life in Louvain, where he became city painter in 1468. His earliest dated work is the portrait of a man (1462, London, NG). There are few documented works, but his style, characterized most obviously by very elongated, calm, reflective figures, is highly distinctive, and there is a fair measure of agreement about the extent of his oeuvre. Van der Weyden, Petrus Christus and the mysterious Haarlem painter van Ouwater were all sources for his style, but Bouts transformed these influences into a very personal manner, and in his lyrical landscape settings, which perfectly match the mood of his quiet figures, and in his exquisite handling of still-life details, he surpasses all his models. His colours are often rich but always controlled, and even when painting grisly subjects, as in the two panels representing *The justice of Emperor Otho* (1470–75, Brussels, Musées Royaux des Beaux-Arts), the treatment is dignified and the emotion understated. Bouts is now recognized as one of the greatest early Netherlandish painters. His two sons, **Dieric** the Younger (*c*.1448–90/91) and **Aelbrecht** (*c*.1460–1549) helped to spread his very influential style. Small devotional panels of subjects such as the *Mater Dolorosa* and *Christ crowned with thorns* deriving from Bouts' designs were especially popular and much copied (examples, London, NG). See vol. 2 p. *95*

Boyd, Arthur Merric Bloomfield born 1920
Australian painter and sculptor. He held his first one-man show before he was 20 and with Sidney Nolan became one of the leading painters in Melbourne. Both artists repeatedly used myths as a basis for their imagery and Boyd's early paintings were strongly moral or religious (*Jacob's dream*, 1946–47, Cambridge, England, Private coll.). He has developed several major themes, such as the celebrated *Half-caste Bride* pictures (1957–59), which take an aboriginal and his white bride as their subject (*Shearers playing for a bride*, 1957, NG of Victoria). Painted in rich, impasto oil, these works are typically expressionistic and naive in character. He moved to London in 1959 and since then his imagery has become more erotic in a gentle, poetic way. See vol. 1 p. *167*

Boydell, John 1719–1804
English engraver and print publisher. He made a fortune with the publication of his engraved views of England and Wales, and from 1786 commissioned artists to provide paintings for the project from which his name is inseparable—the Shakespeare Gallery. More than 30 artists, including Fuseli, Kauffmann, Reynolds and Romney, and more than 150 paintings illustrating Shakespeare's work were involved. They were exhibited at a specially built gallery in Pall Mall in London, and the engravings

after them were published in 1803. Boydell hoped his venture would further "a great national school of history painting", but it failed commercially.

Boys, Thomas Shotter 1804–74
English watercolourist and lithographer. After his apprenticeship he moved to France, where he became a friend of Bonington, and eventually returned to settle in England in 1837. He pioneered colour lithography in England with *Picturesque Architecture in Paris, Ghent, Antwerp and Rouen* (1839). His works are mainly topographical views of urban landscapes, and his views of Regency London are particularly well known.

Boyvin, René *c*.1525–*c*.1598(?)
French engraver, born in Angers and active mainly in Paris. Through his engravings after Rosso's designs he spread the influence of the first school of FONTAINEBLEAU. His engravings are firm, precise and generally rather dry, but his most famous works, illustrations for *The legend of Jason*, 1563, reveal a fertile, even licentious imagination.

Bozzetto
Italian term for a small-scale model, usually in wax or clay, of a larger sculpture. It can also apply to a painted sketch.

Bracquemond, Félix 1883–1914
French etcher of wildlife and portraits. He studied at Gleyre's studio with Whistler, Degas and Fantin-Latour and knew Zola and Manet. He was much influenced by Japanese prints, but his main importance lies in his revival of engraving as a creative medium.

Braekeleer, Henri de 1840–88
Belgian genre, landscape and still-life painter. His early works were influenced by the Dutch genre painters of the 17th century, but in the later part of his short life he studied the problem of light and colour and developed his own Impressionist style.

Bramante, Donato 1444–1514
Italian architect and painter. He is celebrated as the foremost architect of the High Renaissance and in particular as the designer of new St Peter's, Rome (begun 1506), although it was not finished to his plans. His early career, which is rather obscure, seems to have been spent mainly as a painter. He was born near Urbino and the most commonly held view is that he was trained by Piero della Francesca, though other influences, too, are evident in his only certain surviving work as a painter, the frescos of *Armed men* (*c*.1480–85, Milan, Brera). Much more impressive is an attributed work, the half-length *Christ at the Column* (1480–81, also in the Brera). Bramante worked in Milan from about 1480 and after his departure for Rome in 1499 there is no evidence that he continued to paint. According to Vasari, however, he provided the designs for the magnificent classical architectural setting in Raphael's "*The School of Athens*", in which his portrait is introduced as the mathematician Euclid. He was clearly interested in perspective effects and his earliest surviving dated work is the design for an engraving (1481, two known copies, London, BM, and Milan, Private coll.) of a complex architectural setting, so there may well be some truth in Vasari's story.

Bramantino (Bartolomeo Suardi) active 1503–36
Milanese painter and architect. His

nickname derives from the strong influence of Bramante visible in his work. His style is dramatic with exaggerated foreshortening and low perspectives, and his later work contains sombre buildings in a pure classical style (after 1525 he worked as an architect for Duke Francesco Sforza). Much of his work is in Milan, a fine example being *The Crucifixion* (*c*.1520, Brera).

Bramer, Léonard 1596–1674
Dutch genre and history painter. He travelled and worked in France and Italy from 1614 until 1628 when he returned to his native Delft. He is now chiefly remembered for small night scenes with dramatic lighting effects, such as the *Scene of sorcery* (1630s, Bordeaux, Musée des Beaux-Arts). To his contemporaries, however, Bramer was probably best known as a fresco-painter. He was one of the few 17th-century Dutch artists to use the technique, but none of his work in the medium has withstood the Dutch climate.

Brancusi, Constantin 1876–1957
Romanian-French sculptor, one of the greatest and most influential artists of the 20th century. He had an academic training in Crajova and Bucharest, but more important as a formative influence was his upbringing among a peasant community which had a strong tradition of woodworking. In 1904 he went to Paris, where he was to spend most of the rest of his career. He worked briefly with Rodin, but from 1907 onwards, inspired by the primitivist carvings of painter-sculptors such as Gauguin and Derain, he began to reject modelling techniques and naturalism. Instead he began to carve directly into limestone and marble, allowing his materials to dictate stylizations. Thus, in a series of disembodied heads such as *Sleeping muse* (1910, Paris, Musée d'Art Moderne), he progressively reduced organic forms to an essential, almost mystical purity. Later he frequently adapted this approach to the forms of animals, as in *The seal* (1936, New York, Guggenheim). Around 1914 he had begun to work also in wood, creating rugged fetishistic figure pieces such as *Adam and Eve* (1921, Guggenheim) as well as abstract decorative forms which he often used as bases to set off his highly polished sculptures. In 1937 he set up his sculpture for a park at Targu Jiu near his birthplace in Romania, and his work there includes the enormous *Endless column*. He bequeathed his studio, containing his unfinished works, to the French nation (reconstructed in Paris at the Centre Pompidou), and another very fine Brancusi collection is in the Philadelphia Museum of Art. Brancusi's radical simplification and concentration of form and his profound feeling for the qualities of the materials he used have been immensely influential on the development of 20th-century sculpture. Henry Moore wrote of him: "Since the Gothic, European sculpture had become overgrown with moss, weeds—all sorts of surface excrescences which completely concealed shape. It has been Brancusi's special mission to get rid of this undergrowth and to make us once more shape-conscious." See vol. 1 pp. *27, 204*; vol. 3 pp. **146–147**

Brandl, Petr 1668–1735
Bohemian painter of altarpieces and portraits. He was born and trained in Prague, and never travelled, yet his art was open to influences from all over Europe (altar cycle in Brevnov, 1717–19). The technique of his later works

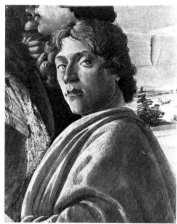
Botticelli: Self-portrait from *The Adoration of the Magi, c*.1476. Florence, Uffizi (Mansell)

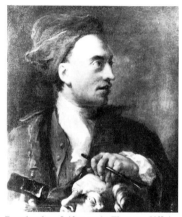
Bouchardon: Self-portrait. Florence, Uffizi (Alinari)

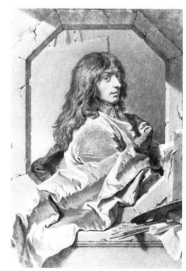
Bourdon: Posthumous drawing by Rigaud. Frankfurt, Städelsches Kunstinstitut

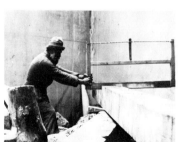
Brancusi: Photograph by the artist of himself working on *Endless column* (David Grob)

became increasingly free (he even used his fingers), notably in the *St Simeon with the Christ Child* (*c.* 1730, Prague, NG).

Brandt, Federico 1878–1932
Venezuelan painter and illustrator. He trained as an engineer and studied briefly with Michelena. In 1902 he travelled to Paris, and on returning to Caracas became increasingly attracted to the intimacy of streets and interiors in the old colonial quarters. These images show his admiration for the French INTIMISTES, Bonnard and Vuillard. He also illustrated literary journals.

Brangwyn, Sir Frank 1867–1956
British painter, etcher and designer. He was born in Bruges, the son of an architect and tapestry designer, and came to England in 1877 where he was apprenticed to William Morris. He was most highly regarded for his large-scale decorative work in England and in America, the culmination of which was the mural cycle on the theme of the British Empire (1924–30), commissioned for the House of Lords and now in the Guildhall, Swansea. In their brilliance of colour and close-fitting spaces they are reminiscent of tapestry. There is a museum devoted to his work in Bruges.

Braque, Georges 1882–1963
French painter, one of the greatest and most influential artists of the 20th century. After experimenting briefly with Fauvism he met Picasso and incorporated the innovations of Picasso's *Demoiselles d'Avignon* into his "*Grand nu*" (Great nude, 1907–08, Paris, Private coll.). In 1908 he exhibited landscapes of L'Estaque which reflected the influence of the shallow spatial effects and denser formal structure of Cézanne's late works, going further, however, in their abstractions from nature. These works, the first to be dubbed CUBIST, are often still considered to be the earliest products of Cubism. Over the next few years Braque collaborated closely with Picasso in exploring this novel anti-naturalistic style. Particular contributions made by Braque to the evolution of Cubism were his concern to visualize forms as interpenetrating with their surrounding space and the first use of stencilled lettering in his "*The Portuguese*" (1911, Basel, Kunstmuseum), a device that served both to provide the spectator with a clue for identifying subject matter and to stress the intrinsic flatness of the picture-plane. To similar effect he also created in 1912 the *papier-collé* technique whereby "collage", invented by Picasso some months earlier, is restricted to the incorporation of strips of paper into the composition. Mobilized in 1914, Braque was discharged two years later after sustaining a severe head-wound. Thereafter he developed a highly personal variant of Cubism, less formal in structure, which featured broad handling of paint often mixed with sand and a distinctively restrained palette of subtly modulated blacks, greys and browns. His career culminated with the *Atelier* series painted from 1948 onwards and of immense complexity and sophistication (*Atelier II*, 1949, Düsseldorf, Kunstsammlung Nordrhein-Westfalen). See vol. 1 pp. *31*, *122*; vol. 3 pp. **148–149**, 179, *228*

Bratby, John born 1928
English painter, the most prominent member of the so-called Kitchen-sink school, at its peak in the 1950s. He paints details of everyday domestic life (and portraits) with a dour vigour, unidealized colour and bold brushwork.

Brauer, Erich born 1929
Austrian painter, a leading exponent of "Fantastic Realism" in Vienna. He was once a folk singer, and has always maintained his interest in folk and especially medieval culture. His paintings and graphic works have many affinities with *fin-de-siècle* Symbolism and, like Jugendstil, contain many floral and other vegetable images, meticulously rendered, often sprouting from the most unlikely places. Everywhere is lavish and luxurious detail—a fairytale world, rich and exotic, painted in a language easily comprehensible to all. There are close links with the painting of Fuchs.

Braun, Matyáš Bernard
1684–1738
The leading Bohemian sculptor of the Baroque period. He was born in the Tyrol, but was forced to make his living further afield, and settled in Prague in 1711. A virtuoso stonecarver, he provided agitatedly expressive sculpture for the Charles Bridge (*St Ivo*, 1711) and the portal of the Clam-Gallas Palace (*c.* 1713) and other sites in the Bohemian capital. The largest collection of his sculpture, however, is at the hospital church at Kucs, for which Braun and his workshop executed numerous allegorical figures for the garden (1712–19).

Breenberg, Bartolomeus
c. 1599–1657
Dutch painter, one of the leading members of the first generation of Italianate landscape painters. He was in Rome, 1619/20–27, and apart from that lived in Amsterdam. His early work is similar in style to that of Poelenbergh, who was in Rome at the same time, and owes much to Paul Bril. His drawings executed in Italy are fresher, and have been mistaken for works by Claude. Mature paintings such as *The finding of Moses* (1636, London, NG), a work bathed in misty light, show a deeper understanding of Claude's art. After about 1645 he forsook landscape for narrative pictures.

Bregno, Andrea 1418–1506
Italian sculptor, born in Lombardy but most active in Tuscany and Rome. A prolific artist, he was head of a large workshop, and collaborated with Mino da Fiesole and others. His output consisted mainly of marble altars and tombs, such as the Piccolomini Altar (1481–85, Siena Cathedral) and the Savelli Monument (Rome, S. Maria in Aracoeli). Though not original, his proficiency and delicacy (and his use of fashionable classical motifs) earned him great praise.

Bregno, Antonio
active 1438–after 1457
Italian sculptor. He came from Lombardy, but was active mainly in Venice, where he is first recorded working on the Porta della Carta under Bartolommeo Buon, 1438–42. His tomb of Francesco Foscari (died 1457) in S. Maria dei Frari, influenced by the Coscia Monument in Florence Baptistery by Donatello and Michelozzo, shows an attempt to rationalize the standard Venetian tomb according to Renaissance principles. Bregno's greatest work was the Arco Foscari in the Doge's Palace, in which Renaissance and Gothic forms are piled in highly decorative mixture.

Breitner, George Henrik
1857–1923
One of the leading Dutch painters of the 19th century. He studied in The Hague, where he met van Gogh, and then in Paris. Horsemen were the favourite subjects of his early work, which was strongly influenced by Maris, but his visit to France in 1884 revealed to him the possibilities of Impressionism. He was invited to participate in an exhibition of Les VINGT in Brussels in 1886, the same year in which he settled in Amsterdam. There he became the leader of the Amsterdam Impressionists. He concentrated on the city centre and its people, painting busy streets by day and night, in a vigorous style (*The Singelbrug near the Paleisstraat*, 1893–95, Amsterdam, Rijksmuseum). He also painted portraits and was a distinguished photographer.

Bresdin, Rodolphe 1822–85
French printmaker. Though admired by the Parisian literary circle of Champfleury and Baudelaire, Bresdin was little appreciated by his artist contemporaries. He admired the graphic work of Rembrandt and Dürer, and his penchant for Gothic subject matter is best revealed in his macabre etching, *The comedy of Death* (1854), which he later transferred with pen on to the lithographic stone, a favourite process with him. Characteristic themes are solitude and flight. Huysmans described Bresdin's prints in his Symbolist novel *A Rebours*, and Odilon Redon, his pupil from 1865, continued his themes.

Breton, André 1896–1966
French writer and critic, the principal founder and theoretician of SURREALISM. Inspired by Apollinaire, the Dada movement and Freudian psychoanalysis, he published his first *Manifesto of Surrealism* in 1924. He continued to oversee the course of the movement until its eventual demise after World War II, contributing poetry and novels, further manifestos and major critical articles on Surrealist painting and sculpture. See vol. 3 p. 174

Brett, John 1830–1902
English painter of landcape and coastal scenes. *The stonebreaker* (1857–58, Liverpool, Walker Art Gallery) impressed Ruskin, who turned Brett to landscapes notable for geological or botanical interest and painted with minute detail and sharp colour. The effect of wind on the sea is often closely observed.

Breu, Jörg the Elder 1475/6–1537
German painter and designer of woodcuts. He worked mainly at Augsburg where he trained under Apt. In 1500–02 he visited Austria and there painted three altarpieces, notably *St Bernard* (1500, Zwettl Art Gallery), which share the deep feeling for landscape of the Danube school painters. In his later work the influence of the Renaissance style is evident, particularly in the two classical history paintings executed for Duke William IV of Bavaria in 1528–29 (Munich, Alte Pinakothek). His son, **Jörg** Breu the Younger (*c.* 1510–47) became court painter at Neuburg.

Bril, Paul 1554–1626
Flemish landscape and marine painter. He trained in Antwerp and was working in Lyons about 1574. By 1582, he had settled in Rome, where he became a pioneer of ideal landscape, forming a bridge between the northern Mannerist style, typically employing bright colours and a high viewpoint, and the much more mellow, naturalistic art of Claude, who studied with Bril's pupil, Tassi. After 1600, Bril's work showed the influence of Elsheimer. He collaborated with Reni on the frescos at the Palazzo Rospigliosi-Pallavicini and executed his own freer decorations at the Vatican. His brother **Matthew** (1550–83) worked in a similar style and also died in Rome.

Broederlam, Melchior
active 1381–1409
Netherlandish painter from Ypres. In 1387 he became court painter to Philip the Bold, Duke of Burgundy, and was commissioned to paint the exterior of the two wings of an altarpiece in the Chartreuse de Champmol, the Duke's major religious foundation. Representing *The Annunciation* and *The Visitation*, *The Presentation* and *The Flight into Egypt* (1396–99, Dijon, Musée des Beaux-Arts), the paintings combine a rich decorative effect with occasional realistic touches in an elegantly linear scheme, typical of Franco-Netherlandish painting of about 1400. They are among the earliest and most delightful examples of the INTERNATIONAL GOTHIC style. See vol. 2 p. **90**

Broken colour
Term in painting describing pure colours applied in small adjacent dabs. When seen from a distance adjoining colours appear to blend, giving an optical hue of greater luminosity than could be obtained by mixing the colours on the palette. It was proposed scientifically by the theoreticians Charles Blanc in 1867 and Ogden Rood in 1879 and was then developed by Seurat and Signac into the technique known as POINTILLISM.

Brokof, Ferdinand Maximilian
1688–1731
The most important Bohemian Baroque sculptor after Braun. He was the son of **Johann** Brokof (1652–1718), a sculptor from northern Hungary who settled in Prague in 1675. Brokof's work is more monumental and naturalistic than Braun's, but without his inner life. His finest works are in Prague, notably the group of *SS. John of Matha and Felix of Valois* on the Charles Bridge (1714); the portal of the Morzin Palace (1714); and the tomb of the Count Mitrowitz in the church of St Jacob (1716).

Bronzino, Agnolo 1503–72
Florentine painter, the pupil and adopted son of Pontormo. His work is thoroughly Mannerist, but has little of his master's sensibility or strangeness. He was court painter to Duke Cosimo I and Eleanora of Toledo, and portraits of them, and the new nobility attached to their court, are extremely polished but cold, stressing the social status of the sitters and revealing this more through detailed depiction of their rich costume than through any penetration of character. The frescos in the Eleanora chapel in the Palazzo Vecchio—the major religious commission of the 1540s—also show his exquisite ornamental style and lack of real feeling. His best-known work, *Venus, Cupid, Folly and Time* (*c.* 1545, London, NG), while sensual in meaning and composition, is passionless with beautiful, bloodless nudes, and clear enamelled colours. See vol. 2 p. **166**

Broodthaers, Marcel 1924–76
Belgian artist and writer. Having worked mainly as a poet and bookseller, in 1963 he suddenly decided to become a visual artist. He began to produce compelling and witty objects aimed at disturbing our normal perception of things. A typical example of his SURREALIST sculpture, somewhat reminiscent of Magritte in its imagery, is *Casserole and closed mussels* (1965, London, Tate), which shows a boiling pot overflowing with mussels surmounted by a lid.

Brooker, Bertram 1888–1955
Canadian self-taught non-objective

painter, writer and music critic, the first Canadian to exhibit abstractions (1927). *Sounds assembling* (1928, Winnipeg Art Gallery) displays the complex spatial composition and tubular forms of Joseph Stella's Futurist paintings.

Brooking, Charles 1723–59
British marine painter, whose detailed knowledge of shipping is said to have been derived from a spell as an apprentice at Deptford, near London. Like all British practitioners of the genre he was initially influenced by Willem van de Velde, but he afterwards developed a style of almost classical lucidity and restraint, with a fine sense of design. Examples of his work are in the National Maritime Museum in Greenwich.

Brooks, James born 1906
American painter. During the 1930s his paintings depicted social realist themes and he developed a monumental, colourful style for murals commissioned by the WPA. He served as an artist-correspondent in World War II, and after the War he turned to a loose, Cubist-based abstraction. By 1951 he had reached artistic maturity with Action Paintings which allied him to the second wave of Abstract Expressionists. His later work reduced the number of forms, increased their scale, and exploited colour contrasts (*Octon*, 1961, Pennsylvania, Allentown Art Museum).

Brosamer, Hans c.1500–c.1554
German painter and designer of woodcuts. Virtually nothing is known of his life, but apparently he worked at Erfurt, Saxony. He produced small woodcuts, strongly influenced by Cranach, and a few paintings, mostly portraits.

Brouwer, Adriaen 1605/6–38
Flemish genre painter. He studied with Hals in Haarlem, and spent his short working life there and in Antwerp, becoming an important link between the Flemish and Dutch schools. He led a colourful, Bohemian life and is best known for his humorously vulgar scenes of peasants in interiors, which initiated the tradition of low-life genre painting in Holland. In *The smokers* (c.1637, New York, Metropolitan) Brouwer shows himself, together with Jan Davidz. de Heem and others, smoking, drinking and merrymaking in a typically abandoned way. He had many followers, most notably Adriaen van Ostade, but they never matched his sparkling brushwork, delicate colour or brilliant characterization. Rubens and Rembrandt greatly admired Brouwer and avidly collected his work. See vol. 2 p. **226**

Brown, Ford Madox 1821–93
English painter of historical, literary, biblical and genre scenes as well as landscapes. Born in Calais, he studied in Belgium and was influenced by the Nazarenes in Rome. He settled in England in 1846, and later became a friend of Rossetti and an important influence on the Pre-Raphaelites, although he was never a member of the Brotherhood. His tight draughtsmanship and brilliant colour are found in his most famous painting, *Work* (1852–65), Manchester City Art Gallery), into which he condensed many of his social beliefs. He was a founder of William Morris' company, for which he designed furniture and stained glass. See vol. 1 p. *87*; vol. 3 p. **83**

Brown, Mather 1761–1831
American portrait and historical painter, most of whose career was spent in England. He was born in Boston and

worked as an itinerant portrait painter before travelling to Paris in 1780 and then to London, where by the late 1780s he had achieved considerable popularity. His later career, however, was a failure. Paintings by Brown have sometimes been wrongly attributed to Gilbert Stuart, but his style is closer to West. There are examples of his work in the National Portrait Gallery, London.

Bruce, Patrick Henry 1881–1936
American painter who settled in Paris in 1903. In 1912 he met Delaunay, his most important influence. By 1916 he had moved to an original abstract style, characterized by thick, bright paint applied with a palette knife. In 1920 he embarked on a series of paintings called *Forms* which are related to Purism and are based on still-life motifs (example, 1925–26, Washington, Corcoran). By 1933 he had given up painting and destroyed most of his works. He committed suicide in New York.

Brücke, Die (The Bridge)
A group of EXPRESSIONIST artists formed in Dresden in 1905–06 by four architecture students, Kirchner, Heckel, Schmidt-Rottluff and Bleyl. The title "The Bridge" did not describe any specific programme; it derived from a phase in Nietzsche's *Thus spake Zarathustra* in which man is seen not as an end in himself, but as a bridge towards a happier future. In this spirit they issued a manifesto declaring their intention to overthrow the concept of art as an end in itself. They wished to integrate art and life, and to use art as a means of communication. They lived and worked as a community, wishing to subsume their individuality in the collective spirit, in emulation of the medieval guild system. Other painters briefly associated with the group were Nolde, Pechstein, van Dongen, and Otto Mueller. In order to reach a wider public they formed a group of associate members who received a portfolio of prints in return for an annual subscription. Their revival of the woodcut as a work of art in its own right was one of their most important innovations. Their early style was strongly influenced by tribal art and van Gogh; they heightened the emotional intensity of their works still further with clashing colour combinations and aggressive distortions and surface textures. Their most common themes were townscapes, informal studio scenes and spontaneous scenes of nudes in the open air. After moving to Berlin (1910) they concentrated on scenes reflecting the stress of urban life, symbolized by cabaret dancers, circus performers and prostitutes. The group lost its common stylistic identity as a result of its differing reactions to Cubism. They exhibited together for the last time at the Cologne Sonderbund exhibition in 1912 and in 1913 the group was formally dissolved. See vol. 3 pp. **134–135**

Bruegel, Pieter the Elder
c.1525–69
The greatest Netherlandish artist of the 16th century, an outstanding engraver and draughtsman as well as a painter. His place of birth is uncertain, as is his training, although van Mander says he studied with Pieter Coecke van Aelst, whose daughter he later married. He became a master in the Antwerp guild in 1551 and at some time between then and 1553 travelled to Italy. Unlike most artists who travelled south he was more influenced by the journey over the Alps than by antique or Italian art. His drawings of Alpine scenery show the com-

mand of detail combined with majestic breadth of vision which were to characterize his later paintings. By 1553 he was back in Antwerp, and in 1555 was designing prints for Jerome Cock. Under the latter's aegis, he produced crowded, narrative compositions with heavily Boschian imagery. These traits were translated on to his panels and reached their high point in the three great compositions of 1562, *"Dulle Griet"* (Mad Meg, Antwerp, Musée Mayer van den Bergh), *The fall of the rebel angels* (Brussels, Musées Royaux des Beaux-Arts) and *The triumph of Death* (Madrid, Prado). Bruegel moved to Brussels in 1563 and in 1565 received a commission from the banker Nicolaes Jonghelinck for his most celebrated works, a series of paintings representing *The Months*, of which five survive, three in the Kunsthistorisches Museum, Vienna, and one each in the Metropolitan Museum, New York, and the National Gallery, Prague. Among them is probably his most famous work, *Hunters in the snow* (Vienna), one of the greatest of all landscape paintings, and one which in its bold, diagonal format broke sharply with the planar recessions of the Patenier tradition. Equally daring were the monumental depictions of proverbs, hitherto a very minor genre (*The blind leading the blind*, 1568, Naples, Museo di Capodimonte). Although popularly known as "Peasant Bruegel" because of his brilliant depictions of rustic festivities (*Peasant wedding dance*, 1566, Detroit Institute of Art), Bruegel was probably a cultured man and the prominence of proverbial themes can be linked to his humanist views and his connections with the quasi-mystical group, The Family of Love. The group advocated moderation in the face of the religious troubles that were tearing the Netherlands apart in the 1560s, and its influence can be seen in Bruegel's pessimistic but strictly non-partisan final works, in particular *The misanthrope* (1568, Naples, Museo di Capodimonte) and *The magpie on the gallows* (1568, Darmstadt, Hessisches Landesmuseum). Bruegel's output was fairly small, but his understanding of the human condition and powers of expression were so great that few artists are now so universally admired. See vol. 1 pp. *42, 48, 61, 107*; vol. 2 pp. **162–163**

Brueghel, Jan ("Velvet" Brueghel)
1568–1625
Flemish painter of landscapes and still lifes, the younger son of Pieter Bruegel the Elder. Like the rest of Bruegel's descendants he retained the "h" in his name, although his father had dropped it in 1559. He was born in Brussels and trained by his grandmother, Mayeken Verhulst. From 1594 to 1596 he travelled to Italy via Cologne and gained the patronage of Cardinal Borromeo. By 1597, he was back in the Netherlands and in 1602 became Dean of the Antwerp guild. His landscapes are very different from those of his father. He concentrated on lush, warm-toned, woodland scenes, densely populated with exotic animals and flowers. Occasionally, biblical themes served as pretexts for these virtuoso pieces—in particular, the Garden of Eden or Noah's Ark. He frequently collaborated with other artists, most notably his close friend Rubens, as in *The Garden of Eden* (The Hague, Mauritshuis), where Rubens painted the figures of Adam and Eve. As a flower-painter he was rated the greatest of his day, and his marvellous skill in painting rich and delicate textures of all kinds earned him the epithet

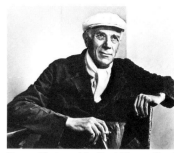

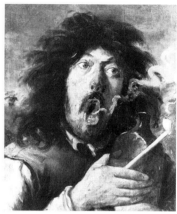

Brouwer: Self-portrait (?), c.1630. Paris, Louvre

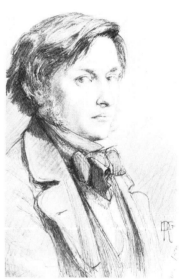

Brown, Ford Madox: Drawing by Rossetti, 1852. London, NPG

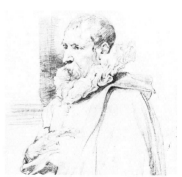

Brueghel, Jan: Drawing by van Dyck, c.1620. Trustees of the Chatsworth Settlement

"Velvet" Brueghel. His sons **Jan II** (1601–78) and **Ambrosius** (1617–75) and many descendants and imitators carried his style on. See vol. 2 p. **200**

Brueghel, Pieter the Younger
("Hell Brueghel") 1564–1638
Netherlandish artist, born in Brussels, the eldest son of Pieter the Elder. He was initially taught by his grandmother and then by Gillis van Coninxloo in Antwerp. Accepted as a master in 1585, Brueghel made his living mainly with copies and reworkings of Pieter the Elder's peasant and *kermis* scenes. They add nothing to his father's achievement, but are often of excellent quality. He was called "Hell" Brueghel because of his predilection for scenes of Hell and fires (*The burning of Troy*, Besançon, Musée des Beaux-Arts). Snyders and Coques were his pupils. His son **Pieter III** (1589–c.1640) also copied Pieter the Elder's work, but was less skilled.

Brullov, Karl 1799–1852
One of the leading Russian painters of the 19th century. He studied in St Petersburg, and in 1822 went to Italy. There he mainly painted portraits for Russian patrons, and his dramatic compositions and brilliant technique won him a considerable reputation. His greatest success, however, came with an enormous history painting, *The last day of Pompeii*, (1830–33, Leningrad, Russian Museum), inspired by a performance of Pacini's opera of that name. Melodramatic, full of reminiscences of the Antique, Raphael and Poussin, and luridly brilliant in colour, it brought him international fame. In 1835, after a visit to Greece, he returned to Russia and in 1839 began his huge *The siege of Pskov by Stefan Batory in 1581*, but this was never finished. He left Russia for Italy in 1849 because of failing health.

Brunelleschi, Filippo 1377–1446
Italian architect and sculptor, one of the group of artists including Alberti, Donatello and Masaccio responsible for the creation of the Renaissance style in Florence. He is principally famous as the first Renaissance architect, and above all as the designer of the superb dome of Florence Cathedral. His original training, however, was as a goldsmith, and his first surviving works as a sculptor are figures in silver on the Altar of St James (1398–1400) in Pistoia Cathedral. He is said to have turned to architecture after being defeated by Ghiberti in the competition for the new doors of the baptistery of Florence Cathedral; the competition panels by both men (1401–02) are now in the Bargello, Florence. One major work of sculpture from later in his career is, however, attributed to him—the polychrome wooden Crucifix (1412) in S. Maria Novella. This is said to have been carved in a private competition with Donatello, and Brunelleschi is reported to have advised him to remember that "Christ was most delicate in every part"—one of the earliest instances of the equation of moral goodness with formal beauty which was to become a commonplace of Renaissance theory. Though not a painter as such, Brunelleschi is important for his contributions to the development of perspective. In the early 1420s he devised on two panels, now lost, the first method for depicting objects in space with a single vanishing point, an invention noted by Alberti in his treatise on painting. See vol. 2 pp. **100**, *105*

Brus, Gunter born 1938
Austrian artist, the co-founder, with Muehl and Nitsch, of the Institute for Immediate Art in Vienna in 1966. He emigrated to West Berlin in 1969. His performances or actions, such as *Test to destruction* (1970), developed the idea of ACTION PAINTING in a morally extreme direction, using real blood and excrement as materials.

Brusasorci, Domenico
(Domenico Riccio) c.1516–67
Italian painter who worked mostly in Verona. His style was affected by the Mannerism of Giulio Romano and Parmigianino, but his decoration of 1556 in the Bishop's Palace, Verona, with its illusionist architectural framework, marks him as a forerunner of Veronese. The later frieze, *Ceremonial cavalcades of Charles V and Clement VII*, a decoration in the Palazzo Ridolfi-Lisca in Verona, is delicate and elegant, and displays the ingenious play with colour for which Brusasorci was famous.

Bruyn, Barthel the Elder
1492/3–1555
German painter, active mainly in Cologne. The leading painter of the Lower Rhine region, he produced a number of altarpieces, including that for Essen Cathedral, 1522–25, as well as portraits. His work was strongly influenced by the Netherlandish artists van Cleve and, later, Jan van Scorel. Probably his most interesting works are his portraits, penetrating depictions of Cologne citizens (*Burgomaster Arnold van Brauweiler*, 1535, Cologne, Wallraf-Richartz Museum). He had two painter sons, **Arnt** (died 1577), and **Barthel the Younger** (died before 1610), who was himself a portraitist of note.

Brygos Painter active c.500–475 BC
Greek RED-FIGURE vase-painter from Athens. He mainly painted cups and is named after the potter of some of those he decorated. His distinct style has been recognized in 170 pieces. A painter above all of movement and indeed violence, he produced many groups of maenads and revellers, with swinging drapery and exuberant gestures, but his masterpiece is perhaps a fine cup depicting the Sack of Troy (Paris, Louvre).

Brymner, William 1855–1925
Canadian painter, born in Scotland. He began to paint in Paris in 1878, returned to Canada in 1885, and directed classes at the Art Association of Montreal, 1886–1921. A number of his female studies show the influence of Bouguereau. He also executed conventional genre scenes (*Two girls reading*, 1898, Ottawa, NG) and naturalistic landscapes often tinged with Impressionism (*Early moonrise in September*, 1899, Ottawa, NG). He was an important influence on the next generation of Montreal painters.

Buchser, Frank 1828–90
Swiss portrait, genre and landscape painter and engraver. Born to a peasant family and of radical political beliefs in his youth, he spent the years from 1847 to 1871 travelling in romantic style round Greece, Spain, Morocco and America. The diversity of his travel is reflected in his painting: Spanish art, particularly that of Velazquez and Murillo, and the exoticism of North Africa had a great effect on works such as *The three friends* (1853, St Gallen Museum). At home he fought consistently for artists' rights and founded the Union of Swiss Painters in 1865.

Buffalmacco (Buonamico Christofani) active 1st half of 14th century
Italian painter. He had a wide contemporary reputation, and is mentioned by the writers Boccaccio and Sacchetti, as well as by Ghiberti and Vasari, but no certain works by him are known. Attempts have been made to connect his name with various paintings, including the frescos of *The triumph of Death* in the Campo Santo at Pisa, usually attributed to Traini. It has also been suggested that he may be identified with the Master of St Cecilia, who is in turn an ill-defined personality. None of these theories has met with general acceptance, and to some critics Buffalmacco is a figure of legend rather than history.

Buffet, Bernard born 1928
One of the best-known contemporary French painters. He was very precocious and had made a considerable reputation by the time he was 20, having by then already evolved his highly distinctive style, which, apart from some brightening of colour, has hardly changed since. Spiky forms with black outlines characterize his portraits, still lifes, townscapes and religious paintings, and his outlook is very pessimistic. His work, which represents a reaction against the prevailing abstraction of the times, is widely popular and much reproduced, but rather slick and repetitive. See vol. 1 p. *111*; vol. 3 p. **250**

Bugiardini, Giuliano 1475–1554
Florentine painter, a pupil of Ghirlandaio and a friend of Michelangelo. His work shows the influence of many contemporary painters, particularly Fra Bartolommeo. His figures are stilted, but at his best, as in *The martyrdom of St Catherine* (1530s, Florence, S. Maria Novella), there is an impressive effect of a great space milling with figures.

Buncho 1763–1840
Japanese painter from Edo (Tokyo), the son of a wealthy Samurai. He studied a great variety of Japanese styles, and apprenticed himself for a time to a Chinese painter. Besides traditional nature subjects he painted a series of landscapes drawn in Western perspective and many portraits (*Kimura Kenkado*, 1820, Osaka Municipal Museum). Both eclectic and conservative, he became a favourite artist of the military caste, wrote a treatise on painting and produced a book with copies of old Japanese paintings. See vol. 3 p. *47*

Buon, Bartolommeo c.1374–c.1465
Italian sculptor and architect. He was the son of the sculptor **Giovanni Buon** (active from c.1382–c.1443), and together they ran the foremost Venetian sculpture workshop of the mid-15th century. Bartolommeo was strongly influenced by the International Gothic sculpture of southern Germany, but his draperies are more naturalistic. His major work was on the Ca d'Oro (1422–34) on the Grand Canal, and the Porta della Carta (commissioned 1438) of the Doge's Palace is his masterpiece.

Burchfield, Charles 1893–1967
American painter of Mid-Western and visionary landscapes. He grew up in Ohio but spent most of his life in Buffalo, New York. His early works are based on childhood emotions and memories, using a vocabulary of grotesquely expressive shapes. *Church bells ringing, rainy night* (1917, Cleveland Museum) exemplifies his haunted imagination. During the 1920s and 1930s he painted more realistic variants of American scene subjects. After 1943 a Nordic mysticism pervaded Burchfield's landscapes. Jagged shapes create a menacing elemental world, as in the apocalyptic *Sun and rocks* (1918/50, Buffalo, Albright-Knox). See vol. 3 p. *206*

Buren, Daniel born 1938
French CONCEPTUAL painter. Since 1966 his work has consisted of vertical stripes alternating white and one colour on paper or canvas. The stripe is always 8.7cm in width. Buren is critical of museums and galleries as privileged refuges for certain forms of art and social groups and his work questions this seclusion. His own paintings are often placed on external walls in New York's SoHo.

Burgin, Victor born 1941
British CONCEPTUAL artist. He has involved himself in semiology and sociology to produce an art of social commentary which is particularly concerned with the way society uses images. He ironically opposes photographs with texts, as in *Lei Feng* (1974, London, Tate), in which a sherry advertisement signifying the competitive ethos of Western capitalism is juxtaposed with a Maoist fable about the denial of personal ambition for the good of society. Burgin adds a theoretical text about the way we understand words and pictures.

Burgkmair, Hans 1473–1531
German painter and designer of woodcuts. He was active chiefly in his native Augsburg, but apparently also worked for Schongauer in Colmar. His earlier works are German in style but hint at the interest in Italian engravings which strongly influenced his later work. This interest was fuelled by a visit to Italy, c.1507. The *Virgin and Child with landscape* (1509, Nuremberg, Germanisches Nationalmuseum), which he painted on his return, was based on a composition by Leonardo and shows his assimilation of Venetian colouring. He received many commissions from the Emperor Maximilian, including several important woodcut series, culminating in his major contribution to the series *The triumph of Emperor Maximilian* of c.1516–18 which was published in 1526. He was also a remarkable portraitist. See vol. 2 p. **155**

Burin
Engraving tool with a short handle which the engraver pushes with his palm while guiding the cutting point over the metal plate with his fingers. The burin leaves a furrow varying in depth and width according to pressure and the different shapes of the cutting edge. The ridge of metal, or burr, thrown up on either side of the gouged line is usually removed with a scraper to leave the clean edges characteristic of metal engravings.

Burlyuk, David Davidovich
1882–1967
Russian painter. He studied in Munich and Paris, then in Moscow (1910–14), where he met and befriended Vladimir Mayakovsky, whom he persuaded to abandon painting for poetry. Burlyuk was one of the first exponents of FUTURIST art in Russia and co-author, with Mayakovsky and others, of the famous Futurist manifesto "A Slap in the Face to Public Taste". He developed a style of painting and illustration in which images are split apart in a manner paralleling the verbal experiments of Futurist poets. He left Russia in 1918, travelling to America by way of Japan and China.

Burne-Jones, Sir Edward Coley
1833–98
English painter, illustrator and designer. As a student at Oxford University

he formed a life-long friendship with William Morris. The major influence on the formation of his style, however, was Rossetti, to whom he apprenticed himself in 1856. Burne-Jones' style, like Rossetti's, was self-consciously aesthetic and dreamlike, but it was also more classical, inspired by antique and Renaissance art, and particularly, in his expressive elongation of forms, by Botticelli. He had a highly successful career as a painter, and also did decorative work for Morris' firm, illustrated certain of his Kelmscott Press books and designed for him some of the finest stained glass and tapestries of his period. His favourite subjects were romantic legends and allegories, and he created a very distinct type of ethereal female beauty, "pale, sickly and wan", as Henry James said of the figures in *Laus Veneris* (1873–75, Newcastle upon Tyne, Laing Art Gallery). He loathed the Impressionists and their followers (he described their subjects as "landscape and whores") and felt a kinship with the French Symbolist painters, on whom he had considerable influence. The best collection of his works is in his native Birmingham. See vol. 3 pp. **83, 123**

Burra, Edward 1905–76
British painter. In 1933 he joined UNIT ONE and in 1936 and 1938 exhibited with the English Surrealists. Works such as *The serpent's eggs* (1934, Gloucester, City Museum) show a macabre fantasy quite comparable to the paintings of Dali or Masson. While his early work is sometimes reminiscent of Grosz, his preoccupations were as much imaginative as social. Apart from collages made in the 1930s in collaboration with Paul Nash, he worked almost entirely in watercolour, concentrating after World War II on landscapes. This did not preclude frequent work on a large scale.

Burri, Alberto born 1915
Italian painter. He studied medicine at Perugia, 1934–39, and during World War II was a medical officer with the Italian army in North Africa. His first paintings were executed at an American prisoner-of-war camp in Texas in 1945, using materials to hand, such as sacking and bandages. He returned to Italy that year and devoted his time to painting, evolving a highly personal and expressive style of collage, incorporating cloth with paint in a way which suggested blood seeping through bandages (*Sacking with red*, 1954, London, Tate). Sometimes the cloth he used was in fact bloodstained. The materials of his later collages, including charred wood and rusty metal, also reflected the horrific carnage of war. See vol. 3 p. **225**

Bury, Pol born 1922
Belgian painter and sculptor. In the 1940s he was involved with the Surrealist movement under Magritte and the writer Scutenaire, and was a member of the JEUNE PEINTURE BELGE group. He was a founder-member of the CoBrA group, but in 1953 he gave up painting for sculpture, and has become one of the most interesting and subtle of KINETIC artists. He exhibited with Calder, Tinguely and Vasarély in the 1955 exhibition, Movements, in Paris, and from 1957 he incorporated electric motors into his work. Whereas Tinguely's mobiles are usually violent and sometimes self-destructive, Bury's make use of slow, gentle movement. Since 1970 he has also made films. See vol. 3 p. **245**

Bush, Jack 1909–77
Canadian abstract painter. He began

painting under the influence of the Surrealists Borduas and Jock MacDonald. As a founder member of PAINTERS ELEVEN in 1953, he participated in group shows with New York Abstract Expressionists. He dropped his Abstract Expressionist mannerisms in 1957, opting for simpler compositions and crude, thinly painted forms. His later abstracts are hard-edge (*Dazzle red*, 1965, Toronto, Art Gallery of Ontario).

Bushnell, John c.1630–1701
English sculptor. He fled from England while still an apprentice (after an unjustified paternity suit), returning probably at the end of the 1660s. During that time he had worked mainly in Venice (monument to Alvise Mocenigo, 1663, S. Lazzaro dei Mendicanti), but also almost certainly visited Rome, as the billowing Baroque draperies which characterize his English work (*Charles I*, 1671, London, Old Bailey) can hardly have been learned from anyone but Bernini. Bushnell was the first English sculptor to work in the Baroque style, but his work is at best competent, and often clumsy, by Italian standards. Although he obtained some important commissions, his arrogant and suspicious nature prevented great success, and he died insane.

Buson, Yosa 1716–83
Japanese poet and painter. Perhaps best known as a writer of *haiku*, Buson was also a talented painter who specialized in landscapes. His style was heavily influenced by the Chinese paintings of the Yuan and Ming dynasties. A representative work is the pair of screens, *Wild horses* (Tokyo, National Museum). He and the calligrapher-painter Ikeno Taiga made a charming set of illustrated Chinese poems, now designated National Treasures of Japan (Kawabata Yasunari memorial collection). See vol. 3 p. 47

Bust
Portrait sculpture or painting showing only the head and neck of the sitter, or including as much as the shoulders, upper arms and chest. The format was exploited above all by the Romans.

Butler, Reg born 1913
British sculptor. He learnt iron forging techniques during World War II and applied them to Surrealist-derived imagery in pieces such as *The birdcage* (1951, London, Kenwood House). His work was never totally abstract and it made sensuous use of the textures created by welding. He received public notice in 1953 when he won an international competition for a monument to *The unknown political prisoner* (version London, Tate). In the 1950s he turned to figurative work in painted bronze.

Buytewech, Willem Pietersz.
c.1591–1624
Dutch genre painter and engraver. He was born in Rotterdam, and entered the painters' guild in Haarlem in 1614. Perhaps because of his early death, few paintings by him are known. He was closely connected with Frans Hals, and his carousing dandies and buxom wenches, of great vitality, set a precedent in genre painting—transposing the traditional *kermis* into a tavern scene (*A merry company*, c.1617–20, Rotterdam, Boymans-Museum). He also painted quieter domestic scenes and etched many costume and fashion plates, as well as Dutch landscapes. See vol. 2 p. **226**

Bylert, Jan van 1598–1671
Dutch painter of biblical and genre subjects. He was born in Utrecht and

studied with Bloemaert, before travelling to France and Italy, 1621–24. Like other painters from Utrecht who travelled to Italy, he adopted a Caravaggesque style. From the early 1630s, however, his palette lightened and his technique became more glossy (*St Matthew and the Angel*, Belfast, Ulster Museum).

Byzantine art
Art of the Byzantine Empire in the Eastern Mediterranean, from AD 330 when Constantinople was dedicated as the capital of the Roman Empire in the East. The early divergence of the imperial artistic traditions of the East and West began soon after the division of the Empire, and was furthered by the decline in the West caused by barbarian disruption. The influence of imperial Rome, the heritage of Hellenistic art, Middle Eastern and oriental art all made their impact in Byzantium. Hellenistic naturalism and vitality distinguish, for example, the remains of the 5th- or 6th-century mosaic floor of the imperial palace in Constantinople. The so-called First Golden Age of Byzantine art reached its climax in the 6th century in Justinian's time, when the capital's architectural masterpiece, Hagia Sophia, was built. Few of its early mosaics survive, but the splendour of metropolitan art in this period is reflected in the mosaic schemes of churches in Ravenna, then under Byzantine rule, miraculously preserved. Hellenism persisted on the outskirts of the Empire (in Syria, Alexandria, Mt Sinai and elsewhere) but art in Constantinople was gradually transformed by stiffening formal values; naturalism lost its place to a heightened spiritual expression, often severe and relatively rigid. Antique work was, however, still admired and copied, notably by artists of the Macedonian Renaissance (following the Iconoclastic period, c.725–843, when idolatrous images were strictly forbidden). In illumination, though styles were sophisticated, technical quality was sometimes poor. Artists used classical and Early Christian models, without imitating their naturalism or convincing spatial settings. Mosaic continued to be the standard medium for decorating churches. The Comnene period, 1057–1185, an era of comparative political strength, proved to be the Second Golden Age of Byzantine art. The mosaics (c.1100) of the church of Daphni in Greece remain to witness its monumental quality. Western Europe was particularly receptive in the 11th and 12th centuries, but the rich art of the Byzantines came to be envied and imitated by Western patrons and artists throughout the medieval period. The mosaic decoration of Venetian and Sicilian churches are obvious examples of direct influence, but transportable artefacts such as fine Byzantine fabrics, icons and reliquaries found their way into more distant countries of Europe. In 1204 Constantinople was sacked by Latin Crusaders and the Empire (greatly reduced) was ruled by Westerners until 1261. The restoration of Byzantine rule saw the Third Golden Age of Byzantine art, 1261–1453, and a freer development of the traditional hieratic styles. Only in the 13th and 14th centuries was the painstaking, expensive medium of mosaic replaced increasingly by the freer medium of fresco. By the 15th century, when Constantinople finally fell to the Turks, Western artists no longer looked to Byzantium for inspiration, but Byzantine influence continued in the Eastern Orthodox Balkan countries and in Russia. See vol. 2 pp. 58–65

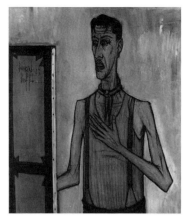

Buffet: Self-portrait, 1954. London, Tate

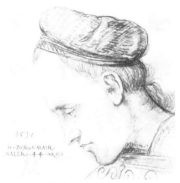

Burgkmair: Self-portrait drawing, 1517. Hamburg, Kunsthalle

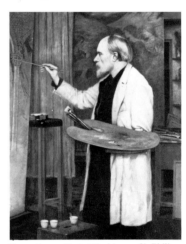

Burne-Jones: Portrait by his son, Sir Philip (1861–1926), 1898. London, NPG

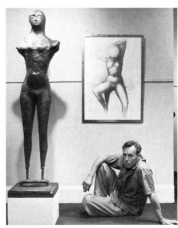

Butler: Photograph taken beside one of his sculptures, 1960 (Popperfoto)

C

Cabanel, Alexandre 1823–89
French painter. He was awarded the Prix de Rome in 1845, and with Bouguereau became the most influential Academician of his day, his sentimentalized style according with Second Empire tastes. Napoleon III was among his patrons, and he received numerous official commissions for historical and allegorical subjects. The erotic *Birth of Venus* (Paris, Louvre) exhibited in the official Salon in the same year as the "Salon des Refusés" (1863), and bitterly attacked by Zola, is typical of his style. See vol. 3 p. **87**

Cabinet painting
Term used for small easel-paintings, essentially those intended to be seen at close quarters in private apartments and domestic interiors. It is particularly appropriate to the genre and still-life scenes popular with the 17th-century Dutch bourgeoisie.

Cadmus, Paul born 1904
American painter. He works in a polished figurative style based upon an admiration of Italian Renaissance art, often using egg tempera. His subject matter is contemporary society viewed with a satirical, even jaundiced eye, and his distortions are in the manner of the Magic Realists (*Bar Italia*, 1952–55, Washington DC, Smithsonian).

Caffiéri, Jean-Jacques 1725–92
French sculptor. He trained under Jean-Baptiste Lemoyne the Younger and won first prize at the Academy in 1748. In the following year he went to Rome, where his stucco group of *The Trinity* in S. Luigi dei Francesi is evidence of the impression made on him by the Baroque. He executed a number of official works after his return to France in 1753, but made his name with a series of portrait busts, both of his contemporaries (*Mme du Barry*, Leningrad, Hermitage) and of great dramatists of the past (Paris, Comédie Française). They are characterized by great liveliness and technical virtuosity.

Caillebotte, Gustave 1848–94
French painter and collector, best known as one of the chief patrons of the Impressionists, whose exhibitions he helped to organize. He is the young man astride a chair in Renoir's *The luncheon of the boating party* (1881, see vol. 1 p. 47). His own paintings, exhibited at five of the Impressionist exhibitions, are in a weaker version of Monet's style (*Sailing boats at Argenteuil*, c. 1888, Paris, Jeu de Paume). His collection was left to a not particularly grateful state.

Calame, Alexandre 1810–64
Swiss landscape painter and etcher. He travelled widely in Europe between 1839 and 1845, but Switzerland was his principal source of inspiration, and he is one of the best-known painters of mountain scenery (*Lake of four cantons* 1842, Basel, Kunstmuseum). Böcklin was his most important pupil.

Calder, Alexander 1898–1976
One of the leading American sculptors of the 20th century. He trained as an engineer, and did not turn to art until he was in his mid-twenties. His early works were witty portraits and set pieces, such as the acrobats of *The brass family* (1929, New York, Whitney), which reflect his interest in the circus and use twisted wire to suggest complex volumes. He also made animated toys prefiguring his most famous creations, "mobiles", a term coined by Duchamp to describe these mechanized or hand-moved sculptures. Both mobiles and their static equivalents, "stabiles", employ the colourful biomorphic shapes found in the work of Surrealists such as Miró and Arp to create a lyrical personal idiom. Calder's sculptures tended to increase progressively in scale, culminating in works such as the 29m (95ft) high stainless steel *Man* for the 1967 Montreal World's Fair and numerous similar civic and corporate commissions. He also worked in many other fields and media including jewellery, tapestry, rug-making, bronze and gouache. See vol. 1 p. *190*; vol. 3 pp. **181, 231**

Callcott, Sir Augustus Wall
1779–1844
English painter. He was a pupil of Hoppner, but rejected portraiture in favour of landscape. One of the most popular artists of his day, he painted in a conventional Italianate manner ignoring the innovations of Constable or Turner. *Diana at the chase* (Bury Art Gallery) is typical. He was elected to the Academy in 1811. His wife, **Maria** (1785–1842), was known for her writings on art.

Calligraphy
Fine handwriting, usually considered a craft, but in some cultures, notably the Chinese, Japanese and Islamic, treated as a branch of art. The strokes of the brush or pen in the individual characters and the overall composition of a piece of writing are the proper concern of their artists. In the 20th century some Western artists, notably Miró and Klee, have practised calligraphy as an art. The term "calligraphic" can be used of flowing or loose brushwork in paintings, and of drawings where the pen has been used for virtuoso loops and strokes.

Callot, Jacques 1592/3–1635
French engraver and draughtsman. He left his native Nancy for Rome at some time after 1607, but his career really began in 1611 when he moved to Florence. There he worked for Duke Cosimo II, producing numerous etchings on court life, mostly in a light-hearted vein. After the death of Cosimo in 1621 he returned to Nancy, where he worked for the ducal court, producing a vast and varied body of work (more than a thousand etchings survive as well as a similar number of drawings). He often worked on a large scale, and showed great compositional mastery in arranging his multi-figure panoramas. Some of his genre scenes (beggars and deformed people were favourite subjects) are close of those of Bellange, who also worked in Nancy, but Callot's style, although elegant, was less Mannerist and more realistic. His most celebrated work is the series of etchings known as *Les Grandes Misères de la Guerre* (The great miseries of war, 1633), inspired by the Thirty Years War and Richelieu's invasion of Lorraine. These devastating appraisals of human cruelty and folly look forward to Goya, who used them as a source.

Caloutsis, Valerios born 1927
Greek artist. His early works were landscapes of his native Crete and abstract relief paintings in monochrome. Since 1966 he has worked on *Kinoptics*, which create changing black and white abstract images through the use of electric currents and reflected light.

Calvaert, Denys
(Dionisio Fiammingo) c. 1540–1619
Flemish Mannerist painter of modest talent but considerable historical importance. He went to Italy in about 1562, remained there for the rest of his life, and founded an academy in Bologna which probably inspired the more famous one of the Carracci. Albani, Domenichino and Reni were among his pupils. His work is well represented in Bologna, in the Pinacoteca and in various churches.

Calvert, Edward 1799–1883
English painter and engraver. On leaving the Navy to study painting, he met Fuseli and, influenced by Palmer and Blake, became one of the ANCIENTS working at Shoreham. He produced visionary woodcuts of Arcadian scenes as well as paintings, but his total oeuvre is small since he destroyed much of it, and after his Shoreham period the quality of his work dropped. *The primitive city*, a watercolour in the British Museum, London, is perhaps his finest work.

Camargo, Sergio de born 1930
Brazilian sculptor. He studied in Buenos Aires under Pettoruti and Lucio Fontana. In 1948 he visited Paris and stayed to study philosophy and then to sculpt, meeting Brancusi, Arp and Vantongerloo. Since 1961 he has lived and worked in France. He is best known for his white relief constructions which use a common module, an angled section of a cylinder, to disperse the flow of natural light upon them (an example is *Relief 35*, 1971, Rio de Janeiro, Gilberto Châteaubriand coll.). The convex-concave relation of the forms and shadows creates a rhythmic vibration.

Cambiaso, Luca 1527–85
Italian Mannerist painter. He worked mainly in Genoa where he was the outstanding painter in the 16th century. His first surviving works are scenes of ancient history and myth (1544) in the Doria Palace, now the Prefettura, and many other decorative schemes in palaces and churches followed before he went to Spain as court painter to Philip II in 1583. His massive figures derive from Michelangelo and his soft modelling from Correggio (*Venus and Cupid*, Chicago, Art Institute). It has been claimed that his poetic night scenes influenced Georges de La Tour, but he is now best known for his drawings, often depicting figures in vigorous movement, using simplified "cubic" shapes.

Camden Town Group
Group of British artists founded by Gilman, Bevan, Ginner and Gore. The name derives from the district of London, at that time a poor area, often painted by Sickert, the senior British artist whom the members of the group most admired. They applied a style derived from Post-Impressionist painters, particularly Gauguin, to often drab scenes of working-class life. They held their first exhibitions in London in May 1911, and in 1913 the group joined Wyndham Lewis and his associates to form the **London Group**.

Camera obscura
Device (literally "dark chamber") used as an aid to accuracy in drawing and based on the same principle as the lens and camera in photography. Light from the object or scene to be portrayed passes through a convex lens in one face of the chamber or box on to the opposite face, where it gives an inverted image which can be corrected with mirrors. The artist then traces the required outlines. The apparatus was in use during the 16th century and became fashionable in the 18th century, when a portable version was especially favoured by landscapists. During the 19th century it was superseded by the **camera lucida** which does not, in fact, involve a "chamber", but uses a prism to reflect the required scene.

Camoin, Charles 1879–1965
French painter. He studied alongside Matisse, Marquet, Rouault and Manguin in Moreau's studio. His *Portrait of Marquet* (c. 1904, Paris, Musée d'Art Moderne) shows the influence of Cézanne, but in 1905 he was identified with Fauvism and exhibited at the Salon d'Automne. He later met Renoir whose influence, with that of Bonnard, came to dominate his brightly coloured landscapes, interiors and nudes.

Campagnola, Giulio
c. 1482–after 1514
Italian artist, known chiefly for his engravings, although he was also a painter, poet and designer of type. Born in Mantua, he trained under Mantegna and worked at the court of Ferrara, but is usually associated with Venice, where he spent the last decade of his life. His importance lies in his copies of Dürer's works, which spread knowledge of these in Italy, and in his pastoral prints which disseminated the idyllic landscape style of Giorgione and Titian. The subject matter of these is frequently obscure and must relate to the tastes of the literary humanists with whom he was friendly. His pupil and adopted son **Domenico** (1500–64) was also a painter and engraver. His drawings have been attributed to Giorgione and Titian, and his prints continue the pastoral vein of Giulio. *The Madonna with the protectors of Padua* (c. 1545, Padua, Museo Civico) is a good example of his eclectic style in painting, a handsome mixture of elements derived from Titian and Pordenone, with brilliant drapery effects reminiscent of Savoldo.

Campania, Pedro de
(Pieter Kempeneer) 1503–80
Netherlandish painter, sculptor, architect and astronomer, born into a wealthy Brussels family. He was versatile, eclectic and much travelled. As a young man, he was employed by Charles V on the decorations for his coronation in Bologna. Leaving Italy, he spent the greater part of his working life around Seville. His work contains a rich fusion of Flemish and Italian motifs and his preferred themes were the Madonna and the Descent from the Cross; one of the finest of the latter (1547) is in Seville Cathedral. In 1563 he returned to Brussels to manage a tapestry workshop for the Duke of Alva.

Campendonck, Heinrich
1888–1957
German painter. In 1911 he exhibited with the BLAUE REITER, and like Marc he aimed to use colour expressively to suggest a pantheistic allegory (*Bucolic landscape*, 1913, St Louis, Morton D. May coll.). He met Chagall in 1914 and his later work, which includes many stained-glass windows, became more dreamlike and decorative.

Campi family
Family of Italian painters based in Cremona. **Galeazzo** (1477–1536) was influenced by Perugino and painted frescos in Cremona. Of his sons **Giulio** (1502–72) was influenced by Romanino and Pordenone and painted works such as *The Madonna in glory* (1540, Crem-

ona, S. Sigismondo), which show an awareness of Mannerism. **Antonio** (*c.*1525–91) was chiefly a portrait painter but also worked at S. Sigismondo, painting several night scenes in a smoky style which seems to prefigure Caravaggio. **Vicenzo** (1536–*c.*1591) seems to have been particularly interested in still life; an example of his work is *Woman with fruit* (Milan, Brera). **Bernardino** (*c.*1522–92), probably a distant cousin, painted frescos in S. Sigismondo (1570).

Campigli, Massimo 1895–1971
Italian painter. He began painting in 1919 while in Paris and was profoundly influenced by his discovery of archaic Greek art. His mature style dates from the late 1920s when he encountered Etruscan art and consists of flat, hieratic figures in relationships of gesture rather than perspective, as in his *Holiday* (1956, New York, Schutz coll.).

Campin, Robert active 1406–44
Netherlandish painter. He was active in Tournai where his life is well-recorded, but, apart from the polychroming of a stone *Annunciation* (1428, Tournai, S. Marie-Madeleine), none of his documented works survives. Most authorities, however, now identify him as the author of a number of paintings grouped as the work of the "Master of Flémalle", who is so called because three of the paintings (*The Virgin and Child*; *The Trinity*; *St Veronica*, *c.*1430, Frankfurt, Städelsches Kunstinstitut) were once believed to have come from Flémalle in Belgium. The identification of Campin with the Master of Flémalle depends on the similarity between the work of Campin's documented pupils, Jacques Daret and "Rogelet de la Pâture" (who is assumed to be Rogier van der Weyden), and the paintings of the Flémalle group. None of the paintings is dated except the wings of the Werl altarpiece (1438, Madrid, Prado), which are thought to be by Rogier even by some who accept the Campin/Flémalle identification. The earliest of the Campin/Flémalle paintings, probably antedating any of Jan van Eyck's extant works, is perhaps the triptych of *The Entombment* (*c.*1415–20, London, Courtauld Institute of Art, Seilern coll.). This has a decorative background, but Sluter's influence is evident in the emphatic plasticity of the figures, and in details such as the angel wiping away a tear with the back of his hand, which is a "quotation" from the Well of Moses in Dijon. The sculptural solidity and the naturalistic (often homely) detail which marks Campin's style are more fully developed in works such as the Mérode Altarpiece (the name "Master of Mérode" is sometimes used rather than "Master of Flémalle") in the Metropolitan Museum, New York, which probably dates from around 1425. His sober skills as a portraitist are evident in the portraits of *A man* and *A woman* (*c.*1430, London, NG), and the emotional power of which he was capable is clear in *The thief on the cross* (*c.*1430–35, Frankfurt, Städelsches Kunstinstitut), a fragment of a work whose complete appearance is recorded in a copy in Liverpool (Walker Art Gallery). Campin has been overshadowed by Jan van Eyck, but although he did not have Jan's supreme technical mastery, he is now recognized as a figure of comparable importance in the founding of the early Netherlandish school. His break with the International Gothic style was convincing and decisive, and his influence, particularly through his great pupil van der Weyden, was widespread. See vol. 2 pp. **90–91**, *94*

Canadian Group of Painters see GROUP OF SEVEN

Canaletto (Giovanni Antonio Canal) 1697–1768
The leading Italian view-painter of the 18th century. Born in Venice, the son of a theatrical scene-painter, he studied for a while under Panini in Rome before returning to his native city in 1730. Apart from a decade spent largely in England (1746–56), he lived in Venice for the rest of his life. In contrast to Guardi he enjoyed remarkable commercial success, and had a virtual monopoly over the tourist trade in Venice. His output was prolific, and he produced etchings as well as paintings. Thanks largely to the endeavours of an English entrepreneur resident in the city, Joseph Smith (the "Merchant of Venice"), he acquired a phenomenal reputation among English visitors; Smith's own extensive collection of the artist's work was sold to King George III of England in 1758, and the British Royal Collection still has the finest collection of Canaletto's paintings and drawings. Although his work had an essentially topographical function (a large number of his views were painted with the aid of a *camera obscura*), at times he showed a poetic responsiveness to the qualities of the individual scene. This is particularly so in early works ("*The stonemason's yard*", *c.*1730, London, NG), and in some of his English views, when he seemed to find the change of scenery refreshing. It was only in later life that ever-increasing demand resulted in stereotyped views painted in a mechanical manner, but even then his gift for composition was unfailing. See vol. 1 pp. *149*; vol. 2 pp. **254–255**

Candle-light Master see BIGOT

Cano, Alonso 1601–67
Spanish painter, sculptor and architect. He was born in Granada, and in 1614 moved to Seville, where he studied painting with Pacheco (Velazquez was a fellow-pupil) and sculpture with Montañés. In 1638 he went to Madrid and in 1652 finally settled in Granada. Cano's life was turbulent (he was in trouble for duelling, and was suspected of the murder of his wife), but his art represents the classical aspect of the Spanish Baroque and is usually fairly restrained. His woodcarvings reflect the influence of Montañés, and in painting he moved from a firmly modelled, strongly lit style derived from Zurbarán to a more painterly one influenced by Velazquez and the work of the Venetian painters he saw in the royal collection in Madrid. In 1667 he designed the façade of Granada Cathedral, one of the finest and most individual pieces of Spanish Baroque architecture, and his work is well represented in the Cathedral with *The Seven Joys of the Virgin* (1652–64) and several statues, including the lovely *Immaculate Conception* (1655). Cano was also the most prolific draughtsman among 17th-century Spanish artists.

Canogar, Rafael Garcia born 1935
Spanish painter. During the 1950s his work developed from landscape to social realism in the manner of Saura, and in the next decade he turned to an aggressive form of abstraction, before once again painting the human figure. He developed a style of political realism, using a number of media such as collage and photography, which places him in the tradition of humanism typical of Spanish painting since Goya. He has travelled widely and has taught in the USA.

Canova, Antonio 1757–1822
Italian sculptor, one of the leading artists of the NEOCLASSICAL movement. He was born at Possagno, near Venice, and settled in Rome in 1781, where he rapidly acquired an international reputation. His first major commission, the tomb of Pope Clement XIV (1783–87, Rome, SS. Apostoli), in its gravity and smooth generalized surfaces contrasts strongly with his early masterpiece, *Daedulus and Icarus* (1779, Venice, Correr), which is marked by naturalistic modelling and agitated movement. He worked for European royalty and aristocracy, as well as the papacy, and made several portraits of Napoleon Bonaparte and his family, including colossal nude statues of Napoleon in bronze (Milan, Brera) and marble (London, Wellington Museum) and a coolly erotic reclining figure of Bonaparte's sister Paulina Borghese (1805–07, Rome, Borghese Gallery). In Paris in 1815 he recovered works of art looted from Italy by Napoleon, and during a subsequent visit to London admired the naturalism of the newly-arrived Elgin marbles. Canova went out of fashion during the Romantic period, when he was accused of being dry and sterile, but now the high quality of much of his work is once again acknowledged. His influence was enormous, and he had a very generous nature, helping young sculptors as much as he could. There is a museum of his work in Possagno. See vol. 3 pp. **60–61**

Čapek, Josef 1887–1945
Czech painter, graphic artist, stage designer, caricaturist, novelist, poet and art critic. He was one of a number of Czech artists (others were Filla and Gutfreund) who were early members of the Cubist movement. He moved from the analytical Cubism of Picasso and Braque to a more personal form which was decorative and colourful (*The organ grinder*, 1913, Nelahozeves, Central Czech Gallery). His later work became Expressionist, characterized by deep human and social concern (*Bad conscience*, 1926, Brno, Moravian Gallery). He was a man of a philosophical nature and like his more famous brother, the writer Karel Čapek, he feared the dehumanizing force of modern civilization. He died in a concentration camp.

Capogrossi, Giuseppe 1900–72
Italian painter. He began painting in 1930 while living in Paris, his early work showing a Cubist influence which he later modified towards more representational ends. After 1949 he broke away with a sudden move to complete abstraction. His mature works employed a comb-like motif as the basic pictorial unit multiplied over the picture surface.

Caporali, Bartolommeo *c.*1420–1508
Umbrian painter, contemporary with Bonfigli and, like him, working in a provincial version of Gozzoli's style. He produced frescos, altarpieces and processional banners. *The compassionate Madonna* (1482, Montone, S. Francesca) is his masterpiece.

Cappelle, Jan van de *c.*1624–79
Dutch painter of seascapes and landscapes. He was a wealthy dyer who painted in his spare time, and assembled a superb private collection including some 500 drawings by Rembrandt, who was his friend, and works by Hals, Rubens, Brouwer and de Vlieger. His few works are mostly river- and seascapes, limpid and monumental compositions deriving from his study of de

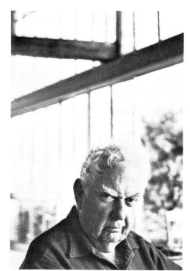
Calder: Photograph by Cartier-Bresson, 1971. Buffalo, NY, Albright-Knox Art Gallery. © Henri Cartier-Bresson

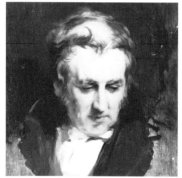
Callcott: Portrait by Landseer, 1834. London, NPG

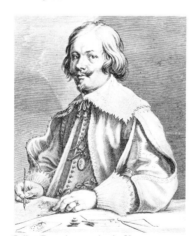
Callot: Portrait engraving by Vorsterman after van Dyck (Mansell)

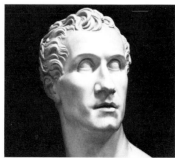
Canova: Self-portrait marble bust, 1812. Possagno, Tempio Canoviano (Alinari)

Vlieger, but he also painted some beach scenes and winter landscapes. Cappelle was outstanding even in a period of great seascape painters (*River scene with vessels becalmed*, *c.*1650, London, NG). See vol. 2 pp. *212*, **223**

Capralos, Christos born 1909
Greek sculptor. He studied in Athens and Paris and is widely travelled. His first works were large, solemn family groups and earthy reliefs of peasant life, but more recently he has worked in an abstract style derived from archaic Greek sculpture, and similar to that of Marini. He works in wood, terracotta, stone and bronze, and is the acknowledged leader of modern Greek sculpture.

Capriccio
Term (from the Italian for caper or caprice) used to describe an imaginary composition in part, at least, based on real scenes. These are usually architectural, as in the townscape *capricci* of Canaletto. Often realistic portrayals of well-known buildings or sites in different locations are juxtaposed. An excellent example is a painting (*c.*1795) by William Marlow in the Tate Gallery, London, in which St Paul's Cathedral is shown at the end of a Venetian canal. The term is also used of other fantasies: Goya's *Los caprichos* are a series of etchings of nightmarish imaginings.

Caracciolo, Giovanni Battista (called Battistello) *c.*1570–1637
Italian Baroque painter, one of the most gifted of CARAVAGGESQUE painters, and the founder of the Neapolitan school of the 17th century. Whereas most of Caravaggio's Italian followers imitated the superficial characteristics of his style, Caracciolo understood the tragic grandeur of his art, and never descended to vulgar realism. *His liberation of St Peter* (1608–09, Naples, Chiesa del Monte della Misericordia) is a worthy companion to Caravaggio's *Seven Works of Mercy* painted in 1607 for the same church. Unlike Caravaggio, Caracciolo also worked in fresco, his finest and best-preserved works in this medium, finished in 1631, being in the Certoso di S. Martino, Naples. They show the more classical direction his art took after 1620.

Caravaggio, Michelangelo Merisi da 1571–1610
The greatest Italian painter of the 17th century. He trained in Milan, and moved to Rome in the early 1590s. Many of his early works are disturbingly erotic, representing fleshy youths in various guises, their bodies painted with the same searching sharp focus as the still-life details in which he delights (*A musical party*, *c.*1593, New York, Metropolitan). With his first two public commissions, however, the direction of his art changed. The three paintings on *The life of St Matthew* in the Contarelli Chapel, S. Luigi dei Francesi (1599–1602) and *The conversion of St Paul* and *The crucifixion of St Peter* (1600–01) in the Cerasi Chapel, S. Maria del Popolo, are startlingly original, with bold, strongly lit, realistically painted figures of intense physical presence emerging dramatically from dark shadow; after this Caravaggio rarely painted anything other than serious-minded religious works. He was often criticized for his supposed lack of decorum in showing biblical characters as ordinary people, and he prided himself on working directly from nature, but the grandeur of his compositions is firmly based in the High Renaissance tradition. In 1606 Caravaggio fled Rome after killing a man, and spent the rest of his life moving around Naples, Sicily and Malta, constantly in trouble because of his violent temperament. In these years, however, he produced his finest works, moving from the violent action of the Cerasi Chapel to a profound contemplative stillness: *The beheading of St John the Baptist* (1608, Valletta Cathedral, Malta) is perhaps the greatest masterpiece in all 17th-century Italian painting. With the Carracci, Caravaggio revived Italian painting from the sterile Mannerism of the late 16th century; their pictorial languages were very different but equally solid and convincing. Unlike the Carracci, Caravaggio had no pupils, but his influence was enormous. See vol. 1 p. *72*; vol. 2 pp. **180–183**

Caravaggisti
Term applied to painters of very different backgrounds and accomplishments, who formed no distinct school, but who adopted to a greater or lesser degree the style of Caravaggio. His immediate Italian followers included Baglione, Orazio Gentileschi, Manfredi, Saraceni and Caracciolo, who was largely responsible for the lasting effect of Caravaggio's style in Naples. A host of lesser painters imitated his realism and dramatic lighting without understanding the deeper aspects of his art. Although Caravaggio's style had wide repercussions in Italy, in Rome itself it lost its appeal in the 1620s, and his influence was more enduring and diverse outside Italy. Artists such as Honthorst and Terbrugghen, who both spent about a decade in Rome, took a sturdy Caravaggesque style to northern Europe, and it was particularly popular in their home town, Utrecht, only dying there in the 1650s, as it did in its other two final strongholds, Lorraine and Sicily. Perhaps the greatest Caravaggesque painter was Georges de La Tour of Lorraine, whose knowledge of Caravaggio probably came via Utrecht. His candle- or torch-lit paintings are close in spirit to the master's last great works, and their still and silent beauty is very far from the horrific violence which was so often the aspect of Caravaggio's art pursued by his Italian followers.

Carducho, Vicente (Vicenzo Carducci) 1576–1638
Spanish painter, and writer on art. Florentine by birth, he came to Spain in 1585 with his brother Bartolomé. Vicente worked chiefly as a religious painter, and was a very fine draughtsman, but is now best known as a writer on art. His *Diálogos de la Pintura* (1633) champions Michelangelo and the Italian classical tradition, in which he was brought up. He sought to encourage a revival of painting in Madrid by reference to the great art of Italy, but this was hardly relevant after the arrival of Velazquez (1623). Whereas Pacheco wrote in favour of the naturalism of Caravaggio, Carducho referred to the latter as "Anti-Michelangelo" and "Anti-Christ". His brother **Bartolomé**, originally Bartolomineo Carducci (1560–1608), helped to introduce a sober tenebrist style to Spain with works such as *The death of St Francis* (1593, Lisbon, Museu Nacional). This still has elongated Mannerist figures, but the lighting and details are naturalistic.

Cariani, Giovanni Busi active 1509–*c.*1548
Italian painter, born in Bergamo but active in Venice. His style depends mainly on the great Venetians of the early16th century—Giorgione, Palma Vecchio, Titian—but he was capable of work of real distinction and vigour, as in the signed portrait of a nobleman (*c.*1525, Ottawa, NG), where the character of the elderly man is tersely expressed, and set off against a stormy sky.

Caricature
Term normally used in art for portraiture in which characteristic features are exaggerated or distorted so that, while still being recognizable, the person portrayed is mocked or ridiculed. Annibale Carracci is generally credited with the invention of caricature in this sense; Bernini and Daumier are among other leading artists who have practised the art. Political caricature, now universal, had its origins and heyday in 18th-century England with the satirical work of Rowlandson and Gillray.

Carles, Arthur B. (Becker) 1882–1952
American painter. He visited Paris in 1907–12, and the Fauvist colours of *The church* (*c.*1910, New York, Metropolitan) show his debt to Matisse. His knowledge of the latest in European avant-garde painting made his reputation in New York, and he exhibited at Stieglitz' "291". He is now best known for his energetically painted abstractions, such as *Abstraction* (1939–41, New York, Graham Gallery), which prefigure the work of the Abstract Expressionists.

Carlevaris, Luca 1665–1730
Italian painter, based in Venice. He was not the first to specialize in view-painting in this city, as has traditionally been claimed, but was the first to approach this genre in a relatively systematic manner; his rational perspectival treatment was to be profoundly important for the art of Canaletto.

Carlone family
18th-century Italian family of frescoists and stuccoists from Lombardy. The most noteworthy member was **Carlo Innocenzo** (1686–1775), the most talented Lombard Rococo painter, who worked in Vienna, Prague, southern Germany and northern Italy.

Carlstedt, Birger 1907–75
Finnish painter, an early advocate of international modernism. Inspired by De Stijl and the Bauhaus, he experimented with interior design, as in the Chat Doré restaurant in Helsinki (1928). After World War II he finally adopted a completely abstract idiom with dynamic intertwining curvilinear and angular forms.

Carmichael, Franklin see GROUP OF SEVEN

Carnovali, Giovanni called **Il Piccio** 1804–73
Italian Romantic painter of landscapes, portraits, religious and mythological works. In Paris in 1845, he met Delacroix and possibly saw Corot's work. The 16th-century Venetian masters influenced his rich chromatic range, as can be seen in *The bather* (1869, Milan, Galleria d'Arte Moderna). His luminous landscapes, mostly painted after 1840, were influenced by Poussin and Claude. Many of the Scapigliati were impressed by his handling of colour and light.

Caro, Anthony born 1924
British sculptor. He initially trained as an engineer but subsequently studied as a sculptor, and from 1951 to 1953 was an assistant to Henry Moore. His early sculptures show a lumpish treatment of the human body and a strong textural interest in the surface of the bronze, both features reflecting the influence of De Kooning and Dubuffet. After meeting David Smith and Noland in the USA in 1959 he started to make sculptures from prefabricated metal shapes, welded and bolted together. An early example was *Midday* (1960, New York, MOMA). Caro's abstract constructions are usually on a large scale, without a base, and painted in a single bold colour. Many explore spatial ambiguities, shapes that seem sprawling from one viewpoint, and become flattened as the spectator moves around the work. In his later sculpture Caro has abandoned smoothly painted surfaces for more weathered, rusted textures. Through teaching in the USA and in London he has exerted a considerable influence on young sculptors. See vol. 1 p. **191**; vol. 3 p. **246**

Carolingian art
Art associated with a period of renaissance in the late 8th and 9th centuries, fostered by emperors of the Carolingian dynasty. Before the Emperor Charlemagne founded the dynasty, the arts of the Franco-Germanic regions had reached a very low ebb; the revival fostered by the Emperor was intended both as glorification of the new Empire and as a kind of reinforcement of authority. Charlemagne was the temporal head of Western Christianity, the champion of Rome and the rival of Byzantine imperialism, and classical and early Christian models were copied by the Carolingians both for their artistic excellence and as symbols of imperial and Christian power. The pattern was set at Aachen (Aix-la-Chapelle), where the court was established. The Palatine Chapel, still largely intact, was firmly modelled on an Eastern plan. A large bronze pine-cone, still in the Aachen chapel, and a small equestrian statue of the Emperor (early 9th century, Paris, Louvre) from Metz, are clear examples of reuse of ancient symbols. Manuscripts, made accessible by the new strong links with Rome, were copied extensively in the court and in monasteries patronized by the Emperor, and the sudden emergence of exceptionally classical, naturalistic works at the court suggests that the Emperor managed to obtain the services of Byzantine painters. The Coronation Gospels (before 800, Vienna, Kunsthistorisches), for example, have finely modelled Evangelist figures in naturalistic settings. Another group of manuscripts related to the court (those associated with Charlemagne's sister Ada) also borrowed extensively, but they are heavily stylized, with more solid lines, richer colour and elaborate ornament. In the lower Rhine and in northern France several monasteries developed vigorous schools of illumination, in which early models were copied assiduously. A particularly influential Hellenistic style flourished in the region of Rheims and in Metz in both manuscript painting and ivory sculpture. The quality of Carolingian murals and mosaic work is more difficult to assess, since little has survived, but the splendid remains of several churches still witness the grandeur of major projects. Despite the disintegration of the Empire a few centres persisted into the 10th century, and the Carolingian achievement proved a strong influence upon Ottonian and early Romanesque art. See vol. 2 pp. 68–69

Carolus-Duran, Emile Auguste 1838–1917
French painter. In his early years he followed Courbet but then visited Italy

and Spain and was profoundly impressed by the Old Masters. *Lady with a glove* (1869, Paris, Louvre), a portrait of his wife, brought him fame and launched him as a successful portrait painter. It reflects his admiration of Velazquez.

Caron, Antoine *c.*1520–*c.*1600
French painter, decorator and festival designer. He is first recorded before 1550 working at Fontainebleau under Primaticcio, and was later employed by Henry III of France and Catherine de Médicis, his work expressing better than that of any other artist the sophisticated but unstable world of the Valois court at the time of the Wars of Religion (1560–98). His exaggerated Mannerist style is characterized by elongated pin-headed figures placed in vast architectural settings with gaudy colour contrasts. Magic and the occult were favourite themes and he also painted allegories based on court festivities, violent battles and massacres (*Massacres under the Triumvirate*, 1566, Paris, Louvre).

Carpaccio, Vittore
*c.*1450/55–1525/26
Venetian painter. His training is uncertain but his early work shows he was influenced by the Bellini, particularly Gentile. He is best known for two great cycles of paintings in Venice, *The legend of St Ursula* (1490–98, Accademia) and *Scenes from the lives of SS. George and Jerome* (1502–07, Scuola di San Giorgio degli Schiavoni). Of all Italian Renaissance painters he is the most fastidiously topographical, representing the exteriors and interiors of houses in detail, notably in *The dream of St Ursula* and in *St Augustine's vision of St Jerome*. His assured command of perspective is clear in *St George killing the dragon*, with its virtuoso foreshortening of the bones of the dragon's victims (rivalling both Uccello's *Battle of San Romano* and Pisanello's *St George* fresco in S. Anastasia, Verona). His meticulous detail, however, is transformed by the miraculous delicacy of his use of light, and his best work exemplifies a supremely Venetian gracefulness. *Two courtesans*, a fragment of a larger painting (Venice, Correr) is perhaps the most widely reproduced work of this extremely popular painter. His altarpieces are less remarkable, though his *Martyrdom of the 10,000* (1515, Accademia) is both gruesome and odd. See vol. 2 p. **122**

Carpeaux, Jean-Baptiste 1827–75
French sculptor and painter, particularly known for the emotional expressiveness of his work. In Italy (1856–62) as winner of the Prix de Rome (1854), he made copies of antique statues and studied works by Raphael and Michelangelo. His lively and naturalistic *Neapolitan fisherboy* (1858, Paris, Louvre), and tormented *Ugolino* (1860, Louvre) established his reputation as the leading sculptor of the day. Returning to Paris in 1862, he executed numerous portrait busts, notably of the imperial family, and began his controversial sculpture group, *The dance* (1866–69, original in the Louvre), for the façade of the Opéra. In his emotional appeal and instantaneity, Carpeaux broke with Neoclassical tradition, and his use of deep shadow in stone was influential on Rodin and Rosso. A collection of his paintings is in the Petit Palais, Paris. See vol. 3 p. **106**

Carr, Emily 1871–1945
Canadian Expressionist landscape painter. She worked in the wilderness of British Columbia, making its native culture and environment her sources of inspiration. Much of her work was executed out of doors, and is characterized by a passionate empathy with nature. Her style is original, although she was undoubtedly influenced by the intensity of expression of the Fauves, whose work she saw in Paris in 1910–11. She had almost stopped painting when in 1927 she saw the work of the Group of Seven, which revitalized her art and led to a deepening spirituality. *Forest landscape II* and *Sky* (1934–35, Ottawa, NG of Canada) attain transcendental grandeur, with lyrically nuanced swirls and streaks of expressive brushwork. She wrote several autobiographical works, and became a national heroine.

Carrà, Carlo 1881–1966
Italian painter. He joined the FUTURISTS in 1909, and his early style, based on Divisionism, depicted the energy of modern life in a surge of colour. After visiting Paris in 1911 and 1912 he imposed a Cubist-type grid on his pictures to produce work such as *The funeral of the anarchist Galli* (1910–11, New York, MOMA), which successfully combines a sense of energy with pictorial order. He published his own Futurist manifesto in 1913. His *Patriotic celebration* (1914, Milan, Gianni Mattioli coll.) was composed entirely of words evoking the heroic spectacle of war. In 1915 he broke away from Futurism, and founded METAPHYSICAL PAINTING with Chirico in 1917. His *Metaphysical muse* (1917, Milan, Emilio Jesi coll.) is a key work. In the 1920s and 1930s he subscribed to the classical principles of the NOVECENTO. See vol. 3 pp. **152–153, 171**

Carracci family
Bolognese painters, the brothers **Agostino** (1557–1602) and **Annibale** (1560–1609) and their cousin **Ludovico** (1555–1619), who played leading roles in the revival of Italian painting around 1600. In about 1585 their studio became a teaching academy, and, in opposition to the prevailing rather vapid Mannerism, revived the High Renaissance practice of drawing from nature, encouraging a realistically solid sense of form. All three were brilliant draughtsmen (more than 500 of their drawings are in the Royal Collection at Windsor), and clear, firm drawing characterizes the work of the leading Bolognese painters of the next generation—notably Domenichino and Reni—who were trained in their studio. Annibale was certainly the greatest artist of the three, the only contemporary Italian painter who ranks beside Caravaggio. His achievements were diverse. He was the inventor of caricature in the modern sense, and his early genre paintings are remarkable in their directness and liveliness of observation (*The butcher's shop*, *c.*1582, Oxford, Christ Church), but his greatest work was the ceiling of a gallery in the Farnese Palace, Rome (1597–1600). The heroic style he perfected here, based on antique sculptures, Michelangelo and Raphael, but with a richness and exuberance which is Annibale's own, was one of the foundations of Baroque painting. He was also the father of ideal landscape, most fully developed by Claude and Poussin (*The Flight into Egypt*, *c.*1604, Rome, Doria Gallery). Poussin was deeply impressed by the economy and precision of composition and gesture of Annibale's work and the Farnese Gallery became a model for history painters throughout the next two centuries. Agostino assisted Annibale in the Farnese Gallery, but painted little, and is principally important as a teacher and engraver. His sys-

tematic studies of the human body, engraved after his death and often republished, were important teaching tools for the next two centuries. Ludovico was the inspiration behind the Carracci academy and directed it alone after his cousins went to Rome. His style was less classical and more painterly than theirs, with flickering lights and rich textures which greatly influenced the young Guercino (*Christ crucified above figures in Limbo*, 1614, Ferrara, S. Francesca Romana). See vol. 2 pp. *182*, **184–187**

Carreño de Miranda, Juan
1614–85
Spanish painter, active in Madrid. With the great exception of his friend Velazquez, he was the most important court painter of 17th-century Spain. His dignified portraits (examples in the Prado, Madrid) owed much to Velazquez, but his religious paintings were often more extravagant and imaginative, as in the huge *Belshazzar's feast* (*c.*1660, Barnard Castle, Bowes Museum). He also worked in fresco: there are examples in Toledo Cathedral and in Madrid.

Carriera, Rosalba 1675–1757
The leading Venetian portraitist of the 18th century. Her sentimental and often insipid portraits (all in pastel) gained her a remarkable international reputation, and she received commissions from such eminent European patrons as Augustus III of Saxony, Maximilian II of Bavaria, and the Elector Palatine. Her greatest moment came when she visited Paris in 1720, accompanied by her mother, sisters and brother-in-law, Pellegrini. Although the French, who had imagined her to be an outstanding beauty, were disappointed by the plainness of her features, she was hailed as the greatest Italian painter of her day; indeed the French found more to admire in her intimate art than in the large-scale decorations by painters such as Pellegrini. She returned to Italy in 1723, went suddenly blind in 1743, and died insane. See vol. 1 p. *160*; vol. 2 pp. **242–243**

Carrière, Eugène 1849–1906
French painter, a pupil of Cabanel. His early paintings show the influence of Rubens and Velazquez, but his later works, usually images of gentleness and love, have a mistiness and melancholy about them. The touching *Motherhood* (Paris, Musée Rodin) represents his favourite theme.

Carstens, Asmus Jacob 1754–98
Danish-German painter and draughtsman, a prophetic upholder of the claims of artistic genius to be accountable to no one. Almost entirely self-taught because of his contempt for academic instruction in Copenhagen, his obsessive goal was Rome. A first attempt in 1783 took him only as far as Mantua. In 1787 he moved to Berlin, where in 1790 he became professor at the Academy. Given a scholarship to Italy in 1792, he spent the rest of his life in Rome, justifying his refusal to return by the claim that he "belonged not to the Berlin Academy but humanity". He painted little, and his novel exhibition of his own works in 1795 largely consisted of cartoons and drawings (illustrations to *The Argonauts*, 1799). A thorough-going Neoclassicist, Carstens exercised a great influence upon the later Nazarenes.

Cartoon
Term usually used in art of a preliminary but fully worked-out sketch of which the outlines could be transferred to establish the design of a fresco or easel-painting.

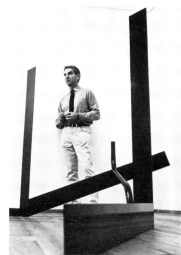

Caro: Photograph taken beside one of his sculptures (J.S. Lewinski, Camera Press)

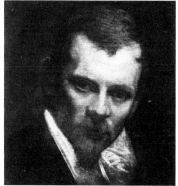

Carracci, Annibale: Self-portrait, *c.*1590. Florence, Uffizi (Alinari)

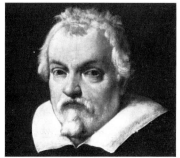

Carracci, Ludovico: Self-portrait? Florence, Uffizi (Alinari)

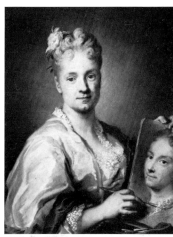

Carriera: Self-portrait, 1709. Florence, Uffizi (Scala)

Thus the famous cartoon by Leonardo (London, NG) is the full-size drawing for Leonardo's proposed *Virgin and Child with St Anne and the infant St John*. In one method of fresco-painting pieces of cartoon appropriate to each day's work were placed on the fresh plaster so that the design could be transferred by pressure of a stylus or by pricking through the paper. The term is now commonly used for humorous drawings.

Cartouche
Scroll-like ornament often used in architecture from the 17th century onwards and also found on prints and maps. It was much favoured for inscriptions and coats of arms by sculptors of funerary and other monuments. The word is also used of those oval or oblong designs in Egyptian hieroglyphics which enclose royal or divine titles.

Caryatid
In decorative sculpture a female figure which acts as a pillar, supporting an architectural member on her head. The most famous are those on the Erechtheion, Athens (421–409 BC). The male equivalent is called an **atlas** (plural atlantes). Whereas caryatids usually stand upright without any suggestion of strain, atlantes are often carved to suggest the effect of carrying a great weight on the shoulders. **Canephorae** are caryatids with baskets on their heads.

Cascella, Pietro born 1921
One of the leading Italian sculptors since World War II. He works in marble and other traditional materials, typically using large, rounded, abstract forms, which in spite of their size often convey a sense of intimacy and sexual curiosity. His sculptures have something of the power and simplicity of archaic Greek art, and his boldness of vision has won him commissions for several large public monuments, on which his brother **Andrea** (born 1920), also a sculptor, has sometimes assisted. Andrea's independent works are also abstract, but smaller and more elegant than Pietro's.

Casorati, Felice 1883–1963
Italian painter whose SYMBOLIST work and teaching in Turin influenced two artistic generations in Italy. In the 1920s he responded to the classical bias of artists such Carrà and Chirico by concentrating on the weight and volume of his subjects in place of his earlier linear and ornamental style. Some of these pictures owe a debt to Metaphysical Painting in their lighting and emphatic perspective. By 1930, however, his interest in line and rhythm had reasserted itself and his subject matter was transformed into decorative lineation.

Cassatt, Mary 1845–1926
American painter. She spent much of her childhood in Europe, and in 1866 settled in Paris, where she became a member of the Impressionist group. She admired the work of Monet, Courbet and, in particular, Degas, working in close collaboration with him from 1879. She is best known for her depictions of mothers with children, such as *The bath* (1892, Chicago, Art Institute). She is also renowned for her graphics, which, like the drypoint *Gathering fruit* (1892), were influenced by Japanese prints. In later life she travelled with collector friends advising them on purchases. See vol. 1 p. *167*; vol. 3 pp. 102, **125**

Casson, Alfred Joseph born 1898
Canadian landscape painter, based in Toronto. He joined the GROUP OF SEVEN in 1926 and was a founder-member of the Canadian Group of Painters in 1933. His clean, crisp manner emerged by 1945, showing an acute sense of structure and surface pattern applied to Ontario landscapes and villages. In *Country store* (1945, Toronto, Art Gallery of Ontario) simple rural architecture is monumentalized, using a system of interlocking rectilinear areas.

Cast
General term for an exact copy of a sculptor's model, made by pouring a molten or liquid substance into a mould. The sculptor first makes his model in clay, plaster, wax or another workable material and then constructs a mould from it to receive the more durable material of the cast, often bronze. In large pieces, the cast is hollow, formed around a core which is usually removed. Methods of producing casts include CIRE-PERDUE, or lost-wax casting, and sand-casting. See vol. 1 pp. **186–189**

Castiglione, Giovanni Benedetto (called Il Grechetto) *c.*1610–65
Italian painter, engraver and draughtsman, born in Genoa. For an Italian artist Castiglione was much influenced by foreigners; Rubens and van Dyck, who both worked in Genoa, helped to form his style in painting, and he was one of the first Italians to admire Rembrandt's etchings. He was at his best with subjects involving a bizarre or fantastic element, as in the exotic *Medea casting a spell* (*c.*1655, Hartford, Connecticut, Wadsworth Atheneum) or his most famous etching, *The genius of Castiglione* (1648). A versatile and prolific artist rather than a profound one, he was highly original technically (the monotype was probably his invention).

Castillo, Antonio del 1616–68
Spanish painter. He was the leading artist of his day in Cordova and was much praised by contemporaries, but because has oeuvre is so ill-defined he is little known today. His style was eclectic, so his work is often confused with that of other artists, and few paintings associated with him are dated. The best works attributed to him are the six *Scenes from the life of Joseph* (*c.*1655) in the Prado, Madrid. Valdés Leal was his pupil.

Castillo, Jorge born 1933
Spanish painter. His first works were inspired by Picasso's Cubism but he soon developed a very personal and idiosyncratic form of Surrealism. His paintings are figurative but in an almost primitive sense, and by their tightly structured designs suggest assemblage. His graphic works, which are numerous, employ a wide range of techniques and create a similar effect.

Catena, Vincenzo
active *c.*1495–1531
Venetian painter. Much of his work is derivative, painted in the mature style of Giovanni Bellini with echoes of Giorgione, Titian and Palma Vecchio. He entered some kind of partnership with Giorgione in 1506 according to an inscription on the back of the latter's *"Laura"* (1506, Vienna, Kunsthistorisches Museum). The signed portrait of a man, also in Vienna, is one of the best examples of his sensitive portraiture.

Catlin, George 1796–1872
American painter, famous for his portrayal of American Indians. He was entirely self-taught, and practised law before turning to portrait painting in 1821. From 1830–36 he lived among Indians, recording them in a colourful, factual style. Unsuccessful in his attempts to sell his paintings at home, in 1839 Catlin, accompanied by a group of Indians, took his "Indian gallery" of 507 pictures to England and France, where they were much praised.

Caulfield, Patrick born 1936
British painter. Initially associated with POP art, his work derives from the stylizations and simplifications of the commercial artist rather than directly borrowing from popular imagery. His early paintings such as *Artist's studio* (1964, Arts Council of Great Britain) parodied the way in which cheap decoration had borrowed from the innovations of modern art. Later he evolved a consistent style using flat, unmodelled colour and a thick black outline, often depicting uninhabited interiors, as in *Dining recess* (1972, Arts Council). In spite of the radical simplifications, these interiors suggest an illusionistic environment. See vol. 3 p. **241**

Cavalcanti, Emilio di born 1897
Brazilian painter, a pioneer of modernism. In 1922 he took part in the *Semana do Arte Moderno* (Week of Modern Art), which marked the beginning of the modern movement in the arts and letters of Brazil. Following a stay in Europe, 1935–40, he became increasingly interested in creating great narrative pictures rooted in the life-styles of Brazilian people. *Brazilian scene* (1937–38, Paris, Musée d'Art Moderne) is a heroic vision of the life, toil and mirth of the common working man and woman.

Cavallini, Pietro active 1273–1308
Roman fresco-painter and designer of mosaics. He is often considered as the Roman parallel to Cimabue, for although his iconography is essentially Byzantine, his figures have a solidity derived from the Antique which looks forward to Giotto. His frescos in S. Paolo fuori le Mura were burned in 1823, but some in S. Cecilia in Trastevere, including an impressive *Last Judgment*, survive, as do the mosaics in S. Maria in Trastevere on *The life of the Virgin*. Cavallini's work in both churches probably dates from the early 1290s. In 1308, at the end of his known career, he worked in Naples, and is probably the author of some of the frescos in S. Maria Donna Regina, although the extent of his contribution is disputed. See vol. 2 p. **78**

Cavallino, Bernardo 1616–56?
Neapolitan painter, chiefly of religious scenes, one of the most individual of Italian Baroque artists. Rejecting the Caravaggism of his master Stanzione, Cavallino developed a subtle and distinctive style which was without parallel in Italian painting of the time. His works are usually sweetly coloured and on a small scale, with graceful and delicate figures expressing great tenderness of feeling, very much in opposition to the prevailing currents in Neapolitan painting. Only one dated work is known (*St Cecilia*, 1645, Naples, Museo di Capodimonte) and his sources and development are not clear.

Cavallon, Giorgio born 1904
American painter. He was born in Italy but emigrated in 1920. In the late 1930s he exhibited with the AMERICAN ABSTRACT ARTISTS group and assisted Gorky on FEDERAL ART PROJECT murals. His hard-edged Cubist and Neo-Plasticist-derived abstraction became more gestural in the 1950s (*Abstraction*, 1950, New York, Egan Gallery).

Cellini, Benvenuto 1500–71
Florentine sculptor and goldsmith, whose life is recorded in his *Autobiography*, one of the most famous ever written. From 1519 to 1540, his activity was centred in Rome, where he made jewellery and medals for Popes Clement VII and Paul III, but little of his work from this period survives. He visited France in 1537, and again in 1540–45, where, for Francis I, he made the celebrated gold salt-cellar (*c.*1540, Vienna, Kunsthistorisches), which, with its elegant figures of *Neptune* and *Ceres*, is a virtuoso piece of Mannerist style and preciousness. In France he also gained experience in bronze-casting, so that on his return to Florence in 1545 he was able, with unmatched skill, to produce his masterpiece and one of the greatest pieces of Mannerist sculpture, the *Perseus* (completed 1554) commissioned by Duke Cosimo I for the Loggia dei Lanzi. Cellini gives an exciting account in his *Autobiography* of the casting of the great bronze figure, effortlessly poised over the body of Medusa and holding aloft her ghastly, but beautiful, head. His bronze busts are in contrast somewhat dry—*Cosimo I* (Florence, Bargello), *Bindo Altoviti* (Boston, Gardner Museum)—and *The Crucified Christ* (1556–72, Escorial) shows his limitations as a sculptor in marble. The *Autobiography* breaks off in 1558 and was not published until 1728. With its tales of imprisonment and flight, quarrels with rivals and authority, and deeds of heroism, it marks Cellini as a prototype of the Romantic conception of the artist. See vol. 1 pp. *186–187*; vol. 2 pp. *167*, **168**

Celtic art
Art of the Celtic peoples of northern and central Europe, extending from about the 5th century BC to the early medieval period. The pagan Celts who spread over Europe in the 5th and 4th centuries BC produced sophisticated metalwork, and decorated their implements, vessels and jewellery with a variety of geometrical and spiral designs, stylized animals and, more rarely, human figures. They took motifs from many sources, from Greece, Italy and the East, and exploited repoussé and inlay techniques, chiefly on bronze and gold. The bronze Basse-Yutz Flagon from France (mid-4th century BC, London, BM) has incised decoration, applied animal figures and coral inserts. A more unusual piece, the silver Gundestrup Cauldron (probably 1st century BC, Copenhagen, Danish National Museum), displays narrative scenes and large, bearded and helmeted heads with other ornament. Between the 1st century BC, when the Celts still had widespread settlements in northern Europe, and the Christian period, when they had moved to the extremities of the British Isles, their art suffered some decline. The metalwork from the medieval period sometimes appears more primitive, but the decorative tendency continued to be predominant even in figurative work (*"The Athlone Crucifixion"*, for example, mid-7th century, Dublin, National Museum). The outstanding achievement of the Christian period was the development of a unique form of manuscript illumination in the monasteries founded in Ireland and in northern Britain. An early example, probably from a northern English monastery, is the 7th-century Book of Durrow (Dublin, Trinity College), with its colourful spiral and geometric patterns, complex interlace, and schematic approach to the human figure. It was an art of ornament, above all, and through the activities of missionaries it exerted a widespread in-

fluence in northern England (as in the ornamental "carpet pages" of the Lindisfarne Gospels, c.700, London, BM) and on the Continent. In sculpture the great Celtic invention was the free-standing stone cross with its fusion of pagan decorative motifs and Christian subjects. See vol. 2 pp. 66–67

Cennini, Cennino d'Andrea
c.1370–c.1440
Florentine painter, a pupil of Agnolo Gaddi. None of his paintings has survived and his fame rests on his book, *Il Libro dell'Arte* (The Craftsman's Handbook), written about 1400. It is the most important source of information on artistic practice in late medieval and early Renaissance times, and contains detailed descriptions of the techniques of fresco and panel painting and of casting.

Cercle et carré (circle and square)
A short-lived artists' association and periodical established by the critic Michel Seuphor and the painter Torrès-Garcia in Paris in 1929 to promote geometric abstract art. One important article which appeared in it was written by Mondrian in 1930—*Realist art and superrealist art*. The movement was superseded in 1931 by the more important and influential ABSTRACTION-CRÉATION group.

Cerquozzi, Michelangelo
1602–60
Italian painter, best known for his battle-scenes, on account of which he was nicknamed "Michelangelo of the battles". He was also one of the few Italian artists to paint peasants and such in the manner of Pieter van Laer.

Ceruti, Giacomo active 1724–38
Italian painter of genre and low-life scenes. He probably originated in Brescia, where most of his work is now to be found. Many of his outstanding renderings of everyday life are grotesquely satirical, while others display a matter-of-fact observation that looks forward to the realism of the 19th century (*Still life*, Milan, Brera).

César (César Baldaccini) born 1921
French sculptor of considerable versatility and inventive power. He began with sharp and witty constructions based largely on animal and fish forms, made from welded scrap metal. His later work has ranged from sculptures created from crushed car bodies (*The yellow Buick*, 1961, New York, MOMA) to soft shiny plastic pieces. He is represented in many important collections of modern art. See vol. 1 p. *191*

Cesare da Sesto 1477–1523
Italian painter. He was born in Milan, but is first recorded in Rome (c.1505), where he collaborated with Peruzzi and no doubt came in contact with the young Raphael. After his return to Milan in 1510 his work shows a fusion of elements drawn from Raphael and from Leonardo, whose work he copied. He perpetuated this synthesis in the work he produced during his most productive period, 1514–20, when he was in Naples (*The Adoration of the Magi*, c.1515, Naples, Museo di Capodimonte).

Céspedes, Pablo de 1538–1608
Spanish painter, scholar and writer on art. Between 1565 (the year after Michelangelo's death) and 1585 he went at least twice to Rome. His few extant writings, including one preserved in Pachecho's *Arte de la Pintura*, show an exaggerated enthusiasm for

Michelangelo, whose *Last Judgment* he saw as the epitome of painting. His high reputation, like Becerra's, was due to his acquaintance with and promotion of Michelangelo's art. Little of his painting is known, but *The Last Supper* in Cordova Cathedral shows him to have been a provincial painter, profiting but little from his acquaintance with Michelangelo's art.

Cézanne, Paul 1839–1906
French painter, of seminal importance to the development of 20th-century art. His early works, in thick, dark paint, often have violent and melodramatic subjects but include some powerful portraits (*Uncle Dominique*, 1865–67, Pasadena, Norton Simon Foundation). On meeting Pissarro and the other Impressionists he lightened his palette and produced works such as "*La Maison du Pendu*" (The suicide's house, 1873, Paris, Jeu de Paume), shown at the first Impressionist exhibition in 1874. However, he reacted against the lack of structure in their paintings and declared his intention to make Impressionism into "something solid and durable, like the art of the museums". He tried to re-create his feelings in front of nature, and his paintings show a painstaking analysis of colour, which replaced light and shade as his means of modelling. Cézanne had an independent income, which enabled him to survive public indifference to his work, and spent much of his life in his native Aix-en-Provence. The death of his father in 1886, when he inherited the family estate, enabled him to marry Hortense Fiquet, his mistress for many years and the subject of many portraits (*Woman with a coffee pot*, 1890–94, Paris, Louvre). Still lifes and landscapes were his other preoccupations; notable are his prolonged analyses of the view at L'Estaque and later of Mont Ste-Victoire. They differ fundamentally, however, from Monet's similar exercises in the *Haystack* and *Rouen Cathedral* series of the 1890s. Cézanne was not concerned with instantaneous effects but with codifying minute variations in tone and colour—observed over a prolonged period—in a form of empirical geometry, the "cylinders, spheres and cones" he mentions in a famous line from a letter to Emile Bernard in 1904. He was given a one-man exhibition by Ambroise Vollard in 1895, and a retrospective show in 1907 had a profound influence on the CUBISTS. Among the works seen were *Bathers* (versions 1906, London, NG, and Philadelphia Museum of Art), in which he treats a traditional subject as a design of interlocking planes covering sky, water and solid forms. Cézanne's objectivity and his rigorous analysis of structure have made him one of the fathers of modern art, an inspiration to pioneers of abstract art, even though his own work never approached complete abstraction. See vol. 1 pp. *33, 51, 75, 119, 125, 150, 157*; vol. 3 pp. **112–113, 118–119,** *126*

Chadwick, Lynn born 1914
British sculptor. He trained as an architect, and began experimenting with mobiles in the late 1940s. Initially he worked in slate, but from 1951 began making sculpture in welded iron in forms often related to animal and insect life. Sometimes, as in *Inner eye* (1952, New York, MOMA), he contrasted the texture of sheet-metal with lumps of raw glass. His sculpture combines a degree of abstraction with a menacing presence.

Chagall, Marc born 1887
French-Russian painter, whose highly

individual style has brought him much popular success. He was brought up in a poor Jewish family in Vitebsk, and studied in St Petersburg. Between 1910 and 1914 he lived in Paris, where he was befriended and encouraged by the poets Cendrars and Apollinaire. Cubist spatial effects and the prismatic colours of Delaunay's Orphism affected his style but he derived his imagery from childhood memories, set in irrational, dream-like juxtapositions. *I and the village* (c.1911, New York, MOMA) is a masterpiece of this early phase. From this basis he developed his characteristically poetic and exuberant style. Returning to Russia in 1914, he held various teaching appointments (after the Revolution), but since 1923 has lived in France and the USA, working prolifically not only as a painter but also as a designer of book illustrations, stage sets, stained-glass windows and decorative commissions. See vol. 1 p. *102*; vol. 3 p. **185**

Chamberlain, John born 1927
American sculptor. In 1955–56 he studied at Black Mountain College, and in the late 1950s, under the influence of David Smith, he began making assemblages from metal taken from wrecked cars. Between 1959 and 1963 he worked exclusively with crushed car bodies, creating crumpled, often sensuous, volumes. In the mid-1960s he turned to other materials for his crushed forms—foam rubber, metals and plexiglass. Since 1967 he has also experimented with videotapes.

Champaigne, Philippe de 1602–74
Flemish-born painter of portraits and religious subjects who became a French citizen in 1629. He trained in his native Brussels, chiefly with Jacques Fouquières, and moved to Paris in 1621, probably with his master. An early work such as *The Adoration of the shepherds* (c.1628, London, Wallace Coll.) clearly shows his Flemish upbringing in its Rubensian composition, but he gradually modified his style to suit more sober French taste, eliminating Baroque flourishes and developing great strength and purity of colouring and sharpness of handling. In 1628 he became court painter to the Queen Mother, Marie de Médicis, and at about the same time began to work for Cardinal Richelieu, of whom he painted several memorable portraits. Two of the finest (both c.1635–40) are in the National Gallery, London—a stunning full-length and a triple view of the cardinal's head intended as a model for a sculpted portrait. In the early 1640s Champaigne came into contact with Jansenism, a very austere Catholic sect, and under its influence his style became even more severe. He developed an original type of bust-length portrait in which his sitters, often Jansenists, are painted with piercing honesty of vision and a complete lack of concern with worldly values (*A man*, 1650, Paris, Louvre). His daughter became a nun at the Jansenist convent of Port-Royal, and his most celebrated work, the *Ex Voto* of 1662 (Louvre), was painted to mark her return from the brink of death by miraculous cure. See vol. 2 p. **193**

Chandler, Winthrop 1747–90
American painter. His portraits, executed in a clearly defined, linear style, are similar to those of Ralph Earl, but somewhat more archaic in appearance (*The Reverend Ebeneezer Devotion*, 1770, Brookline Historical Society).

Chang Hsuan see ZHANG XUAN

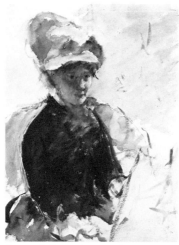
Cassatt: Self-portrait watercolour, c.1880. Washington, DC, Smithsonian, NPG

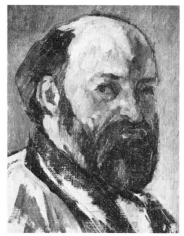
Cézanne: Self-portrait, 1880–81. Paris, Jeu de Paume (Scala)

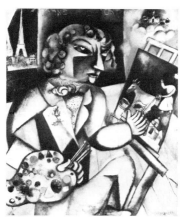
Chagall: *Self-portrait with seven fingers*, 1912–13. Amsterdam, Stedelijk Museum

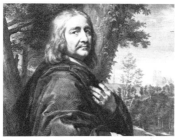
Champaigne: Engraving by Edelinck (detail), 1676, after a lost self-portrait, 1668. Private coll.

Chantrey, Sir Francis Leggatt 1781–1841
English NEOCLASSICAL sculptor. He was largely self-taught and early in his career painted portraits in Sheffield, but in about 1809 he moved to London, where he scored a great success with his bust of the *Rev. J. Horne-Took* (Cambridge, Fitzwilliam), exhibited in the 1811 Royal Academy. He soon succeeded Nollekens as the leading portrait sculptor in England and created numerous monuments more severe than those of Flaxman, executed with large unbroken forms and simple lines. The best-known is *The sleeping children* (1817) in Lichfield Cathedral, probably carved largely by assistants, like much of his output. The equestrian statue of George IV (1828) in Trafalgar Square, London, is his most important work in bronze.

Chao Meng-Fu see ZHAO MENGFU

Chardin, Jean-Baptiste-Siméon 1699–1779
French painter of still life and genre, one of the greatest and most individual artists of the 18th century. He trained under Noël-Nicolas Coypel and was received into the Academy in 1728 with *Rayfish, cat and kitchen utensils* (Paris, Louvre). *The copper cistern* (*c.*1733, Louvre) is an example of the early work in which he rejected the decorative formulae of the Flemish still-life painters to concentrate on the humblest household objects, subtly capturing textural effects by his use of grainy, scumbled paint. From about the mid-1730s he began to concentrate on solemn, unsentimentalized scenes of domestic life, usually on a small scale, and rarely containing more than two figures (*Young governess*, *c.*1739, versions London, NG, and Washington, NG). In the 1760s he returned to still life as his major theme with a less austere but equally compelling style (*Attributes of the Arts*, 1766, Minneapolis, Institute of Arts). Late in life, when failing eyesight forced him to give up painting in oil, he produced some penetrating pastel portraits, including those of himself and his wife (Louvre). Few artists have approached Chardin's directness of vision or his sureness and delicacy of touch in handling oil-paint. He was a contemporary of Boucher and briefly taught Fragonard, but his seriousness and sense of truth are far removed from their fashionable Rococo style. See vol. 1 pp. *74, 117, 136–137*; vol. 2 pp. **246–247**

Charles I, King of England 1600–49
Patron and collector. Throughout his reign (1625–49) he showed a passionate interest in the arts, commissioning works from many artists, including Rubens and van Dyck, both of whom he knighted. Rubens painted for Charles the ceiling of the Banqueting House in London, and van Dyck immortalized the King's appearance in numerous superb portraits. His collection, which included Mantegna's *Triumph of Caesar* series (Royal coll., Hampton Court) and cartoons by Raphael for tapestries woven for the Sistine Chapel (Royal coll., on loan to the V&A, London), was an inspiration to the artists who worked for him.

Charonton see QUARTON

Chase, William Meritt 1849–1916
American painter, primarily important as a teacher. He was born in Indiana and studied in New York and (from 1872) in Munich, thereafter working in a variety of styles, influenced by Velazquez, the Impressionists and Japanese prints. In 1896 he formed the Chase School in New York. Maurer, Demuth, Hartley, Sheeler and O'Keefe were among his many pupils.

Chassériau, Théodore 1819–56
French painter, who successfully combined Romantic and classical ideals. He was precocious, and in 1830 entered the studio of Ingres, whose linear approach is reflected in his own early portraits. His admiration for Delacroix, and visits to North Africa in 1840 and 1846, led him to combine a classicist approach with freer use of colour and to adopt romantic, exotic subjects (*The toilet of Esther*, 1841, Paris, Louvre). He painted portraits, nudes and scenes from North African life as well as large-scale mural decorations, notably for St Merri, Paris (1843), and the Cour des Comptes, Palais d'Orsay, Paris (1844–48, now destroyed). See vol. 3 p. **87**

Chavín art
Art of a highly distinctive culture related to the site of Chavín de Huantar in the northern Andes of Peru and extending from about 1100 BC to 400 BC. The important monumental sculpture from this site depicts a number of fantastic creatures, possibly representing the principal deity. These imposing figures are composed of a series of snarling jaws, fangs and feline heads skilfully interrelated in a complex pattern. The Raimondi Monolith (*c.* 500 BC, Lima, Museo National de Antropologia y Arqueologia) is decorated with such motifs, in low relief. Chavín ceramics are also of exceptional quality, with the emphasis on plastic decoration. Felines, eagles and snakes, as well as geometrical designs, are the most common motifs. The Chavín also made fine hammered and repoussé goldwork, textiles, and personal ornaments of lapus lazuli, turquoise, shell and wood. Chavín ideas and art styles influenced a wide area of Peru and recurred in later cultures.

Chéret, Jules 1836–1931
French printmaker, best known for the posters he designed in the 1880s and 1890s, employing three-colour lithography. Deriving stylistic inspiration from the Japanese print, he used rhythmical linear contours, bold colours and elongated proportions to enliven his figure style. He thus suggested the animated gaiety of the popular entertainments advertised (*The ice palace, Champs Elysées*, 1893, New York, MOMA). His posters were a significant influence upon Art Nouveau designs and such painters as Seurat and Toulouse-Lautrec.

Chiaroscuro
Term from the Italian "bright-dark", used to describe light and shade effects in painting. It is generally applied to a dramatic use of contrasting light and shade, pioneered by Leonardo but particularly associated with Caravaggio and his followers.

Chiaroscuro woodcut
Term used to describe a monochrome woodcut giving an effect of tonal modelling. Light and shade are created by laying the print successively over a number of differently toned blocks in register with the key block, which provides the main outlines of the design. The technique, developed in the 16th century, was, until eclipsed by metal-plate painting, a popular means of reproducing the effects of wash drawing and of copying paintings. Ugo da Carpi was a brilliant early exponent of the chiaroscuro woodcut.

Ch'ien Hsuan see QIAN XUAN

Chillida, Eduardo born 1924
Spanish sculptor. He works primarily in metal in the tradition of González, and is a fine craftsman. His sculpture is abstract and has developed from thin jagged forms to much more solid CONSTRUCTIVIST pieces, in which twisting and interlocking forms often predominate (*Borderline uproar*, 1958, Paris, Galerie Maeght). His drawings show how much his art is initially inspired by the mountainous landscape of his native Basque country. He is often considered Spain's finest living sculptor.

Chimu art
Art of the Chimu kingdom, AD 1200–1470, situated on the North Peruvian coast. Its capital, Chanchan, supposedly the largest city in Pre-Columbian Peru, contained palaces decorated with elaborate clay relief friezes of mythical beings, animals and repetitive geometrical designs. The mass-produced quality of much Chimu art is typified in the burnished black mould-made pottery. It is ornamented with decoration in low relief or figures in the round, with subjects ranging from secular to religious and mythical characters. The Chimu metalworkers created fine objects in gold and silver, much of it cut and hammered with REPOUSSÉ decoration. A splendid example is a large ceremonial knife in gold preserved in Lima at the Museo National de Antropologia y Arqueologia.

Ching Hao see JING HAO

Chinnery, George 1774–1852
English painter of luminous, atmospheric landscapes and line-and-wash sketches of Chinese and Indian scenes as well as portraits. An eccentric character who was unable to cope with his finances, he spent most of his time after 1802 in the Far East and much of his work remains there. *Hau Qua, Senior Hong Merchant at Canton, China* in the Tate Gallery, London, is representative.

Chin Nung see JIN NONG

Chirico, Giorgio de 1888–1978
Italian painter. Born in Greece, he later trained in Munich, where he was influenced by Böcklin's dreamlike landscapes. He went to Italy in 1909 and was in Paris, 1911–15, producing his first "enigma" pictures in 1910. This series was typified by empty Italian townscapes in which was placed a solitary figure or statue, often in conjunction with a modern image such as a train or lighthouse. Typical titles, suggesting the nature of the work, are *Mystery and melancholy of a street* (1914, New York, Resor coll.) and *Nostalgia of the infinite* (1914, New York, MOMA). In 1915 he was posted to Ferrara, where, in 1917, he founded METAPHYSICAL PAINTING with Carrà. His subject matter now incorporated still-life elements such as maps and biscuits as well as enigmatic mannequins whose disconcerting presence evoked a feeling of uneasy expectancy in the spectator. It was pictures like these that caused the Surrealists to recognize him as a forerunner of their movement. After World War I he began the study and imitation of the Old Masters that dominated the rest of his career. After wide fluctuations in direction in the 1920s he repudiated modern art, the remainder of his life being devoted to the production of his own "Old Masters". See vol. 1 pp. *91, 104*; vol. 3 pp. **170–171**

Chiu Ying see QIU YING

Chodowiecki, Daniel Nikolaus 1726–1801
German painter and engraver. He was born in Danzig, but was active in Berlin, where he began by painting on snuff-boxes in enamel. Despite achieving vast acclaim for his Greuze-like picture of *Callas taking leave of his family* (1767, West Berlin, Staatliche Museen), his real strengths were as a draughtsman and engraver. He supplied more than 2,000 engravings to illustrate books and almanacs, and left an incomparable record of the Berlin bourgeoisie, including many touching drawings of his own family.

Chong Son 1676–1759
Korean painter, the great revitalizer of Korean landscape painting. He visited every famous spot in Korea and painted so-called "real landscape" (*chinkyong sansu*). Free from Chinese influence, his brushwork was vigorous and even eccentric, forming patterns of horizontal and vertical lines. Most of his paintings are in museums in Seoul. See vol. 3 p. **43**

Christo (Christo Javacheff) born 1935
Bulgarian-born American sculptor. His art questions the emphasis of today's consumer society on packaging, and central to it is the activity of wrapping. His early wrapped and packaged works, begun in 1958, transform familiar objects into ambivalent presences in a Surrealist manner. By 1961 his approach had become more monumental and environmental; he produced his first project for a wrapped public building and realized it in 1968, when he wrapped the Kunsthalle in Berne. He wrapped other prominent buildings such as the Reichstag, Berlin (1977–79), and an entire rocky bay in Australia (1969). The famous *Valley curtain* (1971–72) at Rifle, Colorado, remained intact only three minutes; the artist, relatively unconcerned with a finished product, is instead preoccupied with the CONCEPTUAL and public implications of his gestures. See vol. 1 p. *204*; vol. 3 p. **248**

Christus, Petrus died 1472/73
Netherlandish painter. He became a master in Bruges in 1444, and is said to have been Jan van Eyck's pupil and to have completed works begun by Jan such as *St Jerome* (1442, Detroit, Institute of Arts). Certainly he was the main channel through which the Eyckian tradition was disseminated, and many of his paintings are copies and variations on themes by the older master, including, probably, his most famous work, *St Eligius and two lovers* (1449, New York, Metropolitan). This has an attractive informality, despite its awkward composition and abundance of iconographical details. A *Madonna* (1452 or 1457, Frankfurt, Städelsches Kunstinstitut) shows the use of Italian geometric perspective and supports the theory that Christus visited Italy. However, his highly personal approach to the description of space is most clearly developed in his portraits, as in *Edward Grimston* (1446, London, NG), where the head is depicted against the angle of a room, giving the portrait solidity and definition. See vol. 2 p. **95**

Chromolithography
see LITHOGRAPHY

Chu-jan see JURAN

Church, Frederick Edwin
1826–1900
American landscape painter, famous for the huge scale and spectacular subjects of his work. He was the only student

of Thomas Cole, in whose household he lived from 1844 to 1846. By 1850 he had shed Cole's Catskill subject matter but retained a mystical feeling towards Nature which led him to distant places in search of scenic grandeur. In 1853 he travelled to South America, making oil-sketches which were the basis of his later epic paintings, the best-known being *The heart of the Andes* (1859, New York, Metropolitan). His *Falls of Niagara* (1857, Washington, Corcoran) established his reputation, and its success in the Paris Universal Exhibition of 1867 led to his subsequent travels in Europe and the Near East.

Churriguera family
Family of Spanish sculptors and architects, active principally in Seville and famous for their elaborate and fantastic altarpieces, which gave rise to the term "Churrigueresque". The best-known was **José Benito** (1665–1725), who designed the high altar and retable (1693) of S. Esteban, Salamanca. He is often credited with inventing the style, but his work was restrained compared to that of other members of the family and he never allowed decoration to become so lavish that it obscured structure. This was the essential feature of the Churrigueresque style as it spread throughout Spain and South America, and the term still sometimes implies decadence.

Chu Ta see ZHU DA

Chu Tuan see ZHU DUAN

Cibber, Caius Gabriel 1630–1700
English Baroque sculptor. Danish by birth, he studied in Italy, and came to England shortly before 1660. He had a successful workshop producing tombs, garden sculpture, and pieces for architectural settings (examples at Hampton Court and St Paul's Cathedral, London). His best-known work is the grand allegorical relief on the Monument, London, built to commemorate the Great Fire of 1666. His sculpture is usually no more than competent, but he produced two strikingly original and powerful works—the figures of *Raving madness* and *Melancholy madness* (c.1675, London, V&A) originally made for the gate of Bedlam Hospital.

Cignani, Carlo 1628–1719
Italian painter, a pupil of Albani, and the first President of the Accademia Clementina in Bologna (1711–19). He was a highly influential but conservative figure painter whose style was based heavily on that of Correggio and Guido Reni. A masterpiece is *The Assumption of the Virgin* in the dome of Forlì Cathedral (1686–1706).

Cignaroli, Giambettino 1706–70
Italian painter. Most of his work is to be found in and around Verona, where he was one of the leading artists of his time, mainly working on historical and religious scenes and decorative commissions. On a visit to Verona in 1769 the Emperor Joseph I described him as "the greatest painter in Europe". His style derives largely from that of Balestra, his teacher.

Cigoli, Lodovico Cardi da
("Il Cigoli") 1559–1613
Florentine painter and architect, a pupil of Alessandro Allori. He was the most powerful and original Florentine painter of his time, but his eclectic art lacked a consistent direction. His *Adoration of the Magi* (1605, Florence, Pitti) looks back to the Renaissance, while the "*Ecce Homo*" (1606, Pitti) shows the influence

of the young Caravaggio. He spent most of the first decade of the 17th century in Rome, where he was an important and progressive influence, excelling in emotional effects and rich, creamy textures. See vol. 2 p. 204

Cimabue (Cenni di Pepi)
active c.1272–1302
Florentine painter. His reputation is based on a passage in Dante's *Divine Comedy* which describes him as having been surpassed by Giotto. Vasari made Cimabue's biography the first in his *Lives* and said he was the teacher of Giotto, so he can be thought to begin the line of great Italian painters. There is, however, very little secure knowledge about him. He is known to have been in Rome in 1272, but his only documented work is a mosaic (1301–02) in the apse of Pisa Cathedral. This is of little help in making attributions, but it seems reasonable to assign to him a group of outstanding pre-Giottesque works, including "*The S. Trinità Madonna*" (Florence, Uffizi), the Crucifix in S. Croce, Florence, and some frescos at Assisi. The design of a stained-glass window in Siena Cathedral has also been attributed to him. His style is a synthesis of Byzantine art and the work of Cavallini and his followers. See vol. 2 pp. **78–79**

Cima da Conegliano, Giovanni
Battista c.1459–c.1518
Italian painter, active principally in Venice. His work resembles that of the mature Giovanni Bellini, though there is also an architectural and scenographic boldness akin to Mantegna, and an accomplishment in dramatic composition derived from the same sources. His rich colouring and subtle shadowing can be seen in late works (*Doubting Thomas*, Venice, Accademia).

Cinquecento
Term (literally "five hundred") used of the 16th century (the fifteen hundreds) in Italian art.

Cione, Andrea di see ORCAGNA

Cire-perdue
French term meaning lost wax, used of a method of casting. A wax model of the sculpture or a wax-lined piece mould made from it is formed around a heat-proof core and enveloped with layers of clay or plaster. The wax between the outer mould and the core (which is held in place by metal pins) is then melted out and replaced by molten metal. Air escapes through vents in the outer mould. Lost-wax casting was used by the Greeks and Romans and by the Egyptians in ancient times. It was revived in the Carolingian period and again in Ottonian Germany by the metalworkers patronized by Abbot Bernward of Hildesheim. It is still the commonest means of hollow casting used by sculptors. See vol. 1 pp. 186–187

Cistercian art
Art of the Cistercian Order of monks, founded 1097/8. Cistercians returned to a stricter monastic life, reacting against Cluniac wealth and laxity, and their early churches were distinctly austere. The first manuscripts from Cîteaux (in Burgundy) are lively, reflecting Anglo-Norman influence, but the influence of St Bernard, Abbot of Clairvaux (died 1153), who promoted austerity in the arts, was soon felt. In his *Apologia* of 1127, St Bernard argued against extravagance in church art, especially in monasteries. Grotesques in monastic cloisters prompted his stern

demand: "What profit is there in those ridiculous monsters?". Luxury books became exceptional, and graver in tone, and rules were made forbidding visual ornament. See vol. 2 pp. 74–75

Citreon, Roelof Paul born 1896
Dutch painter and writer, born in Berlin. His early work was influenced by Corinth and Lieberman, but he then became involved with Expressionist (1914) and later Dadaist (1918) circles in Berlin. He made his first photomontage in 1919 and collaborated in *Dada Almanach* (1920). As a student at the Bauhaus (1922–24) his work became more abstract. Returning to Holland in 1927, he worked on stage sets and portraits and founded the Nieuwe Kunstschool, Amsterdam, on Bauhaus lines (1933–37).

Claesz., Pieter 1597/98–1661
Dutch still-life painter, born in Germany. With Heda he was the greatest master of the almost monochrome breakfast-piece, and founded a school of still-life painting in Haarlem, where he lived from 1617. He developed a remarkably naturalistic style in finely balanced compositions of which the ingredients scarcely vary—foods and wines in pewter, glass and porcelain vessels (*Bread, fruit and glass*, 1647, Amsterdam, Rijksmuseum). The silvery greens and browns of his palette recall the muted tones of van Goyen's landscapes. The landscape painter Berchem was his son. See vol. 2 p. 232

Clará Ayats, Josep 1878–1958
Spanish sculptor. His early work was influenced by Rodin, but it was the example of Maillol that proved decisive. From 1900 onwards he became increasingly concerned with the formal problems of weight and balance as opposed to the symbolism and effects of light that typified his early work. *Goddess* (Barcelona, Plaça de Catalunya) exemplifies his figural style. His studio in Barcelona is now a museum of his work.

Clark, Kenneth (Lord Clark of Saltwood) born 1903
British art historian. He worked with Berenson in Florence and at the Ashmolean Museum, Oxford, before becoming Director of the National Gallery, London, 1934–45. Among his numerous books are monographs on Leonardo da Vinci and Piero della Francesca, and a catalogue of Leonardo's drawings at Windsor Castle. Outside scholarly circles, however, he is best known for his widely popular television series *Civilization* (1969), a survey of European culture. See vol. 3 p. 254

Clark, Lygia born 1920
Brazilian Constructivist sculptress, a co-founder of the Brazilian Neo-Concrete Group in 1959. She studied in Brazil and under Léger in Paris. Following her early abstract reliefs and sculptures made in wood and stone or metal, plastic and rubber, she developed editions of smaller hinged structures made of aluminium, which when moved assume changing forms and relations.

Classicism
Term used to describe the qualities of order, clarity and harmony associated with the art of ancient Greece and Rome. Often the word is used to imply close stylistic dependence on antique models, but it is also used in a much broader sense as the antithesis of Romanticism, denoting art which places adherence to accepted canons of beauty above personal inspiration.

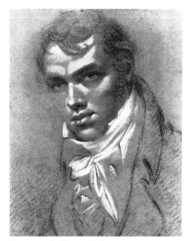

Chantrey: Self-portrait drawing, c.1805. London, NPG

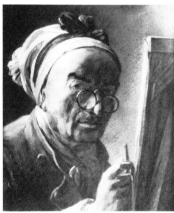

Chardin: Self-portrait pastel, c.1771. Paris, Louvre, Cabinet des Dessins

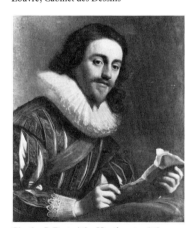

Charles I: Portrait by Honthorst, 1628. London, NPG

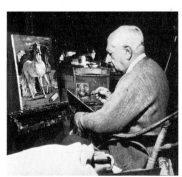

Chirico: Photograph (Fabbri)

Claude Gellée called **Claude Lorraine** 1600–82
French painter, usually known simply as Claude, the most famous and influential exponent of ideal landscape. After an early apprenticeship with Tassi, he visited Naples, whose dramatic and beautiful coastline provided inspiration throughout his career. He spent a year in his native Lorraine in 1626 under Claude Deruet before returning to Rome for the rest of his life. Claude's earliest landscapes and seaports were directly inspired by northern painters who had worked in Rome, especially Elsheimer and Bril, but from about the middle of the 1630s he began to develop his own style. It depended largely on his extraordinary sensitivity to effects of light, which he absorbed through ceaseless drawing from nature (more than 1,000 drawings survive) and used to create a gentle, elegaic mood. In the 1640s, under the influence of the Bolognese painters, particularly Domenichino, Claude's style became more classical and monumental. Always, however, light is of paramount importance, and in his late paintings the figures and buildings are so insubstantial that the air seems to flow through them (*Ascanius and the stag*, 1682, Oxford, Ashmolean). His subjects were often drawn from the Bible or classical myth, but unlike his friendly rival Poussin he was not concerned to recreate the majestic grandeur of the ancient world but rather to evoke the pastoral beauty of Virgil's bucolic poems. To guard against forgeries he compiled his *Liber Veritatis* or "*Book of Truth*" (begun 1635–36, London, BM) in which he made drawings of almost all his paintings, indicating for whom they were painted. Claude's influence was enormous—on numerous Italianate Dutch painters such as Asselyn and Both, and even more so on English painters of the 18th and early 19th century—Lambert, Wilson and Turner. He also inspired a certain type of English landscape gardening in the 18th century, and was so sought after that there are still many more Claudes in England than in any other country. See vol. 1 pp. *62, 159*; vol. 2 pp. **196–197**

Claude glass
Device used by landscape artists, especially during the 17th and 18th centuries, to enable them to see the broad tonal values of their scene by subduing colour and detail. It was basically a black convex glass which reflected the scene in miniature. Claude was said to have used one; Corot is known to have done so.

Clausen, Sir George 1852–1944
British painter. He specialized in agricultural scenes strongly influenced by the *plein-air* realism of Bastien-Lepage and was an original member of the NEW ENGLISH ART CLUB. *Girl at the gate* (1889, London, Tate) displays his solid handling, interest in light and sentimentality.

Clavé, Antoni born 1913
Spanish painter, designer and illustrator. He moved to Paris in 1939 and became a well-respected and innovative theatrical designer. His paintings are less well known. Still lifes or imposing figures are depicted with forceful draughtsmanship in a scheme that contrasts bright colour against a background of darker, more weighty tones (*King and Queen*, Paris, Musée d'Art Moderne).

Clerck, Hendrick de *c.*1570–1630
Flemish painter, mainly of altarpieces, who continued the Mannerist tradition well into the 17th century. He was appointed court painter to Archduke Albert in 1606 and enjoyed a successful career, even though his work must have looked very old-fashioned after Rubens' return from Italy in 1608. *The Holy Family* (1590, Brussels, Musées Royaux des Beaux-Arts), with its elongated crowded figures naively delighting in their complicated poses, is typical.

Clésinger, Jean-Baptiste 1814–83
French sculptor. He studied with his father, **Georges-Philippe** (1788–1852), and also with Thorvaldsen. The overtly sensual and realistic *Woman bitten by a serpent* (Paris, Louvre) created a furore in the 1847 Salon and made his reputation. In Italy (1856–64), he studied the Antique and Michelangelo and at home received numerous public commissions until the fall of the Second Empire. After 1875 he worked mainly on portrait busts. His work is characterized by strong modelling and dramatic poses, and in its eroticism recalls the Rococo.

Cleve, Joos van *c.*1490–1540
Netherlandish painter of devotional works, a master in the Antwerp guild in 1511. He was affected by the Mannerist taste for decoration and precious clothing, but retained a thoroughly conventional subject matter, favouring half-length depictions of the Virgin and Child in a format that derived from van Eyck. *The Holy Family* (1530s, New York, Metropolitan) is a distinguished example, with a characteristic still life on the ledge in the foreground. The influence of Leonardo is sometimes discernible in his modelling. Joos is thought to have worked at the court in Fontainebleau and at Genoa. He may also have collaborated with Patenier on some panels. His son **Cornelis** (1520–67) was also a painter.

Clodion (Claude Michel) 1738–1814
French ROCOCO sculptor. He was the son-in-law of Pajou but was trained by his uncle L.-S. Adam and by Pigalle. In 1759 he won first prize at the Academy and spent the years 1762–71 in Rome at a time when quantities of antique terracottas were being discovered. He made a few large statues such as *St Cecilia* (1775–77, Rouen Cathedral), but his most characteristic works are small-scale terracotta and marble groups of nymphs and satyrs full of warm pagan life (examples are in many museums in France). Clodion was one of the most attractive artists of his age, but the demand for his light-hearted sculptures, like that for Fragonard's paintings, ended with the French Revolution. Unlike Fragonard, however, he came to terms with sterner taste so successfully that he was employed on the decoration of the Arc de Triomphe du Carrousel (1806–09) in Paris, built to celebrate Napoleon's victories. See vol. 2 p. **243**

Cloisonnisme
Style of painting originated by Bernard in the late 1880s. Dark outlines surround flat bright forms, as in stained-glass or **cloisonné** enamelwork. *Cloisonné* derives from the French term for enamelling in which thin strips of metal outline the enamel areas.

Close, Chuck born 1940
American PHOTO-REALIST painter. He paints huge heads using photographs of his friends projected on to canvases inscribed with a grid. The works, which take three to six months to complete, are executed square by square with an air-brush. Close emphasizes that the iconic presence of each portrait-likeness is only incidental to his method; his concern is with perception, and translating "photographic information into paint information". In his avoidance of the painterly stroke, reliance on the grid and interest in the objective nature of photographs, Close, in common with other artists of the 1960s and 1970s, was reacting against the emotionalism of Abstract Expressionism (*Self-portrait*, 1968, Minneapolis, Walker Art Center). See vol. 1 p. *33*; vol. 3 p. **253**

Closterman, Johann Baptist *c.*1660–1711
Anglo-German portrait painter. Born in Osnabrück, he came to London probably in 1681, and worked in partnership with Riley as a drapery painter. After Riley's death (1691) he developed an independent practice. His whole-length and group portraits show compositional skill and originality at the expense of insight into character. A spectacular equestrian portrait of the Duke of Marlborough is at Chelsea Hospital, London.

Clouet, François *c.*1510?–1572
French painter, previously confused under the single name "Janet" with his father, Jean, whom he succeeded as court painter in 1541. The famous portrait of *King Francis I* (Paris, Louvre) in a gorgeously showy doublet is probably his work and painted soon after his appointment. His earliest documented work, the portrait of his friend *Pierre Quthe* (1562, Louvre), is so much more sober and Italianate that it strongly suggests that Clouet visited Italy. The enigmatic *Lady in her bath* (Washington, NG) is his most remarkable work, but his stature as a portraitist can perhaps best be seen in his drawings (more meticulous and detailed than his father's) of which there is a large collection in the Musée Condé at Chantilly. See vol. 2 p. **161**

Clouet, Jean ("Janet") died 1540/1
French portrait painter. He was probably the son of another **Jean** (born *c.*1420), a Flemish artist who came to France in about 1460, but whose life is almost totally obscure. Although Clouet is named in the royal accounts from 1516, and had a great contemporary reputation, there is little secure knowledge about his career. No certainly documented paintings are known, but a handful are generally accepted as his, largely because of their close association with a series of drawings traditionally attributed to him (mainly in the Musée Condé, Chantilly). They are *The Dauphin Francis* (Antwerp, Musées Royaux des Beaux-Arts); *Guillaume Budé* (New York, Metropolitan); *Madame de Canaples* (Edinburgh, NG); *Man with a Petrarch* (Windsor, royal coll.); *Man with gold coins* (St Louis, Art Museum); and a miniature of *The Count of Brissac* in the Pierpont Morgan Library, New York. There are also portrait miniatures in a manuscript celebrating the victory of Francis I at Marignano in 1515 (Paris, BN, and London, BM). These are relatively firmly modelled and show something of the same reflective calmness and sensitive characterization which distinguish his paintings. His drawings (like his paintings invariably three-quarter views) have often been compared to Holbein's for their keenness of observation, but unlike Holbein's they show a concern for mass rather than line.

Clovio, Giulio 1498–1578
Italian miniature painter, born in Croatia, in later life a monk. He went to Rome in 1516 and, influenced particularly by Michelangelo, transferred the prevailing Mannerist style to a miniature scale. Among his famous patrons was Cardinal Alessandro Farnese, for whom he painted his finest work, the Farnese Book of Hours (1536–46, New York, Pierpont Morgan Library). He is best known, perhaps, as the sitter (*c.*1570, Naples, Museo di Capodimonte) and confidant of El Greco. See vol. 2 p. *174*

Cluniac art
Art of the Benedictine Order of Cluny in Burgundy, established in 910. Cluny, a major influence in the Western Church, lavished its wealth on its churches, and the mostly destroyed abbey church of Cluny III was the largest church of its time in Europe. Its highly refined sculpture (ten ambulatory capitals with figures and foliage are in the Musée Farinier at Cluny) was copied even in non-Cluniac churches. The dramatic, linear style of the only surviving Cluniac frescos in the priory church at Berzé-la-Ville, a few miles from Cluny, are derived from Italo-Byzantine art, and possibly reflect lost work in Cluny III. The few remaining Cluniac manuscripts also reflect Ottonian art. See vol. 2 pp. 70–74

CoBrA
Group of artists founded in 1948 by a number of painters from the Netherlands and Scandinavia. The name comes from the initials of the group's members' home cities—**Co**penhagen, **Br**ussels, and **A**msterdam. The main artists involved were the Dutchman Appel, the Belgian Corneille and the Dane Jorn. Others who joined the group were Alechinsky, Atlan and Constant. Their main aim was to develop a directly expressive art freed from intellectual and formal strictures; unrestrained brushwork and wildly gestural forms characterize their work. In many respects CoBrA was a European response to American Action Painting, but in the spontaneous self-expression of the members of the group strange visions of form and colour emerged suggesting fabulous beings, animals, fetishes and masks. In these very strong links with Nordic folklore can be discerned, along with the disturbing goblins found in Dutch and Flemish painting from Bosch to Ensor, the ornamental fancy of Viking art and the grimacing demons of medieval Danish frescos. The group published a review until it disbanded in 1951. See vol. 3 p. **225**

Cochin, Charles-Nicolas 1715–90
French engraver and book illustrator, called "the Younger" to distinguish him from his father **Charles-Nicolas** the Elder (1688–1754), under whom he trained. His very numerous engravings are valuable records of the court festivities of Louis XV and of other aspects of contemporary society. From the time of his appointment as Keeper of the King's Drawings (1751) he exercised an important influence in official artistic circles as a theoretician (accusing French art of being insufficiently classical), biographer and academician.

Cock, Jan de active 1503–*c.*1527
Netherlandish painter who qualified in Antwerp in 1503 and eventually became Dean of the guild in 1520. He worked with Engelbrechtsen and is probably responsible for bringing the exuberant motifs of the Antwerp Mannerists into the latter's painting. A *Lamentation* in Vienna (Kunsthistorisches Museum) is closely related to Engelbrechtsen's Leyden altarpiece. Cock executed

numerous woodcuts and small paintings of hermits and saints, whose sharp profiles and slender forms are strongly reminiscent of Bosch.

Cock, Jerome de 1510–70
Netherlandish etcher, printer and editor, based in Antwerp, the son of Jan de Cock. Fired with enthusiasm from his own trips to Italy, he was foremost in promoting the art of the Romanists in Antwerp, and Floris, Heemskerck and Lambert all produced work for him. The young Bruegel was, however, the most important of those artists who were employed by him. There is evidence that Cock did much to shape the latter's early career by pressing him to exploit the revival of interest in Bosch pastiches.

Cockburn, James Pattison
1779–1847
Canadian topographical artist, born in England. He studied briefly under Paul Sandby before entering the British Army. While posted in Canada, he executed a vast number of watercolour sketches recording urban settings and wilderness with a deft simplicity bordering on naivety. *Quebec and its Environs* was published in 1831.

Coecke van Aelst, Pieter 1502–50
Netherlandish painter, engraver and decorative artist, the husband of Mayeken Verhulst and the father-in-law of Bruegel. He was probably a pupil of van Orley, and was one of the most accomplished Romanist painters in Antwerp (*The Last Supper*, 1531, Brussels, Musées Royaux des Beaux-Arts). His importance lies mainly in his publishing activities. In particular the translation of the celebrated architectural treatise of Sebastiano Serlio which he published in 1545 was very influential in spreading Renaissance architecture in northern Europe, and formed the basis for the English edition (the woodcuts were reused) of 1611. In 1553 he visited Constantinople and his widow issued a fascinating set of woodcuts recording his impressions, *The Manners and Customs of the Turks*, in 1553.

Coello, Claudio 1642–93
Spanish painter. He was a pupil of Careño de Miranda, whom he succeeded as court painter in 1686, working in Madrid and at the Escorial. His most important painting is the large and complex *Charles II adoring the Host* (1685–90, Escorial), one of the finest works of the Spanish late Baroque. It creates impressive spatial effects, and is at one and the same time a devotional picture, a representation of an historical event and a striking gallery of portraits.

Cohen, Bernard born 1933
British painter. His form of abstraction has been dominated by an interest in different processes of mark-making. In his abstracts of the late 1950s and early 1960s he attempted to emphasize gesture by placing it in the context of a rigid formal structure. His use of spray techniques in slightly later paintings such as *Floris* (1964, London, Tate) has resulted in tangled skeins of paint evoking the illusion of depth. He has also experimented with techniques of application.

Coldstream, Sir William
born 1908
British painter, co-founder of the EUSTON ROAD school. In the early 1930s, when contemporaries were experimenting with abstraction, he was painting works such as *The studio* (1934, London, Tate), which combined a radical and

austere simplification with realism. His subject matter has included the nude, townscapes and commissioned portraits, and he has influenced many young British figurative painters.

Cole, Thomas 1801–48
American landscape painter, a pioneer of the HUDSON RIVER school. Cole was born in England and emigrated with his family to Ohio in 1819. He worked as an engraver and portrait painter, living in Philadelphia and then New York City, but it was his landscapes which attracted the notice of Trumbull, Durand and Dunlap, who made him known. In 1826 he was a founder of the National Academy of Design. Between 1829 and 1832 he was in England and on the Continent, where he admired the work of Claude, Poussin and Salvator Rosa and was influenced by Turner and John Martin among living painters. On his return he settled in Catskill, New York, but visited Europe again in 1841–42. His preferred subjects were dramatic scenery and allegorical scenes, sometimes in combination, as in his most famous works, the two series *The Course of Empire* (1836, New York Historical Society) and *The Voyage of Life* (1840, Utica, Munson-Williams-Proctor Institute). These epics are among the major achievements of American painting. See vol. 3 p. **69**

Coleman, Glenn 1887–1932
American painter. He studied under Henri and Shinn and was influenced by the Ashcan school. In the 1920s he reworked many earlier studies, creating lithographs and paintings such as *Downtown street* (1926, New York, Whitney) evoking nostalgia for past times. These works appealed greatly during the Prohibition-ridden 1920s.

Colla, Ettore 1899–1968
Italian sculptor. In 1923 he worked in the studios of Henri Laurens and Brancusi in Paris, and in the next two years was employed as a miner, photographer and elephant trainer in France, Belgium and Austria. He returned to Italy in 1926 and thereafter worked mainly as a teacher of sculpture. In 1941 he ceased figurative sculpture and moved on to metallic abstractions of a Surrealist tendency, for example *Continuity* (1961–63, New York, MOMA). He was also a prolific silk-screen artist. His prints are based on minimal forms and are similar in style to the work of Arp.

Collage
Term derived from the French *coller*, to gum, used to describe works of art created by sticking bits of paper, material or other items on to a flat backing. Though basically a two-dimensional work, it can have a sculptural effect. The Cubists were the first to practise it extensively, extending the accepted boundaries of art by their combination of painted surfaces with real or painted materials. See vol. 1 pp. 154–155

Colombe, Michel *c.*1430–after 1512
French sculptor. Only two documented works survive, but both are of great distinction. His career is almost totally obscure until, in 1502–07, he executed the tombs of Francis II of Brittany and Marguerite de Foix in Nantes Cathedral, jointly with Perréal and Girolamo da Fiesole. The scheme of the recumbent effigy on a raised base and the minutely detailed luxurious costumes and idealized, sweet, sad faces of the attendant Virtues show Colombe continuing in the late Gothic tradition, but his other work, the altar relief of *St George and the*

dragon (1508–09, Paris, Louvre) is much more Italianate. Colombe does not, however, copy specific Italian models, and this enchanting work shows a very personal and successful blending of Gothic and Renaissance elements. The fantastic but homely dragon and St George's classically proportioned horse make a delightful contrast, and both seem completely at home in the exquisite architectural frame carved by Pacherot.

Colombo, Gianni born 1937
Italian artist and designer. He has experimented with various media, including monochrome reliefs, and in 1959 began work on objects which, by allowing their parts to be moved around and by using materials with high reflective qualities, demanded the spectator's participation. Most of his subsequent work has made use of artificial light.

Colonna, Gerolamo Mengozzi
*c.*1688–1766
Italian painter, the most celebrated QUADRATURA specialist of the 18th century. He was born and trained in Ferrara, then settled in Venice, where he worked with many of the city's leading painters. Today he is best known for his architectural settings for Giambattista Tiepolo's frescos. Those in the Palazzo Labia in Venice successfully fuse together influences ranging from the Lombard Rococo to Veronese to Pietro da Cortona. The decorations surrounding frescos (*c.*1757) by Giambattista and Giandomenico Tiepolo in the Villa Valmarana near Vicenza, which include early examples of revived Gothic and chinoiserie, are similarly imaginative, yet always with a restraint in keeping with the art of Tiepolo himself.

Colour-field painting
Term used to describe the paintings of some Abstract Expressionists, notably Newman, Rothko and Still, and also the work of some younger artists including Louis, Noland, Frankenthaler and Olitski. These painters were interested not in forms or gestural textures but in the lyrical or atmospheric effects of vast expanses of colour, often covering the whole canvas. See vol. 3 pp. 218–219

Colquhoun, Robert 1914–62
British painter. In the early 1940s he painted landscapes and figure compositions in a manner initially owing something to Sutherland. By the middle of the decade, in paintings such as *The fortune teller* (1946, London, Tate), he used stylizations deriving from Cubism and the hard-edged portraits of Wyndham Lewis to potent expressive purpose. In spite of a major retrospective exhibition in 1958 he died in relative obscurity.

Colt, Maximilian died 1645
French sculptor and mason who came to England about 1595. His most important commission was for the tomb of Queen Elizabeth I in Westminster Abbey in 1605, with painted decoration by John de Critz. Colt also worked for the Cecil family at the time of the reconstruction of Hatfield House. He became master sculptor to James I in 1608, remaining in this office for the rest of his life, but was little favoured by Charles I.

Colville, Alex born 1920
Canadian painter of contemporary life, an important figure in the development of MAGIC REALISM in Canada. His fastidiously crafted compositions, such as the hypnotic *Horse and train* (1954, Hamilton, Art Gallery), show an ability to infuse mystery into the mundane.

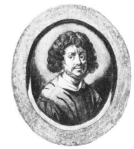

Claude: Self-portrait, frontispiece to his *Liber Veritatis*. London, BM

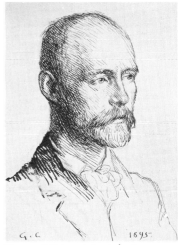

Clausen: Self-portrait drawing, 1895. London, NPG

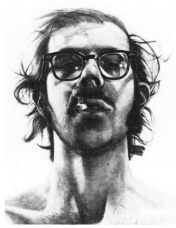

Close: Self-portrait, 1968. Minneapolis, Walker Art Center

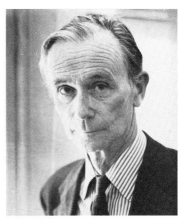

Coldstream: Photograph courtesy of the Slade School, London. © Sara Quill

Combine painting
Work of art which incorporates real objects into the painted surface. Rauschenberg coined the term to refer to works made between 1955 and 1958 which cannot be classified either as painting or sculpture. A good example is his *Monogram* (1959, Stockholm, Moderna Museet) in which a stuffed goat, ringed with a tyre, stands on a painted and collaged platform. Such works show the same desire to integrate art and life which animates Pop art and Happenings. See vol. 1 pp. 154–155; vol. 3 p. 237

Comfort, Charles born 1900
Canadian painter of landscapes and portraits in a boldly Expressionist style. A successful commercial artist and set designer, he favoured the use of arbitrary colour and dramatic back-lighting, as in his striking *Young Canadian* (1932, Toronto, Hart House).

Conca, Sebastiano 1679–1764
Influential Italian painter of religious and historical scenes. After studying under Solimena in Naples, he moved to Rome in 1706, and apart from a stay in Turin in about 1730, stayed there until about 1750; he subsequently returned to Naples. The exuberant and strongly Giordano-inspired element in his work is tempered by a classicism indebted to Maratta (*The crowning of St Cecilia*, 1725, Rome, S. Cecilia). He was known for his teaching and writings on art.

Conceptual art
The primacy of idea over craftsmanship in a work of art as asserted first by Duchamp. Most art movements to emerge in the 1960s—BODY ART, PERFORMANCE, LAND and MINIMAL ART—because they involve questions about the nature of art and attempt to expand its boundaries, can also be called Conceptual. Conceptual art emphasizes the elimination of art objects, or at least, as in the case of EARTHWORKS, of art objects as marketable commodities. ENVIRONMENTS, which are usually temporary and aim to heighten awareness of a site and of spatial and other relationships, are Conceptual in content. The idea and the process of execution are the "art" and not the physical product, which can usually be remade at another time and place and by other hands. Information is a major preoccupation of these artists: Kosuth and others highlight how information alters according to presentation and audience. The Xerox machine is a common tool; the printed page is a popular format. Documentation—in the case of Kawara, of his daily life—becomes art. Plans, diagrams, video and photographic records of sites and projects are a major aspect of Earthworks and Performance. See vol. 3 pp. 246–247

Conder, Charles 1868–1909
Australian painter and lithographer. In Paris in 1890 he became a close friend of Toulouse-Lautrec. His early paintings, mostly Arcadian fantasies, are delicate and tinged with *fin-de-siècle* languor. He also painted Impressionist beach scenes, nocturnal landscapes influenced by Whistler, and designs for fans.

Coninxloo family
Prolific family of Flemish painters, based initially in Tournai and Brussels. By far the most important was **Gillis** van Coninxloo (1544–1607), a landscapist who fled from persecution in Antwerp and travelled in France and Germany before settling in Amsterdam. His dense, airless forest scenes (*The forest*, c.1600, Vienna, Kunsthistorisches Museum) exerted considerable influence on Jan Brueghel and inspired the Dutch realist painters of the 17th century. Other members of the family include **Pieter** (died c.1513), who painted heraldic decorations and portraits of Charles V's court; **Jan** (active c.1520–26), who produced anaemic panels in the manner of van Orley; and **Cornelis** (died 1560), who painted archaic, devotional images. See vol. 2 p. **220**

Consagra, Pietro born 1920
Italian sculptor and designer. His works are iconic reliefs rather than fully three-dimensional sculpture and the main influence on his style is Cubism. His standing screens, however, with their striking colours and ragged forms suggestive of images such as violently torn clouds, show his concern with expressionist and anti-classical form. He works in bronze, steel and aluminium.

Constable, John 1776–1837
English landscape painter. He received limited recognition during his lifetime but is now, with Turner, considered one of the most important landscape artists of the 19th century. Trained at the Royal Academy, he was an instinctive artist who never travelled abroad but took his subject matter from the English countryside, particularly his native county, Suffolk ("Constable country"), Dorset, Brighton, the Lake District and Salisbury. Although admiring Gainsborough, Claude and the Dutch 17th-century landscapists, whose works he copied, he believed in studying directly from nature. His almost "scientific" observation of natural phenomena may be seen in the *Cloud Studies* (1816–22, examples in the V & A, London), but it was the large, finished canvases—"six-footers"—which he considered to be the real test of his art. Constable's brushwork in these finished paintings, and particularly in the full-size sketches for them, was extraordinarily bold and impressionistic, his colour fresh and natural. One of his best-known "six-footers", *The haywain* (1821, London, NG) was exhibited at the 1824 Paris Salon, and received enthusiastic acclaim from French artists, notably Delacroix. His work subsequently became popular in France, influencing the Barbizon school of landscapists. In England official recognition came only in 1829, when he was elected to the Royal Academy. The death of his wife in the previous year deeply affected his work and *Hadleigh Castle* (1829, New Haven, Yale Center for British Art) shows the change in mood from his tranquil landscapes of 1824–28 to more dramatic works showing the full "chiaroscuro of Nature". See vol. 1 pp. *63*, *118–119*; vol. 3 pp. **70–71**

Constant (Constant A. Nieuwenhys) born 1920
Dutch painter, sculptor and architect. He was a member of the COBRA group of painters, but since 1952 he has turned mainly to sculpture and architecture, in particular his ideal urban project, *New Babylon*, for which he has produced numerous designs and models.

Constructivism
Russian art movement founded in 1917–20 by the sculptors Gabo, Pevsner and Tatlin. Their sculptures, constructed from wood, glass and plastic and hung on walls or suspended from ceilings, were intended to be non-representational art-forms for a new industrialized age. Gabo's *Realistic Manifesto* of 1920 set out and made public their ideas. Gabo left Russia in 1922, Pevsner in 1923, and their ideas spread throughout Europe, being picked up in particular by the Bauhaus in Germany, the De Stijl movement in Holland and the Abstraction-Création group in France. Tatlin believed that art should have a more utilitarian function and in this he was joined by Rodchenko. Together with others they pursued the principles of Constructivism into the fields of theatre design, typography and architecture. See vol. 3 pp. 158–159, 180–181

Conté crayon
Exceptionally hard type of crayon, named after the 18th-century French scientist who invented it. It is like hard pastel but is made of graphite and clay and is usually black, red, brown or a mixture of these. See vol. 1 pp. 162–163

Continuous representation
Pictorial narrative featuring two or more successive actions from the same story within one setting. A character may, therefore, appear more than once in the same painting or sculpture.

Contrapposto
Italian term for the interaction of the parts of the body in poses in which the figure maintains balance but twists or turns out of a single plane—the torso and hips, for instance, turning in different directions. It was first used in the Renaissance to describe the pose in antique sculpture in which the weight of the body was shifted on to one leg with consequent realignment of the rest of the body. Michelangelo was a brilliant and daring exponent of *contrapposto* poses and his enthusiastic Mannerist followers perpetrated elaborate contortions in their efforts to emulate him.

Conversation piece
Informal group portrait with the sitters in an appropriate setting. Such paintings were particularly popular during the 18th century in Britain, when artists such as Devis, Hogarth and Zoffany painted groups, usually members of a family, in their domestic surroundings.

Cooper, Samuel 1609–72
One of the greatest English miniature painters. The nephew and possibly the pupil of Hoskins, he was practising independently by 1642, and had soon established a European reputation. His portraits are distinguished by both technical brilliance and psychological insight (*Rev. Stavismore*, 1657, Cambridge, Fitzwilliam). The diarists Evelyn and Pepys both praise him lavishly, and Pepys paid £30 (a large sum) for a miniature of his wife. See vol. 2 p. **207**

Coorte, Adriaen active 1683–1705
Dutch still-life painter who has only lately emerged from obscurity. Active mainly around Middelburg, Coorte concentrated exclusively on small pictures of a few pieces of fruit or vegetables simply arranged on a bare ledge but scrutinized with an almost mystical intensity. Examples of his rare work—both representing *A bundle of asparagus*—are in the Ashmolean Museum, Oxford, and the Fitzwilliam Museum, Cambridge. See vol. 1 p. *73*

Copley, John Singleton 1738–1815
The greatest American painter of the 18th century. By 1755 Copley was established as a painter in his native Boston, and the quality of his work during the next two decades entitles him to rank with the great portraitists of his time. His easy naturalism of conception, power of design, vivacity of characterization and delicacy and sureness of handling far surpassed anything previously achieved by Colonial artists (*Epes Sargent*, 1759–61, Washington, NG). Although the portrait of his stepbrother Henry Pelham, known as *The boy with the squirrel* (1765, Boston, MFA), was warmly received by West and Reynolds in 1766 (it was the first painting produced in America to be exhibited in England), it was not until 1774 that Copley left for London, where he settled permanently after a year travelling in Europe. He was initially successful, becoming a Royal Academician in 1779, but his popularity gradually faded, and after 1800 he sold little work. The most remarkable works of his English period are his history paintings, which followed West's innovation of using modern costume in scenes representing contemporary events (*The death of Major Pierson*, 1783, London, Tate). With their dramatic conviction and mastery of large-scale composition they were much superior to anything produced by British artists in the same field at this period, and some were specially exhibited and won great popular acclaim. Copley's most famous work, *Brook Watson and the shark* (1778, versions in Washington, NG, and Boston, MFA), went further than West by showing in heroic terms an event which was exciting but had no great historical or moral importance, and not until the French Romantic painters was this revolutionary idea developed. See vol. 3 p. **58**

Coppo di Marcovaldo
documented 1260–76
Italian painter. Although Florentine by birth, Coppo spent his working life in Siena and is reckoned a member of the Sienese school, which he and Guido da Siena share the honour of founding. His one signed work is the huge *Madonna and Child* ("*Madonna del Bordone*") in S. Maria dei Servi, dated 1261. Despite the later repainting of the flesh areas, this shows the new element of solidity that he introduced into the Byzantine tradition. Later in the 1260s and again in 1274–76 he was working on frescos and panels for the cathedral at Pistoia. See vol. 2 p. **78**

Coptic art
Art of the Christian Copts in Egypt, who created one of the earliest specifically Christian artistic traditions. Initially based on the Hellenistic art of Alexandria, Coptic art developed in the Nile valley from the early 4th century AD until the Arab conquest in 640. Portraits and mural paintings which survive from the 5th and 6th centuries are often crude, strongly linear and boldly coloured. The elaborate Coptic ornamental motifs, used in architectural decoration and manuscript painting, developed out of organic Graeco-Roman patterns.

Coques, Gonzales 1614/18–84
Flemish genre and portrait painter, who worked in England and Holland as well as his native Antwerp, painting mainly charming, small-scale portrait groups of elegantly dressed figures. He has been called "the little van Dyck", but his meticulous work is closer in style to Dutch painters such as Terborch (*A family group*, c.1665, London, NG).

Corinth, Lovis 1858–1925
German painter. From 1884 to 1887 he studied at the Académie Julian in Paris under Bouguereau. His early style showed this classicizing influence, but by the turn of the century he was combining Impressionist compositional devices with a baroque freedom in the paint surface, as in *Salome* (1899, Harvard

University, Busch-Reisinger Museum). In 1901 he moved to Berlin and became President of the Berlin Sezession in 1911. After suffering a stroke that year, he continued painting with great difficulty, and his style became more Expressionist, as in the Walchensee landscapes (example, *The Walchensee with a yellow field*, 1921, Munich, Neue Pinakothek). See vol. 3 p. **131**

Corneille (Cornelis van Beverloo) born 1922
Belgian painter. He was a founder-member of the COBRA group in 1948, and like the other members he used intense colour and expressive brushwork to release images from the Unconscious. Since 1949 he has lived in Paris, where he studied graphic techniques with Hayter, but he has travelled widely.

Corneille de Lyon active 1533–74
Naturalized French portrait painter, born at The Hague. He was in Lyons, where he mainly worked, by 1534 and became court painter to the Dauphin, later Henri II, in 1540. His only certain work is the strikingly realistic portrait of *Pierre Aymeric* (1533, France, Private coll.). Many paintings, however, are attributed to him, or are in a style close to the Aymeric portrait, bearing out the documentary evidence that he had a great contemporary reputation. They are generally small, with bust or half-length figures, which are modelled naturalistically in the northern manner and portrayed in dark costumes against plain blue or green backgrounds.

Cornelis van Haarlem, Cornelisz. 1562–1638
Dutch biblical and portrait painter. With van Mander, he founded the Academy of Haarlem, and became one of Holland's leading MANNERIST painters. *The Massacre of the Innocents* (1591, Haarlem, Frans Hals Museum) is a characteristic work, crowded with athletic nudes struggling in a grandiose architectural setting. From the 1590s he received a large number of important official commissions, notably group portraits, such as the 1599 *Banquet of the Haarlem guardsmen* (Frans Hals Museum). In this he abandoned the chaotic movement of his Mannerist phase for a more clearly ordered classical style and inspired Frans Hals with his masterly composition. See vol. 2 p. **214**

Cornelisz. van Oostsanen, Jacob c.1470–1533
Netherlandish painter, engraver and decorative artist, born near Amsterdam. He became a master in Antwep in 1507 and remained there till at least 1516 although the city made little impression on his markedly Dutch style. He began by producing woodcuts, notably those for the Lübeck Bible (1494), and these were much freer than his paintings. The latter had the congested, textural quality of Mostaert's work, but with the addition of incongruous, Italianate motifs. *The Adoration* (1512, Naples, Museo di Capodimonte), for example, has a cherubic orchestra in the foreground, further *putti* in the masonry, elaborate inlaid pillars and a marine landscape behind. Van Scorel was his pupil.

Cornelius, Peter von 1783–1867
German painter. He trained in Düsseldorf and in 1811 went to Italy, where he joined the NAZARENES. He had an extremely high-minded conception of art and wished to express the noblest ideals from religion, history and mythology in ideal forms based on the observation of

art rather than nature. The most appropriate medium for such expression was monumental fresco painting, and Cornelius, who became an expert in the technique, directed the Nazarenes' experiments in the field. In 1819 Crown Prince Ludwig of Bavaria (later Ludwig I) summoned him to Munich, where he became Director of the Academy in 1824 and painted a *Last Judgment* mural in the Ludwigskirche. It was unfavourably received, and in 1841 he went to Berlin at the invitation of Wilhelm IV of Prussia, and devoted most of the rest of his career to the preparation of cartoons for a cycle of frescos for a proposed extension to Berlin Cathedral based on the Campo Santo in Pisa. They were never executed, but the cartoons, notably *The four horsemen of the Apocalypse* (c.1845, East Berlin, Staatliche Museen), show at its best the dramatic power of his style, which drew heavily on Raphael's heroic language of gesture. Through his work and teaching Cornelius was the guiding spirit in the 19th-century revival of monumental painting, and his specialist knowledge was held in such high regard that in 1842 his advice was sought in connection with the murals in the Houses of Parliament in London. See vol. 3 p. **75**

Cornell, Joseph 1903–72
American sculptor. Largely self-taught, he began painting and making collages and assemblages in the 1930s, inspired by Ernst's collages. A typical construction, *Medici slot machine* (1942, New York, Reis coll.), is a shallow box, standing vertically, in which collaged images and small objects are arranged in an evocative but enigmatic juxtaposition. In their visual ambiguity and elusive titles his boxes have affinities with works by Duchamp and the Surrealists. All of them are small, some with movable parts inviting viewer participation. Cornell also made Surrealist films.

Corot, Jean-Baptiste-Camille 1796–1875
French landscape and figure painter. From 1822 he studied with the classicizing landscapist Michallon as well as painting out-of-doors in Fontainebleau. In 1825 he visited Italy, and during his stay produced a remarkable series of unaffected, clearly lit landscapes which anticipate the Impressionist achievement (*The Farnese garden*, 1826, Washington, Phillips coll.). He returned to Italy in 1834 and 1843, absorbing the classical tradition which was to be the mainstay of his Salon works. The 1840s saw recognition of his talent, with the award of the Legion of Honour (1846), and from this time he developed romanticized landscape themes, often with blurred outlines, on which he did innumerable variants. Although his popular Salon pieces, such as *Memory of Mortefontaine* (1864, Paris, Louvre), with its nostalgia for an Arcadian past, place him in the older Romantic generation, Corot's earlier luminous paintings from nature greatly influenced the next generation of landscapists and place him amongst the more original artists of the 19th century. His studies of women, begun in 1856, reflect the technical influence of Courbet and Manet and have been unduly neglected. See vol. 1 p. **99**; vol. 3 p. **93**

Corpora, Antonio born 1909
Italian painter. After he had worked in a Post-Impressionist style his paintings in the 1930s became increasingly abstract, using Cubist principles of formal organization. By the late 1940s he had broken

through to a dynamic form of complete abstraction using rich paintwork and iridescent colour. He gradually toned this down to produce a restrained and austere colour field enlivened by luminous ridges of intense colour.

Correggio (Antonio Allegri) died 1534
Italian painter, principally active in Parma, one of the most inventive artists of the High Renaissance. He takes his name from the place of his birth in Emilia. His birth date is unknown but Vasari says he was about 40 when he died. His early paintings are marked by a close knowledge of Mantegna, whose work in Mantua he may well have studied. His earliest documented painting, "*The Madonna of St Francis*" (1514–15, Dresden, Gemäldegalerie), also reveals a thorough grasp of contemporary developments, particularly Leonardo's use of *sfumato* and the inventive approach to composition of both Leonardo and Raphael. Correggio settled in Parma in 1519 and began the first of three fresco decorations there with the vaulted ceiling of the Camera di S. Paolo in the monastery of that name. The type of illusionism he employed was clearly indebted to Mantegna and Melozzo da Forlì, and scarcely anticipated the inventive power he displayed in S. Giovanni Evangelista, 1520–21, and the Cathedral, 1526–30. In the cupolas of these two churches he exploited Mantegna's device of simulating an *oculus* open to a sky, filling it with airborne figures and carrying the illusionism to much greater lengths. His use of foreshortening is extreme and, especially in the Cathedral, the overall effect is one of dizzying emotional ecstasy. His altarpieces and mythological paintings often display a similar fervour. The extreme use of *sfumato* so often associated with his name is particularly apparent in the mythologies painted for Duke Federigo II of Mantua, for instance in *The rape of Ganymede* and *Jupiter and Io* (c.1530), both in the Kunsthistorisches Museum, Vienna. There is no evidence that Correggio travelled widely, but he matched the achievement of the most vaunted painters of his time in Florence, Rome and Venice. His influence was wide and long-lived; his dome paintings were a major source for Baroque artists such as Badalocchio and Lanfranco, and his brilliant handling of erotic subjects was an inspiration for the painters of the Rococo. See vol. 2 p. **148**

Cortona, Pietro da (Pietro Berrettini) 1596–1669
Italian painter and architect. With Lanfranco and Guercino he was one of the founders of the Roman High Baroque style in painting. He ranks second only to Bernini as the all-round Italian artistic genius of the age, for he was also a designer of festival decoration and sculpture, although not a sculptor himself. His most famous painting is the huge fresco *Allegory of divine Providence and Barberini power* (1633–39, Rome, Palazzo Barberini), a triumph of illusionism in which the centre of the ceiling, peopled with brilliantly foreshortened figures, appears to open to the sky. The scarcely less splendid frescos in the dome and apse of S. Maria in Vallicella, Rome (1647–60) are set in Cortona's own rich framework of gilded coffers and stucco figures, and this combination of paint and stucco, seen also in his work in the Palazzo Pitti, Florence (1637–47), was highly influential, in France (where it was taken by his pupil Romanelli) as well as Italy.

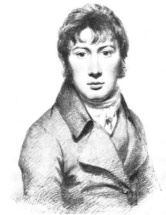

Constable: Self-portrait drawing, c.1800. London, NPG

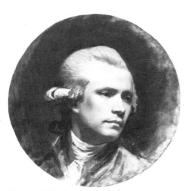

Copley: Self-portrait, c.1780–84. Washington, DC, Smithsonian, NPG

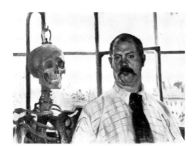

Corinth: *Self-portrait with a skeleton*, 1896. Munich, Städtische Galerie im Lenbachhaus

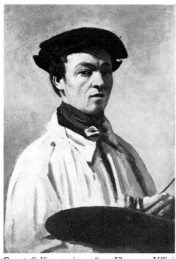

Corot: Self-portrait, c.1835. Florence, Uffizi (Alinari)

Cortona's easel-paintings are less memorable, for he worked best on a large scale. Although he once wrote that he regarded architecture only as a pastime, he was one of the greatest architects of the 17th century. One of his finest buildings is SS. Martina e Luca in Rome (1635–50), and it is typical of Cortona's immense energy that he was working on this at the same time as his Palazzo Barberini ceiling and Palazzo Pitti decorations. See vol. 2 p. **189**

Cosmati work
Term for decorative inlay work using coloured stones and glass. The original Cosmati were a family of 12th-century Roman marble-workers, but all those working in this style were known as Cosmati. They decorated ecclesiastical furniture as well as cloisters and paving with their lively geometric designs. Though mostly Roman, the fashion was widespread until about 1300.

Cossa, Francesco del c.1435–c.1477
Italian painter. He was born in Bologna, but with Cosimo Tura and Ercole de' Roberti ranks as the principal painter of the 15th-century Ferrarese school. All three may have been involved in the decoration (1458–78) of the Duke of Ferrara's Schifanoia Palace with frescos of *The Months*, where Cossa was apparently the leading master. The influence of Piero, who had worked in Ferrara, can be felt in the severe and sturdy figures and harmonious colour schemes, but whereas Piero is invariably solemn the Schifanoia frescos are essentially light-hearted, with much brilliant observation of playful animals and beautiful costumes. Cossa's best-known religious painting is the Griffoni altarpiece (1473), divided between London (NG) and Milan (Brera). His style is less wiry than Tura's, but just as sharply focused.

Costa, Giovanni (Nino) 1826–1903
Italian landscape painter from Rome, also known as a leading patriot. Exiled in Florence, 1858–70, he frequented the Macchiaoli, but his was a more idealized, poetic conception of nature: he preferred dawns and sunsets, as in *The kiss of the dying sun* (1890, Rome, Galleria Nazionale d'Arte Moderna).

Costa, Lorenzo c.1460–1535
Italian painter, born in Ferrara. He worked in Bologna, 1483–1506, and then succeeded Mantegna as court painter to the Gonzagas in Mantua. His early paintings were influenced by Tura and Ercole de' Roberti. His most extraordinary work is the *Triumphs of Death and Fame* (1500) for the chapel of the ruling Bentivoglio family in S. Giacomo Maggiore, Bologna, which contains a myriad of figures in allegorical array. His work for the Gonzagas was mythological.

Cosway, Richard 1742–1821
British miniaturist and draughtsman, a pupil of Hudson. He was the most fashionable miniaturist of his day, pioneering a change from the small, brightly coloured, minutely detailed portrait to a larger format in which the figure would often be shown full-length, drawn in thin, nearly monochromatic washes, with only the face coloured in (*A gentleman*, 1793, London, V&A).

Cotes, Francis 1726–70
British portraitist, best known for his pastels. The fashion for pastel came to Britain from France and Italy, and Cotes took over from French art a modified Rococo manner. In his last decade he was influenced by Reynolds. His pleasing but slightly timid portraits have long been popular in America, where many of the best examples remain (*Frances Lee*, 1769, Milwaukee Art Center).

Cotman, John Sell 1782–1842
English landscape artist, working mostly in watercolour and sepia wash. He was born in Norwich, and in 1798 moved to London, where he worked for Dr Munro and was encouraged by Sir George Beaumont, with whose circle he worked in Wales during 1800. In 1801 he joined Girtin's sketching club. Tours of Yorkshire made in 1803–05 in the area of Helmsley and Rockerby Park were significant for the development of his watercolour technique, where large areas of flat wash broken by the texture of the paper rendered the landscape in simple, almost geometric shapes. His most famous work, *Greta Bridge* (1805, London, BM) was produced at this time, and is one of the finest examples by any artist of the classic English watercolour technique. In 1806 he returned to Norwich, where he became a leader of the NORWICH school. After 1830 his unaffected style changed with the introduction of new techniques, becoming more richly textured. See vol. 3 p. **68**

Cottet, Charles 1863–1924
French painter and etcher. He travelled extensively, but his most characteristic and important works were scenes of Brittany. *The people of Ouessant watching over a dead child* (1899, Paris, Petit Palais) is typical of his dark, sombre paintings in the tradition of regional genre, showing Brittany as a land of poverty, hard work and deep faith.

Coughtry, Graham born 1931
Canadian Expressionist painter. He studied in Toronto, and made Ibiza his retreat. His interest in post-1945 New York painting, fostered by PAINTERS ELEVEN, led him to freely expressionist renderings of the human figure, his exclusive subject. Francis Bacon's influence is evident in much of his work, including his imaginary portraits.

Courbet, Gustave 1819–77
French painter, the foremost exponent of REALISM. Although claiming to be self-taught, Courbet received basic training from several minor masters, attended life classes and intently studied the Old Masters in the Louvre. His early pictures were strongly influenced by literary Romanticism and he made his Salon début in 1844 with the languid *Self-portrait with a black dog* (Paris, Louvre). He established his brilliant and personal Realism in the Salon of 1850–51 with three great socially conscious pictures, *The peasants of Flagey* (Louvre), *The stonebreakers* (formerly Dresden, destroyed in World War II) and *A burial at Ornans* (Louvre). These ordinary scenes from contemporary life, of an epic size normally reserved for history painting, shocked the public and he was criticized for deliberately seeking ugliness. His brand of Realism, evolved from popular pragmatic images rendered in an innovatory technique—bold IMPASTO heavily applied with a palette knife—is distinct from the work of such Realists as Bonvin and Ribot, who depicted daily life in a spiritual manner. A socialist and revolutionary, Courbet, in addition to his controversial genre paintings, treated a wide variety of non-political subjects—landscape, sensuous nudes, still life. In keeping with his defiant attitude towards authority, in 1855 he organized a private pavilion for his work, labelled simply "Le Réalisme", outside the Universal Exhibition which was taking place in Paris. The massive allegory which he showed there, *The artist's studio* (1854–55, Louvre), is open to wide interpretation, and typifies the ambiguity of his art. Elected to the Chamber under the Commune and made Curator of Fine Arts, Courbet was imprisoned in 1872 for his alleged destruction of the Vendôme Column, and in 1873, unable to pay the fine imposed by the French government, he fled to Switzerland, where he died. Described by Redon as "the great realist who was simply a great painter", Courbet, although he did not form a school, exerted an immense influence on modern art by his emphatic rejection of idealization. See vol. 1 pp. *27*, *32*, *39*, *66*; vol. 3 pp. **90–93**

Courtois or **Cortese, Guillaume** 1628–79 and **Jacques** 1621–76
French painters, brothers, both nicknamed "Il Borgognono" or "Le Bourguignon" because of their Burgundian origins. They spent their careers in Italy. Guillaume studied with Pietro da Cortona, and painted numerous altarpieces in churches in Rome in a style close to his master's. Jacques is best known for his prolific output of battle-pieces. In style these are indebted to Salvator Rosa but Courtois had a much lighter touch, favouring light blue skies marked by the puffs of white gun-smoke.

Cousin, Jean the Elder died 1560/1
French painter and designer of stained glass. He was born in Sens and two windows in the cathedral there are attributed to him. In about 1538 he moved to Paris, where he also produced designs for tapestries of *The life of St Geneviève* and of *The life of St Mammès* (two of the latter are in Langres Cathedral). In 1560 he published a book on perspective in Paris. His best-known work is the painting *Eva Prima Pandora* (Paris, Louvre), probably executed before his move to Paris, in which the elegant reclining nude shows the influence of Rosso in the extreme elongation of form and of Leonardo in the soft handling of shadows and contrasts of light and dark. Few other paintings are certainly by him.

Cousin, Jean the Younger c.1522–c.1594
French painter and engraver, son of Jean the Elder. He was also born in Sens, but spent most of his life in Paris, achieving considerable fame in his lifetime. One of his few surviving paintings is *The Last Judgment* (before 1615, Louvre), in which congested masses of puny figures recede into a vast misty space. He produced a book of decorative drawings, *The Book of Fortune*, in 1568, and illustrated editions of Ovid's *Metamorphoses* (1570) and Aesop's *Fables* (1582). The Cousins are among the few who worked largely independently of the school of Fontainebleau.

Coustou family
Family of French sculptors from Lyons, the most important of whom were the brothers **Nicolas** (1658–1733) and **Guillaume** (1677–1746). Their father **François** (c.1657–90) was a minor wood-sculptor who had married the sister of Coysevox, under whom the brothers trained. Like their uncle, they worked mainly for court circles. Both made trips to Rome, and the influence of Bernini is apparent in such works as *Apollo* by Nicolas and *Daphne* by Guillaume (both 1713, Paris, Tuileries). Nicolas was probably the master of Roubiliac, who modelled the figure of *Fame* in his Argyll monument on the *Apollo*. Nicolas's later work remained within the Baroque tradition, but Guillaume moved towards a greater naturalism, first in portraits, culminating in the sardonic tomb effigy of *Cardinal Dubois* (c.1725, Paris, St Roch), then in decorative work. His masterpieces, the two superbly vigorous *Horse-tamers* (originally set up in 1745 at the Château of Marly but now in the Place de la Concorde, Paris) rank among the great sculptural achievements of the age.

Couture, Thomas 1815–79
French history and portrait painter. A pupil of Baron Gros from 1830–35, he later studied in the atelier of Delaroche, achieving notoriety with his enormous *The Romans of the Decadence* (1847, Paris, Louvre), which alluded to contemporary society. Neither a classical nor a Romantic painter, Couture sought a style founded on Greek, Renaissance and Flemish art, and also on "the nature and ideas of our time". From 1847 he received important official commissions and opened a successful atelier where Fantin-Latour, Manet and Puvis de Chavannes all studied. This studio, while generally academic in approach, offered novel technical instruction, significantly including direct landscape study. Couture's own brilliant pictorial technique of lively unmixed colour, free handling of paint and spontaneous brushwork can be seen in his numerous portrait studies. See vol. 3 pp. **86–87**

Couturier, Robert born 1905
French sculptor, friend and follower of Maillol. He later abandoned a Neo-classical style in favour of a freer interpretation of the human figure in which forms are elongated and the medium, often plaster, sensually modelled (*Adam and Eve*, 1945, Paris, Musée d'Art Moderne).

Covert, John 1882–1960
American painter. He studied in Munich and Paris, and on returning to New York in 1915 met Duchamp and Picabia, associates of his cousin, the collector Walter Arensburg. Within months he had abandoned his academic style and identified himself with New York Dada. He was particularly influenced by Duchamp's use of puns in works of art. Covert's *Brass band* (1919, New Haven, Yale University Art Gallery) was, for instance, constructed out of cords painted to resemble brass bands. He gave up painting in 1923.

Cox, David 1783–1859
English landscape painter, a pupil of Varley. He is best known for his broad and vigorously painted watercolours of gathering storms and windy days in North Wales, such as *Going to market* (c.1840, Amsterdam, Rijksmuseum). In 1813–14 he published *Treatise on Landscape Painting and Effect in Water-colour*. From 1840 he turned to oils.

Coypel family
French history and decorative painters, active in the 17th and 18th centuries. **Noël** (1628–1707), a follower of Poussin, worked under Lebrun at Versailles, where he painted the ceiling of the Salle des Gardes de la Reine (c.1675). His son **Antoine** (1661–1722) went to Rome with his father when the latter was appointed Director of the French Academy there in 1672. A friend of the theorist de Piles, he produced a number of works in a Rubéniste manner, includ-

ing an illusionistic ceiling at the Palais Royal in Paris (1702, destroyed), one of the most completely Baroque schemes in French art. But his ceiling of the royal chapel at Versailles (1708) rejects Rubens in favour of an Italian model, Baciccia's nave vault of the Gesù, Rome. He became Director of the Academy in 1714. The works of his half-brother **Noël-Nicolas** (1690–1734), such as *The alliance between Bacchus and Venus* (1726, Geneva, Musée d'Art et d'Histoire), have an easy charm lacking in Antoine's art. Antoine's son **Charles-Antoine** (1694–1752) crowned a career of success with appointment as Premier Peintre du Roi in 1747. Despite a reputation as an energetic Director of the Academy his style was a dull proto-Rococo (*Rinaldo and Armida*, 1725, Paris, Baron Elie de Rothschild coll.).

Coysevox, Antoine 1640–1720
French sculptor. Although there is no evidence that he went to Italy, his work shows a fuller understanding of the Baroque than that of any of his French contemporaries. He worked extensively at Versailles, and his tomb of Cardinal Mazarin (1689–93, Paris, Louvre) is one of the finest of its period, but he was at his best as a portrait sculptor. Even his official works can be very lively, as in the bronze *Louis XIV* (*c*.1680, London, Wallace Coll.), but his talents are shown most fully in informal portraits of his friends, which in their easy naturalism and informality anticipate the Rococo. See vol. 2 pp. **198–199**; vol. 4 p. *103*

Cozens, Alexander *c*.1717–86
British landscape draughtsman, born in Russia of English parents. He visited Rome in the 1740s and afterwards settled in England to become a fashionable drawing-master. He devised a method, which he explained in a pamphlet published about 1785, for composing imaginative landscapes by allowing a brush filled with ink to wander more or less at random over the paper; the resulting blot formed the basis of a finished landscape in brown wash. See vol. 3 pp. **68–69**

Cozens, John Robert 1752–97
British landscape watercolourist, the son and pupil of Alexander Cozens. He specialized in highly atmospheric and poetic views of Swiss and Italian scenery, the sketches for which were made during two tours, 1776–79 and 1782–83. With Pars and Towne he pioneered the Romantic representation of the Alps, emphasizing their grandeur and stillness, with the mountains forming elegant rhythmical shapes. In depicting Italian buildings he was attracted not to their archaeological associations, but to their silhouetted forms when seen in conjunction with trees and hills under a quiet evening sky. He often repeated works—*Lake of Albano and Castel Gandolfo* exists in nine versions (two are in the Yale Center for British Art, New Haven). Turner, Girtin and Constable admired his work. See vol. 3 p. **68**

Craig-Martin, Michael born 1941
British artist. His work in various media is concerned with the intellectual issues involved in the process of representation. For instance, *Conviction* (1973, London, Tate) consists of a series of narrow vertical mirrors displayed so as to reflect only the face of the spectator. Underneath these are handwritten statements about awareness of identity such as "I know who I am". The spectator examines the reflection, as if it were a picture, in the light of these statements.

Cranach, Lucas the Elder 1472–1553
German painter and designer of woodcuts, born in Kronach, South Germany, from which he takes his name. He spent the years about 1501–04 working in humanist circles at Vienna. Here he observed the wooded Danube valley landscape, which appears prominently in works such as his lyrical *Rest on the Flight* (1504, Berlin, Staatliche Museen) and dramatic *Crucifixion* (1503, Munich, Alte Pinakothek). He then became court painter to the Elector of Saxony at Wittenberg, where he established a large workshop. His painted work consisted chiefly of boldly patterned, mannered portraits, such as the innovatory full-length depictions of the flamboyantly dressed *Duke and Duchess of Saxony* (1514, Dresden, Gemäldegalerie), and classical subjects, showing slim female nudes in a landscape background (*Apollo and Diana*, 1530, Berlin, Staatliche Museen). From 1518 he worked for Luther; he painted his portrait several times (examples in Florence, Uffizi) and designed numerous woodcuts in the Protestant cause, notably those for the first German New Testament of 1522. He continued, however, to work for Catholic patrons as well. His son, **Lucas the Younger** (1515–1586), worked in his father's style. See vol. 2 pp. **154–155**

Crane, Walter 1845–1915
English painter, designer and illustrator, best known for his work for the Socialist League and designs for children's books. He was associated with the ARTS AND CRAFTS movement, illustrating books for Morris' Kelmscott Press (Spenser's *Faerie Queene*, for example) in a characteristic, delicate, linear style influenced by Burne-Jones. In 1907 he published *An Artist's Reminiscences*.

Craquelure
Network of small cracks in the surface of a painting which is a normal occurrence when the pigment or varnish has become old and brittle.

Crawford, Thomas 1814–57
American sculptor of official monuments. He was born in New York of Irish parents, served his apprenticeship in New York, then studied with Thorvaldsen (1835) in Rome, where he settled and became a dedicated NEOCLASSICIST. His best-known work is the bronze classical goddess with feathered head-dress *Armed Liberty*, nearly 6m (19ft) high, surmounting the Dome of the Capitol in Washington. She was modelled in his Rome studio, cast in Maryland in 1862, and set in place in 1863.

Crayer, Gaspar de 1584–1669
Flemish portraitist and painter of religious and allegorical subjects, one of the leading artists in Flanders after the death of Rubens. He was particularly distinguished as a painter of altarpieces, many of which are still in churches in Brussels and Ghent. His style owes much to Rubens, but is cooler and more restrained. The dignified and beautifully coloured *Martyrdom of St Catherine* (1622, Grenoble, Musée des Beaux-Arts) is a fine example of his work.

Credi, Lorenzo di *c*.1458–1537
Florentine painter. He trained with Verrocchio at the same time as Leonardo, whose early work formed the basis for Credi's style. His craftsmanship was of a high order, but he had little inventive power, and seems to have been content to remain in Verrocchio's studio until the

latter's death in 1488, looking after the painting side of the business. *The Annunciation* (*c*.1485, Florence, Uffizi) is a good example of Credi's early work, and *The Madonna and saints* (1510, Pistoia Cathedral) of his mature style—when he had absorbed High Renaissance influence, notably from Fra Bartolommeo.

Cremona, Tranquillo 1837–78
Italian painter, specializing in figurative works and portraits. Initially, his academic historical works reflected Faruffini, but, after 1863, he associated with the SCAPIGLIATI. That year, he produced *The kiss* (Rome, Galleria Nazionale d'Arte Moderna), where outline begins to give way to the rapid, fluid brushstrokes typical of later works such as *Ivy* (1878, Turin, Galleria d'Arte Moderna). Portraits of women and children from the 1870s are impressionistic, evocative of Romantic music and many, like *Mme Deschamps* (1875, Milan, Galleria d'Arte Moderna) include musical instruments. The fluidity of his oils is intensified in watercolours such as *High life* (1877, Milan, Galleria d'Arte Moderna). He influenced the Divisionists.

Cremonini, Leonardo born 1925
Italian painter, who since 1951 has lived in Paris. His work is influenced above all by the example of Picasso's *Guernica* and also by the early Italian masters Giotto and Masaccio. He has developed a dramatic figurative style in order to illustrate ideas about the Existential nature of man's life in society. His images are often disturbing in their concern for man's inhuman behaviour and destruction at the hands of evil powers and mechanical accident. He paints his figures in exterior and interior urban settings that employ a distorted perspective and misshapen forms to upset the spectator's spatial balance.

Crespi, Daniele *c*.1598–1630
Milanese painter, chiefly remembered for one work, *The humble repast of St Charles Borromeo* (*c*.1628, Milan, S. Maria della Passione). This expresses better than any other painting the austere piety of the great saint (1538–84), whose Counter-Reformation zeal was still deeply felt in Milan at this time. There are many other paintings by Crespi in S. Maria della Passione, which is almost a museum of his work. His prolific career was cut short by the plague

Crespi, Giovanni Battista
(Il Cerano) *c*.1575–1632
Italian painter, sculptor, architect, engraver and writer, active chiefly in Milan, where he was one of the most important artists of the early 17th century. He painted in a complex late Mannerist style, often morbidly mystical in feeling, with delicate colouring reminiscent of Barocci (*The Virgin of the rosary*, *c*.1615, Milan, Brera). In 1620 he was made the first director of the painting section of Cardinal Federigo Borromeo's Accademia Ambrosiana, and in 1629 appointed head of the statuary works of Milan Cathedral: designs for sculpture by him are in the Cathedral Museum.

Crespi, Giuseppe Maria
1665–1747
Italian painter, the most individual Bolognese artist of his day. He painted religious and historical subjects, but is now best known for his vividly painted genre scenes, such as *The hamlet* (*c*.1705, Bologna, Pinacoteca). These clearly have their roots in the paintings of everyday life by the Carracci, but few artists had attempted to portray, without

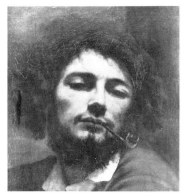
Courbet: Self-portrait, *c*.1849. Montpellier, Musée Fabre (Giraudon)

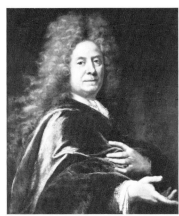
Coypel, Antoine: Self-portrait, *c*.1710. Florence, Uffizi (Alinari)

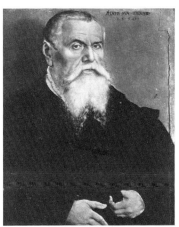
Cranach the Elder: Self-portrait, 1550. Florence, Uffizi (Mansell)

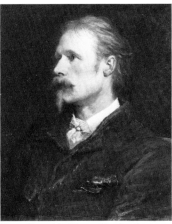
Crane: Portrait by Watts, 1891. London, NPG

recourse to satire, the grime and squalor of contemporary reality. Among his pupils can be counted the Venetian artists Bencovich and Longhi, and probably Piazzetta. After his death his genre works went out of favour in his native Bologna, and by 1787 the historian Longhi could write that his "style of painting had virtually ceased to be valid"; the reappraisal of his art dates from the beginning of this century. See vol. 2 p. 244

Crippa, Roberto 1921–72
Italian painter. In the late 1940s he was the first Italian to practise Abstract Expressionism and Action Painting. He then experimented with reliefs and collages, using newspaper and tree bark in the spirit of Schwitters' *Merz* pictures. His varied and versatile output never deterred him from seeing himself as essentially a colleague of the cool abstractionist Fontana.

Critz the Elder, John de
before 1568–1642
British portrait painter of Flemish origin. In 1605 he was appointed Serjeant Painter to James I jointly with Robert Peake. No signed works are known, but some portraits can be identified on circumstantial evidence. A portrait of *James I* (1610) is in the National Maritime Museum, Greenwich.

Crivelli, Carlo 1435/40–1495/1500
Italian painter. He was born in Venice, but spent most of his career in the Marches. He was trained in Padua, and elaborated the linear approach and meticulous attention to detail which characterized the Squarcione school and the Vivarini workshop. His figures and architectural settings have an extraordinary density, an effect sometimes increased by the use of raised gesso detailing. These qualities can be well seen in the outstanding collection of his paintings in the National Gallery, London, which includes what is perhaps his masterpiece, *The Annunciation* (1486). This work is essentially joyous, but Crivelli had a wide emotional range, as his *Pietàs* show. A fine example (*c.*1500) is in the Brera, Milan. See vol. 1 p. *154*; vol. 2 p. **121**

Crivelli, Vittorio active 1481–1501/2
Italian painter, active in the Marches. He was probably the brother of Carlo Crivelli, whose most faithful follower he was. *The Madonna and Child with saints* (1481, Philadelphia, Museum of Art) is representative of his style—heavier than Carlo's and without his capacity for minute precision of detail.

Crome, John 1768–1821
English landscape painter and etcher, a founder of the NORWICH school. He is known as "Old Crome" to distinguish him from his son of the same name (1794–1842), also a painter. Old Crome largely taught himself by copying the works of Gainsborough, Wilson, Hobbema and Ruisdael in the collection of his first patron, Thomas Harvey of Catton. He subordinated the minor elements of landscape to create works of elegant grandeur, reminiscent of the Dutch 17th-century artists whose work he admired (*The Poringland oak*, *c.*1818, London, Tate). See vol. 3 p. **68**

Cropsey, Jaspar Francis
1823–1900
American architect and painter. As a painter he is regarded as the finest colourist of the HUDSON RIVER school. He visited Europe in 1847–50 and again in 1857–63, when he made his headquarters in London. A founder of the American Watercolour Society in 1866, Cropsey made luminous and realistic views of the Hudson, which were exhibited at their shows (*Autumn on the Hudson*, 1860, Washington, NG). As an architect he is best known for his railway stations on Sixth Avenue—major New York landmarks.

Crosato, Giambattista 1686–1758
Italian figure painter and scenographer, known today almost exclusively for his frescos. Born and brought up in Venice, he spent some time in Turin, where he executed some of his more famous works (most notably in Palazzo Stupinighi). After finally settling in his native city in 1743 he painted the enormous banqueting room of the Ca' Rezzonico. Although his painting is often dismissed as a facile reflection of that of Giambattista Tiepolo, his colourful and lively manner is in fact entirely different in character and owes more to the art of older decorators such as Pellegrini and Amigoni.

Cross, Henry Edmond 1856–1910
French painter. His original surname was Delacroix, which he changed to Cross in 1881, the year he settled in Paris. He studied under Bonvin and then worked in the Impressionist style, being involved in the establishment of the Salon des Indépendants in 1884. In 1891 he moved to Le Lavandou on the Mediterranean and adopted the DIVISIONIST technique. Visiting him there in 1904, Matisse was impressed by his idyllic scenes of naked women by the sea and by his use of brilliant colour. *Nocturne* (1896, Geneva, Petit Palais) is a characteristic figure composition, evoking a certain sadness.

Cross-hatching see HATCHING

Cruikshank, George 1792–1878
English painter, illustrator and caricaturist. He is known principally for his political cartoons and book illustrations to novels such as *Robinson Crusoe* and *Oliver Twist*. He espoused the cause of temperance in many woodcuts of moral themes, for example *The bottle* (1847) and *The drunkard's children* (1848).

Cruz-Diez, Carlos born 1923
Venezuelan Kinetic artist. He studied in Caracas from 1940–45 and worked as a graphic designer, publicity artist and illustrator until 1945. Then he travelled to Spain and Paris, where he began his first intensive researches into the physical properties of colour. These studies evolved over a period of ten years, resulting in his *Physiochromies* (from the words "physical chromaticism".) These are low-relief constructions of parallel strips of colour superimposed at varying angles, which blend and vibrate in the spectator's vision (example, *No. 913*, 1977, Caracas, Galleria de Arte Nacional). Returning to Venezuela in 1957, he founded his own art school. He has lived in Paris since 1960.

Cubism
Movement in 20th-century painting and sculpture. By rejecting the naturalistic tradition, Cubism revolutionized painting and sculpture. Developed jointly by Picasso and Braque, it grew out of explorations inspired by Cézanne's late work and by African tribal sculpture. Picasso first combined these sources in his startling "*Demoiselles d'Avignon*" (1907, New York, MOMA), but the term "Cubist" was first used by the critic Vauxcelles for the geometric simplications of Braque's L'Estaque landscapes of 1908 (*Houses at l'Estaque*, 1908, Bern, Kunstmuseum). Picasso's *Ambroise Vollard* (1910, Moscow, Pushkin Museum) epitomizes the "analytical" phase of Cubism. The sitter is presented from a variety of viewpoints and thus appears fragmented into a crystalline structure of interlocking planes. Variety in colour and texture were sacrificed and perspectival effects replaced by a shallow, ambiguous sense of space. The aim was not complete abstraction, rather a new kind of realism; as their paintings became complex to the point of illegibility the Cubists invented radical new devices to draw the spectator's attention to commonplace subjects such as single figures and still lifes. In the phase known as "synthetic" Cubism they introduced stencilled lettering and then "collage"—the incorporation of extrinsic materials such as fragments of newspaper and printed wall-paper, as in Braque's *Still life with guitar* (1912/13, Philadelphia, Museum of Art). They sought by these means to achieve a balance between the depiction of reality and the autonomy of the painting as a physical object. Picasso and Braque soon developed in independent directions, but the innovations of Cubism stimulated yet further developments by others. Its essential concerns were rigorously pursued by the Spaniard Gris, while Delaunay, Léger and other French artists, many associated with the SECTION D'OR group, adapted the style to different ends, creating for example Orphism, Purism and a host of lesser tendencies. Artists throughout Europe were similarly inspired, some, like Malevich and Mondrian, taking the final step to complete abstraction. See vol. 3 pp. 148–151, 178–179

Cuevas, José Luis born 1934
Mexican painter and graphic artist. In 1954 he held his first major show abroad, at the Pan-American Union in Washington, and in an interview for *Time* magazine criticized the Mexican Muralists. He continued to attack Regionalism and Social Realism through articles, seminars and lectures. In 1959 he took part in a revolutionary movement in Argentina supporting the revived figurative movement. His drawings, made of fine webs of lines and sepia washes, exaggerate the human countenance and explore morality in a social and human context.

Cuixart, Modésto born 1925
Spanish painter. He began painting in 1941, and in 1948 joined the avantgarde Barcelona Dau al Set group, of which Tapiès was also a member. From Surrealist works he moved to canvases incorporating a variety of materials and employing metallic paints. These works have a hieratic, medieval quality. Since 1965 he has developed a more representational mode.

Cullen, Maurice 1866–1934
Canadian landscape painter. He worked in Paris in the 1890s and returned to Canada in 1902. His atmospherically rendered, loosely textured paintings helped to introduce Impressionism to Canada (*Winter evening, Quebec*, *c.*1905, Ottawa, NG of Canada). His snow scenes were admired by the GROUP OF SEVEN.

Currier, Nathaniel 1813–88
American printer and lithographer. In 1857 he formed a partnership with **James Ives** (1824–95), and together they produced cheap lithographs which provide a colourful record of 19th-century life in America. Clipper ships, steamboats, trains, nature scenes and newsworthy events were among the subjects portrayed in the more than 4,000 prints, which the firm of Currier and Ives issued. They were produced by a production line—one assistant to one colour. The sons of Currier and Ives carried on the business until 1907.

Curry, John Steuart 1897–1946
American painter associated with the REGIONALIST movement. After training as an illustrator, he became drawn to indigenous themes such as that of *Baptism in Kansas* (1928, New York, Whitney) and was influenced by Rubens towards a swirling, rumbustious style. During the 1930s he produced murals for the Federal Art Project, emerging as perhaps the most polemical of the major Regionalists. Melodrama often weakens his celebrations of Mid-Western life.

Cuyp, Aelbert 1620–91
The most famous of a family of Dutch painters active in Dordrecht and one of the greatest of Dutch landscape painters. He travelled along the rivers Maas, Rhine and Waal, making sketches from nature, but apparently never went to Italy. His glowing light effects, however, and majestic power of composition, bring him closer to Claude than any of the Dutch painters who had travelled south. Even though he apparently painted little in his last decades, after he had married into a rich family, his output was large. Few of his paintings are dated, and it is very difficult to establish a chronology. His preferred subjects were river scenes (*The Maas at Dordrecht*, Washington, NG) and landscapes with cows—animals which he rendered with a quiet grandeur unmatched by any other painter. The atmosphere created is almost always one of idyllic peace and contentment. Working in provincial isolation, Cuyp had little effect on the development of Dutch painting, but in the 18th and 19th centuries his reputation was very high in England, with the result that he is best represented in England, notably in London (Dulwich College, NG, Wallace Coll.) and at Waddesdon Manor, Buckinghamshire. Cuyp also painted a few portraits, which probably reflect his training with his father **Jacob Gerritz.** Cuyp (1594–1651), who is principally known for his work in this field. He was particularly good at capturing the unaffected charm of children (*Boy with a hawk*, 1649, on loan to Dordrecht Museum). Jacob's half-brother **Benjamin Gerritz.** Cuyp (1612–52) painted biblical and genre scenes influenced by the early work of Rembrandt. See vol. 2 pp. **222–223**

D

Dada
Movement of revolt by European and American artists and writers, first appearing in 1915 and losing impetus by 1923. The title (French for "hobby-horse") was selected at random from a dictionary and symbolized its deliberately anti-rational, anti-aesthetic stance, in part a reaction to World War I. Dadaism first occurred in Zurich (where the main proponents were Arp and Tzara), spread to New York in 1915 (where those involved included Picabia, Man Ray and Duchamp), and to Paris, Berlin, Hanover, Cologne and Barcelona

all before 1918. The original anti-militarist protest developed into a total rejection of the hypocrisy and falseness of established values, of which culture was seen as symptomatic. The Dadaists aimed to destroy art as an aesthetic cult and to replace it by anti-art and non-art, by definition meaningless and shocking. They therefore rejected the artefact, substituting instead the nonsense poem, the ready-made object and the collage, in which arbitrariness dictated the final form rather than creative order. The most notorious Dada statement was Duchamp's *Fountain* of 1917, which consisted of a urinal signed *R.Mutt*. In Paris the tendency to a more whimsical absurdity (as in Picabia's machine configurations) led, by about 1923, to Surrealism. In Germany, during the post-War economic crisis, Dada became socially and politically committed (for example in Grosz's savage caricatures), eventually giving way to NEUE SACHLICH-KEIT. See vol. 3 pp. 166–167

Dadd, Richard 1819–87
English painter. He studied at the Royal Academy Schools, but after extensive travels in Europe and the Middle East began to show signs of mental disorder. In 1843 he murdered his father and for the rest of his life was confined to asylums, where he executed allegorical and fairy pictures crowded with intricate detail (*The fairy-feller's master stroke*, 1855–64, London, Tate).

Daddi, Bernardo
active *c.*1290–1349
The leading Florentine painter of the generation after Giotto. Nothing is known of his training, but his numerous paintings on panel are heavily indebted to Giotto's example, although they also show a marked interest in the patternings of Sienese painting. His single documented work is the altarpiece of *The Virgin enthroned* (1346–47) housed in Orcagna's Tabernacle in Orsanmichele, Florence. He had a large workshop which specialized in the production of small devotional panels, and studio participation seems likely even in his four signed paintings, an example of which is the polyptych showing *The Crucifixion with eight saints* (1348, London, Courtauld Institute Galleries). See vol. 2 p. 85

Daffinger, Moritz Michael
1790–1849
Austrian miniature painter and watercolourist. In the 1820s he became extremely successful as a society miniature painter and executed more than 200 portraits of the Metternich family and their circle alone. In 1841 he abandoned portraiture for botanical watercolours.

Dahl, Johan Christian 1788–1857
Norwegian landscape painter, active mainly in Dresden, where he was a professor at the Academy from 1829–57. He was trained by Eckersburg but his Romantic outlook was shaped more by 17th-century Dutch painters such as Ruisdael, and by his friend Friedrich. His technique was painterly, and his cloud studies recall those of Constable. He discovered Norwegian scenery as a subject, evoking the mountainous countryside with fresh vigour (*Stugnoset*, 1851, Oslo, NG). See vol. 3 p. **74**

Dahmen, Karl Fred born 1917
West German artist, whose highly textured work, roughly characterizable as painting/collage, has close links with TACHISME. He allows his unconventional materials to retain their specific physicality and complex associations.

Dai Jin 1388–1462
Chinese painter, a major figure of the Zhejiang school of Ming painting. He came originally from the provincial capital of Hangzhou, though he is also recorded as having worked in China's extreme south-west, and in Peking. In Peking his work may well have been appreciated by the Xaunde emperor, the most artistically gifted of the Ming rulers and himself an exponent of the coloured style derived from Song and Yuan academic traditions. This was the context of Dai's own work, though he also used a more spacious style in his many genre scenes, such as the handscroll *Fishermen on a river* (Washington, Freer).

Dali, Salvador born 1904
Spanish painter, since Picasso's death probably the most notorious Spanish artist. After early Cubist-inspired work, the influence of Metaphysical Painting and contact with Miró caused him to join the SURREALISTS in 1929, and in collaboration with the director Luis Buñuel he made the first Surrealist films, *Un Chien Andalou* (An Andalusian Dog, 1929) and *L'Âge d'Or* (The Golden Age, 1930). *Accommodations of desire* (1929, Bridgewater, Connecticut, Julien Levy Gallery) reveals the hallucinatory power of his best paintings. By reading psychological case histories Dali hoped to represent neuroses in an ultra-realistic style so as to objectify the irrational with photographic accuracy. Although his early work was based on his own paranoid hallucinations, which he claimed he could induce, his subject matter became increasingly reliant on theoretical rather than personal knowledge and became stereotyped and mannered. This, together with his support for the dictator Franco, led the Surrealists to expel him from their ranks in 1938. Ironically, Dali is identified in the public mind as the Surrealist painter *par excellence* and his eccentric life-style and provocative self-advertising reinforce this. Since World War II he has created jewellery, ceramics and small-scale sculpture as well as painting. From 1940 to 1955 he lived in the USA, and many of his finest works are in American collections. His *Last Supper* (1955, Washington, NG) and other popular late religious works paying homage to the past have been condemned as "academic". His latest, paintings even more meticulous, make the surreal appear three-dimensional. See vol. 1 p. 91; vol. 3 pp. **174–175**

Dalmau, Luis active 1428–60
Spanish painter, an important early exponent of a Netherlandish style which made a considerable impact upon Spanish art. He was court painter to Alfonso of Aragon, who sent him to Flanders in 1431. His greatest work is the *Virgin and Child with councillors* (1445, Barcelona, Museo de Arte de Cataluna), which recalls van Eyck's Ghent altarpiece and includes several solemn portraits.

Dalou, Aimé-Jules 1838–1902
French sculptor, a pupil of Carpeaux. His large-scale monuments and statues, such as the *Triumph of the Republic* (1889–90, Paris, Place de la Nation), are academic and uninventive, but his small-scale sculpture, and particularly his sketches, have refreshing charm (*Woman taking off her stockings*, c.1870–80, plaster, London, Tate). He was a dedicated socialist, and after taking part in the Paris Commune of 1870 he was exiled and spent some years in England.

Dalwood, Hubert 1924–76
British sculptor. His earliest surviving

works are roughly modelled figures, characteristic of the raw, expressive manner of much British sculpture in the 1950s. By the end of the decade, in pieces such as *Icon* (1958, Leeds, City Gallery), a more personal manner emerges. Semi-abstract shapes with organic references suggest patterns of movement or growth. In the early 1960s he made sculptures in painted aluminium, but continued to be preoccupied with associative imagery and suggestions of landscape. In later sculpture accumulations of aluminium rods create an illusionistic space.

Damaphon
active 1st half of 2nd century BC
Hellenistic Greek sculptor from Messene. He repaired Phidias' statue of *Zeus* at Olympia and was himself responsible for a number of monumental groups, including one at Lycosura, where excavation has uncovered three colossal marble heads carved in a rich and classical style (Athens, National Museum).

Danby, Francis 1793–1861
Irish historical and landscape painter, who worked mainly in Bristol and London. During the 1820s his apocalyptic paintings such as *The delivery out of Egypt* (1825, Preston, Harris Museum and Art Gallery) rivalled those of Martin. He was also a painter of pastoral idylls.

Dance, Nathaniel 1735–1811
British painter, the son and brother of architects, both named George. After studying under Hayman, Dance went to Rome (1754–65/6), where he painted historical pictures which are among the earliest examples of Neoclassicism, and also small group portraits of English tourists. He became a founder-member of the Royal Academy (1768). His life-size portraits are forceful but sometimes rather wooden (*Lord Clive*, 1772–73, Wales, Powys Castle).

Daniele da Volterra
(Daniele Ricciarelli) *c.*1509–66
Italian painter and sculptor, born in Volterra, where he was trained by Sodoma. By 1541 he was in Rome, where he became the friend and most gifted follower of Michelangelo, of whom he executed a famous posthumous bronze (numerous versions, for example, Florence, Casa Buonarroti; Paris, Louvre; Oxford, Ashmolean). Daniele's finest work is the noble and moving altar fresco of *The Deposition* (commissioned 1541) in the Orsini Chapel of SS. Trinita dei Monti, but his reputation as a painter has been overshadowed by his most famous (or infamous) work—the painting of draperies over the nude figures in Michelangelo's *Last Judgment*. This, done to suit Counter-Reformation taste, earned him the nickname "Il Bragghettone" (breeches-maker). See vol. 2 p. *205*

Danti, Vincenzo 1530–76
Italian sculptor. He was born in Perugia and active mainly in Florence, his best-known work probably being the bronze group of *The execution of St John the Baptist* (finished 1571) over the south door of the Baptistery. His style was inspired by Michelangelo's, but had more grace and much less power. In 1564 he provided paintings and sculpture for Michelangelo's funeral ceremonies, and in 1567 he published a book on proportion dedicated to Cosimo de' Medici. See vol. 2 p. 128

Danube school
Term used for a number of artists

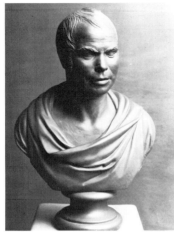
Crome: Plaster cast of bust by Mazzotti (1785?–1870?), *c.*1810. London, NPG

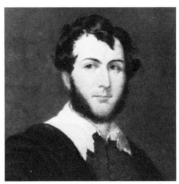
Cruikshank: Portrait by an unknown artist, 1836. London, NPG

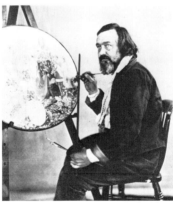
Dadd: Photograph courtesy of The Bethlem Royal Hospital

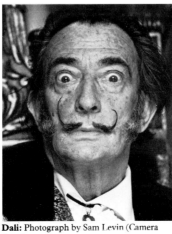
Dali: Photograph by Sam Levin (Camera Press)

working independently in the Danube valley in southern Germany and Austria in the early 16th century. Altdorfer, Cranach the Elder and Huber are among the leading figures. Characteristically their work depicts subjects dominated by a setting of lofty, moss-clad trees and mountains. Their work is important evidence of an interest in depicting landscape and the moods of nature for its own sake, and sometimes their paintings and drawings are entirely without figures. However, the individual artists worked in various styles, and there is no evidence of contact. See vol. 2 pp. **154–155**

Daoji died c.1719
Chinese painter. He was born Zhu Ruoji, a prince of the Ming imperial house, but became a monk after the fall of that dynasty in 1644. He led a wandering life, and gradually won the friendship of artistically-minded members of the Chinese and Manchu élites, despite a notoriously difficult disposition. His views on art, above all his exaltation of spontaneity, ran distinctly counter to orthodox views on the need to imitate earlier work. He had a celebrated, if unfruitful, meeting with the painter Wang Yuanqi, which may have led to his polemical treatise *Words on Painting*, a systematic attack on the orthodox school of painting represented by the successors of Dong Qichang. Much of the work attributed to this master is only dubiously authentic. The famous handscroll *Peach blossom spring* (Washington, Freer), however, bears his distinctive heavy application of ink and rich colour.

Darboven, Hanne born 1941
West German artist, whose work consists almost entirely of playing with numbers. From geometric drawings and constructions in the 1960s, she moved towards a more "pure" presentation of numbers, presented utterly disinterestedly and concretely.

Dardel, Nils von 1888–1943
Swedish painter and draughtsman. He played the morbid dandy, painting a bizarre Surrealist world where agony and idyll are alternating ingredients, and his shimmering paintings often have Pointillist and Naive characteristics. *Visit to an eccentric lady* (1921, Stockholm, Nationalmuseum) is typical.

Daret, Jacques 1406–68 or later
Netherlandish painter from Tournai. He was apprenticed, with "Rogelet de la Pâture" (probably Rogier van der Weyden), to Robert Campin from 1427 to 1432. His style is heavily dependent on the Master of Flémalle—one of the chief reasons for identifying that master with Campin. His major work was an altarpiece for the Abbey of St Vaast, Arras, of which four panels survive (1433–35, *The Presentation in the Temple*, Paris, Petit Palais; *The Adoration of the Magi* and *The Visitation*, West Berlin, Staatliche Museen; *The Nativity*, Lugano, Thyssen coll.). He also worked as an illuminator and tapestry designer, and contributed to the decorations for the marriage of Charles the Bold.

Dasburg, Andrew born 1887
American painter, born in Paris. He emigrated to the USA in 1892, but visited Paris in 1909–10, working closely with Russell. He immersed himself in colour theory and, influenced by the Synchromists' 1914 exhibition, painted some highly abstract works. After 1916 he moved to a more representational style derived from Cubism. In 1930 he settled in Taos, New Mexico.

Dasvanth active 1580s
Indian painter. He was singled out as the greatest of the early MUGHAL artists, but his work is now known only through his draughtsmanship in the great *Razmnameh* manuscript, in progress during the 1580s (Jaipur, City Palace). He was supposedly seen painting figures on a wall by the Emperor Akbar, who immediately entered him in the imperial atelier. His work shows the greatest imagination in reducing to visible shape the complex visions of the *Razmnameh*, the Persian version of the epic *Mahabharata*.

Daubigny, Charles-François 1817–78
French landscape painter and graphic artist, a member of the BARBIZON school. He began his career as an illustrator and first exhibited landscapes in the Salon of 1838, the year he entered Delaroche's studio. Daubigny's early work shows a mixture of styles dominated by the Claudian tradition and by influences assimilated during a visit to Italy, but from the 1850s he moved closer to Dutch art and sought freer, *plein-air* effects. His reputation was established after the Government bought a *View of the Seine* in 1852 (Nantes Museum), followed by Louis-Napoleon's purchase of his *Pond of Gylieu* (Cincinnati Art Museum). In 1857 Daubigny launched his studio-boat, travelling the rivers of France, and from this time water was his principal theme. He had a great impact on the Impressionists through his paintings of pure landscape and devotion to the fleeting aspects of nature. See vol. 3 p. **93**

Daumier, Honoré 1808–79
French caricaturist, painter and sculptor. After a spell as a bookseller he embarked on a career as a political cartoonist and adopted the new technique of lithography. His natural flair for drawing and his strongly Republican stance led quickly to his début in the left-wing press and by 1831 his reputation as a brilliant cartoonist and enemy of the régime of Louis-Philippe was well established. He was even briefly imprisoned for depicting the king as Rabelais's Gargantua (1832). In 1835, when the weekly *Caricature* was suppressed by the state, Daumier abandoned political satire for milder criticism of bourgeois life in *Charivari*. His lithographic output was immense, yet as a painter and sculptor, too, his work shows remarkable originality. From 1848 to 1866 he made a series of paintings of melancholy wanderers—fugitives, clowns, travellers in drab railway carriages. His technique involved building up broad forms from several washes and with strong black outlines in an almost sculptural manner, justifying Balzac's comment: "there is something of Michelangelo in this man". As a sculptor he excelled in a limited field, modelling caricature heads and figures in a rough and spontaneous style. Now considered the "father" of modern caricature, Daumier spent the last years of his life blind and impoverished, in a cottage given to him by Corot. See vol. 1 pp. *87, 167*; vol. 3 pp. **88–89**, *95*

David, Gerard c.1460–1523
Netherlandish painter, born at Oudewater in southern Holland. He qualified as a master in Bruges in 1484 and, apart from a brief stay in Antwerp (1515), spent most of his life there, following in the tradition of van der Weyden and Memlinc. His figures are noble, monumental and reflective, displaying no interest in the material world. *The Marriage at Cana* (c.1503, Paris, Louvre), for

example, has a joyless, ceremonial air, its isolated and statuesque participants acting out a solemn prefiguration of the Sacrament, with the depiction of a wedding a purely secondary concern. David's devout painting was much imitated in Bruges, notably by Isenbrandt, even though a fashion for Italianate painting rapidly superseded his style.

David, Jacques-Louis 1748–1825
French painter, the leading artist of the NEOCLASSICAL movement. After winning the Prix de Rome in 1775, he accompanied his teacher Vien to Italy, where the study of the Antique transformed his earlier Rococo style, learned from his first master, Boucher. A fusion of intense realism with the Antique is seen in his *Oath of the Horatii* (1784, Paris, Louvre), which established him as the leader of the new movement. His severe and remarkably taut compositions, with colour firmly subordinate to line, extolled selfless, civic virtues in episodes taken typically from Livy, and, once the Revolution had begun, he took an active part in it as a Deputy to the Convention. During the Terror he was virtual dictator of the arts, abolishing the Academy and setting up the Institute in its place. He designed processions, and monuments to the Revolution, and painted its martyrs, most memorably *The death of Marat* (1793, Brussels, Musées Royaux des Beaux-Arts). When Robespierre was executed David was twice imprisoned in the Luxembourg, where he painted two remarkable landscapes—unique in his oeuvre—from his window (*View of the Luxembourg Gardens*, 1784, Louvre). In 1799 he began what was perhaps both a plea for humanity and a comprehensive—ultimately rather unsuccessful—statement of the Neoclassical style, *The intervention of the Sabine women* (Louvre), with clear references to Raphael and rather too archaeological ones to the Antique. After the rise of Napoleon he became again official painter, glorifying the Emperor's exploits in epic canvases (*The coronation of Napoleon*, 1805–07, Louvre). The best work of his later career was undoubtedly his portraiture, such as *Mme de Verninac*(1799, Louvre). After Napoleon's defeat at Waterloo, David sought refuge in Brussels and died in exile. His greatest pupils were Gérard, Gros and Ingres. See vol. 1 p. 31; vol. 3 pp. **56–59**

David, Pierre-Jean 1788–1856
French sculptor, known as David d'Angers after his place of birth. By 1808 he was in Paris, where his talent was recognized by J.-L. David, whose humanistic outlook influenced his style. In 1811 he won the Prix de Rome and in Italy he met Ingres, whose idealism he admired above the current Romantic trends. He was also influenced by Canova and Thorvaldsen, and in 1816 studied the Elgin Marbles in London. The classicizing elements in his work, however, were tempered by a vigorous realism. He regarded sculpture as "the recorder of posterity", and his greatest commission (completed 1837) was for the pediments of the Panthéon in Paris, showing France distributing wreaths to distinguished Frenchmen. At his death, he left more than 500 portrait medallions of the major literary, political and artistic figures of the age to his native city.

Davie, Alan born 1920
British painter. He saw Pollock's work in Venice in 1948, although the vigorous handling and visceral imagery of Davie's paintings such as *Male and female* (1956, Buffalo, Albright-Knox) are equally

close to the European CoBrA style. In later paintings the colour has become brighter and the images, suggestive of mythology and magic, have been more boldly outlined. Davie is also a jazz musician and has stressed the role of intuition and improvisation in his work, a concept at one with his interest in Zen and oriental mysticism.

Davies, Arthur Bowen 1862–1928
American artist. His early works drew on such diverse sources as Whistler, Botticelli and Puvis de Chavannes, and he painted fantastic landscape idylls such as *Unicorns* (1906, New York, Metropolitan). In 1908 he exhibited as one of The EIGHT and in 1912 presided over the association which organized the Armory Show. After this his work revealed a superficial influence of Cubism and Synchromism. With his considerable knowledge of European art he helped to form the Museum of Modern Art in New York.

Davis, Ron born 1937
American painter. He received critical attention in the mid-1960s as a POST-PAINTERLY ABSTRACTIONIST. His abstract paintings, featuring elaborate geometric structures, employ two- or three-point perspective (*Five twelves*, 1967, Cologne, Wallraf-Richartz Museum), but the deep illusionistic space is balanced by an emphasis on flat, decorative areas of colour.

Davis, Stuart 1894–1964
American painter. The 1913 Armory Show was a primary influence on his art, and early works such as *Lucky Strike* (1921, New York, MOMA), a painted imitation collage, already show his interest in popular American motifs, partly echoing Léger's imagery. During the 1920s he assimilated late synthetic Cubism and PRECISIONISM in his hard-edged, simplified forms. In the later 1930s he created several murals on the WPA project and was active in artists' politics. His work after 1940 was often quite abstract, evoking jazzy rhythms in a bright, flat, decorative style reminiscent of the later Matisse. Fragments of lettering, realistic motifs or zany titles (as in *Owh! In Sao Pao*, 1951, New York, Whitney) introduce the vitality of modern life to these images. He was probably the most important American artist to explore the Cubist idiom. See vol. 3 p. **210**

Davringhausen, Heinrich 1894–1970
German artist. He studied sculpture and lithography before turning to painting, and exhibited with the NOVEMBER-GRUPPE in 1919, 1923 and 1924. His awkward, anonymous figures express man's isolation and ineffectuality and the precariousness of existence, and Davringhausen's main theme is the corruption of Weimar Germany. *The profiteer*, (1920–21, Düsseldorf, Kunstmuseum) combines a Neue Sachlichkeit approach with the frozen compositional devices of Magic Realism. He emigrated to Spain in 1933, but settled finally at Cagnes-sur-Mer, where he died.

De Andrea, John born 1941
American SUPERREALIST sculptor, who specializes in the nude figure. His works are usually life-size representations of attractive men and women (*Dorothy*, 1969–70, Aachen, Neue Galerie). His medium is moulded fibreglass painted to an extreme degree of lifelikeness—verisimilitude extending to minute details such as body hair. See vol. 3 p. **253**

Decalcomania
Process of transferring an image from a sheet of paper on to a second surface. The technique was used commercially for ceramic decoration but, in the sphere of fine art, it was discovered by Oscar Dominguez, and then by other Surrealists, and used to print from paper painted with gouache. The pressure of the transfer process produces distortions and unusual textures, as in Ernst's *Europe after the rain* (1940–42, Hartford, Conn., Wadsworth Atheneum).

Decamps, Alexandre-Gabriel
1803–60
French painter, a follower of Delacroix. Decamps established his reputation with *The watering-place* (1832, London, Wallace Coll.), a colourful and idealized depiction of the Near East inspired by travels in 1827–29. An important figure in the Romantic movement, he created a new vogue for orientalism and strongly influenced Chassériau and Fromentin. From 1834, after a trip to Italy, he attempted historical and religious subjects, but was still successful with genre and oriental themes.

Decorative art
General term for all arts in which decoration is applied to a functional object. It is often opposed to the fine arts of painting and sculpture, though the distinctions are not hard and fast.

Deesis
The representation in Byzantine art of Christ between his Mother and St John the Baptist. It means "supplication".

Defrance, Leonard 1735–1805
One of the leading Belgian painters of the 18th century. He was trained in the tradition of French classicism and spent several years in Italy, but he is best known for his small anecdotal scenes which are personal reinterpretations of 17th-century Dutch genre painting (*The forge, c.* 1780, New York, Metropolitan). These were very popular in Paris, where Defrance, a friend of Fragonard, made regular visits. There is a fine *Self-portrait* of 1789 in the Musée de l'Art Wallon at Liège, his birthplace.

Defregger, Franz von 1835–1921
Austrian genre and history painter. He studied in Munich under Piloty and visited Paris, where he was influenced by Courbet and the Barbizon painters. He concentrated on Bavarian history and sentimental and highly popular peasant scenes of his native Tyrol, influenced by Leibl, with whose circle in Munich he associated. Between 1878 and 1910 he was professor at the Munich Academy.

Degas, Hilaire Germain Edgar
1834–1917
French painter and sculptor, from a wealthy Parisian family. He studied under one of Ingres's pupils at the Ecole des Beaux-Arts and made an intensive study of the Old Masters in the Louvre, and of Renaissance painting during his stay in Italy, 1854–59. Though his early works were of subjects from ancient history or portraits, by the middle of the 1860s he was turning to modern themes. He came to know Manet and the Impressionist artists who frequented the Café Guerbois, but, although he exhibited at all but one of the Impressionist exhibitions, he differed from his colleagues in the stress he laid on composition and drawing and in the fact that he did not paint out of doors. He was primarily concerned with depicting movement and he often used unusual viewpoints,

with the figure partly cut off at the edge of the canvas. This can be clearly seen in his *Ballet rehearsal* (1874, Glasgow Art Gallery) and probably originated in his interest in photography and Japanese prints. His main subject was contemporary Parisian life, as in *The glass of absinth* (1876, Paris, Jeu de Paume), though this was actually posed for and painted in his studio. He also developed various themes such as racecourses, women ironing, bathing or buying hats and the well-known ballet dancers, all of which show his preoccupation with catching a definitive gesture which gives permanent value to the most transitory subject. For his last 20 years he was almost blind and lived a solitary life, working on very free but lithe wax sculptures which were posthumously cast in bronze. Only one was exhibited in his lifetime, *The little 14-year-old dancer* (1881, casts in London, Tate; New York, Metropolitan, and elsewhere), whose real hair and clothes caused something of a stir. A formidable character, Degas was much admired in his lifetime and he is now one of the most popular 19th-century artists. See vol. 1 pp. *45, 69, 160*; vol. 3 pp. 102, **104–105**.

Degenerate art (Entartete Kunst)
Term coined by the Nazis to discredit all modern art which did not correspond to the theories propounded by Hitler in *Mein Kampf* and by Alfred Rosenberg in *The Myth of the Twentieth Century* (1930). It was also the title given to a propagandist art exhibition held in Munich and other German cities (1937) in which works by artists as varied as van Gogh, Beckmann, Nolde, Chagall, Picasso, Kandinsky and Matisse—compulsorily confiscated from German museums from 1933 on—were shown together with (and by implication on a par with) paintings by the incurably insane.

Degouve de Nuncques, William
1867–1935
French-born Belgian landscape painter. Converted to SYMBOLISM by Toorop, he became a member of Les Vingt and painted symbolic portraits and rather weird landscapes, but after a trip to Spain and the Balearics more Impressionist tendencies emerged. Later he painted quiet and sober landscapes in Brabant such as *Caravan* (1910, Antwerp, Musées Royaux des Beaux-Arts). He may be considered a forerunner of Magritte and Belgian Surrealism.

De Haan, Wim 1913–67
Dutch painter, sculptor and poet. He was a prisoner of war in Thailand, 1942–45, and only started painting in 1953. He began with almost abstract landscapes and in 1957 made his first constructions. His *objets trouvés* and assemblages emphasize totemic and iconic forms, and all his work shows a great interest in texture and symbolic juxtaposition.

Deïneka, Alexander 1899–1969
Soviet painter and graphic designer. He developed a personal realist style in monumental paintings such as *The defence of Petrograd* (1928, Moscow, Museum of the Armed Forces). This owes as much to the flat linear styles of late 19th-century Symbolists, particularly Hodler, as to the manipulation of pictorial space made possible by Cubism and Constructivism. Some of his most appealing works are ink-and-wash drawings, for example *Skaters* (1927, Moscow, Tretyakov Gallery).

Dekkers, Ad (Adriaan) 1938–74
Dutch sculptor. His first works were

precise naturalistic drawings of everyday objects, but he soon moved on to an austere abstract style recalling Mondrian. From 1961 he concentrated on plain geometrical reliefs, mostly white and made from polyester (*Square with sector no. 1–4*, 1968, Amsterdam, Stedelijk Museum). He hoped to attain his ideal for a truly social art in the production of multiples based on his work.

De Kooning, Elaine born 1920
American painter. A member of the New York school of ABSTRACT EXPRESSIONISM, she studied with Marca-Relli and also with Willem De Kooning, whom she married in 1943. Her painterly work has ranged from abstraction to portraiture, and she is also an important writer on the work of her colleagues.

De Kooning, Willem born 1904
American painter of the New York school, one of the major ABSTRACT EXPRESSIONISTS. Born in Rotterdam, he emigrated to the USA in 1926 and in the 1930s began to work on abstract canvases with suggestions of landscape and still life and on a series of male portraits. A close friendship with Gorky encouraged mutual stylistic influence, and by the mid-1940s De Kooning had emerged as a leading Abstract Expressionist. The first of his famous female figure paintings appeared at this time, semi-abstract figures painted in lurid oils (and grimy black recalling Rouault) with full-bodied, slashing strokes. His links with the European Expressionist tradition and parallels with CoBrA work were strong, yet he also developed a more austere abstract style related to Kline, as in *Painting* (1948, New York, MOMA), in black and white enamel paint. In the early 1950s De Kooning again focused on the figure in his *Woman* series (examples in MOMA), and since then, although pure abstraction has re-emerged occasionally, the themes of women and landscapes have continued to preoccupy him. Recently he has made some sculpture. De Kooning's vigorous style had widespread influence on the work of painters in the 1950s. See vol. 1 p. *27*; vol. 3 pp. **216–217**.

Delacroix, Eugène 1798–1863
French painter, one of the greatest artists of the ROMANTIC movement. He trained under Guérin, but was more strongly influenced by the Romanticism of Géricault and his studies of the Old Masters in the Louvre, where he was attracted by the exuberant colour of Rubens and the 16th-century Venetians. He made his Salon début with *The barque of Dante* (1822, Paris, Louvre), Romantic in theme but still indebted in composition and in its muscular treatment of the nudes to the classical tradition to which Delacroix always professed his allegiance. The freely painted *Massacre at Chios* (1824, Louvre), illustrating an incident from the Greek War of Independence, was dubbed by Gros "the massacre of painting", but its purchase by the Government enabled Delacroix to visit England (with Bonington) the following year. There he studied the works of Constable and the English watercolourists, and developed his interest in Shakespeare, Byron and Scott—his chief literary sources. Unlike his great rival, Ingres, he never went to Italy, but his visit to North Africa in 1832 inspired many pictures of oriental subjects which reflect both the exoticism of Islamic Africa and the classical dignity of living antiquity (*Women of Algiers*, 1834, Louvre). From this date a more classical restraint informed his work, while his

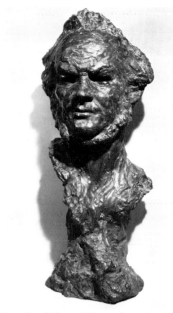

Daumier: Self-portrait bronze bust, 1855. Paris, Bibliothèque Nationale

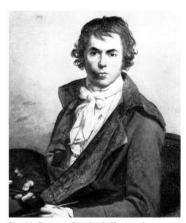

David, Jacques-Louis: Self-portrait, 1794. Paris, Louvre

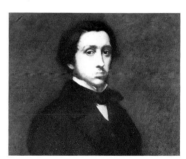

Degas: Self-portrait, *c.*1855. Paris, Louvre

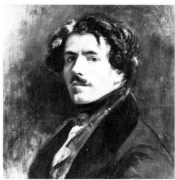

Delacroix: Self-portrait, *c.*1837. Paris, Louvre

palette brightened and his brushwork broadened. During the last 30 years of his life Delacroix received numerous Government commissions for large-scale architectural decorations, best-known of which are his murals for the Chapel of the Holy Angels in St Sulpice (1853–61). His portraits, characterized by their spiritual intensity, include those of *Paganini* (1832, Louvre) and his friends *Chopin and George Sand* (1838, Louvre). A prolific painter, Delacroix also left in his Journal, kept from 1822–24 and from 1847 until his death, a unique record of his own development and the artistic climate of his time. He had no school or direct followers, but was a profoundly influential figure, and Monet, Seurat, Gauguin and van Gogh all felt the impact of his structural use of colour. See vol. 3 pp. **78–81**

Delaroche, Paul 1797–1856
French history painter, a pupil of Gros, who conciliated avantgarde and conservative tendencies in art by combining Romantic themes with academic drawing. His subjects often came from English history; typical are *The children of King Edward imprisoned in the Tower* (1831, Paris, Louvre) and *The execution of Lady Jane Grey* (1833, London, NG)—melodramatic and painstakingly realistic works. See vol. 3 p. 79

Delaunay, Robert 1885–1941
French painter, principally famous as the creator, with his wife Sonia Delaunay-Terk, of ORPHISM. Early in his career he experimented with Neo-Impressionism and Fauvism, but from 1909 began to create an individual style. In 1910 he was working on a series of paintings of the Eiffel Tower which, in accordance with the multiple-viewpoint techniques of Cubism, dynamically fragmented the subject. In his more poetic *Windows* series (1912, example, London, Tate), abstracted views over the Tower and Paris, he combined a planar, grid-like structure deriving from Cubism with the vibrant colour contrasts of Neo-Impressionism. He thus sought to express the dynamic energies of light. These works made a major contribution to Orphism, as did his *Circular Forms* from 1912 (example Zurich, Kunsthaus), radiating compositions of great lyricism and unprecedented abstract purity. Such works were highly influential on groups and artists as diverse as the Italian Futurists and Chagall, the American Synchromists and the German Expressionists Marc, Macke and Klee. However, in monumental figurative images, such as *The Cardiff team* (1912–13, Eindhoven, Stedelijk van Abbe Museum), he celebrated modern urban experience in a more literal manner. Delaunay spent much of the War in Portugal producing bright still lifes and figure paintings. Returning to Paris, he executed many rather uninspired variations on his earlier themes and style. See vol. 3 p. **151**

Delaunay-Terk, Sonia 1885–1979
Russian painter and textile designer. She studied art in Germany and Paris, where she finally settled in 1910 as the wife of Robert Delaunay, with whom she developed ORPHISM to follow from Cubism. An early painting is *Bal Bullier* (1913, Paris, Musée d'Art Moderne). In later paintings and in designs for books and clothes she used bright colours in increasingly abstract forms and the more monumentally abstract approach of her later work, still based on brilliant colour relationships, can be seen in *Triptych* (1963, London, Tate).

Dello di Niccolò Delli
*c.*1404–*c.*1471
Italian painter. He worked in Florence until 1433 and then lived in Spain, apart from a brief return to Florence (1446–47). His work in Spain includes frescos in Old Salamanca Cathedral (1455) and in the choir of Valencia Cathedral (1469–70), in a style close to Bicci di Lorenzo but also reflecting Ghiberti.

Delvaux, Paul born 1897
Belgian painter. His early work was influenced by Neo-Impressionist colour theory and then by Permeke, Ensor and de Smet. Deeply impressed by the work of Magritte and Chirico, which he saw in an exhibition in Brussels in 1934, he became a SURREALIST. A visit to Italy (1939) reinforced an earlier interest in the female nude and in Roman architecture, and he combined these elements with earlier motifs such as railway stations and trains, often seen by moonlight, to create a metaphysical intensity in his views of imaginary cities (*Ladies of the night*, 1937, Antwerp, Musées Royaux des Beaux-Arts).

Delville, Jean 1867–1953
Belgian painter, principal exponent of SYMBOLIST painting in Belgium. In the 1890s he stayed in Paris, and exhibited with the Rose + Croix group, and then returned to Brussels, where he formed an active Symbolist circle with a Salon. He is best known for his portraits but painted murals of a mystical, idealistic conception, and spread the Symbolist message through writing and teaching.

De Maria, Walter born 1935
American sculptor and LAND artist. His Minimal works from the earlier 1960s, featuring elementary, irreducible shapes, are "activated" by viewer participation or response and thus relate to Body art and Performance. Two of his well-known Earthworks are *Mile-long drawing* (1968)—two parallel chalk lines in the Mojave Desert, California—and *Earthroom*, in which 1,600 cubic feet (about 45 cubic metres) of "Pure Dirt/Pure Earth/Pure Land" fill an art gallery. Originally created in Munich in 1968, this was re-created for permanent display in 1980 in the Lone Star Foundation, New York. See vol. 3 p. **249**

Demuth, Charles 1883–1935
American painter. He lived in Paris, 1912–13, where he studied the work of Cézanne, who influenced his delicate watercolour *Acrobats* (1919, New York, MOMA). Another important influence was his friend Duchamp, from whom he took his interest in mechanical forms and Dadaist titles, as in *Box of tricks* (1920, Philadelphia, Museum of Art). Demuth's output was very varied and included illustrations to Henry James' *The Turn of the Screw* and Emile Zola's *Nana*, but he is best remembered as a leading member of the PRECISIONIST movement, painting industrial scenes stripped of all their crudity and presented in a clear decorative manner. His most celebrated work is probably *I saw the figure five in gold* (1928, New York, Metropolitan), based on a poem by William Carlos Williams. See vol. 3 p. **205**

Denis, Maurice 1870–1943
French painter, a central figure of the SYMBOLIST movement. He was a founder-member of the NABIS in 1888 and was thus led to design decorative panels, book illustrations, stained glass and theatre sets, as well as easel-paintings. *Catholic mystery* (1890, France, J.-F. Denis coll.) typifies his concern to express his ardent Catholicism, to echo the pious simplicity of Italian primitives such as Fra Angelico and to reject realism in favour of an emphasis on the decorative possibilities of pure line and colour. In his article *Definition of Neo-Traditionalism*, 1890, he claimed that "a picture—before being a war-horse, a nude woman or some little genre—is essentially a flat surface covered with colours assembled in a certain order." The beginnings of his later reassessment of Cézanne and monumental classicism are evident in *The bathers* (1899, Paris, Petit Palais). See vol. 3 p. 120

Denner, Balthazar 1685–1749
German painter, celebrated in his day for his highly detailed heads of old people (he was originally a miniaturist). Based intermittently in Hamburg from 1701, he was the favoured portraitist of the courts of Brunswick and Denmark. In 1721–27 he lived in London. His most famous work, *Head of an old woman* (Vienna, Kunsthistorisches) was finally bought for a colossal sum by the Emperor Charles VI, who carried the key to its case (such as Denner habitually provided) with him everywhere.

Denny, Robyn born 1930
British painter. While a student he shared the interest of other young British painters in large-scale abstraction. *Baby is three* (1960, London, Tate), shown at the first SITUATION exhibition, was a tripartite composition in which he abandoned his earlier informal handling in favour of a hard-edged geometry, creating subtle visual reactions between interlocking bands of pastel colour. Later paintings have been principally in a vertical format, the compositions often suggesting a doorway.

Derain, André 1880–1954
French painter, whose historical importance outweighs his artistic achievement. In 1898–99 he studied at the Académie Carrière where he met Matisse, and in 1905 they became the joint creators of FAUVISM. Derain's use of bold brush-strokes and strong colours, reflecting an admiration for van Gogh, is epitomized in *Mountains at Collioure* (1905, New York, Whitney). Around 1906 he was one of the first to draw the attention of the avantgarde, including Picasso, to the expressive stylizations of primitive art. However, from 1906 he moved towards a more formally structured style indebted to Cézanne, and later began to look back to early Renaissance art, attempting to revive the classical values of monumentality and solidity of form in a series of still-life and figure paintings (*The bagpiper*, 1910–11, Minneapolis Institute of Arts). In 1914–18 he executed a number of granite masks and took up sculpture again in 1939; his painting style from the 1920s became increasingly dry and academic. See vol. 3 p. **142**; vol. 4 p. 185

Derkinderen, Antonius Johannes (Antoon) 1859–1925
Dutch painter, mainly of murals and decorative glass. He trained with Toorop. His importance lies in his attempt to infuse a new monumentality into art. The unified conception of medieval art represented his ideal and his works have an overtly Catholic bias, though the decorations for the Town Hall at s'Hertogenbosch (Bois-le-Duc), 1889–96, are generally considered his major achievement.

Deruet, Claude 1588–1660
French history painter, portraitist and decorator. He worked both for Cardinal Richelieu and for the ducal court of Lorraine at Nancy, specializing in portraits and decorative designs, but little of his vast output survives. His best-known works are four large canvases of *The Four Elements* (Orléans, Musée des Beaux-Arts), executed for Richelieu. These show his style to have been formally somewhat similar to that of Callot, but without his brilliance or incisiveness.

Deshays, Jean-Baptiste 1721–65
French history painter. He was trained by Restout and strongly influenced by Boucher, whose daughter he married. He studied in Italy in the 1750s and on his return to France was acclaimed by Diderot and others as the leading painter of the day, his *Martyrdom of St Andrew* (Rouen, Musée) causing a sensation at the 1759 Salon. It is now hard to appreciate why his competent late Baroque style should have won such lavish praise.

Desiderio da Settignano
*c.*1430–64
Florentine sculptor, trained by Bernardo Rossellino. Like the Rossellino brothers he was influenced by the gentler aspects of Donatello's style. His major commission, the tomb for Carlo Marsuppini, Chancellor of Florence (*c.*1453, Florence, S. Croce), is indebted to this and to Bernardino Rossellino's Bruni tomb. The subtle delicacy of his marble technique and his sensitivity to individual expression characterize his portrait busts, reliefs (*The Virgin and Child*, *c.*1455–60, Philadelphia, Museum of Art) and free-standing figures (such as the angels of his Tabernacle in S. Lorenzo, Florence, *c.*1460). Assessment of his stylistic development is made difficult by a lack of firmly dated work. See vol. 1 p. *200*; vol. 2 pp. **114–115**

Desiderius, Abbot of Montecassino 1058–87
Italian churchman, one of the outstanding medieval patrons of the arts. He was Abbot of Montecassino in southern Italy, and glorified the Abbey church (destroyed World War II) with bronze doors and other artefacts commissioned from Constantinople. He also summoned Byzantine artists to decorate the church and train his monks in their arts. Montecassino manuscripts are the only evidence of the local style, though the Byzantine-influenced murals of nearby S. Angelo in Formis, where Desiderius is portrayed, may have reflected Montecassino's murals. The manuscripts show strong Byzantine and Early Christian influence.

Despiau, Charles 1874–1946
French sculptor. He collaborated with Rodin, 1907–14, but his best works, such as *Paulette* (1907, Paris, Musée d'Art Moderne), are sensitive female portraits, almost classical in their restraint and far from Rodin's work.

Desportes, Alexandre-François
1661–1743
French painter of still-life and hunting scenes. He painted portraits at the Polish court, 1695, but on his return to France gained royal patronage as a painter of hunts and still life with game, working in a rich painterly style derived from Snyders. Like his main rival, Oudry, he worked for the Gobelins tapestry factory. He produced a remarkable series of landscape studies for the backgrounds of his hunts which prefigure the work of the 19th century, and the splendid *Self-portrait as a huntsman* has imposing details of both still life and landscape.

Detaille, (Jean-Baptiste-) Edouard 1848–1912
French painter, whose patriotic paintings with exact military details were much appreciated after France's defeat in the Franco-Prussian War. He studied under Meissonier and *The dream* (1888, Paris, Musée de l'Armée) has all the precision and finish of the master. He also did an immense fresco in the Panthéon, Paris, *The ride to glory* (1905).

Detroy, Jean-François 1679–1752
French painter of history and genre. In 1706 he returned from study in Italy and had already established a successful career when he came into rivalry with Lemoyne, who eventually became Premier Peintre du Roi while Detroy had to be content with the Directorship of the French Academy in Rome (1738). *Time unveiling Truth* (1733, London, NG) is a fine example of the cool tones and lively rhythms of his large-scale work. More to modern taste are his scenes of elegant social life (*The hunt breakfast*, 1737, London, Wallace Coll.) and the lively sketches (example in the National Gallery, London) for the Gobelins tapestries of *Jason and Medea* (1748).

Deutsch, Niklaus Manuel 1484–1530
Swiss painter, printmaker, designer of stained glass, poet and politician. He was born and worked in Berne. In 1516 and in 1522 he fought as a soldier in Italy. He painted large, colourful works on both religious and classical themes; typical is his *Judgment of Paris* (c.1525, Basel, Öffentliche Kunstsammlung), in which he emphasizes the elaborate head-dresses adorning the somewhat flattened figures.

Devis, Arthur 1711–87
British portrait painter, a leading exponent of the CONVERSATION PIECE. Especially favoured by "first-generation" owners of property, Devis' pictures, such as *The James family* (1751, London, Tate) are of great interest as social documents. His style was conservative and he was not very highly regarded in his own day, but has recently become popular. He became President of the Free Society of Artists in 1768, the year in which the majority of progressive painters joined the newly-founded Royal Academy. Other members of his family were also artists. See vol. 2 p. **245**

Dewasne, Jean born 1921
French artist. First a sculptor, he later turned to abstract painting in the style of Vasarély and Herbin. The large murals for the ice stadium at Grenoble are good examples of his work. He has produced "anti-sculptures" with parts of car bodies covered with broad camouflage patterns, and is also an active architect.

De Wint, Peter 1784–1849
English landscape painter of Dutch extraction, a prominent watercolourist of the early 19th century. Many of his works are of the flat Lincolnshire countryside, which lent itself to his preferred format of great width in comparison to height (*Landscape with harvesters and storm cloud*, c.1820, London, BM).

Dexel, Walter 1890–1973
German painter and writer on art. His work in Munich (1910–14) combined Cubist geometric forms and expressive colours. Through contact with van Doesburg (1921–23) and the Bauhaus artists (1919–25) he turned to CONSTRUCTIVISM, as in *Figuration IX* (1923, Duisburg, Lehmbruck Museum).

Diaz de la Peña, Narcisse Virgile 1807–76
French painter of the BARBIZON school. Influenced by Romantic taste for idyllic pastorals, Diaz's early paintings of nymphs and bathers, strongly reminiscent of the Rococo, recall his beginnings as a porcelain painter. In 1837 he met Théodore Rousseau, a formative influence. Diaz's rich and flickering use of pigment (*Descent of the Bohemians*, 1844, Paris, Louvre) was taken up by Monticelli and Renoir. See vol. 3 p. **93**

Dibbets, Jan born 1941
Dutch artist. He has worked as a painter and draughtsman and produced multiples, but is best known as a CONCEPTUAL artist, particularly for his "perspective correction" photographs, which show areas of grass or sand with lines superimposed to correct any illusion of recession.

Dickinson, Edwin 1891–1978
American painter, who combined an academic style with enigmatic subject matter. The almost grisaille *The fossil hunters* (1926–28, New York, Whitney) has a crowded, sculpturesque atmosphere reminiscent of Baroque *chiaroscuro* effects. He often juxtaposes fragmented shapes in a disquieting mélange. His portraits are more naturalistic.

Dickinson, Preston 1891–1930
American painter. He studied in Paris, where he was influenced by the work of Cézanne and the Fauves' use of colour. In the early 1920s he became associated with the PRECISIONISTS and produced simplified and precise renderings of industrial landscapes. Later works are more personal and richly coloured (*Still life with a yellow-green chair*, 1928, Ohio, Columbus Gallery of Fine Art).

Diderot, Denis 1713–84
French philosopher, dramatist and art critic. He is best known as the editor of the great *Encyclopaedia* (1751–72), which did more than any other work to shape the spirit of rationalism of the 18th century, and contains many interesting articles on artistic topics by Diderot and others (Falconet wrote on sculpture). Diderot's reviews of the Salons of 1759–71, 1775 and 1781 are the foundation of modern art criticism. In them he tried to promote a new seriousness of subject and style to replace the alleged frivolity of Rococo art. See vol. 2 pp. 240, **245**

Diebenkorn, Richard born 1922
American painter. He developed his own style of abstract painting in response to the work of Still and Rothko, fellow-teachers at the Californian School of Fine Arts, where he worked in the 1940s. Subsequently he has alternated between abstract and figurative work but has always used simplified areas of colour and gestural brushwork. In 1967 he began a series of abstracts entitled *Ocean Park*, the name of a coastal area west of Los Angeles. The colours and worked surfaces of these paintings are highly evocative of the open spaces and shaded streets of the district. See vol. 3 p. **251**

Diehl, Hans-Jürgen born 1940
West German painter. Although he paints with photographic realism, his compositions are made up of fragments, invested with symbolic meanings (*The redirected student*, 1968, West Berlin, Neue Nationalgalerie). Eroticism and dehumanization are prevalent themes.

Diepenbeck, Abraham van 1596–1675
Flemish painter and engraver. He

began his career as a glass-painter (there are windows by him in Antwerp Cathedral) and turned to painting altarpieces in about 1630. Many paintings have been attributed to him, but usually on insecure grounds, and his activity in this field remains unclear. His importance as an engraver, however, is beyond question, for as a designer of book illustrations in 17th-century Flanders he was second only to Rubens, by whom he was strongly influenced. His best-known prints are the illustrations to the 1st Duke of Newcastle's treatise on horsemanship, published in 1675.

Dietz, Ferdinand see TIETZ

Diller, Burgoyne 1906–65
American abstract painter and sculptor. In the early 1930s he became aware of Hans Hofmann's theories on abstract compositional balance. His subsequent non-objective style in both painting and sculpture was heavily influenced by Mondrian in its restriction to rectangular vertical-horizontal elements. Works such as *Composition* (1942, New York, MOMA), however, diverge from Mondrian in their simple, free-floating shapes.

Dine, Jim born 1935
American painter and printmaker often associated with POP art. He was a leading organizer of Happenings, 1959–60, and an early creator of Environments. In the early 1960s he began to attach real objects to his canvases, thus establishing a visual dialogue between the concreteness of clothing, tools and household appliances and the energetically painted setting. His wit comes to the fore in juxtapositions which create visual puns, in the aggrandizing of common objects and in the deliberate confusion of sexual and mechanical elements. Since the mid-1970s he has focused increasingly on technique; in a recent series of paintings, he executes a single image on a large scale, employing various compositional devices and colour combinations. He is a masterly printmaker and draughtsman. See vol. 3 pp. **239**, 243

Dioskourides active 1st century BC
Greek mosaic artist active in Southern Italy. He was responsible for a number of signed mosaic panels at Pompeii depicting musicians and old women. *Three street musicians* (Naples, Museo Nazionale) is lively, realistic and finely detailed, and seems to copy a Hellenistic painting. See vol. 2 p. 45

Diptych see TRIPTYCH

Divisionism
Both an alternative term for the technique of POINTILLISM, and a title for Italian Neo-Impressionism. This flourished initially in Lombardy and Piedmont, 1891–1907, then spread to Rome, while a second generation of northern Divisionists was being promoted in Milan in the first decade of the 20th century. Among the first principal exponents were Pellizza da Volpedo and Segantini. They were inspired by the same optical texts as the French Neo-Impressionists but had a minimal knowledge of the latter's works and a far less rigorous application of their scientific principles. They sought to capture the phenomenon of light by juxtaposing pure and complementary colours which were separately applied. The principal Divisionists were influenced by the SCAPIGLIATI's impressionistic brush-strokes yet each evolved a highly personal style, and they never organized a joint exhibition. Their subject matter

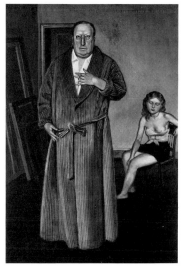
Derain: Portrait by Balthus, 1936. New York, MOMA, Lillie P. Bliss Bequest

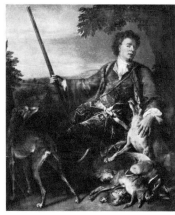
Desportes: *Self-portrait as a huntsman*, 1699. Paris, Louvre (Mansell)

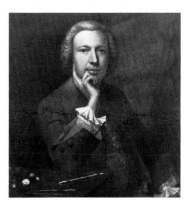
Devis: Self-portrait, c.1750. Preston, Harris Museum and Art Gallery

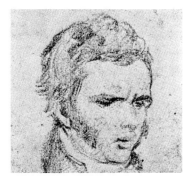
De Wint: Self-portrait drawing, 1810–20. Lincoln, The Usher Art Gallery

was typically Symbolist and Realist, including works demonstrating social concern. Only Segantini was acknowledged internationally. The Futurists, particularly Balla and Boccioni, evolved to some extent out of a Divisionist experience, and echoes of the movement were felt well into the 1920s.

Dix, Otto 1891–1969
German painter and graphic artist, a forceful exponent of the "ugly realism" characteristic of the socially and politically committed approach adopted by some NEUE SACHLICHKEIT painters. In 1920 he contributed a series of paintings of war cripples to the 1st International Dada Fair in Berlin in which collage elements were combined with an aggressive distortion of the figures to create a vehement anti-war statement. An example is *Prague Street (Dedicated to my contemporaries)*, now in the Städtisches Museum, Stuttgart. His other recurrent theme at the time was provided by prostitutes, seen as symbols of society's callousness and moral decadence. He was a brilliant portraitist, merciless in his analysis of character, as in his portrait of the journalist *Sylvia von Harden* (1926, Paris, Musée d'Art Moderne). The work which most completely expresses his vision is perhaps the triptych *The city* (1927–28, Stuttgart, Staatsgalerie), in which he juxtaposed the mythical image of Weimar Germany, symbolized by the hectic gaiety of the jazz club, with the humiliation meted out to the poor and exploited members of that society, symbolized by war cripples and prostitutes. Expressionist distortion is combined with the luminous colours of medieval painting and highly realistic attention to texture and detail. Dix's powers as a graphic artist were most forcefully demonstrated in the series of 50 etchings *The War*, 1923–24. He was forbidden to exhibit by the Nazis, who included his work in their exhibition of Degenerate Art. After World War II he worked in seclusion at Hemmenhofen. See vol. 1 p. *31*; vol. 3 pp. **194–195**

Dobell, Sir William 1899–1970
Australian painter. He studied in London and at The Hague, and on his return to Australia received wide recognition following a court case about his portrait of *Joshua Smith* (1943, Adelaide, Sir Edward Hayward coll.), since damaged beyond repair. The subject was distorted to reveal a creature part-ghost, part-monster. *Mrs South Kensington* (1937, Sydney, NG of New South Wales) shows his mature style, with its Impressionistic brushwork used to caricature in a manner strongly influenced by Hogarth, Daumier and Sickert. Subsequent more academic paintings reveal a loss of confidence.

Dobson, William 1610–46
The greatest English painter of the 17th century. Sixty portraits by him are known, all of royalist sitters, few dated, but all painted in London or Oxford between 1642 and his early death from dissipation in 1646. These lack the elegance of van Dyck, and are more robust in temperament, with rich Venetian colouring and rough impastoed paint, often on coarse canvas. He favoured the half-length with hands (full-lengths are rare), and often included symbolic sculptural reliefs in allusion to his sitter's interests, as in his *Endymion Porter* (London, Tate). See vol. 2 p. **207**

Dobuzhinsky, Mstislav Valeryanovich 1875–1957
Russian painter and theatrical de-

signer. He was a member of the WORLD OF ART group, but diverged from it in his realistic portrayal of the modern city. *Hairdresser's window* (1906, Moscow, Tretyakov Gallery) introduces into his painting the sinister note which characterized his political cartoons for the 1905 Revolution. There are good examples of his set and costume designs in the Victoria and Albert Museum, London.

Doesburg, Theo van (Christian Emil Maries Küpper) 1883–1931
Dutch painter, architect and writer, a major proponent of DE STIJL. His early naturalistic style was gradually replaced by Fauvist and Expressionist works and then by Cubism. In 1915 he met Mondrian and, influenced by him and van der Leck, began to paint his first abstractions; an example is *The cow* (1916–17, New York, MOMA). By 1918 he was painting geometric abstract works. In 1917, in collaboration with Mondrian, he founded the magazine *De Stijl*, which he continued to produce until his death. He was a brilliant polemicist and, as editor of the magazine, played a central role in the dissemination and discussion of abstract art, to which he was totally committed, throughout Europe. His geometric planar paintings were replaced by the introduction of diagonal elements in 1924–25 (*Counter-composition in dissonances no. XVI*, 1925, The Hague, Gemeentemuseum), at which time he had settled finally in Paris. See vol. 3 pp. **186–187**

Doidalsas of Bithynia
active 3rd century BC
Hellenistic sculptor, responsible for the figure of *Aphrodite washing herself* preserved in many Roman marble copies and statuettes (example, Rome, Museo Nazionale). These copies suggest an original remarkable in its compositional sophistication and delicate intimacy.

Dolci, Carlo 1616–86
One of the leading Florentine Baroque painters. He was intensely and neurotically absorbed in religion, and painted mainly devotional works marked by sweet colouring and enamel-smooth handling. These won him an international reputation in his lifetime, but today usually appear merely sickly. The impressive and very precocious portrait of *Fra Arnolfo dei Bardi* (1632, Florence, Pitti) and a fine *Self-portrait* in the Uffizi, Florence, show where his real talent lay.

Domela, César born 1900
Dutch painter and graphic artist. In 1924 he met Mondrian and van Doesburg in Paris and began his first NEO-PLASTIC works. In 1925 he introduced a diagonal element into his paintings, and in 1929 made his first Neo-plastic relief. *Neo-plastic lozenge composition no. 10* (1930, The Hague, Gemeentemuseum) and others used a variety of materials including metal, glass, brass, plexiglass and plastics. His work was published in *De Stijl* and in *Cercle et Carré*.

Domenichino
(Domenico Zampieri) 1581–1641
Bolognese painter, the favourite pupil of Annibale Carracci and one of his most important followers. He trained with Calvaert and in the Carracci academy before going in 1602 to Rome, where he assisted Annibale in the Farnese Gallery. In the second decade of the century he became the leading painter in Rome, the fresco cycle on *The life of St Cecilia* (1611–14) in S. Luigi dei Francesi being the finest example from this period of the

dignified classicism which deeply impressed Poussin. Domenichino's popularity waned in the 1620s, even though his superb pendentives of *The four evangelists* in S. Andrea della Valle (1624–28) showed that he could work convincingly in the Baroque style then coming to the fore. In the 1630s he worked mainly in Naples (frescos and altarpieces in the Cathedral), where hostile local artists were jealous of his success. Domenichino, like Annibale, was a pioneer of ideal landscape painting and was influential on Claude, especially in his sense of scale (compare Domenichino's *Landscape with Tobias and the Angel*, c.1615, with Claude's *Landscape with Hagar and the Angel*, 1646, both London, NG). He was also a fine portrait painter (*Monsignor Agucchi*, c.1610, York, City Art Gallery) and a splendid draughtsman, the finest collection of his drawings being in the Royal Library at Windsor Castle. Domenichino's reputation stood very high in the 18th century, when his *Last communion of St Jerome* (1614, Vatican) was considered one of the supreme masterpieces of painting, but later plummeted with those of other Bolognese painters such as Reni. See vol. 2 pp. **185;** *186*

Domenico del Barbiere (called Dominique Florentin) 1506–1565/75
Florentine painter, sculptor, architect and engraver who went to France with Rosso in 1530 and spent the rest of his life there. He worked at Fontainebleau in the 1530s and in 1541 settled in Troyes, where he had a successful career as a sculptor for churches. In about 1560 he was given the commission for the urn and base of the monument for the heart of Henri II (Paris, Louvre). Primaticcio designed the monument and Pilon sculpted the figures. His sculptural style combines Florentine classicism with certain Mannerist characteristics and his engravings show great verve.

Domenico di Bartolo c.1400–47
Sienese painter, perhaps trained by Taddeo di Bartolo. Almost alone among 15th-century Sienese painters, he was deeply affected by the sculptural modelling of Masaccio, though his drapery style reflects Jacopo della Quercia. His monumental figures remain rather cold and distant (*Madonna and Child before a rose-hedge*, 1437, Philadelphia, Museum of Art). He and Vecchietta painted the major surviving Sienese fresco cycle of the century, the history of the hospital in the Ospedale alla Scala (1441–44), remarkable at such a date for its genre detail and well-articulated nudes.

Domenico Veneziano died 1461
Italian painter of Venetian origin, active in Florence in the mid-15th century. He probably received his early training in Verona, where Pisanello's decorative International Gothic style was dominant. He began his most important commission, the fresco scenes of *The life of the Virgin* at S. Egidio in Florence, in 1439. This is now lost and his greatest surviving work is the highly original St Lucy altarpiece (c.1445). The central panel is in the Uffizi, Florence, and predella panels are in Cambridge (Fitzwilliam), Washington (NG) and West Berlin (Staatliche Museen). The solidity of the figures and their extremely carefully lit and constructed perspectival setting are reconciled with a strong surface pattern. Like his contemporary Castagno, he was strongly influenced by Donatello, but unlike Castagno used soft, bright, atmospheric pastel colours. He influenced Vecchietta, Baldovinetti, Pesellino and,

above all, Piero della Francesca, his assistant at S. Egidio. See vol. 2 p. **107**

Dominguez, Oscar 1906–58
Spanish painter, sculptor and graphic artist. Self-taught, he moved to Paris in 1934 and joined the Surrealists in 1935. His early style, reminiscent of Dali, was replaced by "automatic" pictures suggesting exotic landscapes, executed in the DECALCOMANIA process, which he is said to have invented. Later work incorporated technological objects in bizarre settings in the manner of Ernst.

Domoto, Hisao born 1928
Japanese painter and sculptor. He worked in Paris, 1952–65, and joined the INFORMAL art movement. Besides painting in this style he has produced aluminium sculptures such as *Solution of continuity*, 57 (1963, artist's coll.). He has since developed a more expansive organically geometric abstract art.

Donatello
(Donato di Niccolò) 1386–1466
Florentine sculptor, one of the greatest and most influential Italian artists of the 15th century. After training in the Florence Cathedral workshop and under Ghiberti, he received his first known commission in 1408. From then until 1436, in a series of works for the Cathedral and for the niches of Orsanmichele, he developed an increasingly expressive, monumental, emotionally charged style in which he gradually perfected the articulation and structure of his figures. These statues include the seated *St John the Evangelist*, 1408–15, for the Cathedral façade (now Cathedral Museum), the *St George*, finished 1417 (now Bargello), and the *St Mark*, c.1413, for Orsanmichele, and five prophets for the Cathedral campanile (now Cathedral Museum), including the famous "*Zuccone*", 1423–25, and "*Jeremiah*", 1427–35. The relief beneath the *St George* shows the earliest use of the technique of *stiacciato*, "like drawing in marble", which he invented. There are classical references to be found in these works, and Donatello's study of the Antique certainly assisted his dynamic *contrapposto*, but he was always extremely free in his use of classical sources—much freer than Ghiberti or Nanni di Banco. In the 1420s, in partnership with Michelozzo, he produced the Monument to Anti-Pope John XXIII (c.1425–27) in the Baptistery, which was extremely influential on tomb design; the slightly later "*Cavalcanti Annunciation*" (c.1428–33) in S. Croce and the Cantoria (Singing Gallery) for Florence Cathedral (1433–39, now Cathedral Museum), reveal exuberant *putti* and a profusion of antique architectural ornament—Donatello's "picturesque classicism", developed during a sojourn in Rome, 1430–32. In 1443 Donatello migrated to Padua. There he produced in bronze the first life-size triumphal equestrian statue since antiquity, *Gattemelata*, in the Piazza del Santo, 1443–47, and the now incorrectly re-assembled High Altar of the Santo itself (1446–50). The altar's reliefs, in particular, with their violent perspectival vistas and animated, crowded figures, had a profound influence on artists from Mantegna to Pacher, and the Paduan production of classicizing statuettes (by Riccio and Antico) had its origins in Donatello's residence. The famous bronze *David* (Florence, Bargello) is variously dated between 1430 and 1460 and, like the multiple-viewpoint *Judith and Holofernes* (c.1456–60, Piazza della Signoria), might have been produced for

the Medici. The wooden *Mary Magdalen*, c. 1456, in Florence Baptistery, has a gaunt anguish unparalleled in the 15th century. Donatello's last works, two bronze pulpits, c. 1460–70, in S. Lorenzo, are sublimely disturbing, and no other sculptor before Michelangelo matched such expressive power. See vol. 2 pp. **102–103,** *105, 106, 107, 120, 128*

Dongen, Kees van (Cornelius Theodorus Marie) 1877–1968
Dutch painter. He moved to Paris in 1897 and his early work was strongly influenced by the Impressionists, notably Monet. Between 1900 and 1907 he made several trips to Holland, where he mainly painted landscapes. By about 1905 he had abandoned his earlier style and was gradually introducing bolder, broader brush-strokes and the heightened colour and impasto paint of Fauvism. He particularly favoured nudes and portraits of women, as in *Women on the balcony* (1910, St-Tropez, Musée de l'Annonciade). After 1916 he was principally a painter of Parisian society.

Dong Qichang 1555–1636
Chinese painter, poet, calligrapher and, above all, critic of painting. He was born into a major branch of a distinguished Shanghai official family and became an important Ming statesman. In his later years he employed his immense prestige to promulgate the theory of Northern and Southern schools of landscape painting. These were distinctions not of geography but between the former group of technically advanced but morally deficient professionals, and the latter of amateur scholars of high character. Reduced by his followers to a "gentlemen" versus "players" distinction, this theory dominated all subsequent Chinese ideas of landsape painting. Similarly, Dong's stress on close study of the spirit of Song and Yuan masters tended to degenerate into facile copying and lead to an undistinguished, generalized LITERATI style. His own landscapes depend on a simple composition, which at its best is inspired more by the spirit than the letter of earlier painting, as in a *Landscape* after the 10th-century artist Guo Zhongshu (1599, Stockholm, National Museum). His entire surviving output consists of landscapes, the "scholar's" subject matter. His reputation in his own day spread as far as Japan, and he proclaimed himself the greatest painter since Zhao Mengfu.

Dong Yuan active late 10th century
Chinese painter. He worked at the southern Tang court of Li Yu, and was a key figure in the development of landscape painting towards its pre-eminent position among the arts of China. Retrospectively classed by the connoisseur Dong Qichang as a great master of the "amateur" monochrome landscape style he was also famous for richly coloured landscapes, designed to be viewed from a distance. Most of the work now bearing his name, much of which may consist of copies, is in the form of monumental monochrome landscapes, for example *Clear weather in the valley* (12th-13th century, Boston, MFA).

Donner, Georg Raphael
1693–1741
Austrian Baroque sculptor. He was exceptional in Austria for working in stone and in lead, rather than in wood, and also for his academic enthusiasm for the human body, which gives some of his highly finished works an almost Neoclassical air. His masterpieces are the lead groups of *St Martin and the beggar*

(c. 1735, Bratislava Cathedral) and the *Rivers* from the Mehlmarkt Fountain in Vienna (1737–39, Vienna, Österreichisches Barockmuseum).

Dorazio, Piero born 1927
Italian painter. He studied architecture and classics in Rome and Paris in the 1940s and began painting after he met Prampolini and Severini and became interested in early Futurism. In 1947 he turned to abstraction, producing works of lyrical form and colour, with suggestions of landscape imagery. Apart from painting he has worked in lithography, tapestry and stage design. He has travelled widely and in the 1960s taught at the University of Pennsylvania.

Doré, (Paul) Gustave 1832–83
French book illustrator, painter and sculptor. Doré began his career as a caricaturist on *Le Journal pour Rire*. A prodigious artist, he produced 56 sculptures (the most notable the memorial to Alexandre Dumas, erected 1883, Paris, Place Malesherbes) and large-scale religious and historical paintings, but his graphic work was more successful. Illustrations to Rabelais and Balzac (1855) established his reputation with their romantic style characterized by love of the grotesque, abundance of detail and strong chiaroscuro reminiscent of Goya's graphic work. His masterpiece was his realistic depiction of the London slums (1872), which was even used as evidence in Government reports. He employed woodcutters to do his work at speed and illustrated over 200 books, so the quality of his engravings is often poor. Van Gogh admired his work and his narrative literary approach appealed to the Symbolists and Surrealists.

Dossi, Dosso (Giovanni Luteri) c. 1490–1542
Italian painter, who worked for the Dukes of Ferrara for most of his career. He painted all types of picture—devotional, mythological and portraits—in a style dependent on the lyrical mode of Giorgione and Titian. Landscape was a major element in his work, especially in his mythologies, where there is a charming, almost rococo inventiveness and often a feeling of the exotic, heightened by a resonant, almost arbitrary, use of colour. Dosso probably visited Rome in about 1520, and his later works reveal the impact of contemporary Roman painting, especially Michelangelo's work, as in *Melissa* (c. 1523, Rome, Borghese Gallery), where classicizing grandeur of form is matched by opulence of texture and colour. His brother **Battista** (c. 1497–1548), working in a similar manner, assisted Dosso and took over his workshop after his death. Dosso's work was, however, too idiosyncratic to find much following. See vol. 2 p. **149**

Dou, Gerrit 1613–75
Dutch genre painter, born and active in Leyden. In 1628 he became Rembrandt's first pupil and tried to emulate his master's use of chiaroscuro and draughtsmanship. *The blind Tobit and his wife Anna* (c. 1630, London, NG) is usually thought to be a work of collaboration between them. Dou only discovered his own style when Rembrandt left for Amsterdam in 1631. He developed an extremely polished technique which he used to depict a wide range of subject matter, particularly domestic interiors, with minute attention to detail, sometimes working with a magnifying glass. He was obsessive about materials and tools (he made his own brushes), and never began work before he was sure the

dust had settled in his studio. The works on which he expended such care earned him a fortune, and his paintings fetched massive sums during the 18th and early 19th centuries. Metsu and Schalken were among his pupils, and he influenced Dutch painters working in the detailed *fijnschilder* (fine painter) tradition for two centuries. See vol. 2 p. **227**

Doughty, Thomas 1793–1856
American painter and lithographer. Born in Philadelphia, he taught himself painting and was soon noted for his tranquil views of the Pennsylvania rivers and mountains, among the earliest representations of the American landscape (*A river glimpse*, after 1820, New York, Metropolitan). In the 1820s and 1830s he travelled in Europe and became widely known, partly through numerous engravings of his work. The years 1839–40 were spent at Newburgh by the Hudson River, where his majestic light-filled landscapes anticipated the achievement of the HUDSON RIVER school.

Douris c. 500–470 BC
Greek RED-FIGURE vase-painter from Athens, to whom over 200 vases have been attributed. An accomplished draughtsman with a fine feeling for detail, he painted mainly scenes of revelry, rhythmically composed, animated, but serene. There are, however, some mythological scenes, notably the striking group of *Jason, Medea and the dragon* on a cup in the Vatican.

Dove, Arthur Garfield 1880–1946
American painter, a pioneer of abstract art. He was trained as a commercial illustrator and studied in Paris, 1907–09. After his return to the USA he began working on an astonishing series of abstractions, often based on natural forms, which were shown at Stieglitz's 291 Gallery (*Nature symbolized no. 2*, 1914, Chicago Art Institute). His development towards abstraction was contemporary with Kandinsky's. During the 1920s he worked in collage, exploring the tactile qualities of objects as well as their associations. Many of his paintings were bought by his patron Duncan Phillips and are now in the Phillips Collection, Washington. See vol. 3 p. 205

Dreier, Katherine S. 1877–1952
American painter. As a result of the Armory Show Dreier changed from being an academic painter to an ardent supporter of modern trends. She became friendly with Duchamp and her *Abstract portrait* of him (1918, New York, MOMA) is her best-known work. She was cofounder, with Duchamp and Man Ray, of the SOCIÉTÉ ANONYME. She also lectured extensively on modern art.

Drôlerie
A humorous or comic picture. The term is also used to describe the capricious or grotesque drawings which appear in the margins of medieval manuscripts.

Drouais, François-Hubert 1727–75
French portrait painter. He was the son of a successful miniature and pastel portraitist, **Hubert** (1699–1767), and trained under Carle van Loo and Boucher, rapidly establishing himself as a fashionable court painter in succession to Nattier, his father-in-law. He popularized the new sentimental naturalism in his paintings of aristocratic children in rustic disguise, but his work suffers from an unadventurous handling of paint. The portrait of the elderly *Mme de Pompadour* (1763, London, NG) is his best-known work. See vol. 2 p. **242**

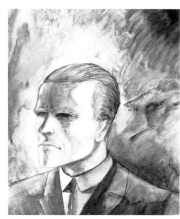
Dix: Self-portrait watercolour, 1922. New York, MOMA, Gift of Richard L. Feigen

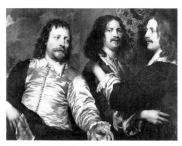
Dobson: *Sir Charles Cotterell, Sir Balthazar Gerbier and the artist* (centre), c. 1643. Alnwick Castle, Duke of Northumberland coll.

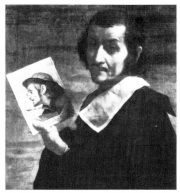
Dolci: Self-portrait, 1674. Florence, Uffizi (Alinari)

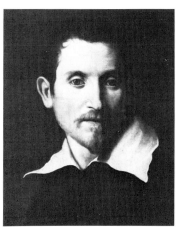
Domenichino: Self-portrait, c. 1620–30. Florence, Galleria Pitti (Mansell)

Drypoint
Direct ENGRAVING technique. A drypoint line, drawn on to a metal plate with a hard steel or diamond point, retains a characteristic fuzziness, deriving from the slightly raised edge thrown up beside the groove made by the point: this is known as the burr, which retains ink. The burr is soon crushed by the pressure of printing, so the number of impressions is necessarily limited. Drypoint is often used—notably by Rembrandt—after etching or engraving to strengthen dark points; areas of dense tone can be built up by repeated scorings. See vol. 1 p. 167

Drysdale, Sir George Russell
born 1912
Australian painter. Born in England, he went to Australia as a child, studied in Melbourne and then in London and Paris. From 1940 he settled in Sydney and pioneered outback Australia as subject material. Early works were stimulated by modern French artists, but later the wartime pictures of Sutherland and Piper encouraged him to express a sense of tragedy and desolation. His series of illustrations for the *Sydney Morning Herald* on the drought of 1944 set the tone for his subsequent work. From the 1950s, he has used aboriginal life as an important theme (*Mullalonah tank*, 1953, Adelaide, NG of South Australia).

Dubois, Ambroise 1542/43–1614
French painter, with Dubreuil and Fréminet one of the leading members of the second school of Fontainebleau. He was born in Antwerp, but seems to have moved to France as a youth, and he became a French citizen in 1601. His most important work was executed at Fontainebleau; his masterpiece, the decoration of the Gallery of Diana, was destroyed in the 19th century and is known only through copies and descriptions, but paintings on the theme of *Theagenes and Chariclea* survive in the Oval Room. Dubois's elaborate style is characterized by rich architectural backgrounds and very elongated figures.

Du Bois, Guy Pène 1884–1958
American painter and critic. Until about 1920 he was mainly a writer. He was a member of the publicity committee for the Armory Show. His paintings of this period are social comments influenced by his former teacher, Henri: *The doll and the monster* (1914, New York, Metropolitan), for example, is a satirical view of the carnality of the rich.

Dubreuil, Toussaint 1560/1–1602
French painter and decorator, one of the most important artists of the second school of Fontainebleau. Very little of his work is still in existence; decorations at Fontainebleau and the Louvre, Paris, have been destroyed, and of the 78 paintings he executed for the royal château of St-Germain-en-Laye, only one, *A sacrifice* (Louvre), survives. There are, however, a number of original drawings in the Louvre, and these, together with copies of other works, show that his style was much more restrained than was usual for his generation, with less distortion and elongation of figures, and to this extent he is a link between Primaticcio and Poussin.

Dubuffet, Jean born 1901
French painter. Born in Le Havre, he moved to Paris in 1918 to study painting, but almost totally abandoned his art between 1924 and 1942 to run the family wine business. When he returned to painting he revealed a determination to turn his back on "Fine Art", and soon provoked public outrage with townscapes of semi-abstract composition and naive figures (*View of Paris: The life of pleasure*, 1944, New York, Mr and Mrs D. Solinger coll.). He was fascinated by the art of children and psychotics, as the Surrealists were, but he went much further in seeking to emulate the naive directness of their scribblings. The "*Art Brut*" collection, begun in 1945, included work by primitives, lunatics, illiterates and children, anything uncontrived and without pretensions. He began, too, to explore mixed-media techniques, which involved building up rough surfaces with materials such as plaster, glue and asphalt. A number of themes have continued to obsess him—landscapes, cities and single human figures—and to inspire a great variety of bold, semi-abstract styles. More recently he has produced large sculptural works and has added to the numerous statements on his art which, with his paintings, have been highly influential in France. See vol. 1 p. *107*; vol. 3 p. **225**

Duca, Giacomo del
*c.*1520–after 1601
Sicilian sculptor and architect, active mainly in Rome. There he assisted Michelangelo on his tomb for Pope Julius II and on the Porta Pia, and Michelangelo's influence can be seen in Giacomo's tomb of Elena Savelli in S. Giovanni Laterano. He is more important as architect than sculptor, as he was the only one of Michelangelo's followers who went beyond superficial imitation. Most of his buildings in Sicily have been destroyed by earthquakes, but the dome of S. Maria di Loreto in Rome is a bizarre surviving masterpiece.

Duccio di Buoninsegna
active 1278–1318
The greatest painter of the Sienese school. Nothing is known of his training, and he is first recorded in 1278 painting cases for account books. In 1285 he was commissioned to paint a large Madonna for S. Maria Novella, Florence, which is now identified with "*The Rucellai Madonna*" (Florence, Uffizi). The only indisputable documented work which survives is his masterpiece, the two-sided *Maestà* of 1308–11 for the high altar of Siena Cathedral, most of which is in the Cathedral Museum. The front shows *The Virgin and Child enthroned* surrounded by angels and the patron saints of Siena; the back carries 26 small scenes of the Passion and Resurrection of Christ. Around the base ran one of the earliest recorded examples of a predella, which is now dispersed: three panels are in London (NG), four in Washington (NG), and others elsewhere. The *Maestà* is one of the largest and most beautiful panel paintings ever made in Italy, and contemporary chronicles describe the public holiday and procession that greeted its installation in 1311. Its impact comes primarily from its wonderful colouring and superb craftsmanship, but the lyrical emotion and grace of line with which Duccio invested Byzantine forms had a profound impact on Sienese painting for the following 200 years: Simone Martini and Barna da Siena are among the painters who are most clearly indebted to him. Duccio seems never to have worked in fresco, but there are numerous panel paintings that can confidently be attributed to him. The best of these are probably the three portable altarpieces (each a triptych and each showing *The Virgin and Child with saints*) in London (NG and Royal coll.) and Boston (MFA). Duccio occupies a position in the Sienese school similar to Giotto's in the Florentine. His paintings are much less three-dimensional than those of his great contemporary, but the exquisite sensitivity with which he represents human relationships marks a clear break from Byzantine traditions. His influence was felt as far afield as France, in the work of illuminators such as Pucelle. See vol. 2 p. **79**

Duchamp, Marcel 1887–1968
French artist and theorist, brother of Raymond Duchamp-Villon and half-brother of Jacques and Suzanne Villon. He is famous above all for *The bride stripped bare by her bachelors, even* (1915–23), now in the Philadelphia Museum of Art, as are almost all his works. Also known as "*The Large Glass*", this is a work of great iconographic and technical complexity. Painted on glass and divided into two horizontal zones, it makes witty use of mechanistic forms to express his sardonic vision of the frustrations of physical love. The upper half, featuring the "bride", grew out of the series of paintings including the notorious *Nude descending a staircase* (1911–12, Philadelphia), which he executed while closely associated with the SECTION D'OR group and in which he progressively moved away from Cubist style. The lower half of "bachelor apparatus", on the other hand, employed traditional linear perspective to incorporate his ensuing interest in "ready-mades" and included, for example, a coffee-grinder and a water-mill. Idiosyncratically he had, since 1912, been elevating such commonplace objects to the status of works of art, thereby cynically repudiating the traditional claims of art to beauty and significance. It appeared that after producing his masterpiece he had abandoned art for the intellectual rigours of chess, but at his death the existence was revealed of "*Etant donnés*" (Given that . . ., 1946–66, Philadelphia), a life-size mixed-media construction, to be viewed through a wooden door, which embodied a realistic and hence more disturbing statement of the erotic theme of "*The Large Glass*". His influence on Dada and Surrealism was immense and his approaches obviously prefigure Conceptual art. See vol 1 pp. *115*, *152–153*; vol. 3 pp. **168–169**, *180*, 246

Duchamp-Villon, Raymond
1876–1918
French sculptor, much admired in Parisian avantgarde circles before 1914. The brother of the painters Jacques Villon and Marcel Duchamp, he was closely involved with the SECTION D'OR group. He was on active service, 1914–18, and died of typhoid. His one masterpiece is *The horse* (1914, New York, MOMA); the inspiration of Boccioni's Futurist sculpture led him to a powerful fusion of mechanical and organic forms. See vol. 1 p. *69*; vol. 3 p. **178**

Dufresne, Charles 1876–1938
French painter and engraver. After World War I he painted in a style indebted to both Fauvism and Cubism, as in *Spahi attacked by a lion* (1919, London, Tate), a typically fantastic image set in an exotic landscape.

Dufresnoy, Charles-Alphonse
1611–68
French painter and writer on art. Between 1633 and 1656 he was in Italy copying works of the Italian Renaissance. His few surviving pictures are pastiches of the work of Nicolas Poussin, and he is chiefly remembered for his poems in Latin, *De Arte Graphica*, which interpret the doctrines of French academic classicism, inspired by Poussin.

Dufy, Raoul 1877–1953
French painter. He studied in Le Havre before going to Paris, where he was first influenced by Fauvism, as in *Posters at Trouville* (1906, Paris, Musée d'Art Moderne). In 1908, with Braque, he painted landscapes at L'Estaque that reveal the influence of Cézanne. Around 1910 he arrived at his characteristic and very distinctive style. In both oil and watercolour he painted race-meetings, fashionable resorts, flowers and landscapes, using bright, luminous colours and linear draughtsmanship to create charming and decorative effects (*Riders in the wood*, 1931, Paris, Musée d'Art Moderne). He also worked as a designer of mural schemes, tapestries and textiles. See vol. 3 pp. **142–143**

Dugento
Italian term (literally "two hundred") used of the 13th century—the 1200s.

Dughet, Gaspard (also called Gaspard Poussin) 1615–75
French landscape painter, draughtsman and etcher. He spent his whole career in Rome and at the age of 15 entered the studio of Nicolas Poussin, who married his sister. Dughet concentrated exclusively on landscapes, even in his frescos on *The history of the Carmelite Order* in S. Martino ai Monti (begun 1647). Apart from these, no works are dated, and his chronology is very difficult to establish. His style combined those of Poussin and Claude, being less heroic and severe than Poussin's, but more solid than Claude's and less concerned with effects of light. He also preferred a somewhat different—more rugged—type of scenery, and was particularly taken with waterfalls and cascades (*Waterfall at Tivoli*, Newcastle upon Tyne, Hatton Gallery). Dughet's style was widely imitated, and in the 18th century he was a revered figure in England, his paintings being used as models for gardens and parks and thus becoming an important element in the Picturesque movement. See vol. 2 p. **197**

Dujardin, Karel 1622–78
Dutch painter, born in Amsterdam. He was probably a pupil of Berchem, and, like him, went to Rome during the late 1640s. In 1650–52 he worked in France before returning to Amsterdam. He painted a variety of subjects including large religious works such as *The conversion of Saul* (1662, London, NG), but is best known for his Italianate landscapes in the tradition of Both and Berchem. Dujardin made no new contribution to the genre, but painted some of the finest examples of the type. The tiny *Italian landscape* (*c.*1652, Cambridge, Fitzwilliam) is so exquisite that in the 18th century it was known as "the Diamond"

Dumonstier (or Dumoustier)
Family of French portraitists who worked in the style of the Clouets. The eldest, **Geoffroy** (*c.*1510–60) was court painter to Francis I and Henri II and worked at Fontainebleau. His eldest son, **Etienne** (1540–1603), was painter to Henri II, Francis II and Henri III and IV. **Pierre** (*c.*1545–1610) and **Cosme** (*c.*1550–1605) were also sons of Geoffroy. The best-known of the family was Geoffroy's nephew **Daniel** (1574–1646), who continued the Clouet tradition into the middle of the 17th century. There were several other members of the family, but their individual oeuvres are generally not well defined.

Dunikowski, Xavery 1875–1964
Polish sculptor. After studying in Warsaw he spent the years 1914–20 in Paris. During World War II he was a prisoner at Auschwitz concentration camp. His sculptures are built up from simplified masses and in them he explores metaphysical themes. A favourite subject is that of motherhood, as in *Pregnant woman I* (1906–08, Warsaw, National Museum). He also sculpted highly regarded portraits.

Dunlap, William 1766–1839
American artist. He was a painter, engraver, playwright and theatrical manager, but is principally remembered as an art historian. His output varied from miniatures to dramatic biblical subjects reminiscent of West, with whom he had studied in London in 1784. He was librarian of the American Academy and a founder of the National Academy of Design, of which he became President. In 1834 he published his *History of the Rise and Progress of the Arts of Design in America*, a valuable source of information and anecdote on the lives of early American artists.

Dunoyer de Segonzac, André
1884–1974
French painter. His early work was influenced by Cubism but he is better known for his contribution to the realistic tendency in French painting in the 1920s. *Nude with a newspaper* (1922–23, London, Tate) typifies his powerfully expressive use of sombre earth colours applied with a palette knife. He later turned to translucent watercolour.

Dupré, Jules 1811–89
French landscape painter of the Barbizon school. Dupré visited England in 1833 and came under the influence of Constable. His work, consisting predominantly of seascapes, was boldly painted in thick impasto and evokes in mood the romanticism of nature. It has affinities with the innovatory painting of his friend, Théodore Rousseau.

Duquesnoy, François
(Il Fiammingo) 1594–1643
Flemish Baroque sculptor. From 1618 he worked in Rome, where he and Algardi were the leading sculptors, apart from Bernini. Like Algardi's, his style was more classical and restrained than Bernini's, showing the influence of his friend Poussin. Only two large-scale sculptures are known, but both are impressive and important works: *St Andrew* (1629–40), for one of the crossing piers in St Peter's, and *St Susanna* (1629–33, Rome, S. Maria di Loreto), praised by Bellori as a perfect blend of nature and the Antique and greatly admired throughout the 17th century. The rest of Duquesnoy's output consisted mainly of small bronzes, which were much imitated, but his popular fame rests on his charming *putti* (as on the tomb of Ferdinand van den Eynde, 1633–40, Rome, S. Maria dell' Anima). Louis XIII invited him to Paris to become court sculptor, but he died on the way. Duquesnoy's father and brother **Hieronymus** (Jerome) I (before 1570–1641) and **Hieronymus** II (1602–54), were also sculptors. His brother worked in Rome with François and introduced a subdued Baroque style into Flanders with his tomb of Bishop Anton Trest in Ghent Cathedral (c.1640–54, probably to his brother's designs), and with his series of *Apostles* in Brussels Cathedral (c.1644–46). He was executed by strangulation for committing sodomy in Brussels Cathedral.

Durand, Asher B. 1796–1886
American painter and engraver. He trained as an engraver, and made his reputation with his print after Trumbull's *Declaration of Independence*. Portraits, landscapes and banknote vignettes established him as one of the leading engravers in America, but during the 1830s he turned increasingly to painting, and especially, under the guidance of Cole, to landscape painting. Durand represented the more naturalistic strain of the HUDSON RIVER school and he stressed acute observation of detail. He studied in Europe, 1840–41, and returned to become known as the "father of American landscape painting" and the President of the National Academy of Design, of which he had been a founder in 1826. His best-known work is *Kindred spirits* (1849, New York Public Library), a memorial to Cole. See vol. 3 p. **69**

Dürer, Albrecht 1471–1528
German painter and printmaker, the greatest artist of the northern Renaissance. He was born in Nuremberg, the son of a goldsmith, and his earliest contacts were with men interested in the new learning of the Renaissance. After an apprenticeship first with his father and then with Wolgemut, he travelled to Colmar hoping to meet Schongauer (who had recently died) and then went to Venice (1494–95). On his journey across the Alps he made a series of outstanding landscape drawings and watercolours. In 1505–07 he returned to Venice and studied the work of the contemporary Venetian painters including Giovanni Bellini, whom he regarded very highly. *The festival of the rose garlands* (1506, Prague, National Gallery), which he painted in Venice, was intended to equal any Italian work in its brilliant colouring. Between the two Italian journeys he had established himself as the leading painter and graphic artist in Nuremberg. The *Self-portrait* of 1500 (Munich, Alte Pinakothek) shows the artist posed to resemble an image of Christ, self-assured and confident of his place in society. He published several albums of woodcuts—particularly innovatory was the Apocalypse of 1498—and also produced single engravings of religious or secular subjects, such as *Melancholia I* of 1514. These are of a more dense and subtle texture than had been seen before, moving away from the purely linear to create a range of tone similar to that of painting. Among his patrons was the Emperor Maximilian; in collaborating with other artists Dürer worked on *The Triumph* woodcuts in 1516–18 (published 1526) and on illustrations to the Emperor's prayerbook. In 1520–21 he travelled to the Netherlands, where he recorded his experience in words and sketches and was received as a great man. In his later years he was preoccupied with the advent of the Lutheran Reformation, to which his last painting, the monumental "*Four Apostles*" (1526, Munich, Alte Pinakothek) refers. In some respects he can be compared to his great Italian contemporary, Leonardo. He was fascinated by all aspects of nature and lavished exquisite care on watercolours of, for example, *A young hare* or *The piece of turf* (1502 and 1503, both Vienna, Albertina). Theoretical study also played a great part in his work and he wrote treatises on measurement and on human proportion. His prints were enormously influential, in Italy as well as northern Europe, and was the first artist of such stature to express himself primarily through engraving. See vol. 1 pp. *24, 32, 36, 69*; vol. 2 pp. **150–153**

Duveneck, Frank 1848–1919
American painter and sculptor of German origin. In 1870 he studied in Munich, where he was influenced by the realism of Leibl and his circle (*Whistling boy*, 1872, Cincinnati Art Museum). In 1875 he showed paintings at the Boston Arts Club which made his reputation, and he returned to Munich to set up a school. He became a major exponent of naturalism, painting in a bold, facile technique reminiscent of 17th-century masters such as Hals combined with the pictorial innovations of Manet.

Duvet, Jean 1485–1561/70
French engraver and goldsmith, one of the most individual artists of his time. His earliest dated engraving, an *Annunciation* of 1520, and other works of the same period, show such a deep understanding of High Renaissance design that it seems almost certain that he had visited Italy. His mature works are completely different in style, and his masterpieces, the 24 illustrations to the Apocalypse (published at Lyons in 1561), have a visionary intensity which looks forward to Blake, who probably knew Duvet's work. There are clear borrowings from Dürer in the Apocalypse series, but the arbitrary sense of scale and space, expressive distortions of the human figure and fantastic imagination are Duvet's own. Apart from the Apocalypse, Duvet's best-known work is his allegorical *Unicorn* series (probably 1540s) and he is sometimes known as the Master of the Unicorn. He lived mainly in Langres and Dijon, but possibly also in Geneva, where his widow is recorded in 1570.

Duyckinck family
Dutch-American family of artists active in New Amsterdam (New York). The founder of the dynasty was **Evert I** (1621–1702), a limner and glazier, who was born in Holland and went to America in 1638. He was followed by his son **Gerrit** (1660–1710), who also produced oil-paintings, and several other members of the family are recorded working in artistic professions until the end of the 18th century. The last of any significance was **Gerardus II** (1723–97), a great-grandson of Evert I. He was a teacher of painting on glass and of drawing. The family provide the best example of the importation of Dutch Baroque taste into the American colonies.

Duyster, Willem Cornelisz.
1599–1635
Dutch genre painter and portraitist. He is said to have been a pupil of his exact contemporary, Pieter Codde, who also specialized in small paintings of soldiers. Duyster's lively *Soldiers fighting over booty in a barn* (London, NG) is representative. He had the ability to characterize individuals and his portraits herald Terborch. His early death cut short a promising career. See vol. 2 p. 226

Dyce, William 1806–64
Scottish painter. Visits to Italy left him profoundly impressed by the work of Raphael and he met the NAZARENES and shared their interests, as can be seen in the simple bold style and seriousness of easel-paintings such as *The Madonna and Child* (1845, Royal coll.). He transmitted his ideas to the Pre-Raphaelite Brotherhood. In 1843 he competed for the commission to decorate the new Houses of Parliament with history paintings, and later completed several of these. He also executed frescos for the Prince Consort at Osborne and was a pioneer of state art education.

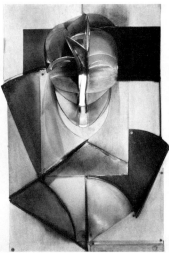
Duchamp: Portrait by Pevsner, 1926. New Haven, Yale University Art Gallery, Coll. Société Anonyme

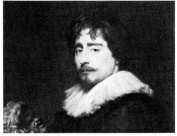
Duquesnoy, François: Portrait by van Dyck, c.1625. Brussels, Musées Royaux

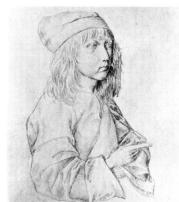
Dürer: Self-portrait drawing at 13 years old. Vienna, Albertina

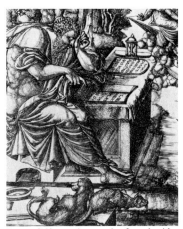
Duvet: Self-portrait engraving from the title-page to the Apocalypse. London, BM

Dyck, Sir Anthony van 1599–1641
The most important Flemish painter of the 17th century apart from Rubens. He trained first under van Balen, but there is no sign of his influence in van Dyck's early work, which was brilliantly precocious. In 1618 he became a member of the Antwerp painters' guild, and at about the same time worked as Rubens' assistant, but he was already active as an independent artist before this. Rubens had a powerful influence on him, but van Dyck's style was always less robust and more nervously sensitive. In 1621–28 he was in Italy, working chiefly in Genoa, where he achieved great success with his grand aristocratic portraits, the most spectacular of which is *Marchesa Elena Grimaldi* (*c.*1625, Washington, NG). The types and poses which he established here, based on Rubens' Genoese portraits, soon became the common property of court painters all over Europe, but few could approach van Dyck's dazzling brushwork or exquisite characterization. He worked in Antwerp again from 1628 to 1632, then at the invitation of Charles I went to England, where he had stayed briefly in 1621. Apart from short trips to the Continent, he remained in England for the rest of his life. He became the perfect court artist, admired by Charles (who knighted him) for his social graces as well as for his skills as a painter. There are 26 van Dycks in the Royal Collection (and many still in the great houses, notably Wilton, Wiltshire, for which they were painted), but the two greatest portraits of the King (both *c.*1638) are in the National Gallery, London, and the Louvre, Paris. Van Dyck also painted religious and mythological scenes, made some remarkably fresh landscape studies in watercolour (London, BM), and began a series of etchings of famous contemporaries, the *Iconography*, which was completed from his drawings and oil-sketches and published in 1645; but it is as one of the greatest of all portrait painters that he has achieved immortality. The effortless elegance and refinement with which he invested his sitters and his incomparable skill in painting rich materials became the model for society portraitists until the time of Sargent. See vol. 2 pp. **200–201, 206–207;** vol. 4 pp. *19, 33, 37, 59, 95*

Dyck, Floris van 1575–1651
Dutch painter, one of the earliest exponents of still life as in independent genre. He was active in Haarlem, where he entered the guild in 1610. His work, which is very rare, exploits a high viewpoint in order to "catalogue" clearly and accurately the objects on a laden table.

Eakins, Thomas 1844–1916
The greatest American painter of the 19th century. He was born in Philadelphia and spent most of his life there, apart from a period in Europe, 1866–70, when he studied with Gérôme in Paris and was deeply impressed by the works of Velazquez and Ribera which he saw in Spain. Uncompromising realism was the basis of his style, but he worked in two distinct manners. His portraits are Rembrandtesque in their subtle chiaroscuro and psychological penetration (*Mrs Edith Mahon*, 1904, Northampton, Mass., Smith College Museum of Art), but his outdoor scenes are strikingly modern and particularly American in their LUMINISM. Boating and bathing on the river were favourite themes and allowed Eakins to display his mastery of light effects (*Max Schmitt in a single scull*, 1871, New York, Metropolitan). In 1876 he began teaching at the Pennsylvania Academy, but was forced to resign in 1886 because he had allowed a class of students of mixed sexes to draw from a nude model. Scientific observation of the human body was one of the bases of Eakins' art (he used Muybridge's photographs in his lectures, and made small wax figures as preparatory studies for his paintings), and his interest in anatomy is reflected in his most celebrated work, *The Gross Clinic* (1875, Philadelphia, Jefferson Medical College). This painting, like his later *Agnew Clinic* (1889, Philadelphia, University of Pennsylvania) occasioned public disfavour because of its harrowingly realistic portrayal of dissection, and the latter part of Eakins' career was spent in neglect. He was, however, awarded some honours at the end of his life, and had considerable influence on the Ashcan school and other American realist painters of the early 20th century. A private income meant that he never had to compromise his vision by courting public favour. His comments on the paintings in the Prado could be applied to his own: "so strong so reasonable so free from every affectation. It stands out like nature itself". See vol. 1 pp. *44, 157*; vol 3 p. **124**

Earl, Ralph 1751–1801
One of the leading American artists of the 18th century, principally active as a portraitist. He was born in Massachusetts and was probably self-taught. His early work is marked by clarity and sharpness of drawing, and by a somewhat naive stiffness of pose which goes well with his forthright presentation of character (*Roger Sherman*, *c.*1775, New Haven, Yale University Art Gallery). He made drawings of some of the earliest events of the American Revolution, which were published as engravings, but his sympathies were with the British and in 1778 he was forced to flee to England, where he remained until 1785. His style became more elegant after his stay in England, but during the rest of his succesful career in New York and Connecticut he retained the sincerity and directness which makes his best works so compelling (*Chief Justice and Mrs Oliver Ellsworth*, 1892, Hartford, Conn., Wadsworth Atheneum). His few landscapes have a similar clarity and sharpness of vision. Earl deserted both his wives and died an alcoholic. His brother **James** (1761–96) and his son **Ralph E.W.** (*c.*1785–1838) were both portrait painters. Ralph married a niece of the future president, Andrew Jackson, and devoted much of his subsequent career to painting portraits of him.

Early Christian art
Art emerging with the growth of the Christian religion in Mediterranean regions of Europe from the 3rd century AD. The earliest remains of Christian painting in the West are in the catacombs in Rome—murals showing the stylistic reliance of the artists on the classical traditions. The Mosaic law forbade the use of divine images, and at first only symbols were used, but Christ and then Mary were introduced and classical motifs such as peacocks and *putti* were adapted to Christian use. Figurative sculpture on early Christian sarcophagi, for example that of Junius Bassus (Rome, Crypt of St Peter's) and on ivory also reveals the adaptation of pagan styles and iconography. Artistic scope was vastly increased with the official recognition of the religion by the Emperor Constantine in AD 313 and the subsequent boom in church building. The great early Roman basilicas, notably Old St Peter's, set a standard for early medieval church architecture. In decoration the basilicas rivalled the classical temples, developing a scheme in which Christ and his saints were represented in the apse and biblical stories were restricted to the nave. The most extensive surviving mosaic scheme, dating from 432 to 440, is in S. Maria Maggiore, Rome. The most celebrated survival of early Jewish art is the fresco scheme (discovered in 1932) of the mid-3rd century in a synagogue at Dura-Europos in Syria. Such work was undoubtedly an important source for the development of Early Christian art, but our knowledge is very fragmentary. Early Christian manuscripts were to play an important part in the emergence of Western and Eastern medieval manuscript illumination, but again, survivals are rare. The 5th-century Vienna Genesis (Vienna, National Library) is the most complete example, and demonstrates a lively, naturalistic style. However, the decline in artistic standards which had been appreciable before the establishment of Christianity was further exacerbated by the disintegration of the Empire. In Western Europe the traditions of Early Christian art were maintained only shakily in a few centres, mainly in Italy, before the Carolingian revival. In Rome by the 6th century artists and patrons were looking to Byzantium for an example. See vol. 2 pp. 52–53

Earth colour
Any pigment found as an earth (for example ochre) or refined from a mineral (as Indian red from iron oxide).

Earthwork see LAND ART

Easel
Stand, often portable, on which an artist can support his canvas or panel while painting. An **easel-painting** is any picture small enough to have been supported on a standard easel.

Eastlake, Sir Charles Lock
1793–1865
English history and genre painter, art historian and arts administrator. Using proceeds from his highly successful *Napoleon on board the Bellerophon* (1815, Earl of Roseberry coll.), he travelled to Italy, living from 1816 to 1830 in Rome, where he was influenced by the NAZARENES' historicism. His history and genre scenes set in the Campagna, such as *The escape of the Carrara family from the pursuit of the Duke of Milan*, 1389 (*c.*1850, London, Tate), influenced by Hubert Robert, were very popular in England, but he became increasingly important as an administrator. He became President of the Royal Academy in 1850, and Director of the National Gallery in 1855, and his interest in early Renaissance painting led to the acquisition of some of the most important works of this kind for the gallery.

Eckersberg, Christopher Wilhelm
1783–1853
Danish painter and portraitist. After studies in Copenhagen and with J.-L. David in Paris, he lived in Rome (1813–16), where he painted topographical scenes in a severely objective, but highly-coloured manner. He executed a series of historical paintings in the Christiansborg palace and had great influence as a teacher; artists such as Købke and Hansen belonged to his school. The portrait of his friend, *Thorvaldsen* (1815, Copenhagen, Royal Academy) is characteristically well painted but without expressive force.

Eclecticism
The practice of selecting different styles, characteristics or features from various artists and combining them. Tintoretto is supposed to have written as a motto above his studio door: "Titian's colour, Michelangelo's line". It has sometimes been supposed that such combinations of the best features would lead to overall excellence, and in the 18th century the Carracci were dubbed eclectics because it was believed that they deliberately followed such a policy. Although the term can be used neutrally, it may have disparaging overtones and suggest lack of originality.

Ecorché
A drawing, print or statue of a figure (human or animal) from which the skin has been stripped to enable study of the muscular construction (*écorché* is the French for flayed).

Eddy, Don born 1944
American SUPERREALIST painter. Since 1971he has worked on a series called *Windows*. The shop windows he meticulously paints contain two worlds—the objects displayed and the reflected street —the artist is concerned with the tension between the two. See vol. 1 p. *145*

Edelfelt, Albert 1854–1905
With Gallen-Kallela the leading Finnish painter of the 19th century. He went to Antwerp to study history painting but moved to Paris in 1874. He first studied with Gérôme, then became a friend of Bastien-Lepage and turned to *plein-air* naturalism, painting sentimental subjects, such as *Funeral of a child* (1879, Helsinki, Ateneum). His portrait of *Louis Pasteur* (1885, Versailles Museum) initiated a revival of the action portrait. Although he never adopted Impressionism Edelfelt allowed his palette to brighten during the 1880s. His last phase was mainly devoted to historical compositions, a genre which assumed renewed importance with the mounting oppression of Finland by Tsarist Russia. Some of his illustrations to J.L. Runeberg's poems relating to the war of 1808–09 were also executed as easel-paintings, and reproductions achieved a widespread, partly clandestine, circulation, symbolizing the resistance against the violation of constitutional rights. There is a museum devoted to Edelfelt at Porvoo (Borgå) near Helsinki.

Edelinck, Gerard 1640–1707
Flemish engraver who spent almost all his working life in Paris. Edelinck was a superb technician, and equally successful in his prints after Old Masters and contemporary artists, notably portrait painters such as Rigaud; indeed as a portrait engraver he rivals Nanteuil, whose daughter he married. His most famous print is *The fight for the standard*, after Rubens' drawing of the central part of Leonardo's *Battle of Anghiari*. See vol. 4 pp. *41, 127*

Egell, Paul *c.*1691–1752
German sculptor, chiefly active in the Palatinate. Nothing is known of his origins or apprenticeship. From 1716 to 1720 he worked under Permoser in Dresden and then spent two years in Italy. In 1723 he was appointed court sculptor in Mannheim, where he stayed

for the rest of his life, providing sculpture and stucco for the Elector's palaces and altar-figures for churches. His sculpture and delicate, flickering drawings influenced Ignaz Günther.

Egg, Augustus Leopold 1816–63
English painter of literary, historical and contemporary scenes, a friend of Holman Hunt. His series *Past and Present* (1858, London, Tate), depicting the consequences of infidelity, was too strong for the Victorian public, who preferred his less controversial scenes such as *The travelling companions* (c.1862, Birmingham City Art Gallery).

Eggeling, Viking 1880–1925
Swedish painter, draughtsman and pioneer of abstract film. In Paris from 1911 he met the avantgarde and was influenced by the Cubists. Then in 1916 he joined DADA in Zurich. With Hans Richter he made *Diagonal-symphonie* (1922), the first abstract film.

Egyptian art
Art of the ancient Egyptians, chiefly of the period between the unification of Egypt, about 3000 BC, and the end of the last dynasty of native rulers, the Ptolemies, 30 BC. Characterized by its descriptive clarity and its magical intention, it developed chiefly in tomb art—in the mastabas (low-lying tombs) and pyramids of the early pharaohs. The Egyptians believed that death was only an interruption in an order created for eternity; indeed, through most Egyptian history a man might acquire immortality if he could only provide himself with a tomb in which his name was recorded and the preservation of his body ensured. Only essential features of the deceased need be shown, and a standard figure was generally made according to a rule of proportion. However, realism in portraiture and in representations of plants and animals was not neglected, and many famous masterpieces witness acute perception and an undeniable ability to imitate nature. Egyptian art emerges in the Predynastic period, about 5000–3100 BC, when objects of carved ivory, glazed steatite and Egyptian faience first appear, together with painted pottery. There followed the first attempts at tomb painting—the subject outlined and filled in with flat colour—and the development of low relief work. From the 1st Dynasty onwards (about 3100 BC) the rich legacy of Egyptian jewellery also reveals high standards of workmanship. The art of MEMPHIS was particularly important in the OLD KINGDOM, when the painting of low reliefs and the production of free-standing, large-scale statues began. In the MIDDLE KINGDOM there emerged a highly sophisticated painting style without the basis of relief, and refined relief work was employed on a large scale, as at KARNAK. In the NEW KINGDOM, when THEBES became the capital city and chief artistic centre, tombs had painted decoration only, and artists displayed a greater freedom in representing human figures and in creating descriptive scenes. This development reached its peak in the 18th Dynasty, and especially in AMARNA art. In the 19th Dynasty the·temples of Ramesses II (at Memphis and ABU SIMBEL for example) achieved· unprecedented scale, but the standard forms had lost their freshness, and there was little originality. See vol. 2 pp. 24–27

Eidophusikon see LOUTHERBOURG

Eight, The
Group of American painters, united by their opposition to the standards and restrictions of the National Academy. Although they exhibited together only once, in February 1908 at the Macbeth Galleries, New York, they became renowned as agitators who opened the way for progressive art in America. The Eight were Glackens, Henri, Luks, Shinn and Sloan—later known as the ASHCAN school—and Davies, Lawson and Prendergast. They were far from being a stylistically unified group but generally portrayed contemporary urban life realistically. See vol. 3 p. 204

Eilshemius, Louis Michel 1864–1941
American painter. During the 1890s he painted conventional Impressionistic landscapes, but after travelling to Europe, North Africa and the South Seas (1892–1903) he turned to an intensely personal, primitive style. Paintings such as *New York at night* (1917, New York, Metropolitan) were noticed by Duchamp and Eilshemius was consequently given a one-man show by the Société Anonyme in 1920. He gave up painting in 1921 and his work fell into obscurity until the 1930s.

Eisen, Ikeda 1790–1848
Japanese UKIYO-E artist. A native of Edo (Tokyo), Eisen learned painting from a Kano master, before taking up print design. He is best known for his designs of women, for instance in his series *Women's Make-up Competition*. The women appear strangely hump-backed and contorted, exuding a perverse eroticism. He was very versatile and produced remarkable landscapes, some of which are done in the "Western" style, with perspective and shading; he invented landscapes printed only with shades of blue.

Eishi, Hosoda 1756–1829
Japanese UKIYO-E artist. The only known case of a high-ranking Samurai who turned to *ukiyo-e*, Eishi was one of the most influential designers of the Golden Age of printmaking. For three years he was painter-companion to the Tokugawa Shogun Ieharu, yet in early middle age he resigned and joined the Torii family. In 1800 he presented a landscape painting of *The Sumida river* (Tokyo, Imperial Palace coll.) to a member of the imperial family; it was accepted into the imperial archives, an honour Eishi commemorated by subsequently adding "seen by Heaven" to his signature. Eishi's prints reflect his breeding and training. His courtesans look like princesses, refined and confident, and his choice of colour and composition suggests the Kano mould.

Eitoku, Kano 1543–90
Japanese painter, fifth in the line of the court-painter family of KANO. He was taught painting by his grandfather, Motonobu, until he was 17. A versatile artist, he was equally at home with landscapes, portraiture, or animal paintings and preferred to work on a large scale. He was patronized by the Shoguns Oda Nobunaga and Toyotomi Hideyoshi, who asked him to decorate their castles in Azuchi and Osaka. Many screens and sliding-door paintings are ascribed to Eitoku but few can be authenticated. Two certain works are the screen with Chinese lions in the Tokyo Imperial Palace collection and those of flowers and birds in the Juko-in, Daito-ku temple, Kyoto. See vol. 3 pp. **46–47**

Ekeland, Arne born 1908
Norwegian painter, influenced by Sur-

realism and German Expressionism. His art has social and political references reflecting contemporary events. He has painted ghostly figures in working-class backgrounds (*The fight*, 1943, Oslo, NG), while other paintings depict an idealized future. His colours are sometimes fiery with shrill dissonances, sometimes deep and saturated, almost monochrome.

Elephanta 8th-9th century
Rock-cut Hindu shrine on the island in Bombay harbour, India. The cruciform cave was excavated to form a shrine to Shiva. The side halls of the cave are adorned with huge scenes in high relief representing the chief episodes in Shiva mythology (for instance, *Shiva's marriage to Parvati*) twice life-size, and a bust of *Shiva Maheshvara* of similar size, showing Shiva with three faces. The front one is sunk in majestic contemplation and those in profile to right and left show him in his benevolent and terrifying aspects. See vol. 3 pp. 16–17

Eliaesz., Nicholaes
(called **Pickenoy**) c.1590–c.1655
Dutch portrait painter whose work was much favoured in Amsterdam before the arrival of Rembrandt in 1631. The portraits of *Gerard Hinlopen* and his wife (Amsterdam, Rijksmuseum) display his fine technique but rather dry approach.

Elsheimer, Adam 1578–1610
German painter and etcher who had an important influence on the development of 17th-century landscape painting despite his short career and small output (fewer than 30 paintings are generally accepted as his, and his drawings and etchings are equally rare). He left his native Frankfurt in 1598, worked in Venice with Rottenhammer, and settled in Rome in 1600. His paintings are always small and on copper apart from a doubtfully attributed *Self-portrait* (c.1606, Florence, Uffizi), which is larger than usual and on canvas. Typically they are of biblical and mythological subjects in landscape settings, with delicate and unusual lighting effects, often nocturnal, creating a sense of poetic melancholy. The quintessence of his art is the exquisite *Rest on the Flight into Egypt* (1609, Munich, Alte Pinakothek), where the lovely device of the moon reflected in still water is introduced. Rubens, a friend of Elsheimer, and Rembrandt painted versions of the same subject obviously inspired by this painting, and Elsheimer's influence on other artists is equally apparent. He had an international reputation in his lifetime, spread by the many copies and prints after his work, but he died in poverty. Sandrart said that Elsheimer's tiny output was due to intense melancholia which often rendered him unable to work; the supremely robust Rubens, who wrote that Elsheimer "had no equal in small figures, in landscapes, and in many subjects", referred regretfully to his "sin of sloth, by which he has deprived the world of the most beautiful things". See vol. 2 p. **196**

Encaustic painting
Method of painting with hot, coloured wax, in common use in the ancient and Early Christian world. After the liquid wax, mixed with powdered pigment, had been laid, heat was passed across the surface to fuse the colours and burn the painting into the wood panel support. The FAYOUM mummy portraits are the best-known surviving examples in this technique, which has been revived by some 20th-century artists using wax emulsions. See vol. 1 p. 140

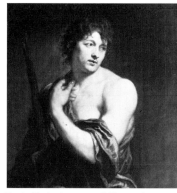

Dyck, Sir Anthony van: Self-portrait, c.1625. London, Wallace Coll.

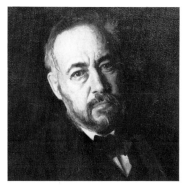

Eakins: Self-portrait, c.1902. New York, National Academy of Design

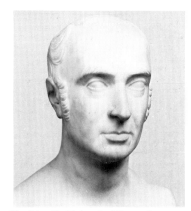

Eastlake: Marble bust by Gibson, 1840s. London, NPG

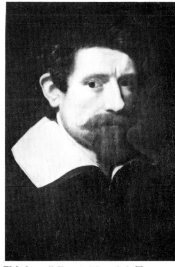

Elsheimer: Self-portrait?, c.1606. Florence, Uffizi (Scala)

Endoios active *c.*550–*c.*500 BC
ARCHAIC Greek sculptor, to whom has been attributed, on the basis of Pliny's description, a seated marble statue of *Athene* recovered by excavation on the Acropolis, Athens. It belongs to a group which reveals a break with earlier perfect symmetry of pose and an advance in naturalism in the way the modelling of the form shows through the drapery.

Engelbrechtsen, Cornelis
1468–1533
Dutch painter from Leyden, who may have trained under Jan de Cock. Cornelis preferred narrative, biblical subjects to purely devotional pictures and adopted many Mannerist traits. Typical works are the altarpieces of *The Crucifixion* and *The Lamentation* (both Leyden, Stedelijk Museum), which depict tall, slender figures in pronounced *contrapposto* poses. Their costumes are exotic, with extravagant swirling drapery. He ran a large studio, his pupils including his sons and van Leyden.

Engraving
Term which refers both to the process of cutting a design into metal or wood and the print taken from a plate or block so cut. Though forms of engraving include the WOODCUT, ETCHING and DRYPOINT, the term is more accurately applied to only two processes of printmaking, metal engraving, or line engraving, and wood engraving. The latter is a relief method in which negative areas of the design are cut away from a block of hardwood sawn across the grain, leaving raised lines and shapes for inking. Metal engraving, characterized by hard, clear lines, is an INTAGLIO process in which the design is cut into a smooth metal plate, usually copper, with an engraving tool and paper is pressed into the inked furrows. Metal engraving was the main method of reproductive printing from the 16th to the 19th centuries, and also itself an art form. See vol. 1 pp. 166–167

Ensor, James 1860–1949
Belgian painter, a forerunner of both Expressionism and Surrealism. He was born in Ostend, where he spent most of his life. His earliest paintings were influenced by Belgian Impressionism and were notable for their vigorous brushwork, thick impasto and strong highlights. Although unexceptional by Parisian standards, these canvases were rejected by the provincially-minded Salons of Brussels and Antwerp and it was only with the creation of the avant-garde exhibiting body Les VINGT that Ensor was able to show his work regularly. Through the group, he came into contact with Symbolist ideas and began producing his disturbing series of bourgeois interiors, where affluent surroundings contrast sharply with the spiritual poverty of the sitters. Moving from this to the study of light as a subject in itself, Ensor then executed a number of daringly Expressionistic canvases, among them *The tribulations of St Anthony* (1887, New York, MOMA), which conveyed its mood through swirling, automatic brush-strokes and intense, unmixed colours. When his most celebrated work, the spectacular *Entry of Christ into Brussels* (1888, on loan to Antwerp, Musées Royaux des Beaux-Arts), was rejected by Les Vingt, he withdrew, a self-styled martyr, into the world of his mother's shop, where he animated her masks, chinoiseries and other carnival trappings, using them as embodiments of the irrational scorn which, he felt, surrounded him. These obsessive images of persecution endeared him

considerably to certain Surrealists. There is a museum devoted to Ensor's work in Ostend. See vol. 3 pp. **130, 133**

Environmental art
Type of modern art in which not merely an object but a total environment is created for the spectator, and in which sight and sound effects may be combined with painted or sculptural elements. The purpose is to involve all his senses in the work of art, of which he is, in some cases, a part. Often the Environment is KINETIC, and the idea closely linked to those of HAPPENINGS or PERFORMANCE. Leading practitioners include Kienholz and Oldenburg. See vol. 3 pp. **242–243**

Epiktetos active late 6th century BC
Greek vase-painter from Athens, working in both red and BLACK-FIGURE techniques. He was a painter mostly of cups, and his repertoire consisted mainly of satyrs and athletes, their forms and poses beautifully adapted to the shape of the cup. The graceful economy of his figures, such as those on the superb cup in the British Museum, London, painted in red-figure outside and black-figure within, shows little concern with anatomical detail, but reveals a fine sense of line and rhythmical composition.

Epstein, Sir Jacob 1880–1959
English sculptor. Born in New York, he studied in Paris and became a British citizen in 1907. His first major commission, a series of figures (1908, destroyed) for the façade of the British Medical Association's building in London, caused immediate controversy on the grounds of indecency. Throughout his career he was to be dogged by such problems and a similar outcry greeted his Monument to Oscar Wilde in 1912 (Paris, Père Lachaise Cemetery), a work derived from the monumental forms of Assyrian art. While in Paris he met Picasso, Modigliani and Brancusi, and his sculpture before World War I, while sharing the harshly mechanistic quality of the paintings of his Vorticist contemporary, Wyndham Lewis, was also affected by their example, in particular by their formal simplifications and awareness of primitive art. Epstein's finest work from this period is the aggressively Cubist *Rock drill* (1913–14, London, Tate), a visored robot-like figure originally displayed on a real drill. Although such radical ideas had no place in his later sculpture he was still popularly identified with all that was most outrageous and offensive in modern art, perhaps because unlike younger, more advanced sculptors he sought a public context for his work, as with his huge bronze group of *St Michael and the devil* (1958) at Coventry Cathedral. His monumental carvings, particularly *Genesis* (1931, Manchester, Whitworth Art Gallery), were widely condemned as obscene, but his portrait busts, including many distinguished men of the 20th century, have been widely admired (examples, London, NPG). See vol. 3 pp. **155, 198**

Erhart, Michael
active late 15th/early 16th century
German woodcarver active in Ulm from 1469. In a series of fine high altars he developed a refined naturalistic style which his son **Gregor** (died 1540), who ran a workshop in Augsburg, continued.

Erichsen, Thorvald 1868–1939
Norwegian painter, a pupil of Zahrtmann in Denmark in the 1890s. Under the influence of the Impressionists, Cézanne and Bonnard, he developed a rich light palette and became a pioneer of

modern art in Norway. His subjects included landscapes (*Fra Telemark*, 1900, Oslo, NG), interiors and flowers.

Erixson, Sven 1899–1970
Swedish painter, inspired by Swedish folk art and Naive painting. His narrative paintings often represent workers, towns and landscapes (*The white walls*, 1935, Oslo, NG). He developed a colourful and explosive Expressionist style, and worked on public monuments, theatre décor and tapestries.

Ernst, Max 1891–1976
German painter, sculptor and collagist. He studied philosophy and psychiatry at Bonn, 1909–14, and was self-taught as a painter. In 1914 he met Arp, with whom he founded the DADA movement in Cologne. His early work was influenced by Chirico's dreamlike scenes, as in the lithograph series *Fiat modes, pereat ars* (1919), and his collages, photomontages and paintings from about 1920 are characterized by a whimsical irrationality in which banal images are combined to make surreal configurations (*The elephant Celebes*, 1921, London, Tate). In his collages, which included the first ones composed of ready-made elements unaltered by the artist, he drew extensively on 19th-century wood and steel engravings from encyclopaedias and technical manuals. After meeting Tzara and Breton he moved to Paris in 1922 and became a founder-member of the SURREALIST group. In 1925 he developed the technique of FROTTAGE, which he used in experiments with "automatic" imagery, and published examples in his book *Histoire Naturelle* (1926, Natural History). In 1938 he left the Surrealist group after a dispute with Breton and in 1941 settled in the USA. The grotesque element becomes more dominant in later works such as *The temptation of St Anthony* (1945, Duisberg, Wilhelm-Lehmbruck Museum). See vol. 1 p. 152; vol. 3 pp. **172–173**

Erro (Gudmundur Gudmundsson) born 1932
Icelandic POP painter. After much travel he settled in Paris in 1958. His output—canvases, collages, frescos and mosaics—has been huge. He paints mainly in series, covering his large canvases with tiny images of banal consumer goods and other objects painted with great precision; *Foodscape* (1964, Stockholm, Moderna Museet) is a characteristic work. He has also taken part in Happenings. See vol. 3 p. **251**

Escher, Maurits Cornelius
1898–1972
Dutch graphic artist, well-known for his prints of fantastic structures based on mathematical premises. They abound with bizarre metamorphoses and optical illusions such as staircases that appear to go both up and down. Critics have slighted his work for its repetitious themes and images but he has acquired wide popularity. See vol. 3 p. **175**

Esquivel, Antonio 1806–57
Spanish ROMANTIC painter, illustrator and art critic, born in Seville and active in Madrid from 1831. He first painted genre and religious works inspired by Murillo, but later turned to historical and mythological works. He was at his best in portraiture: his *Literary meeting in the artist's studio* (1846, Madrid, Museum of Modern Art) depicts more than 40 leading literary figures.

Este family
Aristocratic Italian family, rulers of

Ferrara from 1240 to 1597, among whose members were some of the leading Renaissance patrons of art. Ferrara first became a noted centre for artists and writers during the time of Niccolò d'Este (1384–1441). His two illegitimate heirs were active patrons: **Leonello** (1407–50) of Pisanello, Jacopo Bellini, Piero della Francesca and Rogier van der Weyden; **Borso** (1413–71) of Piero, Tura, Cossa and Ercole de' Roberti. However, the most renowned of Este patrons was Niccolò's granddaughter **Isabella** (1474–1539), who energetically sought the work of most of the famous artists of her time, including Giovanni Bellini, Giorgione, Leonardo (whose profile drawing of her is in the Louvre, Paris), Perugino and Raphael. Her taste, revealed in decorations for the palace at Mantua, was for "sweetness". Her brother **Alfonso** (1476–1539) commissioned five paintings on Bacchanalian subjects, notably Giovanni Bellini's *Feast of the gods* (Washington, NG) and Titian's *Bacchus and Ariadne* (London, NG). Antonio Lombardo also sculpted mythological reliefs for him.

Estes, Richard born 1936
American SUPERREALIST painter. His subject matter is the streets of American cities and towns painted in a scrupulously realist, emotionally neutral manner. His paintings differ from those of other Photo-Realists because they are executed by hand rather than with an airbrush. He slices together aspects of many photographs to create packed, rather shallow compositions with no single focus of interest. His views reveal a preoccupation with perspective illusionism and with the complex play between reflective surfaces (*Foodshop*, 1967, Cologne, Wallraf-Richartz Museum). See vol. 3 p. **252**

Etching
Term which describes the process of biting out a design in a metal plate with acid, and also the print that results. The process was developed in the early 16th century as a rapid means of engraving metal, but in the hands of Rembrandt became a major art form. A polished metal plate, usually copper or zinc, is covered with a dark, acid-resistant, waxy ground and the design is drawn on the ground with an etching needle to expose the metal in fine lines. The plate, with the back protected by a bituminous varnish, is then immersed in nitric acid which bites out the exposed lines. The depth to which the acid is allowed to bite determines the tone of black or grey that will appear in the final print. To vary the tone, areas of the plate may be exposed for a longer time after other areas have been protected with "stopping out" varnish. To take a print, the ground is removed, the plate is inked and wiped clean, and a heavy INTAGLIO press forces paper into the inked lines. The soft ground used in etching enables the needle to be handled almost as freely as a drawing tool, giving greater spontaneity than in engraving and allowing direct sketching from life with a rough-edged line. Etching is often combined with other processes such as AQUATINT and DRYPOINT to produce different tonal or textural effects. See vol. 1 pp. 164–167

Etruscan art
Art of the Etruscans, the earliest recorded inhabitants of the area between the rivers Tiber and Arno in Italy, approximating to modern Tuscany. They were at the height of their power in the 6th century BC but, by the end of the 3rd century BC, the whole of Etruria was

in Roman hands and their culture was on the way to being absorbed by that of the Romans. Surviving works of art and excavation of Etruscan sites have revealed a flourishing artistic tradition, the techniques and style of which were borrowed initially from the Greeks of southern Italy, but which went on to develop in an idiom which is highly individual. Metalwork was particularly outstanding and surviving masterpieces include the famous "*Capitoline Wolf*" (Rome, Museo Capitolino). Stone was used for sculpture when the locality afforded it, but the principal sculptural medium was painted terracotta; the Villa Giulia in Rome contains magnificent examples of Etruscan tomb sculpture, while the splendid tomb paintings at Tarquinia and elsewhere display a bold and rhythmical sense of line and some intriguing parallels with Greek vase-painting. They also provide vivid accounts of Etruscan life, customs and religious belief. See vol. 2 p. *35*

Etty, William 1787–1849
English painter, celebrated for his paintings of the female nude. His weak draughtsmanship sometimes mars his work, but he had great gifts for rendering sensuous textures and voluptuous flesh. His subjects were often drawn from classical mythology and demonstrate his admiration for the work of Titian and Rubens. Etty in turn was admired by Delacroix. The best collection of his work is in York City Art Gallery.

Euphranor active 4th century BC
Greek sculptor and painter, active in Athens. His sculpture included statues of *Paris*, *A priestess* and bronzes of *Philip of Macedon* and his son *Alexander the Great*, but all that has survived is a stately, draped figure of *Apollo Patroos*, without head and arms, which has been found in the Agora at Athens. Among his paintings, classical authors describe one of *The Battle of Mantinea* (418 BC), which used to be in the Stoa at Athens, and they attribute to him two treatises, one on proportion and another on colour. One of the foremost artists of his day, Euphranor is said to have attempted a new system of proportion in the representation of the human figure, in which the head was larger and the body more slender than had been usual.

Euphronios active *c*. 520–500 BC
Greek potter and RED-FIGURE vase-painter from Athens. Regarded, together with his great rival Euthymides, as one of the great pioneers of red-figure vase-painting, he is outstanding in his mastery of line and in his understanding of anatomical structure. A magnificent *krater* in the Louvre, Paris, depicts the struggle between Herakles and the giant Antaios with a monumental force previously unknown in the genre. In another work, a fine *krater* in Arezzo, Museo Archeologico, his originality is apparent in his composition of a powerful battle scene and in his striking use of colour and pattern. See vol. 2 p. *34*

Euston Road school
School of painting and drawing opened in London's Euston Road in 1937 by Coldstream and Pasmore. Influenced by Sickert, Cézanne and the earlier CAMDEN TOWN group, they stressed the value of an objective approach to reality in opposition to the current trends of Abstraction and Surrealism. The school was closed in 1939.

Euthymides *c*. 520–500 BC
Greek RED-FIGURE vase-painter from

Athens, a rival of Euphronios. Some 18 works have been attributed to him. His favourite subjects were athletes and revellers, and by the surety of his line the volume of his figures is lightened with a tripping elegance. He was most innovatory in his mastery of foreshortening and it was alongside a particularly virtuoso piece of drawing, on an amphora in Munich, Staatliche Antikensammlungen, that he made his boast: *As Euphronios could never do*.

Evenpoel, Henri 1872–99
Belgian painter. He moved to Paris in 1892. Influenced by French Impressionism, he changed from sombre-toned history paintings to increasingly colourful genre pictures and portraits with strongly flattened space. He painted many portraits of children (*Henriette with the hat*, 1899, Brussels, Musées Royaux des Beaux-Arts).

Everdingen, Allart van 1621–75
Dutch landscape and marine painter. He was born in Alkmaar, and was probably the pupil of Roelandt Savery and Pieter de Molyn. During the early 1640s he travelled to Scandinavia and returned through Denmark, where he painted for King Frederick IV. He then worked mainly in Haarlem and Amsterdam, but the Scandinavian landscape continued to inspire his densely wooded scenes with spiky fir trees and torrential waterfalls (a fine example is in the Wallace Collection, London). His more romantic and dramatic landscapes were influential on Jacob van Ruisdael. See vol. 2 p. *225*

Everdingen, Cesar Boëtius van 1617–78
Dutch portrait and historical painter, the elder brother of Allart. He worked in Alkmaar, Haarlem and Amsterdam. Although he never went to Italy, his paintings have the spirit of Italian art, and reflect the influence of the Caravaggisti (*Bacchus and two nymphs in a grotto*, Dresden, Gemäldegalerie). He was among the artists who worked on the elaborate decorations in the Huis ten Bosch, the palace near The Hague. Everdingen's refined and graceful *The four muses with Pegasus* (*c*.1650) is perhaps the finest painting in the whole scheme.

Evergood, Philip 1901–75
American painter. He was educated in England, and studied painting there with Tonks. Initially he painted imaginative and biblical themes, but during the Depression of the 1930s he turned to social realist subjects. He retained, however, strong elements of the bizarre and fantastic in his work to create a highly distinctive style. His space tends to be shallow, his figures deliberately awkward, his colours vividly fresh (*Lily and the sparrows*, 1939, New York, Whitney). Later his works became roughly textured and expressionist, but essentially his style was linear.

Eworth, Hans *c*.1520–after 1573
Flemish portrait painter, active mainly in England. His career can be charted from a succession of signed and dated works. Painted in the predominant international Mannerist style of court portraiture, they are notable for strong characterization, careful technique, and a documentary approach to jewels and rich fabric. He was the official portraitist of Mary I (a small portrait is in the NPG, London). See vol. 1 p. *84*; vol. 2 p. **206**

Exekias *c*.550–520 BC
Greek potter and vase-painter from Athens, perhaps the most outstanding

master of the BLACK FIGURE technique. His compositions have astonishing power, elegance and tension, imbuing the image with a deep psychological force, as in the famous scene of *Aias and Achilles playing draughts* (versions London, BM, and Vatican). Elsewhere, as in the cup depicting Dionysos and the dolphins (Munich, Staatliche Antikensammlungen), it is his mastery in the use of colour and texture which is paramount, and his brilliant adaptation to the nature of the space and surface available. Some 31 vases are attributed to him as painter. See vol. 2 p. *34*

Expressionism
Term used in two main senses in the visual arts. In its more general sense (usually spelled with a small "e") it denotes a quality of expressive emphasis and distortion which may be found in the works of art of any place or period. Taken somewhat more narrowly, the term is frequently used to characterize 20th-century north European art, literature and film, in which subjective stress is laid on heightened emotions and the artist's inner vision. This definition can be narrowed still further to refer specifically to the movement which dominated the arts in Germany between about 1905 and 1925, typified mainly by the paintings of Die BRÜCKE and Der BLAUE REITER. However, the term Expressionism was first used in 1911 to describe an exhibition of Fauve and early Cubist paintings at the Berlin Sezession. Only later that year was it first applied to German art, a Die Brücke exhibition at the Sturm Gallery in Berlin. Artistically, Expressionism represented a forceful reaction against the superficiality of late 19th-century naturalism and realism and was anticipated to some extent by van Gogh, Gauguin and Munch. In a self-conscious spirit of rebellion the Expressionist artists insisted on the validity of their emotional response to their subject, from which they developed the concept that genuine artistic form results from inner necessity only and that it can never be imposed by tradition or convention. For this reason they were able to justify the use of any artistic means which gave expression to their feelings. These included distortion, aggressively stylized forms, violent and evocative colour combinations, and the eclectic absorption of such diverse influences as medieval, folk and tribal art. The culmination, in Kandinsky's case, was abstraction. See vol. 3 pp. 131–137, 194–195

Exter, Alexandra Alexandrovna 1884–1949
Russian painter and theatre designer. She brought information about Cubism and Futurism to the Moscow avant-garde after visits to France and Italy, and her own work reveals the influence of Delaunay. In highly influential set designs, she pioneered the use of a cyclorama (*Famira Kifared*, 1916), a raked stage (*Salome*, 1917) and multi-level constructed staging (*Romeo and Juliet*, 1921). Some of the colourful theatre designs are preserved in the Victoria and Albert Museum, London.

Eyck, Jan van died 1441
The most renowned Netherlandish painter of the 15th century. He is first recorded in 1422 in The Hague at the court of John of Bavaria, Count of Holland, and in 1425 became court painter to Philip the Good, Duke of Burgundy, for whom he travelled as an ambassador to Spain and Portugal. All of his dated works belong to the last decade of his life, when he was living in Bruges, and

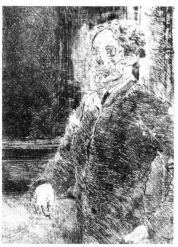
Ensor: Self-portrait etching as a skeleton, 1889. Ostend, Museum voor Schone Kunsten

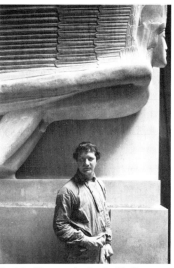
Epstein: Photograph taken beside Oscar Wilde's tomb, 1920 (Mansell)

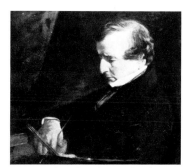
Etty: Portrait (artist unknown). London, NPG

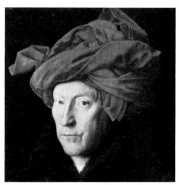
Eyck, Jan van: *Man in a turban* (Self-portrait?), 1433. London, NG

nothing is certainly known of his early career. By the mid-15th century, however, his reputation was widespread—based principally on his most famous work, the massive altarpiece (finished 1432) in St Bavon, Ghent. Early writers, including Vasari, credited van Eyck with the invention of oil-painting, and, although this is not true, he did bring the technique to an unprecedented degree of accomplishment, showing extraordinary skill in the use of layers of pigment and glaze to achieve a translucent luminosity of colour. In the rendering of the tiniest detail, the exact verisimilitude of every texture, and the clarity of his lighting effects, which have not lost their brilliance with time, van Eyck has never been matched. His treatment of space and figures further reveals his unique ability to capture the infinitely small and the infinitely large in an all-embracing vision—Erwin Panofsky wrote of him: "his eye was at one and the same time a microscope and a telescope". Next in fame to the Ghent altarpiece is the double portrait known as *"The Arnolfini Marriage"* (1434, London, NG), which also shows van Eyck's elaborate disguised religious symbolism and his ability to combine objective realism with a feeling of spirituality. His other works include portraits, for example *Timotheos* and *The man in a red turban* (1432 and 1433, both London, NG) and religious works, notably *The Madonna with Chancellor Rolin* (c.1435, Paris, Louvre) and *The Madonna with Canon van der Paele* (1436, Bruges, Musée Communale des Beaux-Arts). *The Virgin in a church* (West Berlin, Staatliche Museen) is generally accepted as an early work of about 1425. Van Eyck's influence was enormous, in other countries as well as Flanders. The contribution of his brother **Hubert** (died 1426?) is tantalizingly obscure. According to the inscription on the Ghent altarpiece, Hubert began it and Jan finished it, but the authenticity of the inscription has been questioned (indeed some scholars have doubted Hubert's existence). Of the few panels which have been attributed to him, the best candidate is *The Annunciation* (New York, Metropolitan). See vol. 1 pp. *36, 61, 72, 93*; vol. 2 pp. **91–93**

Fabritius, Carel 1622–54
Dutch painter. He was the finest of Rembrandt's pupils, but his career was tragically cut short in the explosion of the Delft ammunition depot of 1654. His earliest dated work, *The raising of Lazarus* (1642, Warsaw, National Museum) shows a close dependence on Rembrandt in composition and use of chiaroscuro, but he soon developed a distinctive style. Whereas Rembrandt liked to paint figures emerging from dark shadows, Fabritius preferred dark figures against a light background, and his colours are predominantly cool whereas Rembrandt's are warm. Although very few works exist (it is assumed many perished with him in the explosion), they are remarkably varied in subject, the best-known being the exquisite *Goldfinch* (1654, The Hague, Mauritshuis). Like his other works, this gains its impact from his lovely colour harmonies, effortlessly poised composition, and (even though it is very small) richly satisfying brushwork. Vermeer is supposed to have been a pupil of

Fabritius, and certainly owed much to his influence. Carel's brother **Barent** (1624–73), who mainly painted biblical subjects, may also have been a pupil of Rembrandt. See vol. 2 p. **228**

Fairweather, Ian 1891–1974
Australian painter, born in Scotland and trained in London. An inveterate traveller, he painted for many years in the Far East, arriving in Australia in 1934. Temperamentally unsuited to city life and frustrated at the unsympathetic response to his large mural for a Melbourne hotel, he destroyed it and resumed his wanderings, returning after World War II. A brilliant draughtsman, he combined dense, calligraphic brushwork with a limited yet sensuous range of colour, as in *Monastery* (1960–61, Canberra, Australian NG). His work became increasingly non-figurative and by the 1960s he was considered one of Australia's leading abstract painters.

Faistauer, Anton 1887–1930
Austrian painter. He was essentially a colourist and his still-life and figure paintings show the influence of the Post-Impressionists and Fauves. A typical example of his work is the *Nude on a sofa* (c.1914, Salzburg, Museum Carolino-Augusteum), reminiscent of Matisse.

Faithorne, William 1616?–91
The outstanding 17th-century English portrait-engraver. A Londoner by birth, a royalist in politics, he was in exile in France during the Commonwealth, and is said to have studied with Nanteuil. His drawings and engravings from the life, often published as frontispieces, show an honest sympathy with the sitters.

Falcone, Aniello 1607–56
Neapolitan painter, the first artist to specialize in battle-scenes, a genre in which he was later surpassed by his more famous pupil, Salvator Rosa. They were mostly imaginary—small, multitudinous compositions showing the activity of war rather than individual heroism (*Fight between Romans and barbarians*, Madrid, Prado). Falcone also painted religious works and genre scenes.

Falconet, Etienne-Maurice 1716–91
One of the leading French sculptors of the 18th century. He trained under Jean-Baptiste Lemoyne the Younger. Like his master he never made the customary trip to Italy, and in his *Reflections on Sculpture* (1761) he set out his conviction that the Moderns were superior to the Ancients in the rendering of life and expression. This view is reflected in his admiration for Puget, whose *Milo of Crotona* inspired Falconet's treatment of the same subject, his Academy reception piece (1754, Paris, Louvre). From 1757 to 1766 he worked at the Sèvres factory and many of his small marble statues were reproduced in porcelain. Characteristic of his gently classicizing, delicately erotic style is his *Bathing nymph* (1757, Louvre), the quintessence of French ROCOCO sculpture. In 1766 he was called to Russia by Catherine II, and until 1771 worked on his unexpected masterpiece, the bronze equestrian monument to *Peter the Great* (1766–68, unveiled 1782) in the Square of the Decembrists, Leningrad. This is one of the most imposing of all equestrian statues, and in representing the horse with both forelegs raised is a brilliant technical feat. He wrote prolifically (a six-volume edition of his works was published in 1781) and contributed the article on sculpture to Diderot's *Encyclopaedia*. See vol. 2 p. **243**

Falk, Robert 1886–1958
Russian painter, a founder-member of the KNAVE OF DIAMONDS. His early style is derived from Cubism, as in his portrait of *Midhat Refatov* (1915, Moscow, Tretyakov Gallery), though he kept a sense of colour structure for which he was indebted to Cézanne (whose style provided a constant impetus to Knave of Diamonds artists). After living in Paris from 1928 to 1938 he returned to Moscow. His later work is more lyrical.

Fancelli, Domenico di Alessandro 1469–1519
Florentine sculptor. He was a pupil of Mino da Fiesole and, though employed mainly in Italy, produced much work for the royalty and leading churchmen of Spain. He introduced some of the latest Italian Renaissance ideas to that country and also designed a new type of free-standing tomb—an example is that for the Catholic Kings (1514–17) in the Royal Chapel, Granada.

Fancy picture
Rather vague term used in 18th-century England to describe a type of idealized and sentimental rural genre scene. Gainsborough is the best-known exponent of this type of painting.

Fan Kuan active c.990–1030
Chinese painter of the Song dynasty. He was much influenced by the Taoist Jing Hao, for whom the true rendering of the spirit of nature was more important than the quality of brushwork, and he is said to have abandoned the imitation of Old Masters in favour of observation from the life as a hermit in the mountains. His only certain extant work, however, *Travelling among streams and mountains* (Taichung, Palace Museum), reflects the monumental landscape style of Li Cheng. Several austere northern mountain landscapes are attributed to him, such as *Winter landscape with travellers* (Boston, MFA). See vol. 3 p. **40**

Fantin-Latour, Henri 1836–1904
French painter and lithographer. Apart from the luxurious and sensitive flower-pieces for which he is best known (*Flowers and fruit*, 1865, Paris, Jeu de Paume), he also produced mythological paintings which are freer in handling than his usual rather precise style. A friend of Manet, he frequented the Café Guerbois, becoming intellectually though not artistically involved with the avantgarde, as can be seen in his group portrait, *A studio at Batignolles* (1870, Jeu de Paume), which shows a gathering of artists in Manet's studio. Another famous group portrait is *Homage to Delacroix* (1864, Jeu de Paume), in which Fantin-Latour shows himself, Baudelaire, Manet, Whistler and others grouped round a portrait of Delacroix. See vol. 3 p. **94**

Fantuzzi, Antonio active c.1530–50
Bolognese painter and engraver. He is said to have robbed Parmigianino of engraving plates and drawings before escaping to France, where he assisted Primaticcio at Fontainebleau, designing grotesques for ceiling decorations. One of the first etchers in France, he spread the influence of Rosso and Primaticcio.

Farington, Joseph 1747–1821
English landscape painter and topographical draughtsman, whose diaries (1793–1821) provide a detailed and personal history of the contemporary English art world, particularly the Royal Academy. As an artist he was competent but uninspired.

Farnese family
Aristocratic Italian family from Bolsena, in central Italy. They were among the most important patrons of the 16th century. **Alessandro** Farnese (1468–1549) became Paul III in 1534 and provided Michelangelo with the great commissions of the latter part of his life—*The Last Judgment* in the Sistine Chapel, frescos in the Cappella Paolina; and architectural work on St Peter's and the Palazzo Farnese. Paul III's grandson, Cardinal **Alessandro** (1545–92), saw to the completion of the family palace and formed the collection now in the Museo di Capodimonte, Naples, which includes Titian's portrait of the Pope with himself and his brother **Ottavio** (1521–86). He also commissioned Vasari in 1546 to paint the life of Paul III in the Palazzo della Cancelleria, Rome. His great-nephew, Cardinal **Odoardo** (1573–1626), was responsible for bringing Annibale Carracci to Rome to paint the Farnese ceiling.

Farrokh Beg active c.1585–1615
Indian MUGHAL artist, of Iranian origin. His fully attested work is scarce, being confined to a few pages in the *Akbarnameh* (c.1590, London, V&A) and a couple of portraits. His style is that of 16th-century Safavid Iran, with brilliant, gem-like coloured shapes contained within flat Iranian landscape. Other paintings have been attributed to him, including some from the southern Indian Deccani school of Bijapur, such as the *Yogini* (c.1605, Dublin, Chester Beatty Library). The attribution supposes a stay of some years in Bijapur at the close of Akbar's reign, which is highly contentious.

Faruffini, Federico 1831–69
Italian ROMANTIC painter of historical and religious works, landscapes and portraits. He studied in Pavia, travelled to Rome in 1855 with Carnovali and joined Cremona in Venice (1857–58), before completing his studies at the Brera, Milan. In 1869 he was working in Perugia as a photographer when he committed suicide. Most of his works are in the academic tradition but his colour sketches, derived from Carnovali and the Venetian masters, influenced the Scapigliati. His best-known work is the large *Virgin of the Nile* (1865, Rome, Galleria Nazionale d'Arte Moderna).

Fattori, Giovanni 1825–1908
Italian painter, the leading MACCHIAIOLO. He first experimented with the impressionistic *macchia* technique in studies of French soldiers in 1859. *The Italian camp after Magenta* (1859–60, Florence, Galleria d'Arte Moderna) was the first of many Realist, anti-rhetorical battle scenes. The *Palmieri Rotondo* (1866, Florence, Galleria d'Arte Moderna) explores a radically new treatment of tonal contrasts and brilliant light, developed in Castiglioncello landscapes from 1867 to 1875. Portraits span his long career, from the austere realism of his *First wife* (c.1865, Rome, Galleria Nazionale d'Arte Moderna) to his masterly *Third wife* (1905, Livorno, Fattori Museum). Although Fattori exhibited internationally and won prizes, financial reward came late. He taught in Florence in the late 1880s and was very influential on younger Tuscan artists.

Fautrier, Jean 1898–1964
French painter. His childhood and early student years were spent in England, but he returned to Paris in 1917. His works of the 1920s and 1930s were predominantly still lifes painted in

sombre colours and in an Expressionist style. His output included lithographs illustrating Dante's *Inferno*, but he is best known for the series of paintings *Hostages*, created during World War II and inspired by the horror and suffering of Nazi-occupied France (example, 1943, Paris, Michael Couturier coll.). These are created from built-up layers of cream and pastel coloured paint, the rough impasto evoking the idea of mutilation. In the same manner he painted series of *Objects* and *Nudes*. His work is a prime example of INFORMAL art. See vol. 3 p. **224**

Fauvism

Style practised by a group of artists loosely associated with Matisse around 1905 to 1907. The term "Fauve" (wild beast) was first used by the critic Vauxcelles to describe paintings by Matisse, Derain, Vlaminck, Rouault and others shown at the 1905 Salon d'Automne. The wildness to which he objected lay in their use of brilliant luminous colour and their bold spontaneous handling of paint. Matisse and Derain, working together in the intense light of the Midi at Collioure in 1905, were the first to stress the directness of their perceptions by strong luminous colour. They owed something to Monet, Gauguin, van Gogh and the Neo-Impressionists, but departed radically from literal appearances to express a heightened response to nature. Although short-lived, Fauvism was of fundamental importance for the development of Expressionism throughout Europe. The Dutch painter van Dongen and a group of younger French painters from Le Havre including Dufy, Friesz and Braque were among the artists immediately affected by the style. By 1907, however, many artists associated with Fauvism were taking up new ideas suggested by the Cézanne memorial exhibition in Paris, and only Matisse continued to explore the potential of pure colour. See vol. 3 pp. 142–143

Fayoum portraits

Mummy portraits found in and around Fayoum in Egypt. Dating from the 1st to 4th century AD, they are generally painted in encaustic or tempera on canvas or wood and were set into the wrappings around the face of the corpse. Styles vary, but in general the portraits are extremely vivid and naturalistic, and at times impressionistic in handling. Examples are in London (BM), New York (Metropolitan) and many other museums. See vol. 2 p. *62*

Federal Art Projects

Various government schemes to aid American artists between 1933 and 1943. They were an expression of the increased concern for federal relief in all branches of American society. As early as 1930 a number of minor plans had been made to help artists jeopardized by the growing Depression. In 1933 the Public Works of Art Project (PWAP) was set up, primarily to sponsor the decoration of public buildings. It was replaced in 1935 by the major federal programme, the Works Progress Administration's Federal Art Project, which existed until 1943. The WPA-FAP involved numerous subdivisions including murals, easel-painting, graphics, sculpture, cinematography and photography. Much of the massive quantity of work sponsored by the project was in an illustrative social realist style but abstraction and Surrealism were also embraced. It afforded many artists the unprecedented opportunity to create full-time. It also redefined the relationship of art to

American society by creating a sense of solidarity, professionalism and responsibility among artists that had previously existed only within an academic framework. Nearly all major artists of the era worked or taught on the project.

Fedotov, Pavel Andreevich
1815–52
Russian painter. Starting his career as an officer in the Imperial Guards, he soon became known as a talented amateur portrait painter and with the help of the Tsar was able to retire from the Army and devote himself entirely to painting. His drawings and paintings are mainly genre scenes of the lives of merchants, officers or petty officials, where the element of social satire did not conflict with warm human sympathy. He became insane and died in an asylum.

Feininger, Lyonel 1871–1956
American painter of German parentage. He left for Europe in 1887 in order to study music, but turned to art. In Paris in 1911 he met Delaunay and was strongly influenced by his analysis of light and colour. Increasingly affiliated with German artistic programmes, he exhibited with Der Blaue Reiter, 1913, taught at the Bauhaus, 1919–24, and formed Die BLAUE VIER with Kandinsky, Klee and Jawlensky in 1924. His mature work of the 1930s, such as *Church at Gelmeroda* (c.1936, New York, Metropolitan), is characterized by architectural forms fractured by a prismatic breakdown of light. He produced a considerable amount of graphic work, much of which was also concerned with architectural themes. He returned to America in 1937. See vol. 3 pp. **190–191**

Feke, Robert active 1741–50
American portrait painter. There is considerable documentation on his career during the 1740s, when he worked in Boston, Newport and Philadelphia, but before and after that period there is no secure evidence concerning his life. His work shows the influence of Smibert—compare Feke's earliest dated painting, *Isaac Royall and his family* (1741, Cambridge, Mass., Harvard University) with Smibert's *Bermuda group*—but is much more sophisticated. The clarity of conception and delicacy of handling of works such as *Isaac Winslow* (1748, Boston, MFA) place Feke among the finest of the Colonial painters.

Felixmüller, Conrad born 1897
German painter and graphic artist. After studying at the Dresden Academy he exhibited at the Sturm Gallery in Berlin in 1916. Together with Dix he was a founder-member of the Dresden Sezession (1919) and exhibited with the NOVEMBERGRUPPE in 1929. He developed a highly-charged socially critical style with Expressionist distortion of colour and form (*Fairground boxers*, 1921, Berlin, Private coll.). Towards 1930 his work lost its bite and he drifted back to a gentler naturalism.

Ferber, Herbert born 1906
American sculptor and painter. He made his first wood and stone carvings of nudes soon after a trip to Europe (1927–30), but by the late 1940s he had broken from European influences and begun working with soldered metal. His characteristic work of the 1950s is open and abstract with spiky projections. In the 1960s he launched a new trend with his room-sized environmental sculptures (*Sculpture as environment, interior*, 1961, New York, Whitney), but recently he has turned more to painting.

Fergusson, John Duncan
1874–1961
British painter and sculptor. His early paintings were influenced by the night scenes of Whistler. From 1907 to 1914 he lived in Paris and his work of that period shows an exuberant response to Fauvism. His sculpture, both in bronze and wood, tended towards simplification of form and an emphasis on the specific qualities of the material (*Oak rhythm*, 1925, London, Tate).

Fernandes, Vasco ("Grão-Vasco")
1470/80–c.1541/2
Portuguese painter, the most noted during the reign of Manoel I (1495–1521), a period of great encouragement for the arts. His individual style displays the influence of the Flemish and German artists then extensively employed in Portugal, and also of the Hispano-Flemish style of neighbouring Spain. Later, certain details of his painting show an acquaintance with Italian art. Elements of all these styles appear in his masterpiece, the *St Peter*, c.1535–40, in the Grão-Vasco Museum in Viseu.

Fernández, Alejo c.1470–1543
Spanish painter and miniaturist. He is first mentioned in 1498 in Cordova, and from 1508 worked mainly in Seville, where he had a large workshop. His varied style combines certain Netherlandish or archaic elements (such as inconsistency of scale) with Italian Renaissance perspective and classicizing architecture; his delicacy of touch suggests influence either from Venetian or Umbrian painting. His best-known work is the altarpiece for the Capilla Maese de Rodrigo, Seville, 1516–23.

Fernández or Hernández, Gregorio c.1576–1636
Spanish Baroque sculptor, active in Valladolid from about 1605. He was one of Spain's greatest masters of polychromed wooden sculpture, and brought to the genre a new intensity based on naturalistic colour (he abandoned the use of gold) and an expressive realism of gesture and characterization. There are several works in Valladolid Museum, including a *Pietà* (1617) and a *Baptism of Christ* (1630), and his workshop was responsible for several large altarpieces, notably those of S. Miguel, Valladolid (1606), and of Plasencia Cathedral (1624–34).

Fernández-Muro, José Antonio
born 1920
Argentinian painter, born in Spain. In 1960 with his wife and others he formed an avantgarde group which was recognized as the corner-stone of new painting in Argentina. Since 1962 he has lived in New York surrounded by a large group of Latin American expatriate artists. He uses relief textures found in the city (for example, man-hole covers and grates) in conjunction with boldly geometric shapes, vibrantly coloured, to create imposing, almost hieratic forms.

Ferrari, Gaudenzio c.1475–1546
Italian painter, who worked in Piedmont and Lombardy. He was an individualist and his work is difficult to place. He drew heavily upon northern art, Dürer and Pacher particularly, but his elaborate compositions also recall Raphael's last paintings. His most extraordinary works are *The Stations of the Cross* (shortly before 1520) in a series of shrines leading to the church of Sacro Monte at Varallo Sesia, in which painted statues are placed before a frescoed background in a life-size tableau.

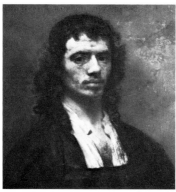

Fabritius: Self-portrait, c.1645–50. Rotterdam, Boymans-van Beuningen

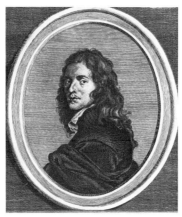

Faithorne: 18th-century engraving after a self-portrait (Courtauld Institute)

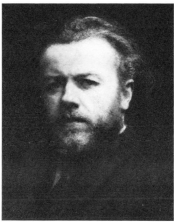

Fantin-Latour: Self-portrait, exhibited 1883. Florence, Uffizi (Alinari)

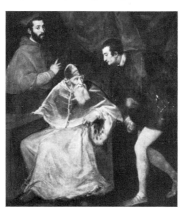

Farnese family: *Pope Paul III and his grandsons* by Titian, 1545–46. Naples, Museo di Capodimonte (Scala)

Fête champêtre
Type of genre scene with romantic figures pictured in an idealized park or garden setting. The theme, which may derive from the medieval Garden of Love, enjoyed a lasting vogue in European painting. The *Concert champêtre* (*c*.1510) in the Louvre, Paris, traditionally by Giorgione but often now attributed to Titian, is the best-known example from the Renaissance, and in the 18th century Watteau's elegant variations on the theme, his **fêtes galantes**, prolonged its popularity.

Feti (Fetti), **Domenico** 1588/9–1623
Italian painter. He is usually classed as a member of the Venetian school, though he was born in Rome, worked from 1613 to 1622 as court painter to Vincenzo Gonzaga at Mantua, and lived in Venice only in the last two years of his life. He was a fine portraitist, but is best known for his small-scale paintings of subjects drawn from the Parables. These, broadly painted and usually with landscape settings, are highly original—a kind of Venetian version of Dutch genre. They were very popular, and often exist in several versions with only slight variations (*The blind leading the blind*, *c*.1620/3, versions in Alnwick Castle, Northumberland; Birmingham, Barber Institute; Bologna, Pinacoteca Nazionale; Dresden, Gemäldegalerie).

Feuchtmayer, Joseph Anton
1696–1770
South German ROCOCO sculptor and stuccoist. A member of a family of sculptor-stuccadors from Wessobrunn, he settled and worked around Lake Constance. He stuccoed, carved choir-stalls, built altars, and provided sculpture for numerous churches—all of these together in his masterpiece, the pilgrimage-church of Neu-Birnau (1746–53), which contains the most celebrated of his winsome *putti*, the "*Honey-licker*".

Feuerbach, Anselm 1829–80
German painter of history, mythology and portraits, one of the leading exponents of a classicizing, idealistic trend in 19th-century German painting. He trained in Düsseldorf and Munich, and then in Antwerp and with Couture in Paris. From 1858 to 1873 he lived in Italy, where he was a friend of von Marées and Böcklin, and where he developed his characteristic style of ideal figure composition. Feuerbach was brought up amidst the ideals of ancient humanism and he tried to express these through noble subjects depicted in the style of Raphael and the great Venetian masters of the 16th century (*Plato's Symposium*, 1869, Karlsruhe, Kunsthalle). Feuerbach's skill seldom matched his ambitions, and his best works are now considered to be his portraits of the model Nanna Risi, who was his ideal of womanhood. These portraits, of which a good example (1861) is in the Staatsgalerie, Stuttgart, have, in his own words, a "truly majestic, forbidding tranquillity". Feuerbach was professor of history painting at the Vienna Academy from 1873 to 1876, then, discouraged by criticism of his ceiling painting for the Academy, *The fall of the Titans*, he returned to Italy, where he died. He thought he was a misjudged and unappreciated genius and expressed his feelings in his self-pitying autobiography, published posthumously in 1882.

Fiammingo
Italian word meaning "Fleming", applied, especially in the 17th century, to Flemish artists working in Italy.

Field, Erastus Salisbury
1805–1900
American artist, working in the LIMNER tradition. His conservative portraits are in the vein of his teacher Morse, but more delicate are his numerous treatments of *The Garden of Eden*. On the 100th anniversary of American Independence (1876) he painted a massive *Historical monument of the American Republic* (Springfield, Mass., MFA), an allegorical architectural fantasy.

Fielding, Anthony Vandyke Copley 1787–1855
English watercolourist. He was born in Yorkshire and in 1809 settled in London, where he studied under Varley. His early subjects were landscapes of Wales and the Lake District, but after 1814 he increasingly painted seascapes. Although his works were brilliantly executed with a vivid sense of colour, they were often repetitive as he turned from *plein-air* painting to studio productions to meet the demands of the market.

Figari, Pedro 1861–1938
Uruguayan painter and statesman. Although he took up painting only at the age of 60 his work is neither naive nor amateurish. His simple drawing, strong sense of colour and almost complete rejection of any perspective were deliberate pictorial devices used to emphasize the processional manner of his figure compositions—portraits of the life of the Pampas and the bustle of streets, sometimes containing humorous overtones. An example is *Candombé*, a dancing scene (Buenos Aires, Federico Vogelbaum coll.). He moved to Paris in 1925.

Figurative art
Art which represents figures, animals or other recognizable objects. The term representational art is used more or less interchangeably, and both contrast with non-figurative or ABSTRACT art.

Filarete (Antonio di Pietro Averlino)
c.1400–69?
Florentine sculptor, architect and theorist. His best-known work is the pair of bronze doors for Old St Peter's (*c*.1433–45, Rome, St Peter's), in which the figure types and the use of champlevé enamel decoration are distinctly archaic. But on the same doors Filarete made use of antique motifs, and he also produced small bronzes after the Antique: his *Marcus Aurelius* (1465, Dresden, Albertinum) was inspired by the antique equestrian statue in the Campidoglio, Rome. Accused of stealing a relic, he left Rome in 1447 and finally settled in Milan as sculptor and architect to Duke Francesco Sforza. In Milan he designed the Ospedale Maggiore and other buildings, and made terracotta reliefs (1451–65) for the Castello Sforzesco. In 1465 he completed his *Treatise on Architecture*—a fascinating jumble of old and new, of medieval and Renaissance ideas.

Filla, Emil 1882–1953
Czech painter, graphic artist, sculptor and art theorist. He made several journeys to France, Italy and Germany, 1907–14, and his early work was influenced by Expressionism and Symbolism. He soon, however, adopted Cubism, of which he was to become the Czech pioneer and leading exponent. Under the influence of the Dutch Old Masters (he spent World War I in Holland), he developed a highly personal form based on bright colours and sharply defined surfaces (*Basket of fruit*, 1916–17, Prague, NG). In the 1930s he began working in a more objective figural style, and his movement towards realism was intensified by his experiences in a concentration camp during World War II.

Filliou, Robert born 1926
French artist. In the 1950s he travelled in the USA, the Far East, Egypt and Spain. His ideas are influenced by Zen Buddhism and this is reflected in his witty CONCEPTUAL art, often deliberately absurd. He is best known for his neon tubing attached to incongruous objects.

Filonov, Pavel 1883–1941
Russian painter and graphic designer. He developed a highly individual, proto-Surrealist style in reaction to avantgarde art in St Petersburg and Europe (which he visited 1911–12). His graphics are found in Russian Futurist publications, while paintings, such as *Faces* (1919, Moscow, Tretyakov Gallery), reveal people and objects of varying sizes arranged in multi-layered compositions with social and religious themes. In the 1920s he ran a teaching studio exploring painting as a communal enterprise, but he excited official disapproval and was unable to exhibit after 1929.

Finch, Alfred William 1854–1930
Finnish painter, etcher and ceramic artist of British-Belgian extraction. He worked with Seurat and adopted a modified POINTILLISM. In 1897 he moved to Finland, where his paintings helped to transmit Neo-Impressionist influences and he exerted a decisive influence on the Finnish craft industry.

Fine arts
General term for the "higher" arts, traditionally painting, sculpture and architecture, as opposed to the decorative or applied arts.

Finiguerra, Maso 1426–64
Florentine goldsmith, trained in Ghiberti's workshop. Little of his work survives, but he was much praised in the writings of Filarete and Cellini. He worked in a style akin to Baldovinetti and Filippo Lippi and was especially expert at niello, an inlay technique; the earliest known Florentine engravings (1450s)—tiny scraps of paper with one or two *putti*—are attributed to him.

Finson, Louis (Ludovicus Finsonius)
before 1580–1617
Flemish painter, one of the earliest northern followers of Caravaggio. He was born in Bruges, made two trips to Italy, and died in Amsterdam, but worked mainly in southern France. He collected and copied Caravaggio's work as well as basing his own sombre style on it, and was important in introducing the Caravaggesque manner to France (*The Resurrection*, 1610, Aix-en-Provence, St Jean de Malte). He painted mainly religious scenes and portraits, but also occasionally genre scenes. There is a fine *Self-portrait* (a rarity by a Caravaggesque painter), signed and dated 1613, in the Musée des Beaux-Arts, Marseilles.

Fitzgerald, Lemoine 1890–1956
Canadian landscape and still-life painter. *Doc Snider's house* (1931, Ottawa, NG of Canada) shows the smooth finish and sensitive spatial interrelationships of American PRECISIONISM, with the muted colour typical of his developed manner.

Fjell, Kai born 1907
Norwegian painter and draughtsman. He studied under Revold and was influenced by Munch, by German Expressionism and by Surrealism. His early painting featured macabre dark-coloured subjects. Later, inspired by Norwegian folk art, he produced rhythmically decorative narrative compositions. Village fiddlers and women (as symbols for fertility and life) are his central motifs, as in the dreamlike *Violin* (1947, Oslo, NG).

Flanagan, Barry born 1941
British sculptor. He came to public attention with sculpture in unconventional materials, such as canvas and sand, which prevent the artist from determining a precise form. *June (2)* (1969, London, Tate) consists of a large sheet of raw flax propped against the wall by three branches. Since 1973 he has worked principally in stone, usually carved roughly, and sometimes covered with incised lines (*Figures*, 1976, Eindhoven, Van Abbemuseum).

Flandrin, Hippolyte 1809–64
French academic painter, working in the Neoclassical tradition. He studied in Lyons before starting an apprenticeship with Ingres. In 1830 he won the Prix de Rome, and in Italy, influenced by Florentine monumental painting, began to specialize in religious subjects. He returned to Paris in 1838 and received numerous decorative commissions for churches, culminating in frescos for the nave of St Vincent-de-Paul (1849–53) and St Germain-des-Prés (1856–61). He also painted histories, mythologies and portraits. See vol. 3 pp. **86–87**

Flannagan, John Bernard
1895–1942
American sculptor, an isolated and original figure. He gradually moved to free-standing pieces from painted reliefs. His early work concentrates on religious themes in an attenuated Expressionist style. After 1926 he carved almost exclusively in stone, and felt that he was expressing a living, mystical image contained within the material. As a self-taught carver he revealed considerable sensitivity to the expressive properties of the medium. He usually represented animals which, as in *Jonah and the whale* (1937, Minneapolis Institute of Fine Arts), have a sense of foetal or primordial simplicity.

Flavin, Dan born 1933
American sculptor. Since 1963, he has created coolly disquieting sculptures using light fixtures. His works range from a single fluorescent tube fixed to the wall to several in a geometric construction (such as *Pink and gold*, 1968, Chicago Museum of Contemporary Art) and more elaborate environmental pieces. His preference for simple geometric compositions and standard units is shared by the Minimal sculptors and his experiments with luminous fields of colour cast by fluorescent tubes have affinities with colour-field painting.

Flaxman, John 1755–1826
English NEOCLASSICAL sculptor, illustrator and designer, one of the earliest English artists to exercise an important influence on the development of art outside his own country. In 1770 he entered the Royal Academy Schools (forming a life-long friendship with Blake), and in 1775 began working for the potter Josiah Wedgwood. The designs which he produced for translation into the silhouette technique of Wedgwood's pottery brought out his exquisite sensitivity to line—the salient characteristic of his art. From 1787 to 1794 he was in Rome, where he produced his illustrations to the *Iliad* and the *Odyssey* (published 1793), outline drawings of

great purity and clarity, which established his fame on the Continent. Ingres and the Nazarenes are among the artists most obviously influenced by them. In England his free-standing Monument to the Earl of Mansfield (1793–1801, London, Westminster Abbey) established his reputation as a sculptor and from then he was constantly employed on private and public commissions. His free-standing monuments—the most prestigious was that of Nelson (1808–10, London, St Paul's Cathedral)—are generally less successful than his reliefs, in which he showed the grace and sensitivity of his line (Monument to Agnes Cromwell, 1800, Chichester Cathedral). In 1810 he was appointed the first Professor of Sculpture at the Royal Academy and his lectures were posthumously published. A large collection of his drawings and models is at University College, London, and his monuments are in churches throughout England. See vol. 3 p. **62**; vol. 4 p. *27*

Flegel, Georg 1563–1638
German still-life painter, one of the earliest artists to specialize in the genre. His paintings have an almost naive simplicity of composition, and show careful attention to the realistic depiction of individual objects (*Still life*, 1589, Kassel, Staatliche Kunstsammlungen).

Flinck, Govert 1615–60
Dutch portrait and history painter. With Backer, he left an early apprenticeship in Leewarden to study with Rembrandt in Amsterdam. In his work of the later 1630s and 1640s he revealed a gift for imitating his master and indeed was said to have sold his paintings as Rembrandts. He soon became highly successful himself, painting portraits closer to the style of van der Helst and receiving public commissions, including work for Amsterdam Town Hall.

Floris, Frans *c*.1517–70
Netherlandish painter. He was a pupil of Salviati and then of Lambert Lombard from 1538 to 1540, when he qualified as a master in Antwerp. In 1541 he left for Italy, where he made drawings after Michelangelo, Giulio Romano, Tintoretto and classical statuary, before returning home in 1547. He was the first Fleming to devote as much study to Venetian art as to that of Rome and Mantua, but it was Michelangelo's recently finished *Last Judgment* which exerted the greatest influence, inspiring the turbulent, muscular nudes in the large-scale history and religious paintings which earned him his reputation. A comparison between his celebrated *Fall of the angels* (1554, Antwerp, Musées Royaux des Beaux-Arts) and Bruegel's archaically Gothic version of the same theme painted eight years later is as telling an indication of his devotion to the new trends as it is of Bruegel's aversion to them. Floris, who ran a large workshop, also excelled in portraits, but they are more naturalistic than his history paintings; *The falconer's wife* (1558, Caen, Musée des Beaux-Arts) has a robust directness of characterization which looks forward to Hals. His brother **Cornelis** (1514–75) was a sculptor and architect and is principally famous as the designer of Antwerp Town Hall, the greatest Flemish building of the time.

Flötner, Peter *c*.1495–1546
German sculptor and engraver, an important figure in the spread of the Renaissance in his country. Arriving from Ansbach in 1522, he established himself as the leading sculptor in Nuremberg.

His style was strongly influenced by the Antique, and he visited Italy at least once, in 1530. His most famous work is the elegantly classical Apollo Fountain (1532, Nuremberg, Germanisches National Museum). See vol. 2 p. **159**

Folk art
Term describing art based on traditional designs, and often produced by peasant communities. Although it may include painting, it more generally pertains to decoration, as in weaving, metalwork, woodcarving and embroidery. The designs and execution are often highly complex and skilful, but it is the lack of sophistication that has impressed many artists of the 19th and 20th centuries seeking to achieve similar freshness and directness in their own work. See vol. 3 p. 126

Fontainebleau school
Term applied to artists associated with the French court at Fontainebleau during the 16th century. A first and a second school of Fontainebleau are recognized, the first being the more important. Francis I (ruled 1515–47), a great patron of Italian artists, was responsible for bringing together the first group, above all Rosso and Primaticcio, who created the system of combining painted panels with extensive surrounds of stucco sculpture which is particularly associated with the school. Heroic mythology formed the subject of most of the painted scenes, and these were treated in an elegant Mannerist style. Rosso's principal work, the Gallery of Francis I, 1530–40, still survives. Primaticcio's graceful figure style, influenced by that of Parmigianino, is seen in the Room of the Duchesse d'Etampes and the Gallery of Henri II. Through etchings after these first school works, the style became widespread. A distinctive decorative motif used in the stuccowork, strapwork, became very popular also in Flanders and England. The third important figure of the first school, Niccolò dell'Abbate, is in particular noted for his panoramic landscape paintings. Most of the panel paintings associated with the school are anonymous, but some are of very high quality, notably the famous *Diana the huntress* (*c*.1550, Paris, Louvre). The second school of Fontainebleau was developed during and after the interruption of the Wars of Religion under the patronage of Henri III and Henri IV. The style of painting was more academic, the leading artists being Dubois, Dubreuil and Fréminet. See vol. 2 pp. 161, 167

Fontana, Lucio 1899–1968
Italian painter and sculptor, born in Argentina. He came to Italy in 1905, and produced abstract painting and sculpture from 1930. During World War II he lived in Argentina and issued *The White Manifesto* (1946), introducing a new conception of art, **Spatialism**, in which artists and scientists would co-operate to express new ideas in a total art form synthesizing colour, sound, movement, space and time. In 1947 he founded the Spatialist association in Milan and issued *The Technical Manifesto of Spatialism*. In direct contrast to his earlier style of spontaneous calligraphy on roughly painted backgrounds, his work became increasingly empty of content and the materiality of the canvas was emphasized with knife-slashes and projections.

Fontana, Prospero *c*.1512–97
Italian Mannerist painter. He worked with Perino del Vaga in Genoa, assisting him with the decoration of the Palazzo

Doria, then was active in Florence and Rome, but most of his large output is in his native Bologna, where he settled in the 1540s. His rather flaccid and derivative Mannerist style typifies the trends to which the Carracci were opposed and can be seen in his *Crucifixion* of 1580 (Bologna, S. Giuseppe). Fontana's daughter **Lavinia** (1552–1614) had a considerable reputation as a portraitist in her day (*Lady with a lap dog*, Baltimore, Walters Art Gallery).

Fontanesi, Antonio 1818–82
Italian painter of Romantic and Realist landscapes. From 1849 to 1865 he painted Romantic landscapes in Geneva in the style of Calame. In 1855, in Paris, he admired works by Corot and the Barbizon school, whose influence is found in his brownish palette, depiction of trees grouped against the light, and close observation of nature at particular moments, as in *After the rain* (*c*.1870, Turin, Galleria d'Arte Moderna). In London (1865–66), he was impressed by Constable, Gainsborough and Turner. He was an influential teacher.

Foppa, Vincenzo *c*.1428–*c*.1515
Lombard painter, born in Brescia, probably a pupil of Squarcione. Active in Genoa, Milan and Pavia as well as Brescia, he was the leading painter in Lombardy before Leonardo arrived in Milan. He developed a simple monumental style exemplified in his frescos for the Cappella Portinari, S. Eustorgio, Milan (*c*.1467–68), with their understated realism. His later work combines broad handling with bold perspectival effects reminiscent of Mantegna.

Forain, Jean-Louis 1852–1931
French painter and printmaker. He received an academic training in Paris, but was influenced particularly by Degas in his scenes of dancers, racecourses and brothels. He produced many etchings and lithographs and made his living by contributing cartoons to Parisian illustrated magazines. His *Counsel and accused* (1908, London, Tate) focuses on the injustices of the legal system, emulating Daumier, but Forain was not motivated by Daumier's moral conscience. His works were shown in four of the Impressionist exhibitions.

Forner, Raquel born 1902
Argentine painter. Her works reflect dramatic events such as the Spanish Civil War and World War II, and in 1974 she completed a series of more than 30 works entitled *Space Mythology*, in homage to man's exploration of space and the moon landing (example, Washington, Corcoran). She paints broadly, with strident colour contrasts and vigorous gestures.

Fortuny y Carbò, Mariano 1838–74
Spanish genre painter, much of whose career was spent in Italy. His elaborate, detailed paintings, often costume pieces set in the 18th century (*Marriage in the priory*, 1870, Barcelona, Galleria d'Arte Moderna) fetched extremely high prices. Their influence in Spain and Italy was much contested by the Macchiaioli and other Realists.

Foster, Myles Birket 1825–99
English watercolourist and engraver, best known for idyllic pastoral scenes. He made wood engravings for *Punch* and the *Illustrated London News*, then turned to painting around 1859. His watercolour style, combining crumbling textures with sweet sentiment and honest skill, was much imitated.

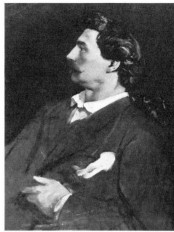
Feuerbach: Self-portrait, 1878. Karlsruhe, Gemäldegalerie (Mansell)

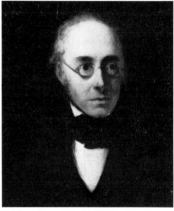
Fielding: Portrait by Sir William Boxall (1800–79), 1843. London, NPG

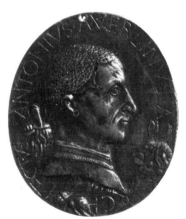
Filarete: Self-portrait bronze medal, *c*.1466. London, V&A

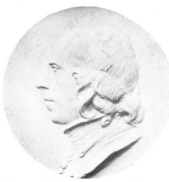
Flaxman: Self-portrait plaster medallion, *c*.1790–95. London, NPG

Foucquières (Fouquier), **Jacques**
*c.*1580/90–1659
Flemish landscape painter, who moved to Paris in 1621 and worked for Louis XIII. His style was influenced by Joos de Momper, and his work sometimes conveys an impressive sense of vast distance (*Mountainous landscape*, 1620, Nantes, Musée des Beaux-Arts). Philippe de Champaigne was his pupil.

Found object
Object selected and displayed as art, without material alteration to the form in which it was found. The idea originated with the DADAISTS and SURREALISTS. The object may be a natural form, such as a shell or stone, or a manufactured one, usually called a READY-MADE.

Fouquet, Jean or **Jehan** *c.*1420–81
The leading French painter of the 15th century and the first well-defined personality in French art. Between 1443 and 1447 he travelled to Rome, where he painted a portrait, now lost, of Pope Eugenius IV. In the workshop of Filarete he acquired some knowledge of Italian theories of perspective and classical architecture, which he later used to great advantage in the lavish miniatures for the manuscript of the *Jewish Antiquities* of Josephus (1470–76, Paris, Bibliothèque Nationale). He returned to his native Tours in 1448 to enter the service of Charles VIII, and in 1475 became court painter to Louis XI. All his work, whether miniatures or panel paintings, is clearly drawn, sober and poised. Convincing solidity of form and sense of space are clearly seen in his best-known work, the Melun diptych, a devotional altarpiece representing the *Madonna and Child* (*c.*1450) with Fouquet's wealthy patron Etienne Chevalier and St Stephen. The *Virgin and Child* is now in West Berlin (Staatliche Museen) and the other wing in Antwerp (Musées Royaux des Beaux-Arts). His masterly miniatures for the Hours of Etienne Chevalier (*c.*1455, Paris, Bibliothèque Nationale and Louvre; Chantilly, Musée Condé) demonstrate an original use of perspective and a remarkable sensitivity to landscape. See vol. 2 p. **97**

Fowler, Daniel 1810–94
Canadian watercolour painter, born in England. He emigrated to Canada in 1843, settling on Amherst Island near Kingston. He is noted particularly for his sensitive and animated depictions of the countryside around his island home.

Fragonard, Jean-Honoré 1732–1806
French painter of mythology, gallantry and landscape, one of the greatest of ROCOCO artists. He studied under Chardin and Boucher and won the Prix de Rome in 1752. After three years' further study with Carle van Loo he went in 1756 to the French Academy in Rome. There he particularly admired the work of Giambattista Tiepolo, and drew landscapes with Hubert Robert. He returned to Paris in 1761 after touring Italy (in 1773 he made a second trip) and his first Salon exhibit, *Coroesus sacrificing himself to save Callirhoe* (1765, Paris, Louvre) was a great success. Soon, however, he gave up history painting and turned to light-hearted and erotic subjects to which his gifts for witty characterization, delicate colour and vivacious brushwork were ideally suited. His dislike of court patronage was confirmed when Madame du Barry, one of Louis XV's mistresses, rejected his masterpieces, the four *Progress of Love* canvases (1771–73, New York, Frick), and he preferred to work for private patrons. His most celebrated work, *The swing* (1769, London, Wallace Coll.), is one of the quintessential works of Rococo art. The demand for such frothy, titillating paintings ceased with the Revolution, and Fragonard died virtually forgotten. See vol. 2 p. **240**

Franceschini, Marcantonio
1648–1729
Italian decorative painter, along with his teacher Carlo Cignani the leading Bolognese decorative painter of the late 17th and early 18th centuries. His art follows on from the Bolognese tradition stemming from the Carracci, and was also strongly influenced by the works of Carlo Maratta.

Francesco di Giorgio Martini
1439–1501/2
Sienese painter, sculptor, architect and inventive military engineer, active in Milan, Naples and Urbino as well as his native city. He trained under Vecchietta and shared a studio with Neroccio de' Landi, 1469–75. Despite Francesco's contemporary fame, few works survive which are certainly by him. *The Nativity* (1475, Siena, Pinacoteca), painted in an animated, lyrical, linear style, is his only signed and dated painting. Most of the other paintings attributed to him are small works such as *cassone* panels. As a sculptor his best-known works are the two bronze angels (completed 1497) on the high altar of Siena Cathedral, which reflect the influence of Donatello, who had worked in Siena in the late 1450s. By 1477 Francesco was working as an architect for Duke Federico da Montefeltro in Urbino, and he also wrote an influential architectural treatise.

Francia (Francesco Raibolini)
*c.*1450–*c.*1518
The leading Bolognese painter of his period. His gentle graceful style was based on the Umbrians Perugino and Raphael, but his figures are sometimes elongated in a manner recalling Lorenzo Costa, with whom he worked in partnership from 1483 to 1506. He is best known for his Madonnas (*"The Felicini Madonna"*, 1494, Bologna, Pinacoteca), but also produced some strikingly refined portraits (*Federico Gonzaga as a child*, 1510, New York, Metropolitan).

Franciabigio (Francesco di Cristofano) *c.*1482/3–1525
Florentine painter, a pupil of Piero di Cosimo. He was a collaborator of Andrea del Sarto and Fra Bartolommeo and painted in the new Raphaelesque classical style with great assurance but little depth. His spacious architectural settings are particularly impressive, but his figures tend to have a rather unnatural stiffness. He was at his best in portraits, which have something of the romantic dreaminess of Andrea's (*A Knight of Rhodes*, *c.*1520, London, NG).

Francis, Sam born 1923
American painter. In the late 1940s he studied under Park and Still and became one of the leading members of the second generation of ABSTRACT EXPRESSIONISTS. Since then he has been based in Paris and made several extended visits to Mexico and Japan—the calligraphy and use of space in Japanese art have had a considerable effect on his painting. By 1949 he was working with thinned pigment in irregular blot shapes seemingly thrown on the canvas in the manner of Pollock (*Big red*, 1953, New York, MOMA). Towards the end of the 1950s he began to leave large areas of open canvas, moving to an emptied centre in the 1960s. See vol. 3 p. **215**

Francken family
Flemish painters, active in the late 16th and early 17th centuries, mainly in Antwerp. It is not easy to disentangle the contribution of the many artist members of the family, but **Frans I** (1542–1616) and his son **Frans II** (1581–1642) are the two best known. Both painted Italianate religious scenes, and Frans II, the most talented, also painted landscapes and genre subjects; his charming *Adoration of the Magi* (*c.*1620, Soissons, Musée Municipal) combines elements of all three types, with its splendid winter landscape and homely rustic details. Frans II was also one of the first artists to paint the interior of picture galleries, a genre subsequently popularized by David Teniers the Younger. The best collection of the works of the family as a whole is in the Musées Royaux des Beaux-Arts, Antwerp.

François, Guy *c.*1578–1650
French CARAVAGGESQUE painter. He spent the early part of his career in Rome where he came under the influence of Saraceni as well as Caravaggio. On his return to his native Le Puy (by 1613) he supplied a large number of altarpieces for local churches, mostly still *in situ*.

Frankenthaler, Helen born 1928
American painter, whose work marks the transition between Abstract Expressionism and colour-stain painting. She studied with Tamayo and, in 1950, with Hofmann. In 1952 she painted the seminal work *Mountains and sea* (Artists's coll.) which was seen by Louis and Noland the following year. An abstract work with suggestions of landscape, it employs washes of thinned paint poured and stained into unprimed canvas. From 1958 to 1971 she was married to Motherwell. A change from oil to acrylic paint in the early 1960s allowed for more intensely saturated colour and her work has developed from an internal figuration with landscape suggestions to a treatment of the whole canvas as a field for inflection. See vol. 1 p. *133*; vol. 3 p. **219**

Freake Master
Name sometimes applied to the unknown painter of the pair of portraits (1674) of *John Freake* and his wife *Elizabeth Freake and baby Mary* in the Art Museum at Worcester, Mass. The mother and child portrait is considered one of the finest paintings of the Colonial period, with a naive charm and bold composition much superior to the average work of the period. A few other portraits, including the three of the Gibbs children (1670, Boston, MFA) and that of *Alice Mason* (1670, Quincy, Mass., Adams National Historic Site) have been attributed to this master.

Fréminet, Martin 1567–1619
French painter, a leading member of the second school of FONTAINEBLEAU. He went to Italy in the late 1580s and worked mainly in Rome, where he came under the influence of Il Cavaliere d'Arpino. He was summoned back to Paris by Henry IV in 1602 on the death of Dubreuil. Of his few surviving works, the most important is the ceiling of the Chapel of the Trinity (begun 1608) at Fontainebleau, where his heavy colour and the violent torsion of his figures combine effectively with the sophisticated stucco decoration.

French, Daniel Chester
1850–1931
American academic sculptor, well-known for his numerous public commissions. His large statue of *The minute man* (1875) for the city of Concord, Mass. (representing an eager young man, ready to defend his country in a minute) made his reputation, but his most famous work is the monumental seated figure of Abraham Lincoln (1922), for the Lincoln Memorial in Washington.

Fresco
Italian word meaning "fresh", used to describe a mural painting technique using water-based paint on lime plaster. For the true method of fresco, known as "buon fresco", a rough coat of plaster, the **arricciato**, is laid on the wall and the outlines of the design are traced on it in charcoal, and sometimes elaborated with red iron oxide pigment to complete the SINOPIA. Fresh plaster mixed with lime is laid over a small area suitable for a day's work and the painting is done, with pure pigments dispersed in water, while this layer, the **intonaco**, is still damp. Paint and plaster fuse as they dry, forming a matt, stable surface which in suitably dry climates does not flake or rub off. To complete the day-piece before the plaster dries the fresco-painter must work swiftly and decisively. By the mid-15th century, the design was often scored or retraced in charcoal on the *intonaco* by means of a full-size cartoon. Fresco colours usually dry to light tones, creating clear, airy harmonies. The large scale, together with the limited range of tones used, created, particularly in the Italian Renaissance, works of great simplicity and grandeur. As the technique is susceptible to damp, fresco-painting is confined mainly to Mediterranean areas, where it is an ancient art probably used by the Minoans and Greeks and certainly by the Romans. In his treatise of about 27 BC Vitruvius describes a fresco method similar to that explained by Cennini, *c.*1400. During the Middle Ages, **fresco secco** (painting in tempera on dry plaster) was often used as a guide for the mosaic artist, and the less durable *secco* technique continued to be used to add or to retouch details in some true frescos. The great era of true fresco painting began with Giotto and was carried on by Masaccio, Piero della Francesca, Michelangelo and others. The technique became much less common in the 18th century (Giambattista Tiepolo was the last great Italian exponent), but it was revived in the 19th century by German painters such as Cornelius and in the 20th by the Mexican muralists. See vol. 1 pp. 142–143

Freud, Lucian born 1922
British painter. Born in Berlin, the grandson of Sigmund Freud, he came to England in 1931. His early paintings are marked by a tightly linear quality expressive, as in *Girl with roses* (1947–48, British Council), of an extreme yet unspecific psychological intensity, emphasized through the staring eyes and tight grip of the figure's hands. In later portraits such as *Francis Bacon* (1952, London, Tate) the execution remains rigid with more emphasis on volume than contour. From the late 1950s he employed a looser handling of paint to convey a vital palpability in the depiction of flesh equalled by few contemporary painters. He paints his sitters either in extreme close-up or in barren interiors; the most frequent prop is a bed. Although his technical precision has led to frequent descriptions of his work as "realist", its concern with transmitting experience as opposed to appearance places him outside the "objective" tradition which has dominated most British figuration since the Euston Road school. See vol. 3 p. **252**; vol. 4 p. *17*

Freundlich, Otto 1878–1943
German painter and sculptor. He was influenced by Orphic Cubism and his aim was a balanced composition of interwoven geometric colour planes. He lived from 1924 to 1939 in Paris where he was associated with the ABSTRACTION-CRÉATION group. His sculpture *The new man* featured on the catalogue cover of the DEGENERATE art exhibition in 1937 and many of his works were destroyed by the Nazis. He died in a concentration camp.

Friedrich, Caspar David
1774–1840
German landscape painter, one of the greatest of Romantic artists. From 1794 to 1798 he studied in Copenhagen with Juel and Abilgaard, then settled for life in Dresden. From there he made journeys to his birthplace on the Baltic coast, the Harz mountains and elsewhere, but not even his friend Goethe could persuade him to visit Italy. His first works were topographical landscapes in pencil and sepia wash, but in 1807 he began painting in oils, and immediately created a sensation with *The Cross in the mountains* (1807–08, Dresden, Staatliche Kunstsammlungen). This work, painted for the chapel of Count Thun's castle at Tetschen, was the first landscape to be used as an altarpiece, and critics accused Friedrich of sacrilege. His paintings are never of biblical subjects as such, but his scenes of ruined Gothic churches, cemeteries, desolate landscapes and silent figures set in vast spaces are deeply spiritual, and create a sense of awe in front of nature hitherto unknown in painting. The monumental simplicity of these images, bathed in mist and hazy light and often painted in mauve and silver tones of great delicacy, reflects the essential melancholy of Friedrich's outlook, and he was sad, lonely and poor at his death. By 1835 he was almost paralysed, and had to return to the small sepia landscapes with which he had started his career. His importance lies in his being the first artist single-mindedly to imbue the natural phenomena of landscape, light and weather with emotional and symbolic content, but his art was too personal to find much of a following and his immediate influence was confined to some of his students at the Dresden Academy (notably Kersting and J.C. Dahl), where he taught from 1816. At the end of the century, however, his greatness was again recognized. Very few of Friedrich's paintings are outside Germany; the best collection is in Dresden. See vol. 1 p. *93*; vol. 3 pp. **74–77**

Friesz, Othon 1879–1949
French painter who studied in Le Havre alongside Braque and Dufy. Settling in Paris in 1899, he met Matisse and Rouault and exhibited as part of the FAUVE group at the 1905 Salon d'Automne. His *Landscape at Ciotat* (1907, Troyes, Pierre Lévy coll.) recalls Braque's contemporary pictures of the same view in its use of curvilinear contours and bright colours. He looked to Cézanne in 1908 but his later work was conservative.

Frink, Elisabeth born 1930
British sculptor and printmaker. She works mainly in bronze and made her reputation with angular, menacing sculpture in which the bird becomes a particularly potent image (*Harbinger bird*, 1960, London, Tate). She has also made over-life-size heads, often roughly finished but with highly polished "goggles" suggesting blindness. More recent sculptures of horses and the human figure are blander in mood and texture. See vol. 1 p. *177*

Frith, William Powell 1819–1909
English narrative painter. He first made his reputation as a history painter, then, with undisguised commercialism, turned to contemporary subjects made popular by the Pre-Raphaelites. The popular success of paintings such as *Derby day* (1856–58, London, Tate) was such that barriers had to be erected in front of them when they were exhibited at the Royal Academy. His *Reminiscences*, published in 1888, give an excellent insight into the artistic life of his day. See vol. 1 p. *49*; vol. 3 p. **82**

Froment, Nicolas active 1450–90
French painter from Languedoc, who worked in Avignon after 1468. *The Raising of Lazarus* (1461, Florence, Uffizi) clearly reveals the influence of Rogier van der Weyden in the sculptural quality of the modelling and the exaggerated edges he gave his forms. His masterpiece, the triptych of *Mary in the burning bush* (1476, Aix-en-Provence, Cathedral), executed in 1476 for René of Anjou, is more lyrical in style, and the extremely intricate nature of the religious symbolism is matched by a minutely observed landscape vista.

Fromentin, Eugène 1820–76
French painter, novelist and art critic. The Orientalist painters of the 1830s inspired his interest in North Africa, which he visited in 1846, 1848 and 1852. His own Orientalist works were greatly admired in his own time, but in the Bacchanalian *Centaurs* (1868, Paris, Petit Palais) and later in his Venetian scenes, he tried unsuccessfully to break away from the genre. Fromentin is now best known for his book *Masters of Past Times*, published in 1876, a penetrating critique of earlier Netherlandish painting and its influence on French artists such as Théodore Rousseau.

Fronte Nuovo delle Arti
(New Art Front)
Group of Italian artists formed in 1947 to combat post-War pessimism by advocating art with a more human content than that which was current. The artists involved, among them Birolli and Guttuso, included abstractionists and realists and represented many styles and ideologies. The group split up in 1948.

Frost, Terry born 1915
British painter. He began painting in 1943 when a prisoner of war. In the late 1940s and 1950s he was concerned with abstract painting which related to the experience of landscape. *Winter 1956, Yorkshire* (London, Tate) was inspired by "a strong, cold, black and white environment"—a snow-covered hill with black figures. Characteristic of his paintings are sliced elliptical shapes, firmly outlined yet not rigidly geometric.

Frottage
Technique of making patterns from the surface of objects by rubbing them through paper. A textured surface such as wood grain or coarse cloth is covered with paper and an impression taken by rubbing over the surface with pencil or crayon. The method was pioneered for use in art by Max Ernst and taken up by a number of other Surrealists. The rough design was used to stimulate the imagination and hints of form were worked up by drawing, collage and other media.

Frueauf, Rueland the Elder
died 1507
Austrian painter, active mainly in Salzburg and after 1497 in Passau. He had a large workshop producing altarpieces

with monumental figures recalling those of Netherlandish painters. His son, **Rueland the Younger** (died *c.*1545), is recorded in Passau from 1497. His *Boar hunt* and other scenes from the St Leopold altarpiece of 1507 (Klosterneuburg, Stiftsmuseum) are close to the DANUBE school in their calm and spacious landscape and backgrounds.

Fry, Roger 1866–1934
British art critic and painter. He was appointed Curator of Painting at the Metropolitan Museum, New York, in 1906, but in the same year discovered the work of Cézanne and turned his attention from Renaissance to contemporary art. His two exhibitions of Post-Impressionism (a term coined for the occasion), held in 1910 and 1912, showed the work of painters such as Cézanne, van Gogh and Matisse in London for the first time. As a critic his belief in formal values made him responsive to non-European, particularly African art. His own work as a painter was influenced by Fauvism and in 1915 he exhibited totally abstract paintings. The Courtauld Institute Galleries, London, has paintings by Fry, and furniture and pottery produced by the OMEGA Workshops which he founded in 1913, with Grant and Vanessa Bell. His books include *Vision and Design* (1920) and *Cézanne* (1927). See vol. 3 p. *112*

Fuchs, Ernst born 1930
Austrian painter, with Brauer one of the main figures associated with Viennese "Fantastic Realism". He revived certain medieval craft techniques and applied them to magical and alchemical subjects. After his conversion to Christianity he painted religious works, equally bizarre and fantastically detailed (*Mystery of the Holy Rosary*, 1958–61, egg tempera and gold-leaf on parchment, Vienna, Rosenkranzkirche).

Fuhr, Xaver born 1898
Self-taught German painter. His early Mannheim townscapes use subtle shifts in perspective to reveal the magical character and essential ambiguity of reality (*Chapel by the lake*, 1929, Duisburg, Wilhelm Lehmbruck Museum). After 1945 his work became more abstract, based on dynamic rhythms.

Führich, Joseph van 1800–76
Austrian draughtsman, graphic artist and painter. He was deeply influenced by Dürer's woodcuts and by Overbeck's graphic work, and shared the Nazarenes' longing for the pure poetry of the medieval world. The monumentality of his figure drawings (*Eliezar and Rebecca*, 1828, East Berlin, NG) was also influenced by his extensive travels in Italy. In 1840 he was appointed professor of history painting at the Vienna Academy and he painted frescos for several churches in the city.

Fuller, Isaac died 1672
English painter of decorative schemes and idiosyncratic portraits. His altarpiece in All Souls College Chapel, Oxford, was described by the diarist Evelyn in 1644 as "too full of nakeds for a chapel", but this, like most of the work on which his reputation was based, has disappeared. His major surviving works are five large canvases showing incidents from the Battle of Worcester, with Charles II's celebrated escape (London, NPG). His *Self-portraits* (*c.*1670, NPG, and 1670, Oxford, Bodleian Library) are characterized by a larger-than-life bravura which make it easy to believe the stories that he led a dissolute life.

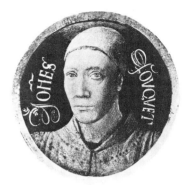
Fouquet: Self-portrait on a Limoges enamel, *c.*1450. Paris, Louvre

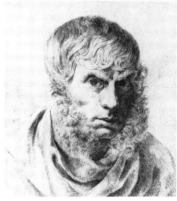
Friedrich: Self-portrait drawing, *c.*1810. East Berlin, Staatliche Museen, Kupferstichkabinett

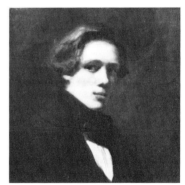
Frith: Self-portrait, 1838. London, NPG

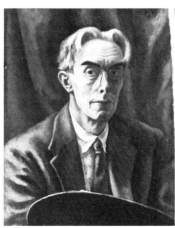
Fry: Self-portrait, 1930–34. London, NPG

Fulton, Hamish born 1946
British artist. His work is concerned with recapturing the experiences of travelling through landscape. He records his journeys both in Britain and abroad in the form of photographs which he presents captioned in heavy wooden frames suggestive of the relics of a Victorian explorer. His work has been compared to that of Richard Long but his methods are less schematic and his response to landscape more overtly romantic. See vol. 3 p. **248**

Fulton, Robert 1765–1815
American engineer and inventor, who in his early career worked mainly as a painter. He had humble beginnings painting miniature portraits in a jewellery shop in Philadelphia, but his work attracted such attention that in 1787 local businessmen sponsored him to study in London. He became a pupil of West and exhibited at the Royal Academy, but abandoned painting in 1793 to devote himself to his scientific interests, becoming the most remarkable naval engineer of his time. There are examples of his paintings in the Pennsylvania Academy of Fine Arts, Philadelphia.

Furini, Francesco *c.* 1600–46
One of the most distinctive Florentine painters of the 17th century. His only securely dated works are two impressive allegorical frescos (1636/37) on Medici history in the Pitti Palace, which show the influence of Raphael and Reni in their firm drawing and idealized types. The paintings for which he is best known, however, show morbidly sensual female nudes emerging mysteriously from dark backgrounds. These are sometimes rather sickly in flavour, but at their best display melodious draughtsmanship and a poignant eroticism (*Faith*, *c.* 1635, Florence, Pitti).

Fuseli, Henry
(Johann Heinrich Füssli) 1741–1825
Swiss painter and draughtsman, whose career was spent in England where he was a key figure of Romanticism. His father, the portrait painter **Johann Caspar** Füssli (1707–82), forced him to become a Zwinglian minister, but he never practised as a priest. Early drawings impressed the British Ambassador in Berlin, at whose suggestion Fuseli moved to England (1765) where Reynolds encouraged him to devote himself to painting. From 1770 to 1778 he studied in Rome where, responding powerfully to Michelangelo and the Mannerists, he became virtual head of a group of Scandinavian and British artists inspired by Romantic literature and the classics. After his return to England in 1779, he exhibited strikingly mannered, often grotesque and unpainterly works, inspired by literary sources and northern myths, with heavily-muscled figures in strained and violent poses. International acclaim came with his still enigmatic *Nightmare* (1781, Detroit Institute of Art), and his illustrations to the work of the Swiss physiognomist Lavater. During the 1780s and 1790s he was preoccupied with a series of paintings for two major projects—Boydell's Shakespeare Gallery (launched in 1786) and his own Milton Gallery, which opened in 1799. Highly influential in his lifetime, his work was largely ignored thereafter until the 20th century, when his disturbing imagery made him a rich quarry for psychoanalytical interpretation. See vol. 3 pp. **62–63**

Futurism
Italian art movement founded in 1909 by the poet Marinetti. Initially a literary group, its key artist members were the painters Balla, Boccioni, Carrà, Russolo and Severini and the architect Sant'Elia. Manifestos were published on painting (1910), sculpture (1912) and architecture (1914) as well as photography, cinema and music. Futurism was concerned with incorporating the dynamism of modern technological society into art. As Marinetti declared in 1909: "The splendour of the world has been enriched with a new form of beauty, the beauty of speed." To this end the group opposed *fin de siècle* pessimism on the one hand and the deadening weight of artistic tradition on the other. The first major exhibition was held in Milan in 1911, followed by a tour through France, England, Germany and Holland in 1912. After exposure to Cubism the art of the Futurists approached abstraction, using Cubist instead of Divisionist devices for new, dynamic purposes. Although Marinetti formed a new group after the war, it had little in common with the initial group that had broken up. See vol. 3 pp. 152–153

Fyt, Jan 1611–61
Flemish painter and etcher, primarily of still-life and animal subjects. He was a pupil of Snyders, and was active mainly in Antwerp, but he also travelled in Holland, France and Italy. Fyt had a delicate feeling for the texture of the objects he depicted, but he was able to combine this with a grandeur of design suitable to the large scale (for still life) on which he often worked (*Still life with a page*, 1644, London, Wallace Coll.).

Gabo, Naum
(Naum Neemia Pevsner) 1890–1977
Russian sculptor. He became a medical student in Munich in 1910 but in 1913 and 1914 he visited his brother Antoine Pevsner in Paris and on the outbreak of World War I retired to Oslo, where he made his first sculptures in about 1916. In the same year he was joined by his brother Antoine, and in 1917 both returned to Russia, where they came into contact with Tatlin and Malevich in the Moscow College of Art. These artists had begun to postulate new materials and forms for sculpture, and Gabo himself produced a series of *Sculptural models*, which explored the "forms of space and time" which he discussed in his *Realist Manifesto*, posted up all over Moscow in 1920. Finally, with the *Kinetic construction* of the same year (London, Tate)—basically a piece of wire set vibrating by an electric motor in the base—he incorporated a new element, kinetic rhythm. Although he left Russia in 1922 in reaction to the materialism and utilitarianism of the Moscow Constructivists, his sculptures, made of metal and glass, were received as Constructivist in the West. His later writings, however, (published for example in *Circle*, 1937, an international survey of Constructivist art) reveal the gulf between his humanist approach and the pragmatic "laboratory studies" of his Russian counterparts. In his later linear constructions, such as *No.1.1943* (London, Tate), he used thin rods arranged in a fashion which he described as related to the growth patterns of the natural world, enclosing space and often implying movement. He lived in Germany, England, and finally America, and is recognized as the founder of CONSTRUCTIVISM in the West. See vol. 1 p. *192*; vol. 3 pp. **158–159, 180**

Gaddi, Agnolo active 1369–96
Florentine painter. He was the son and pupil of Taddeo, and thus perpetuated a direct line of descent from Giotto to the end of the 14th century. His most important work is the cycle of frescos of *The story of the Cross* in the choir of S. Croce, Florence, painted in the early 1380s. Later works are the frescos of *The story of the Virgin and her girdle* in Prato Cathedral (1392–95) and the altarpiece for S. Miniato al Monte, Florence (1396). Many panel paintings are attributed to him, including examples in Florence (Uffizi), London (NG), New Haven (Yale University Art Gallery) and Philadelphia (Museum of Art). His main contribution to Florentine art was his use of light colours, especially white and yellow, which influenced later painters such as Lorenzo Monaco. See vol. 2 p. 85

Gaddi, Taddeo, *c.* 1300–*c.* 1366
Florentine painter, the son of **Gaddo** Gaddi, also known as Gaddo di Zanobi (*c.* 1250–1327/30?), a painter and mosaicist. Taddeo was the closest follower of Giotto, for whom he is said to have worked for 24 years. In 1347 he was described as the best painter in Florence. His most important surviving work is a cycle on *The life of the Virgin* in the Baroncelli Chapel of S. Croce, painted between 1332 and 1338. These frescos are typical of the period in turning away from Giotto's logical clarity in favour of a more dramatic presentation. Among the panel paintings attributed to him is an impressively sombre *Pietà* in Yale University Art Gallery. See vol. 2 p. **85**

Gainsborough, Thomas 1727–88
British portrait and landscape painter. He was born in Suffolk, and trained as a painter in London from about 1740, probably under the French artist Gravelot, by whom he was introduced to the Rococo style of Watteau. In addition, he learnt much from 17th-century Dutch landscape paintings, which he restored and copied for dealers. Gainsborough maintained that landscape was his first love, but the bulk of his output consisted of more financially rewarding portraits. From 1748 to 1759 he worked in Suffolk, painting a number of small portraits of full-length figures in landscape settings in the manner of Hayman, the most splendid example of which is *Mr and Mrs Andrews* (*c.* 1748, London, NG). In 1759 he moved to Bath, where his style became much freer and more dashing, reflecting, as in his most famous work, *"The Blue Boy"* (*c.* 1770, San Marino, Huntington Art Gallery), his profound appreciation and understanding of van Dyck and, in landscape, of Rubens. Gainsborough settled in London in 1774, and became a founder-member of the Royal Academy. His late works include, besides portraits and landscapes, a number of FANCY PICTURES—pastoral scenes with life-size genre figures, usually children (*Peasant girl gathering sticks*, 1782, Manchester City Art Gallery). Gainsborough's art is in strong contrast to the ideals of his great rival Reynolds. He was not attracted to literary or historical subject matter and his work has no moral implications. Unlike most contemporary portraitists he painted his own draperies and gained his effects from his feeling for rhythm, colour and the texture of paint, combined with an extraordinary ability to evoke mood. See vol. 1 pp. *62*, *147*; vol. 2 pp. **252–253, 255**

Galimberti, Sándor 1883–1915
Hungarian painter. In 1914, in Holland, he painted a large and important work called *Amsterdam* (Pécs, Jannus Pannonius Museum). It shows the influence of Fauvism, Cubism and German Expressionism. The spectator is given a bird's-eye view of the town, reminiscent of medieval images, and painted mainly in dark browns outlined in black. On the outbreak of World War I he returned to Hungary, where he committed suicide.

Gallait, Louis 1810–87
Belgian painter. His enormous eclectic paintings of national subjects are more or less forgotten, though in his day they won him great fame at home and abroad. An excellent example is *The abdication of Charles V* (1841, Brussels, Musées Royaux des Beaux-Arts).

Gallego, Fernando
c. 1440–after 1507
Spanish painter, active mainly in his native Salamanca. His impassive figures show some familiarity with the work of Dirk Bouts, although he is not known to have travelled to the Netherlands. Painstaking naturalistic detail and a dynamic use of line are other characteristics of his style. Major works include the Retable of S. Ildefonso of 1467 in Zamora Cathedral, and the now decaying ceiling frescos in the Old Library of Salamanca Cathedral. He was the leading Castilian painter of the second half of the 15th century and had a large following in the provincial workshops of Salamanca, Castile and Zamora.

Gallen-Kallela, Akseli
(originally Axel Gallén) 1865–1931
The greatest artist and prime mover in the revival of a national Finnish art. A precocious realist prior to his first Paris trip in 1884, he admired Bastien-Lepage, but later rejected naturalism as inadequate for the rendering of Finnish myth, which was to be his principal inspiration. In 1890 he first visited Karelia in search of original folk culture, and the large Aino triptych (1891, Helsinki, Ateneum) is no longer consistently realistic. A Symbolist phase, 1893–95, brought contacts with Scandinavian artists and writers in Berlin, where he exhibited with Munch (1895). By this time he had succeeded in adapting Synthetist stylization to mythical subjects: *The defending of Sampo* (1896, Turku Art Museum) and other works of this period on the theme of *Kalevala*, the Finnish national epic, represent the climax of his career. He produced a series of illustrations for the poem in 1922. His monumental work includes frescos in a mausoleum at Pori (1903) and in the Finnish National Museum (1928). He was also highly influential as a designer. His house in Helsinki is now a museum devoted to his work.

Gambara, Lattanzio *c.* 1530–73/4
Italian painter, born in Brescia. He was a pupil of the Mannerist Antonio Campi in Cremona, but later returned to Brescia to collaborate with the aging Romanino on the decoration of the Palazzo Averoldi. His most important surviving works are in the Cathedral at Parma, where he decorated the nave with scenes from *The life of Christ* (executed at intervals between 1567 and 1572). He died after falling from scaffolding.

Gao Kegong 1248–after 1310
Chinese painter. His family originated in Central Asia, and may well have been of non-Chinese origin. If so, he was one

of many such who rose to political eminence under Kubla Khan at the Peking court. Later he moved south to Hangzhou, and it is the soft scenery of this region which dominates his work. The mist-shrouded mountains he painted owe much to Mi Fei, whom he consciously followed, but he was also a student of pre-Song landscape, and the massiveness of his peaks is a legacy of Dong Yuan and Juran (*Clearing after spring rain*, 1299, Taiwan, National Palace Museum).

Garofalo (Benvenuto Tisi) *c.*1481–1559
Italian painter, active in Ferrara, possibly a pupil of Boccaccino. He formed a personal idiom from a variety of sources including Rogier van der Weyden, Giorgione, Leonardo, Michelangelo and Raphael, but acquired only the outward indices of these great masters' styles, often producing a stiff and over-sophisticated effect, as for instance in the turbulent *Massacre of the Innocents* (1519, Ferrara, Pinacoteca).

Gatch, Lee 1902–66
American painter. He was taught by Lhôte and Kisling in Paris in 1924. Their influence and Klee's is evident in the mixture of School of Paris abstraction and Expressionism which marks his Pennsylvania landscapes of the 1930s. He tended to loosen and blur his Cubist planes during the next decade and approach a Nabi-like richness of colour (*Dances*, 1955, Washington, Hirschorn).

Gaudier-Brzeska, Henri 1891–1915
French sculptor. He died in the trenches during World War I aged only 23, but his few finished works were highly influential. After travelling around Europe he went to Paris, where he added the name of his Polish companion Sophie Brzeska to his own. In January 1911 they went to London, where he began to work as a sculptor and was included in major avantgarde exhibitions. Turning away from the influence of Rodin around 1913, he began to make carvings that show instead the inspiration of Brancusi, Epstein and tribal art. He was a close friend of Wyndham Lewis and the poet Ezra Pound, and became particularly associated with VORTICISM. *Red stone dancer* (1913, London, Tate) is a fine example of his final style. See vol. 3 p. **155**

Gauguin, Paul 1848–1903
French painter, sculptor and printmaker, with Cézanne and van Gogh the greatest of the POST-IMPRESSIONISTS and one of the founding figures of modern art. He spent his childhood in Peru, and started painting only around 1873, when he was working as a stockbroker. He met the Impressionists and painted with Pissarro and Cézanne, before spending long periods at PONT-AVEN in Brittany. Fascinated by the daily life and religious feelings of the peasants there, he painted *The vision after the sermon*, also called *Jacob wrestling with the angel* (1888, Edinburgh, NG), a key work marking Gauguin's break with Impressionism and discovery of his own style (see SYNTHETISM). It shows the unsophisticated Breton peasants' vision after a sermon, the non-naturalistic red ground highlighting the fact that the scene takes place in the imagination. Gauguin's rejection of the naturalism of the Impressionists in favour of a subject matter provided by the imagination and depicted by expressionist means was his most influential contribution to the development of Western art. In this he

was allied with the Symbolists, with the Nabis—the artists who surrounded him in Brittany—and with van Gogh, whose friendship with Gauguin broke up dramatically at Arles in 1888. Gauguin also pioneered appreciation of the simple and primitive, a taste which led him to Martinique in 1887, Tahiti in 1891–93 and 1895–1901, and finally to the Marquesas Islands, where he died. He also widened artistic horizons by using postcards of works of art of many different cultures—Javanese, Greek, Egyptian—as inspiration for his paintings. His Breton style, with its flat contoured figures, gradually matured into the richly coloured, subtly modelled and allusive works of his South Sea period. Native and European myth are woven into highly personal visions of the human condition, as in his celebrated allegory of life *Where do we come from? What are we? Where are we going?* (1897, Boston, MFA). A forceful personality, Gauguin's influence has been equally dominating. See vol. 1 p. *79*; vol. 3 pp. *103*, **112–113, 116–117,** 120

Gaulli, Giovanni Battista (Il Baciccio) 1639–1709
Italian painter, celebrated for his *Adoration of the name of Jesus* (1674–79), a ceiling fresco on the nave vault of the Gesù, Rome. This is one of the greatest masterpieces of Baroque decoration, and in its sense of tumultuous, joyous movement it is equalled in Italy only by Pozzo's ceiling in S. Ignazio, Rome. Gaulli was a protégé of Bernini, and the stucco figures so brilliantly married to his Gesù painting are by Bernini's favourite pupil, Raggi. Although Gaulli's fame is inseparable from this work, he carried out other fine decorations in Rome (pendentives in S. Agnese in Piazza Navona, *c.*1670) and was also a distinguished painter of altarpieces and portraits (*The death of St Francis Xavier*, *c.*1675, Rome, S. Andrea al Quirinale; *Clement IX*, *c.*1667, Rome, Galleria Nazionale).

Gavarni, Paul (Guillaume-Sulpice Chevalier) 1804–66
French caricaturist. He made fashion sketches and a few unsigned political caricatures after the Revolution of 1830, but specialized in humorous, graceful satires of the bourgeoisie. In 1847 he was in London, where he published a series of plates depicting life among the poor. He returned to Paris in 1851.

Geertgen tot Sint Jans active *c.*1480–90
Northern Netherlandish painter, born in Leyden, one of the most attractive artists of his time, but relatively obscure. Van Mander says that he was the pupil of Ouwater and that he died at the age of 28. He was a lay-brother of the Order of St John in Haarlem, from which he takes his name (little Gerard of St John). Two panels (originally two sides of a wing) showing *The Lamentation* and *The burning of St John the Baptist's bones* (Vienna, Kunsthistorisches) are all that remain of a triptych of *The Crucifixion* painted for the Brotherhood, and form the basis for further attributions. About 15 paintings are now given to him, their most distinctive feature being innocent, doll-like figures with smooth, almost egg-like heads. Geertgen's other salient characteristics are his deep feeling for nature and his sensitivity to light, the former shown particularly in *St John the Baptist in the Wilderness* (West Berlin, Staatliche Museen); the latter in *The Nativity* (London, NG), a radiantly joyous nocturnal scene. See vol. 2 pp. **98–99**

Gelder, Aert de 1645–1727
Dutch painter of portraits, histories and landscapes. He studied with Hoogstraten in Dordrecht, his native town, then became one of Rembrandt's last pupils, working in his studio from about 1661 to 1663. For the rest of his life he practised Rembrandt's style—the only Dutch artist to do so in the 18th century. His palette, however, was lighter and more varied than his master's. *Jacob's dream* (London, Dulwich College Picture Gallery), a good example of his work, was very popular during the 19th century, when it was attributed to Rembrandt.

Gemito, Vincenzo 1852–1929
Italian sculptor, born and active in Naples. His pleasing naturalism is seen in early terracotta heads of children and his numerous portraits, including Giuseppe Verdi and fellow-artists Fortuny and Meissonier. Of several versions of the enchanting *Boy fishing*, the most famous is the bronze in the Bargello, Florence (1879). Numerous drawings, pastels and watercolours survive, but after 1881 he became insane.

Geneleos active mid-6th century BC
Greek sculptor from Ionia, known from an inscription on a group of marble statues found at the Temple of Hera on Samos and now in the Vathy Museum, Samos. The group consists of four standing figures—three girls and a young boy—and a seated and a reclining figure, and most probably represents the family of the dedicator. The figures are fluent and graceful in the ARCHAIC mode, with a softness in the forms suggested beneath the drapery which contrasts with the solidity of mainland works of the time.

Generalić, Ivan born 1914
Yugoslav painter from the village of Hlebine (north Croatia), where he was discovered by Hegedušić. He is now the leading member of the school of peasant-painters which developed in Hlebine, where he still lives as the veteran of Yugoslav NAIVE painting. The inspiration he draws from everyday scenes of village life is best seen in his early masterpiece, *The funeral of Štef Halaček* (1934, Zagreb, Gallery of Modern Art).

Genovés, Juan born 1930
Spanish painter. His work is realist and concerned, like Canogar's, with an almost photo journalistic criticism of society. The most significant influence upon him is that of the film-maker Eisenstein, and he bases his imagery on photographs of moving crowds. His concern with these anonymous configurations of frightened humans seems to be less political than philosophic. His forms are minute and structured in narrative sequences which use cutting and montage techniques in order to relate the images to film.

Genre painting
Term used to describe paintings depicting everyday life. Genre painting flourished most notably in Holland in the 17th century, when the prosperous, comfortable citizens of the newly independent country took delight in representations of their ordered, peaceful daily round. The tradition, however, goes back to classical times, and Pliny describes paintings of market stalls, barber's shops and other low-life subjects. In academic theory genre painting was placed among the lowest categories of painting. The word genre is also used more broadly to mean a category of art: thus landscape, portraiture and still life are all genres.

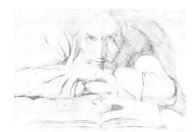
Fuseli: *Self-portrait drawing, c.*1820. London, NPG

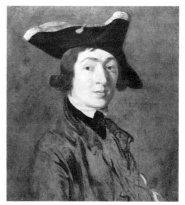
Gainsborough: *Self-portrait, 1754.* Lord Cholmondeley coll.

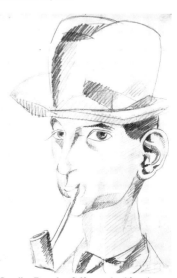
Gaudier-Brzeska: *Self-portrait with a pipe, no. 1, c.*1913. Cambridge, Kettles Yard

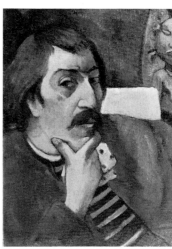
Gauguin: *Self-portrait, 1893.* A. Sachs coll. (Mansell)

Gentile da Fabriano c.1370–1427
Italian painter, with Ghiberti the outstanding representative in Italy of the INTERNATIONAL GOTHIC style. He came presumably from Fabriano in the Marches, but soon reached Venice, where his frescos in the Doge's Palace (now lost) established his fame. He is recorded in Brescia in 1414 and in the early 1420s began a highly influential journey south, reaching Florence in 1423, then Siena, Orvieto and, in 1427, Rome, where he was painting frescos (also lost) in S. Giovanni Laterano at the time of his death. His early style—his exquisite use of gold and of rich colours, of graceful figures in floating, quietly curvilinear drapery—is represented by the Valle Romita polyptych (c.1410, Milan, Brera). His greatest surviving work is *The Adoration of the Magi* (1423, Florence, Uffizi), famous not only for the splendour of its main panel but also for the naturalistic narrative and revolutionary handling of light (including a night scene with three light sources) in the predella, and even for the beautifully painted flowers in the pilaster panels. The influence of Masaccio has been seen in the main figures of his Quaratesi polyptych (1425, Florence, Uffizi; Vatican; Washington, NG, and Hampton Court, Royal coll.) and it would be wrong to oppose Masaccio's Renaissance painting to Gentile's Gothic too rigidly—the earliest known drawings after the Antique are by Gentile (Milan, Ambrosiana, and elsewhere). Whereas Masaccio's reputation was largely posthumous, Gentile was recognized as the leading painter of his day, and his work provided an inspiration for numerous and diverse artists. He was assisted by Pisanello in Venice and Rome, and by Jacopo Bellini in Florence, and profoundly influenced Giovanni di Paolo and Sassetta. His greatest follower was perhaps Fra Angelico. See vol. 2 pp. **88–89**

Gentileschi, Artemisia 1593–c.1652
Italian CARAVAGGESQUE painter, the daughter of Orazio. She was born in Rome, and worked mainly there and in Florence before settling in Naples in 1630. Apart from a visit to her father in England, 1638–40, she was based in Naples for the rest of her life, and her most distinctive works are powerful and sombre. She was very precocious—the highly accomplished *Susannah and the Elders* (Pommersfelden, Schloss Weissenstein) is dated 1610. Her favourite subject was the story of Judith and Holofernes, of which she painted at least seven pictures (examples, Detroit Institute of Arts, and Florence, Uffizi). Her seeming obsession with the theme of female decapitating male has been explained on feminist grounds (she was allegedly raped by Agostino Tassi).

Gentileschi, Orazio 1563–1639
Italian painter, one of the best and most individual of Caravaggio's followers. He was born in Pisa and settled in Rome in about 1576. His early style was Mannerist, but he came under Caravaggio's influence around the turn of the century, and was one of the few Caravaggesque painters to have close personal acquaintance with the master. His work lacks Caravaggio's power, but is distinguished by clear, graceful draughtsmanship, noble, stately figures and poetic feeling (*The Annunciation*, probably 1623, Turin, Pinacoteca). He left Rome in 1621 and worked in Genoa and France before settling in England in 1626. His travels helped to spread the Caravaggesque manner, but by the time he painted his main works in England, the ceiling paintings commissioned by Charles I for the Queen's House at Greenwich (probably after 1635, now in London, Marlborough House), his colours had become very light and his links with Caravaggio minimal.

Geometric art
Art of the period of pre-classical Greece (9th to 8th centuries BC) named after the decoration characteristic to its pottery. The style progresses from early simple bands of pattern to complex schemes in which friezes of stylized animals and humans may occur. See vol. 2 p. 34

Gérard, Baron François-Pascal 1770–1837
French painter. He was born in Rome and was a pupil there of J.-L. David. Gérard was principally a portraitist, and scored his first great success at the 1796 Paris Salon with his portrait of *Jean-Baptiste Isabey and his daughter* (Paris, Louvre). Thereafter he rapidly became the leading society and court portraitist of his day (*Madame Recamier*, 1802, Paris, Musée Carnavalet). He also painted elegant mythological paintings, of which the best-known is *Cupid and Psyche* (1798, Louvre).

Gerhaerts von Leyden, Nicolaus active 1462–73
Netherlandish sculptor. He was one of the most original sculptors of his period in northern Europe, and several signed or documented works, in stone and wood, survive; the earliest is the tomb of Archbishop Jacob von Sierck (1462, Trier, Bischöfliches Museum). The Crucifixion group in polychromed walnut from a dismantled altarpiece (1462, Nordlingen, Georgskirche) is characteristic of the vitality and warmth of his style, the figures garbed in voluminous drapery reflecting the strong influence of Sluter. Gerhaerts travelled from Trier to Strasbourg and to Vienna, and his style was highly influential in the flowering of late Gothic sculpture in Germany, though his great altarpiece for Constance Cathedral, 1465–67, is lost. The expressive sandstone bust of a man (c.1476, Strasbourg, Musée de l'Oeuvre Notre-Dame) is held to be a self-portrait. See vol. 2 p. **158**

Géricault, Théodore 1791–1824
French painter, one of the founders of ROMANTICISM. He first studied with Carle Vernet and frequented the Louvre, emulating the exuberance of Rubens in copies of his work. In 1810–11 he received a thorough classical training as a pupil of Guérin but his visit to Florence and Rome (1816–17) proved more decisive for his style, awakening an enduring admiration for Michelangelo and Baroque art. A brilliant horseman himself, Géricault made numerous studies in Rome on the theme of the race in the Corso of the riderless horses for a projected painting, later abandoned. His most famous work, *The raft of the Medusa* (1819, Paris, Louvre), painted after his return to Paris, caused a political scandal and was to prove highly influential on the younger generation of Romantic artists. In 1820 he took this work for exhibition in England, where he remained until 1822, painting *The Derby at Epsom* (Louvre), executing many lithographs and absorbing the impact of Stubbs' animal paintings and Constable's landscapes. In the two years preceding his early and tragic death, he began monumental projects, never realized, and executed a series of penetrating portraits of mental patients in the care of Dr Georget, a pioneer of humane treatment for the insane. Géricault made wide use of the oil-sketch and painted directly on to the canvas with the power and spontaneity that became hallmarks of the Romantic style. His influence was profound on his successors, of whom Delacroix was one. See vol. 1 p. *69*; vol. 3 pp. **78–79**

Gérôme, Jean-Léon 1824–1904
French painter and sculptor. He studied under Delaroche, whom he accompanied to Italy in 1844, and with Gleyre, who first inspired his interest in the Middle East. Between 1856 and 1875 he paid regular visits to Egypt, and became recognized as one of the leading painters of oriental subjects. His paintings are highly finished and painstakingly realistic (*The guard of the harem*, 1859, London, Wallace Coll.). Anti-innovatory, especially anti-Impressionist, Gérôme was a pillar of the art establishment. From 1878 he turned mainly to sculpture. See vol. 3 pp. **86–87**

Gerstl, Richard 1883–1908
Austrian painter. His first works show the strong influence of Klimt's Sezession style in their elaborate decorative patterns. The style for which he is best known, however, anticipates the painterly Expressionism of painters such as Kokoschka in its often anguished psychological study of the human face and body. *The sisters* (c.1907, Vienna, Osterreichische Galerie) shows a grotesque pair of women seen as if about to metamorphose into bird-like mannequins. One of his finest paintings is a group portrait of the composer Schoenberg's family (c.1908, Vienna, Museum der 20 jahrhunderts). Gerstl committed suicide after running off with Schoenberg's wife. See vol. 3 p. 195

Gerstner, Karl born 1930
Swiss painter. Interested in philosophy and in music, he admires logical thinking and aspires to produce an exactitude of sensation to match the exactitude of mathematical models. The relationship of art with science concerns him greatly and his work, in its geometrical purity, has obvious links with the Constructivist tradition.

Gertler, Mark 1891–1939
British painter, of Polish-Jewish parentage. An early painting such as *The artist's mother* (1911, London, Tate) is based on drawing and close observation, but his later work was strongly affected by folk art. A notable example is *Merry-go-round* (1916, London, Ben Uri Gallery), a fiercely coloured painting, probably to be understood as a satire on militarism. It shares a mechanistic quality with his one sculpture, *Acrobats* (1917, London, Tate). He committed suicide on the failure of an exhibition.

Gertsch, Franz born 1930
Swiss PHOTO-REALIST painter. His large paintings, usually, but not always, containing people, do in a sense reproduce the objectivity of the photograph, but what is immediately striking is that they add a revelatory quality, a heightened perception of reality—superrealist is an appropriate adjective.

Gesso
Brilliant white coating of gypsum and glue used on rigid supports as a ground for painting. In medieval tempera paintings it was usually polished to give a smooth surface imparting luminosity to subsequent colour layers. Though unsuitable on canvas it is also used as a ground for oil-painting on panels or boards. See vol. 1 pp. 140–141

Gheeraerts the Younger, Marcus 1562–1636
Flemish portrait painter, the son of the engraver **Marcus the Elder** (c.1530–c.1590), with whom he came to London in 1568. He married the sister of de Critz, and his own sister married Isaac Oliver. In the 1590s he became the most fashionable portraitist in London, producing ambitious but rather impersonal portraits of great splendour. He painted Elizabeth I and James I, and was the favourite painter of Anne of Denmark. After about 1615 he ceased to be fashionable at the highest levels of society. His most famous work is the "Ditchley" Elizabeth I (c.1592, London, NPG).

Gheyn, Jacob II de 1565–1629
Dutch painter, engraver and draughtsman. He studied under his father **Jacob I** (c.1530–82), a history painter, glass painter and miniaturist working in Antwerp, and in the late 1580s under Goltzius. Jacob II worked in Haarlem, Amsterdam, Leyden and The Hague and was an important figure in the transition from Mannerism to realism. His drawings and etchings were more advanced than his paintings, and in his informality and spontaneity as a draughtsman he looks forward to Rembrandt. *Woman and child looking at a picture book*, a pen-and-wash drawing in West Berlin (Kupferstichkabinett) shows him at his best. His son **Jacob III** de Gheyn (c.1596–1641) was an engraver, chiefly of mythological subjects.

Ghiberti, Lorenzo 1378–1455
Florentine sculptor, goldsmith, stained-glass designer, architect and writer. He was a major figure in the transition between Gothic and Renaissance, essentially an INTERNATIONAL GOTHIC artist of the highest order. Though he executed several life-size bronzes, notably *St John the Baptist* (1412–16), *St Matthew* (1419), and *St Stephen* (1425–29), for Orsanmichele, Florence (still *in situ*), and the Shrine of St Zenobius in the Cathedral (1439–42), he is most widely celebrated for his two pairs of richly gilded bronze doors for the Baptistery in Florence. In 1401 he won the commission for the first set of doors against Brunelleschi, Jacopo della Quercia and others with his relief of *The sacrifice of Isaac* (Florence, Bargello). These doors (1403–24) featured 28 quatrefoils of the life of Christ and Evangelists and Doctors of the Church, in which Ghiberti gradually concerted the grace and flow of the earlier scenes with fuller articulation of the figures in the later; even in the earliest scenes he borrowed from the Antique. The second set, known as the Gates of Paradise (1425–52), comprised 10 large squarish plaques of Old Testament scenes. Here the relief is pictorial, making use of perspective: each plaque contains a number of episodes in continuous representation. These Ghiberti himself called "effects", and the second doors, for all their Renaissance motifs, are above all supremely decorative. Ghiberti's *Commentaries*, both an account of his own career and an analysis of Italian art history, is fascinating and the first autobiography of an artist. He had greater prestige in the first half of the 15th century than any other sculptor, and his flourishing workshop produced designs for tombs, altars and stained glass. It also provided the principal training ground for the younger generation of Florentine artists including Donatello, Masolino, Uccello, Michelozzo and Benozzo Gozzoli. See vol. 1 pp. **194–195**; vol. 2 pp. **100–101**

Ghika, Nicolas born 1906
Greek artist. He studied in Paris, 1922–25, and in 1934 returned to Athens, where he was Professor of Painting at the Architecture School, 1941–57. He has travelled widely. In the 1930s he adopted a Cubist style and later began to paint Mediterranean landscapes of a lyrical quality. His colours emphasize the dry, bright light of the south, while his composition skilfully adapts architectural motifs to his own semi-abstract design. He has written on art, illustrated the poetry of Cavafy, and designed for the theatre.

Ghirlandaio, Domenico 1449–94
Florentine painter. He was a pupil of Baldovinetti and possibly also of Verrocchio. With his younger brothers **Benedetto** (1458–97) and **Davide** (1452–1525) he established a large workshop producing frescos and altarpieces for a great many Florentine churches. In them he left a vivid record of his contemporaries, their cultures, faces, furniture and manners. His concentration on descriptive detail (reflecting Netherlandish influence) gives *St Jerome* and *The Last Supper* (1480, Florence, Ognissanti) a slightly pedestrian air, but his *Life of St John the Baptist* cycle (1485–90, Florence, S. Maria Novella) seems to reveal without exaggeration or sentiment an era in Florentine social history. Ghirlandaio also painted frescos in Pisa, San Gimignano and in Rome in the Sistine Chapel (*The Calling of the Apostles*, 1481–82). He also made intimate small tempera portraits (*The old man and his grandson*, undated, Paris, Louvre), but most of his meticulous portrayals are cooler in tone, such as *Lucrezia Tornabuoni* (c.1475, Washington, NG). There, in an inscription, he confesses his inability to convey the beauty of the soul as of the face—the great difference between him and his contemporary Leonardo. His son **Ridolfo** (1483–1561) was also a competent portraitist, and a friend of Raphael. Michelangelo was Domenico's pupil. See vol. 2 pp. **116–117**

Ghislandi, Giuseppe
(Fra Galgario) 1655–1743
The most distinguished Italian portrait painter of the late Baroque. He was born in Bergamo and trained in Venice, where he lived for about 25 years and became a lay-brother of the Order of S. Francesco di Paola. In about 1700 he settled permanently in his native city. His straightforward and sober portraiture is characteristic of much Brescian and Bergamesque art, in the tradition established by Moroni. There are good examples in the Accademia Carrara in Bergamo, and the Accademia in Venice.

Giacometti, Alberto 1901–66
Swiss sculptor and painter, one of the most original of the 20th century. From 1922 to 1925 he studied sculpture at the Paris Academy under Bourdelle. In 1930 he joined the Surrealist group and until 1935 made witty Surrealist constructions similar to those of other members of the group; an example is *The palace at 4 a.m.* (1923, New York, MOMA). In the mid-1930s he returned to the human figure in both painting and sculpture, but it was not until 1948 that he received public acclaim with an exhibition of his work in New York. Giacometti's sculptures are of stick-like figures of varying scale often placed in dramatic groups. Some of the early ones become so slight and attenuated that they seem to be disappearing; this tendency changed after World War II, when the figures became larger. However,

Giacometti is always concerned with the apparent capacity of light to eat away at the confines of matter. His figures are alienated and emphasize an Existential sense of immobility and isolation; he was, in fact, friendly with the Existentialist philosopher Jean-Paul Sartre, who wrote an influential introduction to the catalogue of the New York exhibition. Sartre saw Giacometti's work as revealing perfectly the sense of *Angst* typical of modern man. His paintings and drawings are almost entirely portraits of friends and relations. In an extended series of drawings, *Caroline* (example, 1965, London, Tate), Giacometti showed his creative "inability" to find a finished form. Although Giacometti's works are figurative they seem to question deeply the possibility of a realistic aesthetic. See vol. 1 p. *175*; vol. 3 pp. *181*, **232–233**

Giacometti, Giovanni 1868–1933
Swiss painter, father of Alberto Giacometti. He studied in Paris with Bouguereau and Robert-Fleury and was closely associated with Hodler and Buchser. He took part in several important avantgarde exhibitions, such as the Die Brücke show in Dresden in 1908, his work combining the decorative sinuous line of Jugendstil with the strong local and expressive colour of Post-Impressionism (*Rainy atmosphere at Maloja*, 1908, Chur, Kunsthaus).

Giambologna (Giovanni Bologna) 1529–1608
Italian sculptor of Flemish origin, the most important sculptor in Italy between Michelangelo and Bernini, and one of the leading figures of MANNERISM. He was trained in his native Flanders but came to Rome in the early 1550s, finally settling in Florence. His first major project (1563–66) was the Fountain of Neptune in Bologna, with its powerful bronze statue of the god dominant. The monumental two-figure marble sculptures, *Samson and the Philistine* (1565–67, London, V&A) and *Florence triumphant over Pisa* (completed 1570, Florence, Bargello), lead up to the apogee of his Mannerist virtuosity, *The rape of the Sabine* (1579–83, Florence, Loggia dei Lanzi). The latter depicts three figures linked into a single twisting composition, the perfect exposition of the Mannerist *figura serpentinata*. For Medici villas he provided works ranging from dainty bronze birds (modelled in the late 1560s for the Villa Reale at Castello, now in Florence, Bargello) to the mighty *Appennine* (1570), a mountain-like garden sculpture seeming to emerge like a natural eruption from a rock face in the garden of the Medici villa at Pratolino. His northern origin is apparent in his more restrained religious reliefs, such as the six panels of *The Passion* (finished 1585) for the Grimaldi Chapel in S. Francesco di Castelletto, Genoa. Giambologna was a consummate modeller of small bronzes and through the many replicas of his small statuettes, his style was spread widely. The best known is his *Mercury* of c.1564. See vol. 1 pp. *86, 185, 205*; vol. 2 pp. **168–169**

Giambono, Michele di Taddeo active 1420–62
Venetian painter and mosaicist. He was influenced by the International Gothic of Italy and Bohemia and the persisting Byzantine current in Venetian painting. The signed *Presentation of the Virgin* mosaics in the Mascoli Chapel, S. Marco, which reflect the influence of Guariento, are his best-known works, but he also painted altarpieces.

Giaquinto, Corrado 1702–65
Neapolitan painter of religious and historical subjects. He trained under Solimena before moving to Rome in 1723. Later he worked in Turin and Madrid, where he became court painter to Ferdinand VI; his last three years were spent in his native city. His art represents the most light-hearted and colourful extreme of the Neapolitan Rococo (*Prophets, Heroines and Sibyls*, 1749, Naples, Museo di Capodimonte). His frescos in Spain influenced the palette of the young Goya. See vol. 3 p. 64

Gibbons, Grinling 1648–1721
Dutch woodcarver and sculptor, who settled in England about 1667. He was discovered by the diarist John Evelyn in 1671, and introduced to Charles II and the architect Wren. He was a virtuoso craftsman, and his *forte* was the carving in limewood of swags of fruit, flowers, birds and so on, for interior architectural settings. Such is his fame that most good English woodwork of roughly the right date has been attributed to him at one time or another, but there are documented examples at Burghley House, Lincolnshire; Petworth House, Sussex; Windsor Castle; and St Paul's Cathedral, London.

Gibson, John 1790–1866
English NEOCLASSICAL sculptor. A protégé of Flaxman, he moved to Rome in 1818 and became a pupil of Canova. For the rest of his life he was based in Rome, although he made several visits to England and regularly exhibited at the Royal Academy. He became recognized internationally as a leading Neoclassical artist, and, in his desire to imitate the ancient Greeks as closely as possible, experimented with polychromy, as in his most famous work *Tinted Venus* (1851–52, Liverpool, Walker Art Gallery). See vol. 3 p. **106**; vol. 4 p. *61*

Giersing, Harald 1881–1927
Danish painter and writer. He was trained by Zahrtmann in Copenhagen and inspired by Bonnard, Vuillard and Manet in Paris. He painted concentrated and simplified landscape compositions, and worked with a few deep, saturated colours. Portraits, such as *The three sisters* (1923, Århus Art Museum), are heavily linear and sombre. One of the founders of the Grønningen artists' group in 1915, he has been of great importance for younger generations as a teacher at his own school.

Gierymski, Aleksander 1850–1901
Polish painter. He followed his brother **Maksymilian** (1847–74) to Munich, where they both studied under Piloty. Aleksander visited Rome in 1875, returning to Warsaw in 1880, and in the following decade painted open-air scenes, such as the *Sand-diggers* (1887, Warsaw, National Museum), a dazzling display of sunlight on rippling water and gleaming piles of sand. In his most famous painting, *The Jewish Festival of Trumpets* (1884, Warsaw, National Museum), he uses the same means—the greying twilight reflecting on the still waters of the river—to highlight the poverty and isolation of ghetto life. Gierymski spent the years 1890 to 1893 in Paris, and his seseqent works are influenced by Seurat and the IMPRESSIONISTS (*Bridge over the Seine*, 1893, Cracow, National Museum). He spent his last years wandering about Europe in virtual obscurity, but is now considered the forerunner of 20th-century Polish Impressionism.

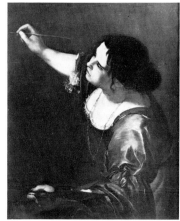
Gentileschi, Artemisia: Self-portrait, mid-1630s. Royal Collection, by permission of Her Majesty The Queen (Mansell)

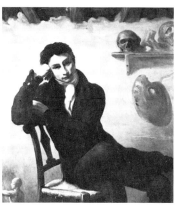
Géricault: Self-portrait, c.1818–19. Paris, Louvre (Mansell)

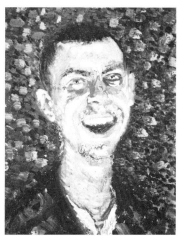
Gerstl: *Laughing self-portrait*, 1908. Vienna, Osterreichische Galerie

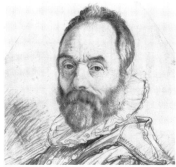
Giambologna: Portrait drawing by Goltzius, 1591. Haarlem, Teylers Museum

Gilbert, Sir Alfred 1854–1934
British sculptor. An enthusiasm for Italian art is apparent in his early sculpture, but later, more individual work, in which he often made use of polychrome, shares stylistic features with Art Nouveau, which he professed to despise. He is best remembered for his Monument to Lord Shaftesbury, the Eros Fountain (1887–1893) in Piccadilly Circus, London, in which he exploited the light weight of aluminium, then a new material for sculpture, to achieve a delicately balanced figure.

Gilbert and George
(Gilbert Proesch, born 1943, and George Passmore, born 1942)
British artists. They call themselves "sculptors", but since the late 1960s they have worked together in various media—photography, painting, performance and video. They are concerned with the projection of their assumed personalities, archetypally English, rather old-fashioned and, except in the context of avantgarde art within which they work, conformist. In *Underneath the Arches*, 1969, they mimed mechanically to the old song of that name for eight hours at a stretch.

Gilduin, Bernard
active late 11th century
French ROMANESQUE sculptor. He signed the high altar of S. Sernin, Toulouse, and the seven large marble plaques in the ambulatory of the church (the earliest preserved Romanesque figure sculpture on a large scale) are also attributed to him. Their low-relief style, showing classical and Carolingian features, is close to that of the altar.

Gill, Eric 1882–1940
British sculptor, engraver and typographer. He became a Roman Catholic in 1913 and tried to revive a medieval religious attitude towards art. His advocacy of the importance of the artist's handwork and his rejection of realism as a criterion of judgment were part of a larger mistrust of the mechanistic bent of 20th-century culture. He worked principally in low relief, as in his directly carved, simply stated *Stations of the Cross* (1914–18, London, Westminster Cathedral), and even his free-standing carvings such as *The sower* (1931, Manchester City Art Gallery) tend to be composed on a single plane. Gill was also a prolific writer and book illustrator and designed alphabets and printing types.

Gilloli, Emile 1911–77
French painter and sculptor, born in Paris of an Italian family. He developed a monumental Cubist style, which turned into abstraction of a type popular with architects for the decoration of buildings. Using semi-precious materials such as gilt bronze, onyx and agate he produces harmonious, highly polished surfaces, as in *Belltower* (1958, Washington, Hirschorn). He is a fine draughtsman and a maker of tapestries daring in simplicity of colour and form.

Gillot, Claude 1673–1722
French painter, draughtsman and etcher. He began as a decorative painter, then took up etching and book illustration, in which fields, like Audran, he developed the arabesque style of Bérain into a free and elegant Rococo idiom. His paintings are very rare, but his favourite subject matter, the *Commedia dell' arte* (example, *Quarrel of the cabmen*, Paris, Louvre), was taken up by his pupil Watteau, although in an incomparably more subtle and poetic manner.

Gillray, James 1757–1815
English caricaturist. Most of his political works were done between 1780 and 1811, before mental illness ended his successful career. His witty but often coarse style, influenced by Hogarth, lampooned leading contemporary personalities including the royal family. Under the influence of his patron, Pitt the Younger, he published many vicious political cartoons, those of Napoleon I being very popular. See vol. 1 p. *31*

Gilman, Harold 1876–1919
British painter, a founder-member of the CAMDEN TOWN GROUP, and first president of the London Group. He was an admirer of Sickert, and in paintings such as *Eating house* (*c.*1914, Sheffield, City Art Gallery) he emulated the older artist in the choice of working-class subject matter and unconventional, informal composition. Sickert's drab coloration, however, was rejected in favour of brilliant oranges and reds which Gilman combined with an emphasis on outline derived from Gauguin.

Gilpin, Sawrey 1733–1807
British painter of horses, a pupil of Samuel Scott. Gilpin tended to endow his animals with human emotions, a trait which differentiated him from the more scientifically minded Stubbs. He often painted animals and figures in landscapes by other artists. *Horses frightened by a thunderstorm* (1798, London, Royal Academy) is typical of his somewhat melodramatic style. His brother, the Reverend **William** (1724–1804), was an amateur draughtsman and an influential writer on the PICTURESQUE.

Ginner, Charles 1878–1952
British painter. He studied painting in Paris and was a founder-member of the CAMDEN TOWN GROUP. His favoured subject matter was the townscape, usually drab industrial scenes (*Leeds canal*, *c.*1916, Leeds, City Art Gallery). These are depicted in ordered, slab-like brushstrokes repeating the structural process by which the city itself is built up.

Giordano, Luca 1634–1705
The most important Neapolitan painter of the later 17th century, known as "Luca fa presto" (Luke quick-hand) for the speed at which he produced his enormous output in oil and fresco. Giordano absorbed a great variety of influences, and he was renowned for his ability to imitate the styles of other painters. He travelled widely in Italy, and in 1692 was summoned to Madrid by Charles II of Spain as the only man who could tackle the vast area of ceilings in the Escorial. He spent ten years as court painter and in 1702 returned to Naples, where many churches have examples of his work: the huge fresco *Christ driving the merchants from the Temple* (1684) in the Chiesa del Gerolomini is one of the most impressive. His light airy style anticipates the Rococo. See vol. 2 pp. **234–235**

Giorgione da Castelfranco
1476/78–1510
Venetian painter. Giorgione is one of the most extraordinary figures in the history of art, for although almost nothing is known of his life and only a handful of paintings are universally accepted as his, his importance is enormous. He probably trained in the studio of Giovanni Bellini, whose influence is most clearly apparent in *The Castelfranco altarpiece* in the cathedral of Castelfranco, Giorgione's home town. In 1507/09 he worked in the Doge's Palace, and in 1508 painted frescos on the exterior of the Fondaco dei Tedeschi in Venice; the former paintings, however, have disappeared, and the latter are known only through ruinous fragments (Venice, Accademia) and engravings. Apart from these public commissions, Giorgione seems to have worked mainly for a small circle of humanists, and he was one of the first artists to paint small pictures for private collectors. His subject matter is often enigmatic, as in *The tempest* (Venice, Accademia) or *The three philosophers* (Vienna, Kunsthistorisches), and his intellectual puzzles probably appealed to his cultivated audience. Both these works show to the full Giorgione's great contribution to the history of painting, the integration of figures and landscape to create a mood—usually one of poetic reverie—that is more important than the subject. He had a very powerful influence on Venetian painting in the generation after his death, most notably on the young Titian, who is said to have completed some of Giorgione's paintings including the *Venus* (Dresden, Gemäldegalerie), the source of Titian's reclining nudes. "*The Concert Champêtre*" (Paris, Louvre) is still disputed between Giorgione and Titian. Even the aged Bellini was influenced by Giorgione's innovations, and many younger painters imitated the Giorgionesque mood in pastoral paintings. A type of dreamy, romantic male portrait also derives from Giorgione, who himself is said to have been handsome and amorous: examples in West Berlin (Staatliche Museen) and San Diego (Fine Arts Gallery) are reasonably attributed to Giorgione himself. Vasari thought Giorgione's contribution was so momentous that he placed him with Leonardo as one of the founders of "modern" painting. See vol. 2 pp. *139*, **140–141**, 142

Giotteschi or **Giottesques**
Name given to the 14th-century followers, often anonymous, of Giotto. Many painters imitated Giotto's physical types, but few could approach his human understanding and expressive powers. Of his followers, Maso di Banco was probably truest to the master's spirit, and among other leading Giotteschi were Bernardo Daddi, Taddeo Gaddi and the Master of St Cecilia. See vol. 2 p. 85

Giotto di Bondone *c.*1267–1337
Florentine painter and architect. The greatest of the early Italian painters, Giotto can also be considered the founder of the main tradition of Western painting because of the way he broke away from Byzantine tradition and introduced the concern with an illusionistic pictorial space. The momentous quality of his work was recognized in his lifetime: Dante and Boccaccio praised him lavishly, and Cennino Cennini, writing in about 1400, summed up his stylistic revolution in the words "Giotto translated the art of painting from Greek to Latin." He was greatly in demand and worked all over Italy (for Old St Peter's in Rome he designed a huge mosaic, now altered beyond recognition, of the Ship of the Church—the "*Navicella*"), but no documented paintings survive, and there is considerable scholarly debate about the works attributed to him. In particular, whether he painted the frescos on *The life of St Francis* in the Upper Church of S. Francesco at ASSISI (1290s?) is one of the most controversial problems in art history, but the later frescos in the Arena Chapel in Padua (completed by 1313) are universally accepted as his, and form the basis for any study of his work. The main scenes represent the story of the Virgin and her parents (St Anne and St Joachim) and the Life and Passion of Christ, combining a simple grandeur of composition and drawing with intense human feeling. Probably in the 1320s, he painted four chapels in S. Croce, Florence, of which two (the Bardi and Peruzzi) survive. Between 1329 and 1333 he was court painter to Robert of Anjou in Naples (Simone Martini had earlier worked for the same patron), but almost nothing survives from this period. In 1334 he was put in charge of the building operations of Florence Cathedral, for which he designed the celebrated campanile. Several panel paintings are attributed to Giotto in addition to his frescos. The finest is the large and majestic "*Ognissanti Madonna*" (*c.*1305–10), which hangs with similar works by Cimabue (traditionally Giotto's teacher) and Duccio in the Uffizi, Florence, and demonstrates how much more three-dimensional Giotto's style was than those of his two greatest contemporaries. Giotto's influence on Florentine painting, which was overwhelming in the generation after his death, declined with the onset of the International Gothic style, but was revived by Masaccio, who was the true heir to Giotto's heroic grandeur. See vol. 2 pp. **79, 82–83**

Giovanni d'Alemagna active 1440s
Venetian painter of supposed German origin, of whom little is known. He was the brother-in-law of Antonio Vivarini and collaborated in his workshop at Murano. His signature often appears with Vivarini's and his style is to be identified with the shop's richly detailed ensembles of architectural framework and decorated figures, as in *The coronation of the Virgin* (Venice, S. Pantaleone).

Giovanni da Maiano
active first half of the 16th century
Italian sculptor, active in England. In 1521, he produced a set of medallions and reliefs for the exterior of Hampton Court Palace (still *in situ*) and in 1527, stucco and woodcarvings for the Banqueting House in London (now destroyed). From 1531 to 1536, he worked on a splendid black marble sarcophagus, ordered by Cardinal Wolsey, but eventually used to house the remains of Lord Nelson in St Paul's Cathedral, London. He was a competent artist who played an important role in introducing the Renaissance style to England.

Giovanni da Milano active 1360s
Italian painter, Milanese by birth, but active in Florence, where he was one of the outstanding artists working around the middle of the 14th century. His major surviving work, the splendid series of frescos in the Rinuccini Chapel of S. Croce, Florence (begun 1365), shows no signs of his origins in Milan and is in an elegant Giottesque style. His only other dated work is the exquisite *Pietà* (1365, Florence, Accademia), remarkable for its delicacy of handling and depth of feeling, as well as for being one of the earliest representations of the subject to be painted in Florence. He became a citizen of Florence in 1366, but is last documented in 1369 in Rome.

Giovanni da San Giovanni
(Giovanni Mannozzi) 1592–1636
Italian Baroque painter. An isolated figure, he was the only Florentine artist of the 17th century to work mainly in fresco. His masterpiece, full of homely rustic detail, is the captivating *Holy Family arriving at an inn* (1621, Florence, Istituto di Belle Arti).

Giovanni da Udine 1487–1564
Italian painter and stucco modeller. He worked in Raphael's workshop, reinventing antique processes for modelling stucco and developing this mode of ornament. His work is mainly to be seen in his native Udine, for example *The coronation of the Virgin* (c.1506–12, Udine, Museo Communale).

Giovanni di Paolo
active late 1420s–1460s
Sienese painter. He was trained by Taddeo di Bartolo and influenced early in his career by Gentile da Fabriano (who was working in Siena 1425–26) and, later, by his Sienese contemporary Sassetta. Essentially, however, he continued the tradition of Duccio, Simone Martini and the Lorenzetti. His oeuvre is composed entirely of small-scale religious works, elegant and lively, and often verging on the fantastic, evoking enchanting dream worlds. Among the best known are the *Paradiso* (1445, New York, Metropolitan), *The Presentation in the Temple* (1447–49, Siena, Pinacoteca) and two late series of scenes from the life of St John the Baptist (Chicago, Art Institute, and London, NG).

Giovannino de' Grassi
active 1389–98
Italian architect, sculptor, painter and illuminator, the most remarkable member of the 14th-century Lombard school. He is first documented as an engineer at Milan Cathedral and a sculpted relief in the sacristy can be ascribed to him. His most important surviving work is a medicinal book now in the Biblioteca Civica at Bergamo, containing some of the earliest known drawings of flowers, animals and people made directly from nature. His delightful and newly naturalistic style was an important constituent in the formation of International Gothic in northern Italy.

Girardon, François 1628–1715
With Coysevox, the leading French sculptor of Louis XIV's reign. His style was more severe and classical than Coysevox's, and he represented the ideal of the French Academy more completely than any other sculptor. He worked extensively at Versailles, and made one of the most impressive French monuments of the 17th century in his tomb of Cardinal Richelieu (1675–77, Paris, Church of the Sorbonne). His equestrian statue of Louis XIV (1683–92) for the Place Vendôme in Paris was destroyed during the Revolution. See vol. 2 p. **199**

Girodet de Roucy, Anne-Louis
(called Girodet-Trioson) 1767–1824
French painter. He studied under J.-L. David, and in 1789 won the Prix de Rome with *Endymion sleeping* (1791, Paris, Louvre). This was inspired by an antique bas-relief, but in its atmospheric lighting and mannerist elongation of the figures shows a move towards Romanticism, later more fully developed in the immense *Deluge*, 1806, and *Atala's Entombment*, 1808 (both in the Louvre). On his return to Paris from Italy in 1795 he executed numerous portraits and created a scandal in the 1799 Salon with the satirical sexual references in his *Mlle Lange as Danäe* (Minneapolis, Institute of Arts). In 1812 he gave up painting and devoted himself to writing tedious poems on aesthetics. See vol. 3 p. **59**

Girolamo da Fiesole
active early 16th century
Italian sculptor, whose known career was spent in France. In 1500 he was commissioned to work on the tomb of Francis II, Duke of Brittany, in the Cathedral at Nantes. Colombe and Perréal also worked on the tomb, but Girolamo probably contributed the Italian-type sarcophagus with its twelve *Apostles* standing in the niches traditionally occupied by weepers.

Girtin, Thomas 1775–1802
British landscape watercolourist. With Turner he was chiefly responsible for freeing watercolour from its dependence on line-drawing and making it into an independent medium, capable of conveying broad effects of space and light. He made almost annual sketching expeditions in England and Wales, and began with fairly objective renderings of picturesque views or buildings. Later he developed his characteristic style, based on the use of broad and luminous washes which created an effect of majestic and poetic serenity, as in *Kirkstall Abbey: evening* (c.1800, London, V&A). In 1801–02 he visited Paris to draw views which were published in aquatint after his death, and in 1802 he exhibited a vast panorama of London—the Eidometropolis—painted in oils (lost). Turner is said to have paid tribute to his friend with the words "If Tom Girtin had lived, I should have starved." See vol. 3 p. **69**

Gislebertus
active 1st half of 12th century
French ROMANESQUE sculptor, active in Burgundy. He signed *The Last Judgment* (begun about 1120) on the tympanum of the west portal of Autun Cathedral, and more than 50 capitals in the church display his style. His figures are elongated, angular and highly expressive, carved in deep relief, their drapery articulated with delicately incised parallel lines. Gislebertus may well have trained at Cluny, and possibly worked at Vézelay before arriving at Autun. He was also influenced by classical art, as is evident, for example, in the famous reclining *Eve*, originally from the Cathedral's north transept portal (now in the Musée Rolin, Autun). The impact of his art on Burgundian sculpture was immediate; close copies of scenes are found in several churches, including those at Beaune, Moûtiers St Jean and Saulieu. But the greatest tribute to his influence was the central tympanum of the inner doorway at Vézelay, c.1130, where his dramatic expressiveness was raised to new heights. See vol. 2 pp. **72–73**

Giuliano da Maiano see BENEDETTO DA MAIANO

Giulio Romano 1499?–1546
Italian painter and architect, the chief pupil and assistant of Raphael and one of the most important MANNERIST artists. He was born in Rome, and by about 1515 was working on Raphael's *Stanza del Incendio* in the Vatican. After Raphael's death, Giulio completed several works the master had left unfinished, including *The Transfiguration* and the *Sala di Costantino* frescos. In 1524, he left Rome for Mantua, where he became court painter and architect to the Dukes. His most important work in Mantua is the Palazzo del Tè, begun in 1526 for Federigo Gonzaga. In this, one of the first Mannerist buildings, Giulio deliberately broke the conventions of classical architecture to create surprising and bizarre effects. His painted decorations in the Palace are similarly witty and inventive in their illusionism, most notably the frescos in the *Sala dei Giganti* (The Hall of the Giants, 1532–34). This room is shaped like a beehive and the spectator is completely surrounded by an illusion of hurtling figures and crashing stone as the gods destroy the giants. From 1536 to 1539 he carried out a similarly ambitious and energetic decorative scheme, also for Federigo, at the Ducal Palace, Mantua. The Riding Court of the Palace and Giulio's own house in Mantua (1544–46) show the culmination of his rich, inventive architectural style. Giulio's painting, which extends the Mannerist tendencies of Raphael's late work and combines them with a muscularity derived from Michelangelo, was widely influential. An indication of his fame is that he is the only modern artist mentioned in Shakespeare ("That rare Italian master Julio Romano", *The Winter's Tale*, v, 2, 105). Shakespeare, however, made the mistake of thinking that Giulio was a sculptor. See vol. 2 pp. **164–165**

Giunta Pisano
documented 1229–54
Pisan painter, known from three signed Crucifixes, all undated, painted for churches in Assisi, Bologna and Pisa. The distance between these towns proves his wide contemporary fame. Compared with the earlier Crucifix by Berlinghiero Berlinghieri, those by Giunta show a quite new Franciscan-inspired concern with Christ's suffering and humanity.

Giusti or **Juste** brothers
Italian sculptors, **Antonio** (1479–1519) and **Giovanni** (1485–1549), who in about 1504 settled in France, where they changed their surname to Juste. Antonio was back in Italy between 1508 and 1516; he had a house at Carrara where Michelangelo is known to have sometimes stayed when visiting the quarry there. The most important work of the brothers (signed only by Giovanni, but probably the work of both with the help of assistants) is the tomb of Louis XII and Anne of Brittany (1515–31) at St-Denis. This large and imposing monument has seated *Apostles* and *Virtues* and sensitively observed kneeling figures and recumbent effigies of the King and Queen set in a graceful framework of classical architecture. The *Apostles* are derived from Michelangelo's Sistine Ceiling *Prophets*. With Girolamo da Fiesole and Guido Mazzoni, the brothers helped introduce the Renaissance style to France. See vol. 1 p. *201*

Giusto de' Menabuoi
active 1363/4–1387/91
Italian painter. He was born and trained in Florence and for this reason is often considered a member of the Florentine school, but his surviving work was done elsewhere. During the 1360s he worked in Milan but by 1370 he had moved to Padua, where he spent the rest of his life. His principal surviving work there is the huge fresco cycle (completed in 1376) that covers the interior of the Baptistery. The vigour of his teeming scenes makes him, with Altichiero, the leading figure in the resurgence of the Paduan school.

Glackens, William James
1870–1938
American painter, one of The EIGHT. He worked as a newspaper illustrator before meeting Henri (1891), who encouraged him to paint. His work reflects the concern with topicality and vitality typical of the ASHCAN school. However, Glackens' greatest stylistic debt was to the Impressionists and, in particular, Renoir, as can be seen in his most famous work, *Chez Mouquin* (1905, Chicago, Art Institute)—a New York restaurant frequented by The Eight.

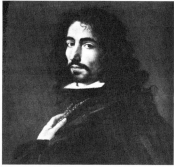
Giordano: Self-portrait, c.1665. Florence, Uffizi (Alinari)

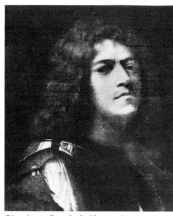
Giorgione: Copy? of self-portrait, c.1506–10. Brunswick, Herzog Anton Ulrich Museum

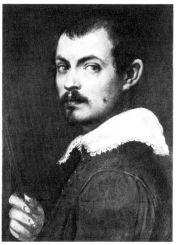
Giovanni da San Giovanni: Self-portrait, c.1620. Florence, Uffizi (Alinari)

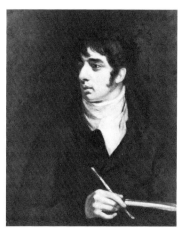
Girtin: Portrait by Opie, c.1800. London, NPG

Glarner, Fritz 1899–1972
American abstract painter born in Switzerland. In Paris after 1923, Glarner became familiar with avantgarde abstractionists such as van Doesburg. He arrived in New York in 1926 and was associated with the AMERICAN ABSTRACT ARTISTS group. He has created numerous works entitled *Tondo* or *Relational painting*, which explore the relationship between form and space. His style is indebted to Mondrian but his hard edges usually depart from the horizontal-vertical axes and create a shifting, dynamic impression.

Glaze
A thin layer of transparent oil-paint brushed over dried underlayers of oil or tempera to modify tones and hues and give luminosity and depth to the work. The term is also applied to the glassy coating fused to pottery.

Gleizes, Albert 1881–1953
French painter, chiefly remembered as co-author with Metzinger of *Of Cubism* (1912), the first book on Cubism. He exhibited works in the Cubist room at the 1911 Salon des Indépendants and was a member of the SECTION D'OR group. A typical work of this period, *Harvest threshing* (1912, New York, Guggenheim), derives its style from Picasso and Braque but displays great originality in its imagery. During World War I, which he spent in New York, he responded to the bright colours and dynamism of Delaunay's work. After a religious experience in 1917, Gleizes became preoccupied with the expression of spiritual meaning in art.

Gleyre, Charles 1808–74
Swiss-born painter, active in Paris. Largely supported by private patronage, he remained independent of the Academy. He painted anecdotal and often enigmatic scenes in antique settings, exemplified in the meticulously painted, melancholy *Evening, or lost illusions* (Paris, Louvre) which made his reputation at the Salon of 1843. This success led him to take over Delaroche's studio and he became the teacher of many Impressionists, notably Bazille, Monet, Renoir and Sisley. One of the most original teachers of his age, Gleyre stressed free compositional sketches and *plein-air* painting.

Goerg, Édouard born 1893
French painter and engraver. He was born in Sydney, Australia, but was in Paris by the age of seven. Taught by Denis and Sérusier at the Académie Ranson, he first exhibited in 1924. A sentimental realist, he has specialized in portraits of young girls (*The pretty flower-girl*, 1929, Paris, Musée d'Art Moderne). His book illustrations, such as those for Baudelaire's *Les Fleurs du Mal*, are well-known.

Goes, Hugo van der died 1482
Netherlandish painter, the greatest northern master of the later 15th century. He was probably born in Ghent, and joined the painters' guild there in 1467, becoming dean in 1475. Soon afterwards he entered a monastery in Brussels but he continued to paint and to travel. Hugo assimilated the achievements of his great predecessors and carried them to new heights of expressiveness. In early works such as the diptych of the early 1470s representing *The Lamentation* and *The Fall* (Vienna, Kunsthistorisches) and *The Adoration of the Magi* (West Berlin, Staatliche Museen), he combined the compositions and figure types of Rogier van der Weyden with the representational means of van Eyck. His masterpiece is the gigantic Portinari altarpiece representing *The adoration of the Child* (*c.*1474–76, Florence, Uffizi), a tremendous achievement in its combination of maximum surface ornament with spatial depth. It was executed for the Italian merchant Tommaso Portinari, and immediately shipped to Florence, where the brilliant technique and the prominence given to the rustic shepherds startled artists and had a lasting impact on Italian art. Its most novel quality in the context of Netherlandish painting, however, is a feeling of unease, presaging the fate of the Child. The remaining pictures attributed to Hugo tend to be rather more loosely painted and less colourful, testifying to the artist's increasing melancholy. *The death of the Virgin* (*c.*1480, Bruges, Musée Communale des Beaux-Arts)—his last known picture—is set in a room with no real depth, although the figures are most carefully observed; the whole effect is thoroughly personal and disquieting. In 1481 he became insane, and died the next year. See vol. 1 p. *100*; vol. 2 p. **96**

Goethe, Johann Wolfgang von 1749–1832
German writer and amateur artist, one of the key figures of ROMANTICISM. Though a passionate draughtsman (he left about 2,000 drawings), Goethe's importance for art lay not in these, but in his theories. His *Concerning German Architecture* (1772), extolling Strasbourg Cathedral, founded the Romantic appreciation of Gothic art. His first Italian journey (1786–88) brought friendships with J.H.W. Tischbein, Hackert and Kauffmann, and led him to proclaim the necessity of rules and the value of classical models, so that study of the particular could be elevated by synthesis into universal statements about humanity. His attempts to influence artists included publishing an art journal, *Propyläen* (1798–1800), and establishing an annual painting competition on a set theme (1799–1805). In 1810 he published his *Theory of Colour*, which stimulated Turner. See vol. 3 pp. 62, 74

Gogh, Vincent van 1853–90
Dutch painter, one of the greatest and most influential artists of the 19th century. He worked in London for a firm of picture dealers in 1873 but in 1875 moved to Paris before returning to Holland to study theology. In 1878 he went to the Borinage in Belgium as a lay preacher to the coal miners (his father was a Protestant pastor) but suffered an acute psychological crisis, abandoned preaching and in 1880 began to paint, taking instruction in anatomy and perspective. On the advice of his uncle, Antoine Mauve, he moved to Antwerp, where he studied at the Academy. Academic art, however, had little to offer him; his work continued expressionistic in style and realist in its choice of working-class subjects (*The potato eaters*, 1885, Amsterdam, National Museum Vincent van Gogh). In 1886 he moved to Paris, where his work changed dramatically under the various influences of Degas, Gauguin, Seurat, Toulouse-Lautrec and Japanese woodcuts, becoming concerned with aesthetic rather than social problems, though still broadly humanist. Under Seurat's influence he began to incorporate elements of Pointillism, but retained his characteristically vibrant colour and his stress on the thickness and opacity of paint. In February 1888 he moved to Arles in southern France, where he lived in poverty, sold no works and suffered from depression and hallucinations. Gauguin joined him at the end of the year with the idea of founding an artists' colony, but by this time van Gogh was living permanently on the verge of clinical insanity and after a quarrel with Gauguin he cut off part of his right ear, an incident recorded in his disturbing *Self-portrait with bandaged ear* (1889, London, Courtauld Institute Galleries). Soon after, he voluntarily entered an asylum at St Rémy and there painted a series of extraordinarily intense landscapes, typified by the *Cornfield with cypresses* (1889, London, NG). In May 1890 he moved to Auvers-sur-Oise, where a burst of creativity preceded his suicide on 29th July. His art, dependent upon often violently interacting colours and forms, and a strong expressionist line, created a new concept of the artist's relationship with the material world. His influence on Symbolism, Fauvism and Expressionism, upon early abstraction and Surrealism, was enormous and he virtually initiated the line of descent to the Abstract Expressionism of the 1940s and 1950s. See vol. 1 pp. *33*, *43*, **70–71**, *119*, *159*; vol. 3 pp. **112–115**

Goings, Ralph born 1928
American painter. Unlike other SUPERREALISTS such as Close, whose concerns are primarily process-oriented, Goings gives prime consideration to subject matter. His major image is the automobile at a drive-in or service station, as in *Paul's Corner* (1970, New York, O.K. Harris Gallery). In celebrating these "icons" of American materialism, the meticulously realist, generally spacious views of shiny vehicles recall POP art. See vol. 1 p. *118*; vol. 3 p. **253**

Golden Mean or **Golden Section**
Proportion in which a line or rectangle is divided into two unequal parts in such a way that the ratio of the smaller to the larger part is equal to the ratio of the larger part to the whole. It cannot be expressed in rational numbers, but an approximation is 8:13. It has been considered a mystical proportion with inherent aesthetic value and has been found in natural forms as well as art. The idea was discussed by classical writers such as Euclid and Vitruvius and was taken up again in the Renaissance, most notably by the mathematician Luca Pacioli. This friend of Leonardo and Piero della Francesca wrote a book on the golden section called *Divine Proportion* (1509), illustrated by Leonardo. See vol. 1 p. 131

Goltzius, Hendrik 1558–1617
Dutch engraver and painter, active in Haarlem. His early work, peopled by monstrously muscular men and elongated pin-headed women, was thoroughly Mannerist, but after a brief trip to Rome (1590–91) his style became much more classical and naturalistic. Although his right hand was crippled, he was a technician of unsurpassed virtuosity. His portrait engravings are especially delicate and his imitations of Dürer and Lucas van Leyden passed as originals. In the context of 17th-century Dutch art his most important works are his landscape drawings, among the earliest *plein-air* representations of the Dutch countryside (*Dune landscape near Haarlem*, 1603, West Berlin, Kupferstichkabinett). See vol. 4 p. *73*

Gombrich, Sir Ernst born 1909
Austrian-born British art historian, from 1959 to 1976 director of the Warburg Institute, London, and Professor of the History of the Classical Tradition. He has made many contributions to the theory of perception and representation, and to the study of Renaissance symbolism, but he is best known for *The Story of Art* (1950). This reached its 13th English edition in 1978, and, translated into numerous languages, has probably introduced more people to art history than any other work. See vol. 2 p. 119

Gonçalves, Nuño active 1450–71
Portuguese painter. He is recorded as court painter to Alfonso V in 1463, and is known to have painted a *St Vincent* altarpiece for Lisbon Cathedral (destroyed in the earthquake of 1755). Another work showing *St Vincent with members of the Portuguese Court* (Lisbon, Museu Nacional de Arte Antiga), the outstanding Portuguese painting of the 15th century, is attributed to him. The stiff and uninvolved figures are similar to those of Dirk Bouts but the paint is handled more broadly and the portrait heads are strongly individualized and sculptural in effect.

Goncharova, Natalia 1881–1962
Russian painter and designer. She trained as a sculptor in the Moscow College of Art, and only later turned to painting. Up to 1915, when she left her home country for good, Goncharova was one of the leaders of Russian avantgarde art, and with Larionov she developed RAYONNISM. In 1919 they settled in Paris, but her later paintings did not fulfill the promise of such early works as *Laundry* (1913, London, Tate) or her outstanding lithographs in Russian Futurist publications. She is now perhaps best-known for her scenery and costume designs, of which there is a collection in the Victoria and Albert Museum, London. See vol. 3 pp. **156–157**

Gong Xian *c.*1660–1700
Chinese landscape painter. He worked in the austere style of the northern Song, and was active in the Nanking area. In the neat classifications of which traditional Chinese critics were so fond, he is one of the "Eight Masters of Nanking", an eccentric character who died in poverty but who also exercised considerable influence through his numerous pupils and his posthumously published treatise *Secrets of Painting*. A certain number of leaves from his annotated sketchbook have been published, giving a relatively rare glimpse of a Chinese artist's working method. They show strikingly the all-pervasive awareness of past styles and codification of imitative techniques which are so characteristic of Qing painting, and present in all Gong Xian's works, for example a monochrome *Landscape* scroll (Kansas City, Nelson Gallery).

Gonzalès, Eva 1849–83
French painter. She was taught by Manet, whose life-size portrait of her at the easel (1870) is in the National Gallery, London. She mainly painted scenes of contemporary Parisian life (*Box at the Théâtre des Italiens*, *c.*1873, Paris, Jeu de Paume) and tended to use dark colouring reminiscent of the young Manet's. She also worked in pastel.

González, Julio 1876–1942
Spanish sculptor and painter. Despite the delicacy and refinement of his early work, González's importance stems from his technical innovations in sculpture after 1926, when he decided to abandon painting. His use of industrial techniques such as welding and riveting had profound implications for the de-

velopment of modern sculpture for with them he transformed iron into a viable artistic medium. *Woman arranging her hair* (1936, New York, MOMA) reveals his mature style, in which linear elements are assembled in a way which has been described as "drawing in space". However, his most famous work, *Montserrat* (1937, Amsterdam, Stedelijk Museum), is a comparatively naturalistic piece. It is formed of sheet-metal and shows a woman holding a child in her arms. Named after Spain's holy mountain, it symbolizes the suffering of the Spanish people in the Civil War. In the 1930s González taught Picasso to construct iron sculpture, and the contact enriched his own iconography. In the *Cactus People* of the late 1930s, for example, the components that stand for limbs, torso or head are derived from non-human elements, including forms reminiscent of cactus plants and mechanical objects (*Cactus man no. 2*, Paris, Musée National d'Art Moderne). González's work has been so influential (notably on British and American sculptors such as Reg Butler and David Smith) that it is hard to realize how original it must have once seemed to his contemporaries. See vol. 1 p. *190*; vol. 3 p. **181**

Gore, Spencer 1878–1914
British painter. He was a founder-member of the CAMDEN TOWN GROUP and exhibited in the second Post-Impressionist exhibition in 1912. He took the example of van Gogh and Gauguin further towards abstraction than his Camden Town colleagues and in certain works such as *The beanfield, Letchworth* (1912, London, Tate) employed a radical simplification, the subject being depicted in a series of broad multi-coloured strips.

Gorgon Painter
active early 6th century BC
Greek BLACK-FIGURE vase-painter from Athens, named after the superb vase of the *dinos* type in the Louvre, Paris, depicting Perseus and the Gorgons. Some 29 vases have been attributed to this artist. While Corinthian influence is apparent in his animals and decorative motifs, his lively and expressive narrative style marks a new departure.

Gorky, Arshile (Vosdanig Manoog Adoian) 1905–48
American abstract painter, a major link between European Cubism and Surrealism and American Abstract Expressionism. He was born in Armenia and taken to the USA in 1920. His early work, such as *The artist and his mother* (c.1926–36, New York, Whitney), employs the shallow, broad planes of Cubism but is also suggestive of the work of his close friend, De Kooning. In the 1930s he assimilated the styles of Cézanne, Miró and particularly Picasso, whom he much admired. In 1934 he executed murals (now destroyed) at Newark Airport for the Federal Art Project. His definitive, unique style began to be established early in the 1940s; fluid, brilliant washes of paint held or bursting out of black lines typify his fully abstract yet often biomorphic idiom, as in *The liver is the cock's comb* (1944, Buffalo, Albright-Knox). His colours tended to greys and browns in the last years of his life, accompanying a series of personal disasters which culminated in his suicide. See vol. 3 p. **211**

Goshun, Matsumura 1752–1811
Japanese painter. A native of Kyoto, Goshun became a pupil of Yosa Buson,

and joined the studio of Maruyama Okyo, where he concentrated on sketching. In 1788, after the fire which devastated Kyoto, he opened his own school in the Shijo area. Goshun was a polymath: he composed poems with Buson, was a man of affairs, literature and music, and was said to have a phenomenal memory. He is best-known for his landscapes, for instance the *Countryside* screen in the Ohashi collection.

Gossaert, Jan (called Mabuse) c.1478–c.1533
Flemish painter. He came from Maubeuge and is recorded as a master in the Antwerp guild in 1503. His earliest panels followed in the tradition of van Eyck and van der Goes, but a trip to Italy with his patron, Philip of Burgundy, in 1508, made him change direction. Van Mander cited him as the first painter to bring nude painting to the Netherlands, though in this Gossaert was influenced by Dürer rather than by Italian work. However, his Italian sojourn was more evident from the pot-pourri of architectural styles and the borrowed classical poses which he married to conventional Flemish figures. Hence his *St Luke* paints the Virgin in an incongruous environment of pillars, friezes and statuary (c.1515, Prague, NG) and his *Danaë* (1527, Munich, Alte Pinakothek) is a Flemish model in an outlandish and exotic loggia. Unlike later Mannerists, Gossaert did not aim for movement and the figures in his *Adoration of the Magi* (c.1507–08, London, NG), for example, have a dignified, trance-like quality and clearly show his skill at portraiture. Royal commissions of this nature took him to Middelburg, Brussels, Malines and Utrecht, and his work had wide influence. See vol. 2 p. **160**

Gothic art
Style of sculpture, architecture and painting which succeeded Romanesque art in Europe. Gothic developed first in northern France in the mid- and late 12th century, in the architecture and sculpture of a number of churches and cathedrals. The key monument was the abbey church of St-Denis near Paris, rebuilt by Abbot Suger from 1137 to 1144. The new choir and west front were distinguished by a novel architectural style, with relatively thin walls, large windows, and a systematic use of pointed arches and ribbed vaulting. Narrative sculpture was concentrated on the west front in a triple portal of closely-integrated design. Much of the early Gothic sculpture of St-Denis has been badly damaged or destroyed, but an almost contemporary masterpiece survives at Chartres, in the Royal Portal, revealing the elements of the Gothic style. The sometimes almost abstract, hieratic style of the Romanesque sculptors was disappearing, replaced by a more natural, humanistic manner, and the programme itself was becoming more coherent. By the early 13th century the new architecture and sculpture reached a climax, at Chartres (in the choir, nave, and transept portals) and at Rheims and Amiens—the great "High Gothic" cathedrals. At Rheims a distinctly classical style was manifest, particularly in the figures flanking the Judgment Portal of the north transept, about 1230, with their deeply folded swathes of drapery and solemn, philosophical expressions. The sweet courtly grace of the Virgin and Archangel Gabriel on the west front belonged to a more lasting trend, one soon widespread, and reflected also in increasingly sophisticated small-scale sculpture. New stan-

dards were set in the wealth of decoration of cathedrals, with their soaring vaults, great schemes of stained glass and extraordinarily delicate tracery patterns. The mature Gothic style spread to Spain, where it was often faithfully imitated, to England and to Germany, where it made a greater impact and, in sculpture, stimulated a strongly expressive, realistic style. In Italy, Gothic was never whole-heartedly accepted, and a more classically rooted style of sculpture and architecture prevailed. The transition from Romanesque to Gothic was more gradual in painting and emerged slightly later in the 12th century. The chief vehicles were manuscripts, which were produced in increasing numbers, stained glass (rather than mural painting) and, somewhat later, panel painting. The more naturalistic style apparent by the mid-12th century in sculpture was emerging in manuscript painting by the close of the century (The Souvigny Bible, Moulins, Bibliothèque Municipale), but a graceful linear stylization gained ground in the early 13th century. As in architecture and sculpture, the lead was taken in France: the decorative style of illumination which emerged in Paris in the reign of Louis IX (1226–70) soon spread throughout Europe, and played an important part in the development, in the later 14th century, of the International Gothic style. See vol. 2 pp. 76 ff

Gotlib, Henryk 1890–1966
Polish painter. He studied in Cracow, Munich, Amsterdam and Paris and in 1919 was a co-founder of the avantgarde "Formist" movement in Cracow. The years 1923 to 1930 were spent mainly in France and the influence of Bonnard is clear in his works of this period, both in their choice of subject matter—nudes and domestic scenes—and in their colouring. In 1939, trapped by the War, he settled in England, where he executed a triptych, *Poland at war* (1940, Warsaw, National Museum), in which he expressed his fear of the effect of the war on his native country.

Gottlieb, Adolph 1903–74
American ABSTRACT EXPRESSIONIST. After a brief period with WPA in the 1930s, he came under the influence of the European Surrealists. Jungian Archetypes, south-west American Indian art and the automatic techniques pioneered by the Surrealists all had a formative impact on his development. From 1941 to 1951 he painted "pictographs" in which evocative abstract emblems, anatomical fragments and natural elements are organized within the flat picture space by a loose, grid-like matrix of dark lines (*Voyager's return*, 1946, New York, MOMA). In the 1950s, Gottlieb began to paint *Imaginary Landscapes*. These canvases, generally large, feature one or more orbs above and a thatch of heavy gestural strokes below. Later, in a prolonged series of *Bursts*, similar compositions take on a vertical emphasis. See vol. 3 p. **215**

Gouache
Watercolour paint made opaque by the admixture of white pigment (sometimes now marketed as designer's or poster paint). It is fast-drying, denser and more reflective than transparent watercolour, and was used widely by manuscript illuminators and by miniature painters, especially in Persia and India. As corrections can be made readily it was also popular for rapid preparatory sketching, and in France it has often been the preferred watercolour medium. See vol. 1 pp. 160–161

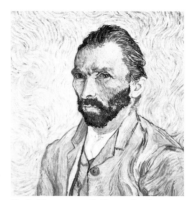
Gogh, Vincent van: Self-portrait, 1890. Paris, Jeu de Paume (Scala)

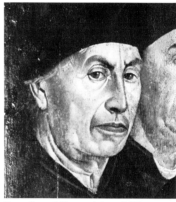
Gonçalves: Self-portrait from *St Vincent with members of the Portuguese Court*, c.1460–70. Lisbon, Museu Nacional de Arte Antiga

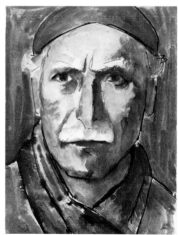
González: Self-portrait, 1941. London, Tate

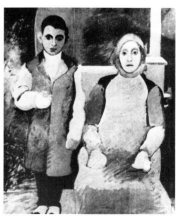
Gorky: *The artist and his mother*, c.1926–36. New York, Whitney

Goujon, Jean c.1510–68
The leading French sculptor of the mid-16th century. Nothing is known of him before 1540, when he is recorded in Rouen. The columns he made for the organ in the church of St Maclou there, however, are so classical in style that a visit to Italy seems probable. By 1544 he was in Paris, working on the rood screen of St Germain l'Auxerrois, of which reliefs of *The Entombment* and *Four Evangelists* survive in the Louvre, Paris. The influence of Parmigianino and Rosso is evident, but Goujon places more emphasis on decorative patterns, especially in the exquisite drapery. Goujon's elegant and highly personal classicism had its finest flowering in the decoration of the Fountain of the Innocents (1547–49), most of which is now in the Louvre. From 1549 to 1562 Goujon is documented working for the architect Lescot at the Louvre, sculpting allegorical reliefs on the ground floor and attics on the exterior of the building, and caryatids in the Salon. The caryatids (1550–51) are his most thoroughly classical works—more solid than most of his sculpture—and his scholarship in matters of the Antique is brought out in his illustrations to the first French edition of Vitruvius (1547). No work of Goujon's is recorded after 1562, and there is evidence that he died in Bologna, perhaps as a Protestant exile. See vol. 2 p. 167

Gower, George died 1596
English portrait painter. A gentleman by birth, he was established as an artist by 1573, and for two decades dominated fashionable portraiture. In 1581 he was appointed Serjeant Painter to Elizabeth I, and in 1584, with Hilliard, he tried to obtain a monopoly in the production of royal portraits. Good examples of his style are the portraits of *Sir Thomas* and *Lady Kytson* (1573, London, Tate).

Goya y Lucientes, Francisco de 1746–1828
Spanish painter and printmaker, the greatest and most original European artist of his period. The early years of his career were spent at Saragossa, and in Madrid under Bayeu, whose sister he later married. He visited Italy briefly in 1771 and settled in Madrid in 1775. One of the early influences on him was Mengs, then working for the Spanish court, who gained Goya the commission for a number of cartoons for tapestries for the royal family (Madrid, Prado), in which he blended elements of Neoclassicism with Rococo gaiety and vivid colour. Tiepolo's importance in his development can be seen in the frescos Goya painted for the church of San Antonio de la Florida (begun 1798). These are painted with extraordinary freedom and show his mastery of *trompe-l'oeil*. The looseness of his technique owes much to Velazquez, and like him Goya ranks among the world's greatest portraitists. He became a court painter in 1786 and First Court Painter in 1799, and many of his most memorable portraits are of the royal family, either singly or together (*Charles IV and his family*, 1800, Prado). A severe illness in 1792 which left Goya stone-deaf is thought to have turned him in upon his own imaginative resources, inspiring the fantastic and increasingly sinister visions of *Los Caprichos*, a series of etchings published in 1799, private expressions of distaste for a corrupt and fanatical Establishment (particularly the Church) which he was bound, in his official capacity of Court Painter, to endorse. Goya's liberalism, which led him at first to welcome the overthrow of Charles IV by the French,

was soon outraged by the invaders' barbarity. He recorded them in the etchings *The Disasters of War* (1810–20) and in two paintings of the events of *May 2nd, 1808* and *May 3rd, 1808* (1814, Madrid, Prado), the latter a work of unparalleled drama, pathos and immediacy which had a notable influence on Manet. In his old age, Goya retired to Quinta del Sordo, a house near Madrid, which he decorated with the so-called "Black Paintings", grim and powerful visions that seem to express both horror at human cruelty and understanding of the fear that often inspires it. Goya's last years were spent in France, for though his own country had long recognized his genius, his bitter opposition to tyranny finally made him an exile. Goya was a prolific artist and many major galleries have examples of his work; most of his key masterpieces, however, are in the Prado. See vol. 1 pp. *57, 90, 115, 164*; vol. 3 pp. **64–67**; vol. 4 p. *21*

Goyen, Jan van 1596–1656
Dutch landscape painter born in Leyden, a pioneering figure in the development of Dutch realistic landscape. He studied under Esaias van de Velde, and worked in Leyden, The Hague and Haarlem. His early works reflect the influence of Esaias, but subsequently his colours became muted and his picturesque views, marked by luminous light effects and sense of airy freshness, acquired a distinctive poetic tranquillity. Often they are virtually monochromatic, and with Salomon van Ruysdael he is recognized as the great master of the "tonal" phase of Dutch landscape painting, when the rendering of atmosphere was of prime importance. Tonal contrasts became stronger in his late works, such as *River scene*, 1656 (Frankfurt, Städelsches Kunstinstitut), but, once he had established his distinctive style in the 1630s, his outlook was fairly consistent, and he often repeated popular motifs. His output was huge and he was highly influential. See vol. 2 p. **222**

Gozzoli, Benozzo c.1421–97
Florentine painter. In his youth he worked for Ghiberti on the Baptistery doors and then for Fra Angelico on frescos in the Vatican. His fame rests on one work, his decoration of the small chapel of the Medici Palace in Florence with frescos representing *The journey of the Magi* (1459–61). This, with a splendour and courtly elegance recalling the International Gothic style, is a work of captivating brilliance, and set a standard for comparable decoration elsewhere, for instance by Bonfigli in Perugia. Portraits of the Medici family are included among the cavalcade, and its secular outlook is very different from that of Fra Angelico. None of his other frescos or altarpieces (*Madonna and Child with saints*, 1461, London, NG) approaches this in quality. See vol 2 p. **110**

Grabar, Igor 1871–1960
Russian painter. After studying painting in Greece and in Munich, he developed bright landscapes, executed in clear colours applied in small brushstrokes (*February, sky blue*, 1904, Moscow, Tretyakov Gallery). He exhibited with the WORLD OF ART group from about 1906. In 1913 he became director of the Tretyakov Gallery.

Graeco-Roman art
Term applied to the art of the late republican and Imperial periods produced by Greek artists, or at least according to Greek style and prototypes, but under Roman patronage.

Graevenitz, Gerhard von
born 1934
West German KINETIC artist, who uses geometrical shapes—squares, circles, ellipses. Derived ultimately from Constructivism, his art nevertheless requires a new relationship with the spectator, as in his *Kinetic room with movable walls* (1969, Nuremberg, and 1973, Milan). His light boxes are programmed in various complex mathematical ways, including in one case a programme designed to be random and free from any recognizable structure.

Graf, Urs c.1485–1527/8
Swiss painter, engraver, goldsmith and designer of stained glass, active at Basel from 1509. He trained as a goldsmith, but his virtuoso drawings (usually signed and dated) and prints are his main achievement. Many were based on his experiences as a mercenary in Italy, while others, for example the drawing *Pyramus and Thisbe* (1525, Basel, Kunstmuseum) have classical themes. His lively, curling strokes invest his subjects with an air of fantasy as well as a vivid sense of reality.

Graff, Anton 1736–1813
German painter. Born in Switzerland and trained largely in Augsburg, he settled in Dresden in 1766. Graff was almost exclusively a painter of portraits, many of them for the courts of Saxony and Prussia. He worked in an elegant style similar to that of English painters such as Gainsborough, but also had a gift for psychological penetration without frills, which emerges most clearly in his portraits of literary and artistic figures and of himself (*Self-portrait*, 1765, Dresden, Gemäldegalerie).

Graffiti
Scratched or scribbled designs on walls, commonly humorous or obscene (from the Italian *graffare*, to scratch). Graffito or sgraffito is also the term used for a medieval and Renaissance technique of scratching a design through a layer of gilt or paint on to a ground which is of a different colour.

Graham, John (Ivan Dambrowsky) 1881–1961
Russian-born artist, who went to the USA in the early 1920s. His eccentric paintings straddle realism, abstraction and Surrealist biomorphism. His writings, especially the book *Systems and Dialects of Art* (1937), and his stress on the importance of the Unconscious, may have influenced young Abstract Expressionists such as Gorky.

Gran, Daniel 1694–1757
Austrian fresco-painter, a representative of the classical strain of the Baroque. Gran was not interested in illusionism, but was celebrated for his ability to devise and organize complex groups of allegorical figures in the heavens—most notably in the vaults of the Hofbibliothek in Vienna (1730).

Granacci, Francesco 1469–1543
Florentine painter. He was a pupil of Lorenzo di Credi and later of Domenico Ghirlandaio, though he was strongly influenced by the painters of the High Renaissance, particularly Fra Bartolommeo. His mature work is characterized by smoothness of modelling and a deft use of chiaroscuro, as for instance in *The Madonna with SS. Francis and Zenobius* (c.1515–16, Florence, Accademia). He was one of the assistants on the Sistine Ceiling before Michelangelo decided to do the work entirely himself.

Grand Manner
Elevated style of history painting showing heroic figures in idealized settings. In academic theory the Grand Manner was the only suitable way to treat the loftiest themes from the Bible or from ancient history and mythology. The classic exposition of its principles is to be found in Reynolds' *Discourses*.

Grand Tour
Extended Continental journey, lasting often a year or more, undertaken by young aristocrats, particularly British, during the 18th century. The purpose was to complete a broad education by viewing at first hand the classical glories of Italy and, increasingly, the "sublime" landscape of the Alps. Artists such as Batoni, Canaletto and Piranesi successfully catered for this "tourist" trade.

Grandville (pseudonym of Jean-Ignace-Isidore Gérard) 1803–47
French caricaturist and illustrator. In Paris, his first works were light-hearted lithographs of bourgeois life, but he achieved notoriety with the political *The metamorphoses of day* (1828), in which human beings have the physiognomy of animals. He was a republican and a contributor on *Charivari* and *Caricature* (1830–35), until the Press Laws of 1835 made him turn to book illustration—notably for the *Fables* of La Fontaine (1838). In his last years he became obsessed with macabre, dreamlike images and he died insane.

Granet, François-Marius 1775–1849
French painter of interior scenes and landscapes. He attended J.-L. David's atelier in 1799, and spent the years 1802–19 in Rome. Apponted Curator at the Louvre in 1826 and at Versailles in 1830, he devoted only part of his time to painting, specializing in romantic interiors, often of religious inspiration. An example of his detailed technique, recalling Dutch and Flemish masters, is *The choir of the Capuchin church in Rome* (1815, New York, Metropolitan). During the 1848 Revolution, he returned to his native Aix-en-Provence and founded the Musée Granet there.

Grant, Duncan 1885–1978
British painter and designer, a close associate of Roger Fry. His work before World War I represents an early English response to advanced French painting. *The Queen of Sheba* (1912, London, Tate), for example, was influenced by Pointillism. A pioneer of abstract painting, in 1914 he made an *Abstract kinetic collage painting* (London, Tate), devised so as to be gradually unrolled to the accompaniment of music by Bach. His later paintings were more traditional. He worked on many decorative projects and was co-director of the OMEGA WORKSHOPS. See vol. 4 p. *23*

GRAV see GROUPE DE RECHERCHE D'ART VISUEL

Gravelot, Hubert 1699–1773
French painter and engraver. His paintings are rare but he was an important book illustrator, working in a charming Rococo style. From 1732 to 1735 he was in London, where he ran a drawing-school, and he is perhaps best known for his engravings for Richardson's *Pamela* (1742) and Fielding's *Tom Jones* (1750), which are among the earliest illustrations to novels. He was a friend of Hogarth, and an important channel of influence for the Rococo style in England. Gainsborough was probably his pupil.

Graves, Morris born 1910
American painter. His lyrical sensibility usually focuses on single diminutive natural presences such as birds, painted in gouache or tempera amidst a shallow but ambiguous space. Intense, mystical images (*Bird in the spirit*, 1940–41, New York, Whitney) reveal his awareness of Tobey's "white writing" and perhaps of Klee's delicate linearity. They may also reflect his study of oriental thought.

Greco, El (Domenikos Theotokopoulos) 1541–1614
Painter, sculptor and architect, born in Crete and trained in Italy, but considered one of the greatest artists of the Spanish school. The signatures on his paintings always use his real name in Greek characters, and he often appended *Kres* (Cretan) to his name. He was probably first trained in the Byzantine style of icon painting current in Crete, then went to Italy, where he was said to have been one of Titian's last pupils in Venice. Tintoretto, however, is a much more obvious influence on his style. In about 1570 he moved to Rome. *Christ driving the money-changers from the Temple* (*c.*1572, Minneapolis, Institute of Arts) and the portrait of the miniaturist *Giulio Clovio* (*c.*1570, Naples, Museo di Capodimonte) date from his Italian period. By 1577 he was in Toledo, where he lived for the rest of his life. He apparently failed to win Philip II's patronage but his religious compositions were much sought after by ecclesiastics in the Jesuit city of Toledo and many were repeated by himself or his studio. He also painted portraits of Church dignitaries, for instance the sensitive *Felix Paravicino* (1609, Boston, MFA), and of other distinguished persons. *The burial of Count Orgaz* (1586, Toledo, S. Tomé) and *Christ stripped of his garments* (1577–79, Toledo Cathedral) are generally considered his masterpieces. It was after his move to Spain that he developed his highly individual, almost febrile, style—brilliantly reflecting the atmosphere of intense religious zeal in his adopted country. The distortions of his elongated flame-like figures, usually painted in cold bluish colours, have sometimes been attributed to astigmatism, but they perfectly express the emotion of his themes. Apart from religious works and portraits, he also painted two views of Toledo (New York, Metropolitan, and Toledo, Casa y Museo del Greco), and one mythological work, *Laocoön* (Washington, NG). El Greco is also known to have made wax models as preparatory studies for painting and some polychrome wooden sculpture by him survives (*The bestowal of the chasuble on St Ildefonso*, 1583, Toledo Cathedral). He also designed altarpieces, working as architect, sculptor and painter, as at the Hospital de la Caridad, Illescas (1603). The inventory of his library shows he was a man of culture, and Pacheco says that he wrote on painting, sculpture and architecture. Velazquez owned several works by him but El Greco's art was too personal to establish much of a following, and after his death he was largely forgotten for two centuries. See vol. 1 pp. *79*, *92*; vol. 2 pp. **174–175**

Green, Anthony born 1939
British painter. He uses bizarre perspectives, frequently aided by shaped canvases, to present an idealized view of middle-class life which usually stresses the eroticism beneath the surface of bourgeois respectability. His paintings are often autobiographical (*Our tent, 14th wedding anniversary*, 1975, Rochdale, Art Gallery).

Green, Valentine 1739–1813
British mezzotint engraver, well known for his reproductions of Reynolds' work. He made his first mezzotint after Reynolds in 1778, but a quarrel ended their association in 1783. Green also made fine mezzotints after West and Romney.

Greene, Balcomb born 1904
American painter, first chairman of the AMERICAN ABSTRACT ARTISTS group. His sparse, non-objective work during the 1930s reveals an assimilation of Constructivism and Mondrian in its use of geometric, shifting planes. After about 1943 his work changed radically to a fragmented, almost expressionistic figuration involving hazy and dramatic washes of colour.

Greenhill, John *c.*1644–76
English portrait painter in oils and pastels. His early work is in the English provincial style, but in the late 1660s he entered Lely's studio and thereafter worked in a simplified version of his master's manner. *Mrs Cartwright* and a *Self-portrait*, both in the Dulwich College Picture Gallery, London, are good examples of his style.

Greenough, Horatio 1805–52
American Neoclassical sculptor, active mainly in Italy. He studied in Rome with Thorvaldsen, and while in Florence met the writer James Fenimore Cooper, who commissioned *The chanting cherubs* (1828–30, now lost), the first major work in marble by an American. In 1832 he received the commission for a statue of George Washington for the rotunda of the Capitol (1833–41, now in Washington, Smithsonian Institution), the first important state commission given to an American sculptor. Greenough based the head on Houdon's portrait of Washington, and the body is derived from reconstructions of Phidias' Olympian Zeus—a mixture of realism and idealism generally thought unsuccessful. Greenough's theoretical writings, which stressed functional considerations, were perhaps of more significance than his rather pedantic statues.

Greenwood, John 1727–92
American painter. He was born in Boston and, after an apprenticeship as an engineer, began a career as a portrait painter in 1745. In 1752 he moved to Surinam in the Dutch East Indies, where he painted many stiff and undistinguished portraits and one remarkable work, *Sea captains carousing in Surinam* (1758, St Louis, Art Gallery). Greenhill represented himself and some of his friends in this spirited scene, which looks like a rather naive reflection of Hogarth's work and ranks as one of the first examples of genre painting in American art. From Surinam Greenwood moved to Holland, and in 1762 he settled in London.

Greuze, Jean-Baptiste 1725–1805
French painter. He is best known for his anecdotal genre scenes such as *The Bible-reading* (1755, Paris, Louvre), which made him the most popular painter in mid-18th-century France. He was in Italy, 1755–57, and had ambitions as a history painter, but *Septimius Severus rebuking Caracalla* (1769, Louvre) was a humiliating failure. His popularity faded with the growth of Neoclassicism, and he turned increasingly to titillating and mawkishly sentimental pictures of young girls to try and capture a different market. By the end of his career he was virtually forgotten, but one of his last commissions was for a portrait of Napoleon (1804–05, Versailles), when he shared the sitting with Ingres. His output was enormous; there is a museum dedicated to him in Tournus (his native town) and large collections in the Louvre, the Musée Fabre, Montpellier, and the Wallace Collection, London. See vol. 2 p. **245**; vol. 3 p. **56**

Grimaldi, Giovanni Francesco
(Il Bolognese) 1606–80
Italian painter, engraver and architect, best known for his classical landscapes in the manner of Annibale Carracci. These, less heroic and severe than Annibale's or Poussin's, were very popular in painted and engraved form and helped to spread the tradition of ideal landscape. He was active chiefly in Rome (frescos, 1644–48, in the Villa Doria Pamphili, where he also worked as an architect), but in 1649–51 he carried out decorations at the Mazarin Palace (Bibliothèque Nationale) and the Louvre in Paris.

Grimmer, Jacob *c.*1526–*c.*1590
Flemish painter. He was a pupil of Mathys Cock, and entered the Antwerp guild in 1546/47. He painted several versions of the *Seasons* (for instance, the signed series in the National Museum, Budapest) and went some way towards treating landscape as an autonomous genre. In his scenes of peasant *kermises*, he shows himself a follower of Bruegel. He collaborated with Gillis Mostaert in his biblical paintings. His son **Abel** (*c.*1573–before 1619) was also a painter, specializing in landscapes and small religious and genre paintings.

Grimshaw, John Atkinson 1836–93
English painter of landscapes, townscapes and dockyards, usually seen by moon or lamplight or at sunset. Whistler said of him: "I considered myself the inventor of *Nocturnes* until I saw Grimmy's moonlit pictures." He painted in London, Glasgow, Leeds, Scarborough and Liverpool, developing a highly personal style, often using photographs as a compositional aid. His rather acidic colours are particularly distinctive. Though he exhibited only five paintings at the Royal Academy, he sold well and imitations and forgeries appeared in his own lifetime. A fine collection of his work is in the City Art Gallery of his native Leeds.

Gris, Juan (José González) 1887–1927
Spanish painter. He studied in Madrid, and went to Paris in 1906, at first working in a decorative Art Nouveau style, but then coming under the influence of Picasso. Although his contribution to CUBISM dates only from 1911, it had a radical influence on the style's subsequent development. His pictures emphasized constructive rhythms and abstract components in opposition to the more intuitive methods of visual analysis of Braque and Picasso (*Homage to Picasso*, 1911–12, Chicago, Art Institute). Gris himself encapsulated the difference of approach when he wrote: "I try to make concrete that which is abstract . . . Cézanne turns a bottle into a cylinder, but I make a bottle—a particular bottle—out of a cylinder." By 1913 he had introduced colour into his work and was experimenting with *papier collé*, both of which developments shaped the emergence of synthetic Cubism. His later paintings have a classic poise and are more painterly in handling (*Violin and fruit dish*, 1924, London, Tate). Gris also made book illustrations and polychrome sculpture, but more important are his stage sets and costumes for the great ballet impresario, Diaghilev. See vol. 1 p. *75*; vol. 3 pp. **150**, *179*

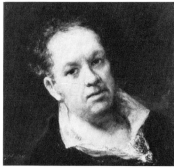
Goya: Self-portrait, 1815. Madrid, Academia de San Fernando (Scala)

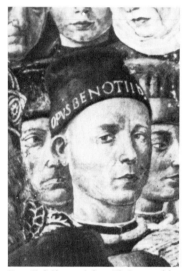
Gozzoli: Self-portrait from *The journey of the Magi*, 1459. Florence, Palazzo Medici-Riccardi (Mansell)

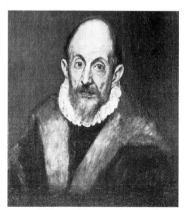
Greco: Self-portrait? *c.*1604. New York, Metropolitan, Joseph Pulitzer Fund

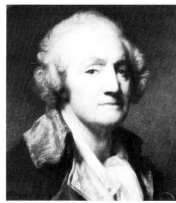
Greuze: Self-portrait, *c.*1760. Paris, Louvre

Grisaille
Painting executed entirely in tones of grey or neutral greyish colours. Grisailles may be used to imitate the effects of sculpture, as a sketch for a proposed work or as an underpainting.

Gropper, William 1897–1977
American cartoonist and social realist painter. Between 1912 and 1915 he studied with Henri and Bellows. As a graphic artist for numerous periodicals, including the *New York Tribune*, he transformed their realism into a radical political weapon. He began painting seriously in 1921 and his approach, as in *The senate* (1935, New York, MOMA), has the crudeness and vitality of an artist primarily recording social injustice.

Gros, Baron Antoine-Jean
1771–1835
French painter, a major precursor of the Romantic movement in France. He studied with J.-L. David, and in 1793 set out for Italy, where his meeting with Napoleon set the course of his career. As official war painter he travelled with Napoleon and painted epic scenes recording his campaigns, the most celebrated of which is *The plague at Jaffa* (1804, Paris, Louvre). After the fall of Napoleon, Gros turned mainly to portrait painting, although he also decorated the dome of the Panthéon in Paris. Unsuccessful in his attempt to reinstate in his work the classicism of his early training, he committed suicide. Géricault, Delacroix, Barye and Bonington, his pupils, were all strongly influenced by his dramatic subject matter and bold technique, which was partly derived from his study of Rubens and the great Venetian masters. See vol. 3 p. **78**

Grosz, George 1893–1959
German illustrator, painter and caracaturist, who became an American citizen in 1938. During World War I he contributed satirical drawings such as *Fit for active service* (1918, New York, MOMA) to anti-war periodicals. In 1917 he and Heartfield (who anglicized their names in World War I as a war protest) published a series of illustrated books and journals savagely critical of German militarism and the capitalist corruption of post-War Berlin. His style at this time consisted of a collage-like assemblage of sharply outlined anonymous figures focusing attention uncomfortably on a given social or political abuse, as in *Suicide* (1916, London, Tate). He joined the Communist Party in 1918 and in 1919 became a member of the Berlin Dada group. In 1920 he organized and exhibited at the First International Dada Fair. He was prosecuted several times for blasphemy and obscenity between 1921 and 1930. After 1924 he produced a series of Expressionist yet painterly nudes and café and street scenes which are curiously lacking in the social bite of his other work. Despairing of the political developments in Germany, in 1933 he accepted a teaching position at the Art Students' League in New York. In the USA he painted New York street scenes and nudes in a more lyrical vein (*New York Harbour*, 1936, New York, Metropolitan), while still continuing his savage attack on Fascism. After World War II his work took on a nightmarish, surreal quality, as, for example, in *The pit* (1946, Kansas, Wichita Art Museum). See vol. 3 pp. **194–195**

Grotesque
Term for a kind of fanciful decoration dominated by linked festoons and delicately decorative frames incorporating figurative or floral ornament. It derived from the Italian word "*grotta*", meaning cave, and was coined after the discovery of the decorated rooms of Nero's Golden House in Rome. In the 15th century artists such as Crivelli, Filippino Lippi, Mantegna, Signorelli and Tura exploited similar antique decorative forms. In the 16th century Raphael and members of his workshop, such as Perino del Vaga and Giovanni da Udine, were inspired by the recently discovered grotesques of the Golden House. The fashion spread throughout most of Europe, and was a strand in the delightful decorative fantasies of early French Rococo. It was as part of the reaction against Rococo that the word grotesque began to be used to suggest something monstrous or abnormal.

Ground
The surface on which a design or painting is made, but also specifically the prepared surface or the substance with which it is prepared. In painting the ground provides a durable barrier between the support and the paint, reducing absorbency and chemical interaction. It may be brittle and smooth, as is gesso, damp, as in the final plaster layer used for fresco, or elastic and textured, as in the oil-based priming layers used to prepare canvas for oil-painting. In etching, the ground is the acid-resistant wax rolled on to the plate.

Group of Seven
Group of landscape painters, based in Toronto, who created the first important national movement in Canadian painting. The name dates from the first group exhibition, held at the Art Museum in Toronto in 1920, although some of the artists involved had been working together since 1913. Tom Thomson, one of the early leaders, died in 1917, and the seven who gave their name to the 1920 exhibition were Franklin Carmichael, Lawren Harris, A.Y. Jackson, Frank Johnston, Arthur Lismer, J.E.H. Macdonald and Frederick Varley. Edwin Holgate was among the painters who joined later. They participated in group sketching expeditions, sometimes to remote parts of Canada, and expressed their national pride in a style characterized by brilliant colour, expressionist brushwork, stylized curvilinear forms and a disdain for spatial relationships. Their work initially suffered much critical abuse, but their undeniably patriotic feelings eventually won them public favour. In 1933 the Group of Seven changed its name to the **Canadian Group of Painters**, and the members' work developed more individualistically; Harris, for example, eventually turned to pure abstraction.

Groupe de Recherche d'Art Visuel (GRAV)
Group of kinetic artists formed in Paris in 1959 by Le Parc, Vasarély's son Yvaral and others. The group was greatly influenced by Vasarély's ideology of an anonymous, impersonal art and aimed to involve the public in experiments designed to question commonly held assumptions about the environment. The first group exhibition was held in 1960, and as well as individual works the members produced joint projects. Elaborate labyrinths were constructed containing optically disturbing effects—distorting mirrors, moving floors—encouraging public participation. These ideas were largely Le Parc's; others in the group were more interested in purely visual problems. The group split up in 1968. See vol. 3 p. 245

Groux, Charles de 1825–70
Belgian painter. He studied in Brussels with Navez and in Düsseldorf, at first working in a Romantic manner but later, with Rops and Meunier, becoming more involved with Realism. He painted daily life in a realistic vein with moralistic overtones, as in his *Drunkard* (1853) in the Musées Royaux des Beaux-Arts, Brussels.

Grund, Norbert 1717–67
Bohemian painter of small-scale genre scenes and idylls, painted for sale to a wide variety of collectors in Prague rather than commissioned. The finest collection of his paintings (which are mostly on metal or wood) is in the National Gallery in Prague.

Grundig, Hans 1901–58
German painter. He belonged to the politically-oriented group of NEUE SACHLICHKEIT artists working in Dresden in the 1920s, which included Dix. His style was a fusion of Expressionist elements with the urban and industrial themes associated with Neue Sachlichkeit (*Hunger march*, 1932, Dresden, Gemäldegalerie).

Grünewald, Isaac 1889–1946
Swedish painter and designer. He studied with Bergh and in Paris with Matisse, under whose influence he developed a sensual Expressionism in rhythmic decorative compositions dominated by rainbow colours. His work varied from portraits and town views to stage designs and monumental projects; in 1926, for example, he decorated an auditorium in the Stockholm Concert Hall. He was Professor at the Academy in Stockholm, 1932–42, directed his own art school there, 1942–46, and published his theories of art in various writings.

Grünewald (Mathis Gothardt-Neithardt) *c.*1470/80–1528
German painter, one of the greatest and most individual artists of his time. He was active in the Middle Rhine area, mainly in Aschaffenberg as a court painter to two successive Archbishops of Mainz, for whom he also worked as an architect and engineer. The small body of his work which survives is exclusively on religious themes. His masterpiece is the altarpiece for the hospital chapel of the monastery at Isenheim, Alsace (finished *c.*1515, Colmar, Musée Unterlinden). This is a large polyptych with two sets of wings, and includes representations of the Crucifixion, Resurrection and Annunciation. The scenes are composed with a full mastery of perspective, but the imagery is essentially late Gothic. Grünewald's colouring is both splendid and subtle, but the most impressive aspect of the work is the astonishingly intense emotion, brought about by expressionist distortion, and in *The Crucifixion* by an unprecedented depiction of the horrors of physical suffering. The terrible lacerations of Christ's body also occur in Grünewald's smaller paintings of *The Crucifixion* in Basel (Kunstmuseum) and Washington (NG). Unlike most of his great German contemporaries, Grünewald seems not to have worked as an engraver, though a number of drawings survive, and he remained little known through succeeding centuries, so much so that his real name was not discovered until the 1920s—"Grünewald" is a mistake of Sandrart's. His influence, however, is clearly to be found in the work of contemporaries such as Baldung Grien, Ratgebe and Holbein the Younger. See vol. 1 p. *78*; vol. 2 p. **151**

Guan Tong active early 10th century
Chinese painter, the rival (and possibly a pupil) of Jing Hao. Guan Tong enjoyed in the Song dynasty the reputation of being the greatest landscape painter of the Five Dynasties. The works attributed to him today are of doubtful authenticity, but they do show the strong sketchy brushwork in monochrome ink thought to be the hallmark of the early landscape style, as for example in a hanging scroll entitled *Awaiting a crossing* (Taiwan, National Palace Museum). Originally from Chang'an, the Tang capital in the North, he subsequently worked at the Nanking court of the later Liang dynasty.

Guanxiu 832–912
Chinese painter. He entered a Zen Buddhist monastery as a child but later travelled widely, before settling in Chengdu in the early 10th century. He specialized in paintings of *Lohan*, a group of Buddhist sages with grotesque ascetic appearance. Several series attributed to him exist, but almost certainly they are not by his hand. The development of a lively tradition of idealized religious portraiture, which continued through to the Yuan dynasty in both painting and wood sculpture, owes much to his reputation.

Guardi, Francesco 1712–93
The best-known member of a family of artists who worked in Venice. He painted a wide range of subject matter, from historical and devotional pictures to flower-pieces and still lifes, but is now principally remembered for the view paintings to which he largely devoted himself after the death of his brother **Giovanni Antonio** (1699–1760), the head of the family studio. Francesco lived a life of considerable obscurity: his patrons were to be found among minor dealers whose support proved insufficient to prevent him from dying in poverty. His style was remarkably free and expressive, and his views of Venice, in contrast to the minutely detailed ones of Canaletto, evoke rather than record the topography of the city. Towards the very end of his life he painted an increasing number of purely imaginary views (*capricci*). His output was enormous, and there are examples in most major collections; the National Gallery, London, for example, has seventeen; the National Gallery, Washington, eight. Opinion is divided as to whether Francesco or Giovanni Antonio is responsible for the parapet of the organ with representations of *The story of Tobit* (after 1753) in the church of S. Raffaele, Venice. This explosive work is painted with such astonishing freedom that the forms are almost dissolved, and if it is indeed by the elder brother, he, too, must rank as a great innovator. See vol. 2 p. **255**

Guariento di Arpo
documented 1338–70
Paduan painter. His one signed work, a Crucifix in the Museo Civico at Bassano, shows him to have been the closest of Giotto's immediate Paduan followers. In 1365/8 he painted a huge fresco of *The coronation of the Virgin* in the Doge's Palace in Venice; this was badly damaged in the fire of 1577, but the sinopia is preserved and is still impressive. Its influence is clear in works by Jacobello del Fiore and Antonio Vivarini. His most important surviving works in Padua are the scenes from the Old Testament in the Cappella del Capitano in the former Palazzo Carreresi. The extensive cycle of frescos in the choir of the Eremitani church was destroyed in 1944.

Guayasamin, Oswaldo born 1919
Ecuadorian Expressionist painter. His studies of deprivation, sorrow and abandon, devoid of any explicit political comment, earned him a considerable following in the 1950s. He has travelled extensively and has executed a number of important mural commissions including ones in Quito and Caracas. They are allegorical groups expressing anger, agony and fraternity.

Gude, Hans 1825–1903
Norwegian painter. He was Professor at the Academies in Düsseldorf (1854–62), Karlsruhe (1864–80) and Berlin (1880–1901). In Germany he painted many of his best-known pictures from memory, especially the atmospheric landscapes of his native fjords. *Høyfjell* or *Mountain heights* (1857, Oslo, NG) is a fine example of his realistic style.

Gudnason, Svavar born 1919
Icelandic painter working in Reykjavik and Copenhagen. In the late 1930s he studied in Paris with Léger and was strongly influenced by Picasso. He soon evolved a lively abstract style and became a pioneer of non-figurative painting in Iceland and Denmark, and joined the COBRA group. He used strong clear colour and vigorous lines in powerful, rhythmical compositions.

Guercino, Il (Giovanni Francesco Barbieri) 1591–1666
One of the most individual of Italian BAROQUE painters. His nickname, "Guercino", means "squint-eyed". He was born in Cento, near Ferrara, and was largely self-taught. His early work, strongly influenced by Ludovico Carracci and Venetian painting, and perhaps indirectly by Caravaggio, is highly original, with grand forms, dramatic lighting, rich colour and distinctive soft modelling (*Erminia and the shepherd*, 1620, Birmingham, City Art Gallery). In 1621 he was summoned to Rome by Gregory XV, for whose nephew he painted his most celebrated work, *Aurora*, a ceiling fresco in the Casino of the Villa Ludovisi, far more Baroque in style than Guido Reni's equally famous treatment of the subject of 1613–14. On Pope Gregory's death in 1623, Guercino returned to Cento, where he enjoyed a highly successful career, mainly as a painter of altarpieces. His style became more classical as a result of his stay in Rome and his originality gradually faded, but he never lost his painterly skill. After Reni's death in 1642, Guercino moved to Bologna, taking over his studio and position as the city's leading painter. His late works are very close in style to Reni (*The Cumaean Sibyl*, 1651, London, Denis Mahon coll.). Guercino was a brilliant and original draughtsman, and there is a fine collection of his drawings at Windsor Castle. See vol. 2 p. **185**

Guérin, Baron Pierre-Narcisse 1774–1833
French painter. A pupil of J.B. Regnault, Guérin continued the Neoclassicism of J.-L. David in epic scenes from Roman history and French classical drama, combining gracefulness with disciplined form, as in his mannered *Hippolytus and Phaedra* (1802, Cambridge, Mass., Fogg). As the teacher of Géricault, Delacroix, Delaroche and Scheffer, he was an important transitional figure in the Romantic movement.

Guggenheim, Peggy 1898–1979
American patron and art dealer. She spent much of her life before World War II in Europe and brought back important works of modern European artists when she returned to the USA during the War. In New York she founded the Art of This Century gallery (1942), which gave one-man shows (often the first) to many leading painters of the New York school. She returned to Europe in 1947 and opened a gallery for her art collection in Venice. See vol. 3 p. 210

Guglielmi, Louis 1906–56
American painter. He was born in Cairo, but his family moved to New York in 1914. His earlier work concentrates on urban and architectural motifs. From the mid-1930s onwards he assimilated Surrealism, especially Chirico's bleak Metaphysical cityscapes, whilst conveying overtones of social reference, particularly to the inhabitants of Brooklyn's "mean streets".

Guglielmo della Porta died 1577
Italian sculptor. He is first recorded in 1534 in Genoa working on the Altar of the Apostles in the Cathedral. In 1537 he went to Rome, where he made a great reputation as a bronze sculptor, executing several papal busts. His masterpiece is the tomb of Paul III (1549–75) in St Peter's, with a solemn, seated effigy in bronze and two reclining marble female figures of *Virtues* below. He was an avowed follower of Michelangelo, and the influence of Michelangelo's *Day* and *Night, Dawn* and *Evening* in the Medici Chapel in S. Lorenzo, Florence, is evident in the *Virtues*. Guglielmo was a fairly prolific artist and many other tomb sculptures by him are in Roman churches; a typical narrative relief in gilt bronze is *The Flagellation* (c.1575, London, V&A).

Guido da Siena active c.1260–80
Italian painter, with Coppo di Marcovaldo the founder of the Sienese school. He was heavily influenced by Byzantine art, both in his forms and in his iconography. Several paintings are attributed to him, but his only signed work is a much repainted altarpiece of *The Madonna and Child* in the Town Hall of Siena. This has been the subject of much controversy because it bears the date 1221, which seems impossible on stylistic grounds. The lettering is old and unaltered, but was probably added for commemorative purposes when the picture was repainted in the early 14th century (possibly by Duccio).

Guillaumin, Armand 1841–1927
French landscape painter. Largely self-taught, he exhibited regularly with the Impressionists, but it was only in 1891, when he won a lottery, that he was able to devote himself fully to painting. His work shows a use of Impressionist technique and vivid, near-Fauve, colour but he chose industrial themes. He often painted working people on the banks of the Seine (*Charcoal thieves on the Quai de Bercy*, c.1882, Geneva, Petit Palais).

Gu Kaizhi c.344–406
Chinese painter. He is the earliest named Chinese painter of whose style we may still gain some impression, though only through copies of his scrolls of considerably later date: *The nymph of the Luo river* (versions in Peking, Palace Museum, and Washington, Freer); *The admonitions of the court instructress* (London, BM) and *Biographies of eminent women* (Peking, National Palace Collection). Opinions differ as to the dating of these copies, but they do seem to preserve a distinctively pre-Tang painting tradition of lines of unvaried thickness, even areas of colour and open composition against a plain ground. Later traditions about Gu Kaizhi's life are numerous, and it seems that the centre of his activity was the aristocratic Jin dynasty court in Nanking. See vol. 3 p. **40**

Gulbransson, Olaf 1873–1958
Norwegian draughtsman and painter. A brilliant caricaturist, he began working for the Press at 16 and from 1902 to 1923 worked for *Simplizissimus* in Munich, where he was later professor at the Academy (1929–34). He won international fame for his economical draughtsmanship and satirical perception of the foibles of the famous and bourgeois narrow-mindedness.

Günther, Ignaz 1725–75
The outstanding Bavarian sculptor of the Rococo. In 1754 he settled in Munich, and devoted his career to carving wooden (usually polychrome or white and gold) sculpture and furnishings for churches in Bavaria, notably Weyarn (1755–65), Rott am Inn (1759–62) and Starnberg (1766–68). The elegance and the exquisite refinement of his sculpture, with its sharp linear folds and delicate colours, are translated from his pen and watercolour drawings, which are among the finest ever made.

Günther, Matthäus 1704–88
South German fresco painter. Born near Wessobrunn and a pupil of C.D. Asam, Günther spent his life based in Augsburg, frescoing numerous churches, mostly in Bavaria and the Tyrol (notably Amorbach, 1745–57, and Rott am Inn, 1760–63). He worked in a light, somewhat schematized development of his teacher's idiom, modified by Venetian influences.

Guo Xi active c.1060–75
Chinese painter, the foremost northern Song landscape painter of the later 11th century. His activity centred on the court, where he held a post in the Painting Academy and wrote a treatise on landscape painting. He was best known for compositions of mountains, which were on an unprecedented scale, in particular his murals in the Imperial Palace, in which he may have used the rough wall surfaces to deliberate effect. The murals, however, have not survived, and the large silk scroll *Early spring* (1072, Taichung, Palace Museum) is the only work which is generally considered to be from his own hand. It reveals a breathtaking world of rugged grandeur, with towering swollen crags and twisted trees painted with agitated lines. There are many attributed works, and the Song dynasty copy of his *Clearing autumn skies over mountains and valleys* (Washington, Freer) is perhaps the best surviving example of the large-scale romantic early Song landscape from the tradition of Li Cheng, Dong Yuan, Fan Kuan and Guo Xi himself. See vol. 3 p. **40**

Guston, Philip 1913–80
American painter. As a result of his mural works for the WPA, he was recognized as an important figurative artist by the early 1940s. In 1949 he turned from political and social themes to abstraction. Paintings of his first mature style, characterized by a build-up of luminously coloured overlapping brushstrokes towards the centre of an airy whitish field, are sometimes called "Abstract Impressionist". By the 1960s, lyricism gives way to an air of doom and sobriety, and a dense, crude manner of execution. A return to figuration is evident in later paintings attacking social injustice. See vol. 3 p. **215**

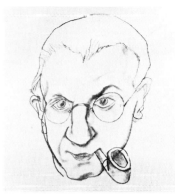

Grosz: Self-portrait drawing, 1916. Private coll.

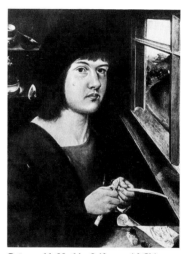

Grünewald, Mathis: Self-portrait? Chicago, Art Institute of Chicago

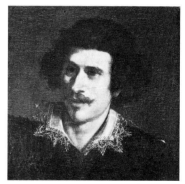

Guercino: Presumed self-portrait, early 17th century. Florence, Uffizi (Scala)

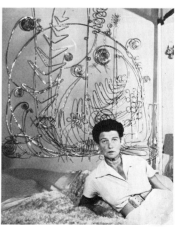

Guggenheim: Photograph taken beside a silver sculpture by Calder, 1961 (Popperfoto)

Gutai group (Gutai Art Association) Japanese group of artists founded in 1954 by Jiro Yoshiwara and 15 other artists. It flourished in the 1950s and early 1960s, and realized 22 group shows and 14 numbers of its magazine before Yoshiwara's death in 1972 and its demise. In the early period there were two different phases of activity—first neo-Dadaist works and remarkably early Happenings (preceding the Japanese Pop art and Junk art movements of the late 1950s and early 1960s); secondly, somewhat later, abstract paintings, such as Yoshiwara's circular shapes on plain painted grounds. This abstract movement was inspired by Informal art, which was introduced to Japan in 1957, and led almost all the Gutai painters to adopt Abstract Expressionism.

Gutfreund, Otto 1889–1927
Czech sculptor. He was one of the first artists to apply the principles of Cubism to sculpture, only Picasso and Archipenko working in the field as early as he did. He came into contact with the most modern trends in art when studying with Bourdelle in Paris, 1909–10, and Cubist tendencies are present in his sculptured details on Hlávka Bridge, Prague, as early as 1911. His more fully developed style can be seen in such works as *Cubist bust* of 1912–13 in the Tate Gallery, London. His Cubist phase lasted until the end of the decade, and his later work became more naturalistic. He committed suicide. There is a good collection of his works in the National Collection of Czech Modern Sculpture at Zbraslav.

Guttuso, Renato born 1912
Italian painter. In the early 1940s he founded a group with Birolli and others in order to fight the official Fascist cultural policy, and after World War II he was a founder-member of the FRONTE NUOVO DELLE ARTI. Like Cremonini he is essentially an Expressionist painter of social realist subjects. His early works are Cubist in style and show the influence of Picasso's *Guernica*. The colours are bright and aggressive and his design is based on complex linear patterns into which he compresses his realist imagery. This latter, however, is often complex and symbolic and lends his work a disturbing Surrealist atmosphere. See vol. 3 p. **250**

Guys, Constantin 1805–92
French draughtsman and watercolourist. He was born in Holland of French parents, and little is known about his vagabond life. From 1848 he worked in London for the *Illustrated London News*, recording the fashions of Victorian life, and was sent in 1854 as a war artist to the Crimea. He returned to Paris during the 1860s, and his circle of friends included Daumier, Delacroix, Gavarni and the photographer Nadar. Guys recorded with the eye of a dandy the pleasurable world of the Second Empire, and many of his elegant drawings have affinities with Impressionist draughtsmanship. Manet, Gavarni, Forain and Toulouse-Lautrec were all influenced by him. Baudelaire devoted his most celebrated article, a modernist manifesto, to Guys as *The Painter of Modern Life* (1863). See vol. 3 p. **88**

Gwathmey, Robert born 1903
American painter. He frequently depicts southern black workers, and his work is characterized by simplified areas of colour frequently placed within an almost *cloisonné* linear framework (*Workers on the land*, 1947, Norman, University of Oklahoma).

H

Haacke, Hans born 1936
West German artist, who has been active principally in the USA. He is a prominent exponent of "systems" art, concentrating on the process of making a work rather than on a finished object. From 1963 he made transparent boxes and tubes containing fluids which responded to changes in temperature, air pressure, etc. The behaviour of water in all its forms, including snow, ice and steam, has been a major interest, as have wind and air, and his documentation has contained detailed meteorological data. Several projects have involved animals, for example *Chickens hatching* (1969). Increasingly interested in spectator participation, he has moved into political and sociological areas: in *Proposal: Poll of MOMA visitors* (1970, New York, MOMA), visitors cast votes into transparent boxes. He made no explicit comment but much of his recent work has taken a clearly left-wing and critical stance. See vol. 3 p. **249**

Hackert, Jacob Philipp 1737–1807
German painter, the best-known of a large family of artists. He was chiefly active in Italy, one of the last exponents of the classically composed landscape in the manner of Claude. After early years in Berlin and Paris (1765–66) he travelled in 1768 to Italy. There he remained, painting highly-finished views of famous sites for German, Russian and English travellers. From 1786 he was court painter in Naples. Goethe, whom he met in 1787, admired him and wrote his biography. He was very prolific and his paintings were widely collected; ten are at Attingham Park, Shropshire.

Haese, Gunter born 1924
West German sculptor. His constructions are personal, lyrical, sometimes witty and always reveal great skill (*Oasis*, 1964, Cologne, Wallraf-Richartz Museum). Haese originally used bits of machinery, then began to create machine sculptures entirely from wire. Although made of metal, they never seem to belong to the industrial sphere but rather to that of biomorphic, indeed somewhat anthropomorphic, fantasy.

Hagenau, Nicholas von (Niclas Hagnower) documented 1493–1526
German sculptor working in Strasbourg from 1493 to 1526. His most important work is probably the high altar of Strasbourg Cathedral (*c.* 1501), but better known is the wooden shrine of Grünewald's Isenheim altarpiece (1505, Colmar, Musée Unterlinden), which is usually attributed to him. His style was strongly influenced by that of Gerhaerts.

Hagesandros see PERGAMENE SCHOOL

Hague school
Group of Dutch landscape painters working in The Hague from the mid-19th century until around 1900. Drawing inspiration from Ruisdael, Potter, Constable and the Barbizon school, the members aimed at a lyrical but faithful representation of their locality and excelled at atmospheric light effects. Paradoxically, the best-known member, Josef Israels, was not a landscapist but a peasant painter in the vein of Millet, his canvases advocating a patient acceptance of life's hardships. Other noteworthy members were Bosboom, the Maris brothers, Mauve, Mesdag and Weissenbruch. Good collections of their work are in the Mesdag Museum and the Gemeentemuseum, both in The Hague.

Hains, Raymond born 1926
French artist, photographer and filmmaker, best known for his *affiches lacérées* (torn posters), first exhibited in 1957, which he used to criticize the ephemeral values of advertising.

Half tones
Those tones which fall between the absolutes of black and white, or dark and light. In the half-tone printing process different tones are achieved by varying the distance between dots – the further apart they are the lighter the tone.

Haller, Hermann 1880–1950
Swiss sculptor. He began studying painting but in 1905 decided to dedicate himself to sculpture. In 1907 he travelled to Paris, where he saw the work of Rodin and Maillol. His work has varied in style but has always remained naturalistic, focusing mainly on the female nude. A fine example of his mature style is *Female nude* (1918, Düsseldorf, Nordrhein-Westfalen), a perfectly poised slender form.

Hals, Dirk 1591–1656
Dutch painter, the younger brother of Frans and, like him, active in Haarlem. He mainly painted small interior scenes of great charm. The early ones owe much to Buytewech, but around 1630 he abandoned crowded compositions for pictures showing one or two figures engaged in everyday activities (*Woman tearing up a letter*, 1631, Mainz, Gemäldegalerie). See vol. 2 p. **226**

Hals, Frans 1581/85–1666
The first great painter of the 17th-century Dutch school, and one of the most celebrated of all portraitists. He was probably born in Antwerp, but by 1591 his parents had settled in Haarlem, where he studied with van Mander, and spent all his career. His earliest dated work is the sober and unexceptional portrait of *Jacobus Zaffius* (1611, Haarlem, Frans Hals Museum), and he suddenly emerges as a major artist in 1616 with *The banquet of the St George Civic Guard* (Hals Museum), the first of his six such group portraits. This brilliant work, celebrating the healthy optimism of the new Dutch Republic, broke away from the stiff conventions of earlier group portraits to present a vivid picture of lively and varied personalities in naturalistic action. The brushwork is as fresh as the composition and Hals' unprecedented ability to capture a sense of fleeting movement and spontaneous expression is the key to the tremendous vivacity of his portraits (and of his genre scenes, which always have a portrait character). The joyful exuberance associated with Hals is nowhere more clearly shown than in his most famous work, "*The Laughing Cavalier*" (1624, London, Wallace Coll.). Here the brushwork, of dazzling virtuosity, is finely detailed, but in other works Hals (by whom no drawings are known) painted *alla prima* with exceptional freedom. During the 1630s his style began to grow more sober, and his greatest works, group portraits of *The regents* and *The regentesses of the Almshouse* (*c.* 1664, Hals Museum), are in their sombre grandeur and feeling for the frailty of flesh surpassed only by Rembrandt. Hals was constantly in financial difficulties (probably because of his large family) and apparently died destitute. He had numerous pupils, including Brouwer, Leyster, Wouwermans, and several of his own sons, but he established no school and true appreciation of his genius came only in the second half of the 19th century. See vol. 1 p. *148*; vol. 2 pp. **214–215**

Hamel, Théophile 1817–70
Canadian Romantic portrait painter, active in Quebec. From 1838 to 1840 he was apprenticed to Plamondon and studied in Italy and France, 1843–46. He returned to Quebec accomplished in the current Romantic idiom, as his *Self-portrait* (1843, Quebec, Musée) shows. He became popular, and was commissioned by Parliament to paint the present and past Speakers of the legislative council and assembly. During his best period, 1852–55, he painted *L'Abbé Edouard Faucher* (1855, Lotbinière, St Louis), with the substantiality and impassivity of Plamondon's religious portraits.

Hamen y Leon, Juan van der 1596–1633
Spanish painter, the leading still-life specialist in Madrid in the early 17th century. He was of Flemish descent and his bodegones show something of the influence of Aertsen (*The cook*, *c.* 1630, Amsterdam, Rijksmuseum). His pure still lifes, of which the finest example (1627) is in the National Gallery, Washington, are similar to Beert's in their high viewpoint and straightforward arrangement of objects.

Hamilton, Gavin 1723–98
Scottish history painter, classical archaeologist and art dealer, a notable contributor to Neoclassicism. Born and educated in Scotland, he settled permanently in Rome about 1755, making occasional visits to Britain. He was trained as a painter but earned his living chiefly by selling Old Master paintings and classical antiquities to British collectors making the GRAND TOUR. From 1762 onwards he sent back large canvases, with subjects from Homer's *Iliad*, for exhibition in London. These are characterized by hard outlines, frieze-like compositions and formal borrowings from Poussin and Guido Reni (*Achilles lamenting the death of Patroclus*, 1763, Edinburgh, NG of Scotland). Internationally renowned, he was one of the few British artists to receive commissions from foreigners. See vol. 3 p. **56**

Hamilton, Richard born 1922
British POP painter. At an early age he worked in advertising, studying art in the evenings at the Academy and the Slade School in London. In the 1950s he made paintings which reflected his interest in marketing styles. Works such as *$he* (1958–61, London, Tate), depicting a refrigerator and a toaster with a woman styled to match, were a major inspiration for the younger British Pop painters. In the 1960s he made paintings on the theme of the impact of photography. *Portrait of Hugh Gaitskell as a famous monster of filmland* (1964, Arts Council of Great Britain), a protest against the socialist leader's opposition to nuclear disarmament, is a blown-up newspaper photograph overlaid with the image of Claude Rains in the film *Phantom of the Opera*. Recent paintings by Hamilton have revived the old theme of *memento mori*. See vol. 3 pp. **240–241**

Hammershøi, Vilhelm 1864–1916
Danish painter. He was influenced by Vermeer and his contemporaries, and painted spartan and serene indoor scenes with few colours, often moderated tones of grey. *The collector of coins* (1904, Oslo,

NG) is a sombre, sensitive portrait of a solitary man.

Handling
The painter or sculptor's manipulation of his or her material. It is one of the most personal parts of the act of creation, and a chief factor in distinguishing one artist's work from another's.

Han Gan active mid-8th century
Chinese painter. He was associated as a court painter with the circle around the Tang Emperor Xuanzong (reigned 712–56), and the spirited paintings of horses for which he is famous were imperial commissions. Only later copies of his compositions survive, the best and earliest of which is probably the so-called "*Night Shining White*" (c.750, New York, Metropolitan).

Han-Kan see HAN GAN

Hanly, Patrick born 1932
New Zealand painter. He studied and worked in Europe from 1957 to 1962. Early influences were Chagall's naive lyricism, Picasso, and the technical bravura of Francis Bacon. In the important series *Figures in Light*, 1964, he successfully adapted intense Pop art colours to the harsh light and shade on Auckland beaches. From 1969 he developed a splatter technique in pure colour, and has also shown a bold grasp of local idiom in public commissions, notably in murals for Auckland International Airport.

Hansen, Constantin 1804–80
Danish painter and book illustrator, a pupil of Eckersberg. He began by specializing in portraits of amiable-looking middle-class subjects, displaying a strong sense of colour and grasp of plastic form. From 1835 to 1844 he lived in Italy, where he painted genre scenes of Rome and its environs. He also painted mythological frescos for the University of Copenhagen (1844–53).

Hanson, Duane born 1925
American sculptor, well known for his life-size figures made of fibreglass resin which are realistic to the smallest detail. Starting in an expressionistic vein, Hanson found that he could more effectively comment on the contemporary scene through a seemingly objective approach. He "re-creates" lower and middle-class Americans, generally focusing on tasteless modes of dress, as in *Supermarket lady* (1970, Aachen, Neue Galerie), an overweight woman with curlers in her hair, or an elderly couple of *Tourists* (1970, Private coll.) in Hawaiian shirts. The figures are dressed in real garments and real objects are often included as props. See vol. 3 p. **253**

Happening
An art form in which the artist performs or directs an entertainment which combines elements of theatre, music and the visual arts. This can take place in a specially created environment and the audience be asked to participate. Although the course of events may be carefully planned, the execution is usually intended to include an element of spontaneity. The "event" experiments of the musician John Cage at the Black Mountain College in the USA in the 1950s had a profound influence on such artists as Kaprow and Dine. **Performance art** is sometimes used synonymously, though it can be applied to more theatrical and more carefully programmed events, in which the audience seldom participates. See vol. 3 pp. **242–243**

Hard-edge painting
Type of abstract painting in which the shapes within the composition, whether organic or geometric, are executed in flat colour with sharply defined edges. The technique was facilitated by the development of quick-drying acrylic paints. Two of its main pioneers were Albers and Reinhardt. Their followers include Held and Elsworth Kelly. The term "hard-edge" was coined by the American critic Langser in 1958.

Hare, David born 1917
American sculptor. Before taking up sculpture in 1942 he had worked as a photographer, developing his own automatist procedures in photography. During the early 1940s he was closely involved with Surrealist ideas, being editor of the magazine *VVV*. In his first sculptures he experimented with various materials. *Juggler* (1950–51, New York, Whitney) explores the interpenetration of a figure with space and its transformation through its depicted activity.

Harnett, William Michael 1848–92
Irish-born American still-life painter. Harnett worked in Philadelphia and New York, but also in Europe (1880–86), mainly in Munich. He originally trained as a silver engraver, and brought something of the precision required in the technique into his *trompe-l'oeil* paintings (*Old cupboard door*, 1889, Sheffield, Graves Art Gallery). With Peto he is the major American specialist in still life in the 19th century. See vol. 3 p. **125**

Harpignies, Henri 1819–1916
French landscape painter. His *Autumn scene* (1884, Grenoble, Musée des Beaux-Arts) shows him as a follower of the BARBIZON school. His soft and lyrical treatment of trees was particularly appreciated and from 1870 onwards he achieved fame and success.

Harris, Lawren Stewart
1885–1970
Canadian landscape painter and abstractionist. He was a founder of the GROUP OF SEVEN and its most original and sophisticated member. From 1904 to 1908 he studied in Berlin, employing bold Expressionist colour in his subsequent studies of Toronto buildings. Painting with Group members on Lake Superior and in the Arctic in the late 1920s, he produced impeccably finished works, dominated by primeval shapes towering upward, and bathed in unearthly light (*Icebergs, David Strait*, 1930, Kleinburg, McMichael coll.). His transcendental geometric abstractions produced after 1936 are infused with Kandinskian mysticism.

Harris, Robert 1849–1919
Canadian portrait and history painter, born in Wales. He studied in Boston, 1873–74, in London and with Bonnat in Paris in 1877. He arrived in Toronto in 1879 and in 1883 he moved to Montreal. His facility in monumental history painting prompted a Government commission to paint the famous *Fathers of Confederation* (1883–84, destroyed 1916). His work transcends academic formulae, achieving a warm presence in spite of painstaking naturalism.

Hartigan, Grace born 1922
American painter. A second generation ABSTRACT EXPRESSIONIST, under the influence of De Kooning she abandoned a painterly figuration for complete abstraction. Her first works were exhibited under the name George Hartigan in 1951. Since 1952 she has painted works

with a mythological content and abstract versions of paintings by Rubens, Goya and other masters.

Hartley, Marsden 1877–1943
American painter. He was regarded as a progressive artist even before visiting Paris and Berlin, 1912–13. Once in Europe, he visited Kandinsky and Marc and exhibited at Der Sturm. He was particularly attracted to Germany and lived in Berlin from 1914 to late 1915. It was here that he painted his most accomplished works, including the brightly coloured and decorative *A German officer* (1914, New York, Metropolitan), based on military emblems organized in an abstract pattern. His later paintings, mainly landscapes such as *Lobster fishermen* (1940–41, Metropolitan) have a mournful quality due to the heavy outlines and massive forms with which they are painted. See vol. 3 p. **205**

Hartung, Hans born 1904
German-born painter who settled in France in 1935. Before studying at the Leipzig Academy in 1922 he had developed an abstract style fusing the intense colours of Nolde with the expressive improvisations of Kandinsky and Klee in a series of freely flowing watercolours. In the early 1930s he was influenced both by the formal geometric vocabulary of the Abstraction-Création group in Paris and by Miró's spontaneous Surrealist configurations. The result was his "*Taches d'encre*" (inkspots) series (1934–38) and subsequent paintings in which a subtle network of calligraphic brush-strokes charge the surface with emotional vibrancy. He gave all his works a "T" number (for *toile*—French for canvas), for example *T1949–49* (Düsseldorf, Kunstsammlung Nordrhein-Westfalen). He is usually associated with Informal art, indeed his work seems to pre-empt Abstract Expressionism. See vol. 3 p. **224**

Harunobu, Suzuki 1724–70
Japanese UKIYO-E artist. Harunobu became famous for being the first to market the polychromatic print, the *nishiki-e*. He was a pupil of Sukenobu in Kyoto, and moved to Edo (Tokyo) around 1759. He gained enormous popularity only about six years before his death, when he was able to publish the *nishiki-e*. He was also the first print designer to use women from ordinary walks of life as models, although he depicted everybody, male and female alike, with a delicate, childlike grace. His influence was so great in those six years that all other designers copied his style, often making it impossible to differentiate between them. See vol. 3 p. **50**

Hasior, Vladislav born 1928
Polish sculptor. His works are assemblages of broken or redundant materials constructed and painted like totem-poles or banners. They are much influenced by folklore, myth and ritual and sometimes incorporate fire and water. He also created monuments (*Monument to partisans*, 1964, Zakopane).

Hassam, Childe 1859–1935
American painter. He discovered French Impressionism on a visit to Europe in 1866 and became one of the leading American exponents of the style. As his *Boston Common at twilight* (1885–86, Boston, MFA) shows, he was profoundly influenced by the Impressionist depiction of light, use of eccentric viewpoints and rapidly executed brush-strokes. In 1905 he exhibited his work with the Sezession in Munich.

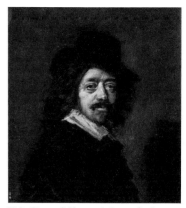
Hals, Frans: Self-portrait (copy after lost original, late 1640s). New York, Metropolitan, Michael Friedsam coll.

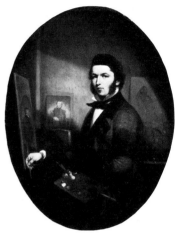
Hamel: Self-portrait, 1843. Musée de Québec

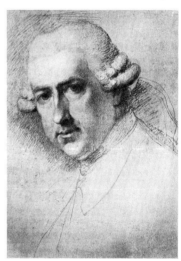
Hamilton, Gavin: Self-portrait drawing, 1767. Edinburgh, Scottish NPG

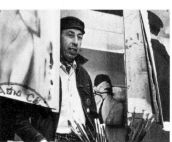
Hamilton, Richard: Photograph by J. S. Lewinski, Camera Press

Hatching
Technique of shading used in drawing, etching, engraving, and also with quick-drying paints such as tempera. A series of fine lines is laid close together or intersecting (**cross-hatching**).

Hausmann, Raoul 1886–1971
Austrian painter and writer. He worked as an illustrator and critic, 1907–12, and then associated with Richter and the future DADAISTS. He became known as the Dada philosopher or Dadasophe. In 1918 he met Schwitters and began to produce aggressive photomontages and a year later he founded the *Der Dada* review in Berlin. At this time he met Arp, Moholy-Nagy and Eggeling and organized the first Dada exhibition with Grosz. After 1923 he stopped painting and became interested in photography but during World War II, while living in France, he returned to gouaches and produced pictograms. See vol. 3 p. **167**

Haydon, Benjamin Robert 1786–1846
English ROMANTIC history and genre painter. His *Autobiography* (1847) and journals contain superb accounts of the contemporary scene. He continually promoted the cause of history painting, demanding that it should receive state patronage. He was a severe critic of the Royal Academy, and a brilliant teacher, whose lectures in the provinces on the social purpose of art anticipated those of Ruskin and Morris. His history paintings, often clumsy and out of scale, were too ambitious for his limited talents (*Curtius leaping the gulf*, 1842, Exeter, Royal Albert Memorial Museum), and his advocacy of fresco painting to decorate the Houses of Parliament resulted in bitter disillusionment when he failed to gain a premium in the 1843 competition. He committed suicide.

Hayez, Francesco 1791–1882
Italian painter of religious, historical and mythological works and portraits. He led the Lombard school from Neoclassicism to Romanticism and exerted great influence through teaching at the Brera in Milan (1822–79). From 1809 to 1817 he lived in Rome, where he was influenced by Canova and Ingres and where, with Minardi, he met the Nazarenes. On exhibiting *Pietro Rossi charged with command by the Venetians* (1820, Milan, Private coll.), he was hailed in Milan as the leader of Romanticism. His works, however, are more Romantic in subject than technique and retain a sharp academic outline. *Matilda Juva Branca* (1851, Milan, Galleria d'Arte Moderna) is an excellent example of his gift for portraiture.

Hayman, Francis 1708–76
British painter and book illustrator. As a young man Hayman was employed as a scene-painter at Drury Lane Theatre, and as a mural decorator. He later became well known as a painter of conversation pieces and small informal portraits, which influenced the early work of Gainsborough. His decorations for the pavilions at Vauxhall Gardens, the fashionable London pleasure park, were inspired by scenes from everyday life, and the popular sports and amusements of the time (*The milkmaid's garland*, c.1743, London, V&A). Hayman was a Foundation Member of the Royal Academy and its Librarian from 1771 until his death. See vol. 2 p. **245**

Hayter, Stanley William born 1901
British printmaker and painter. In 1927 he founded in Paris the Atelier 17, an etching studio which was to become a focal point for the 20th-century revival of print as an art form in its own right. His own work as an etcher has been influenced by the more abstract forms of Surrealism, and Automatism has been a stimulus to the improvisatory quality of his art, as can be seen in his etching *Myth of creation*, 1940. His books, *New Ways of Gravure* (1949) and *About Prints* (1962), are useful for the history as well as the technique of printing.

Heartfield, John
(Helmut Herzfelde) 1891–1968
German painter, typographer, photomonteur and journalist, a co-founder of the Berlin Dada group in 1919. He waged an ardent life-long battle against capitalism, war and Nazism by means of the bitingly satirical photomontages he designed as illustrations, book covers and as explicitly political posters. For example, *Hurrah, the butter is finished* (1935) shows a family in a room festooned with swastikas greedily consuming bicycle chains and handles, hatchets and spades—a literal interpretation of Goering's dictum that "iron makes a country strong" whereas "butter and lard only make people fat". With Grosz he founded the anti-war journal *Neue Jugend* (1916–17). From 1938 to 1950 he lived in London, thereafter in Leipzig. See vol. 3 p. **194**

Heckel, Erich 1883–1970
German EXPRESSIONIST painter and graphic artist, a founder-member of Die Brücke. Influenced by the bright colours and agitated linear style of van Gogh and Munch, he painted nudes and landscapes (*Reclining girl*, 1909, Munich, Staatsgemäldesammlungen) and produced starkly expressive woodcuts in which forms are greatly simplified in order to set up dramatic contrasts. After moving to Berlin (1911) his colour became more sombre and his drawing more angular, as can be seen in *Two men at a table* (1912, Hamburg, Kunsthalle). In 1913 he saw works by Delaunay and his subsequent style was influenced by the crystalline forms of Orphism. After World War I he remained in Berlin until 1944, when he settled at Lake Constance. See vol. 3 pp. **134–135**

Heda, Willem Claesz.
1599–1680/82
Dutch still-life painter, with Pieter Claesz. the foremost master of the Dutch *ontbijt* or breakfast-piece. Both were active in Haarlem. Heda tended towards greater detail and a higher degree of finish than Claesz., and favoured more refined and elegant subject matter—oysters rather than herrings, silver rather than pewter (*Still life*, 1648, Leningrad, Hermitage). Both artists developed from depictions of a few simple objects in a horizontal display to fuller, richer and more complex pieces, with strong vertical and diagonal accents, although their palettes remained subdued and almost monochromatic, greygreens and browns predominating. Heda's son **Gerrit** (died 1702) was his major pupil. See vol. 2 p. **233**

Heem, Jan Davidsz. de 1606–83/4
The best-known and most brilliant member of a large family of Dutch still-life painters. He was born in Utrecht, where he was taught by van der Ast, who inspired his early paintings of flowers, fruit and shells. In the late 1620s he worked in Leyden, painting *vanitas* subjects and also modest monochrome still lifes in the manner of Claesz. and Heda.

After 1636 most of his career was spent in Antwerp, where he formed a link between the traditions of Dutch and Flemish still-life painting, the latter being much more exuberant. His compositions became more elaborate and colourful, and his lavish flower-pieces and banquet arrangements earned him an enduring reputation as one of the greatest of still-life painters. The *Still life* of 1640 in the Louvre, Paris is more than 2 metres (6 ft) wide and shows de Heem at his most opulent. His work inspired many imitators, including his son **Cornelis** (1631–95). See vol. 2 pp. **232–233**

Heemskerck, Maerten van 1498–1574
One of the leading Netherlandish MANNERIST painters. He was born near Haarlem and studied there and in Utrecht with van Scorel, who fired his enthusiasm for Italian trends. In Heemskerck's *St Luke painting the Virgin* (1532, Haarlem, Frans Hals Museum), for example, St Luke is sitting on what appears to be an antique sarcophagus. From 1532 to 1535 he was in Rome, where he made numerous drawings of classical buildings and statuary, which are valuable records of contemporary knowledge of the Antique (West Berlin, Kupferstichkabinett and Rome, Palazzo Venezia). The influence of Giulio Romano and Salviati are evident in the crowded compositions he made back in Haarlem, while memories of Michelangelo clearly inspired the muscular and heroic *Christ crowned with thorns* (Hals Museum). His elegantly elongated, fashionably dressed and brilliantly coloured figures sometimes seem to lack real feeling, but the tragic *Lamentation* (Delft, Prinsenhof) shows the depth of emotion of which he was capable. Heemskerck was also an excellent portraitist in the manner of van Scorel. See vol. 2 p. **161**

Heerup, Henry born 1907
Danish sculptor, painter and engraver. His interest in Romanesque and primitive art is revealed both in his paintings and in his painted monolithic granite sculptures of humans, animals and plants. *Boys bathing* (1907, Skive Art Gallery) is typically crudely painted with emphasis on the pattern of outlines.

Hegedušić, Krsto 1901–75
Yugoslav painter. One of the founders, in 1929, of the Zagreb group, The Earth, advocating art with a social message, he also co-founded the now world-famous school of peasant-painters in the North Croatian village of Hlebine. From 1936 he taught in Zagreb. He went through various phases, always in search of a bold transposition of reality, and was influenced by Expressionism, Surrealism and Naive art. One of his best-known paintings is *Dead waters* (1956, Belgrade, Museum of Contemporary Art).

Hegenbarth, Josef 1884–1962
Austrian painter and illustrator. He studied in Dresden and then travelled to Prague, where he joined the Sezession and was influenced by Art Nouveau illustrations. He returned to Dresden in 1921 and began to work for the magazines *Jugend* and *Simplizissimus* as a cartoonist. During the 1930s he spent most of his time painting and developed a style of caricatural expressionism incorporating images from his graphic work, such as fairy-tale scenes and episodes from the circus and theatre.

Heidelberg school
Group of late 19th-century Australian painters, who met (1888–1900) at Eaglemont, in Heidelberg, Victoria. Their work was based on *plein-air* and Impressionist painting. In August 1889 they launched the most famous local exhibition in Australia's history, the 9 × 5 Impression Exhibition in Melbourne. Although the group had virtually disbanded in 1900, its vision of the Australian landscape was the dominant influence in Australian art of the 1920s and inspired many landscape and social realist painters in later decades.

Heiliger, Bernhard born 1915
West German sculptor. His early figurative work was influenced by Maillol, whom he met on a visit to Paris in 1939. In 1949 he began teaching at the Berlin Academy of Art, and gradually developed a more animated semi-abstract style, sometimes with a rhetorical quality well suited to his numerous public commissions (*The flame*, West Berlin, Ernst Reuter Platz).

Heine, Thomas Theodor 1867–1948
German graphic artist and painter from Leipzig. From 1889 he drew for the magazines published in Munich (including *Simplizissimus* and *Jugend*) which promoted ART NOUVEAU ideas in Germany. He developed a powerful, Beardsley-like linear style concentrating on social abuses. In 1933 he had to leave Germany; he settled in Sweden in 1942.

Heizer, Michael born 1944
American sculptor. Heizer, son of a geologist, is one of the several LAND artists to work in the vast spaces of the American south-western desert. He is interested in manipulating materials on a monumental scale and in the impact of natural forces on his works. In *Nevada depressions* (1968) he created negative space by the direct removal of earth. Unlike most other Land artists, he also constructs pieces small enough to be exhibited indoors—generally solid but dynamic compositions of faceted forms. The architectural aspect of such shapes is apparent when executed on the huge scale of *The city, complex one* (1972, Central East Nevada), made of concrete, steel and earth. See vol. 3 pp. **248–249**

Held, Al born 1928
American painter. His heavily pigmented canvases of the 1950s were influenced by Abstract Expressionism, but in the 1960s he moved towards cleaner edges and flatter, geometrical planes. Scale and shape were his prime concern in the 1960s; *Greek garden* (1964–66, New York, André Emmerich Gallery) is a gigantic tripartite work made up of triangular, rectangular and circular elements. In 1967 he began his black and white paintings—canvases crowded with linear projections of overlapping and interlocking forms seeming to bulge and recede. See vol. 3 p. **223**

Heldt, Werner 1904–54
German painter. His early anecdotal scenes of sleepy Berlin suburbs (*Pink wall*, 1930, Hamburg, Kunsthalle) gave way to townscapes dominated by endless, anonymous façades. He often adopted a high viewpoint. After 1946 his style became more abstract, in the manner of Gris' "architectonic" works.

Hélion, Jean born 1904
French painter. He studied architecture and engineering before turning to art in 1922. From 1926 onwards he was in close contact with Mondrian and was strongly influenced by his work. In the 1930s, when associated with the

ABSTRACTION-CRÉATION group, he produced imposing and highly distinctive abstract paintings such as *Ile de France* (1935, London, Tate), in which metallic, powerfully modelled forms, recalling Léger's work, are floated against a ground of geometric shapes. From 1936 to 1940 and from 1942 to 1946 he lived in the USA and played an important role in transmitting ideas from Europe.

Helst, Bartholomeus van der
1613–70
Dutch portrait painter. Born in Haarlem, he moved to Amsterdam in 1636, when Rembrandt was at the height of his popularity. As Rembrandt's style grew deeper and more personal, patrons demanding a more elegant but less intense form of portrait turned to van der Helst, who became the most popular portraitist in the city. His groups and individual portraits, with their virtuoso display of finery, show Flemish influence, especially that of van Dyck. The portrait of *Abraham del Court and his wife* (1654, Rotterdam, Boymans-van Beuningen Museum) is characteristic of the gentle sentiment and rich detail of his portraiture. See vol. 2 p. **227**

Hemessen, Jan Sanders van
*c.*1504–*c.*1575
Netherlandish painter, active in Antwerp and probably Haarlem, where he is said to have died. He painted religious scenes and portraits, and was also a pioneer of genre. His satirical portraits and scenes illustrating proverbs and religious parables link him with Marinus and Massys. *The prodigal son* (1536, Brussels, Musées Royaux des Beaux-Arts), a rather uneasy mixture of Italian motifs and Flemish moralizing (sturdy courtesans with heroic gestures are set in a palatial, classical structure), is typical.

Henri, Robert 1865–1929
American painter. He visited Paris, 1888–91, and was influenced by the European realist tradition—by Manet in particular. On his return to Philadelphia he became convinced that artists should not only be socially aware but should paint what they saw. He worked closely with the former newspaper illustrators Luks, Shinn, Sloan and Glackens, and together they formed the nucleus of The Eight, later known as the ASHCAN school because of their urban genre paintings. Henri's *West 57th Street, New York* (1902, Yale, University Art Gallery), a representative work, shows the poor picking their way through the slush and snow of New York. His portraits, having something of the style and dash of Sargent, are probably his finest paintings but he is best known as a teacher and crusader. He organized the 1910 Exhibition of Independent Artists as an alternative to the artistically sterile Academy. See vol. 3 p. **204**

Hepworth, Barbara 1903–75
British sculptor. She studied at the Royal College of Art, London, where she was a contemporary of Henry Moore, and shared his interest in carving, as opposed to the modelling technique preferred by most older sculptors. Her early works in wood and marble are remarkable for their sensitivity to the natural qualities of the material, so that *Figure in sycamore* (1931, Orkney, Pier Gallery) is far more fluid in form than comparable pieces in stone and hardwood. From the early 1930s she was attempting an abstract synthesis between natural and geometric forms. By 1935 her work was completely abstract. Her late sculpture employed a more extended range of materials. Woodcarvings such as *Pelagos* (1946, London, Tate) contrast painted surfaces with the natural wood-grain and curved hollowed-out volumes with the tautness of strings. After World War II she began working in bronze, although she retained a special regard for what she called the "natural and affirmative art" of direct carving. She became one of the most celebrated of contemporary sculptors and had many important public commissions, including the Dag Hammerskjold Memorial *Single form* (1963, New York, United Nations). After her death her studio and garden at Barnoon Hill, St Ives, were dedicated as a museum to her work. See vol. 1 pp. *174, 199*; vol. 3 pp. **198–199**

Herbin, Auguste 1882–1960
French painter. Living near Picasso in 1909, he began to experiment with Cubism and was subsequently influenced by Delaunay's Orphism. He started to work in a planar, fully abstract manner around 1917–18. As a founder-member of the ABSTRACTION-CRÉATION group in the 1930s he went through a more organic, curvilinear phase. *Air, fire* (1944, Paris, Musée d'Art Moderne) typifies his work after 1939, in which rigidly hieratic compositions are built up out of bright geometric shapes.

Hering, Loy *c.*1484/5–1555
German sculptor. He was trained in Augsburg as a stone sculptor, and headed a workshop in nearby Eichstätt from 1513. Most of his work consisted of epitaph reliefs carved in a gently rounded style, but he seems also to have produced small limestone reliefs with nude figures. Many of his compositions were based on the prints of Dürer and other Germans, but he drew his primary inspiration from northern Italy, which he may have visited early in his career. He was among the first German sculptors to master the Italian style and his work was influential in spreading it.

Herkomer, Sir Hubert von
1849–1914
Bavarian-born English painter. He painted social realist scenes, such as *Hard times* (1885, Manchester City Art Gallery), when such subjects were rare in English art. He also specialized in group portraits in Dutch 17th-century style.

Herm (or Term)
Sculpture consisting of head or bust of armless nude male surmounting a rectangular column tapering downward. Though the column is usually plain the Greek herm (named after Hermes) exhibited a phallus.

Herman, Josef born 1911
British painter. He was born in Poland and came to Britain in 1940. He paints sombre, monumental pictures of workers, particularly peasants and miners (*Three miners*, 1953, London, Tate).

Herman, Sali born 1898
Australian painter. He was born in Switzerland and studied widely in Europe before going to Australia in 1936. He is best known for his depictions of street scenes and old houses in Sydney, which he treats with a muted range of colour and carefully worked tactile surfaces, as in *McElhone stairs* (1944, Australia, Private coll.), criticized at the time for portraying one of Sydney's slummiest aspects.

Heron, Patrick born 1920
British painter. Works painted in Cornwall from the late 1940s reflect the influence of contemporary French painters, especially Braque, in the way that the subject emerges from intertwining lines, although the formal structure is looser and the colour bolder. In the late 1950s his work became entirely abstract. Particularly notable are the vigorously gestural stripe paintings of 1957 such as *Scarlet, lemon and ultramarine* (London, Tate). The title of this and later paintings emphasizes his concern with the interaction of colour as the primary preoccupation of painting.

Herrera, Francisco the Elder
*c.*1590–1656?
Spanish painter and engraver. He was one of the leading artists in Seville in the early 17th century, and an important figure in the transition from Mannerism to Baroque. His masterpiece, *St Basil dictating his rule* (1639, Paris, Louvre), shows the bold composition and vigorous brushwork of his mature work. Velazquez is said to have been his pupil for a brief period, and to have left him because of his unbearably bad temper. From about 1638 he worked in Madrid.

Herrera, Francisco the Younger
1622–85
Spanish painter and architect, son of Francisco the Elder. He fled from his father's temper and studied in Rome, returning after his father's death. He, too, worked in Seville, where in 1660 he was appointed Murillo's deputy in the newly-founded Academy of painting, and in Madrid, where he became court painter in 1672. His airy paintings, full of movement and bright colours, owe much to Murillo (*The triumph of St Hermengild, c.*1665, Madrid, Prado). As an architect his most important work is the huge church of El Pilar at Saragossa.

Hertevig, Lars 1830–1902
Norwegian painter, a pupil of Gude in Düsseldorf. After 1854 he became mentally deranged and was forgotten, but he was still productive, especially as a romantic landscape painter of western Norway. *Herring fishing in spring* (*c.*1865, Oslo, NG) illustrates his style; painting in rich and subtle colours midway between reality and fantasy, he creates a strange visionary world.

Hesse, Eva 1936–70
American sculptor, born in Germany. Hesse's short career as a sculptress of what have been called "Eccentric Abstractions" lasted from 1964 to 1970. Her work unites apparently contradictory impulses: it features both irregular organic forms evocative of sexual imagery and also characteristics more commonly associated with Minimal sculpture —repetition and severely limited colour. Her use of materials, which include rubber tubing, synthetic resins, wood, papier-maché, wire, cloth and cord, is inventive and suggestive (*Repetition 19 (III)*, 1968, New York, MOMA).

Hesselius, Gustavus 1682–1755
Swedish-born American painter. He went to America in 1712 after studying in England, and was active chiefly as a portraitist in and around Philadelphia, recording his sitters in a sober and direct way. His best-known works, the pair of portraits of the Delaware chieftains *Lapowinsa* and *Tishcohan* (1735) in the Historical Society of Pennsylvania in Philadelphia, are the first serious representations of American Indians as individual personalities. In the same collection are portraits of himself and his wife (1740). Hesselius also executed religious and mythological scenes, which again

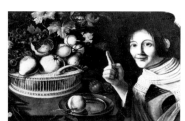
Heem, Jan Davidsz. de: Self-portrait? (detail), *c.*1630. Private coll.

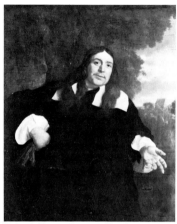
Helst: Self-portrait, 1662. Hamburg, Kunsthalle

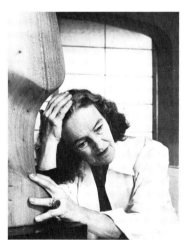
Hepworth: Photograph by J. S. Lewinski, Camera Press

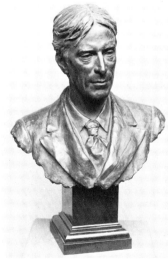
Herkomer: Bronze cast of bust by E. O. Ford (1852–1901). London, NPG

were pioneering works in colonial America (*Bacchus and Ariadne*, c.1720, Detroit Institute of Arts). His son **John** (1728–78) was also a portrait painter, working over a wide area before he settled in 1763 in Annapolis, Maryland, where he was the first teacher of Charles Willson Peale. John studied under his father, but his style, influenced by Feke and Wollaston, was more Rococo (*Charles Calvert and his slave*, 1761, Baltimore Museum of Art).

Hessing, Leonard born 1931
Australian painter. He was born in Austria, studied in Paris under Léger in 1950, and then travelled extensively before settling in Sydney. His Abstract Expressionist paintings manipulate line and a complex range of colour with controlled vitality. *Fata Morgana* (1959, Artist's coll.) was the first of many experiments in enamels.

Heyden, Jan van der 1637–1712
With Saenredam, the most distinguished Dutch painter of town views. He apparently travelled in Flanders and Germany, but was active mainly in Amsterdam, where he was also involved in civic administration. The fire hose, on which he published an illustrated book in 1690, is said to have been his invention. His paintings are marked by an astonishing attention to detail, every brick being rendered with precise neatness. In spite of this, his work is never dry, nor does the detail detract from the harmony of his compositions or their sense of atmosphere (*The Dam in Amsterdam*, Amsterdam, Rijksmuseum). He also painted purely imaginary views, mainly architectural fantasies (examples in the National Galleries of London and Washington), and his sense of the picturesque foreshadowed Italian architectural painting of the 18th century.

Heysen, Sir Hans 1877–1968
Australian painter. He was born in Hamburg, but settled in Adelaide as a child. He studied in Paris and from the time of his first exhibition (Melbourne, 1908) gained steadily in popularity. Mainly a watercolourist, he is best known for landscapes, meticulously recording the gum trees of the Australian outback, for example, *Red gold* (1913, Adelaide, NG of South Australia).

Hicks, Edward 1780–1849
American primitive painter, trained as a coach and sign painter. He made some 100 variants (none of which was sold) on the subject of *The peaceable kingdom*, reflecting the pacifism of the Quaker society in which he was a preacher. They show animals living peaceably with children in a vision of brotherly love—a symbolic presentation of the prophecy in the 11th chapter of Isaiah.

Higgins, Eugene 1874–1958
American painter and draughtsman. He is often associated with the Ashcan school, but his sentimental depictions of the poor owe more to the French Realist tradition, which he encountered while studying in Paris, than to his American contemporaries. The influence of Millet and Daumier is particularly evident in his most powerful painting, *The gamblers* (c.1917, New York, Metropolitan).

Highmore, Joseph 1692–1780
British painter. Highmore enrolled at Kneller's Academy in 1713 and became a successful portrait painter. In the 1730s he began to respond to the newly-fashionable Rococo style, and visited Paris in 1734. His series of 12 paintings

illustrating Samuel Richardson's novel *Pamela* (c.1744–45, London, Tate; Cambridge, Fitzwilliam; Melbourne, NG of Victoria) reveal the influence of Gravelot in their lightness and elegance.

Hildebrand, Adolf von 1847–1921
German sculptor and aesthetician of the classical tradition. He was closely associated with von Marées, whom he met in Florence in 1867 and whom he helped with the frescos at the Zoological Institute in Naples in 1873. His sculpture tends to appear bland and monumental (The Wittelsbach fountain, 1844, Munich, Maximilian Platz), belying the theory behind it. In 1893 he published his famous and influential treatise, *The Problem of Form*, advocating direct carving and understanding of materials.

Hill, Anthony born 1930
British artist. After a brief period of Informal abstraction in the early 1950s he began work in 1954 on relief constructions in which he used industrial materials such as standardized aluminium parts and rigid vinyl laminate, without added colour (*Relief construction*, 1960, London, Tate). He has also worked as a mathematician and his *Co-structures* of 1970 onwards, his first fully free-standing three-dimensional works, reflect his interest in graph theory.

Hill, Carl Fredrik 1849–1911
Swedish landscape painter and draughtsman. He studied first in Stockholm and later in Paris, where he was interested initially in the Barbizon painters and then in Impressionism. In 1876 the Impressionists asked him to participate in their exhibitions, but he refused. His failure to win acceptance at the Paris Salon depressed him, and he became incurably insane at 28, although he remained prolific until his death. A fantastically imaginative strain is apparent in his paintings and his many drawings.

Hilliard, Nicholas 1547–1619
English miniaturist, the greatest English painter of the 16th century. A goldsmith by training, he became limner and goldsmith to Elizabeth I about 1569, and later worked for James I. In his treatise *The Arte of Limning* (written in about 1600) he states that he based his style, which is linear and shadowless, on the miniatures of Holbein. He fastidiously records the details of elaborate costumes and jewels, and the miniatures often bear inscriptions in his exquisite calligraphy. Their elaborate jewelled cases are presumably often his own work. He considered miniature painting the occupation of a gentleman, and it is clear that he moved with ease at court. He is known to have worked occasionally on a large scale, and portraits of Elizabeth in the National Portrait Gallery, London, and the Walker Art Gallery, Liverpool, are attributed to him. There is a fine collection of his miniatures in the Victoria & Albert Museum, London. His son **Lawrence** (1582–after 1640) was also a miniaturist, and Isaac Oliver was his pupil. See vol. 1 p. *122*; vol. 2 p. **206**

Hillier, Tristram born 1905
British painter. In 1933 he became a member of UNIT ONE. At this time he painted hallucinatory landscapes such as "*Ecole Communale*" (1932, Kettering, Art Gallery), with irrational accumulations of objects reminiscent of illusionistic Surrealism. Later paintings in tempera such as "*Las Lavanderas*" (1965, Rochdale, Art Gallery), a beach scene with women washing clothes, have a vivid Mediterranean clarity.

Hilton, Roger 1911–75
British painter. He studied in Paris (1931–39) under Bissière and gained a strong feeling for the sensual qualities of paint. His most uncompromising abstract work dates from the early 1950s. Paintings such as *June 1953 (Deep cadmium)* (1953, Edinburgh, Scottish NG of Modern Art) are composed of interlocking coloured shapes. Later there are suggestions of landscape and the nude, and sometimes much of the canvas is left bare to emphasize the shiny tackiness of the paint. At the end of his life he worked entirely in gouache, with a gaily coloured exuberance belying his declining health.

Hiltunen, Eila born 1922
Finnish sculptor. In the late 1950s she began to use welded metal and steel in strips and plates. Her subjects include dancers and impersonal, generalized human shapes. Her major work is the Sibelius Monument (1967, Helsinki, Sibelius Park), consisting of hundreds of tubular elements made of stainless steel welded together to form a towering W-shaped structure.

Hind, William George Richardson 1833–89
Canadian painter, born in England. He acted as official artist on an exploration trip to Labrador and later joined a group travelling to the gold fields of western Canada, 1862–65, sketching the scenery of human activity of the regions. On returning to eastern Canada he completed a sketchbook of coastal life in 1876. A small but striking *Self-portrait* (c.1865, Montreal, McGill University, McCord Museum) reveals his uncompromisingly realistic approach.

Hiroshige, Ando 1797–1858
Japanese UKIYO-E artist, the son of an Edo (Tokyo) fireman. At 17 he became a pupil of Toyohiro, although he was officially a government employee. In the 1830s he went on business from Edo to Kyoto, and his first masterpiece, *The 53 stations of the Tokaido Highway*, was based on the sketches made on this voyage. Published in 1833, it was an instant success. The print-buying people of the cities were curious about the rest of the country, and they loved Hiroshige's affectionate observation of the people he met on his travels. His publishers made him repeat the travel theme over and over again, sometimes teaming him with other popular artists. His last great series, 118 prints of *A hundred famous views of Edo*, was one of the first to arrive in Europe, quite by chance. Van Gogh, among many others, was fascinated by it, and made copies of two prints. See vol. 3 p. **51**

Hirschfeld-Mack, Ludwig 1893–1965
German abstract painter. While a student at the Bauhaus (1920–25) he carried out experiments with light as an art medium, using various devices to produce moving patterns of coloured light. He aimed to create a synthesis of movement, light, colour and form. These ideas were further developed by Moholy-Nagy, though they were not to find widespread appeal until the Kinetic art movement of the 1950s.

History painting
Paintings depicting scenes from history, real or imaginary. As well as representations of historical events, the term includes ancient myths, religious legends, and scenes from great literature, such as Dante and Shakespeare. History painting was taught in the

academies from Renaissance times, and, in the hierarchy of acceptable subjects, was considered the noblest, demanding the GRAND MANNER. Modern history with figures in contemporary dress made its appearance in the 18th century, in the work of West and Copley.

Hitchens, Ivon 1893–1979
British painter. He came close to abstraction during the 1930s by way of Cubist-influenced works such as *Autumn composition, flowers on a table* (1932, London, Tate). By 1939 he had evolved a distinctive manner of landscape painting, as seen in *Damp autumn* (1941, Tate). The scene is evoked in broad brush-strokes on a wide canvas forming a semi-abstract panorama. He painted in this way for the rest of his life, although, as he grew older, his palette changed from naturalistic greens and browns to bright purples, yellows and reds.

Hittite art
Art of the Hittite state of central Anatolia, flourishing in the second half of the 2nd millennium BC. The art of this Indo-European people is remarkable only for stone reliefs depicting religious beliefs. They are not of great quality, but are notably original in showing scenes of ritual procession on the outer walls of buildings, for example the palace at Alaça Huyuk (probably 14th century BC). The "art gallery" cut into the natural rock in the sacred complex of Yazilikaya, near the capital Hattusas (modern Boghazkoy), is a major shrine showing the deities of the Hittites in two formal processions, males to the left, females to the right, converging on a central panel which depicts the meeting of the great gods Hatti, Teshub, Hepa and Sharruma. Hittite sculptors were also employed on the carving of gate figures to guard cities; good examples are the Sphinx Gate at Alaça Huyuk and the Royal or Herald's Gate at Hattusas itself. This latter may show the influence of a Babylonian sculptor known to have been employed by the Hittite king. Carvings of gods and kings are to be found on natural rock surfaces wherever the Hittite Empire spread.

Hjørth, Bror 1894–1968
Swedish sculptor, painter and draughtsman. He was a pupil of Bourdelle in Paris, and studied Cubism and Naive and Primitive art, although his works are mainly rooted in Swedish folk art. Earthy sensualism and a sense of creative joy characterize his often highly expressive sculptures, polychrome wooden reliefs and paintings. Country dances, weddings and village fiddlers are frequent subjects. He had his own school for sculptors in Stockholm, 1931–34, and was Professor at the Academy in Stockholm, 1949–59. His studio at Uppsala is now a museum.

Hobbema, Meindert 1638–1709
Dutch landscape painter active in Amsterdam, the leading pupil of Jacob van Ruisdael. For some years he imitated his master closely and even based his compositions on Ruisdael's. By the early 1660s, however, he had gained greater independence, and moved from Ruisdael's dramatic representations of nature to the much-loved works with which his name is always associated—sunlit summery woodland scenes and views of water-mills, themes which he repeated again and again. In 1668 he took a post as a wine gauger with the Amsterdam customs and excise, and painting seems to have become a part-time occupation. His most celebrated work, however, the

justly famous *Avenue at Middelharnis* (London, NG) is dated 1689. Hobbema was very popular in England in the 18th and 19th centuries and is very well represented in English collections. His influence is particularly apparent in the work of Gainsborough. See vol. 2 p. **223**

Höch, Hannah 1889–1978
German painter, a member of the Berlin DADA group and a close associate of the Dadaists Hausmann and Schwitters. She made her first abstract collages and photomontages in 1917, the same year in which she started to make Dada dolls and puppets with crudely distorted proportions. Her photomontages, such as *Cut with the kitchen knife through the first Weimar beer-belly epoch* (1919, East Berlin, Nationalgalerie), combine Dada formal anarchy with trenchant social criticism. She also painted Surrealistic pictures. Banned by the Nazis, she spent the post-war years in seclusion experimenting with printing techniques.

Hockney, David born 1937
British painter and printmaker, one of the most colourful figures in British art since the 1960s. His early work was superficially related to Pop art in its use of lettering and references to popular culture. His sources were graffiti, the style of which he emulated in scratchy oil-paint on raw canvas. *We two boys forever clinging* (1961, Arts Council of Great Britain) is characteristic both of this manner and of the frank homosexual content found in much of his work. After visiting California in the mid-1960s his painting acquired a flatter, more hard-edged quality, coinciding with a technical change from oils to acrylic. The swimming-pool has been a consistent theme, not only because, as in *Peter getting out of Nick's pool* (1966, Liverpool, Walker Art Gallery), it provides an appropriate context for the nude figure, but also for its technical problems of depicting the surface of the water in sunlight. The most striking of his later works are his portraits in spacious interiors. *Mr and Mrs Clark and Percy* (1970–71, London, Tate) captures the style and affluence of the London of the 1960s in a manner which now touches a note of nostalgia. See vol. 3 p. **241**

Hodges, William 1744–97
British landscape painter, draughtsman and engraver. He was Richard Wilson's pupil, assistant and imitator. Much of his career was spent in recording the landscapes of distant countries, first as draughtsman to Captain Cook, 1772–75, then in India, 1778–84, and finally Russia in 1790. His most original works are undoubtedly those based on his voyage to the South Pacific with Cook, which, although rooted in the language of classical landscape painting, are remarkable for their subject matter (*The monuments of Easter Island*, c.1774, London, National Maritime Museum).

Hodgkin, Howard born 1932
British painter. His paintings are semi-abstract, broadly painted and in intense colours. Their subject matter includes landscape and interiors, usually with friends whose appearance and character are defined by simple shapes encompassed by bold sweeps of the brush. His admiration for Indian miniatures is reflected in his flat colour and frequent inclusion of a decorative border.

Hodgkins, Frances 1869–1947
New Zealand's most significant expatriate painter. She settled in England in 1913. Her first oils date from this period,

the most striking, *The Edwardians* (1918, Auckland City Art Gallery), recalling the CAMDEN TOWN school. From the 1920s she developed a broader, more adventurous style echoing Matisse and Dufy. Her reputation, especially as a watercolourist, was consolidated when she joined the progressive Seven and Five Society. *Flatford Mill* and *Wings over water* (1930–32, London, Tate) were among the most original figurative works to be exhibited with the group. Later, like Hitchens, she arrived at a near-abstraction based on fluid colour.

Hodler, Ferdinand 1853–1918
Swiss painter, rivalled only by Böcklin as his country's major artist in the 19th century. The success of his early realistic genre paintings, deeply influenced by Courbet and his teacher Barthélemy Menn, enabled him to travel to France and Spain, after which he began evolving a powerfully individual style. His monumental allegories, such as *Night* (1890, Berne, Kunstmuseum), can be seen as Symbolist in their non-realistic treatment of nature and use of colour to evoke specific emotions—in his great cycles depicting the times of day and seasons he emphasizes the state of mind implied by the subjects (*Day*, c.1900, Zurich, Kunsthaus). His precise and sinuous linear rhythms are clearly related to Jugendstil. Hodler was immensely popular in the Germanic world and was honoured with exhibitions in Germany and Austria. In the last decade of his life he transferred his preoccupation with unity and uniformity in pictorial space to an increasing interest in landscape painting. His glowing, stark and unpeopled Alpine and lake scenes concentrate on powerful and luminous colour to evoke a vision of cosmic order. See vol. 1 p. **45**

Hoefnagel, Joris 1542–1600
Flemish miniaturist, watercolourist and engraver, born in Antwerp. He was a pupil of Hans Bol and inherited his taste for sensitive and detailed landscapes. He travelled widely, to France, Germany and England in the 1560s and later to Prague, Munich and Vienna. These visits were recorded in the *Civitates Orbis Terrarum* (*Cities of the world*, 1572), an influential collection of city views which paved the way for the development of topographical art in the following century. He also produced numerous watercolour studies of butterflies and insects, which "Velvet" Brueghel copied.

Hoerle, Heinrich 1895–1936
German painter. He was a member of the Cologne DADA movement, contributing to the Dada magazine *Ventilator* published by the poet and painter Baargeld and by Ernst. He was a founder of the Cologne Progressive Artists' Association (1924), whose journal *a–z* he helped to produce. Influenced by Metaphysical painting (*Factory scene*, c.1926, Düsseldorf, Kunstmuseum) and then towards geometric simplifications drawn from Léger, he depicted the soulless anonymity of industrialized man.

Hofer, Carl 1878–1955
German Expressionist painter. He lived in Rome, 1903–08, working in the idealized symbolist style of Böcklin and von Marées, but his mature style was most deeply affected by his visits to India, 1909 to 1911, and time spent in Paris, between 1908 and 1913, where he absorbed the solid structure of Cézanne's compositions. Thereafter his figures lost their classical appearance and became stiffly angular, sometimes seeming frozen in disillusioned remoteness

and melancholy (*Circus performers*, 1921, Essen, Folkwang Museum). He remained in Berlin from 1913, and gradually moved towards semi-abstraction. See vol. 3 pp. **194–195**

Hofmann, Hans 1880–1966
German-born American painter and teacher. Before World War I he lived in Paris and was close to the Fauves, Cubists and particularly Delaunay. He emigrated to the USA in 1932 and founded schools in New York and Provincetown, Mass., where he taught a number of students who were to become prominent painters in the 1950s, most notably Helen Frankenthaler. Hofmann's own style began to develop in the 1930s in a series of landscapes and still-life interiors which amalgamated the influence of Matisse with that of Cubism. His 1940s canvases often included areas of dribbled and poured paint and were crucial in the development of Abstract Expressionism; *Effervescence* (1944, Berkeley, University of California) is a notable example. In later paintings of the 1960s he sited sharp-edged rectangles against a more open field. See vol. 3 p. **211**

Hogarth, William 1697–1764
One of the most original and influential of British artists. He was the son of a London schoolmaster who, during the artist's boyhood, was imprisoned for debt: this experience of the seamy side of life marked Hogarth permanently, while it gave him material for his art. He was trained in engraving, which he continued to practise throughout his life. Among his first paintings, dating from the late 1720s, were small portrait groups or CONVERSATION PIECES. He then turned to a new genre of moral narrative. These paintings, for which he became famous, were picture-stories in six or eight scenes, exposing the follies and vices of the age in realistic, albeit theatrical, terms. Titles include *The Rake's Progress* (1733–35, London, Soane Museum), and *Marriage à la Mode* (1743–45, London, NG). Both reached a wide public through engravings, most of which were executed by Hogarth himself. He made some half-hearted attempts at historical painting, but his other main activity was portraiture. Although he did not set much store by this work, he was in fact the finest and liveliest British portraitist of the period, being especially successful with sitters from his own educated middle-class background (*Captain Coram*, 1740, London, Foundling Hospital). He ran the first effective drawing academy in Britain, in St Martin's Lane, 1735–55, and made an important contribution to aesthetics with *The Analysis of Beauty* (1753). He was the first British artist to be widely admired abroad. See vol. 1 pp. *39, 54*; vol. 2 pp. **248–249**

Hoitsu, Sakai 1761–1828
Japanese painter and printmaker, the younger brother of a feudal lord. He was extremely versatile in all the arts and excelled in poetry (*haiku* and *kyoka*) and acting as well as calligraphy and painting. He entered Kano Eitoku's studio, joined the Tosa school and worked with Okyo to perfect his sketching. Finally, he adopted the Korin style as his own. So devoted did Hoitsu become to this long-dead master that he published a set of prints as a memorial to him, called *Korin hyakuza* (A hundred pictures according to Korin). One of his large, six-sided screens in colour on gilded paper, *Autumnal grasses* (Asahi Kogaku Shoji Company coll.), has been designated an Important Cultural Property of Japan.

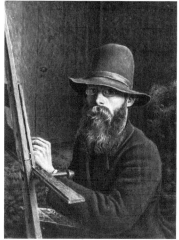
Hind: Self-portrait, c.1865. Montreal, McCord Museum, McGill University

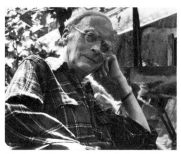
Hitchens: Photograph by J. S. Lewinski, Camera Press

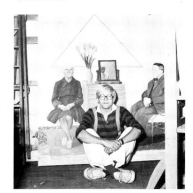
Hockney: Photograph by Robert Workman

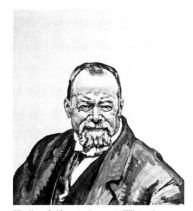
Hodler: Self-portrait, 1916. Winterthur, Kunstmuseum

Hokusai, Katsushika 1760–1849
Japanese painter and printmaker, the most exciting and original of the 19th-century Japanese UKIYO-E artists. He turned his hand to every possible subject, apprenticing himself to as many printmakers and orthodox artists as he could, and produced masterpieces in every genre—landscapes, legends, Kabuki theatre scenes, plants and animals, erotica. His book illustrations are also exceptional and his 13-volume book simply called *Manga* (sketches or drawings) is an extraordinarily rich compendium of figure studies, cartoons, descriptions of objects and fabulous beasts. Manet owned a copy of at least one *Manga* volume, as did Degas, who derived some of his subjects from it. Hokusai sometimes experimented with European methods of perspective but his best-known works are landscapes in the Japanese manner, and the finest of these are in the series *Thirty-six views of Mount Fuji*, which show the mountain from unusual viewpoints or in unusual weather conditions. Figures appear in the foreground of most of these prints, sawing wood, riding by or performing other mundane tasks. The richness of his imagination, the sureness of his technique and the quality of his wit and humour made Hokusai not merely one of the greatest Japanese artists, but one of the greatest artists of the world. In his personal life he was, as one of his pen-names, Gakyojin (old man mad about drawing), suggests, totally dedicated to his art. He quarrelled with most of his business associates in his relentless pursuit of perfection and died when almost 90, begging the heavens to grant him five more years to reach his goal. See vol. 1 pp. *32*, **58–59**, *122*; vol. 3 pp. **50–51**

Holanda, Francisco de
1517/18–84
Portuguese miniaturist, draughtsman and writer on art, son of **Antonio** (active c.1495–c.1540), a miniaturist from Holland. As court artist in Lisbon he was sent to Rome to study fortifications, 1538–39, when he met Michelangelo and studied antique remains (sketchbook in the Escorial library). His *De Pintura* (On painting) was intended as propaganda for the new art of Rome and to encourage the patronage of painting and architecture in his own country—on the decline after the great reign of Manoel I. He is probably best known for the dialogues, in *De Pintura*, purporting to be his discussions with Michelangelo.

Holbein, Hans the Elder
c.1465–1524
German painter, a native of Augsburg and father of the painters Hans the Younger and **Ambrosius** (1494–c.1519). He was principally a painter of altarpieces and his work for the Dominican convent of St Catherine at Augsburg in 1499 and about 1504 (Augsburg, Museum) shows his careful compositions and use of rich colour. Later works, such as the altarpiece of *St Sebastian* (1516, Munich, Alte Pinakothek), show the influence of Italian art. He was also a sensitive portraitist and draughtsman, and a designer of stained glass. Ambrosius Holbein painted portraits and designed book illustrations.

Holbein, Hans the Younger
1497/8–1543
German painter and designer of woodcuts, the greatest portraitist of the northern Renaissance. He was born in Augsburg, the son of Hans Holbein the Elder, and by 1515 was active in Basel. His learned patrons included the great humanist Erasmus, whom he portrayed several times, most impressively in the painting (1523) in the Louvre, Paris. In his portraits Holbein combined intense and minute scrutiny of physiognomy, costume and accessories with an unerring line. His religious paintings are usually much less memorable, but *The dead Christ* (1521, Basel, Kunstmuseum) is remarkable for its harrowing realism. The satirical *Dance of Death* woodcuts (designed c.1525) were widely popular and influential. In 1526 he left for England, where he painted Sir Thomas More and his family in the earliest domestic group portrait. This is now lost, but is known through copies (one is in London, NPG) and a preparatory drawing in the Kunstmuseum, Basel. He also painted a superb portrait of More as Lord Chancellor (1527, New York, Frick). In 1528 he returned to Basel, but settled in England permanently in 1532. As court painter to Henry VIII his masterpiece was the life-size dynastic portrait (1537) in Whitehall Palace, before which contempories felt "abashed and annihilated". This also is destroyed, but part of the cartoon survives (London, NPG) and shows a formidable full-length, directly frontal portrayal of the King. A bust-length portrait of the King from Holbein's own hand is in the Thyssen collection at Lugano. Holbein portrayed many other members of the court in paintings and in a series of delicate yet unrelenting drawings (mainly at Windsor Castle). He was one of the greatest of miniaturists—an inspiration for Hilliard—and also produced numerous designs for objects ranging from fireplaces to jewellery. Holbein's influence on English painting was enormous. See vol. 1 p. *166*; vol. 2 pp. **156–157**

Holgate, Edwin born 1892
Canadian figure and landscape painter. He trained in Paris and joined the GROUP OF SEVEN in 1930. His style is brisk and direct, his reputation based on a series done in the 1930s of female nudes posed outdoors (*Nude*, 1930, Toronto, Art Gallery of Ontario).

Holguín, Melchor Pérez
c.1660–c.1725
Leading Spanish colonial painter of the 17th century. He was born in Bolivia, and worked mostly at nearby Potosí, then a city of 30 churches and monasteries. Despite its pre-eminence in a South American context, his old-fashioned art is crude and eclectic, combining Flemish, Italian Mannerist and even Indian influences. See vol. 3 p. 208

Hollar, Wenceslaus or **Wenzel**
1607–77
Bohemian engraver, active mainly in England. He was born in Prague and trained under Merian the Elder in Frankfurt. In 1635 he was brought to England by the Earl of Arundel, and fought on the Royalist side in the Civil War. More than 2,000 prints by him are known, covering a great variety of subjects. They form an invaluable record of 17th-century England, especially of London before the Great Fire of 1666.

Hölzel, Adolf 1853–1934
German painter. Having encountered Impressionism in Paris in 1887, he settled in Dachau and in 1891 founded an art school attended by Nolde and Kerkovius. In 1896 he began experimenting with colour harmonies, which, according to his theory, contained both mystical and musical qualities. While teaching at the Stuttgart Academy (1906–19) he greatly influenced Baumeister, Schlemmer and also Itten, who was later to incorporate Hölzel's theories in his teaching at the Bauhaus. The stylized figures in Hölzel's landscapes (*Before the sunset*, 1917, Berlin, Staatliche Museen) and religious compositions were gradually reduced to abstract ornaments or "colour sounds" characteristic of his work in later years and culminating in his designs for stained-glass windows (1928–33).

Holzer, Johann Evangelist
1709–40
South German fresco painter from the Tyrol. Admired as "the German Raphael" by adherents of Rococo and Neoclassicism alike, his enormous promise was cut off by premature death. Unfortunately, neither of his masterpieces, the façade fresco of *The country dance* in Augsburg and the frescos in Münterschwarzach Abbey (1737–40), survives, and we have only engravings after the former, Holzer's brilliant oil-sketches for the latter, and one major fresco, in St Anton, Partenkirchen (1739) by which to judge him.

Homer, Winslow 1836–1910
One of the most powerful and original American painters of the 19th century. He trained as a lithographer and began painting fairly late, when he was recording scenes of the American Civil War for *Harper's Weekly*. *Prisoners from the front* (1866, New York, Metropolitan) is one of his first major paintings, and is reminiscent of the work of contemporary war photographers in its straightforwardness and lack of romanticization. In 1867 he visited Paris, where he seems to have been influenced by Manet's broad tonal contrasts; they occur in Homer's clearly drawn and vivid outdoor scenes (*Breezing up*, 1876, Washington, NG). The sea was his favourite subject and in 1881–82 he lived on the rugged coast of north-east England at Cullercoats near Tynemouth, where the scenery and life of the fisherfolk inspired works such as the watercolour *Inside the bar, Tynemouth* (1883, New York, Metropolitan). On his return to America, Homer, a solitary character, settled in isolation at Prout's Neck on the Maine coast, and turned increasingly to dramatic representations of stormy seas (*Northeaster*, 1895, New York, Metropolitan). His watercolours are fresh in technique, and sometimes as strong as his oils. See vol. 3 p. **124**

Hondecoeter, Melchior de
1636–95
Dutch painter of birds and still life, active in Utrecht, The Hague and Amsterdam, a pupil of his uncle Jan Baptist Weenix. He achieved an international reputation with large-scale, brilliantly coloured canvases of domestic and exotic birds grouped in landscapes and gardens (often hinting at grand environs). His technique was exquisite, and his subjects strongly characterized; *Fight between a cock and a turkey* (Munich, Alte Pinakothek) is a lively example. His father **Gysbert** (1604–53) painted birds and his grandfather **Gillis** (died 1638) landscapes. See vol. 2 p. **233**

Hone, Nathaniel 1718–84
British portraitist, born and brought up in Ireland. After moving to London, he studied in Italy, 1750–52, then settled permanently in London. He became a founder-member of the Royal Academy in 1768. His most interesting work is *The conjuror* (1775, Dublin, NG of Ireland), a skit on Reynolds' practice of cribbing poses from the Old Masters—Hone was compelled to withdraw it from exhibition at the Academy.

Honthorst, Gerrit van 1590–1656
Dutch painter. He was a pupil of Bloemaert in his native Utrecht before going to Italy in about 1610/12. In Rome he gave himself over completely to Caravaggio's style and became known as Gherardo delle Notti (Gerard of the night scenes). He was particularly skilful in depicting dramatic scenes lit by a single candle, as in *Christ before the High Priest* (c.1617, London, NG) or *Samson and Delilah* (c.1620, Cleveland Museum of Art). In 1620 he returned to Holland, and with Terbrugghen became a leading figure of the Utrecht school. He soon abandoned his Caravaggesque manner, however, and adopted a much lighter palette. In 1628 he was in England working for Charles I, whose portrait he painted (London, NPG), and most of the rest of his career was spent as court painter in The Hague. The last three decades of his life were largely devoted to portraits—a fine collection is at Ashdown House, Berkshire, including several of members of the Danish royal family. Honthorst's portraits made him one of the few 17th-century Dutch artists to have an international reputation but now seem less interesting than his Caravaggesque works, which probably influenced Rembrandt and Georges de La Tour. See vol. 2 p. **213**; vol. 4 p. *43*

Hoogh, Pieter de 1629–84
Dutch genre painter. He was born in Rotterdam and is said to have studied with Berchem, presumably in Haarlem. His fame and popularity rest on a small number of tranquil masterpieces created in Delft, where he lived for about a decade from about 1652. In warm but unsentimental works such as *The courtyard of a house in Delft* (1658, London, NG), de Hoogh seems to sum up more completely than any other artist the peaceful order and well-being of 17th-century Holland. His relationships with his great Delft contemporary Vermeer are unclear, but de Hoogh may have anticipated him in some respects, and in lucidity of composition and delicate observation of the fall of light approaches him more closely than any other Dutch genre painter. After his move to Amsterdam (c.1661) de Hoogh began working for wealthier patrons and his paintings declined sadly in quality as they became grander (*A musical party*, c.1675–77, London, Wellington Museum). See vol. 1 pp. *50*, *106*; vol. 2 p. **229**

Hoogstraten, Samuel van
1627–78
Dutch painter, active in Amsterdam, The Hague, London, Rome and Vienna as well as his native Dordrecht. He became a pupil of Rembrandt in 1640, and his great admiration for his master is shown in his book *Introduction to the Art of Painting* (1678). As a painter, however, he is best known as a virtuoso of perspective effects. One of his "perspective boxes" (London, NG) shows a miniature world visible through peep-holes, and at the opposite extreme is his large *Perspective view down a corridor* (1662), still where it was placed in the 17th century, at the end of a suite of rooms at Dyrham Park, Gloucestershire, conveying a brilliant illusion of the extension of the real space. He also painted genre scenes, landscapes, portraits and still lifes. See vol. 2 p. *212*

Hopper, Edward 1882–1967
One of the leading American figurative painters of the 20th century. During

early trips to Europe he was impressed by Manet and Degas and by Meryon's disquieting prints of the urban scene. His etchings and watercolours between 1915 and about 1923 announced the concerns which were to preoccupy his mature work. Although the everyday subjects are partly inherited from Ashcan school realism (he was a pupil of Henri) they are imbued with a peculiarly melancholy romanticism. Isolated individuals avert their gaze from the viewer towards the empty space of a window; deserted streets and buildings convey boredom or loneliness. His themes in the early 1930s were superficially shared with Regionalist painters such as Burchfield but he was unaffected by the fervid optimism associated with that movement. Urban compositions increasingly emphasize architectonic stillness (*Early Sunday morning*, 1930, New York, Whitney). Hopper's bland, luminous surfaces consistently eschewed psychological involvement but created tension through their very impassivity. See vol. 1 p. *63*; vol. 3 pp. **206–207**

Hoppner, John 1758–1810
British portraitist. He was one of the chief successors of Reynolds and, for 20 years, a rival to Lawrence. He was brought up in the royal household and later became painter to the Prince of Wales (afterwards George IV). His male portraits are very reminiscent of Reynolds but his women and children have a more obviously unaffected charm (*Princess Mary* and *Princess Sophia*, both 1785, Royal coll.).

Horn, Rebecca born 1945
West German artist, working in performance art, film and video. She seeks to remove any distinction between performer and spectators, and to extend the psycho-physical experiences of the participants by the use of props which encourage their fantasies, as in *Cockfeathermask for Dieter* (1973) and *Fingergloves* (1972).

Hoskins, John *c.*1595?–1665
English miniaturist, the uncle and probably the teacher of Samuel Cooper. His early work, with its sensitive response to character, is close in feeling to the portraits of Gheeraerts and Cornelius Johnson. He later specialized in miniature copies of van Dyck's portraits, and his originality, if not his technical brilliance, suffered. The Victoria and Albert Museum, London, has fine examples.

Høst, Oluf 1884–1966
Danish painter. He was a pupil of Giersing and was strongly influenced by Karl Isakson. He painted his native island of Bornholm in a lyrical manner showing sensitivity to light and colour; a representative example is *Farmhouse* (1932, Rønne, Bornholm Museum).

Houbracken, Arnold 1660–1719
Dutch painter and writer on art, a pupil of Hoogstraten. His rather dry and academic paintings are now forgotten, but he is important as the author of *The Great Theatre of Dutch Painters* (1718–21), the successor to van Mander and the most important source of information on 17th-century Netherlandish art. His son **Jacobus** (1698–1780) was the finest Dutch 18th-century portrait engraver, and made illustrations for *The Great Theatre* after his father's designs.

Houdon, Jean-Antoine 1741–1828
The greatest French sculptor of his period. He was a pupil of Michel-Ange

Slodtz and of Pigalle, and in 1761 won the Prix de Rome. From 1764 to 1768 he was in Rome, where he became famous with two works—an *écorché* (1767, Gotha, Schlossmuseum), which was widely copied and used for anatomical instruction in art academies, and the marble statue of *St Bruno* (1767, Rome, S. Maria degli Angeli). Houdon, however, was to gain his greatest celebrity for his portraits. He portrayed many of the leading men of his times with an astonishing vivacity and psychological perception, displaying a brilliant gift for capturing quirks of gesture and expression—*Denis Diderot* (1771, Paris, Louvre), *Benjamin Franklin* (plaster, 1786–91(?), Boston, Athenaeum). Voltaire sat to him several times, most notably in a seated marble statue (1781, Paris, Comédie Française), and Houdon succeeded as no other portraitist in suggesting the liveliness and brilliance of his mind. Houdon's fame was such that he was called to America (1785) to make a marble statue of George Washington, and the work, executed in France, was set up in the Virginia State Capitol at Richmond in 1796. Houdon narrowly escaped imprisonment during the French Revolution, but returned to favour under Napoleon. From 1815, however, he produced little, and became senile five years before his death. See vol. 1 p. *185*; vol. 3 p. **60**

Hoyland, John born 1934
Influential British abstract painter. His paintings are usually on a large scale and concerned above all with colour. In work of the 1960s acrylic paint soaked the canvas with simple but slightly irregular shapes against a single colour field. Later paintings are more thickly painted with layers of brilliant colour (*Saracen*, 1977, London, Tate). He has taught at the Chelsea School of Art in London and promoted British abstract art through touring exhibitions. See vol. 1 p. *153*

Hsai Kuei see XIA GUI

Hsieh Ho see XIE HE

Hsü Hsi see XU XI

Hua Yan 1682–1765
Chinese painter. He came from the rather backward province of Fujian, worked in the prosperous lower Yangtze cities of Hangzhou and Yangzhou, and is usually included in the group of "The Eight Eccentrics of Yangzhou". The majority of his many surviving works are in the form of album leaves, a small-scale and intimate context well suited to his preferred subject matter of birds, flowers and insects, as is the fan-painting *The dirge of autumn* (1730, Boston, MFA). These, together with his studies of peasant life and his comparatively few landscapes, make frequent use of the "boneless" technique, an ink wash without the use of any outline.

Hua Yen see HUA YAN

Hubbuch, Karl born 1891
German painter. He studied in Berlin at the same time as Grosz (1912–13) and belonged to the NEUE SACHLICHKEIT movement. He frequently emphasized the contrast between social classes in his work, and many of his paintings depict power-hungry men and sexually assertive women, all rendered with unmerciful frankness (*Twice Hilde I*, 1923, Munich, Staatsgemäldesammlungen).

Huber, Wolfgang *c.*1485–1553
German painter, printmaker and archi-

tect, a leading painter of the so-called DANUBE school. Born in Feldkirch, he became court painter (before 1515) and later architect to the Bishop of Passau. His tours in the Danube valley were the inspiration for contemplative delicate landscapes, such as his drawing of *Mondsee* (1510, Nuremberg, Germanisches Nationalmuseum). Landscapes form the backgrounds of many of his religious paintings (*The Flight into Egypt*, *c.*1525, West Berlin, Staatliche Museen).

Hudson, Thomas 1701–79
British portrait painter, a pupil of his father-in-law, Jonathan Richardson. Hudson was the most fashionable London portraitist of the 1740s and early 1750s, with a busy practice necessitating the help of drapery painters. At his best, as in *George Frederick Handel* (1756, London, NPG), Hudson was a highly competent if unimaginative painter.

Hudson River school
Loosely-knit group of American landscape painters who flourished in the mid-19th century. Cole is usually considered the founder, and other leading artists involved included Cropsey and Durand. They had a Romantic approach to nature, and emphasized the scale, beauty and nobility of the Hudson River Valley and of the Catskill, Berkshire and White Mountains. The writings of Washington Irving and James Fenimore Cooper and the influence of European painters such as Turner and John Martin also played a part in shaping their vision and attitudes, for their work is often not "pure" landscape and has moral implications or literary associations. The painters of the Hudson River school found an appreciative public, for as the frontier moved westward the mystique of nature became part of American culture. See vol. 3 p. 69

Huet, Christophe died 1759
French Rococo painter and engraver. He was a pupil of Oudry, and is best known for his whimsical engravings and decorative paintings (examples, 1735, Chantilly, Musée Condé) involving animals, often dressed up and engaged in human activities. Huet also painted still lifes. See vol. 2 p. *240*

Huet, Paul 1803–69
French landscape painter and graphic artist. He trained with Guérin and Gros, but his direct study of nature places him as a forerunner of the Barbizon group. He was closely associated with the Romantic entourage surrounding Delacroix and many of his landscapes are subjective and turbulent interpretations of nature (*Equinoctial seas*, 1861, Paris, Musée Delacroix), but Bonington's lucid naturalism also affected his style.

Hughes, Arthur 1830–1915
English PRE-RAPHAELITE painter and illustrator. In the 1850s his paintings were among the most poetic and brilliantly coloured Pre-Raphaelite creations; *April love* (1855–56, London, Tate) is the best-known. He worked with Burne-Jones, Morris and Rossetti on the Oxford Union murals, but soon lapsed into journeyman illustration, occasionally producing highly imaginative drawings such as those for Christina Rossetti's *Sing Song* (1872). See vol. 1 p. *55*

Hugo, Victor 1802–85
French poet, dramatist and novelist, also a painter and graphic artist. Closely linked with the artists of the Romantic movement, Hugo developed his own expressive style after a journey to the

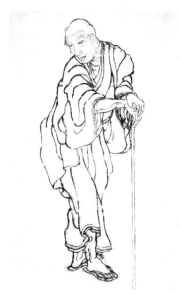

Hokusai: Self-portrait, 1840. Paris, Guimet

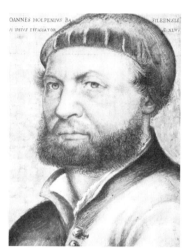

Holbein, Hans the Younger: Self-portrait, 1540–43. Florence, Uffizi (Scala)

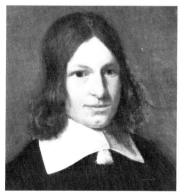

Hoogh: Self-portrait?, 1649. Amsterdam, Rijksmuseum

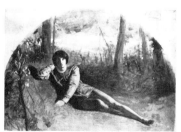

Hughes: *A young poet* (Self-portrait), *c.*1849. Birmingham Museums and Art Gallery

Rhine in 1840. These drawings from memory of romantic landscapes, some strongly allegorical (*Le Burg à la Croix*, 1850, Paris, Musée Victor Hugo), mirror the development of his poetry.

Huguet, Jaime active *c.* 1448–92
Spanish painter of the Catalan school. *St George and the Dragon* (Barcelona, Museum) is attributed as an early work, and documented paintings include *The Epiphany* (1463, Barcelona, Cappella Reale) and *The consecration of St Augustine* (1463–85, Barcelona, Museo de Arte de Cataluña). He was one of the creators of the typical Spanish retable, usually of sumptuous decorative effect with an elaborate carved frame. Continuing the Netherlandish-inspired style of Bernardo Martorell, Huguet described form by contour rather than modelling, and paid great attention to details of dress and ornament. However, he had a great gift for characterization and his faces are highly individualized.

Hui Tsung see HUIZONG

Huizong 1082–1135
(reigned 1101–26)
Chinese painter, an emperor of the Northern Song dynasty. Huizong (Beauteous Ancestor) was the posthumous "temple name" of this the most talented painter and calligrapher of all Chinese emperors, whose personal name was Zhao Ji. He carried to a new height the aesthetic enthusiasms of the Song ruling house, and was the moving spirit behind the Imperial Academy of Painting, and himself one of the most distinguished practitioners of the small, exquisitely worked renderings of birds and flowers which were one of its principal products. *Five-coloured parakeet* (early 12th century, Boston, MFA) in luminous colours on silk, is the epitome of courtly refinement, and may be from the emperor's own hand. Many copies in Huizong's style are extant, and his distinctive calligraphy, in a style known as "slender gold", is found on several supposedly Song paintings. Carried off to die in captivity at the fall of his capital in 1126, he remains the Chinese ideal of the artistically sensitive but politically feckless ruler. See vol. 3 p. 40

Humphrey, Jack 1901–67
Canadian figurative painter. He worked in St John, New Brunswick and studied in 1929 with Hans Hofmann. He used dynamic planes of colour to build compositions based on local scenery. Though small, his works seem monumental (*Draped head*, 1931, Toronto, Hart House). His example encouraged many Canadian East Coast artists.

Humphry, Ozias 1742–1810
British portrait painter, active in Bath before moving to London in 1763. He lived there for the rest of his life apart from visits to Italy (1773–77) and India (1784–87). A miniaturist until an accident in 1772 affected his eyesight, he later worked successfully in oils and then crayon. There are examples of his rather conservative work in the National Portrait Gallery, London.

Hundertwasser, Friedensreich
born 1928
Austrian painter. His work is figurative but the primary impact is strongly decorative. Influenced by the artists of the Vienna Sezession, his art has a characteristically Viennese quality: along with its decorative richness, it has links with the fairy-tale quality of "fantastic realists" such as Brauer and Fuchs. Very ecologically conscious, Hundertwasser elevates the "vegetative" and opposes it to the hard, mechanical lines of modern technology, which he sees as both dangerously alienating and dangerously wasteful. He wants his art to fulfil a magical and religious function. His self-portrait *House born in Stockholm* (1965, New York, J.J. Aberbach coll.) is characteristically highly coloured.

Hunt, William Holman
1827–1910
English painter, one of the founders of the PRE-RAPHAELITE Brotherhood. His deep religious convictions and rigid adherence to Pre-Raphaelite ideals resulted in a strong didactic element and an almost microscopic rendering of detail in paintings crowded with symbolism (*The awakening conscience*, 1853, London, Tate). He made three trips to the Middle East in his fanatical pursuit of accurate background for his religious paintings and was the only one of the original Pre-Raphaelites to maintain such idealism. The paintings which resulted (*The scapegoat*, 1854, Port Sunlight, Lady Lever Art Gallery) show, however, that sincerity is not a substitute for talent. In 1905 he published *Pre-Raphaelitism and the Pre-Raphaelite Brotherhood*, a basic source book. See vol. 3 pp. **82–83**

Hunt, William Morris 1824–79
American painter. In 1847, he studied with Couture in Paris before becoming closely linked with Millet and the BARBIZON SCHOOL, Returning to America in 1856, he established a market in Boston for Barbizon artists, and his own broad, atmospheric portraits, landscapes and figure studies considerably influenced his contemporaries. Hunt was instrumental in making Paris the centre of study for American artists, and Lafarge and the author Henry James were among his many pupils. Most of his work was destroyed in a fire of 1872, and he is now remembered for the unattractive mural decorations in the New York State Capitol at Albany, heroic compositions close to the grandiose type of 19th-century French academic painting.

Huszar, Vilmos 1884–1960
Hungarian-born artist, who settled in Holland in 1906. His early work was influenced by Israëls and van Gogh. Through his friendship with van Doesburg he was introduced to Cubism and developed geometric abstraction (1916–18) in works such as the lithograph *Composition* (1918, Otterlo, Rijksmuseum Kröller-Müller). With Mondrian, van der Leck and van Doesburg he was a founder of De STIJL in 1917. He specialized in designing abstract stained-glass and interior decoration. He left De Stijl in 1923 and returned to geometricized figurative painting.

Huysum, Jan van 1682–1749
Dutch flower-painter, the eldest son of the flower and landscape painter, **Justus** (1659–1716). Ruysch was the only flower-painter of comparable skill working at the same time, and Jan's contemporaries thought he brought the genre to the peak of perfection; subsequent taste has been less in his favour. His lavish compositions are painted in a highly detailed manner, using pale colours against even lighter grounds, often on copper or mahogany. Whilst insistent upon painting each flower from the life, he paid no regard to their seasonal compatibility. He is well represented in collections in London—Dulwich College Picture Gallery, NG and Wallace Coll. See vol. 2 p. **233**

Ibbetson, Julius Caesar
1759–1817
British painter of landscapes with figures. He worked in oils and watercolours, and began by copying Dutch landscape paintings for dealers. He also imitated the works of Gainsborough and de Loutherbourg. A kind of artificial picturesque rusticity clings to even his best works—broad scenes of the moors and fells of his native Yorkshire or of the Lake District (*Ullswater*, 1801, Leeds City Art Gallery).

Icon
Image of a saint or other religious figure. Derived from the Greek *eikon*, meaning likeness, the word is applied particularly to those images of the Byzantine Church, and subsequently the Greek and Russian Orthodox Churches, which are believed to be sacred in themselves and to facilitate contact with the personage portrayed. Often they have wide-staring eyes which seem almost to hypnotize the worshipper into veneration. They vary in size and medium, but typically take the form of fairly small panels, and certain rules and criteria have dictated their form and use. By the 6th century Christian buildings were full of them on walls, ceilings, floors and in shrines, but in the 8th century there was a reaction against them. **Iconoclasts** ("image breakers") believed that icons were closer to idolatry than true worship and that the image of the human form could not embody spiritual presence. Icons are still produced in Greece and Russia. See vol. 2 pp. 62–63

Iconography
Branch of art history which deals with the subject matter of the figurative arts. The identification of a saint in a painting through the attribute with which he is represented—St Lawrence with the gridiron on which he was martyred, for example—is a straightforward instance of the use of iconography. In his book *Studies in Iconology* (1939) the art historian Erwin Panofsky proposed that the term "**iconology**" should be used distinctly from iconography to denote the related but wider field of study which extends the approach on a broader historical and philosophical basis by examining the meaning and tradition of pictorial motifs. In this way an attempt is made to understand a work of art in terms of its cultural environment. An older meaning of the term "iconography" was a collection of portraits, as in van Dyck's series of etchings of contemporaries, the *Iconography*. The word can be used in the classification of portraits of individuals —"the iconography of Charles I".

Iconostasis
A screen which, in Byzantine, Greek and Russian Orthodox churches, divides the sanctuary from the public areas and on which icons are placed.

Ife art
Art from the ancient religious capital of the Yoruba people of Western Nigeria. Ife masks and sculpted commemorative heads of the classical period, *c.* 1100–1400, in both bronze and terracotta, can be remarkably naturalistic and beautiful. See vol. 2 p. 15

Illumination
Decoration of manuscripts, whether with ornamental letters, with borders or with miniatures. Illumination was practised by the Egyptians (as witnessed in their *Books of the Dead*), the Greeks and the Romans, and became widespread in Europe during the Middle Ages. Manuscripts were generally written on parchment or vellum, although from the 14th century paper was also employed for less lavish copies. The medium used for the illumination was usually tempera. Because manuscripts have survived from many areas better than wall-paintings or sculpture, the illumination in them is often the main source of knowledge concerning the art of particular periods. Illumination declined with the invention of printing (although illuminations were added to printed books), and comparatively little of great merit was produced after the end of the 15th century.

Illusionism
The use of pictorial techniques to create an illusion of real space and form on a two-dimensional surface. Perspective and minute naturalistic painting are the means most commonly used to attain it; QUADRATURA and TROMPE L'OEIL are specialized branches of these methods.

Impasto
Thick, opaque paint applied with a brush, knife or fingers, creating various textural features on the surface of the painting. It is suited only to oil-paints and certain forms of acrylic. Artists renowned for their use of impasto include Rembrandt, Manet, van Gogh and Auerbach. The latter's impasto is so thick that the paint is almost modelled.

Impressionism
Movement in painting originating in France in the 1860s. The artists involved were not a formal body, but to varying degrees they shared related outlooks and techniques, and they grouped together for the purpose of exhibiting. Cézanne, Degas, Manet, Monet, Camille Pissarro, Renoir and Sisley were the most important artists associated with Impressionism, but their involvement and commitment varied greatly. They reacted against academic doctrines and the Romantic idea that art should be a vehicle for personal emotion, and tried to depict contemporary life in a new objective manner by rendering an "impression" of what the eye sees in one particular moment rather than what the mind knows to be there. In this they were influenced by scientific study which demonstrated that colour was not inherent in an object but the outcome of the way light is reflected from it, and thus a matter of constant change and modification. Landscape offered the most obvious channel for studying such effects, and painting out of doors became one of the hallmarks of Impressionism, although Degas, for example, never subscribed to the idea. Constable, Turner and the painters of the Barbizon school were seen as precursors. Monet, after whose *Impression: sunrise* (1873, Paris, Musée Marmottan) the movement was named, is often considered the Impressionist *par excellence* because his commitment to its ideas was total throughout his career and he developed them most single-mindedly. Pissarro, however, was the only artist who exhibited at all eight Impressionist exhibitions (1874, 1876, 1877, 1879, 1880, 1881, 1882 and 1886), and as a figure much respected by all his associates was also central to the movement. The Impressionists were at first generally mocked and attacked because of their high-keyed colour and lack of finish; a

contemporary critic of 1876 referred to them as "lunatics" and wrote: "Someone should tell M. Pissarro forcibly that trees are never violet, that the sky is never the colour of fresh butter, that nowhere on earth are things to be seen as he paints them . . ." After the final Impressionist exhibition the group dissolved, but the influence of the movement was enormous; indeed it was the most radical artistic phenomenon of the 19th century. Most obviously it caused painters everywhere to lighten their palettes and the term Impressionism is sometimes used to cover the work of painters in countries outside France, that of Steer in England, for example, and Hassam in America. Reactions against it were also far-reaching. The lack of intellectual content was seen as a major drawback, and the Post-Impressionists were concerned to bring back "meaning"—emotional or symbolic—to painting. See vol. 3 pp. 98 ff

Imprimatura
Thin layer of colour applied to a white ground, sometimes over a preliminary drawing, to establish a middle tone for an oil-painting. It is usually a green or grey colour, though some artists prefer a warmer hue. It can be applied together with oil resin, glue size and other media.

Inca art
Art of the Inca Empire, flourishing about 1430 to 1580 in the southern central highlands of Peru and later extending from Ecuador to Chile. There are extensive remains at Quito, Cuzco, Chanchan, Machu Picchu, Ollantaytambo, Pisac and elsewhere. Generally, Inca art and architecture had an austere quality with an emphasis on repetitive geometrical decoration and meticulous attention to detail and finish. Some of the most impressive remains are Inca walls of tightly fitting and beautifully dressed blocks of masonry, notably at Machu Picchu and Cuzco. Small stone carvings have an inert and detached air although some animal figures, such as those of llamas, have a great deal of charm. Almost all the pottery is polychrome with a great variety of surface decoration, and painted wooden vessels have inlaid designs. Very fine textiles, often decorated with checkerboard patterns, were woven with considerable skill. Of the renowned wealth of objects in gold and silver, little survives other than a few simply styled human and animal figurines. See vol. 2 p. 19

Inchbold, John William 1830–88
English landscape painter. He imitated the detailed, brightly coloured style of the Pre-Raphaelites and earned Ruskin's praise. He travelled widely and his style gradually loosened, but never lost its poetry. *Lake of Lucerne, Mount Pilatus in the distance* (1857, London, V&A) shows him at his most intense.

Indépendants, Salon des see SALON DES INDÉPENDANTS

Indiana, Robert (Robert Clark) born 1928
American painter and graphic designer. Like other POP artists he has adopted the language of commercial billboards, plaques and traffic signs for the purposes of art, but his attitude is more celebratory than that of most of his contemporaries. He composes with geometrical shapes and boldly coloured sign lettering. See vol. 3 pp. **238–239**

Induno, Domenico 1815–78 and Gerolamo 1825–90
Italian painters, brothers from Lombardy. They were patriots and are famous for their depictions of Risorgimental subjects, such as Domenico's *Arrival of news of the Peace of Villafranca* (1859, Milan, Museum of the National Risorgimento). Their luminous interiors, for instance Gerolamo's *Sad presentiment* (1862, Milan, Brera), reflect Dutch influence and possibly that of the Macchiaioli. Together, they brought an unprecedented dignity to Italian genre painting.

Informal art
Term coined by the French critic Michel Tapié in his book *Un Art Autre* (1952) to describe paintings in which figurative and geometric forms are rejected in favour of the use of totally spontaneous techniques. It was a major style in European art in the 1940s and 1950s: its chief exponents were Wols, Fautrier, Hartung, Soulages and Mathieu. TACHISME and Art Autre are synonymous terms and the style is in many ways similar to American ABSTRACT EXPRESSIONISM.

Inglés, Jorge active mid-15th century
Painter active in Castile. His name means "George the Englishman", but nothing is known of his origins or life. His style, vaguely reminiscent of Rogier van der Weyden, suggests he trained in the Netherlands. The only documented work by him is a retable commissioned for the Hospital of Buitrago by the Marquess of Santillana (1455, Madrid, Duke of Infantado coll.). Unusually, the donor portraits occupy the main panels. He was one of the first artists to work in a Hispano-Netherlandish idiom.

Ingres, Jean-Auguste-Dominique 1780–1867
French history and portrait painter, one of the leading, but also most personal, exponents of NEOCLASSICISM. The son of **Jean-Marie-Joseph** Ingres (1755–1814), a minor sculptor and painter from Montauban, he was first taught drawing by his father before studying at the Académie Royale in Toulouse. In 1796 he entered David's studio and won the Prix de Rome with *The ambassadors of Agamemnon* (1801, Paris, Louvre), much praised by Flaxman for its stylized line. Political upheavals delayed his stipend for five years, and during this time his paintings, with their linear rhythms based on Greek and Etruscan models, departed from Davidian Neoclassicism. In Rome (1806–24), he studied Renaissance art, especially the work of Raphael, whom he idolized, but the paintings he sent back to the annual Salon were considered bizarre, particularly *Roger and Angelica* (1819, Louvre). After the collapse of the Napoleonic Empire, Ingres was forced to make a living by drawing pencil portraits of English tourists (more than 450 are known), finely observed studies which closely resemble outline engraving. Although he was a superb portraitist, his preferred subjects were grandiose religious and historical themes and his reputation at the Salon was secured on his return to Paris in 1824 with *The vow of Louis XIII* (Montauban Cathedral), which is strongly reminiscent of Raphael. It marked him out as the champion of Neoclassicism against the rising Romanticism of Delacroix and his followers, a position which Ingres consolidated as director of the French Academy in Rome from 1834 to 1841. His famous dictum "Drawing is the probity of Art", and his championship of line before colour, exerted a wide influence over his many pupils. However, many of Ingres's paintings were at variance with his severe classicist teaching, and are notable for their mannered gracefulness. This is particularly so in his representations of the female nude, which are anatomically distorted to increase their sensuous elegance (*The Turkish bath*, 1859–62, Louvre), but is also evident in his portraits, among the most outstanding of which are two of *Mme Moitessier* in the National Galleries of Washington (1851) and London (1856). Chassériau was the only one of Ingres's pupils to attain lasting distinction, but Degas, Picasso and Matisse as well as the Nabis were strongly influenced by his supreme draughtsmanship. Ingres left many works to the museum in Montauban which is named after him. See vol. 1 pp. *119, 162*; vol. 3 pp. **84–86**

Innes, James Dickson 1887–1914
British painter. He was a friend of Augustus John, with whom he painted in north Wales. His work, always on a small scale, reflects the influence of Matisse and in some of his landscapes there is a degree of abstraction and decorative refinement recalling Japanese prints (*The waterfall*, 1910, London, Tate).

Inness, George 1825–94
American landscape painter. His early work was influenced by the Hudson River school (*The Delaware Valley*, 1865, New York, Metropolitan). Later, after contact with the Barbizon school in Fontainebleau and a stay in Italy (1870–74), he abandoned precise detail for a broader style, using glowing light and indistinctly massed forms (*The monk*, 1873, Andover, Mass., Addison Gallery of American Art). Despite a surface resemblance to Impressionism, his later work retained a mystical view of nature and gained wide popularity.

Intaglio
A method of printing where the design is cut or etched into the surface of the metal plate and the ink is held in the incisions or pits, as in METAL ENGRAVING, DRYPOINT, ETCHING, AQUATINT and MEZZOTINT. See vol. 1 p. 167

International Gothic
Style of painting and sculpture in Europe, emerging in the late 14th century, and continuing in many areas of Europe well into the 15th century. It was the background against which the Renaissance style was formed in Italy and the new realism emerged in the Netherlands. The mingling of international styles which gave rise to the term was encouraged by the peripatetic careers of several influential artists, the close communications and rivalry of court centres and an increase in the trade of works of art. The dominant styles were Franco-Netherlandish and Italian, and works were characterized by decorative detail, rich colour, a frequently lyrically linear manner, and, occasionally, a refined naturalism. A trend towards stronger naturalism was evident by the mid-14th century in Italy and in France (as in the portrait of *King John the Good*, pre-1364, Paris, Louvre). By the late 14th century northern masters (such as Jean Pucelle in France and Master Theodoric and others at Karlstein Castle in Bohemia) were following the Italian example in attempting to convey convincingly three-dimensional pictorial space. The strongest Italian influence was the decorative fluent style of Simone Martini, who had worked in Avignon. International Gothic reached its peak by the early 15th century. Amongst its master-

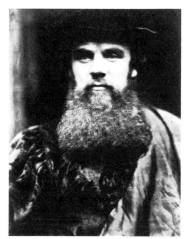

Hunt, William Holman: Photograph by D. V. Wynfield, *c.*1860. London, NPG

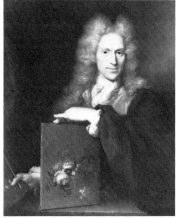

Huysum, Jan van: Self-portrait, *c.*1739. Oxford, Ashmolean

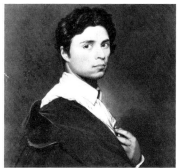

Ingres: Self-portrait, *c.*1804. Chantilly, Musée Condé (Giraudon)

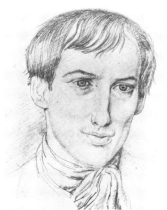

Innes: Drawing by Ian Strang (1886–1952), 1913. London, NPG

pieces were the *Très Riches Heures* painted in Burgundy by the Netherlandish Limbourg brothers (1413–16, Chantilly, Musée Condé) and *The Adoration of the Magi* by Gentile da Fabriano (1423, Florence, Uffizi). The stronger strain of realism in the sculpture of Sluter in Burgundy heralded the gradual demise of the style in northern Europe, though sculptors such as Multscher in Germany continued working in it well after 1450. See vol. 2 pp. 88–89

Intimisme
Term applied to the intimate domestic interiors painted by Bonnard and Vuillard from the 1890s on. Their styles were different but owed much to the colouring and the move away from naturalism of the Nabis. See vol. 3 p. 120

Intonaco see FRESCO

Ipoustéguy, Jean Robert
born 1920
French artist. He has worked in various media, notably stained glass and painting, but since 1954 has concentrated on sculpture. Like many European artists after World War II, he rejected pure abstraction in order to produce compositions expressive of humanity. He developed a highly individual technique of shattering heavy, blackened bronze, and achieved a strong Surrealist flavour, particularly in his craggy megaliths with head-like tops, and large ensembles (*Alexander before Ecbatana*, 1965, Paris, Galerie Claude Bernard).

Isaac Master see ASSISI

Isabey, Jean-Baptiste 1767–1855
French painter, the most celebrated miniaturist of his day. He was a pupil of J.-L. David from 1786 and was patronized by Marie-Antoinette. After the Revolution, he sought to convey its heroism with popular army scenes and established a close liaison with Napoleon I and the Empress Josephine. Following the fall of the Empire, after a short exile in England, he returned to France and regained the patronage of subsequent French monarchs. His brilliant and detailed miniatures were painted in a technique resembling watercolour and he was one of the first artists to publish lithographs.

Isabey, Louis Gabriel Eugène
1803–86
French painter and lithographer, the son of Jean-Baptiste. He studied with his father, but was more strongly influenced by Delacroix's Romanticism. He was patronized by Louis-Philippe, for whom he painted contemporary historical events, and his costume genre scenes, set in the 17th and 18th centuries, were highly popular. Much of his later work was dramatic marine painting which was influential on his pupils, Boudin and Jongkind (*Etretat in a storm*, 1851, Hamburg, Kunsthalle).

Isakson, Karl 1878–1922
Swedish painter who worked mainly in Denmark. He studied in Stockholm, with Zahrtmann in Italy and in Copenhagen, and with Le Fauconnier in Paris. He was influenced by Cézanne, Matisse and Cubism. His nudes, portraits and still lifes are painted in subtly juxtaposed areas of complementary and contrasting colour (*Standing model from the back*, 1918–20, Denmark, Louisiana Museum). Towards the end of his life, he painted visionary, biblical compositions. His art strongly influenced later Swedish and Nordic painters.

Isenbrandt (Ysenbrandt), **Adriaen**
died 1551
Netherlandish painter. He became a master in the Bruges guild in 1510, and is said to have been a pupil of Gerard David. No documented paintings by him are known, but a considerable body of work continuing David's style of devotional painting is attributed to him, outstanding among which is the diptych *The seven sorrows of the Virgin* (divided between the church of Notre-Dame, Bruges, and the Musées Royaux des Beaux-Arts, Brussels). Much of his output was once attributed to Mostaert.

Islamic art
Art of the Islamic religion. From the 7th century Islam embarked on the conquest of the Mediterranean world, moving northwards from the Arabian heartland into the Byzantine Empire and westwards into North Africa and Spain, bringing with it a distinctive style of art, based to a great extent on the decorative elaboration of Koranic calligraphy. Besides its achievements in architecture and architectural sculpture, Islamic art embraces and raises to a high level arts which in the West might be classed as minor—pottery, metalworking and carpet-making—while painting was largely an aspect of the arts of the book. In all branches a strongly decorative sense prevails; calligraphic, floral and geometric patterns are dominant. Figural representation is rare, for while the Koran does not specifically forbid the representation of human figures, it is possible to infer such prohibition from Chapter V and the ban became enshrined in Islamic custom virtually from the first. In pottery, the most celebrated wares were the 10th-century slip-painted calligraphic wares, the 13th-century Kashan lustre pots and the 16th-century Iknik wares, characterized by lively floral decorations. Metalwork reached great heights in the 13th century with the development of sophisticated inlay techniques, while carpet-making was at its most sumptuous in the 16th century, particularly the rugs of Tabriz. Miniature painting is considered to have reached its peak in the 15th century, when a distinctive Persian style developed out of the mixed styles of the previous period. However, more is known of the great painters of the 16th century, particularly Bihzad and his pupils who worked in Tabriz for the great libertine and sage, Shah Tahmasp. See vol. 3 pp. 22 ff

Israëls, Jozef 1824–1911
Dutch painter. He studied in Amsterdam and Paris, was influenced by Scheffer, and travelled widely. He started as a painter of historical themes in a Romantic style but while living in Zandvoort (1855) he began to paint large-scale genre scenes of fishermen (*Passing his mother's grave*, 1857, Amsterdam, Stedelijk Museum). His sentimental psychological treatment of humble subjects made him very popular all over Europe. About 1870 he established himself in The Hague, where he became a leading member of the HAGUE school.

Itcho, Hanabusa 1652–1724
Japanese painter, the son of an Osaka physician. When he was 15 the family moved to Edo (Tokyo), where he began to learn painting. He excelled in depicting people, flowers and birds in pure KANO style, and was friendly with all the fashionable *literati* and dilettanti of the city. He is considered one of the greatest *giga* (cartoons/caricature) artists in Japanese history. In 1697 he was sentenced to 12 years of exile on a remote island for insulting a government official in an illustrated book of poems lampooning the famous of the day. He continued to paint and publish and on his release he returned to a welcoming public and a prosperity which enabled him to live an eccentric and extravagant life. He painted almost to the last day of his life, even though he had to steady his hands with weights. A set of highly-coloured ink paintings, *Scenes of Takao and Kurama*, are in the Tokyo University of Arts Exhibition Hall.

Itten, Johannes 1888–1967
Swiss painter and designer. He studied with Hölzel in Stuttgart and from 1915 practised a form of Constructivism. He was one of the first teachers at the Weimar BAUHAUS, where he introduced the first-year Basic Course—its elements are still an important part of most art college education. His interest in Indian philosophy and introduction of a vegetarian diet to the Bauhaus canteen gave him the reputation of being a crank. His attitudes were opposed to the technological ones of Gropius and in 1923 he was replaced by Albers. He was a painter of Delaunay-influenced colour compositions, but is best remembered as a teacher. See vol. 3 pp. **190–191**

Ivanov, Alexander 1806–58
One of the leading Russian painters of the 19th century. He went to Rome in 1827 and spent almost all his career there. Inspired by the success of *The last days of Pompeii* by his countryman Brullov and by his own deep religious convictions, he dedicated his life to the production of an epic painting which he hoped would have greater spiritual depth and truth to nature than any hitherto produced. His subject was *Christ's first appearance to the people*, for which he made more than 600 preparatory studies. He sought the advice of the Nazarenes, and his desire for historical accuracy led to plans (unsuccessful) to visit the Holy Land. The enormous painting (now in the Tretyakov Gallery, Moscow) was eventually exhibited (1857) in St Petersburg to a mixed reception. It is an heroic failure—the figures, full of learned quotations from the Antique and Renaissance art, conflicting with the naturalistic setting. The studies he made for it, however, are often remarkably fresh, and his other religious works sometimes have a very impressive, if somewhat cold grandeur (*Noli me tangere*, 1835, Leningrad, Russian State Museum).

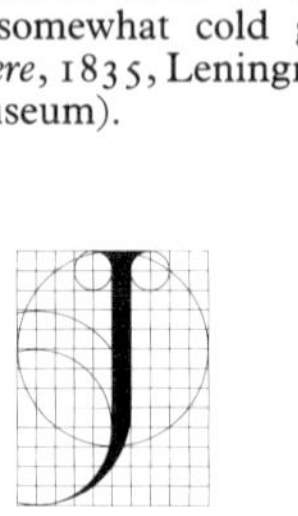

Jackson, Alexander Young
1882–1974
Canadian landscape painter, a founder-member and dedicated propagandist of the GROUP OF SEVEN. He was converted to Impressionism by a period of study in Paris (1907). In 1913 he shared a Toronto studio with Tom Thomson, then painted in Algoma with Lawren Harris and on the St Lawrence shore, where his technique and style crystallized in the 1920s. Typical are the simple undulating contours and muted intermediate tones accented by vivid colour in his snow scenes (*First snow, Algoma*, 1920, Kleinburg, McMichael coll.). He became a venerated senior figure to Canadian landscape painters.

Jackson, Gilbert active 1622–40
English portrait painter. Although based in London, he travelled the provinces, working in an unambitious style influenced by Cornelius Johnson. The portraits are two-dimensional, with strongly frontal poses, often garish colouring, and a fascination with the detail and pattern of dress. Some 20 signed works are known; the most impressive may be *Lord Keeper Williams* (1625, Oxford, St John's College).

Jacobello del Fiore active 1401–39
The first important Venetian painter of the 15th century. He practised a version of the International Gothic style, and his early *Madonna and Child* panels (many in private collections) combine colouristic refinement with weighty modelling. In 1408 he met Gentile da Fabriano, whose graceful style influenced such later work as *The coronation of the Virgin* (*c.*1432, Venice, Accademia).

Jacobi, Otto Reinhold 1812–1901
Canadian painter, born in Prussia. He studied and worked in Berlin and Düsseldorf, where he was known as a portrait painter. He moved to Montreal in 1860 and later settled in Toronto. *A forest stream* (1869, Ottawa, NG of Canada) displays his predilection for majestic scenery depicted with an eye for naturalistic detail and romantic effects.

Jacobsen, Egill born 1910
Danish painter. He was influenced by Danish folk art, by Matisse, Picasso and Kandinsky, and painted expressive abstracts with strong and brilliant colour contrasts. He joined COBRA and established himself as one of the leading modern artists in Denmark.

Jacobsen, Robert born 1912
Danish self-taught sculptor. In the late 1940s his works were made of granite, marble or limestone and were often heavily voluminous and wholly abstract, sometimes reminiscent of Arp's work. From 1949 he produced geometric iron constructions such as *Statique II* (1959, Århus Art Museum). He has also made surrealistic works of scrap-iron.

Jacquemart de Hesdin
died after 1409
French painter and manuscript illuminator, documented in Poitiers and Bourges as painter to Jean, Duc de Berri, from 1384 to 1409. His style is indebted to Jean Pucelle and French court painting in general, but reveals Italian influence in details of landscape and architecture. None of his large-scale paintings survives. Illuminations in two Books of Hours have been attributed to him (one in Brussels, Bibliothèque Royale, and one in Paris, Bibliothèque Nationale). There are doubts, however, about the identification of the Brussels Hours, and the full-page miniatures have been cut from the Paris *Les Grandes Heures du Duc de Berri* (but *The way to Calvary*, Paris, Louvre, painted by Jacquemart, may be a detached folio). Jacquemart's style forms a link between Pucelle and the Limbourgs, who succeeded Jacquemart as court painters to the Duc de Berri.

Jakac, Božidar born 1899
Yugoslav painter and graphic artist. He is probably best known for his series of portraits (mainly in pencil, sepia or red chalk) of Tito and the partisan leaders which he made during World War II. He has given the major part of his works to

the gallery at Kostanjevira in Slovenia which is named after him.

Jakuchu, Ito 1716–1800
Japanese painter from Kyoto. He first trained under a Kano master, but later studied Chinese Yuan and Ming works and Korin's paintings. He evolved a distinct style, specializing in flowers and birds, and above all domestic fowl, which he kept himself and constantly observed. One of his most famous fowl paintings is on some sliding doors of the Saifuku temple in Kyoto.

Jannsen, Horst born 1928
West German artist, mainly known for his drawings and graphic work. There is throughout an atmosphere of sexual malaise, of disturbing memories and obscure desires. Of his recurring imagery, the female nude is relatively clearly depicted, while other motifs are less recognizable, their ambiguity relating to the symbolism of dreams.

Janssens, Abraham c.1575–1632
Flemish figure and portrait painter, one of the most distinctive and important contemporaries of Rubens. He was in Italy in 1598 and back in his native Antwerp by 1601. His earliest dated work, *Diana and Callisto* (Budapest, Museum of Fine Arts), is of that year and thoroughly Mannerist. A second visit to Italy at some time in the first decade of the century seems likely, for from 1609 (*Scaldis and Antwerpia*, Antwerp, Musées Royaux des Beaux-Arts) his work shows a sober and solid classicism, with clearly and powerfully modelled figures, suggesting direct contact with the most up-to-date Italian models, especially Caravaggio. The noble *Calvary* (c.1620, Valenciennes, Musée des Beaux-Arts) is perhaps his masterpiece. During the 1620s Janssens fell under the spell of Rubens, like almost all other Antwerp painters, and the quality of his work declined. Rombouts and Gerard Seghers were among his pupils.

Janssens van Ceulen, Cornelis
see JOHNSON, CORNELIUS

Jawlensky, Alexei von 1864–1941
Russian painter. He settled in Munich in 1896, where he met Kandinsky. Though loosely associated with the Blaue Reiter group, Jawlensky developed an independent style, characterized by flattened, abstract forms and strong colouring (*Girl with peonies*, 1909, Wuppertal, Von der Heydt Museum). He continued to produce simplified line and colour paintings which resist the dynamic effects of post-Cubist developments, despite re-establishing links with Kandinsky after 1923, when he exhibited with him as one of Die BLAUE VIER. Later paintings are more mystical, and from 1929 on he did an icon-like series (*Night*, 1933, Bonn, Städtisches Kunstsammlungen).

Jeanneret see LE CORBUSIER

Jegher, Christoffel 1596–1652/3
Flemish woodcut engraver, best known for his prints after Rubens, with whom he worked in close collaboration in the 1630s. His bold technique was ideally suited to Rubens' virile style and enabled him to work on a large scale: his masterpiece, *The garden of love* (paintings of the subject by Rubens, early 1630s, in the Prado, Madrid, and at Waddesdon Manor, Buckinghamshire), printed from two blocks, is 120 cm (4 ft) wide. Apart from his work with Rubens, he worked mainly as a book illustrator.

Jen Jen-fa see REN RENFA

Jenkins, William Paul born 1923
American painter. He studied in New York (1948–52) and since 1953 has spent much of his career in Paris. In 1963, influenced by Wols and Tobey, he began to work with poured paint: the irregular configurations seem to depend on the paint flow (*Phenomena red wing*, 1962, New York, D. Kluger coll.).

Jeune Peinture Belge
Group of Belgian artists founded in 1945, with the aim of holding exhibitions of contemporary Belgian art all over Europe. Most of the artists involved produced abstract work, but many tendencies were represented. Alechinsky and Bury were leading members of the group, which dissolved in 1948.

Jihei, Sigimura
active late 17th century
Japanese UKIYO-E print artist. Very little is known of his life, but most of his prints and albums appeared between 1685 and 1698 and their content is chiefly erotic. His style reveals the influence of Moronobu and his use of sweeping lines is particularly effective. See vol. 3 p. 49

Jing Hao
active late 9th–early 10th century
Chinese painter. He was one of the first great masters of monochrome landscape painting and his career bridged the gap between the Tang and the succeeding Five Dynasties period. No authentic example survives, but his influence was transmitted through the first full treatise on the art of landscape entitled *A Treatise on Landscape (Records of Brushwork)*, wherein he develops the ideas of Xie He in dialogue form, stressing spontaneity and vitality over painstaking craftsmanship within a Taoist framework.

Jin Nong 1687–after 1764
Chinese painter, a leading figure of the group of painters classified as "The Eight Eccentrics of Yangzhou". Yangzhou was a wealthy centre on the lower Yangtze where, in the 16th and 17th centuries, a distinct, if unorthodox, culture was sustained by the rich salt merchants of the region. Jin began to paint seriously only in his fifties, having been previously famed as a poet, philosopher and calligrapher. Indeed, a highly individual calligraphy, with angular characters achieved by cropping the tip of the brush, is an integral part of most of his painting, in which themes such as bamboos and plums predominate. The hanging scroll of *Plum blossom* (1759, Washington, Freer), in ink and colour on paper, is a typical example.

Joest van Calcar, Jan c.1450–1519
Netherlandish painter, probably born in Wesel but living in Calcar by 1480. His major work, *The life and Passion of Christ* (1505–08, Calcar, St Nicholas) has an impressive dignity, and in its delicate landscape and chiaroscuro effects carries echoes of Geertgen and Joos van Cleve. From 1509 to 1519 he worked in Haarlem.

John, Augustus 1878–1961
British painter. One of the most colourful figures of his generation, he was identified in the first quarter of the 20th century with all that was most rebellious in British art. Much of his early work was devoted to depictions of gypsy life, and from 1911 to 1919 he led a nomadic existence in Ireland, Dorset and his native Wales. Paintings of this period such as the Symbolist *The way down to the*

sea (1909–11, Exeter, New Hampshire, Lamont Art Gallery) show sympathy with the stylizations of advanced French art in their simplicity of colour and form. In his later work bravura often seemed to degenerate into bombast, but he could still be formidable as a portraitist, especially when the subject suited his style, as in *Marchesa Casati* (1919, Ontario Art Gallery), a wild red-haired beauty. See vol. 3 p. **154**; vol. 4 p. *131*

John, Gwen 1876–1939
British painter, sister of Augustus John. She studied at Whistler's studio in Paris, the city in which she lived for most of her life. The very opposite, both artistically and in personality, of her exuberant brother, she shunned any publicity and worked in muted, almost monochromatic tones on a small scale. She painted portraits of young girls, posed against a neutral background, quiet and self-absorbed, and her *Self-portrait* in the same format. During her life her work was little appreciated, though her brother was not alone in believing that her painting surpassed his. See vol. 3 p. **154**

Johns, Jasper born 1930
American painter, printmaker and sculptor, an outstanding figure in post-1945 art. He began in an ABSTRACT EXPRESSIONIST mode, but after meeting Rauschenberg and the avantgarde composer John Cage his approach altered radically. The first *Target* and *Flag* paintings date from 1954–55. They are emblematic and flat and painted in a flourishing Abstract Expressionist manner, sometimes with wax encaustic to emphasize texture. In *Target with four faces* (1955, New York, MOMA), the flat target is combined enigmatically with plaster casts of faces. These seemingly representational works indicate the extremely self-conscious, ironic directions American art would take in the next decades; Johns is often seen as the father of POP art and a forerunner of CONCEPTUAL art. His sculptures—beer-cans, a flashlight, a can of paint-brushes—are all highly realistic in detail and scale. Paintings of the 1960s and early 1970s frequently incorporate real objects: they are large and complex canvases featuring a mesh of verbal and visual contradictions which raise questions about artistic preconceptions. His latest paintings and prints, in which the disturbingly awkward juxtapositions have been eliminated, highlight his virtuoso technical abilities and growing subtlety. See vol. 1 pp. *75, 140*; vol. 3 p. **236**

Johnson or **Jonson, Cornelius**
(Janssens van Ceulen) 1593–1661
English portrait painter and oil miniaturist. He was born in London of Dutch parents, and possibly trained in Holland. From 1617 until his departure for Holland in 1643 he produced an unbroken series of signed and dated portraits, of sound craftsmanship, delicate sense of colour, and shy characterization. He often used the short half-length in a feigned stone oval. *The Capel family* (c.1639, London, NPG) is his most ambitious work.

Johnson, Eastman 1824–1906
American portrait and genre painter, born in Maine and trained in Düsseldorf, The Hague and Paris. He returned to America in 1855 and had his first popular success in 1859 with *Old Kentucky home* (New York Historical Society), a typically detailed, naturalistic and sentimental picture. Later works feature luminous landscapes with figures, and vivid portraits. See vol. 3 p. **124**

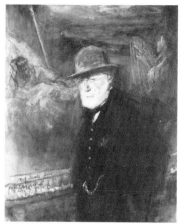

Israëls: Self-portrait watercolour, 1908. Toledo Museum of Art

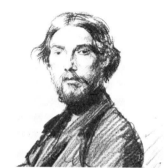

John, Augustus: Self-portrait drawing, c.1901. London, NPG

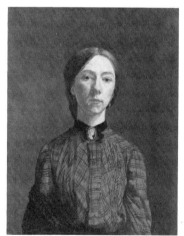

John, Gwen: Self-portrait, c.1899–1900. London, Tate

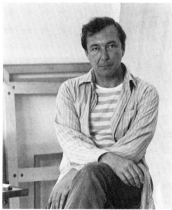

Johns: Photograph courtesy of Leo Castelli, New York

Johnston, Frank 1888–1949 see GROUP OF SEVEN

Jones, Allen born 1937
British painter and sculptor. He was associated with POP art in the early 1960s although his relationship to commercial sources lay in his bright, synthetic colour as opposed to his subject matter. *Battle of Hastings* (1961–62, London, Tate) was a tribute to the pioneering abstracts of Kandinsky and tried to recapture the Russian artist's sense of open space and improvisation. In later works he has treated the female figure superrealistically within colourful semi-abstract settings with fetishistic accompaniments such as high-heeled shoes or leather gear (as in the ensemble of figures *Hatstand, table, chair*, 1969, Aachen, Neue Galerie). He has been frequently attacked for presenting woman as an object. See vol. 3 p. **241**

Jones, Arne 1914–76
Swedish sculptor. He worked as a stone-mason before training at the Stockholm College of Art. His work was marked by an awareness of space and environment, as is evident in his *Cathedral* (1948, Norrköping Museum), a soaring rib construction suggestive of human forms. His fountain designed for the Norrköping Museum in the 1950s employs a characteristic spiral form.

Jones, David 1895–1974
British painter, writer and calligrapher. His work, mostly in pencil and delicate watercolour, includes references to Catholic symbolism and Arthurian legend and often has a mystical quality (*Chalice with flowers and pepperpot*, c.1950, London, Tate). During the 1920s he worked with Gill.

Jones, Inigo 1573–1652
British architect, stage designer, draughtsman and painter. He is principally famous for revolutionizing English architecture by introducing a fully mature classical style to a still half Gothic country, but he is first recorded as a "picture-maker" in 1603, and he was the finest British draughtsman of his time. His drawings for court masques (more than 450 of them are at Chatsworth House, Derbyshire) show his inventiveness as a costume and set designer as well as his lively style, developed during his two journeys to Italy, one of them in company with Arundel. His immense prestige as Charles I's artistic expert helped to raise the status of the visual arts in England. His greatest building is the Banqueting House (1619–22) in Whitehall, London, for which Rubens provided ceiling paintings.

Jones, Thomas 1742–1803
British landscapist in oil and watercolour, noted chiefly for his spirited oil-sketches made in and around Rome and Naples. Although oil-sketching in the open air had been practised in Italy since the 17th century, Jones' are the earliest British examples to survive in any quantity. He lived in Italy from 1776 to 1783 and left a lively account of his stay there (published 1948). There is a good collection of his works in Cardiff (National Museum of Wales).

Jongkind, Johan Barthold
1819–91
Dutch painter and etcher who spent much of his life in France, and was an important precursor of Impressionism. He studied in The Hague under Schelfhout, but it was L.G.E. Isabey who persuaded him to visit France in 1846. His studies of the Normandy coast, made directly from nature, capture light and movement with even more spontaneity than the Barbizon school painters, with whom he exhibited. He moved frequently between France and Holland, painting both street scenes and seascapes, and it was the freshness of his sketches which particularly impressed Boudin and the young Monet. Jongkind also made many fine etchings, recording atmospheric effects in broken, delicate line. Although he was acclaimed by such critics as Baudelaire and the Goncourts, he lived on the verge of poverty, aggravated by mental instability and alcoholism, and died destitute. See vol. 3 p. 98

Jordaens, Jacob (Jacques)
1593–1678
Flemish painter, etcher and tapestry designer, the leading figure-painter in Flanders after the death of Rubens. He was the pupil of Adam van Noort, whose daughter he married in 1616. His style is based on Rubens, but Jordaens is much more down-to-earth, using stronger, often harsh, chiaroscuro and thicker impasto. From the early 1620s he had a large and prosperous workshop in Antwerp, but also often assisted Rubens, as with the paintings for Philip IV's Torre de la Parade in Madrid, 1636/7. His prolific output included altarpieces, portraits and genre and mythological scenes, and although he rarely left Antwerp he received numerous commissions from outside Flanders. The most notable was from Amalia van Solms, widow of the Stadtholder Frederik Hendrik, for whom Jordaens painted *The triumph of Frederik Hendrik* for the Huis ten Bosch, her villa near The Hague (1652, *in situ*). See vol. 2 p. **201**

Jorn, Asger 1914–73
Danish painter and engraver. In the 1930s he was influenced by Klee and Ensor and inspired by Negro masks and tribal art. He studied briefly under Léger in Paris, 1936, and collaborated with Le Corbusier at the Paris International Exhibition in 1937. Returning to Denmark and reacting against the cool classicism of the Paris school, Jorn developed an increasingly bold and expressive style, and in 1948 became a founder-member and a dominant figure in the COBRA group. He settled in Paris in 1955. During the late 1950s and 1960s he painted highly coloured abstracts, executed with savage brushwork, and also experimented with automatism. *Green ballet* (1960, New York, Solomon R. Guggenheim Museum), with its wild implosion of smeared and textured colour, is a fitting reflection of an exuberant personality. See vol. 1 p. *151*

Josephson, Ernst 1851–1906
Swedish painter and draughtsman. He studied in Stockholm, Holland, Italy, Spain and France. During the early 1880s, he came in contact with Impressionism, but was also interested in Nordic nature myths, which inspired a series in the 1870s and early 1880s, for instance the colourful and fresh *Water sprite* in Prince Eugen's Palace, Stockholm. In 1888 he became mentally deranged, but was intensely productive in a less realistic, more playful manner.

Jouvenet, Jean 1644–1717
French history painter. He worked in Lebrun's studio in the 1660s, and his decorations in the Salon de Mars at Versailles (1671–74) are entirely in his master's manner. His later style, well represented by the huge *Miraculous draught of fishes* (before 1706, Paris, Louvre) is in a more Baroque idiom, though one deriving ultimately from the late works of Raphael rather than from Rubens. Although his work was soundly academic, he placed unusual emphasis on observation from nature.

Juanes, Juan de 1523–79
Spanish painter, son of Juan Vicente Masip. He was the leading painter of his generation in Valencia and in an individual way combined elements from the Italian high Renaissance (first introduced into Valencia by Yañez and Llanos) with a meticulous Flemish technique. His most significant works, the five paintings relating the *Life of St Stephen* (Madrid, Prado), are carefully wrought compositions that today appear impaired by their exaggerated figures.

Judd, Donald born 1928
American sculptor, a CONCEPTUAL artist who came to prominence in the mid-1960s. He aims to make basic statements about form and order, believing "A shape, a volume, a colour, a surface is something in itself," and should become the subject of a work of art. Much of his work consists of boxes or other solid geometric units, fabricated in metal or metal and plexiglass and often painted; more recently he has begun using plywood. He places these units on the floor in simple rows or displays them in vertical or horizontal progressions (*Untitled*, 1965, New York, Henry Geldzahler coll.). See vol. 3 p. **247**

Juel, Jens 1745–1802
One of the leading Danish painters of the 18th century, principally famous as a portraitist. He studied in Hamburg and from 1772 to 1780 travelled throughout Europe, enjoying distinguished patronage wherever he went. Returning to Copenhagen, he was appointed court painter in 1782 and in 1784 Professor at the Academy, where Friedrich and Runge were among his pupils. Apart from portraits, Juel also painted still lifes, genre scenes, and landscapes (*The Little Belt, seen from a height near Middlefart*, c.1800, Copenhagen, Thorvaldsens Museum). His delicate, highly sensitive style marks a transition from Rococo to Biedermeier. See vol. 3 p. **74**

Jugendstil
German term for ART NOUVEAU, deriving from the review *Die Jugend*, founded in 1896 in Munich.

Junayd Naggash al-Sultani
active 1396
Persian or eastern Turkish painter, the first to whom a picture can be given with certainty. His signature, with an epithet indicating his status as a royal servant, appears in the *Masnavi* of *Khwaju Kirmani* of 1396 (London, BL), a work produced in Baghdad for Sultan Ahmad Jalayr. Junayd's style ushers in the smaller figures and a sweeter colour range typical of the 15th century. His compositions are complex, with accents most carefully placed, though the impression is of freshness and romance.

Juní, Juan de c.1510–77
Spanish sculptor, born in Burgundy, with Alonso Berruguete the greatest sculptor of 16th-century Spain. He appears to have visited Rome and worked in Oporto (1531–32). In 1533 he is recorded in Leon, and by 1541 had settled in Valladolid. His individual style, which stems from his training in Burgundy and Italy, combines a strong emotive quality, expressive of the fervent spiritual atmosphere of Spain in his time, with an almost aristocratic grace. Among his outstanding works are two versions of *The Lamentation* (1539–44, Valladolid, National Museum of Sculpture, and 1571, Segovia Cathedral).

Junk art
20th-century art form in which urban debris is used for both aesthetic and polemical purposes. It might be called the modern still life. Junk art was first seriously attempted by Schwitters in the 1920s and developed out of the Cubist experiments with collage. In the 1950s the idea was revived and developed in Europe and the USA in the assemblages of Rauschenberg, Nevelson and Paolozzi and also featured in the Happenings of Kaprow and others.

Juran active c.960–80
Chinese painter, a contemporary of Dong Yuan at the court of Nanking. He was a cloistered Buddhist monk, painting monochrome ink landscapes. His particular importance lies in the fact that he lived on to work at the Northern Song court in Kaifeng, carrying the southern Tang tradition into the new dynasty. Such works as bear his name are Song or Yuan copies, showing the massive composition and careful brushwork believed in later times to be the characteristic feature of 10th-century painting.

Juste brothers see GIUSTI

Justus of Ghent (Joos van Wassenhove) active c.1460–after 1475
Netherlandish painter who also worked in Italy. He entered the painters' guild in Antwerp in 1460 and in 1464 became a master in Ghent, where he was a friend and associate of van der Goes. Two paintings are attributed to the late 1460s, *The Crucifixion* (Ghent, St Bavon) and *The Adoration of the Magi* (New York, Metropolitan). The style of these shows links with Dirk Bouts and Albert van Ouwater. From 1473 to 1475 Justus was in the service of Federigo da Montefeltro, Duke of Urbino, and *The Institution of the Eucharist* (1473–75, Urbino, Galleria Nazionale) was an important agent in the dissemination of Netherlandish technique in Italy. Justus was also commissioned, with Pedro Berruguete, to paint two series of figures for studios in the Ducal Palaces, *Famous Men* (c.1476, Paris, Louvre, and Urbino, Galleria Nazionale) and *Liberal Arts* (c.1480, London, NG). See vol. 2 pp. **97**, 113

K

Kaigetsudo, Ando active 1700–14
Japanese UKIYO-E artist. "Kaigetsudo" is the name of a print shop-cum-studio, famous for the mass production of prints and hand-painted designs of standing courtesans. The school was very popular for a short period, before its founder Ando was exiled in 1714, apparently after a palace scandal. Only hand-painted examples of his own work, of remarkably fine quality, survive. The style is distinguished by powerful contour brush-strokes and the *yamato-e*-like designs on the clothes. See vol. 3 p. **50**

Kakemono
Japanese term for long vertical scroll painting, about 76 cm (30 inches) high or taller, and about 25 cm (10 inches) wide. A horizontal scroll of these dimensions is called a **makemono**.

Kakuyu 1053–1140
Japanese painter, also known as Toba sojo, meaning "priest of Toba". He was a talented amateur whose activities ranged from restoring old Chinese-style religious paintings (such as the *Eight Shining Kings*, c.1120, Kyoto, Daigo temple) to making story-telling scroll paintings, done in a free, vivacious style which was the forerunner of *yamato-e*. The first two of the delightful *Frolicking animal* scrolls in the Kozan monastery in Kyoto are attributed to him.

Kalamis active c.475–450 BC
Greek sculptor of the early Classical period. According to ancient authors he was one of the greatest sculptors of the age, ranking with Myron and Pythagoras, but it is not possible to attribute any extant work to him.

Kalf, Willem 1619–93
Dutch painter, born in Rotterdam, perhaps the most celebrated of all still-life specialists. His early works were modest kitchen interiors and farmyard scenes, but he soon devoted himself to the richer still lifes which enjoyed a lasting vogue—pictures of gold vessels, glassware, porcelain and fine rugs. After a stay in Paris, 1642–46, he settled in Hoorn and then in Amsterdam, in 1653. *Still life with a nautilus cup* (c.1660, Lugano, Thyssen coll.) is a splendid example of his mastery of delicate highlights and rich colour schemes painted against deep, dark backgrounds. The chiaroscuro may owe something to Rembrandt, while the exquisite yellow-blue contrast of the lemon peel and china bowl (favourite Kalf motifs) and the rich texture of the carpet recall Vermeer. Kalf's marvellous painterly skills, however, never obscure the noble grandeur of his compositions. See vol. 2 p. **233**

Kalinowski, Horst Egon born 1924
West German artist, since 1950 resident in Paris. Starting as an abstract painter, he moved towards collage, incorporating diverse materials, and then made glass-topped boxes like reliquaries containing found objects. His *caissons*, wall-hung leather-covered boxes, were non-objective but often included forms suggestive of the human anatomy. Their poetic titles add to a deliberate air of mystery and many are intended to evoke the function of the sexually-charged fetishes of primitive cultures. The *stelae* are similar but free-standing constructions, while in his *ensachements*, pendulously-shaped sacks, he entirely abandons hard-edged geometrical forms.

Kandinsky, Wassily 1866–1944
Russian-born painter, one of the most prominent pioneers of abstract art in the early 20th century. He gave up a career in law to study painting in Munich, and settled there in 1896. After participating in various avantgarde exhibitions he organized his own show with Franz Marc, Der BLAUE REITER (The Blue Rider), in 1911. By this time he had passed through Art Nouveau and Fauvist styles, and had established his personal expression, at first in highly-coloured semi-abstract work (*Blue mountain, no. 84*, 1908, New York, Guggenheim) and then in the series of *Compositions*, *Improvisations* and *Impressions* which are often claimed to be the first purely abstract paintings. In 1912 he published his famous statement *Concerning the Spiritual in Art*, expressing his belief in non-objective art based on the harmony of colour and form, and revealing the influence of Theosophy and mysticism on his thinking. Widely exhibited both in

Europe and Russia, his first abstract paintings were not immediately imitated, but they provided a strong stimulus for many artists seeking a way towards abstract art. After a brief return to Russia (1917–20), where he inaugurated a teaching programme for art schools, Kandinsky emigrated and taught in Germany at the Bauhaus, first in Weimar and then in Dessau, whence his pupils spread his ideas to Europe and America. In 1933 he settled in France, where he continued to develop the formal, geometric style he had begun after leaving Russia in 1920. His essays, including *Reminiscences* (1913) and *Point and Line to Plane* (1926), are among the classics of 20th-century artists' writings. See vol. 1 pp. *132, 161*; vol. 3 pp. **138–141**, *158*, **190**

Kändler, Johann Joachim 1706–75
German sculptor, the most celebrated of all porcelain modellers. He was chief modeller at the Meissen factory near Dresden from 1733 until his death, and the factory's world-wide success (its influence was felt even in China) owed much to his brilliance. His Rococo style was marked by great vivacity, delicacy and wit, and his animals and birds, based on sketches he made in a zoo, are particularly spirited. He often worked on a large scale, but had to abandon his greatest project, a monument to Augustus III of Saxony featuring a life-size equestrian figure. Kändler's work is in many museums, notably the Porzellansammlung, Dresden. See vol. 1 p. *185*

Kane, John 1860–1934
American NAIVE painter. Born in Scotland, he emigrated to America in 1879. He took up painting in his spare time and at the age of 67 had his work shown in an important exhibition. From that time Kane's reputation grew. He painted reminiscences of childhood, townscapes and industrial scenes in a complex detailed manner (*The Monongahela Valley*, 1931, New York, Metropolitan).

Kane, Paul 1810–71
Canadian painter, born in Ireland. From 1846 to 1848 he travelled in Canada under the auspices of the Hudson Bay Company, producing a remarkable series of sketches. These resulted in his first Indian canvases, painted in his Toronto studio. One, *The man that always rides* (1849–55, Toronto, Royal Ontario Museum), seems an imaginary work with its orchestrated drama in the tradition of European Romanticism. He published accounts of his travels and died a legendary figure.

Kang Hui-an 1419–65
Korean amateur painter, scholar-official in the reign of King Sejong (1418–50). He was Second Counsellor of the Hall of Worthies (*Chiphyonjon*), a centre of scholarly and scientific inquiry which was famous for poetry, calligraphy, and painting. He travelled to Peking and was influenced by the Southern Song Academy style. *Contemplating the water* (Seoul, National Museum) displays his characteristically broad, swift brush-line. See vol. 3 pp. **42–43**

Kanoldt, Alexander 1881–1939
German painter. After an early Cubist phase, he was influenced by the classicism of Derain and Carrà. From this he developed the highly stylized, architectonic realism which has come to be associated with NEUE SACHLICHKEIT. Objects are depicted with absolute precision and clarity, the sense of immediacy

being further strengthened by the use of a dominant unifying colour, as in *Still life with guitar* (1926, Stuttgart, Staatsgalerie). In a series of Italian landscapes this objectivity was imbued with a sense of Romantic idealism.

Kano school
School of Japanese painting founded by Kano Masanobu in the mid-15th century. Masanobu served under the Shogun in Kyoto and developed the ink-painting style traditionally associated with Zen monk-painters. His school was firmly established by his son Kano Motonobu, and with the official support of the shogunate it persisted into the 19th century and exercised a considerable influence on Japanese art. The characteristic Kano ink style is linear, sharply defined and finely balanced in composition; the subjects are those of the Chinese ink-painters. Among the greatest members of the school was Eitoku, active in the 16th century when the school was at its zenith. See vol. 3 pp. **46–47**

Kantor, Tadeusz born 1915
Polish artist. His work has been very varied and he is considered one of the leaders of Polish avantgarde art. He moved from Expressionist paintings during the 1940s to work influenced by Matta and then by Tachisme. In the 1960s, under the influence of Pop art, he began to make assemblages (or *emballages*) which explored the idea of packaging. They incorporated real objects, such as the umbrella in *Emballages, objects, personages* (1969, Cracow, National Museum). He organized Poland's first Happenings and was involved in experimental theatre; more recently he has worked in the field of Conceptual art.

Kao K'o-kung see GAO KEGONG

Kaprow, Allan born 1927
American artist and theorist, best known as the inventor of HAPPENINGS. Abstract Expressionism, with its emphasis on the act of painting, was a vital early influence, and studies with the composer John Cage, who uses notions of chance and randomness in his music, encouraged Kaprow to venture further into the realm of unconventional aesthetics. He moved from painting to elaborate assemblages and in 1957–58 began to create ENVIRONMENTAL works. The first Happening—*Eighteen happenings in six parts* (October 1959, New York)—provided a loosely planned framework of time and space in which participants acted out fantasies and responded spontaneously to incidents as they occurred. Since 1960, he has devoted himself to promoting this new art form in the USA and Europe. Segal, Oldenburg, Samaras and others cite Kaprow as a crucial formative influence. See vol. 3 p. **242**

Karfiol, Bernard 1886–1952
American painter, born in Hungary. As a student in Paris he was influenced by Matisse and Picasso but as his work matured it grew more conservative. He is best known for his nude studies which, like *Seated nude* (1929, New York, MOMA), reveal a great debt to Renoir.

Karnak
Site of vast complex of Egyptian temples in the area of Thebes, one of the greatest religious complexes of antiquity. Of the MIDDLE KINGDOM, the famous Kiosk of Senusert I (1971–1929 BC) contains exquisitely cut hieroglyphic texts in low relief. In the NEW KINGDOM an intensive period of building was launched by King Thuthmosis I (1525–

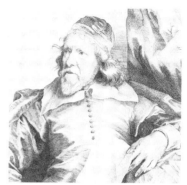
Jones, Inigo: Engraving after the drawing by van Dyck, c.1640 (Mansell)

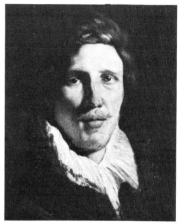
Jordaens: Self-portrait, c.1615–18. Florence, Uffizi (Scala)

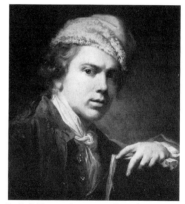
Juel: Self-portrait, c.1775. Copenhagen, Statens Museum for Kunst

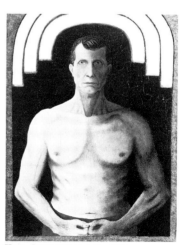
Kane, John: Self-portrait, 1929. New York, MOMA

1512 BC), Queen Hatshepsut (1503–1482 BC) and Thuthmosis III (1505–1450 BC). The great temple of Amun (the principal state god of the New Kingdom) was enlarged and a series of pylons (gateways consisting of two mighty uprights—first appearing in the Middle Kingdom) added by several rulers. Obelisks (tall, tapering pillars) of rose-coloured granite and colossal statues were also built. The vast complex is approached through an avenue of sphinxes built by Ramesses II (1304–1237 BC). The Hypostyle Hall, built by Seti I (1318–1304 BC) and Ramesses II, was originally resplendent with 134 closely-spaced floral columns with brightly painted incised relief decoration. See vol. 2 pp. 26–27

Karsten, Ludvig 1876–1926
Norwegian painter living in Copenhagen from 1907. He was one of the few close followers of Munch, and early works, such as *The consumptive* (1907, Oslo, NG), reflect Munch's intense and dramatic approach. Karsten, however, tended increasingly to dissolve form in strong and vivid colours.

Kassák, Lajos 1887–1967
Hungarian-born painter, sculptor and writer. From 1910 he was a central figure in cultural life in Budapest before moving to Vienna, where he wrote concrete poetry, made collages, sculpted, and from 1924 produced architectural models. Returning to Hungary, he became an important figure among young avantgarde Hungarian artists. After World War II he worked mainly as an organizer of cultural events. He returned to painting in the 1950s and became the main inspiration for Hungarian HARD-EDGE abstractionists.

Kauffmann, Angelica 1741–1807
Swiss NEOCLASSICAL painter. She travelled with her father in Italy from an early age and in 1766 went to England. There she began as a fashionable portraitist, but branched out to paint pioneering pictures illustrating Homer, Shakespeare and English history, which nonetheless retain a Rococo prettiness. The architect Robert Adam often employed her to decorate the houses he designed. She was the darling of Reynolds and a founder-member of the Royal Academy. After an unfortunate first marriage, in 1781 she married the painter Antonio Zucchi (1726–95) and left England to spend most of the rest of her life as a prominent figure in Roman artistic society. Reynolds, Winckelmann and Goethe sat for her. There is a collection of her works at Saltram Park, Devon. See vol. 4 p. *189*

Kaulbach, Wilhelm von 1805–74
German painter in the heroic and Romantic style of the Munich school of history painting. A fine example is the fresco *World history* executed in the 1840s (Berlin, Neues Museum). His highly idealistic paintings, with their theatrical lighting, completely disregarded the move towards naturalism that Leibl and his Munich circle were achieving in the 1860s and 1870s. Kaulbach was immensely popular during his life, and dominated the Academy.

Kaus, Max born 1891
German painter and etcher. He turned to fine art after meeting Heckel during World War I, and developed a style fusing an expressive tendency with a desire to create decorative surface patterns (*Self-portrait in blue jacket*, 1925, Berlin, Brücke Museum).

Kawaguchi, Tatsuo born 1940
Japanese artist. In 1965 he organized a group of artists questioning the basis of art and he began to make Environmental works using the energy of light and electricity (*Interrelation energy*, 1972, Artist's coll.). Recently he has made more sculptural work of lead lumps.

Kawara, On born 1933
Japanese CONCEPTUAL artist. In his striking *Bathroom* and *Lumber Closet* paintings of 1953–54 he created telling images of the Japanese predicament after World War II—wrecked human beings in claustrophobic interiors. In 1959 he left Japan and travelled in the USA, Mexico and Europe, settling in New York in 1965. A number of series in the 1960s, *Date painting*, *I met* and *I went*, illustrate an obsession with the passing of time day by day and with the artists's continued existence. There are also series of *I got up* and *I am still alive* postcards and telegrams, sent to friends from many places. See vol. 3 p. **246**

Kelly, Ellsworth born 1923
American painter. He employs regular, irregular, geometric and curved formats, sometimes with multiple panels (for example *Blue, green, yellow, orange, red*, 1966, New York, Guggenheim). His preferred pigments, applied in a flat, uniform manner, are bright colours, black and white and, more recently, shades of grey. His large, simple, hardedged forms are derived from nature—both the shape of the canvas and the divisions within each composition—rather than geometry. His work with positive and negative space and with shape extends into three dimensions and in the late 1970s his experience with metals has informed his "painting". The colour and texture of large flat panels of steel, hung on the wall like canvases, derives from rust impressions in the metal. See vol. 3 p. **223**

Kemény, Zoltán 1907–65
Hungarian-Swiss sculptor and designer. In the 1930s he became renowned as a designer of wrought-iron household articles and also as a couturier but after World War II he began work on collages using material such as sand, iron slag and dried vegetables. In the 1950s he produced a striking series of electrically lit kinetic reliefs and later metallic mural reliefs which are among the most powerful organic abstractions produced in the post-War period (*Zephyr*, 1964, Paris, Mme Kemény coll.).

Kennington, Eric 1888–1960
British sculptor and painter. The *Monument to the 24th Division* (1924, London, Battersea Park) has a compact, dignified form, far from the sentimental imagery or pedantic details of most British war memorials of the period. His smaller scale, more personal sculptures such as *The earth child* (c.1936, London, Tate) reflect the influence of Gill. He was an official artist in both World Wars.

Kensett, John Frederick 1816–72
American landscape painter, a follower of Cole and a member of the HUDSON RIVER school. He is noted for his serene and luminous open vistas (*Along the Hudson*, 1852, Washington, Smithsonian). From 1840 to 1848 he worked in Italy, Germany and England, and thereafter sought inspiration within the United States.

Kent, Rockwell 1882–1971
American painter and illustrator. He studied under Henri, 1903–04, and organized an Exhibition of Independent Artists in 1910 with him. Kent's early work, such as the vigorously painted *The road roller* (1909, Washington, Phillips coll.), reflects the Ashcan school's concern with depicting American life. However, he is best remembered for his black and white illustrations, such as those in his book *Voyaging Southward* (1924), which depend on flowing lines and contrasting tones to express feelings of isolation and tension. He went on several scientific expeditions, enabling him to paint scenes of Alaska and Patagonia.

Kent, William 1685(?)–1748
British architect, interior designer, landscape gardener and painter. Painting was the first but least important of his activities. He studied painting in Rome, where he had gone in 1709 as an agent to buy pictures, and was brought back to England in 1719 by his patron Lord Burlington, who gained him commissions for decorative murals in Burlington House and Kensington Palace, London. By about 1725, however, he had given up painting for architecture.

Kenzan, Ogata 1663–1743
Japanese potter and painter. His elder brother Korin decorated some of his pottery. He formulated a method of firing which came to be known as Kenzan-*yaki*, and painted many pots with his own poems. As a devotee of the tea ceremony, he made tea bowls which were avidly collected by other enthusiasts; many survive. Two of his paintings have been designated Important Cultural Properties of Japan—an eight-fold screen, *Bridge on the iris pond*, and *Mynah bird*, in the Egawa Art Museum. See vol. 3 p. 47

Kephisodotos
active early 4th century BC
Greek sculptor from Athens, probably the father of Praxiteles. No original work survives, but a group of *Eirene holding the infant Ploutos*, generally attributed to him, is known in Roman copies. If this work is indeed by Kephisodotos and is as early as 375 BC, then in both its conception as an allegory of peace and wealth and in the technique of its deeply cut drapery it heralds the manner in which 4th-century sculpture was to develop: the composition and the subtle interaction of the two figures suggest the work of Praxiteles himself. Praxiteles' son was also a sculptor named **Kephisodotos**, active around 300 BC. With his brother, **Timarchos**, Kephisodotos the Younger was responsible for statues on the altar of the Asclepeion on Cos, fragments of which reveal a delicate, sensuous and emotive style. A fine portrait head of *Menander* (Boston, MFA), may be a copy from a seated statue which the brothers made for the theatre at Athens.

Kersting, Georg Friedrich
1785–1847
German painter. He studied in Copenhagen, 1805–08, and then moved to Dresden, where he was closely associated with Friedrich, of whom he painted two portraits. In 1818 he became director of the painting department of the Meissen china factory. His art, especially his portraits in interiors, for example, *Man reading by lamplight* (1814, Winterthur, Oskar Reinhart Foundation), combines the yearning and melancholy mood of Romanticism with the meticulous observation and detail of Biedermeier. See vol. 3 p. *77*

Kessel, Jan van 1626–79
Flemish still-life and flower-painter. He is most noted for small paintings, often on copper, of insects or shells, highly finished in the manner of his grandfather, "Velvet" Brueghel. He was popular and prolific: the Prado, Madrid, has 40 of his paintings, and there are many in the Fitzwilliam, Cambridge, and the Ashmolean, Oxford.

Key, Willem c.1515–68
Netherlandish painter. He was apprenticed to Coecke in Antwerp in about 1529 before moving to Liège to study under Lambert. In 1542, he entered the Antwerp guild as a master. His *Susannah and the Elders* (Pommersfelden, Gemäldegalerie), with its Roman sarcophagus and sphinx, shows the antiquarian influence of Lambert, but Key earned a wider reputation as a portraitist. Although overshadowed in this field by Floris and Mor, he gained important commissions from Hapsburg court circles and his portrait of the Duke of Alva (1568, Madrid, Alva Palace) is in the arch, correct style that won him popularity. His nephew **Adriaen** (c.1544–after 1589) was a fine portraitist.

Keyser, Hendrik de 1565–1621
The leading Dutch sculptor and architect of the early 17th century, active mainly in Amsterdam. His most important work as a sculptor is the tomb of Prince William I (began 1614) in the Niewe Kerk, Delft. He is perhaps best known, however, for his sober realistic portrait busts (*Unknown man*, 1608, Amsterdam, Rijksmuseum). His most important work as an architect is the Westerkerk in Amsterdam (begun 1620), and several of his church towers are still landmarks in the city. Nicholas Stone was his major pupil. Two of Hendrik's sons, **Pieter** (1595–1676) and **Willem** (1603–c.1674) were also sculptors, mainly of monuments.

Keyser, Thomas de 1596/7–1667
Dutch portrait painter and architect, the son of Hendrik. He spent all his life in Amsterdam where, with Eliasz., he was the leading portraitist before the arrival of Rembrandt in the winter of 1631–32. Inevitably his work has suffered from comparison with Rembrandt's, and his *Anatomy lesson of Dr Sebastian Egbertsz.* (1619, Amsterdam, Rijksmuseum) looks stiff and posed next to Rembrandt's famous *Anatomy lesson of Dr Tulp*. De Keyser was at his best on a small scale, as in his portrait of *Constantijn Huygens* (1627, London, NG), which looks forward to the 18th-century conversation piece. In his later years he introduced a new type, the small equestrian portrait (*Pieter Schout*, 1660, Amsterdam, Rijksmuseum). He was city architect for Amsterdam from 1662 until his death.

Khajuraho
Capital of the Chandella dynasty of Jejabhukti in the Madhya Pradesh province of India, famous for its temple sculpture. A group of some 25 temples, datable 950–1050, survives. The main temples—Kandarya, Mahadeva, Lakshmana, Visvanatha and Devi Jagadamba—have at least two and sometimes three bands of sculpture, half life-size, running round the assembly hall and the shrine, depicting the gods in their various iconic manifestations and the *Apsaras*, or nymphs of heaven, in the most alluring poses, as well as scenes of explicit eroticism. In all these the human form is deftly stylized with brittle, tapering limbs combined with voluptuous female curves, sharp pointed features and elongated eyes. See vol. 3 pp. 18–19

Khalil Mirza Shahrukhi
active *c.* 1420–30
Persian or eastern Turkish painter working in Herat for the great bibliophile Shah Rukh (1405–46), son of Tamurlane. No extant works are known, but several are recorded, including a *Battle between Timur and Tuqtamish Khan*, which was owned by the Mughal Emperor Jehangir.

Khnopff, Fernand 1858–1921
Belgian SYMBOLIST painter, illustrator and sculptor. He studied in Brussels and later with Moreau and Delacroix in Paris, and was also influenced by the Pre-Raphaelites, especially Rossetti and Burne-Jones. A founder member of Les VINGT, he was closely connected with other members of the group, such as Ensor and Toorop. He belonged to the Rose + Croix and illustrated several of Péladan's books. His paintings are mainly of the Symbolists' ideal woman in her guise either of sphinx or angel, as in two well-known works, *The caress* (1896) and *The silence* (1890), both in the Musées Royaux des Beaux-Arts, Brussels. See vol. 1 p. *51*; vol. 3 p. **123**

Kienholz, Edward born 1927
American sculptor. Since 1961 Kienholz, who began as a painter, has created three-dimensional tableaux. These life-sized environments include real objects, plaster or plastic figures and once even a canary. His subjects—street bums, hospital rooms, American small town scenes—are generally infused with the artist's bitter disapproval of the superficiality and materialism of American life. The *Portable war memorial* (1968, Cologne, Wallraf-Richartz Museum), which includes a working coke machine, a recorded version of *God bless America*, and a hot dog stand, also has a blackboard which can be inscribed according to where the piece is exhibited. See vol. 1 pp. *49, 192–193*; vol. 3 p. **242**

Kim Chong-hi 1786–1856
Korean painter and calligrapher, a prominent scholar in archaeology. At the age of 24 he accompanied his father to Peking on a government mission, and met Chinese scholars. He painted in Chinese-style monochrome ink (a fine example is *Orchid* in the Chun Hyong-pil collection in Seoul) and became famous for his own vigorous calligraphic style.

Kim Hong-do 1745–*c.*1818
Korean painter, with Chong Son one of the major exponents of the typical Korean landscape style. He was also proficient in figure, flower and animal painting, and humorous, realistic genre scenes. His work, both albums and paintings, is well represented in the National Museum, Seoul.

Kim Myong-guk born 1600
Professional Korean court painter. His landscape and figure paintings were influenced by Chinese Ming work, but he established his own style, which was dominated by a bold, energetic brushline (*Bodhi dharma*, Seoul National Museum). Between 1636 and 1643 he made several visits to Japan as a diplomat, and left many paintings there.

Kinetic art
Term broadly used to describe art which incorporates real or apparent movement using artificial light, optical illusion or a motor. It has been used to define works as dissimilar as Calder's mobiles and Julio Le Parc's reflected lights. Their chief characteristic is a concern with temporality and the movement of forms in space. These concerns were fostered by the "accelerated Impressionism" of Futurism and the experiments of the Constructivists in the 1920s. Duchamp's *Rotative plaques* (1920, New Haven, Yale University Art Gallery) and Moholy-Nagy's *Light-space modulation* (1922–30, Harvard University, Busch-Reisinger Museum) anticipated the more recent work of Takis and Tinguely. Takis uses the possibilities of magnetism and Tinguely those of electric motors to produce Kinetic sculptures. In its widest sense Kinetic art may encompass Happenings and any art form that invites the spectator to take part. See vol. 3 pp. 244–245

King, Phillip born 1934
British sculptor. In the 1960s he followed the example of Caro in making large-scale coloured abstract sculpture. He worked in synthetic materials such as plastic or fibreglass to gain a smooth impersonal surface as opposed to the expressive, pitted textures common in sculpture of the 1950s. Sometimes, as in *Rosebud* (1962, New York, MOMA), the sculpture is a compact cone-shape. In his other pieces the components are physically separate and unified only by subtle visual rhythms. More recent works such as *Within* (1978–79, London, Tate) have a rugged appearance through the use of materials such as slate and wood.

Kiprensky, Orest Adamovich
1782–1836
One of the leading Russian painters of the Romantic period. He studied in St Petersburg, then worked around Moscow until 1816, when he went to Italy. In 1823 he went back to Russia, but returned to Italy in 1828 and remained in Rome until his death. His best works are his portraits, sometimes dashing, but often lyrical or melancholy in mood. There are examples of his work, including self-portraits, in the Russian Museum at Leningrad.

Kirchner, Ernst Ludwig
1880–1938
German EXPRESSIONIST painter and graphic artist. He studied painting in Munich and architecture in Dresden. In 1905, with Heckel and Schmidt-Rottluff, he founded Die BRÜCKE. He was influenced initially by Neo-Impressionism, and also by van Gogh, and in 1904 discovered the expressive possibilities of tribal sculpture in the Ethnographical Department of the Zwinger, Dresden. In his early paintings he used disquieting juxtapositions of brilliant colours combined with large, simple forms to express "feeling and experience" (*Self-portrait with model*, 1909–10, Hamburg, Kunsthalle). Influenced by both primitive and medieval prototypes, he achieved a similar intensity of feeling in his woodcuts and woodcarvings, characterized by aggressively incised contours and extreme distortion. In 1910 he moved to Berlin, where he depicted his reactions to life and strife in a big city in a series of paintings and woodcuts of cabaret dancers, circus performers and prostitutes (*The street*, 1913, New York, MOMA). These were executed in more sombre colours and with even more frenzied angularity. Conscripted in 1915, he was discharged after six months, suffering from tuberculosis, and moved to Switzerland in 1917. In the 1920s his pictures, many of them landscapes, gained in serenity and by 1930 had become semi-abstract. In 1937 the Nazis condemned him as a Degenerate artist and seized some 600 of his works. These events exacerbated his chronic depression and the following year he committed suicide. See vol. 3 p. **134**

Kisling, Moïse 1891–1953
French painter, born in Poland. He arrived in Paris in 1910 and soon came under the influence of Cubism. An exhibition in 1919 established him and thereafter, inspired by Derain, he contributed to the realist tendency in French painting of the 1920s (*Woman in a Polish shawl*, 1928, Paris, Musée d'Art Moderne).

Kitaj, Ron B. born 1932
American painter and printmaker who works in England, with Hockney a leader in the British POP art movement. His paintings, prints and mixed-media works, featuring celebrities, friends, American sports heroes and political figures, express both sociological issues and the artist's personal feelings (*Walter Lippmann*, 1966, Buffalo, Albright-Knox). He employs a collage method in his complex works, splicing together incidents, references to literary and philosophical texts and sometimes to art history. He paints in flat, soft-edged areas of bright colour, often on very large canvases. In the 1970s he became known as a champion of figurative, as opposed to abstract art. See vol. 3 pp. **240–241**

Kitsch
German word meaning vulgar or worthless, used for art objects, sometimes mass-produced, displaying bad taste, sentimentality and low artistic quality. The ambiguous state of kitsch reflects the instability of aesthetic values in 20th-century Western society.

Kivijärvi, Harry born 1931
Finnish sculptor. In the early 1960s he adopted a non-representational idiom, specializing in black granite or diabase (a kind of basalt) blocks with subtly curved smooth sides contrasting with the rough surfaces of the unworked stone.

Kiyohiro, Torii active 1750–76
Japanese UKIYO-E artist. Not much is known of Kiyohiro's life, except that he died young. Although he belonged to the Torii family, which specialized in actor prints, Kiyohiro excelled in the *bijin-ga* or pictures of beautiful women. His erotic prints are famous for their youthful energy. All remaining examples are *benizuri-ga*, prints coloured by a cruder method which preceded the polychromatic *nishiki-e* invented by Harunobu. An example is *Suruga-machi*, a view of a street in Edo (Tokyo).

Kiyonaga, Torii 1752–1815
Japanese UKIYO-E artist, the arch-rival of Utamaro. A native of Edo (Tokyo) and the son of a bookseller, he entered the Torii family of printmakers which specialized in theatre prints. Kiyonaga did not make theatrical prints, however. He played an important part in the development of the polychromatic *nishiki-e* into a major art form, and, after studying the works of such masters as Harunobu, Koryusai and Buncho, developed a masterly style, especially in *bijin-ga* (pictures of beautiful women). See vol. 3 p. **50**

Kiyooka, Roy born 1926
Canadian abstract painter. He made contact with Jock MacDonald before studying in Mexico in 1955, and subsequently developed a lyrical hard-edge idiom in large-scale colour paintings of primal appeal. *Barometer no.2* (1962, Toronto, Art Gallery of Ontario) set a standard for Vancouver painting in the 1960s, when he settled there.

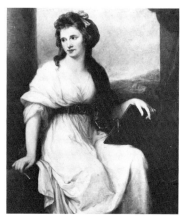
Kauffmann: Self-portrait, 1787. Florence, Uffizi (Scala)

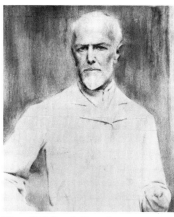
Khnopff: Self-portrait, 1918. Florence, Uffizi

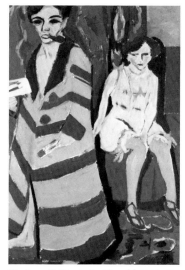
Kirchner: *Self-portrait with model*, 1909–10. Hamburg, Kunsthalle (Cooper-Bridgeman)

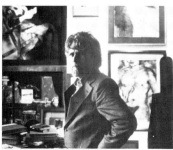
Kitaj: Photograph by Roger Perry/*The Sunday Times*

Kjarval, Johannes Sveinsson 1885–1972
Icelandic painter, originally a fisherman. He studied in England, where he was influenced by Turner, and in Copenhagen. Returning home in the 1920s, he painted the Icelandic mountains in a lyrically Expressionist style. His central motifs are moss and blown-up lava-blocks, for which he used a rich palette and vigorous brushwork akin to that of van Gogh.

Klapheck, Konrad born 1935
West German painter. He first made his reputation in 1955 with a precisely realistic painting of a typewriter, a motif which recurred frequently. His other motifs are also man-made objects, often household ones such as sewing-machines, which he invests with an extraordinary human significance. He does not, however, use them as symbols, but gives them an existence absurdly their own. The precision of rendering he sees, along with humour, as his principal weapon (*The mother-in-law*, 1967, Milan, Galleria Schwarz). Related to Surrealism and to Existentialism, his art can also be seen as a forerunner of early 1970s Superrealism.

Klee, Paul 1879–1940
Swiss painter and graphic artist, one of the most original and inventive artists of the 20th century. As a child he showed an aptitude for all the arts, especially music. He studied painting in Munich, 1898–1901, and then travelled in Italy. The years 1902–06 were spent in his native Berne, but he then moved back to Munich where, in 1911, he became involved with the artists of Der BLAUE REITER, in particular Marc, Macke and Kandinsky. He was influenced by the Cubists and Orphists in Paris in 1912 and made a visit to Tunisia with Macke and Moilliet in 1914. In 1920 he began his career as a teacher at the Bauhaus. He also taught at the Düsseldorf Academy in the early 1930s until he was dismissed by the Nazis, when he returned to Berne, remaining there until his death. Klee's early works were Symbolist, inspired by Ensor, and almost entirely black and white. He also painted on glass and achieved early fame as an engraver. After his meeting with Der Blaue Reiter and the visit to Tunisia he became concerned with the chromatic construction of pictures. He constantly absorbed the influences around him and his style ranged freely between abstraction and figuration; but his work is almost always immediately recognizable. His small, exquisitely painted canvases have often been likened to the work of children because of their apparent simplicity and and extreme unpretentiousness. In his last years, troubled by illness and the anticipation of war, his paintings became a little larger and more sombre in tone. No single work can illustrate his genius, but *The vocal fabric of the singer Rosa Silber* (1922, New York, MOMA) shows his inspired use of colour, his wit and the joyous spirit of his art. Klee was also an excellent teacher and writer on art. His son created the Felix Klee Foundation, Berne, which owns the largest collection of his works. See vol. 1 pp. *117*, *130*, *157*; vol. 3 pp. **136–137, 190, 192–193**

Klein, César 1876–1954
German painter and stage designer, a founder-member of the NOVEMBERGRUPPE in 1918. His early style was influenced by Die BRÜCKE but the 1920s saw the return to a calmer, more classical approach with an interest in creating decorative effects (*Spanish girl*, 1927, Pansdorf, Private coll.). In the 1920s he also executed many stage designs and large murals and mosaics. His later works became increasingly abstract.

Klein, Yves 1928–62
French painter, one of the most revolutionary artists in the period since World War II. His work constantly challenged accepted ideas. He studied oriental languages and worked as a jazz pianist and judo instructor (he won a black belt in Tokyo) and had no formal training as an artist. His bizarrely original works ranged from pictures produced with a blow-torch (*Fire-colour-picture*, 1962, New Orleans, Louisiana Museum) to his *Anthropometries*, a form of Action Painting in which he directed nude models pressing their paint-covered bodies against a plain canvas. His exhibition of empty rooms, *The void*, at the Galerie Iris Clert in Paris in 1958 almost caused a riot. Although Klein died young, his ideas exercised an enormous influence on other artists of his generation, such as Aubertin and Jean Tinguely. See vol. 3 pp. **242–243**

Kleitias 575–560 BC
Greek BLACK-FIGURE vase-painter from Athens, responsible, with the potter Ergotimos, for the famous volute *krater* in Florence known as the François Vase (*c.*570 BC, Museo Archeologico). The richness and invention of his design and the liveliness of his figure-drawing mark a shift away from the more static Corinthian style of vase decoration.

Kleophrades Painter (Epiktetos)
active *c.*500–480 BC
Greek RED-FIGURE vase-painter from Athens, a pupil of Euthymides. His nickname is used to avoid confusion with his namesake, Epiktetos the cup-painter. More than 100 vases have been assigned to him and he is regarded as one of the finest exponents of the red-figure technique. Though a superb draughtsman, he was less concerned than the previous generation with experimental poses and foreshortenings and preferred to develop the dramatic and expressive possibilities of his mythological scenes.

Klimt, Gustav 1862–1918
Austrian painter, a founder-member of the Vienna SEZESSION. After an Impressionist phase, his art showed an eclectic assimilation of English Pre-Raphaelitism, Toorop's Symbolism and Glasgow Art Nouveau, as can be seen in his regular early contributions to the Sezession's magazine *Ver Sacrum*. He created an expressionist, decadent art which combined grandiose feeling with refined form and allegorical subject matter. His paintings describe a neurotic and erotic world of nudes trapped in a brilliant and bejewelled background. His line is extremely mannered and he had an unusual gift for subtle colour chords and abstract ornamental forms. One of his most famous commissions was the mosaic mural for the Palais Stoclet in Brussels (finished by 1911, still *in situ*), influenced by Byzantine mosaics. His work influenced Schiele and Kokoschka. See vol. 1 pp. *162–163*; vol. 3 p. **121**

Kline, Franz 1910–62
American ABSTRACT EXPRESSIONIST painter. Until the late 1940s he produced impastoed cityscapes and landscapes, but in 1948, under the influence of De Kooning, he began painting and drawing more abstracted works. After seeing an enlarged projection of his drawings, he switched to large-scale paintings in which a broadly drawn black scaffolding divides its white ground into sections. *Chief* (1950, New York, MOMA), named after a train, combines rectilinear and curvilinear drawn marks, while other works suggest a more architectonic structure. The starkness of the black and white is modified by the dry brushing, scumbling and overpainting. During the late 1950s he began to paint in colour but his calligraphic black and white paintings are usually considered his best works. See vol. 3 p. **214**

Klinger, Max 1857–1920
German painter, sculptor and graphic artist. After early studies in Berlin and Brussels and several sojourns in Italy, he began evolving his own highly individualistic solutions to the conflict between fantasy and reality which he saw as one of the central issues in the rejuvenation of German art in the 1880s and 1890s. Under the influence of antique sculpture he began creating polychromatic figures, culminating in the Beethoven monument (1899–1902, Leipzig, Museum der Bildenden Künste), in which 17 different materials are used in the gigantic and heroically posed figure. He continued such experiments in large-scale paintings in which he incorporated the frame as a decorative element (*The Judgment of Paris*, 1885–87, Vienna, Neue Galerie). In retrospect his graphic work seems to have achieved his aims more successfully; cycles such as *Adventures of a Glove* of 1881 combine surreal symbols with erotic undercurrents which accurately express *fin-de-siècle* romanticism and disenchantment.

Klucis (Klutsis), **Gustave**
1895–1944
Latvian painter. He studied art in Riga and St Petersburg before moving permanently to Moscow in 1918. First as a student, then as a teacher he pioneered the technique of photomontage, using photographically produced textures (instead of colours) and tiny, cut-out photographs of people to put back "reality" into abstract art (*Dynamic city*, 1919, present whereabouts unknown). He made typographical experiments and posters for Soviet exhibitions.

Knapton, George 1698–1778
British portraitist. He is chiefly known for his 23 portraits (1741–49), mostly in fancy dress, of members of the Society of Dilettanti, a club for gentlemen with aesthetic tastes who had made the Grand Tour. A pupil of Richardson, he was in Italy himself between 1725 and 1732.

Knaus, Ludwig 1829–1910
German genre painter of the Düsseldorf school. Although they show some influence of the French and German Realism which had become influential in the 1860s, his scenes of peasant life remain both sentimental and anecdotal (*The cheat*, 1851, Düsseldorf, Kunstmuseum). It was left to the more talented of his pupils to elevate the painterly detail from its subservience to the pictorial narrative.

Knave of Diamonds
Short-lived avantgarde movement in Russian art, founded in 1909 in Moscow. Larionov was briefly a leading spirit, and Falk and Lentulov were prominent members. The first exhibition, in 1910, made a great impact, bringing recent European paintings to Russia, and work by Kandinsky.

Kneller, Sir Godfrey (Gottfried Kniller) 1646–1723
German-born portrait painter who studied in Amsterdam with Rembrandt's pupil Bol, and in Italy, before settling in England in 1674. By the mid-1680s he had become the leading English portrait painter, the successor of Lely. He and Riley were Principal Painters to William and Mary at their accession in 1689. Kneller was enormously prolific, and the many products of his well-organized studio often seem mechanical, but his best works show great vitality. Three well-known series are the *British Admirals* (Greenwich, National Maritime Museum), the *Hampton Court Beauties* (Hampton Court, Royal coll.) and the *Kit-Cat Club* (London, NPG). See vol. 2 p. **207**

Knight, Dame Laura 1877–1970
British painter. Her subject matter included gypsy life—which she treated less romantically than Augustus John—the circus and the ballet. She regarded herself as a painter of modern life and her finest works are probably those she made as a war artist, recording the war effort on the home front (*Ruby Loftus screwing a breech ring in the Bofors Gun*, 1942, London, Imperial War Museum).

Kobell, Ferdinand 1740–99
German landscape painter and engraver. Intended for an official career, he largely taught himself to paint imaginary landscapes in the Dutch manner. It was only in the 1780s that he developed his own technique of realistic views executed in a strongly linear technique with bright local colour (*View of Goldbach*, 1785–87, Munich, Bayerische Staatsgemäldesammlungen). Such works freed German landscape painting from its dependence on Dutch models and laid the foundations of the realist Munich school of landscape painting of the Biedermeier era.

Kobell, Wilhelm von 1766–1855
German painter of panoramic landscapes and historic battle scenes who served as painter to the Bavarian court from 1792. His huge horizontal compositions, in which the landscapes and atmospheric effects dominate the numerous, tiny human figures, still reflect the sense of order and idealism of classicism, although the detailed observation and clear light are consistent with Biedermeier preoccupations (*The siege of Kosel*, 1808, Munich, Neue Pinakothek).

Købke, Christian 1810–48
Danish artist and engraver, a pupil of Eckersberg and a fine representative of the BIEDERMEIER style. He painted fresh and modest nature scenes on the outskirts of Copenhagen with a fine feeling for colour, atmosphere and distribution of light. He also represented his family and close artist friends in penetrating and tender portraits (*The artist's wife*, 1835, Copenhagen, NG).

Koch, Joseph Anton 1768–1839
Austrian painter of landscape and literary themes. He studied in Stuttgart and painted Alpine landscapes in Switzerland. In 1795 he settled in Rome, where he became close to Carstens and the Nazarenes, under whose influence he started including elements of antiquity and poetry in his grand landscapes (*Heroic landscape with rainbow*, 1805, Karlsruhe, Kunsthalle). After a period in Vienna he returned to Rome in 1815 and became leader of the German colony of painters there. Between 1824 and 1829 he painted four murals in the Dante room of the Villa Massimo, Rome. He was an important influence on young German Romantics. See vol. 3 p. **74**

Koekkoek, Barend Cornelis
1803–62

The outstanding member of a large and prolific family of Dutch landscape painters. He travelled much in Germany and Belgium before settling in Kleef, where he established a drawing school (1841). The Koekkoek family is chiefly associated with seascapes but Barend Cornelis' speciality was forest scenery, often painted with rosy light effects in the manner of Jan Both. Together with Schelfhout and Bakhuyzen he was one of the leading Dutch landscape painters of the first part of the 19th century.

Koetsu, Honnami 1558–1637
Japanese painter. He excelled in calligraphy and decorative lacquerwork as well as painting. He apprenticed himself to Kano Eitoku for painting, but also studied the Tosa style. His paintings reflect his talent for decoration; together with Sotatsu he is believed to have perfected the ancient art of decorating paper with gold and silver to form a background for calligraphy. Their work provided inspiration for the Korin school of the late 17th and early 18th century. Examples are a silver painting of ivy, over which the artist wrote words from a No song (Tokyo, Hatakeyama coll.), and the *Deer* scroll with gold and silver ornament in the Atami Museum, Shizuoka-ken. See vol. 3 pp. **47**, 49

Kohn, Gabriel 1910–78
American sculptor. From 1935 to 1942 he worked as a Hollywood set designer. He studied sculpture first in the USA and then under Zadkine in Paris, and worked mainly in France and Italy until the late 1950s. His mature work dates from the early 1950s, when he began to carve and later construct in wood. A typical later work, *Acrotere* (1960, New York, MOMA), has a clear, blocky form made from laminated and dowelled sheets of wood; it tilts precariously on two pegs.

Kokoschka, Oskar 1886–1980
Austrian painter and writer. He came under the influence of the Sezession painters, particularly Klimt, at the Vienna School of Applied Art, 1904–07. Between 1908 and 1924 he travelled around Europe and fought for the Austro-Hungarian Army; he gained a reputation as a wild exhibitionist and was known as "Mad Kokoschka". In 1934 he emigrated to Prague but fled from the Nazis to London in 1938; after World War II he lived in Salzburg and Switzerland. His earliest works are portraits, which with nervous wiry lines and luminous colour are intended to show the sitter's psychological make-up (*Le Marquis de Montesquiou*, 1909–10, Stockholm, Nationalmuseum). He also produced a large amount of graphic work, in particular illustrations for the avant-garde Berlin magazine *Der Sturm*. Between the Wars he came to specialize in "portraits" of towns, often painted from an unusually high viewpoint (*Jerusalem*, 1929–30, Detroit Institute of Arts). After 1938 he painted a series of political allegories while continuing with portraits and landscapes. He established a reputation as one of the major EXPRESSIONIST painters of this century and also wrote several plays, one of which, *Sphinx and Strawman*, was produced by the Dadaists in the early 1920s. See vol. 1 p. *33*; vol. 3 pp. **195**, 229

Kolbe, Georg 1877–1947
German sculptor. He trained as a painter in Germany and France, but during a stay in Rome (1898–1901) he began to to create his expressive sculptures, mainly of the female nude. Stylistically he was influenced by Rodin and Maillol. In 1903 he settled in Berlin, where he belonged to the Sezession. His classicizing nudes (*Standing nude*, 1926, Minneapolis, Walker Art Center) made him into one of the most highly regarded sculptors of the Nazi regime.

Kollwitz, Käthe 1867–1945
German graphic artist and sculptor. Her etchings, woodcuts and lithographs focus with powerful, compassionate intensity on human suffering and tragedy. Her famous etching cycles *Weavers' Revolt* (1897–98) and *Peasants' War* (1902–08) are vehement protests against contemporary working conditions, set in an historical perspective. From 1910 she preferred to use lithography to create sparse yet extremely moving, haunting images for her cycles *The War* (1923) and *Death* (1934–35). She is equally well remembered for her sensitive and gentle images of motherhood in both drawings and sculpture, such as the bronze *Mother and Child* or *Pietà* (1936, Washington, Hirschhorn Museum). See vol. 1 p. *163*; vol. 3 p. **131**

Konarak
Site of a temple in Orissa, East India, sacred to the sun-god, Surya. Built by Natasimha I of the Eastern Ganga dynasty in the first half of the 13th century, it was conceived as a gigantic representation of the chariot of the sun-god, pulled by his seven horses and with huge wheels decorating the temple's plinth. The plinth, the assembly hall, the base of the tower and the separate dancing hall survive together with groups of gigantic free-standing statuary, unique in India. They include some of the most moving depictions of human relationships in Indian art and are often explicitly erotic. Important groups from the site are in London (BM) and New Delhi (National Museum). See vol. 3 p. 18

Koninck, Philips de 1619–88
Dutch painter active in Amsterdam, and according to Houbraken a pupil of Rembrandt. He painted a variety of subjects, but he is remembered solely for his landscapes, which are among the most majestic in Dutch art. He usually shows extensive scenes of flat country with the sky occupying half or more of the painting. Four superb examples are in the National Gallery, London. They are somewhat reminiscent of the work of Seghers, but Koninck is more naturalistic. His paintings are not very numerous, and he apparently painted little late in life. He was, however, a prolific draughtsman, and his drawings have sometimes been confused with Rembrandt's. See vol. 2 p. **225**

Kore see KOUROS

Korin, Ogata 1658–1716
Japanese painter, brother of Ogata Kenzan. Korin was a native of Kyoto and a dyer by trade. He became obsessed by the genius of Sotatsu and determined to emulate and surpass him. He also admired Koetsu, and like him studied calligraphy and lacquer designs. A keen observer of nature, he sketched from life and produced naturalistic ink-paintings, but at the same time, he could produce the stylized decorative works which are associated with the influential school which he founded—scroll paintings, and designs for lacquer boxes, lavishly endowed with gold and silver. His richly coloured *Iris* screens in the Nezu Museum in Tokyo are a National Treasure. See vol. 3 pp. **48–49**

Korovin, Konstantin Alexeivich
1861–1939

Russian painter and theatre designer. He early adopted French Impressionism (*Paris at night*, 1908, Moscow, Tretyakov Gallery), and was influential as a teacher in the Moscow School of Painting, 1901–18, and the Free State Studios, 1918–19. He was principal artist for the Bolshoi Theatre, 1903–10, and in 1924 he settled in Paris.

Koryusai, Isoda active 1765–84
Japanese UKIYO-E artist. Koryusai's early life is obscure, but there is a theory that he was one of the few *ukiyo-e* artists of Samurai origin. He was a friend of Harunobu, and during the latter's popularity, their work was almost indistinguishable. Koryusai's later subjects, however, have an earthier quality and his colours are more subdued. After Harunobu's death he began to work in a new larger size of print and produced much erotic and, later, pornographic work. Backed by the publishers Eishudo, he produced a 60-piece series of prints depicting the courtesans of the Yoshiwara which assured his success. See vol. 3 pp. **50–51**

Kosice, Gyula born 1924
Argentine sculptor and KINETIC artist. He was responsible for bringing Constructivism to Argentina, but is known principally for his perspex and aluminium constructions called *Hydrosculptures*, which use jets or sheets of water to simulate weather conditions in an enclosed environment. He has written from an ideological point of view on the relation between art and life and has travelled widely propagating his views.

Kossak, Juliusz Fortunat von
1824–99

Polish painter. He received his early training in Russia and Poland, travelled to Vienna in 1853, and visited Paris several times between 1856 and 1862. He settled in Warsaw and specialized in battle scenes and pictures of animals—mostly stud horses—in a style which sparkles with life and movement. He was also an outstanding watercolourist.

Kossoff, Leon born 1926
British painter. His training as an artist included classes with Bomberg, and, like that of Auerbach, another Bomberg pupil, his work is characterized by exceptionally thick paint. His style, however, is more linear and his general approach more expressionist and emotive. His themes include portraits and views of London, particularly railways. *Children's swimming pool, autumn* (1972, Arts Council of Great Britain) is one of a number of paintings of this subject, which, in spite of the dense and tacky paint, have an extraordinary feeling of spontaneous movement.

Kosuth, Joseph born 1945
American CONCEPTUAL artist. A leading writer on Conceptual art, he is concerned with art as information. His focus is on language and syntax, or how information is altered in its presentation. In *The seventh investigation, art as idea as idea, proposition one, 1970* (documented in Software Exhibition, 1971, New York, Jewish Museum) a graphic blow-up of an ambiguous, quasi-dictionary definition is placed in four different contexts including a billboard in New York's Chinatown (in English and Chinese) and an advertisement in a newspaper. Such a project is "art" because the activity is placed "in an art context" by an artist. See vol. 3 p. **246**

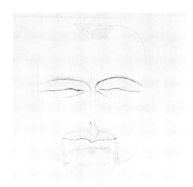

Klee: *Lost in thought*, self-portrait drawing, 1919. Pasadena, The Norton Simon Museum, Galka Scheyer coll.

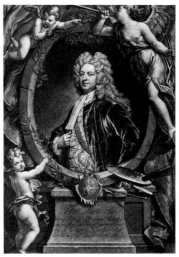

Kneller: Engraving after a self-portrait, from a set of 18th-century engravings of *The Hampton Court Beauties* (B. T. Batsford Ltd)

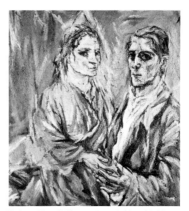

Kokoschka: *Self-portrait with Alma Mahler*, 1912. Hamburg, Horstmann coll. (Cooper-Bridgeman)

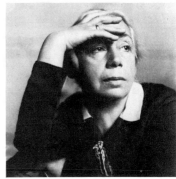

Kollwitz: Photograph (Mansell)

Kounellis, Jannis born 1936
Greek-born artist who works in Rome. In his earliest works he used public notices from streets, endowing the signs with an epic quality, and more recently his work has become Surrealistic. In his *Table* (1963) the artist was seen sitting behind a Greek mask taken from a piece of antique sculpture, the fragments of which were arranged on the table. A flute was played by a musician at the end of the table. This is typical of his mixture of Surrealism and PERFORMANCE art.

Kouros (plural **Kouroi**)
Greek work meaning "young man" applied to a type of nude male statue typical during the ARCHAIC period. The figure is shown looking straight ahead with his hands, thumbs forward, against his thighs and his left leg advanced. The pose is derived from Egyptian art, but gradually became more naturalistic as the Greek artists' mastery of anatomy increased. The female equivalent is the **Kore** (plural *Korai*), which, however, is clothed and more statically posed. See vol. 2 pp. 34–35

Kraft, Adam *c.*1460–1508
German sculptor, a native of Nuremberg, where he had an important workshop executing stone sculpture. In his most famous work, the tabernacle in St Lorenz, Nuremberg (1493–96), a towering steeple of Gothic tracery contrasts with the sturdy, life-size figures within, crouching to support the structure, who are so weighty and realistically carved that they have often been seen as portraits of the artist and his assistants. Much of his work consisted of monumental reliefs, carved with great clarity and simplicity, and often achieving vivid effects of emotion, as in the seven reliefs of *The Stations of the Cross* (1508, Nuremberg, Germanisches Nationalmuseum). See vol. 2 p. **159**

Kraljević, Miroslav 1885–1913
Yugoslav painter. He studied in Munich and Paris, returning to his native Zagreb in 1912. In the years preceding World War I, he introduced the new trends of French painting to Zagreb, and he is acknowledged as the master of Croatian Impressionism. *The artist with a pipe* (1912, Zagreb, Gallery of Modern Art) shows the psychological insight of his portraits.

Kramskoy, Ivan Nikolaevich
1837–87
Russian painter. In 1856 he entered the Academy of Fine Arts in St Petersburg, but left in protest against academic strictures. After the failure of an artistic commune he helped to found the WANDERERS. Kramskoy's work consisted mainly of portraits, serious in approach and often of penetrating insight (*Leo Tolstoy*, 1873, Moscow, Tretyakov Gallery). His early training in photography is evident in their sharply detailed realism and lack of interest in colour. He was a deeply spiritual man, and in his religious paintings tried to give visible expression to universal truths, as in his well-known work *The Temptation of Christ* (1872–74, Tretyakov Gallery).

Krasner, Lee (Leonore) born 1911
American painter. In the 1930s she worked on the Federal Art Projects and from 1938 to 1940 studied with Hofmann. She received serious recognition only after the death of her husband Jackson Pollock in 1965. Her mature works are thinly painted with a crowded, all-over gestural drawing occasionally suggesting figuration.

Kresilas active mid-5th century BC
Greek sculptor from Crete, active in Athens. No original work survives, but a Roman copy of a statue of an *Amazon* in the Capitoline Museum in Rome has been identified with a figure which Pliny describes as having been made by him in a competition with other sculptors, who included Phidias and Polykleitos. Two copies of the head of a statue of Perikles by Kresilas have also been identified (London, BM, and Vatican Museum). See vol. 2 pp. **36–37**

Kricke, Norbert born 1922
West German sculptor. Shortly after finishing his studies in Berlin he produced his first abstract sculptures in space, a major theme of his art. He uses tubes and wire for his space constructions, and his forms reflect both his admiration for Malevich and his awareness of the planet and the universe (*Large space sculpture*, 1965, Los Angeles County Museum of Art). His best-known works are his *Water Forests*, fountains made of plexiglass tubes (examples in Düsseldorf).

Krieghoff, Cornelius 1815–72
Canadian landscape and genre painter who spent his boyhood in Düsseldorf. By 1853 he was established in Quebec City, after a spell in America. His work, rich in details of local life and meticulously painted sweeps of landscape, reflects Germanic Academic influences. *Merry-making* (1860, Fredericton, Beaverbrook Gallery) displays many tiny figures locked in a masterly composition of unified atmosphere and colour. He was much imitated and forged.

Kritios early 5th century BC
Greek sculptor of the early Classical period. He is best known for the group of the tyrannicides *Harmodios and Aristogeiton*, which he and Nesiotes were commissioned to make in 477 BC to replace the group by Antenor. The complete copy of this work in the Museo Nazionale, Naples, displays a vigorous and convincing rendering of dynamic action which is new to the art of the time. On the basis of this work a number of others have been attributed to Kritios, including a male nude known as "*The Kritios Boy*" (Athens, Acropolis Museum). See vol. 2 pp. *35*, *36*

Krohg, Christian 1852–1925
Norwegian painter. He studied in Karlsruhe and Berlin and was influenced by the art of Menzel and Liebermann. During the period 1879 to 1884, he settled at Skagen and painted the fishing population. In 1886 he published *Albertine*, a novel that deals with a prostitute's life, and he painted many canvases on the same theme; *Albertine* (1886–87, Oslo, NG) shows prostitutes in a police doctor's waiting-room.

Krohg, Per 1889–1965
Norwegian painter and book illustrator, the son of Christian Krohg. Trained by his father and Matisse and interested in Cubism and contemporary French trends, he developed a bizarre and subtle realist style, specializing in scenes from the big city. *Kiki* (1928, Oslo, NG) is an evocative portrait of a sexy French model. His output also included murals and monumental works for many public buildings in Norway and abroad.

Krøyer, Peder Severin 1851–1909
Danish artist. He studied French *plein-air* painting in Paris, and was especially interested in the effects of sunlight and artificial light (*Italian village hatters*, 1880, Copenhagen, Statens Museum for Kunst). He travelled in Spain and Italy and settled at Skagen in Denmark in 1882, becoming the central figure in the Skagen group of artists and painting the fishing population and his artist friends. In 1900 he became mentally deranged and ceased painting. He is richly represented at the Skagen Museum.

Kršinić, Frano born 1897
Yugoslav sculptor. He has taught and worked in Zagreb since 1924. In spite of a number of official commissions, the serenity of his work has been unperturbed by ideological considerations. The Mediterranean sensuality of his simple volumes and pure lines is best seen in his female nudes (*Girl*, 1928, London, Tate).

Kruseman, Cornelis 1797–1857
Dutch painter much praised in his day for his portraits, religious subjects and Italian scenes. He spent many years in Italy and based his technique on the Italian High Renaissance. *Piety* (Amsterdam, Rijksmuseum) is typical of his idealizing style. His nephews, the cousins **Jan Adam** Kruseman (1804–62) and **Frederik Marinus** Kruseman (1817–*c.*1860), were also painters, Jan specializing in portraits and history scenes, and Frederik in landscapes.

Krushenick, Nicholas born 1929
American painter. During the 1950s he worked as an Abstract Expressionist, but by 1962 had evolved a hard-edged style. The bands of bright colour edged with thick black lines share Pop art's brashness, but the images are abstract, suggesting close-up diagrams of twisting spaces and bulging surfaces.

Kuan Hsiu see GUANXIU

Kuan T'ung see GUAN TONG

Kubin, Alfred 1877–1959
Austrian illustrator and engraver, member of Der Blaue Reiter. Kubin appears to have had an extremely disturbed and traumatic childhood and his work constantly portrays a haunted and mysterious world. In 1906, while using a microscope, he realized the possibilities of an abstract art based upon minute natural structures magnified into decorative ornament. He published several portfolios of drawings as well as illustrating a number of books; he also published a "dream novel", *The Other Side*, in 1909. He had considerable influence on German abstract painters and on Chirico. See vol. 3 p. *137*

Kubín, Otakar (Othon Coubine)
1883–1969
Czech painter and graphic artist. Much of his career was spent in France, and his style was more French than Czech. His early work was influenced by Fauvism, but thereafter he developed a cool, classical, anti-modernist style which showed his reverence for the great masters of the past, whose work he studied intensely on journeys through Europe. He is best known for his landscapes of Provence and genre scenes.

Kudo, Tetsumi born 1935
Japanese sculptor, living in Paris since 1962. He participated energetically in the Yomiuri Independent Show in 1958–62 with anti-artistic works and HAPPENINGS. In Paris he began creating the series of erotic objects which illustrated his "Philosophy of Impotence", violent and grotesque images which criticize himself as much as modernized society. *Your portrait—T* (1965–66, Paris, Galerie Mathias Fels) is characteristically disturbing, an open-ended cube or die with an egg-box-like interior stuck with wires and brain-like masses

Kuhn, Justis Englehardt died 1717
German painter who became a naturalized American in 1708. He settled in Annapolis, Maryland, where he painted portraits of several local families in a style which brought elements of European Baroque to the limner tradition (*Eleanor Darnell*, *c.*1710, Baltimore, Maryland Historical Society).

Kuhn, Walt 1877–1949
American painter, best-known for securing loans of contemporary European art for the New York Armory Show. His own paintings are relatively conservative, for example, his studies of clowns and acrobats in which the private sadness of the sitters is contrasted with their jovial appearances (*Clown with black wig*, 1930, New York, Metropolitan).

Kuindzhi, Archip Ivanovich
1842–1910
Russian landscape painter, a member of the WANDERERS. From 1875 he painted large South Russian landscapes with unusual sun and particularly moonlight effects (*Ukrainian night*, 1876, Moscow, Tretyakov Gallery). These pictures won him immense popularity and a great fortune, but aroused much controversy among critics and painters. From 1892 he was a professor in the Academy of Fine Arts in St Petersburg, where his exceptional kindness made him a very popular and influential teacher.

Ku k'ai-chi see GU KAIZHI

Kulmbach, Hans Suess von
*c.*1480–1522
German painter and designer of engravings and stained glass, active mainly in Nuremberg. His early style indicates that he was an assistant of Jacopo de' Barbari in Nuremberg in about 1500, before joining Dürer's workshop in about 1503. Between about 1509 and 1516 he executed a number of altarpieces for churches in Cracow, Poland, which he may have visited. His altarpiece for the church of St Sebald, Nuremberg, 1513, was carried out after Dürer's designs, but, as one of his most gifted pupils, he developed his own stylistic tendencies, notably in his use of bright colour and elongated figures clothed in sweeping draperies.

Kung Hsien see GONG XIAN

Kunisada, Utagawa 1786–1864
Japanese UKIYO-E artist, a pupil of Toyokuni I. The most prolific of all the printmakers of the 19th-century Utagawa family, Kunisada illustrated most of the popular stories published in his time and made commercial portraits of all the star Kabuki actors of the day—the works for which he is best known. He also perfected the depiction of the strangely hump-backed, curiously sensual and vivid type of woman which became the fashion. Kunisada is said to have designed more than 10,000 prints. Often they are of poor quality, but he also left many excellent hand-painted pictures, and these give a better idea of his genius.

Kuniyoshi, Utagawa 1797–1861
Japanese UKIYO-E artist. The son of an Edo (Tokyo) dye merchant, at the age of 15 he was accepted as a pupil by Toyokuni I, who trained him in calligraphy as well as in print design. Popularity

came with the publication, in 1827, of his series of prints illustrating the Chinese classic *The Water Margin*. From then on Kuniyoshi was regarded chiefly as a designer of warrior prints, but his reputation did not discourage him from expanding his technique. He apprenticed himself to a master of the Chinese school, studied the works of Hokusai, and also experimented with Western perspective and shading. Kuniyoshi was an extroverted, courageous individual who dared to depict historical characters in recognizably contemporary settings in order to criticize corruption. Two of his prints were banned as seditious by the government. See vol. 3 p. **51**

Kuniyoshi, Yasuo 1893–1953
American-Japanese painter. His work evinced a deliberate primitivism in the 1920s and early 1930s with fanciful and often pastoral or idyllic imagery. During the 1930s his art became more sober and was influenced by Pascin and Derain in its choice of languid female subjects and in its elegant handling (*I'm tired*, 1938, New York, Whitney). Later work, however, moved towards harsher colouring and a rather disquieting, possibly hermetic, imagery where carnival motifs are prominent.

Kuo Hsi see GUO XI

Kupecký, Jan 1667–1740
Bohemian Baroque portrait painter. Kupecký escaped a training as a weaver to learn painting in Vienna, followed by more than two decades in Italy (1686–1709). On his return he worked from 1709 to 1723 in Vienna, but his desire for artistic and religious freedom finally led him to settle in Nuremberg. Despite his popularity and prolific output, he made few concessions to the vanity of his sitters, whom he presented with the same intensity as in his own numerous self-portraits (examples in the National Galleries of Prague and Budapest). There is a museum devoted to his work at Pezinok in Czechoslovakia.

Kupka, Frank (František)
1871–1957
Czech painter and graphic artist, a pioneer of ABSTRACT art. After training in Prague and Vienna he settled in Paris in 1895, where he worked as a book illustrator and associated with leading avantgarde artists such as the Duchamp brothers. In 1908 he began to explore the problems of conveying movement in a series of works representing a *Girl with a Ball* (mostly New York, MOMA). This series, paralleling the development of Futurism, culminated in *Amorpha, fugue in two colours* (1912, Prague, NG), one of the earliest completely abstract paintings. At this stage of his career his work, like that of the closely related Orphists, was often mystical in feeling. His later work was also often in the vanguard of abstract developments, and in the 1920s he produced paintings which are among the finest of their kind in evoking Machine-Age power and energy (*Working steel*, 1921–29, Paris, Musée National d'Arte Moderne). See vol. 3 p. **151**

Kuznetsov, Pavel Varfolomeevich
1878–1968
Russian painter, an early admirer of Borisov-Musatov. He evinced a personal subject matter and style from travel in Khirgiz and Kazakhstan, catching the poetry of nomadic life in pastel-coloured canvases, with figures outlined in blue (*Evening on the steppes*, 1908, Leningrad, Russian Museum). After 1930 he adapted his style to socialist realism.

Kylberg, Carl 1878–1952
Swedish painter and draughtsman. He developed a strong sense of colour in his early landscapes, and during the 1920s used only a few dominant deep tones, omitting all descriptive details to leave a general emotive impression of his subject. In later compositions the visionary, symbolic and religious traits of his art stand out clearly (*A new day is dawning*, 1933, Paris, Musée d'Art Moderne).

Lacasse, Joseph born 1894
Belgian painter. Originally a quarry worker and stone-cutter, he was fascinated by the structure and changing colour of rocks in the evening light. The influence of Cubism led him to paint abstract compositions, but in 1915 he returned to figurative works—principally scenes of quarrymen and miners and religious subjects. He settled in Paris in 1925 and met Delaunay there. After 1931 he returned to abstract painting, producing lyrical, brilliantly coloured formulations of flat shapes (*Red canvas*, 1961, Paris, Galerie Jacques Massol).

Lachaise, Gaston 1882–1935
French sculptor, born in Paris. In 1906 he emigrated to the USA, where he executed reliefs in New York for the Telephone Building, 1921, and for the Rockefeller Center in 1931 and 1935. He is best-known for his voluptuous female nudes, bulging and smoothly modelled (*Standing nude*, 1927, New York, Metropolitan), reflecting ancient Hindu influences as well as Brancusi and Nadelman. With the latter, Lachaise was one of the most important figures in the transition in American sculpture between late 19th-century academicism and more expressive formalism.

Laer, Pieter van 1592–1642
Dutch genre painter, known as Bamboccio ("clumsy baby") because of his deformed body. He was born in Haarlem, and in 1625 went to Italy, where he specialized in Roman street scenes. His paintings reveal a sympathetic approach to the poor, whom he treated in a dignified manner, with realistic details and sombre lighting which owe something to Caravaggio (*The quoit seller*, Rome, Galleria Nazionale). His career is obscure and his paintings rare and difficult to date, but he inspired a host of followers—the BAMBOCCIANTI. He was admired by painters as diverse as Claude and Velazquez, and his figure style was adopted by many landscapists for their staffage. His *Self-portrait* (Rome, Galleria Pallavicini) is typically direct, presenting his deformities without bitterness or self-pity. See vol. 2 p. 192

Lafarge, John 1835–1910
American painter and decorative artist. He studied with Couture in Paris and was open to diverse influences, writing influential articles on Japanese and Chinese art. His first major scheme was in the neo-Romanesque Trinity Church in Boston (1876), where he organized the mural decorations and revived the use of stained glass. In his spiritual attitude towards art, he had much in common with the Pre-Raphaelites and with William Morris, whom he met in 1856. His easel-paintings varied from landscapes to illusionist still life, and, following a journey to the Far East in

1880, exotic subjects (*Maua our boatman*, 1891, Andover, Mass., Addison Gallery of American Art).

La Fosse, Charles de 1636–1716
French painter of history and mythology. Although a pupil and collaborator of Lebrun, he was—perhaps due to three years at Venice in the 1660s and friendship with the Rubeniste theorist de Piles—an early exponent in France of a free colouristic Baroque idiom (*Rape of Proserpine*, 1673, Paris, Ecole des Beaux-Arts). By the time of his dome fresco at the church of Les Invalides, Paris (1700–02) and the *Bacchus and Ariadne* (c.1699, Dijon, Musée), however, he had developed a lighter proto-Rococo style. François Lemoyne, Boucher's master, was among his pupils.

La Fresnaye, Roger de 1885–1925
French painter. He trained in Paris and was taught by Denis and Sérusier. In 1910 he began to experiment with Cubism and was a member of the SECTION D'OR group. *Conquest of the air* (1913, New York, MOMA) shows a use of prismatic colours applied in transparent planes recalling Delaunay, while the flight theme relates to Italian Futurism.

Laguerre, Louis 1663–1721
French decorative painter. After working under Lebrun he came to England in 1683–84, collaborating with Verrio at Christ's Hospital, Horsham, Sussex, at Chatsworth, Derbyshire, and at Hampton Court. Among his independent works is his masterpiece, the saloon at Blenheim Palace (c.1714). His work is generally weak and derivative compared with the best decorative painting of his day, but he enjoyed a successful career, mainly because of the lack of native talent in England in his field. He also painted a number of histories and portraits.

La Hyre, Laurent de 1606–56
French painter of landscapes, portraits and religious and mythological scenes, born and active in Paris. His style was influenced initially by the second school of Fontainebleau, but gradually became more purely classical. *The birth of Bacchus* (1638, Leningrad, Hermitage) is modelled on the early work of Poussin, but La Hyre's treatment of the landscape—the most individual aspect of his work—is softer and more poetic. The severer aspect of his later work is well represented by *Allegory of music* (1648, New York, Metropolitan). He also produced engravings.

Lairesse, Gérard de 1641–1711
Dutch painter and writer on art theory, born in Liège. In 1665 he moved to Amsterdam, then in 1684 settled in The Hague. He was the most popular decorator in Holland at the end of the 17th century, producing classicizing allegorical, historical and mythological canvases for town and country houses and for civic buildings (*Allegory of Amsterdam trade*, 1672, The Hague, Peace Palace). In about 1690 he went blind, and thereafter lectured on art theory. His talks were collected in two books: *Foundation of Drawing* (1701) and *The Great Painting Book* (1707), both of which were translated and frequently reprinted throughout the 18th century. In them he shows a strictly academic approach and repudiates his early admiration for Rembrandt. Rembrandt had painted his portrait (1665, New York, Metropolitan), showing his disfigured face sympathetically.

Lam, Wilfredo born 1902
Cuban painter. He studied in Madrid,

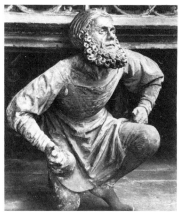

Kraft, Adam: Self-portrait from the Shrine of the Sacrament, St Lorenz, Nuremberg, 1493–96 (Bildarchiv Foto Marburg)

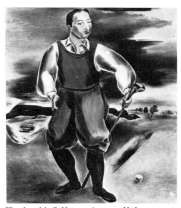

Kuniyoshi: *Self-portrait as a golf player*, 1927. New York, MOMA, Abby Aldrich Rockefeller Fund

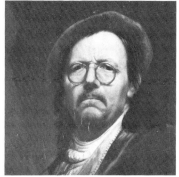

Kupecký: Self-portrait, c.1735. Stuttgart, Staatsgalerie

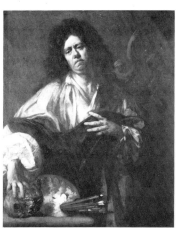

Lairesse: Self-portrait, c.1685. Bayonne, Musée Bonnat (Giraudon)

1924–36, and from 1937 to 1941 lived in Paris, where he was influenced by Surrealism. Lam developed a personal and highly charged symbolic iconography which was rooted in the ritual fetishes, mythologies and traditions of the Caribbean. In 1941 he travelled to Martinique and Haiti, where he encountered voodoo, and was inspired to begin his Jungle series (*Large jungle*, 1943, New York, MOMA). His mature work reveals a world of semi-abstract images, sometimes highly coloured—demons, animals and vegetation in metamorphosis—and full of suppressed menace.

Lambert, George *c.* 1700–65
British landscapist, the leading practitioner of the genre in his day. A pupil of Wootton, he was strongly influenced by the classical landscapes of Gaspard Dughet, and sometimes inserted views of English country houses into settings derived from these sources. However, he also painted two unusual, realistic views of the English countryside, *Hilly landscape with a cornfield* and *Extensive landscape with four gentlemen on a hillside* (1733, London, Tate).

Lami, Eugène-Louis 1800–90
French painter, watercolourist and lithographer, famed for his elegant illustrations of Parisian high society. A pupil of Horace Vernet (1813) and Gros (1817–20), he began as a military painter, but from 1837 concentrated on depicting contemporary society, with much detail and emphasis on costume (*Visit of Queen Victoria to Versailles*, 1855, Versailles, Musée National). Lami followed Louis-Philippe into exile in London, where he produced numerous watercolours. In 1852, he returned to Paris and received court patronage.

Lanceley, Colin born 1938
Australian painter and sculptor, born in New Zealand. He first emerged as a follower of American POP art in 1962 and his ASSEMBLAGES were among the most significant statements made in the 1960s against the "poetic" elements of Australian painting. At first his disquieting images of generals, orators, or nightclub strippers were distinctly narrative, but since 1962 his work has become tighter and more abstract. Always provocative, its intellectual content is matched by an element of spontaneous discovery which displays a deep appreciation of Miró. He left Australia for London in 1965.

Lancret, Nicolas 1690–1743
French painter of genre and FÊTES GALANTES, with Pater the chief of Watteau's imitators. His *fêtes galantes*, which were very popular in his time, are ravishing in colour, but he never approached Watteau's psychological penetration. He is well represented in the Wallace Collection, London.

Land art
Type of art pioneered in the late 1960s and using for materials the land itself, earth, stones, wood and other natural objects. Some artists, such as Heizer, work in the desert or on the seashore, moving tons of earth and rock. Others, including Long and De Maria, introduce the outside world into the gallery by bringing in earth or stones and arranging them there. Aerial photography has complemented these activities. See vol. 3 pp. 248–249

Landseer, Sir Edwin Henry 1802–73
English painter, sculptor and engraver, best known for his treatment of animals. Although he had great natural gifts, his work suffered from a tendency to humanize animals in order to point a moral or tell a story (*The old shepherd's chief mourner*, 1837, London, V&A). His sentimental paintings, however, were very popular, and became widely known in engravings; Queen Victoria was among his many admirers. His best-known painting is *The monarch of the glen* (1850, London, Dewar House) and he was the sculptor of the lions in Trafalgar Square, London (1867). See vol. 3 p. **82**; vol. 4 p. *37*

Lane, Fitz Hugh 1804–65
American seascape painter, an exponent of LUMINISM. He worked as a lithographer in Boston for 20 years specializing in architectural views, then in 1849 returned to his native Gloucester, Mass., where he produced elegant, stylized marine paintings, reminiscent of the English topographical tradition (*Owl's Head, Penobscot Bay, Maine*, 1862, Boston, MFA).

Lanfranco, Giovanni 1582–1647
Italian painter, with Pietro da Cortona and Guercino one of the founders of the Roman High BAROQUE style. He was a pupil of Agostino Carracci in Bologna, and in 1602 moved to Rome, where he assisted Annibale Carracci in the Farnese Palace. Principally important as a fresco painter, his greatest work is *The Assumption of the Virgin* in the dome of S. Andrea della Valle, Rome (1625–27), where he combined the Carracci figure style with the illusionistic foreshortening of Correggio's dome paintings, which he had studied in his native Parma. This was a key monument in the development of Baroque decoration and marked the end of the dominance of Bolognese classicism in Rome. Lanfranco was in Naples (1633–46), and his influence there was as great as in Rome. As an easel-painter his finest work is *The ecstasy of St Margaret of Cortona* (*c.* 1620, Florence, Pitti), which looks forward to Bernini's *St Theresa*. See vol. 2 p. **185**

Lang, Nikolaus born 1941
West German artist. His art combines elements of landscape and rural sociological history, displayed almost like archaeological evidence in a museum, but not without a feeling of magic.

Lanier, Nicholas 1588–1666
English connoisseur and amateur painter of French origin. A musician by training, appointed Master of the King's Music in 1625, Lanier was a notable connoisseur of works of art, and was employed by Charles I to buy pictures on the Continent. A self-portrait is in the Faculty of Music, Oxford.

Lanyon, Peter 1918–64
British painter and sculptor. He was born in St Ives, where he met Ben Nicholson and Gabo. In the early 1940s he made constructions influenced by the latter, but became more interested in painting. His work, however abstract, was always related to the spirit of a particular place. Often, as in *Porthleven* (1951, London, Tate), the piling up of the elements of the scene radically reverses the traditional horizontal format of landscape. Other paintings evoke space with multiple layers of vigorously applied colour.

Lapicque, Charles born 1898
French painter. Until 1928 he worked as an engineer and produced a thesis on optics in 1938. Since about 1940 he has employed a style influenced by his scientific researches and by Fauvism and Cubism. He combines allusions to the visual world with more abstract interests in bold colour and formal simplification, as in his portrait of *The Duc de Nemours* (1950, Paris, Musée d'Art Moderne).

Laprade, Pierre 1875–1932
French painter, best known for his poetic representations of landscapes and intimate domestic or garden scenes. *The musicians* (1907, Paris, Private coll.) shows his preference for pastel shades and his ability to capture atmospheric effects. He provided delicate illustrations for the French poet Verlaine's *Fêtes Galantes*.

Lardera, Berto born 1911
Italian sculptor. He was self-taught and worked in Paris after 1947. From 1946 he produced a series of abstract sculptures made from iron, copper and aluminium, using two dimensional geometric shapes and wire, and rejecting traditional concerns with mass and volume. By the mid-1950s he was working in three dimensions, experimenting with geometry in space (*Heroic rhythm III*, 1957, Hamburg, Kunsthalle).

Largillière, Nicolas de 1656–1746
French painter, with Rigaud the most successful portraitist of the last years of Louis XIV's reign. He was born in Paris but spent his youth in Antwerp, and in the 1670s worked in London in Lely's studio, where he developed a rather flashy version of van Dyck's style. On his return to France in 1682 he adapted the strong colour and billowing drapery of the Flemish Baroque to the tastes of his rich Parisian patrons. Although he abandoned the formality of his portrait of *Lebrun* (1686, Paris, Louvre) in favour of more relaxed pose and costume, the air of intimacy is somewhat contrived in his *The painter with his wife and daughter* (*c.* 1700, Louvre). Many of his female portraits of a lightly mythologizing character are faintly absurd, though *Elizabeth Throckmorton as a Dominican nun* (1729, Washington, NG) shows that he could be vigorous and direct to striking effect. Largillière also painted a number of *ex votos*, religious works and still lifes. See vol. 2 p. **242**

Larionov, Mikhail Fedorovich 1881–1964
Russian painter, who until 1914 was at the forefront of modernism in Moscow. In about 1911 he began to develop a non-objective style called RAYONNISM, typified by such paintings as *Glass* (1912, New York, Guggenheim), but at the same time he continued to paint in the restrained style which characterized his slightly earlier work and which owed much to Russian folk art (*Summer*, 1912, Paris, Musée d'Art Moderne). Invalided out of the Army in 1915, he joined Diaghilev in Switzerland and began work for the Ballets Russes, producing exciting stage designs and working on choreography. From 1919 he lived in Paris with Goncharova, continuing to produce book illustrations but, like his companion, failing to fulfil the promise of his early work. This had a great impact on the development of CONSTRUCTIVISM. See vol. 3 pp. **156–157**

Larkin, William died 1619
English portrait painter who has only recently emerged from total obscurity. Two full-length portraits at Charlecote Park, Warwickshire, are the only certain works by him, but others have been attributed to him because of their similarity to these, including a group at Ranger's House, Blackheath, London, characterized by minutely observed details, particularly of costume, and the presence of elaborate Turkey carpets and pairs of curtains in metallic folds. If Larkin is indeed responsible for all these, then his stature is considerable.

Larsson, Carl 1853–1919
Swedish painter, draughtsman, engraver and book illustrator. He studied in Stockholm and France, 1877–85, where he established his reputation. Returning to Sweden in 1889, he began painting murals, of which the most remarkable are six gigantic frescos on episodes in the history of Swedish art in the National Museum, Stockholm, 1896. Larsson's first book, *A Home*, was published in 1897 and contained watercolours of his own home in Dalecarlia. Such delicate, decorative paintings, recalling Rococo effects and Japanese designs, initiated a new style of interior decoration (still popular) related to the ideals of Morris.

Larsson, Marcus 1825–64
Swedish painter. He studied in Stockholm and Düsseldorf, and was influenced by Ruisdael. He painted dramatic landscapes, often with waterfalls, stormy skies, cliff coastlines and shipwrecks—scenes of destruction reflecting his passion and unease. After success in Sweden, Finland and Russia, he died destitute in London at the age of 39.

Lascaux
Site of a complex of caves in the Dordogne region of southern France containing masterpieces of Palaeolithic art. The paintings tend to be bolder than those at Altamira, and some of the animals, such as those in the Hall of the Bulls, are over life-size. Besides these silhouetted and coloured animal paintings there are engravings cut in the rock. The Lascaux caves were probably in use about 15000 BC, and were excellently preserved when found. See vol. 2 p. 13

Lassaw, Ibram born 1913
American sculptor, born in Egypt. He was a founder-member of the AMERICAN ABSTRACT ARTISTS' group and one of the first Americans to make abstract sculpture. In the 1930s he produced biomorphic works with a Surrealist influence. He took up welding in 1938, and after a brief period of rectilinear works influenced by Mondrian in the early 1940s he integrated his two early styles. His mature style—organic, open grids and lattices—did not emerge until 1950. *Kwannon* (1952, New York, MOMA) resembles a tiny fantasy scaffolding.

Lastman, Pieter 1583–1633
Dutch painter of biblical, historical and mythological scenes, remembered principally as the teacher of Rembrandt and Lievens. He travelled in Italy (before 1607), and was influenced particularly by Elsheimer and Caravaggio. On his return to Amsterdam he became one of the most influential Dutch painters of his period. His pictures tend to be small with lively, very highly coloured figures, and he often chose unusual subjects (*Juno discovering Jupiter with Io*, 1618, London, NG). Rembrandt's early works are very heavily indebted to Lastman in their sense of scale, lighting and vivid characterization. See vol. 2 p. **213**

Latham, John born 1921
British artist. He made his first "book sculptures" such as *The burial of Count Orgaz* (London, Tate) in 1958, and in the 1960s participated in HAPPENINGS,

for instance *The Skoob Tower ceremonies*, which involved the destruction of towers of books. His thinking as an artist has emphasized the event rather than the object and in the late 1960s he chewed up a library copy of Clement Greenberg's *Art and Culture* as a gesture of opposition to its formalist views, at that time enormously influential on British artists.

La Tour, Georges de 1593–1652
French painter, perhaps the greatest of CARAVAGGESQUE artists. He worked from 1620 in Luneville in Lorraine, somewhat away from the court of his patron, the Duke of Lorraine, at Nancy. His studio flourished, and he may have been patronized by Louis XIII, but he passed into virtually complete oblivion for almost three centuries after his death. Of the 40 or so surviving paintings only two are dated (*St Peter penitent*, 1645, Cleveland, Ohio, Museum of Art; *The denial of St Peter*, 1650, Nantes, Musée des Beaux-Arts), and his chronology is difficult to establish. The works which are considered his earliest, however, are brightly-lit genre scenes (*Peasant* and *Peasant's wife*, c.1620, San Francisco, California Palace of the Legion of Honor), very different from the majestic and sombre religious paintings, often lit by a single candle, with which he is chiefly associated. In these he developed an increasing simplification of forms so that, for example, in *St Sebastian tended by the holy women* (version, c.1650, Broglie, Parish Church) a tree-trunk looks almost like a classical column. The sources of La Tour's style are also problematic. It has been suggested that he went to Rome, but it seems more likely that his knowledge of Caravaggio's style was gained via Utrecht painters such as Honthorst and Terbrugghen. His finest works, however, transcend any models, and in their grandeur, serenity and exquisite handling of light rank among the greatest paintings of the 17th century. See vol. 2 pp. **192–193**

La Tour, Maurice-Quentin de 1704–88
The most successful French pastellist of the 18th century. He arrived in Paris at the time of the visit of the Venetian pastel portraitist Rosalba Carriera in 1720–21 and it was her success which persuaded him to adopt the medium. He was a regular exhibitor at the Salon and his eccentric personality and the brilliant virtuosity of such portraits as the *Mme de Pompadour* (1755, Paris, Louvre) made him in demand at all levels of society. His vivacious and rather theatrical presentation of his sitters can best be studied in the museum at his native Saint-Quentin. Perronneau and Liotard were among his rivals. See vol. 2 p. **243**

Laurana, Francesco c.1430–1502?
Italian sculptor of Dalmatian birth. Though he is recorded working in Naples from 1453 on Alfonso I's triumphal Arch at Castelnuovo, the extent of his contribution there is uncertain. He worked in the south of France, 1461–66, and in Sicily in 1467. The best testament to his art is his series of portrait busts of women, which reveal a subtle and sensitive response to shape and surface and were sometimes polychromed to achieve a highly naturalistic effect (*Isabella of Aragon*, Vienna, Kunsthistorisches). Laurana's visit to Urbino, where the architect Luciano Laurana (perhaps related) had been active, is witnessed by a bust of the Duchess of Urbino (c.1475–76, Florence, Bargello). He was back in France, 1477–83, and eventually died there about 1502.

Laurencin, Marie 1885–1956
French painter and designer. She became the mistress of Apollinaire in 1908 and celebrated their relationship in a group portrait which included their artistic friends such as Picasso (*The guests*, 1908, Baltimore Museum of Art). Influenced superficially by the latter, her art is repetitive yet charming, employing soft pastel shades to represent doe-eyed young girls with simplified oval faces (*The rehearsal*, 1936, Paris, Musée d'Art Moderne).

Laurens, Henri 1885–1954
French sculptor. His early work was influenced by Rodin, but he became friendly with the Cubist painters and was one of the first to adapt their style to sculpture (*Bottle and glass*, 1915, Paris, Galerie Louise Leiris). During World War I he produced relief carvings, and, following Picasso, made constructions from wood, plaster and sheet-iron. In the mid-1920s he reverted to a more sensuous, figurative, organic style to depict monumental female figures, as in *The farewell* (1940, Paris, Musée d'Art Moderne). Many of his works are polychrome and he made important innovations in the use of colour in sculpture.

Law, Bob born 1934
British painter and sculptor. His drawings of the late 1950s used simple, schematic hieroglyphs, but since 1960 his work has been predominantly abstract and he has produced extremely uncompromising examples of Minimal art. Some paintings appear at first sight to be entirely black, though on further acquaintance colouristic subtleties become apparent at the edges. In the *Castle* series of 1975 onwards, totally white canvases are bounded by a single thin line in biro or pencil. The idea is to make the spectator acutely aware of the artist's intervention through the minute variations in the outline.

Lawrence, Jacob born 1917
One of the first important black American painters. He studied at WPA classes and was influenced by the atmosphere of social conscience of the 1930s. He has drawn on black culture for his subjects, and did a series of 60 paintings on *The Migration of the Negro*, 1940–41, New York, MOMA, and Washington, Phillips Coll.). He frequently works in tempera, and his simplified handling combines flattened forms with a primitive angularity reminiscent of Ben Shahn.

Lawrence, Sir Thomas 1769–1830
English portrait painter. He was very precocious, established his reputation with a portrait of *Queen Charlotte* (1789, London, NG), and rapidly became the most fashionable portraitist of the day. In 1792 he succeeded Reynolds as Painter to the King, was knighted in 1815 and became President of the Royal Academy in 1820. After the 1814 allied victory over Napoleon he was asked to paint a series of portraits of the leaders of the campaign for the Waterloo Chamber, Windsor Castle. The 24 full-length portraits, completed in 1818, are a unique historical document as well as Lawrence's greatest achievement. His style was rooted in the 18th-century tradition of British portraiture, but his fluid, glossy technique won Delacroix's admiration and allies him with Romanticism.

Lawson, Ernest 1873–1939
American painter who worked in the Impressionistic style of Twachtman, with whom he studied. Although a member of The EIGHT, he lacked the vigour usually associated with the group and is best remembered for his winter landscapes (*Winter on the river*, 1907, New York, Whitney).

Lear, Edward 1812–88
British writer, painter and ornithologist. He was a fine watercolourist—especially of topographical Mediterranean and Middle Eastern scenes.

Lebrun, Charles 1619–90
French painter, the most important artist of Louis XIV's reign and the chief formulator of French academic doctrine. He was a pupil of Vouet, and in 1642 went to Rome, where he worked with Poussin. In 1646 he returned to Paris, and worked mainly on large decorative commissions. By 1661 he was established in Louis's favour, and in 1663 he was appointed Director of the Academy and of the Gobelins factory. The factory produced everything needed for the furnishing of royal palaces, and a good idea of its activities can be gained from the famous tapestry after Lebrun's design, *Louis XIV visiting the Gobelins* (1663–75, Paris, Gobelins Museum). Much of this energy was directed into the palace of Versailles, and Lebrun's best-known work there is the decoration of the Galerie des Glaces (Hall of Mirrors), 1679–84. His lectures at the Academy influenced French art for generations. His own paintings are often more interesting and personal than his theories would lead one to expect. He never entirely lost the vigour of his early masterpiece, *Hercules and the horses of Diomedes* (c.1640, Nottingham, Art Gallery), and was a lively portraitist and brilliant draughtsman. See vol. 2 p. **198**

Leck, Bart van der 1876–1958
Dutch painter. His earliest work was Symbolist and showed the influence of Toorop. By 1913 he had developed a simplified hieratic style with figures on a white ground, and by 1915, in *The storm* (1915, Otterlo, Kröller-Müller), he had reduced his range of colours to red, blue, yellow, black and white. Between 1916 and 1918 he worked closely with Mondrian and in 1917 he joined De STIJL, painting abstract compositions with small geometric shapes of primary colour, such as *Composition* (1917, Kröller-Müller). His colour analysis and interior colour schemes were an important component of the movement's aesthetic. After 1918 he also painted figurative works. See vol. 3 p. **187**

Le Corbusier (Charles Edouard Jeanneret) 1887–1965
French architect and artist of Swiss parentage. He is principally famous as one of the greatest and most influential architects of the 20th century, but early in his career he painted, and with Ozenfant was the founder of PURISM.

Leduc, Ozias 1864–1955
Canadian painter, active in St-Hilaire, Quebec. His artistic concerns reflected his adherence to the traditional union of art and religion in his community, and his output included programmes of decoration in 27 churches. The easel-paintings he made for himself are composed in earth colours and have an intense, almost mystical, aura, even in a simple genre scene such as *Child with bread* (1892–99, Ottawa, NG of Canada). In 1907 he went to Paris, though this affected his work less than later readings of Symbolist theory. He encouraged Borduas, and was greatly respected by many Canadian artists.

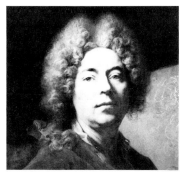

Largillière: Self-portrait, c.1704. Paris, Louvre

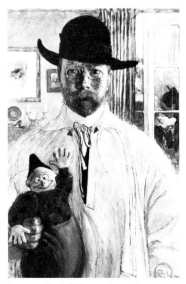

Larsson, Carl: Self-portrait, 1906. Florence, Uffizi (Scala)

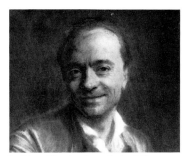

La Tour, Maurice-Quentin de: Self-portrait, c.1770. Paris, Louvre (Alinari)

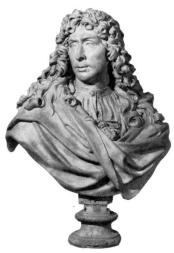

Lebrun: Terracotta bust by Coysevox, 1676. London, Wallace Coll.

Le Fauconnier, Henri 1881–1945
French painter. Between 1909 and 1913 he was in close contact with the SECTION D'OR group, producing works such as *Plenty* (1910/11, The Hague, Gemeentemuseum), in which Cubist devices are superficially applied to an allegorical theme. Around 1914 he developed a figurative expressionistic style which made a considerable impact upon younger painters in the 1920s.

Lega, Silvestro 1826–95
Italian artist active in Tuscany, a leading member of the MACCHIAIOLI. From 1856 he painted landscapes and portraits at Modigliana; then, from 1859, he associated with the Macchiaioli and painted with Signorini in 1861. Landscapes with figures from this period are particularly successful: *The pergola* (1869, Milan, Brera), with its filtered sunlight, is the best-known. Later works, such as *Grandmother's lesson* (1881, Peschiera sul Garda, Comune), concentrate more on the figure and reflect his interest in portraiture. In the late 1880s he painted superb landscapes using new creamy and rosy tones.

Le Gac, Jean born 1936
French painter and illustrator. In his illustrative work he joins text and visual image in an intimate way, and shows a persistent ironic interest in the notion of the "great" painter. In the way in which he elevates the insignificant to a position of great dramatic importance his work has been compared to the novels of Robbe-Grillet and the films of Rohmer.

Légaré, Joseph 1795–1855
Self-taught Canadian painter, active in Quebec. He is known for his many Romantic historical paintings dealing with incidents in Indian life. One of his documentary works, *The burning of the Quartier St-Roch* (1845, Quebec, Musée), represents an innovation in urban landscape, with its horrific drama reminiscent of Salvator Rosa. Plamondon studied under him until 1825.

Léger, Fernand 1881–1955
French painter who created one of the most distinctive styles of any 20th-century artist. His first major work, *Nudes in the forest* (1909–10, Otterlo, Kröller-Müller Museum), inspired by Cézanne and by early Cubism, asserted his life-long preoccupation with formal simplification and monumental structure. Aware of Cubism and associated with the Section d'Or group, he evolved a more fragmented style, as in *The wedding* (1911–12, Paris, Musée d'Art Moderne) and in 1913 arrived at the concentrated dynamism of his *Contrasting Forms* series (example, 1913, Paris, Musée d'Art Moderne), consisting of improvised abstractions expressing his enthusiasm for the polished metallic surfaces of machinery. *Three women* (1921, New York, MOMA) epitomizes his return, after the War, to an explicitly figurative tradition. His purpose was to celebrate modern urban and technological culture by means of heroic scale and popular imagery, as in his series of paintings of people at work and play (*The builders*, 1950, Biot, Musée Léger). *The great parade* (1954, New York, Guggenheim) employs a more informal structure typical of his late style. He also designed theatre sets, films and decorative schemes, and taught at Yale University. See vol. 1 p. 45; vol. 3 pp. **150–151, 179, 229**

Legros, Alphonse 1837–1911
French painter, etcher and sculptor. In 1863 he came to England on Whistler's encouragement. His religious scenes and church interiors are notable for their pious mood and careful delineation. He had considerable influence as a teacher of etching in London. See vol. 4 p. *171*

Lehmbruck, Wilhelm 1881–1919
German graphic artist and sculptor, an outstanding figure in the revival of German sculpture in the early 20th century. He trained in Düsseldorf and visited Italy before settling in Paris, 1910–14. A reflection of Maillol's style may be seen in the smooth masses of Lehmbruck's bronze and stone nudes, but Rodin's example and Minne's expressionist style made a deeper impression on him. The graceful, attenuated *Kneeling woman* (completed 1911, New York, MOMA) also recalls Gothic sculpture, not only in its stylized distortion, but in its sweet, sad sentiment. After 1912 a stronger tendency towards abstract form is apparent both in his etchings and in his nude figures (*Seated youth*, 1918, Duisberg, Wilhelm-Lehmbruck Museum). See vol. 3 p. **131**

Leibl, Wilhelm Maria Hubertus 1844–1900
German painter of peasant genre scenes. He studied in Munich under Piloty and, after meeting Courbet in Munich in 1869, moved to Paris until the Franco-Prussian War of 1870. In the 1870s he abandoned Munich and went with his followers to live in a small Bavarian village where he could better observe the community. *Three women in church* (1882, Hamburg, Kunsthalle) is probably the best-known of his masterly renderings of village life.

Leighton, Frederic, Lord 1830–96
English painter and sculptor of historical and mythological subjects. Queen Victoria bought the first painting he exhibited at the Royal Academy, and thereafter his career flourished, and he became the prime exponent of a fashionable classicism. He made numerous studies of nude and draped figures in preparation for such polished paintings as *Captive Andromache* (c.1888, Manchester, City Art Gallery). He became President of the Royal Academy in 1878 and a peer in 1896. The elaborate home he built in Kensington is now the Leighton Museum. See vol. 3 p. **87**

Leinberger, Hans
documented 1510–30
German sculptor. He is first documented at Landshut, Bavaria, where he later worked for the court. He seems early to have been influenced by the painters of the Danube school and translated their interest in landscape into sculptured wooden reliefs. In his important altarpiece for the Collegiate church at Moosburg, 1513–14, representing the Virgin, saints and Crucifixion, he demonstrated his mastery of space and movement; his innovatory sculpting of deeply cut, swirling draperies is highly personal. His later works continued to develop this new freedom in large, free-standing figures of emotional intensity.

Lely, Sir Peter 1618–80
English portrait painter of Dutch origin. His real name was van der Faes, but early on he took his nickname from the lily carved on his father's house in The Hague. He studied in Haarlem, and came to England in the mid-1640s. He first painted landscape and historical compositions (*Sleeping nymphs*, early 1650s, London, Dulwich College Picture Gallery), but quickly turned to portraiture. His early work is Dutch in temper, but was soon transformed by the influence of van Dyck's portraits. He is, however, usually coarser in technique, more brightly coloured and bolder in mood than van Dyck. Though he painted Charles I, Cromwell and the leading figures of the Commonwealth, Lely is particularly associated with the luxurious Restoration court of Charles II, and with the King's mistresses. The series of female portraits at Hampton Court known as *The Windsor Beauties* is typical of his subject matter and style. He operated a highly organized studio, and often painted no more than the head in works which bear his name, as in the series of *Flagmen* (c.1666, Greenwich, National Maritime Museum). Greenhill and Largillière both worked in his studio. See vol. 2 p. **207**

Lemieux, Jean Paul born 1904
Canadian painter of figures and landscapes, working in Quebec. He evolved a Symbolist style of poetic reticence, conveyed in monumental figures, often set in front of stark landscapes (*Cardinal Leger*, 1962, Paris, J. Leger coll.).

Lemmen, Georges 1865–1916
Belgian painter, graphic artist and designer. The influence of Seurat converted him to Pointillism and together with van Rysselberghe he was an advocate of Neo-Impressionism in Belgium. Apart from his paintings in all genres, he designed posters, textiles, wall-paper and ceramics, which won him an important place in Belgian Jugendstil.

Le Moal, Jean born 1909
French abstract painter who was taught by Bissière. A typical example of his work is *Feast of St John, midsummer day* (1955, Paris, Musée d'Art Moderne), in which a loose linear grid defines freely applied patches of strong colour.

Lemoyne, François 1688–1737
French painter of history and mythology, an important figure in the transition from Baroque to Rococo. His colourful, illusionistic *Apotheosis of Hercules* ceiling at Versailles (completed 1736) was a great contemporary success and led to his appointment as Premier Peintre du Roi. It was, however, the swan-song of the Baroque decorative tradition in France and was soon outmoded by the intimate and graceful Rococo style of his pupils Boucher and Natoire. *Time revealing Truth* (1737, London, Wallace Coll.) was completed a few hours before his suicide.

Lemoyne family
French sculptors active in the reigns of Louis XIV and Louis XV, 1654–1774. *The Companion of Diana* (1724, Washington, NG) is typical of the graceful Baroque ornamental work of **Jean-Louis** (1665–1755), though he is better known for his portrait busts in the manner of his master Coysevox (*Jules Hardouin Mansart*, 1703, Paris, Louvre). His brother **Jean-Baptiste the Elder** (1679–1731) was a minor figure whose *Death of Hippolytus* (1715, Louvre) shows the influence of Rubenisme on sculpture. Jean Louis's son, **Jean-Baptiste the Younger** (1704–78), was the most important artist of the family. His vivacious naturalism made him the most successful portrait sculptor of his generation (*Louis XV*, 1757, New York, Metropolitan). His monumental work included a *Baptism of Christ* (1731, Paris, St Roch) and his bravura equestrian *Louis XV* (Bordeaux, destroyed),

which invited comparison with the classicizing work of Bouchardon who, unlike Lemoyne, had been to Rome. He was an influential teacher; Falconet, Houdon, Pajou and Pigalle were among his pupils.

Le Nain brothers
French painters, **Antoine** (c.1588–1648), **Louis** (c.1593–1648) and **Mathieu** (1607–77) born in Laon, but all active in Paris by 1630. The demarcation of the oeuvres of the three brothers is one of the most controversial problems in the history of art, for all their signed paintings bear only the surname, and those that are dated are from 1648 or earlier, when all three were alive. Ultimately we are still dependent on the distinctions made by the novelist du Bail, writing in 1643. According to him Antoine made "miniatures and portraits in small", Louis "little pictures in which a thousand different attitudes which he copies from nature attract the eye", and Mathieu "portraits and big pictures". The paintings associated with Louis are the most important—sober genre scenes of peasants painted with great dignity and an almost classical simplicity (*The peasants' meal*, 1642, Paris, Louvre). They are entirely different in feeling from contemporary Dutch or Flemish paintings of peasants, and historians have often wondered who bought such works. Examples of paintings given to the other two brothers are *The little singers* (Rome, Palazzo Venezia) by Antoine and *The guardroom* (1643, Louvre) by Mathieu, and the three collaborated on religious works. See vol. 2 p. **192**

Lenbach, Franz von 1836–94
German painter, who dominated the artistic life of Munich in the last two decades of the 19th century and was the most popular German portrait painter of the period. He studied under Piloty in Munich and travelled in Italy, where he came under the influence of the Venetian school. Combining the colours of Titian with detailed realism, he achieved a style of festive and highly flattering portraiture which led to commissions from leading European statesmen, fashionable society and the court, and to numerous portraits of Bismarck. A collection of his works is housed in the Lenbachhaus, Munich.

Lenk, Kaspar-Thomas born 1933
West German sculptor, specializing in convoluted forms created from layers of thin plates of wood, aluminium or plastic, occasionally brightly coloured. These forms are inspired by Constructivist ideals and, like his graphic work, they reflect a deep belief in technology and art's integration into modern commercial society (*Stacking*, 1966, Stuttgart, Galerie Müller).

Lens, Andreas Cornelis
1739–1822
One of the earliest Neoclassical painters in Belgium. He was a pupil of Mengs in Rome and a devotee of Winckelmann's ideas. He published a book on ancient costume (1776) and a treatise *On Good Taste and Beauty in Painting* (1811), which were more influential than his smooth and rather vapid paintings, examples of which are in the Musées Royaux des Beaux-Arts, Antwerp.

Lentulov, Aristarkh Vasilevich
1882–1943
Russian painter, a founder-member of the avantgarde KNAVE OF DIAMONDS Moscow exhibiting group (1910). Cézanne was an important inspiration,

and Lentulov invented a distinctive method of abstracting form, in a series of more and more imaginary architectural townscapes, constructed from overlapping planes of colour, as in *Nizhny Novgorod* (1915, Moscow, Tretyakov Gallery). In the 1920s he returned to Cézanne-based landscapes.

Leochares active *c*.370–325 BC
Greek sculptor, known to have worked for Philip of Macedon and Alexander the Great. He collaborated with Skopas and others on the sculpted friezes of the Mausoleum at Halicarnassus about 353 BC (though his part in it is not certain). The famous "*Apollo Belvedere*" in the Vatican is sometimes said to be a Roman copy of an original by him. See vol. 2 p. **41**

Leonardo da Vinci 1452–1519
Florentine artist, scientist and thinker, one of the greatest Renaissance painters and perhaps the most versatile genius who has ever lived. The range of his accomplishments was astonishing, for he was an anatomist, engineer, mathematician, naturalist and philosopher, as well as a painter, sculptor and architect. He trained in Verrocchio's studio and according to Vasari gave the first great demonstration of his prowess by painting in his master's *Baptism of Christ* (*c*.1472, Florence, Uffizi) the left-hand angel, which indeed makes the other figures look prosaic. In 1481/2 he went to Milan, leaving unfinished his early masterpiece *The Adoration of the Magi* (Uffizi), a work of great originality and complexity in its sense of movement and in its variety of gesture and expression. In Milan he worked chiefly at the court of Duke Ludovico Sforza. His two most important artistic undertakings before he left in 1499 were an abortive project for a huge equestrian statue of Ludovico's father, and his mural painting of *The Last Supper* (*c*.1495, S. Maria delle Grazie). This is now a sad ruin because Leonardo's technical experiments with his medium failed, but it still retains some of the authority which made it the most celebrated painting of its time. Leonardo's drawings and notes indicate the immense care taken in its design. "That figure is most praiseworthy", he wrote, "which, by its action, best expresses the passions of the soul." This psychological approach was revolutionary, and the idea of the artist as a creative thinker rather than a skilled artisan stems chiefly from Leonardo. In 1500 he passed through Venice, then looked mainly to Florence until 1506. From this period dates the *Mona Lisa* (Paris, Louvre), innovatory in the subtlety and naturalness of its pose and expression, and the wall-painting of *The Battle of Anghiari* in the Palazzo Vecchio. This is destroyed but copies show that its dynamic energy anticipated the Baroque. From 1506 to 1513 Leonardo was based in Milan, although he made two lengthy visits to Florence. In 1513 he went to Rome, and in 1516, at the invitation of Francis I, settled in France, where he died. His later years were taken up increasingly with scientific work (which largely remained hidden in his notebooks). Leonardo's contemporary reputation was colossal and has never faded. He was a generation older than the other two supreme artists of the High Renaissance, Michelangelo and Raphael, and with his nobly balanced designs and heroic figures can virtually be said to have created the style. Another immensely influential aspect of his work (notably on Giorgione's style) was his SFUMATO modelling through light and shade which suggested rather than de-

lineated the form. No sculptural or architectural works are certainly known to be by Leonardo, but his ideas had wide influence in both fields. Although his paintings are so few, more drawings exist by Leonardo than by any other contemporary Italian artist (mainly at Windsor Castle), and in them is revealed his insatiable quest for knowledge and the range and power of his extraordinary genius. See vol. 1 pp. **28–29**, *68*, *142*, *159*; vol. 2 pp. **128–131**

Leoni, Leone *c*.1509–90
Italian sculptor. He worked in Venice and Padua as a medallist, then in 1537 moved to Rome as engraver at the papal mint. He was condemned to the galleys for a murder conspiracy, but was freed and became master of the mint in Milan. His work has a clear monumentality combined with Mannerist smoothness and in the late 1540s he achieved wide fame with his large-scale bronzes, producing portraits of Emperor Charles V and the imperial family. Later he moved to Spain, where his son **Pompeo** (*c*.1533–1608) also settled. Father and son collaborated in several works, including the production of 27 statues for the high altar of the Escorial, near Madrid, completed in 1582. Pompeo created the lifelike and majestic statues of Charles V, Philip II and their families on each side of the altar. See vol. 2 p. **174**

Le Parc, Julio born 1928
Argentine artist, major contributor in the developments of KINETIC art in the 1960s. He took an early interest in Lucio Fontana's Spatialist movement and in 1958 he moved to Paris, where he currently resides. There, with Yvaral Vasarély, Soto, Tinguely, Bill and other leading members of the Paris avantgarde, he founded the GROUPE DE RECHERCHE D'ART VISUEL, 1960. Le Parc's work emphasizes technological means, spectator participation and movement and has become increasingly environmental. He is best known for mobiles using reflected light (example London, Tate) and for motorized works, such as *Visual games: forms in movement* (1966, Paris, Galerie Denise René). See vol. 3 p. 245

Lépicié, Michel-Nicolas-Bernard 1735–84
French painter of history and genre. He is best known for his genre paintings, which were influenced by Greuze. In a work such as the charming *Fanchon arising* (1773, St-Omer, Musée-Hôtel-Sandelin) simplicity and sentiment combine to produce a surreptitious erotic frisson typical of the early phases of the anti-Rococo reaction.

Lépine, Stanislas Victor Edouard 1835–92
French painter, a pupil of Corot. *Rue de l'Abreuvoir in Montmartre* (Edinburgh, NG) is a typical simple, street scene. His delicacy of colouring and light touch in some ways anticipated the Impressionists, with whom he exhibited in 1874.

Le Sueur, Eustache 1616–55
French history painter born and active in Paris, and a founder-member of the French Academy in 1648. He was a pupil of Vouet, but his Baroque style was soon discarded and he turned to Poussin for inspiration. Le Sueur, however, is less heroic and more tender and reflective than his model. His most important work is the series of paintings depicting *The Life of St Bruno* (begun 1648, Paris, Louvre), executed for the Chartreuse of Paris, but since they originally decorated

the cloister these are now in rather poor condition. His late works are dull imitations of Raphael. See vol. 2 p. **198**

Le Sueur, Hubert *c*.1595–*c*.1650
French sculptor who settled in England in 1625. He was patronized by Charles I and is remembered chiefly for his bronze equestrian statue of the king (1633) at Charing Cross, London. He had great skill as a bronze-caster, but his works are rather empty in feeling and their smooth dead surfaces give them the curious impression of having been inflated from within rather than modelled. Immensely conceited, he sometimes signed his busts (which helped to popularize the form in England) "Praxiteles Le Sueur".

Letin or **Lestin, Jacques de** 1597–1661
French painter. In the 1620s he was in Rome but by 1626 he had returned to his native Troyes, bringing back a Baroque style with Caravaggesque overtones. Most of his best pictures were executed for local churches, a good example being the signed *Presentation of the Virgin* (Troyes, Musée des Beaux-Arts).

Leu, Hans the Younger *c*.1490–1531
Swiss painter and designer of woodcuts. He was born in Zurich, but worked under Dürer in Nuremberg and Baldung-Grien in Freiburg-im-Breisgau, returning to Zurich in 1514. His work is notable chiefly for his interest in landscape, as in his monochrome *Orpheus* (1519, Basel, Kunstmuseum).

Leutze, Emanuel Gottlieb 1816–68
American history painter. He was born in Germany, but lived in Virginia before returning to study in Düsseldorf. In 1859 he settled permanently in America. He is remembered almost solely for his *Washington crossing the Delaware* (1851, New York, Metropolitan), a large and flamboyant canvas, which characterizes his contemporary type of history painting, modern in technique but based on the Grand Manner of the 18th century. See vol. 1 p. 57

Levi, Carlo 1902–75
Italian painter and writer. He began painting in 1923 in association with the NOVECENTO but soon reacted against its academicism and adopted an Expressionist style in treating scenes from Lucanian peasant life. After World War II he worked as a writer and politician before resuming painting in the 1950s. With Guttuso, he was seen as the leading Italian social realist.

Levine, Jack born 1915
American painter. He began his career by working for the Federal Art Projects in 1935. During the 1940s he continued in a figurative Expressionist tradition, related to Rouault and Soutine, painting social themes with a sharp, satirical vision. His *Gangster funeral* (1952–53, New York, Whitney) makes a cynical political comment. Later works turn their attention to the middle class.

Levitan, Isaak Ilyich 1861–1900
Russian landscape painter. From 1884 he started to exhibit with the WANDERERS and his fresh landscapes full of intimate feeling struck a new note in Russian painting (*Grey day*, 1888, Moscow, Tretyakov Gallery). He visited Paris in 1889, and was familiar with the French Impressionists, but his innumerable studies from nature place him firmly among the Russian realists. These

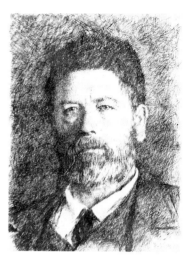
Leibl: Self-portrait drawing, 1896. Cologne, Wallraf-Richartz Museum

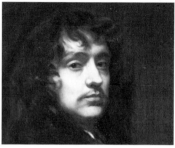
Lely: Self-portrait, *c*.1660. London, NPG

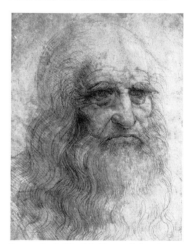
Leonardo da Vinci: Self-portrait drawing, *c*.1512. Turin, Royal Library (Alinari)

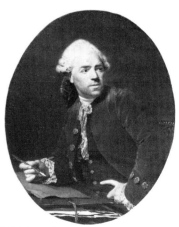
Lépicié: Self-portrait, *c*.1770. Lisbon, Calouste Gulbenkian Foundation

studies were the basis for pictures with a social message conveyed by an emotional reading of nature (*Vladimirka—Road to Siberia*, 1892, Tretyakov Gallery).

Levy, Rudolf 1875–1944
German painter, born in Poland. From 1903 to 1931 he was in Paris, where for many years he worked in Matisse's studio, and with Purrmann formed "the German Matisse School". He began as a *plein-air* artist but then tried to absorb the Fauves' palette (*On the Seine*, 1910, Duisburg, Wilhelm-Lehmbruck Museum). He died in a concentration camp.

Lewis, Percy Wyndham 1884–1957
British painter and writer. He was the central figure in the VORTICIST movement and the vociferous editor and principal contributor to the magazine *Blast* (1914), a violent outcry against the moribund legacy of Victorian England. His harsh, angular paintings such as *Workshop* (1914, London, Tate) often recall Italian Futurism in their rhythmic repetition of form and their attempts to express the mechanistic quality of the modern world; at times they approached abstraction. In his later career Lewis created some of the finest British portraits of this century, painted with an almost Ingres-like clarity of outline and in harsh colour (*T.S. Eliot*, 1938, Durban, Municipal Art Gallery). See vol. 3 pp. **154–155**

LeWitt, Sol born 1928
American CONCEPTUAL sculptor. He is fascinated with the infinite combinations inherent in the most radically reduced formal vocabulary, and serialization and the creation of systems are his prime concern. This is evident in his many white and black cubes—displayed as open or closed forms, singly, in series and as three-dimensional projections of the grid (*Open modular cube*, 1966, Toronto, Art Gallery of Ontario). He also creates prints, "bookworks" and wall-drawings, which he plans and leaves others to execute. Since the later 1970s he has used not only black, white and grey but also the three primary colours. See vol. 3 p. **247**

Leyden, Lucas van 1494–1533
Netherlandish engraver and painter, an outstanding artist of the northern Renaissance, and one of the greatest of all engravers. He was a boy prodigy and soon outstripped his master Engelbrechtsen. His earliest dated engraving, *Mohammed and the murdered monk* (1508) is astonishingly mature—inventive and of the highest technical accomplishment. There are dated engravings throughout his career, but there is no clear stylistic development. The strongest influence on him was Dürer, whom he met in Antwerp in 1521, but Lucas was less single-minded and often included anecdotal features in his prints. His paintings, which are more variable in quality than his engravings but often highly original, place him among the pioneers of the great Dutch genre tradition; *The game of chess* (*c*.1510, West Berlin, Staatliche Museen) and *The card players* (*c*.1516, Wilton House, Wiltshire), both masterly character studies, are outstanding. His masterpiece in painting, however, is the large *Last Judgment* triptych (1526–27, Leyden, Stedelijk Museum), which demonstrates to the full his power of invention, dramatic and unusual light and colour effects and brilliant fluid brushwork. Van Mander says that Lucas was a dilettante and an Epicurean, but he was remarkably prolific. His reputation was enormous (Vasari rated him above Dürer) and his engravings had wide influence. See vol. 2 p. **161**

Leyster, Judith 1609–60
Dutch painter of portraits, genre scenes and still lifes. She was the pupil of Frans Hals in Haarlem in 1629 and at times imitated her master very closely (*The serenade*, 1626, Amsterdam, Rijksmuseum). She was also, more briefly, influenced by the work of the Utrecht Caravaggisti. In 1636 she married Jan Molenaer, whose style was also influenced by Hals, and the two of them worked together, sharing models and props in their studio. See vol. 2 p. **226**

Lhôte, André 1885–1962
French painter and sculptor. In a typical painting such as *Rugby* (1917, Paris, Musée d'Art Moderne) the composition is an academic mixture of flat, drily handled planes of colour, inspired by Cubism, and more literal descriptive passages. His teaching and writing on the aims and techniques of painting were more influential than his paintings.

Liang Kai active early 13th century
Chinese painter. After beginning his career as a painter of orthodox Confucian subjects at the Hangzhou imperial academy, he retired to a monastery to produce a series of works inspired by the intuitive, anti-rational philosophy of Chan (Zen) Buddhism. His two masterpieces are both in Japan (private collections), since Chinese Chan art was to be more appreciated there than in its homeland. One is an imaginary portrait of the Tang poet *Li Bai*, in which three or four strokes of amazing spontaneity and confidence suffice for the outline of the figure. The other is *Sixth Patriarch cutting bamboo* (also monochrome ink on paper), in which he equally emphatically rejects the decorative academic style in favour of a sparse, dry style which has great dynamism.

Liberale da Verona *c*.1445–*c*.1529
Italian painter and illuminator from Verona. He worked as an itinerant journeyman in Siena and Venice before returning to Verona in 1487. Here, in 1490, he painted frescos in the Bonaveri Chapel, S. Anastasia. His illuminations are more accomplished than his paintings. They are exquisitely coloured and richly ornamented, combining a wide variety of border decorations with illusionistic apertures into biblical scenes.

Li Chao-tao see LI SIXUN

Li Cheng active *c*.960–990
Chinese painter. He came from an élite family of the old Tang capital Chang'an, and settled in Shandong province, where he was active as a landscape painter under the early Song dynasty. Mi Fei in the 11th century doubted whether any of his works survived, but his fame was such that 159 pieces attributed to him were found in the Song imperial household collection. Those that survive today are mostly wintry, desolate scenes (*Travellers among snowy hills*, Boston, MFA). See vol. 1 p. *60*

Lichtenstein, Roy born 1923
American painter, sculptor and graphic artist, one of the best-known POP artists. In his most characteristic works he parodied pulp magazines about romance, war and sports heroes by blowing up one or a few isolated frames from a cartoon narrative in paintings such as *As I opened fire* (1963, Amsterdam, Stedelijk Museum). The dots of the printing process in the originals are reproduced by hand in the paintings. By the mid-1960s Lichtenstein's focus shifted from the mannerisms of the media to those of art. In his painted and graphic work the Greek temple, De Stijl, Picasso and the Abstract Expressionist brush-stroke are his subjects, treated in a bright, linear, Pop manner. Witty sculptures expand his treatment of this theme. See vol. 1 pp. *54–55*; vol. 3 pp. **238**, *254*

Licini, Osvaldo 1894–1958
Italian painter. His figurative subjects and portraits of the 1920s gave way to CONSTRUCTIVIST works in the 1930s that established his reputation as one of the pioneers of the modern movement in Italy. In the 1950s his work was influenced by Surrealism.

Licinio, Bernardino *c*.1491–before 1565
Venetian painter. His early work is in the style of Giovanni Bellini, but he soon adopted Titian and Palma Vecchio as his models. He is best known for his group portraits (*Family group*, 1524, Hampton Court, Royal coll.).

Liebermann, Max 1847–1935
German painter, one of the first artists of his country to absorb the lessons of French Impressionism. He studied in Berlin and at the Weimar Academy; then travels in France and Holland brought him into contact with the Barbizon school and with Israëls and the Dutch school of open-air painting. Holland not only gave him stylistic inspiration but also much of his subject matter of the 1880s, when he painted scenes of peasant rural life and of community life in institutions such as orphanages. On moving back to Berlin he became the moving force in promoting new trends. He was a founder-member of the Berlin SEZESSION (1898–99) and his influence in the art world continued after his appointment as President of the Berlin Academy (1922–33). See vol. 3 p. **130**

Liège, Jean de died 1382
Flemish sculptor, employed by Charles V of France (1364–80) for most of his career. His many projects are mostly known only from records and descriptions. His grandest works, royal tombs at St Denis and elsewhere, were sculpted in marble, recumbent effigies under ornate canopies on elaborate bases. That of Philippa of Hainault, Queen of England (*c*.1365–67, London, Westminster Abbey), a plump 50-year-old lady, is characteristic of his mildly realistic style.

Lievens, Jan 1607–74
Dutch painter, etcher and wood-engraver, born in Leyden. Lievens was a prodigy, and after training with Lastman in Amsterdam was working as an independent artist by the age of 13. He became a close friend of Rembrandt and shared a studio with him in Leyden during the 1620s. *The raising of Lazarus* (1631, Brighton Art Gallery), with its dramatic low viewpoint and daring representation of Lazarus only by his arms emerging from the tomb, shows Lievens' power at this stage of his career. His brilliant early promise, however, was not fulfilled. He spent about a decade in Antwerp before returning to Amsterdam in 1644, and his later work, influenced by Rubens and van Dyck, was elegant but facile. Dividing his time between Amsterdam and The Hague, he received numerous commissions for historical and allegorical paintings and was also a popular portraitist.

Li Gonglin *c*.1040–1106
Chinese painter, a major figure painter of the northern Song period, whose importance in his field matches that of Guo Xi in landscapes. Li is the acknowledged originator of the technique, closely linked to that of calligraphy, of *bai miao*, "writing" his paintings with rhythmic strokes of a brush only lightly loaded with paint, but few works from his own hand survive. His immense prestige occasioned great numbers of copies, over-optimistic attributions and fakes, and even the best-documented compositions such as the *Classic of Filial Piety* (Princeton, University Museum) have at times been under suspicion. His famous painting of *Five horses* was destroyed in Japan World during War II.

Liljefors, Bruno 1860–1939
Swedish animal and landscape painter, draughtsman and writer. He studied in Germany and France and was inspired by Japanese art and by photographs. His feeling for nature is displayed in his bewitching image *The owl* (1895, Gothenburg Museum).

Li Lung-mien (Li Po-shih) see LI GONGLIN

Limbourg brothers
Netherlandish illuminators, nephews of Jean Malouel. There were three brothers, **Herman**, **Jean** and **Pol** de Limbourg, all of whom were dead by 1416, probably victims of an epidemic. Jean and Herman were apprenticed to a goldsmith in Paris in 1400, and in 1402 Jean and Pol were illuminating a Bible Moralisée (probably that in Paris, BN) for Philip the Bold of Burgundy. Some time after Philip's death in 1404 they moved into the service of his brother, Jean de Berri. All three continued in his service until their deaths. Pol was probably head of the workshop, but it is very difficult to differentiate their work. The *Belles Heures* (*c*.1408, New York, Metropolitan) was the first completed major work which they illuminated for the Duke. Their most famous manuscript, *Les Très Riches Heures* (Chantilly, Musée Condé) was unfinished at their death. Though the figure style is strongly influenced by Italian art (there is good evidence that they had been to Italy), this exquisite book is the archetype of French INTERNATIONAL GOTHIC art: the elegant and refined miniatures combine a decorative use of colour and pattern with naturalistic detail. The calendar miniatures reflect contemporary life, each month being illustrated with an appropriate scene of peasants at work or courtiers at leisure, and several feature one of the Duke's castles in the background. In the complexity and accomplishment of composition and landscape, the Limbourgs surpassed their contemporaries. They were famous in their own time and had a privileged position at the Duke of Berri's court. See vol. 1 pp. **40–41**; vol. 2 p. **89**

Limner
In the general sense, a now archaic term for an artist. It was first used of manuscript illuminators, then in the 16th century came to describe portrait miniaturists—Hilliard's treatise was called *The Arte of Limning*. The word is now used to describe the untrained sign-painters and portraitists of Colonial America in the 17th and 18th centuries.

Lindner, Ernest born 1897
Vienna-born Canadian landscape painter, who has made a highly individual and imaginative contribution to

Superrealism. Encouraged in 1964 by Jules Olitski and the critic Clement Greenberg, he intensified his focus on the phenomena of generation. Amongst his intricate studies of tree-trunks, the watercolour *Decay and growth* (1964, Regina, Norman MacKenzie Gallery) is an outstanding example.

Lindner, Richard 1901–78
German painter, who left Germany for Paris in 1933 and settled in the USA in 1941. He illustrated books and contributed graphic work to magazines, but abandoned illustrations in 1950 to devote himself to painting. His disturbing, often erotic, images are painted in bright, hard-edged colour (*Rock-Rock*, 1966–67, Dallas, Museum of Fine Arts). Elements of his style derive from Cubism and Surrealism but also seem to anticipate Pop art.

Linear perspective see PERSPECTIVE

Linnell, John 1792–1882
English landscape painter, a pupil of West and Varley, friend and patron of Blake, and father-in-law of Samuel Palmer. His early landscapes, both oil and watercolour, have the freshness of Constable's sketches, but his mature paintings of the Surrey countryside are done in a fleecy pastoral manner influenced by Palmer, but without his intensity of vision (*The last gleam before the storm*, c.1847, Liverpool, Walker Art Gallery). He also painted portraits and did Bible illustrations.

Linnqvist, Hilding born 1891
Swedish painter. He was influenced by Munch and Persian miniatures and his naive style, often representing town life, still lifes and flower-pieces, became more decorative and brightly coloured after visits abroad (*Market scene in a small French town*, 1921–25, Stockholm, Moderna Museet). He also worked on monuments and was Professor at the Academy in Stockholm, 1939–41.

Linocut
Relief printing process introduced in the 20th century using a piece of thick linoleum on a block of wood, and tools similar to those employed in woodcutting. The smooth, easily worked surface allows bold, simple images to be made by cutting away negative lines and areas. After the block is inked, prints are taken in a press or by hand. Polychrome prints can be made by using separate blocks for each colour or by progressively cutting away and re-inking a single block. A popular teaching medium, the linocut has been effectively used by artists such as Matisse, Picasso and Gaudier-Brzeska. See vol. 1 p. 166

Liotard, Jean-Etienne 1702–89
Swiss portrait painter, active throughout Europe. Liotard's paintings, most of which are pastels, are very distinctive in their lucid clarity and high finish. After working in Paris and Rome, he went to Constantinople for four years (1738–42), and adopted Turkish dress and beard to promote himself thereafter. His bizarre appearance is recorded in several *Self-portraits*; examples are in the Uffizi, Florence, and the Museum of Art and History, Geneva, which has an outstanding collection of his work. His sitters included the Empress Maria Theresa (1744–45) and children of the French (1749–52) and English (1754–55) royal families. His most celebrated work is the utterly straightforward *Girl serving chocolate* (1744–45, Dresden, Gemäldegalerie). See vol. 1 p. 160

Lipchitz, Jacques (Chaim Yakob) 1891–1973
Russian sculptor, born in Lithuania. He studied engineering before moving permanently to Paris in 1909 to take up art. From 1914 he began to invent sculptures with interlocking planes, in which he explored the possibilities of using CUBIST principles in three dimensions (*Head*, 1915, London, Tate). During the 1920s he developed a freer, linear approach, closer to Surrealism and often using skeletal forms. After emigrating to America in 1941 he readopted his early Cubist approach, which he used in an almost expressionist manner; the best-known example is *Sacrifice* (1948, Buffalo, Albright-Knox Art Gallery). See vol. 3 p. **178**

Lippi, Filippino c.1457–1504
Florentine painter, the son of Filippo Lippi. He produced altarpieces, portraits and *cassone* paintings, but his best works are his frescos. By 1472 he was the pupil of Botticelli, from whom he learnt his fine draughtsmanship. His first major painting, *The vision of St Bernard* (c.1480, Florence, Badia) displays his more robust version of Botticelli's linear expressiveness and sweet sentiment. In 1484 he completed Masaccio's and Masolino's frescos in the Brancacci Chapel, S. Maria del Carmine, Florence, imitating the former's style with great faithfulness. In 1488 he went to Rome to decorate the Caraffa Chapel in S. Maria sopra Minerva, with frescos depicting *The life of St Thomas Aquinas* (1488–93), remarkable for their free handling and powerful movement. His most important work, however, was the fresco cycle of *The lives of SS. Philip and John* for the Strozzi Chapel in S. Maria Novella, Florence (1495–1502). The imaginatively and elaborately detailed classical architecture, and more so the breadth of composition, the conviction of movement and the ringing colours foreshadow the monumental grandeur of the High Renaissance. Filippino's drawings are also fine. See vol. 2 p. **117**

Lippi, Fra Filippo c.1406–69
One of the leading Florentine painters of the generation following Masaccio's death. An unwanted child, he was entered in the Carmelite monastery of the Carmine and took his vows in 1421. Religion was not his vocation, and he later caused scandal because of his love affair with a nun, Lucrezia Buti, who bore his son Filippino. They were allowed to marry, but Filippo still signed himself "*Frater Philippus*". According to Vasari, Filippo decided to become a painter after watching Masaccio at work in the Brancacci Chapel in the Carmine church, but in his earliest dated work, "*The Tarquinia Madonna*" (1437, Rome, Galleria Nazionale), he has already gone far towards translating Masaccio's modelling into line, though the Virgin and Child are still robust, even clumsy. The picture is compelling in its wistful melancholy, created by the handling of light, which probably reflects Netherlandish influence. Also in 1437 Filippo began the Barbadori altarpiece (Paris, Louvre), an early example of a *sacra conversazione*, uniting in one coherent space the compartmentalized elements of the standard Gothic scheme. In the 1450s Filippo's mature style, with its supreme elegance of line and magical aura of pale white light, emerged, notably in the exquisite *Madonna and Child* tondo (1452, Florence, Pitti). Some of his most delicate works were panels for the Medici: *The Madonna adoring her Child* (late 1450s, West Berlin, Staat-

liche Museen) was painted for the Medici Palace Chapel; but Filippo also painted frescos, notably *The feast of Herod*, with its lightly tripping Salome, in the cycles of SS. Stephen and John the Baptist (1452–65) in Prato Cathedral. His delicate, decorative style was continued above all by Botticelli, but finds reflection also in artists such as Desiderio. See vol. 2 p. **107**

Lippold, Richard born 1915
American abstract sculptor. His work stems from his training as an industrial designer and his interest in Constructivism. He is best known for his "space cages", suspended constructions of thin wire and sheet-metal tautly stretched, as in *Variation no. 7: Full moon* (1949, New York, MOMA), based on a double cone. He uses symmetrical arrangements of geometrical shapes, often illuminated within dark surroundings giving an illusion of weightlessness.

Lipton, Seymour born 1903
American sculptor. Largely self-taught, he took up sculpture in 1928. In the mid-1940s he turned from wood and stone to sheet-metal, molten alloys and soldering. His images of these years suggest Surrealist mythic figures, while in the later 1940s they relate to cages. The curving, shell-like forms of *Sea King* (1956, Buffalo, Albright-Knox Art Gallery) alternately scoop out and bulge into space. His shapes are generally oppressive—abstract, yet suggestive of the human anatomy or organic growths.

Li Sixun 651–716
Chinese painter. He was a member of the Tang imperial family, and was identified in later ages as a founder of the so-called "professional" manner of painting in a highly coloured and decorative mode. In this style mineral pigments of blue and green predominate, with a lavish use of vermilion and gold outlining. As no authentic works by Li or his important son **Li Zhaodao** (c.670–730) survive, it is impossible to determine the extent to which such later conventional interpretations are a true reflection of their art. The subjects associated with both Lis are landscapes, or elaborate palaces and pavilions, often set against towering mountains.

Lismer, Arthur 1885–1969
Canadian landscape painter, a founder-member of the GROUP OF SEVEN. He evolved a densely patterned and intimate approach to landscape composition (*Bright land*, 1938, Kleinburg, McMichael coll.), and is known also for brilliant reed-pen drawings.

Liss (Lys), **Johann** c.1597–1631
Apart from Elsheimer, the most important German painter of the 17th century. His career is obscure at many points but he probably trained in Amsterdam, possibly under Goltzius. He then visited Paris, and moved to Italy, where he is documented in Venice in 1621. He died in Verona, but worked mainly in Rome and Venice. His early style was very robust, at times almost Rubensian, and in Rome he was influenced by the Caravaggisti (*Judith and Holofernes*, c.1625, London, NG). It is his Venetian works, however, that display his greatness and originality. The looseness and freedom of his brushwork, dissolving outlines, and his brilliant high-keyed colour look forward to, and undoubtedly influenced the great Venetian painters of the 18th century. The popularity of *The vision of St Jerome* (c.1628, Venice, S. Nicolo da Tolentino) is obvious from copies.

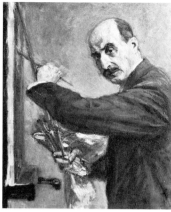

Liebermann: Self-portrait, c.1885. Cologne, Wallraf-Richartz Museum

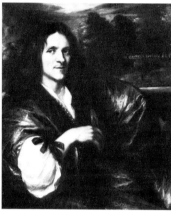

Lievens: Self-portrait, c.1644. London, NG

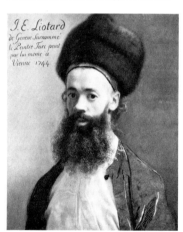

Liotard: Self-portrait, 1744. Florence, Uffizi (Scala)

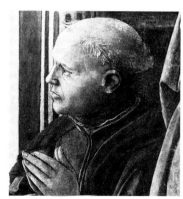

Lippi, Fra Filippo: Presumed self-portrait from *The coronation of the Virgin*, 1441–47. Florence, Uffizi (Mansell)

Lissitzky, El (Lazar Lisitsky)
1890–1941
Russian painter and designer. He trained as an architect in Germany until 1914, and was an expert lithographer, which no doubt explains why Chagall invited him to take charge of printing as well as architecture at the art school in Vitebsk. He worked there from 1919 to 1921, printing several books for Malevich. Although strongly influenced by Suprematism, he invented a rival approach to geometric painting which he named *Proun*—"the name we have given to the station of the path of the construction of new form". His *Prouns*—compositions suggesting an aerial view of modern architecture—are characterized by muted colours and rectilinear forms, for instance *Proun 99* (1924–25, New Haven, Yale Art Gallery). In the 1920s he travelled widely in Europe, disseminating information about Russian art. He also continued to produce fine prints, for example the lithograph portfolio *Victory over the Sun* (1923, London, Tate) with its semi-abstract figures. He designed many Constructivist books, of which *For the Voice*, poems by Mayakovsky turned into purely visual conceits, is outstanding. From the 1920s he organized a series of exhibitions revealing his many talents. See vol. 3 p. **159**

Li Ssu-hsün see LI SIXUN

Li Tang *c.*1050–after 1130
Chinese painter, a key figure in the preservation of the northern Song academic painting tradition after the fall of the capital at Kaifeng in 1126. Li was first Director of the Imperial Academy of Painting on its reformation at Hangzhou, and is known chiefly as a landscape painter, for whom Fan Kuan was a major influence. He used new techniques, involving a stiff, dry brush (*Landscape with snow*, Peking, Palace Museum). Many figure paintings of rural scenes have been wrongly attributed to him.

Literati
Oriental scholar painters, amateurs for whom painting was part of the pursuit of culture. Their subjects tended to be closely related to literature, especially poetry, and they held the professionl painter in contempt. The Chinese *literati* dominated painting in the MING period (1368–1644) and strongly influenced Korean and Japanese attitudes.

Lithography
A method of surface printing in which a design is drawn or painted directly on to a limestone block or metal plate. It was invented in 1798 by the Bavarian playwright Aloys Senefelder, who discovered that the natural antipathy of grease and water could be used to produce prints without cutting into the block as in relief or intaglio printing. The design, brushed or drawn on the stone with ink or a greasy crayon, is chemically fixed before the stone is wetted down and then rolled with an oil-based ink which adheres only to the greasy image, being repelled by the negative areas that have absorbed the water. Alternatively, the design can be drawn on paper and transferred to the stone at the start of the process. Reverse prints are taken on paper in a lithographic press or, in offset lithography, the image can be transferred to a rubber cylinder from which a positive print is taken. Early masters of the medium were Géricault, Delacroix and Daumier, and later its immense range of expressive effects was extended by Manet, Degas, Whistler, Redon and Bonnard. See vol. 1 p. 167

Li Zhaodao see LI SIXUN

Llanos, Fernando see YAÑEZ

Lochner, Stephan (active 1442–51)
German painter, active in Cologne, where he was the leading painter of the day. His most important work is *The Adoration of the Magi* (*c.*1448), now in Cologne Cathedral, but originally painted for the Town Hall Chapel, where it was seen by Dürer "with wonder and astonishment". Stylistic evidence suggests that Lochner trained in the Netherlands, for his work combines traditional elements and the soft modelling of the International Gothic with the realism of detail associated with Campin. With his bright colours and innocent expressions Lochner creates an air of radiant sweetness. See vol. 2 p. **97**

Lohse, Richard born 1902
Swiss painter. His paintings are primarily systematic explorations of colour, yet his systems are grounded in intuition. Connections have been seen with Op art of the kind produced by Bridget Riley, but his art belongs more properly in the tradition of Delaunay and Albers. It also relates to the concerns of serial and even Conceptual art. See vol. 1 p. *133*

Lomazzo, Giovanni Paolo
1538–1600
Italian painter, poet and art theorist, active in Milan. He went blind in 1571 and turned to writing on art. His *Treatise on the Art of Painting, Sculpture and Architecture* (1584) is a complete embodiment of Mannerist theory, containing sections on proportion, motion, colour, light, perspective, practice, and history, which last is a guide to iconography. In 1598 an English translation appeared, containing new information on native painters such as Hilliard.

Lombard, Lambert 1505–66
Flemish painter and engraver from Liège, said to have worked with Gossaert in Middelburg. An antiquarian and scholar, he was inspired by Roman monuments in France and Germany and this interest was reinforced by a trip to Rome in 1537. Many of his drawings from the Antique were engraved by Jerome de Cock's workshop. His subject paintings were dry and academic, but his portraits were livelier, notably the *Flute player* (Liège, Musée de l'Art Wallon). He is best remembered as a teacher; among his many pupils were Floris, Key and Goltzius.

Lombardo family
Leading Venetian sculptors of the late 15th and early 16th centuries. Originally from Lombardy, **Pietro** Lombardo (*c.*1435–1515) and his sons **Tullio** (*c.*1455–1532) and **Antonio** (died 1516) established a successful workshop producing monuments and chapel decorations in Venice, Padua and Treviso. Pietro's early work, such as the Capella Maggiore, S. Giobbe, Venice (1470), shows strong Florentine influences. His best-known work is the monument of Doge Pietro Mocenigo (*c.*1476–81, Venice, SS. Giovanni e Paolo), executed with assistance; virile soldiers with crisply chiselled features stand within a classical arch and lateral niches. Pietro was also an architect, responsible for designing the church of S. Maria dei Miracoli in Venice. Tullio's more fluent and original classical style is evident in the ensemble of marble figures in the Vendramin Monument (*c.*1493, SS. Giovanni e Paolo), which created a new standard in monumental sculpture. The sensuously beautiful *Adam* (New York, Metropolitan Museum of Art) from this tomb exemplifies its very faithful evocation of antique sculpture. Antonio's work is less well documented and apparently subsidiary to his brother's. He and Tullio both worked on the strongly classicizing reliefs of St Anthony's shrine commissioned in 1501 (Padua, Santo), and Antonio later produced mythological reliefs for Alfonso d'Este at Ferrara, 1506–16. See vol. 2 p. **147**

Long, Richard born 1945
British LAND artist. He has brought the countryside physically into the gallery in works such as *119 stones* (1976, London, Tate), in which found objects are arranged across the floor in a pattern; he has made similar arrangements and photographed them outdoors (often in remote places); and he has documented his walks in the countryside by means of maps, photographs and objects he has picked up. His installations can be regarded as a fusion of the English landscape tradition and the preoccupation of sculptors such as Caro and King, who have taken sculpture from the pedestal on to the ground, while his outdoor Land art often recalls prehistoric earthworks. See vol. 3 p. **248**

Longhi, Pietro 1702–85
Italian genre painter. He began his career as a frescoist, painting in 1734 the grandiose *Fall of the giants* in the Palazzo Sagredo in Venice, but later specialized exclusively in small genre scenes of Venetian life. His name is invariably linked with the playwright Carlo Goldoni, who also abandoned the pompous costume drama of his time in favour of direct observation of everyday life, and with the journalist Gaspare Gozzi, who once wrote that he preferred Longhi's "representation of what he sees around him to Tiepolo's grand scenes of the imagination". Longhi's paintings, modest in intention, were filled with bland doll-like figures, often revealing the artist's considerable technical limitations, and were not as revolutionary as Gozzi would lead us to suppose. There is an extensive collection in the Ca' Rezzonico, Venice. See vol. 2 p. **244**

Lorenzetti, Ambrogio
active *c.*1319–1348?
Sienese painter, the younger and greater brother of Pietro. He is first recorded in Florence in 1321, and entered the guild there in 1327. His first documented works are the frescos on the theme of good and bad government (1338–39) in the main chamber of the Palazzo Pubblico at Siena. These masterpieces include one of the earliest realistic landscapes in Italian art, which already shows an intuitive understanding of perspectival recession. Other dated works are *The Presentation in the Temple* (1342, Florence, Uffizi) and *The Annunciation* (1344, Siena, Pinacoteca). Ambrogio, even more than Pietro, succeeded in bridging the gap between the surface decorativeness of the Sienese school and Giotto's concern for realism. Their influence was limited due to their early deaths, probably in the Black Death of 1348. See vol. 2 pp. **85–87**

Lorenzetti, Pietro
active *c.*1319–1348?
Sienese painter, the elder brother of Ambrogio. His first dated work, the 1320 polyptych of *The Virgin and Child with Saints* in the Pieve di S. Maria at Arezzo, though deriving from Duccio, shows a remarkable interest in Florentine concerns for modelling and weight. This is even more apparent in later works, such as the triptych of *The birth of the Virgin* (1342, Siena, Cathedral Museum). His finest works are the undated frescos in the Lower Church at Assisi, which include a *Descent from the Cross* of a frozen intensity difficult to parallel in Italian art. See vol. 2 p. **85**

Lorenzo Monaco *c.*1370–*c.*1425
Sienese painter and miniaturist working in Florence, where he entered the Camaldolite monastery of S. Maria degli Angeli in 1391. His style was rooted in the great 14th-century Sienese tradition stemming from Duccio. The miniatures attributed to him in choir-books in the Biblioteca Laurenziana, Florence, and his altarpieces, are radiant with softly modulated high-key pinks and blues and acidic greens and yellows; the figures are elegant and slender in decoratively looped and folded drapery, though they have also a rather rubbery look. Early works include the triptych *The coronation of the Virgin with angels and saints* (*c.*1406–10, London, NG). Later works, for instance *The Adoration of the Magi* (*c.*1423, Uffizi), show the influence of International Gothic currents, of Gentile da Fabriano and of Ghiberti. Lorenzo's late frescos of *The life of the Virgin* in the Bartolini Chapel, S. Trinità, Florence, of about 1425, witness the continued vitality of his by then outmoded style.

Loscher, Sebastian 1480/85–1548
German sculptor. Apprenticed at Augsburg, he visited northern Italy and perhaps Tuscany before returning to Augsburg in 1510. His most important work was the decoration (1510–18) of the Fugger Chapel in St Anne's Church, Augsburg. The work was carried out by many sculptors but Loscher seems to have been the most important. It was strongly influenced by Italian designs, as surviving pieces show; *Putti* from the choir-stalls (Vienna, Kunsthistorisches Museum) recall those produced by the Della Robbia workshop. He also executed a number of small-scale reliefs such as *The Virgin and Child with a female donor* (*c.*1520, Munich, Bayerisches Nationalmuseum), which show his serene style and feeling for the play of solid against void. See vol. 2 p. **159**

Lost-wax process see CIRE-PERDUE

Lotto, Lorenzo *c.*1480–after 1556
Venetian painter. According to Vasari he trained in Giovanni Bellini's studio at the same time as Giorgione and Titian. His early work is closely dependent on Bellini, but he later developed an eclectic but distinctive style, which at its best (he was a very uneven artist) is of great distinction. His finest works are his portraits, usually bold in design and moody in atmosphere. He often used a horizontal format, as in *Young man in his study* (*c.*1528, Venice, Accademia). His finest work on a large scale is *The Crucifixion* (1531, Monte San Giusto, S. Maria in Telusiano), in which he handled the dramatic possibilities of deep space and complex lighting with great panache. He worked in Rome and the Marches as well as in Venice and ended his days as a lay-brother in the monastery at Loreto. See vol. 2 p. **147**

Louis XIV 1638–1715
French king, whose reign, beginning in 1643, is associated with the establishment of the French Académies and the creation of grandiose palaces, notably Versailles, on an unprecedented scale. He used all the arts in ensembles to propagandize his monarchical glory,

and to this end employed the most famous artist of his time, Bernini, and teams of French masters led notably by Lebrun. See vol. 2 pp. 198–199

Louis, Morris 1912–62
American painter, the leader of the development of colour-stain painting in the late 1950s. Living in Washington, he remained apart from the New York school, although his early works developed through Cubism and collage, and showed an interest in Pollock's automatism. In 1953, together with Noland, he saw Frankenthaler's *Mountains and sea*, in which coloured pigment was soaked directly into the unprimed canvas. Within the following year Louis developed his own mature style. The *Veil* series (1954 and 1958) consists of thinned floods of paint successively poured on to the unstretched canvas, resulting in a subtly billowing shape which occupies nearly the entire picture surface. The *Unfurled* series (1960–61) restricts the brilliant colour to diagonally flowing, parallel trickles across the lower corners, opening out a wide central expanse of bare canvas. His last major series, the *Stripe* paintings (1961–62), consist of bands of vivid colour placed next to each other. Louis profoundly influenced Noland and other American painters in the 1960s. See vol. 1 p. *153*; vol. 3 p. **219**

Loutherbourg, Philippe Jacques de 1740–1812
French painter, primarily of dramatically charged landscapes. In 1771, after eight admired years exhibiting in the Paris Salons, Loutherbourg settled in England, where he became a friend of Gainsborough. The great actor Garrick introduced him to stage design, and Loutherbourg is most famous for his invention of the **Eidophusikon** (1781), a theatrical presentation of scenic effects of nature. His later years were spent depicting picturesque British scenery, famous battles, and literary and biblical episodes. He is well represented in London collections (Dulwich College Picture Gallery; National Maritime Museum; Tate; V&A). See vol. 3 p. **68**

Lowry, Lawrence Stephen 1887–1976
One of the most popular and distinctive of 20th-century British painters. He lived almost all his life in Salford, an industrial city in the North, and his most characteristic work was a highly personal response to this environment. Sticklike figures are set against gaunt, almost monochromatic buildings which dominate the composition. The earliest date from the 1920s and frequently have some semi-humorous anecdotal content, as in *The arrest* (1927, Nottingham, Castle Museum). In other paintings the figures are dwarfed by the bleak urban panorama. In spite of the primitive quality of Lowry's drawing he was in no way a naive painter and studied art for several years. See vol. 3 p. **250**

Lubarda, Petar 1907–74
Yugoslav painter, who lived in Paris for most of the inter-War period. From the figurative and dramatic realism of his early works he evolved towards increasingly abstract Expressionism, drawing his inspiration from the landscape of his native Montenegro and from historical legends (the largest and best-known instance being *The Battle of Kosovo*, 1953, a mural in the Executive Council Building of the Republic of Serbia, Belgrade). He had a considerable influence on younger Yugoslav painters.

Ludius (Studius)
active 1st century BC–1st century AD
Roman wall-painter of the Augustan period, painting in a style since known as the Second POMPEIAN. He was one of the few painters of the Roman period whom Pliny thought worthy of mention—he describes him as having invented the genre of pleasant rustic scenes in a landscape setting. On this basis some have identified him as the painter of the splendid decoration of a house near the Villa Farnesina in Rome, known as the Farnesina Master.

Luini, Bernardino active 1512–32
Milanese painter. His style was formed by such Milanese artists as Bramantino but later he became one of Leonardo's most prominent followers. He vulgarized Leonardo's style, turning his enigmatic smiles into sickly smirks, but his paintings were very popular. His output was enormous, and there are many examples in Milan.

Lukasbrüder see NAZARENES

Luks, George Benjamin 1867–1933
American painter. Originally he worked as a newspaper illustrator but Henri persuaded him to take up painting. He exhibited with The EIGHT and is associated with the ASHCAN school. His flamboyant personality is reflected in paintings such as *The wrestlers* (1905, Boston, MFA), which is painted from the level of a ringside spectator. Both the style of this work and its subject matter—a scene of lower-class urban life—reveal his debt to Henri. See vol. 3 p. **204**

Luminists
Group of mid-19th-century American landscape painters whose concern with light and atmosphere relates them to the BARBIZON school and IMPRESSIONISM. Cole evolved his treatment of light before visiting Europe. Other artists, including Church, Durand, and Lane, who all painted the natural wonders of America and concentrated on atmospheric effects, are also termed Luminists.

Lundstrøm, Vilhelm 1893–1950
Danish painter, one of the pioneers of modern art in Denmark. During the 1920s, under the influence of Picasso and Braque, he became interested in problems of pure form and evolved a monumental classicism, evident in the figure of *Thusnelda* (1925–30, Oslo, NG). He became Professor at the Academy in Copenhagen in 1944.

Lüthi, Urs born 1947
Swiss PERFORMANCE artist. The principal theme of his art is ambiguity, of which androgyny is the prime symbol. An inveterate poser, as photographs in his teens show, he projects himself in a variety of guises, frequently transvestite, sometimes comic, sometimes unsettling. While his effect on audience has been strong, he is known to most people only through his copious photographic documentation and this has arguably become his main medium.

Lysippos active 370–312 BC
Greek sculptor from Sicyon, famous for introducing a canon of proportion for the human body in which the head was small and the limbs slender and firmly knit. No originals survive, but a Roman copy of his "*Apoxyomenos*" (Athlete scraping down, *c*.325 BC, Vatican Museum) demonstrates his canon, and also offers a contrast with the work of earlier sculptors in the momentary nature of the pose

with limbs and torso disposed in shifting planes to provide no single viewing point. As a portraitist, he made a statue of Socrates, of which some 30 copies exist, and a series of portraits of Alexander the Great, begun when the king was a boy. He made a number of colossal statues for various Greek cities, and was responsible for some complex figure compositions, such as one of Alexander hunting lions, of which there is a relief version in the Louvre. The realism for which he was famed can be seen in this and in the copy in the Naples Museum of a statue known as "*The Farnese Hercules*", with its virtuoso rendering of texture and muscular detail. These various innovations exerted a considerable influence over the development of Hellenistic sculpture. See vol. 2 pp. **40–41**

Ma Ben
active late 11th–early 12th century
Chinese painter, famed for his skilful renderings of birds and animals. He held an official post in the academy of the Emperor Huizong, and was the founder of a virtual dynasty of court painters. Though he is associated with the decorative academic manner, the scroll attributed to him in the Honolulu Academy of Arts entitled *One hundred geese* shows a much freer style than that usually ascribed to Huizong's circle.

Mabuse see GOSSAERT

McCahon, Colin born 1919
New Zealand painter. He is often linked with Rita Angus and Woollaston in a trio of native-born artists who led the move away from conventional figuration. In numerous works of crude, visionary power, often incorporating word imagery, he sought to integrate the theme of the Passion with the indigenous landscape. The emotive series *Stations of the Cross*, for example, uses the rise and fall of the North Otago hills to represent Christ's suffering. He was much influenced by the ideas of Mondrian after a visit to America, and called one of his *Gate* series *Here I give thanks to Mondrian* (1961, Auckland City Art Gallery).

Macchiaioli
Group of late 19th-century Italian painters. Fattori, Lega and Signorini were among the principal exponents of the movement, which started when a group of artists began to paint *plein-air* landscape sketches using *macchie* (patches) of colour to capture light effects by means of sharp tonal contrasts. They worked chiefly in Florence, but some visited Paris, where they were impressed by the BARBIZON school. The full *macchia* technique was first used in Morelli-inspired historical works, then in small, horizontal landscapes. Its practitioners have been termed Proto-Impressionists, but the spontaneity of their sketches is lacking in their finished works, where they paid close attention to form, and their palette retains the brownish tones of the Barbizon painters. Boldini also painted bourgeois interiors, while Fattori, Lega and Boldini made a significant contribution to portraiture. They were not recognized internationally at the time, nor did they achieve a rewarding financial market at home, but they are now considered the most important 19th-century Italian school.

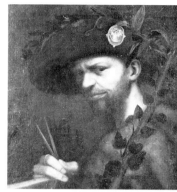

Lomazzo: Self-portrait, 1568. Milan, Brera

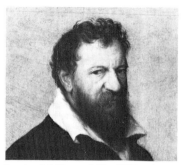

Lombard: Self-portrait (detail)? Kassel, Staatliche Kunstsammlungen

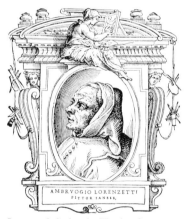

Lorenzetti, Ambrogio: Woodcut from Vasari's *Lives of the Artists*, 1568

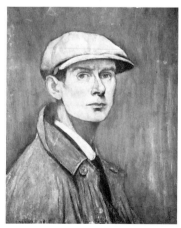

Lowry: Self-portrait, 1925. Salford Museum and Art Gallery

Macció, Romulo born 1931
Argentine figurative painter. In 1960 he went to study in Europe, and settled in Paris in 1963. His works portray seated figures with generalized or incongruous features painted in broad, gestural strokes against flat areas of colour suggesting interiors, as in the work of Francis Bacon. Later he developed a lyrical style more his own, which places emphasis on the sinuous contours of the figure with erotic overtones (*Painter's model*, 1973, Private coll.).

MacDonald, James Edward Hervey 1873–1932
Canadian landscape painter, the senior founder of the GROUP OF SEVEN. He hoped to embody a specifically Canadian spirit in his paintings, as in the dynamic *The elements, Georgian Bay* (1916, Toronto, Art Gallery of Ontario), with its heavy cloud formations treated as solid counterparts of the primeval rock masses below. His brash canvases assumed a flatter, more finished look when he returned to commercial design and teaching in the late 1920s. A sensitive teacher, MacDonald also defended the Group of Seven against reactionary criticism.

MacDonald, Jock (J.W.G.) 1897–1960
Canadian landscape and abstract painter, born in Scotland. He produced his first "automatic" abstract in 1934, and from this evolved a series of "modalities", semi-abstract mood paintings alluding to landscape subjects. His theosophical inclination was reinforced by friendship with Emily Carr and Lawren Harris. From 1947 to the early 1950s he specialized in "automatic" painting in watercolour and encounters with Hofmann and Dubuffet led him to adapt experimental watercolour techniques to oil on perspex. In 1956 he became an associate of PAINTERS ELEVEN. *Nature evolving* (1960, Toronto, Art Gallery of Ontario), abstract yet profoundly suggestive of organic processes, completes a series of such works. An inspiring teacher, he advanced the cause of modernism in Canada.

MacDonald-Wright, Stanton 1890–1973
American painter, a co-founder of SYNCHROMISM. He moved to Paris in 1907 and in 1911 met Russell, with whom he launched Synchromism in 1913. Although all their paintings were based on similar colour theories, Russell exhibited completely abstract works whereas MacDonald-Wright's were generally based on a representational motif. His *Sunrise synchromy in violet* (1918, Pittsburgh, Carnegie Institute), for example, is based on a figure of Michelangelo's. In 1919 he moved to California, where he became involved in teaching and colour film experiments and also developed a great interest in oriental art. He resumed Synchromist painting in 1953.

Machuca, Pedro died 1550
Spanish architect and painter. With Alonso Berruguete, also from Castile, Machuca was one of the first Spanish artists to break free entirely from late Gothic precedents. His early career is obscure, but he probably spent about 10 to 15 years in Italy before returning to Spain by 1520. *The Virgin with the souls of Purgatory* (1517, Madrid, Prado), his earliest dated work, shows his understanding of Correggio and Perino del Vaga. Machuca is most important as the architect of the Palace of Charles V, built in the grounds of the Alhambra in Granada from 1527, with its well-known circular court. It, too, shows a mature knowledge of Italian work.

MacIver, Loren born 1909
American painter. She was largely self-taught and was influenced by Marin and also by Klee. She paints both figurative and abstract compositions, usually in pale colours which create a misty, atmospheric effect. Apart from her paintings of European cities, her best-known motifs are of the transitory—the iridescent, rainbow-like appearance of oil slicks or marks on street pavements (*Hopscotch*, 1940, New York, MOMA).

Mack, Heinz born 1931
West German artist, an important exponent of KINETIC art and co-founder, with Piene, of Group ZERO (1957). His main concerns are movement and light and his creations are intended as catalysts for the articulation of light and space. He made paintings based on repetitive rhythms, before beginning to work with light directly, and his interest in the imprints of mechanical patterns on reflective metal surfaces led to his *Light reliefs*. Also based on the distortion of light are his rotating discs, such as *Silberroter* (1967, Cologne, Wallraf-Richartz Museum), from which light is reflected through corrugated glass. He has more recently been fascinated by the possibilities offered by working in vast open spaces, for example the Sahara.

Macke, August 1887–1914
German painter, a founder of Der BLAUE REITER. He studied with Corinth in 1907 and encountered both Fauvism and Cubism during visits to Paris, 1907–08. By the time he met Marc in 1909 he was beginning to develop a style fusing elements of Cézanne's multiple space and Cubist analysis of objects with Fauve colours and simplification of forms (*Church in Bonn*, 1911, Bonn, Städtische Kunstsammlung). In 1911 he participated in the *Blaue Reiter* exhibition, and also contributed an essay to the *Blaue Reiter Almanac*. After he and Marc visited Delaunay in Paris in 1912 his style was influenced by the gentle colour harmonies of Orphic Cubism (*Walk on the bridge*, 1912, Darmstadt, Hessisches Landesmuseum). In April 1914 he, Klee and Moilliet visited Tunis, which inspired him to paint a series of jewel-like watercolours. These greatly influenced Klee. Macke was killed in World War I. See vol. 3 pp. **136–137**

Maclise, Daniel 1806–70
Irish painter and lithographer, living in London after 1827. He achieved eminence in two very different fields. His 84 lithographs for *Fraser's Magazine* (original drawings mainly London, V&A) are among the best caricatures of English literary figures (Charles Dickens was a close friend), but he also painted history and genre subjects. The most notable were two heroic frescos for the House of Lords, London: *The death of Nelson* and *The meeting of Wellington and Blucher*. Worn out by these vast works, Maclise painted little in his final years.

Maderno, Stefano 1576–1636
Italian sculptor. One of the leading sculptors in Rome in the early 17th century until the emergence of Bernini, he is now remembered for only one work: *St Cecilia* (1600, Rome, S. Cecilia in Trastevere). The recumbent figure has a moving simplicity, but its fame rests also on the legend that it shows the body of the Early Christian martyr exactly as it was found in 1599.

Madrazo y Agudo, José 1781–1859
Spain's foremost NEOCLASSICAL painter and illustrator. He studied in Madrid and for two years in Paris with David. From 1806 to 1818 he was a successful portraitist in Rome and his *Princess Carini* (Madrid, Private coll.) compares well with Ingres's portraits. Canova's influence dominates his dry, sculptural historical works such as *The death of Viriato* (Madrid, Prado). His influence was widely felt, not least by his son **Federico** (1815–94), a history and portrait painter who succeeded his father as director of the Prado.

Maes, Nicholaes 1634–93
Dutch genre and portrait painter, born in Dordrecht, a pupil of Rembrandt, *c.*1648–54, in Amsterdam. He is best known for his anecdotal genre scenes painted during the 1650s, such as *The listening maid* (1656, London, Wallace Coll.). These display a sentimental approach and a love of deep velvety contrasts of light and shade, and are less obviously influenced by Rembrandt than his portraits, such as *A young boy* (*c.*1650, Cincinnati, Art Museum), which may be a portrait of Rembrandt's son Titus. From about 1660 Maes painted nothing but portraits, and especially after a trip to Antwerp between 1665 and 1667 his style changed and became much more elegant—nearer to van Dyck than to Rembrandt, but closest of all to French painters such as Rigaud (*A man*, *c.*1670, Hanover, Niedersächsische Landesgalerie). In 1673 he moved from Dordrecht to Amsterdam, where his stylish and well characterized society portraits were very successful and were influential well into the next century. See vol. 2 p. **227**

Maestà
Italian word meaning majesty, used to describe a work of art portraying the Virgin and Child enthroned, surrounded by saints or angels. The most famous is the one painted for Siena Cathedral by Duccio in 1308–11.

Mafai, Mario 1902–65
Italian painter. After initially painting highly-coloured abstract works he turned to paintings akin to Soutine in their sombre mood and Expressionist handling. In the 1940s he produced his *Fantasies* series. The tragic intensity within these visions of twisted bodies in a macabre setting has been compared to Ensor's (*Fantasy*, 1942, Genoa, Della Ragione coll.). After World War II his style modulated into a delicate lyricism of subtle colour harmonies, giving a bitter-sweet melancholy to his landscapes and street scenes.

Ma Fen see MA BEN

Maffei, Francesco *c.*1600–60
Italian Baroque painter. He was born in Vicenza and worked mainly in the Veneto, drawing on the great Venetian masters, especially Veronese, for his inspiration and rejecting the prevailing academic Mannerism. His refreshingly unorthodox style, a source for his slightly younger and more brilliant contemporary Sebastiano Mazzoni, was characterized by nervous brushwork and strangely elongated, at times ghostly, figures (*Parable of the workers in the vineyard*, *c.*1650, Verona, Museo di Castelvecchio). Maffei settled in Padua in 1657, and the paintings of his last three years are much quieter in mood than his Venetian works (*The Annunciation*, Hull, Ferens Art Gallery).

Magic Realism
A vague term initially applied to the work of the French Surrealist Pierre Roy and also to German Neue Sachlichkeit. It gained currency in the USA with the exhibition in New York (MOMA, 1943), *American Realists and Magic Realists*. Artists as diverse as Albright, Guglielmi, Shahn and Wyeth were subsequently associated with the term. It therefore implies the depiction of disquieting, fantastic or surreal themes in a sharply focused style.

Magnasco, Alessandro 1667–1749
Italian painter of religious paintings and fantastic landscapes. At an early age he went to Milan, and apart from a brief stay in Florence, about 1709–11, and in Bergamo, 1723, he remained in Milan until his final return to his native Genoa in 1735. The extraordinary freedom of his technique and the drama of his windswept landscapes owes something to the work of Salvator Rosa (*Sea painting*, 1712, Bologna, Pinacoteca). Like Rosa, he was especially appreciated in the Romantic era.

Magnelli, Alberto 1888–1971
Italian painter. He was self-taught, but his early work reveals the influence of his contacts with the Cubists and Futurists in 1910 and 1914 on his development from naturalism to vividly-coloured abstraction. After World War I he reverted to a semi-representational style influenced by METAPHYSICAL PAINTING, before turning to abstraction again in the 1930s with works of ordered arrangement and muted colour (*Oceanic round*, 1937, Paris, Musée d'Art Moderne).

Magritte, René 1898–1967
Belgian painter, one of the leading SURREALISTS. A variety of influences from Impressionism (1915) to Futurism and Cubism (1920–23) are apparent in his early work. In 1922 he saw Chirico's *Song of love*, which profoundly influenced him, and in 1925 he collaborated with Mesens on the Dadaist review *OEsophage*. He then began to paint his first Surrealist works, such as *The menaced assassin* (1926, New York, MOMA). Between 1927 and 1930 he lived in Paris in close contact with Breton, Dali and other Surrealists and, apart from a brief period in the 1940s when he returned to Neo-Impressionism, he remained a Surrealist. The main emphasis of his work is on the analysis of pictorial language, the relationship between various juxtaposed man-made and natural objects and particularly, between words and images—often he creates effects of disturbing ambiguity. In *The key of dreams* (1930, Paris, Claude Hersaint coll.) six objects (hat, shoe, candle, hammer, glass and egg) are given contradictory definitions, provoking reflection on their true nature. Magritte painted in a scrupulously precise technique derived from advertisements and popular illustrated detective stories, and pursued problems of paradox and the nature of perception with rigorous logic. See vol. 1 p. *87*; vol. 3 pp. **174–175**

Maillol, Aristide 1861–1944
French artist, celebrated for his sculptures of the female nude. His early career was devoted largely to tapestry design, and he also painted, but in the 1890s, troubled by an eye disease, he gave up tapestry and turned to sculpture. He had his first one-man exhibition in 1902 and thereafter received many commissions for public monuments. Maillol's sculptures consisted almost entirely of representations of the mature female nude,

and he attempted to continue the tradition of Greek and Roman sculpture. His figures tend to be calm and monumental, with a sense of classical dignity (*The Mediterranean*, c.1901, New York, MOMA). Only occasionally did he show the nude figure in action, or represent a male figure (*The young cyclist*, 1907–08, Paris, Musée d'Art Moderne). Maillol also made woodcut illustrations for editions of classical and modern poems. As an outstanding figurative sculptor, he had wide influence. See vol. 3 p. **107**

Maitani, Lorenzo active c.1302–30
Sienese sculptor and architect. He is first recorded working on Siena Cathedral. In 1308 he was called to Orvieto, becoming superintendent of all building operations of the cathedral in 1310, and remaining there for the rest of his life. The main work of this period at Orvieto was on the façade, and its rich sculptural decoration is usually credited to him. Small-scale figures are set in strips in a highly original way; most show a charming Gothic lyricism which gives way to expressionistic drama in the terrifying scenes of The Last Judgment. See vol. 2 p. **81**

Makart, Hans 1840–84
Austrian painter of history and grandiose allegorical compositions. He studied in Vienna, with Piloty in Munich, and travelled widely throughout Europe and the Middle East. His academic style was strongly influenced by Titian, Veronese and Rubens (*The triumph of Ariadne*, 1873, Vienna, Österreichische Galerie). Makart's position in Vienna was unrivalled in the 1870s and 1880s, when his festive and decorative style influenced the visual arts, interior decoration and fashion to such an extent that this era became popularly known as "the Makart Period".

Makemono see KAKEMONO

Malbone, Edward Greene
1777–1807
America's best-known miniature painter. Born in Newport, Rhode Island, he studied under West at the Royal Academy, London) after graduating from Harvard University. He began his career in Providence, where he painted *The hours* (1801, Providence, Athenaeum), one of his best-known works. His delicately painted portraits were pleasing likenesses, and popular. He moved about the country, painting in Boston, New York, Philadelphia, Charleston and Savannah, where he died.

Malevich, Kasimir Severinovich
1878–1935
Russian painter of Polish parentage, one of the pioneers of abstract art. Between 1910 and 1913 he painted pictures on peasant themes which reflect Cubist and Futurist influence (*The knife grinder*, 1912, New Haven, Conn., Yale Art Gallery), but he came to the forefront of the Moscow avantgarde in December 1915 when he launched SUPREMATISM. Canvases such as *Black square* (1915, Leningrad, Russian Museum) present a more absolute abstraction than had been achieved by any of the current abstract practitioners in the East or West, supported by theory which he expounded in his book *The Non-objective World*, 1915. Malevich progressed to richer geometrical constructions in the next few years, consisting of coloured geometrical forms painted on white grounds, often overlapped to convey a type of space derived from his previous study of Cubism and arranged dynamically, with dominant

diagonals (*Suprematist composition*, 1917, London, Tate). The culmination (c.1918) was the seminal series of *White on White* paintings (examples, New York, MOMA). In 1919 he took over the Vitebsk School of Art from Chagall and was thereafter active as painter, teacher and writer. At the school he developed Suprematist principles, in rivalry with the pragmatism of the Constructivists. His first visit to Europe took place in 1927 on the occasion of a retrospective exhibition of his works shown in Warsaw (by Strzemiński) and in Berlin; the work exhibited is now in the Stedelijk Museum, Amsterdam. Afterwards he returned to painting peasant themes using brilliant colours and simplified forms—most of these are in the Russian Museum, Leningrad—and shortly before his death he adopted a neo-Renaissance style, perhaps appropriate to the new doctrine of Socialist realism. See vol. 1 pp. *99*; vol. 3 p. **157**

Maliavin, Philip Andreevich
1869–1940
Russian painter, best known for his spectacular portrayals of peasant subjects; typical is *The red whirl* (1906, Moscow, Tretyakov Gallery), which combines brilliant colouring with a free technique. Maliavin's brand of celebratory realism remained popular in the Soviet era, though he himself emigrated to Paris in 1922.

Ma Lin active mid-13th century
Chinese painter. He was the son of Ma Yuan, and almost certainly began his career in his father's workshop at the southern Song court in Hangzhou. It is often difficult to separate his output from that of his more famous and admired father. Landscapes attributed to Ma Lin are extant, for example *Three officers proceeding on inspection* (mid-13th century, Peking, National Palace coll.), but he appears also to have revived the flower-and-bird style of his more distant ancestor Ma Ben. If the religious figures bearing his signature are genuine he may have been a precursor of late Song Chan-influenced paintings depicting patriarchs and sages.

Malouel (Maelwael), **Jean**
active 1386–1415
Netherlandish painter. He came from a family of artists from Nimwegen in Guelders. By 1396 he was in Paris, designing cloth of gold and velvet for Queen Isabella of Bavaria. From 1397 until 1415 he was painter to the Dukes of Burgundy, where his early commissions were for heraldic work and five altarpieces for the Chartreuse of Champmol, Dijon. None of his documented work survives, but "*Le Grand Pietà*" (c.1404, Paris, Louvre) seems to come from Champmol and is attributed to Malouel. This work shows the elegant lyricism and soft modelling of the INTERNATIONAL GOTHIC style, as do certain portions of *The martyrdom of St Denis* (finished 1416, Paris, Louvre), a painting which is probably the one known to have been begun by Malouel and finished by Bellechose.

Malton, Thomas 1748–1804
British topographical watercolourist. He painted precise and detailed city views, and might almost have served as a publicity agent for the speculative builders of the period, so clean and handsome are his streets and houses and so elegant the passers-by. He was influenced by Sandby and knew enough about perspective to teach Turner. He published *A Picturesque Tour through the Cities of London and Westminster* (1792).

Mancini, Antonio 1852–1930
Italian painter. Born in Rome, he studied in Naples under Palizzi and Morelli and demonstrated a precocious talent for genre and portraiture. Using a dense impasto, freely worked, he created a colourful, shimmering, luminous surface which surpasses the painterly virtuosity of his masters. He travelled widely in Europe and met the Impressionists in Paris in 1875 and 1878. Manet's influence can be seen in *The coral seller* (1878, Milan, Sacerdoti Gallery).

Mandala
In Buddhist and Hindu art, a symmetrical design symbolizing the harmony and indivisibility of the universe. Based usually upon a circle or series of concentric rings, it may be used as an aid to meditative concentration.

Mander, Karel van 1548–1606
Flemish painter and art historian. From 1573 he travelled in Italy, meeting Vasari and also Spranger, who helped him find employment with Rudolf II on his return through Austria in 1577. By 1583 he was back in Haarlem, where he founded an academy with Goltzius and Cornelis Cornelisz. Frans Hals was one of the pupils there. The principles of Mannerism, evident in his paintings, were expounded to greater effect in *Het Schilderboeck* (The Book of Painters, 1604), a part-theoretical, part-biographical study which made his reputation as the Vasari of the North.

Mandorla
An almond-shaped aura of light surrounding the figure of Christ or the Virgin. It was generally used to portray Christ in his divine manifestation, as he appeared at the Transfiguration and Resurrection and in heavenly glory.

Mandyn, Jan van Haarlem
c.1500–c.1560
Netherlandish painter, born in Haarlem, who moved to Antwerp in about 1525 and worked there for the remainder of his life. He was one of the principal exploiters of the Bosch revival which took place in the 1540s. Boschian imagery and themes—particularly *The temptation of St Anthony*—dominate his oeuvre, but his sturdier figures, occasional nudes and the greater verve of his landscapes show Mannerist influence. Gillis Mostaert and Spranger were his pupils.

Mané-Katz 1894–1962
French painter, born in Russia of Jewish parentage. Before World War I he studied in Paris, settling there in 1921. He travelled extensively in the Middle East between 1927 and 1937. His work, like that of Chagall, celebrates Jewish life and customs. There is a museum devoted to his work at Haifa.

Mánes, Josef 1820–71
Czech painter and graphic artist, regarded as the founder of Czech national painting. He travelled round the Slav lands of the Austrian monarchy, painting peasants, national folk costumes, homes and customs, some of which he used as sketches for his monumental drawings and paintings. His work includes illustrations for collections of Czech folk poems, designs for banners for leading patriotic societies and the series of paintings of *The Months* (1866) for the dial of the clock in the Prague Old Town Hall (originals now in the Museum of the Capital at Prague). There is a good collection of his work in the National Gallery, Prague.

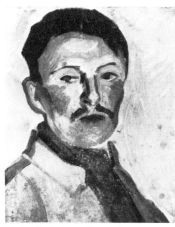
Macke: Study for a self-portrait, 1910. Private coll.

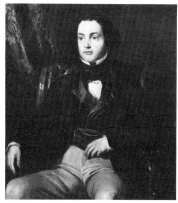
Maclise: Portrait by E. M. Ward (1816–79), 1846. London, NPG

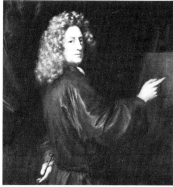
Maes: Self-portrait, 1680s. Dordrecht Museum

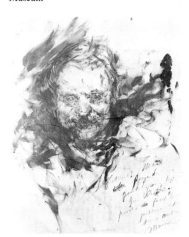
Mancini: Self-portrait, c.1906. London, Tate

Manessier, Alfred born 1911
French painter, a pupil of Bissière, 1940–41. Since 1943 his art has been dominated by religious themes and a search for spiritual meaning in abstract art. *The Crown of Thorns* (1950, Paris, Musée d'Art Moderne) typifies his use of strong colours within a loose linear grid, creating a vibrant luminosity reminiscent of stained-glass windows, a medium in which he has also worked extensively.

Manet, Edouard 1832–83
French painter and graphic artist, one of the most important artists of the 19th century and often regarded as the father of modern painting. He studied under the successful academic painter Couture, but was more affected by his own observations of Spanish and Dutch painting, as is evident in the subject matter and dramatic lighting of his early work, for example *The guitarist* (1861, New York, Metropolitan), his first Salon success. Although he incorporated many motifs from the Old Masters into his works, they often gave an overall impression of shocking modernity to the public who regarded him, much against his will, as leader of the avantgarde, especially after his *"Le Déjeuner sur l'Herbe"* (The picnic, 1863, Paris, Jeu de Paume) caused an uproar at the Salon des Refusés. One of the reasons for the outrage that greeted this work and his *Olympia* (1863, Jeu de Paume) was the directness of Manet's approach, showing contemporary women nude and unidealized, and the freshness of his technique, in which he abolished half-tones and irrelevant details. Following a visit to Spain in 1865, the influence of Velazquez on his art was strengthened, as he himself indicated by including a print of Velazquez's *The topers* in the background of his portrait of *Emile Zola* (1868, Jeu de Paume). Also included in the same work is an Utamaro print—Japanese art had a profound impact on Manet's spatial organization and flattening of surfaces. His later paintings show the influence of his pupil Berthe Morisot, and of Monet. In 1874 he joined the latter in painting out of doors at Argenteuil, where his work became lighter and freer. The sheer painterly brilliance of his late work is marvellously demonstrated in *The bar at the Folies-Bergères* (1881, London, Courtauld Institute Galleries). Throughout his life he took an active part in Parisian life, notably in café discussions with his friends Zola and Baudelaire and the Impressionist circle. Manet never exhibited with the Impressionists, but was looked upon by them as an inspiration. See vol. 1 p. *85*; vol. 3 pp. **94–95**

Manfredi, Bartolommeo
*c.*1587–1620/1
Italian Baroque painter. One of the closest followers of Caravaggio, he occupied an important role in the dissemination of the CARAVAGGESQUE style. Early sources show that it was Manfredi who popularized genre scenes of taverns, fortune-tellers and soldiers in guardrooms, subjects which were particular favourites of northern artists who visited Rome. In view of Manfredi's position, it is ironic that not a single surviving work is securely documented, but about 40 paintings are attributed to him, including the well-known *Concert* (Florence, Uffizi). Like many of these this was once attributed to Caravaggio himself.

Manguin, Henri Charles
1874–1943
French painter. He entered Moreau's studio in 1894 and there met Matisse, Marquet and others who later painted in his private studio. Exhibiting at the Autumn Salon from 1904 onwards, he was identified with FAUVISM. *St Tropez* (1905, Paris, Galerie de Paris), executed in the south of France, where he painted regularly, exemplifies his preference for bright colours in an orderly structure.

Mannerism
Art-historical term implying the pursuit of a heightened, often artificial sense of style. The word *"maniera"* was in this sense used by Vasari, but its usage has become much more widespread in the present century and it is now used generally to denote the period between the High Renaissance and the emergence of Baroque, that is to say from the death of Raphael in 1520 until the end of the 16th century. Primarily, the term is applied to those artists who developed or exaggerated the styles of Michelangelo and Raphael in a desire for striking visual effects. Mannerist painting is often characterized by elongated or overmuscular figures set in extravagantly contorted poses; the themes are often abstruse and are rendered more obscure by the crowding of the canvas or an oblique approach to composition; colour is frequently harsh or lurid, designed to create an intense, emotional response. Mannerism has been equated with decadence, but the positive aspects of the style are now recognized, and the greatest Mannerist artists—Giulio Romano, Parmigianino, Pontormo, Rosso, or in sculpture Giambologna—achieved effects of great emotional and formal power as well as of sophistication. In less capable masters, however (for example the so-called ANTWERP Mannerists), there was a tendency to portray exaggerated gestures, distorted facial expressions and needless *contrapposto*. None the less, when finally allied to a genuine taste for naturalism, the Mannerist search for movement formed the basis for the development of the Baroque. See vol. 2 pp. 164 ff

Manolo (Manuel Martinez Hugué)
1872–1945
Spanish sculptor. The influence of Maillol on him was crucial, as on his compatriot Clará Ayats. The weighty, volumetric style he employed for female nudes, peasants, *toreros* and dancers gives his works a classical flavour, although they are popular in character (*Young woman seated*, 1929, Dortmund, Museum am Ostwall). He was associated with Picasso's circle from 1900.

Manship, Paul 1885–1966
American sculptor. He executed ornamental sculpture, especially for architecture, in numerous public commissions during the 1920s and 1930s. *Prometheus*, for the Rockefeller Center, New York, (1932–33), is amongst his best-known works. His flowing style was influenced by Egyptian, Greek and Roman models but rarely transcended a superficial elegance.

Mansueti, Giovanni
active 1485–1527(?)
Venetian painter. He was a pupil of Giovanni Bellini, but his work also has intriguing affinities with Gentile Bellini's. Mansueti depicted scenes with crowds of exquisitely painted figures set against an elaborate perspective background (*The miracle of St Mark*, 1499, Venice, Accademia).

Mansur active 1590–1630
Indian Mughal artist, principally of animal subjects. He first worked on manuscripts of the late Akbar period, in particular the natural history section of the *Baburnameh* manuscript (now dispersed). Under Jehangir this aspect of his work was developed until, by 1610, he was doing nothing else. His best work is distinguished by a sharpness of observation that captures the subject precisely, as in the *Turkey* of 1612 and the *Zebra* of 1621 (both London, V&A). His work was much copied, even in his lifetime, so that precise attribution is difficult.

Mantegna, Andrea *c.*1430–1506
Italian painter and engraver, one of the most celebrated of early Renaissance artists. He grew up in Padua, then the leading centre of humanism in north Italy, as the adopted son and apprentice of Squarcione, from whom he acquired a profound knowledge of classical antiquity, a devotion to the study of perspective, and a sharp precision of draughtsmanship. His first major work, the frescos for the Ovetari Chapel of the Eremetani church, Padua (1448–57), now largely destroyed, showed his early command of classical motifs and his mastery of foreshortening, which surpassed that of any contemporary artist. This was put to use more fully in his illusionistic fresco decoration (*c.*1474) of the *Camera degli Sposi* (Bridal Chamber) in the Ducal Palace, Mantua. Here, for the first time since antiquity, there was created with brilliant virtuosity by Mantegna the illusion of an extension of the real space of the room. The centre of the ceiling appears to open to the sky, and this device was later taken up by Correggio and was the starting point for much Baroque decoration. The Bridal Chamber was painted in Mantegna's capacity as court painter (from 1459) to Lodovico II Gonzaga, Duke of Mantua, and Lodovico's grandson Francesco commissioned the artist's late masterpieces, the nine large canvases representing *The Triumph of Caesar* (1486–94, Hampton Court, Royal coll.). This was the ideal subject for Mantegna's archaeological tastes, but his treatment, here as elsewhere, is never dry, and the animals, for example, are handled with remarkable liveliness. Mantegna was also one of the earliest artists in Italy to experiment with engravings, and the first to use them in large numbers as a means of propagating his compositions. His impact was decisive not only on artists of Padua and Ferrara, but on his brother-in-law Giovanni Bellini and on Dürer. Bellini's reciprocal influence is apparent in two of Mantegna's most sophisticated paintings, *Parnassus* and *The triumph of Virtue* (Paris, Louvre), painted for Isabella d'Este's *studiolo*. When Mantegna died, the Gonzaga court went into mourning and tributes came from all over Italy; the acclaim was greater than that previously accorded to any artist. See vol. 1 pp. *120–121*; vol. 2 pp. **120–121**, *182*

Manzoni, Piero 1933–63
Italian experimental artist. Until 1956 he produced traditional figurative work, but he then began to include in his canvases impressions from objects dipped in paint. In 1957 he met Yves Klein, who was a profound influence, and in the same year he produced the first of his *Achromes*. These were intended to be both anti-material and anti-colour; he called them "primary spaces". They were initially made from canvas dipped in lime and kaolin, but later incorporated fibreglass, cotton wool and other materials. He also began to produce works of a Performance nature; he signed people's bodies, proclaiming them genuine works of art, sold his breath and also signed thumbprints. In 1961 he created *The magic base*; when anyone stood on it he became a work of art. His neo-Dadaist *Lines* (example, *Line 1000m*, 1961, New York, MOMA), first shown in 1959, were lines of different lengths drawn on pieces of paper and sealed in cans. One of his last works was *The base of the world* (1961, Denmark, Herning Park), a block on which is inscribed, upside down, *The base of the world*. He died from a "fatal combination of cirrhosis and extreme cold".

Manzù, Giacomo born 1908
Italian sculptor. His work in the 1930s was influenced by Rodin, but after 1940 he simplified his formal vocabulary to produce works of classic calm and stability. Much of his work is religious, and in the 1950s he made bronze doors for St Peter's, Rome, and Salzburg Cathedral. A famous series of *"Cardinals"* was begun in 1937 (example, London, Tate). His career demonstrates the possibility of producing traditional figurative sculpture relevant to the concerns of the 20th century. He has also worked as a painter and book illustrator. See vol. 1 p. *195*; vol. 3 pp. **230–231**

Maori art
The art of the Polynesian inhabitants of New Zealand. At the time of European discovery the Maoris possessed a well-developed tradition of woodcarving which survives in modified form to the present. Buildings, canoes and utilitarian objects were decorated with sophisticated curvilinear and spiral designs with stylized human figures. The Maoris were also highly skilled tattooists and makers of textiles. See vol. 2 p. 23

Maquette
French term for a small model, usually in clay or wax, made by a sculptor as a rough sketch for a large work.

Mara, Pol born 1920
Belgian painter. Although he has produced lyrical abstract paintings, his most characteristic works are very aggressive in their attack on conventional notions of female beauty. He uses blown-up photographs of varying textures and sizes that play tricks with perception. His art is contrived as a sort of static and ambiguous striptease.

Maratta or **Maratti, Carlo**
1625–1713
The leading painter in Rome in the second half of the 17th century. Through his master Sacchi he inherited the classical tradition of Raphael, and like Sacchi he was a fine portrait painter (*Pope Clement IX*, 1667–69, Vatican Gallery). In 1650 he established his reputation with *The Adoration of the shepherds* (Rome, S. Giuseppe dei Falegnami), and thereafter was continuously successful. He became internationally famous for his *Madonnas*, which are academic Baroque reworkings of types established during the High Renaissance (*Madonna and Child*, *c.*1695, Vatican Gallery). Like Guido Reni, another painter who suffered from excessive adulation, Maratta later plummeted in critical esteem and suffered from the failure to distinguish his work from that of his numerous and often very banal pupils and imitators. His finest paintings, however, are among the most impressive of his time, and it is easy to appreciate why the nobility of bearing and calm dignity of his simply-draped figures seemed refreshing to his contemporaries amidst the sometimes excessive rhetoric of Baroque art. See vol. 2 p. **234**

Marc, Franz 1880–1916
German EXPRESSIONIST painter, a leading member of Der BLAUE REITER. After studying in Munich he visited Paris in 1903 and 1906 and was briefly influenced by Impressionism and by van Gogh. In 1908, searching for simpler, symbolically powerful forms, he began to make small bronze animal figures. His pantheistic belief in the spirituality of animals led him to evolve a highly personal Expressionist style, using colour symbolically, as in *The blue horse* (1911, Munich, Lenbachhaus). In 1910 he met Kandinsky and joined the New Artists' Association, out of which the Blaue Reiter group developed in 1911. He contributed three essays to the *Blaue Reiter Almanac*, which he and Kandinsky co-edited. His meeting with Delaunay and the Cubists in Paris (1912) prepared the way for his later symbolic abstract works, the best-known of which is *Fighting forms* (1913, Munich, Staatsgemäldesammlungen). He was killed on active service in World War I. See vol. 3 pp. **136–137**

Marca-Relli, Conrad born 1913
American painter. He began drawing in the 1920s while in Italy and worked on the Federal Art Projects during the mid-1930s. Further study abroad in the late 1940s produced stark cityscapes reminiscent of Chirico. During the early 1950s he worked in an abstract, biomorphic manner and turned to collage in 1953. By the 1960s he was working on a large scale using cut-out shapes of painted canvas with only vague figurative suggestions. He continued to experiment with relief sculpture and collage using metal and vinyl sheets.

Marcks, Gerhard born 1889
German sculptor. His figure sculptures, mostly of the nude, combine the hieratic stylization of ancient Greek sculpture with the expressive severity and simplification of medieval sculpture (*Melusine II*, 1949, Minneapolis, Walker Art Center). He was also influenced by Lehmbruck and Kolbe, and because of this stylistic link with Expressionism he completed Barlach's series of figures on the gable of St Catherine's, Lübeck (1947). He spent much of his life teaching, including five years at the Bauhaus (1919–25) in charge of pottery.

Marcoussis, Louis (Louis Markous) 1878–1941
French painter, born in Poland. He came to Paris in 1903 and met the Cubists and Apollinaire, who suggested his pseudonym. An example of his work when associated with the SECTION D'OR group is *Still life with draughts board* (1912, Paris, Musée d'Art Moderne). His style thereafter remained a derivative variant of Cubism.

Marées, Hans von 1837–87
German painter of landscapes and mythological scenes who spent most of his life in Italy. His major theme is the human figure in landscape, but he refused to use narrative to make his paintings more accessible. As a result his highly theoretical and cerebral compositions were virtually unknown during his lifetime and it was only at the beginning of the 20th century that the art critic Meier-Graefe took Marées up as his symbol for the German spirit of modernity and simple monumentality. The well-known series of wall-paintings at the Zoological Institute, Naples (1873) serve as an example of Marées' desire to portray contemporary everyday scenes in the monumental style of antiquity.

Margarito or **Margaritone of Arezzo** active 2nd half of 13th century
One of the earliest Italian painters by whom signed works survive: there are examples in the National Galleries of London and Washington. He was a minor, provincial painter, sometimes charming in his clumsiness, but the chance survival of signed works which have found their way to major galleries, together with the fact that Vasari, who also came from Arezzo, included his biography in his *Lives*, has given him a certain measure of fame.

Mari, Enzo born 1932
Italian sculptor and industrial designer. He studied classics and literature in Milan, 1952–56, and began researches into the psychology of perception. The methods he employs in his CONSTRUCTIVIST sculptures are often stimulated by new technological means (*Structure in aluminum, black steel and rubber*, 1964, Veneto, Torviscosa). He has exerted considerable influence on the younger modern designers in Italy and also on foreign artists such as Max Bill.

Marin, John 1870–1953
American painter. After training as an architect, he studied painting and spent the years 1905 to 1910 in Europe. He is best known for his watercolours, influenced by Cézanne's work in this medium and by the colouring of the Fauves. In 1914 he started painting the coastal regions of Maine and his work gradually became more abstract. In the 1930s he began to work more in oils and employed a watercolour style so that areas of the canvas are left blank. *Beach, Flint Island* (1952, New York, Marlborough Gallery) shows his complete assimilation of Cézanne's planar construction. See vol. 3 p. **205**

Marini, Marino 1901–80
Italian sculptor, painter and graphic artist. His early paintings and graphics reveal the influence of antique and Renaissance models and this trait is shared by his sculpture, in particular, his *Horse and Rider* series (examples in London, Tate; Minneapolis, Walker Art Center; and elsewhere). He made this theme his own, and it became his principal means for exploring the pathos of the human condition. Bronze was his favourite medium, and his exploitation of the varied surface qualities of the material is best seen in his brilliant portraits (*Igor Stravinsky*, 1951, casts in Milan, Galleria d'Arte Moderna; Minneapolis Institute of Arts; and elsewhere). See vol. 1 pp. *69, 184*; vol. 3 p. **230**

Marinus van Reymerswaele *c*.1495–*c*.1567
Flemish artist, trained in Antwerp but apparently working in the provinces. In 1556 he was banished from Middelburg for his part in iconoclastic riots. He is best known for his painstaking depiction of tax-gatherers and bankers, a genre in which he followed Massys. Marinus, however, introduced an obsessive realism into the portrayal of crumbling papers and spent candles, and savagely distorted the expressions of his greedy subjects (*Two tax-gatherers*, *c*.1530, London, NG). Such paintings were evidently popular (many versions and copies exist), but it is not known what kind of patron or collector bought them.

Maris brothers
Dutch painters. The eldest and best-known was **Jacobus Hendricus** or **Jacob** (1837–99), one of the leading members of the HAGUE school. He was strongly influenced by the Barbizon school painters, although he never followed their practice of working in the open air. His colour schemes were sombre, with a marked preference for greys. **Matthijs** or **Thijs** (1839–1917) worked in an entirely different vein, painting figure compositions, portraits and visionary subjects evocative of dreams and fairy tales. He moved to Paris in 1869, and in 1877 settled in London, where he was influenced by the Pre-Raphaelites. A third brother, **Willem** (1844–1910), like Jacob, was a leading member of the Hague school. Landscapes with cattle and ditches with ducks were his favourite subjects. Good examples of their work are in the Gemeentemuseum in The Hague.

Marisol (Escobar Marisol) born 1930
Venezuelan sculptor living in the USA. Her startling, brightly painted sculptures of single figures and groups satirize contemporary *mores* and manners by freezing and transforming such events as a New York cocktail party or a gathering of art dealers. These *assemblages*, sometimes over life-size, are essentially angular painted wood constructions incorporating plaster casts and found objects.

Marlow, William 1740–1813
British marine and view painter. A pupil of Samuel Scott and possibly of Wilson, he was also influenced by Canaletto. He painted country house views (four are at Castle Howard, Yorkshire), landscapes in England and Wales, views in France and Italy (where he travelled, 1765–68), and occasionally CAPRICCI. His work was usually fairly prosaic, but very accomplished, and his silvery quality of light is often very attractive.

Marmion, Simon *c*.1425–89
Franco-Flemish illuminator and painter, probably born in Amiens. By 1458 he had moved to Valenciennes and he established a workshop there, but in 1468 he is recorded in the Tournai guild. His reputation as a great illuminator lasted into the 16th century but no signed or documented manuscript survives. However, a Book of Hours (1475–81, London, V&A) and the shutters from an altarpiece of *The death of St Bertin* (1455–59, London, NG, and West Berlin, Staatliche Museen) are generally accepted as his work. His style was very delicate and tender.

Marquet, Albert 1875–1947
French painter. In 1897 he joined the studio of Moreau, where Matisse and Rouault were fellow-students. Though he collaborated closely with Matisse at the start of his career he never developed the more radical possibilities of FAUVISM. He aimed to portray light and atmosphere by means of large areas of unmodulated colour set within firm contours and an orderly composition, as in *The Pont Neuf* (1906, Washington, NG). See vol. 3 p. **143**

Marsh, Reginald 1898–1954
American painter of the urban scene. Throughout the 1920s he was a prolific newspaper illustrator. He took up painting seriously in 1923, and worked mainly in tempera; he also produced prints. The blowsy or pinched figures usually crowding Marsh's work seem to express the strain of city life in the Depression, and their squalor suggests his awareness of German Neue Sachlichkeit (*Pip and flip*, 1932, New York, B. Danenberg coll.). After the late 1930s his art declined sharply in quality.

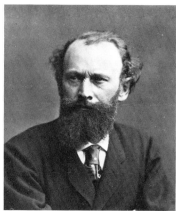
Manet: Photograph (Mansell)

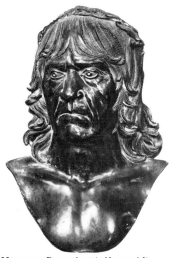
Mantegna: Bronze bust (self-portrait?), *c*.1490. Mantua, S. Andrea (Mansell)

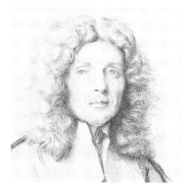
Maratta: Self-portrait drawing, 1684. London, BM

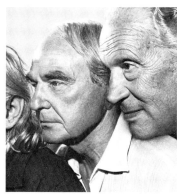
Marini: Photograph, with Henry Moore on his right, by Karsh, 1970 (Camera Press)

Marshall, Benjamin 1767–1835
English sporting painter, a follower of Stubbs. After early training as a portrait painter, he concentrated almost exclusively on horse racing and hunting scenes, particularly following his move to Newmarket in 1812.

Martin, Agnes born 1912
Canadian-born American MINIMAL painter. Her paintings, in which the square or near square picture field was based on a grid, first appeared in the 1960s (*Bones no. II*, 1961, New York, Betty Parsons coll.). These restrained, meditative works proved profoundly influential on younger artists working toward systematic and reductive approaches. Her canvases had become more colourful by 1967, when she moved from New York to New Mexico and stopped painting temporarily. Since 1974 she has featured broad, horizontal or vertical pastel pink and blue or all white stripes, varying subtly in width.

Martin, Homer Dodge 1836–97
American painter. He was a member of the HUDSON RIVER school in the early part of his career, but was influenced by Impressionism during a stay in France, 1881–86. On returning to America he synthesized the two approaches in works such as the once-famous *Harp of the winds* (1895, New York, Metropolitan).

Martin, John 1789–1854
British ROMANTIC painter and mezzotint engraver. He specialized in intensely melodramatic scenes depicting cataclysmic events, often from the Bible or Milton. They are usually crowded with tiny figures and convey a sense of vast distance. Martin not only made mezzotints after his paintings, but also, unusually, made original compositions in the medium for his illustrations to the Bible and Milton's *Paradise Lost*, which are among his finest works. During his lifetime Martin was famous (he was honoured by several European academies and influenced American artists such as Cole), but was subject to the greatest extremes of critical response, being hailed as a mighty genius and reviled as a vulgar hack. He was later forgotten to such an extent that his three last great paintings, *The great day of his wrath*, *The Last Judgment* and *The plains of Heaven* (1851–53, London, Tate), which toured Britain and America for 20 years after his death, were bought in 1935 for only £7. His reputation has gradually revived. See vol. 3 p. **68**

Martin, Kenneth born 1905
British painter and sculptor. He worked as a figurative painter until the late 1940s, when he turned to abstraction. *Composition* (1949, London, Tate) points to a subsequent preoccupation with movement in the way in which the interlocking geometric forms subtly suggest rotation. In 1951 he began making mobiles, initially influenced by Calder. In these works a sequence of brass bars is organized as a spiral, so as to present a constantly changing profile and pattern of light when rotated (*Screw mobile*, 1953, London, Tate).

Martin, Mary 1907–69
British artist. She was a figurative painter until the beginning of the 1950s, when she turned to geometric abstraction, and soon began working on reliefs. At first these were entirely in white, but later, in pieces such as *Spiral* (1963, London, Tate), she used polished steel to create light reflections. She was married to Kenneth Martin.

Martini, Arturo 1889–1947
Italian sculptor and painter. He studied under Hildebrand in Munich. Unresponsive to Cubist and Futurist discoveries before World War I, he was associated with the classicizing trend which was a major force in Italian art in the 1920s. His work is typified by a reworking of antique ideals derived from Roman sculpture and ranges from historical subjects to formal investigations such as his *Girl under water* (1941, Milan, Private coll.). In 1945 he abandoned sculpture for painting, calling sculpture a "dead language".

Martini, Simone see SIMONE

Martorell, Bernardo died *c.*1453
Spanish painter and illuminator, active in Barcelona from 1443. The presentation miniature in the *Comentario* of Jaime Marquilles (1448, Barcelona City archives) is an authenticated work. The altarpiece of St Peter (1437, Gerona Museum) and the panels from a St George altarpiece (Chicago, Art Institute and Paris, Louvre) are generally accepted as his; these works show close links with Borrassá and Netherlandish art, especially Campin.

Marzal de Sax, Andrés died 1410
Painter of German origin (the Sax of his name probably means Saxony), active in Valencia. Of a series of documented works of 1393 to 1405 only one fragment remains, *The incredulity of St Thomas* (*c.*1400, Valencia, Cathedral Museum), a work which suggests the influence of Master Bertram. The very large St George Retable (*c.*1400–10, London, V&A) is the most important work attributed to him. The grisly representations of the various trials of the Saint contrast with the sumptuous effect of the whole.

Masaccio (Tommaso di Ser Giovanni di Mone) 1401–28?
Florentine painter, one of the great innovators of the early Renaissance. Although his career was brief and his commissions relatively modest, his work had a revolutionary impact. Nothing is known of his training; he is first recorded in Florence in 1422, and from this year dates his earliest known work, the S. Giovenale triptych (Reggello, S. Giovenale in Cascia), which shows *The Madonna and Child with saints*. This is an immature, somewhat clumsy work, but already shows an astonishing individuality in the bulk and weight of the figures, which completely reject Gothic elegance. His three major surviving works are the Pisa polyptych (1426) for the church of the Carmine there (central panel London, NG, other main parts West Berlin, Staatliche Museen and Naples, Museo di Capodimonte); the fresco cycle (*c.*1425–28) in the Brancacci Chapel of S. Maria del Carmine, Florence, done in collaboration with Masolino; and the *Trinity* fresco (probably 1428) in S. Maria Novella, Florence. The great innovations of the Pisa altarpiece were the consistency of viewpoint in the foreshortening of the figures and the consistency of the fall of light; only one source is used and the shadows it casts are accurately plotted. The Brancacci Chapel frescos represent *Scenes from the life of St Peter*, and there are additional scenes of *The temptation* and *The expulsion from Paradise*. Masaccio's masterpiece is generally acknowledged to be *The tribute money*, in which his grave and monumental figures, with their heads derived from Roman busts, are placed convincingly in a realistic setting, and show a concentration on essentials which recalls Giotto. In *The expulsion*, which makes *The temptation*, painted by Masolino, seem limp, Masaccio conveys a mood of tragic intensity; among contemporary artists only Donatello could match the grandeur and solidity of his figures or his ability to convey emotion, and Alberti's injunction in his *On Painting* that a painter should imitate sculpture surely reflects Masaccio's work. *The Holy Trinity*, perhaps Masaccio's last work, reveals most completely his concern with the creation of a realistic pictorial space, the majestic architectural setting reflecting his friendship with Brunelleschi. In 1428 Masaccio went to Rome, and there is no certain evidence of any work he might have done there before his death. Masaccio's role in Renaissance painting was crucial. His mastery of perspective and understanding of light provided the first great advance in naturalism in painting since Giotto, and his innovations were soon taken up by artists such as Fra Angelico, Filippo Lippi and Piero della Francesca. Vasari records the names of many great artists who drew from the Brancacci Chapel frescos, among them Michelangelo, Masaccio's true spiritual successor. See vol. 2 pp. **104–106**

Masanobu, Kano 1434–1530
Japanese painter, the founder of the prestigious court painting school of KANO. He first learned to paint from his father, a painter from the village of Kano in Izu province, who became a retainer of the Shogun. Masanobu also studied with Shubun, and after becoming independent he entered the service of the Shogun Ashikaga Yoshimasa, who was having his Silver Pavilion in Kyoto decorated; the great ink-painter Sesshu recommended that Masanobu complete the work, and thereafter he received many commissions for decorative schemes. His speciality was the depiction of people and he succeeded in giving a Japanese flavour to the Song Chinese painting style. A good example is *Chou Mao-shu cherishing lotuses*, now designated a National Treasure of Japan (Tokyo, T. Nakamura coll.). See vol. 3 p. 47

Masegne brothers
Venetian late Gothic sculptors. The greatest work of **Jacobello** dalle Masegne (died *c.*1409) and **Pierpaolo** (died 1403?) was the iconostasis in S. Marco in Venice, 1391–94, with its bronze half-life-size saints in graceful, animated poses. They also worked in Bologna, Pavia and Milan, and were the dominant sculptors in northern Italy between about 1380 and 1400. Their tomb of Doge Antonio Venier (died 1400) in SS. Giovanni e Paolo, Venice, echoes in design and style Nino Pisano's Cornaro tomb in the same church.

Masereel, Frans 1889–1972
Belgian painter and graphic artist. He gained an international reputation with his woodcut series *The Dead Awaken*, which began to appear in 1917. The prints are executed in a style derived from tribal art, folk art and Expressionism. The main theme of both his paintings and graphic work is human suffering and deprivation caused by war or the pressures of city life.

Masip, Juan Vicente
*c.*1475–before 1550
Spanish painter from Valencia. He was a contemporary of Fernando Yañez and Fernando Llanos, from whom he probably derived the Italian element in his work, which he passed on to his son, the better-known Juan de Juanes.

Maso da San Friano (Tommaso Manzuoli d' Antonio) *c.*1532–71
Italian painter active in Florence. He was a member of Vasari's sizeable studio and assisted in the decoration of the *studiolo* (*c.*1570) in the Palazzo Vecchio, for which he produced the exquisite MANNERIST fantasies *The fall of Icarus* and *The diamond mine*. Later he retreated from this exaggerated Mannerism to a more painterly naturalism (*The Holy Family*, *c.*1570, Oxford, Ashmolean).

Maso di Banco active *c.*1330–50
Florentine painter, the most mysterious and interesting artist of the generation after Giotto. It is only a tradition which credits him with the authorship of the frescos of *The life of St Sylvester* in the Bardi Chapel of S. Croce. The monumental clarity of their design and the solid masses of their colouring reveal him as the most profound of Giotto's Florentine followers. It has, however, been argued that much of their effect is due to restoration. See vol. 2 p. **85**

Masolino da Panicale
1383/4–1447
Florentine painter. His early training in the Starnina and Ghiberti workshops, and the influence of Gentile da Fabriano, informed his lyrical INTERNATIONAL GOTHIC style. His earliest known work, a *Madonna and Child* (1423, Bremen, Kunsthalle), displays the unusual softness of his idealized faces, and his gently decorative use of line. 16th-century sources suggest that Masolino was the master of Masaccio, but this idea is now discounted, and when they worked together on the frescos (*c.*1425–28) in the Brancacci Chapel of S. Maria del Carmine, Florence, the influence was the other way around, as Masolino developed a greater awareness of pictorial space and of volume. They also collaborated on *The Virgin and Child with St Anne* (*c.*1425, Florence, Uffizi), in which Masolino's Virgin has nothing like the density or weight of Masaccio's Child. There are still reflections of Masaccio in Masolino's frescos (1428–31) in S. Clemente in Rome, especially in *The Crucifixion*, but Masolino returned later to his more decorative, less sculptural style. He still, however, retained an interest in perspective, as for example in a version of *The Annunciation* (Washington, NG) and in frescos in the Baptistery and Collegiata of Castiglione d'Olona near Como (mid-1430s), perhaps his finest surviving work, and his influence is clear in the work, for instance, of Domenico Veneziano and Uccello. See vol. 2 pp. *105*, **106**

Masson, André born 1896
French painter, a major contributor to the SURREALIST movement. By 1924 he had become a close friend of Breton, Miró and Ernst. Concerned with the spontaneous expression of unconscious mental life, he first improvised "automatic" linear drawings and then began to build up the surfaces of his canvases with randomly applied glue, sand and pigment (*Painting (figure)*, 1927, New York, MOMA). In 1929 he dissociated from the Surrealists and in the 1930s he turned his attention to mythical imagery. During World War II he lived in New York, painting influential works such as *Meditations on an oak leaf* (1942, New York, MOMA), in which patches of glowing colour are evocatively distributed across a dark ground. See vol. 3 p. **176**

Massys (Matsys, Metsys), **Quentin**
1464/5–1530
Flemish painter, probably born in Lou-

vain. He qualified as a master in Antwerp in 1491 and became one of the foremost artists there. His earliest authenticated works are the St Anne altarpiece (1509, Brussels, Musées Royaux des Beaux-Arts) and *The Lamentation* (1511, Antwerp, Musées Royaux des Beaux-Arts). Both are composed in the manner of tapestries, with large, refined figures spread across the panels and little attention paid to the diffusion of light or spatial recession. Massys may have travelled to Italy and certainly demonstrates some knowledge of Leonardo in his style of modelling, but the character of his work is purely Flemish—as in *A banker and his wife* (1514, Paris, Louvre), with its depiction of human greed, the wife diverted from her open prayerbook. He was a fine portraitist and is best known in this field for the pair (1517) representing *Erasmus* (Rome, Museo Nazionale) and *Petrus Egidius* (Longford Castle, Wiltshire). This new type—the scholar in his study—was very influential, notably on Holbein, who probably met Massys in Antwerp on his way to England. See vol. 2 pp. **160–161**

Master Bertram active 1367–1414/5
German painter, one of the leading masters in Hamburg in the late 14th century. His most important work was the altarpiece known as the Grabow altarpiece (1379, Hamburg, Kunsthalle), which reflects the influence of Bohemian artists, notably Master Theoderic.

Master E.S. active 1450–67
German engraver active in the upper Rhine valley, named from the monogram on 18 of his surviving prints. He was the most important graphic artist in northern Europe in the mid-15th century, and a pioneer of copper-plate engraving. Except for early prints which are clearly influenced by the Master of the Playing Cards—a *Nativity* (c.1450, Hamburg, Kunsthalle) and an *Ars moriendi* (c.1450, Oxford, Ashmolean)—his works are engraved and characterized by crisp, firm outlines and rich ornament. He evolved a system of cross-hatching to model form, and many of his engravings were models for goldsmiths' work (*St John the Baptist in the wilderness, surrounded by Evangelists and Church Fathers*, 1466, Boston, MFA). His work reflects the influence of van der Weyden and Gerhaerts' sculpture, in particular the latter's elaborate drapery style. It was in turn an important source for German artists.

Master Francke
active 1st half of 15th century
German painter, the leading artist of his day in Hamburg. His rich colour, delicate linear rhythms and richly-clad aristocratic types are characteristic of the INTERNATIONAL GOTHIC style. He also reveals an unusual interest in dramatic narrative, and in the humorously realistic portrayal of human types (St Thomas à Becket altar of 1424, Hamburg, Kunsthalle).

Master Honoré died before 1318
French miniaturist, head of a great Parisian workshop. Honoré was a highly paid and respected painter, employed by King Philippe IV le Bel (1285–1314), and is first documented in 1288. The Breviary of Philippe le Bel (Paris, BN) displays his carefully modelled figures and decorative backgrounds. His Book of Hours (Nuremberg, Stadtbibliotek) initiated a new, widely-copied arrangement of text and illumination, closely integrated, with freely drawn marginal ornament of ivy-leaves. See vol. 2 p. **77**

Master Hugo
active early 12th century
English illuminator of the Romanesque period. Between 1121 and 1148 he was paid for work on the Bury St Edmunds Bible (Cambridge, Corpus Christi College), a lavish volume written and illuminated in the monastery of Bury St Edmunds. The earliest of a series of great illuminated Bibles in 12th-century England, it displays heavily stylized, richly-coloured and monumental figures in clearly drawn scenes, setting a new standard for English illumination. Master Hugo is also recorded working as a bronze-caster. See vol. 2 p. **74**

Master Jacomart see BAÇO, JAIME

Master Mateo
active 2nd half of 12th century
Spanish or French sculptor and architect, active in northern Spain. He signed the triple Portico de la Gloria, on the west façade of Santiago Cathedral, dated 1188, and portrayed himself in prayer at the base of a jamb. Both in the crypt, which he built from 1168, and in the portals Mateo borrowed from Burgundian and southern French example, and his style is more closely related to Romanesque than to Gothic.

Master of . . .
Expression used by art historians as a convenient label for anonymous artists who seem to have a distinct artistic personality. The custom originated amongst 19th-century German scholars. The invented name is nowadays usually taken from the most important or typical work by the artist (The Master of The St Bartholomew Altarpiece), but formerly much more poetic names were preferred, as in The Master of the Pearl of Brabant, now identified as Dirk Bouts.

Master of Alkmaar active 1504–20
Dutch painter, trained and active in Haarlem. His oeuvre is based around the altarpiece of *The Seven Mercies* (Amsterdam, Rijksmuseum), which was produced for the church of St Lawrence in Alkmaar in 1504. This work is remarkable for the unifying quality of its light effects, although the figures are stiff and awkward, reminiscent of Geertgen.

Master of Flémalle see CAMPIN

Master of Mary of Burgundy active 1476–c.1490
Netherlandish illuminator named after two Books of Hours owned by Mary of Burgundy, heiress of Duke Charles the Bold (c.1477–82, Vienna, Kunsthistorisches and West Berlin, Kupferstichkabinett). Other works have been attributed to him, notably a Book of Hours in the Bodleian Library, Oxford, which shows a new type of border, with items of still life on a rather larger scale replacing the traditional framing foliage. The Master's love of spacious vistas and fascination with still life are apparent in the most famous illumination in the Vienna Book of Hours, which shows Mary, with all her everyday possessions from small pug to vase of flowers, reading before a view into a spacious church. See vol. 1 pp. **18–19**

Master of Moulins
active c.1480–1500
One of the finest French painters of the 15th century, named after the exquisite triptych of *The Virgin and Child* in Moulins Cathedral (c.1498). The portraits of Pierre, Duke of Bourbon and his wife Anne de Beaujeu, the principal patrons of the Master of Moulins, appear

on the wings. *The Nativity with Cardinal Jean Rolin* (c.1480, Autun, Rolin Museum) is generally accepted as the Master's earliest surviving work; the cold flesh tones, the rustic shepherds and the composition in half-length all show the influence of Hugo van der Goes, and suggest a training in Flanders. He is sometimes identified with Jean Hay, who signed an *Ecce Homo* (Brussels, Musées Royaux des Beaux-Arts).

Master of René of Anjou see MASTER OF THE CUER D'AMOUR ESPRIS

Master of St Cecilia active c.1304
Italian painter named after the St Cecilia altarpiece in the Uffizi, Florence, which came from the church of S. Cecilia, burnt in 1304. Attempts have been made to attribute other paintings to the author of this impressive Giottesque work, including several of the frescos on the life of St Francis in the Upper Church of S. Francesco at ASSISI, and some criticis have tried to identify him with the mysterious Buffalmacco.

Master of St Francis see ASSISI

Master of the Aix Annunciation
active c.1445
French painter named after the altarpiece made for St Sauveur de la Madeleine, Aix-en-Provence (*The Annunciation*, 1445, central panel, Aix, la Madeleine; wings, Brussels, Musées Royaux des Beaux-Arts; Rotterdam, Boymans Museum; Paris, Louvre). The weighty figures and rigid draperies point to the influence of Netherlandish painting and Burgundian sculpture but the painting is assumed to be the work of a Provençal artist as yet unidentified.

Master of the Bambino Vispo
active c.1400–30
Florentine Painter. His name, meaning "Master of the lively Child", describes his spontaneous treatment of the Christ Child in panels which are attributed to him (for example "The Lederer Madonna", Geneva, Lederer coll.). His art, as far as it can be judged, was an expressive fusion of International Gothic elegance and a more decorative style suggestive of Spanish activity or influence.

Master of the Bedford Hours
active 1st half of 15th century
Name given to an artist illuminating manuscripts in Paris during the first half of the 15th century. Many manuscripts can be associated with his workshop, but those once owned by John Lancaster, Duke of Bedford, Regent of France 1422–35, form the central group—the Bedford Hours (c.1424, London, BL), the Salisbury Breviary (left unfinished 1435, Paris, BN) and a Missal (destroyed). The style is based on that of the Boucicaut Master but is more animated.

Master of the Cuer d'Amour Espris active 1435–65
French illuminator who illustrated a romantic allegory written by René of Anjou in 1457, *Le Livre du Cuer d'Amour Espris* (The Book of Heart Smitten by Love; Vienna, Nationalbibliothek). A masterpiece of French illumination, the book displays a lively and naturalistic narrative style and remarkably early night scenes (notably that in which Love gives the King's heart to Desire). *Le Livre des Tournois* (The Book of Tourneys; Paris, BN) has an inscription to the effect that it was written and painted by René himself, but there is now little doubt that the artist was not René. See vol. 2 p. **97**

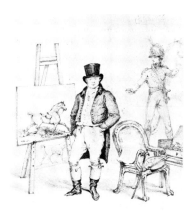

Marshall: Drawing attributed to I. R. Cruikshank (1789–1856). London, NPG

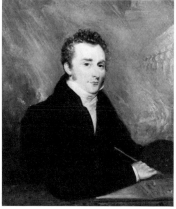

Martin, John: Portrait by H. Warren (1794–1879), c.1839. London, NPG

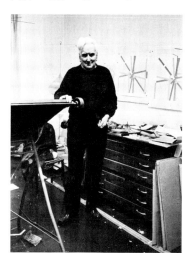

Martin, Kenneth: Photograph, 1976 by Derek Smith (Waddington Galleries Ltd.)

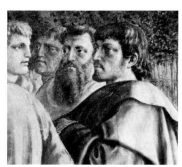

Masaccio: Self-portrait? from *The tribute money*, 1425–28. Florence, S. Maria del Carmine (Scala)

Master of the Life of the Virgin
active c.1460–90
The most influential Cologne painter of his time, named after eight panels from St Ursula, Cologne (Munich, Alte Pinakothek, and London, NG). The strong influence, particularly of Bouts, on his work, as in *The vision of St Bernard*, (c.1480, Cologne, Wallraf-Richartz Museum), suggests that he may have trained in the Netherlands.

Master of the Playing Cards
active c.1430–50
German engraver named after his finest work, a set of 60 cards in Dresden (Kupferstichkabinett) and Paris (BN). Whilst not the originator of the technique, he is one of the first distinct artists in the history of engraving. He showed a minute attention to naturalistic detail, using a characteristic technique of short, thin parallel lines.

Master of the Registrum Gregorii
see OTTONIAN ART

Master of the Rohan Hours
active c.1410–30
French illuminator whose workshop produced *Les Grandes Heures de Rohan* (c.1420–25, Paris, BN) and other manuscripts. The singular, expressive power of his style has led to much speculation over his origins. It is likely that he worked in Troyes, 1410–14, and was later employed by Yolande of Aragon, for whom *Les Grandes Heures* were originally made. Although he draws upon the work of the Limbourgs and the Boucicaut Master for figures and settings, his miniatures rely on strong colour, violent changes of scale and swirling line for their effect.

Master of the St Bartholomew Altarpiece
active c.1470–1510
Painter and illuminator named after an altarpiece from St Colomba's, Cologne, of about 1505–10, of which three panels survive in the Alte Pinakothek in Munich. He is generally thought to have trained in the Netherlands and the Book of Hours of Sophia of Bylant (Cologne, Wallraf-Richartz Museum), which he illuminated, is dated 1475, while the panels from a dismembered altarpiece (*The journey of the Magi*, Munich, Alte Pinakothek, and *The Nativity*, Paris, Petit Palais) are also from this early period. He settled in Cologne about 1480. His mature works, including the panels of the St Bartholomew altarpiece, a *Deposition* (Paris, Louvre), and the *Crucifixion Triptych* (Wallraf-Richartz Museum), all combine a refined attention to detail and rich enamel-like colour with an animated figure style. See vol. 2 p. **155**

Master of the View of St Gudule
active c.1470–c.1490
Netherlandish painter named after a panel in the Louvre, Paris, depicting a scene from *The life of St Géry* (c.1485) which includes a view of the façade of St Gudule, Brussels. The north tower is shown unfinished, which would fit with a date of about 1485. The works attributed to this painter, such as the *Young man* (c.1480, London, NG), show an Eyckian style owing much to van der Weyden. See vol. 1 p. *144*

Master of the Virgo inter Virgines
active c.1470–1500
Northern Netherlandish painter and designer of woodcut illustrations, named after a painting, *The Virgin with SS. Barbara, Catherine, Cecilia and Ursula* (c.1480–90, Amsterdam, Rijksmuseum). He lived and worked in Delft and dominated book illustration in that town. The *History of the Seven Wise Men*, with woodcuts attributed to this Master, was published there about 1483. *The Entombment* (c.1480–90, Liverpool, Walker Art Gallery) and *The Crucifixion* (c.1480–90, Barnard Castle, Bowes Museum) are amongst his most characteristic works, and attest to this master's loose technique and the strange, feverish pathos of his distinctive and expressive style. See vol. 2 p. *99*

Master of Třeboň
active late 14th century
Bohemian painter named after three panels from an altarpiece in the southern Bohemian monastery of Třeboň (c.1390, Prague, NG). They are regarded as one of the peaks of Bohemian achievement and witness the dawn of the International Gothic style.

Master of Vyšši Brod active c.1350
Bohemian painter named after the nine panels from an altarpiece in the Cistercian monastery of Vyšši Brod (Hohenfurth), now in the National Gallery, Prague. They are amongst the finest of their time and their linear style reflects the Sienese influence then current in Bohemian art.

Masterpiece
Term now generally used to mean a work of acknowledged greatness or the most important work by a particular artist. It was originally used of a work produced by an artist or craftsman on the completion of his apprenticeship to qualify him for the rank of master in a Guild.

Master Theodoric active 1348–70
Bohemian painter patronized by Emperor Charles IV. He executed 135 panels between about 1360 and 1365, nearly all still *in situ* in the Holy Cross chapel in Karlstein Castle, Czechoslovakia. He brought a firm sense of volume and a taste for naturalistic detail to the current fluent line and soft colours of Bohemian art. See vol. 2 p. **89**

Matejko, Jan 1838–93
The leading Polish painter of the second half of the 19th century. He studied in Munich and in Vienna, 1859–60, thereafter returning to Cracow, where he became Director of the School of Fine Arts there in 1873. The vast historical canvases which form the greater part of his oeuvre are rich in colour and detail, zealously instructing the spectator in the great events of Polish history (*The arrest of the deputy Thaddäus Rejtan at the Diet of Warsaw in 1773*, 1866, Warsaw, National Museum).

Mathieu, Georges born 1921
French painter. He began painting in 1942, and under the influence of Wols and De Kooning developed an abstract style of sweeping line which came to be known as Lyrical Abstraction. He has created Action Paintings before an audience in a theatre and has produced a large oeuvre including stage sets, tapestries, mosaics and architectural designs. His paintings are often very large and have pompous historical titles (*The crowning of Charlemagne*, 1956, Champaign, University of Illinois, Krannert Art Museum). See vol. 3 p. **224**

Matisse, Henri 1869–1954
French painter, one of the greatest and most influential artists of the 20th century. Quitting his law studies, he entered the studio of Moreau in Paris in 1892. After cautious beginnings, he was stimulated by Signac's Neo-Impressionism and began to apply his new-found high-key colour with increasing spontaneity while working with Derain at Collioure during the summer of 1905 (*The open window*, 1905, New York, Whitney). His works, with those of Derain, Vlaminck and others, were to provoke the term FAUVISM when exhibited at the Salon d'Automne in Paris in 1905. Subsequently he sought to eliminate the traces of illusionistic description of volume and space which remained in his Fauvist work, emphasizing instead the flatness of the picture plane and the abstract purity of line, decorative pattern and colour. He explored such concerns in a series of Arcadian figure paintings (*Joie de vivre*, 1906, Merion, Barnes Foundation) that culminated in the great images of *Dance* and *Music*, intended as decorations for a staircase (1909–10, Leningrad, Hermitage Museum). He then began to adopt a more formal structure, resulting around 1916–17 in a series of pictures of austere, monumental grandeur, for example *Bathers by a river* (1916–17, Chicago, Art Institute). From 1920 on he lived mainly in Nice, and turned to a more naturalistic style, painting particularly a series of *Odalisques*. His late work is exemplified by *Memory of Oceanie* (1953, New York, MOMA), in which he uses a "cut-out" technique in simple compositions made from pieces of brightly coloured paper, which express his hedonistic response to light and colour. His work culminates in the decorations for the Chapel of the Rosary at Vence, for which he designed the windows, ceramic tiles and vestments. He continued to work until his death, although crippled by arthritis. Matisse was also a forceful sculptor and an illustrator; of particular note are his relief bronzes, *Back I-IV* (1909–30, London, Tate). He summarized his artistic ideas in *Notes of a Painter* (1908). See vol. 1 pp. *49, 122–23, 124, 155*; vol. 3 pp. **142–145**, *184*, **228–229**

Matsys see MASSYS

Matta Echaurren, Roberto
born 1912
Chilean SURREALIST painter. He trained as an architect and worked, 1934–37, with Le Corbusier in Paris. In 1937 he joined the Surrealist movement and became a principal exponent of biomorphism along with Tanguy, Masson, Miró and others. The paintings of this period are entitled *Psychological morphologies*, a numbered serial progression of free pictorial abstractions in which galaxies of tremulous bodies whirl and combine with vaporous clouds of colour in unfathomable space (*No. 37*, 1938, California, Mill Valley, Gordon Onslow-Ford coll.). In 1939 Matta emigrated to the USA, retaining his Automatism and symbolic iconography and becoming a significant influence on the future Abstract Expressionists, especially Arshile Gorky. They particularly admired his intellectual perspicacity. He formed a bridge between them and the older generation of Tanguy, Ernst and Duchamp. See vol. 3 pp. **210–211**

Matteo de' Pasti active c.1441
Veronese artist, whose wide-ranging activities included manuscript illumination, medals, sculpture and architecture. He may have been trained by Pisanello, and is first recorded in 1441 illustrating a copy of Petrarch's *Triumphs* for Piero de' Medici. He spent the greater part of his career in Rimini as the friend and court artist of Sigismondo Malatesta, whom he served at least from 1449. He was closely involved with Alberti and Agostino di Duccio in the architectural and sculptural transformation of S. Francesco, the Tempio Malatestiano, and carvings attributed to him reveal strong antique influences. See vol. 2 p. *115*

Matteo di Giovanni c.1435–95
Sienese painter. He was the pupil of Vecchietta, but was influenced more noticeably by Donatello and the Pollaiuoli, for example in his powerful *Assumption of the Virgin* (1475, London, NG) and his designs for the marble inlay floor of Siena Cathedral (1814). His *Madonna and Child with two saints* (c.1490, Birmingham, Barber Institute) is typical of late 15th-century Sienese painting in its flat patterning and bland, blond colours.

Maulbertsch or Maulpertsch, Franz Anton 1724–96
The foremost Austrian fresco painter of the Rococo, one of the greatest masters of the spontaneous oil-sketch, and an accomplished etcher. Born by Lake Constance, he arrived in Vienna in 1739 and during his prolific career he was active in Austria, Bohemia, Moravia and Hungary. He was variously influenced by the tenebrism of Piazzetta and the painterly *brio* of Pittoni, as mediated through Troger. His frescos develop from agitated chiaroscuro in the church of Maria-Treu in Vienna (1752–53), through bright pageantry in the church at Sümeg (1757–58) and in the Archiepiscopal Residence at Kromeriz (1759–60), to classic harmony in the library of Strahov, Prague (finished 1794). They are always distinguished by their vivacity and vivid colours, and by expressiveness verging on the bizarre.

Maurer, Alfred Henry 1868–1932
American painter. In the 1890s he visited Paris and established contact with the Paris avantgarde, consequently developing from Impressionism to a Fauvist style (from 1908) influenced by Matisse. In 1909 Stieglitz gave Maurer his first one-man show. Later, he evolved a Cubist style (*Still life with fish*, 1927–28, New York, Metropolitan). He was a tragically unhappy man, beset by family problems, and this comes across in his work. He finally hanged himself shortly after his father's death.

Mauve, Anton 1838–88
Dutch landscape painter, a leading figure of the HAGUE school. Millet and the Barbizon school were important influences on his style. He painted dunes during his time in The Hague, where he was once visited by his nephew, van Gogh (*Scheveningen*, 1874, Glasgow Art Gallery). After 1886 he moved to Laren, where his main subjects were heathlands with cattle.

Mayan art
Art of the Mayan civilization of southern Mesoamerica, in the classic period, c.200–900. Amongst many widespread ceremonial centres, some of the best-known are Tikal, Copán, Chichén Itzá, Palenque and Bonampak. The magnificence of these sites attests the superb skill of the Mayan architects and sculptors. In sculpture they tended to cover surfaces with a profusion of both figurative and symbolic decoration and hieroglyphic inscriptions. Human heads were frequently portrayed, illustrating the classic Maya profile with its artificially deformed skull. The Maya are also noted for their fine lapidary work, particularly in jade, and for their elaborately painted

polychrome pottery, often depicting animated scenes of ceremonial life and religious practice; murals have also survived at Bonampak. They also produced pottery with modelled, excised and appliqué decoration and lifelike figurines. A few finely carved lintels and three beautifully painted manuscripts (in Dresden, Sacchsische Landesbibliothek, Paris, BN, and Madrid, Museo de America) have survived. Metalwork was practised only to a limited extent—a few objects in copper and gold have been found. See vol. 2 pp. **18–19**

Mayno (Maino), Juan Bautista
1578–1649

Spanish painter. Although he is said to have been a pupil of El Greco, his colouring is so clear and his draughtsmanship so firm that it seems likely that he trained in Italy in the circle of Bolognese painters such as Reni. He worked for Philip III, was the drawing-master of his son, the future Philip IV, and continued in royal favour until his death. He was also a priest, and his output was fairly small. His best works are his penetrating portraits, outstanding among them *A Dominican monk* (*c*.1635, Oxford, Ashmolean), which conveys an astonishing sense of plastic bulk and physical presence. He was a friend of Velazquez and helped to advance his career at court.

Ma Yuan active *c*.1190–1224

Chinese painter, one of the most famous landscape painters of the Song court tradition. His work (for example the tiny *Landscapes* on fans in the Boston Museum of Fine Arts) in monochrome ink shows the strong brushwork of "academic" landscape, which was to go out of fashion in the Ming dynasty under the influence of literati notions. He and Xia Gui painted in a similar manner, leaving much of the surface of the painting untouched, in carefully worked asymmetrical compositions. These patches of "nothingness" are often the true subject of the painting. *Landscape in rain* (Tokyo, Seikado Foundation) is a characteristic work, displaying the knarled pine-trees which were reputedly one of Ma Yuan's trade-marks. See vol. 3 p. 40

Mazo, Juan Bautista Martínez del
c.1614–67

Spanish painter, the pupil and son-in-law of Velazquez and his successor as court painter. His paintings, principally portraits, imitate Velazquez's mature style in an accomplished but uninventive way. Very few works are signed (one is *Queen Mariana*, 1666, London, NG), and some of the best now given to him are rejections from Velazquez's oeuvre (*Don Adrian Pulido Pareja*, London, NG).

Mazzoni, Guido active 1473–1518

Italian sculptor, painter and miniaturist from Modena. In Italy he specialized in life-size terracotta *Lamentation* groups, not quite so strident in their emotionalism as those of Niccolò dell'Arca, but powerfully realistic—notably that in S. Giovanni della Buona Morte in Modena, 1477–80. He was a court artist in Naples from 1489, then in 1495 King Charles VIII brought him to France, perhaps having been impressed by his *Entombment* in Naples (Church of Monte Oliveto). In France his tomb for Charles VIII of 1498, destroyed but known from engravings, influenced the design of future French royal tombs. After a brief return to Modena in 1507, he is known to have made a lost equestrian statue of Louis XII at Blois, and was active in France until 1515; he died in Modena.

Mazzoni, Sebastiano *c*.1611–78

Italian Baroque painter of bizarre originality, also a poet and architect. He was born in Florence, where the exotic art of Furini helped to form his style, and moved to Venice in 1648. He was highly imaginative in his choice of subject matter, and even more so in his treatment of it (*The sacrifice of Jephthah*, 1660, Kansas City, Nelson Gallery). Mazzoni's unique approach to form and movement, as shown in this work and in what is perhaps his masterpiece, *The Annunciation* (*c*.1650, Venice, Accademia) found no successors, but his brilliantly free brushwork looks ahead to the great 18th-century Venetian painters, and according to some early sources he was the teacher of Sebastiano Ricci.

Meadows, Bernard born 1915

British sculptor. From 1936 to 1940 he was assistant to Henry Moore, and early pieces such as the elmwood *Standing figure* (1951, London, Tate) reflect the influence of Moore's organic forms. Later, in works such as *The crab* (1954, Cambridge, Jesus College) a more angular aggressive mood enters his work and persists in his armed bronze figures of the early 1960s. More recent works are smoother in texture but remain sinister in their human and animal imagery.

Medici family

Italian family that ruled Florence and later Tuscany for most of the period 1434 to 1737 and included in its members some of the greatest art patrons of their time. The fortunes of the banking family were founded by **Giovanni di Bicci** de' Medici (1360–1429), who employed Brunelleschi as an architect. For his son, **Cosimo** (1389–1464), Michelozzo built the family's city residence, now the Palazzo Medici-Riccardi; Cosimo's favourite painter was Fra Angelico. **Piero**, his son (1416–69), was a much more active patron of painters and sculptors: his commissions went to Domenico Veneziano, Uccello, Gozzoli, the Pollaiuoli brothers, Verrocchio and Mino da Fiesole, who sculpted his portrait (1453, Florence, Uffizi); his favourite artist was perhaps Filippo Lippi. Piero's son, **Lorenzo** (1449–92), called the Magnificent, was the most celebrated Medici, and himself a humanist poet. He was the first recorded patron of Michelangelo, but his main collecting interests seem to have been in antique coins and gems. His second cousin **Lorenzo di Pierfrancesco** (1463–1503) was the principal patron of Botticelli. The Medici lost power in 1494, but regained it in 1512. Two of the great patron popes of the 16th century were Medici—**Leo X** (1513–21) and **Clement VII** (1524–43), employing Giulio Romano, Michelangelo, Raphael, Rosso and Sebastiano del Piombo amongst others. The most celebrated Medici commission from Michelangelo was the Medici Chapel (1519–34), containing his tombs of Lorenzo de' Medici, and his brother Giuliano, in S. Lorenzo, Florence. **Cosimo I** (1519–74) became the first Grand Duke of Tuscany in 1569 and patronized many celebrated Mannerist painters and sculptors including Giambologna: his *studiolo* in the Palazzo Vecchio is a Mannerist shrine. Vasari built the Uffizi (now the art gallery) for him and painted huge frescos of the history of Florence and the ruling family in the Palazzo Vecchio. Cosimo also acquired the Pitti Palace in 1549, had additions made by Ammanati, and made it the Medici residence. The tradition of collecting and patronizing artists was maintained by Cosimo's successors, in particular the most enterprising 17th-century Medici patron, **Leopoldo** (1617–75), chiefly remembered for beginning the celebrated collection of artists' self-portraits in the Uffizi. Pietro da Cortona carried out sumptuous decorations in the Pitti Palace in the 1630s and 1640s, but by 1683, when Luca Giordano painted *The apotheosis of the Medici* in the Medici Palace, the zenith of their power was long past, and the Grand Duchy fell from their hands in 1737.

Medieval art

Art in Europe from early Christian times, after the fall of the Roman Empire, until the Renaissance. The Middle Ages were regarded as an era of artistic and cultural debasement during the Renaissance, and the appreciation of the great variety and comparative sophistication of medieval styles dates only from the 18th century. Three great international styles emerged in Europe after the so-called Dark Ages: ROMANESQUE, GOTHIC, and INTERNATIONAL GOTHIC. In sculpture and painting forms ranged from the ornamental and abstract (highly developed in CELTIC, ANGLO-SAXON and MOZARABIC art) to the figurative and heavily stylized.

Medium

Term applied in general to the various methods and materials of art, painting being a different medium from sculpture and, within the broad category of painting, tempera being a different medium from fresco. In **mixed-media** works, more than one technique is used, as when oils are added to a tempera underdrawing, or collage materials to oils. Medium is also used in another sense to designate the substance—often water, oil, turpentine or varnish—added to paint to extend it, alter its consistency or drying speed, or influence its matt or glossy appearance.

Meidias Painter active *c*.420–400 BC

Greek RED-FIGURE vase-painter from Athens, named after and possibly identical with the potter Meidias who signed one of his vases. He was a late exponent of the red-figure technique, and the influence of contemporary wall-painting is apparent in his use of perspective and in his ability to arrange his slightly mannered figures on different spatial levels, as in the *hydria* in the British Museum, London, which depicts the rape of the daughters of Leukippos.

Meidner, Ludwig 1884–1966

German painter, lithographer and engraver. Although an archetypal EXPRESSIONIST, he never belonged to any of the major groups. Originally from Silesia, he moved to Berlin in 1905, and a visit to Paris (1906) resulted in the lasting influence of van Gogh on his work. Although he was an atheist, his most powerful pictures were prompted by mystic visions, as in his famous series of apocalyptical landscapes and Berlin scenes (*Burning city*, 1913, St Louis, Morton D. May coll.). They are painted in a style combining Expressionist distortion and Futurist shifting perspectives, creating a frenetic sense of impending disaster.

Meissonier, Ernest 1815–91

French painter, engraver and sculptor. Meissonier began his career as an illustrator and established his reputation with painstaking historical genre paintings inspired by Dutch cabinet pictures. Often they evoke the world of Dumas's *Three Musketeers* or are of Napoleonic subjects. He was immensely successful

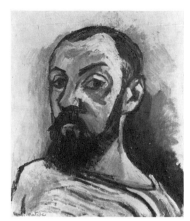

Matisse: Self-portrait, 1907. Copenhagen, Statens Museum for Kunst

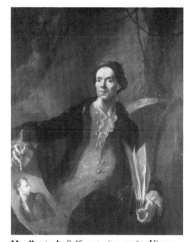

Maulbertsch: Self-portrait, *c*.1760. Vienna, Osterreichische Galerie

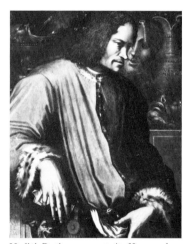

Medici: Posthumous portrait of Lorenzo by Vasari, 1533. Florence, Uffizi (Scala)

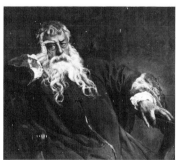

Meissonier: Self-portrait, 1889. Paris, Louvre (Alinari)

and showered with honours, and his conceit was enormous—with his long white beard he saw himself as a latter-day Leonardo. His paintings (of which there are large collections in the Louvre, Paris, and the Wallace Collection, London), now often seem ridiculous, but his *Barricade, Rue de la Martellerie* (1848, Louvre), portraying the revolutionary events of 1848, and showing corpses lying like paving-stones, is very different in spirit from most of his work, and was much admired by his friend Delacroix. See vol. 3 pp. **86–87**

Meit, Conrad died 1550/1
German sculptor, a native of Worms. In the early 16th century he worked at the Saxon court at Wittenburg with Cranach, but spent most of his career as court sculptor to the Hapsburg rulers of the Netherlands. His work for them included tombs for the Regent Margaret of Austria and her family (1526–32, Bourg, Notre-Dame-de-Brou), incorporating outstanding portrait figures. Much of his work consisted of small pieces on classical themes and portrait busts, bronzes and alabasters executed with a masterly smoothness and simplification drawn from study of both Italian and Netherlandish art. See vol. 2 p. **159**

Melanesian art
The art of the inhabitants of the South-West Pacific islands from New Guinea to Fiji. Melanesian peoples have many local cultures with varied artistic traditions. Various combinations of sculpture, modelling and painting were used to embellish architecture, costume and objects of everyday use. The most elaborate artistic efforts were usually devoted to esoteric religious ceremonies, generally concerned with the spirits of ancestors. Masks, elaborate costumes and figurative sculptures, often of ephemeral materials, were created for these occasions, and are among the most striking and powerful examples of tribal art admired in the West. See vol. 2 pp. 22–23

Meléndez, Luis Eugenio 1716–80
Spanish still-life painter, sometimes called "the Spanish Chardin", active mainly in Madrid. In spite of the high quality of his work his life was spent largely in poverty. There are good examples of his still lifes in the Prado, Madrid; and there is a striking *Self-portrait* in the Louvre, Paris. It shows the artist holding a drawing of a male nude, and has something of the imaginative power and emotional impact of a portrait by Goya.

Mellan, Claude 1598–1688
French painter and engraver. Very few of his paintings survive and he is mainly important as one of the founders of the French school of portrait engraving, of which Nanteuil was the leading representative. Mellan was particularly celebrated for his technical virtuosity, which is shown most clearly in *The sudarium of St Veronica*, which became famous immediately it was published in 1642. It is made up of one continuous line which goes round like the groove on a gramophone record.

Mellery, Xavier 1845–1921
Belgian painter and illustrator. His subjects were portraits, landscapes and small-scale allegorical scenes and monochrome interiors which evoke a meditative silence and the inner life of things (*The awakening*, undated drawing, Brussels, Musées Royaux des Beaux-Arts). His more monumental ambitions were never realized. He exerted a profound influence on his pupil, Khnopff.

Melozzo da Forlì 1438–94
Italian painter from the Romagna, chiefly active in Loreto, Urbino and Rome. His sensitive portraiture and solid sense of pictorial structure were developed in contact with Piero della Francesca and Netherlandish artists such as Justus of Ghent. Like Mantegna, he became interested in illusionistic spatial setting and virtuoso foreshortening, exemplified in his fresco, *Sixtus IV founding the Vatican Library* (1474, Vatican) and his spectacular *Ascension* for SS. Apostoli, Rome (1478–80, now Quirinal Palace, fragments Vatican), with its dramatically foreshortened Christ and beautiful angels. See vol. 2 p. *128*

Memlinc or **Memling, Hans**
*c.*1430/40–94
German-born Netherlandish painter. He worked in Bruges from 1465 until his death and became the most popular Netherlandish painter of his time. His output was prolific and his patrons included several Italian merchants. In this way his works were important in spreading Netherlandish influence in Italy. In composition and repertory of figures Memlinc's style is closely dependent upon Rogier van der Weyden, with whom he is thought to have trained, but without the emotional intensity of that master. The Donne triptych (*c.*1480, London, NG) reveals the static charm, pious restraint and interest in surface detail characteristic of Memlinc's work throughout his career. Other altarpieces show little variation in style. A greater freshness and originality is found in his numerous portraits. In several, he copied a formula invented by van der Weyden—a diptych with the *Madonna and Child* on one side and a donor on the other. He brought the type to a peak of harmony and definition in the diptych of Martin van Nieuwenhove (1487) in the Hospital of St John, Bruges, which is now a Memlinc museum. Memlinc was very popular as a portraitist with the wealthier classes of Bruges, developing a distinctive single portrait type with the head shown half-face against a landscape vista (*A young man*, Venice, Accademia). See vol. 1 p. *144*; vol. 2 p. **96**

Memmi, Lippo active 1317–57
Sienese painter, the brother-in-law of Simone Martini. Memmi's main claim to fame lies in *The Annunciation* (1333, Florence, Uffizi), which he signed jointly with Simone Martini. No one has yet managed satisfactorily to distinguish their respective shares. Memmi's independent work can best be seen in his paintings of the *Virgin and Child*, of which there are good examples in Boston (Gardner Museum) and in the Church of the Servites at Siena—the so-called "*Madonna del Popolo*".

Memphis
City in Lower Egypt, founded about 3000 BC, one of the major centres of Egyptian art. Memphite art was particularly influential in the OLD KINGDOM, when the court style maintained uniformity of expression during several Dynasties. The city's burial grounds, with their royal pyramids and lesser tombs, preserve a great legacy of Old Kingdom painting and sculpture, notably at Giza, Saqqara and Dahshur. See vol. 2 pp. 24–25

Mena, Pedro de 1628–88
Spanish Baroque sculptor, working chiefly in polychromed wood. He was an assistant of Cano in his native Granada from 1652 to 1658, then spent most of the rest of his life in Malaga, where he carved a set of choir-stalls (1658–62) for the Cathedral. The best-known of his statues, which tend to be pious and emotionally direct but with a dignified restraint, is *St Francis* (1663, Toledo Cathedral). His prosperous workshop sold sculptures throughout Spain.

Mengs, Anton Raffael 1728–79
Bohemian-German history painter and portraitist, the apostle of the Neoclassical reform in painting. He was the son of a miniaturist, **Ismael Mengs** (died 1764), who "pummelled him into art" by forcing him to draw after classical models incessantly. Appointed court painter in Dresden for his portraits in 1745, he nevertheless spent his formative years in Rome, where he derived much of his theoretical inspiration from his friendship with Winckelmann. His ceiling painting *Parnassus* in the Villa Albani (1761) broke with Baroque illusionism to become a manifesto of the classical revival. Invited to Spain, where he spent most of 1761–77, he painted portraits and ceilings in the royal palaces of Madrid and Aranjuez, and turned the tide against his rival, Giambattista Tiepolo. With the exception of *Parnassus*, his works were less influential than his theories—partly set down in *Considerations on Beauty and Taste in Painting* (1762). His history paintings are rather flimsy and he was at his best in portraiture, in which field he was rival in Rome to Batoni. See vol. 3 p. **56**

Menn, Barthélemy 1815–93
Swiss painter of landscape, genre and figure scenes. He spent the years 1838 to 1843 in Paris in contact with Corot, Ingres and Delacroix. On returning to Geneva he did much to gain recognition for these painters and organized several major exhibitions of their work. *Bathers at Leman* (Winterthur, Musée des Beaux-Arts) shows the influence of Corot in the soft colour sketching of the landscape, and that of Ingres in the fine detail of the portraiture. In later years Menn was to discover and teach Hodler.

Mense, Carlo 1889–1965
German painter. He studied at Düsseldorf and at Berlin under Corinth, 1905–09. His early work, exploring colour resonances, shows the influence of Der Blaue Reiter and in 1918 he was a member of the NOVEMBERGRUPPE. In Munich during the 1920s he developed a stylized, simplified form of Neoclassical realism, similar to that practised by the other painters in the group, Davringhausen, Kanoldt and Schrimpf. His portraits and still lifes, while detached and impersonal, have a warmth and naive quality (*Mother with children*, *c.*1927, Marburg, Universitätsmuseum).

Menzel, Adolph von 1815–1905
German painter and engraver, the first of the great German Realist painters of the 19th century. His early international reputation arose from his 400 illustrations for the historian Kugler's *History of Frederick the Great* (1840–42). These combine the acute observation of Realism with grace and inventiveness. His unique position in Germany during this period is due both to his subject matter, which veers towards the everyday without literary or allegorical overtones, and his technique, which is astonishingly free in brush-stroke and explores the values of colour and light in a proto-Impressionist manner.

Mercier, Philippe 1689–1760
German-born painter of French origin who settled in England by 1725. He painted portraits and fancy pieces, but is remembered chiefly for his conversation pieces, which he was probably the first artist in Britain to paint (*A music party*, *c.*1737–40, London, Tate). George II's son, Frederick Prince of Wales, was among his patrons, and his rather diluted Rococo style was popular and widely spread through engravings.

Merian family
Family of German artists, active in the 17th and 18th centuries. The two best-known members were **Matthaeus the Elder** (1593–1650) and his daughter **Maria Sibylla** (1647–1717). Matthaeus was an engraver and publisher, who produced a large number of topographical prints, of historical rather than artistic interest. Hollar was his principal pupil. Maria Sibylla made watercolours of insects and butterflies, remarkable both for their delicacy and for their scientific accuracy. She worked in Holland as well as Germany, and travelled to Surinam in South America to study the insects there, on which she published a book in 1705. The best collection of her work is in the Academy of Sciences in Leningrad.

Merida, Carlos born 1891
Guatemalan painter, especially of murals. He studied in Paris, 1910–14, under Modigliani and van Dongen and settled in Mexico after 1919. He developed from a politically conscious figurative style applied to local subjects towards an abstract manner. He used the recurring linear motifs and decorative borders characteristic of Mayan art and worked on traditional bark paper. The quiet but insistent power of his work was suited to murals. He undertook numerous commissions in later years, including those at the Municipal Palace in Guatemala City, where he used coloured mosaics instead of traditional fresco.

Meryon, Charles 1821–68
French painter, etcher and draughtsman. Discovery of his colour-blindness finished his career as a painter, but he then became the most important figure in the revival of the art of etching in France. Buildings formed his principal subject and his greatest series was *Etchings of Paris*, 1850–54, a romantic, subjective portrayal evocative of medieval Paris, which exists in many states. From 1857, when he began to suffer periodic bouts of mental illness, fantastic apparitions, recalling those of Hieronymous Bosch, appeared in his work (*Ministry of the Marine with flying devils*, 1865); in 1866 he finally entered an asylum. Both Victor Hugo and Baudelaire greatly admired his city etchings. See vol. 3 p. **89**

Merz see SCHWITTERS

Mesdag, Hendrik Willem
1831–1915
Dutch marine painter and art collector. He established himself in The Hague in 1869, and became an important member of the HAGUE school. His fame rests on the *Panorama* (1881, The Hague, Mesdag Museum), a huge illustration of the beach at Scheveningen.

Mesens, E.L.T. 1903–71
Belgian poet, musician and painter. He was an important member of both the Belgian and, after 1938, British SURREALIST groups. From 1924 he made witty, poetic collages in the vein of Man Ray and Picabia (*The completed score for Marcel Duchamp's band*, 1945, Brussels, Musées Royaux des Beaux-Arts).

Mesopotamian art

Art in Mesopotamia over a period of some 3,000 years, from the early domination of the SUMERIAN civilization to the last flowering of the Neo-Babylonian era in the 6th century BC. A variety of artistic styles and media were employed by successive cultures. The first notable period after the Sumerian decline is the Akkadian (24th–22nd centuries BC), from which two major works survive: the bronze *Head*, perhaps of King Sargon, found at Nineveh (Baghdad, Iraq Museum), and the Stela of Naram-Sin (Paris, Louvre), remarkable for its free use of space and its flowing composition. Later, in Old Babylonian times (18th century BC), a magnificent palace at Mari flourished, with outstanding murals in gesso technique, such as *The investiture of Zimri-Lim* (Louvre). Then came the ASSYRIAN period, and lastly the Neo-Babylonian era, when the ancient city of Babylon was rebuilt and made resplendent by Nabopolassar and his son Nebuchadnezzar. The fabled Hanging Gardens and the great *ziggurat* (the biblical Tower of Babel) are largely lost to us, but enough remains of the Palace, the Ishtar Gate and the Processional Way, with their splendid moulded and glazed tiles in the form of lions, bulls and the mythical dragons of the gods, to give us a hint of the greatness that has been lost. Both the Ishtar Gate and the Processional Way have been reconstructed, using many original tiles, in the Pergamon Museum, East Berlin. Mesopotamia as a cultural and political entity reached its end when it was conquered by Cyrus the Great, the ACHAEMENIAN king, in 539 BC, but it influenced early Ionian art. See vol. 2 pp. 28–29

Messagier, Jean Félicien Emile
born 1920

French artist. He began in a Cubist style but since the early 1950s his work has become far more fluid. His graphic art is based on meshes of thin lines, while his sculpture uses found objects. His portraits of art dealers and film stars are well known. Recently he has moved on to works of vast dimensions.

Messerschmidt, Franz Xaver
1736–83

Austrian sculptor. He was a fine portrait sculptor, but is now remembered almost solely for his profoundly original studies of facial expression, which border on the pathological. He became a pupil at the Vienna Academy in 1752, and after travelling to Rome and London in 1764, returned to Vienna, where he taught at the Academy (1769–74), until madness began to afflict him. In 1777 he retreated to Pressburg (Bratislava), where he lived like a hermit, obsessively modelling his "character heads"—studies in temperament (predominantly in lead), inspired partly by the contemporary researches of the physiognomist Lavater and partly by his persecution mania. The Österreichische Barockmuseum in Vienna has examples of Messerschmidt's work.

Meštrović, Ivan 1883–1962

Yugoslav sculptor, a shepherd boy who became his country's leading artist. In 1900 he moved to Vienna, and by 1914 he had a European reputation. His best heroic figures belong to his early period, when he worked in an eclectic but powerful classicizing style (*Miloš Obilić*, 1908, Zagreb, Meštrović Studio). After World War I he worked mainly on large-scale official commissions such as the Monument of Gratitude to France (1930, Belgrade, Kalemegdan). In 1946 he emigrated to the USA and taught at

Syracuse and Notre Dame Universities. His large monuments now appear somewhat dated, though always marked by powerful idealism. His more moving lyricism is to be found in his smaller and more intimate works.

Metaphysical Painting
(Pittura Metafisica)

Italian art movement. When Carrà met Chirico in Ferrara in 1917 their allied response to the role of modern art led to the foundation of the Metaphysical school. They wished to present an alternative reality which could communicate with the Unconscious by dislocating objects from the real world and presenting them in incongruous relationships that seemed to depend on extramundane logic. A group of *Metaphysical Interiors* and *Muses*, using mannequins, resulted. Within six months Carrà had left, ending their collaboration, and by the early 1920s both were painting in other styles. Although not a group like Futurism, other artists were associated with it, notably Sironi, Soffici, Savinio, de Pisis and Morandi. See vol. 3 pp. 170–171

Metsu, Gabriel 1629–67

Dutch genre painter, born in Leyden and active there until he moved to Amsterdam (by 1657). He is said to have been taught by Dou, but his early paintings, mainly of mythological and religious subjects, have a broad touch very unlike his supposed master's. The works for which Metsu is best known are refined and delicately painted bourgeois interiors. Very few are dated, which makes his development and relationships with other artists difficult to assess. It seems likely, however, that *The music lesson* (late 1650s?, London, NG), one of his most charming works, predates Vermeer's paintings of the same type. Metsu's finest painting is perhaps *The letter reader* (*c*.1665?, Blessington, Ireland, Beit coll.). This includes a figure of a maid pulling back a curtain to look at a painting, an interesting example of how art appealed to all levels of society in 17th-century Holland. See vol. 2 p. **227**

Metsys see MASSYS

Metzger, Gustav born 1926

German-born artist who moved to Britain in 1939 and is now without nationality. He is the originator of auto-destructive art: his works are made only to be destroyed, either immediately, as in his painting with acid on nylon (performed before an audience), or over several years. Partly this reflects his interest in processes, especially chemical ones, of change and decay; partly it is a protest against the idea of art as the creation of precious objects and against consumerism in general; most fundamentally, it is an attempt to emphasize the destructive nature of technological society.

Metzinger, Jean 1883–1956

French painter. He settled in Paris in 1903 to study art and worked at first in a Neo-Impressionist style. From 1906 he also wrote poetry and art criticism. Meeting Picasso and Braque in 1910, he was one of the first to respond to Cubism in both his paintings and writings. A friend of Gleizes and Le Fauconnier, he became a central figure in the SECTION D'OR group and is chiefly remembered as co-author with Gleizes of the first full account of the movement, *Of Cubism* (1912). In paintings such as *Tea time* (1911, Philadelphia, Museum of Art) he applied Cubist fragmentation and multiple viewpoint techniques in a superficial and academic manner.

Meulen, Adam Frans van der
1632–90

Flemish painter and tapestry designer, noted for his military subjects. He trained in Brussels, and entered the service of Louis XIV in 1664, becoming the chief recorder of his military glory. He travelled with the French Army, and his paintings and designs for the Gobelins tapestry works showing the King's campaigns (numerous examples at Versailles) are marked by great accuracy and detail. Van der Meulen was one of Lebrun's principal assistants in his giant decorative schemes for Louis, but was also happy working on a small scale and with less heroic subject matter (*Hunting party*, 1662, London, NG).

Meunier, Constantin Emile
1831–1905

Belgian painter and sculptor, influenced by de Groux in his choice of the working class as his subject. His painting is realistic, later Impressionist, and tends to glorify labour. After a journey through the mining district (1888) with Mellery and Rops he began to take the life of miners as a theme first for painting and then for sculpture. One of his most important works is *Monument of Labour* (1901, Brussels, Place de Trooz).

Mezzotint

Term for a tonal rather than linear engraving process, and for a print produced by means of it. Developed in the 17th century, mezzotint was used widely as a reproductive printing process, especially in England, until the mid-19th century. A copper or steel plate is first worked all over with a curved, serrated tool called a "rocker", raising a burr over the surface to hold the ink and print as a soft dark tone. The design is then created in lighter tones by scraping and burnishing areas of the roughened plate so that they hold less ink, or none in highlights. Details may be sharpened by engraving or etching in a "mixed mezzotint"

Michallon, Achille-Etna
1796–1822

French landscape painter, a pupil of David and later of Valenciennes. He was the first recipient of the Prix de Rome in the Historical Landscape category established in 1817. Michallon's landscapes, classical in composition and with their serene mood and silver-grey tonality, influenced his pupil, Corot.

Michalowski, Piotr 1800–55

Polish painter. He visited Paris in 1831–35, where he copied some of Géricault's works, but otherwise was active mainly in his native Cracow. He was the leading Polish Romantic, specializing in paintings of soldiers and animals, rendered with spontaneous brush-strokes, in dark twilight landscapes (*Blue Hussars*, 1836, Vienna, Kunsthistorisches).

Michaux, Henri born 1899

Belgian-born artist and writer. He acquired French citizenship in 1955, but travelled widely before settling in Paris in 1940. Michaux is difficult to categorize: he experiments freely and has produced a large body of work, both figurative and abstract, as a painter and draughtsman (*Painting in India ink*, 1966, Paris, Galerie Point Cardinal). His work is often visionary in feeling, and in the 1950s he produced drawings under the influence of the drug mescalin.

Michel, Georges 1763–1843

French landscape painter. Michel worked as a restorer at the Louvre, Paris, and the inspiration for his paintings,

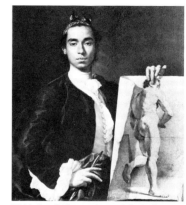

Meléndez: Self-portrait, 1746. Paris, Louvre

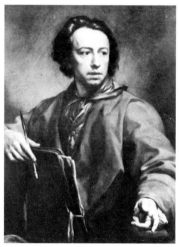

Mengs: Self-portrait, 1773. Florence, Uffizi (Scala)

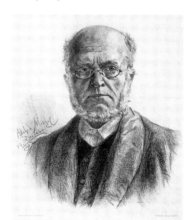

Menzel: Etching by A.-I. Gilbert (1828–99) after a self-portrait drawing (Mansell)

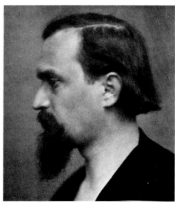

Meštrović: Photograph, *c*.1914 (Mansell)

often romantic in mood, was drawn partly from Dutch Old Masters such as Ruisdael. He was, however, one of the earliest artists to paint out of doors, and in this he was an important influence on members of the Barbizon school, notably Dupré. He exhibited at the Salon from 1791 to 1821, but had little popular success and died virtually unknown. He is well represented in the Louvre. See vol. 3 p. **92**

Michelangelo Buonarroti
1475–1564
Florentine painter, sculptor, draughtsman, architect and poet, one of the greatest figures of the Renaissance, indeed of world art. In 1488 he entered Ghirlandaio's workshop but transferred after a year to the tutelage of Bertoldo in the Medici antique sculpture garden, a kind of academy, about which little is known. One of his earliest works, *The Battle of the Lapiths and Centaurs* (*c.*1492, Florence, Casa Buonarroti), was based on a relief by Bertoldo. During the upheavals which followed the death of his patron, Lorenzo the Magnificent, Michelangelo left Florence, arriving in Rome in 1496. There, he completed his first major sculptures, *Bacchus* (1496–97, Florence, Bargello) and a *Pietà* (completed 1499, Rome, St Peter's). The latter, with its brilliant mastery of the difficult problems involved in depicting a full-length male figure stretched across a woman's lap, and its flawlessly beautiful finish, established his reputation and ensured that his return to Florence in 1501 was greeted with important commissions. The fresco of the *Battle of Cascina*, which was intended to complement Leonardo's *Battle of Anghiari* in the Palazzo Vecchio, now survives only in fragmentary copies, but the *David* (1501–04, Florence, Accademia), symbolizing the civic pride of the Florentines, still exudes its formidable sense of latent power. Once more in Rome, in 1505, Michelangelo came under the patronage of Julius II. An exacting taskmaster, the Pope launched him on two Herculean projects. The first, a massive tomb monument for the Pope, calling for 40 figures, brought forth the unfinished *Slaves* (before 1513, Paris, Louvre), but eventually had to be completed on a vastly reduced scale by assistants, nearly four decades later. Of the finished tomb in S. Pietro in Vincoli, Rome, only the *Moses* (1513–16) is entirely from Michelangelo's own hand. The Sistine Ceiling (1508–12) proved an equally daunting but more fruitful commission. Working virtually unaided, under the most testing conditions, Michelangelo revealed his vision of human aspirations to divine nature with an awesome combination of Florentine grace and Roman grandeur. Here, the Creation, the Deluge and the Drunkenness of Noah were witnessed by Prophets, Sibyls and the elegant *Ignudi*—examples of perfect human beauty—in a marriage of Christian and classical elements that may have stemmed from the Neoplatonic theories circulating at Lorenzo's court. Michelangelo worked in Florence from 1516 to 1534, his main undertaking in this period being the Medici Chapel (1519–34) in S. Lorenzo with his tombs of Lorenzo and Giuliano de Medici. He returned to Rome in a more pessimistic frame of mind and his *Last Judgment* fresco (1536–41) on the altar wall of the Sistine Chapel reflected a post-Reformation gloom, with its wrathful Christ and its emphasis on the terrible punishments inflicted on the damned. Muscular, contorted figures replaced the earlier, more graceful nudes. Architectural commissions—in particular the rebuilding of St Peter's—took up much of Michelangelo's time in later years, but he also produced some deeply religious drawings of the Crucifixion and the Holy Family for his friend, Vittoria Colonna. The same intense piety pervades his frescos (1542–50) for the Pauline Chapel in the Vatican, and is present again in "*The Rondanini Pietà*" (Milan, Castello, Sforzesco—left unfinished at his death), where the figures of the Virgin and Christ merge together in a starkly modern image of frailty and grief. Michelangelo's art inspired awe in his contemporaries, who called him "divine", and his effect on European art has been incalculable. For three centuries after his death hardly any artist of consequence who expressed himself through the medium of the human body remained untouched by his influence. See vol. 1 pp. **22–23,** *90, 111, 176–177, 178–179*; vol. 2 pp. **132–135, 164,** *180*

Michelena, Arturo 1863–98
Venezuelan genre painter. His repertoire ranged from the anecdotal realism of his Paris period, 1885–89, to the battle scenes, official portraits and religious frescos commissioned by the Venezuelan State. He completed several public commissions, for example in Caracas Cathedral, before his death.

Michelino da Besozzo
active 1388–1445
Lombard painter and miniaturist, of the highest reputation in his day. His frescos painted in 1388 in S. Pietro in Ciel d'Oro, Padua, have been lost, but illustrated Books of Hours survive (in Avignon and Cologne). His signed *Mystic marriage of St Catherine* (Siena, Pinacoteca) epitomizes the extreme delicacy and colouristic refinement of his late INTERNATIONAL GOTHIC style.

Michelozzo, Michelozzi
1396–1472
Florentine sculptor and architect. He was trained by Ghiberti and by Donatello, with whom he worked in partnership, 1425–33. They produced together several important tomb designs, including the influential wall-tomb of the schismatic Pope John XXIII (*c.*1425–27, Florence, Baptistery). There is no evidence, however, that Donatello had any hand in the Aragazzi Monument (*c.* 1427–38, dismembered, parts in London, V&A, and in Montepulciano Cathedral), which is often designated the first humanist tomb. Michelozzo subsequently worked for Ghiberti and for Luca della Robbia, but became active, predominantly as an architect, working in particular for Cosimo de' Medici, for whom he designed the Palazzo Medici-Riccardi (begun 1444), one of the most influential buildings of the Quattrocento. His marble sculpted figures, freestanding and in relief, are sturdy and classical with an appealing individuality.

Micronesian art
The art of the peoples of the small Pacific islands north of Melanesia. Some islands supported strong traditions of figurative sculpture in restrained and abstract style. Others produced finely ornamented utensils, or undertook elaborate tattooing. In general, however, Micronesian art is less ostentatious than that of other Pacific regions, and is marked by functionalism and a striking clarity of design. See vol. 2 p. 23

Middle Kingdom 2052–1786 BC
Art of the period when Egypt re-emerged as a unified kingdom, following the collapse of the Old Kingdom and 130 years of chaos. Instability and loss of confidence seem to have stimulated a more varied and experimental art. The reliefs from the mortuary at THEBES (built by Mentuhotep II, *c.*2050 BC), those on the sarcophagi of Queens Kawit and Ashayat (Cairo, Egyptian Museum), and the reliefs from the Kiosk of Senusert I, 1971–1929 BC, at KARNAK, are perhaps the finest of the Middle Kingdom period; executed in low relief, they show great sensitivity of line and detail, whether in formal representations, such as those of King Mentuhotep, or in the intimate scenes of Queen Kawit's toilet. Amongst the best-preserved tomb paintings from the period, those at Beni Hasan demonstrate the improved quality of art and the liveliness which gradually transformed older, hieratic modes. Humorous paintings of everyday life decorate the rock-cut tombs of the nobles Amenemhat and Khnum-hotep; from the latter the *Birds in an acacia tree* scene is deservedly well-known. The developed style of the 12th Dynasty painting is revealed in painted coffins from Deir el-Bershed, such as that of Prince Djehutynekht (*c.* 1850 BC, Boston, MFA). The fine craftsmanship and subtle modulations of colour in scenes depicting offerings for the dead anticipate the refinement of New Kingdom techniques. This relatively brief period of stability came to an end with the invasion of the Hyksos or Shepherd Kings, who introduced their own culture. See vol. 2 p. 25

Miel, Jan 1599?–1663
Flemish painter, active chiefly in Italy, where he was one of the chief painters of BAMBOCCIATE (*Roman carnival*, 1653, Madrid, Prado). He was more versatile than most *bamboccianti*, however, and also painted elegant mythological scenes (*Dido and Aeneas*, *c.*1655, Cambrai, Musée Municipal).

Miereveld, Michiel Jansz. van
1567–1641
Dutch portrait painter, born in Delft. He studied in Utrecht and adopted a late Mannerist idiom in history painting, but soon devoted himself entirely to portraiture, in which field he enjoyed enormous success. According to Sandrart, Miereveld made more than 10,000 portraits. They are meticulous, conventional and usually rather dull, of more value as historical records than as works of art. He was active mainly in Delft and The Hague, where he worked for Dutch statesmen and the House of Orange.

Mieris, Frans van 1635–81
Dutch genre painter, active mainly in Leyden. With Schalken he was Dou's most important pupil, and painted in a highly finished, precise style derived from his master. His subjects were mainly genteel interior scenes, but they often contain sexual allusions (*The oyster meal*, 1659, Leningrad, Hermitage). Frans' sons, **Jan** (1660–90) and **Willem** (1662–1747) and grandson, **Frans II** (1689–1763) continued the *fijnschilder* (fine painter) tradition. See vol. 2 p. **227**

Mi Fei 1051–1107
Chinese painter. Like his contemporary Su Shi, he fulfilled the Chinese ideal of the scholar-painter, achieving high bureaucratic rank at the northern Song court of Kaifeng. He was a famous eccentric, who dressed in the archaic robes of the Tang dynasty, was obsessive about cleanliness, and reputedly preferred the company of curiously shaped rocks to that of men. No undoubtedly authentic work survives, but the small landscapes in a loose style using a heavily-loaded brush which went under his name, for instance *Grassy hills and leafy trees in mist* (Washington, Freer), were greatly admired in the Yuan and Ming periods, even if not to the taste of his academic contemporaries. A major calligrapher and a highly important collector, Mi's writings on works he owned or had seen are important for any study of the now largely vanished painting before the Song dynasty. See vol. 3 p. **40**

Mignard, Pierre 1612–95
French Baroque painter. He trained with Vouet, then worked in Rome from 1635 to 1657. On his return to France he became the rival of Lebrun and succeeded him as director of the French Academy in Paris in 1690. Mignard painted in a cold classicizing style much influenced by Nicolas Poussin. His best works are his portraits, in which his sitters, often members of Louis XIV's court, are often fitted out with allegorical trappings (*The Marquise de Seignelay and two of her children*, 1691, London, NG). His brother **Nicolas** (1606–68) was also a popular painter of portraits and religious subjects. See vol. 2 p. 199

Miki, Tomio 1937–78
Japanese artist. He studied at the Tokyo School of Hygiene Technology before joining the Japanese neo-Dadaist group, and in 1963 began his famous series of *Ear* sculptures. The cast aluminium (*Untitled*) *Ear* (1964, New York, MOMA) is one of many variations. The ear is presented realistically, in isolation and as a repeated module, and symbolizes a state between communication and non-communication.

Millais, Sir John Everett 1829–96
English portrait, landscape, genre and history painter. A child prodigy, he met Holman Hunt at the Royal Academy Schools and with him and Rossetti founded the PRE-RAPHAELITE Brotherhood. The Pre-Raphaelites' sharp detail, bright colour, moral purpose and poetic feeling are evident in such early works as *Lorenzo and Isabella* (1849, Liverpool, Walker Art Gallery), reviled by the critics until Ruskin came to their support in 1851. Millais later married Ruskin's wife Effie. With growing success he gradually lost his revolutionary fervour, and his paintings were often sentimental, as in his most famous work, *Bubbles* (1886, A. & F. Pears, Ltd), which became well-known through its subsequent use as a soap advertisement. *Bubbles* shows the lovely creamy touch which Millais developed when he had abandoned his Pre-Raphaelite manner. By the end of his career he had immense prestige (he became President of the Royal Academy in 1896). He painted many of the leading figures of his day including Carlyle and Gladstone (London, NPG). See vol. 3 pp. **82–83**

Millares, Manuel 1926–72
Spanish painter. He was self-taught, and after briefly working in a Surrealist style he turned to abstract painting in 1949. On a coarse canvas support, taut or clumped, he used a red, white and black palette, creating the effect of an organized network of roping. This violent surface is rooted in a highly emotional criticism of social oppression. His *Antropofaunas* series (1969) shows his interest in the theme of man as beast.

Milles, Carl 1875–1955
The greatest of Swedish sculptors. He

studied in Paris, where he was strongly influenced by Rodin, and with Hildebrand in Munich, 1904–06. He experimented with a number of styles, from monumental Classicism to a sophisticated naturalistic manner. He even borrowed from Ottonian art (specifically from Bernward of Hildesheim's bronze doors) for his *Bronze doors* for Saltsjobaden church, 1911–12. He became Professor at the Academy in Stockholm, 1920–31, and taught from 1931 to 1945 at the Cranbrook Foundation in the USA. He made many official sculptures both in Sweden and the USA, such as the onyx Peace Monument (1936, Minnesota, St Paul, City Hall) with its god-like figure inspired by Pre-Columbian art. His studio and garden at Lidingö, Stockholm has become the museum of Millesgården, displaying his sculptures (including the Orpheus Fountain of 1930–36, with its slim, almost floating figures).

Millet, Jean-François 1814–75
French painter and graphic artist. Of peasant stock, Millet received his first training in Cherbourg, but in 1837 a scholarship enabled him to study in Paris under Delaroche. Until 1846 portraits were his main means of suport. In 1849, the year after he exhibited his first large-scale painting of peasant life in the Salon, *The winnower* (1848, Paris, Louvre), Millet settled in Barbizon where, apart from a brief return to Cherbourg during the Franco-Prussian War, he remained until his death. There he devoted himself to scenes of rural life, moving from his earlier prettified Arcadian style to a more robust, realistic approach. In the 1850 Salon, his *Sower* (Boston, MFA), exhibited with Courbet's epic realist canvases, won him the label of "Socialist revolutionary", but, although he was involved in the social consciousness of 1848, Millet's depiction of rural labourers was fatalistic rather than political. After 1863, through the influence of his friend Théodore Rousseau, he turned increasingly to pure landscape. See vol. 1 pp. *43*, *109*; vol. 3 pp. **89**, *93*

Mills, Clark 1810–83
American sculptor. Self-taught, he made his reputation in the 1840s with portrait busts done from life masks, but his equestrian statue of Andrew Jackson (Washington, Lafayette Square) is his best-known work. Although crude in technique—it was completed in 1852 only after six attempted castings—its conception of the General seated on a rearing horse was daring.

Milne, David 1882–1953
Canadian painter of landscape and still life, who worked in Ontario and New York. He could convey a profound sensibility with economical means—dry, descriptive line and discreet use of colour. *Water lilies, Temagami* (1929, Toronto, Hart House) displays characteristic surface patterning.

Minardi, Tommaso 1787–1871
Italian painter and illustrator. In Rome he associated with the NAZARENES, and in 1834, with Overbeck and others, he signed the *Purist Manifesto* calling for a return to the spiritual purity of 14th-century Italian art. In fact, Fra Bartolommeo, Andrea del Sarto and Perugino are more obviously reflected in his work. His strongest quality was his draughtsmanship (*Michelangelo's Last Judgment*, 1818–27, Vatican).

Mincho 1352–1431
Japanese painter. Mincho was a native of Awaji, and joined the Zen monastery of Tofuku in Kyoto. He was first and foremost a devout priest who painted edifying subjects for the uplift of his own soul, but while other Zen priests preferred landscape painting, Mincho liked to honour his superiors by painting their portraits. One such is that of *Shoitsu Kokushi* in Tofuku-ji, an Important Cultural Property of Japan.

Ming dynasty 1368–1644
Chinese dynasty, established following the civil wars and anti-Yuan uprisings of the 14th century, which succeeded in driving the Mongols back to the steppe and re-establishing native Chinese rule. From the early 15th century the capital was fixed at modern Peking, but it was from the wealthy and cultured cities of the lower Yangtze region that most of the dynasty's great artists came. Following an 11th-century precedent artists were divided into two categories: skilful but less morally worthy professionals; and gentleman-scholars—amateurs who put more stress on personal statement than on facility of brushwork. These categories were never as rigid as Chinese works of criticism suggest; a "professional" painter like Qiu Ying was also at home in the supposedly LITERATI styles of monochrome painting, and was a personal friend of the great "amateur" painters of his day. This distinction, however, remained influential through the Ming dynasty and succeeding centuries. The professional style decayed into decoration, and the scholar style tended towards a great body of indistinguishable monochrome landscapes—copies of great masters and utterly lacking in the self-expression which had been the avowed aim of the school's earlier and more eminent practitioners. Other arts, particularly the production of a characteristic blue and white porcelain, flourished during the Ming dynasty, while there were also notable achievements in the fields of philosophy and literature. See vol. 3 pp. 36–41

Miniature
A very small painting, usually a portrait. The word derives from the practice of illuminating initial letters in manuscripts, the decorations executed in red-lead paint or "minium" by a miniator. The meaning "tiny" has become attached to the word by confusion with the word "minute". Later miniatures were on vellum, card or ivory and kept safe in a small frame which could be worn as a locket or personal ornament.

Minimal art
Art, principally sculpture, involving strictly geometric, elemental forms. The term was first used in the early 1960s Minimal artists—Tony Smith, LeWitt, Judd, Andre, Morris and others—wanted to reassert the physical reality of the art object in reaction to the metaphysical preoccupations of artists in the 1940s and 1950s. The methods they use are also antithetical to the expressionistic, autographic techniques of the Abstract Expressionists. LeWitt, Andre and Judd all depend on industrial foundries to fabricate their works. The nature of the material used is an important concern; Andre's floor-pieces heighten the viewer's awareness of the copper, lead or fire bricks which he uses (for example, *Lever*, 1966, Ottawa, NG). Judd's use of interchangeable units or modules is characteristic of much Minimal art. These seemingly simple works signal a complex network of aesthetic issues. Perception is a key one. The artists present art works as simple "informa-tion"; the "meaning" depends on the viewer's experience and interpretation which varies according to scale, viewpoint and setting. The placement of the object, in a gallery or outdoors, is calculated to trigger perceptions about dynamic relationships between forces, forms and spaces. The late 1950s and 1960s paintings of Stella, Noland, Kelly and others, concerned with strict definition of the medium and favouring simple shapes, colours and systematic compositions, can also be called Minimal. See vol. 3 pp. 223, 246–247

Minne, George 1866–1941
Belgian sculptor, draughtsman and illustrator, predominantly self-taught, a member of Les VINGT. The mother and child relationship was a common theme in his work, and he also often depicted young boys (*Fountain with five boys kneeling*, 1898, Brussels, Senate).

Mino da Fiesole 1429–84
Florentine sculptor. The early deaths of his more distinguished contemporaries, Desiderio da Settignano, under whom Mino possibly trained, and Bernardo Rossellino, assisted his career. In Florence and Rome he executed a series of portrait busts inspired by Roman models; early examples, such as *Piero de' Medici* (1453, Florence, Bargello) are realistic but rigid whereas later busts, for instance *Diotisalvi Neroni* (1464, Paris, Louvre), are more sensitively handled. In the 1460s he received two major commissions, the tombs of Bernardo Gigni and Count Ugo of Tuscany (Florence, Badia). He spent most of his later years in Rome (1474–80) collaborating on a series of unremarkable monuments. See vol. 2 p. **114**

Minton, John 1917–57
British painter and illustrator, one of a group of Neo-Romantic artists following the English tradition of visionary landscape. In drawings such as *Sunflowers* (1945, London, V&A) he came close to the vision of Palmer's Shoreham period. His attempts to revive the academic subject picture in modern terms were less happy (*The death of Nelson after Daniel Maclise R.A.*, 1952, London, Royal College of Art). See vol. 3 p. *252*

Mirak Naqqash Khurasani, Amir Ruh Allah died c. 1507
Persian or eastern Turkish painter. His chief importance is as the master and guardian of Bihzad, whom he taught while himself librarian to Sultan Husayn Bayqara in Herat. Mirak's work in the *Khamseh* of 1494 (London, BL), with thick-set, haggard-faced figures, seems rather stiff and old-fashioned.

Mir Musavvir Sayyid
active c. 1530–50
Persian painter of Badakhshan or Sultaniyeh, working in the library of Shah Tahmasp in Tabriz. It seems that he worked on the Houghton *Shahnameh* (New York, Metropolitan), and the British Library *Khamseh* of 1539–43, and a signed drawing depicting *Rustram killing the dragon* is preserved in the British Museum. His work shows a preference for interior settings, revealing a meticulous attention to architectural detail, and a gentle view of humanity in the figures. He followed his son, Mir Sayyid Ali, to India and died there.

Miró, Joan born 1893
Spanish painter, one of the most versatile and original of 20th-century artists. His early work in the period after World War I reveals the influence of

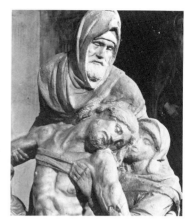
Michelangelo: Self-portrait as Nicodemus, detail of *Pietà*, c.1550–55. Florence, Cathedral (Scala)

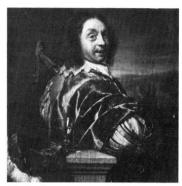
Mieris, Frans the Elder: Self-portrait, 1674. London, NG

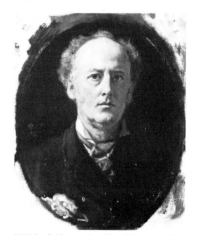
Millais: Self-portrait, 1883. Aberdeen, Art Gallery and Museum

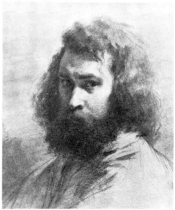
Millet: Self-portrait drawing, 1845–46. Paris, Louvre, Cabinet des Dessins (Mansell)

Cubism and the strong legacy of Catalan art, which he experienced before moving to Paris in 1917. *Catalan landscape* (1923, New York, MOMA) represents his artistic coming of age, with its abstracted figures and freedom of line combining a naive and sophisticated vision in one work. In 1924 he signed the Surrealist manifesto and increasingly turned to a more spontaneous form of painting in line with Breton's "psychic automatism". *Dog barking at the moon* (1926, Philadelphia Museum of Art) reveals his new concern for large areas of pure colour with forms placed against them in intuitive rather than logical order. His most characteristic paintings show brightly coloured amoeba-like forms against a largely plain background, creating a vivid sense of restless motion, but the political events of the 1930s, in particular the Spanish Civil War, led to a series of pictures of which the sombre colouring and savage forms were in marked contrast to his earlier work. In 1940, however, he painted a series of *Constellations* that offered a vision of man in harmony with nature. Constantly inventive, his murals for the UNESCO building in Paris (1955–58) and Harvard University (1960) are in a novel ceramic technique. He lives in Spain, producing small-scale work. See vol. 1 pp. *132–133*; vol. 3 pp. **176–177**, *255*

Mir Sayyid Ali
active mid-16th century
Persian painter, the son of Mir Musavvir. He worked in Tabriz for Shah Tahmasp. A page from the British Library *Khamseh* of 1539–43, depicting an incident from the story of *Majnun and Laila*, is attributed to him; the scene is characterized by exquisite observation and rich ornamental detail. He followed the Mughal Humayun to India and is thus a founder of the Mughal school. He was joined by his father, whose portrait he painted (c.1565, Paris, Musée Guimet). See vol. 3 p. 27

Mirza Ali active mid-16th century
Persian painter, the son of Sultan Muhammad. He worked for Shah Tahmasp in Tabriz. His style is close to that of Aqa Mirak, as is shown in the two pages for which he was responsible in the *Khamseh* of 1539–43 (London, BL). These elegant scenes are characterized by a delight in graceful ornament and slightly ruffled textures. See vol. 3 p. 27

Mitsunaga, Tosa
active late 12th century
Japanese painter. Little is known of his life, except that he was a member of the Tosa family of imperial court painters, and had a rank at court. His paintings are remarkable for the realism of their human figures, both important personages (whom he painted on the screens in the imperial palace) and common people (on the scrolls which are attributed to him). Mitsunaga is considered one of the greatest *yamato-e* (Japanese style) painters, and one of the most prominent of the Tosa school. The National Treasure scrolls, *Ban Dainagon* (Tokyo National Museum) and *Yamaizoshi* (Aichi Prefecture, A. Sekido coll.), are attributed to him. See vol. 3 p. **48**

Mitsunobu, Tosa 1434–1525
Japanese painter, a member of the Tosa family. When young he wished to travel to China and study under the Ming masters. As this proved impossible, he decided to concentrate on the purely Japanese styles, for which his family had been renowned for generations. He came to be equally at home with ink or with colour, and produced his best work on screens and scrolls. His style is delicate, with fine brushwork, and a lavish use of gold-leaf. Mitsunobu was also a poet and a designer. His portrait of *Monoi Naonori* is in the Tokyo National Museum. See vol. 3 p. 49

Mixed media see MEDIUM

Mixtec art
Art of the Mixtec people of Oaxaca in Mexico, from about 1200 to 1521. They were noted for their excellent craftsmanship. Mixtec lapidarists excelled in working in jade and turquoise as well as jet, amber, coral and rock crystal. Fine featherwork and textiles and elaborately painted polychrome pottery were also produced. Some of the most notable existing Mixtec objects are the fine pieces of delicate gold jewellery made by the *cire-perdue* method and decorated with false filigree. Several screenfold Mixtec manuscripts in deerskin have also survived, with pictographic representations of ritual, historical, and genealogical matters. The Zouche Nuttall Codex (London, BM), for example, is in an angular and rhythmic style and highly coloured. See vol. 2 pp. 18–19

Miyiwaki, Aiko born 1929
Japanese painter and sculptor. Until the mid-1960s she painted in oils, using constantly repeated tiny organic forms, the impasto paint reflecting light and creating textural patterns. She has continued to employ small repeated motifs in sculpture. In *Untitled* (1966, New York, Guggenheim), tiny brass squares reflect light in different directions.

Mobile
Type of kinetic sculpture, composed of shapes, often flat and cut from sheet-metal, suspended from wire and horizontal rods so that it is balanced and responds to movements in the air; alternatively it can be motorized. In this sense the term was first used by Duchamp to describe the moving sculptures made by Calder in the early 1930s. However, Duchamp himself had introduced the term in describing his ready-made *Mobile: Bicycle wheel* of 1913, and in 1920 Man Ray created a hanging sculpture made from coathangers. Similar constructions with static component parts are called **stabiles**.

Moche art
Art of the Moche people on the northern coast of Peru from about AD 1 to 600. Remains of Moche adobe (mud-brick) pyramids, palaces, fortifications and irrigation canals have been found there, particularly in the Moche and Chicama valleys, of which the largest is the Moche stepped pyramid, known as the Sun Temple. Beautiful examples of metalwork, woodcarving, mural painting and a small amount of weaving have been found, but the most important art form of the Moche still extant is their pottery. Some pots are decorated with lively painted scenes or abstract designs, while others are modelled in the round or in low relief. Vegetation, animals, houses, humans, inanimate objects, and mythical characters and events are all vividly represented. Perhaps best known are the very beautiful portrait vessels in the form of carefully modelled, realistic heads (*Laughing man vessel*, c.500 AD, Lima, National Museum of Anthropology and Archaeology). See vol. 2 p. 19

Mochi, Francesco 1580–1654
The most original Italian sculptor of the early 17th century until eclipsed by Bernini. His energetic *Annunciation* group (1603–08, Orvieto Cathedral) has justifiably been called the first piece of BAROQUE sculpture, and his magnificently proud *Alessandro Farnese* (1620–25, Piacenza, Piazza Cavalli) is one of the finest of all equestrian statues, marking in its vigorous movement a decisive break with the tradition of Giambologna. After his move to Rome in 1629, Mochi lost most of his creative fire, and his last important sculpture was *St Veronica* (1629–40), one of the four huge statues for the crossing piers of St Peter's and a work of pointlessly vehement movement. See vol. 1 p. *202*

Modello
Italian term for a painting or drawing carried out as a proposal for a larger work, usually to be shown to a potential patron. It is not merely a first sketch, being more detailed and considered.

Modersohn-Becker, Paula
1876–1907
German painter and graphic artist. After studying in London and Berlin she moved to an artists' colony at Worpswede near Bremen in 1898. Her early work there—landscapes and scenes of peasant life—was influenced by highly detailed naturalism, though she avoided idealized sentimentalism. In 1900 she spent six months in Paris, where she was especially impressed by the "great simplicity of form" she found in Millet, Gauguin and Cézanne. Further visits to Paris led to the evolution of a style in which the linear configurations she had admired in Gauguin were fused with the emotional intensity associated with Expressionism (*Old woman by the poorhouse duckpond*, c.1906, Bremen, Roseliushaus). From about 1900 her subject matter was mostly single figures, self-portraits (many in the nude) and still lifes. See vol. 3 p. **131**

Modigliani, Amedeo 1884–1920
Italian painter and sculptor, one of the most original artists of the early 20th century. His artistic education was based on the study of the Italian Renaissance masters in Florence and Naples, but from 1906 he lived in Paris, and is often considered French by adoption. Apart from a few early landscapes, his paintings consist of portraits (*Jeanne Hébuterne*—his last and most famous mistress—1919, New York, Guggenheim) and female nudes which are often highly erotic (*Reclining nude*, c.1919, New York, MOMA). His finest paintings belong to his last five years, and show an archaic simplification and distortion of form, a superb sense of linear design, and a sensitive, if limited, use of colour. Cézanne, Picasso and African sculpture were among his sources. His friendship with Brancusi resulted in a series of sculpted figures and heads of primitive power (*Head*, c.1911–12, London, Tate), and sculpture was for several years his preferred medium until World War I made it impossible for him to get the necessary materials. Modigliani's popular fame rests on his amorous, dissolute life and early death as well as on the quality of his work. See vol. 1 p. *111*; vol. 3 pp. **182–183**

Mohlzahn, Johannes 1892–1963
German painter, engraver and photographer. A member of the STURM circle in Berlin, in 1919 he published his *Manifesto of Absolute Expressionism*, in which he sought to establish the meditative character of colours and forms used symbolically. His style became increasingly abstract, using forms and space in such a way as to suggest a sense of spirituality (*Janus*, 1930, Duisberg, Wilhelm Lehmbruck Museum). Dismissed by the Nazis as a teacher, he lived in the USA from 1933 to 1959.

Moholy-Nagy, László 1895–1946
Hungarian-born painter, sculptor and experimental artist. In 1919 he became interested in Cubist art and in 1920 moved to Berlin. The Russian Constructivist Lissitzky inspired his abstract sculptures in metal, exhibited in his first one-man show in 1922. In 1923 Moholy-Nagy joined the Weimar Bauhaus as head of the metal workshop and the preliminary course. He announced his commitment to experimental media in his book *Painting, Photography, Film* (1925) and produced his documentary film *Berlin Still Life* in 1926. His famous kinetic object *Light prop* (1922–30, recreated in the Stedelijk van Abbesmuseum at Eindhoven) also demonstrated his pioneering spirit and his lifelong fascination with light, abstract form and movement. After leaving the Bauhaus in 1928, he worked in commercial design, made sets for the theatre and worked extensively as a photographer. He lived in Paris, Amsterdam and London before settling in 1937 in Chicago, where his New Bauhaus was soon replaced by the Institute of Design, which he directed until his death. One of the most influential teachers of his time, he worked for an art which would be the visual counterpart of a new co-operative society. He said that art was part of the "total work". See vol. 3 pp. **190–191**

Moilliet, Louis 1880–1962
Swiss artist. In 1911 he became closely associated with Macke, Klee and the BLAUE REITER group. He exhibited at the Sonderbund exhibition in Cologne in 1912 and in 1914 travelled to Tunis with Klee and Macke. During the 1930s he produced a set of stained-glass windows for the Lukaskirche in Lucerne. Like his fellow Blaue Reiter artists, he based his work on chromatic harmonies which approach, at times, pure abstraction.

Moillon, Louise c.1609–96
French still-life painter. Influenced by contemporary Flemish painting, her work has a freshness of vision combined with great accuracy of detail. Most of her few surviving paintings depict fruit (*Grapes, apples and melons*, 1637, Chicago, Art Institute).

Mola, Pier Francesco 1612–66
Italian painter. With Rosa and Testa he was one of the leading representatives of the romantic strain in Roman painting which ran alongside Pietro da Cortona's Baroque and Sacchi's classicism in the mid-17th century. He trained with Il Cavaliere d'Arpino in Rome, but his style was formed in north Italy, where he worked from about 1633 to 1647, the soft modelling of Guercino being a particularly important influence. His most characteristic works are small idyllic scenes with biblical figures or saints in landscapes, reminiscent in style of Albani (*The rest on the Flight into Egypt*, c.1630–35, London, NG). He was also, however, an accomplished fresco-painter (*Joseph making himself known to his brethren*, 1657, Rome, Quirinal Palace), and his best-known work is the unusual and splendid *Barbary pirate* (1650, Paris, Louvre).

Molenaer, Jan Miense c.1610–68
Dutch genre painter, born in Haarlem. His early works (mainly genre scenes) reflect the art of Frans Hals, and in 1636

he married Hals' most successful pupil, Judith Leyster. From 1637 to 1648 he was in Amsterdam. His finest genre pieces, such as the *Musician* (London, NG), date from the early 1630s. They reveal a fine technique and careful attention to detail. Later, under the influence of Adriaen Ostade, Molenaer painted interiors, but without his earlier vitality. He also painted a few portraits and religious works.

Molinari, Guido born 1933
Canadian abstract painter and sculptor, committed to formal statement rather than intuitive expression. Managing a Montreal gallery until 1957, he was influenced by the formal purism of Les PLASTICIENS. In 1963 he abandoned use of variable geometric forms, as in *Rhythmic mutation* (1965, Artist's coll.), and concentrated on surface optics, using brilliant colour.

Molvig, Jon 1923–70
Australian painter, who came to prominence in the mid-1960s with his highly individual portraits. His early savage yet sensuous paintings, such as *The lovers* (1957, Artist's coll.), have been compared with De Kooning. A powerful draughtsman, he was also one of the few original colourists in Australia. Violent juxtapositions of brilliant hues appear in his figure subjects and landscapes. After 1961 his style changed abruptly and his forms became hard-edged and totemic.

Molyn, Pieter de 1595–1661
Dutch landscape painter, born in London, and active for most of his working life in Haarlem. He was influenced by Esaias van de Velde and, like van Goyen and Salomon van Ruysdael, painted monochromatic landscapes with dunes and cottages. Early works, such as *The sandy road* (1626, Brunswick, Herzog Anton Ulrich Museum), are remarkably advanced for their time in their naturalism and mastery of relatively austere composition, but his later work did not fulfil this promise.

Momper, Joos (Jodocus) **II de** 1564–1634/5
Flemish landscape painter, active mainly in Antwerp, the best-known of a family of artists. He was the greatest Flemish landscape painter of his period, a worthy successor to Bruegel. Like Bruegel he usually employed a high viewpoint, and his majestic panoramas, often mountainous scenes, doubtless inspired by his travels in Italy and in Switzerland, convey a sense of immense distance. Again like Bruegel, he was a marvellous painter of snow scenes (*The Flight into Egypt*, Oxford, Ashmolean). Very few of his works are dated, and a chronology is difficult to establish; he seems to have found his distinctive style early and changed little. The figures in his paintings are sometimes the work of other artists such as "Velvet" Brueghel.

Mondrian, Piet 1872–1944
Dutch painter, one of the most important abstract artists and the major proponent of De STIJL. His earliest works, predominantly landscape subjects, were in a Symbolist vein, but by 1906 he had discovered Fauvism and began to paint in a brightly coloured Expressionist manner (*The red tree*, 1908, The Hague, Gemeentemuseum). Between 1911 and 1914 he lived in Paris, where he was greatly influenced by Cubism. His work was becoming increasingly abstract although still based on natural images. In the *Pier and Ocean* series of 1913 onward (example of 1915 in Otterlo, Kröller-

Müller) the ebb and flow of waves against land is represented by small horizontal and vertical lines. In 1917, together with van der Leck and van Doesburg, he founded De Stijl and in its magazine expounded his theory of Neo-Plasticism. His paintings became more severely geometric, building on a repertoire of black lines on a white ground bounding rectangles of primary colour. By 1925 he had arrived at his definitive statement, as typified by a work such as *Composition in yellow and blue* (1929, Rotterdam, Museum Boymans-van Beuningen). In rejecting the traditional qualities of painting—representation, texture, illusion of three-dimensionality—Mondrian was seeking to create a "pure reality" based on a harmonious, expressionless sense of order. His compositional structure developed with complete consistency, varying only with the introduction of lozenge-shaped paintings, and the abandonment of colour. He moved to New York in 1940 and a new rhythm and excitement entered his last works, based on his experience there; *Broadway Boogie-Woogie* (1942–43, New York, MOMA) is one of his greatest accomplishments. See vol. 1 pp. *63*, *93*, *114*, *132*; vol. 3 pp. **186–189**

Monet, Claude Oscar 1840–1926
French painter, often regarded as the greatest of the IMPRESSIONISTS, whose *Impression: sunrise* (1873, Paris, Musée Marmottan) gave the movement its name. He was brought up in Le Havre, where Boudin, his early mentor, encouraged him to paint out of doors and to render atmospheric effects as accurately as possible. He went in 1859 to Paris, where he met Pissarro at the Académie Suisse and later (1862–63) studied under Gleyre. There he found among his fellow-students, Renoir, Sisley and Bazille, a common desire to paint directly from nature and to try to record their impressions of the transient effects of light; for this purpose they went painting together in the forest of Fontainebleau. Much influenced by Manet during these years, Monet yet showed in such paintings as *Women in the garden* (1867, Paris, Jeu de Paume) a unique and experimental concern with the fall of light. During the Franco-Prussian War, 1870–71, he stayed with Pissarro in London, where they saw the work of Turner and Constable and where Monet made studies of the Thames. Returning to France, he rented a house at Argenteuil on the Seine, where Renoir joined him for painting sessions, but in 1883 he settled at Giverny. The Japanese-inspired water-garden that he constructed there became the theme of much of his later work. He spent much time painting the coast of Brittany and from 1890 onwards concentrated on series of pictures of the same subject under different lights—*Poplars*, 1890–91; *Haystacks*, 1891; *Rouen Cathedral*, 1894; *Mornings on the Seine*, 1896–97; *The Thames*, 1899–1901; in all these, light and the shifting colours it created was his central preoccupation. Labouring under increasing blindness, Monet painted his last series, the *Waterlilies*, 1899–1926, many of which now hang in the Orangerie, Paris. Their enormous size and vibrant colours, in which form all but disappears, have been seen as anticipating later developments in abstraction. But however indistinct the subject, it always remained integral to Monet's art, and these works more accurately represent the final, most sophisticated and most evocative stage of Impressionism. See vol. 1 p. *117*; vol. 3 pp. **98–99**, **100–101**, *103*, **126**

Monnier, Henri Bonaventure 1805–77
French artist and caricaturist, playwright and actor. He studied briefly under Girodet and Gros and his watercolours were influenced by Bonington, but it was as a cartoonist that he achieved sudden fame. He was a friend of Cruikshank and dedicated the *Distractions* (1832) to him, but is best known as the creator of Joseph Prudhomme, the epitome of the complacent *bourgeois*.

Monnoyer, Jean-Baptiste the Elder 1636–99
French painter. His early career in France as a decorative painter working under the direction of Lebrun was particularly successful. He specialized in elaborate flower-paintings, much imitated, and executed several dozen for Lord Montague, with whom he went to London in 1677 (most of them now at Boughton House, Northamptonshire).

Monochrome
Term (literally "one colour") used of a work drawn or painted in a single colour.

Monory, Jacques born 1934
French painter. He is an independent artist, although his work shows the influence of Surrealism. He paints in monochrome, generally blue—the blue of television light in a darkened room—his scenes are adapted from photographs and are usually of urban subjects. His figures, in ambiguous or threatening situations, seem silent and frozen as if in a dream or in a world in which there is no distinction between fantasy and reality. He tends to work in series—a major one was *The Velvet Jungle* of 1969–71. See vol. 3 p. 252

Monotype
Method of printing in which a print is taken from a flat surface, either metal or glass, on which a design has been freshly painted. A sheet of paper is pressed down over the still-wet plate. It is usually only possible to take one print using this process, hence the term monotype.

Monro, Dr Thomas 1759–1833
British physician and amateur painter in the 18th-century PICTURESQUE manner. As a collector and patron he encouraged and employed several young artists, including Turner, Girtin, De Wint and Cotman, who often used his rooms in the Adelphi, London, or his house in Bushey, Hertfordshire, as a place to meet and work.

Montage
Picture made by piecing together ready-made images; the term derives from the French for "mounting". Newsprint and photographic images are widely used, often to achieve surreal effects or to make political or social points. Montage differs from COLLAGE in that the prime reason for choosing the element is its subject matter, whereas in collage material is used primarily for formal reasons. Photomontage dates back to the early days of photography. It made considerable impact on commercial art.

Montañés, Juan Martínez 1568–1649
The most celebrated Spanish sculptor of the 17th century, known as "the god of wood". Almost all his life was spent in Seville, where he occupied a position comparable to that of Fernández in Valladolid in bringing a new realism to the polychromed statue. Whereas Fernández sometimes tended towards vulgarity, however, Montañés was aristo-

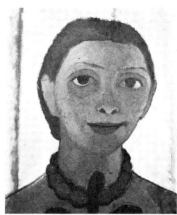
Modersohn-Becker: Self-portrait (detail), 1907. Essen, Folkwang Museum

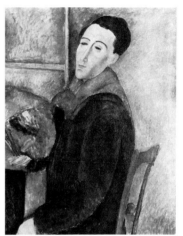
Modigliani: Self-portrait, 1919. São Paolo, Museu d'Arte Contemporanea (Giraudon)

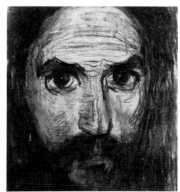
Mondrian: Self-portrait drawing, 1908–09. The Hague, Gemeentemuseum

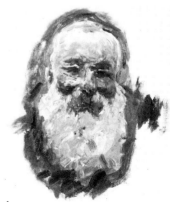
Monet: Self-portrait, 1917. Paris, Louvre, Jeu de Paume

cratic and dignified, even when expressing intense emotion. His most famous work is the *Christ of Clemency* (1603–06, Seville Cathedral). Montañés ran a prolific workshop, which sold work to South America as well as to various parts of Spain. His influence was felt not only by sculptors whom he trained, such as Cano, but also by painters of the stature of Velazquez and Zurbarán, who were moved by the sober realism and the powerful but controlled emotion of his work. See vol. 2 p. 209

Monticelli, Adolphe 1824–86
French painter of landscape, portraits and still life. His career was divided between Marseilles, where he was born, and Paris. He began by copying Old Masters in the Marseilles Museum and the Louvre, but his meeting with Diaz de la Peña in 1856 and his discovery of Delacroix's work rapidly transformed his classical manner. He was drawn to romantic themes and his most prolific and original period dated from 1871 to 1884, when he worked in thick impasto and brilliant, high-key colours which influenced van Gogh (*Walk in a park at twilight*, 1883, Paris, Louvre).

Moon, Jeremy 1934–73
British painter. His abstractions were uncompromisingly hard-edged and impersonally painted so as to exploit to the utmost the interaction of colour. Many of his works are on shaped canvases, and most are based on a single pictorial device. An extreme and effective painting is *Crusader* (1968, Belfast, Ulster Museum), a shaped canvas covered with a black grid over shades of orange.

Moore, Albert Joseph 1841–93
English painter. He began with Pre-Raphaelite works, but in the 1860s turned to classical subjects. His most characteristic paintings depict statuesque Grecian maidens, singly or in groups, usually elaborately draped (*Blossoms*, 1881, London, Tate). They can be rather sentimental, but are distinguished by fine draughtsmanship and exquisite colouring. Moore's friend Whistler was influenced by his work.

Moore, Henry born 1898
British sculptor, draughtsman and graphic artist. He studied in Leeds and at the Royal College of Art, London, 1921–24, where he rebelled against the academic tradition of modelling in favour of direct carving, inspired especially by the example of Gaudier-Brzeska. In 1924 he spent several months in Italy, where he discovered the frescos of Masaccio. The influence of their stark monumentality is apparent in his carvings, but more radical in its effect was his discovery of African and Mexican art, which seemed to provide a robust alternative to the over-refined surface realism of the European tradition. The pose and block-like masses of *Reclining figure* (1929, Leeds City Art Galleries) are clearly inspired by Pre-Columbian Chacmool figures. In the 1930s Moore was close to the mainstream of European avantgarde art. His carvings in wood and stone took elements both from Surrealism, particularly the biomorphism of Arp and Miró, and from current tendencies in abstract art, although at the time the two groups were bitterly opposed ideologically. A work such as *Two forms* (1934, New York, MOMA) is totally abstract in form and yet suggests through its relationships a certain human aspect. The most characteristic features of his art emerge in this period, the hollowing out and piercing of volume and his perennial theme of the visual relationship of the human form to landscape, as in *Reclining figure* (1938, London, Tate). The humanist aspect of his work came to the fore during World War II with his series of drawings of figures sheltering from air-raids in underground stations (examples, Tate). These brought him widespread popularity and after the War he became the best-known contemporary British artist and has had many commissions in Britain and elsewhere (*Reclining figure*, 1957–58, Paris, UNESCO). See vol. 1 pp. *31*, *170–171*, *182–183*; vol. 3 pp. **200–201**; vol. 4 p. *113*

Mor, Anthonis 1519–75
Netherlandish portrait painter, born in Utrecht, where he trained with van Scorel. In 1547 he became a master in the Antwerp guild, and in 1549 became court painter in Brussels. For the next two decades he travelled widely around the courts of Europe—Augsburg, Lisbon, London, Madrid, Rome—and became the leading international portraitist of his day (he is also known by the Spanish and English versions of his name—Antonio Moro and Sir Anthony More). His dignified formal style owed much to Titian, but his detailed treatment of dress and accessories reveals his northern origins. At his best he had great power of design and a vivid sense of characterization (*Man with a dog*, 1569, Washington, NG). He was particularly influential in Spain, his style being well suited to the stiff etiquette and ceremony of the Spanish court. Sánchez Coello was his pupil, and Beuckelaer one of his drapery assistants. See vol. 2 p. **174**

Morales, Luis (El Divino)
*c.*1520–84
One of the outstanding and distinctive Spanish painters of the 16th century. Born in Badajoz, on the Portuguese border, he worked away from the official art of the court or of the great religious centres, Toledo and Seville. He developed an unostentatious style that brought together the devotional approach of Spanish and Netherlandish 15th-century painting, Mannerist attenuation of forms, and a modelling apparently derived from Leonardo's Milanese following (possibly also from the work of Yañez and Llanos). His simple, devotional images, notably of the *Ecce Homo* and the *Mater Dolorosa*, all half-length, for which he is best known, express their piety with directness and intensity. His *Pietà* (Madrid, Academia de San Fernando) is one of the most original and moving masterpieces of Spanish 16th-century painting.

Moran, Thomas 1837–1926
English-born American landscape painter and engraver. One of the late exponents of the HUDSON RIVER school of painting, he achieved great success with his dramatic views of the far West (*The Grand Canyon of the Yellowstone*; 1872, Washington, Smithsonian). His recognition was official as well as popular, and interest in his work was a factor in establishing the National Parks.

Morandi, Giorgio 1890–1964
Italian painter. He was briefly associated with Futurism, but soon turned to still-life painting as his principal means of expression. Initially, under the influence of METAPHYSICAL PAINTING, his pictures had a hallucinatory intensity produced by artificial light and distorted perspective; but as his work developed he discarded these for a more profound investigation of the interrelations of form, light and colour. *Still life* (1938, New York, MOMA) shows the mute colour, clarity of design and hypnotic solemnity of his mature work. See vol. 3 pp. **170–171**

Moreau, Gustave 1826–98
French painter, one of the leading SYMBOLISTS. Apart from a significant visit to Italy (1857–59), where he was impressed by the work of Carpaccio, he spent almost his entire life in Paris and for the last years of his life led a secluded existence. His early work was influenced by Delacroix but, above all, by the romantic exoticism of his close friend Chassériau. Moreau's allegorical mythological and fabulous scenes are peopled, or haunted, by an ambiguous image of a powerful, seductive, evil woman, and are some of the finest Symbolist evocations of the *femme fatale*. They are painted in rich, jewel-like colours, and the works in oil have a glistening, impastoed surface; the watercolours are swiftly painted, and some are almost abstract. Moreau taught at the Ecole des Beaux-Arts, where his students included Matisse and Rouault; Rouault was the first curator of the Musée Moreau in Paris, where many of the artist's finest works, such as *Salome dancing* (1876), can be seen. See vol. 3 p. **122**

Moreau brothers
French artists. **Louis-Gabriel** (1740–1806), called Moreau the Elder, was a landscape painter and etcher whose works, such as the fresh and delicate *View from the outskirts of Paris*, 1782, Paris, Louvre), seem to anticipate the naturalism of the 19th century. **Jean-Michel** (1741–1814), called Moreau the Younger, was a designer, engraver and book illustrator. His engravings give an intriguing picture of fashionable manners and modes in 18th-century France.

Moreelse, Paulus 1571–1638
Dutch painter and architect, born in Utrecht. He was the pupil of Miereveld and like him early abandoned MANNERIST history painting for portraiture. In the 1620s he produced a series of charming shepherds and shepherdesses in romantic costume (example in the Rijksmuseum, Amsterdam).

Morelli, Domenico 1823–1901
Italian ROMANTIC painter from Naples. His early works betray the influence of the Nazarenes, and these and such historical works as *Torquato Tasso and Eleonora D'Este* (1865, Rome, Galleria Nazionale d'Art Moderna) initially impressed the MACCHIAIOLI. Fortuny's influence is reflected in works after 1870, while later paintings demonstrate an expressive use of light and spontaneous brushwork culminating in *The love of the angels* (1885, Santiago, Private coll.).

Moretto (Alessandro Bonvicino)
*c.*1498–1554
Italian painter, born in Brescia. He worked mainly there and in Bergamo, but visited Venice and Verona in the 1540s. His output consisted mainly of religious works, which are in the manner of Giorgione and the late work of Giovanni Bellini, but his portraits are considered to be his most interesting works. They are strong and direct and Moretto seems to have introduced the independent full-length portrait to Italy (*A gentleman*, 1526, London, NG). Moroni was his pupil. See vol. 2 p. **149**

Morgner, Wilhelm 1891–1917
German EXPRESSIONIST painter. From 1908 to 1911 he studied at Worpswede. In 1911 he went to Berlin, where he attempted to absorb the pointillist technique and joined the Sezession. He was greatly influenced by the BLAUE REITER works shown at the 1912 Cologne Sonderbund exhibition. Aiming to find abstract forms that could give expression to emotions, he transformed figures into symbolic ornamental patterns, as in *Entry into Jerusalem* (1912, Dortmund, Museum am Ostwall).

Morisot, Berthe 1841–95
French IMPRESSIONIST painter. She was the first woman to join the group and was influential in persuading her one-time mentor and brother-in-law, Manet, to take up *plein-air* painting. She shared the Impressionists' love of iridescent light, but not their use of a short, broken brush-stroke, and the influence of her early teacher Corot remains apparent in her fragile, feathery technique. From about 1885 she was increasingly influenced by Renoir. Apart from quiet family scenes, such as *The cradle* (1873, Paris, Louvre), she is also famous for the delicate series of marine pictures and watercolours done at Pontrieux in the summer of 1894. See vol. 3 p. **99**

Morlaiter, Giovanni Maria
1699–1781
German-born Italian sculptor. He was the leading 18th-century sculptor in Venice, where, at the peak of his success, he received virtually all the major sculptural commissions. His innumerable clay models have a vitality that suggests a knowledge of contemporary Austrian or German sculpture; his finished works are more academic and austere and look forward to Canova (*Two angels*, 1750–53, Venice, S. Maria delle Fava).

Morland, George 1763–1804
British painter of rustic scenes. His work was very popular in his own lifetime and throughout the 19th and early 20th centuries. His style was imbued with Dutch influences, with a hint of Greuze in the figures (*Outside the alehouse door* 1792, London, Tate).

Morley, Malcolm born 1931
British painter, living in New York since 1964. In the 1960s he made meticulous copies of colour photographs using a grid system. More recently he has been concerned with the reproduction on a flat surface of crumpled or torn postcards. There is sometimes an implicit political comment, as in *Race track* (1970, Aachen, Ludwig coll.), a South African tourist poster defaced with a red cross. See vol. 3 p. **252**

Moro, Antonio see MOR, ANTHONIS

Moroni, Giovanni Battista
*c.*1525–78
Italian painter, active mainly in Bergamo. He was a pupil of Moretto in Brescia, and continued his master's sober, thoughtful style of portraiture. His paintings often have a very distinctive, delicate silvery tonality, as can be seen in the outstanding collection of his works in the National Gallery, London, which includes the well-known "*Tailor*". Moroni's religious and allegorical paintings are by contrast very pedestrian. See vol. 2 p. **149**

Moronobu, Hishikawa
*c.*1618–*c.*1694
Japanese UKIYO-E artist. Moronobu is credited as the first artist to design *ukiyo-e* prints. He came from a family of embroiderers and worked in Edo (Tokyo) from around 1660, illustrating

printed books and publicity material for actors and courtesans. This prepared him for the genre prints for which he became famous, and, as his popularity grew, he received commissions for hand-painted pictures, which he signed *yamato eshi* (master of Japanese painting) in an attempt to elevate his status to that enjoyed by artists of the Tosa or Kano schools. See vol. 3 p. **49**

Morrice, James Wilson
1865–1924
Canadian landscape painter, working principally in France. He painted the Breton coast and Paris streets, becoming something of a café personality. His sensitive INTIMISTE approach recalls Bonnard and Vuillard. In 1911 he visited North Africa where, under Matisse's influence, his muted palette brightened (*Tangiers, the window*, c.1911, Montreal, L.M. Hart coll.). A second generation Impressionist, Morrice made Canadians aware of the movement.

Morris, George Lovett Kingsland 1905–75
American abstract painter and critic. Morris studied with Léger and Ozenfant in Paris and then helped found the AMERICAN ABSTRACT ARTISTS' group in 1936. During the 1930s his art typified the international non-objective style of the period. *Mural composition* (1939, Dallas, MFA) displays his hard-edged forms, which synthesize geometric abstraction and biomorphism. His later paintings are composed of many small colour blocks set within diagonal grids.

Morris, Robert born 1931
American sculptor and CONCEPTUAL artist whose major concerns are perception, natural forces and "process"—the procedure of making the artwork. His first works were in a neo-Dadaist vein but in the mid-1960s his MINIMAL sculptures drew attention to scale, shape and spatial relationships that change according to the viewer's expectations and viewpoint. His "anti-form" pieces, made in felt, are "sculpted" by the forces of gravity, as in *Untitled* (1967–68, Ottawa, NG of Canada). He also created earthworks in which natural forces are a vital component. His interest in process is further expressed in film and Performance work. See vol. 3 p. **247**

Morris, William 1834–96
English writer, painter, designer and printer. One of the great Victorian reformers, he looked to medieval traditions to restore art as an integral part of human well-being and progress. He believed beauty could be found in utility and in 1861 he founded the firm Morris and Company to make carvings, fabrics, tapestries, stained glass, furniture and wallpaper—anything that satisfied his credo: "Have nothing in your home that you do not know to be useful or believe to be beautiful." Outstanding artists, notably Burne-Jones, his life-long friend, worked for the firm, which produced some of the finest decorative art of the 19th century, domestic and ecclesiastical. Morris' graceful use of the S-curve, especially in wallpaper design, anticipated ART NOUVEAU. In 1890 he founded the Kelmscott Press with the intention of improving both the quality and elegance of English book printing.

Morse, Samuel Finley Breese
1791–1872
American painter and inventor. He trained in London under Allston and West as a history painter, but was forced to make a living by portraiture: *Lafayette*

(1825, New York, Brooklyn Museum) is one of the finest American Romantic portraits. His landscapes were stylistically similar to the Hudson River school. Following his invention of electric telegraphy (hence Morse code) in 1832, his scientific interests became predominant.

Mortenson, Richard born 1910
Danish painter, a pioneer of abstract art in his country. He paints in pure cheerful colours using sharp lines to create a surface tension and an impression of fragmented perspective.

Mosaic
Picture or decorative pattern made by setting small fragments of marble, glass or ceramic materials into cement or plaster. These fragments are known as tesserae and are usually irregular in shape. Though usually applied to a smooth wall or floor, their uneven surfaces create the reflective glitter so characteristic of Byzantine mosaics. The earliest known mosaic is Sumerian, with terracotta tesserae; the Egyptians, Minoans, Greeks and Romans used glass. Originally mosaic was mostly used on floors and pavements, but mural mosaics, both internal and external, became more common with the rise of Christianity, and became the principal feature of Byzantine art.

Moser, Kolomann 1868–1918
Austrian painter, designer and co-founder of the Vienna Sezession with Klimt and others. He was important mainly as a painter and book designer but also produced jewellery, glass, textiles and furniture. His work represents the Viennese style as influenced by the architects Mackmurdo and Mackintosh, with its interlocking geometrical patterns based on natural forms.

Moses, Grandma
(Mary Anne Robertson) 1860–1961
American NAIVE painter. Her first works were embroideries, often copying illustrations, showing the landscape and way of life in her native New York State. She took up painting seriously only after the death of her husband and was entirely self-taught. She was discovered by the collector Louis Calder and had her first one-man show in 1940 (when she was 80). She rapidly became successful and her 100th birthday was declared a national holiday. Her works, which are painted in generally bright colours, are decorative and yet intimate evocations of country life. See vol. 3 p. **250**

Mostaert, Gillis the Elder
c.1534–98
Netherlandish landscape painter, active mainly in Antwerp. He was a follower of Bruegel. Many works go under his name but authenticated ones are rare. His brother **Frans** (died 1560?) and his son **Gillis the Younger** (born 1588) were also painters and there has been confusion between the three.

Mostaert, Jan c.1472/3–1555/6
Netherlandish painter. According to van Mander, he spent 18 years in the service of the Regent Margaret, who was based at Brussels and Malines. This royal patronage is most evident from the care he lavished on the finer details of costumery and from his rich local colouring. His figures are stiff and doll-like, owing much to Geertgen, as *The Tree of Jesse* (Amsterdam, Rijksmuseum) shows. His portraits, however, are enlivened by small, narrative scenes in the background (*Man with the legend of St Hubert*, Liverpool, Walker Art Gallery).

Motherwell, Robert born 1915
American painter and theorist. He has been an influential figure since World War II through both his painting and his writing. Of the painters of the New York school Motherwell was particularly close to the Surrealist wartime expatriates, and he edited a book on Dada. He was a pioneer of ABSTRACT EXPRESSIONISM, and his early work reflects the impact of Picasso—among his generation he was unique in his development of collage techniques. Matisse, too, was an important touchstone for Motherwell's French sensibilities. In the late 1940s his work became more abstract, although the shapes in his paintings continue to have figurative overtones. In 1949 he painted the first of his *Elegies to the Spanish Republic*—with their recurrent motif of vertical bands and oval shapes in black, white, and colour (*Elegy to the Spanish Republic XXXIV*, 1953–54, Buffalo, Albright-Knox). In 1968 in his *Open* series he produced large fields of saturated colour inflected spatially by spare charcoal lines. He was married to Frankenthaler. See vol. 3 p. **215**

Motonobu, Kano 1476–1559
Japanese painter. First trained by his father, Kano Masanobu, he was already reputed a genius when presented to the Shogun Ashikaga Yoshimasa at the age of ten. Motonobu travelled widely in his youth, sketching wherever he went. On his return to Kyoto, he married the daughter of the court artist Tosa Mitsunobu and thus secured a place at court, where he served under three Shoguns. At 50 he entered the Buddhist priesthood. He was equally at home with the Chinese style of painting, having studied the works of Chinese masters of the Song, Yuan and Ming dynasties, and in the decorative YAMATO-E style of Nobuzane and his father-in-law's studio. His works found their way to the Ming Chinese court, where they were profoundly admired. Many paintings are attributed to Motonobu although their authorship is not always agreed. However *Eight views of Hsiao-hsiang* in the Tokai-n temple, and *Landscape with a pavilion* in Konchi temple, are clearly his own work. See vol. 3 pp. **46–47**

Moynihan, Rodrigo born 1910
British painter. He was the most radical member of the OBJECTIVE ABSTRACTIONISTS. In 1937 he was associated with the EUSTON ROAD Group and turned to figurative painting. He worked as an official war artist, documenting the daily life of the troops. In the late 1950s and 1960s he again worked as an abstract painter, this time on a scale reflecting the influence of American painting. Since the early 1970s he has painted still lifes and portraits in pale muted colours with a traditional concern for the placing of objects in space.

Mozarabic art
Art of the Christians of Muslim Spain (known as *Mozarabes*), especially from the 9th to the 11th century. They developed a highly sophisticated and original style, chiefly associated with a large group of illuminated manuscripts of the Beatus Apocalypse, the earliest known dating from the early 10th century (New York, Pierpont Morgan Library). The heritage of the Christian Visigoths and influence from Muslim art effected a calligraphic style of painting, with flat unmodelled figures forming patterns on background bands of bright colour. It is a decorative art, free from classical influence. It was gradually superseded by Romanesque styles.

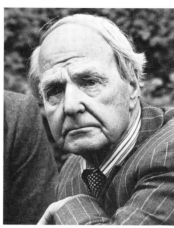

Moore, Henry: Photograph, 1980 (Popperfoto)

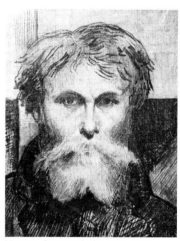

Moreau, Gustave: Self-portrait, 1850. Paris, Musée Gustave Moreau (René Roland)

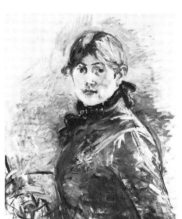

Morisot: Self-portrait, 1885–86. Paris, Private coll.

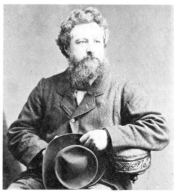

Morris, William: Photograph (Mansell)

Mucha, Alfons 1860–1939
Czech painter, graphic artist and designer, one of the leading exponents of ART NOUVEAU. He is best known for his poster designs, characterized by luxurious, flowing lines and light, clear colours. Many were made in the 1890s in Paris for the actress Sarah Bernhardt, for whom he also designed sets and costumes. Although his fame is based on his association with Paris, where he was popularly taken to be a Hungarian, Mucha was an ardent Czech and Slav patriot. He decorated the Burgomaster's room in the Prague Municipal Hall, designed a window in Prague Cathedral and the first Czechoslovak stamps and banknotes. He worked on his series of vast paintings, *The Slav Epic*, during the 1910s and 1920s. Some were shown in the USA, but they are now stored in a disused castle in Czechoslovakia.

Muche, Georg born 1895
German painter, architect and textile designer. He was called to the Bauhaus in 1920 to assist Itten in the foundation course and also to run the weaving workshop. While there he was influential as an architect, especially with his ideas for modular houses. However, painting was his first love. Influenced initially by the abstract tendencies of Der Blaue Reiter, he later returned to figuration, though modified by synthetic Cubism (*Two buckets*, 1923, Darmstadt, Bauhaus Archive). His weaving experience added an organic, rhythmic element.

Mu Ch'i see MUQI

Muehl, Otto born 1925
Austrian ex-artist (he has now renounced art, consistent with his dictum that "it is the assignment of the artist to destroy art"). He had started with painting, then moved on to Junk art, which temporarily provided a vehicle for his aggression, and finally proceeded to his Material Actions, in which materials (often edible—eggs, flour, ketchup) and objects (balloons, needles) were combined with nude performers.

Mueller, Otto 1874–1930
German painter. He trained as a lithographer before studying painting at the Dresden Academy. In 1907 he settled in Berlin, where he met Heckel and Kirchner. The latter found in him a fellow-admirer of Cranach and Dürer and was intrigued by the distemper technique he had developed. Although he was much older than the other members, he was invited to join Die BRÜCKE in 1910. He invariably painted idyllic scenes of bathers or gypsies in a limited range of cool pastel tones, which, combined with the attenuated bodies, convey a sense of unrelieved melancholy (*The large bathers*, 1910–11, Bielefeld, Städtisches Kunsthaus). See vol. 3 p. 135

Mughal painting
The court painting of the Mughal Emperors of India, flourishing from about 1550 to the end of the 18th century. It originated in a blend of the Safavid style of Iran, imported into India, with the indigenous style, and was firmly established by the artists, both Persian and Indian, brought together at the Mughal court by the Emperor Akbar (ruled 1556–1605). The style of the atelier was rapidly homogenized under the vigorous encouragement of the Emperor, for whom the atelier produced illustrations, of flawless technique, for manuscripts of history and literary classics. Influenced by European engravings from about 1580 onwards, Mughal painting tended, in contrast to its Iranian and Indian progenitors, to a realistic portraiture, perspective and modelling of objects, though retaining the general conventions, and glowing colours, of Persian painting. Under Jehangir (ruled 1605–27), the academy was much reduced in numbers, and far fewer illuminated manuscripts were produced, the emphasis being now on portraits, formal court scenes, and studies of animals and birds, to be mounted into albums (*muraqqas*). It was under Jehangir that the school reached its technical zenith in a series of penetrating portrait studies of the Emperor by artists such as Abu'l Hasan. Under the later Emperors, the style slowly atrophied, although the technique remained superb. With the collapse of the central power of Delhi in the 18th century, and the establishment of autonomous states out of former provinces, various provincial centres such as Hyderabad and Lucknow extended the style's life and vitality, before they, too, withered when the powers of patronage passed mainly to British officials of the East India Company around 1800. See vol. 3 pp. 20–21

Muhammadi
active 2nd half of 16th century
Persian painter from Herat. He may have worked for Isma'il II. Opinions differ as to the extent of his oeuvre, there being quite a number of attributed drawings. He appears to have worked in a fine line with touches of light colour, treating rustic or dervish scenes with delicate humour. A *Scene of village life* is in the Louvre, Paris, and is dated 1578.

Muhammad Zaman
active c.1670–1703
Persian painter, working in Isfahan and Ashraf. He is sometimes identified with a Christian convert, Paolo Zaman, but this is uncertain. Shah Abbas II sent him to Venice, and his painstaking illuminations in a *Shahnameh* (c.1675, Dublin, Chester Beatty Library) and a *Khamseh* (1675–77, New York, Pierpont Morgan Library) reflect the influence of Western engravings in their treatment of space and volume. His copy of an engraving after Rubens is preserved in the Fogg Art Museum (Cambridge, Mass.).

Mu'in Musavvir active 1638–1707
Persian painter, working in Isfahan. He was a pupil of Riza Abbasi, and painted a portrait of the latter (Princeton, University Library). Mu'in's single paintings suggest European or Mughal influence, though the proportions of his figures are more traditional than his master's. He added notes to his drawings.

Mulready, William 1786–1863
Irish painter of genre subjects, who worked in England. His early watercolours were influenced by Varley, but from 1808 he concentrated on sentimental scenes in the manner of Wilkie and Dutch masters. With their light, clear colours and precise drawing, these anticipated the Pre-Raphaelites (*The sonnet*, 1839, London, V&A).

Multscher, Hans active 1427–67
German sculptor, one of the most important and influential of the mid-15th century. Although he was a rather conservative artist, his refined and restrained style revitalized the stock formulae of earlier German sculpture by relating the drapery folds to the limbs and movement of his figures and to the entire composition. The stone carvings for Ulm Minster, for instance the *Man of Sorrows*, dated 1429, reveal his contact with Sluter. His large Ulm workshop produced paintings and wood and stone sculpture, but it seems his own activity was restricted to sculpture. His elaborate altarpiece in the Frauenkirch at Vipiteno in the southern Tyrol combines wooden reliefs and figures in the round with painted wings. It is his last known work.

Munch, Edvard 1863–1944
The greatest Norwegian painter and graphic artist, allied to the Symbolists and a forerunner of Expressionism. He trained at the School of Design in Oslo and belonged, for a time, to the Bohemian circle of artists led by Christian Krohg. Visits to France in his twenties brought him into contact with Impressionist and, more significantly, Symbolist trends. Gauguin's example was particularly important, demonstrating the possibilities of distilling intense emotions into universal experiences through the use of simplified, sinuous forms and evocative blocks of pure colour. Symbolism also gave direction to Munch's neuroses—his morbid preoccupation with the sickroom, his voracious *femmes fatales*, his lonely figures set against the shore in attitudes of solitude or despair. In 1892, an exhibition of Munch's work in Berlin caused an uproar. It was closed within a week and the resulting disputes led to the formation of the Berlin Sezession. Munch's next 16 years, largely spent in Germany, were his most creative. He conceived his idea for a *Frieze of Life*, a compilation of his most powerful studies of love and death, which, he hoped, would produce a symphonic effect when shown together. The most celebrated item from the series is *The scream* (1893, Oslo, NG), an archetypal depiction of *Angst*, where a violently red sunset and the inky waters of a fjord are transformed into shock waves, pressing in on the shrieking victim. Munch's images were like recurrent nightmares, which he sought to exorcise through constant reworking. For this, the printmaking mediums of lithography and colour woodcuts were invaluable. *The kiss*, for example, began as a naturalistic oil-painting, but gained a new intensity in its woodcut version (Oslo Municipal Art Collections). In 1908, Munch suffered a nervous breakdown and much of the obsessive imagery vanished from his repertoire. Where it reappeared, it did so only as bloodless repetition. Instead, his later career was marked by impressive winter landscapes and vigorous studies of workmen. See vol. 1. pp. *39, 98, 151;* vol. 3 pp. **128–129;** vol. 4 p. *173*

Munnings, Sir Alfred James
1878–1959
British painter, specializing in scenes with horses. He was President of the Royal Academy, 1944–49, making full use of his position for attacks on modern art more notable for their force than their cogency. The vigorous handling and colour of his best work, such as the atmospheric *Their majesties return from Ascot* (1925, London, Tate), show that his popularity was not unjustified.

Münter, Gabriele 1877–1962
German painter. She studied under Kandinsky in Munich from 1902 to 1903 and subsequently became his mistress. Her early work was Impressionist (*Kandinsky painting in a landscape*, 1903, Munich, Lenbachhaus), but by 1908 she had developed an EXPRESSIONIST style, using non-naturalistic colours and heavy outlines in a manner similar to the Fauves (*Listening, portrait of Jawlensky*, 1909, Munich, Lenbachhaus). After separating from Kandinsky in 1916 she travelled a great deal and from 1931 lived in seclusion. See vol. 3 pp. **136–137**

Muqi 1180–1270?
Chinese painter, originally from Sichuan, perhaps the greatest of all Chan (Zen) monk-painters. He spent his life in the famous Chan Buddhist temple set amidst the inspiring scenery of the West Lake at Hangzhou. His finest work is now preserved in Japan: one of the best-known examples is in Daitoku-ji, Kyoto, a triptych of *The white-robed Guanyin* framed by *A crane in a bamboo grove* and *A mother Gibbon and baby* (c.1250?). Its fluent brushwork contrasts with the stark minimalism of *Six persimmons* (in the same temple), where simple blobs of ink form the globular fruit, a perfect realization of the Chan theory that as much of the Buddha-nature is revealed in the humble fruit as in the most splendid icon of a demi-god. Muqi's major influence was on Japan, but his temple at Hangzhou remained a centre of the Chan school at least into the succeeding Yuan dynasty. See vol. 3 pp. **40–41**

Murillo, Bartolomé Esteban
1618–82
Spanish painter, born and active in Seville. His earliest known works are in a tenebrist style influenced by Zurbarán, then the leading painter of the city (*The Flight into Egypt*, c.1645, Detroit, Art Institute). Murillo achieved sudden fame with a cycle of 11 paintings executed in 1645–46 (now widely dispersed) for the Franciscan monastery in Seville, and overtook Zurbarán in popularity. He became first Director of the Academy in Seville (founded 1660) and ran a flourishing workshop. His work continued to influence painting in Seville throughout the 18th century. He is best known for two types of painting—sentimental genre scenes of peasant children (particularly good examples in London, Dulwich College Picture Gallery and Munich, Alte Pinakothek) and devotional paintings appealing to popular piety and painted with the fluttering draperies, soft colours and melting forms which go to make up his famous *estilo vaporoso* (vaporous style). His most frequent subject was *The Immaculate Conception* (examples, Madrid, Prado; Paris, Louvre, and elsewhere). He also painted a few excellent and rather severe portraits. In the 18th century Murillo's reputation stood exceptionally high. See vol. 2 p. 209

Muybridge, Eadweard 1830–1904
British-born pioneer of motion photography. In his youth he emigrated to the USA where, in 1872, he began a study of animal motion, seeking to show the varying positions of a horse's limbs while galloping, in a series of still photographs. Five years later he developed the technique, using a fast camera shutter, which conclusively proved that at a certain point all four legs are in the air; he went on to evolve a method which reproduced motion by projecting the photographs at high speed on to a screen. In the 1880s he transferred his attention to the human figure, nude and clothed, and his analysis of sequential motion had a decisive impact on artists as diverse as Eakins, the Impressionists, the Futurists and Bacon. See vol. 1 pp. *68–69;* vol. 3 pp. 125, 127

Muzaffar Ali active 1456–80/88
Persian painter, working in Herat. He was a pupil of Bihzad, and is accredited with the fine miniatures in the *Khamseh of Mir Ali Shir Nawa'i* (1485, Oxford,

Bodleian Library). According to a contemporary historian, Muzaffar Ali was "a master of group pictures".

Muziano, Girolamo 1532–92
Italian painter. He was born in Brescia, studied in Padua and Venice, and in about 1549 settled in Rome. There he studied so assiduously that he is said to have shaved his head to avoid amorous distractions. *The Raising of Lazarus* (1555, Rome, Vatican Museum), with weighty, emphatic figures rendered with the painterly fluency of his Venetian training, was the first of many impressive altarpieces for churches in Rome and the surrounding towns. He was distinguished from his Roman contemporaries by his interest in landscape.

Muzika, František 1900–74
Czech painter, stage designer and book illustrator. He believed that "a picture is a painted poem", and his lyrical instincts led him from Cubism to a highly individual and poetical Surrealism. His later paintings revealed a world of strange cellular formations.

Myers, Jerome 1867–1940
American painter who helped to organize the ARMORY SHOW. He is best remembered for his romantically sympathetic paintings of the New York poor, such as *The night mission* (1906, New York, Metropolitan).

Myron *c*.480–440 BC
Greek sculptor, active in Athens. He was perhaps the most distinguished sculptor of the early Classical period, when the mastery which had been gained in the graceful and convincing representation of the human figure was being extended into a new range of stances and positions. No original work has survived, but his skill is apparent in the complex but harmonious pose of the "*Diskobolos*" (Discus thrower, *c*.450 BC), the work for which he was most famed in antiquity and of which the best Roman copy is in the Terme Museum in Rome. Another important work was a group of *Athene and Marsyas*, also preserved in Roman copies, in which the startled movement of Marsyas is subtly countered by the calm stability of the goddess. See vol. 1 p. *50*; vol. 2 p. **38**

Myslbek, Josef Václav 1848–1922
Czech sculptor, a leading representative of 19th-century monumental realism. Inspired with the ideals of the Czech national revival, he created most of the historic commemorative statues erected in Prague at the turn of the century, for instance *Bedřich Smetana* (1894, National Theatre) and *St Wenceslas* (1912–13, Wenceslas Square).

Mytens, Daniel *c*.1590–1647
Anglo-Dutch portrait painter. He was born in Delft, trained in The Hague, and was in London by 1618. He soon gained royal patronage, and was appointed an official "picture-drawer" by Charles I on his accession (1625). Until the arrival of van Dyck, Mytens dominated court portraiture with his confident technique, sure sense of colour and character, and ability to orchestrate a grand full-length. He left England probably in 1634 and died in The Hague. There is a good collection of portraits, including James I and Charles I, in the National Portrait Gallery, London, but his finest achievement, the masterpiece of the period before van Dyck in English painting, is *The first Duke of Hamilton* (1629, Duke of Hamilton coll., on loan to NG of Scotland, Edinburgh). See vol. 4 p. *15*

Nabis
Group of French painters, active in the 1890s, who took their name from the Hebrew word meaning prophets. They were attracted by the advice Gauguin gave Sérusier in 1888 at PONT-AVEN to paint in flat areas of pure colour, rejecting naturalistic representation. Redon was also influential. The Nabis felt that a painting should not be an imitation of reality but a parallel to nature, stressing subjective, sometimes mystical perceptions. Beside painting, they worked in theatre design, book illustration, posters and stained glass and were, to various extents, indebted to contemporary Japanese prints. Bonnard and Vuillard were probably the best painters of the group and eventually reverted to a modified style known as INTIMISME. Other members included Denis, Ranson and Sérusier. See vol. 3 p. 120

Nadelman, Elie 1882–1946
Polish-born American sculptor. He emigrated from his native country in 1914. His sculpture is elegant and self-conscious, revealing a limited invention despite his involvement with a wide range of materials including ceramic, papier-maché and metal-plated plaster. His tapered or bulging figures often have a classical air, but their deliberate naivety indicates an awareness of American folk art. The incongruous details of his mannequins, such as the bowler hat of *Man in the open air* (*c*.1915, New York, MOMA), often convey a slightly absurd aura. Nadelman ranks with Lachaise as an important figure in the break away from the academic attitudes which dominated American sculpture in the 19th and early 20th centuries.

Nagarjunakonda see AMARAVATI

Naive art
Painting in a childlike or untrained fashion, characterized by a careful, simplifying style, non-scientific perspective, simple bright colours and, often, an enchantingly literal depiction of imaginary scenes. Naive painters do not follow any particular movement or aesthetic, but have been a continuing international phenomenon and influence since the beginning of the 20th century. The exhibition of naive painting organized by Wilhelm Uhde, The Painters of the Sacred Heart, 1928, was a turning point in critical recognition. Amongst many well-known naive artists are Hicks, Grandma Moses, Bombois, Vivin and Rousseau. Professional artists have found in their art a directness and freshness of vision often lacking in more sophisticated art. See vol. 3 p. 141

Nakian, Reuben born 1897
American sculptor. After acquaintance with Lachaise he produced representational works including a number of portraits of politicians in the 1930s. By the late 1940s his style had undergone drastic revision, with an abstract, roughly textured treatment of mythological themes, perhaps influenced by his friend Gorky, the writer. After using steel rods and sheets in the 1950s he then moved to crusty, jagged, fluttering forms (*Olympia*, 1961, New York, Whitney).

Nanni di Banco died 1421
Florentine sculptor. He is first recorded as a member of the Stonemasons' Guild in 1405, and worked on the Porta della Mandorla of the Cathedral in 1408. His subsequent career unfolded side by side with Donatello's, in a series of works for the Cathedral and for Orsanmichele. His *St Luke* for the Cathedral (1408–13, now Cathedral Museum) antedates Donatello's *St John* and shows a desire for harmony and richly rounded volume, in contrast to Donatello's emphatic articulation. Subsequent work, however, shows him struggling to absorb Donatello's remarkable innovations; these are successfully reconciled with his own natural fullness and serenity in *The Asumption* in the gable of the Porta della Mandorla (1414–21). The three marble works for Orsanmichele (*St Philip, St Eligius, Four martyr saints*) have not been dated precisely, and his development is hard to reconstruct. He was influenced not only by the Antique and by Donatello but also by Jacopo della Quercia (in *The Assumption*) and by Ghiberti (in the *St Eligius*). Because his *St Philip* and *Four martyr saints* are undated, it is difficult to assess how original their extremely accomplished use of the Antique really was; his *St Philip* is clearly related to Donatello's *St Mark*, but whether it came later or earlier is controversial. See vol. 2 p. **101**

Nanteuil, Robert *c*.1623–78
French draughtsman and engraver. Nanteuil was the finest portrait engraver of the 17th century, and the only contemporary French portraitist to stand comparison with Philippe de Champaigne. He engraved the work of Champaigne and other artists, but also his own original compositions. In 1658 he was appointed royal draughtsman by Louis XIV and he executed many pastel portraits of the King and royal family.

Naonobu, Kano 1607–50
Japanese painter, somewhat overshadowed by his more prolific brother Tan'yu. They were both summoned to Edo (Tokyo) from Kyoto, to be appointed official painters to the Tokugawa Shogun's court. This was a change of direction for the Kano family, who were until then painters to the imperial court. Naonobu was first trained by a pupil of his grandfather Mitsunobu, and soon became at home in a multitude of subjects. An example of his lyrical style is the screen with *Eight scenes of Sosho* in the Tokyo National Museum.

Nash, Paul 1889–1946
British painter and printmaker. After being wounded in World War I he worked as an official war artist. The most memorable of his war pictures, such as *We are making a new world* (1918, London, Imperial War Museum), commemorate the devastation done to the land. His subsequent discovery of Surrealism and in particular the work of Chirico confirmed his tendency to isolate the mysterious and threatening aspects of landscape (*Monster field*, 1939, Durban Art Gallery). In spite of his interest in continental modernism (he founded the avantgarde association UNIT ONE), he was in many ways a conservative artist with a deep attachment to the countryside. In World War II he was again a war artist, this time documenting the war in the air; one of his greatest pictures is "*Totes Meer*" (Dead sea, 1940–41, London, Tate), in which the "waves" are wings of shot-down aeroplanes. His book illustrations were outstanding, notably his visionary woodcuts for Genesis (1924) and coloured drawings for Sir Thomas Browne's *Urne Burial* (1928). See vol. 3 p. **198**

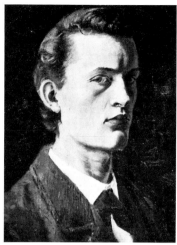

Munch: Self-portrait, 1881–82. Oslo, Munch Museet (Scala)

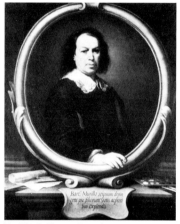

Murillo: Self-portrait, early 1670s. London, NG

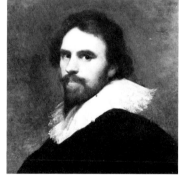

Mytens: Self-portrait, *c*.1630. Hampton Court, Royal coll.

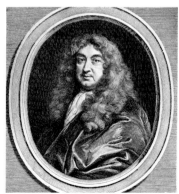

Nanteuil: Engraving by Edelinck after a self-portrait (Mansell)

National Academy of Design
Self-governing New York institution founded in 1826 by American artists in opposition to the academic and European-dominated American Academy of Fine Arts. Morse was its first President. Its members stressed study from nature, and the Academy exhibited only work by living New York artists. In the wake of Impressionism, it grew reactionary.

Natoire, Charles-Joseph 1700–77
French history painter and decorator. He was a pupil of François Lemoyne and was in Italy, 1723–28. His prettily coloured ROCOCO development of Lemoyne's idiom was well suited to tapestry cartoons and decorative schemes such as the *Cupid and Psyche* series at the Hôtel de Soubise, Paris (1737–38); serious subjects such as his series on *The History of Clovis* (c.1736, Troyes, Musée) are less successful. He was appointed Director of the French Academy in Rome in 1751 and took up landscape, encouraging Robert and Fragonard, and producing elegant views of Rome.

Nattier, Jean-Marc 1685–1766
Fashionable French portrait painter at the court of Louis XV. *A lady as Diana* (1756, New York, Metropolitan) is an example of the pastel-like delicacy of his female portraits, which, though marked by an air of intimacy, convey little sense of character. *Marie Leczinska* (1748, Versailles) is the best of a series of full-lengths in which he combined an air of ease with the requirements of the Baroque state portrait. See vol. 2 p. **242**

Naturalism
Term generally used to describe a style in which the artist attempts to render the qualities of an object as empirically observed, rather than stylizing or applying intellectual and extraneous considerations to the work. In literature, more specifically, the term Naturalism was used by and applied to the works of Emile Zola, being distinguished from Realism in that it presupposed art mirroring in a virtually photographic way detailed natural beauty rather than a more metaphysically real beauty or truth. The two terms, however, are often confused in criticism. Courbet might be called Realist while Meissonier might be called Naturalist.

Nauen, Heinrich 1880–1941
German Expressionist painter. His early naturalism gave way to the influence of van Gogh and Matisse during his years at the academies in Stuttgart and Düsseldorf. He was more interested in creating decorative surface patterns than in exploring the expressive possibilities of forms and colours. In 1921 he was called to a post at the Düsseldorf Academy, where he taught Dix.

Nauman, Bruce born 1941
American artist, a protagonist of BODY art and PERFORMANCE. His early work, which explored the idea of the art work as an extension of the artist's physical self, took the form of performances, wax casts of parts of his body (for example *From hand to mouth*, 1967, New York, Joseph Helman coll.) and even holographic self-images. More recently, Nauman has set up sculptural "situations" which require viewers to participate physically. Audio and video mechanisms are often incorporated in his environments, as in *Live taped video corridor* (1968–70, Italy, Varese, Giuseppe Panza di Biumo coll.), a space with a video monitor in which the spectator sees himself upside down and from the back. See vol. 3 p. **246**

Navarrete, Juan Fernández
c.1526–79
Spanish painter from Navarre, known as El Mudo (the mute), perhaps the most significant painter of his generation in Spain. He was trained in Italy—in Venice (where he may have been a pupil of Titian), and probably Rome. In 1568 he was made painter to Philip II in order to work on the Escorial, where his works are still *in situ*. He developed an individual, monumental style, remarkably attuned to the Escorial and the spirit of Philip II, that combined Spanish traditional naturalism with something of the heroic style of Rome. In 1576 he was commissioned to provide 36 paintings for the altars of the church of the Escorial, and had completed eight when he died. Certain of his later paintings, including *The burial of St Lawrence* (his last work, 1579, Escorial), prefigure, in their naturalism and dramatic use of chiaroscuro, something of Caravaggio.

Navez, François Joseph
1787–1869
Belgian portrait and history painter. He studied in Brussels and in Paris, where his teacher, David, exerted a profound influence over his style. His biblical and mythological scenes are treated in a Neoclassical manner, influenced by Ingres, whom he met during his stay in Rome (1817–22). However, Navez achieved his greatest success in portraiture (*The de Hemptinne family*, 1816, Brussels, Musée Royal d'Art Moderne). He was Director of the Academy in Brussels from 1835 to 1862.

Nay, Ernst Wilhelm 1902–68
German painter and engraver. From 1925 to 1928 he studied under Hofer, whose strain of classical idealism influenced his early work. In the early 1930s he produced a series of pictures based on mineral and organic imagery similar to that invented by Ernst. After his dismissal by the Nazis (1933) he changed to a figurative style characterized by Expressionist pathos and with colours used symbolically (*Departure of the fishermen*, 1936, Hanover, Niedersächsische Landesgalerie). From 1937 to 1938 he was with Munch in Norway. After 1945 he turned to abstraction, creating complementary and contrapuntal colour accords in compositions dominated by circles or triangles.

Nazarenes
Group of early 19th-century German and Austrian painters who worked in Italy. Formed in Vienna in 1809, the Brotherhood of St Luke (Lukasbrüder), on which the Nazarene movement was based, intended to work co-operatively with a joint programme reminiscent of the medieval guild system. The aim was a revival of Christian art. Late medieval painting in Germany provided much of the inspiration, but the strong contours and clear local colours associated with the group were derived from Italian Renaissance art. The most important members were Cornelius, Overbeck, Pforr and Wilhelm von Schadow. Their major joint venture was the frescos at the Casa Bartholdy in Rome (1816–17), where they executed scenes from the story of Joseph. See vol. 3 p. 75

Neefs or **Neeffs family**
Family of Flemish painters, active in Antwerp, of whom the most important were **Pieter the Elder** (c.1578–1656/61) and his son **Pieter the Younger** (1620–after 1675). Both specialized in paintings of church interiors, and their works are virtually indistinguishable.

Their style is more mechanical than that of the Steenwycks, and figures in paintings from the Neefs studio were often added by others (Bonaventura Peeters the Elder in Neefs the Elder's *An evening service in a church*, 1649, London, NG).

Neer, Aert van der 1604–77
Dutch landscape painter, born in Amsterdam and active there from the mid-1630s. He is best known for two types of pictures—frozen winter landscapes with skaters on ice, and moonlit scenes, of which he was the foremost exponent of his time. Both display his mastery of atmosphere and light effects. His moonlit scenes, which often show canals or rivers—the reflections in the water treated with great subtlety—are particularly romantic in feeling. He seems to have been a slow deliberate worker and had trouble making a living, but his paintings were much copied and imitated in the 17th and 18th centuries. The full range of his work (he also painted conventional landscapes) is represented in the Rijksmuseum, Amsterdam, and the National Gallery, London. His son and pupil **Eglon** (1634–1703) turned to genre painting in the style of Terborch and Metsu. He was during his life much more famous than his father and had an international career, ending as painter to the Elector Palatine at Düsseldorf.

Negret, Edgar born 1920
Colombian sculptor. The success of his work rests on his logical development of a system of assemblage, and an understanding of the malleable and structural properties of his material, normally sheet-metal painted black, white or vermilion. A fine example of his public work is *Coupling* (1966, Bogota, Public Gardens). He now lives in Bogota, but has had two periods in New York, 1948–50 and 1956–63.

Neizvestny, Ernst born 1925
Soviet sculptor. He has been forced to work unofficially, and the small scale of his work is probably due to reduced means. He survived a bullet exploding inside his chest during World War II and all his figure-sculptures and drawings celebrate themes of life, death and metamorphosis, particularly the suffering of the Russian people, through powerful distortions of the human body. He is renowned for a public confrontation with Krushchev in 1962.

Nelli, Ottaviano active 1400–44
Italian painter of the Umbrian school, active in central Italy. Nelli's old-fashioned altarpieces and frescos have freshness and charm, fusing International Gothic costume and decoration with motifs from 14th-century masterpieces in Assisi. The small panels of *The Adoration of the Magi* (Worcester, Mass., Art Museum) and *St Francis marries Lady Poverty* (Vatican Gallery) illustrate the appeal of his style, which had many local imitators.

Neoclassicism
Movement which dominated European art and architecture in the late 18th and early 19th centuries. It was marked by an heroic severity of tone—a reaction against the frivolity of the ROCOCO—and by a desire for archaeologically correct details, in part stimulated by the discovery of Herculaneum and Pompeii. Whereas the BAROQUE had been the style of Absolutism, Neoclassicism was an expression of the Enlightenment and the Age of Reason, and classical forms were seen as embodying a reason and order corresponding to the prevailing philosophical and social outlook. In France it is particularly associated with the Revolution and a desire to instil ancient Roman virtues into civic life. Not surprisingly, Neoclassicism generated more theoretical writing than any previous movement in the arts, Winckelmann being the most important contributor. He thought that the outstanding characteristics of ancient art were "noble simplicity and serene grandeur", qualities which one indeed finds in the works of the greatest Neoclassical artists such as Canova and David, though with lesser exponents the results could be merely ponderous or cold. Neoclassicism, however, could also embrace a proto-Romantic dream of antiquity (often known as Romantic Classicism) or much less high-sounding, more decorative, even pretty, aims. See vol. 3 pp. 56–62

Neo-Impressionism
Movement in French painting, both a development out of Impressionism and a reaction against it. The critic Félix Fénéon coined the name in 1886 when Seurat, Signac and Pissarro exhibited works in the Pointillist technique at the last Impressionist exhibition. This technique extended the flecked colour of Monet and Renoir into a deliberate system of applying pure colours so divided and balanced that, according to current theory, they would mix not on the canvas but in the eyes of the spectator with matchless luminosity. The Neo-Impressionists considered themselves to be extending and correcting Impressionism by making it more rational and scientific. With some notable exceptions, posterity has often found their works disappointingly dull and rigid. See vol. 1 p. 126; vol. 3 pp. 110–111

Neo-Plasticism see DE STIJL

Neo-Romanticism
Term applied to two distinct, yet related tendencies in 20th-century painting. In France in the 1930s a number of painters including Berman, Bérard and Tchelitchew exploited the fantastic effects of exaggerated perspective in a glamorized view of Mediterranean poverty. There are stylistic affinities with the work of Dali, although there is none of his sensational imagery. In the late 1930s and 1940s many British painters turned back to a Romantic tradition of painting and illustration, regarded as distinctively national. Examples were the sinister landscapes of Sutherland, Piper's revival of topographical painting and the attempts to recapture the spirit of Samuel Palmer's Shoreham period in paintings by Minton and Ayrton. These latter two artists were also strongly influenced by French Neo-Romanticism.

Neri di Bicci 1419–after 1491
Florentine painter, the son of Bicci di Lorenzo. He was the head of a productive workshop where many minor artists were trained. His stilted altarpieces, such as *The Annunciation* (1464, Florence, Accademia) variously reflect the styles of Masolino, Fra Angelico, Filippo Lippi and Baldovinetti.

Neroccio de' Landi 1447–1500
Sienese painter. He collaborated with Francesco di Giorgio but surpassed him in painting, creating distinctive masterpieces. The sparse, elegant figures, refined colour and meditative expressions in works such as *The Madonna and Child with saints* (c.1495, Washington, NG) recall in some degree Verrocchio, but also look back to Duccio and the 14th-century Sienese tradition.

Nesiotes see KRITIOS

Nesterov, Michail Vassilevich
1862–1942
Russian painter. His first pictures were genre scenes in the manner of the Wanderers, but he soon found his own individual style in poetical renderings of subjects taken from Russian Orthodox teaching. The decorative side of his deeply emotional, lyrical art brought him into Diaghilev's WORLD OF ART circle. After 1918 he stayed in Russia and painted several very fine portraits of famous scientists and artists.

Netscher, Caspar c.1635–84
Dutch genre and portrait painter. He was the leading pupil of Terborch in Deventer and settled in The Hague in 1662. His career parallels that of Maes, since he abandoned genre scenes (The lace maker, 1664, London, Wallace Coll.) for elegant society and court portraits. He was particularly skilled at depicting rich materials, and his sitters were often placed against the background of a park with decorative sculpture (Maria Timmers, 1683, The Hague, Mauritshuis). His sons **Theodoor** (1661–1732) and **Constantijn** (1688–1723) imitated his style. See vol. 4 p. 159

Neue Sachlichkeit
(New Objectivity)
Term first used by Gustav Hartlaub, director of the Mannheim Kunsthalle, as the title of an exhibition of post-War figurative art he planned there in 1923. Neue Sachlichkeit was not a coherent movement, nor does the term describe a unified style; rather, it designates a new, objective way of seeing and commenting upon the banality of everyday reality. It represents a decisive attempt to exorcise the EXPRESSIONISTS' obsession with subjectivity. The main tendency within Neue Sachlichkeit was represented by the so-called "Verists" such as Grosz, Dix, Heartfield and the NOVEMBER-GRUPPE, who adopted a blatantly aggressive political attitude to social abuses in a style combining Expressionist distortion, a collage-like compositional structure and a meticulously rendered surface texture. Another major artist associated with Neue Sachlichkeit was Max Beckmann, though he concentrated less on objective reality than on complex allegorical interpretations of the forces underlying contemporary life. The term MAGIC REALISM has also been used to describe the work of some Neue Sachlichkeit artists, including Schrimpf and Kanoldt. See vol. 3 pp. 194–197

Nevelson, Louise born 1899
Russian-born American sculptor who settled in the USA in 1905. She studied briefly with Hofmann in Munich and by the mid-1940s was making assemblages. Her most characteristic works, such as Sky cathedral (1958, Buffalo, Albright-Knox) form whole walls or even rooms consisting of shallow box-like units sprayed in a uniform colour (frequently black, sometimes white or gold). Each unit is filled with found wooden forms—pieces of furniture, parts of balustrades and so on. The effect is one of a strange iconic shrine or altar. In the later 1960s she took up new materials—aluminium, steel and plexiglass—and made some exterior sculptures. She is one of the best-known contemporary sculptors. See vol. 1 p. 196; vol. 3 p. 246

Nevinson, Christopher Richard Wynne 1889–1946
British painter. He was the leading British exponent of FUTURISM and a disciple of the poet Marinetti. In 1914 they published together the English Futurist manifesto Vital English Art. However, Nevinson's most enduring achievements are his depictions of World War I, which employ a harsh angular style, more reminiscent of Wyndham Lewis' VORTICISM than Italian models, and evoke the depersonalizing effects of modern warfare (Returning to the trenches, 1914–15, Ottawa, NG of Canada). His subsequent work was more traditional and included ponderous allegories on the human condition.

New English Art Club
Artists' club founded in London in 1886 to exhibit paintings reflecting some degree of French influence. It exhibited twice a year and attracted a wide range of artists. One notable group was the Newlyn school, which practised a naturalism inspired by Bastien-Lepage's plein-air approach. The club became associated with English Impressionism and was seen to challenge the traditions of the Royal Academy. See vol. 3 p. 154

New Kingdom c.1554–332 BC
The arts of Egypt in the New Kingdom period when Pharaohs of the 15th Dynasty created an empire stretching eastwards to the Euphrates and southwards along the Upper Nile. From the time of Thuthmosis I (1525–1512 BC) until the Late Period, royalty were buried in the famous "Valley of the Kings" near Luxor, ancient THEBES. The expansive spirit of the New Kingdom is manifest in the celebrated temple of Queen Hatshepsut (1503–1482 BC) in western Thebes, with its elongated terraces and spacious colonnades. The painted reliefs preserved in the temple maintain the traditional use of outline, flat colour and system of horizontal registers, but with an unprecedented attention to detail and locality. Theban tomb-painters developed a greater freedom of technical approach and an expanded repertoire of subjects painted on flat, plastered surfaces. Illustrated papyrus manuscripts (Books of the Dead) were introduced, placed in the coffin with the mummy. Coloured glass also came into extensive use: not only in jewellery but for goblets and vases. The art of the 18th Dynasty reached its zenith in the reigns of the heretic Akhenaten (1379–1361 BC), the founder of AMARNA, and Tutankhamun (1361–1352 BC). Though succeeding dynasties failed to develop the Amarna trend of naturalism, there were great achievements in the Rammeside period, when Ramesses II (1304–1237 BC), built many temples, notably at ABU SIMBEL, and in the Saite period, 664–525 BC, when OLD and MIDDLE KINGDOM art was copied with consummate elegance. However, in general the years 1085–332 BC saw a decline due to foreign domination. See vol. 2 pp. 26–27

Newman, Barnett 1905–70
American painter, a leading figure in the development of COLOUR FIELD painting and a powerful theoretician and polemicist. Although he was a contemporary of, and closely connected with, the ABSTRACT EXPRESSIONIST painters, Newman's paintings are more austere and less painterly. He is more closely associated with Rothko, Gottlieb and Still, with whom he also shared a common interest in mythological subjects during the 1940s. The technique and cosmic preoccupations of his paintings of the late 1940s relate to Surrealism. He arrived at his mature style with Onement I (1948, New York, Annalee G. Newman coll.), in which an orange vertical band crosses an Indian-red canvas. From then on his characteristic works consist of coloured fields sectioned by "zips" (as he preferred to call the bands). Scale became increasingly important to the sheer spread of colour—"Vir Heroicus Sublimis" (1950–51, New York, MOMA) is more than 5 m (17 ft) wide. Occasional pieces of sculpture and several triangular-shaped canvases appeared in his last years. Newman's painting had a strong impact upon the next generation of artists. See vol. 3 p. **218**

New York school
Name often given to a loosely associated group of avantgarde artists based in New York in the middle years of the 20th century. The broad characteristics which define the group are a determination to find a uniquely American mode of expression, a general rejection of representational images and the frequent use of huge canvases. Many of the artists were influenced by and worked with the European émigrés, Gorky and Hofmann; also influential was the Surrealism of Miró and Masson. Two main tendencies can be discerned among the artists—on the one hand Pollock and De Kooning developed a gestural mode of abstraction often called ACTION PAINTING; on the other painters such as Rothko, Newman, Motherwell and Still worked in a more lyrical and philosophic idiom. Also associated with the New York school and occupying a ground between these groups were Baziotes, Tomlin, Kline, Guston, Gottlieb and Tworkov. See vol. 3 pp. 210 ff

Niccolo active early 12th century
Italian ROMANESQUE sculptor, the heir to the achievements of Wiligelmo. He was active in Lombardy and his first known work (c.1120) is the Zodiac portal (which he signed) of the Sacra di S. Michele near Turin. Southern French Romanesque sculpture influenced his work, and his elaborately figured portals with sculpted tympana at the cathedrals of Piacenza and Ferrara were new to Italian art. Softly sculpted drapery figures with large heads and tender expressions are characteristic of his style, which was propagated by his workshop, and proved widely influential.

Niccolò dell'Arca (or d'Apulia) c.1435–94
Sculptor of South Italian origin, active in Bologna after 1463. He takes his name from the shrine of St Dominic (Arca di S. Domenico) sculpted in the 1260s by Nicola Pisano in S. Domenico Maggiore, Bologna, for which he carved a marble canopy and statuettes (1469–73), later completed by the young Michelangelo. His masterpiece is an emotionally charged ensemble of realistic terracotta figures, The lamentation over the dead Christ (1480s?, Bologna, S. Maria della Vita). The Nicodemus is traditionally held to be a self-portrait.

Nicholas of Verdun
active late 12th–early 13th century
Mosan metalworker and enameller, the most distinctive personality of the TRANSITIONAL style which superseded Romanesque in a few areas of northern Europe. Two signed works by him survive, the altarpiece (finished 1181) for the abbey church at Klosterneuburg, Austria (Klosterneuburg, Stiftsmuseum), and the Shrine of St Mary (1205) in Tournai Cathedral. His masterpiece, the Klosterneuburg altar, was originally a pulpit, but was remodelled after a fire in the 14th century. Despite this and later restorations, it is perhaps

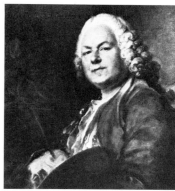

Nattier: Self-portrait. Private coll.

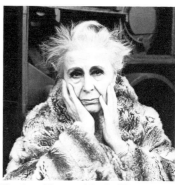

Nevelson: Photograph by Cecil Beaton (Camera Press)

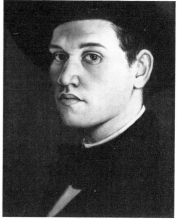

Nevinson: Self-portrait, 1911. London, Tate

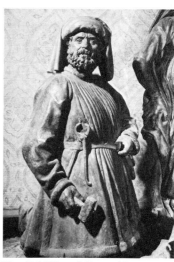

Niccolò dell'Arca: Self-portrait? as Nicodemus from The lamentation, 1480s. Bologna, S. Maria della Vita (Scala)

the greatest surviving piece of medieval enamelwork, its plaques, arranged in three rows, forming a complex iconographical programme with episodes from the Life of Christ presaged in Old Testament scenes. Figures are individualized, and dramatized by their antique-style drapery, which has both volume and rich linear articulation. Attributed to Nicholas is the Shrine of the Three Kings in Cologne Cathedral. This, made of gold, silver gilt, bronze gilt, gems, pearl and enamel, is the largest reliquary shrine of its age, and has some particularly powerful and expressive free-standing figures of prophets. See vol. 2 p. **76**

Nicholson, Ben born 1894
British artist, the son of Sir William Nicholson. He painted his first abstract in 1924, but his subjects during the 1920s and early 1930s were mainly landscapes and still lifes, in which he gradually formulated his own response to Cubism. A painting such as *Fireworks* (1929, Orkney, Pier Gallery) has a certain naive quality, reflecting his interest in the Cornish naive painter Wallis, whose improvised use of rough surfaces he admired and emulated in his own work. *At the Chat Botté* (1932, Manchester, City Art Gallery), represents the high point of his debt to Cubism. While in Paris in 1933 he made his first carved relief, and the subsequent series of works in white plaster were the most uncompromisingly abstract art made by an English artist to that date (*White relief*, 1935, London, Tate). Composed in right angles and circles, they were intended to create for the viewer the sense of a mysteriously receding space. During the war years figurative references returned to his work and later he created suggestions of still life and landscape from a complex network of arabesques. He was married to Barbara Hepworth until 1951. See vol. 3 pp. **198–199**, *227*

Nicholson, Sir William 1872–1949
British painter and poster designer. As a painter he usually worked on a small scale, and is best known for his still lifes, such as *Silver* (1938, London, Tate), which employ limited muted tones with great sensitivity.

Nielsen, Kai 1882–1924
Danish sculptor and ceramicist. Influenced by Rodin and Baroque art, his works both renewed and revitalized Danish sculpture. A new Scandinavian preoccupation with hard stone, especially granite, is reflected in the hugely swollen and smoothly polished figure of *Mads Rasmussen* begun in 1914 (Fåborg Museum). He is best known for his exuberant and sensual representations of mother and child.

Nihal Chand active 1730–50
Indian artist of Rajputana, who worked for the outstanding ruler Raja Savant Singh (1748–57). He produced paintings of brilliant technique depicting *Radha and Krishna* as the ideal lovers in landscape or palace settings. Radha is represented as an exquisitely stylized type with a long narrow face and upturned sweeping eyes. Nihal Chand infused the rather cold formal style of the imperial Mughal atelier, then in a state of decline, with Rajput passion. His work was imitated in the school of Kishangarh, but never equalled. See vol. 3 p. **21**

Nikias active *c*.350–*c*.310 BC
Athenian painter of great repute, said to have favoured large compositions with well-modelled figures. Though his work is now lost, there are a number of Roman paintings of his subjects which may well be copies, even if they do not reflect the quality of the originals. See vol. 2 p. **45**

Niobid Painter active *c*.465–450 BC
Greek RED-FIGURE vase-painter from Athens, so called from his famous *calyx krater* in the Louvre, Paris, depicting the slaughter of the children of Niobe by Apollo and Artemis. Influenced by contemporary wall-painting, especially that of Polygnotos, he seems to have preferred to work on big vases suitable for large-scale compositions, such as battle scenes and the Sack of Troy. Some 90 vases are attributed to him.

Niten 1584–1645
Japanese painter. Niten is also known as the "invincible" Miyamoto Musashi, the master of double-sword fighting. A cultured military man, he wrote several important books on the art of war and swordsmanship, wrote poetry, and left some fine ink-paintings, a good example of which is *Bird on a branch* (Philadelphia Museum of Art). See vol. 3 p. **47**

Ni Tsan see NI ZAN

Nitsch, Hermann born 1938
Austrian Performance artist, the co-founder, with Brus and Muehl, of the Institute for Immediate Art in Vienna in 1966. He is probably the most prominent of all the Viennese Actionists: certainly his is the most articulate and fully developed philosophy. Typical Actions have included the crucified corpses of recently slaughtered lambs, which are then disembowelled and their innards, with buckets of blood, poured over nude performers. He aims at liberation from violence through catharsis.

Nittis, Giuseppe de 1846–84
Italian painter of landscape, bourgeois interiors and contemporary city life. In 1866, he visited the MACCHIAIOLI in Florence and in 1867 moved to Paris, where he resumed *plein-air* landscape and befriended Manet and Degas. He exhibited with the Impressionists in 1874. After 1879, he experimented in etching and pastels (*Races at Auteuil*, 1881, Rome, Galleria Nazionale d'Arte Moderna). A large collection of his work is in the Pinacoteca Communale of his native Barletta.

Ni Zan 1301–74
Chinese painter, the dominating figure of 14th-century Chinese painting, and one of the supreme geniuses of monochrome ink landscape painting at any period. He lived a life of luxurious seclusion on his estate in Jiangsu province. His family had traditionally had Taoist associations, however, and from about 1350 he began to divest himself of his wealth, wandering the region's numerous lakes and rivers in a houseboat with only his wife as company. Most of his painting dates from the years of his travels and concentrates almost obsessively on a limited repertoire of subjects endlessly reworked—landscapes, painted with a minimum of ink, showing desolate scenes of water, shore and gnarled pines. Often a hut is depicted, invariably without sign of human occupation, as a symbol of withdrawal, solitude and the rejection of worldly concerns. This moral and literal fastidiousness made Ni a hero to the scholar élite, both in his own time and subsequently. There are major problems surrounding the authenticity of his surviving work, but a typical genuine example is *A pavilion among pines* (1354, Taiwan, National Palace Museum). See vol. 3 p. 41

Noami, Shinno active 1450
Japanese painter, a native of Kyoto. Noami was a favourite of the Ashikaga Shogun Yoshimasa, whom he served as a court artist. He first learned to paint still lifes and landscapes from Shubun, but when he was exposed to the works of the Chinese Song artist Muqi he changed his style completely. His *White-robed Kannon*, an ink-painting in the Asano collection in Tokyo, is in his new Chinese-inspired style. A highly cultured man, Noami was also an accomplished poet, a sword-evaluator, a tea ceremony master, and a garden designer.

Nobuzane, Fujiwara 1177–1265
Japanese painter. A consummate courtier, Nobuzane held high office in the imperial court; besides painting, he compiled a poetry anthology. Most of his paintings are scrolls illustrating stories—two attributed works are designated National Treasures: a portrait of *Emperor Go Toba* (1221?, Osaka, Minase shrine), and a scroll in a gently mocking style of *Courtiers on prancing horses* (1247? Tokyo, Okura coll.).

Noda, Tetsuya born 1940
Japanese printmaker. He is concerned with representing daily life through the medium of print. He makes much use of photographs—*Diary, 22 August 1968* (1968, Japan Foundation) is a silk-screen print of a photograph of his family.

Noguchi, Isamu born 1904
American sculptor, born in Los Angeles of Japanese parentage. In the late 1920s he studied with Brancusi, whose influence is visible in his highly polished works of the period. He subsequently became involved with brush-drawing and pottery in the Far East and also created numerous gardens and theatrical sets. A passing encounter with social realist themes in the mid-1930s was followed by an assimilation of Surrealist biomorphism and a series of constructions, such as *Monument to heroes* (1943, Artist's coll.), which involve paper, wood, bones and string, suggesting the precedent of early Giacometti. Noguchi's work gained in austerity and grandeur towards the end of the 1950s, as when he exploited rough-hewn stone masses alternating with severe monumental cubic blocks as in the aluminum *Sesshu* (1958, Hartford, Wadsworth Atheneum). See vol. 1 pp. *204*

Nolan, Sidney born 1917
The best-known contemporary Australian painter. He had little formal training before becoming a professional artist at the age of 21 after a varied career including periods as a racing cyclist and goldminer. His earliest works were abstract, but his reputation was made with paintings of themes from Australian history and folklore, in particular the career of the 19th-century bushranger Ned Kelly, on which he began a series in 1946 (*Kelly at Glenrowan*, 1955, New York, Metropolitan). These attain a Surrealistic, hallucinatory intensity. His style is original and highly distinctive, employing broad washes of paint to create opalescent colour effects. He sometimes paints on unusual smooth materials—even glass—which accentuates the fluidity of his brushwork. See vol. 3 p. **251**

Noland, Kenneth born 1924
American painter. He is a prominent second generation ABSTRACT EXPRESSIONIST artist who has developed methods emphasizing the basic components of painting—colour and the two-dimensional canvas support. The geometric orientation of Bolotowsky, with whom Noland studied, and the staining technique used by Frankenthaler, were crucial to the formation of Noland's mature HARD-EDGE style. In his "target" paintings begun in 1958 (*Song*, 1958, New York, Whitney), the artist uses the centre of the canvas as a structuring device. From 1962 his compositional repertoire expanded to include ovals, chevrons, horizontal stripes and, from 1975, irregularly shaped canvases. See vol. 3 p. **222**

Nolde, Emil (Emil Hansen)
1867–1956
German EXPRESSIONIST painter and graphic artist. He trained as a wood-carver, then studied painting at the Académie Julian, Paris (1898–99), and under Hölzel (1899), from whom he learned the expressive potential of colour. He was a deeply religious man, and his aim was to express his religious feeling through colour, using violent colour clashes and grotesque distortion, as in *Dance round the golden calf* (1910, Munich, Staatsgemäldesammlungen). A mystic pantheism also pervades his landscapes, still lifes and "mask-like" figures (*Masks and dahlias*, 1919, Seebüll, Nolde Foundation). Although briefly a member of Die Brücke, 1906–07, he was essentially a solitary figure among the Expressionists. His interest in tribal art was further stimulated by an expedition to New Guinea via Russia and China in 1913–14. From 1926 he lived at Seebüll on the North German moorlands. Declared "Degenerate" by the Nazis and forbidden to paint, he painted small watercolours in secret—these are known as the "unpainted pictures". See vol. 1 pp. *157*, *165*; vol. 3 pp. **132–133**

Nollekens, Joseph 1737–1823
English NEOCLASSICAL sculptor, the most distinguished member of a family of artists originally from Antwerp. He was apprenticed to Scheemakers in 1750, and from 1760 to 1770 worked in Rome, copying and repairing ancient sculpture. His output included monuments (several are in Westminster Abbey, London) and statues, often gently erotic in feeling (*Venus chiding Cupid*, 1778, Lincoln, Usher Art Gallery), but he is best known for his brilliantly characterized portrait busts, of which a superb example is *Charles James Fox* (1792, Holkham Hall, Norfolk). He was immensely successful and a notorious miser.

Noort, Adam van 1562–1641
Flemish history and portrait painter, whose chief claim to fame is that he was one of the early teachers of Rubens. His early paintings are very rare, as are works by Rubens before he moved to Italy, so it is difficult to know what influence he may have had on his pupil. Van Noort's later work was strongly influenced by Jordaens, who was also his pupil, and became his son-in-law in 1616.

Nordström, Lars Gunnar
born 1924
Finnish painter and sculptor, a leading exponent of Constructivism. His two-dimensional works are composed of distinct areas of black, white and one primary colour, creating a tension between figure-ground effects and the sense of surface flatness. His work in welded steel often lays stress on diagonals.

Norwich school
Regional school of British painters, established in Norwich by "Old" Crome in 1803. It held annual exhibitions from 1805 to 1825 with Crome and Cotman as

its principal contributors. Their oils and watercolours depicting the Norfolk countryside are reminiscent of Dutch 17th-century landscape artists such as Hobbema and Ruisdael. See vol. 3 p. 68

Notke, Bernt c.1440–1509
German sculptor and painter, first recorded as a painter with a workshop in Lübeck in 1467. He was the most important woodcarver in the Baltic area in the late 15th century. The over life-size polychromed and lavishly decorated group of *St George and the dragon* (1489, Stockholm, Storkyrka) shows very well how he liberated his sculpture from earlier Gothic limitations by using additional blocks of wood to create dramatic and expressive movement. Other major works include the Triumphal Cross (1477) for Lübeck Cathedral and altarpieces for the cathedrals at Reval (1482/3) and Aarhus (by 1482). He had a large workshop and wide influence.

Novecento Italiano
Group of Italian artists formed in 1922 to oppose prevailing artistic trends. Many important Italian artists, such as Campigli, Carrà and Marini, were initially associated with the group, which called for a return to classical discipline in composition and the revival of large-scale figurative works. The first exhibition was held in 1926 and the group broke up in 1943. From the start it was associated with politics and nationalism, and soon became identified with the promotion of Fascist propaganda.

Novembergruppe
Group of leading German Expressionists and Dadaists formed in Berlin in December 1918, including Klein, Pechstein, Mueller and Campendonck. They were closely linked with the "Workers' Council for Art" founded in the same year by the architect Gropius. The two groups amalgamated in November 1919. Both were socialist in orientation, calling for a reconciliation between art and the masses; however, their proclamations had more to do with group consciousness than with political action, and many of their aims were realized only at the BAUHAUS. The group finally broke up in 1929.

Nussberg, Lev born 1937
Russian KINETIC artist. After working for a time in films and publishing, he started the new kinetic movement "Dvijenie" in 1962 with a group of other artists. Under the pretext of its scientific nature the group could show its abstract constructions of light and movement widely both in the Soviet Union and abroad. Nussberg emigrated in 1976 and now lives in Paris.

Objective Abstractionists
Group of British painters who exhibited together in London in 1934. They included Graham Bell, Moynihan, Richards, Pasmore and Hitchens. The work ranged from the semi-abstract (Hitchens, Richards) to the radically non-representational paintings of Moynihan which affirmed the material qualities of pigment in a manner prophetic of later abstraction. Though diverse, the artists were united in their rejection of the geometric style which dominated international abstraction at the time.

Objet trouvé see FOUND OBJECT

Obregon, Alejandro born 1920
Colombian painter, a leading exponent of ABSTRACT EXPRESSIONISM in his country. His techniques resemble that of New York Action Painting but his emphasis on the actual paint and deep sonorous colours recall the Paris TACHISTES, especially Soulages. Obregon adds a narrative element drawn from the Colombian setting, its flora and fauna as well as its contrasting geographical features (*The birth of the Andes*, 1965, New York, David Rockefeller coll.).

O'Brien, Lucius Richard 1832–99
Canadian painter of landscapes in oils and watercolours. He was principally active in Ontario, but visited the Rocky Mountains in 1882 and returned to paint a series of western Canadian landscapes for the Canadian Pacific Railway. His style was influenced by Bierstadt's Luminism, also practised in Montreal by Jacobi. *Sunrise on the Saguenay* (1880, Ottawa, NG of Canada) is notable for its heroic scale and the use of light to introduce a spiritual element.

Obrist, Hermann 1863–1927
Swiss sculptor, designer and naturalist. He was a leading exponent of Art Nouveau, and his experiments in abstract ornament and colour had a profound influence on the future leaders of abstraction. Perhaps his most famous design is the embroidered *Whiplash* (1895, Munich, Stadtmuseum) in gold on pale turquoise. Its calligraphic and natural forms blend to represent a cyclamen. His sculpture had some influence on the Futurist work of Boccioni.

Oceanic art
The art of Australia and the Pacific islands east of Indonesia. This area can be divided into four major cultural and artistic regions: Melanesia (including New Guinea); Polynesia; Micronesia; and Australia. All Oceanic peoples originally employed a simple non-metal technology to produce a wide variety of art forms, usually for decorative or religious purposes. See vol. 2 pp. 22–23

Ochtervelt, Jacob 1634–82
Dutch genre painter, born and mainly active in Rotterdam. According to Houbracken he was a pupil of the landscape painter Berchem (at the same time as de Hoogh), but his paintings are almost all upper-class interior scenes, in which field he was Rotterdam's leading specialist. Ochtervelt's figures, often shown making music, are slender and elegant, and sometimes of a rather overrefined fragility. His colour sense is very delicate, and like Terborch he had consummate skill in the rendering of fine materials (*The music lesson*, c.1670, Birmingham, City Art Gallery).

O'Conor, Roderick 1860–1940
Irish painter who worked principally in France. He was influenced by the work of van Gogh and met Gauguin in Pont-Aven. His paintings, such as *Field of corn, Pont-Aven* (1892, Belfast, Ulster Museum) are characterized by heavy diagonal striations of bold colour.

Oelze, Richard born 1900
German painter, a student at the Bauhaus under Itten (1921–25). His early works, still lifes of everyday utensils and objects, are in the dry, emotionless manner of MAGIC REALISM. From 1932 to 1936 he lived in Paris and was involved with the Surrealist movement. He painted ghost-like figures and faces

and fantastic landscapes with incongruously placed crowds (*Expectation*, 1935–36, New York, MOMA). From 1946 his fantasies became more macabre and abstract (*Neuland*, 1959, Hanover, Niedersächsische Landesgalerie).

O'Gorman, Juan born 1905
Mexican nationalist painter and architect. His reputation as an easel-painter was established long before his first involvement with murals in 1937, when he executed *Man's conquest of the air* at the International Airport in Mexico City. His *History of Michoacan*, 1942, in the apse of the old church of San Augustin, Patzcuaro, is an outstanding example of narrative symbolism in mural painting, rich in detail and in colour, in the generation after Rivera, Orozco and Siqueiros, and his mural mosaic on all four sides of the University Central Library, Mexico City (1951–53) made a sensation. As an architect he was an enthusiastic exponent of Functionalism and admired Le Corbusier.

Oil-paint
Paint produced by mixing pigment and a medium of drying oils. Because it can be used to create a wide variety of effects, from enamel smoothness to the most violently expressive impasto (it is slower drying than water-based paints), it has been the dominant medium in European painting from the late Renaissance until the present day. Its origins cannot be precisely dated, but there is evidence of the use of oil as a paint base as well as a varnish in the 12th century. Netherlandish painters, including the van Eycks, developed its use during the 15th century as a glazing medium over tempera, and it was well established as a medium in its own right by the 16th century. Since the 19th century oil-paint has been produced commercially in metal tubes. Such changes allowed artists to work more freely in the open air, and new paints also allowed a greater range of effects. See vol. 1 pp. 144–151

Okada, Kenzo born 1902
Japanese painter. He studied in Tokyo and Paris before settling in the USA (1950). There he developed a personal style of semi-abstract painting in which distinctive Japanese images, such as curved roofs and fans, are painted hazily in delicate pastel colours (*Dynasty*, 1956, Buffalo, Albright-Knox).

O'Keeffe, Georgia born 1887
American painter, a pioneer of modernism in her country. From 1912 to 1918 she worked at intervals in Texas, where she was deeply impressed by the landscape. In 1915 she began a series of innovatory drawings and watercolours which approach abstraction while suggesting natural forms in a sparse, emblematic style. Stieglitz began to exhibit these at the 291 Gallery and she married him in 1924. Her mature style crystallized in the 1920s; almost abstract images, often of a luminous emptiness suggesting landscape, alternated with more representational motifs, especially flowers (*Black iris*, 1926, New York, Metropolitan). Her cityscapes of New York have affinities with Precisionism. Her work reveals an austere sense of design allied to a lyrical handling of arid and luscious tones. See vol. 3 p. 210

Okyo, Maruyama 1733–95
Japanese painter. Okyo was taught by a KANO master, and was unusual in that he came from peasant stock. He lived in dire poverty until he was discovered by the Kyoto aristocracy, then learned to read

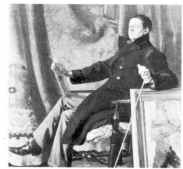
Nicholson, William: Portrait by Augustus John, 1909. Cambridge, Fitzwilliam (Mansell)

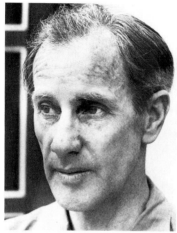
Nolan: Photograph by Dominic/Camera Press

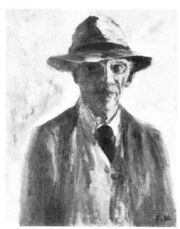
Nolde: Self-portrait, 1947. Seebüll, Nolde Foundation

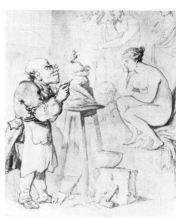
Nollekens: *Preparations for the Academy—Joseph Nollekens and his Venus* by Rowlandson, c.1800 (Courtauld Institute)

and write and studied the Chinese and Japanese masters (as well as some Western models, examples having filtered in from Nagasaki). His style, an eclectic mixture of Chinese and Japanese modes and naturalism, became very popular; the Emperor commissioned work from him but he turned down a permanent post. He finally founded his own school of painting, based on his belief: "If a shape is correctly copied, the painting will come alive", and any aspiring painter wishing to train in sketching from nature came to the Maruyama school. One of Okyo's paintings is designated a National Treasure of Japan: *Pine trees in the snow* (Tokyo, Mitsu coll.).

Oldenburg, Claes born 1929
American sculptor, born in Sweden. Along with Kaprow, Oldenburg was a leading participant in HAPPENINGS from 1960 to 1965. With the large *Dual hamburger* (1962, New York, MOMA) he was hailed as one of the founders of POP art. This work became the centrepiece of a wider array of painted plaster food and other commodities offered for sale at his New York shop, "The store". Giant foodstuffs, soft versions of normally hard objects such as typewriters and bathroom appliances, enormous metal and soft plastic cigarette butts are disturbing but comical contradictions of the nature of ordinary things. His use of shiny vinyl, rough-painted plaster and other materials reveals a delight in sensual values. He also conceives fantastic public monuments such as the unexecuted, colossal *Good humour bar* to span New York's Park Avenue (1965). See vol. 1 p. *193*; vol. 3 pp. **239, 242**

Old Kingdom 2686–2181 BC
Art of the first period of Egyptian unification. Near the capital of MEMPHIS at the royal cemetery of Saqqara the first developments of the unique Egyptian tomb art and architecture began. The stone Step Pyramid of Djoser (3rd Dynasty) anticipated the appearance of the first true pyramid, at Meidum (4th Dynasty), which was followed by the Great Pyramids at Giza north of Memphis. Fine low reliefs were carved on the walls of corridors beneath the Step Pyramid and on wooden panels from the brick tomb of Hesy-ra (Cairo, Egyptian Museum), whence came the first known Old Kingdom paintings, representations of funerary furniture. Figures, in their horizontal registers, tend to be well-spaced and clearly depicted, if not always well proportioned in themselves or in relation to other figures. For tombs and temples numerous statues of kings, nobles and servants were produced, ranging from life-size (the limestone statue of King Djoser, for instance, Cairo Museum) to tiny. In the 4th, 5th and 6th Dynasties all tombs of nobles and temples of kings were decorated with painted low reliefs. Although Old Kingdom styles and subject matter were generally inspired by royal monuments, by the 5th Dynasty a distinct imagery for humbler citizens sometimes emerged, as in the tombs of Mereruka and Ti at Saqqara, which offer a remarkable variety of painted relief scenes of everyday life. The gradual collapse of the regime occasioned a decline in standards, revived only two centuries later in the MIDDLE KINGDOM. See vol. 2 pp. 24–25

Olitski, Jules born 1922
American COLOUR-FIELD painter, born in Russia. His family moved to America in 1923, and he studied in New York and Paris in the late 1940s and early 1950s. His works of the 1950s have thickly impastoed surfaces with pictorial incident occurring near the edge. In 1960 he began to make paintings stained with dye and by 1964 he had moved from an imagery of circles and concentric arcs to stained spreads of acrylic paint with drawing and gesture confined to the edge zone. Paintings executed with a spray-gun in 1965 display entire fields covered with colour particles, which appear to condense and dissolve. The edges again became emphasized with thickly drawn brush-strokes (*Pink alert*, 1966, Washington, Corcoran Gallery). Since the late 1960s he has occasionally made sculpture, both polychromed and in unpainted steel. See vol. 3 pp. **222–223**

Oliver, Isaac before 1568–1617
English miniaturist of French origin. The child of Huguenot refugees, he arrived in England in 1568, and became the pupil and then rival of Hilliard. His work, however, is broader in technique, with bold use of naturalistic shadow, and strong characterization. He is well represented in the Victoria and Albert Museum. His son **Peter** (*c.*1594–1647) was also a miniaturist. See vol. 2 p. **206**

Olivier, Ferdinand 1785–1841
German Romantic painter, a member of the Brotherhood of St Luke (the NAZARENES), though he never worked in Italy. Trained in Dessau, he and his brother, the painter **Friedrich Waldemar** Olivier (1790–1859), moved to Dresden, where they met Friedrich, and in 1811 to Vienna, where they met Koch and came into contact with the Brotherhood. Ferdinand painted and engraved seasonal nature themes, landscapes and city views (*Imaginary Salzburg landscape*, 1829, Dessau, Staatliche Galerie), executed in graceful contours and delicate colour. In 1830 he moved to Munich, where Cornelius arranged for him to become professor of art history at the academy.

Olmec art
Art of the earliest great civilization in Mesoamerica, *c.*1200–600 BC, centred in the southern coastal regions of the Gulf of Mexico. The Olmec possessed many of the features of later Mesoamerican cultures—a calendar system, ceremonial centres and massive pyramids. A distinctive feature of Olmec art is the representation of a part feline, part human figure, perhaps an important deity. Some of the finest examples of Pre-Columbian lapidary work are Olmec figurines, pendants and ceremonial objects, often carved in a blue jadeite. The Olmec were also adept at executing monumental sculpture, exemplified by massive lifelike stone heads. Other enigmatic features are the votive offerings such as giant jaguar masks of blocks of serpentine. Many Olmec stone monuments and finely executed cave-paintings have been found, each differing in iconography but often having jaguar-featured humans as motifs. The influence of Olmec art spread as far afield as Costa Rica. See vol. 2 p. 18

Olsen, John born 1928
Australian painter, who studied in Europe before returning to Sydney in 1960. His Abstract Expressionist style was based on the work of the COBRA group in Paris, and of the British Abstract Expressionist Davie. With a strong native sense of place he fuses a child-like primitivism with technical expertise. A lively calligraphy imposed on rich, colourful passages is characteristic, as are colloquial titles, such as the rollicking series of 1961, "*Journey into You Beaut country*" (*Journey no. 2*, Queensland Art Gallery). He also designs tapestries and in 1972 painted a mural for the Sydney Opera House.

Omega Workshops
Company formed in 1913 by Roger Fry in order to provide regular employment for young painters in the decorative arts. The work was concerned more with surface decoration than product design and was characteristically applied to existing manufactured objects. Fry intended Omega design to be expressive and non-utilitarian and the painted surfaces had a deliberately hand-made look. The work produced was theoretically anonymous so that prospective purchasers would not be influenced by the name attached. Artists employed included Duncan Grant, Vanessa Bell, Gaudier-Brzeska and Lewis, although the last-named quickly quarrelled with Fry. Never a financial success, the workshops were closed in 1919.

Onley, Toni born 1928
Canadian painter of lyrical landscapes, and a collagist, who with Kiyooka revitalized West Coast painting in the 1960s. In Vancouver from 1959, he produced freely abstracted contemplative landscape studies in watercolour. His white-on-white canvas collages are more innovative.

Onosato, Toshinobu born 1912
Japanese painter. His work before World War II was influenced by Picasso but during the War he was imprisoned in Siberia by the Russians, and after this he developed a more personal style. His principle motif is the circle, painted in a manner similar to some Op art. He composes his paintings from tiny rectangular coloured shapes arranged in an arabesque manner. *Four circles* (1960, Nagaoka, Museum of Contemporary Art) shows his interest in movement between foreground and background.

Op art
Type of abstract art which exploits the optical effects of pattern. It uses hard-edged black-and-white or coloured patterns which appear to vibrate and change their shape as the viewer watches them. Its most famous exponents are Victor Vasarély, Albers, Poons and Riley. Its predecessors include the "iridescent interpretations" of the Futurist Balla and some of the experiments of the Bauhaus painters in the 1920s. See vol. 3 p. 244

Opie, John 1761–1807
British portrait, history and genre painter. At the age of 20 he was launched in London society by an unscrupulous self-appointed agent as a supposedly untutored genius, "the Cornish Wonder". His early works do have a certain natural ruggedness, clothed in Rembrandtesque chiaroscuro, and his freshness won him great popularity. As his career advanced, however, his portraits tended to become repetitive and insipid. His rather stagey paintings for Boydell's Shakespeare Gallery were very popular in engravings and influential on, for example, Delaroche. See vol. 4 p. *75*

Oppenheim, Meret born 1913
Swiss artist, born in Berlin. She moved in 1932 to Paris, where she met Arp and Giacometti. In 1933 she exhibited her paintings and strange woodcuts with the Surrealists. She is best remembered for *Object* (1936, New York, MOMA) a fur-lined tea cup and saucer, which caused a stir when shown at the London Surrealist exhibition of 1936.

Orcagna (Andrea di Cione)
active 1343–68
Italian painter, sculptor and architect, the most important Florentine artist in the third quarter of the 14th century. The only painting certainly by him is the powerful altarpiece of *The Redeemer with the Madonna and saints* in the Strozzi Chapel of S. Maria Novella, 1354–57. Its forbidding and hieratic quality, denial of a sense of depth and brilliant colours are far removed from the humanity and naturalism of Giotto and his successors, and mark a reversion to Byzantine ideals. These, however, are expressed through Gothic forms and individual figures are strongly modelled. The surviving fragments of a colossal trilogy of *The triumph of Death*, *Last Judgment* and *Hell*, painted in fresco at an uncertain date in S. Croce, are also attributed to him. His most important work as a sculptor is the richly decorated Tabernacle in Orsanmichele (finished 1359), built to house Daddi's *Virgin enthroned*. Between 1358 and 1362 he was in charge of the works at Orvieto Cathedral, and also worked as an architectural adviser for Florence Cathedral. His two brothers, **Nardo** di Cione (active 1343/6–65/6) and **Jacopo** (active 1365–98), worked in his style. Nardo's main work is, perhaps, the series of frescos of *The Last Judgment*, *Hell* and *Paradise* (probably 1350s) in the same chapel of S. Maria Novella as Andrea's great altarpiece. Among the panel paintings given to him the finest is the wonderfully well-preserved triptych *Madonna and Child with saints* (*c.*1360, Washington, NG). Jacopo, who completed the St Matthew altarpiece (Florence, Uffizi) which Andrea left unfinished, was the least talented of the three. Attributions to him are often rejections from the oeuvre of his brothers. There is also a large group of anonymous paintings which can be described as Orcagnesque. See vol. 1 pp. *140–141*; vol. 2 p. **85**

Orchardson, Sir William Quiller
1835–1910
Scottish painter, who settled in London in 1862. He began with historical genre subjects but later specialized in scenes of psychological tension in upper-class married life. Using thin paint, muted colour, lamplight effects and subtle placing involving large empty spaces, he created a sense of drama and despair, as in his best-known works, the scenes illustrating *A Marriage of Convenience* (1883, Glasgow, City Art Gallery).

Orley, Bernard van *c.*1488–1541
Netherlandish painter and designer of stained glass and tapestries, born into a family of painters in Brussels. He became the leading painter of his day in Brussels and after 1518 he was the official court painter to the Regent, Margaret of Austria, painting mainly court portraits. His work was influenced by Dürer, whom he met in 1520, but owed a greater debt to Raphael. The latter's Sistine cartoons were in Brussels from 1516 to 1519 and left such a mark on Orley that he became known as the "Raphael of the Netherlands". His masterpiece is *The ordeal and patience of Job* (1521, Brussels, Musées Royaux des Beaux-Arts), a turbulent assemblage of Romanist elements with violent movement, bold foreshortenings and Italianate architecture, which shows that his understanding of Italian art was more superficial than that of his rival Gossaert. The latter part of his career was devoted to tapestry and stained-glass design, including windows for Brussels Cathedral. See vol. 2 p. **160**

Orozco, José Clemente
1883–1949

Mexican painter, one of the great muralists along with Diego Rivera and Siqueiros. Unlike these great contemporaries, Orozco was never an advocate for a political movement, but his devotion to the humanist mission of his painting was absolute throughout his career. Early paintings, genre scenes depicting street life, bars, cafés and brothels, express the misery of pre-Revolutionary Mexico, while his graphic work for various Revolutionary papers suggests Posada's influence in its crude expressive strength. He lived in the USA between 1917 and 1918, and undertook his first major murals in 1922, at the Mexico National Preparatory School, where Rivera was also employed. The didactic, monumental style which Orozco discovered there matured in the late 1920s, and was sustained in a number of mural decorations in the USA between 1927 and 1934—characteristically grand narrative scenes heavy with humanitarian symbolism. The Pomona College murals in California, those for Dartmouth College, New Hampshire and for the New School for Social Research, New York, were among his most important commissions. Following his return to Mexico he undertook a number of large mural schemes. In the 1940s he showed a growing interest in geometrical abstraction and Léger and developed the emotive power of his style to an extraordinary extreme, as in the magnificent *Hidalgo and Castillo* (heroic figures raising the torch of rebellions against Spain) in the Palace of Government, Guadalajara, completed in the last year of his life. See vol. 3 pp. **208–209**

Orpen, Sir William 1878–1931
British painter, born in Dublin, who had great success as a fashionable portraitist. His society portraits are painted in a vigorous style, but are rather flashy and superficial (like those of his friend Augustus John), and his skill in the depiction of character is better revealed in *Homage to Manet* (1910, Manchester, City Art Gallery), which shows a number of his artist friends with Manet's painting of Eva Gonzalès. The Imperial War Museum, London, has a collection of his paintings done as an official war artist, and his best-known work, *The signing of the Peace Treaty at Versailles*, 1919–20. Some show a different side to his talent in their grim objectivity and realism (*Dead Germans in a trench*, 1918).

Orphism or Orphic Cubism
Term coined by Apollinaire in 1912 to define a development of CUBISM found in the work of Delaunay, Léger, Picabia and Duchamp. Kupka, though not named by Apollinaire, was also part of the movement. Apollinaire described Orphism as "The art of painting new structures out of elements which have not been borrowed from the visual sphere, but have been created entirely by the artist himself, and been endowed by him with the fullness of reality. The works of the Orphic artist must simultaneously give a pure aesthetic pleasure, a structure which is self-evident, and a sublime meaning, that is, the subject. This is pure art." The term "Orphic", from the singer and poet of Greek mythology, reflected the concern of the artists involved to adapt the innovations of Cubism to a more lyrical purpose. They considered that Cubism was tied too closely to the object depicted and that it lacked colour. Inspired partly by Italian Futurism, they sought to express the "simultaneity of the modern world"

using dissonant juxtapositions of form and dynamic interactions of strong colour. Orphism was short-lived, but it had a strong influence on German artists such as Macke and Marc and on the Synchromists. See vol. 3 p. 151

Orsi, Lelio probably 1511–87
Italian Mannerist painter and architect, active mainly in his native Novellara and in nearby Reggio Emilia. His style was based on Correggio and Giulio Romano, and, after a visit to Rome in 1555, Michelangelo. Orsi worked extensively as a secular decorator, especially as a painter of façades, but almost all his work in this field has perished. His surviving paintings are cabinet pictures of religious scenes marked by considerable energy and an often bizarre expressive power (*The martyrdom of St Catherine*, c.1560, Modena, Galleria Estense).

Os family
Family of Dutch painters active in the later 18th and 19th centuries. The founder **Jan** van Os (1744–1808) and his son **Georgius Jacobus Johannes** (1782–1861) and daughter **Maria Magrita** (1780–1862) were still-life painters specializing in lavish flower- and fruit-paintings in the tradition of Jan van Huysum. Another son, **Pieter Gerardus** (1776–1839), was well-known in his time as a painter of cattle. He drew inspiration from Paulus Potter, as in his life-size *Cow with calf* (c.1810, The Hague, Gemeentemuseum). His son and pupil **Pieter Frederik** (1808–92) was Mauve's teacher.

Ossorio, Alfonso born 1916
American painter, born in the Philippines. He was involved in the first wave of Abstract Expressionism but proceeded in the 1950s and 1960s to create thickly impastoed canvases bristling with inset shells, stones and other materials. The emphasis on primitivist expression recalls Dubuffet. More recent works feature assemblages of incongruous objects (*Multiflora*, 1969, Brandeis University, Mass., Rose Art Museum).

Ostade, Adriaen van 1610–85
Dutch painter and engraver, mainly of genre scenes. He worked in Haarlem and he may have been the pupil of Frans Hals, but in his earlier works—usually somewhat vulgar, but brilliantly painted interior scenes of peasants carousing or brawling—Brouwer's influence is much more apparent. It is also possible to detect Rembrandt's influence in Ostade's chiaroscuro, but later his palette lightened and his subject matter became more respectable. Ostade was widely popular and much imitated, most notably by his brother and pupil **Isaac** (1621–49). Had he not died so young Isaac might have been the greater figure, for his genre scenes are a match for his brother's and he also painted excellent landscapes, in particular very fine winter scenes. Both brothers are well represented in the National Gallery, London. See vol. 2 pp. **226–227**

Otero, Alejandro born 1921
Venezuelan Constructivist painter, active in Paris as well as his native country. His early compositions, Cézannesque landscapes and Cubist still lifes, belong to the first flowering of modern art in Venezuela, and his transition from figurative to abstract painting may be seen in his *Cafeteras* painting (*Cafetera rosa*, 1947, Caracas, Galleria de Arte Nacional). In 1951 he moved into the field of optical art, and in 1955 began his most celebrated and influential series,

Coloritmos (Colour-rhythms)—vertical panels divided by parallel bands of changing colour.

Ottonian art
Medieval art in Germany under the Ottonian dynasty. Otto the Great (936–73) re-established the strong royal authority which had lapsed with the decline of the Carolingian Empire. He paved the way for an artistic revival fostered by several successors and by many remarkable churchmen, amongst them Bernward, Abbot of Hildesheim. The influence of the Carolingian heritage is manifest in the earliest Ottonian works, including the celebrated Gero Codex, painted before 976 (Darmstadt, Landesbibliothek). Its strong colours, use of gold and heavy majestic figures owed much to the tradition of the Carolingian Ada school. Archbishop Gero also commissioned the earliest surviving example of monumental sculpture in this period, the life-size Gero Crucifix in Cologne Cathedral. It is remarkably naturalistic in comparison with most contemporary figure sculpture, but with a sombre weightiness characteristic of Ottonian art. The essential features of Ottonian low-relief sculpture tend to be unnaturally squat figures, and simple, generally symmetrical composition. Although Ottonian churches afforded opportunities for architectural sculpture, the chief medium of Ottonian sculptors was metalwork and ivory for altar reliefs, book covers and devotional images. In manuscript painting in the 10th century an individual art appeared in the works of the **Master of the Registrum Gregorii** (manuscript in Trier, Stadtbibliothek, and Chantilly, Musée Condé). His clearly arranged compositions, painted in delicately shaded pastel colours, were profoundly influential. Late classical illumination influenced his miniatures. The Ottonian period saw the emergence of several important manuscript centres at Reichenau, Trier, Cologne and elsewhere. Byzantine influence on manuscript painting and sculpture was reinforced in the late 10th century by the marriage of Otto II (972–80) to the Byzantine Princess Theophanu. Ottonian art reached its climax in the reign of Henry II (1002–24), and proved to be an important influence on emerging Romanesque styles. See vol. 2 p. 69

Oudry, Jean-Baptiste 1686–1755
French painter. He painted a few portraits (Largillière was his teacher) and histories, but he is best known as a painter of royal hunts and still life, rivalled only by Desportes. His essentially decorative talent was well used at the Beauvais and Gobelins tapestry factories, where he was Director from 1726 and 1736 respectively. He published a treatise on painting in 1752. Many of his paintings are in the State Museum, Schwerin, and he is also well represented in the Wallace Collection, London, and the Louvre, Paris. See vol. 2 p. **244**

Ouwater, Albert van
active 2nd half of 15th century
Netherlandish painter. Only one documentary reference to him (in 1467) is known but van Mander considered him the founder of the Haarlem school of painting and said he was the master of Geertgen tot Sint Jans. Van Mander praised him particularly as a landscapist, but from his descriptions the only work which can be securely identified is a scene set within a church, *The Raising of Lazarus* (West Berlin, Staatliche Museen). With its slender unemotional

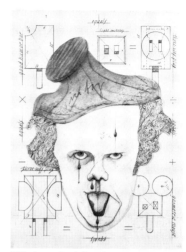

Oldenburg: *Symbolic self-portrait*, 1969. Stockholm, Moderna Museet

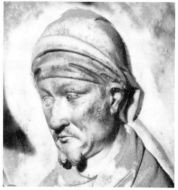

Orcagna: Self-portrait from *The Assumption of the Virgin*, c.1359. Florence, Orsanmichele

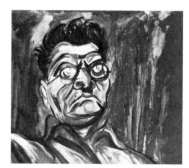

Orozco: Self-portrait, 1940. New York, MOMA

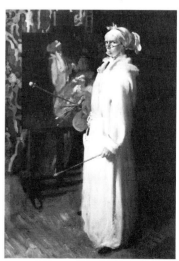

Orpen: Self-portrait, 1908. Newcastle upon Tyne, Laing Art Gallery

figures, this has affinities with the work of Dirk Bouts, also from Haarlem.

Overbeck, Friedrich Johann 1789–1869
German painter, one of the founders of the NAZARENES. He studied in Vienna and in 1810 moved to Rome, where with his fellow-Nazarenes he executed frescos at the Casa Bartholdy in Rome (1816). He was based in Italy for the rest of his life but made some short trips to Germany. Apart from some portraits, his output was almost exclusively of religious subjects (*The rose miracle of St Francis*, 1829, Assisi, Portiuncula Chapel). His consciously archaic and often rather insipid style was based on Perugino and Raphael, employing bright colours and very clear outlines. He exercised considerable influence on other high-minded painters such as Dyce and the Pre-Raphaelites. See vol. 3 p. **75**

Overpainting see UNDERPAINTING

Ozenfant, Amédée 1886–1966
French painter and writer on art, with Le Corbusier the founder of PURISM. He taught in Paris, London and New York, and his books *Modern Painting* (1925) and *Foundations of Modern Art* (1928) were widely read. See vol. 3 p. **179**

P

Paalen, Wolfgang 1907–59
Austrian/Mexican painter. During the 1930s he lived in Paris, where he was associated with the Surrealist and Abstraction-Création groups. In 1939 he moved to Mexico, where, in 1940, he organized an international Surrealist exhibition. His early works were hard-edge abstractions but his Surrealist works of the late 1930s dwelt upon strange semi-abstract forms inspired by biological shapes and painted in phosphorescent tints (*Untitled*, 1938, New York, MOMA). He committed suicide.

Pacheco, Francisco 1564–1654
Spanish painter, poet, scholar and writer on art, active mainly in Seville. He was a mediocre painter, but in sympathy with the new interest in naturalism and was a very able teacher; Velazquez, who became his son-in-law, and Cano were his most important pupils. Pacheco is best known for his book *The Art of Painting*, published in 1649 but prepared much earlier. This contains biographical as well as theoretical matter (including an account of Pacheco's meeting with El Greco in Toledo in 1611), and is the most important source for the study of Spanish art of the period. In 1618 Pacheco had become official art censor to the Inquisition, and his iconographical prescriptions were often followed with great exactness by Sevillian artists. Most of Pacheco's paintings are still in Seville; *The Immaculate Conception* in the cathedral (probably 1621) is one of his finest works.

Pacher, Michael active *c.*1465?–98
Austrian painter and sculptor, a citizen of Bruneck in the southern Tyrol between 1467 and 1496. A rapid development in style is suggested by the contrast between one of his earliest works, the altarpiece of Gries, near Bozen (1471–75), with its traditional, symmetrical arrangement, and the complex, magnificent altarpiece of St Wolfgang (completed 1481). The St Wolfgang altarpiece has the intricate traceried canopy and abundant decorative detail typical of the late Gothic tradition, but the carved, richly painted figures are more carefully co-ordinated in their architectural frame, and the play of drapery suffuses them with gentle movement. Pacher's painting style was extraordinarily advanced, notably in his *Four Doctors of the Church* (*c.*1483, Munich, Alte Pinakothek), showing effective manipulation of space and a good knowledge of Italian artists, particularly Mantegna. His colourful, dramatic style, exploiting the advances of Gerhaerts and also the drapery patterns of Master E.S., was highly influential in Austria and south Germany. See vol. 2 pp. **154, 158**

Pacherot, Jérôme 1463–*c.*1540
Italian sculptor, recruited with other artists by Charles VIII of France from Naples in 1495 and retained by Louis XII and Francis I. In 1503 he settled in Tours. He specialized in ornamental sculpture, and was an important figure in the spread of Renaissance decoration in France. His best-known work is the frame for Colombe's altar-relief of *St George* (1507–09, Paris, Louvre), the marble pilasters and cornice of which are decorated with arabesques of the greatest delicacy. As he was a maker of cannons, he presumably also worked in bronze.

Padovanino, Il (Alessandro Varotari) 1588–1648
Italian painter, born in Padua, more important as a teacher than for the quality of his work. He derived his style from Titian, and encouraged the many pupils he trained after settling in Venice in 1614 to return to 16th-century models, thus greatly influencing late 17th-century Venetian art. He painted religious and often unusual mythological subjects, such as *Penelope bringing the bow of Odysseus to her suitors* (*c.*1620?, Dublin, NG of Ireland).

Painterly
Term first used by the Swiss art historian Wölfflin in his *Principles of Art History* (1915) to denote an approach to form the opposite of linear. Thus painterly artists (Rembrandt, Titian, Velazquez) see in terms of areas of mass and light and shade. Botticelli, Bronzino and Holbein are among the least painterly of artists, and treat form in linear terms.

Painters Eleven
Group of Canadian non-objective artists who banded together in Toronto in 1953. Diverse in their styles, they were united by the need to promote their work in an unfavourable environment. Their exhibited work, influenced by Abstract Expressionism, was regarded as revolutionary. Once the barrier of distrust had been lifted, the group lost cohesion, and finally broke up in 1960. Its most spectacular personalities were Ronald and Town. A major collection of paintings by the group exists in the Robert McLaughlin Gallery, Oshawa.

Paionios late 5th century BC
Greek sculptor from Thrace. The damaged figure of his *Nike*, or *Winged Victory* (Olympia Museum), was recovered in excavation at Olympia in 1875. With its free movement and fluttering, transparent drapery it is a fine example of the sculptural style of the final decades of the 5th century. See vol. 2 p. **39**

Pajou, Augustin 1730–1809
French sculptor trained under Jean-Baptiste Lemoyne the Younger and in Rome, 1752–56. He was patronized by Mme du Barry, Louis XV's mistress, but his busts of her are less successful than those of friends, such as *Hubert Robert* (1789, Paris, Ecole des Beaux Arts). His large statue of *Jacques Bossuet* (1778–79, Paris, Institut de France) is one of the finest works commemorating great Frenchmen, but a royal commission for a pendant to Bouchardon's *Cupid* produced the insipid *Psyche abandoned* (*c.*1790, Paris, Louvre). Pajou's essentially decorative art is best seen in his reliefs at the Opera, Versailles (*c.*1768).

Palencia, Benjamin born 1902
Spanish painter. His vibrant landscapes are imbued with emotion expressed through his sensitive handling and use of colour. Recognition of his poetic Expressionism and individual development has made him a deeply respected and influential figure among artists working in Madrid.

Palermo 1943–77
West German artist (his pseudonym was taken from the Mafia gangster Blinky Palermo), a student of Joesph Beuys. He was interested in colour and how shapes of colour (for example a band going round the edge of a wall) modify architectural space. In a sense, he practised a new kind of mural painting, but it was one which had strong links with MINIMAL art.

Palette
Shaped board with a thumb-hole grip on which the painter arranges and mixes colours. The term also applies to the range of colours used by an artist, so that Leonardo may be said to have had a restricted palette whereas Monet painted with a rich palette.

Palette knife
A flexible spatulate blade fixed in a wooden handle. It is used for mixing oil- or similar paint on the palette, scraping it off canvases, or applying impasto.

Palizzi brothers
Italian painters, active in the 19th century. Of four brothers, all of whom studied in Naples, **Filippo** (1819–99) and **Giuseppe** (1812–88) are the best-known. They specialized in naturalistic genre, landscape and animal paintings. Giuseppe moved to Paris in 1814 and was influenced by the Barbizon school, while Filippo remained in Italy (though he visited Paris) and became Director of the Naples Academy, 1878–80, and President after 1891. He encouraged young artists to study nature, and was recognized as the master of Neapolitan Realism. *Landscape after the rain* (1869, Rome, Galleria Nazionale d'Arte Moderna) is typical of his gentle poetry.

Palma, Jacopo (called Palma Giovane) 1544–1628
Venetian painter, the great-nephew of Palma Vecchio. He probably trained with Titian, and completed the master's great *Pietà* (Venice, Accademia), intended for his tomb and left unfinished at his death. Apart from a period of about three years in Rome in the 1560s, Palma spent all his career in Venice. In the redecoration of the Doge's Palace after the 1577 fire, he worked alongside Tintoretto, and after the latter's death in 1594 was left the dominant personality in Venetian painting. His style was an amalgam of the late Titian and Tintoretto, in which soft atmosphere was sometimes overlaid by violent chiaroscuro (*Venus enthroned*, Venice, Doge's Palace). He was very prolific; many churches in Venice have examples of his work, and he received commissions from various parts of Italy and abroad.

Palma Vecchio (Jacomo Negreti) *c.*1480–1528
Italian painter, active in Venice from 1510, when he is first documented. He had adopted the name Palma by 1513. Nothing is known for certain of his early years (Vasari's statement that he died aged 48 is the only evidence for his birthdate), and no paintings given to him are indisputably signed or documented. However, the traditional attribution to him of a group of richly sensuous paintings, similar in style to early Titian, is never contested. He is particularly noted for his superbly voluptuous blonde-haired women, who are found not only in portraits or allegories, but also as saints in his religious works. *"La Bella"* (Lugano, Thyssen coll.) is perhaps his best known work. See vol. 2 p. **146**

Palmer, Erastus Dow 1817–1904
The most important American sculptor of the 19th century to work in his native country rather than in Europe. Self-taught, he began by carving shell cameos before turning to marble. His best-known work is *The white captive* (1859, New York, Metropolitan), inspired by Powers' *Greek slave*, and showing a young girl captured by Red Indians. The smooth generalized forms of her naked body are typically Neoclassical, but the head is an arresting portrait of the sculptor's daughter.

Palmer, Samuel 1805–81
English painter and etcher of pastoral scenes. In 1822 he met John Linnell, Mulready, Stothard and Varley and was introduced to Blake. Influenced by Blake's illustrations to Virgil's *Eclogues* and responding fully to his mystical teaching, he settled in Shoreham, Kent, and produced landscapes such as *A hilly scene* (*c.*1826, London, Tate), inspired with a pantheistic vision of fecundity. His emotional directness and use of spatial elision to condense his designs placed him outside the accepted traditions and not until Surrealism popularized the hallucinatory was the visionary nature of his art fully appreciated. His later work lacks the intensity of his "Shoreham period", which lasted only seven years. See vol. 3 p. **63**

Palomino, Antonio 1655–1726
Spanish painter and writer. Until 1680 he lived mostly in Cordoba, where he studied briefly under Valdés Leal; thereafter he was principally based in Madrid, becoming court painter in 1688 to Charles II. He painted frescos in different parts of Spain, and numerous easel-pictures in a style largely indebted to Coello and Carreño, but he is now chiefly remembered for his writings on art. His collection of biographies, both of leading Spanish painters and of foreigners who worked in Spain, is a valuable source for the history of Spanish painting.

Pane, Gina born 1939
Italian BODY artist, living in Paris since 1960. She abandoned conventional art for Body work in 1968. Her performances, often recorded on video, usually involve discomfort, sometimes physical injury, and incorporate a symbolism of fire, milk, blood and pain. An example of her work is *Nourishment: slow and difficult absorption of 600 grammes of minced meat which disturb the usual digestive operations*, performed in Paris in 1971, in which she forced herself continuously to regurgitate the meat. See vol. 3 p. **243**

Panel painting

A painting on a rigid support of wood, metal or, more commonly now, board. Though canvas, parchment and leather were sometimes stretched over wood in the Middle Ages, most panel paintings were executed on smooth grounds of size and gesso applied to a wide range of woods, which had been well seasoned to reduce the risk of warping and splitting. Panels were the most popular supports for easel-paintings until canvas became predominant during the 16th century. For large works, panels could be made up from several pieces of wood glued together with casein.

Panini (Pannini), Giovanni Paolo
*c.*1692–1765

Italian view-painter and decorator. He was born in Piacenza and around 1755 settled in Rome. There he studied initially as a figure painter but soon specialized exclusively in perspective decorations and view-paintings. The latter were of various sorts—view of ruins, sometimes populated with biblical figures, *capricci* and scenes of contemporary Rome, notably interior views of St Peter's (London, NG, and Washington, NG). He taught perspective at the French academy in Rome and had other strong links with France; accordingly he influenced French view-painters as well as Canaletto and other Italians. See vol. 2 p. **254**

Panofsky, Erwin 1892–1968

German art historian, professor at the universities of Hamburg and New York, and from 1935 at the Institute for Advanced Study, Princeton. He devoted himself principally to medieval and Renaissance art, and is particularly noted for his great erudition in matters of iconology. His many books include *Albrecht Dürer* (1943), *Early Netherlandish Painting* (1953) and *Meaning in the Visual Arts* (1955). Kenneth Clark called him "unquestionably the greatest art historian of his time".

Pan Painter, active *c.*480–450 BC

Greek RED-FIGURE vase-painter from Athens, perhaps the most accomplished of the early Classical period. He is named after a scene of Pan pursuing a shepherd boy on a bell *krater* in Boston. His decorative scheme is generally limited to two or at most three figures on each side of a vase, elegantly composed in relation to one another. His drawing is delicate and fluent.

Pantoja de la Cruz, Juan
*c.*1553–1608

Spanish painter, a pupil of Sánchez Coello, whom he followed in 1596 as court painter to Philip II, and later to Philip III. He continued the type of formal court portraiture created by Titian and developed in Spain by Mor and Sánchez Coello. He also painted religious works; examples of these and of his portraits are in the Prado, Madrid.

Paolo Veneziano active 1321–62

The most important Venetian painter of the 14th century, and the earliest named artist of that school whose work has survived in any quantity. In about 1345 he painted the cover for the Pala d'Oro (a celebrated altarpiece of Byzantine enamels) in S. Marco, perhaps the most significant state commission of its time. His characteristic products were large polyptychs, many of which were exported to the Venetian colonies of the Adriatic coasts. In his use of sumptuous materials and glowing colours he is closer to Byzantine artists than to his Italian contemporaries. His work was continued by his sons and collaborators, **Luca** and **Giovanni**. With Giovanni, Paolo signed his last dated work, *The coronation of the Virgin* (1358) in the Frick Collection, New York. His earliest dated work (1324, Washington, NG) shows the same subject.

Paolozzi, Eduardo born 1924

British sculptor and printmaker. In Paris in the late 1940s he discovered the legacy of Dada and Surrealism which was profoundly to influence his subsequent work. In particular a consistent scepticism about exclusive fine art values was manifested in his *Bunk* collages, which marked an acceptance of transatlantic commercial imagery. His sculptures of the 1950s, such as *St Sebastian no.2* (1957, New York, Guggenheim), were figures, heads or animals made from old machine parts cast in bronze, exuding an air of expressive dilapidation. His manner changed radically in the early 1960s, in some ways following the brighter, more optimistic, Pop tendencies which he had himself anticipated in his collages. Sculptures such as *City of the circle and the square* (1963–66, London, Tate) were colourful totems suggesting humanized machines. See vol. 1 p. *189*; vol. 3 p. **240**

Papiers collés

Term deriving from the French for "pasted paper" referring to a form of COLLAGE in which pieces of different kinds and colours of paper are incorporated into a painting or constitute the work itself. A Chinese invention, taken up as a popular pastime in the 10th century, it became a fine art in the hands of Braque and Picasso, who incorporated it in works of theirs from 1912—pieces of paper simulating chair-caning or wood-graining used to *trompe-l'oeil* effect. The best known *papiers collés* are those of Matisse's late years (*Memory of Océanie*, 1953, New York, MOMA).

Pareja, Juan de *c.*1610–*c.*1670

Spanish painter. He was of Moorish origin and is sometimes called El Esclavo, as he was thought to have been Velazquez's slave. He was in fact his pupil and assistant, and accompanied the master on his second visit to Italy (1649–51), where Velazquez immortalized him in the portrait now in the Metropolitan Museum, New York. Pareja is recorded as painting portraits in the manner of Velazquez, but his few remaining pictures are religious works. They are totally unlike Velazquez in style, being more animated and high-pitched emotionally, rather in the manner of Tintoretto (*Baptism of Christ*, *c.*1667, Huesca, Museo Provincial).

Paret y Alcázar, Luis 1746–99

After Goya the outstanding Spanish painter of his period. Born in Madrid, he studied under a mediocre French pupil of Boucher, and then in Italy, during which period he seems to have visited both Rome and Venice. Amorous involvements with members of the Spanish aristocracy led to banishment to Puerto Rico (1775–78) and thus the distinction of being the first major 18th-century European painter to have visited America. He was exceptionally learned, well-versed in humanist writings, and an expert on oriental languages. As an artist he showed a comparable versatility, ranging from religious, historical and mythological scenes to landscapes and still lifes. Perhaps his most appealing works today are his genre scenes with their Rococo charm and vivid technique reminiscent of Fragonard.

Paris, Matthew died 1259

English miniaturist and chronicler, head of the St Albans scriptorium from 1236 until his death. His one signed miniature, in his *History of the English* (London, BL), is a gentle and fluent tinted line-drawing, a self-portrait with the Virgin and Child. Amongst attributed work is a painting of an elephant (Cambridge, Corpus Christi College) from the life. It is remarkable for its fresh observation in contrast to his usual stylized approach. See vol. 2 p. **77**

Paris, school of

Term often used to refer to the large community of artists who made Paris the major centre of avantgarde artistic activity during the first half of the 20th century. The supremacy of Paris was unchallenged until the emergence of the New York school after World War II. A lively and competitive atmosphere and the presence of writers, critics and dealers willing to support innovation and experiment attracted to Paris not only French artists but also many major figures from abroad. Amongst the latter were the Spaniards Picasso, Gris and Miró, Modigliani from Italy, Brancusi from Romania, the Dutchmen Mondrian and Vantongerloo, Calder from the United States and a large group of Russians including Chagall, Sonia Delaunay-Terk, Archipenko, Pevsner, Kandinsky and Soutine. No single style unified the school of Paris but artists grouped themselves into a succession of movements, such as Fauvism, Cubism, Orphism, Purism, Abstraction-Création and Surrealism. These made an enormous impact upon the international development of modern art, but the school of Paris also nurtured tendencies of more localized significance, producing a tradition of humanist-realism which included Dunoyer de Segonzac and later Buffet and Balthus. See vol. 3 pp. 184–185

Park, David 1911–60

American painter, working mainly in San Francisco. In the late 1930s he came under the influence of Picasso and began to paint in an abstract manner. In 1950 he abandoned Abstract Expressionism for a return to the figure, yet retained his painterly brushwork and bright colour.

Parker, Raymond born 1922

American painter. He was a second generation Abstract Expressionist, but in the late 1950s turned to simpler, more disciplined shapes and muted colours. In these works several soft-edged rectangular blocks of opaque pigment float discretely over a field of uniform colour (*Untitled*, 1959, London, Tate). Recently his shapes have become harderedged and more organic in form.

Parler, Peter died 1399

German architect and sculptor, the best-known member of a distinguished family of masons. In 1353 he became architect of Prague's new Gothic cathedral, but he also ran a large and highly successful sculptural workshop, responsible for tombs and a series of celebrated portrait busts in the triforium of Prague Cathedral, including one of the Emperor and a *Self-portrait* of about 1378–79. His weighty, realistic style, recalling the art of Master Theoderic, was influential in Bohemia and southern Germany.

Parmigianino (Girolamo Francesco Maria Mazzola) 1503–40

Italian painter and etcher, one of the most elegant and distinctive of MANNERIST artists. He was born in Parma (from

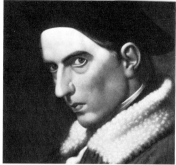

Overbeck: Self-portrait, 1844. Florence, Uffizi (G. Brogi)

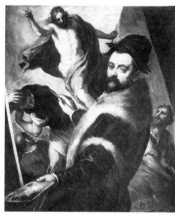

Palma Giovane: Self-portrait. Milan, Brera (Mansell)

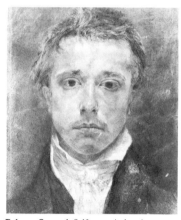

Palmer, Samuel: Self-portrait drawing, *c.*1828. Oxford, Ashmolean

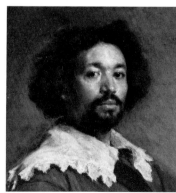

Pareja: Portrait by Velazquez, 1650. New York, Metropolitan

which he takes his nickname) and was very precocious, decorating two chapels in S. Giovanni Evangelista at the age of 19. They show the influence of Correggio, who had also recently worked in the church. In about 1523 Parmigianino moved to Rome, and his style became more powerful and graceful under the influence of Michelangelo and Raphael. *The vision of St Jerome* (1526–27, London, NG) is his masterpiece from this time, and with Pontormo's closely contemporary *Deposition* set a new standard in sophisticated expressiveness. After the Sack of Rome in 1527 Parmigianino moved to Bologna for four years, then returned to Parma. In 1531 he undertook to decorate a vault and apse in S. Maria della Steccata, but eventually failed to fulfil the contract, for which default he was imprisoned. The greatest work of his final period is *"The Madonna of the Long Neck"* (*c.*1535, Florence, Uffizi), a work of extraordinary grace and refinement. Apart from his religious works, he also made some of the most striking portraits of his time (two superb examples are in the Museo di Capodimonte, Naples) and painted a memorable mythological work, *Cupid carving his bow* (1535, Vienna, Kunsthistorisches Museum), in which the often scarcely veiled eroticism of his religious works is made more explicit. He was also one of the first Italian artists (perhaps the first) to practise etching, and through this and engravings after his work his style had wide influence, not least on the FONTAINEBLEAU school. See vol. 2 p. **165**

Parodi, Filippo 1630–1702
Italian BAROQUE sculptor, Genoa's first and greatest. He worked in a dynamic and expressive manner (tomb of Bishop Francesco Morosini, 1678, Venice, S. Nicola da Tolentino) reminiscent of Bernini, under whom he studied in Rome for six years (1655–61).

Parrhasios late 5th century BC
Greek painter, reputed by his contemporaries a master of line-drawing. Born in Ephesus, he lived and worked in Athens, where he depicted chiefly mythological subjects. See vol. 2 p. 44

Parri Spinelli 1387–1453
Italian painter, born in Arezzo, the son and pupil of Spinello Aretino. He assisted his father on the frescos of the Palazzo Pubblico, Siena (1407–08). Most of his work, in an increasingly nervous mannered version of his father's late Gothic style, is still in Arezzo. His drawings (some in Florence, Uffizi) are rare survivals from the first half of the 15th century.

Parrocel, Charles 1688–1752
French painter of battles. He came from a long line of painters, and his father **Joseph** (1648–1704) had studied in Italy with Jacques Courtois and was also a noted battle painter. Charles spent a year in the cavalry, and his knowledge and love of horses is shown not only in his paintings of Louis XV's campaigns (examples in the Louvre, Paris, and at Versailles), but also in his illustrations for *The Cavalry School*, 1733.

Pars, William 1742–82
British landscape watercolourist, a pioneer of both Grecian and Alpine views. He visited Greece and Switzerland and also worked in Rome, where he died. His style tends to be precise, factual and rather dry, but he successfully conveyed the spaciousness and grandeur of the scenery he depicted. Many Grecian and Alpine watercolours are in the British Museum, London.

Pascin, Jules (Julius Pincas) 1885–1930
Bulgarian-born painter. He lived a Bohemian life, settling temporarily in Paris before becoming an American citizen. Taking his inspiration from Degas and Toulouse-Lautrec, though without their sharpness of observation, he concentrated on female figure studies in which delicacy of line and colour compensate for a certain repetitiveness. A typical example of his work is *Young girl seated* (*c.*1929, Paris, Musée d'Art Moderne). He was a tragically disturbed man who committed suicide. See vol. 3 p. **184**

Pasmore, Victor born 1908
British painter. He exhibited with the Objective Abstractionists in 1934 and in 1937 was a founder of the EUSTON ROAD school. However, he was less interested in documentary realism than in poetic, almost Whistlerian effects of light (*Evening, Hammersmith*, 1943, Ottawa, NG). Later in the decade the application of a pointillist technique pushed Pasmore closer to abstraction and by 1949, in a work such as *Triangular motif in pink and yellow* (Hull, Ferens Art Gallery), a painting with collage, he had abandoned the subject entirely. In the 1950s he was the leading British Constructivist, making geometric reliefs in painted wood and perspex. The austerity of this work is modified in later paintings which, though still entirely abstract, are freer and more organic in their forms. See vol. 3 p. **199**

Passarotti, Bartolommeo 1529–92
Italian painter, active mainly in his native Bologna, where he had a flourishing studio. His religious paintings and portraits are in an accomplished but generally unexceptional eclectic Mannerist style, and his fame now rests principally on a few genre scenes of butchers' shops (example, Rome, Galleria Nazionale). These fresh and lively works, inspired by northern painters such as Aertsen, broke free from Mannerist formulae, and in their naturalistic observation looked forward to the Carracci—Agostino was his pupil.

Pastel
Stick of colour made from powdered pigment and bound with gum. Though pastels are applied dry and their effect is instantly ascertainable they can be handled in the manner of paint by blending and mixing the colours on the paper. They can also be used for drawing. Their greatest drawback is that the dusty substance does not adhere closely to the paper and is liable to smudge and fall off, but this has to a great extent been overcome in recent years with the development of fixatives. French artists of the 18th century were brilliant users of the medium.

Pasternak, Leonid 1862–1945
Russian painter, a member of the WANDERERS. He taught at the Moscow College of Art, coming under attack from the more avantgarde students. Many traditional portraits and landscapes, in rather drab colours, are in Moscow (Tretyakov Gallery), but there are also examples of his work in London (Tate) and Oxford (Ashmolean Museum), where he lived after emigrating in 1920.

Pastiche
Forgery or imitation in which various parts from genuine works by a particular artist are copied and recombined so as to give the impression of being an original work by the artist.

Patch, Thomas 1725–82
British painter, best known for his caricature groups of Grand Tourists painted in Florence in the late 1750s and 1760s. Patch, who lived in Italy from 1747 to his death, also painted conventional landscapes and made etchings of frescos by Giotto and Masaccio.

Patel, Pierre *c.*1605–76 and **Pierre-Antoine** 1648–1707
French landscape painters, father and son, active mainly in Paris. Pierre's landscapes are very much in the manner of Claude, especially in their treatment of golden light (*River scene*, 1650s, Cambridge, Fitzwilliam Museum). Pierre-Antoine is fairly close to his father in style, but anticipated the Rococo decorative manner with his picturesque ruins.

Patenier, Joachim *c.*1485–1524
Netherlandish painter, a master in Antwerp by 1515. Dürer, whom he met, referred to him as "a good landscape painter" and his importance lies in his pioneering of landscape as an autonomous genre. Several of his paintings are signed, but none is dated. He developed his jutting crags, pointed promontories and fantastic plant-life from the example of Bosch, but shifted the emphasis away from the figures. In his versions of *The Flight into Egypt* (Antwerp, Musées Royaux des Beaux-Arts) and *St Christopher* (Madrid, Prado), for example, the religious theme was a mere pretext. He employed an archaic form of dual perspective, the scenic features being viewed from above, while his figures were shown head-on, without foreshortening. The latter were sometimes supplied by others, among them Massys and Cleve. See vol. 2 p. **161**

Pater, Jean-Baptiste 1695–1736
French painter of FÊTES GALANTES, the pupil of Watteau and, with Lancret, his principal imitator. Much of his work, painted with a mannered flickering touch, is so close to Watteau as to be pastiche, but his characterization was much less penetrating and his works often have a note of suggestiveness quite foreign to the master. Many of his paintings are in the Wallace Collection, London. See vol. 2 p. 239

Pater, Walter 1839–94
English essayist and critic, one of the chief spokesmen of AESTHETICISM. He established his reputation with *Studies in the History of the Renaissance* (1873), written in exquisitely polished, rather mannered prose, and including his celebrated description of the Mona Lisa—"She is older than the rocks among which she sits . . ." See vol. 1 pp. 14, 28

Pavlović-Barilli, Milena 1909–45
Yugoslav painter who also lived in France, Italy and, from 1939, in the USA. *Venus with lamp* (1938, Belgrade, Museum of Contemporary Art) epitomizes her poetic Surrealist dreamworld.

Peake, Robert *c.*1551–1619
English portrait painter. He was established as a fashionable portraitist by 1590, and on the accession of James I became principal painter to Prince Henry. He was appointed Serjeant Painter jointly with de Critz in 1607. A prolific artist in the linear English tradition, his works can often be identified by a distinctive form of inscription. He was assisted and succeeded by his son **William** (*c.*1580–1639).

Peale family
Family of American artists, active in the 18th and 19th centuries. The founder and most important member was **Charles Willson** Peale (1741–1827). He studied briefly with John Hesselius and then in London with West (1767–69). In 1775 he settled in Philadelphia, becoming the leading portraitist in the colonies, working in a dignified Neoclassical style. He was active in the American Revolution, and in 1784 opened a portrait gallery of Revolutionary heroes which later expanded into a natural history museum. Peale celebrated the prize exhibit, the skeleton of the first mastodon found in America, in *The exhumation of the mastodon* (1806, Baltimore, Peale Museum). He married three times and had 17 children, several named after artists. Five became painters. **Raphaelle** (1774–1825), **Rembrandt** (1778–1860) and **Titian Ramsay** (1799–1885) were the most distinguished. Raphaelle was one of America's finest still-life painters. His masterpiece is *After the bath* (1823, Kansas City, Nelson Gallery—Atkins Museum), a brilliant and witty piece of *trompe l'oeil* painting (see vol. 1 p. 75). Rembrandt mainly painted portraits, including several of George Washington, but also achieved fame with his huge moralizing allegory *The court of Death* (1821, Detroit Institute of Arts). Titian Ramsay was a naturalist and animal artist. Charles Willson's brother **James** (1749–1831) was also a painter, mainly of still lifes and portraits, as were his son and four daughters.

Pearlstein, Philip born 1924
American painter associated with the SUPERREALIST trends of the 1960s and 1970s. His preoccupation with volume and mass—early expressed in densely painted images of craggy mountains—resulted in an illusionistic technique notable for its powerful sculptural effects. His subject is the nude figure, singly or in pairs. The sitters are treated more as still-life objects than as living beings. Such brutally objective works as *Seated nude on a green drape* (1969, New York, Whitney) show his use of high intensity lights, his predilection for oblique angles of view and his tendency to crop heads and other parts of the anatomy. See vol. 3 p. **252**

Pechstein, Max 1881–1955
German painter. A founder-member of Die BRUCKE, he was the first of the group to move to Berlin, where he helped to found the Neue Sezession in 1910 and later the NOVEMBERGRUPPE. His early works show the influence of Post-Impressionism, especially van Gogh, though expressiveness is heightened by the use of unnaturalistic colours (*River landscape*, *c.*1907, Essen, Folkwang Museum). From 1909 on his forms became simplified, with large colour patches contained by expressive contours (*Portrait in red*, 1909, Darmstadt, Hessisches Landesmuseum). After a visit to the Caroline Islands in 1914 his work showed an increased interest in primitive, exotic elements. After World War I his style became softer and more decorative. See vol. 3 pp. **134–135**

Pedersen, Carl-Henning born 1913
Danish self-taught painter, influenced by Klee and Nolde. He was originally an abstract artist but now paints pictorial visions where primitive figures are combined with magic animal forms. In this and in his use of vivid colours he reveals concerns in common with other artists of CoBrA, of which he was a founder-

member (*Red boat*, 1948, Åalborg, Nordjyllands Kunstmuseum).

Peel, Paul 1860–92
Canadian genre painter. He studied in Paris and eventually settled there, but he exhibited regularly in Canada. His association with Gérôme and others influenced his later genre scenes, for which he attained a considerable reputation. Works such as *Reading the future* (1883, Vancouver Art Gallery) were very popular for their self-conscious sweetness.

Peeters, Josef 1895–1960
Belgian painter. His early work was influenced by Futurism but he became known for his geometric abstractions, painted after 1919. He was a vociferous advocate of contemporary art. He stopped painting in 1927 but resumed his abstract work in 1956.

Peeters family
Family of Flemish painters. The most important was **Bonaventura the Elder** (1614–52), the leading painter of seascapes in 17th-century Flanders, where the genre was much rarer than in Holland. He worked in a style similar to that of Simon de Vlieger, and is well represented in the National Maritime Museum, Greenwich. He also painted landscapes, and added figures to the works of other artists, for example Neefs. His brothers **Gillis** (1612–53) and **Jan** (1624–80) painted mainly landscapes and seascapes respectively, and Gillis was the father of **Bonaventura the Younger** (1648–1702), another marine painter. **Catharina** (1615–76), the sister of Bonaventura the Elder, painted seascapes and still lifes; she is sometimes confused with **Clara Peeters** (1594–after 1657?), a distinguished Antwerp still-life painter but no relation.

Pelaez, Amelia born 1897
Cuban painter. She studied in New York, 1924–25, and from 1927 to 1934 in Paris, where she encountered the art of Picasso and Braque and worked under the Russian Constructivist and set designer Alexandra Exter. From then on her work adhered to certain Constructivist principles, later adapted to the subjects and colouring of the Caribbean. Employing a system of broken patches of colour and webs of lines reminiscent of stained glass, she developed a decorative style which is reminiscent of Matisse and Braque (*Still life in red*, 1938, New York, MOMA).

Pelham, Peter 1697–1751
British-born American portrait painter and mezzotint engraver. He migrated to Boston in 1726, and his mezzotint of *Rev. Cotton Mather* (1727) was the first to be produced in America. Pelham's original painting on which it is based is in the American Antiquarian Society at Worcester, Mass. His collection of engravings of European works was an important source for Boston artists, not least Copley, whose widowed mother he married in 1748.

Pellegrini, Giovanni Antonio 1675–1741
Italian artist, a prolific and slap-dash Venetian decorator of the early 18th cetury, who worked in Austria, England, Holland, Germany and France. He was brought to England in 1708 by Charles Montagu, later Duke of Manchester, for whose country seat at Kimbolton he painted perhaps his most attractive decorations. In France, which he visited in 1720 with his sister-in-law, Rosalba Carriera, he executed an enor-

mous ceiling fresco in the Banque Royale in Paris; this met with a largely negative critical response, and was shortly afterwards destroyed. See vol. 2 p. 235

Pellizza da Volpedo, Giuseppe 1868–1907
Italian painter of portraits, landscapes and works reflecting his social commitment. One of the most rigorous of Italian DIVISIONISTS, he generally applied a myriad of pure colours with tiny brushstrokes on to a pale ground. His *magnum opus* is *The fourth estate* (1901, Milan, Galleria d'Arte Moderna), evolved over eight years and depicting the inexorable advance of the working classes towards social justice. At the same time he was painting Symbolist works such as *The mirror of life* (1896–98, Turin, Galleria d'Arte Moderna). After 1901 he concentrated on landscapes and innovatory studies of light (*Sun*, 1903–04, Rome, Galleria Nazionale d'Arte Moderna).

Pencz, Georg (Jorg Bencz)
c.1500–50
German painter and engraver. He worked at first in Nuremberg under Dürer, painting murals in the Town Hall after the latter's designs. In 1525 he and the Beham brothers were expelled for their extreme Protestant views. Later he worked for the Duke of Prussia. His engravings, like the Behams', were inspired by Dürer, but also influenced by Italian Mannerism, like his painted mythologies and portraits (*Jorg Herz*, 1545, Karlsruhe, Kunsthalle).

Penni, Giovanni Francesco
c.1496–c.1528
Florentine painter active mostly in Rome, where with Giulio Romano he was Raphael's principal assistant. He is said to have specialized in decorative brocades, backgrounds and architectural settings, and to have been responsible for much of the work on Raphael's tapestry cartoons (1515–16, London, V&A), particularly the borders. Numerous drawings from Raphael's shop have been attributed to him.

Penthesileia Painter
active c.465–440 BC
Greek vase-painter from Athens, mainly in RED-FIGURE, though some white-ground works are known. More than 150 vases have been attributed to him, mainly cups, among which is his masterpiece, and the vase after which he was named, showing the slaughter of Penthesileia by Achilles (Munich, Staatliche Antikensammlungen). His typical works depict everyday scenes, youths conversing or in the wrestling yard, drawn in an easy economical line, but with a good sense of interaction between the figures. His mythological scenes, and especially *Penthesileia*, with its large struggling figures filling most of the ground, have a force and a sense of emotional encounter which some have related to the influence of contemporary tragedy. See vol. 2 p. 39

Pentimento
Italian word for repentance, used to refer to evidence of a painter's change of mind when areas of a picture which he has overpainted become visible through the fading with age of the overpaint.

Pereda, Antonio de c.1608–68
Spanish painter, active in Madrid. He painted a variety of subjects, but is now remembered mainly for his still lifes and moralizing allegories, the best-known of which is *"The Dream of Life"* (c.1655, Madrid, Academia de San Fernando),

This brilliant depiction of the vanity of worldy goods, appropriately painted with great sensuousness, inspired similar works by Valdés Leal.

Pereira, Irene Rice 1907–71
American abstract painter. Her involvement with mechanistic imagery during the 1930s led to technical experiments, especially with glass panels, and a vocabulary of sharp geometric forms allied to fine linear patterning (*White lines*, 1942, New York, MOMA). In the 1950s she interspersed her complex, usually rectilinear grids with loosely brushed textures evoking mysterious spatial effects.

Performance art see HAPPENING

Pergamene school
Name applied to a tradition of Hellenistic sculpture identified with the city of Pergamum in Asia Minor, which rose to prominence in the 3rd century BC under the Attalids. Works associated with the school can, in many ways, be seen as a culmination of the general trend of Hellenistic sculpture and are characterized by a virtuoso realism and an almost theatrical intensity of effect. Of these, an early group consists of a number of figures of *Dying Gauls*, Roman copies of bronzes dedicated by Attalos I (241–197), in which the emotions of weariness and despair are rendered with great pathos. In the frieze of the Great Altar of Zeus at Pergamum, built by Attalos' successor, Eumenes II (197–159), an extraordinary virtuosity in the representation of form and emotion is revealed in the images of struggle and pain. Associated with the style of the Pergamene school, though not of it, are a number of other works of the period, most notably the *Laocoön* (Vatican), signed by three sculptors from Rhodes, **Athenodoros**, **Hagesandros** and **Polydoros**. When it was rediscovered in 1506 it made a great impression on the artists of the time, notably Michelangelo, inspiring a new intensity in the rendering of emotion and movement. In 1957 several groups of Hellenistic sculptures were discovered in a cave at Sperlonga, near Naples, and there is reason to believe that they are by the sculptors of the Laocoön. These dramatic discoveries are now in the museum at Sperlonga. See vol. 2 p. 42

Perilli, Achille born 1927
Italian painter and theatre designer. He had close associations with Arp, Picabia and Pevsner in Paris in 1948, and during the 1950s he travelled extensively in Europe. His early work included gestural paintings related to TACHISME, and comic-strip compositions with linear figures on coloured zones. He developed large-scale versions of the comic-strip figures, concentrating on spatial problems, and produced splendid prints showing precise draughtsmanship.

Perino del Vaga (Piero Buonaccorsi)
1501–47
Florentine painter, the pupil of Ghirlandaio's son. As a youth he was employed by Raphael in the decoration of the Vatican Loggie. One of the principal followers of Raphael, he developed during the period up to 1527 a Mannerist style far more ornamental that his master's, and remarkable for its assertive grace and movement. After the Sack of Rome, 1527, he went to Genoa, where he decorated the Palazzo Doria, and until the late 1530s he divided his time between there and Pisa. His last years were spent in the service of Pope Paul III; he executed, among other important large-

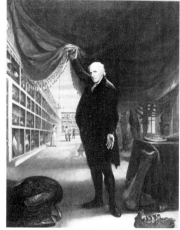

Peale, Charles Willson: *The artist in his museum*, 1822. Pennsylvania Academy of the Fine Arts, J. and S. Harrison coll.

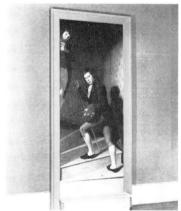

Peale family: *Staircase group*. Titian I (above) and Raphaelle (below) by Charles Willson Peale, 1795. Philadelphia Museum

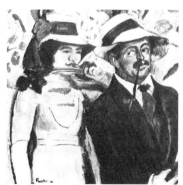

Pechstein: *Self-portrait with Lotte*, 1910. Cologne, Private coll.

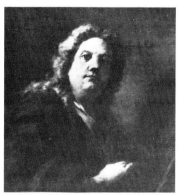

Pellegrini: Self-portrait, 1716–17. Florence, Uffizi

scale commissions, the monochrome paintings below Raphael's frescos in the *Stanza della Segnatura* and, in the Castel S. Angelo, the opulent decoration of the Sala Paolina with its frescos of *The deeds of Alexander the Great*.

Permeke, Constant 1886–1952
Belgian painter and sculptor. His early work moved from Impressionism to a form of expressive realism. After World War I, partly spent in England, he returned to Belgium and became one of the most important Belgian EXPRESSIONISTS. His subjects were principally of peasant life, fishermen and sailors with their women and he treated them in a simple, monumental style in dark sombre colours (*The fiancés*, 1923, Brussels, Musée d'Art Moderne). His concern with plasticity led him to create figurative sculptures in 1935–36. See vol. 3 p. **195**

Permoser, Balthasar 1651–1732
German Baroque sculptor in stone, wood and ivory. Together with the architect Pöppelmann, he was responsible for the uniquely sculptural architectural ensemble of the Zwinger in Dresden (begun 1711, badly damaged in World War II). Trained in Salzburg and Vienna, he spent 14 years in Italy, mostly in Florence. Invited to Dresden as court sculptor in 1689, he spent the rest of his life there, apart from occasional absences—for example in Vienna in 1721, to deliver *The apotheosis of Prince Eugene* (Vienna, Osterreichische Barockgalerie). His sculpture is noteworthy for its painterly complexity and vigour.

Perov, Vassily Grigorievich 1833–82
Russian painter. He studied in Arzamass and later in Moscow. In the 1860s he became known for his tragic scenes of peasant life (*Easter procession*, 1861; *Funeral of a peasant*, 1865; *Last inn near the town gate*, 1868, all Moscow, Tretyakov Gallery). In 1870, with Kramskoy, he founded the society for travelling art exhibitions (WANDERERS), and his strongly critical paintings became synonymous with the movement. Some of his later works are trivial anecdotes, but he remained an excellent portraitist (*Fyodor Dostoevsky*, 1872, Moscow, Tretyakov Gallery).

Perréal, Jean (called Jean de Paris) c.1455–1530
French painter and architect. By 1483 he was in the service of the city of Lyons, where he carried out decorations for the entry of Charles of Bourbon. In about 1530 he moved to Paris. He accompanied Charles VIII to Naples and returned to Italy with Louis XII, and met Leonardo. He worked on the tomb of Francis II of Brittany in Nantes Cathedral and in 1509–12 he was working on tombs at Brou for Margaret of Savoy. Perréal's mastery of naturalism is seen in his portrait of Louis XII (1512, Windsor, Royal coll.) and in portrait miniatures (examples, Paris, Louvre).

Perronneau, Jean-Baptiste 1715?–83
French portraitist and engraver. He was a pupil of Natoire, and is best known for his vigorous pastel portraits, though he also worked in oils. He eschewed the technical virtuosity of Maurice Quentin de La Tour, whose popularity in Paris led Perronneau to seek work in Italy, Holland and Russia. The charming *Girl with a kitten* (1745, London, NG) is a typical and popular work.

Perspective
The means by which an illusion of three-dimensional space is created on a flat picture surface. Scientific or geometric perspective, also known as Renaissance, optical or **linear** perspective, is based upon a fixed, central viewpoint. It relies on the optical illusion that parallel lines converge as they recede towards a **vanishing point** on a horizon line level with the viewer's eye, and that objects become smaller and closer together in the distance. Scientific perspective applied to a single form is known as foreshortening. Alberti in his *On Painting* (1435) was the first to formulate perspective rules for painters, based on the pioneering work of Brunelleschi in the early 1420s. Not in Alberti's system, but quite frequently in the Renaissance, two or more vanishing points rather than one may be introduced. Not all methods of perspective are based on optical laws. Some imply a moving rather than a fixed eye, though illusions of depth may still be created by overlapping of forms, vertical or oblique recession of parallel lines, and differences of scale. A further method of creating illusory depth, often used together with linear perspective, is **aerial** perspective, in which background tones or colours are made progressively paler or cooled towards blue to suggest intervening atmosphere. Many 20th-century artists have either abandoned perspective altogether or adopted non-scientific and inconsistent forms of perspective as being truer to everyday spatial experience than the fixed "window" view of Renaissance painting. See vol. 1 pp. 102–105

Perugino, Pietro (Pietro Vannucci) c.1445–1523
Italian painter, active mainly in Perugia, from which he takes his nickname, but also successfully in Florence, where he trained. His early life is obscure, but he probably trained in Verrocchio's workshop, and by 1481 he was well enough known to be commissioned to work on the frescos in the Sistine Chapel, Rome, alongside Botticelli, Ghirlandaio and others. Perugino's main contribution was *The giving of the Keys to St Peter*, a composition of majestic and ordered spaciousness. He painted several other frescos throughout his career, and was also a fine portraitist, but is best known for his altarpieces, peopled by gentle, graceful, rather sentimental figures. A fine example is *The Crucifixion with saints* (Washington, NG), probably painted at about the same time as his work in the Sistine Chapel. The figures are symmetrically arranged across the picture plane, the heads of the saints expressively tilted and foreshortened and the eyes deeply yearning. Even in his lifetime Perugino was criticized for the excessive sweetness of his work, but the clarity and harmony of his compositions, as well as his idealized physical types, had an overwhelming influence on the young Raphael, his pupil, and to this extent Perugino played an important role in the formation of the High Renaissance style. Though by about 1500 his style was obsolete in Florence, he continued to run a flourishing workshop in Perugia until his death. His work was a major inspiration for the Pre-Raphaelites. See vol. 2 p. **116**

Peruzzi, Baldassare 1481–1536
Sienese artist, active mainly in Rome. He is best known as one of the leading architects of his period, but he was also an accomplished painter, and in particular a master of elaborate perspective illusions, which reflected his interest in ancient stage design. His masterpiece in this vein is the Sala delle Prospettive (c.1515) in the Villa Farnesina, a building which he designed.

Pesellino, Francesco c.1422–57
Florentine painter. During his short career, he produced small panels in a delicate, courtly style, chiefly influenced by Filippo Lippi and Fra Angelico. Several *cassone* panels survive, for instance *The triumphs of Petrarch* (Boston, Isabella Stewart Gardner Museum), crowded with detail. His late work, such as the large altarpiece of *The Trinity and saints* (1455–57, London, NG), finished by Filippo Lippi, is more individual. His paintings of animals were especially appreciated, notably by the Medici.

Peto, John Frederick 1854–1907
American painter. He was almost totally neglected in his lifetime and for many years afterwards, but is now considered, with Harnett, the outstanding American still-life painter of the late 19th century. Harnett was his major inspiration, but Peto's works were more anecdotal and convey a distinctive sense of introspection and nostalgia (*The poor man's store*, 1885, Boston, MFA). In tonality and expressive use of light he is sometimes close to Eakins.

Petrović, Nadežda 1873–1915
Yugoslav painter. She studied in Belgrade and Munich, and on returning home in 1903 introduced modern European conceptions, from Impressionism to Expressionism, to the Serbian art world. She also worked as a critic and played an important role organizing exhibitions. Her *Shepherd* (c.1912, Belgrade, National Museum) shows her intensely Expressionistic use of colour.

Petrović, Zora 1894–1962
Yugoslav painter. After 1918 she taught in Belgrade, except for a period in Paris in the mid-1920s. Her characteristic Expressionistic style, reinterpreted through native motifs, developed gradually. She is best known for her massive female figures, nude or in peasant dress and increasingly distorted throughout her career (*Nude women*, 1956, Belgrade, Museum of Contemporary Art).

Petrov-Vodkin, Kuzma 1878–1939
Russian painter. He travelled in 1905 to Africa, where he was impressed by both the art and harsh quality of light. His early large-scale works boldly juxtapose colour contrasts (*Bathing of the red horse*, 1912, Moscow, Tretyakov Gallery). He evolved a system of painting based on the idea that space could be represented by means of a curved horizontal axis (*Boys playing*, Leningrad, Russian Museum). After the Revolution, he became a professor at the Leningrad Art Academy. His personal realistic style was widely imitated by the early Soviet painters.

Pettenkofen, August von 1822–89
Austrian painter of genre and military scenes. He studied in Vienna, 1834–40. In Hungary and France, where he came into contact with the Barbizon school, he observed peasant and gypsy life and this became his favourite subject matter. His early graphic BIEDERMEIER style changed to one with poetic and picturesque qualities and his use of colour became so free that he can be seen as an early precursor of Impressionism in Austria (*Austrian infantrymen crossing a ford*, 1851, Vienna, Osterreichische Galerie).

Pettie, John 1839–93
Scottish history and genre painter, who moved to London with Orchardson in 1862. His vigorous, naturalistic style well suited his narrative subjects. He specialized in scenes of the theatre, always imaginatively composed and expressively handled; a large selection is in the Mappin Art Gallery, Sheffield.

Pettoruti, Emilio 1892–1971
Argentine painter. He studied in Florence, Rome and Milan, 1912–21. As a close associate of Gris and Severini, he developed a more methodical treatment of CUBIST principles than either Picasso or Braque. In 1930, as Director of the Museum of Fine Art in La Plata, he showed current European art amid great controversy and drew a large following of young artists. His large *Harlequin* compositions, which were the climax of his middle period (*Harlequin with accordion*, 1928, Chile, Asuar, Pedro Gonzalez coll.), recall Picasso's *Three musicians*. His later work showed a logical and meticulous approach to formal design, reaching abstraction in the late 1940s.

Peverelli, Cesare born 1922
Italian painter. His earliest paintings are Cubist and Futurist in manner, but by 1960 he had met Matta and Bacon and adopted a style related to theirs. In his paintings he creates a disquieting space, sometimes peopled with beings seemingly without substance.

Pevsner, Antoine 1886–1962
French painter and sculptor of Russian origin, one of the major CONSTRUCTIVISTS. Trained first in Kiev and St Petersburg, he was influenced by Cubism during protracted stays in Paris (1911–14). He made his first sculptures during World War I, which he spent in Oslo with his brother Naum Gabo. In 1917 both returned to Russia, where they taught and published their *Realistic Manifesto* (1920). In conflict, however, with the social Productivist movement led by Tatlin and Rodchenko, they left for Berlin. Pevsner then moved in 1924 to Paris, where he transmitted Constructivist ideas to other artists and was a founder-member of the ABSTRACTION-CRÉATION group. His works employ modern materials such as sheet-metal and celluloid in figurative constructions (*Torso*, 1924–26, New York, MOMA) and, later, fully abstract, spiralling forms (*Development column*, 1942, MOMA). See vol. 3 p. **180**; vol. 4 p. 59

Pforr, Franz 1788–1812
German painter, a founder-member of the NAZARENES. He studied at the Vienna Academy, 1805–1810, and in 1810 moved to Rome with the other Nazarenes, settling at the monastery of San Isidoro. His many history paintings, such as *Rudolf of Hapsburg and the priest* (c.1809, Frankfurt, Städelsches Kunstinstitut), have a naïve and fairy-tale quality enhanced by detailed drawing and vivid colour and showing the influence of Uccello. See vol. 3 p. **75**

Phidias died c.432 BC
Greek sculptor from Athens, perhaps the most celebrated artist of antiquity. No original work is known to have survived, but some idea of his style can be gained from copies and descriptions, and from the surviving sculpture of the Parthenon. In antiquity he was most admired for his enormous cult statues of *Athene* inside the Parthenon, Athens, and of *Zeus* in his temple at Olympia. A number of copies of the *Athene* exist and the *Zeus* is known from representations on coins. Both were worked in gold and ivory, and their power seems to have

resided in their religious majesty rather than in the idealized naturalism which characterized the rest of his oeuvre. This is perhaps best seen in the copies of his life-size "*Lemnian Athene*" (a head of the statue in the Museo Civico Archaeologico, Bologna, is particularly sensitive). Phidias oversaw the sculptural decoration of the Parthenon, Athens, from 447 to 432 BC. This, the greatest sculptural undertaking of the Classical age, included a low-relief frieze 155 m (500 ft) long, 92 metopes in high relief, and free-standing groups on both pediments. Most of the remaining sculpture is in the British Museum, London. A team of sculptors was involved in the carving, and the quality is uneven, but as a whole the Parthenon sculpture represents one of the summits of ancient art, and is the greatest testimony to Phidias' genius. It reveals a development from the severe Classical style of the earlier Temple of Zeus at Olympia (in the metopes) to the supreme grace, calm authority and rich harmony (in the pediment sculptures) for which he was famed, and which is reflected in contemporary vase-painting and the sculpture of his successors. See vol. 2 pp. **38–39**

Phillip, John 1817–67
Scottish painter of genre scenes in the manner of Wilkie. He worked in Aberdeen, London and Spain. His paintings depicting scenes of Spanish life were executed in brilliant colours with great attention to detail (*La Gloria*, 1864, Edinburgh, NG of Scotland).

Phillips, Peter born 1939
British painter, an exponent of POP art. His early paintings such as *The entertainment machines* (1961, London, Tate) are derived from the style and imagery of pin-ball machines and juke-boxes. Later paintings have played paradoxically with the illusionistic techniques of commercial art: images painted with a photographic realism are fragmented into sections and reorganized across a grid.

Philoxenos of Eretria
active 2nd half of 4th century BC
Greek painter of the Hellenistic period. He is almost unanimously thought to have painted the original of the famous and dramatic Alexander mosaic from Pompeii (Naples, Museo Nazionale). See vol. 2 p. **44**

Phoenician art
Art of the Phoenician people, established perhaps from prehistoric times (c.5000 BC) in the north Levant. The independent Phoenician city states of the 1st millennium BC seem to have been full of artists and craftsmen of the highest calibre, but we have to rely mainly on literary evidence for our knowledge of their work. They were employed on contract throughout the Near East. David and Solomon hired men of Tyre to build the Palace and the Temple of Jerusalem; the latter was filled with bronze ritual apparatus and embellished with ivory panels overlaid with gold-leaf and inlaid with precious stones and glass pastes, all created by men of Tyre. In bronze, and especially in ivory, the craftsmen of Phoenicia were recognized as supreme. Motifs drawn from all over the Near East were given a new character, with the sphinx of Egypt transformed in Solomon's Temple into the winged cherubim guarding the Ark. Some pieces of Assyrian royal furniture in the *Nimrud Ivories* (Baghdad, Museum, and London, BM) were either taken to Assyria as booty, or made there by Phoenician slaves.

Photorealism see SUPERREALISM

Piazzetta, Giovanni Battista
1683–1754
Venetian painter of religious, historical and genre scenes, one of the most individual Italian artists of his period. In many ways he was an old-fashioned artist, who rejected the growing fashion for the colourful style of Veronese, persisting in the sombre dramatic manner characteristic of Venetian 17th-century painting. He painted almost exclusively in oils when fresco was becoming popular, though his frescoed ceiling in the chapel in SS. Giovanni e Paolo is a gem. He was meticulous in technique and serious in approach; his profundity is most fully revealed in his genre scenes, which have a haunting, enigmatic quality closer in spirit to Giorgione than to any Venetian artists of his own day. Although he painted extremely slowly ("He is a snail", wrote a Swedish visitor in 1736), Rococo tendencies are apparent in his later work, which has a freedom belying its laborious execution (*Isaac and Rebecca*, c.1740, Milan, Brera). See vol. 2 pp. **235, 244**

Picabia, Francis 1879–1953
French painter, who played an important role in disseminating avantgarde ideas amongst the proto-Dada circles in Zurich, the USA and Paris by means of the magazines he founded. At first successful as a late Impressionist, he changed course around 1911 after meeting Apollinaire and Duchamp and contributing to the intellectual theorizing of the SECTION D'OR group. In 1913 he visited New York for the opening of the Armory Show, and went again in 1915, when he collaborated with Stieglitz. The inspiration of Duchamp's mechanistic style and introspective, erotically charged imagery is apparent in, for example, the monumental *I see again in memory my dear Udnie* (1914, New York, MOMA). Also influential were the sardonic drawings and collages he executed during and after the war years. See vol. 3 p. **166**

Picasso, Pablo 1881–1973
Spanish painter, sculptor, graphic artist and stage designer, the most renowned artist of the 20th century, whose protean development encompassed the majority of its progressive movements. The son of a drawing-master, he was very precocious, and by the time of his first trip to Paris in 1900 had already shown a brilliant gift for draughtsmanship and absorbed a wide variety of influences. His "Blue" period of 1901–04, named from the dominant colour of his paintings, concentrated on the pathos of the life of the poor expressed through a restrained Symbolism. In 1904 he moved to Paris and developed his "Rose" period as a stylistic extension of his earlier work, but with a warmer tonality and more enigmatic meaning. At this time circus performers were among his favourite subjects. His discovery of Cézanne's formal organization and of the austere simplicity of African and ancient Iberian art influenced the proto-Cubist breakthrough of "*Les Demoiselles d'Avignon*" (1907, New York, MOMA). His meeting with Braque provided mutual inspiration and together they developed CUBISM over the next seven years with crucial results for most European art. "*Ma jolie*" (1911, New York, MOMA) reveals in its complexity of form and clarity of pictorial discipline the measure of the Cubist achievement. From 1911 Picasso allowed a more decorative feeling to enter his art, culminating in the 1921 *The three musicians* (New York, MOMA). Between 1920 and 1925 he painted in a classicizing style, producing pictures of massive weight, poise and authority (*Mother and child*, 1921, Chicago Art Institute), and also was affected by SURREALISM (*The three dancers*, 1925, London, Tate). In the 1930s he worked in a variety of styles, with an emphasis on the curvilinear or the sculptural. His experiments with metal sculpture, stimulated by González, date from this decade, when he was also very active as a graphic artist and book illustrator. In 1937, in response to the Spanish Civil War, he produced his most famous painting, *Guernica* (now in New York, MOMA, bequeathed conditionally to Spain by the artist), a devastating attack on man's cruelty and folly. His later career was equally productive but more sporadic in its achievements. Yet even as late as 1963 he could answer the criticisms of playfulness with a work such as *The large profile* (Düsseldorf, Nordrhein-Westfalen), which synthesized his whole development. No artist has been more fecund or had a greater influence on his contemporaries: much of the history of 20th-century art can be written around him. See vol. 1 pp. **27, 57, 67, 85, 109, 189**; vol. 3 pp. **148–149, 178, 202–203, 228–229**; vol. 4 p. **171**

Pickett, Joseph 1848–1918
American NAIVE painter. A carpenter and grocer, he took up painting towards the end of his life (about 1914). The few canvases he painted record the history of his native town, New Hope, Pennsylvania. *Coryll's Ferry* (c.1914–18, New York, Whitney Museum of American Art), which is painted in high relief, represents Washington at his headquarters before crossing the Delaware.

Picture plane
The surface of a picture, the plane from which the illusory space created by perspective appears to recede or, in some *trompe l'oeil* effects, to project.

Picturesque
Term which became popular in Britain in the 18th century to describe an aesthetic approach which took pleasure in roughness, curiousness and irregularity of forms. It was applied particularly to rustic landscapes and crumbling buildings. The Picturesque occupied a position between the concepts of the "Sublime" and the "Beautiful", having neither the awe-inspiring grandeur of the first nor the order and regularity of the second. A large body of literature grew up around the concept, which had great influence on landscape painting, architecture and gardening.

Piene, Otto born 1928
West German KINETIC artist. In 1957 he founded Group Zero with Mack, and from this year date his first "light paintings" (light projected through stencils). Choreographed performances of these became his "light ballets", and were eventually mechanized. His use of light stresses its crucial role, since Einstein, in the mapping of space and time. He has also created a number of "sky events", using balloons and inflated tubes—thus escaping from the limitations of galleries into the public sphere. He is fascinated by air as an element, as he is by fire: his "fire paintings" incorporate smoke and soot. Piene's art is an ambitious attempt to fuse the scientific with the visionary.

Pieneman, Jan Willem 1779–1853
Dutch portrait and history painter, in his time famous for such works as *The battle of Waterloo* (1824, Amsterdam,

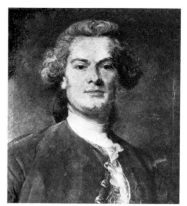
Perronneau: Self-portrait, c.1745. Tours, Musée des Beaux-Arts

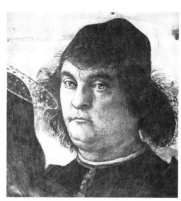
Perugino: Self-portrait from *The giving of the Keys to St Peter*, 1481–82. Vatican, Sistine Chapel (Mansell)

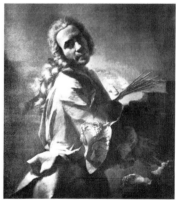
Piazzetta: Self-portrait, 1730s. Venice, Accademia (Mansell)

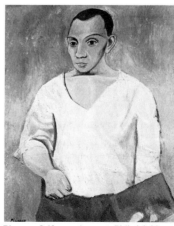
Picasso: Self-portrait, 1906. Philadelphia Museum of Art, A. E. Gallatin coll.

Rijksmuseum). He had some formal training, but was mainly self-taught. In 1820 he became the first Director of the Amsterdam Academy. Jozef Israëls was one of his pupils.

Pierce (Pearce), **Edward** c.1635–95
English sculptor and architect. He worked extensively on the City of London churches built after the Great Fire of 1666, both as a decorative sculptor and a mason-contractor. His best works, however, are his portrait busts, including one of *Christopher Wren* (Oxford, Ashmolean), probably carved to commemorate the architect's knighthood in 1673. This is one of the finest pieces of English sculpture of the 17th century, and conveys a feeling of Wren's brilliant mind more vividly than any of the painted portraits of him.

Pierfrancesco Fiorentino
1444/5–after 1497
Italian painter, active mainly in the area of San Gimignano. A huge output of stereotyped altarpieces, panels and frescos came from his workshop. His style, with its dry, linear modelling, idealized, standardized faces and repetitious compositions, was strongly influenced by his masters Gozzoli, Baldovinetti and, above all, Filippo Lippi. *Madonna with Child and saints* (1476, San Gimignano, Palazzo Communale) is representative.

Piero della Francesca 1416?–92
Italian painter, long neglected after his death, but now perhaps the most revered painter of the early Renaissance. He was born in Borgo San Sepolcro, and is first documented in 1439, assisting Domenico Veneziano on frescos in S. Egidio in Florence. This, his only recorded visit to the city, allowed him to witness the monumentality of Masaccio's painting and the result is evident from his altarpiece of *The Compassionate Madonna* commissioned in 1445 (Borgo San Sepolcro, Pinacoteca Communale). It is a solid, old-fashioned design and the fact that payment for it was completed only in 1462 suggests that, in keeping with his style, Piero was a slow, deliberate worker. Following projects in Ferrara and Rimini, he embarked on his most celebrated series of frescos, *The history of the true Cross* (1452–64, Arezzo, S. Francesco). Taken from the *Golden Legend*, the complex narrative of the painting was put across with Piero's customary stillness and meditative grandeur. His liking for sharp profiles and rigid frontality was clearly shown and can be seen to full effect also in *The Resurrection* (c.1463, Borgo San Sepolcro), where the starkly symmetrical pose of Christ and the severe angularity of the tomb creates a majestic aura of holiness. Piero, however, was also influenced (mainly in his interest in light) by Netherlandish painting and probably by Greek vases (notably in *The old age and death of Adam* in the Arezzo frescos). During the 1460s, if not before, Piero was a leading light in the humanist court of Federigo da Montefeltro at Urbino. Here he developed his interest in mathematical precision and the problems of perspective, which culminated in his treatise *On Perspective in Painting*, 1482, with drawings of foreshortened heads. *The Flagellation* (Urbino, Ducal Palace) and the double panel of *Federigo and his wife* (c.1472–73, Florence, Uffizi) are two famous examples painted at Urbino. Some detect a diminution of his powers in late works such as *The Madonna and saints with Federigo da Montefeltro* (c.1475, Milan, Brera), with its complex architecture. Piero's pupil, Signorelli,

soon moved away from his influence, but it is apparent in the spatial clarity and foreshortened heads of Perugino. See vol. 1 p. *127*; vol. 2 pp. **110–113**

Piero di Cosimo 1462–1521
Florentine painter, a pupil of Cosimo Rosselli, whose name he took as a patronym. One of the most charming and idiosyncratic artists of his time, Piero is the subject of one of Vasari's most vivid biographies, in which he is portrayed as an eccentric and self-conscious primitive living on hard-boiled eggs, disdaining civilized behaviour and fascinated by pre-history and mythology. None of his paintings is dated and it is difficult to establish a chronology. He is most famous for his humorous and whimsical paintings in which Lapiths, centaurs, fauns and all manner of wild and fantastic beasts and men are disposed in wooded or strange landscapes (examples New York, Metropolitan, and Oxford, Ashmolean). He painted animals with great sympathy, for all his usual hard, tight modelling. The delightful portrait of *Simonetta Vespucci* (Chantilly, Musée Condé), shown as Cleopatra with the asp around her neck, and the exquisitely poignant *Cephalus and Procris* (London, NG) show other aspects of his unique genius. He also painted more conventional, though still highly personal religious scenes which influenced his pupil Andrea del Sarto. Piero's *Immaculate Conception* (Florence, Uffizi) seems to have inspired the disposition of the figures in Andrea's "*Madonna of the Harpies*". See vol. 2 p. *119*

Pietà
Italian word meaning "pity", applied to a painting or sculpture of the Virgin supporting the dead Christ on her lap, occasionally surrounded by other mourners. This moving development of the mother and child relationship originated in Germany in the 14th century, where it was called *Vesperbild*. Perhaps the best-known *Pietà* is that by Michelangelo in St Peter's, Rome.

Pigalle, Jean-Baptiste 1714–85
The most successful French sculptor of his time. He was a pupil of Jean-Baptiste Lemoyne and studied in Rome, 1736–39. In 1744 he became famous with his marble *Mercury* (Paris, Louvre; the preparatory terracotta model is in the Metropolitan Museum, New York), the most successful reception piece in the history of the Academy. The naturalism apparent in this is also seen in Pigalle's brilliantly lively portraits (*Self-portrait*, 1780, Louvre), and his famous naked *Voltaire* (1770–76, Paris, Institut de France). He was very versatile, creating with equal skill such charming genre pieces as the *Child with a birdcage* (1750, Louvre) and monumental works such as the majestic tomb of Maurice of Saxony (designed 1753, Strasbourg, St Thomas), one of the greatest pieces of tomb sculpture of the century. Added to his versatility were a formal invention and technical accomplishment which place him among the greatest sculptors of the 18th century. See vol. 3 p. **61**

Pigment
The finely-ground, coloured powder which, when suspended in a medium such as oil, egg emulsion or water, forms paint. Pigments are also the colouring in dyes and inks but there they are dissolved rather than suspended in the medium. The first pigments used were ground from earth and vegetable matter or minerals but now they are made chemically and are more permanent.

Study of pigments can be useful in the dating and attribution of paintings.

Pillement, Jean-Baptiste
1728–1808
French painter of landscape and marine subjects, designer and engraver. His elegant landscapes owe much to Boucher, but they show a greater sensitivity to atmospheric effect than is usual in 18th-century decorative painting. He travelled widely in search of work, visiting Poland, Austria, England, Spain and Portugal. His extravagant Rococo and chinoiserie designs exercised a powerful influence on the decorative arts through the medium of engravings.

Pilon, Germain 1527–90
The greatest French sculptor of the 16th century, born and mainly active in Paris. His first recorded work (1558) was with Bontemps on the tomb of Francis I at St Denis, but Pilon's figures are now lost. In 1560, however, he was commissioned to make the three marble figures of *Graces* on the monument for the heart of Henry II (Paris, Louvre), and these reveal that his early style was based on the decorative manner of Primaticcio and the Fontainebleau school. Subsequently his work became more naturalistic, but his figures always tended to be expressively elongated. His naturalism at its most poignant is seen in the tomb of Henry II and Catherine de' Medici at St Denis, 1563–70, for which Pilon executed kneeling bronze effigies of the King and Queen and marble figures of their corpses. Pilon was appointed Controller General of the Mint in Paris in 1572, and in the 1570s produced mainly medals and portrait busts (Charles IX, London, Wallace Coll.). In the 1580s he returned to large-scale works and his style became increasingly emotional. Most of his late works are in the Louvre, including *The Virgin of Piety* (c.1585), and the tomb of Valentine Balbiani (before 1583). Such works were too personal to find much of a following, but French sculptors of the late 16th century were greatly influenced by Pilon's earlier manner. See vol. 1 p. *174*; vol. 2 p. *167*

Piloty, Karl Theodor von
1826–86
German painter of historical compositions. His dramatic and opulent historical paintings show the strong influence of the Venetian school and Titian in particular. As a professor and later Director of the Munich Academy he influenced many young painters, the most famous of whom are Lenbach, Makart and Defregger.

Pineau, Nicolas 1684–1754
French ROCOCO designer and decorator. After his return to Paris from the Russian court in 1726 he was one of the most fashionable practitioners of Rococo design. The wall-decorations of the Hôtel de Villars (1732–33, now at Waddesdon Manor, Buckinghamshire) are typical of his elegant, asymmetrical style, widely known to his contemporaries through engravings.

Pintoricchio (Bernardino di Betto)
c.1454–1513
Italian painter from Perugia, probably a pupil of Perugino. His style is similar but more sumptuous and his more secular subjects were suited to the lavish decoration of rooms. His best surviving masterpiece is the Piccolomini Library in Siena (1506–07), which commemorates the life of the Sienese Pope, Pius II. Through a brilliantly decorated series of illusionistic arches, important scenes from the

Pope's life are portrayed in marvellous detail and bright colour. He painted many other fresco cycles, notably those in the Borgia appartments in the Vatican (1492–94). His works reflect the delight in pageantry of late 15th-century Italy. See vol. 2 pp. **128–129**

Piper, John born 1903
British painter, designer and printmaker. In the 1930s he was one of the leading British abstract painters, but by the end of the decade he had become disillusioned with what he saw as the limitations of abstraction. Works such as *Up the gorge, Hafod, North Wales* (1939, London, V&A), attempted to revert to an English tradition of a subjective response to nature. He defined this tradition in his influential book *British Romantic Artists* (1942), a key text for the NEO-ROMANTICISM of the 1940s. His most enduring works were his paintings of bomb damage made as an official war artist (1940–42), and his images of country houses such as Castle Howard (c.1944, Norwich, Castle Museum). The stormy atmosphere evoked in these paintings suggests a threat not only to the buildings, but to a way of life.

Pippin, Horace 1888–1946
American NAIVE painter who was "discovered" in the late 1930s. Among his most evocative works is his first oil-painting, the highly detailed and sombre *End of the war; starting home* (1933, Philadelphia, Museum of Art), a cynical reflection of the artist's experiences in World War I.

Piranesi, Giovanni Battista
1720–78
Italian artist, known principally today for his highly influential etchings of architectural views. He was born in Venice, where he was trained in the arts of perspective and stage-design, but moved to Rome in 1740, and, apart from a brief return to Venice in 1744, remained there for the rest of his life. His etched views, which first established his reputation, are characterized by a grandeur of scale which thoroughly transforms their subjects; but his extraordinary imagination is best displayed in his two series of engravings of imaginary prison scenes (the *Carceri d'Invenzione*). In their vividness of technique, abrupt changes in scale, and wealth of architectural inventiveness, these have a visionary intensity. Despite the fantastic dimension to his art, and the fact that only one of his architectural projects (the church of the Priorato di Malta) was ever realized, he greatly influenced the Neoclassical architects of his day, and was regarded as the most eloquent spokesman for classical Roman architecture. His influence was wide (his son **Francesco** (1748–1810) continued his work) and profoundly important for the Romantic era. See vol. 2 pp. *189*, **254**

Pisanello (Antonio Pisano)
c.1395–1455/56
Northern Italian painter and medallist. He was probably a pupil of Stefano da Verona. He worked in the prevailing International Gothic style of Gentile da Fabriano, with whom he collaborated in Venice and Rome on frescos, since lost. Rich colour, surface texture and naturalistic details make up the sumptuous tapestried effect of his frescos, notably *St George and the Princess* (c.1435, Verona, S. Anastasia), and of the painted panel *The vision of St Eustace* (London, NG). His drawings of sharply-observed animals, birds, people and costumes are the finest surviving drawings of the early

15th century and indicate the new tendency both to draw from the life and to make studies for particular commissions, rather than to use old formulae. Economical use of line and physiognomic accuracy characterize his famous portrait medals (examples in Washington, Milan, Florence and elsewhere), dating from 1438. He worked for a number of Italian courts, notably that of the Gonzaga in Mantua (newly discovered frescos of jousting with virtuoso glimpses of foreshortened knights in the agony of battle in the Ducal Palace are attributed to him). He was praised just after his death for the "poetry" of his naturalistic world. See vol. 1 p. 76; vol. 2 pp. **88–89**

Pisano, Andrea
active before 1330–c.1348
Italian sculptor, goldsmith and architect, unrelated to Giovanni and Nicola Pisano. He was probably born in Pisa, but is first recorded in Florence between 1330 and 1337, making the gilded bronze doors for the south entrance to the Baptistery. In 1340 he was put in charge of operations on Florence Cathedral and supplied various statues and reliefs for the upper part of the campanile. His style was basically Gothic, but was influenced by Giotto's clarity of design. See vol. 2 pp. **81,** *100*

Pisano, Giovanni
active c.1265–1314
Pisan sculptor, the son of Nicola. He is first documented as his father's assistant on the Siena pulpit and the fountain at Perugia. Between 1284 and 1296 he worked as architect and sculptor on the façade of the cathedral at Siena. This is the first of the great Italian Gothic façades and contains an outstanding series of life-size figures, highly expressive and deeply undercut. Notable also are those over the entrance to the Baptistery in Pisa, c.1295, now in the Museo Nazionale. Afterwards he carved pulpits in S. Andrea, Pistoia (1300–01) and in the cathedral at Pisa (1302–10). These are modelled on the two great pulpits of his father, but Giovanni's work is more elegant and Gothic in style. He also made various free-standing Madonnas, the most famous of which is on the altar of the Arena Chapel in Padua. Giovanni was the greatest Italian sculptor of his time, breathing a quite new drama and movement into the forms of Nicola, but his expressiveness was too personal to find much of a following. See vol. 2 pp. **80–81,** *82, 100*

Pisano, Nicola active c.1258–84
Pisan sculptor. He stands at the head of the Pisan and thus the entire Italian tradition of sculpture. His earliest known work is the pulpit in the Baptistery at Pisa, finished in 1260. This large, free-standing work was revolutionary in its tremendous vitality, its powerful relief panels and majestic architectural forms making most earlier pulpits look timid. A second, more elaborate pulpit in the cathedral at Siena followed in 1265–68. Both this and his last work, the Fontana Maggiore (completed 1278) at Perugia, were made in collaboration with his son Giovanni. Two documents prove that he was born in Apulia, in the south of Italy, where he would have been trained among the classicizing sculptors employed by the Emperor Frederick II (died 1250). On arriving in Pisa, his interest in the Antique was decisively reinforced by the numerous Roman sarcophagi that he found displayed in the Campo Santo. Several of the figures on his pulpits have been shown to be di-

rectly modelled on these. For this reason Nicola is sometimes held to herald the Renaissance, but this is somewhat misleading. Nicola only revived the forms of classical antiquity within a generally Gothic or even Romanesque style, and showed none of the interest in classical civilization itself which later characterized the true Renaissance. See vol. 1 p. *200*; vol. 2 pp. **80,** *87*

Pisano, Nino active 1349–?1368
Pisan sculptor, goldsmith and architect. He was the son and pupil of Andrea, whom he succeeded as architect in Orvieto. Later, 1357–58, he worked on a silver antependium for the cathedral in Pisa. He followed his father's style, but was much less talented. His chief significance is that he was one of the earliest sculptors to specialize in life-size free-standing figures.

Pisis, Filippo de 1896–1956
Italian painter. Recognized as one of the leading Italian landscape painters of this century, he is often compared with Utrillo in the individuality of his achievement. After dissatisfaction with his Dada and Metaphysical work, in the 1920s he united the structural strength of Cubism with the light and colour of Impressionism and the 18th-century Venetians to produce a style in which bravura handling and vibrant colour were used to express his sensations rather than record the landscape motif.

Pissarro, Camille 1830–1903
French painter, one of the leading IMPRESSIONISTS. He was born in the West Indies, and went in 1855 to Paris, where he studied with Corot. He met Monet in 1859, and again in 1870–71 in London, where they were introduced to the dealer Durand-Ruel. In London he studied Turner and Constable and painted atmospheric views of the area in which he lived (*Lower Norwood, snow scene*, 1870, London, Tate). An anarchist, he enthusiastically helped to establish the revolutionary Impressionist exhibitions and exhibited at all eight. His *Red roofs* (1877, Paris, Jeu de Paume) is characteristic in its rural subject matter, solidity of form and high horizon line. At the last Impressionist exhibition in 1886 he presented POINTILLIST works clearly influenced by Seurat, but by about 1890 he felt that this methodical approach was not suited to his temperament and he returned to a freer style, though it was more subdued in colour than his earlier Impressionist paintings. He was a kindly father figure who greatly helped younger artists such as Gauguin and Cézanne and introduced them to his Impressionist friends, among whom he had an important role as a peacemaker. See vol. 1 pp. *150–151*; vol. 3 pp. **98–99, 102–103**

Pissarro, Lucien 1863–1944
French painter, the eldest son of Camille Pissarro. His early work progressed from Impressionism to Pointillism. In 1890 he settled in London and for a time both his paintings and his book illustrations reflected the influence of the English Arts and Crafts movement. He played a significant role in transmitting French avantgarde concerns to young English painters. *The rue Sainte Victoire, winter sunshine* (1890, Michigan, Flint Institute of Arts) is an example of his Neo-Impressionist work.

Pistoletto, Michelangelo
born 1933
Italian painter and Performance artist. He had his first show in 1960 and in 1962 started to incorporate photographs into

his paintings. He turned to abstract sculpture in 1964 and in 1970 to "actions" and Happenings. He is best-known for his work with mirrors: a large sheet of highly polished steel is partially covered with a life-size monochrome figure, leaving the other areas to reflect the viewer. He has been associated with Superrealism. See vol. 3 p. **252**

Pittoni, Giovanni Battista
1687–1767
Italian painter of religious, historical and mythological scenes. He spent most of his life in his native Venice, and was a founder member of the Venetian Academy. In his youth he painted in a style indebted to both Sebastiano Ricci and Piazzetta, but in later life he fell heavily under the influence of his younger Venetian contemporary, Giambattista Tiepolo (*The sacrifice of Jephtha*, 1733, Genoa, Palazzo Reale).

Pittura Metafisica see METAPHYSICAL PAINTING

Pizzolo, Niccolò 1421–53
Italian sculptor and painter of the Paduan school, one of the most gifted pupils and the assistant of Squarcione. With Mantegna he was commissioned to decorate the Ovetari Chapel of the Eremetani Church at Padua, but completed not much more than the terracotta altarpiece before being murdered. He had been an assistant of Donatello in Padua and his work strongly reflects his influence.

Place, Francis 1647–1728
English amateur draughtsman and engraver. He painted an oil self-portrait, drew crayon portraits and was a pioneer mezzotint engraver, but is best known for his architectural and topographical drawings. Many of these show views in and around York, and the best collection is in the City Art Gallery there.

Plamondon, Antoine 1804–95
Canadian portrait painter who began by assisting Légaré in restoration work. He developed an austerely classical approach under Guérin in Paris, 1826–30, and returned to a plethora of portrait and church commissions in Quebec, many of which were free adaptations of Rubens and Raphael. His series of nuns' portraits is outstandingly sensitive. *Sister Saint-Alphonse* (1841, Ottawa, NG of Canada) has the psychological penetration of a Géricault, combined with delicate modelling and exquisite colour. Hamel was his most important pupil.

Plasticiens, Les
Group of Canadian painters in Montreal, including Molinari and Tousignant, who were proponents of "pure" painting. In the 1955 *Manifesto*, they announced a quest for perfect forms in a perfect order, opposing hidden meanings and humanitarian overtones in abstract art. Their austerely geometric work contrasts with the freely-executed paintings of their fellow-Canadian abstractionists, Les AUTOMATISTES.

Plasticity
Word used in sculptural contexts in connection with materials which have a great quality of manipulation, for example clay and wet plaster. It is also a term used in art criticism to describe sculptural, three-dimensional qualities in painted works.

Plastov, Arkady 1893–1972
Russian painter. He spent most of his life in his small country village where,

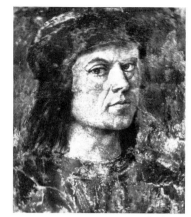
Pintoricchio: Self-portrait from Baglioni chapel frescos, 1501. Spello, S. Maria

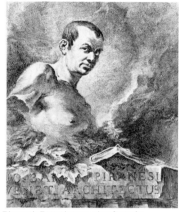
Piranesi: Portrait engraving from the frontispiece to *Opere Varie*, 1750. London, BM

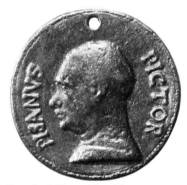
Pisanello: Self-portrait? medal, c.1440–43. London, BM

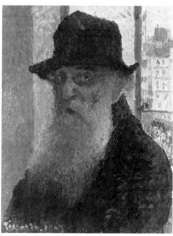
Pissarro, Camille: Self-portrait, 1903. London, Tate

until 1931 when he took up painting full-time, he was a farmer. His paintings celebrate, in bright, cheerful colours, the way of life of the Russian countryside. Works such as *Haymaking* (1945, Moscow, Tretyakov Gallery) present in a realistic style an idealistic view of labour. He also painted many portraits and did book illustrations. See vol. 3 p. **251**

Plein air
Term meaning "open air", chiefly used to describe paintings that have actually been executed outdoors, rather than in the studio. *Plein-air* painting was first taken up mainly by the English painters, Bonington and Constable and the French 19th-century BARBIZON school, and it became central to IMPRESSIONISM. Its popularity was aided by the development of lightweight painting materials and equipment.

Pleydenwurff, Hans died 1472
German painter. He had a workshop in Nuremberg from 1457, and his style, which was strongly influenced by van der Weyden and Bouts, brought a new realism to Nuremberg painting. This is seen, for example, in the diptych of *The Man of Sorrows adored by Georg von Löwenstein* (*c*.1456, Nuremberg, Germanisches Nationalmuseum) and in *The Crucifixion* (*c*.1465, Munich, Alte Pinakothek). Wolgemut worked with him and married his widow. His son **Wilhelm** (died 1494), a painter and engraver, also worked in Nuremberg.

Poccetti, Bernardino 1548–1612
Florentine artist, trained as a painter of house façades and grotesque ornament. In 1580 he painted frescos of saints in the cloister of S. Maria Novella, and then in the monastery at Val d'Ema, where his *Funeral and translation of St Bruno* (1592–93) is full of sharp naturalism. He belonged to the post-Vasarian generation of artists who moved from Mannerism towards a more restrained, naturalistic style, though in his *Massacre of the Innocents* in the Ospedale degli Innocenti, Florence (1610), he retains some of the decorative intonation of Mannerism.

Poelenburgh, Cornelis van
c.1586–1667
Dutch painter, with Breenberg the outstanding artist of the first generation of Italianate landscapists. He studied with Bloemaert in his native Utrecht and was in Italy from about 1617 until 1625. *The rest on the Flight to Egypt* (Cambridge, Mass., Fogg Art Museum) is a typical work, probably dating from his Italian period, in which romantic ruins and fragments of antique statuary decorate the spacious setting in which the biblical characters are placed. On his return to Utrecht he became very successful and had imitators even in the 18th century. He sometimes added the figures to the work of other artists, for example Jan Both. See vol. 2 p. **221**

Pointillism
Technique adopted by the NEO-IMPRESSIONISTS. It was based on Seurat's research into the findings of Chevreul (who had published his *Laws on the Simultaneous Contrasts of Colour* in 1839) and of Delacroix and others, and was possibly influenced by contemporary chromotypogravure—a form of early photomechanical colour printing used in France in the mid-1880s. The aim rarely achieved, was to give greater luminosity by placing pure pigments of primary colours on the canvas, leaving the dots to fuse at a distance to create an optical mixture and thus give the spectator a more luminous, vibrant image. Signac's book *From Delacroix to Neo-Impressionism*, 1899, codified the theories behind the term Divisionism, which is now frequently used for the Italian Neo-Impressionist movement, though the French Neo-Impressionists themselves preferred this name to that of Pointillism. See vol. 3 pp. 110–111

Pointing machine
Device invented in the early 19th century for the production of exact replicas of sculptures. A simple method based on callipers was used by the Romans when copying Greek statuary, and this was gradually refined in the Renaissance and thereafter. See vol. 1 p. 181

Poirier, Anne and **Patrick** born 1942
French LAND artists. They have been working together since 1970. In this year they visited Angkor, Cambodia, where they were struck by the Cambodians' use of their ancient temples as living and working places. Their models of archaeological sites such as *Ostia Antica* (1973, no fixed location) are intended to capture pieces of the past that are still "living" and create a bond between past and present. See vol. 3 p. **249**

Polack, Jan died 1519
German painter, perhaps of Polish origin, active in Munich, where he was Town Painter from 1488. He painted wall-paintings and altarpieces in a vigorous and expressive, if conventional, late Gothic style (St Peter altarpiece, *c*.1490, Munich, Bayerisches Nationalmuseum).

Polenov, Vassily Dmitrievich
1844–1927
Russian painter. He studied in St Petersburg, 1863–71, and at the Academy in France, 1872–76. He painted religious, historical and genre pictures but his most memorable works were his poetical landscapes (*Moscow courtyard*, 1878, Moscow, Tretyakov Gallery). He was an active member of the WANDERERS. Combined with his teaching in Moscow (1882–95), his personality as well as his art had a great influence on the artists of the next generation.

Poleo, Hector born 1918
Venezuelan REGIONALIST painter. He studied at Caracas and in Mexico City, where he was taught the techniques of mural painting, and his first exhibition in Caracas in 1941 shows the influence of the Mexican muralist tradition. He travelled extensively through Latin America and settled for a while in New York (1944). Working in Spain, Italy and Paris, he was influenced by Surrealism and Italian frescos. There followed a period of geometric clarity and heightened colour figuration, and then experiments with vaporous forms and veils of colour suggesting dreamlike forms.

Poliakov, Sergei (Serge Poliakoff)
1906–69
Russian painter, who left his country in 1919, settling in Paris in 1923. He had trained as a musician and began to study painting in 1930, spending two years in London (1935–37). His mature style, seen in *Abstract composition* (1954, London, Tate), is based on relationships set up between colour patches of organic shape, with further underlying layers of colours still visible under the surface.

Polidoro da Caravaggio (Polidoro Caldara) *c*.1500–1543?
Italian painter born in Caravaggio, Lombardy. At 18 he was working with Raphael in the Vatican Loggie. Inspired by Peruzzi, he decorated many house façades in Rome with monochrome ancient histories in the manner of antique relief sculptures, but with much energy and grace in the figures. One façade, on the Palazzo Ricci, survives; others are known through prints and drawings. These friezes were influential and much copied. His scenes in S. Silvestro al Quirinale, illustrating events from *The lives of Mary Magdalen* and *St Catherine of Siena* were innovatory in the domination of landscape over subject. After the Sack of Rome, 1527, he fled to Naples and thence to Messina, where his work became more violent in emotional content, for example *The road to Calvary* (before 1534, Naples, Capodimonte).

Polke, Sigmar born 1942
West German artist, one of the most articulate of the group of younger artists who, under the spiritual guidance of Beuys, made Düsseldorf a major centre of artistic activity at the end of the 1960s. He has worked in a variety of styles, always stressing the importance of freedom and individual creativity.

Pollaiuolo, Antonio del 1431/2–98 and **Piero del** 1441–96
Florentine artists, brothers who ran a workshop together. Antonio was trained as a goldsmith, while his younger brother was trained as a painter, perhaps in Castagno's workshop. Antonio's first commission (with two other artists) was the silver Crucifix for the altar of the Baptistery, 1457–59. The figures are tiny, but already show the sinewy vigour of Antonio's mature style, which in fact changed very little throughout his long career. His commission to paint large canvases of *The Labours of Hercules* for the Medici Palace (1460, lost) is assumed to be reflected in two little panels and a free-standing statuette, an early example of its kind, *Hercules and Antaeus*, *c*.1475–80, in the Uffizi, Florence. Piero's first commission was for a series of *Virtues* (1469, Uffizi). Their graceful linear style reflects not only Castagno but Filippo Lippi; however, the sense of structure is not strong, and the general tendency has been to attribute the weaker parts of their subsequent joint productions to Piero, the better parts to Antonio. The fresco altarpiece in the Cardinal of Portugal's Chapel in S. Miniato in Florence, 1469, and *The martyrdom of St Sebastian* (1475, London, NG) have been analysed in this way. The latter especially is remarkable for its atmospheric evocation of the Arno in its spacious landscape, and it reflects the preoccupation with the human figure in movement that informs Antonio's early and only engraving, *Ten nudes fighting*, *c*.1460, and his many, superbly expressive, pen drawings (Uffizi, London, BM, and elsewhere). Both brothers were summoned in 1483 to Rome, where they designed first the bronze tomb of Sixtus IV (1484–93, St Peter's Museum), with its deliciously elongated and sinuous *Liberal Arts*, and secondly the tomb of Innocent VIII (1492–98), with its dramatic life-size figure of the Pope blessing. Both were original designs; the latter had lasting influence—on the papal tombs of Michelangelo, Bernini and Canova. Important figures of the late 15th century, the Pollaiuoli continued the tradition of Donatello and Castagno, extended it to new media and concentrated it on the nude male figure. See vol. 2 p. **115**

Pollock, Jackson 1912–56
American painter, the leading member of the New York school of ABSTRACT EXPRESSIONISM. He studied with Benton but the main influences on his early work were Siqueiros and American Indian art. Between 1935 and 1940 he worked in the easel division of the Federal Art Projects. In 1939, he entered therapy with a Jungian analyst. Mythic imagery, which can be associated with a Surrealist-inspired interest in both Jung and Freud, appears in paintings such as *Guardians of the secret* (1943, San Francisco, Museum of Art); in the early 1940s he gradually developed a painterly abstract style. From 1946 to 1950 he worked with the canvas on the floor, pouring skeins of paint across the surface from all four sides creating an all-over texture of lines and splatters. This has frequently been taken as an example of Action Painting, but Pollock maintained control over the flow of paint, deliberately absorbing chance effects, and his poured paintings have remarkable monumentality. In the 1950s his work became much larger, and he produced explosive works such as *Blue poles* (1953, Canberra, National Museum), involving huge swirling networks of colour. He also executed a series in entirely black and white enamelized paint. Throughout his life Pollock enjoyed a notorious reputation, to which his therapy, alcoholism and premature death in an accident all contributed. His style was a breakthrough for modernist painting and he stands at the front of a generation of American painters who achieved international fame. See vol. 3 pp. **212–213**

Polydoros see PERGAMENE SCHOOL

Polyeuktos active 3rd century BC
Greek sculptor from Athens. A fine bronze portrait statue of the orator Demosthenes, dating from *c*.280 BC and surviving in a Roman copy (Copenhagen, Ny Carlsberg Glyptothek) may be ascribed to him. See vol. 2 p. **42**

Polygnotos active *c*.475–447 BC
Greek painter from Thasos, later an Athenian citizen, described as the first great painter of Greek art. His chief works were murals at Delphi and in the Stoa Poikile at Athens. His subjects seem to have been drawn mainly from Homer and his figures are praised for their nobility and expression. Technically, he is acclaimed as the first artist to master spatial depth and foreshortening. Although no work has survived, his poses and groupings may be identified in the works of later vase-painters, notably in the Argonaut *krater* of the Niobid Painter. See vol. 2 p. 44

Polykleitos
active 2nd half of 5th century BC
Greek sculptor from Argos, a contemporary and rival of Phidias. He is said to have written a book on proportion and to have set out his theories in a statue of a youth holding a spear. The best of the Roman copies of this "*Doryphoros*" is in the Museo Nazionale, Naples. The figure shows a fine mastery of naturalistic detail and, although it is solid and broad-shouldered, its proportions are harmonious and the pose is conceived in a rhythmic counterpoint of muscular tension and relaxation. Another athlete, the "*Diadoumenos*" (Youth binding his head), has also been identified in copies, as has an *Amazon*, with which Polykleitos is said to have defeated Phidias in a competition and of which the pathos contrasts with the remote calm of the latter's works. Polykleitos' most celebrated work was his colossal gold and ivory statue of *Hera* for her temple

at Argos, said to be comparable to Phidias' *Zeus* at Olympia.

Polynesian art

The art of the easternmost Pacific islands, from Tonga to Easter Island and from Hawaii to New Zealand—areas inhabited by peoples of similar language and culture. Polynesians produced finely crafted objects in wood, shell and fibrous materials for everyday use and for chiefs' courts and insignia of rank. Figurative sculpture portraying gods and spirits was well developed on some islands. Few such artistic traditions survived European contact in the 18th century. See vol. 2 pp. 22–23

Polyptych see TRIPTYCH

Pomodoro, Arnaldo born 1926

Italian sculptor and designer. He began working as a stage designer and gold and jewellery worker in 1950. During the 1950s he travelled in Europe and the USA. He was a professor at the University of California in 1968, and in 1971 returned to Italy. He is a master of bronzecasting and his work is on a huge scale. It has a sense of drama originating from his theatrical work. His characteristic forms are split or broken to reveal jagged and irregular material (*Sphere*, 1964, New York, Marlborough-Gerson Gallery).

Pomodoro, Gio born 1930

Italian sculptor and designer. Like his elder brother Arnaldo he began working in precious metals and jewellery, and with him was one of a remarkable group of artist-jewellers in the early 1950s. Many of his later ideas were originated then. He uses fibreglass and bronze in his regular and contained forms (*Borromini square II*, 1966, New York, Marlborough-Gerson Gallery).

Pompeian styles

Painting styles identified in murals of the south Italian town of Pompeii, painted between the 2nd century BC and AD 79, when the town was buried. Three major styles are commonly accepted, the first and earliest being a purely decorative painting simulating marble revetments. The second style introduced illusionistic landscape and figure scenes with well modelled, solid forms (as at the Villa of the Mysteries). The third style, enthusiastically imitated by European painters and designers after the rediscovery of Pompeii in the 18th century, is distinguished by its exquisitely painterly figurative scenes and fantastic illusionistic architectural decoration. It reached its peak in the 1st century BC and was succeeded only briefly by the less easily defined fourth style, 63–79 AD, in part a revival of the second style.

Pont-Aven, school of

Group of artists who surrounded Gauguin at the small picturesque town of Pont-Aven in Brittany between 1886 and 1891. In their treatment of Breton peasant subjects, they reacted against the naturalistic representation of the external world found in Impressionist paintings in favour of a non-naturalistic style based on ideas and emotions, and known as SYNTHETISM or CLOISONNISME. The group included Bernard and Anquetin. They held their first exhibition in Paris at the Café Volpini in 1889. Gauguin's *Vision after the sermon* (1888, Edinburgh, NG of Scotland) was the most important painting to come from Pont-Aven. See vol. 3 p. 120

Pontius, Paul 1603–58

Flemish engraver. He began his career as a painter, but was already working as an engraver in Rubens' studio in 1623/4. He lived in Rubens' house until 1631 and became his favourite engraver. His technique was precise and highly finished, as in his best-known print, that after Rubens' self-portrait of 1623.

Pontormo (Jacopo Carucci) 1494–1557

Italian painter, a leading early MANNERIST. His nickname comes from the village of his birth. He studied with Piero di Cosimo and possibly Leonardo in Florence and entered Andrea del Sarto's workshop there in 1512. *Joseph in Egypt* (c.1515, London, NG) shows that his distinctive style was formed early in his career. It is full of restless movement and incident and has the vivid colours—crimson, pink, apple green and celestial blue—which appear in many later works. Between 1520 and 1521 he worked for the Medici at their villa at Poggio a Caiano, where he painted a lunette of *Vertumnus and Pomona*, for which some of his most beautiful drawings exist. His swooping, swirling line, extraordinary colours and elongated bodies with animated drapery reach a climax in *The Deposition* (c.1526–28, Florence, S. Felicità). One of the masterpieces of the period, this is a work of astonishing formal sophistication and great majesty, but it also conveys intense spiritual feeling. By this time Pontormo may have visited Rome and seen the Sistine Chapel ceiling; certainly he had absorbed the lessons of Michelangelo's *contrapposto*. He was also an admirer of Dürer and his *Supper at Emmaus* (1525, Florence, Uffizi) is based on an engraving by the German master. Pontormo's nervous, taut portraits, such as that of a young man thought to be Alessandro de' Medici (c.1525–27, Lucca, Pinacoteca), must have influenced his pupil Bronzino. Pontormo was a deeply disturbed, paranoid character who, in the last years of his life, kept an exhaustive diary from which we understand something of the origin of his strange, haunting paintings. See vol. 2 pp. **164–165**

Poons, Larry born 1937

American painter, born in Tokyo. *Orange crush* (1963, Buffalo, Albright-Knox)—an orange field speckled with blue-green dots—is a characteristic early work, and links him with Op art. He exploits the optic effects of complementary colours to activate the surface of his canvases. He studied music before turning to painting; the staccato rhythms of the apparently moving dots are visual transcriptions of musical themes. The seemingly random placement of dots, later to become ellipses, is in fact controlled by an underlying grid. Later canvases are covered with thick layers of cracked and blistered pastel pigments.

Pop art

Artistic movement arising in the mid-1950s in Britain and the USA which reached a peak in the early 1960s. The term was coined by the critic Lawrence Alloway to describe ironic works celebrating the imagery and techniques of the mass media, advertising and popular culture. Pop art is a reaction against the high seriousness of Abstract Expressionism. In England the leading practitioners were Hamilton, Kitaj and Blake. In the USA the 1950s works of Rauschenberg and Johns form the link between Abstract Expressionism and Pop art. Warhol, Lichtenstein, Oldenburg, Wesselman, and Rosenquist created variations on popular American cultural icons, employing collage techniques, air-brush, the industrial printing press or, ironically, duplicating commercial silk-screen effects by hand. Pop art, which presents the everyday object as art (as in Warhol's *100 cans of Campbell's soup*, 1962, Buffalo, Albright-Knox), keeps alive the spirit of Dada; Oldenburg's giant soft sculptures and other works rely on the Dada technique of altering the accustomed scale and physical properties of an object. The movement shares concerns with other trends of the 1960s: for example, its predilection for serial imagery and the preference for impersonal means of execution reappear in Minimal art. See vol. 3 pp. 238–241

Popova, Lyubov Sergeevna 1889–1924

Russian painter and designer. Returning to Russia in 1913 deeply imbued with Cubist principles after studies in Paris, she worked alongside Tatlin, taking part in the most extreme avant-garde exhibitions. She worked briefly as a Suprematist in 1916, before turning to studies in form and colour which led to her characteristic linear Constructivist paintings; *Architectonic painting* (1917, New York, MOMA) is an early example. From 1921, she developed Constructivist artefacts, including scenery for Vsevolod Meyerjold's revolutionary stage productions; best-known are her designs for *The Magnanimous Cuckold* (1921, reconstructed model, Norwich, University of East Anglia).

Porcellis, Jan c.1584–1632

Flemish marine painter active in Holland. In the development of marine painting, his work marked a turning point from the earlier busy, brightly-coloured seascapes of Vroom to a more tonal, naturalistic approach. His favourite subject was the study of a stormy sea and sky with a modest fishing boat (*Rough weather*, 1629, Munich, Alte Pinakothek). Such atmospheric scenes may well have influenced van Goyen, and Porcellis' works were collected by Rembrandt and van de Cappelle.

Pordenone (Giovanni Antonio de Sacchis) 1483/4–1539

Italian painter, born in Friuli but active mostly in the small towns of the Veneto. His early work is much in the style of Titian and the pupils of Giovanni Bellini, for instance *The Compassionate Madonna* (after 1515, Pordenone, Cathedral). But after 1520, possibly due to the impact of the Roman High Renaissance, he developed a style of great bravura, with startling illusionistic effects of figures lunging into the spectator's space, and dramatic foreshortenings. Among his finest surviving works are the frescos in Cremona Cathedral, where he completed the decoration of the nave begun by Girolamo Romanino: in the vast *Crucifixion* scenes (1520–21) he treats the narrative in a dense dramatic manner, the figures closely packed on a narrow stage in a rotating composition which seems to enclose the spectator. See vol. 2 p. **149**

P-Orridge, Genesis (Megson, Neil Andrew) born 1950

British artist. The performances, films and other artworks of his group, Coum transmissions, use violent and sexual imagery as a protest against industrial society. To reach a larger audience he formed the rock band Throbbing Gristle, including his female companion, Cosey Fanni Tutti. He was co-editor of *Contemporary Artists* (1977)—an international dictionary of some 1,300 artists.

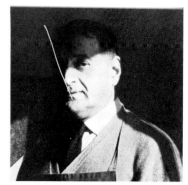

Poliakov: Photograph courtesy of Redfern Gallery, London

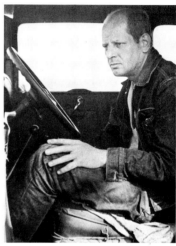

Pollock: Photograph, 1952 (courtesy of Hans Namuth, New York)

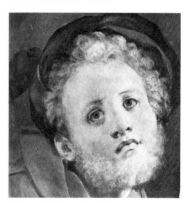

Pontormo: Self-portrait from *The Deposition*, c.1526–28. Florence, S. Felicità (Mansell)

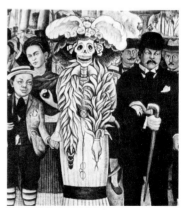

Posada: Portrait (as a boy and man with bride) by Rivera from *A dream in Alameda Park*, 1947. Mexico City, Hotel del Prado

Portinari, Cândido 1903–62
Brazilian painter. Like Cavalcanti he portrayed the lives of Brazilian peasants and workers in their rural surroundings. His large compositions, at once intimate and monumental, are reminiscent of Picasso's classicizing period on the one hand and the work of the American Regionalists Benton, Curry and Grant Wood on the other. He dissociated himself from the social realism of his Mexican contemporaries, adhering to an individual and expressionist style of drawing. He gained a considerable reputation as a society portrait painter, and won important public commissions, including large canvases on *War* and *Peace* for the United Nations Building in New York, 1950–56.

Posada, José Guadalupe
1851–1913
Mexican graphic artist and caricaturist. During his lifetime 15,000 lithographs were commissioned from him by the conservative publishing house of Vanegas Arroyo. His drawings appeared in three or four publications antagonistic to the regime of Porfirio Diaz. His images variously edified, amused and offended the Mexican public; he concentrated on political and social crises, the social contrasts of the epoch, the pretentions of the upper classes and the appalling living conditions of the poor. A recurring theme in his drawings is the *calavera* or animated skeleton. His work has been compared with that of Goya and Callot and he was an important influence on 20th-century Mexican painting, notably on the muralists Orozco and Rivera. See previous page and vol. 3 p. **208**

Post, Frans 1612–80
Dutch landscape painter. He went on the Dutch West India Company's voyage of colonization to Brazil, 1637–44, and became the first European artist to paint landscape in the New World. Post was stimulated by the new environment to paint works of a remarkably vivid freshness and naive charm (*São Francisco River and Fort Maurice*, 1638, Paris, Louvre). Such paintings were evidently popular, for Post continued to paint New World scenes after he settled in Haarlem in 1644, including a *Sacrifice of Manoah* (1648, Rotterdam, Boymans Museum), set in a Brazilian landscape complete with exotic flora and fauna, including an armadillo.

Post-Impressionism
Term coined by Roger Fry for his exhibition, *Manet and the Post-Impressionists*, held at the Grafton Galleries, London, in 1910. It was used primarily to link the highly individual styles of the three artists who dominated the show, Cézanne, Gauguin and van Gogh. Fry agreed that the term was negative—he wanted to call them "expressionists"—but argued that they shared a dissatisfaction with the naturalistic aims of Impressionism and a common need to convey the essence of their subject matter through formal simplifications. Members of the Nabis also conformed to these tendencies and Fry later broadened the definition to include Seurat and the Pointillists. Post-Impressionism, thus, overlaps with Symbolism, Neo-Impressionism, the beginnings of Expressionism and even Fauvism, and can be applied to any of the reactions against Impressionism that emerged in the period between about 1880 and 1905. See vol. 3 pp. 112ff

Post-Painterly Abstraction
Term invented by the American critic Clement Greenberg to refer to the work of a group of painters who came to public attention in the 1960s. Noland, Stella, Olitski, Kelly and others, though working in a broad range of abstract styles, all sought alternatives to the extreme painterliness and subjectivity of ABSTRACT EXPRESSIONISM. Their canvases tend to feature hard-edged areas of high-key colours. The two-dimensionality of the picture plane is emphasized at the expense of tactile effects.

Potter, Paulus 1625–54
Dutch painter of landscapes with animals. Born in Enkuizen, he worked in Delft, The Hague and Amsterdam before his premature death. His most famous painting, *The young bull* (1647, The Hague, Mauritshuis) is a life-size, almost reverent portrait of a cheerful-looking beast with a placid cow and an admiring cowherd. Potter's approach was, however, more sentimental than that of his contemporary Aelbert Cuyp. Most of his works were smaller scenes of pigs, cows and sheep in sunlit summery landscapes. See vol. 2 p. **223**

Pougny, Jean (Ivan Puni)
1894–1956
French painter of Russian origin. He became aware of Cubism during stays in Paris between 1910 and 1914. In St Petersburg on the outbreak of World War I, he became an active member of the Russian avantgarde, responding both to Malevich's abstractions and to Tatlin's relief constructions. He later reverted to a more naturalistic style close to Bonnard and Vuillard (*The violin*, 1919, Paris, Musée National d'Art Moderne) and settled in Paris in 1923.

Pouncing
A method, used predominantly in FRESCO painting, of transferring a CARTOON or drawing on to a wall or other painting surface. A powder (pounce) is dabbed through perforations in the outline of the drawing, thus producing on the surface a series of dots by which the outline can be reconstructed.

Pourbus family
Family of Flemish painters of the 16th and 17th centuries. The first was **Pieter** (*c.*1523–84), born in Gouda but active in Bruges from 1543. He married one of Blondeel's daughters and had something of the artist's verve, as his biblical panels show. Benson was a greater influence, however, as can be seen from the allegorical *Love feast* in the Wallace Collection, London. He also painted portraits, and it is in this field that his son **Frans I** (1545–81), a pupil of Frans Floris, and active in Antwerp, is best known. His style was more Italianate than his father's. Frans I's son **Frans II** (1569–1622) is perhaps the best-known member of the family. He had a successful career as a court portraitist, working in Flanders, France and Italy. His output was prolific and his style typical of international court portraiture of the period—formal, highly accomplished technically, with great attention paid to details of costume but without much analysis of character.

Poussin, Nicolas 1593/94–1665
French painter and draughtsman, the chief formulator of the French classical tradition in painting. After an unsuccessful early career in France he worked mainly in Italy, travelling there first in 1624. He established himself in Rome, where he studied the Antique, but he was also inspired by the Venetian painters of the 16th century, chiefly Titian and Veronese. *The poet's inspiration* (*c.*1628–29, Paris, Louvre) marks the height of this Venetian influence, but in the 1630s his style, though still sensuous, became more classical as he strove to produce pictures more closely resembling the tightly-knit compositions found on classical sarcophagi (*Bacchanalian revel*, *c.*1635, London, NG). In 1640 Poussin was invited to Paris by Louis XIII in order to decorate the Grande Galerie of the Louvre, but two years later he returned to Rome, having failed to complete his task. Large decorative compositions were alien to his temperament and he preferred to work on easel-paintings for a circle of highly cultivated private clients. His working procedure was very elaborate and methodical, the final painting being based on numerous drawings and wax models which Poussin arranged on a kind of miniature stage-set to work out the lighting and composition. In the late 1640s, when his work had reached a stage of pure and monumental classicism (*The Holy Family on the steps*, 1648, Washington, NG), he turned to ideal landscape painting, perhaps initially influenced by his brother-in-law Dughet. Poussin's landscapes are much more heroic and severe than Dughet's or Claude's (*The burial of Phocion*, 1648, Earl of Derby coll., Knowsley Hall, Lancashire) and the work of the three men provided sufficient range to form the basis for almost all classical landscape painting for the next two centuries. In his last years, Poussin's style became less rational, reviving the Venetian influences of his youth and taking on an almost mystical intensity, as in his four paintings of *The Seasons* (1660–64, Louvre). His influence was enormous. Lebrun's academic doctrines, which shaped French art for generations, were based on his work, and the great masters of Neoclassicism looked to his example. See vol. 1 pp. *124–125*; vol. 2 pp. **194–196**

Poussinisme
Term given to a movement in painting in late 17th-century France, when artists who declared their allegiance to Poussin disputed the claims of their rivals, the **Rubenistes**. The Poussinistes, led by Lebrun, put their faith in formal, classical values, and above all claimed the superiority of *disegno* or draughtsmanship. The Rubenistes admired the colouristic brilliance and free, painterly style of Rubens. Their disputes, which sometimes became acrimonious, centred on the Academy, which veered between the two sides. The famous dispute between Ingres and Delacroix was on much the same lines.

Powers, Hiram 1805–73
American sculptor, the most celebrated of such in the 19th century. He lived in Italy from 1837. His success originally came with naturalistic portrait busts (*Andrew Jackson*, *c.*1835, New York, Metropolitan), but his fame was established by, and still depends on, *The Greek slave* (1843, original version in Washington, Corcoran). This nude female figure toured America to great acclaim and was one of the sensations of the 1851 Great Exhibition in the Crystal Palace in London. To modern eyes it seems a rather slick and tepid piece of Neoclassicism, but its contemporary success depended on the way in which its sentimentality subtly cloaked its eroticism. See vol. 3 p. **106**

Poynter, Sir Edward 1836–1919
One of the leading English artists in the High Victorian period, chiefly known for his large historical canvases. He trained under Gleyre in Paris, with Whistler. By 1865 he was enjoying great success in London with elaborate reconstructions of historical events; *Israel in Egypt* (1867, London, Guildhall) is the largest. From the late 1860s he was much occupied with decorative schemes for the Houses of Parliament and elsewhere, and then with teaching and administration. He confined himself to small classical genre scenes, close in style and subject to those of Alma-Tadema.

Pozzo, Fra Andrea 1642–1709
Italian painter, architect and stage designer, one of the greatest of illusionist ceiling decorators. He was a Jesuit lay-brother (he is often given the courtesy title of "Padre") and his masterpiece is *Allegory of the missionary work of the Jesuits* (1691–94) on the nave vault of S. Ignazio, one of the most important Jesuit churches in Rome. This huge ceiling is an astonishing feat of QUADRATURA illusionist painting, the architecture and teeming figures surging towards the heavens with unprecedented energy and bravura. In 1702 he went to Vienna, where his decoration in the Jesuit church and elsewhere in the city indicated the direction Austrian Rococo would take. His influence was further spread by his treatise on perspective for painters and architects (1693), translated into English in 1707, and into Chinese by Jesuit missionaries in 1737. See vol. 2 p. **234**

Prampolini, Enrico 1894–1956
Italian painter, sculptor and designer. He joined the Futurists in 1912, producing abstract pictures such as *Lines of force in space* (1914, Venice, Peggy Guggenheim coll.) and mixed-media works called *Polimaterici*. After a Dadaist phase during World War I he returned to Futurism and designed for the theatre. From 1925 to 1937 he lived in Paris, joining the abstract art groups and developing his interest in materials and spatial structures with the *Dialogues with Material* and *Cosmic Pictures* series (*Cosmic anomalies*, 1955, Milan, Galeria Schwarz). With Magnelli, he was one of the pioneers of Italian abstract art.

Prassinos, Mario born 1916
French artist, born in Istanbul. He moved to Paris in 1922. He was scenographer for theatres in Paris and for La Scala in Milan, 1948–72. In 1949 he began making tapestries for Mobilier National des Gobelins, Paris, and he has also made designs for Sèvres ceramics. In his painting he has been obsessed by the image of his grandfather Pretextat, which he explains in his book *Les Pretextats* of 1973. His main body of work is in the graphic media and is heavily influenced by Surrealism.

Pratt, Christopher born 1935
Canadian High Realist painter. A student of Colville, Pratt works in Newfoundland, and depicts evocative images of isolation, often in architectural subjects (*Demolition on the south side*, 1961, Halifax, Dalhousie University coll.). His work is avidly collected in Canada.

Pratt, Matthew 1734–1805
American painter, active mainly in his native Philadelphia. From 1765 to 1768 he visited England, where he studied with West, and Pratt's masterpiece, *The American school* (1765, New York, Metropolitan) shows West instructing his pupils. The elegance and crisp draughtsmanship of this arresting work held great promise for the future, but Pratt's later works tended to be conventional society portraits.

Praxiteles active mid-4th century BC. Greek sculptor from Athens, among the most celebrated artists of antiquity. He was a prolific artist, and many of his works have been identified in Roman copies, among them the *Aphrodite* which he made for the Cnidians, the work for which he was most famed. Copies of this, the first statue to represent the goddess wholly nude, may reproduce to some extent the soft fluidity of its pose, but otherwise give little sense of the delicate sensuality for which the original was famous. The most notable of the works associated with him, however, is *Hermes with the infant Dionysos*, found at Olympia in 1877 and now in the museum there; it may be original, though the matter is controversial. The pose of the Hermes is characteristic of 4th-century sculpture in its rhythmical balance, soft transitions and flowing curves, while the refined modelling of the features imparts an expression of almost feminine grace to the god. This softening of the forms of the 5th century marks a shift away from the remote idealization of the Classical period towards an art which, though still (for a time) ideally beautiful, was growing more concerned with expression and human emotion. In Praxiteles' work this is apparent in the meditative absorption in the faces of his statues, in his development of allegorical works such as *Persuasion* and *Consolation* and in his conception of intimate groups such as the *Hermes* already mentioned. It was this almost picturesque aspect of his work which was to influence the development of Hellenistic sculpture more than the purely formal qualities. See vol. 2 p. **40**

Precisionism
A specifically American style of painting, at its height during the 1920s, in which urban and industrial scenes are rendered in a precise, clean-edged, simplified manner. Those associated with the style, Demuth, Dickinson, O'Keeffe, Sheeler and Spencer, do not form a coherent group, but were linked by their emphasis on mechanical, industrial forms. Demuth's *Buildings, Lancaster* (1930, New York, Whitney) is typical of the style, which seems rather cold and lacking in any human element. The group were also known as the Sterilists, Cubist-Realists and Immaculates.

Preda or **Predis, Ambrogio da**
*c.*1455–after 1508 and **Evangelista da** active 1483–after 1490
Milanese painters, half-brothers. They are best known for their association with Leonardo da Vinci in the contract (1483) for *The Virgin of the rocks* (London, NG). The brothers are usually accredited with the wings, which depict angels with musical instruments, although some also claim to detect their hands in the central panel, which is of much higher quality. Ambrogio has the greater substance as an independent artist and worked mainly as a portraitist. His style is a rather mechanical imitation of Leonardo's.

Predella
One or more small panels affixed to the bottom of an altarpiece. The scenes shown generally relate to, or comment on, the main scene above.

Prendergast, Maurice 1859–1924
American painter, a member of The EIGHT. He studied from 1891 to 1894 in Paris, where he encountered the work of Vuillard and Bonnard and the Nabis. Their influence is apparent in the brilliant colours and highly decorative patterns of his paintings (*The promenade*, 1913, New York, Whitney).

Pre-Raphaelite Brotherhood
Small but influential group of English painters, formed in 1848 and so named because they wanted to recapture the simplicity and moral content of painting before Raphael. The original members were Rossetti, Hunt, Millais, Woolner, James Collinson (1825?–81), the critic F.F. Stephens and the writer W.M. Rossetti, the painter's brother. At first violently attacked, in 1851 they gained the support of Ruskin, but two years later the group had virtually disbanded. They sought to combat what they considered the sterile English academic tradition and the prevalence of trivial genre painting. They stressed the importance of painting from nature, paying careful attention to detail. To achieve a brilliant purity of colour they painted on a white ground. The achievement of the Brotherhood is not to be confused with the second wave of Pre-Raphaelitism, notably the pseudo-medieval subjects and languorous female beauties produced by Burne-Jones and Rossetti in the 1860s and after. See vol. 3 pp. 82–83

Preston, Margaret Rose
1883–1963
Australian painter and graphic artist who travelled widely in Europe until 1920. Her absorption of Fauvism distinguishes her early, highly decorative still-life paintings with their bright Australian flora. Her later, more austere manner, using sober colours and simple block-like shapes bounded with crisp contours, reached a high point in works such as *Implement blue* (1927, Sydney, NG of New South Wales). She was the first Australian painter to recognize the quality of Aboriginal bark-paintings.

Preti, Mattia (Il Calabrese) 1613–99
Italian Baroque painter, who travelled widely in Italy and had a prolific output. His early easel-paintings are Caravaggesque, but his frescos, on which his reputation rests, are modelled mainly on Lanfranco, whom he succeeded in the decoration of S. Andrea della Valle, Rome (1650–51). He worked successfully in Naples after the great plague of 1656 had carried off many of the city's artists, and in particular was given the commission for two huge frescos commemorating the plague for the city gate: these have not survived, but the sombre and powerful *modelli* for them are in the Museo di Capodimonte there. He lived in Malta from 1661, and many churches on the island have examples of his work.

Previtali, Andrea active 1502–28
Italian painter, active in his native Bergamo and in Venice, where he trained with Giovanni Bellini. His eclectic, uneven, but sometimes highly attractive work (mainly on religious subjects) was also influenced by Lotto and Palma Vecchio. He is well represented in the National Gallery, London.

Prieur, Barthélemy
active *c.*1573–1611
French sculptor, working in Paris. Around the base of the monument for the heart of Constable Montmorency (Paris, Louvre) he made three life-size, highly-finished bronze *Virtues*, using classical models but imposing Mannerist elongation of proportion. In 1594 he was sculptor to Charles VIII of France and engaged on decoration for the part of the Louvre built by the architect Lescot. In 1610 he carried out festive decorations for the entry into Paris of Queen Marie de Médicis. His work can be seen as a kind of sculptural equivalent to the paintings of the second school of Fontainebleau.

Primary colour
Term used in painting of red, yellow and blue, since they cannot be created by a mixture of other colours and are themselves the bases for these colours. Thus red and yellow make orange, red and blue make purple and blue and yellow make green. These mixtures are called **secondary** colours.

Primaticcio, Francesco
1504/5–70
Italian painter and architect, born in Bologna. In 1526 he joined Giulio Romano in Mantua and assisted in the decoration of the Ducal Palaces. In 1532 he went to FONTAINEBLEAU and collaborated with Rosso on the decoration of the great royal residence there. On Rosso's death he took over the direction of the work. The Ballroom and the Chamber of the Duchesse d'Etampes show Primaticcio's elegant Mannerist figure types, derived from Parmigianino and embellished with gorgeous decoration. For Francis I he went to Rome in the 1540s to buy antiquities and casts of famous statues. With Rosso he introduced Italian Mannerist features into French decorative art, and his engravings had far-reaching influence. See vol. 2 p. **167**

Primitive see NAIVE

Prix de Rome
A four-year travelling scholarship to Rome which was initiated under Colbert with the foundation of the French Academy in Rome, the "Villa Médicis", in 1666. In the 18th and 19th centuries it was the most coveted prize in official artistic circles in France.

Profil perdu
French term meaning "lost profile", referring to the image presented when a head is turned so far from the spectator that the profile is no longer visible as, for example, in Ingres's *Valpinçon bather* (1808, Paris, Louvre).

Prout, Samuel 1783–1852
English watercolourist. His picturesque views of Europe promoted the popular romantic vision of the continent through such publications as Robert Jennings' *Landscape Annual, the Tourist in Switzerland and Italy* (1830), where they appeared as engravings. His carefully worked designs of local scenes were particularly admired by Ruskin.

Provenance
The history of a work of art from its creation through to the present day. A full provenance includes details of all the previous owners and locations.

Provost, Jan *c.*1462–1529
Netherlandish painter, born at Mons and working initially in Valenciennes, perhaps as a pupil of Marmion. After a brief stay in Antwerp, he qualified in 1494 as a master in Bruges. There he conformed to the popular taste for soft brushwork and a smooth finish, as exemplified by the docile *Madonnas* of Gerard David. His panels often suffer from overcrowding—witness the *Legend of St Catherine* (Antwerp, Musées Royaux des Beaux-Arts)—but his powers of pictorial invention can prove quite startling. The nocturnal *Nativity* scene at Banbury (Upton House), dominated by a large ox in the foreground, provides a very fresh approach to a familiar theme.

Prud'hon, Pierre-Paul 1758–1823
French painter, a leading figure in the transition from Neoclassicism to Romanticism. In 1784, Prud'hon won the

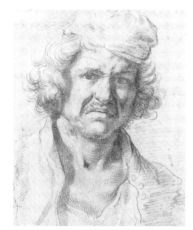
Poussin: Self-portrait drawing, *c.*1630. London, BM

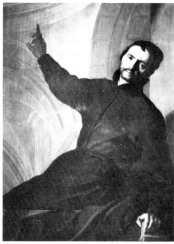
Pozzo: Self-portrait, 1685. Florence, Uffizi (Scala)

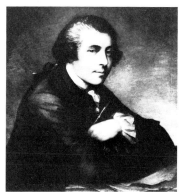
Pratt: Self-portrait, 1764. Washington DC, Smithsonian Institution, NPG

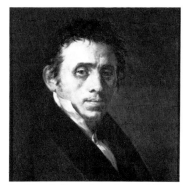
Prud'hon: Self-portrait, *c.*1803–05. Dijon, Musée Magnin

Prix de Rome and in Italy was deeply impressed by the SFUMATO of Leonardo and, above all, by Correggio. Prud'hon received numerous official commissions under the Consulate and became a favourite painter of the wives of Napoleon I, the Empresses Josephine and Marie-Louise. His greatest work, *Justice and Divine Vengeance pursuing Crime* (1808, Paris, Louvre), is notable for its moral content and successful combination of Correggio's style with Baroque and Classical elements. See vol. 3 p. **59**

Pucelle, Jehan active *c.*1300–*c.*1355
An outstanding French miniaturist of the early 14th century. Records of his work begin with an account entry of 1319–24, and include the names of many assistants in his Parisian workshop (and the high prices paid for his pictures). His most famous work is the Book of Hours of Jeanne d'Evreux (1325–28, New York, Cloisters Museum), which has delicate, graceful monochrome scenes framed by prominent marginal ornament—an arrangement which soon became popular. His rendering of pictorial space and iconography reflects contemporary Italian achievements. See vol. 2 p. **89**

Puget, Pierre 1620–94
The most powerful and individual French sculptor of the 17th century, active mainly in his native Marseilles and in Toulon. From 1640 to 1643 he worked in Rome and Florence with Pietro da Cortona, and the emotional intensity of his work is based on Italian Baroque and on Michelangelo, whose influence is clearly seen in the physical and mental anguish of Puget's *Atlantes* (1656) for the doorway of Toulon Town Hall, his first important commission. Puget made several visits to Genoa, and also worked in Paris, but although his most famous work *Milo of Crotona* (1672–82, Paris, Louvre) was accepted for the gardens at Versailles, his style was too personal and Baroque for him to achieve the success at court he desired. His headstrong temperament—almost that of a Romantic artist—also hindered his career, and his final years were embittered. Puget was a splendid draughtsman, and also occasionally painted. See vol. 2 p. **199**

Pulzone, Scipione *c.*1550–98
Italian painter, born near Naples. In Rome he portrayed Popes Gregory XIII and Sixtus V and many notables, and painted altarpieces such as the *Crucifixion* in the Chiesa Nuova, clearly ordered in composition but slight in feeling. About 1589 he was called to Florence to paint Ferdinando de' Medici and his wife (portraits in Florence, Pitti Gallery). Described as well-paid and of princely aspect, he regarded himself as an authority on the theory of painting.

Purism
French avantgarde art movement founded by Le Corbusier and Ozenfant. Their theoretical programme was set out in their book *After Cubism* (1918), in which they criticized the tendency within Cubism toward facile decorative effects and advocated a return to its original order, clarity and objectiveness. Art, they believed, should be in tune with the Machine Age and their paintings contain predominantly machine-made objects rendered in cool, restricted colours with an impersonal finish. Typical examples are Ozenfant's *Composition* (1920, Basle, Kunstmuseum) and Le Corbusier's *Still life* (1920, New York, MOMA). They expounded their views in the periodical *L'Esprit Nouveau*, published between 1921 and 1925—the years during which Purism was at its height. By 1930 both men were pursuing different goals. The Purist aesthetic, however, has since been influential on much design work. See vol. 3 p. 179

Purrmann, Hans 1880–1966
German painter, a member of the Berlin Sezession. He went to Paris in 1906 to study Impressionism but was more influenced by the Fauves. Gertrude and Leo Stein introduced him to Matisse, with whom he shared a studio and whose light airy touch and rich tone he tried to emulate (*Factory landscape in Corsica*, 1912, Cologne, Wallraf-Richartz). He also helped to organize the Académie Matisse until his return to Berlin in 1914. His style from then on was a fusion of Matisse's graceful gaiety with German introspection. Dismissed by the Nazis, he settled in Switzerland in 1943.

Putto (plural **putti**)
Term from the Italian for "little boy", applied to the plump, naked children, sometimes winged, who appear in works of art. They are commonly found as decorative motifs in 15th- and 16th-century Italian art, but first appeared in antique art.

Puvis de Chavannes, Pierre
1824–98
French painter. His non-naturalistic work and use of the formal means of line and colour to convey the message of the painting were influential for the SYMBOLISTS. *The poor fisherman* (1881, Paris, Louvre), much admired for its static, timeless, soulful qualities, is a good example of his Symbolist work. He carried out many large decorative commissions, but worked in oil rather than fresco—though his pale tonality imitates its effects, as in *The inspiring Muses* painted for Boston Public Library, 1893–95. He was immensely popular in his day and very influential on younger artists. See vol. 1 p. *125*; vol. 3 p. **122**

Pynacker, Adam 1622–73
Dutch landscape painter born in Pijnacker near Delft, and active principally in Delft and Amsterdam. He is said to have spent three years in Italy, and he was one of the finest of the Italianate Dutch landscapists. Among his contemporaries he is closest to Asselyn and Jan Both, but Pynacker sometimes excels them in boldness of invention, and his work is often marked by a distinctive silvery blue tonality. A particularly large and splendid example is *Landscape with sportsmen and game* (1660s, London, Dulwich College Picture Gallery).

Pythagoras
active 1st half of 5th century BC
Greek sculptor. He is named by ancient authors with Kalamis and Myron as one of the outstanding sculptors of the period. No extant work of his is known.

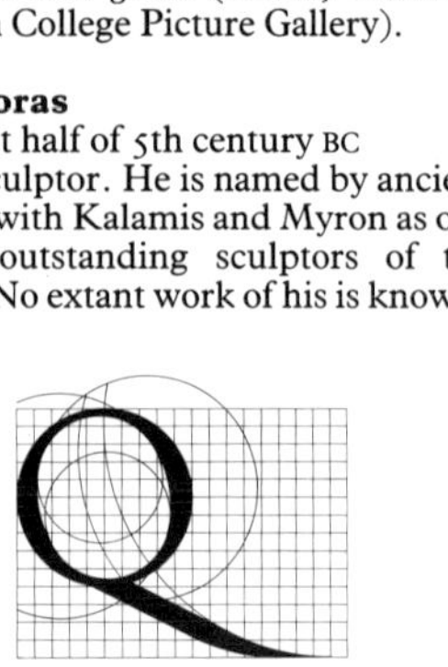

Qasim Ali Chikrehayshay
active last quarter of 15th century
Persian or eastern Turkish painter working in Herat, where his patrons were Mir Ali Shir Navai and Sultan Husayn Bayqara. His work closely resembles that of his master, Bihzad, though his epithet indicates that he was a celebrated painter of faces. He was responsible for several pages in the 1485 *Sadd-i Iskandari* (Oxford, Bodleian Library) and the 1494 *Khamseh* (London, BL). It seems that he was a learned and religious man, and that he retired to teach in Sistan.

Qian Xuan *c.*1235–1300
Chinese painter, an important agent in the transmission of Song academic ideals into the Yuan dynasty. Qian worked in both the flower-and-bird tradition and that of figure painting, producing an idealized version of the lost Tang figure style. Despite invitations to the Mongol court at Peking he remained in isolation, both from the new court tradition of Zhao Menfu, and from the art of those scholars who were denied access to power under the new regime. His elegantly coloured works such as *Crab-apple and gardenia* or *Yang Guifei mounting a horse* (both early Yuan dynasty, Washington, Freer Gallery) must have looked increasingly old-fashioned as the 14th century wore on, and the more austere monochrome painting gained greater acceptance.

Qiu Ying died 1552(?)
Chinese painter, a leading professional of the mid-Ming dynasty. Qiu was of lowly origin, and his career was set entirely in the prosperous lower Yangtze region, where he was frequently patronized by wealthy collectors, as much for his skill as a copyist of old masters as on his own account. In later centuries, he was famed almost solely for his detailed, highly-coloured scenes of élite life, and in particular beautiful women, but extant works demonstrate a much wider range, from the controlled brushwork of *Spring morning in the Han Palace* (Taiwan, National Palace Museum), to freer renderings of gentlemanly pursuits. He was much imitated and forged.

Quadratura
Illusionistic architectural decoration of walls or ceilings which appears to extend the real architecture of a room into an imaginary space. Mantegna pioneered its development in his *Camera degli Sposi* in the Ducal Palace, Mantua, and it reached its fullest expression in Baroque Italy, when there were specialists known as quadraturisti who supplied the architectural framework for other painters' figures. Colonna and Tassi are two well-known examples. Pozzo's huge, dizzying ceiling in S. Ignazio, Rome (1691–94), is perhaps the most celebrated of all feats of quadratura. As with other similar examples, the illusion works properly only from a single central viewing point.

Quadro riportato
Italian term meaning "carried picture", used to describe a picture on a ceiling which does not attempt illusionistic foreshortening, and is painted with the same perspective system as an easel-painting seen at eye level. A classic example is the central panel of the Farnese Gallery by Annibale Carracci.

Quarton (Charonton), **Enguerrand**
*c.*1410–66
French painter, born in Laon and active at Aix, Arles and Avignon. Two surviving works are documented as his, *The Virgin of Mercy* (1452, Chantilly, Musée Condé), painted in collaboration with the obscure **Pierre Villatte** (active 1452–95) and *The Coronation of the Virgin* (1454, Villeneuve-les-Avignon, Musée de l'Hospice). They are characterized by angular figures and harsh lighting, and are similar to the Avignon *Pietà* (Paris, Louvre), which has been attributed to Quarton. See vol. 2 p. **97**

Quattrocento
Term, literally the "400s", used of the 15th century, the "1400s", in Italian art. It is often used by art historians adjectivally: a work may show Quattrocento, or early Renaissance characteristics.

Queirolo, Francesco 1704–62
Italian sculptor, born in Genoa and active mainly in Rome and Naples. His style was based ultimately on Bernini and he was a virtuoso technician, as is best seen in his *Allegory of deception unmasked* (after 1750) in the Cappella Sansevero de' Sangri, Naples. This chapel is famous for its ambitious and intricate sculptural decoration, but even in such surroundings Queirolo's group, which features a net carved from marble, stands out as a *tour de force*.

Quellin (Quellinus) **family**
Flemish family of sculptors. **Artus** (Arnoldus) **I** (1609–68) was the most talented and important. He studied with Duquesnoy in Rome and developed an impressive classical style, which he employed magnificently in the decoration of Amsterdam Town Hall. Quellin was in charge of this, one of the great sculptural ensembles of the 17th century, from about 1650 to 1664. He was also a fine portrait sculptor (examples in Amsterdam, Rijksmuseum), and capable of deep feeling in his religious work (*St Peter*, 1658, Antwerp, St Andreas Kerk). **Artus II** (1625–1700), his cousin, worked in a more full-blooded Baroque style, exemplified in his figure of *God the Father* (1682) for the rood screen of Bruges Cathedral, an impressive rhetorical piece, with magnificent, deeply undercut draperies. Artus II's son, **Artus III** (1653–86), usually called Arnold, came to England in about 1678, and worked successfully with Grinling Gibbons, notably on the great altarpiece for James II's chapel at Whitehall Palace (1686, fragments survive at Burnham Church, Somerset). His most important independent work is the tomb of Thomas Thynne (1682) in Westminster Abbey, with its famous relief below the reclining effigy showing Thynne's murder by highwaymen.

Quercia, Jacopo della
1374/5–1438
The greatest Sienese sculptor of the 15th century. His style was rooted in the Gothic manner of Giovanni Pisano, but in its robust realism also reflects Northern sculpture, perhaps that of Sluter. His career was peripatetic: for much of it he was working on more than one commission in different places at the same time, and both his personal and professional life seems to have been turbulent. He first appears competing for the Florence Baptistery doors in 1401, but his piece is lost and his earliest surviving work is the tomb of Ilario del Carretto (1406, Lucca Cathedral), one of the most distinguished early Renaissance tombs. No longer complete, it comprises a life-size recumbent effigy, in the northern manner, on a deep base classically decorated with plump *putti* and swags of fruit and flowers. *The Madonna* of 1408 in Ferrara Cathedral offered more scope for lively representation and his use of full, sensuous, heavily folded drapery. Also brilliantly animated are the fragments of reliefs and figures for a fountain in Siena, The Fonte Gaia (1414–19, Siena, Palaz-

zo Pubblico), including some superb draped female figures and a relief of *The Expulsion from Paradise*, which, although severely battered, retains immense power. He also contributed, with Donatello and Ghiberti, to the Siena Baptistery font (1417–30). His masterworks are the reliefs for the doorway of S. Petronio in Bologna, begun in 1425 and left unfinished at his death. The dramatic and heroic nudes in these vigorous panels impressed Michelangelo, who visited Bologna in 1494. See vol. 1 p. *42*; vol. 2 p. **101**

Quidor, John 1801–81
American painter. He made his living mainly as a sign-painter, since the humorous genre pieces in which he specialized were generally ignored. Quidor's subjects came mostly from romantic literature, especially the work of Washington Irving (*The Return of Rip van Winkle*, 1829, Washington, NG). His lively and sometimes grotesque imagination seems to have been stimulated by 17th-century Netherlandish painting and by English pictorial satirists such as Hogarth and Rowlandson.

Rabin, Oskar born 1928
Russian painter. One of the major figures of so-called "unofficial art" in the Soviet Union, Rabin works in a highly personal manner with his roots in the Symbolist art of the beginning of the century. Suburban landscapes and still lifes, where every object seems to live its own sinister life, have brought him wide international acclaim.

Räderscheidt, Anton 1892–1970
German painter, one of the foundermembers, with Hoerle, of the Cologne Progressive Artists' Association after World War I. Influenced by Chirico, he developed a MAGIC REALIST style in which he depicted the isolation and alienation of urban man as a puppet-like figure in a deserted townscape (*Young man with yellow gloves*, 1921, Private coll.). In the 1930s his mood softened, and after World War II he turned to abstract painting.

Radziwill, Frans born 1895
German painter. He trained as an architect, and after World War I settled in Berlin, where he joined the NOVEMBERGRUPPE (1920) and began to paint in the style of Magic Realism. In the mid-1920s his works acquired a Surrealist overtone. He was fascinated by the alienation of man in the technical age; machines and buildings are seen as autonomous, no longer dependent on man for their meaning (*The strike*, 1931, Münster, Landesmuseum). An atmosphere of impending chaos is created by the sudden appearance in these eerie landscapes and urban scenes of comets or low-flying aircraft.

Raeburn, Sir Henry 1756–1823
Scottish portrait painter who achieved a status in the Scottish art world similar to that of Reynolds in England. He moved in 1784 to London, where he met Reynolds, but after a trip to Italy in 1787 he returned to Edinburgh. His portraits of leading literary and legal worthies and Highland chiefs were painted without preliminary drawings in an original, bold and direct style often called his

"square touch". At times this led to rather empty technical bravura, but it was also very well suited to his more rugged masculine sitters (*Sir John Sinclair*, c.1794–95, Edinburgh, NG of Scotland). See vol. 1 p. *131*

Raffaëlli, Jean-François 1850–1924
French painter, engraver, lithographer and sculptor. He was known for his paintings of working-class life on the outskirts of Paris, and was particularly interested in characteristic gestures and physiognomies. Even though he exhibited with the Impressionists in 1880 and 1881 he remained unaffected by their use of bright colour. *Blacksmiths drinking* (1885, Douai, Musée Chartreuse) is typically dark-toned. His work was admired in the late 19th century.

Raffaellino del Garbo c.1479–c.1527
Florentine painter. It is now thought that this artist, written about by Vasari, is the same person as Raphael Capponi, the "*pictor nel Garbo*" and Raffaele Carli, all of whom are documented. If the paintings associated with them are all by Raffaellino then he was highly eclectic—painting in a style derived from Botticelli, Ghirlandaio and Perugino. The one painting unanimously accepted by critics as his work is *The Resurrection* (c.1496–1505?, Florence, Uffizi).

Raggi, Antonio 1624–86
Italian sculptor, initially trained in Algardi's studio, but later Bernini's favourite pupil. By 1647 he was working under Bernini on the decoration of the interior of St Peter's, and remained with him for more than 30 years, although he also had independent commissions. He was at his best working in stucco, as in the great cycle of decoration in Il Gesù (1669–83), notably the clerestory of the nave and transepts, where his intense, nervous figures are a perfect accompaniment to Gaulli's ceiling. See vol. 2 p. **234**

Raimondi, Marcantonio c.1480?–c.1534
Italian engraver, who pioneered the use of prints as a means of reproducing the work of other artists. He was a pupil of Francia in Bologna and worked in north Italy until about 1510, when he moved to Rome. There he became particularly associated with Raphael, of whose work he issued numerous prints which played an important role in the dissemination of Raphaelesque classicism throughout Europe. See vol. 1 p. *84*

Rainer, Arnulf born 1929
Austrian artist. He works mainly with photographs of his own body, often in hysterical poses, overlaid with violent and apparently cancelling marks, owing something to Abstract Expressionism.

Rajput painting
Painting produced at the Hindu Rajput courts of Rajasthan, Bundelkhand and the Punjab Hills of north-west India from about 1600 to the 19th century. Principally concerned with Hindu subjects, in which the god Krishna and his adventures figure predominantly, it is distinguished from contemporary Mughal painting by simpler compositions, hotter colours and sophisticated stylizations of form. Recent discoveries have now made it clear that early Rajput painting, so far from being an offshoot of Mughal painting produced at Rajput courts imitating that of the Emperors, in fact predates the Mughal school and developed out of the highly stylized

western Indian paintings cultivated by the Jains from about the 15th century, probably under the influence of imported paintings from Iran, or out of lost Hindu examples in a similar style. The principal centres, so far as we know, for the production of Rajput painting were Mewar, Bundi, Kotan, Bikaner, Jaipur, Kishangarh (where Nihal Chand was active) and Jodhpur in Rajasthan, and in the Punjab hills Basohli, Kulu, Guler and Kangra. Originally concerned with the illustration of manuscripts, in the course of the 17th century the schools began to produce portraits and genre scenes, as well as frescos to decorate palace walls. Perhaps under the influence of the frescos, very much larger paintings, in which hunting scenes were predominant, were produced in the 18th century. After about 1800, European influence undermined the subtle basis of Rajput stylizations. See vol. 3 p. *21*

Ramirez-Villamizar, Eduardo born 1923
Colombian sculptor and exponent of geometric abstract painting. In the 1950s with others, including Rayo, Negret and Rojas, he advanced the spatial and constructive concerns of geometric painting, and went on to develop a group of monumental designs for outdoor spaces such as his *Architectural labyrinth* of 1973 in Bogota, Public Gardens. In their rectilinear purity and scale they recall the non-utilitarian architectural projects of Malevich and the Italian Futurist architect Sant'Elia.

Ramsay, Allan 1713–84
Scottish painter, active mainly in London, one of the most sensitive portraitists in the history of British art. After practising briefly in Edinburgh he worked in Rome and Naples, 1736–38. The experience must have enhanced his innate good taste and decorative sense, both of which find a reflection in his portraits, such as *Rosamund Sargent* (1749, Bath, Holburne of Menstrie Museum), painted in London on his return. In the early 1750s, partly under the influence of French pastellists, his art entered a second, more ambitious phase. His modelling became softer, his colours lighter and his poses more varied. He revisited Rome, 1754–57, partly to improve his skill in drawing, and while there painted his masterpiece, *The artist's wife* (c.1755, Edinburgh, NG of Scotland), a work of exquisite delicacy in characterization and execution. For the next ten years he was a serious rival to Reynolds, at any rate in portraits of women, but, after executing the coronation portraits of *George III* and *Queen Charlotte* (1761/2, Royal coll.) he gradually retired from painting and devoted himself to political studies and archaeology. See vol. 2 p. **250**

Ranson, Paul 1864–1909
French painter, a founder-member of the NABIS. As well as painting, he also designed tapestry cartoons, ceramics, book illustrations and costumes for puppets and founded the Académie Ransom in Paris, which his widow continued to run after his early death. His *Christ and Buddha* (c.1890, Private coll.) shows his deep commitment to theosophy.

Ranzoni, Daniele 1843–89
Italian painter, associated with the SCAPIGLIATI and best known for his portraits of women and children. His small, feverish brush-strokes, delicate tonalities and introvert nature, exemplified in *Girl in white* (c.1887, Milan, Galleria d'Arte Moderna), distinguish his work

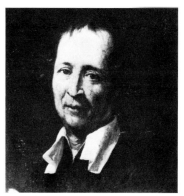

Puget: Self-portrait, 1650s. Aix, Musée Granet

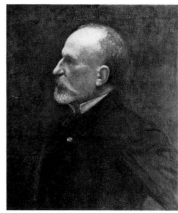

Puvis de Chavannes: Self-portrait, 1887. Florence, Uffizi (Mansell)

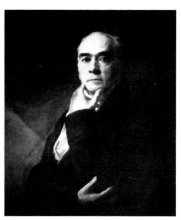

Raeburn: Self-portrait, c.1815. Edinburgh, NG of Scotland

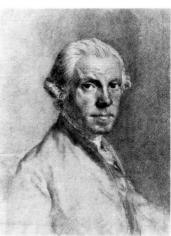

Ramsay: Self-portrait, 1776. London, NPG

from that of Cremona. His search for luminosity influenced the Divisionists.

Raoux, Jean 1677–1734
French portrait painter, a pupil of Rigaud. *Mlle Prévost as a Bacchante* (1723, Tours, Musée) is representative of his portraits of women in classical guise, a genre more sympathetically practised by Nattier.

Raphael (Raffaello Sanzio) 1483–1520
Italian painter and architect, in whose works are found the most complete expression of the ideals of the High Renaissance. He was born in Urbino, the son of Giovanni Santi, who gave him his first instruction in art. According to Vasari Raphael then trained with Perugino, and his early work is so overwhelmingly influenced by Perugino that there is little reason to doubt it. Raphael was very precocious, and in *The marriage of the Virgin* of 1504 (Milan, Brera), which is closely based on a painting of the same subject by Perugino, the lucidity, solidity and easy grace surpass that of his teacher. Between the years 1504 and 1508 Raphael was working widely in Tuscany and Umbria, and absorbed the impact of Florentine art, particularly of Leonardo, whose compositional devices he developed in a series of lovely paintings of *The Virgin and Child*, exuding a sense of well-being foreign both to Leonardo and to Michelangelo. (Leonardo and Michelangelo were essentially solitary figures, while Raphael was renowned for his sociable courtesy and charm). In 1508 he was called by Pope Julius II to Rome (where he was to remain for the rest of his life) and took over the fresco decoration of a series of rooms (the Stanze) in the Vatican. The first room, the *Stanza della Segnatura*, contains one of his most celebrated works, "*The School of Athens*", which, though on a larger scale than his previous work, already demonstrated the harmony, serenity and majesty which characterized his mature style. By the time he completed the second room, the *Stanza d'Eliodoro* in 1514, Raphael was in such demand that from then on much of his work was executed by assistants, as, for example, were the celebrated cartoons (1515–16, London, V&A) for tapestries for the Sistine Chapel. Exceptions include some portraits, in which he rivalled Leonardo's subtlety of characterization (*Baldassare Castiglione*, c.1516, Paris, Louvre). Extremely adaptable, always ready to absorb new influences (from Michelangelo, from Sebastiano del Piombo), Raphael was highly influential on early Mannerism and even, for instance, on the young Titian in Venice; his designs became widely known through Raimondi's engravings. His subsequent influence has been perhaps even greater, as for three centuries after his death he was almost universally regarded as the greatest of all painters—the artist who had expressed the loftiest ideals of Christianity with the grace and grandeur of the Antique. Among High Renaissance architects he ranks second only to Bramante, whom he succeeded as architect to St Peter's in 1514, but little of his work survives as designed. See vol. 1 pp. *25*, *79*, *81*, *105*; vol. 2 pp. *129*, **136–137**, *164*

Ratgeb, Jörg c.1480–1526
German painter, active in Swabia—in Frankfurt, 1514–17, and Stuttgart after 1520. The *Flagellation* from the Herrenberg altarpiece (1519, Stuttgart, Staatsgalerie) shows his liking for somewhat cramped compositions, and the influence of Grünewald is apparent in the exaggerated expressionism of the figures. He was executed for his part in the Peasants' Revolt.

Rauch, Christian Daniel 1777–1857
German NEOCLASSICAL sculptor. He studied under Schadow and was deeply influenced by Thorvaldsen during his stay in Rome between 1804 and 1811. After moving to Berlin in 1812 he received many commissions for monuments commemorating royal figures, such as that of Queen Luise (1814, East Berlin, Charlottenburg). His style is characterized by an extremely smooth treatment of his material and a strong tendency toward decorativeness and courtly elegance.

Rauschenberg, Robert born 1925
American artist who emerged as an influential leader of the avantgarde in the 1950s. He studied at Black Mountain College with Albers, whose reductive, structural concerns are evident in Rauschenberg's early black, white and red paintings. Around 1954 he began to incorporate everyday objects in his paintings; among the earliest of these "combine-paintings" is *Bed* (1955, New York, Mr and Mrs Leo Castelli coll.)—a quilt-covered bed hung on the wall and splashed with paint in a manner parodying Abstract Expressionism. Another is perhaps his most famous work, *Monogram* (1963, Stockholm, Moderna Museet), in which a stuffed angora goat girt with a tyre is painted in a similar fashion. The artist has stated his intention to "act in the gap between life and art", and his work acts as a hinge between the self-consciously arty inward-looking Abstract Expressionists and the Pop artists' exploration and adulation of the external world. For Rauschenberg paint, reproduced images and common objects carry equal weight and significance. This is also true in his silk-screen work of the 1960s. These complex, collage-like compositions, full of references to current events, art history and literature, combine newspaper images and fine art reproductions with floating planes of colour and flourishing abstract scrawls (*Retroactive*, 1964, Hartford, Wadsworth Atheneum). Rauschenberg is continually experimental and a recent series, *Jammers* (1975–76), features cloth panels and poles, diaphanous fabric silk-screens and wall panels suggestive of interiors. He has been involved in Happenings, Performance, theatre design and choreography. See vol. 1 p. *155*; vol. 3 p. **236**

Ray, Man 1890–1977
American painter, photographer and film-maker. His early works are in a Cubist style, but after meeting Duchamp in 1915 his sophisticated Dadaist spirit was revealed by paintings such as *The rope dancer accompanies herself with her shadows* (1916, New York, MOMA), with its schematic mechanical forms. He was an indefatigable technical experimenter, and in 1917 invented the Rayograph, a device whereby light affects negative film without the use of a camera. He also created a number of Dada-Surrealist objects such as the absurd *Gift* (1921, Chicago, Mr & Mrs Newmann coll.), an iron with an attached row of nails. From 1920 to 1940 he lived in Paris, where he was prominent in Surrealist circles and made four films. His later work is more academic. See vol. 3 p. **166**

Rayo, Omar born 1928
Colombian painter and printmaker. His style stems from enquiries into geometrical grids and formalist methods of design. He uses illusionistic devices to upset the planar dimensions of his work, and many of the images are based on the repetition of a single element which is carried through to the periphery of the shaped canvas and restated in the form of a three-dimensional object. His prints consist only of the relief impression of the object on the paper.

Rayonnism (Rayonism, Rayism)
Non-objective painting style, conceived in Moscow by Larionov about 1911. The first documentary mention of the term *Luchizm* (literally "ray-ism") dates from autumn, 1912, although Larionov insisted on much earlier dates for his invention of non-objective painting. Larionov and Goncharova, the chief exponents of Rayonnism, painted a number of canvasses in which the objects are distorted, apparently by the action of different rays of light, as in his *Glass* (1912) and her *Cats* (1913, both New York, Guggenheim). This construction of a non-objective painting through the exploration of "colour, light and texture" provided a solution for Russian artists searching in 1916–17 for a pragmatic alternative to Suprematism and thus contributed to the evolution of Constructivism. See vol. 3 pp. 156–157

Raysse, Martial born 1936
French painter. He began by painting abstract canvases and constructing Surrealist assemblages, but has become best known as a leading exponent of POP art. His compositions, which include real objects, are usually produced with spray paints, often using stencils. They celebrate the mundane aspects of daily popular culture (*Simple and tranquil painting*, 1965, Cologne, Wallraf-Richartz). He has also produced theatre designs.

Read, Sir Herbert 1893–1968
British art critic and poet. His book *Art Now* (1933) presented to the British public a much broader view of the modern movement in art than had been previously available, so effectively ending the dominance of Fry and Bell. Subsequently he espoused both Surrealism and abstraction at a time when they were generally regarded as antithetical. *Education through Art* (1943), which used the insights of psychoanalysis to justify the teaching of art as an aid to the growth of the individual personality, was still more far-reaching in its impact.

Ready-made
Term used by Marcel Duchamp to describe his designation of certain objects of everyday use as works of art. His first "assisted" ready-made was a bicycle wheel placed upside-down on a chair (1912); his first true ready-made was *Bottle rack* (1914, formerly Paris, Man Ray coll., now Milan, Private coll.).

Realism
Term used in a general sense to describe unidealized and objective representation, and more specifically (often with capital R) applied to a movement in 19th-century art, particularly in France. French Realist painters rebelled against the idealized subjects of mythical and historical painting and turned to contemporary ones. Caricaturists such as Daumier, and genre painters such as Bonvin and Ribot, led the way in the 1830s, but it was Courbet who became the leading Realist, creating a coherent and revolutionary movement with his massive compositions (*The burial at Ornans*, 1850, Paris, Louvre). Courbet's own dictum, that "painting is essentially a concrete art and must be applied to real and existing things", sums up French 19th-century Realism. See vol. 3 p. 88–91

Rebeyrolle, Paul born 1926
French painter. He first worked as an enameller and began to paint after he moved to Paris in 1944, his early work being influenced by Picasso, Soutine and Chagall. His output consists chiefly of landscapes and genre scenes painted in a realistic manner. His use of heavy impasto as well as his subject matter made a great impact on the young British realists of the 1950s.

Red-figure vase-painting
Technique of Greek vase-painting, developed at Athens around 530 BC, in which the figures were reserved in the basic red colour of the pot, while the background was filled in around them in black. The advantage of this technique over the BLACK-FIGURE style which it came to replace was that the details of the figures could be drawn with a brush rather than incised into a black silhouette. See vol. 2 p. 34

Redgrave, Richard 1804–88
English landscape and genre painter. During the 1840s he specialized in contemporary social issues, for example *The seamstress* (1846, Forbes Magazine coll.), depicting the plight of women forced to stitch shirts for a pittance. Under the influence of the Pre-Raphaelites he took up landscape painting, combining it with social themes, as in *The emigrants' last sight of home: Leith Hill, Abinger, Surrey* (1859, London, Tate). His brother **Samuel** (1802–76) was a writer on art, known for his *Dictionary of Artists of the English School* (1874).

Redon, Odilon 1840–1916
French painter and lithographer. He is often associated with Moreau and Puvis de Chavannes as a major exponent of SYMBOLISM. He went to Paris in 1859 and studied under Gérôme, but suffered a nervous breakdown and had to return to his home town, Bordeaux, where he was taught by Bresdin. From 1879 he worked mostly in charcoal and lithography, producing fantastic images often inspired by the poetry of Edgar Allen Poe, and he embarked on his highly-coloured paintings and pastels only about 1892 (*The cyclops*, 1898, Otterlo, Kröller-Müller). He kept a remarkable journal, which has been published under the title *To himself*. See vol. 1 pp. *75*, *160*; vol. 3 p. **122**

Redouté, Pierre Joseph 1759–1840
Belgian flower-painter, active mainly in Paris. His delicate use of watercolour coupled with scientifically exact observation were new contributions to botanical art. He had connections with the Bourbon court and in 1805 became flower-painter to the Empress Josephine. A professor at the Jardin des Plantes, he wrote and illustrated several botanical books, notably on roses.

Rees, Otto van 1884–1957
Dutch painter. Principally self-taught, he first worked in a Neo-Impressionist style with small block-like strokes of pure colour. His friendship with van Dongen undoubtedly influenced his work until around 1919, when an admiration for the work of Bernard led to his introduction of broad planes of colour and crisp cloisonniste outlines. He then introduced collage to his work under the

influence of Cubism. In 1914 he moved, with his wife **Ada Dutilh-van Rees** (1876–1959) to Zurich, where they became involved in Dada activities at the Cabaret Voltaire. Both worked with Arp and explored abstract forms in their collages and embroidery.

Regionalism

Movement in American 20th-century art which was at its strongest in the Depression of the 1930s. The most important adherents, Benton, Curry and Wood, were all from the mid-west and their paintings tend to celebrate the life of small-town, rural America. Their styles were often traditional and in the hands of figures such as Benton and the critic Thomas Craven, Regionalism had conservative, nationalistic implications.

Regnault, Henri Alexandre Georges 1843–71

French painter of history and genre subjects. In 1866 he went to Rome, having won the Prix de Rome, and in 1868 he studied the works of Goya and Velazquez in Spain. His magnificent *Automedon with the horses of Achilles* (1868, Boston, MFA) has heroic subject matter, violent action and a suitably draped male nude holding two rearing horses in a style very similar to that of Delacroix. A career of brilliant promise was cut short when he was killed in the Franco-Prussian War. See vol. 3 p. **87**

Regnault, Jean-Baptiste, Baron 1754–1829

French painter. He painted mostly historical and mythological subjects and was received as an Academician in 1783 with his *Education of Achilles* (Paris, Louvre). His style was based on the Antique but his luminous palette and soft brushwork distinguish his work from current Neoclassical trends.

Reichlich, Marx

documented 1494–1508
Austrian painter working around Salzburg and the Tyrol. He executed altarpieces in a style which was strongly influenced by Pacher, his master, and showed evidence of direct contact with Italy; he almost certainly visited Venice. His interest in architectural construction and the effects of light and his depictions of landscape parallel those of the Danube school (three scenes from *The life of the Virgin*, 1502, Munich, Alte Pinakothek).

Reid, George Agnew 1860–1947

Canadian painter and art teacher. He studied at the Pennsylvania Academy under Eakins. *The call to dinner* (1887, Hamilton, McMaster University Art Gallery) epitomizes Reid's sympathetic approach to the simple values of country living, depicted with grace and strength.

Reiner, Václav Vavřinec 1689–1743

The most important Bohemian fresco and landscape painter of the late Baroque. From a family of artists and dealers, but with an obscure training and no direct experience in Italy, Reiner nonetheless succeeded in raising Bohemian fresco painting to a European level, using all the devices of illusionism, as in his frescos in St John Nepomuk on the Hradschin (1727). His vigorous ideal landscapes are strongly indebted to Salvator Rosa and Marco Ricci.

Reinhardt, Ad (Adolf) 1913–67

American painter. He joined the group of American Abstract Artists in 1937, producing paintings of simple geometric form in bright colours, reflecting the influence of Mondrian and Stuart Davis. In developing his abstract style Reinhardt exploited succeeding trends in American art; he was a strong protagonist of abstract painting, and in the 1940s caricatured the conservative art world in a series of satirical cartoons. During these years his style became less rigid, and he formed close friendships with Abstract Expressionist artists, but he rejected their free application of paint, and gradually began to reduce the colour and form in his paintings. He also studied Oriental art. By 1953 he was producing monochrome paintings (usually red or blue) with a rectilinear or cruciform structure, and by 1960 he arrived at his final reduction of colour and structure—his *Black Paintings*, square canvases divided into nine smaller squares of black so subtly distinguished as to approach imperceptibility. Although these anticipated Minimal art, Reinhardt's polemical theories were closer to the grandiose utterances of contemporaries such as Newman. See vol. 3 p. **222**

Reixach, Juan see BAÇO, JAIME

Relief

A sculpture in which the forms are created on or against a background surface of stone, wood, ivory or metal rather than being free-standing. Reliefs are classified usually as low (*basso relievo* or bas-relief), medium (*mezzo relievo*) or high (*alto relievo*) according to whether forms project from the background by less than half, about half, or more than half their natural depth. In many reliefs—particularly the extremely flattened kind developed by Donatello and known as *stiacciato*—the background is carved to create atmospheric or perspective effects, making relief partly a sculptural and partly a pictorial art. Though associated mainly with architecture, reliefs are also common on coins, medals, furniture and other objects. In the reverse form of relief known as sunken relief the carving is executed on an area hollowed out from the surface plane. See vol. 1 pp. 194–197

Rembrandt Harmensz. van Rijn 1606–69

Dutch painter, etcher and draughtsman, one of the supreme geniuses in the history of art. He was born in Leyden, and had his principal training (c. 1624) in Amsterdam with Lastman, who imparted his taste for religious and allegorical subjects, along with the stylistic lessons of Elsheimer and Caravaggio. Rembrandt's first dated work, *The stoning of St Stephen* (1625, Lyons, Musée), well illustrates his debt to his master. In 1625, Rembrandt was once more in Leyden, working in collaboration with Lievens, before returning permanently to Amsterdam in 1631/2. His brilliant, sharp technique and ability to convey a sense of physical presence enabled him rapidly to overtake Eliasz. and Thomas de Keyser as the city's leading portraitist. *The anatomy lesson of Dr Tulp* (1632, The Hague, Mauritshuis) established his reputation, and the fact that more than 40 of his portraits are dated 1632 or 1633 shows the extent of the demand for his work. His marriage to the wealthy Saskia van Uylenburgh, in 1634, ushered in a period of prosperity and contentment, epitomized by the opulent *Self-portrait with Saskia* (c.1635, Dresden, Gemäldegalerie). Rembrandt's religious paintings from these years were equally exuberant (*The blinding of Samson*, 1636, Frankfurt, Städelsches Kunstinstitut). In the 1640s his fortunes began to decline. Blame for this used to be attached to his famous group portrait, *"The Night Watch"* (1642, Amsterdam, Rijksmuseum), in which he did not, as was traditional, give equal prominence to all the sitters (who shared costs), but created a drama of light and shade and movement, but it is now thought that it was not so unfavourably received. This was the year Saskia died and Rembrandt's financial problems did increase, culminating in near-bankruptcy in 1656, when he was obliged to sell his extensive art collection. As he became more introspective and expressed himself with growing technical freedom, bourgeois clients who demanded a high degree of finish turned to artists such as van der Helst for their portraits. Rembrandt, however, continued to have perceptive supporters such as the rich Amsterdam Burgomaster Jan Six, whose portrait he painted in 1654 (Amsterdam, Six coll.). The deepening spirituality which the Six portrait exemplifies was paralleled in all aspects of his art. *Bathsheba* (1654, Paris, Louvre), for example, displays none of the dramatic qualities of his earlier biblical scenes but presents a starkly honest portrayal of the bodily imperfections and quiet despair of the sitter. The development of this unmatched psychological penetration is best witnessed in the marvellous series of *Self-portraits*, spanning 40 years. The studies of facial expressions, confident stares and flamboyant costumes of the earlier ones give way to the unflinching patience and dignity of the mature portrayals, which include some of the most moving portraits ever painted. Two date from his final year (London, NG, and The Hague, Mauritshuis). He died alone, in poverty, having survived both his mistress, Hendrickje Stoffels, and his son, Titus. Rembrandt's output was enormous and, unlike most of his specialist Dutch contemporaries, he treated virtually every type of subject. He was an inspiring teacher and taught some of the leading painters of his day, from Dou (his first pupil in 1628) to de Gelder, who continued his style into the 18th century. Fabritius was his greatest pupil and among the others were Bol, Flinck, Hoogstraten and Maes. See vol. 1 pp. 26, 32, 37, 44, 67, 74, **76–77**, 117, 121, 149; vol. 2 pp. 212, 213, **216–219**, 221, 225, 227, 233, 246; vol. 4 p. 17

Remington, Frederic 1861–1909

American painter, famous for his lively depictions of contemporary Western life. They project a heroic, showmanlike image of the "Wild West" that profoundly influenced American culture. He turned to bronze sculpture in 1895, and the *Bronco buster*, his first completed bronze, of which there are more than 300 castings, was very popular.

Renaissance

Term meaning "rebirth" and variously defined as: a revival of art and letters in imitation of classical models; a humanist movement reflecting a new conviction in the dignity of man and a confident assertion of his role in the natural world; or a general but ultimately inexplicable upsurge in the human spirit occurring initially in Italy and extending from about 1400 to 1600. In 1550, Vasari was using the word *rinascita* to describe what he felt was an organic development in painting from Giotto to Michelangelo. However, the widest application of the term stemmed from Jacob Burckhardt's enormously influential *Civilization of the Renaissance in Italy* (1860), which, somewhat romantically, treated the entire period as a cultural coming of age

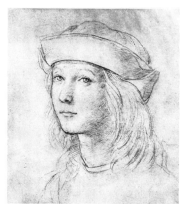
Raphael: Self-portrait drawing, c.1496–98. Oxford, Ashmolean (Mansell)

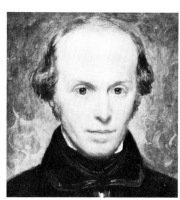
Redgrave: Self-portrait, c.1835. London, NPG

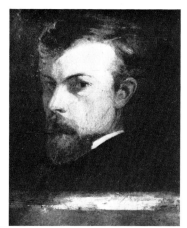
Redon: Self-portrait, 1867. Paris, Ari Redon coll.

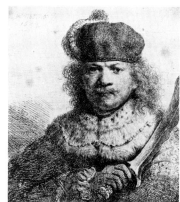
Rembrandt: Self-portrait etching, 1634. Cambridge, Fitzwilliam

and blossoming forth of aesthetic values. Inevitably, in using such a generalized term, constant qualifying statements have to be made. In architecture, the emphasis was on a return to antique sources, combined with an ordered, scientific approach. The simplest forms were employed—the circle and the square, linked, in Vitruvian fashion, to the proportions of the human body—and rational guidelines were devised by Alberti and Brunelleschi. With sculpture, the earliest resurrection of ancient forms is ascribed to Nicola Pisano, while Donatello is usually credited as the first to re-create the spirit of antique art. Painting is more problematic, as virtually no early Roman models were available for artists to emulate. Instead, it was Pliny's description of the classical search for truth to nature and the perfection of human forms that prompted the rejection of Gothic conventions and ideals. Within the movement as a whole, there are certain subdivisions. The High Renaissance denotes the brief period, lasting from about 1500 to 1520, when the aims and innovations of the early Renaissance found their fullest expression. The canons of harmony and proportion were recognized and interpreted with a new-found freedom and mastery of technique. The late works of Leonardo and the mature offerings of Raphael and Michelangelo all date from this short span of time. The transmission of Italian ideals and imagery to the rest of Europe is known as the Northern Renaissance. See vol. 2 pp. 100ff

Reni, Guido 1575–1642
Bolognese painter. He was a pupil of Denys Calvaert (*c.*1584–93), then came under the influence of the Carracci, whose classicizing style was his early inspiration. Most of Reni's life was spent in Bologna, but he made several visits to Rome, and it was there that he executed his most famous painting, the ceiling fresco *Aurora* (1613–14, Casino Rospigliosi), a captivatingly lovely work based on a study of Raphael and ancient relief sculpture. After the death of Ludovico Carracci in 1619, Reni's large and productive studio dominated the Bolognese school, producing mainly idealized religious paintings which spread his fame throughout Europe. In the 18th and 19th centuries Reni was placed by many critics second only to Raphael, but his reputation crumbled with the fall from favour of the Bolognese painters, whom Ruskin in 1847 considered had "no single virtue, no colour, no drawing, no character, no history, no thought", and it is only fairly recently that a just appreciation of his status, based on a study of original works rather than those of his numerous pupils and imitators, has been possible. He is now considered one of the greatest Italian artists of the period for the beauty of his colouring, in which he surpasses all other 17th-century Italian painters, and the grandeur and grace of his figures (*St John the Baptist*, *c.*1625, London, Dulwich College Picture Gallery). See vol. 2 p. **185**

Renier de Huy
active early 12th century
Mosan metalworker of the Romanesque period, first mentioned in a 15th-century document. The only work assigned to him is a bronze font, commissioned by Abbot Hellinus (1107–18), *c.*1110, for Notre Dame des Fonts, Liège (now in St Bartholomew, Liège). This large, skilfully modelled bowl has five scenes related to the sacrament of baptism, with unusually well-proportioned figures in gently-flowing classical drapery. The work inaugurates the exceptionally naturalistic, classicizing tradition of art around the mouth of the river Meuse, known as the Mosan region. See vol. 2 p. **71**

Renoir, Pierre Auguste 1841–1919
French painter, one of the greatest of the IMPRESSIONISTS. In 1854 he went to Paris to work as a decorator in a porcelain factory. He entered Gleyre's studio in 1862 and met Sisley, Bazille and Monet, with whom he associated, often painting with Monet in the open air and sharing the same subject matter. The sombre and weighty style of his early canvases gave way to light-filled scenes built up in characteristically Impressionist broken brush-strokes (*La Grenouillère*, 1869, Stockholm, Nationalmuseum). He exhibited at the first three Impressionist exhibitions before his portraits (such as *Mme Charpentier and her children*, 1879, New York, Metropolitan) won him success and acceptance at the Salon. In 1881, feeling that he had taken Impressionism as far as he could, he visited Italy, where the Renaissance masters had a decisive influence on his style. More interested than most other Impressionists in the human figure, and less detached from his sitters, he rejected the idea of disintegrating form simply to achieve effects of spontaneity. *The Umbrellas* (*c.*1881–84, London, NG) marks his transition from Impressionism to a more classical structure, its areas of feather brush-strokes contrasting with smoother patches giving greater solidity of form. As one who travelled much, studying the Old Masters, he was never committed to the doctrines of instantaneity and often made many preliminary sketches, as, for instance, for the carefully constructed *The bathers* (*c.*1884–87, Philadelphia Museum of Art). His sensuous appreciation of colour and light, his ample, glowing nudes, the charm and poetry of his works, have made him one of the best-loved of the Impressionists. Beautiful women, children and people enjoying themselves remained his favourite subjects even in old age, when he realized his earthy female nudes in sculptures "dictated" to his assistants. See vol. 1 pp. *10*, **46–47**, *121*; vol. 3 pp. **98–99**, **102–103**

Renqvist, Torsten born 1924
Swedish painter, engraver and draughtsman in an Expressionist style. He paints everyday objects and landscapes, but his art has become decreasingly figurative, and highly personal. Water and rivers are favourite subjects, and since the 1960s he has also made several tree sculptures. *Animals*, 1952, a portfolio of woodcuts, is representative.

Ren Renfa 1254–1327
Chinese painter. Like Zhao Mengfu, he is renowned for his paintings of horses, a theme which presumably found an appreciative audience at the court of the hitherto nomadic Mongols. His closeness to Zhao is seen in the handscroll *Horses and grooms* (Cambridge, Mass., Fogg Art Museum) and in *Feeding horses* (London, V&A), but he could also make use of this theme to put across an ideological point; in the handscroll *The lean horse and the fat horse* (Peking, Palace Museum), an artist's colophon makes explicit the allegory of the honest official facing starvation, while the arrogant and corrupt enjoy a life of comfort.

Repin, Ilya Efimovich 1844–1930
Russian painter, generally considered the greatest of his period. He became closely involved with the WANDERERS and *Boat haulers on Volga* (1870–73, Leningrad, Russian Museum) established him as their leader. In 1873–76 he travelled to France and Italy and greatly enriched his technique without changing his ideals. His huge *Procession of the Cross in the region of Kursk* (1880–83, Moscow, Tretyakov Gallery) was meant to show a broad spectrum of Russian society with special sympathy for the poor and oppressed, while other paintings of modern life showed direct sympathy with the Revolutionary movement. In popular historical pictures such as *Ivan the Terrible kills his son* (1885, Moscow, Tretyakov Gallery) the emotional and melodramatic side of his art can be overpowering, and his portraits (among them many of his famous contemporaries—Tolstoy, Mussorgsky, and many others) remain his best achievements. In 1894 he became a professor in the reformed Academy, where he taught many of the painters of the next generation.

Repoussé
A technique of metalwork, in which a malleable metal such as silver or copper is hammered over a block of wood carved to the requisite design.

Repoussoir
Term from the French *repousser*, to push back, describing an object or figure placed in the extreme foreground of a painting, usually at the side, with the intention of creating spatial depth and drawing the spectator into the picture.

Representational art see FIGURATIVE ART

Reredos see ALTARPIECE

Restout, Jean 1692–1768
French history painter. He studied under his father **Jean the Elder** (1663–1702), a minor religious painter, and his uncle Jouvenet. A highly successful career culminated in his appointment as Chancellor of the Academy in 1761. He painted accomplished portraits and scenes from mythology and history, but it is his religious painting which makes him stand out from his contemporaries. His masterpiece, *The death of St Scholastica* (1730, Tours, Musée), is conceived with a gravity and intensity which bear out his pronouncement to the Academy in 1755 that it was necessary for a painter "to have noble feelings, an elevated mind, an excellent character, to treat his subjects worthily".

Retable see ALTARPIECE

Rethel, Alfred 1816–59
German painter, draughtsman and engraver. He studied under Schadow and made frequent trips to Italy. In his best-known work, the series of woodcuts *Another Dance of Death in the Year 1848* (1849), he uses symbol and allegory in the depiction of contemporary events, as he did for historical ones. The realistic detail and social commentary inherent in his work make his position in German art similar to that of Daumier in France. Like earlier German Romantics, he was much involved in attempting to revive the late medieval symbolism and woodcutting technique of Dürer.

Revere, Colonel Paul 1735–1818
American artist, best known as a hero of the American Revolution. He trained in Boston as a silversmith, and his "Sons of Liberty" punchbowl (1768, Boston, MFA) is probably the most famous piece of silver in America. During the Revolutionary years he produced prints and broadsides denouncing British imperialism. The best-known is the crude but vigorous *Bloody massacre perpetrated in King Street, Boston* (1770), copied from a print by Pelham.

Reverón, Armando 1889–1954
Venezuelan painter and latter-day Impressionist. He studied in Caracas, 1908–12, travelled to Spain and France and on his return to Caracas in 1916 played an important part in introducing Impressionism to Venezuelan art. In 1921 he settled in a quiet coastal district and devoted himself to local subjects. These works are monochrome, often painted out of doors on raw flax. Reverón suffered from periods of mental disorder, and built himself a fortress-like dwelling with seashells and stones where he lived with his companion and model Juanita. *Reclining woman* (1938, Caracas, Galleria de Arte Nacional) is a fine example of his art in this period. Following Juanita's death, he made a group of life-size dolls and masks of ritual appearance.

Revold, Axel 1887–1962
Norwegian painter, a pupil of Matisse. The latter's influence and that of Cubism are evident in the first of his many frescos on Norwegian public buildings, for example at the Exchange in Bergen, 1921–23. He depicted the countryside and everyday life of Norway in bright strong colours and clearly arranged compositions (*Fishing boats on the way out*, 1935, Oslo, NG). He was Professor at the Academy in Oslo, 1925–46.

Reynolds, Sir Joshua 1723–92
British painter, writer on art and first President of the ROYAL ACADEMY, the central figure of British art in the second half of the 18th century. The son of a Devon clergyman, he trained under Hudson in London, 1740–43, then painted portraits in Devon. In 1750–52 he was in Italy, where he assiduously studied classical sculpture and Italian Renaissance and Baroque painting, and developed the ideas of the GRAND MANNER, which he applied to his own portraiture on his return to London. The pose of *Commodore Keppel* (1753, Greenwich, National Maritime Museum), for example, is based on a famous classical statue, "*The Apollo Belvedere*". Between 1769 and 1790 he delivered to the Royal Academy his 15 *Discourses on Art*, the main purpose of which was to encourage history painting and which gave British painters a standard for excellence which could also be applied to other fields. This is certainly true of Reynolds' own portraits, on which he often sought to bestow what he called a "senatorial dignity" and something of the quality of historical painting—a lofty aim which conflicted both with the mechanical "face-painting" of his predecessors and with the gradual development during the 18th century of the "natural" portraiture of Hogarth, Ramsay, Gainsborough and Reynolds himself in his more relaxed moods. Reynolds' output was enormous and he showed great versatility as a portraitist ("Damn him, how various he is!" said Gainsborough). He could capture equally convincingly a soldier's bluff strength (*Lord Heathfield*, 1788, London, NG), an aristocratic lady's grace (*Mrs Francis Beckford*, 1756, London, Tate) or a child's innocent charm (*Miss Jane Bowles*, 1775, London, Wallace Coll.). His history paintings are much less convincing, but his advocacy of the lofty nature of his art and his social success (he was a friend of leading liter-

ary figures such as Goldsmith and Johnson) did much for the prestige of English art. See vol. 1 p. 45; vol. 2 p. **250**

Ribalta, Francisco 1565–1628
Spanish painter, active primarily in Valencia. He was in Madrid in 1582, and his early, Mannerist, style was influenced by Navarrete and other court painters (*The nailing to the Cross*, 1582, Leningrad, Hermitage). In the late 1590s he settled in Valencia, where his style changed and became impressively sombre; his latest works seem to show the influence of Caravaggio, perhaps conveyed to him by Ribera. *St Bernard embracing Christ* (c.1620–28, Madrid, Prado) is characteristic in its chiaroscuro, its still and powerful figures suffused with strong golden light and placed in an almost empty darkness. Ribalta was one of the first artists in Spain to work in such a realistic tenebrist manner, and had considerable influence. See vol. 2 p. **208**

Ribera, Jusepe (José) **de** (called Lo Spagnoletto) 1591–1652
Spanish painter, etcher and draughtsman, all of whose known career was spent in Italy. His early life is obscure and it is not known when he went to Italy. There is evidence that he worked in Parma and Rome before settling in Naples in 1616. No works are known to date from before this. His large output consisted mainly of religious works, but he also painted mythological and genre scenes and some portraits. His earliest works are in a powerful tenebrist style owing something to Caravaggio, but Ribera is distinguished from most Caravaggesque painters by his vigorous scratchy brushwork. He is perhaps best known for his harrowing scenes of martyrdom (*The martyrdom of St Bartholomew*, c.1630, Madrid, Prado), but this side of his art has tended to obscure other aspects of his work. In his respect for an individual's personality, for example, he comes close to Velazquez, as is memorably shown in *The clubfooted boy* (1642, Paris, Louvre). This painting also shows the lighter palette which he developed during the 1630s. His late works are often richly coloured, with soft broad modelling, and in them the expression of spirituality became a primary concern (*The mystic marriage of St Catherine*, 1648, New York, Metropolitan). Ribera was one of the few Spanish artists to be well known outside his native country before the Napoleonic Wars. His influence was wide, both in Naples (for example on Rosa) and Spain, where many of his paintings were exported during his lifetime. See vol. 2 p. **208**

Ribot, Théodule Augustin
1823–91
French painter, essentially self-taught. His intimate genre paintings and still-life studies place him among the lesser-known Realists linked to Courbet. In his major Salon paintings, the influence of Spanish and Neapolitan painting and the Baroque tradition is manifest, especially in his use of dramatic chiaroscuro (*St Sebastian*, 1865, Paris, Musée du Luxembourg), but his genre canvases caused him to be described as "the Velazquez of kitchens".

Ricci, Marco 1676–1730
Italian landscape painter. A nephew of Sebastiano Ricci, he was active in Venice before embarking on a peripatetic career; in 1705 he was working in Milan with Magnasco, who influenced his free handling of paint and fantastical effects, and he proceeded to Florence, then to

Rome, where his city views were influenced by Panini. In London in 1708, he worked with Pellegrini as a decorative painter. He made a second trip to London with his uncle, initiating a successful partnership which continued when they returned to Venice in 1717. Amongst their many shared works is *Moses striking the rock* (1720s, versions in Hampton Court and Venice, Accademia). See vol. 2 p. **235**

Ricci, Sebastiano 1659–1734
Italian late Baroque painter of religious, historical and mythological subjects whose works were influential in encouraging a lighter and more colourful style among Venetian artists. He was trained in Venice and Bologna; thereafter he led an itinerant life, working in Piacenza, Parma, Rome, Florence, Milan, Germany, France, Flanders and England, before finally settling in Venice in 1717. As a painter he is exceptionally uneven, the speed at which he worked often leading to extreme carelessness. He was strongly influenced by Veronese (*Esther before Ahasuerus*, c.1733–34, London, NG), borrowing his costumes and settings as well as assimilating his style, and inspiring a revival of Venetian interest in him. See vol. 2 p. **235**

Riccio, Il (Andrea Briosco)
1470/5–1532
Italian sculptor from Padua, a great master of the bronze statuette. His earliest attributed works are three figures on the Roccabonella monument in San Francesco, Padua, begun by Bellano, his probable teacher, and completed by Riccio after 1496. He made a huge, bronze Easter Candlestick for the Santo in Padua, about 1507–15, richly encrusted with figures in an antique style, and with reliefs owing much to Donatello's altar in the same church. He is most famous, however, for his small bronzes (examples in Parma, Galleria Nazionale, and elsewhere), which reproduce on a small scale the qualities of Roman statuary. Their subject matter, reflecting the tastes of Paduan and Venetian humanists, ranges from elegant nude fauns to frogs serving as inkwells, and they possess great vivacity, though chased with precision. See vol. 1 p. *207*; vol. 2 p. **147**

Richards, Ceri 1903–71
British painter, born in Wales. In the 1930s he made Surrealist-inspired wood reliefs. In the 1940s the influence of Picasso and Miró on his work was the source for a less insular and inhibited romanticism than that practised by his contemporaries. *Cycle of nature* (1944, Cardiff, National Museum of Wales) is a frenzied and colourful composition of visceral semi-abstract forms. Much of his later work reflects his love of music: he made a series of paintings and reliefs inspired by a Debussy prelude.

Richardson, Jonathan the Elder
1665–1745
British portraitist, working in the period between the decline of Kneller and the rise of Hogarth. He was more interesting as a writer on art and collector of drawings. His *Theory of Painting* (1715) was a standard work until superseded by Reynolds' *Discourses*, which it helped to inspire. *An Account of Some of the Statues, Bas-reliefs, Drawings and Pictures in Italy* (1722), based on information supplied by his son **Jonathan the Younger** (1694–1771), also a portrait painter, was an excellent tourists' guidebook.

Richier, Germaine 1904–59
French sculptor, pupil of both Rodin

and Bourdelle. Around 1940, under the influence of Giacometti, she moved from an early classicizing phase into her characteristic style, creating a new kind of macabre sculptural imagery. She was trying to find a response to the horror and destruction which man inflicts upon himself and his world; her figures are often half-human, half-insect, decomposing, torn and withered (*The bat-man*, bronze, 1946, Hartford, Wadsworth Atheneum). She concentrated on this harrowing figurative sculpture apart from a period of abstraction in the mid-1950s. See vol. 3 p. **230**

Richier, Ligier c.1500–67
French sculptor chiefly employed by the Dukes of Lorraine. He visited Rome about 1515, and returned to Lorraine five or six years later. His first major surviving work, the tomb of the Duchess of Lorraine (Nancy, Church of the Cordeliers) dates from the late 1540s. The recumbent effigy displays a particularly grim late Gothic naturalism, which was exceeded in his tomb for the Duchess's husband, René of Nassau, with its free-standing marble skeleton (now at Bas-le-Duc, St Pierre). In the 1550s he produced a sepulchre with 12 over-life-size figures for St. Pierre, St Mihiel. He became a Protestant and fled to Geneva.

Richmond, George 1809–96
English painter, son and pupil of the miniaturist **Thomas** Richmond (1771–1837) and father of the late Victorian classical painter **Sir William Blake** Richmond (1842–1921). In 1824 he was a pupil of Fuseli. Through Samuel Palmer, his life-long friend, he met Blake and became one of the ANCIENTS. His early poetic and religious subjects are inspired by Blake, but after 1830 he earned his living as a highly successful portrait painter.

Richter, Adrian Ludwig 1803–84
German painter, illustrator and engraver. He was influenced by Koch's heroic landscape painting in his youth, and arrived at his own style in the 1840s. This was a naive and pious Romanticism, deeply rooted in an idyllic interpretation of the lives of the peasants and petit-bourgeois. His numerous illustrations to children's fairy tales and depictions of serene domestic scenes or idyllic shepherdesses consciously avoid the still dominant Biedermeier realism.

Richter, Gerhard born 1932
West German painter, chiefly remarkable for the number of different styles in which he has worked. These range from a painterly Abstract Expressionism, to grid paintings of colour squares and transcriptions of photographs—early manifestations of Superrealism (*Emma—nude on a staircase*, 1966, Cologne, Wallraf-Richartz Museum).

Richter, Hans 1888–1976
German painter, sculptor, film-maker and writer. He was influenced by the Fauves and the Cubists, in whose manner he painted until 1914. In 1917 he joined the Zurich Dadaists and began to paint purely abstract geometrical canvases. In 1918 he met Viking Eggeling, with whom he conducted film experiments, and in 1921 he made his first abstract film, the seminal *Rhythm 21*. From 1940 he lived in the USA, making films, paintings and collages. He has written many books on film and Dada.

Rickey, George born 1907
American painter and sculptor. Born in Indiana, he trained in London and with

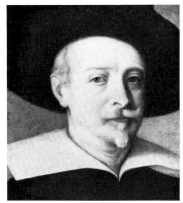
Reni: Self-portrait, c.1630. Florence, Uffizi (Scala)

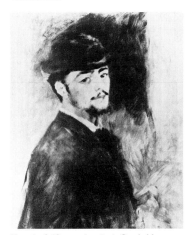
Renoir: Self-portrait, 1876. Cambridge, Mass., Fogg (Mansell)

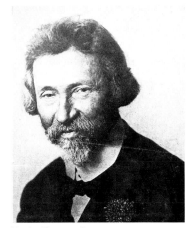
Repin: Photograph, 1912 (Novosti Press Agency)

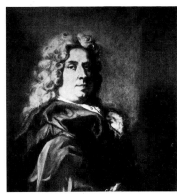
Ricci, Sebastiano: Self portrait, 1704. Florence, Uffizi (Alinari)

Lhôte in Paris. Returning to the USA in 1930, he began his career as a painter and not until 1945 did he make his first mobile. During the 1950s he continued to explore movement, and by the end of the decade he was producing more simplified works in which thin planes and blades are set rocking by the force of wind. *Two lines-temporal I* (1964, New York, MOMA) consists simply of two spears swivelling on a thin shaft.

Riemenschneider, Tilman died 1531
German sculptor. He was trained in Ulm, but in 1485 became a citizen of Würzburg, where he ran a flourishing workshop virtually until his death. He mainly produced altarpieces in limewood, though he also made free-standing figures and designs for stone carvings, and seems to have been the first German sculptor in wood to have finished his sculpture in a dark-brown varnish rather than in colour—concentrating the interest on texture, lighting and expression. His style shows an assimilation of Gerhaerts but its serenity reflects the tradition of Multscher; his figures are repetitive, made up of a limited number of recurring elements—curls of hair, sharp noses, characteristically broken planes of drapery—and are quietistic, but imbued with considerable strength of feeling. His surviving works include his altarpieces in St Jakob, Rothenburg, with its famous *Last Supper* (1501–05), and in the Herrgottskirche at Creglingen (*c.*1505–10), with an *Assumption of the Virgin*. He is now regarded as the leading German sculptor, with Stoss, of the period before the Reformation. See vol. 2 pp. **158–159**

Rigaud, Hyacinthe 1659–1743
With Largillière the most successful French portrait painter of the last years of Louis XIV's reign. After obscure beginnings in Montpellier, he came to Paris in 1681. In 1688 the success of his portrait of the King's brother (lost) brought him a flood of commissions and he became almost exclusively a court artist. His style, though derived from Flemish Baroque, has a greater air of restraint. His best-known work is the great state portrait of the aging *Louis XIV* (1701, Paris, Louvre) but a less formal aspect of his style can be seen in *The artist's mother* (1695, Louvre), in which the sitter is shown twice, and which indicates in its sympathetic treatment of old age an interest in Rembrandt. See vol. 2 p. **199**; vol. 4 p. *31*

Riley, Bridget born 1931
British painter. An early interest in Pointillism and the possibilities of working within strict visual limitations led her, in the early 1960s, to the form of abstraction which was to become known as OP art. Initially she worked entirely in black and white; *Fission* (1963, New York, MOMA) is a progression of dots which becomes compressed towards the centre, so creating an illusion of space and movement. In other works the close-packed curving lines in parallel create a more violent retinal impact. Later in the 1960s she began using colour, and more recent paintings such as *Zephyr* (1976, Manchester, City Art Gallery) suggest a subtle rippling motion. See vol. 3 p. **244**

Riley, John 1646–91
English portrait painter. His early work is ill-defined, and it is only after the death of Lely in 1680 that he emerges as a distinctive personality. His portraits show a genuine sympathy for the reticent aspects of the English character, and he is at his best with sitters from the humble walks of life, as in his two best-known works, *Bridget Holmes* (1686, Royal coll.) and *The scullion* (Oxford, Christ Church). He was appointed Principal Painter to William and Mary jointly with Kneller in 1688. In much of his later work he collaborated with Closterman.

Rimmer, William 1816–79
English-born American sculptor, active in Boston and, later, New York. A remarkable character, he taught himself medicine as well as art and believed he was the son of the pretender to the French throne. His medical knowledge comes out in his powerful command of anatomy, which he used, as in his most famous sculpture, *Falling gladiator* (1861, Boston, MFA), to express the Romantic theme of tormented, tragic isolation. Rimmer also painted (the mysterious *Flight and pursuit*, 1871, Boston, MFA, is his best-known work in this field), but is remembered chiefly as a teacher and for his books *Elements of Design* (1864) and *Art Anatomy* (1877).

Ring the Elder, Ludger Tom 1496–1547
German painter, working in Münster. His work was influenced by that of nearby Netherlandish painters and included decorative work for Münster Cathedral. His few surviving portraits show flat but colourful figures (*Anna Romp*, *c.*1540, Cologne, Wallraf-Richartz). His sons **Herman** (1521–96) and **Ludger Tom the Younger** (1522–84) were both painters.

Rinke, Klaus born 1939
West German CONCEPTUAL artist, especially interested in structures of time and space. He has used photographs of himself, in which the gesture he makes, or the angle from which he is photographed, or the way the photograph is cropped, progresses through a tightly preordained mathematical system. In three-dimensional work he has also investigated physical forces such as expansion and gravitation. His work reveals relationships between conceptual understanding and physical perception that are unexpected.

Riopelle, Jean Paul born 1923
Canadian abstract painter and sculptor, a member of Les AUTOMATISTES. Since 1946 he has lived in Paris, although he returned to Canada in 1948 to sign Borduas's manifesto *Universal Refusal*. His early paintings were in a lyrical style, but during the 1950s his work became more powerful with a greater concern for texture. The dense, faceted surface of the large-scale *Knight watch* (1953, Ottawa, NG of Canada) suggests Pollock's work. His hard, rough sculptures echo this concern with mass and density. Riopelle has made important contributions to Abstract Expressionism in Canada and in Europe.

Rissanen, Juho 1873–1950
Finnish painter. Originally a decorator, he studied painting from 1897. His scenes from rural life are populated by robust figures with expressive character heads and gesticulating hands. He first visited Paris in 1908, lived there from 1918, and finally settled in the USA in 1939. His late style tends to simplified serenity and lacks his earlier vigour.

Rivalz family
Family of French history painters, active in Toulouse in the 17th and 18th centuries. **Jean-Pierre the Elder** (1625–1706), a pupil of Vouet, spent nine years in Italy in the circle of Poussin, possibly painting the architecture in his works. He spent the rest of his life in Toulouse, where he decorated the Hôtel de Ville and practised as an architect. His son **Antoine** (1667–1735) returned from Rome in 1700 influenced by Maratta, and from 1726 ran an academy which was the centre of a Toulouse school quite independent of Parisian influence and inspired by the Roman rather than the Flemish Baroque. Among his pupils were his son **Jean-Pierre the Younger** (1718–85) and Subleyras. There are many works by the Rivalz in Toulouse.

Rivera, Diego 1886–1957
Mexican painter, one of the founders of the Mexican mural renaissance, along with David Siqueiros and Orozco. His first one-man show in 1907 earned him a travel scholarship abroad to Madrid and Paris. Early experiments with Cubism were followed in 1920 by a renewed interest in Mexican traditions. He returned to Mexico in 1922, and there he completed his first mural, an allegorical picture called *Creation* (Mexico City, National Preparatory School). Then, with a knowledge of folk traditions and the Pre-Columbian art of Mexico, he evolved a narrative style which glorified its history, the peasants, workers and their revolutionary fervour. This was the mainspring for the movement which followed. His murals at the Detroit Institute of Art and the Rockefeller Center, New York, were commissioned in the 1930s and became influential in American artistic circles. The frescos for the Lerma Water Works and the mosaic murals in the National Stadium, Mexico City, remain outstanding examples of his later work. See vol. 1 p. 55; vol. 3 p. **208**; vol. 4 p. *143*

Rivera, José de born 1904
American sculptor. His early pieces were smoothly crafted, as in the sleek, Brancusi-like shapes of *Flight* (1938, New Jersey, Newark Museum). He subsequently exploited the volumetric curves of bent sheet-metal. Since the early 1950s he has created tubular stainless steel constructions which outline space in swift, glinting curves.

Rivers, Larry born 1923
American painter, sculptor, designer and graphic artist, associated with the second generation of the New York school. He was trained as a musician and took up painting seriously in 1945, studying with Hofmann and Baziotes. Influenced both by Abstract Expressionism and by the work of such artists as Bonnard, observed during a visit to Europe in 1950s, Rivers developed a free, painterly style applied to figurative imagery. He draws upon a wide range of subject matter—historical figures (for example *Washington crossing the Delaware*, 1953, New York, MOMA), advertising images, reproductions of paintings, maps, stamps, money—and has also experimented with different styles and techniques. He is often associated with Pop art because of his eclectic subject matter, but his approach is more painterly. See vol. 3 p. **238**

Riza Abbasi died 1635?
Persian painter, in the employ of Shah Abbas I in Isfahan. The possible identity of the artist with **Aqa Riza ibn Ali Asghar al Kashani** has been hotly debated, though a note on a portrait of the former by his student Mu'in Musavvir that the subject is Riza Abbasi Ash'ar (*sic*) would seem to confirm the identity. The artist left a considerable number of signed paintings and drawings dated from 1598 to 1643, most often of single figures executed in ink or body colour, in which line is used to describe volumes and textures expressively (*Day-dreaming youth*, Cambridge, Mass., Fogg). The curvy poses convey elegant languor, combined with an intense sense of presence, as in Riza Abbasi's most famous painting, *Amorous couple* (New York, Metropolitan). See vol. 3 pp. *23*, *27*

Rizi, or **Ricci, Francisco de Guevera** 1608–85 and **Juan Andrés** 1600–81
Spanish painters, brothers, the sons of an Italian painter, **Antonio Ricci** (died after 1631), who settled in Spain. Juan became a Benedictine monk in 1627 and painted mainly for Benedictine monasteries in Castile in a direct tenebrist style which sometimes recalls Zurbarán. He was also an accomplished portrait painter (*Fray Alonso de San Vitores*, *c.*1659, Burgos, Museo Provincial) and wrote a treatise on painting. Francisco was an expert in perspective and stage designer for the theatre. *The Adoration of the Magi* (1645, Toledo Cathedral) is his earliest dated work and a good example of his lively, somewhat Rubensian style.

Rizzo, Antonio active 1465–1499/1500
Veronese sculptor, active in Venice. Though he collaborated with Antonio Bregno, his style was more classical. His Niccolò Tron monument (1476, Venice, S. Maria dei Frari), together with Pietro Lombardo's contemporary Mocenigo monument, applied the Florentine Renaissance architectural style to Venetian tombs for the first time. His figures, however (such as the *Adam* and *Eve* in the Palazzo Ducale, Venice, *c.*1483–85), show distinctly Gothic proportions and sensuous qualities.

Robbia, Luca della 1400–82
The best-known member of a family of Florentine sculptors specializing in ceramics. He may have been trained under Nanni di Banco in the Florentine Cathedral workshop, but is first recorded as an artist in 1431, working on the first of two *Cantorie* (Singing Galleries) for Florence Cathedral—the other was Donatello's. Luca's lively marble relief plaques of dancing and music-making children were partly inspired by classical reliefs, and are both idealized and naturalistically spontaneous. The earliest dated use of polychrome glazed terracotta is on a tabernacle (now in Peretola), 1443, for S. Egidio, and this invention, apparently involving a formula the della Robbia workshop successfully kept secret, came to dominate Luca's career. First used as a decoration, the technique was soon applied to medallions and tympana, such as *The Resurrection* and *The Ascension* (late 1440s) in Florence Cathedral, medallions in the Pazzi Chapel of S. Croce in Florence (*c.*1444), those on Orsanmichele (*c.*1455–65), and the ceiling of the funerary chapel of James, Cardinal of Portugal (1459–66) in S. Miniato al Monte. Until about 1465 these works are consistently of high quality—often delightful *Virgin and Child* reliefs in rectangular or tondo form. Luca was assisted by his son **Giovanni** (1469–1529) and his nephew **Andrea** (1435–1525), who carried on the workshop, relying heavily on his designs, their own tending to facility. See vol. 2 p. **101**

Robert, Hubert 1733–1808
French landscape painter. He went to Rome in 1754 and obtained a place at the

French Academy there. He studied landscape in company with Fragonard, whose late Rococo style had much in common with his own, and in 1761 they travelled together to southern Italy. Robert evolved a romanticized version of the work of the view-painters Panini and Piranesi, and introduced it to France on his return in 1765. He became a member of the French Academy in 1768 and achieved great popularity with his topographic works and fantastic ruinpieces. The two genres are combined in such works as the delicately melancholic *Pont du Gard* (c.1787, Paris, Louvre). See vol. 2 p. **241**

Robert, Léopold Louis
1794–1835
Swiss painter of genre scenes, who spent most of his life in Italy. He studied in Paris, 1810–16, with David and Gros. Although a classicist in style, he nevertheless founded the Italian school of genre painting depicting peasant and bandit life in the early 19th century. His four great compositions of peasants outside the major Italian cities at different seasons of the year were acquired by the Louvre, Paris, when completed in 1830.

Robert-Fleury, Joseph Nicolas
1797–1890
French painter and lithographer. The pupil of Vernet, Girodet and Gros, he became a successful artist and director of the Ecole des Beaux-Arts. His accurately detailed historical scenes often had contemporary relevance. *Jane Shore* (1850, Fontainebleau, Musée National du Château) was a state commission.

Roberti, Ercole de' c.1450–96
Italian painter from Ferrara. His mannered linear style is reminiscent of Cossa, with whom he studied (1473–78), and of Mantegna, but a distinct development from them. In about 1470 he contributed *September* to the frescos of *The Months* in the Duke of Ferrara's Schifanoia Palace. He also worked with Cossa in Bologna, where he painted companion portraits of *Giovanni II* and *Ginevra Bentivoglio* (c.1480, Washington, NG), half-length profile views in brilliant, clear colours. He succeeded Tura as court painter to the Este in 1487. One of his finest works is the *Pietà* in Liverpool, Walker Art Gallery, which is part of a predella; the contemplative mood is enhanced by an austere composition, colouristic subtlety and a softer treatment of figures and landscape.

Roberts, Goodridge born 1904
Canadian figurative painter. He studied in New York under Max Weber, 1927–29. He paints directly from the model, exploiting the fluidity of the paint and rapidly setting out the entire work, using Matisse-like compositional devices. *Marian* (1946, Toronto, Art Gallery of Ontario) displays the lightness and lyricism of his touch.

Roberts, William 1895–1980
British painter. He was a member of the VORTICIST group. Early paintings such as *The return of Ulysses* (1913, Nottingham, Castle Museum) were close to the work of Bomberg in their extreme geometric simplification of the figure. However, he was less interested in abstraction than Lewis or Wadsworth and after World War I applied a geometric style to scenes of everyday life. The monumentality of his later work has been compared to Léger, but a painting such as *The common market* (1963, Preston, Harris Art Gallery) is sharper and less idealized. See vol. 3 p. **155**

Rocky Mountain school
Name given to a 19th-century group of American artists, otherwise unconnected, who painted scenes of the Rocky Mountains, often on large canvases. Bierstadt and Moran are the best-known artists covered by the term.

Rococo
The style, characterized by intimacy of scale, asymmetry and grace, which in the early 18th century superseded the formal plastic grandeur of the Baroque. Born in France as a style of extravagant decoration characterized by scroll, rock and plant motifs, it became a mood and a manner that soon spread to all the fine and decorative arts. The finest manifestations came in south Germany and particularly in France—in the work of French painters such as Fragonard who, already freed from restraint by the influence of Rubenisme, lightened their palettes, introducing an easy elegance into their compositions, and, following Watteau, exploited the new genre of the *fête galante*. Boucher's hedonistic mythologies are the most characteristic expression of French Rococo painting, but, as the style spread through Europe, by the mid-century its idiom is recognizable in the work of artists as disparate as Hogarth in England and Giambattista Tiepolo in Italy. By the 1760s, in France and in most of Europe, the tide of taste was moving away from what had come to seem a frivolous style towards Neoclassicism, but the Rococo continued in parts of Germany until the end of the century, most notably in the decoration of palaces and churches. In a distinct form, having more in common with the Baroque tradition of Italy than of France, it reached its most extravagant, colourful and labyrinthine heights in Germany. See vol. 2 pp. 240–243

Rodakowski, Henryk 1823–94
Polish painter, who worked in Paris from 1846 until 1867. His work is characterized by broad handling and a sombre palette, as for instance in the early portrait of *General Dembinski* (1852, Cracow, National Museum), which established his reputation. He was more concerned to achieve fame as a painter of histories, however, and realized this aim in 1870 with the monumental *War without combat: the confirmation of the nobles' privileges* (Warsaw, National Museum).

Rodchenko, Alexander Mikhailovich 1891–1956
Russian artist, graphic designer and photographer, a member of the CONSTRUCTIVIST movement. His first pure abstractions of 1914, made with a ruler and compass, showed the influence of Malevich's Suprematist paintings, but by 1919 Rodchenko had coined the term "Non-objectivism" to define his more rigorous, less other-worldly approach to abstract art, which was more in line with Larionov's Rayonnist theory. In the same year he sent his painting *Black on black* (1918, New York, MOMA), a reply to Malevich's *White on white*, to the Suprematist-Non-Objectivist exhibition in Moscow. From 1920 to 1922 he worked in the Constructivist idiom, producing austere, "minimal" line constructions, some of which, translated into three dimensions, formed graceful hanging sculptures (example, 1920–21, Athens, Costakis coll.). However, like Tatlin, he was soon to reject fine art and after 1922 concentrated on utilitarian work, designing textiles, posters and exploring photomontage. See vol. 3 pp. **158–159**

Rodhe, Lennart born 1916
Swedish painter, draughtsman and engraver. He adopted a Cubist style in painting under the influence of Picasso, and demonstrated an acutely objective realism in drawing, before turning entirely to abstract painting in the late 1940s during a visit to North Africa. Since 1948 most of his work has been for public buildings, geometrical abstracts with dot and line motifs (enamel work for the University of Uppsala, 1961–63).

Rodin, Auguste 1840–1917
French sculptor. In the history of sculpture Rodin occupies a place even more important than that of his contemporaries Cézanne, Gauguin and van Gogh in painting, for single-handedly he brought sculpture back to the mainstream of art and the centre of public attention after it had occupied a secondary position since the days of Canova and Flaxman. Unlike them, Rodin was primarily a modeller rather than a carver, a Romantic in spirit, with a masterly ability to create movement through the play of light on broken surfaces. He came from a lowly background and his early career was unsuccessful: for 20 years he earned his living performing menial sculptural tasks and suffered three rejections from the Ecole des Beaux-Arts. The turning point came in the mid-1870s, when he made a visit to Italy and felt himself liberated from the bonds of academic art by the example of Michelangelo, who inspired his first major work (1875–76), *The Age of Bronze* (many casts of this work were made; like most of Rodin's work it can be seen in the Rodin museums in Paris and in Philadelphia). Rodin's realistic figure broke so completely from conventional stylizations that he was accused of having made it from a cast taken from a live model. It made his reputation and in 1880 was bought by the State. In the same year he received a commisson from the State for a project which obsessed him for most of the rest of his life, a large bronze door, *The Gates of Hell*, for a future museum of decorative arts. This large and complex project was still unfinished at Rodin's death, but many of the individual figures which are part of the door (there are almost 200) were enlarged to form independent pieces. Among them are his famous works, *The kiss* and *The thinker*, both of which exist in several versions, the marble ones being carved by assistants. The expressive power of these figures, gained through formal simplification and exaggerations and an often rough "unfinished" quality in the modelling, was taken even further by Rodin in his most powerful individual figure, the monument to Balzac (1897). This was so radical that it was rejected by the commissioning committee, but in 1900 a pavilion was devoted to Rodin's work at the Paris World Fair, and from then on his genius was increasingly recognized. In his last years he turned to drawing and produced many pencil-and-wash sketches of dancers and nudes, whose fluid beauty contrasts with the brutal power of much of his sculpture. Although the literary and symbolic associations of Rodin's work have been antithetical to much 20th-century art, his place in its development is crucial. He made sculpture once more a vehicle for personal expression after it had largely lapsed into the areas of decoration and bombastic public monuments. His assistant Bourdelle and Maillol were among those most directly influenced by his work. See vol. 1 pp. **34–35,** *172, 176, 189*; vol. 3 pp. **106–109**

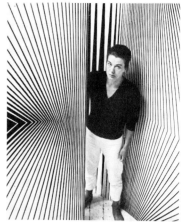
Riley, Bridget: Photograph by the entrance to her painting *Continuum* (Thomas Picton, Camera Press)

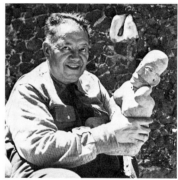
Rivera, Diego: Photograph, 1954 (Camera Press)

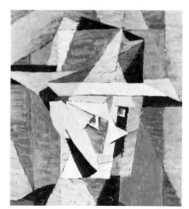
Rodhe: Self-portrait, 1943. Private coll. (Stockholm, Statens Konstmuseer)

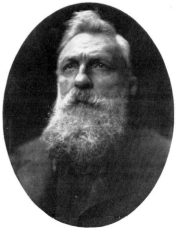
Rodin: Photograph, 1913 (Mansell)

Roeder, Emy born 1890
German sculptor. From 1912 to 1914 she studied in Darmstadt and, in 1918, joined the NOVEMBERGRUPPE. She lived in Italy, 1937–49, and since 1950 has lived at Mainz. Her early Expressionist sculptures, especially her portraits, show the influence of Barlach. She carved animals as well as figures, but her mature style is abstract.

Roelas, Juan de las 1558/60–1625
Spanish painter, active mainly in Seville, where he was the leading painter of his day. He was a priest who painted mainly for churches and religious houses, and most of his work is still in and around Seville. His skilfully orchestrated, large, colourful scenes (*The martyrdom of St Andrew*, 1609, Seville Museum) have been likened to Veronese's. Roelas' style, however, was altogether more fervent, and his combination of realism and mysticism had a lasting influence in Seville.

Roerich, Nikolai Konstantinovich 1874–1947
Russian artist and designer, a member of the WORLD OF ART group. His paintings of imaginary scenes of the distant past, set in vast landscapes of the steppes, such as *Battle in the heavens* (1912, Leningrad, Russian Museum), led the great ballet impresario Diaghilev to invite him to design for his dance company Les Ballets Russes. Typical is the set for *Polovtsian Dances* (1909, London, V&A). He lived briefly in America but settled in India in 1928 as Director of a Himalayan Institute of Studies. The majority of his paintings are in Leningrad (Russian Museum).

Roger of Helmershausen
active late 11th/early 12th century
German goldsmith, whose work marks the introduction of the Romanesque style into northern Germany. His signed portable altar (Paderborn, Cathedral Treasury) was given to Paderborn in 1100 by Bishop Heinrich (1084–1127). The metal sides of the small chest are incised with heavily stylized figures conceived in linear patterns, clearly influenced by Byzantine art. Roger is sometimes identified with the monk **Theophilus**, the author of three books, *De Diversibus Artibus* (Of Diverse Arts), which were probably written in the early 12th century in northern Germany. Theophilus was clearly well-travelled, and a master of several crafts. His books contain a rich store of instruction for painters and craftsmen.

Rohlfs, Christian 1849–1938
German painter and engraver. He began painting in an intimate naturalistic style until influenced by the Post-Impressionists, especially van Gogh, in the 1890s. By 1905, then in his mid-50s, he had discovered and absorbed the principles of Expressionism. In 1905 and 1906 he painted with Nolde in Soest, producing townscapes in pure, luminous colour (*St Patroclus in Soest*, 1906–07, Essen, Museum Folkwang). In later works he sought to give an ethereal, almost visionary quality to his brilliant colour combinations. He also painted flowers and religious themes.

Rojas, Cristóbal 1857–90
Venezuelan painter. He was apprenticed to **Herrara Toro** (1857–1914), who was then completing the religious murals for Caracas Cathedral. In 1884 he travelled to Paris, studied at the Académie Julian and shared a studio with his compatriot Michelena. By

1886, when Rojas exhibited *Misery* (Caracas, Galleria de Arte Nacional) at the Paris Salon, he had acquired a remarkable mastery of 17th-century genre painting techniques, working on a large scale with a heightened sense of realism. In 1889 he returned to Caracas, where he enjoyed considerable public success.

Roldán, Pedro 1624–99
Spanish sculptor. He trained in Granada, and by 1656 had settled in Seville, where he was the leading sculptor of the late Baroque. His greatest work is the reredos (begun 1670) for the high altar of the church of the Hospital de la Caridad. This is one of the most spectacular and colourful examples of its period. The framework is by the architect Bernardo Simón de Pineda and Roldan's elegant figures were polychromed by Valdés Leal. Roldan's daughter **Luisa** (c.1656–1704) was also a sculptor.

Rolfsen, Alf 1895–1979
Norwegian painter, book illustrator and one of the pioneers of modern mural painting in Norway. Modern French art, especially Cubism, and Italian Renaissance frescos inspired his art. His large figurative works decorate many public buildings, including Oslo Town Hall.

Romako, Anton 1832–89
Austrian history, genre and portrait painter. He studied in Vienna and lived in Rome between 1857 and 1874. Romako's tragic personal life, worsened by illness and endless financial difficulties, and his disastrous attempt to compete against the immensely popular Makart with his own isolated and uncomfortable society portraits, meant that he died totally unrecognized. Only at the beginning of the 20th century was he seen to be one of the precursors of Expressionism. His *Battle of Lissa, 1866* (1880, Vienna, Österreichische Galerie) shows his dismissal of conventional composition and pictorial space for the sake of expression and spontaneity.

Romanelli, Giovanni Francesco c.1610–62
Italian Baroque painter and tapestry designer, the leading pupil of Pietro da Cortona, and like him much patronized by the Barberini. Romanelli softened Cortona's bravura with the classicism of Domenichino, his first teacher, and Sacchi, producing a style which was rather facile, but often of great charm; his masterpieces are the enchanting frescos in the Sala della Contessa Matilda in the Vatican (1637–42). He paid two visits to France, and his restrained version of Baroque was influential in the development of the Grand Manner of history painting promoted by Louis XIV at Versailles and elsewhere. The sweet colouring and graceful physical types of his more intimate works deeply influenced Eustache Le Sueur.

Romanesque art
First widespread European style of art in the medieval era, maturing in France in the late 11th century and dominating Europe by the 12th century. The revival followed a century of barbarian invasions which destroyed much of the Carolingian culture. Romanesque was principally a church art (though it should be remembered that secular expressions have survived less well). Romanesque church architecture, foreshadowed in buildings of northern Spain and Lombardy in the 10th century, is commonly distinguished by the use of rounded arches and well-integrated ground plans and elevations. It gave birth to an extra-

ordinary sculptural art—carved portals (the earliest known example is at St Genis des Fontaines in southern France, about 1019–20) and figured capitals with religious and profane subjects. The developed portal featured a carved tympanum with figures in its archivolts and columns and reliefs beneath: masterpieces were produced in Burgundy (notably by Gislebertus) and in southern France, as at Moissac, c.1115–20. The early examples of Romanesque church sculpture show a strong preference for abstract forms, linear styles and a highly imaginative approach; the classical naturalism which had survived in some areas of Carolingian and Ottonian art was rarely imitated, though Carolingian and Ottonian models were clearly influential. A remarkable exception was the art of the Mosan region of north-eastern France, epitomized by the bronze sculpture of Renier de Huy. Generally, the intention to instil a fearful respect for divine power was served by stylized images of holy figures, nightmarish demonic creatures and humble, caricature-like figures of men. The direct influence of classical sculpture tended to be superficial, though the art of Wiligelmo in Italy and the sculpture of the façades of St Trôphime in Arles and of St Gilles du Gard, both in Provence, came close to Roman art. Many of the monastic scriptoria of France began once more to produce illuminated manuscripts of high quality in the Romanesque period: 11th-century manuscripts echo Carolingian and Ottonian art, but Byzantine influence became increasingly strong. France also possesses the most remarkable surviving Romanesque murals and some of the earliest stained glass in Europe. Among the masterpieces of 12th-century painting are English productions, for example the Bury Bible of Master Hugo (Cambridge, Corpus Christi College) and the Winchester Bible (Winchester, Cathedral Library), both superbly executed in brilliant colour. The transition from Romanesque to Gothic was less startling (and later) in painting than in architecture and sculpture. By the mid-12th century the first characteristics of early Gothic were emerging in the churches and cathedrals of northern France. See vol. 2 pp. 70–75

Romanino, Girolamo c.1484–after 1559
Italian painter, born in Brescia, and active there and elsewhere in northern Italy. Giovanni Bellini, Giorgione and Titian were important influences on him, and his style combined Venetian colour with the descriptive realism typical of Brescian art. The four noble frescos depicting *The Passion of Christ* (1519–20) in the nave of Cremona Cathedral are good examples of his work.

Romanists
Term applied to artists from northern Europe who imported Italian ideas to their countries. It is particularly used of Netherlandish painters of the early 16th century, in whose work there is a profusion of often half-understood Renaissance ornament and exaggerated poses based on Michelangelo and Raphael.

Romano, Antoniazzo c.1461–1512
Italian painter. Though fairly undistinguished, he was perhaps the most notable native Roman painter of the late 15th century and worked on many papal commissions, often in collaboration with others, including Melozzo da Forlì, Ghirlandaio and Perugino. *The Virgin and Child* (Florence, Uffizi) is representative of his eclectic style.

Romantic classicism
Movement within NEOCLASSICISM in which the interest in antiquity is tinged with Romantic feeling. The term fits best the fervid and almost mystic reaction of foreign artists—among them Fuseli, Carstens and Romney—to the dream or sight of Rome in the second half of the 18th century, but it is also used to describe works transitional between Neoclassicism and established Romanticism—those, for instance, of Girodet.

Romanticism
Movement in art flourishing from the late 18th until the mid-19th century. Nourished by Romantic literature (Rousseau, Byron, Ossian, Goethe), it was a reaction to classicism and the rational Encyclopédistes, although itself having a classical foundation. Reaction against the growing industrialization of Europe can be found in the Romantics' intense identification with nature in its untamed state and, often, in their emphasis on the past. Although nostalgic, this attitude differed fundamentally from the idealized Arcadian visions of a classicist like Poussin. Melancholy, even melodramatic tragedy tends to underlie the Romantic view of the past, while natural phenomena become infused with human feeling. This first emerges perhaps in English Romanticism, notably in the poetry of Wordsworth, but in German landscape painting, too, trees, rocks and sky all become forms invested with emotion. For Friedrich and Runge landscape was a manifestation of the Divine, and Runge's images of children in landscapes are quintessential expressions of the Romantic belief in the near-sanctity of infancy; artists struggled to recapture the clarity and unselfconsciousness with which the child experiences the natural world. Spontaneity and belief in the primacy of feeling and self-expression were central tenets of the Romantic belief. In France, Géricault, objecting to the rigid training of the Ecole des Beaux-Arts, wrote: "Genius is the fire of a volcano which must and will break forth", an ideal embodied in Delacroix with his rich, brilliant colour, energetic brushwork and dramatic and emotive subject matter. In England the Romantic tradition in painting, which began with Fuseli and concluded with Constable and Turner, produced in Blake an artist of exceptional originality. His hatred of tyranny and support for revolution, and his assertion of artistic independence are of his time, yet in his portrayal of an inner, non-naturalistic vision he is unique, even among Romantic artists. See vol. 3 pp. 62–81

Rombouts, Theodore 1597–1637
Flemish painter, one of the most impressive of the northern CARAVAGGISTI. He trained with Abraham Janssens in Antwerp, and went in 1616 to Italy, where he stayed for about a decade. He painted religious and genre scenes in a bold, sharply-focused style (*Two musicians*, c.1620–25, Lawrence, Kansas, University of Kansas Museum of Art), which made his reputation. Later, influenced by Rubens and van Dyck, he used a lighter palette and more painterly technique (*Marriage of St Catherine*, 1634, Antwerp, St Jakobskerk).

Romney, George 1734–1802
British painter, principally a portraitist, once considered almost the equal of Reynolds and Gainsborough. He was active in the north of England until 1762, then mainly in London apart from a visit to Italy, 1773–75. His best portraits, which are usually of young people, have

un elegance based on clear, flowing lines, the avoidance of confusing shadows and a distinctive and appealing combination of greys, pinks and blacks. His heart was not in portraiture, and he lived almost a double life, associating privately with those of romantic temperament such as the sculptor Flaxman and the poet Hayley, and making quantities of pen-and-wash drawings of historical and literary subjects, much like Fuseli's. He also painted historical pictures and a series of "history" portraits of Emma, Lady Hamilton. Romney was long a favourite with American collectors and many of his best paintings are in the USA (Washington, NG, and New Haven, Yale Art Center). See vol. 2 p. **251**

Ronald, William born 1926
Canadian painter, whose example was crucial to the development and acceptance of abstract art in Toronto. In New York in 1948–49, he discovered the Abstract Expressionists, who influenced the vigorous handling of *In dawn the heart* (1954, Toronto, Art Gallery of Ontario). In 1953 he organized a group show of Toronto artists who were to form PAINTERS ELEVEN. Ronald moved to New York in 1955, producing *Central black* (1955–56, Oshawa, Robert McLaughlin Gallery), a painting suffused with suppressed energy, its slashing brushwork reminiscent of Kline's.

Rops, Félicien 1833–98
Belgian SYMBOLIST painter and draughtsman, most of whose career was spent in Paris. He is best known for his graphic work, which in general is satirical, and often highly erotic, indeed consciously pornographic. Much of it was published in his own magazine *Uylenspiegel*, in which he poked fun at society. He painted subjects much like those of his graphic work, and also some Impressionist portraits and landscapes.

Rosa, Salvator 1615–73
Italian painter, born in Naples and active mainly in Rome. He was a poet, actor and musician as well as an artist, and his colourful life and egotistic conception of his own genius made him for the 18th and 19th centuries the prototype of the ROMANTIC artist as a rebel against society. His output was varied, and included battle-pieces derived from his master Falcone. Rosa considered his history paintings to be his most important works, but his major achievement was the creation of a new type of wild, rugged landscape, which had, in Reynolds' words, "the power of inspiring sentiments of grandeur and sublimity". He had a strong sense of the bizarre and macabre and often chose unusual subjects (*Landscape with the crucifixion of Polycrates*, 1665, Chicago, Art Institute). In about 1660 he took up etching, in which medium he became one of the finest artists of his day. See vol. 2 p. **197**

Rosai, Ottone 1895–1957
Italian painter. A precocious artist, he exhibited with the Futurists in 1914. After World War I he was briefly influenced by METAPHYSICAL PAINTING, but by 1920 he was painting the pictures of urban working-class life that would remain his usual subject matter. His compositions combine structural coherence with a quasi-Naive simplification of form which avoids the sentimental without sacrificing the poetic.

Rosati, James born 1912
American sculptor. Originally a musician, he taught himself to sculpt and had his first one-man show in 1954. His work

can be compared with that of Minimal sculptors such as Tony Smith in that it is abstract and constructed in a rather monumental, block-like fashion.

Rose + Croix, Salon de la
Title of art exhibitions held in Paris in the 1890s by the esoteric, mystic brotherhood of the Rosicrucians. A lodge of the brotherhood was founded in France by the critic Joséphin Péladan between 1892 and 1897, when his Order held a series of exhibitions of art with mystical, often specifically Catholic, themes. Prosaic and modern subjects were not accepted and the Salons became a focal point of the SYMBOLIST movement, exhibiting works by both French and foreign painters.

Rosenquist, James born 1933
American painter. He worked as a commercial artist painting billboards from 1954 to 1960. Although his earlier paintings were abstract, in 1960 he began to paint some of the first works to bring the style and subject matter of commercial art into fine-art painting. Throughout the 1960s he continued to be associated with the other POP artists. His paintings, such as the famous *F-111* (1955, New York, Mr and Mrs Robert Scull coll.), use a montage of the blown-up, sharp images of billboards juxtaposed in unfamiliar, suggestive arrangements. This work was designed to cover four walls of a room, thus creating a total environment and a visual bombardment of images in brilliant, glossy colours. See vol. 3 p. **239**

Roslin, Alexander 1718–93
Swedish portraitist in oils and pastel, mostly active in France. Roslin arrived in Paris in 1752, after stays at the courts of Bayreuth (1745–47) and Parma (1751–52). His facility in painting stuffs and complexions rapidly made him one of the most sought-after and prolific portrait painters in Paris. He was a favourite portraitist with artists and his most famous work is his portrait of his pastellist wife, **Marie Suzanne**, née Giroust (1734–72), as *The lady in a black veil* (1768, Stockholm, Nationalmuseum).

Rosselli, Cosimo di Lorenzo 1439–1507
Florentine painter, the pupil of Neri di Bicci, 1453–56, and probably of Benozzo Gozzoli. Though he lacked originality, his facility and craftsmanship resulted in many official commissions. In 1481 he was part of the team of artists decorating the walls of the Sistine Chapel, where he painted *The Last Supper* and *Moses receiving the Law*. He employed a linear, decorative style in somewhat cluttered compositions enriched with a quantity of gold and rich ultramarine. Late in his career he developed a stately, mannered style reminiscent of Filippino Lippi (*The Madonna and Child with Saints*, 1492, Florence, Accademia). Fra Bartolommeo, Andrea del Sarto and Piero di Cosimo were among his pupils.

Rossellino, Bernardo (1409–64) and **Antonio** (1427–79)
Florentine sculptors. Bernardo, also a distinguished architect, trained both his brother Antonio and Desiderio da Settignano as sculptors. His greatest work, the tomb of Leonardo Bruni, Chancellor of Florence (1444–50, Florence, S. Croce), combined architecture and sculpture in the classical vein and became a model for many later funerary monuments. In architecture he was influenced by the designs and ideas of

Alberti. Antonio's first dated work is the marble bust of *Giovanni Chellini* (1456, London, V&A); he used a life mask to attain unprecedented realism. His major work, in which he was assisted by his brother, was the tomb of the Cardinal of Portugal, in S. Miniato al Monte, Florence, 1460–66, the sculpture being designed as an integral part of the architecture of the funerary chapel, which was also decorated by Luca della Robbia, Baldovinetti and the Pollaiuoli. Antonio's reliefs there and his *Madonna and Child* have a lively and graceful idealism. See vol. 2 p. **114**

Rossetti, Dante Gabriel 1828–82
English painter and poet, a founder of the PRE-RAPHAELITE Brotherhood. He trained at the Royal Academy Schools, but, rejecting their classical aridities, went briefly to Ford Madox Brown's studio. He then shared a studio with Holman Hunt which became the cradle of the Brotherhood. In 1855 he met Burne-Jones and William Morris and later involved them in the murals in the Union building of Oxford University. He married his mistress Elizabeth Siddal in 1860, just two years before she died. He drew her continuously, putting her into several paintings, including *Beata Beatrix* (1864, London, Tate). When the Brotherhood disbanded he worked mainly in watercolour, but in the 1860s returned to oils and produced painting after painting of heavy-lidded sensual women, frequently using the same model, one favourite being Jane Morris, wife of William. Rossetti's personality and romantic aestheticism made him a potent influence on late 19th-century art. See vol. 3 pp. **82–83, 123**; vol. 4 p. *33*

Rossi, Gino 1884–1947
Italian painter. He visited Paris in 1907 and responded to the Post-Impressionists, particularly Gauguin and the Nabis, with pictures such as *Springtime in Brittany* (1908, Treviso, Museo Civico). After World War I the influence of Cézanne and early Cubism is detectable. He became insane in 1926.

Rosso, Medardo 1858–1928
Italian sculptor. From his student days his aim was to produce sculpture that portrayed the effect of light and atmosphere on his subjects. His work can be seen as Impressionist and rivals that of Rodin in its innovatory quality and influence. Rosso's subject matter ranged from solitary women and children to figure groups in contemporary settings and highly accomplished portrait busts. His preference for modelling in wax reinforced his view of solid matter as essentially malleable by atmosphere. The lack of detail and blurred forms in, for example, *The bookmaker* (1894, New York, MOMA) give a sense of movement and incorporeity that contrasts with the tangibility of traditional sculpture. See vol. 1 p. *185*; vol. 3 p. **107**

Rosso Fiorentino (Giovanni Battista di Jacopo) 1495–1540
Florentine painter, possibly a pupil of Andrea del Sarto, and one of the greatest of the Florentine MANNERISTS. His work has close affinities in colour, composition and atmosphere to that of Pontormo. His elegant, brittle figures are strangely suspended in a dreamland, acting out their roles with something approaching self-adulation, which does not preclude intensity of emotion and powerful characterization, as in the *Dead Christ with Angels* (c.1525, Boston, MFA). In the last decade of his life he was chief among the Italian artists to be

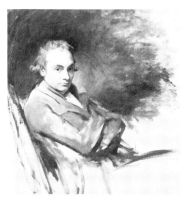
Romney: Self-portrait, 1782. London, NPG

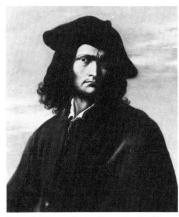
Rosa: Self-portrait (detail), c.1640. London, NG

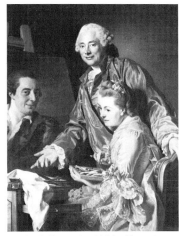
Roslin: Self-portrait with his wife, 1760s. Private coll. (Stockholm, Nationalmuseum)

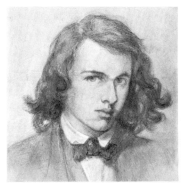
Rossetti: Self-portrait drawing, 1847. London, NPG

employed by the French monarchy in the decorations at FONTAINEBLEAU. See vol. 2 pp. **165–167**

Roszak, Theodore born 1907
American painter and sculptor, born in Poland. His family emigrated to the USA in 1909. In 1929 he went to Europe and came under the influence of the Bauhaus. He turned seriously to sculpture in the Constructivist idiom in 1936, and in the mid-1940s his work became freer and rougher and he adopted brazing and welding techniques. Mythical and literary themes are developed into powerful images suggestive of skeletal plants and primordial creatures.

Rotella, Mimmo born 1918
Italian painter. During the 1950s he taught in the USA before returning to Rome, where he developed the technique known as "décollage", in which posters stripped from walls are transferred to a canvas and then further mutilated. Rotella introduced direct moral messages into the medium through his use of photographic images, and his art reveals a desire to relate artistic statements and methods to urban society.

Roth, Dieter born 1930
Swiss artist, the creator of some of the most sophisticated graphic work produced since World War II. He was born in Germany, arrived in Switzerland in 1943 and moved to Iceland in 1950. A major part of his oeuvre is contained in his series of books, such as *The Seas of Tears and their Relatives* (1973–77). These combine verbal poetry with images of extraordinary poetic power which both exploit and comment on the printing process. Layer succeeds layer: images are reworked again and again in different ways and with different colours. He has frequently collaborated with other artists, most notably Richard Hamilton. He has also worked in other media, including music and film.

Rothenstein, Sir William
1872–1945
British painter. He studied in Paris, where he came under the influence of Degas and Whistler. He is best known for his early work in sombre colours, portraits such as *Augustus John* (1899, Liverpool, Walker Art Gallery) or figure compositions such as *A doll's house* (1899, London, Tate), an enigmatic study of a man and woman on a staircase inspired by Ibsen's play of that name.

Rothko, Mark 1903–70
American painter, one of the leading members of the NEW YORK school and, with Newman and Still, one of the first to create COLOUR FIELD painting. Rothko was born in Russia and arrived inthe USA in 1913. In 1935 he founded, with Gottlieb, the Expressionist group The Ten and from 1936 to 1937 worked on the Federal Art Project. His early paintings depicted urban scenes with isolated figures but in the mid-1940s, influenced by Surrealism, he turned to more primordial imagery, often painted in delicate watercolour. In the late 1940s he began to move toward his definitive style—blurred colour patches became more strictly ordered and his familiar format of a vertically suspended stack of shifting rectangles was arrived at by 1950. The surfaces of these soft-edged expanses of colour seem to breathe and the frequently warm colours open up the pictorial surface. In the late 1950s Rothko's palette darkened in accord with his growing state of depression. His murals for the ecumenical chapel in Houston, Texas (1967–69), completed shortly before his suicide, are hypnotically mystic canvases of black, dark brown and sombre purple. See vol. 1 pp. **88–89**, *120*; vol. 3 p. **218**

Rottenhammer, Hans (or **Johann**)
1564–1625
German painter, who between 1589 and 1606 worked in Italy. He painted small mythological scenes with landscape backgrounds, often on copper, in the manner of Paul Bril, and these in turn may have influenced Elsheimer, with whom he worked in Venice.

Rottmann, Carl 1797–1850
German landscape painter, much travelled in Greece and Italy. He attempted landscape painting in monumental format (including murals for the Hofgarten in Munich), with high stylization and literary and much emotional content.

Rottmayr, Johann Franz Michael
1654–1730
The founding figure of Austrian High Baroque painting. After 13 years in Venice, he worked in Salzburg (1688–95), where he began his association with the architect Fischer von Erlach. His fresco over the Jesuit Church in Breslau (1704–06) was the first in the German Empire to unite the entire vault of a nave. His oil-sketches were also a novelty. Settled in Vienna from 1696, and ennobled in 1704, he painted major frescos both there (Karlskirche, 1725) and further afield (Melk, 1716) in a robust, painterly idiom.

Rouault, Georges 1871–1958
French painter who, through his expressionist religious work, achieved a special place in 20th-century art. The exotic style and imagery of his teacher Moreau remained a powerful influence throughout his career, as did the formal values which he had learned as an apprentice in a stained-glass workshop. In 1905 he exhibited at the Salon d'Automne in the next room to his fellow-students from Moreau's studio, the Fauves—Matisse, Marquet and Camoin. Like them he used wild brushwork and glowing colours, but his subject matter sets him apart from them. In common with Daumier he expressed a vision of the fallen condition of humanity by means of powerful images of judges, prostitutes and tragic clowns (*Little Olympia*, 1906, Copenhagen, Statens Museum for Kunst). Much of his work was inspired by the Catholic theology of his friend Léon Bloy (*Christ mocked*, c.1932, New York, MOMA), and from 1918 his works were almost entirely religious. He also designed tapestries, prints and book illustrations and in 1929 drew cartoons for the windows of the Church of Assy. See vol. 3 p. **143**

Roubiliac, Louis-François
*c.*1705–62
French sculptor, whose career was spent almost entirely in England. He was born in Lyons and arrived in London in the early 1730s; before then his life is largely obscure, although he is said to have studied with Permoser in Saxony and with Coustou in Paris. His first success was the statue of *George Frederick Handel* (1738, London, V&A), the beginning of a long line of brilliantly vivacious portraits, both full-lengths and busts (*William Hogarth*, *c.*1741, London, NPG). Apart from portraits he was principally active as a tomb sculptor and, beginning with the Argyll monument (1745–49, London, Westminster Abbey), he established his superiority over his leading contemporaries, Rysbrack and Scheemakers. In 1752 Roubiliac made a brief journey to Rome, where he was greatly impressed by the work of Bernini, compared to which he said his own sculptures looked "meagre and starved, as if made of nothing but tobacco pipes". Bernini's influence is apparent in Roubiliac's most celebrated work, the startlingly dramatic Nightingale monument (1761, Westminster Abbey). Although he was very productive, the quality of his work is unfailingly high, and in his formal inventiveness, sensitive characterization and technical virtuosity he ranks as one of the greatest sculptors of his time. See vol. 2 pp. **243**, *248*

Rousseau, Henri Julien
("Le Douanier") 1844–1910
French painter, the most famous of all NAIVE painters. He worked as a toll inspector before devoting himself to art in 1885. Through the anarchic dramatist Alfred Jarry he entered the circle of Apollinaire and Picasso, who admired the purity of vision of his art. He is best known for the jungle scenes of 1900–10 such as *The dream* (1910, New York, MOMA), in which the stylized, minutely detailed lush foliage and the mysterious lurking figures are endowed with an extraordinary conviction and intensity. As well as depicting rural and modern urban landscapes he painted portraits and enigmatic studies of children such as *Child on rocks* (1895, Washington, NG). See vol. 1 p. *87*; vol. 3 pp. **140–141**

Rousseau, Théodore 1812–67
French landscape painter, a leading figure in the BARBIZON school. He began painting at an early age, but his talent was first recognized in 1833 by Scheffer, who exhibited his romantic and expressive *plein-air* studies of the Auvergne landscape. Always controversial for his intense and boldly executed landscapes, Rousseau's *Descent of the cattle* (1835, Amiens) was a *cause célèbre*, and from 1836 until the Revolution of 1848 his work was consistently excluded from the Salon, earning him the sobriquet "le grand refusé". From 1848 until his death he settled in Barbizon, working closely with Millet, Daubigny, Dupré and Diaz. Described by Baudelaire as "tormented by a thousand devils and not knowing which one to heed", Rousseau ranged in his landscapes from the translucent and realistic to the intense and melancholic. See vol. 3 pp. **92–93**

Rowlandson, Thomas 1756–1827
English draughtsman, printmaker and caricaturist, the finest pictorial satirist of his period. He worked mainly in ink and watercolour washes to create illustrations of contemporary life and bawdy social commentaries. Though his subjects were often coarse, his sense of line and colour were very delicate. Little is known of his life; he entered the Royal Academy Schools in 1772 and during the 1770s spent some time in France. His output was enormous and he produced numerous series for publishers, notably *The Comforts of Bath* (1798) and *The Tours of Dr Syntax* (1812–20). See vol. 1 pp. *84–85*; vol. 4 p. *131*

Roy, Pierre 1880–1950
French painter and designer. He was associated with the early phase of Surrealism, exhibiting at the first Surrealist exhibition in 1925. Influenced by Chirico, he created disturbing and mysterious effects by setting realistically observed objects in bizarre juxtapositions, as in *The dangers of the stairway* (1927–28, New York, MOMA).

Royal Academy of Arts
The leading British art institution from its foundation in 1768 until the late 19th century. Like virtually all academies of art before the 20th century, it had two main aims—to improve the professional, social and economic status of artists and to promote the grand style of history painting. It succeeded in the first, but only very partially in the second. It imitated the longer-established academies of France and Italy in securing royal patronage (though British sovereigns have only shown benevolent interest, never tried to dictate policy) and in establishing schools, where for a long time only drawing from the life and from casts was taught. A key activity was the holding of large annual exhibitions, another practice borrowed from France. The giving of lectures by prominent academicians was also not new, but such was the success of the *Discourses* of Reynolds, its first President, that such lectures became, unprecedently, an annual, or twice-yearly, event.

Rozanova, Olga Vladimirovna
1886–1918
Russian avantgarde painter and graphic designer, and author of an influential article on *Non-objective Painting* (1913). A series of illustrations for Russian Futurist publications culminated in a set of collages for *Universal War* (1916), made of coloured tissue-paper, glued on deep blue paper. She was a leading member of the Oganization for Proletarian Culture—committed to the creation of a mass culture—and after the Revolution this group set about putting their ideas into practice on the lines of a socialist realist programme she drew up. Her pioneering work was recognized by an enormous retrospective exhibition in Moscow (1919).

Rubenisme see POUSSINISME

Rubens, Sir Peter Paul 1577–1640
The greatest Flemish painter of the 17th century and the dominant figure of Baroque art in northern Europe. He was born at Siegen in Westphalia, but in 1587 moved to Antwerp, where he studied with three fairly mediocre artists, Tobias Verhaecht, Adam van Noort and Otto van Veen. In 1600 he went to Italy, where, apart from a trip to Spain, 1603–04, on behalf of Vincenzo Gonzaga, Duke of Mantua, he remained until 1608. From 1605 he worked principally in Genoa and Rome. In Genoa he developed a new type of grand aristocratic portrait (*Marchesa Brigida Spinola-Doria*, 1606, Washington, NG), which was to form the basis of van Dyck's Genoese work. It was in Rome, however, that Rubens' style was chiefly formed. His drawings show how thoroughly he studied the Antique, the great masters of the Renaissance and the leading contemporary artists, particularly Annibale Carracci, and on this basis he developed a style of heroic grandeur and amplitude. On his return to Antwerp, Rubens was immediately successful. In 1609 he became court painter to the Spanish Viceroys, Albert and Isabella, and in the same year married Isabella Brandt: his portrait of himself and his wife (Munich, Alte Pinakothek), undated but presumably painted to mark their marriage, gives a wonderful picture of the young artist's vitality and self-confidence. The works which established his reputation are the two triptychs of *The raising of the Cross* and *The Descent from the Cross* (1610–11 and 1611–14, Antwerp Cathedral). Both are works of epic grandeur, and *The raising* shows the dy-

namic energy which was to be one of the leading characteristics of Rubens' work. After these triumphs, Rubens was showered with commissions, and was able to execute them all only because of his extraordinary energy and highly organized studio. Among great artists perhaps only Picasso has matched his sheer fecundity and only Raphael his ability to organize a team of assistants. Many of the leading Flemish artists of the time worked with him as pupils, assistants or collaborators (van Dyck, Snyders, "Velvet" Brueghel, Gerard Seghers) and his output included not only paintings on virtually every subject but also book illustrations, designs for tapestries and festival decorations. Because of his courtly manners, great intelligence and linguistic skills, Rubens was also entrusted with diplomatic missions to Spain and England, where he was knighted by Charles I. It was for Charles that he provided canvases (completed 1634) for the ceiling of the Banqueting House in London, the only one of his large decorative commissions still in its original position. Although Rubens' career was so public, there was also a personal dimension to his art, which found expression chiefly in his landscapes and paintings of his family (*Hélène Fourment with two of her children*, *c*.1637, Paris, Louvre). (Isabella had died in 1626, and he married Hélène in 1630.) Rubens was such a dominant personality that hardly any 17th-century Flemish artist remained untouched by his influence, and he employed engravers such as the Bolswert brothers, Jegher and Pontius to reproduce his work and increase his international reputation. His achievement was so diverse that artists of very different temperaments could respond to his work; Watteau, Gainsborough and Delacroix are three artists who testify to his posthumous influence. See vol. 1 pp. *26, 30, 54, 56, 84, 106, 134, 147*; vol. 2 pp. **202–205**

Rublev, Andrei *c*.1370–1430
The most celebrated of Russian painters, and the most famous of icon painters. Little is known for certain of his life. There is written evidence that he worked with Theophanes in the Cathedral of the Annunciation, Moscow, in the late 14th century, and on other wall-paintings, but the only icon given to him on the same grounds is *The Holy Trinity* (*c*.1411, Moscow, Tretyakov Gallery). In this he infused the hieratic stylized forms of late Byzantine painting with a gentler, more lyrical spirit, and other icons are attributed to him because of their stylistic similarities. See vol. 2 p. **62**

Rude, François 1784–1855
French sculptor. Although he was an admirer of classical principles, his sculpture is clearly Romantic, especially in his greatest work, the dramatic high relief for the Arc de Triomphe, *The departure of the volunteers in 1792* (1833–36, Paris). His portraits were not idealized but were individual and dramatic, embodying the dynamic heroism of both the Revolutionary and Napoleonic eras; his allegiance to Napoleon led him to leave Paris on the Emperor's abdication and to go with J.-L. David to Brussels, where he worked from 1814 to 1827. Rude's ability to capture movement and emotion found its fullest expression in his monument *Napoleon awakening to immortality* (1845–47, Paris, Louvre). See vol. 1 p. *57*; vol. 3 p. **79**

Rude, Olaf 1886–1957
Danish painter. Influenced by Gauguin, van Gogh, Matisse and Picasso during a visit to Paris in 1911, he turned to CUBISM in 1918. He painted Cubist landscapes, portraits and still lifes for the rest of his career. *Old woman with a dish* (1924, Denmark, Randers Art Gallery) uses colour expressively. Many landscapes are of the island of Bornholm.

Ruisdael, Jacob van 1628/9–82
The greatest Dutch landscape painter of the 17th century. He was born in Haarlem, the son of a frame-maker and the nephew of Salomon van Ruysdael (the difference in spelling occurs in their signatures). Little is known of his training, and he seems a mature artist even in his earliest works (*Dunes*, 1646, Leningrad, Hermitage). He is distinguished from most Dutch landscapists by the range and power of his work, which often shows an emotional response to the dramatic aspects of nature. Landscapists of the previous generation had largely been concerned with atmospheric purity, but Ruisdael used powerful forms and dense colours, as in the mighty view of *Bentheim Castle* (1653, Blessington, Ireland, Beit coll.), where the romantic silhouette of the castle crowns a rugged hill which sweeps diagonally across the picture. In his most famous work, *The Jewish cemetery* (1660s, versions in Detroit Institute of Arts and Dresden, Gemäldegalerie), he takes his subjectivity further and creates a mood of tragic intensity. In 1657 Ruisdael moved to Amsterdam and remained there for the rest of his life, teaching Hobbema amongst others. He did some notable paintings of waterfalls (examples in London, NG, and Wallace Coll.) influenced by Everdingen's Scandinavian scenes, but his chief subject remained the Dutch landscape, its forests, flats and shores. Ruisdael's contemporaries were profoundly affected by his achievement, and in later centuries he was widely revered. Gainsborough, Constable and the painters of the Barbizon school were among those who appreciated the majestic power and intensity of his art. See vol. 1 p. *61*; vol. 2 pp. *222*, **224–225**

Runciman, Alexander 1736–85 and **John** 1744–68/9
Scottish painters, brothers, who belonged to the phase of Romantic Classicism in British art chiefly associated with Fuseli. They travelled to Italy but John died in Naples aged 24, having completed some unusual biblical and Shakespearean paintings in the style of Rubens. Alexander studied the Antique and the Old Masters and returned to Scotland to decorate Penicuik House near Edinburgh with subjects from the poems of Ossian (the paintings were burnt in 1899). His masterpiece is generally given as *King Lear in the storm* (1767, Edinburgh, NG of Scotland).

Runge, Philipp Otto 1777–1810
With Friedrich, the greatest of the German ROMANTIC painters. Whereas Friedrich was a landscapist, Runge concentrated on figures within landscape. After studies in Copenhagen and Dresden he settled in Hamburg, where he started work on the allegorical cycle *The Four Phases of Day* (1803–09, Hamburg, Kunsthalle). A mystical apprehension of the harmony of man and nature underlaid his art, in which he strove to convey the essential divinity of all created forms. This spirit he most often embodied in images of children and flowers, culled from both pagan and Christian sources, but amalgamated to express his complex personal version of Romantic pantheism. Although he attached a primarily symbolic meaning to

colour, a more objective attitude is evident in his treatise *Colour Spectrum* (1810), and growing naturalism can be found in the landscape backgrounds of certain portraits and in *Morning* (1809, Hamburg, Kunsthalle). Studies of his family and friends convey a strong sense of physical likeness, but are always informed by an intense spirituality. See vol. 3 pp. **74–75**

Rusconi, Camillo 1658–1728
Italian sculptor, the most powerful personality in sculpture in Rome in the early 18th century. His masterpieces are four huge statues of the *Apostles* (1708–18) in S. Giovanni in Laterano. These heroic figures have something of the dynamic life of Bernini but are more classical and restrained, forming a kind of sculptural equivalent to the work of his friend, the painter Maratta. Another well-known work by Rusconi is the tomb (1719–25) of Pope Gregory XIII in St Peter's.

Rush, William 1756–1833
American sculptor, born and active in Philadelphia. He was the son of a ship's carpenter, and wood was his favourite medium, his work representing the culmination of the folk tradition of carving before Neoclassicism came to dominate American sculpture. His best-known sculptures are the figures of *Comedy* and *Tragedy* (1808, Philadelphia, Pennsylvania Academy of Fine Arts), for the Chestnut Street Theater, Philadelphia. His style was very lively, with expressive use of deep undercutting.

Ruskin, John 1819–1900
English writer, critic and artist. Through his voluminous writings (the complete edition of his work occupies 39 large volumes) he exercised a greater influence on taste in Victorian England than anyone else. He came to public attention with the first volume of *Modern Painters* (1843), a defence of Turner, which subsequently expanded into a general survey of art. His successful defence of the Pre-Raphaelites is another example of the hold he had over public opinion. In *The Seven Lamps of Architecture* (1849) and *The Stones of Venice* (1851–53) he extolled Gothic art and architecture, finding in it evidence of the craftsman's delight in his labour. His personal life was tragic (his wife left him for Millais) and in the 1870s he began to go insane. In 1878 he lost a celebrated libel case against Whistler. The last years of his life were spent in the Lake District. He was a talented artist whose watercolours and drawings reflect his scientific interest in botany and geology as well as in architecture. See vol. 3 p. 73

Russell, Morgan 1886–1953
American painter, a co-founder of SYNCHROMISM. He studied sculpture with Matisse in Paris, 1908, and became interested in colour theory. In 1913 he and MacDonald-Wright launched Synchromism. His *Synchromy in orange: to form* (1913–14, Buffalo, Albright-Knox), one of the earliest pure abstract paintings, attracted great attention in Paris. It is a composition of pure colours arranged according to forms suggested by Michelangelo's *Dying slave*. From 1915 Russell worked in a more representational vein, but returned to his abstract Synchromies in 1922.

Russolo, Luigi 1885–1947
Italian painter. Trained as a musician, he began painting in 1908 and signed the FUTURIST manifestos of 1910. His work at this period investigated the interaction of space and matter, as in his *Interpene-*

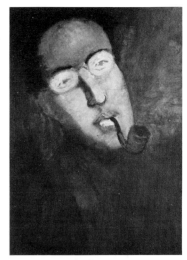
Rothko: Portrait by Avery, 1933. Providence, Rhode Island School of Design, The Albert Pilavin coll.

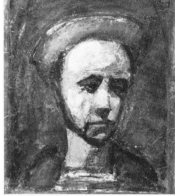
Rouault: Self-portrait, 1925–26. Paris, Musée National d'Art Moderne

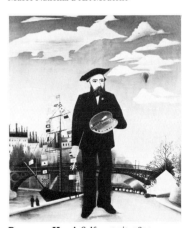
Rousseau, Henri: Self-portrait, 1890. Prague, National Gallery

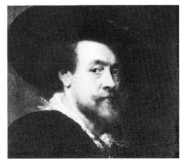
Rubens: Self-portrait, *c*.1630. Florence, Uffizi (Alinari)

tration of house and light and sky (1912, Basel, Kunstmuseum). He also published a manifesto of *Noise Music* in 1913. After the War his work became less abstract and he evolved a representational style that incorporated Surrealist elements. See vol. 3 p. **153**

Ruthenbeck, Reiner born 1937
West German sculptor. After being a photographer, specializing in scenes of desolate stillness, he studied under Joseph Beuys at Düsseldorf. His first sculptures were of recognizable objects (cupboards, spoons and so on) but he altered the scale and exaggerated certain formal properties in such a way that the object's function was totally denied. He then progressed to sculptures exploring the properties of materials and, more recently, the architectural setting.

Ruysch, Rachel 1664–1750
Dutch still-life painter, primarily of flower-pieces. The daughter of a botanist, she was a pupil of Willem van Aelst. A painstaking painter (only some 100 works are known), she adhered to the darker palette of the preceding generation (unlike van Huysum). From 1708 to 1716 she worked solely for the Elector Palatine. She was one of the best flower-painters—combining Rococo delicacy with precise naturalism (*Bouquet*, 1715, The Hague, Mauritshuis).

Ruysdael, Salomon van *c.*1600–70
Dutch landscape painter, born and active in Haarlem. With van Goyen he ranks as the leading master of the tonal phase of Dutch landscape painting, when the subtle depiction of atmosphere rendered with muted colours was a primary concern. Both van Goyen and Ruysdael were early influenced by the unaffected country views of Esaias van de Velde. Ruysdael settled in the 1630s to a prolific output of river scenes in a lyrical manner so close to van Goyen's that their work of this period has been confused. In the 1640s his colours became somewhat fresher (*River scene*, 1644, The Hague, Mauritshuis), and the greater sense of substance found in his later work may owe something to his nephew, Jacob van Ruisdael. In the 1660s he painted a few still lifes and hunting trophies. See vol. 2 p. **222**

Ryckaert, David III 1612–61
The most important member of a family of Flemish painters. He was one of the principal followers of Adriaen Brouwer, and painted mainly scenes of peasants in interiors (*The operation*, 1638, Valenciennes, Musée des Beaux-Arts). His grandfather, father and son, David I, II, and IV, were all painters, but better known is his uncle **Marten** Ryckaert (1587–1631), who painted landscapes in the manner of Joos de Momper.

Ryder, Albert Pinkham
1847–1917
American painter, one of the most individual artists of his period. Apart from a few short trips to Europe, from 1870 he led a solitary life in New York, painting his intensely subjective, at times almost mystical works. Often they show scenes of the sea, recalling the fishing port of New Bedford, Massachusetts, where he was born. They are painted very thickly, with bold, highly simplified forms and strange, often yellowish lighting, producing an effect of haunting intensity. He was deeply read in Romantic literature, and his work has often been compared to the writing of Edgar Allan Poe, which he greatly admired. The most macabre and

famous of his paintings is probably *The race track*, also known as *Death on a pale horse* (Cleveland Museum of Art). Ryder was largely self-taught and his eccentric technical methods have caused many of his paintings to deteriorate. He tended to work his paintings over a long period, so they are often difficult to date. Although he was such a solitary figure, his work was appreciated in his lifetime, and there are said to have been more fakes of his work than of any other American painter. See vol. 3 pp. **124–125**

Rysbrack, John Michael
1694–1770
English sculptor. He came from a family of Antwerp artists and in about 1720 settled in England, where he became undoubted head of his profession until Roubiliac and Scheemakers began to overtake him in popularity in the 1740s. In style his work lies somewhere between that of his two rivals; he was more sombre and classical than Roubiliac, but his interpretation of antique forms was more personal and lively than that of Scheemakers. His prolific output included tombs, statues and busts, and he introduced the vogue for portraits done in the Roman manner. Several of his monuments are in Westminster Abbey, London, including one to Sir Isaac Newton (1731), perhaps his best-known work. *William III* (1735, Bristol, Queen Square), his chief work in bronze, is the noblest equestrian statue produced in England in his century.

Rysselberghe, Theodoor van
1862–1926
Belgian painter and illustrator, also active in applied arts. He studied in Ghent and Brussels, travelled widely, and was a founder-member of Les VINGT. In 1888 he adopted a Pointillist style, after seeing paintings by Seurat and Signac. In 1897 he moved to Paris, but maintained close contact with Brussels. As a decorator he was closely associated with the architects of Art Nouveau, such as Henry van de Velde. Some of his best work can be seen in the Rijksmuseum Kröller-Müller, Otterlo (*A family gathering in an orchard*, 1890, and *Portrait of Mrs van Rysselberghe*, 1894).

Sacchi, Andrea 1599–1661
Italian painter. He was a pupil of Albani, but his inspiration came chiefly from Raphael, and he became the leading exponent of classicism in painting in Rome in the mid-17th century, his work forming a parallel to that of Algardi and Duquesnoy in sculpture. In the 1630s he had a controversy with Pietro da Cortona in the Accademia di S. Luca over whether history paintings should be represented with few figures (Sacchi) or many (Cortona). Sacchi and his circle won the dispute, but the work which gave him the best opportunity to put his ideas into practice, the large ceiling fresco of *Divine wisdom* (1629–33, Rome, Palazzo Barberini), compares very unfavourably with Cortona's celebrated ceiling in the same building, being ponderous and dull. Sacchi was much happier working on a smaller scale, as in his finest work, the serious and pensive *Vision of St Romuald* (*c.*1631, Vatican, Pinacoteca). He was also a talented portraitist. His principal pupil was Maratta.

Sacra conversazione
Italian term meaning "holy conversation" describing a representation of the Virgin and Child with saints where the figures (usually symmetrically disposed) are united in a single scene rather than occupying the separate compartments of a polyptych. Filippo Lippi's Barbadori altarpiece (begun 1437) is sometimes cited as the first example.

Sadiqi Beq (Sadiq) 1533–1609
Persian painter, active in Qazvin and Isfahan. He was a pupil of Muzaffar Ali and was also a writer and a soldier. For a time in the 1590s he was librarian to Shah Abbas I, but had been dismissed by 1598. His first dated work in the 1573 *Garshaspnameh* (London, BL) shows a definite taste for action. His single-figure drawings are executed in an elegant calligraphic style, with lines of varying thickness (*Bearded man*, *c.*1600, Dublin, Chester Beatty Library).

Saenredam, Pieter 1597–1665
Dutch painter of architectural subjects, active in Haarlem. He was the first to break away from the fanciful Mannerist tradition and specialize in accurate representations of specific buildings or sites. A hunchback, he lived a reclusive life, working slowly and deliberately, and only about 50 paintings by him are known. His perspective was precise and his palette mostly restricted to the palest of tones, but he invested the barest Protestant churches with atmosphere and sometimes added small figures to animate the scene and increase the sense of scale (*St Bavo, Haarlem*, 1660, Worcester, Mass., Art Museum). Many Dutch artists continued the tradition of view-painting which Saenredam initiated, but only de Witte and van der Heyden approach him in quality. See vol. 2 pp. **212, 222**

Sage, Kay 1898–1963
American SURREALIST painter. She lived during 1937–39 in Paris, where she met Tanguy whom she later married; they fled to America in 1941. She was clearly impressed by the organic, osseous shapes set in a mysterious space which Tanguy employed. To this Surrealistic scenery she added fantastic mineral and architectural elements, which give her paintings a slightly less remote quality than his. She also made some Surrealist, mixed-media constructions.

Saint-Aubin brothers
Four French ROCOCO draughtsmen and designers. **Charles-Germain** de Saint-Aubin (1721–86) began as a designer of embroidery and later produced volumes of engravings after his delicate watercolour flower studies. **Gabriel-Jacques** (1724–80) was the most talented of the quartet. His etchings of Parisian life are among the most charming works of the 18th century, and he painted a few canvases of similar themes, such as *A street show in Paris* (*c.*1760, London, NG). His views of contemporary Salons and picture auctions are valuable for their art historical information (*The Salon of 1765*, Paris, Louvre). **Louis-Michel** (1731–79) was a porcelain painter at the Sèvres factory, while **Augustin** (1736–1807), though a fine draughtsman, is best known as an engraver of the works of Boucher, Fragonard and Greuze among others.

Saint-Gaudens, Augustus
1848–1907
The outstanding American sculptor of his generation. Born in Ireland and brought to America as a child, he trained

as a cameo cutter and studied in Paris and Rome. His reputation was established with the heroic bronze and stone Admiral Farragut Monument (1878–81, New York, Madison Square Park), which is typical of his work in its blending of realism and idealism. His masterpiece is the bronze Adams memorial (1891, Washington, Rock Creek Cemetery), a monument to the suicide Marian Hooper Adams, wife of a friend of the sculptor. The highly original seated effigy, swathed in voluminous draperies, seems caught in an almost mystical reverie. Saint-Gaudens' home at Cornish, New Hampshire, is a museum of his work.

Saint-Phalle, Niki de born 1930
French sculptress. She became well-known in the early 1960s for her assemblages incorporating bags of paint which she burst with shots from a pistol. Her most famous work was *Hon* (Swedish for "she"), a brightly coloured model of a woman, over 25m (80ft) long, 6m (20ft) high and 9m (30ft) wide, shown in the Moderna Museet at Stockholm in 1963. Visitors were able to enter the body via the crutch, and inside were an aquarium, a bar, a cinema, a gallery of fake paintings and music rooms. This was closely related to her series of *Nanas*—fat ladies covered in ornaments similar to those found on primitive sculpture. She has also worked as a painter and since 1973 she has been making films.

Saito, Yoshishige born 1904
Japanese artist. In the 1930s he produced works which show the influences of Russian Constructivism and Dada. In 1953 he secluded himself in a fishing village near Tokyo, but he returned to art in 1957. During the first half of the 1960s he constructed many works from painted blocks of wood, some incised with lines. He then moved to relief works, also in wood, sometimes with movable pieces. A large-scale relief is that made in mahogany in the Royal Hotel, Kyoto (1972). His influence as teacher and member of the avantgarde has been considerable.

Salimbeni da Sanseverino, Lorenzo 1374–1416/20 and **Jacopo** active 1400–27
Italian painters, brothers, working in the Marches, collaborating on frescos and altarpieces. Their attractive but old-fashioned INTERNATIONAL GOTHIC style was heavily dependent on Lombard and Sienese models. The *St John the Baptist* frescos (1416, Urbino, S. Giovanni Battista) are their most notable works.

Sallinen, Tyko 1879–1955
The most important Finnish Expressionist painter. He founded and was the leader of an influential Finnish group called the November Group who exhibited together from 1916 to 1924. Originally a tailor, he studied painting from 1902, and stays in Copenhagen (1904) and Paris (1909 and 1914) acquainted him with French modernism. At home he aroused violent controversies with *Washerwomen* (1912, Helsinki, Ateneum) and *The hunchback* (1915, Vaasa, Museum). His early phase is characterized by impasto application of crayon-like paint and by bright colours liberated by Munch and Fauvism. During his middle period the colour becomes sombre and the brushwork regular: large, visionary canvases such as *The devil's dance* (1919, Vaasa, Museum) are restatements of his traumatic childhood experiences. His late period includes subdued figural compositions and landscape watercolours.

Salon
Name given to the annual art exhibition of the Académie Française. Although from the 17th century informal exhibitions were held in the Salon d'Apollon in the Louvre, not until the 19th century did the Salon assume its paramount importance. Exhibits were selected by a jury and acceptance generally secured an artist's sales and reputation, while further prestige attached to the medals awarded for painting, sculpture and engraving. As the century progressed, the academic and increasingly conservative jury rejected many innovatory artists until in 1863 Napoleon III established a **Salon des Refusés** in response to the protest against the number of works rejected by the official Salon that year; it was here that Manet's *Olympia* caused an uproar. By 1870 the Salon had become synonymous with conventional art and had declined in importance. It was taken over in 1881 by the Société des Artistes Français.

Salon d'Automne
Annual exhibition in Paris, founded in 1903 as an alternative to the official Salon and to the Salon des Indépendants. The first exhibition was a memorial showing of Gauguin's work and helped to establish his reputation with leading avant-garde artists, but in 1905 the Salon became notorious when the brilliant, non-naturalistic canvases of Matisse, Derain and Vlaminck were dubbed by an outraged critic the work of "wild beasts" (*fauves*). Two years later the Salon was the venue of Cézanne's memorial exhibition and for the first time the breadth of his achievement was made public. The exhibition is now regarded as a milestone in 20th-century art.

Salon des Indépendants
Title of exhibitions held by the Société des Artistes Indépendants. Seurat and Signac were the principal founders of the society, which was formed in 1884 following the intransigence of the selection committee at the official Salon. Their Salon had no selection committee and the rules allowed any artist to enter a painting on payment of a fee. The society lasted until the outbreak of World War I and was important in allowing progressive works to be shown in public.

Salviati, Francesco (Francesco de' Rosso) 1510–63
Florentine MANNERIST painter. He first trained as a goldsmith then studied painting, partly with Andrea del Sarto. In about 1530 he went to Rome, where he entered the service of Cardinal Salviati, whose name he adopted, and for whom he painted a richly complex fresco of *The Visitation* (1538, Oratory of S. Giovanni Decollato), the work which secured his reputation. He was restless and itinerant, working in France as well as Florence and Venice. His peak period was 1547–54, in Rome, when with exuberant invention he painted grandiloquent fresco cycles in palaces, notably the scenes of *David* in the Palazzo Ricci-Sacchetti, which are framed by virtuoso illusionistic painted architecture. Salviati was also a tapestry designer and an accomplished portraitist. The name Salviati was also adopted by his principal pupil **Giuseppe Porta** (*c*.1520–73). See vol. 2 pp. **166–167**

Samaras, Lucas born 1936
Greek-born artist living in the USA. Samaras is a versatile artist, early involved in HAPPENINGS, who keeps alive the Surrealist spirit. His exploration of two major themes—self-examination and object fascination—is not confined to any single medium or approach. His work includes precious, bizarre assemblages in boxes (*Untitled box no. 3*, 1963, New York, Whitney); decorative, disturbing *Transformations* of ordinary objects; full-scale rooms, textile collages and, for the last ten years, a series of *Autopolaroids*—provocative photographic self-portraits involving chemical and manual manipulation of the print.

Sánchez Coello, Alonso 1531/2–88
Spanish painter. He studied in Portugal and Flanders, where he was a pupil of Anthonis Mor. By 1555 he was back in Spain as painter to Philip II. He is best known for his portraits, in which he continued the tradition of court portraiture begun by Titian and Mor, and later carried on by his pupil Pantoja de la Cruz. A number of his portraits of Philip II and his court are in the Prado, Madrid. On Navarrete's death, he was one of those commissioned by the King to complete the series of paintings begun by him for the church of the Escorial (*in situ*).

Sánchez Cotán, Fray Juan 1560–1627
Spanish painter. He became a lay-Carthusian in 1603 and painted distinguished religious works, but he is best known for his very individual still-life paintings, produced before 1603 in Toledo. They display a few humble fruits and vegetables, the separate objects characteristically arranged in a descending parabola, but the artist's concentration on them is such that his work takes on a mystical intensity (*Quince, cabbage, melon, cucumber*, 1602, San Diego, Fine Arts Gallery). The same naturalism, use of a quiet light and insistence on texture are also apparent in his large religious paintings for the Cartuja in Granada (*in situ*), some of which include telling still-life details (*Rest on the Flight into Egypt*; *The Last Supper*). He infused spiritual content into detailed, realistic forms, and in this inspired Velazquez and Zurbarán.

Sanchi
Site of a Buddhist *stupa* (a shrine commemorating the Nirvana of the historic Buddha) in Western Madhya Pradesh, India, dating from about the 2nd century BC to the 2nd century AD. The site was established as a pilgrimage centre by the great emperor Ashoka (3rd century BC). The main *stupa*, dating about 50 BC, has been beautifully restored and is the most complete surviving example of a Buddhist *stupa* in the country. It is enclosed by a severe plain stone railing, with four monumental and elaborately carved gateways more than 10m (34ft) in height. The carving in low relief on the limestone represents scenes from the life of the Buddha and of his former lives (Jatakas). On top of each of the three lintels of each gateway some free-standing sculpture has survived (mostly elephants and horses), while hanging underneath the bottom lintel supported by the uprights are the famous *Yakshis* or tree goddesses, only a few of which are still *in situ*. All bear witness to the vigour of early Indian Buddhist sculpture, particularly the narrative panels with their lively figures and backgrounds of lush foliage. See vol. 3 p. 12

Sandby, Paul 1725–1809
British watercolour painter and etcher of topographical scenes. He was technically very accomplished and versatile, and one of the first artists to achieve real distinction and a large output as a water-

colourist. There are collections of his work in the royal collection at Windsor Castle and in the Victoria and Albert Museum, London. His brother **Thomas** (1721–98) worked in a similar vein.

Sandrart, Joachim von 1606–88
German painter, engraver and writer. The wide knowledge of art he gained in his extensive travels in Europe bore fruit in his *Teutsche Akademie* (German Academy), published in 1675, on which his fame rests. This treatise has sections on art theory, iconography and Eastern art, but is primarily important for its biographies, a rich fund of information on 17th-century painting. Sandrart was highly prized as a painter in his lifetime but is now considered academic and derivative. In his striking *Self-portrait* in Frankfurt (*c*.1670, Historisches Museum), he presents himself as a grand and cultured gentleman.

Sano di Pietro (Ansano di Pietro di Mencio) 1406–81
Sienese painter, head of a large workshop producing a huge number of stereotyped *Madonnas* and polyptychs for local churches. His personal style is a weak version of Sassetta and Giovanni di Paolo and his simple, pious compositions and naive presentations of miracles in predella scenes reflect an unsophisticated taste. His most important work is *The coronation of the Virgin* (1445, Siena, Palazzo Pubblico) painted in collaboration with Domenico di Bartolo.

Sanraku, Kano 1559–1635
Japanese painter, one of the finest Kano school painters of his time. He was a Samurai, retainer first to a feudal lord, then to the Shogun Toyotomi Hideyoshi, who apprenticed him to the most prestigious artist of the day, Kano Eitoku. Sanraku developed a restrained version of his master's style. He became court painter to Hideyoshi, and supervised most of the decorations of his new castle in Osaka. When the Toyotomi family was defeated in 1603, Sanraku retired to Kyoto, and his art lost its vitality. Amongst his best works, done earlier in Kyoto, is *Peonies* on the sliding doors of the Daitoku temple.

Sansovino, Andrea 1467/70–1529
Florentine sculptor and architect. His first documented work is *The Baptism* on the East Portal of the Florence Baptistery, 1502–05, which combines the gracefulness of Ghiberti with the figure composition of Verrocchio's *Christ and Thomas* group at Orsanmichele. In 1505 he moved to Rome, where he executed two wall monuments in S. Maria del Popolo. Their form emulates that developed by Florentine sculptors of the previous century, but the figures are more elegant and indicate knowledge of Michelangelo's early work. In 1513 Pope Leo X appointed him *capomaestro* (master of works) of the Holy House in the basilica of Loreto (in the Papal states). This shrine was designed by Bramante. Andrea's sculpture is very competent without being exciting. The Holy House occupied him for the remainder of his life. See vol. 2 p. *128*

Sansovino, Jacopo (Jacopo Tatti) *c*.1486–1570
Florentine sculptor and architect of the High Renaissance period, the pupil of Andrea Sansovino, whose name he took. He accompanied the latter to Rome in 1505, and gained a close knowledge of ancient Roman styles through work restoring ancient sculptures. His master's style, and the achievements of

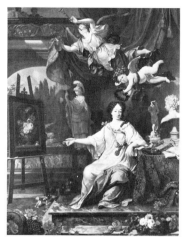

Ruysch: *Rachel Ruysch in her studio* by Constantijn Netscher. Raleigh, North Carolina Museum of Art

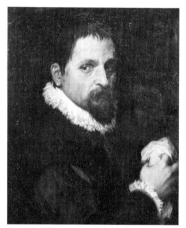

Salviati: Self-portrait. Florence, Uffizi (Scala)

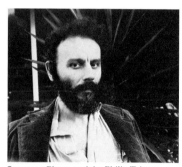

Samaras: Photograph by Philip Tsiaras, 1978 (New York, The Pace Gallery)

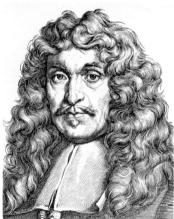

Sandrart: Portrait engraving (Mansell)

Michelangelo and Raphael, influenced his work of this period, both in Florence, 1511–17, and in Rome again until 1527 (*Madonna del Parto*, 1519, Rome, S. Agostino). After the Sack of 1527 Sansovino moved to Venice, where he was appointed state architect (1529) and he was soon busily engaged on the city's major sculptural and architectural commissions (notably St Mark's Library). He contributed four free-standing bronzes and a number of fluent, graceful reliefs in his mature style to his Loggetta at the base of the S. Marco Campanile (1540–45) and in 1546 began work on his sculptural masterpiece, the bronze doors for the Sacristy of S. Marco. The large reliefs depict events from the Passion of Christ, and effectively combine vitality with refinement. Sansovino's most famous sculptural works, however, are the colossal *Neptune* and *Mars* commissioned for the staircase of the Ducal Palace in 1554. He was a great friend of Titian, and with him and the poet Aretino formed a "triumvirate" in the Venetian art world. See vol 2 p.**147**

Santi, Giovanni died 1494
Umbrian painter, the father of Raphael. He worked mainly for the court at Urbino, and was a man of considerable culture, who would have introduced Raphael to humanistic ideas as well as giving him his first instruction in art. Santi, however, is remembered less for his paintings than for his verse chronicle about the Dukes of Urbino, which contains useful comments on contemporary artists. His house in Urbino is now a museum; it contains a wall-painting of the Virgin and Child said to portray the infant Raphael and his mother.

Santi di Tito c.1536–1603
Italian painter, born in Borgo San Sepolcro. At the age of 22 he went to Rome, where he painted some extravagantly Mannerist decorations in the Vatican. He was back in Florence by 1564, when he painted a panel for the obsequies of Michelangelo. In 1565–70 he worked under Vasari on altarpieces in S. Croce: his *Resurrection* is based on a composition of Michelangelo's. However, his later religious works are restrained and relatively realistic, in reaction against extreme Mannerism.

Saraceni, Carlo c.1580–1620
Italian painter, born in Venice, and active mainly in Rome. His style was formed on the examples of Elsheimer and Caravaggio; in *The rest on the Flight into Egypt* (1606, Frascati, Calmadolese Hermitage), for example, he places figures derived in type from Caravaggio against a poetic Elsheimer landscape. The lighting owes something to both of them. Elsheimer and Caravaggio both died in 1610, and Saraceni seems to have taken some of their market. He painted the replacement for Caravaggio's *Death of the Virgin* (Paris, Louvre), which had been rejected by the church of S. Maria della Scala in 1606. Saraceni's painting is still in the church. His early death cut short the career of one of the most sensitive painters of his generation.

Sargent, John Singer 1856–1925
American painter, the most celebrated society portraitist of his time. Sargent was born in Florence and was much travelled in his youth. In Paris (1874–76) he studied under the fashionable society portraitist Carolus-Duran. He painted some Impressionist landscapes, but his portrait style, with its virtuoso handling of paint, was based on masters of the loaded brush such as Hals, Manet and Velazquez. He became famous with his portrait of *Madame Gautreau*, also called *Madame X* (New York, Metropolitan), exhibited at the 1884 Paris Salon. The scandal caused by what was considered its overt eroticism persuaded him to move to London, where he settled for the rest of his life, although he made frequent trips to America. His success was phenomenal, and his work has formed the popular image of the life of the rich and privileged of his time. None of Sargent's rivals could equal the way in which he captured a sense of aristocratic refinement and hauteur, his dazzlingly rich brushwork or his brilliant flattery. He was also highly inventive in composition and responded to each sitter as an individual. In about 1910 Sargent turned again to watercolour landscapes. He also painted murals in the Public Library and Museum of Fine Arts in Boston and was an official war artist in World War I. See vol. 3 p. **125**

Sarrazin, Jacques 1588–1660
The most important French sculptor of the mid-17th century. From 1610 to about 1627 he was in Rome, where he formed a dignified classical style modelled on the Antique and on artists such as Domenichino and Duquesnoy. On his return to France he became the leading sculptor of his day, and most of the noteworthy sculptors of the next generation (those employed by Louis XIV at Versailles) either trained in his workshop or based their style on his. His best-known works are the caryatids (1641) which decorate the Pavillon de l'Horloge of the Louvre, Paris. From 1652 to 1660 he directed the decoration of the Château de Maisons, designed by the architect François Mansart and perhaps the finest example of French classical architecture of the 17th century. See vol. 2 p. **198**

Saryan, Martiros Sergeevich 1880–1972
Russian-born painter. His travels in Egypt and Turkey encouraged a profound love of intense colour, which he used in simplified schemes, such as *Date-palm, Egypt* (1911, Moscow, Tretyakov Gallery). He found his greatest inspiration in Armenia and is honoured by his own museum in Erevan.

Sassanian art
Art of Iran centred on the homeland of the Sassanian dynasty, whose empire flourished from the 3rd to the 7th century AD and was the political equal of Rome and Byzantium. Great emphasis was placed on nationalism, and traditions current over four millennia found a refined, late expression. Most famous is the palace at Ctesiphon, the capital, which was embellished with mosaics, murals, marble and stuccowork, and (according to literary sources) splendid carpets. Sassanian rock-carved reliefs are noteworthy (examples at Naqsh-i-Rustam), and were sometimes incorporated in audience halls, as in the cave of Taq-i-Bustan, where the figure of a king in full armour on horseback is carved in deep relief. The workmanship of silver, gold and rock-crystal vessels reached great heights of sophistication in the 3rd and 4th century AD. Kings enthroned or at the hunt were depicted, and dancers, animals and floral designs. Silk imported from China or produced locally was woven into carpets and textiles of traditional designs (medallions and hunting scenes). Such goods were traded with Byzantium and Rome, and Sassanian motifs were reused in both Islamic and medieval European art. See vol. 2 p. 29

Sassetta (Stefano di Giovanni) 1392/1400–50
A major Sienese painter of the 15th century. He was trained in the late 14th-century Sienese manner, but by 1432, the date of his first extant work, "The Madonna of the Snow" (Florence, Contini Bonacossi coll.), he had acquired a vigorous decorative style, reflecting a study of the great Sienese 14th-century painters and the influence of Gentile da Fabriano. The predella scenes show a fine narrative technique, which reached its peak in the great St Francis altarpiece (1436–44, main panel in Paris, Louvre, panels of the saint's life in London, NG, and Chantilly, Musée Condé). This was once in Borgo San Sepolcro, and its monumental *St Francis* surely influenced Piero della Francesca. See vol. 2 p. **88**

Sassoferrato (Giovanni Battista Salvi) 1609–85
Italian painter, active mainly in Urbino, Perugia and Rome. He painted almost exclusively religious works in an archaizing style of Peruginesque sweetness. His drawing and colouring are very pure, and his style, based on Bolognese classicism, so little affected by the Baroque that his paintings could almost be mistaken for works by a Nazarene artist. His paintings were evidently popular, for they often occur in numerous versions by himself or his assistants; the Wallace Collection, London, has two versions of a much repeated *Virgin and Child* design, almost identical except that one is rectangular, the other circular.

Saura, Antonio born 1930
Spanish painter. He went to Paris in 1953 and painted in a Surrealist manner, but after his return to Madrid in 1957 he developed an expressionist style, in which thick textures and the use of intense red and black colours create a violent effect. The iconography is of mutilated and agonized humanity, often painted on a torn canvas. His art has since become more openly polemical (*Portrait of Philip II (no. 3)*, 1967, Paris, Galerie Stadler).

Savery, Roelandt 1576–1639
Flemish painter and etcher of flowers, landscapes and animal subjects. He travelled widely and enjoyed a highly successful career, working successively for Henry IV in France, Rudolf II in Prague and the Emperor Matthias in Vienna before settling in Utrecht in 1619. Rudolf II had a menagerie, and here Savery studied the exotic animals which became a distinctive feature of his paintings—brightly coloured, highly finished works reminiscent of "Velvet" Brueghel but more archaic in style. His favourite subject, which he treated several dozen times, was *Orpheus with the animals* (example, 1628, London, NG). He is said to have died insane. Other members of the Savery family were painters and engravers, principally of animal subjects and landscapes, the earliest known being **Jacob I** (c.1545–1602), who was either the father or brother of Roelandt. Others were **Jacob II** (c.1593–1627), the son of Jacob I; **Jan** or Hans (1597–1665) and **Salomon** (1594–1655), nephews of Roelandt; and **Jacob III** (1617–66), the son of Salomon. See vol. 2 p. 220

Savinio, Alberto 1891–1952
Italian painter and writer. The brother of Chirico, he helped formulate the principles of METAPHYSICAL PAINTING. After moving to Paris in 1926 he began to paint Surrealist works using Metaphysical elements but without the reticence characteristic of the movement.

Savoldo, Gian Girolamo active 1508–after 1548
Italian painter, born in Brescia and active mainly in Venice. He painted mainly religious scenes, and mythological works, related to Venetian developments and indicating some knowledge of Flemish work. He had an individual poetic sensibility, which comes out particularly in his realistic and sombre nocturnal scenes. The best-known of these is probably *Mary Magdalen approaching the sepulchre* (version in London, NG, c.1540), in which the Magdalen's shimmering mantle is a virtuoso piece of painting. His surviving output is small. See vol. 2 p. **149**

Scapigliatura
Italian ROMANTIC movement, principally literary but also artistic, centred on Milan in the 1860s and 1870s. The term means "dishevelled", and refers to a Bohemian way of life. Among the principal artistic exponents were Bianchi, Carnovali, Cremona, Faruffini and Ranzoni. United by discontent with Risorgimental politics, the Scapigliati were opposed to the Academy and their researches into light and atmosphere brought a loosening of outline. The Italian DIVISIONISTS owed much to them.

Schad, Christian born 1894
German painter. He was a member of the Dada movement in Zurich and Geneva, 1915–20, producing woodcuts, wood reliefs and "Schadographs", prints made from the exposure of objects directly to sensitive paper. He was in Italy, 1920–25, and in 1921 he began to paint portraits in a precise Neue Sachlichkeit manner (*Woman from Pozzuoli*, 1925, Private coll.). In 1925 he went to Vienna and in 1928 to Berlin. The portraits from this period are painted with a meticulous detail which creates an effect that is both highly realistic and disturbingly remote and alien (*Graf St Genois d'Anneaucourt*, 1927, Private coll.).

Schadow, Gottfried 1764–1850
German NEOCLASSICAL sculptor, also a draughtsman, engraver and lithographer. In 1785–87 he travelled in Italy, where he met Canova, and in 1788 settled in Berlin for the rest of his career. His largest work is the *Quadriga* (1793, damaged in World War II and recast, 1950s) on the Brandenburg Gate in Berlin, but his sculpture consisted largely of tombs and portraits, including busts of Goethe and Kant. In both fields his classicism is enlivened by naturalism, and the effect is particularly harmonious in his celebrated and charming group of *The Princesses Luise and Frederike* (1795–97, East Berlin, Staatliche Museen). His statue of *Marshall Blücher* at Rostock (1815–19) was the first monumental bronze to be cast in Germany since Schlüter. With the progressive deterioration of his sight after 1821, he turned increasingly to graphic work and writing on art theory. His sons **Felix** (1819–61), **Rudolf** (1786–1822) and Wilhelm were artists. See vol. 3 p. **61**

Schadow, Wilhelm von 1788–1862
German sculptor and teacher. The son of Gottfried Schadow, with whom he began his studies, he travelled to Italy in 1811 and became closely involved with the NAZARENES. He participated in their fresco work at the Casa Bartoldy (1816–17) and in 1819 returned to Germany, where he taught at the Berlin Academy. In 1826 he became the Director of the Düsseldorf Academy and helped to make it a great centre of German history painting in the 19th century.

Schaeffer, Carl born 1903
Canadian landscape painter, primarily a watercolourist, who exhibited in GROUP OF SEVEN shows in the 1930s. Using a minimal palette of earth tones with silvery touches, he created canvases of heroic breadth, epitomized by the moody *Storm over the fields, Hanover* (1937, Toronto, Art Gallery of Ontario).

Schalken, Godfried 1643–1706
Dutch painter, active mainly in Leyden, where he was one of the principal pupils of Dou. The small scale and exquisite detail of his work are taken from his master, but Schalken had a penchant for candlelit scenes, often showing coquettish women (*Girl with a candle*, 1662, Florence, Pitti). In the 1670s he introduced classical themes to his repertoire, as in *Lesbia weighing her sparrow against her jewels* (c.1675, London, NG). Schalken was very popular in his day and in the 18th century.

Schamberg, Morton 1881–1918
American painter. He studied in Paris, 1908–10, where he was joined by Sheeler. Encouraged by both Sheeler and Stieglitz, he took up photography as a career. He is best remembered, however, for his Dada-inspired portrait of *God* (1916, Philadelphia, Museum of Art), an assemblage of plumbing pipes.

Schäufelein, Hans c.1480–c.1540
German painter and designer of woodcuts. From about 1503 he was active in Dürer's workshop in Nuremberg, often working from Dürer's designs. In 1512 he was at Augsburg, where he collaborated on woodcuts for the Emperor Maximilian, including the *Triumphs* of about 1516–18. The Ziegler altarpiece (1521, Augsburg, National Galerie) shows his flat, loosely painted figures. Perhaps more interesting are his numerous incisively drawn biblical woodcuts.

Scheemakers, Peter 1691–1781
Flemish sculptor, active mainly in England, where, with Roubiliac and Rysbrack, he was one of the leading sculptors around the middle of the century. He twice visited Rome and his style was nobly but rather coldly classical. Tomb sculpture accounted for the bulk of his large output, but his best-known work is the statue of *William Shakespeare* (1740) in Westminster Abbey, London. His brother **Henry** (died 1748) and his son **Thomas** (1740–1808) were also sculptors active in England. Henry's masterpiece, much more relaxed and Baroque than most of his brother's work, is the brilliantly characterized monument to Sir Francis and Lady Page (c.1730, Steeple Aston Church, Oxfordshire). Thomas is well-known for the enchanting monument to Mary Russell (1787, Powick Church, Worcestershire).

Scheffer, Ary 1795–1858
Dutch painter, active mainly in France, the favourite painter of King Louis-Philippe. In 1811 he entered Guérin's studio, where he became close friends with Géricault. Much of his early work is sentimental and anecdotal (*Paolo and Francesca appearing to Dante and Virgil*, 1822, Paris, Louvre). During the 1830s literary themes formed the basis of his work, but by the 1840s he was the leading painter of devotional art, stylistically drawing closer to the classicism of Ingres. He was also a prodigious portraitist. A collection of his work is in the museum of his native Dordrecht.

Schelfhout, Andreas 1787–1870
Dutch landscape painter. He worked in The Hague, specializing in winter landscapes, and is considered one of the precursors of the HAGUE school. His reputation has suffered because of his limited and repetitious subject matter, but his work was widely imitated. Jongkind was among his many pupils.

Schiavone, Andrea (Andrea Meldolla) 1522?–1563
Venetian painter, born in Dalmatia. His work was strongly influenced by Parmigianino, whose prints he copied, and by the painterly handling of Bonifazio Veronese. He created a Venetian Mannerist mode enlivened by an ornamental use of colour. From 1556 to 1560 he was painting in St Mark's Library, where two *tondi* survive. Mostly he painted small format mythological subjects with landscape backgrounds for private patrons.

Schick, Gottlieb 1776–1812
German painter, primarily of portraits. He worked in David's studio in Paris between 1789 and 1802 and adopted many of the qualities of NEOCLASSICAL portraiture. His years in Rome (1802–11) brought him into contact with Koch and helped him achieve a stylistic synthesis between the classical tradition and a poetic view of nature. The combination of clearly delineated figures against a lush and romantic landscape had great success in Rome (*Willelmine von Cotta*, 1802, Stuttgart, Staatsgalerie).

Schiele, Egon 1890–1918
Austrian draughtsman and painter, the greatest EXPRESSIONIST artist of early 20th-century Vienna. He studied at the Vienna Academy, where he met Klimt, and adopted an Art Nouveau manner which he soon transformed into a highly personal and expressive language. He is famous for his drawings of nudes silhouetted in disturbed, angular lines and trapped in erotic poses; these outraged contemporaries, and he was briefly imprisoned in 1912, charged with disseminating indecent drawings. His concern with sexuality was not wholly decadent, however, but reflected a fascination with passion and neurosis, influenced by Freudian psychology. He also painted landscapes, fantasies and portraits; the watercolour *The artist's mother sleeping* (1911, Vienna, Albertina) reveals Klimt's influence in the juxtaposition of an almost abstract background with the realistic head; *Paris von Gütersloh* (1918, Minneapolis, Institute of Art) is a mature work, every bone and line of the figure twisted to express personality. Schiele died just as he was achieving recognition. See vol. 1 p. 39; vol. 3 p. **195**

Schindler, Emil Jakob 1842–92
Austrian landscape painter. He studied in Vienna, 1860–69, and travelled widely in France, Italy and the Netherlands, coming under the influence of the Barbizon school. Between 1885 and 1892 he lived in the Vienna Woods and became head of the Viennese school of Impressionist landscapists (*Beech wood near Goisern*, 1884, Vienna, Nieder-Österreichisches Landesmuseum).

Schjerfbeck, Helène 1862–1946
Finnish painter. She went to Paris in 1880 and worked under Gérôme, Bastien-Lepage and Puvis de Chavannes. Among her favourite themes are children; another *leitmotiv* is the seated woman. From about 1900 her realistic phase was followed by works in a softly lyrical style with silvery greyish tones and subdued colour accents. During her last years this refined aloofness was followed by a more vigorous mood, especially in a series of *Self-portraits* of compelling intensity.

Schlemmer, Oskar 1888–1943
German painter, sculptor, stage designer and writer. He studied under Hölzel at Stuttgart. His interest in Cubism led first to abstract experiments, but by 1916 he had developed his figurative Constructivism (*Homo*, 1916, Stuttgart, Staatsgalerie). From 1920 to 1929 he taught at the Bauhaus, where he was head of the stage workshop. He saw the stage as a Constructivist fusion of space and building, as the abstract space in which the human form, transfigured by mask and costume, can express form and colour in motion, particularly in dance. His ideas were published by the Bauhaus in 1925 in *Man as Art Figure*. He also painted monumental murals, such as the frescos in the Bauhaus at Weimar (1923). See vol. 3 p. **191**

Schlichter, Rudolf 1890–1955
German painter and draughtsman. After studying in Stuttgart and Karlsruhe he worked as an independent painter in Berlin (1913–32), exhibiting with the NOVEMBERGRUPPE. He also belonged to the Berlin Dadaist group, adopting the socially critical outlook and style of Dix and Grosz. In the 1920s he painted brothel scenes, street scenes and portraits (*Berthold Brecht*, c.1926–27, Munich, Lenbachhaus), showing his awareness of Neue Sachlichkeit. He settled in Munich in 1939 and developed a Surrealist style.

Schlüter, Andreas c.1660–1714
German Baroque sculptor and architect, active chiefly in Prussia. Born in Danzig, Schlüter originally gravitated to Poland. In 1694 he arrived in Berlin, where his first major work as a sculptor—the *Dying warrior* keystones on the Zeughaus (1696)—led to his earliest efforts as an architect, on the same building. His architectural career was blighted by a series of collapses, but his bronze equestrian monument to the Great Elector Friedrich-Willem (1696–1708, Charlottenburg Castle) survives as one of the most powerful realizations of this supreme challenge for the sculptor. He died seeking work in Russia.

Schmidt-Rottluff, Karl 1884–1976
German EXPRESSIONIST painter. He met Kirchner in 1904 and became a founder-member of Die Brücke. The influence of Post-Impressionism, especially van Gogh, can be discerned in his early works and in subsequent years the influence of Munch, Toulouse-Lautrec and Fauvism is apparent, as the famous Norwegian landscapes of 1911 show (*Loftus*, Hamburg, Kunsthalle). In 1911 he settled in Berlin, after which he discovered the emphatic, stylized forms of African tribal art, as seen in the portrait of *Dr Rosa Schapire* (1919, London, Tate). He was a prolific graphic artist; his woodcuts, with their bold contrasting areas, constitute one of the high points of Expressionist graphics. From 1918 on he began to reintroduce a more naturalistic element into his works. See vol. 3 pp. **134–135**

Schnorr von Carolsfeld, Julius 1794–1872
German painter and illustrator. He studied in Vienna, where he met Koch, and later with Ferdinand Olivier. In Rome in 1817 he joined the Nazarenes and worked with them on the frescos in the Casa Massimo (1818–27). From

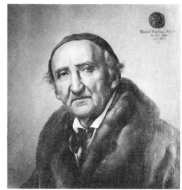
Schadow, Gottfried: Portrait by J. Hubner (1806–82), 1832. Berlin, Staatliche Museen

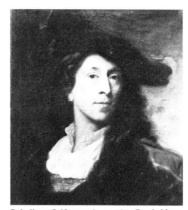
Schalken: Self-portrait, c.1685. Cambridge, Fitzwilliam (Mansell)

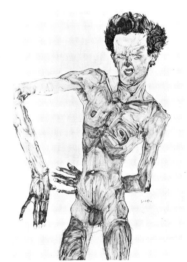
Schiele: Self-portrait, 1910. Vienna, Albertina

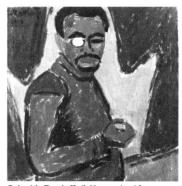
Schmidt-Rottluff: *Self-portrait with eyeglass*, 1910. West Berlin, Staatliche Museen

1827 he lived in Munich and painted frescos for the Residenz. His preoccupation with historical themes, severe linearity and clear colour are a legacy of his association with the Nazarenes (*Flight into Egypt*, 1828, Düsseldorf, Kunstmuseum). The exquisite and ornamental quality of his line in drawing was particularly suited to his illustrations to the Bible and to romantic tales.

Scholderer, Otto 1834–1902
German painter, primarily of still-life and figure compositions. He was one of the first German artists to go to Paris and come into contact with Courbet and Fantin-Latour. A close friend of Thoma, he was instrumental in acquainting him with the achievements of Courbet and French Realism while they were both working together in Munich in the 1870s. His own work combines lyrical Romanticism and the detail of Biedermeier painting with the new textural ruggedness he discovered in Paris (*Violinist at a window*, 1861, Frankfurt, Stadtisches Kunstinstitut).

Scholz, Georg 1890–1945
German painter, an exponent of NEUE SACHLICHKEIT. He painted still lifes, landscapes and socially critical themes. The latter are not wholly successful, owing to his literary approach, and his best works are probably his still lifes, in which he created tense contrasts between hard and soft textures (*Still life with cacti*, 1925, Kaiserslautera, Pfalzgalerie). Towards the end of the 1920s he became disillusioned and forsook social realism for a softer style based on Derain.

Scholz, Werner born 1898
German painter. He belonged to the second generation of Expressionists. His early work depicts the harsh conditions and suffering of the post-War years, but has none of the overt social criticism of Dix or Grosz. Banned by the Nazis in 1933, he sought refuge in a Tyrolean village, where he painted mythical and religious themes, including several triptychs (*Antigone*, Essen, Museum Folkwang) in a Rouault-like style. In the mid-1950s he began painting industrial Ruhr landscapes, in a lighter palette.

Schönfeld, Johann Heinrich 1609–82/3
German painter and etcher, active mainly in Augsburg. He travelled extensively in Italy in his youth, absorbing a wide variety of influences, and was very versatile, painting religious, historical and genre subjects with invention and wit, but without ever reaching great heights (*The life-class in the Augsburg Academy*, *c.*1670, Graz, Johanneum).

Schongauer, Martin died 1491
German artist, the greatest northern engraver of the 15th century and also an accomplished painter. He lived and worked in Colmar for most of his life. In engraving he carried further the advances of Master E.S. and his technique became increasingly sophisticated and subtle in the description of texture and light. It is clear that he had studied the work of Rogier van der Weyden and the influence of Netherlandish art in general is apparent throughout his work, but he had an original imagination, as his *Temptation of St Anthony* (*c.*1470) reveals—St Anthony hovers stoically in the air amidst meticulously fantasized demons. Schongauer's engravings became an important source for artists throughout Europe. The young Dürer travelled to Colmar in 1492 with the intention of entering his workshop, only to find he had recently died. The *Virgin of the Rose bower* (1472, Colmar, St Martin's) is Schongauer's most securely attributed painting. See vol. 2 p. **154**

School
Collective term for a group of painters allied by style and period, or attached to a specific country, city, town or even village. The term is also used to describe artists working in close contact with a master, as in the school of Raphael.

Schrimpf, Georg 1889–1938
German painter. After extensive travel throughout northern Europe and Italy he lived in Berlin and Munich, establishing contact with the Expressionists. His early Expressionist works were exhibited at the STURM Gallery. In Italy again (1922) he absorbed the current trends of classical realism. He became an important exponent of the idealized, magic realist form of Neue Sachlichkeit favoured by Munich artists in the 1920s. His small, intimate pictures of women, children and landscapes, in which all forms are smoothly rounded in the manner of Piero della Francesca, convey a sense of permanent idyll beneath the outward banality of appearances (*Girl at the window*, 1925, Basle, Kunstmuseum). See vol. 3 p. **195**

Schuch, Carl 1846–1903
Austrian still-life and landscape painter. After studying in Vienna, 1866–68, he moved to Munich and spent several years with Trübner and the painters of the Leibl circle. Extensive travels in Italy were followed by several years in Paris (1882–94), where he came under the influence of Courbet and the French Impressionists. *Houses in Ferch* (1881, Bremen, Kunsthalle) illustrates his fusion of German Realism and French Impressionism.

Schut, Cornelis 1597–1655
Flemish painter, engraver and tapestry designer, on stylistic grounds thought to be a pupil of Rubens. Although he is mentioned in numerous contemporary documents and several undoubted engravings have long been known, it is only recently that a group of paintings has been convincingly attributed to him. Foremost among these is the large and powerful *Massacre of the innocents* (Caen, Eglise de la Trinité), and it seems possible that as Schut's oeuvre is clarified he will emerge as one of the outstanding Flemish artists of the 17th century.

Schuyler Limner active 1715–25
Anonymous American portrait painter active in the Albany area, named after one of the families he portrayed. The artist is also often called the Aetatis Suae Limner, because this Latin inscription, followed by the artist's age, is often found on his work. Up to 80 portraits have been given to him, but some authorities discern more than one hand at work in the group. European features are grafted on to earlier limner conventions and details are sharply rendered, but the figures are still stiff and two-dimensional (*Mrs David Ver Planck*, *c.*1717, Albany, Institute of History and Art).

Schwarzkogler, Rudolf 1940–69
Austrian Performance artist and co-founder, with Brus, Muehl and Nitsch, of the Institute for Immediate Art in Vienna in 1966. His particular concern was with the human body seen in an art context. He presented himself in extremely violent situations and gained notoriety by reputedly having cut off his own penis bit by bit.

Schwind, Moritz von 1804–71
Austrian painter. He studied philosophy in Vienna and joined a circle of Romantics including the composer Schubert, the novelist Grillparzer and the Olivier brothers. In 1828 he was invited to paint the ceiling of the library in the Munich Residenz, and this was followed by commissions for frescos at the Karlsruhe Gallery, the Wartburg and the Vienna Opera House among others. He also painted romantic panels (*The rose*, 1847, East Berlin, Nationalgalerie) and was a prolific illustrator of popular fairy tales.

Schwitters, Kurt 1887–1948
German DADAIST painter, poet and sculptor. In 1918 he produced his first collages and in 1919 he was a founder of the Hanover Dadaist group. He is best known for his **Merz** constructions. This meaningless syllable, included at random in a collage of 1919, became a generic term describing haphazard combinations of materials, including rubbish, arranged on a flat surface or as a relief (*Merz 32*, 1924, New York, MOMA). *Merz* was also the title of an influential Dada magazine (1923–32) which he founded. In 1923 he began his first *Merzbau*, a house in Hanover completely filled with junk constructions; it was unfinished when he left Germany in 1935 and was destroyed by bombing in 1943. He settled in England in 1940 and in 1947 he began his third and final *Merzbau* at Ambleside. It was uncompleted on his death and is now in the Hatton Gallery, Newcastle upon Tyne. See vol. 1 p. *154*; vol. 3 p. **167**

Scipione (Gino Bonichi) 1904–33
Italian Expressionist painter, whose early death curtailed a career of great promise. His paintings are similar in their visionary intensity to those of Rouault and Ensor. His violent handling and restless colour composition, as in his *Apocalypse* (1930, Turin, Museo Civico), come close to destroying his subject matter. These ecstatic visions of modern Rome had a profound influence on later Italian painting.

Scorel, Jan van 1495–1562
Netherlandish painter, born near Alkmaar. He studied in Haarlem and under Jacob Cornelisz. in Amsterdam before ging to work with Gossaert in Utrecht. In 1519 he journeyed south through Germany to Venice and then on, via Crete and Cyprus, to Jerusalem. Subsequently, on his arrival in Rome, he was appointed Keeper of the Belvedere by the Utrecht-born Pope, Hadrian VI. He swiftly absorbed the lessons of Raphael and Michelangelo and, on his return to Utrecht, produced some of the most successful combinations of Flemish and Italian elements. *The discovery of the Cross* (Breda, Grote Kerk), for example, is a masterly exercise in the depiction of physical effort, while *Mary Magdalen* (*c.*1540, Amsterdam, Rijksmuseum)—a reworking of a van der Weyden composition—sets an Italian woman, bathed in an airy, southern atmosphere, within the framework of a Pateniersque landscape. Mor and Heemskerck were among his pupils. See vol. 2 p. **161**

Scott, Samuel 1702/3–72
British marine and topographical artist. Until the 1740s he was mainly a marine painter in the tradition of Willem van de Velde, but he turned to painting London views following Canaletto's successful 1746 visit to Britain. *An arch of Westminster Bridge* (*c.*1750, London, Tate) is typical of Scott's clear if prosaic style.

Scott, William born 1913
British painter. From 1937 to 1939 he was in France and is one of the British painters of his generation closest to French art, particularly the still-life tradition of Chardin and Braque. The high degree of abstraction in his work often creates ambiguity in subject matter. *Yellow and black composition* (1953, New York, Guggenheim) could be read as a figure or as a still life on a table.

Scrotes, William (Guillim Stretes) active 1537–53/4
Netherlandish portrait painter. He was appointed painter to Queen Mary of Hungary, Regent of the Netherlands, in 1537, and came to England in 1545, succeeding Holbein as King's Painter. Only a handful of his Holbeinesque works, all from the English period, are known, including whole-length portraits of Edward VI in the Louvre, Paris, and at Hampton Court.

Scumble
A broken passage of opaque or semi-transparent paint dragged or skimmed across the canvas in such a way that it is modified by the colour underneath.

Sebastiano del Piombo (Sebastiano Veneziano) *c.*1485–1547
Venetian painter, active mainly in Rome. He probably trained with Giovanni Bellini, but Giorgione was a deeper influence on his early work. Sebastiano is said to have completed works Giorgione left unfinished at his death and some works are still disputed between them. The painterly and colouristic brilliance and poetic feeling of Sebastiano's early work is well represented by *Salome* (1510, London, NG). In 1511 he was invited to Rome by the banker Agostino Chigi, for whom he painted the colossal *Polyphemus*, the companion to Raphael's *Galatea* in the Villa Farnesina. After this initial contact with the Raphael circle, Sebastiano gravitated towards Michelangelo, entering into direct competition with Raphael on their respective commisions for two altarpieces for the Cathedral of Narbonne. Raphael produced *The Transfiguration* and Sebastiano, with the help of drawings by Michelangelo, *The Raising of Lazarus* (1517–19, London, NG), an ambitious composition in which Sebastiano combined the rich colouring of his early training with Roman grandeur of form. In later years Sebastiano confined himself mainly to portraiture, producing images of a very grand type (*Clement VII*, 1526, Naples, Museo di Capodimonte), and after the death of Raphael he was unrivalled as the leading portraitist in Rome. In 1531 Clement VII appointed him keeper of the papal seals (they were made of lead—Italian "piombo"—from which his nickname derives), and thereafter he painted little. See vol. 2 p. **146**

Secco
Term meaning "dry" in Italian, used to describe a wall-painting technique in which tempera or casein colours are applied to dry lime plaster, either to retouch or finish a FRESCO or to execute an entire work. Though the surface was sometimes wetted down beforehand, painting *a secco* is a less permanent method than fresco, in which the colours are bound by the drying plaster.

Section d'Or
Loose association of French painters which existed between autumn 1912, when they held their first exhibition, and the outbreak of war in 1914. Metzinger,

Gleizes, La Fresnaye, Léger, Picabia and Kupka, and others less closely involved such as Gris, Herbin, Lhôte and Marcoussis, gathered at the studios of the Duchamp brothers at Puteaux (near Paris). United by a common stylistic debt to Cubism and their deep admiration for Cézanne, their purpose was to promote group exhibitions and theoretical discussion of their aesthetic principles. This distinguished them from the more private, intuitive procedures of Picasso and Braque, as did their interest in harmonic systems of proportion and, under Futurist inspiration, epic themes celebrating the dynamism of the modern world. See vol. 3 p. 151

Sedgley, Peter born 1930
British painter, working in the field of OP and KINETIC art. Since the early 1970s he has divided his time between England and Germany. He experiments with light and colour and, more recently, their interrelationship with sound. He was self-taught and his earliest works used Ernst's *frottage* techniques. In 1964, influenced by Vasarély and Riley, he began to experiment with optical movement and created the series *Targets*, in which circles of ultraviolet light expand, change colour and blend into one another. Since the early 1970s he has been creating large-scale works of coloured light in which any movement triggers off photo cells, causing the projected colour to change. When sound is included as another dimension the spectator is involved in a constantly changing colour- and sound-filled environment (*Sound/light installation*, 1973, Bordeaux Festival). See vol. 3 pp. **244–245**

Segal, George born 1924
American sculptor. He shifted from Abstract Expressionist painting to figurative sculpture after becoming acquainted with Kaprow. He freezes and distils everyday activities in his "sculptural situations", comprised of life-sized plaster casts, often of his friends and family, and props suggestive of specific environments. His work, for example *Cinema* (1963, Buffalo, Albright-Knox), emphasizes spatial relationships, bodily postures and the contrasting anonymity of the figures with specific situations. Since 1975, he has often worked with fragmentary figures and bright colour. See vol. 3 p. **242**

Segall, Lasar 1891–1957
Brazilian painter and graphic artist, of Lithuanian descent. Before finally settling in Brazil in 1923, he had lived in Germany, where he met Dix and Grosz and developed an Expressionist style marked by deep human feeling. He is particularly noted for his moving depictions of refugees from Nazi oppression (*Ship with immigrants*, 1939–41, São Paolo, Museum of Art).

Segantini, Giovanni 1858–99
Italian DIVISIONIST painter, whose early works reflect the SCAPIGLIATI. He retired to the Swiss Alps in 1881, and stylistic developments correspond with his changes of residence there. He gradually developed a divisionist technique of long, filamented brush-strokes, used directionally to create form and colour and applied in heavy, superimposed layers; he was at his best in pastoral idylls. In the 1890s literary Symbolism determined such works as *The punishment of Luxury* (1891, Liverpool, Walker Art Gallery), but he returned to a more straightforward, pantheistic view of nature in *The triptych of Nature* (1896–99, St Moritz, Segantini Museum).

Seghers, Daniel 1590–1661
Flemish flower-painter, active mainly in his native Antwerp, where he trained with "Velvet" Brueghel. Seghers' technique was broader than Brueghel's but his lovely creamy paint was applied with unerring sureness and he was considered the finest flower-painter of his day. His paintings usually take the form of garlands around a cartouche containing a religious subject (*Garland of flowers round a statue of the Virgin*, 1645, The Hague, Mauritshuis). Often the figure element was painted by another artist, notably Seghers' friend Rubens. Much rarer than paintings of this sort are his single vases of flowers, which attain a truly noble simplicity and are now perhaps the most prized of all flower-paintings.

Seghers, Gerard 1591–1651
Flemish painter, said to have been a pupil of Janssens. He travelled in Italy and probably Spain, about 1611–20, and his early work is in a Caravaggesque style derived from Manfredi (*The denial of St Peter*, c.1620–25, Raleigh, North Carolina Museum of Art). From 1620 he built up a successful practice as a painter of altarpieces in his native Antwerp, and from the late 1620s he turned to a Rubensian style (*The Assumption of the Virgin*, 1629, Grenoble, Musée des Beaux-Arts). Seghers is a minor but attractive painter, and noteworthy as one of the few Flemish artists to work in a convincing Caravaggesque style.

Seghers, Hercules 1589/90–c.1635
Dutch landscape painter and etcher, the most original and remarkable artist in the transition from Mannerism to naturalism in Dutch landscape. A native of Haarlem, he was a pupil of Gillis van Coninxloo in Amsterdam, and also worked in Utrecht and The Hague. He was almost forgotten until 1871, when a landscape (c.1630–35) in the Uffizi, Florence, which had previously been given to Rembrandt, was identified as his work. Like most of his few surviving paintings it is small in scale but conveys a sense of vast distance, and the grand and desolate panorama is characteristically charged with emotional tension. His etchings are perhaps even more original. He made many experiments and innovations in technique, printing in colour on both paper and linen, attaining effects of haunting delicacy and intensity which have caused his work to be compared with Chinese art. From the little that is known of him, Seghers seems to have lived in melancholy poverty, and Rembrandt is one of the few contemporaries who appreciated his work. See vol. 2 p. 220

Segui, Antonio born 1934
Argentine POP artist, living in Paris since 1963. He is known for his nostalgic references to past art and his use of depersonalized media imagery, rendering his subject anonymous, as if mass-produced. His work of the 1960s was reminiscent of British Pop art of the same period. In the mid-1970s he explored a number of stylistic avenues which confirmed his resourcefulness and eclecticism as a painter. In recent work, 1978–79, Segui made corrections and added graffiti to Rembrandt's *The anatomy lesson of Dr Tulp* (much as Duchamp had used Leonardo's *Mona Lisa*). *Doctor Nose-Squeeze* (1979, New York, Lefebre Gallery) is an example.

Seisenegger, Jacob 1504/5–1567
Austrian painter, primarily of portraits. He was court painter to the Hapsburgs, and although his talent was modest his

development of the full-length portrait, the figure posed elegantly before a drawn-back curtain, had a great influence on court portraiture throughout Europe. One such portrait of *Charles V* (1532, Vienna, Kunsthistorisches) was the model for a painting by Titian.

Sekine, Nobuo born 1942
Japanese artist. His earthworks of the 1960s were an exciting new development for younger artists in Japan. Since 1969 he has made sculptural works from soil and clay. *Emptiness* (1970, Tokyo, Ministry of Foreign Affairs), in which a large piece of volcanic stone is placed on a post of polished steel, is another characteristic creation. The steel reflects its surroundings so that the stone seems suspended in space.

Seligmann, Kurt 1900–61
Swiss painter and graphic artist. He studied in Geneva and Florence. In the 1930s he lived in Paris and was a member of ABSTRACTION-CRÉATION as well as being influenced by the Surrealism of Arp and Miró. In 1939 he moved to the USA, where he painted a series of *Cyclonic Landscapes*, visionary and apocalyptic pictures concerned with the metamorphosis of objects and surroundings. Many of his works reveal his deep interest in the occult, of which he wrote a history, *The Mirror of Magic*, in 1948. *The alchemists* (1949, Private coll.) combines specific magical symbolism with imagery derived from Surrealism.

Sepia
A brown pigment made from the ink sacs of marine creatures such as cuttlefish. It has a semi-transparent quality and is used for line and wash drawings.

Sequeira, Domingos Antonio de 1768–1837
Portuguese painter and illustrator of religious, historical and mythological scenes and portraits. His historical works, such as *The allegory of Casa Pia* (1792, Lisbon Museum), reflect the influence of Mengs, while his portraits recall those of Ingres. In later works, he moved towards a bolder handling of light and colour (sketch for *Dom Joao VI*, 1825, Lisbon Museum).

Séraphine (Séraphine Louis) 1864–1934
French NAIVE artist. She worked as a daily woman and only began to paint when aged about 40. She was discovered and encouraged by the critic Wilhelm Uhde, who exhibited her work in 1928 alongside that of Bombois, Bauchant, Vivin and Le Douanier Rousseau. Her densely filled compositions of fruit, leaves and flowers express her rich imaginative powers and religious attitude (*Tree of Paradise*, 1929, Paris, Musée d'Art Moderne). See vol. 3 p. *141*

Sergel, Johann Tobias 1740–1814
German-born sculptor and draughtsman, active mainly in Sweden, where he was the leading exponent of NEOCLASSICISM. After 10 years' study in Stockholm he went to Rome in 1767. He immediately vowed to renounce "the abominable French manner" he had been taught, and formed important friendships with Fuseli and his circle. After 1779, when he was recalled to Stockholm as court sculptor, he was virtually restricted to portrait sculpture. He never ceased to regret leaving Rome, where he had modelled most of the spirited clay and terracotta sketches on which his reputation now rests (*Mars and Venus*, Stockholm, Nationalmuseum).

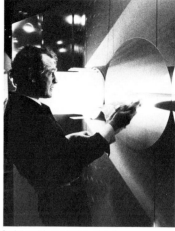
Sedgley: Photograph by Ingeborg Lommatzsch (Redfern Gallery)

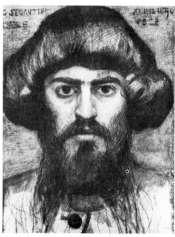
Segantini: Self-portrait drawing, 1890.

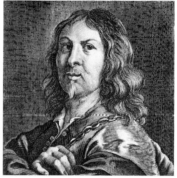
Seghers, Gerard: Engraving after a self-portrait (Courtauld Institute)

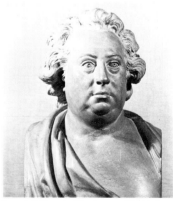
Sergel: Self-portrait bust, 1793. Stockholm, Nationalmuseum

Serov, Valentin 1865–1911
Russian painter. He studied privately under Repin and was admitted to the St Petersburg Academy at the unusually early age of 15. After graduation he moved to Moscow, where he painted his first famous portraits (*Girl with peaches: Vera Mamontova*, 1887, and *Girl in the sun: Maria Simonovich*, 1888, both Moscow, Tretyakov Gallery). Through his uncompromisingly serious approach to his art and despite his tribute to Art Nouveau stylization (*Ida Rubinstein*, 1910, Leningrad, Russian Museum), Serov remained appreciated and sought after both by the WANDERERS and by Diaghilev's World of Art circle.

Serpotta, Giacomo 1656–1732
Sicilian sculptor in stucco, in which medium he was an unsurpassed virtuoso. He may have trained in Rome, but almost all his life was spent in Palermo, where he decorated numerous churches with his ravishingly delicate and often playful work. The figure of *Fortitude* (1720) in the Oratorio di S. Domenico, dressed with a courtly Rococo flamboyance, is perhaps his masterpiece.

Sert y Badia, José Maria
1876–1945
Spanish painter and mural designer. He was in popular demand as a decorator, and his work was sought for private and public buildings in Europe and the USA. Examples of his essentially conservative style can be found in the Waldorf Astoria Hotel, New York, and the League of Nations Assembly Hall, Geneva.

Sérusier, Paul 1863–1927
French painter, a founder of the NABIS. He met Gauguin at PONT-AVEN in 1888 and was given a painting lesson which resulted in a landscape called "*The Talisman*" (1888, Paris, J.F. Denis coll.). The panel was painted in pure unmodulated colours and aimed to express experienced sensation rather than to represent the external world naturalistically. Sérusier showed it to his friends at the Académie Julian and with them formed the Nabis. In 1897 he joined the school of religious painting at the Benedictine abbey at Beuron in Germany and in 1921 published his *ABC of Painting*, concerning systems of proportion and colour relationships. See vol. 3 p. **120**

Servranckx, Victor 1897–1965
Belgian painter, sculptor and designer. His work included interior designs, tapestries and furniture. An exhibition of his work in 1917 was the first to feature abstract art in Belgium. It was based on curvilinear abstract forms derived from his work with a wall-paper manufacturer. By 1920 he was producing geometric abstractions, in the vein of Mondrian but more decorative (*Opus 47*, 1923, Brussels, Musées Royaux des Beaux-Arts).

Sesshu 1420–1506
Japanese painter and priest. A native of Bichu province, Sesshu was sent as a boy to a Zen monastery, where his artistic genius manifested itself. He moved to Kyoto, but by the age of 40 set up a school of painting in Yamaguchi. In 1467–68 he went to China to learn from the Ming masters at first hand. He spent his stay absorbing a great variety of styles, travelling widely and sketching. His twin triumphs in China were to obtain the commission to paint a mural (lavishly praised) in a Peking government office and to be accorded the honour of sitting beside the abbot in the temple of Tianting. Sesshu is best known for his ink landscapes, executed with an angular, calligraphic hand (*Autumn* and *Winter*, Tokyo, National Museum), but he was equally at home in a softer style, which he used for *Flowers and birds of the four seasons* (Toyama, Shinagawa coll.), and in portraiture. The designs of some gardens in Yamaguchi are attributed to him. See vol. 3 pp. **46–47**

Sesson 1504–89?
Japanese painter and priest. Sesson spent all his working life in the northern province of Aizu Wakamatsu, to which he was invited by the Daimyo. Though he admired the work of his fellow-painter-priests, Sesshu and Shubun, he developed in his distant studio a unique style of ink-painting, with a finer line and gentle colouring. He always worked on a special kind of paper manufactured in the Nasu area, which became famous as Sesson paper. An example of his mastery of ink- and colour-paintings is his *Self-portrait* with his own calligraphy (Nara, Yamato Bunkakan Museum).

Seuphor, Michel born 1901
Belgian painter, poet and historian of abstract art. He was influenced by the theories of De Stijl, met van Doesburg in 1922 and was a close friend of Mondrian. In 1926 he began his first geometric abstract work. He collaborated with Torres-García, Vantongerloo and Arp on the review and exhibitions CERCLE ET CARRÉ (1929–31) and published many writings on abstract art, including the first biography of Mondrian (1957). He has also produced tapestries.

Seurat, Georges 1859–91
French painter, the instigator and most important practitioner of NEO-IMPRESSIONISM. He had an academic training and was a superb draughtsman; his tonal drawings, usually in black conté crayon, were his first important works. He exhibited for the first time at the 1883 Salon, but the following year *A bathing scene at Asnières* (1883–84, London, NG), painted in POINTILLIST technique, was rejected and shown instead at the Salon des Indépendants. In his minute analysis of the visual world, and particularly in his exhaustive application of optical theory, Seurat differed markedly from the Impressionists. Rather than conveying the sense of brevity attached to a particular moment, he sought to make that moment into something enduring. He devoted himself to the development of a few very large canvases, which, in their conscious monumentality and highly formalized composition, reflect his long analysis of the Old Masters and, in technique, the influence of Eugène Chevreul's and Charles Blanc's theories on colour. *La Grande Jatte* of 1884–86 (Chicago, Art Institute) was exhibited with Pissarro's support at the last Impressionist exhibition. In 1887–88 he painted *The parade* (New York, Metropolitan) and from 1889–90 he worked on *The uproar* (Otterlo, Kröller-Müller), while *The circus* (Paris, Jeu de Paume) was left unfinished at his death in 1891. All these illustrate his pursuit of a theory of composition that would ensure balance and harmony and convey a specific mood through form; in a letter of 1890 he outlined the psychological properties of line, colour and tone. His work and ideas had great influence in his lifetime and after, and attracted several disciples, the best-known of whom is Signac. See vol. 1 pp. *126*, *162–163*; vol. 3 pp. **110–111**; vol. 4 p. *165*

Severini, Gino 1883–1966
Italian painter. He began his career as a copyist before moving to Paris in 1906 and joining the avantgarde there. He joined the FUTURISTS in 1910 and played a crucial role in transmitting French artistic theory to them. His paintings reveal a stronger Cubist influence than his compatriots', especially in their concentration on abstract form as opposed to movement (*Dancer, sea and vase of flowers*, 1913, New York, Private coll.). In the 1920s he adopted a more classical style before turning to a quasi-abstract, decorative style based on synthetic Cubism. See vol. 3 p. **152**

Sezession (Secession)
The name taken by several groups of painters in Germany and Austria in the 1890s who broke away from what they considered the restrictive environment of the official academies. They sought the freedom to work unimpeded in contemporary modern styles—chiefly IMPRESSIONISM, SYMBOLISM and ART NOUVEAU—and to mount their own exhibitions. The first Sezession took place in Munich in 1892, led by von Stuck and Trübner. The Vienna Sezession under Klimt followed in 1897, and the Berlin Sezession in 1899 under Liebermann. In 1910 the Berlin Sezession rejected the work of a group of die Brücke artists, who then formed the Neue Sezession.

Sfumato
Term deriving from the Italian for "smoke" and used to describe the blending of tones so subtly that the transition is imperceptible. Leonardo, who said that light and shade should blend "without lines or borders, in the manner of smoke", is the artist most closely associated with *sfumato*. See vol. 2 p. 130

Sgraffito see GRAFFITO

Shadbolt, Jack born 1909
Canadian painter of Abstract Expressionist and surreal landscapes. He works in Vancouver, where he knew Carr and studied with Varley. Using biomorphic shapes derived from landscape, he evokes inchoate states of nature. *Winter theme* (1962, Ottawa, NG) is typically dark and rich chromatically.

Shahn, Ben 1898–1969
American social realist painter, printmaker, photographer and calligrapher. He emigrated to New York from Lithuania in 1906. Significant early works are those devoted to political scapegoats such as Dreyfus, Sacco and Vanzetti and Tom Mooney, which combine angular, intentionally dead-pan colour planes with an incisive line. He worked on Federal mural schemes during the 1930s and photographed rural poverty in the Mid-West. Towards the end of the decade he began to seek more universally symbolic images, and in paintings such as *Pacific landscape* (1945, New York, MOMA) he created moving images of wartime alienation. In his late work he continued to explore tragic themes with emblematic sparseness. Written scripts or commentaries are sometimes incorporated into these images, which are patterned in a delicate, nervous manner recalling Klee. See vol. 1 pp. *51*, *141*; vol. 3 p. **205**

Sharaku, Toshusai active 1794–95
Japanese UKIYO-E artist. Scarcely anything is known of the life of this brilliantly original portrayer of Kabuki actors. The 158 known designs by Sharaku were produced during a mere 10 months, 1794–95. They are unique in their almost caricature-like exaggerations, and are distinguished by brilliant use of colour and of shining backgrounds made by means of metallic powders. Questions about Sharaku remain: was he an actor himself who briefly made prints as a hobby, did he fail as a print designer because his portraits were too grotesque, or did he simply die after his brief spate of activity? See vol. 3 p. **51**

Shaykh Zadeh'
active 1st half of 16th century
Persian painter from Khurasan. As a pupil of Bihzad he shows the closest affinity among Shah Tahmasp's painters with the style of late 15th-century Herat. From about 1520 to 1530 he worked in Tabriz; his *Episode in a mosque* (Paris, Louis Cartier coll.) is a well-known work from this period. On the basis of this the first 13 illustrations of a *Khamseh* of Nizami, 1525, in the Metropolitan, New York, have been attributed to him. By 1538 he had moved to Bukhara.

Shee, Sir Martin Archer
1769–1850
Irish portrait painter, working in London from 1788. He became the leading society portraitist of the day apart from Lawrence, whom he succeeded as President of the Royal Academy in 1830. His work, which has less bravura than that of Lawrence, is well represented in the National Portrait Gallery, London. He published *Rhymes on Art* in 1805 and *Elements of Art* in 1809.

Sheeler, Charles 1883–1965
American painter, whose name is identified with PRECISIONISM. Although influenced by Cubism and Synchromism after the Armory Show, two quite different influences contributed to the characteristics of his mature work—the mechanical forms used in the work of his friends, the New York Dadaists, and his own photographic experiments. His paintings of the Ford factory on the River Rouge, such as *River Rouge plant* (1932, New York, Whitney) and his earlier photographs of it, did much to popularize the industrial landscape as a worthy subject for American art.

Shen-Chou see SHEN ZHOU

Shen Zhou 1427–1509
Chinese painter and calligrapher. Born of a prosperous family of the Suzhou region, with long traditions of interest in poetry, calligraphy and painting, Shen, versatile and prolific, was the epitome of a gentleman-artist. Early influences were the Yuan scholar painters such as Wang Meng, though later study of Dong Yuan, Juran and other 10th-century masters produced a shift in the direction of more monumental landscapes. Many of his works take the famous scenery of his native area as their subject, for example the handscroll *A complete view of the Suzhou landscape* (1480s, Taiwan, National Palace Museum). Equally famous as a poet and calligrapher, Shen was highly influential, his most important disciple being Wen Zhengming.

Shinn, Everett 1876–1953
American painter. Like the majority of the ASHCAN painters with whom he was associated, he originally worked as a newspaper illustrator. In 1908 he exhibited as one of The EIGHT. He was an extremely sociable man and his enjoyment and love of the theatre are evident in many of his works. *The London Hippodrome* (1902, Chicago, Art Institute) is reminiscent of Degas.

Shinoda, Morio born 1931
Japanese sculptor, who spent much of

the 1960s in the USA. He has executed more than 400 works in his *Tension and Compression* series. In one of these, *Universe* (1966, Tokyo, Railway Co.), metal shapes are held by wires between cones standing in water. Recent works have used light, sound waves and electricity.

Shin Saimdang 1512–59
Korean landscape and nature painter, mother of the Neo-Confucian scholar Yulgok Yi Yi. She said she learned landscape painting from An Kyon. Her other subjects such as grapes, insects and flowers (a fine example is in Seoul, Ewha Women's University Museum) are painted with delicate feminine sensitivity to colours and composition.

Shishkin, Ivan Ivanovich 1832–98
Russian landscape painter. Between 1862 and 1865 he lived in Germany and Switzerland. His favourite subjects were very closely observed and minutely executed trees and his monumental images of Russian forests exhibited with the WANDERERS show a response to the growing feeling of national identity. Most of his famous landscapes are in the Tretyakov Gallery in Moscow—*Distant forest* (1884); *Oaktree grove* (1887); *Morning in the pine forest* (1889).

Shterenberg (Sterenberg), **David Petrovich** 1881–1948
Russian painter. After the October Revolution he was appointed Commissar for Art (1917–18); he also taught in Moscow until 1930. His *Meal* (1916, Leningrad, Russian Museum) shows the play he made on the paradox of "realism" and "abstraction" by placing evocative, everyday objects on a completely plain, coloured background.

Shubin, Fedot 1740–1805
The foremost Russian sculptor of the 18th century. He studied abroad, 1767–73, partly in Paris with Pigalle, but also in Rome, Turin and London (where he was influenced by Nollekens). He specialized in marble portrait busts, notably those of Catherine I, much praised for their psychological expressiveness. A marble figure of Queen Catherine is in the Tauride Palace, Leningrad.

Shubun, Ekkei active 1430–60
Japanese painter and priest. A leading figure in the revival of the Chinese style of painting, Shubun succeeded Josetsu as the leader of the Zen academic school. Little is known of his life: he held executive office in the influential Shokoku temple in Kyoto, and worked closely with the Ashikaga shoguns, whom he served faithfully. He is believed to have been a member of an official mission to Korea in 1423. The only authenticated work by Shubun is a wooden statue of the saint *Daruma* (Nara, Daruma temple), which he is said to have coloured (1430?). A representative painting attributed to him is *The hermitage of the three worthies* (1418, Tokyo, Seikado coll.).

Shunman, Kubo 1757–1820
Japanese UKIYO-E artist. A native of Edo (Tokyo), Shunman produced excellent examples of *bijin-ga* (prints of beautiful women). He preferred, however, to concentrate on *surimono*, luxury prints, with which he decorated his *kyoka* poems. Many examples of his hand-painted *ukiyo-e* remain, and his imitation of the "limited-colour" print is a unique achievement. One of many Edo artists versatile in all forms of art, Shunman also wrote plays and poetry, and was proficient in shell-work and carving.

Shunsho, Katsukawa 1726–92
Japanese UKIYO-E artist. Shunsho is arguably the greatest print-designer of the first part of the Golden Age of *ukiyo-e*. He was the first to portray star Kabuki actors realistically both on and off stage. Though he was forced by Harunobu's popularity to design *bijin-ga* (pictures of beautiful women) in his style, most of the time he wisely concentrated on his favourite subjects, actors and warriors, to which his strong, masculine line and colouring were best suited. Only in his genre paintings can Shunsho's ease with a smoother style be seen—as in his *hashirakate* (pillar-print) series *Twelve Months of Women's Customs*.

Siberechts, Jan 1627–1700/3
Flemish landscape painter, born in Antwerp, and active in England from about 1672 until his death. He mainly painted landscapes with peasants, but he is best known as the first professional painter of "portraits" of country houses; among the earliest are two views of Longleat, Wiltshire, 1675 and 1676, still in the house which they represent. His later work became more naturalistic, and his *View of Nottingham and the Trent* (c.1695, Birdsall House, Yorkshire) stands at the beginning of the British tradition of landscape painting.

Sickert, Walter Richard 1860–1942
British painter. Born in Munich of Danish parents, he came to England in 1868. He was a pupil of Whistler and from 1885 onwards knew Degas well. Both these painters were important influences, Degas for his emphasis on the tradition of drawing and the pursuit of spontaneous effects deriving from photography, Whistler for his modulation of tones. After he settled in London in 1905, Sickert's studio became a centre for many younger painters, including those who were to found the CAMDEN TOWN Group. In this period he concentrated on urban subject matter, the music-hall and often quite sordid scenes of working-class life, partly in reaction against the aestheticism of Whistler; in 1910 he wrote: "The more our art is serious, the more will it tend to avoid the drawing-room and stick to the kitchen." His best-known work, *Ennui* (version c.1913, London, Tate), depicts a middle-aged couple in their home in a potent image of a dead marriage. Sickert's later work was more broadly handled and more dependent on the photographic sources he had always used—the monumental *Raising of Lazarus* (c.1929–32, Melbourne, NG of Victoria), for example, was derived from a photograph of a lay-figure being carried upstairs. See vol. 3 p. **154**; vol. 4 p. *171*

Sidur, Vadim born 1924
Russian sculptor. Experiments in different techniques stimulated a tendency to the abstract in his fundamentally expressionist style, and the profoundly pessimistic and tragic context of his art brought him into deep conflict with official Russian attitudes towards sculpture. Violence is the dominant theme of his art, as in *Martyrs of violence*, erected in 1973 in Kassel, West Germany.

Sieverding, Katharina born 1944
West German Performance artist. She uses films and still photographs and is interested in exploration of aspects of herself and others which contradict conventional definitions. In *Motor-kamera* (1973) she aimed at an interchange of identity with a male artist and in 1974 she took part in the "Transformer" exhi-bition (Lucerne, Kunstmuseum), which centred around the themes of androgyny and sexual ambiguity.

Signac, Paul 1863–1935
French NEO-IMPRESSIONIST painter. He was associated with Seurat in 1884 at the Salon des Indépendants, which he had helped to found. Two years later he exhibited POINTILLIST works at the last Impressionist exhibition. He was important as the theoretician of Neo-Impressionism and in 1899 he published *From Delacroix to Neo-Impressionism*, in which he advocated painting with scientific precision. His own best work, however, was produced later when his style became more spontaneous and his colours more brilliant. By 1892 he had moved to St Tropez, where in 1904 he was visited by Matisse, on whom he had a profound influence. His *Railway junction at Bois-Colombes* (1866, Leeds City Art Gallery) is a fine early example of his pointillist work. See vol. 3 p. **111**

Significant form
Concept introduced by Clive Bell in his book *Art* (1914) to denote "the quality that distinguishes works of art from all other classes of objects", a quality which exists independently of any representational or symbolic content.

Signorelli, Luca active 1470–1523
Italian painter from Cortona, active in central Italy. The circumstances of his training and the chronology of his early work are uncertain, but there are both iconographic and stylistic reasons to believe Vasari's report that his master was Piero della Francesca. The *Madonna and Child* in Boston (MFA), for example, is remarkable for the weightiness of the figures and the sensitive treatment of light and shade, while *The Flagellation* (c.1480, Milan, Brera) echoes the composition of Piero's *Flagellation*. In this work, however, and in the large-scale altarpiece of *The Madonna and Child with saints* (1484, Perugia, Museo dell'Opera del Duomo) the dramatic style cultivated by Florentine artists, and especially the wiry athleticism of the Pollaiuoli, also exerted an influence. In 1483 Signorelli was called in to finish the series of Sistine Chapel frescos begun by Perugino and others: his contribution, *The last days of Moses*, features a mysterious nude that may have inspired Michelangelo's *Ignudi* on the ceiling of the Sistine some 25 years later. Signorelli's masterpiece is *The Last Judgment* fresco cycle in Orvieto Cathedral (1499–1502), where his fascination with movement and muscular contortion is consummated in a vast drama of nude bodies surpassed in terrible grandeur only by Michelangelo's *Last Judgment* in the Sistine Chapel. See vol. 2 pp. **116–117**

Signorini, Telemaco 1835–1901
Italian painter and art critic, a leading member and defender of the MACCHIAIOLI. He first experimented with the *macchia* technique in landscape painting at La Spezia in 1858 and 1861. In 1861 he visited Paris and was impressed by Corot and the BARBIZON school, reflections of whose work are found in his Piagentan landscapes from this period. He often returned to Paris and visited London and Scotland. Inspired by the philosopher Proudhon, he revealed his interest in social reform in works such as *The violent madwomen's ward* (1865, Venice, Galleria d'Arte Moderna), which was admired by Degas. He is best remembered for his landscapes executed around Florence in the 1880s and at Riomaggiore after 1881.

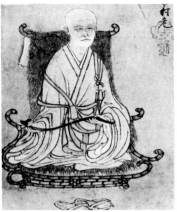

Sesson: Self-portrait (detail). Nara, Yamato Bunkakan Museum

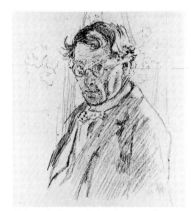

Sickert: Self-portrait drawing, c.1908. Oxford, Ashmolean

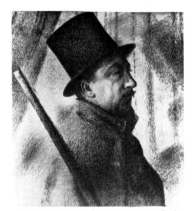

Signac: Drawing by Seurat, 1889–90. Paris, G. Cachin-Signac coll.

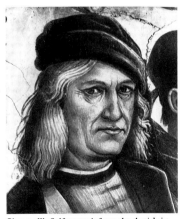

Signorelli: Self-portrait from the *Antichrist* fresco, (1499–1502). Orvieto Cathedral, (Anderson)

Silk-screen printing
A method of colour printing first developed commercially but now used to make works of art. A stencil is stuck, painted or drawn on a stretched screen of fine-mesh fabric through which ink, paint or dye is forced on to a printing surface of paper or board, leaving blank the areas covered by the stencil. Separate stencils are made for each colour run. See vol. 1 p. 167

Siloë, Diego de c.1495–1563
Spanish architect and sculptor. He was strongly influenced by Italianate achievements, and may have studied in Italy—numerous projects reveal a personal combination of late Gothic and Renaissance features. His masterpiece, the Escalera Dorada (Golden stairway) of 1519–23 at Burgos Cathedral, is elaborately decorated with florid reliefs, originally richly painted and gilded. He also worked in wood and marble, and collaborated with Bigarny on an altarpiece for Burgos Cathedral. In 1528 he became master of works of Granada Cathedral, and erected a grand Renaissance church on Gothic foundations.

Silverpoint
Drawing made by a fine silver rod, pointed at the tip, on paper covered in a tinted layer, now zinc white but formerly powdered bone. The rod is either held directly in the hand or consists of a hollow shaft into which a pointed piece of silver wire is inserted. Fragments of metal are deposited along the drawn lines; these gradually darken as they tarnish. Very delicate effects can be achieved with silverpoint, and it was widely used in Italy and the north during the 15th century, though it later became rarer, probably because it permits little variation and cannot be erased. Many silverpoint drawings are touched with white highlights or overdrawn with other media. See vol. 1 p. 162

Silvestre, Israel 1621–91
French etcher. He was much patronized by Louis XIII and was drawing-master to the young Louis XIV. Most of his work consists of architectural views of Rome, Florence and Paris. His style was almost entirely derived from Callot, but Silvestre's work is generally more important for its historical information than for its artistic quality.

Šima, Josef 1891–1971
Czech painter and graphic artist, who moved to Paris and became a French citizen. He was influenced by Surrealism, but his style was highly original, particularly in portraiture. After 11 years inactivity he spent his last twenty years painting poetic fantasies of great spaces, unaffected by contemporary art.

Simberg, Hugo 1873–1917
Finnish painter. He was a pupil (1895–97) of Gallen-Kallela, who taught him graphic techniques and tempera painting. He worked mainly on a small scale and in his watercolours, coloured drawings and etchings he used figures from popular tradition to produce novel, bizarrely naive images, where Death and devils, angels, Frost and other personifications mingle with wretched humans. He did murals in the Johannes Church (now Cathedral) at Tampere, 1904–06.

Simone Martini c.1285–1344
Sienese painter. His training is unknown, but his work shows him to have been Duccio's principal successor, and after him he was the greatest artist of the Sienese school. His first known work is the large frescoed *Maestà* (1315) in the Town Hall of Siena. In 1317 he went to Naples, where he painted a politically charged image of *St Louis* resigning his crown to Robert of Anjou (1317, Naples, Capodimonte). His experience there of the linear elegance of French Gothic decisively affected his later style, which was essentially courtly. His other major works include an equestrian portrait in fresco of *Guidoriccio da Fogliano* (1328, Siena, Palazzo Pubblico) and a series of frescos at Assisi on *The life of St Martin* (probably 1320s). The large and sumptuous *Annunciation* (1333, Florence, Uffizi), made in collaboration with his brother-in-law Memmi, was his last major work in Italy. In 1340–41 he moved to the papal court, then in refuge at Avignon, where he died. The chief works of these years are the small panel of the very unusual subject *Christ reproved by his parents* (1342, Liverpool, Walker Art Gallery) and the frontispiece in a volume of a commentary on Virgil (Milan, Ambrosiana) which belonged to his friend Petrarch, for whom Simone painted a portrait (now lost, but mentioned in a sonnet) of the poet's beloved Laura. He also painted frescos in the cathedral at Avignon, of which the sinopie survive. Simone's exquisite grace of line and decorative richness were influential on French manuscript illuminators as well as Italian painters. See vol. 2 p. **84**

Sim Sa-jong 1707–69
Korean painter, one of the major artists of the Middle Yi Dynasty. He learned painting from Chong Son and the Chinese Old Masters, and deployed a Chinese style in traditional late Ming subjects. He was also well-known for light and delicate colours, as in the famous *Tiger* (Seoul, National Museum).

Singier, Gustave born 1909
French painter. He was born in Belgium, but moved to Paris in 1919 and became naturalized. From 1936 he exhibited regularly at all the main avantgarde Salons. His first works show Cubist influences, but were essentially Expressionist canvases painted with a Fauvist palette. Since World War II he has painted abstract compositions marked by large areas of flat colour. He has also made a number of tapestries, which are in the Palace of Justice, Paris.

Sinopia
A reddish-brown earth, named after Sinope in Asia Minor, one of its sources, used to make preliminary drawings for FRESCO. The term is now used to describe any such preliminary drawing, properly on the layer immediately beneath the *intonaco*, even if it is in another medium (such as charcoal).

Sintenis, Renée 1888–1965
German sculptor and painter. She owed her early success to the support of the poet Rilke. Her speciality was small bronze sculptures of women, children and animals executed in a lively, imaginative manner (*Daphne*, 1913, New York, MOMA). She also painted portraits, and did numerous book illustrations.

Sin Yun-bok
active 2nd half of 18th century
Korean painter, a member of the state Bureau of Painting. A master of genre painting, he created erotic, playful scenes of aristocrats and beauties with delicate line and subtle colour. Albums and paintings, such as *Standing lady in Korean dress*, are in the National Museum, Seoul.

Siqueiros, David Alfaro
1896–1974
Mexican painter, one of the three great Mexican muralists. From 1912 to 1922 he travelled through Europe making contact with the avantgarde. As editor of the magazine *Vida Americana* in Barcelona, 1921, he appealed to artists to take up the social realist cause; indeed his militant commitment to Marxism deeply affected his art. On his return to Mexico he took part, along with Orozco and Rivera, on the murals of the National Preparatory School, Mexico City, where the new thematic and stylistic possibilities of muralism became manifest for the first time. His style revealed a strong feeling for volume and an affinity with the forms of Pre-Columbian art, applied to strongly-felt socialist themes. He founded the Syndicate of Technical Workers, Painters and Sculptors in 1922, and organized painting teams to work with air-guns on large outdoor murals. His experiments, such as substituting silicates for pigments and curved for flat surfaces, won him renown and when, in 1936, he founded the Experimental Workshop in New York, he met with the admiration of many young and established artists. His last work, the *Polyforum Siqueiros* (1971, re-erected in Mexico City), was his most experimental—a vast purpose-built auditorium which successfully integrated architecture, sculpture and mural painting with themes of great portent. It was violently expressive and brilliantly coloured, and was subtitled *The march of humanity on earth* and *Towards the Cosmos*. See vol. 3 p. **209**

Sironi, Mario 1885–1961
Italian painter. He joined the Futurists in 1914 and later became associated with Metaphysical Painting. In both these phases he kept an interest in urban and industrial images, which became the distinctive feature of his art after 1920. He was a founder of NOVECENTO, and his work in fresco and on canvas was consistently strong in construction and feeling (*Law between Justice and Strength*, 1936, Milan, Palace of Justice).

Sisley, Alfred 1839–99
French-born IMPRESSIONIST painter, of English parentage. He spent most of his life in France painting landscapes, and occasional portraits and still lifes. His early works were chiefly influenced by Corot, and his conversion to Impressionism was gradual. He met Renoir, Monet and Bazille when he was studying with Gleyre (1860–63) and his friendship with Monet was particularly important. His landscapes near Paris in the 1870s display a careful organization of patch-like brush-strokes, a fine sense of colour and composition, and a distinctive quiet serenity (*Floods at Marly*, 1876, Cambridge, Fitzwilliam Museum). Though the bolder pioneers of Impressionism were more influential, few matched Sisley's sensitivity as a landscapist, his delicacy of touch and sureness of composition. See vol. 3 p. **99**

Situation
Exhibition held in London in 1960 by younger British painters who were frustrated by the lack of opportunity given to their kind of work by the commercial galleries. Conditions for entry were that the paintings should be totally abstract, and at least 30 feet square, a stipulation reflecting the admiration young British painters felt for the scale of the American Abstract Expressionists. Artists taking part included Turnbull, Denny, Cohen, Ayres, Law and Richard Smith. In retrospect the exhibition, together with Caro's first welded sculptures of the same year, marks a watershed in British art, in a move towards a more international context and a brighter, more optimistic tone. A second "Situation" exhibition was held in 1961.

Size
Form of glue used to prevent paint soaking into canvas. Much diluted before application, size does not render the surface completely impermeable, because too thick a coating would prevent the paint adhering to the canvas and cause flaking and cracking.

Skeaping, John 1901–80
British sculptor. In the late 1920s and early 1930s he made carvings which, like those of Hepworth (to whom he was for a time married) and Moore, attempted to exploit the natural properties of wood and stone. His later work was more traditional and he became principally known as an animal sculptor.

Sköld, Otte 1894–1958
Swedish painter, draughtsman and engraver. Influenced by Cubism and Futurism, he began painting scenes of detailed realism, dance halls and bars (*Bistro*, 1920, Oslo, NG), and became the foremost Swedish Neue Sachlichkeit painter. He lived in Paris from 1919, working in fresco, mosaic and stained glass. He was Professor at the Academy in Stockholm, 1932–42, its Director, 1941–50, and Director of the National Museum, Stockholm, 1950–58.

Skopas active 4th century BC
Greek sculptor from the island of Paros, regarded by ancient authors as one of the foremost artists of his age. He is known to have worked on the Temple of Athene Alea at Tegea, the Temple of Artemis at Ephesus and the Mausoleon at Halicarnassus. Surviving fragments from Tegea include several heads now in the National Museum at Athens. Remarkable in the intensity of expression of the features and deep-set eyes, these correspond well with descriptions of Skopas' work, and on the same basis other pieces have been attributed to him, including a relief slab from Halicarnassus, now in the British Museum, London. Other works have been recognized in copies, including the ecstatic figure of *A maenad* at the Albertinum, Dresden. Skopas' influence is thought to be most evident in later works which represent violent movement and emotion, especially in those of the PERGAMENE school. See vol. 2 p. **40**

Slevogt, Max 1868–1932
German painter of the Impressionist school. After studying in Munich he spent two years in Paris at the Académie Julian (1889–90), where he first came into contact with French Realism and Impressionism. On returning to Germany he became close to the Leibl circle through his friendship with Trübner. Much of his work shows a strong Baroque influence and a preoccupation with theatre and music (*The singer d'Andrade as Don Juan*, 1902, Stuttgart, Staatsgalerie). His move to Berlin in 1901 brought him in contact with Liebermann and the Sezession, and resulted in a considerable lightening of his colour, looser brushwork and a much greater freedom in the choice of casual, everyday subject matter. With Liebermann and Corinth he is considered the strongest exponent of naturalism in Germany, while his decorative extravagance and dazzling use of light ensured him great popularity and a wealth of commissions.

Sloan, John 1871–1951
American painter, a leading light of The EIGHT. Originally a newspaper illustrator, he was encouraged to paint by Henri, whom he met in 1892 in Philadelphia. In 1904 he moved to New York, and in 1908 he and Henri organized The Eight, opposing Academic hegemony, and promoting a modern realistic art. Later Sloan was elected President of the Society of Independent Artists. His contribution to the modern American stream lay in an unpretentious, colourful view of everyday, lower-class life in New York—the back-street districts portrayed by contemporary novelists such as Theodore Dreiser (*Hairdresser's window*, 1907, Hartford, Wadsworth Atheneum). See vol. 3 p. **204**

Slodtz family
Family of French sculptors and decorators, originating from Antwerp. **Sébastien** (1655–1726), a pupil of Girardon, specialized in ceremonial decorations in a refined, classical style. He trained his two elder sons, **Sébastien-Antoine** (c.1695–1754) and **Paul-Ambroise** (1702–58), each of whom, in turn, held the post of Dessinateur de la Chambre du Roi (king's decorator). Both worked in a Rococo manner, typified by Paul's lyrical *Dead Icarus* (1743, Paris, Louvre). The best-known member of the family is the youngest son, René-Michel, better known as **Michel-Ange** (1705–64), who also trained briefly with his father before joining the French Academy at Rome in 1728. There he was particularly impressed by Bernini and by the tortuous figures of Michelangelo's late period—thus earning his nickname. He also drew on the example of Puget for his animated *St Bruno* (1744, Rome, St Peter's), the work which made his reputation. Michel-Ange finally returned to France in 1747, bringing an exuberant Baroque style that reached its height in the tomb of Languet de Gergy (1750–57, Paris, St-Sulpice), with its swirling drapery and animated depiction of Death. His chief pupil was Houdon.

Sluter, Claus died c.1406
Netherlandish sculptor, chiefly active in Burgundy, the pioneer of a realistic trend in northern European sculpture which superseded Gothic. He was born in Haarlem and worked in Brussels (1380–85) before joining the group of artists (several of them Netherlandish) in the service of Philip the Bold, Duke of Burgundy. Two of Sluter's masterpieces are in the Chartreuse de Champmol at Dijon, a monastery founded by Duke Philip. The portal of the abbey, completed in 1397, bears large stone figures, exceptionally solid and voluminously draped, simply arranged and practically independent of the portal's architectural framework. The Well of Moses (1395–1403), originally a towering structure, survives only in part, but its six prophets (originally richly coloured by the painter Malouel) are fully three-dimensional and each prophet is individualized with an expressive face and expansive gestures. In 1404 he began work on his last commission, the Duke's funerary monument (Dijon, Musée). This was left unfinished at Sluter's death, but the figures of *Mourners* or *Weepers* around the sarcophagus are from his hand, and although small in size they have a massive solemnity. Sluter's powerful style was a major influence, not only on sculptors but on painters such as Campin, and he ranks as one of the most important artists of his time in northern Europe. See vol. 2 p. **90**

Sluyters, Jan (Johannes Carolus Bernardus) 1881–1957
Dutch painter. His early work was Symbolist, but following a visit to Paris in 1904 he developed a Fauvist palette of heightened colour and dabbing strokes, as in *Flowers in a vase* (1912, Otterlo, Kröller-Müller). After a short period of abstract work in 1914, he returned to brisk, eclectic paintings of interiors and figure studies, principally of children and the female nude.

Smart, Jeffrey born 1921
Australian painter. His studies in Europe included a period with Léger. His SURREALIST paintings, formal in design, rely on incongruous incident to present chilling scenes of suburban life (*After the meeting*, Holbrook, Australia, Mr and Mrs Douglas Carnegie coll.). Since 1965 he has exhibited regularly in London and in Italy, where he lives.

Smart, John c.1742–1811
British portrait miniaturist, whose bright, pretty style and porcelain-like finish epitomize the popular idea of late 18th-century elegance. *An unknown man* (1776, London, V&A) is typical.

Smet, Gustave de 1877–1943
Belgian EXPRESSIONIST painter. His early work was Impressionist, but in Holland between 1914 and 1922 he met Sluyters, Toorop and Le Fauconnier and was influenced by Expressionism. In 1922 he settled near Ghent. His broadly painted interiors and scenes of rural life, for example *Village kermis* (1930, Ghent, Musée des Beaux-Arts), are rendered in a powerful range of deep reds and browns. His figure studies and portraits, after 1939, were less abstract.

Smibert, John 1688–1751
British-born portrait painter who became one of the leading artists in colonial America. Smibert came to study in London from his native Edinburgh and in 1717 left for Italy, returning three years later to paint rather stodgy portraits in the style of Kneller. He was brought to America as a teacher in 1728, and settled in Boston, where his work and his collection of engravings were important in promoting European styles among artists such as Copley. His best-known work is the portrait of *Dean George Berkeley and his family*, usually called *The Bermuda Group* (1728–29, New Haven, Yale University Art Gallery), which clearly influenced Feke.

Smith, David 1906–65
The foremost American sculptor of the post-World War II period. In the 1920s he studied painting and became familiar with European Cubism. Around 1930 he saw illustrations of Picasso's welded metal sculptures and also those of González; their use of iron and steel as sculptural media had a great impact on him. He acquired a knowledge of metal-working techniques while employed in the car industry in 1925 and this training was of immense significance to him when he began sculptures in metal in 1933, after a period of making collages and constructions. His first welded sculptures incorporated objects and machinery parts, a practice which he continued regularly through his career. Although non-representational, virtually all the sculptures evoke suggestions of figure, landscape or still life; the surface quality—polished, burnished, painted or left rough—is always of extreme importance. Many of his works have an open, skeletal structure, as if they were three-dimensional drawings (*Australia*, 1951,

New York, MOMA). From the late 1950s until his death (in a road accident) he worked on several series of more opaque or volumetric works, of which the best-known is the *Cubi* series (examples in many modern collections). These are mostly vertical constructions built up from boxes and cylinders of polished stainless steel. A few of the *Cubis* form gateways or course across a horizontal expanse, suggesting fresh approaches to one of Smith's recurrent preoccupations, sculpture's relationship to the environment. Smith's structural sense and his adaptation of industrial materials and techniques have had a profound influence on post-War sculpture. See vol. 1 pp. *177*, *191*; vol. 3 p. **231**

Smith, Jack born 1928
British painter. In the early 1950s he became known for dour, almost monochromatic paintings of everyday life (*Mother bathing child*, 1953, London, Tate). An interest in the symbolic was to lead him to abstract paintings such as *Shimmer, red and orange* (1962, Manchester, City Gallery). More recent work has involved complex sequences of semi-abstract forms on a white ground suggesting musical development.

Smith, Sir Matthew 1879–1959
British painter. Gauguin and Matisse (in whose studio Smith spent a few weeks in 1910) were formative influences on his work. The two *Fitzroy Street nudes* (1916, London, Tate, and British Council) echo Matisse in their bold unnaturalistic, Fauvist colour, but Smith used the daring juxtapositions of green shadow with yellow flesh to impart information about the volume of the figure. His finest paintings were perhaps the Cornish landscapes of 1920 such as *Cornish church* (Tate). In these his personal sense of colour came to the fore, and his ability to extract the utmost intensity from predominantly dark, saturated tones, particularly purples and reds. His later depictions of the nude are marked by a unique lush opulence.

Smith, Richard born 1931
British painter. His early work combined an interest in the vigorous handling of Abstract Expressionism with a concern for the scale and visual impact of advertising. He used shaped canvases, as in *Staggerly* (1963, Cardiff, National Museum of Wales) or even projections from the wall, as in *Giftwrap* (1963, London, Tate), which could also be called Pop. In later work he became more involved in the formal possibilities of experimentation with the support and recent paintings have exploited a kite-like format so that the stretcher becomes part of the visible structure of the work (*Mandarino*, 1973, London, Tate). See vol. 1 p. *153*; vol. 3 p. **240**

Smith, Thomas
active last quarter of 17th century
American painter, the earliest artist in colonial America whose identity is reasonably certain. He is mentioned in an account book of Harvard College in 1680 and a number of portraits have been attributed to him on the basis of an impressively stern and strongly individualized *Self-portrait* (c.1690, Worcester, Mass., Art Museum), signed with his initials. In its severity and simplicity of handling it relates to provincial English family portraits of the same date.

Smith, Tony born 1912
American sculptor, painter and architect. After an apprenticeship with the architect Frank Lloyd Wright, Smith

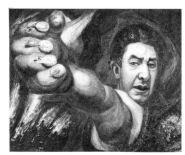

Siqueiros: Self-portrait, 1943. Mexico City, Museo de Arte Moderno (René Roland)

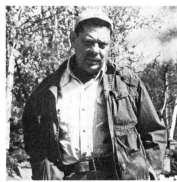

Smith, David: Photograph by Sam Meulendyke (Archives of American Art, Smithsonian Institution)

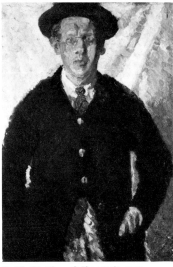

Smith, Matthew: Self-portrait, 1909. London, Guildhall (Cooper-Bridgeman)

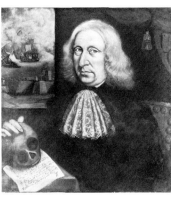

Smith, Thomas: Self-portrait c.1690. Massachusetts, Worcester Art Museum

worked as an architect and painter until 1960, when he turned to sculpture. He was hailed as one of the pioneers of MINIMALISM. His concern that art should have a public context is expressed in such huge courtyard and plaza sculptures as *Gracehoper* (1961, Detroit Institute of Arts), which one can walk round and through. Characteristically, this black metal piece unites the seemingly antithetical properties of imposing solidity and agile grace. See vol. 3 p. **247**

Smithson, Robert 1938–73
American sculptor, a major proponent of LAND art. In the mid-1960s, he first exhibited Minimal sculptures based on geometric progressions. He then shifted from making objects to expressing concepts through various earthworks. In 1968 he began the series of *Sites* and *Non-sites*, the latter involving earth or rocks put in bins and displayed with an aerial map of the site from which it was "displaced" (an example is *Non-Site, Palisades-Edgewater, N.J.*, 1968, New York, Whitney). *Spiral jetty* (1970, Great Salt Lake, Utah), his best-known work, is a colossal manifestation of his preoccupation with the processes of time and erosion. See vol. 3 p. **249**

Smits, Jacob 1855–1928
Belgian/Dutch painter and draughtsman, known for his landscapes and scenes of rural life. He studied in Rotterdam and Brussels and travelled to Munich, Vienna and Rome, also having contacts with the HAGUE school. His deep sympathy with the poverty of the farming population inspired the development of a personal symbolism in which he depicted their plight (*The father sentenced*, 1901, Brussels, Musées Royaux des Beaux-Arts). He also painted his local landscape and religious subjects, and was a precursor of Flemish Expressionism.

Snow, Michael born 1929
Canadian painter, sculptor, film-maker and musician. His work is a witty intellectual commentary on art and social mores, as in his *Walking Woman* series of paintings and sculptures, begun in 1960 (Toronto, Art Gallery of Ontario).

Snyders, Frans 1579–1657
Flemish painter of animals, hunting scenes and still life, born and mainly active in Antwerp. He was a pupil of Pieter Brueghel the Younger and a frequent collaborator with his close friend Rubens and other painters. In a letter of 1616 Rubens mentions a painting of *Prometheus* (Philadelphia Museum of Art): "original, by my own hand, the eagle painted by Snyders", and it is clear that Snyders was prized as the finest animal painter of his day. His best independent works are his hunting scenes, which have tremendous energy (*The boar hunt*, c.1640, Poznan, National Museum). Curiously, in view of the robustness of his preferred subjects, Snyders appears from van Dyck's portraits of him to be a man of almost fragile sensitivity, and the fact that he made his will four times suggests that he suffered from ill-health. See vol. 2 p. **200**

Soami died 1525
Japanese painter of the third generation of a family of artists, retainers to the last of the Ashikaga shoguns. They were made courtiers purely on their artistic merit and they contributed much to cultural and artistic development in the Shogunal court, particularly as experts on Chinese art. Soami practised Chinese style ink-painting but he was proficient in any other style requested. His sliding doors of the Daisen in the Daitokuji monastery, Kyoto, were executed in a style reminiscent of Sesshu's.

Sobrino, Francisco born 1932
Spanish sculptor. He studied in Madrid and Buenos Aires before moving to Paris in 1959, where he was a co-founder of the GROUPE DE RECHERCHE D'ART VISUEL the following year. He specializes in abstract geometrical sculptures assembled in aluminium and plexiglass (*Indefinite spaces C*, 1963, Paris, Galerie Denise René). These vary from kinetic, experimental works, and essays in light and colour, to free-standing, totemic structures.

Social realism
Branch of REALISM in which the subject has social or political content. It is distinct from **socialist realism**, which is the approved style in certain socialist countries (notably the USSR) and does not involve a critical approach to society.

Société Anonyme Inc.
Gallery of modern art in New York, founded by Duchamp, Man Ray and the collector and amateur painter, Katherine Dreier, with the intention of educating the American pubic about recent developments in art. It was opened in 1920 and in certain respects replaced Stieglitz's 291 Gallery, which had closed in 1917. Its name derived from the founders' intention to deal with art—particularly abstract art—rather than personalities. It had a programme of travelling exhibitions and lectures and was responsible for introducing the work of such artists as Ernst, Klee, Léger, Malevich and Schwitters to America. Its activities slackened during the Depression and it was dissolved in 1950 when its fine collection was donated to Yale University.

Society of Independent Artists
American society, established in New York in 1917 to organize annual exhibitions to which artists could submit works without selection by jury and without the incentive of prizes; it was in fact based on the ideas of the French Salon des Indépendants. It had no artistic policy, and, unlike Henri's 1910 Independents exhibition, was open to foreigners. Its first officers included such diverse figures as Duchamp, Glackens, Prendergast, Schamberg and Stella. The first exhibition, held in 1917, included some 2,200 works by 1,300 artists hung in alphabetical order. The only work rejected was Duchamp's urinal *Fountain* (1917, Milan, Galleria Schwartz); Duchamp resigned.

Sodoma, Il (Giovanni Antonio Bazzi) 1477–1549
Italian painter, born in Vercelli, and active mainly in and around Siena but also in Rome. His style was bizarrely eclectic—old-fashioned and up-to-date elements mingling in an often very attractive manner. According to Vasari, his personal life was also odd, and he is said to have kept a troupe of exotic animals. Among his major works are frescos of *The life of St Catherine* (1526) in S. Domenico, Siena, and *The marriage of Alexander and Roxane* (1516–17) in the Villa Farnesina, Rome. In his lifetime Sodoma was considered the leading painter in Siena, but the more powerful Beccafumi is now generally preferred.

Soffici, Ardengo 1879–1964
Italian painter and critic. His articles helped introduce modern artistic theory to Italy before World War I. At first hostile to the Futurists, he joined them in 1913, although his painting owed more to Cubism in the last analysis. He introduced "free word" painting, which exploited the visual and aural potential of words included in a picture (*Still life, melon and bottle*, 1914, Venice, Cardazzo coll.). After 1920 his painting and criticism shared the classicizing aesthetic of those involved with NOVECENTO.

Soft style see BOHEMIAN ART

Solana, José Gutiérrez 1885–1945
Spanish painter. His pictures depict the daily life of Madrid in a highly Expressionist manner, at times shot through with a dark pessimism reminiscent of Goya. Thick, heavy pigment with vibrant touches of bright colour, and a vigorous unrefined drawing style, transform his subjects into significant statements of life and death in the 20th century (*Reunion at the Café Pombo*, 1920, Madrid, Museo d'Arte Moderna).

Solario, Andrea active 1495–1524
Italian painter, active mainly in Milan. His work was influenced by Leonardo and also by Netherlandish art, perhaps partly through the work of Antonello da Messina. Solario, however, had a distinctive bright colouring, as can be seen in *The Madonna with the green cushion* (1507, Paris, Louvre).

Solario, Antonio de (lo Zingaro) active 1502–18?
Venetian painter, active in the Marches and in Naples. His gentle style is based on the work of Giovanni Bellini. It is possible that he visited England, for his finest surviving work is the Withypoll triptych (1514, Bristol, City Art Gallery, wings on loan from London, NG), showing the English merchant Paul Withypoll flanked by SS. Catherine of Alexandria and Ursula. He also painted frescos.

Soldati, Atonasio 1896–1953
Italian painter. Trained as an architect, be began painting in 1922. At first his work was influenced by Cézanne and analytical Cubism, but during the 1930s his style passed through a Metaphysical phase before finally settling into geometric abstraction akin to the international style of the Bauhaus and De Stijl (*Spiritual architecture*, 1950, Legnano, Ernesto Crespi coll.).

Solimena, Francesco 1657–1747
Italian painter, unchallenged head of the Neapolitan school in the first half of the 18th century. His compositions owe much to the art of his great Neapolitan predecessor, Luca Giordano, and also to that of Cortona, Lanfranco, and Mattia Preti. Underlying these Baroque influences and his own personal and very theatrical handling of light and shade is an academic figure style derived from classical authorities such as Raphael, the Carracci and Domenichino (*The fall of Simon Magus*, 1690, Naples, S. Paolo Maggiore). His art was highly influential, not only in Naples and elsewhere in Italy, but also, through the work that he sent to such important patrons as Prince Eugene of Savoy and Louis XIV of France, in many other European countries. See vol. 2 p. **235**

Solis, Virgil 1514–62
German engraver and designer of woodcuts, active in Nuremberg, where he had a large workshop. He produced many book illustrations on classical and biblical themes, which owe much to the Beham brothers, and did a series of influential ornamental pattern engravings.

Somer, Paul van c.1577–1622
Flemish portrait painter and engraver. He worked throughout the Netherlands before settling in 1616 in London, where, with Mytens and Cornelius Johnson, he became the leading painter at the court of James I. His style is similar to Mytens', but more archaic (*Queen Anne of Denmark*, 1617, Royal coll.).

Somov, Konstantin Andreevich 1869–1939
Russian painter. Son of a curator of paintings in the Hermitage in Leningrad, he studied at the Academy under Repin. Somov belonged to the impresario Diaghilev's art circle and his small pictures with scenes of French court life, often with erotic overtones, made a strong impact on the whole WORLD OF ART movement. He was an excellent portraitist with just a hint of retrospective nostalgia to add special poignancy (*Lady in blue: Elisaveta Martinova*, 1897–1900, Moscow, Tretyakov Gallery). He left Russia in 1924 and later settled in Paris.

Sonderborg, Karl Horst born 1923
Danish painter of German extraction. In the late 1940s he studied painting in Hamburg and discovered his subject in the city's dockland, translating mechanistic motifs into almost abstract geometrical compositions. In 1953 he went to Paris and studied graphic art, which inspired a dramatic monochrome abstract style, the paint manipulated with windscreen wipers and razor blades in a manner recalling Kline and Soulages. He was also influenced by oriental techniques (as in the ink *Untitled, Hamburg, 3.10 1951*, 1951, Artist's coll.).

Sonderbund
Title of an exhibition held in Cologne in 1912 which included for the first time all the avantgarde developments in European art. It drew together Expressionist art from all over Europe and from different periods. Thus El Greco was shown in a room close to works by Cézanne, Munch, Die Brücke and Blaue Reiter artists. The exhibition also included Gauguin, van Gogh, Picasso and Signac.

Song Dynasty 960–1279
Chinese dynasty during which the arts, and particularly landscape painting, flourished. Even at the time of its greatest strength, when it was founded, the Song dynasty never exercised the control over far-flung territories enjoyed by its predecessor, the Tang. However, even though northern China remained occupied by peoples from the north, the Song emperors had a far firmer control on the provinces than any previous rulers, and the warlordism which had destroyed the Tang was never a serious threat. The capital at Daifeng was chosen for its commercial rather than strategic value, for this was an age of unprecedented economic development, too, and the ideal of the Chinese élite turned from the virile horse-riding Tang aristocrat to the scholar of perhaps humble origins but of dazzling literary and artistic talents. A dichotomy came to be established between court taste and that of the scholar-gentry, embodied artistically in the gap between the meticulous academic artistic style patronized and practised by Emperor Huizong, and the monochrome bamboo paintings of Wen Tong. Landscape was elevated to become the major subject matter of Chinese painting, and this tendency may have been accelerated in the 12th century. In 1127 Kaifeng fell to the non-Chinese Jurchen, the Song Empire was reduced to the

provinces south of the Yangtze River and the capital moved to the beautiful city of Hangzhou. Many of the élite fled south to this lush area, once backward but now the richest and most populous in the Empire, and its scenery may have given a fresh impulse to landscape painting. The decorative arts, especially ceramics, flourished in both the Northern and Southern Song Empires, with a keen interest in China's own past. In later centuries, the period was viewed as one of great cultural eminence, undermined by the military weakness which was to deliver China over to conquest by the Mongols. See vol. 3 pp. 36–41

Sophilos c.580–560 BC
Greek vase-painter and potter from Athens, by whom four signed vases are known. Although not a fine draughtsman, he was one of the pioneers of the Attic BLACK-FIGURE technique and his *dinos* depicting the marriage of Peleus and Thetis (London, BM), while showing many Corinthian characteristics in drawing and use of colour, marks a clear departure in its expressiveness and vivid narrative technique.

Sørensen, Hendrik 1882–1962
Norwegian painter and book illustrator, a pupil of Zahrtmann in Copenhagen and Matisse in Paris. His *Inferno* (1924–25, Oslo, NG) reflecting the horrors of World War I, is dramatically subjective and expressive. He painted romantic landscapes, portraits and murals for public buildings, notably those for the Oslo Town Hall.

Sorge, Peter born 1937
West German painter. He was originally influenced by Neue Sachlichkeit of the 1920s, but around 1963 he began to incorporate images from newspapers and these became progressively more central to his art. In works such as *Several voyeurs (woman's year)* (1975, West Berlin, Neue Nationalgalerie) he juxtaposes the themes of sex, media reporting and violent death; but he is more concerned with the aesthetics of photography and media presentation than with a straight treatment of such subjects. Thus he is linked to Pop art and Superrealism.

Sotatsu, Nonomura died 1643
Japanese painter. Sotatsu was the proprietor of the Tawaraya fan shop in Kyoto, a vast treasury of fans, scrolls, screens and sliding doors for the rich merchant class and the nobility. Together with Koetsu, he brought about an artistic renaissance, looking back to the Heian period when Kyoto had been Japan's centre of government and culture. A great number of works are attributed to him, from *The elephant and lion* (c.1621) on the cedar doors in the Yogen temple, to the opulent Bugaku screens in the Samboin temple (both in Kyoto). Two dated works are certainly his—a fan depicting *Hamamatsu* (1607) and a scroll *Life of the priest Saigyo* (1630, formerly in the Mori collection). Sotatsu and his atelier completely revitalized the colourful YAMATO-E style and exerted an enormous influence on later artists, particularly Ogata Korin. See vol. 3 p. **47**

Soto, Jesus-Raphael born 1923
Venezuelan KINETIC artist, who with Cruz-Diez and Alejandro Otero pioneered the abstract art movement in Venezuela. In Paris from 1950, he was drawn to Russian Constructivism and the spatially suggestive works of Mondrian and Malevich. He began with relief constructions, using wood, wire and superim-

posed layers of perspex to suggest movement and optical vibration (as in *Spiral*, 1955, Krefeld Museum). He used kinetic elements for the first time in the series entitled *Vibrations*, begun in 1958, in which lengths of curved wire or fine metal rods are hung spatially in front of a field of closely meshed parallel lines. In the series *Penetrables* there are veils of hanging nylon threads or metal rods through which the spectator may walk. Soto has received numerous public commissions: the kinetic sculptures for the Venezuelan pavilion, Expo 67, Montreal, and the mural for UNESCO, in Paris, are among his finest. See vol. 3 p. **245**

Sotto in su, di
Italian term, meaning "from below upwards", used to describe foreshortening in ceiling painting when figures appear to be suspended in space above the viewer. It first occurs in 15th-century Italian art, notably in Mantegna's work at the Palazzo Ducale, Mantua.

Soulages, Pierre born 1919
French abstract painter. He began to paint seriously only in 1946, but he rapidly became one of the leading exponents of TACHISME. His first works were entirely in black and white but he began to introduce colour, albeit sombre greys, browns and blues, in 1953 (*May 23rd, 1953*, 1953, London, Tate). His paintings are built up with broad, powerful strokes; the effect is one of aggression and dynamism. Some of the monolithic forms Soulages uses resemble those of the Romanesque sculpture in his home region of the Massif Central, and his work is highly individualistic and distinctive. He has also worked as a theatre designer. See vol. 3 p. **224**

Soutine, Chaim 1893–1943
Russian EXPRESSIONIST painter, active in France from 1913. His intensely hard childhood in a Jewish town in Lithuania, and his difficult personality, are reflected in a strongly expressive, often highly coloured style, influenced by European Expressionist developments but also by his study of Old Masters in the Louvre. In Paris he studied at the Ecole des Beaux-Arts, and developed his characteristic style between 1919 and 1921 while staying in the South of France, using thick impasto to evoke energy and pathos in landscapes and portraits which sometimes recall Kokoschka (*The madwoman*, 1920, Tokyo, Rokubin Hayashi coll.). In the 1920s and 1930s in Paris he was associated with a circle of expatriate artists, including Chagall, Zadkine and Lipchitz. His portraits are particularly potent (*Self-portrait*, c.1922, Paris, Musée d'Art Moderne), often seeming to disintegrate the sitter to find the soul. His paintings have particularly influenced one of his great admirers, Francis Bacon. See vol. 3 p. **184**

Soyer, Moses 1899–1975
American painter, born in Russia. With his brother **Raphael** (born 1899) he concentrated on social realist subjects, portraits and intimate figure scenes. His quiet, unassuming style reflects the naturalism he admired in Rembrandt, while his ballet dancers of the 1940s recall Degas. Many of his figures seem to be imbued with a gentle air of melancholy. Raphael was also deeply involved with urban imagery. His style from the late 1920s onwards is naturalistic, with a restrained, loosely brushed handling, but during the Depression he favoured more overtly social realist themes (*Office girls*, 1936, New York, Whitney).

Spatialism see FONTANA

Spazzapan, Luigi 1890–1958
Italian painter. He moved to Turin in 1928 and came under the influence of Casorati. His early paintings were Fauvist in style but he gradually developed a form of visionary Expressionism characterized by vivid colour and light. He later controlled the violence of his colours with linear structures that organized and articulated his landscapes, still lifes and figure compositions.

Spencer, Niles 1893–1952
American PRECISIONIST painter. He is remembered for his austere canvases, such as *City walls* (1921, New York, MOMA), inspired by the formal relationships he saw in the cityscapes of New York, and painted in flat, bold colours.

Spencer, Sir Stanley 1891–1959
One of the most original, eccentric and distinctive of 20th-century British painters. The visionary quality of his paintings was apparent in his earliest work, which is distinguished by a combination of archaism and simplified sculptural modelling. His subjects were often from the Bible, but he set the scene in his native village of Cookham, Berkshire, using its inhabitants as protagonists. During World War I he worked with the Medical Corps and commemorated his experiences in a cycle of murals filling the Oratory of All Souls, Burghclere, Hampshire, 1927–31, and culminating in a depiction of mass resurrection. He rejected the concept of eternal damnation and in his vast canvas *The Resurrection, Cookham* (1923–27, London, Tate) the righteous merely rise from the grave with greater ease than the sinful. He painted a number of searching self-portraits and their tortured realism is also found in nude portraits painted between about 1929 and 1939 which express the sexual frustrations of his second marriage. *Double nude portrait: the artist and his second wife* (1936, Tate), which also contains a leg of mutton, is both erotic and repellent. His landscapes, which were for sale rather than for personal satisfaction, are more conventionally naturalistic. Spencer's brother **Gilbert** (1892–1979) was also a painter. See vol. 3 p. **199**

Spillaert, Leon 1881–1946
Belgian painter, chiefly a watercolourist. He was self-taught and adopted a style similar to that of the Nabis, with broad surfaces and undulating wavy lines. His works are dreamlike and he favoured sea and beach scenes (*Woman on the sea-wall*, 1908, Brussels, Musées Royaux des Beaux-Arts).

Spinello Aretino
documented 1385–1410
Italian painter, born in Arezzo. He was possibly a pupil of Agnolo Gaddi in Florence, but sought much of his inspiration directly from Giotto. He was one of the most productive painters of his period, filling numerous churches in Arezzo, Florence, Pisa and Siena with fresco cycles, often in collaboration with his son Parri Spinello. The best-known is perhaps the life of St Benedict in S. Miniato al Monte, Florence.

Spitzweg, Karl 1808–85
German painter, one of the main exponents of the BIEDERMEIER style. He was a self-taught painter who began by producing caricatures for the satirical magazine *Fliegende Blätter* (Flying leaves) in 1844. His comic and extremely human characters poke gentle fun at social

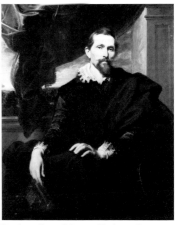
Snyders: Portrait by van Dyck, c.1620. New York, Frick

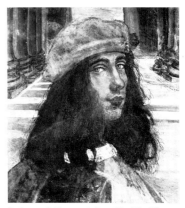
Sodoma: Self-portrait from *The life of St Benedict* fresco, 1506/07. Siena, Monte Oliveto Maggiore (Mansell)

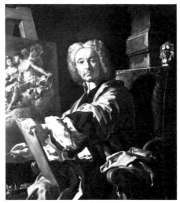
Solimena: Self-portrait, 1730–31. Florence, Uffizi (Alinari)

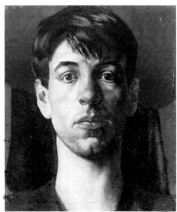
Spencer: Self-portrait, 1913. London, Tate

stereotypes and banal situations. Although his art did not aspire to great heights, his painterly use of light and colour and his ability to maintain mood without sentimentality show the influence of French painting and in particular the Barbizon school (*The laundresses*, c.1880, Darmstadt, Hessisches Landesmuseum).

Spranger, Bartholomeus
1546–1611
Flemish MANNERIST painter. He was born and trained in Antwerp, then had an international career, working in France, Italy and Vienna before settling in Prague (1581) in the service of Rudolf II. His paintings are highly polished and usually complex in composition, the figures deriving from a number of sources including Correggio and Parmigianino. Mythologies and allegories formed the bulk of his work, which became widely known through engravings. There is a fine collection of his paintings in the Kunsthistorisches Museum, Vienna, including an *Allegory of Rudolf II* (1592).

Squarcione, Francesco
1397–1468
Italian painter from Padua. His life is obscure but his workshop helped to make Padua an important artistic centre. As a determined collector and dealer in antiquities Squarcione disseminated interest in classical sculpture, a trend reinforced by the presence of a university in Padua, and by the influence of contemporary Florentine artists there, above all Donatello. His many pupils and assistants included Mantegna, Zoppo (who both broke their apprenticeships with him), Pizzolo, Cosimo Tura and perhaps Foppa. The lack of securely attributable works disallows firm assessment of his art, but works from his studio (such as a polyptych of 1449–52 in Padua, Museo Civico) are generally characterized by elaborate detail and a very dry, linear approach. See vol. 2 p. 120

Stabile see MOBILE

Staël, Nicolas de 1914–55
French/Russian painter, one of the most gifted and influential artists to emerge in France after World War II. He was born into a noble Russian family which emigrated to Poland in 1919. Brought up in Brussels, he attended the Academy of Fine Arts there, 1932–33, and settled in France in 1937 but continued to travel widely. Stimulated by his friendship with Braque, he began in the 1940s to develop his characteristic style in which juxtaposed patches of thick paint, subtly varied in colour, offer a pictorial equivalent for the experience of light and texture in nature. Arriving at a point of complete abstraction around 1950, he then reintroduced explicit references to landscape and still life, but was unable to reach to his satisfaction a compromise between representation and abstraction; but *The roofs* (1952, Paris, Musée d'Art Moderne) is outstanding. He committed suicide. See vol. 3 pp. **224–225**

Staffage
Figures and animals included as animating details in a painting which is essentially topographical. Especially in 17th-century Flanders and Holland, landscape painters often did not paint their own staffage; Poelenburgh and Teniers the Younger are two well-known artists who frequently performed this function for other painters.

Stamos, Theodoros born 1922
American painter of Greek parentage. Like Baziotes he began with evocative, biomorphic images suggestive of shells and flotsam, handling the paint with soft, subtle nuances (*Sounds in the rock*, 1946, New York, MOMA). His work of the 1950s became more abstract, suggestive rather than symbolic. In the *Infinity* series of the late 1960s he used sweeping, open washes of colour, but he later returned to more complex forms.

Stanfield, William Clarkson
1793–1867
English marine and landscape painter. After an early career as a sailor he became a stage designer, creating spectacular dioramas for Drury Lane Theatre. From 1829 he devoted himself to seascapes, which, although rather flat and conventional in composition, are notable for their renderings of the nuances of colour and light of the sea (*On the Dogger Bank*, 1846, London, V&A). His Romantic seascapes and naval paintings were popular but never achieved Turner's unity of composition or power.

Stanzione, Massimo 1586–1656
One of the leading Neapolitan painters of the first half of the 17th century. His style was formed on that of Caravaggesque painters such as Caracciolo and Ribera, but was modified to such an extent by Bolognese classicism that he has been called "the Neapolitan Guido Reni". Most of his work is still to be found in Naples, in churches and in the Museo di Capodimonte. Cavallino was his most important pupil.

Starnina, Gherardo died 1413
Italian painter, trained in the International Gothic manner. He was chiefly active in Florence, where he is first documented in 1387. Vasari regarded him as an innovator, and his surviving oeuvre does not adequately represent his achievement. His work in Spain (in Toledo, 1398, and Valencia, 1401) is lost. He painted frescos (badly damaged) in S. Stefano, Empoli and in S. Maria del Carmine and S. Croce in Florence. The fragments of the Florentine frescos demonstrate a reverence for Giotto which may have influenced or anticipated Masaccio. A panel painting of *The Thebaid* (Florence, Uffizi) is often attributed to Starnina—monastic figures are scattered in an artificial landscape of rocks and crags.

State
Term used in printmaking to identify the working stage of a plate or block at the time a print or trial proof is taken. Editions may be made from a number of successive states, each of altered design.

Stażewski, Henryk born 1894
Polish artist. In 1924 he helped to found the group and magazine *Blok*, which was based on Constructivist principles. His work at this time was geometrically abstract and showed the influence of Neo-Plasticism. In the 1930s he spent much time in Paris, where he met Mondrian. In 1929 he joined CIRCLE ET CARRÉ and in 1932 ABSTRACTION-CRÉATION. He moved from Constructivist black and white works to white reliefs, and in the 1960s began to introduce brilliant colour to his geometrical compositions. *White-black relief* (1962, London, Tate) is a small panel.

Steadman, Ralph born 1937
British illustrator. He has provided witty, satirical cartoons for many leading political magazines and has also illustrated a number of books. His drawings are swiftly yet precisely executed, the figures distorted often to the point of grotesqueness. See vol. 3 p. *255*

Steen, Jan 1626–79
One of the most prolific Dutch genre painters of the 17th century, whose robust good humour has won him great popularity. He was born in Leyden, the son of a brewer (Steen later ran a tavern), and seems to have studied with Adriaen van Ostade in Haarlem and Jan van Goyen (his future father-in-law) at The Hague. Steen led a varied life and worked in several Dutch towns, although not, so far as is known, in Amsterdam. This restlessness is reflected in his paintings, which vary greatly in subject from lyrical outdoor scenes such as *The skittle players* (c.1660, London, NG) to genteel interiors such as *The morning toilet* (1663, Royal coll.), and to riotous festive gatherings such as *The egg dance* (c.1675, London, Wellington Museum). They vary also in quality (about 800 paintings are attributed to him), but at his best he showed remarkable powers of invention and composition (particularly in his multi-figure scenes) and a technique of sparkling freshness. Although Steen's paintings often seem anything but serious, many include moralizing allusions. He was a Catholic, and throughout his life painted some religious paintings, which usually have a genre quality. See vol. 2 p. **227**

Steenwyck, Hendrick van the Elder died 1603? and **Hendrick van the Younger** died 1649
Flemish painters of architectural views, father and son. The peripatetic careers of both men are obscure at many points, but Hendrick and Elder is usually considered to be the first artist to have specialized in views of church interiors. Among them are fairly factual renderings of real buildings (*Aachen Cathedral*, 1573, Munich, Alte Pinakothek), but more often they are invented views, sometimes night scenes of considerable poetic feeling. Both types were taken up by his son, one of whose outstanding works is *The liberation of St Peter* (1621, Vienna, Kunsthistorisches), an eerie nocturnal scene in which the prison is a church crypt.

Steer, Philip Wilson 1860–1942
British painter. A founder-member of the NEW ENGLISH Art Club in 1886, he was profoundly influenced by Impressionism and took part in the 1889 London Impressionist exhibition organized by Sickert, a close associate at this time. His most enduring paintings are the beach scenes and seascapes of the late 1880s, and early 1890s, in which he absorbed the influence of Whistler, Manet and Degas and suffused his work with subtle effects of light (*The beach at Boulogne*, 1892, London, Tate). Some of this freshness is lost in the paintings after 1895, which look self-consciously back to older styles. See vol. 3 p. **154**

Stefano da Verona or **da Zevio**
c.1375–after 1438
Italian painter of the Veronese school, a pupil of Altichiero. Unlike most of his contemporaries he adopted a style shaped by northern INTERNATIONAL GOTHIC art without any marked local accent. His figures, as in his *Adoration of the Magi* (Milan, Brera) and *The Virgin in a rose garden* (c.1405, Worcester Art Museum, Mass.) lack substance, their tiny heads and sweeping draperies accentuating already elongated proportions. See vol. 2 p. **89**

Stein, Leo (1872–1947) and **Gertrude** (1874–1946)
American collectors, brother and sister, whose salon at 27 rue de Fleurus was, between 1903 and the outbreak of World War I, one of the most distinguished in Paris. Through the Steins (Gertrude was a writer), many American artists studying in Paris were introduced to modern French art and met such painters as Matisse, Picasso and Delaunay.

Steinberg, Saul born 1914
American painter, graphic artist and cartoonist, born in Romania. He studied architecture in Milan and has lived in New York since 1942. He is best known for his cartoons, especially those which have appeared regularly in the *New Yorker* magazine. His drawings are precise and fine with a somewhat whimsical distortion of reality and an often biting, satirical intent.

Steinlen, Théophile-Alexandre
1859–1923
French painter and graphic artist, who was born in Switzerland but took French citizenship. He worked on social subjects, especially satirical pieces for socialist periodicals. Now dated, like *The laundresses* (c.1900, Washington, NG of Art), his paintings are rarely seen today.

Stella, Frank born 1936
American painter. He began in an Abstract Expressionist mode, but then led the way toward the systematic, rigorously formal methods which dominated painting of the 1960s. Elementary pictorial structure is at issue in his first exhibited all-black paintings, in which successive diamond-shaped stripes echo the central lozenge (*Jill*, 1963, Buffalo, Albright-Knox). The idea of the abstract painting as an object rather than a metaphor for a metaphysical or emotional state is clearly expressed in his shaped canvases, which he developed in the 1960s. As he explored other geometric shapes and combinations—concentric circles, irregular polygons, protractors—he reintroduced colour. The potential exuberance of his bright, artificial colours, highly controlled in the striped paintings, came to the fore in the early 1970s, when he introduced three-dimensional supports. More recent works, such as *Guadalupe Island* (1979, London, Tate), are composed of curved and angular wood and metal planes splashed with paint and glitter, exhibiting growing freedom and wit. See vol. 1 p. *153*; vol. 3 p. **223**

Stella, Jacques 1596–1657
French history painter and engraver. From 1619 to 1634 he lived in Florence, where he worked for Duke Cosimo II, and later in Rome he came under the influence of Poussin. On his return to France he became one of Poussin's most faithful followers, producing competent but rather cold works such as *The Adoration of the shepherds* (1639, Barnard Castle, Bowes Museum).

Stella, Joseph 1877–1946
American painter. Born in Italy, he emigrated to the USA in 1896. In 1909 he revisited Italy and he was in Paris from 1911 to 1912, where he met the Futurists. Their influence on his work is clear in one of his most famous paintings, the dynamic *Battle of lights, Coney Island* (1914, Yale, University Art Gallery). Although soon rejecting Futurism, Stella remained attracted to mechanical and city themes. *The bridge* (1926, Newark Museum of Art) is painted in a Precisionist style. See vol. 3 p. **205**

Stenberg, Georgii 1900–33
and Vladimir born 1899
Russian artists, brothers who worked closely together until the accidental death of Georgii. In post-Revolutionary Moscow they were among the founders of the Society of Young Artists (*Obmokhu*), the members of which followed Tatlin's non-utilitarian approach to sculpture, but the Stenbergs exhibited their *Structures* independently under the label CONSTRUCTIVIST in 1921. Some of these have been reconstructed (Canberra, NG of Australia) and show an investigation of the dynamic properties of materials such as iron and glass. They are surprisingly monumental considering their small scale. The brothers also made a significant contribution to Constructivist graphic design with their lively film and theatre posters of the 1920s.

Stern, Irma 1894–1966
South African painter. She studied in Germany from 1913 to 1920 (she was a founder-member of the NOVEMBER-GRUPPE), and her work was influenced by the Expressionists, particularly Pechstein, whom she met in 1916. On her return to South Africa she became established as a major painter and introduced current European trends. Her paintings recall van Gogh in their use of warm, vibrant colours and vital, rhythmic forms (*Fishing boats*, 1931, Pretoria Art Museum).

Sterne, Maurice 1878–1957
American painter and sculptor. In the mid-1930s he worked on murals for the Department of Justice, Washington DC, but is best remembered for his decorative paintings of Bali such as *Bali bazaar* (1913–14, New York, Whitney), which are reminiscent of Gauguin's work. In 1933 he was the first American artist to be given a one-man show at the Museum of Modern Art, New York.

Stevens, Alfred 1817–75
English sculptor, painter, decorator and architectural designer, one of the greatest artists of the Victorian period. He studied in Italy from 1833 to 1842, working with Thorvaldsen for a year. His stay instilled his style with the monumental grandeur of High Renaissance art, and many of his drawings reflect a deep admiration for Raphael. On his return to England he gained little recognition until in 1858 he began work on the monument to the Duke of Wellington in St Paul's Cathedral, London. This structure, to which he devoted most of the rest of his life, was adorned with massive figures exuding calm. It was uncompleted at his death. Also for St Paul's, he designed some splendid mosaics. See vol. 3 p. **106**

Stevens, Alfred Emile 1823–1906
Belgian painter, active mainly in Paris. He was at first influenced by narrative painting and realism, and *Vagabondage* (1855, Compiègne, Musée National) caused a political stir when it was exhibited. By 1857, however, he was concentrating on depicting refined young ladies, in elegant interiors, admiring pictures or oriental *objets d'art* (*The visitors*, Williamstown, Clark Art Institute), and was immensely successful. His work seems highly conventional to later eyes, but Stevens responded to Baudelaire's call for modern subjects and also promoted the work of Manet, Jongkind and Boudin. He also influenced Tissot, Whistler and Sargent. After 1880 he moved to the coast for the sake of his health and painted numerous marine pictures.

Stieglitz, Alfred 1864–1946
American photographer and gallery owner who contributed more than any other individual to the development of modern art in America. The pages of his photographic journal *Camera Work* (1903–17) were open to articles relevant to contemporary art and, between 1908 and 1917, he showed the work of some of the most advanced European artists at his gallery in Fifth Avenue, New York (known as the **291 Gallery**). Here the American public was introduced to the work of Matisse, Rodin and Le Douanier Rousseau, and to major one-man shows of Picasso (1911), Picabia (1913) and Brancusi (1914). After World War I Stieglitz continued to support the work of such native artists as Hartley, Marin and O'Keeffe (his wife) at his Intimate Gallery and An American Place. Much of his collection was donated to the Art Institute of Chicago. See vol. 3 p. 205

Stifter, Adalbert 1805–68
Austrian painter, better known as a writer. He was self-taught and began painting and drawing mainly for the purpose of illustration. His painting was not admired during his lifetime, partly because his small-scale works lacked the heroic and monumental spirit admired in Vienna during the Romantic period, and partly because of their unusual freedom, which can be seen in his various cloud studies and landscapes in the museum devoted to his work in Vienna.

Stijl, De
Dutch group of artists and architects, formed in 1917. The members included the painters Mondrian, van der Leck, Huszar and van Doesburg—who edited their journal, also called *De Stijl*—and the architects Oud, Rietveld and Wils, the sculptor Vantongerloo and the poet Kok. The ideology on which De Stijl (meaning "the style") was based was **Neo-Plasticism**—a theory evolved by Mondrian for a "new plastic art" expressive of universal harmony. The painters restricted themselves to pictorial elements which they felt had universal validity and could convey the order and harmony which they saw as the goal of life. These were the straight line and the rectangle, the primary colours and the non-colours—black and white and grey. All their work was austerely abstract. Although committed to Neo-Plasticism, the journal also published Dadaist contributions as well as discussions of film, architecture, poetry and prose. It continued until 1932. In painting and architecture De Stijl exerted a profound influence throughout Europe and America. See vol. 3 pp. 186–187

Still, Clyfford 1904–80
American painter, associated with both Abstract Expressionism and colour-field painting. Still's work resists categorization. His early landscapes and distorted figures gave way to more abstract paintings with mythical, even apocalyptic, suggestions. By 1947 he had arrived at his mature style, in which jagged-edged areas of knifed-on colour interlock and completely cover the picture plane. The texture in a single painting can range from glossy to matt, and colour accents may be widely contrasting in hue, as in *Painting* (1951, New York, MOMA). Still, however, was also one of the first artists to produce monochromatic paintings, sometimes almost completely black. About 1950 he moved towards extremely large-scale works. His distinctive style began to be assimilated by younger painters only in the late 1960s. See vol. 3 p. **215**

Stimmer, Tobias 1539–84
German painter and designer of woodcuts. He was strongly influenced by Italian Mannerist art, and may have visited Italy, but he is first recorded at Schaffhausen, where he decorated the exteriors of houses with illusionistic mythologies, 1568–70. In 1570 he went to Strasbourg and produced woodcut illustrations in a bold, broadly outlined style. He also painted many portraits.

Stone, Nicholas 1587?–1647
English sculptor, mason and architect. He trained in London and in the Amsterdam workshop of Hendrik de Keyser, whose daughter he married. On his return to England (1613) he rapidly became the most prolific and distinguished English sculptor of his day, producing a series of monuments of notable originality (Bodley monument, 1615, Oxford, Merton College). His later work (Lyttelton monument, 1634, Oxford, Magdalen College) shows an increasing awareness of classical and Italian Renaissance sculpture. The shrouded effigy of the poet John Donne (1631) in St Paul's Cathedral, London, is his most famous work. His sons **John** (1620–67) and **Nicholas** (1618–47) worked as his assistants. We are exceptionally well informed about Stone's practice, as a notebook and account book survive (London, Soane Museum).

Stoss, Veit c.1450–1533
German sculptor of Swabian origin, with Riemenschneider the leading German late GOTHIC sculptor. After initially working in Nuremberg, in 1477 he left for Cracow, where he carved the massive polychromed altarpiece of *The death of the Virgin* (completed 1489) for St Mary's, the church of the German merchants there. This, his most famous work, is less elaborate in form than the altarpieces of his contemporaries, concentrating on the emotional characterization of the figures. While in Cracow he also carved the red marble tomb of King Casimir IV (1492, Cracow Cathedral). In 1496 he returned to Nuremberg, where he ran a successful workshop and received many commissions for monuments and altarpieces. However, his career was severely upset by his trial for fraud and forgery, which resulted in the restriction of his freedom by the city fathers. One of his last great works is the huge altar for the Carmelite Church of Nuremberg (1520–23, now in Bamberg Cathedral), carved in his characteristic highly ornate and calligraphic style. Towards the end of his life, however, in the religious uncertainties of the 1520s, he seems to have turned to making small wooden statuettes of religious subjects in a more subdued, personal manner. Vasari recorded the admiration which the brilliant, late Gothic virtuosity of his St Roch (c.1520–21, Florence, SS. Annunziata) aroused even in Italy. See vol. 1 p. *176*; vol. 3 pp. **158–159**

Stothard, Thomas 1755–1834
English NEOCLASSICAL painter. Highly prolific, he was also a book illustrator and a designer of stone monuments, metalwork and jewellery. His history paintings tended to be small-scale narrative pieces in the conventional Neoclassical manner, influenced in style by his friend Flaxman, particularly in the use of line, although in general they are sweeter. Two major decorative pieces were *The horrors of war* (1799–1802) for the walls of the staircase under the Verrio ceiling at Burghley House, and the painted cupola of the Upper Hall of the Advocates' Library, Edinburgh (1822).

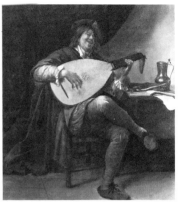

Steen: Self-portrait, c.1661–63. Lugano, Thyssen-Bornemisza coll.

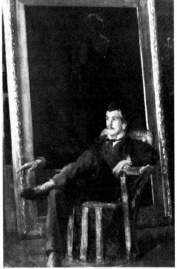

Steer: Portrait by Sickert, c.1895. London, NPG

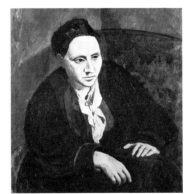

Stein: Portrait by Picasso, 1906. New York, Metropolitan

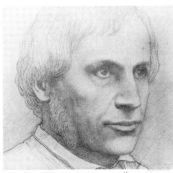

Stevens, Alfred: Posthumous silverpoint portrait by Legros, 1907 (Mansell)

Streeter the Elder, Robert (Streater) 1624?–79
English painter. He painted various types of pictures, but was best known for his decorative work. Most of this has been destroyed, but the largest survives, the allegorical ceiling (1668/9) in the Sheldonian Theatre, Oxford. This is a rather ponderous work, but noteworthy as the most ambitious piece of Baroque decoration by an Englishman before Thornhill. Other surviving paintings include landscapes in the Royal Collection and at Dulwich College Picture Gallery, and a portrait of *Sir Francis Prujean* in the Royal College of Physicians, London. Streeter was appointed Serjeant Painter in 1660, and his son **Robert** (died 1711) followed him in this office.

Stretes, Guillim see SCROTES

Strigel, Bernhard *c.*1460–1528
German painter. Nothing is known of his training, but in the 1490s he worked with Zeitblom and is documented at Memmingen from 1508. Later he became court painter to the Emperor Maximilian and his profile portrait of the Emperor became the official likeness. The full-length group portrait of *Conrad Rehlinger and his family* (1517, Munich, Alte Pinakothek), in which the flat, elongated figures are closely grouped together, shows his late Gothic style. He also painted religious works.

Strindberg, August 1849–1912
Swedish writer and painter. He is best known as one of the greatest European dramatists of his period, but he also wrote art criticism and painted landscapes. He regarded landscape as reflecting a state of mind. His art originated from Turner and tended towards later trends such as Expressionism (*The town*, Stockholm, Nationalmuseum).

Strozzi, Bernardo 1581–1644
The leading Genoese painter of the early 17th century. He was a Capuchin monk (hence his nicknames "Il Prete Genovese" and "Il Cappucino"), but in 1610 he gained permission to leave his convent to support his widowed mother. After her death in 1630 he resisted pressure to return and in 1631 moved to Venice, where he continued his successful career, there being little native competition at this time. The distinctive richness of his colour and handling was influenced by Rubens and van Dyck, who both worked in Genoa, and, after his move to Venice, by Feti and Liss. The other main characteristic of his work is the vein of tenderness which ran through almost everything he did (*Pietà*, *c.*1620, Genoa, Palazzo Bianco). Apart from religious works, he also painted genre scenes and was a fine portraitist.

Strzemiński, Vladislav 1893–1952
Polish painter and theoretician. He was born in Russia, studied in Moscow and met Malevich in Vitebsk. In 1915 he was wounded, losing an arm and a leg, and while in hospital met **Katarzyna Kobro** (1898–1950), a prominent sculptress, whom he married. They moved to Poland in 1922, became involved in Polish avantgarde activities and were founder-members of the CONSTRUCTIVIST group Blok. Strzemiński's earliest work was influenced by Cubism, but he moved on to Neo-Plasticism. After 1945 he explored the after-image of the sun in a series of vividly coloured canvases (*The sun's afterglow*, 1948–49, Warsaw, NG).

Stuart, Gilbert 1755–1828
With Copley the most celebrated American portrait painter of his period. His career was peripatetic and he worked in England, Scotland and Ireland as well as in various cities in America. When he settled permanently in America in 1792, his fluid painterly technique and convincing characterization (West said he "*nails* the face to the canvas") quickly established him as the finest portraitist of his day—"court painter" to the leading figures of the new republic. Above all he is famous for his portraits of George Washington. He originated three types, all of which were produced in numerous versions in his studio; the "Vaughan" type (1795, Washington, NG), the "Lansdowne" type (1796, Philadelphia, Pennsylvania Academy of Fine Arts), and the "Athenaeum" type (1796, Boston, MFA). They all became national icons, and it is the Athenaeum head which is used on the American one dollar bill. See vol. 3 pp. **58–59**

Stubbs, George 1724–1806
British animal painter and engraver, celebrated chiefly as the greatest of horse painters. He was almost entirely self-taught as an artist, and while earning his early living as a portraitist in the north of England devoted himself to his real passion, which was anatomy. In 1759 he settled in London, and after a journey to Italy and Morocco published in 1766 his book *Anatomy of the Horse*, illustrated with his own engravings, which are remarkable for their accuracy as well as their beauty. The book's successful reception made his career, and he was soon in demand for his "portraits" of horses, often shown with their owners or grooms. Stubbs, however, stood far above the average sporting painter of his day. Apart from his matchless command of anatomy, he was also supreme in depicting the beauty of horses' glossy coats, and he was able to convey the nobility of animals without sentimentalizing them. Stubbs was also varied in mood, for while *Mares and foals in a river landscape* (1763–68, London, Tate) is lyrical in feeling in keeping with its Neo-classical purity of line, *Horses attacked by a lion* (1770, New Haven, Yale University Art Gallery) strikes a highly Romantic chord. Among the other animals Stubbs painted were a kangaroo, a rhinoceros and a zebra, and he also made preparations for *A Comparative Anatomical Exposition of the Human Body with that of a Tiger and a Common Fowl* (1795–1805, Public Library, Worcester, Mass.). Stubbs also experimented with painting on enamel, and the great potter Josiah Wedgwood made some fine panels from his designs. See vol. 1 pp. *42*, *69*, *167*; vol. 2 p. **251**

Stucco
Light, malleable type of reinforced plaster, used for architectural decoration and for sculpture. It was used in Roman and medieval times for both purposes, but it was fully exploited only in the Mannerist, Baroque and Rococo periods when architectural decoration and figurative sculpture were fused in elaborate schemes.

Stuck, Franz von 1863–1928
German painter, the most prominent exponent of the Munich school of JUGENDSTIL. He studied in Munich and was one of a group of avantgarde painters who founded the SEZESSION in 1892. His chief motif was the female nude, rendered with highly academic draughtsmanship but always endowed with a quality that is at once decorative, erotic and mysterious. The sinuous linearity of his work, so typical of Jugendstil art, can be seen in *The sphinx* (1904, Darmstadt, Hessisches Landesmuseum), portraying against a mysterious landscape not the half-bird, half-woman of myth, but a sultry, naturalistic nude with forearms extended in the pose of an Egyptian sphinx. Very popular in his day, he lived in a house of his own design (today the Stuck Museum, Munich) in an ambience of sensuous Jugendstil decor.

Sturm, Der (The assault)
Name of a periodical and also a gallery, both founded in Berlin by Herwarth Walden (1878–1941?), a composer and man of letters, to promote avantgarde developments in the arts in Germany. The first edition of the magazine featured drawings by Kokoschka; in 1911 works by Die Brücke, and in 1912 works by Der Blaue Reiter artists. The year the gallery opened, 1912, Walden showed Der Blaue Reiter and other German Expressionists, in addition to introducing the German public to Futurism and Orphism. The "First German Salon d'Automne" held at the gallery in 1913 was his crowning achievement, bringing together 85 avantgarde artists from 12 countries. See vol. 3 p. 135

Subleyras, Pierre-Hubert 1699–1749
French history painter. After winning the Prix de Rome he left for Rome in 1728 and never returned. He was a fine portraitist but his fame rests on his religious works, which owe much in technique to Solimena and have a seriousness rare in French art of this period (*The mass of St Basil*, Rome, S. Maria degli Angeli). Many of his works appear in *The painter's studio* (after 1740, Vienna, Akademie).

Sugai, Kumi born 1919
Japanese painter, living in Paris since 1952. In the 1950s he moved towards colourful abstract paintings made of simple forms on a plain background. *Festival of Tokyo* (1969, Tokyo, National Museum of Modern Art) is a tripartite composition of curvilinear striped and rectangular shapes.

Suger, Abbot 1081–1151
French churchman, one of the most celebrated patrons of his day. In rebuilding the abbey of St-Denis near Paris he was practically responsible for the introduction of the GOTHIC style in sculpture and architecture. Unusually, he wrote a detailed account of the rebuilding and decoration of his abbey church, but with few comments on its novel stylistic features. Among the liturgical vessels he ordered for St-Denis, the Eagle Vase (Paris, Louvre) shows clearly his love of antique art. His rapturous contemplation of the beauties of his church, which led his thoughts to a higher world, contrasts with the contemporary Cistercian ideals of austerity. See vol. 2 p. 76

Sukenobu, Nishikawa 1671–1751
Japanese UKIYO-E artist, born in Kyoto and active there all his life. He took lessons from Kano and Tosa masters and studied the works of designers in Edo (Tokyo), Kyoto, and Osaka. His prints remain mostly in book illustrations, but he has left many hand-painted *ukiyo-e*. His album *Spring Rain* has rare *beni-e* prints (hand-coloured, predominantly in a tawny yellow shade). On achieving popularity, he often gave himself the title *yamato eshi* (master of Japanese paintings), wanting to promote the pure Japanese style in place of the Chinese styles more highly regarded by connoisseurs. He illustrated erotic and pornographic books, but fell foul of government censorship in 1723. There is a theory that Harunobu was his pupil.

Sully, Thomas 1783–1872
The leading American portrait painter of his generation. He was born in England and made trips there in 1809 (when he visited West) and 1838 (when he painted Queen Victoria), but was active mainly in Philadelphia. His fluid brushwork and expressive use of light and shade, derived from Lawrence, won Sully deserved popularity. He painted more than 2,000 portraits and also history paintings, of which *Washington crossing the Delaware* (1819, Boston, MFA) is the best-known.

Sultan Muhammad active *c.*1520–45
Persian or eastern Turkish painter working in Tabriz, where he gave lessons to the young Shah Tahmasp. His signature is incorporated into illustrations in a *Divan* of Hafiz of about 1530 (Cambridge, Fogg). His authorship of the page depicting *The court of Gayumars* in the *Shahnameh* in the Houghton Collection (Queenstown, Md) is also virtually certain, while certain pages of the *Khamseh* of 1539–43 (London, BL) are attributed to him. His style is characterized by a unique combination of majesty of conception and humour in the rendering of detail which owes much to the great master Bihzad. See vol. 3 p. **27**

Sumerian art
Art of the Sumerian people in southern Mesopotamia. The Sumerian civilization of the 3rd millennium BC was that of an urbanized and literate people whose ancestors had already inhabited the region for about 2,000 years. In the late 4th millennium the Sumerians were already master craftsmen in stone, as the *Head of Inanna* from Uruk shows (East Berlin, Pergamon Museum). Their expertise in mosaic inlay, using coloured mud to simulate woven hangings, is still evident in the decoration of the Pillar Court at Uruk. In the 3rd millennium Sumerian artists excelled in many fields, making attractive votive statuettes in stone, for example the group of figures from the Abu temple at Tell Asmar (Baghdad, Iraqi Museum, and University of Chicago, Oriental Institute). They also used the lost-wax method to create charming figures in bronze. Their skill in stone relief carving is seen at its best in the Stela of the Vultures (Paris, Louvre), the record of a king's victory in battle. Most famous of all, the royal tombs of Ur of about 2600 BC, excavated in the 1920s, have given us magnificent works in silver and gold; the Helmet of Meskalam-dug (Baghdad, Iraqi Museum) is only one. The Standard of Ur (London, BM) shows us the full beauty of mosaic inlay on wood, as do several of the great harps, such as the one in the University of Pennsylvania Museum, Philadelphia. The care lavished on these and on the intaglio designs of that peculiarly Sumerian invention, the cylinder seal, shows us how much each tiny piece of imported stone was prized in the stoneless south. Many aspects of Sumerian civilization were emulated by their MESOPOTAMIAN successors, but their skill and vigour were not surpassed. See vol. 2 p. 28

Sung Dynasty see SONG DYNASTY

Superrealism
Style of figurative painting or sculpture prominent in the USA and Britain during the late 1960s and the 1970s. Its subject matter is usually banal, static and con-

temporary, and reproduced with minute exactitude, a high finish and a smooth and bland surface. Superrealist paintings often resemble photographs, hence the alternative term **Photorealism**. Superrealism, however, is not naturalism: its aim is to generate an acute sense of unreality by presenting its subject with hallucinatory particularity. Thus the scale is often altered—Chuck Close magnifies small snapshots while Duane Hanson makes slightly less than life-size facsimiles of contemporary American bourgeois. Other important Superrealists are Eddy, Estes, Goings and Morley. See vol. 3 pp. 252–253

Suprematism
Radical, non-objective style of painting, evolved in Russia by Malevich around 1913. In contrast to CONSTRUCTIVISM, which was developing in Russia at the same time, Suprematism stressed the spiritual values of abstract art: "By Suprematism I mean the supremacy of pure feeling or perception in the pictorial arts", stated Malevich. The first paintings in the style were exhibited in 1915—they are characterized by geometric shapes on a white background and range from the austere, startling *Black square* (1915, Leningrad, Russian Museum) to others suggestive of movement in an infinite space (*Suprematist painting*, 1916, Amsterdam, Stedelijk). Malevich recognized a relationship between Suprematism, the Neo-Plasticism of Mondrian and the architecture of Gropius and Le Corbusier. See vol. 3 p. 157

Surikov, Vassily Ivanovich
1848–1916
Russian painter. He was born in Siberia and studied at the St Petersburg Academy. In 1877 he moved to Moscow, where he worked on the decoration of the Cathedral of Our Saviour but soon embarked on his first important historical picture, *The morning of the Streletz execution under Peter the Great* (1881–83, Moscow, Tretyakov Gallery). In this and others which followed he assembled huge crowds of individuals, each reacting in their own way, to create a psychological drama on an enormous scale. Surikov was also a strong colourist, and achieved universal recognition as the best historical painter of his period.

Surrealism
French avantgarde movement, literary in origin and led by the poet André Breton. Its sources of inspiration were the nihilistic ideas of the Dadaists and a French poetic tradition including Lautréamont and later Apollinaire, which acknowledged the supremacy of irrational association and imaginative insight. The aims of the movement, set out in Breton's *Manifesto of Surrealism* (1924), stimulated two approaches amongst affiliated artists, both influenced by Freud's theories of psychoanalysis. Some, on the one hand, pursued "automatism". In their work of the mid-1920s, Miró, Ernst and Masson, for example, on the analogy of the psychotherapeutic procedure of "free association", invented unorthodox spontaneous techniques as a means to eliminate conscious control and so express the workings of the unconscious mind. On the other hand, an interest in dreams, for Freud "the royal road to the Unconscious", inspired Magritte, Dali and Tanguy to look back to Chirico's Metaphysical painting and adapt a "realistic" style to the precise delineation of bizarre, dislocated imagery. Surrealism was a vital force in European art of the 1920s and 1930s. Then, during the War

years, many adherents moved to the USA, where they made a profound impact upon New York painters such as Gorky and Pollock. See vol. 3 pp. 172–177

Su Shi 1036–1101
Chinese statesman, poet, calligrapher and amateur artist. Although no authenticated examples of his work survive, he played a key role in Chinese painting, as the embodiment of Song-dynasty scholarly sensibilities. He was a leading member, and a friend of most of its great men, of the brilliant 11th-century generation which set the seal on the transition from Tang ideals of a vigorous, aristocratic culture to the more humanistic, more literary ideals of the Song. He possessed a mastery of numerous skills while avoiding the vulgarity of being a specialist in any one of them. He was a great poet, and a great calligrapher whose colophons are an integral part of the monochrome bamboo paintings of his friend Wen Tong. See vol. 3 p. 41

Su Shih see SU SHI

Sustermans or **Suttermans, Justus**
1597–1681
Flemish painter of portraits and religious and historical scenes, active chiefly in Florence. He was born in Antwerp and worked in the studio of Frans Pourbus II in Paris, before going (1619/20) to Italy, where he was employed as court painter to the Grand Dukes of Tuscany. He worked in a glossy international court style derived from van Dyck, and he had an enormous reputation as a portraitist, being called to Austria and possibly Spain, as well as to numerous Italian capitals, to execute commissions. He is well represented in Florence.

Sutherland, Graham 1903–80
British painter and graphic artist, whose varied achievements made him one of the leading figurative artists of the 20th century. He first studied engraving, and his etchings of the 1920s are reminiscent of Palmer's work. From 1934 onwards he embarked on a series of oils and watercolours, often exploiting vivid reds and oranges, based on the landscape around Pembroke, Wales. These combined observation of the unusual local effects of light with an awareness of Continental modernism. He exhibited at the 1936 London Surrealist exhibition. Toward the end of the 1930s he evolved a kind of landscape painting based not on the view but on a selective and heightened response to individual features, as in *Entrance to a lane* (1939, London, Tate). His anthropometric treatment of trees and plants culminated in *The Crucifixion* commissioned for St Matthew's, Northampton, in 1948, and Sutherland is also well-known for his religious work, above all for the huge tapestry of *Christ in glory* (completed 1962) in Coventry Cathedral. During World War II he was an official war artist. After 1947 he worked mainly on the French Riviera, his painting showing the influence of Mediterranean subject matter. His many portraits, for instance that of *Somerset Maugham* (1949, Tate), often verge on caricature. The most notorious, that of *Winston Churchill* (1954) was hated by its subject and subsequently destroyed by Lady Churchill. See vol. 3 pp. **198–199**

Suvero, Mark di born 1933
American sculptor, born in China. In 1941 he moved to San Francisco, but left for New York in the late 1950s. His first one-man show in New York was held in 1960. Until the mid-1960s he was

known for his huge constructions made of weathered wooden beams, rope, chains and tyres, some of them with mobile seats inviting spectator participation (*Hankchampion*, 1960, New York, Whitney). In the later 1960s he began to turn to steel constructions with clean lines, and his work of the 1970s is even more pared down.

Swart van Groningen, Jan
c.1500–*c*.1555
Netherlandish painter and engraver. He came to Antwerp from the north-east in about 1520. In Antwerp, he made a name for himself through his book illustrations, particularly those for a Dutch Bible published in 1528. These were heavily influenced by Dürer and Lucas van Leyden, although Swart's technique was far more cursory. In about 1530 he moved to Gouda, and concentrated on stained-glass painting. A distinctive feature of his work is his predilection for giving his figures bizarre headgear.

Sweerts, Michiel 1624–64
Flemish painter, one of the most charmingly idiosyncratic artists of his time. He was born in Brussels, and in the 1640s and 1650s spent about a decade in Rome. There he came into contact with the Bamboccianti, but Sweerts' paintings in their manner stand out above those of any of his contemporaries because of their exquisite tonality and mood of gentle melancholy (*Peasant scene*, The Hague, Mauritshuis). In Rome he also painted interior views of artists' studios which give a fascinating insight into studio practice of the time (examples, Amsterdam, Rijksmuseum, and Detroit Institute of Arts). By 1656 Sweerts was back in Brussels, then is documented in Amsterdam in 1661, before he left for the Orient as a missionary, only to be dismissed as unsuitable. He died at Goa in India. In his later years Sweerts seems to have concentrated on portraits, which like his other work are distinguished by a restrained lyricism of mood and colour harmonies—pale blues, lilacs, greys and browns—of the greatest delicacy. *Portrait of a boy* (*c*.1660, Hartford, Wadsworth Atheneum) stands comparison with Vermeer.

Symbolism
Movement in art providing an intellectual alternative to the purely visual painting of the Impressionists. It flourished principally in France during the 1880s and 1890s, although its currents spread throughout Europe—and admitted the Romantics and the Pre-Raphaelites as its spiritual ancestors. Symbolist painting should be distinguished from allegory: its iconic forms were not intended as concrete equivalents of ideas or emotions, but rather as ambiguous evocations of them. The subject matter of a picture was to be suggested rather than understood. To this end, two distinct methods were employed. Literary painters, such as Moreau, Redon and Puvis de Chavannes, were inspired by the striking imagery of Symbolist writers—in particular, the *femme fatale*, the severed head, the androgyne and the gaudy trappings of esoteric religious sects. In time, the imaginative juxtapositions in these works inspired the Surrealists. Alternatively, there was the formal approach, in which decorative, linear stylizations and evocative pure colours were used to create emotional effects. Gauguin, van Gogh and the Nabis were the chief practitioners of this process and their studies paved the way for the development of Expressionist and abstract art. See vol. 3 pp. 122–123

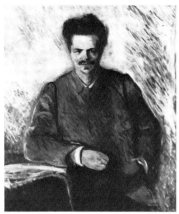

Strindberg: Portrait by Munch, 1892. Stockholm, Moderna Museet

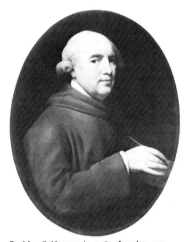

Stubbs: Self-portrait, 1781. London, NPG

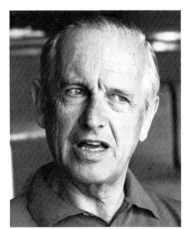

Sutherland: Photograph by Francis Goodman (Camera Press)

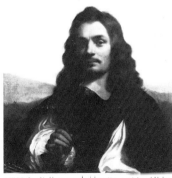

Sweerts: Self-portrait (detail), *c*.1660. Ohio, Oberlin College, Allen Memorial Art Museum

Synchromism

American movement in painting, the term meaning literally "colours together". It was conceived by Russell and MacDonald-Wright, who exhibited together as the Synchromists in Munich and Paris in 1913 and New York in 1914. Their concern with harmoniously arranged pure colours is apparent in Russell's *Synchromy in orange: to form* (1913–14, Buffalo, Albright-Knox). Although Synchromism was criticized in Paris for being too close to Orphism, it influenced several young American painters, including Dasburg and Benton, and was the first American avantgarde movement to attract attention in Europe.

Synthetism

Word used to describe the works of Gauguin, Bernard and other artists from the school of PONT-AVEN at the 1889 Café Volpini exhibition. Although Bernard's *Breton women in a meadow* (1888, St-Germain-en-Laye, M. Denis coll.) is regarded as the first Synthetist painting, both Bernard and Gauguin claimed individual credit for developing the style. In Synthetist paintings objects are represented in large unmodulated areas of colour confined by a bold, dark contour—a technique related to CLOISONNISME, which stood for a rejection of naturalistic interpretation in favour of the expression of ideas, moods or emotions. The pictures were intended to be abstractions or syntheses of the ideas which inspired them.

Syrlin, Jorg died 1492

German joiner and sculptor, active in Ulm from 1449. He made an altarpiece (destroyed) and carved furnishings for Ulm Minster. The most famous of these are the choir-stalls (1469–74), which incorporate lively and realistic carved wooden busts. They reveal the influence of Gerhaerts and one of them is a supposed self-portrait. His son, also called **Jorg**, was also a joiner and sculptor in Ulm (active 1475–1521).

Szyslo, Fernando de born 1925

Peruvian painter of Polish descent, a pioneer of abstract art in Peru. He has lived in Europe and New York, and currently lives and works in Lima. The cultural heritage of Peru and its varied geography have been a constant stimulus and he has strongly defended the preservation of a national identity. His works are painted with veils of vibrant colour and with some latent figuration.

Tacca, Pietro 1577–1640

Florentine bronze sculptor, the principal pupil and follower of Giambologna. He succeeded the latter as sculptor to the Dukes of Tuscany, and completed several works which the master had left unfinished at his death. His sculpture, is mostly in Florence, but his two best-known works are elsewhere—the four *Slaves* (1615–24) at the base of Bandinelli's Ferdinand I monument in Leghorn, and the equestrian statue of *Philip IV* (1634–40) in the Plaza de Oriente, Madrid.

Tachisme

Term used to describe a style in European art of the 1940s and 1950s, somewhat similar to American Abstract Expressionism. It derives from the French word *tache*, meaning "blob", and refers to the dabs and blotches the artists used to present a powerful, simple and direct expression of abstract, psychic states. Major artists practising this style were Wols, Mathieu and Fautrier. INFORMAL ART is a broader term covering the same group of artists. See vol. 3 p. 224

Tada, Minami born 1924

Japanese artist, who since the 1950s has made chiefly ENVIRONMENTAL sculpture. She uses mirrors and transparent materials which reflect and distort their surroundings, as in *Space terminal* (1971, Tokyo, Keio Plaza Hotel).

Taddeo di Bartolo c.1362/3–1422

Italian painter, active in Siena, San Gimignano, Pisa, Perugia and Volterra. His conservative style was dependent upon Simone Martini and the Lorenzetti, as his frescos for the Collegiata in San Gimignano (1393) show. From 1406 to 1414 he and his workshop executed frescos in the Chapel of the Virgin in the Palazzo Pubblico of Siena—early surviving examples of the typically Renaissance cycles of *Famous Men*.

Taeuber-Arp, Sophie 1889–1943

Swiss painter and decorative artist. She met Arp in 1915 and married him in 1921; she was also associated with the Dadaists—Richter, the poet Tzara, and Picabia. In the 1920s she worked on puppets and stage decoration for Swiss and French dramatic groups. Her work shows consistent progress toward an abstract art based on rhythmic, geometric shapes, using pure colours in a manner similar to Delaunay's (*Triptych*, 1918, Zurich, Kunsthaus). One of her best-known works was the result of her collaboration with her husband and van Doesburg on the interior of the Café Aubette in Strasbourg, an exercise in abstraction (now destroyed). She also made embroideries, collages, murals and relief sculpture.

Tai Chin see DAI JIN

Taiga, Ikeno 1723–76

Japanese painter, a native of Kyoto. Taiga excelled in calligraphy from childhood. He travelled to Kii province and to Yamato, to study painting, and then taught himself Chinese methods. A lover of mountains, he climbed and sketched most of the famous peaks of Japan. Unusually for one of the LITERATI, he did several large paintings, such as the sliding doors of the Henjokoin temple in Wakayama (c.1755), and the six-sided screen *Pavilions in a landscape* (c.1770, Tokyo, National Museum), both National Treasures.

Takamatsu, Jiro born 1936

Japanese artist. In 1961–63 he exhibited his *Points* and *Strings* series and also realized a number of Happenings. His work has explored distance and perspective and, as in his *Shadow* paintings, the relationships between objects and ideas. Such experiments led him to Conceptual works such as *Oneness of 16* (1970, Artist's coll.), which consists of 16 tree-trunks of a similar size but with slightly differently carved tops. These have influenced his film sets.

Takanobu, Fujiwara 1141–1204

Japanese painter and courtier, also a renowned poet. In the imperial court (which had recently lost political power) Takanobu belonged to a group which sought to preserve cultural supremacy over the *parvenu* shogun court. He studied painting with Mitsunaga and excelled in portraiture. Works have been attributed to him but none bears his signature, although records in the Jingo temple, Kyoto, state that the portrait of *Shogun Minamoto Yoritomo*, one of its treasures, is one of his four portraits of prominent people. See vol. 3 p. 48

Takis (Panayotis Vassilakis) born 1925

Greek artist, best known for his original experiments in KINETIC sculpture. His *Signals* of the late 1950s consist of modelled forms on the end of long rods of steel, an extremely pliable and light material which allows them to remain in constant vibration. They were suggested by railway signals seen at Calais. In 1959 he made magnetic and telemagnetic sculptures in which balls, cones or needles are suspended in an electromagnetic field in which they move and change, and in 1960 at the Galerie Iris Clert, Paris, he suspended the poet Sinclair Beiles in a magnetic field. He invented and patented a device to extract power from sea oscillation in 1970 and patented electromagnetic musical instruments in 1974. There is a huge and marvellous Takis at the Pompidou Centre, Paris. See vol. 3 p. 245

Tamayo, Rufino born 1899

Mexican painter, muralist and graphic artist. He was self-taught and his style combines elements of European paintings such as Cubism and Surrealism with a profound sense of the native traditions of Mexican Indian and Pre-Columbian art. During the 1920s he was head of the ethnographic department of the National Archaeological Museum, Mexico City, with responsibility for sustaining folk art traditions in the country. From 1926 he made frequent visits to New York. He created his first mural in 1933 for the Conservatory in Mexico City. Both his murals and easel-paintings possess a free sense of Mexican themes, escaping the often narrowly political and social aspects of the famous Revolutionary muralists. See vol. 3 p. 209

Tang dynasty 618–907 AD

Major Chinese dynasty, one of the most culturally and artistically vigorous periods in Chinese history. It was viewed in retrospect by the Chinese as a Golden Age. Building on the unification of the long-divided country achieved by the brief Sui dynasty, the Tang went on to push Chinese hegemony deep into central Asia, to continue the assimilation of China's deep south and to assert a cultural domination over Japan, Korea and parts of South-East Asia. The capital city of Chang'an (modern Xi'an) was the most populous city in the world and was in Chinese terms uniquely opened to influences from across Asia and as far west as the Byzantine Empire. This cosmopolitan climate is reflected in the ceramics, metalwork and textiles of the period, and also in the painting and sculpture produced for the increasingly rich and influential Buddhist religion. A great deal of magnificent sculpture survives from this period, notably at the famous Buddhist sites of northern China, Yungang and Longmen. Little Tang painting survives, however, with the exception of the wall-paintings at certain outlying sites, such as the great pilgrimage centre in central Asia, Dunhuang, and the murals from the subterranean tombs of the Tang aristocracy. From literary records, we know that this was the period when Chinese landscape painting came into its own and for centuries after Chinese artists and critics were absorbed in the search for an authentic Tang style. The work of the almost legendary Tang masters, however, then as now, was known only through copies, and though the division of landscape painting into the northern and southern schools was traced back to the divergent manners of the great Tang masters Li Sixun and Wang Wei, it is doubtful that such an antagonism existed at the time. See vol. 3 pp. 35–41

Tanguy, Yves 1900–55

French painter. He was self-taught and his discovery of the work of Chirico around 1924 was a formative influence. In 1925 he met Breton and became closely involved with the Surrealist movement. Thereafter he discovered his characteristic style, employing minute detail to depict desolate mental landscapes populated by enigmatic forms, at once organic and mechanical, which cast sharply defined shadows upon the infinite expanse of their surroundings (*Indefinite divisibility*, 1942, Buffalo, Albright-Knox). He settled in America in 1939 and married the Surrealist Kay Sage. Though Tanguy's style evolved over the years his distinctive motifs remained constant. See vol. 3 p. **176**

Tang Yin 1470–1523

Chinese painter. He is often seen as the epitome of the Ming professional painter, but was a close friend of the scholarly, amateur painter Wen Zhengming (which shows the dangers of accepting too rigidly the antagonism between amateur and professionals portrayed by Chinese critics). He came to painting as a career only after the collapse of his hopes for office in an examination scandal in 1499, and was a pupil of the Suzhou academic artist Zhou Chen (1450–1535). His name is associated with a great many portraits of elegant maidens, not all of them from his hand, but he was also well enough versed in the best work of preceding centuries to produce pieces such as *A recluse*—after Liang Kai (c.1520?, Taiwan, National Palace Museum). As a hero of the picaresque novels inspired by his colourful life, he is possibly the best-known of all Chinese artists. See vol. 3 p. **41**

Tan'yu, Kano 1602–74

Japanese painter. The grandson of Kano Eitoku, Tan'yu is credited with reviving the fortunes of the KANO school. At the age of 11, already having mastered the styles of the Chinese and Japanese schools, he demonstrated painting in front of the future Tokugawa Shogun Ieyasu. At 16, he was appointed official painter in the shogunal court, and was later commissioned to decorate rooms in Nijo castle in Kyoto in preparation for a visit by the Emperor Go-Mizunoo. Of his many surviving works one of the most impressive is the great *Landscape* on a decorated sliding door in the Daituko temple in Kyoto, an Important Cultural Property of Japan.

Tao-Ch'i see DAOJI

Tàpies, Antonio born 1923

Outstanding Spanish painter in the period since World War II. He studied law in the 1940s and is largely self-taught, studying art in his travels about the world. His earliest work was wittily Surrealistic in the manner of Miró and Klee, but his most original contribution has been his use of mixed media, which he began to develop in 1953. In an influential essay, *Nothing is Mean* (1970), he explained his belief in the validity of all materials, and he frequently uses glue and plaster on his canvases, and even objects such as parts of doors, furniture, wire and cloth. His scratched, cracked, impastoed works, often resembling walls ravaged by time, seem to reflect on the transitory and frail nature of human existence (*Large painting*, 1958, New York, Guggenheim). Generally sombre in colour, they are extremely powerful, poetic and meditative, sometimes with a trace of humour. He has had an enormous influence on artists throughout the world. See vol. 1 p. *152*; vol. 3 p. **225**

Tassel, Jean 1608–67
French painter, the best-known member of a family of artists active mainly in Langres. He was in Rome in the 1630s and back in Langres by 1647, but little is known for sure of his early work. In France he produced small pictures strongly influenced by the Bambocchianti and also religious works which have an unadorned simplicity. His masterpiece, however, is a portrait, *Catherine de Montholon* (Dijon, Musée des Beaux-Arts), which in its austerity is reminiscent of Philippe de Champaigne.

Tassi, Agostino c.1580–1644
Italian painter, born and mainly active in Rome. He was one of the leading *quadratura* specialists of his day, being responsible, for example, for the illusionistic architectural setting of Guercino's ceiling fresco *Aurora*. Tassi also painted small landscapes, and for many years his significance as a decorator was largely forgotten and he was remembered chiefly as the teacher of Claude. He was once accused of raping Artemisia Gentileschi.

Tatlin, Vladimir 1885–1953
Russian artist and theatre designer. He began to make highly original CONSTRUCTIVIST sculptures after seeing Picasso's Cubist works during a visit to Paris in 1913. The abstract *Painting reliefs* (1913) and the projectile *Corner* and *Counter reliefs*, which were intended to be hung in the corner of a room or suspended from wires, used everyday materials—metal, glass, wood and wire (unfortunately most of this early work is known only from photographs). In 1919 he was commissioned to create a *Monument to the Third International* by the Revolutionary Department of Fine Arts. Had this work been executed it would have been an ambitious monument to Constructivist principles, unifying sculpture with architecture. In the 1920s Tatlin became concerned with the production of utilitarian goods—clothing and household items—and was deeply opposed to the spiritualist stance of the Suprematists, led by Malevich. One work of a non-utilitarian nature was the *Letatlin* (1932, Moscow, Central Museum for Aviation), an air-bicycle. His early theatre designs were innovatory, but after 1930 they were more conventional in line with the official Socialist Realism. See vol. 3 pp. 157, **158–161**

Tchelitchew, Pavel 1898–1957
Russian painter. He fled from Russia during the Revolution and in 1923 settled in Paris, where he came to be regarded as the leading exponent of NEOROMANTICISM. In the 1920s he painted circus themes in a manner reminiscent of the Blue period of Picasso, and later exploited extreme perspectival distortions of the human figure. After moving to the USA in 1934 he became interested in the use of multiple images. *Hide and seek* (1940–42, New York, Museum of Modern Art) represents the simultaneous representation of a group

of children's heads and a gnarled tree-trunk containing analogies with the hand and foot. Such works were followed by X-ray-like studies of the human body.

Tempera
The usual medium in which easel-pictures were painted in the West until the 15th century, when it began to be superseded by oil. In true tempera, the binder is white or yolk of egg, mixed with water, giving a smooth fast-drying paint very suitable for fine work, which retains a bright, permanent surface. It is not as malleable as oil-paint, and it can readily be combined with other media. Its popularity has revived somewhat in the 20th century: Wyeth is a contemporary exponent. See vol. 1 pp. 140–141

Tenebrism
Term deriving from the Italian "tenebroso" (obscure) used to describe the use of a very dark overall tonality in painting. Leonardo is perhaps the first painter who could be called a *tenebrist*, but the term *tenebristi* is normally used of some 17th-century painters.

Teniers, David the Younger
1610–90
Flemish painter, born in Antwerp and active there and in Brussels. He painted almost every kind of picture (about 2,000 works have been attributed to him), but is best known for his peasant scenes, which are similar in style to Brouwer but less vigorous, and scenes with bourgeois characters which owe more to Rubens. In 1651 Teniers was appointed court painter to Archduke Leopold Wilhelm in Brussels. He also looked after the Archduke's superb picture collection (now mainly in the Kunsthistorisches Museum, Vienna) and painted several fascinating views of the gallery in which it was housed (examples, Brussels, Musées Royaux des Beaux-Arts; Madrid, Prado; Vienna, Kunsthistorisches). Teniers also made copies of individual paintings from the collection; several are in the Wallace Collection, London. His father, **David the Elder** (1582–1649), was also a painter. There are many speculative attributions to him, but almost nothing is known for certain about his work. See vol. 2 p. **201**

Teotihuacan
Large urban settlement in the Valley of Mexico, flourishing in the first six centuries AD. At the heart of the site two large pyramids, called the Sun and Moon, dominate a grand ceremonial complex. Painted murals found on several structures provide an important source of information on local religious beliefs. Perhaps the best-known objects are stone masks, usually plain with rather expressionless features, deeply-cut eyes and half-open mouths. Amongst the decorative techniques used were incising and low relief work, painting, fresco and mould-made ornamentation. Thousands of pottery figurines have been found, the earlier pieces modelled, the later ones mould-made and progressively more elaborate.

Terborch, Gerard 1617–81
Dutch genre and portrait painter. He studied with his father **Gerard the Elder** (1584–1662) in his native Zwolle and then with Pieter de Molyn at Haarlem. Unlike most 17th-century Dutch painters Terborch was widely travelled, visiting England, Italy and possibly France and Spain, as well as Germany, where he worked in 1646. It was there that he painted the group portrait representing *The swearing of the oath of*

ratification of the Treaty of Münster (London, NG). By 1654, however, he had settled permanently in Deventer, and it was there that he produced the works which have made him justly celebrated as one of the finest of Dutch genre painters. He specialized in genteel interior scenes, exquisitely delicate in their drawing, characterization and wonderful depiction of fine materials. His refinement was such that one of his best-known works has since the 18th century been called *"The Parental Admonition"* (c.1655, West Berlin, Staatliche Museen), even though it represents a brothel scene, the coin which the "father" offers to the "daughter" having been partially erased. Terborch's portraits, which like his genre scenes are usually on a small scale even when full-length (*A young man*, c.1663, London, NG), are also highly sophisticated. His most important pupil was Caspar Netscher. See vol. 1 p. *51*; vol. 2 p. **229**

Terbrugghen, Hendrick
1588–1629
Dutch painter, the first Dutch exponent of the CARAVAGGESQUE style to return to Holland from Rome. He was born in Deventer, and trained with Bloemaert in Utrecht before going to Rome, probably in 1604. By 1614 he was back in Utrecht, and he and Honthorst became the chief exponents of the Caravaggism associated with the city. No certain works are known from his Italian period, and very few from before 1620. Curiously, his later paintings are the more Caravaggesque, which has led some critics to believe that he made a second trip to Italy. *The calling of St Matthew* (1621, Utrecht, Centraal Museum), for example, is clearly indebted to Caravaggio's celebrated painting of the same subject in the expressive hand gestures of the two main protagonists, but the delicate colour scheme recalls Bloemaert, and the highly individualized heads look back to 16th-century Netherlandish painters such as Marinus and Massys; much more thoroughly Caravaggesque are works such as the sombre *Liberation of St Peter* (1629, Schwerin, Staatliches Museum). Terbrugghen also painted genre scenes, and the subtle tonality of, for example, *The flute player* (1621, Kassel, Staatliche Gemäldegalerie), in which he places a dark figure against a light background, seems to have influenced painters of the Delft school such as Fabritius and Vermeer. See vol. 2 p. 213

Term see HERM

Tessai, Tomioka 1836–1924
Japanese painter. He was originally trained for the Shinto priesthood, but was instructed in the *nanga* (LITERATI) and TOSA styles. During the political upheavals before the Meiji Restoration, he was involved with some of the imperialist militants, but afterwards returned to restore important shrines. He joined in the formation of an association for the revival of the *literati* style. He used rough, strong brush-strokes and usually incorporated a quotation in his paintings, with calligraphy in a similar style (*The hermit's landscape*, 1924, Seicho temple, near Takarazuka).

Testa, Pietro 1611–50
Italian etcher and painter, born in Lucca and active mainly in Rome. He trained with Domenichino and moved in Poussin's circle but, although he based individual figures on classical models, his work has a bizarre and romantic quality of imagination which places him temperamentally with artists such as

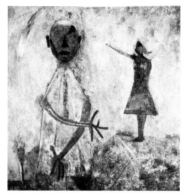
Tamayo: Self-portrait (detail), 1967. Mexico City, Museo de Arte Moderno (René Roland)

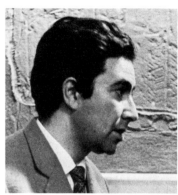
Tàpies: Photograph by McCullin/OBS (Camera Press)

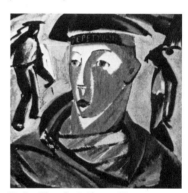
Tatlin: *The sailor* (self-portrait), 1911. Leningrad, Russian Museum

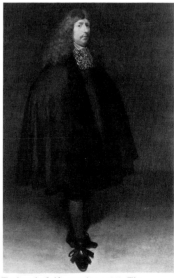
Terborch: Self-portrait, 1668. The Hague, Mauritshuis

Castiglione and Rosa. Few paintings survive and he is best known for his etchings, among the finest and most complex of which is his *Allegory of Reason* (*c.*1640–50). His death by drowning was probably suicide.

Thebes
Present-day Luxor, a city in the Upper Kingdom of Egypt which emerged as a major religious centre, and capital, in the NEW KINGDOM period. Royalty were buried in the nearby Valley of the Kings, and the city itself contained many mortuary temples, notably that of Queen Hatshepsut, 1503–1482 BC, and the Ramesseum of Ramesses II, 1304–1237 BC. A great painted palace anticipating the AMARNA style was built there by Amenhotep II, 1417–1379 BC, who also began the famous temple of Luxor. See vol. 2 pp. 26–27

Theophanes the Greek (Feofan) *c.*1330–after 1405
Byzantine painter and illuminator, active chiefly in Russia. His earliest known and best-preserved work, the frescos of the church of Our Saviour of the Transfiguration, Novgorod, is dated 1378. Theophanes' style relates to contemporary work in Constantinople in its dramatic use of line and tone but his figures are more convincingly individualized. In Moscow, from 1395 to 1405, he worked on murals in three churches, collaborating with Rublev. Little of his Moscow murals and no illuminations by him survive, but it is evident that he exercised a strong influence on Russian art at the time. A tradition of Byzantine-influenced painting was established at Novgorod and flourished throughout the late medieval period. See vol. 2 p. **61**

Theophilus see ROGER OF HELMERSHAUSEN

Theus, Jeremiah *c.*1719–74
Swiss-born American portrait painter. He was active in South Carolina from the late 1730s, and became the leading portraitist in the southern states. His genteel sitters are portrayed in pleasing soft colours (*Elizabeth Rothmaler*, 1757, New York, Brooklyn Museum).

Thoma, Hans 1839–1924
German painter of landscape and genre scenes. He studied at Karlsruhe (1859) and Düsseldorf (1867), and then travelled to Paris, where he saw the work of Courbet and the Barbizon school. On returning to Munich in 1870 he came into contact with the Leibl circle and with Böcklin. Although there were strong influences of Realism in his work, much of which was painted out of doors (*Laufenburg*, 1870, West Berlin, Staatliche Museen), it had poetic intensity.

Thomson, Tom 1877–1917
Canadian landscape painter. It was not until 1914 that he was able to paint full-time. His major works date from the last years of his life—virtuoso oil-on-wood sketches produced in Algonquin Park, which embodied the essence of Canadian landscape, and larger canvases produced in the studio which reveal him as a painter of commanding stature. *The jack pine* (1917, Ottawa, NG of Canada) is one of the most famous and popular paintings by a Canadian artist. His career was tragically cut short when he drowned in Canoe Lake, Algonquin Park, but his ideals lived on in the GROUP OF SEVEN.

Thoré, Théophile (W. Burger)
1807–69
French lawyer, critic and art historian. With Baudelaire, he is now considered the most perceptive art critic of his age. Thoré's Salon reviews (1832–48, 1860–68) acclaimed the avantgarde painters Courbet, Daumier, Millet and Manet, and he was also a brilliant historian of Dutch art, largely responsible for the rediscovery of Vermeer.

Thornhill, Sir James
1675/6–1734
British decorative painter in the Baroque style. He was the only native painter who competed successfully with visiting foreign artists during the brief period, about 1690 to about 1725, when large-scale decorative painting was fashionable in Britain. He worked in several country houses, but his greatest achievements are the *grisaille* paintings on *The Life of St Paul*, 1716–19, in the dome of St Paul's, London (a commission won in competition with Pellegrini and Sebastiano Ricci), and the ceiling of the Great Hall of Greenwich Hospital, 1708–27, which illustrates, with energetic bravura, constitutional events in the reigns of William III, Anne and George I. Hogarth was his pupil and son-in-law.

Thorn Prikker, Johan 1868–1932
Dutch SYMBOLIST painter, also active in the applied arts. His treatment of religious themes is highly subjective, painted in flowing Art Nouveau style and often charged with erotic overtones (*The bride*, 1893, Otterlo, Kröller-Müller). From 1896 he concentrated on the design of stained glass, monumental murals and furniture, continuing his practice after his move to Germany eight years later. He taught at Krefeld, 1904–10, and Campendonck was his pupil.

Thorvaldsen, Bertel 1770–1844
Danish sculptor, with Canova and Flaxman one of the triumvirate of internationally famous figures who dominated sculpture in the NEOCLASSICAL period. He was born in Copenhagen, where he studied in the Academy. In 1796 he went to Rome and, apart from a visit to Denmark in 1818–19, remained there until he returned home in 1838. His career was successfully launched with his statue of *Jason with the golden fleece* (1802–03, Copenhagen, Thorvaldsens Museum), which was based on Roman copies of the "*Doryphoros*" (Spear-carrier) by Polykleitos, and his work became so sought after that by 1820 he was employing 40 assistants. Major commissions (which came from all over Europe) included *The lion of Lucerne* (1819–21, Lucerne, Gletscherpark), a monument commemorating the Swiss who died during the French Revolution, the statues of *Christ* and *The apostles* (1821–27) and other work in the Church of our Lady, Copenhagen, and a monument to Lord Byron (1829, Cambridge, Trinity College Library). Thorvaldsen's style was more severely classical than Canova's, in his dependence on antique models, his tendency to compose his work around frontal planes with little movement in depth, and his complete disregard for surface animation. Only for his portrait busts did he use living models. His work is almost uniformly calm and austere; his contemporaries found it noble and moving, but to many modern eyes it is frigid and empty. The finest collection is in the Thorvaldsens Museum in Copenhagen, begun in 1839 after his triumphant return, and appropriately an outstanding piece of Neoclassical architecture. See vol. 3 p. **61**

Thulden, Theodor van 1606–76
Flemish painter, engraver and tapestry designer, active chiefly in Antwerp, where he was a pupil, and later a collaborator, of Rubens. He was popular and prolific, and had an international clientèle, for whom he painted religious, historical and genre subjects in an attractive, watered-down and sweetened version of Rubens' style (*The martyrdom of St Barbara*, *c.*1633, Dijon, Musée des Beaux-Arts).

Tibaldi, Pellegrino 1527–96
Italian painter and architect, one of the leading MANNERISTS of the second half of the 16th century. His style, forceful but somewhat ponderous, was formed in Rome in the late 1540s, when he worked with Perino del Vaga on frescos in Castel S. Angelo, taking over the commission after the latter's death in 1547. In the 1550s his most important work was done in Bologna, most notably frescos on *The story of Ulysses* (*c.*1555) in the Palazzo Poggi, now the University. From the 1560s he worked largely as an architect, principally in and around Milan, where he was architect to the Cathedral. In 1587, however, he was invited to Spain by Philip II, and in a last explosion of effort as a painter produced a huge quantity of frescos in the Escorial which had a powerful influence on Spanish Mannerist painting.

Tichý, František 1896–1961
Czech painter and graphic artist. He was the leading EXPRESSIONIST in Czech art of the 1940s, but his work suffered from the restrictive political doctrines in his country after 1948. He is particularly noted for his scenes of circus life.

Tidemand, Adolph 1814–76
Norwegian painter. He settled in 1846 in Düsseldorf, where his guidance was important to the Scandinavian artists there. He took up the Norwegian peasantry as subject matter in detailed compositions of idyllic and romantic character (*The sect*, 1852, Oslo, NG).

Tiepolo, Giambattista 1696–1770
The greatest Italian painter of the 18th century, the last in the line of fresco decorators and a fine graphic artist. He was brought up in Venice and his early work shows him favouring the dark and exaggerated style characteristic of most Venetian art of this time. His great series of fresco cycles begins with the decoration of the Church of the Gesuati (contracted 1737), in which all the crudities of his earlier style have given way to a remarkably clear and restrained rendering of a celestial vision. In the mid-1740s he painted a series of works devoted to the story of *Anthony and Cleopatra*, culminating in the frescoed ceiling of the *salone* of the Palazzo Labia. The rich surfaces and brilliant decorative effects of Tiepolo's work of this period are strongly reminiscent of Veronese; but his sources are in fact wide-ranging, and his religious canvases of the 1740s and 1750s derive elements from such disparate artists as Bellini, Tintoretto, Piazzetta, Rembrandt, Titian, Poussin and Rubens. His most glorious period was his two years in Würzburg. In the *Kaisersaal* (1751) of the Prince-Archbishop's Palace he depicted two incidents in Frederick Barbarossa's life in an extravagant Rococo setting of white and gilt stucco. The major frescos of his last Italian years (1753–61) were for the Villa Valmarana near Vicenza (1757) and the Villa Pisani at Strà (1761–62). The latter was a massive showpiece, for which he painted yet another grandiloquent apotheosis; but the former was a modest country retreat, designed for relaxation and entertaining guests, and Tiepolo's work there is appropriately more delicate and sensitive in character. In 1762 he went to Madrid, where he spent the rest of his life working for the Spanish royal family. The most outstanding of his Spanish works are his religious canvases—notably the oil-sketches (London, Courtauld Institute, Seilern coll.) for a series of works for the Royal Chapel at Aranjuez. These convey a very genuine pathos and show both a love for simple still-life details and also an acute responsiveness to the Spanish landscape. His sons Giandomenico Tiepolo and **Lorenzo** (1736–before 1776) worked as his assistants. See vol. 1 pp. *86*, *126–127*; vol 2 pp. **236–237**

Tiepolo, Giandomenico
1727–1804
Italian artist, the more talented of Giambattista Tiepolo's two sons. He worked with his father on many of his major fresco cycles, accompanied him to Germany and Spain, and spent his last years as an eminent figure in the Venetian art establishment. He successfully assimilated Giambattista's style and, despite a predilection for genre scenes (notably in the guest rooms of the Villa Valmarana), worked in the latter's Grand Manner to the end of his life. See vol. 2 p. **244**

Tietz or **Dietz, Ferdinand** 1708–77
South German ROCOCO sculptor, born in Bohemia but active in Franconia. Primarily a carver of garden sculpture in stone, Tietz succeeded in reproducing the sprightly merriment of porcelain on a monumental scale. Sometimes his figures were indeed painted to look like porcelain. His chief patrons were the Prince-Bishops of Würzburg and Bamberg, for whom he carved the garden sculpture of Veitscöchheim (begun 1763, originals now mostly in the Mainfränkisches Museum at Würzburg).

Tillemans, Peter 1684–1734
Flemish topographical painter. He came to England in 1707, and worked first as a copyist, but soon turned to views of country houses, landscapes with sporting scenes, especially horses, and small portraits of delicate character.

Tilson, Joe born 1928
British painter and printmaker. He has made brightly coloured POP wood reliefs such as *Space trophy* (1962, Arts Council of Great Britain). More recent work has dealt with the theme of the maze and included occult and alchemical symbolism. As a printmaker he has used colour photography and developed a form of three-dimensional printmaking in vacuum-formed plastic.

Timanthes late 5th century BC
Greek painter from Cynthus, a contemporary of Zeuxis. It was said that in his *Sacrifice of Iphigenia* the varying degrees of grief of the onlookers' faces were movingly expressed, but none so movingly as Agememnon's, which was veiled. No work has survived.

Timarchos see KEPHISODOTOS

Tinguely, Jean born 1925
Swiss artist whose work comments ironically on technology and mechanization. He started making moving mechanical objects—water-wheels with sound effects—when aged about 11. He was attracted to the work of Klee and Miró but above all to Duchamp's irreverent, anarchistic attitude to art. In 1959 he created his first *Métamécanique*; made from scrap metal, these delightfully

absurd machines move with erratic jerks and scribble on yards of paper (*Métamatic no. 9*, 1959, Houston, MFA). His most famous creation was the self-destroying *Homage to New York* (1960, remnants in New York, MOMA). Assembled from an old piano, a baby's pram, bits of metal, an orange meteorological balloon and a "money-thrower" donated by Rauschenberg, this blew itself up in front of a crowd of distinguished spectators. See vol. 3 p. **245**

Tino di Camaino c.1285–1337
Italian sculptor and architect. He was born in Siena, but trained in Pisa, most probably under Giovanni Pisano, whom he succeeded in 1315 as master of the works at Pisa Cathedral. In 1318 he moved to the equivalent position in Siena, and in 1321 transferred to Florence, where he carved the della Torre tomb in S. Croce and the Orso tomb in the cathedral. In 1323/4 he entered Angevin service in Naples, working on a series of royal tombs and various architectural projects. Tino was the greatest sculptor of the generation after Giovanni Pisano. His important sepulchral monuments were impressively dignified and highly influential. See vol. 2 p. **81**

Tintoretto, Jacopo (Jacopo Robusti) 1518–94
Venetian painter, with Veronese the leading artist in the city after the death of Titian. His father was a dyer (*tintore*), hence his nickname. He is reported to have studied for a few days with Titian, but more probably he was a pupil of either Bordone or Schiavone. Titian, however, was the exemplar for his colour, as Michelangelo became for his drawing. He was a qualified master by 1539 and secured his reputation nine years later with *The miracle of St Mark rescuing a slave* (1548, Venice, Accademia); the frieze-like composition and brilliant coloration were typically Venetian while the astonishing foreshortenings and obvious taste for theatricality suggested a more personal style. Tintoretto's development, particularly in his striking perspective effects and manipulation of space, is visible in *The finding of the body of St Mark* (1562, Milan, Brera). Here the heroic, Michelangelesque poses and the eerie, sepulchral lighting combine to produce a masterpiece of dramatic urgency. The style was well suited to large-scale decorative painting and Tintoretto found an important outlet in his long association with the Scuola di San Rocco (1564–87). In the upper hall he painted scenes from the Life of Christ; in the lower room scenes from the Life of the Virgin range from the genre-type *Annunciation* to the *Magdalen* placed in a shimmering landscape. As official painter to the Republic he executed many canvases for the Doge's palace—among them the huge *Paradise*. His power did not diminish with age; a late version of *The Last Supper* (1592–94, Venice, S. Giorgio Maggiore) is arguably his finest work. The scene unfolds with all the mystery of a séance; its startled participants, barely materialized, emerge from the darkness into a dim, spectral light. Tintoretto also painted portraits, though some attributed to him may be by his workshop or by his sons **Domenico** (1562–1635) and **Marco** (1561–1637), who took over the workshop after Tintoretto's death. His daughter **Maria** (c.1556–90) was also a painter. See vol. 1 pp. *26, 101, 106, 115*; vol. 2 pp. **170–173**

Tischbein family
A dynasty of German portrait painters,

the most famous of whom were nicknamed after their places of residence or—in the case of the best-known—most celebrated sitter. **Johann Heinrich the Elder**, "Kassel" Tischbein (1722–89), painted both portraits and mythological and genre scenes. His pupils included his nephews **Johann Friedrich**, "Leipzig" Tischbein (1750–1812), who was strongly influenced by English portraiture, and the Neoclassicist **Johann Heinrich Wilhelm**, known as "Goethe" Tischbein (1751–1829) from his celebrated portrait *Goethe in the Campagna* (1787, Frankfurt, Städelsches Kunstinstitut). Johann Wilhelm studied in Paris under Carle Van Loo and then in Italy under Piazzetta. He became Director of the Naples Academy in 1789, and was famous less for his paintings than for his outline engravings after classical antiquities. See vol. 2 p. **254**

Tissot, James Jacques Joseph 1836–1902
French painter and engraver. He first exhibited at the Salon in 1857, beginning with portraits and then in 1864 moving to scenes of contemporary life. After taking part in the Siege of Paris and the Commune he found it advisable to retreat to London, remaining there for ten years. He became very popular for his highly-finished society scenes, which cleverly capture nuances of social behaviour (*The last evening*, 1893, London, Guildhall). In their extensive use of black and white they show his debt to Manet and Whistler, but he was also a brilliant colourist. His last 20 years, spent in Palestine and France, were devoted to religious scenes. See vol. 1 pp. *126–127*

Titian (Tiziano Vecellio) died 1576
The greatest painter of the Venetian school, and one of the most celebrated names in the history of art. He trained with Giovanni Bellini, but was more deeply influenced by Giorgione, whom he assisted with the lost frescos of the Fondaco dei Tedeschi (1508). His debt is clearly evident in such early works as *The three ages of man* (c.1512, on loan to Edinburgh, NG of Scotland), with its mood of gentle lyricism suffusing both landscape and figures. Titian is said to have completed several paintings left unfinished at Giorgione's death, and their relationship was so close that a number of works are still disputed between them. Fortune cleared the way for Titian's advancement. The death of Giovanni Bellini in 1516, following closely on the departure of Sebastiano del Piombo and the premature demise of Giorgione, left Titian without a serious rival in the Venetian scene, a dominance he maintained for 60 years. He established his fame with *The Assumption of the Virgin* (1516–18, Venice, Frari), a work of astonishing energy and power. The grandeur of its forms was matched by the finest contemporary painting in Rome, but Titian's rich expressive colouring was already unrivalled. Commissions rapidly followed this success, among them the Bacchanalian scenes for Alfonso d'Este of Ferrara. They were probably intended to complement Bellini's *Feast of the Gods*, although this work seems positively sedate when compared with the surging figures and earthy paganism of *Bacchus and Ariadne* (1523, London, NG). This painting is one of the finest demonstrations of the sheer sensuous richness of Titian's work, his ability to depict any colour or texture of the natural or man-made world with complete conviction. By the 1530s he was famed throughout Europe, and in 1533

was made a Count by Charles V, one of his greatest patrons. In the Emperor's service, he developed his portraiture, combining his incisive characterization with an opulent treatment of accessories and a remarkable pictorial inventiveness. *Charles V at Mühlberg* (1548, Madrid, Prado), for example, is one of the earliest equestrian portraits and prefigures the achievements of Velazquez and van Dyck. It was painted at the imperial court at Augsburg, and it was on a second visit in 1550 that Titian met the great patron of his latter years, Philip II of Spain. Philip's preference was for the erotic mythologies described by the artist as *poesie*, in which Titian rose to new heights in the painting of succulent flesh, his colours now glowing in mellow harmony rather than contrasting boldly as in his youth. *The rape of Europa* (1562, Boston, Gardner Museum) is perhaps the most celebrated of the series. By this time Titian's technique had become very free, exploiting to the full the possibilities of oil-paint. His pupil Palma Giovane reported that in the final stages of his work Titian "used his fingers more than his brush", and his paint indeed has an expressive life of its own, independent of any representative function. Until the end his powers remained undimmed; the *Pietà* (Venice, Accademia), intended for his own tomb and unfinished at his death, is awe-inspiring in its majesty and depth of feeling. No artist has left a greater final testament to the world. Titian reigned supreme in every department of painting and revolutionized its technique. His reputation as a supreme artist has never wavered, and his influence has been incalculable. See vol. 1 pp. *20, 38*, **96–97**, *113, 129, 131, 147*; vol. 2 pp. **142–145**; vol. 4 p. *65*

Tobey, Mark 1890–1976
American painter. Largely self-taught, Tobey was originally a commercial artist. In 1918 he was converted to the Baha'i faith and his interest in oriental philosophy, religion, calligraphy and woodcuts subsequently dominated much of his work. In the mid-1930s he visited China and Japan, after which he developed the "white writings" for which he is most famous. *Broadway* (1935, New York, MOMA) is characteristic of this calligraphic style, which is painted with free, white brushwork over a faintly coloured background. See vol. 1 p. *118*; vol. 3 p. **211**

Tocqué, Louis 1696–1772
French portraitist, active in Paris and at the courts of Russia and Denmark. He was the son-in-law of Nattier but admired the more masculine style of Rigaud. He produced portraits in the fashionable mythologizing vein popularized by Nattier, but his best works are of a more natural kind (*A man*, 1747, London, NG). See vol. 2 p. 243

Tohaku, Hasegawa 1539–1610
Japanese painter. He joined the KANO school in Kyoto, then at the zenith of its prestige, but decided that the Sesshu school of Unkoku offered greater opportunities; he styled himself Sesshu's grandson-in-painting. He also studied the Song Chinese paintings of Muqi. Tohaku was specially famed for his portraits. In an effort to counter the powerful Kano school he teamed up with the celebrated tea-master Sen no Rikyu, and founded the rival Hasegawa school of arts. Many of Tohaku's works have been designated National Treasures of Japan, amongst them the screens with *Pine trees* in the National Museum, Tokyo. See vol. 3 p. **47**

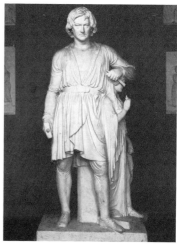
Thorvaldsen: Self-portrait marble statue, 1839. Copenhagen, Thorvaldsens Museum

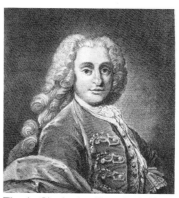
Tiepolo, Giambattista: Engraving by P. Monaco (1707/10–after 1775) (Mansell)

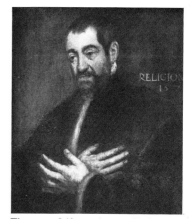
Tintoretto: Self-portrait, 1573. Venice, Scuola di S. Rocco (Mansell)

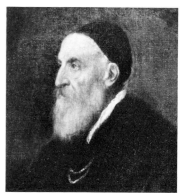
Titian: Self-portrait, c.1565–70, Madrid, Prado (Scala)

Toltec art
Art of the militaristic Toltec people of central Mexico from about the early 10th century to the end of the 12th. Originally from North Mexico, they settled further south at Tula in about 856. This was their chief centre. Toltec art is stiff and geometrical in style, and even the free-standing sculpture, such as the colossal "Atlas figures" at Tula and the reclining *Chacmools*, possess a squared, two-dimensional quality. Toltec architecture is decorated with somewhat repetitive relief carvings, mostly of eagles and jaguars. See vol. 2 p. 19

Tomé, Narciso *c.* 1690–1742
Spanish artist, one of a family of sculptors, who is remembered almost solely for his *Transparente* (1721–32) in Toledo Cathedral. This extraordinary chapel mingles painting, architecture and sculpture in a dazzling illusionistic confection. An inscription proudly records that Tomé himself was responsible for the conception and execution of the entire work.

Tomlin, Bradley Walker
1899–1953
American painter, associated with ABSTRACT EXPRESSIONISM. He studied in Paris, where he was influenced by the Post-Impressionists, but little of his early work survives because he systematically destroyed it. In the late 1930s he developed a form of Cubism derived from Braque, but in 1944, influenced by Gottlieb and other Abstract Expressionist friends, he developed a more distinctive idiom. His late work is typified by *Number 20* (1949, New York, MOMA), in which white calligraphic lines writhe across a huge, vaporous canvas.

Tondo
Italian word for "round", used to describe a circular painting or sculpture.

Tonks, Henry 1862–1937
British painter, more influential as a teacher than a practitioner. His own painting has a dry powdery quality due to the technique of "Tonking", covering the canvas with an absorbent surface after work each day to extract the oil and present a dry surface for subsequent work. An element of humour and caricature sometimes takes over in his paintings such as "*Sodales, Mr Steer and Mr Sickert*" (1930, London, Tate). He influenced a generation of art students during his 30 years at the Slade School of Art.

Tooker, George born 1920
American painter, a pupil of Marsh and Cadmus. His figurative style is tight and finished (he usually employed egg tempera) and evokes nightmarish visions of the predicaments of man in modern society. *Subway* (1950, New York, Whitney) exemplifies his Kafkaesque outlook: anxious figures inhabit an inhuman urban world of hallucinatory repetitions and isolation.

Toorop, Charley 1891–1955
Dutch painter. She trained as a musician but taught herself to paint, with the guidance of her father Jan Toorop. Her early work was influenced by the Symbolist elements in his work, but these were gradually replaced by a profound respect for the paintings of van Gogh. Between 1930 and 1940 she painted monumental realist compositions. An example of her work is *Women among the ruins* (1943, Amsterdam, Stedelijk).

Toorop, Jan 1858–1928
Dutch painter, graphic artist and designer, a major figure in the ART NOUVEAU movement. Born in Java, he lived in Holland from 1872 onwards, and studied in Amsterdam and Brussels. His early work—portraits, landscapes, and figure paintings—was chiefly influenced by French and Belgian Post-Impressionism, but during his stay in Belgium he met many avantgarde poets and artists, notably Ensor, and during the 1890s he joined the Symbolist movement. He adopted more literary subjects and he exploited a distinctive version of the characteristic Art Nouveau linear style (*The three brides*, 1893, Otterlo, Kröller-Müller). After his conversion to Catholicism in 1905 his subjects were mainly religious. He exhibited with Les Vingt and gained international renown. See vol. 3 p. **130**

Torii family
Japanese school of UKIYO-E printmakers, devoted to the production of actor prints and theatre posters. They dominated this genre from the 1660s to the late 18th century, but their work became tediously stereotyped. Kiyonaga was the last great master of the school.

Torres-García, Joaquín
1874–1949
Uruguayan painter and art theorist, the founder of Uruguayan CONSTRUCTIVISM. He studied in Barcelona until 1895 and worked out of doors with Spanish colleagues. Later he worked with the architect Gaudí on stained glass for Palma Cathedral, Majorca. In 1920 he moved to New York, where the pace and complexity of the city marked his work. His Constructivist phase began in Paris around 1924, and his meeting with Mondrian in 1929 proved vital in his development. In 1930 he founded the review *Cercle et Carré* (Circle and Square) with Seuphor and finally returned in 1934 to Uruguay, where he published numerous theoretical texts.

Torrigiani, Pietro 1472–1528
Florentine sculptor. He studied in the Medici "academy" under Bertoldo (where he broke the nose of Michelangelo, a fellow-student). After a varied career, including a period as a soldier, he arrived in England and while there he executed his most outstanding works, the finest and most important of which is the tomb of Henry VII (1512–18) in Westminster Abbey, London. The sensitive effigies have a Gothic elegance, but the four angels at the corners of the tomb and the exquisite decorative work are purely Italian in style. At some point before 1522 Torrigiani moved to Spain, where he was imprisoned by the Inquisition and perished at their hands. See vol. 1 p. *188*

Tosa school
School of Japanese painting which dominated imperial court art from the 15th to the 19th century, controlling the *E-dokoro* or Painting Office. Founded by Tosa Mitsunobu, the school's principal aim was to follow the traditional Japanese YAMATO-E style, but it was not unaffected by the prevalent taste for Chinese-inspired art. The Tosa school rivalled the Kano school in importance. See vol. 3 pp. 48–49

Tosi, Arturo 1871–1956
Italian painter. Throughout his career he concentrated on landscapes, at first in an Impressionist manner. His serenity of vision, couched in a personal interpretation of Post-Impressionism, gained him recognition as one of Italy's leading painters of landscape.

Toulouse-Lautrec, Henri Marie Raymond de 1864–1901
French painter, an aristocrat by birth and one of the most colourful figures in late 19th-century art. Poor health and an accident in childhood left him stunted and the misery of this deformity may have influenced his preferences for the low life of Montmartre, his acid wit and his alcoholism. He studied in a Paris studio, where he met Anquetin, Bernard and van Gogh. Much influenced by Degas, he painted perceptive, unidealized recordings of contemporary life. *In the parlour at the Rue des Moulins* (1894, Albi, Musée Toulouse-Lautrec) shows the prostitutes sitting around, bored and glamourless, waiting for clients. Most of his paintings are in thinned oil-paint on unprimed cardboard, but he is perhaps more famous for his posters and lithographs of dance halls and cabarets. In 1895 he made the first of many visits to London, where he met Oscar Wilde, Whistler and Beardsley. He was a superb draughtsman, with the ability to convey rapid movement, while trying always to catch the truth of his subject matter, particularly the seedy side of life. His oblique angle of vision, bold translation of an everyday object into a near-abstract shape and calligraphic line were all inspired by Japanese prints but made wholly original and unequivocally European in style and content. The innovative vividness of his colour lithography established a style which was to shape the future of graphic art. See vol. 1 p. *167*; vol. 3 p. **121**

Tournier, Nicolas 1590–1638/9
French CARAVAGGESQUE painter. He was in Rome from 1619 to 1626, and a group of genre scenes of eating, drinking and music-making parties rather in the manner of Manfredi and Valentin has been attributed to him from this period (*A musical party*, St Louis, City Art Museum). On his return to France, where he worked mainly in Toulouse, he turned to religious subjects such as *The Deposition* (Toulouse, Musée des Augustins). He is distinguished from most Caravaggesque artists by his elegance and rather refined physical types.

Tousignant, Claude born 1932
Canadian abstract painter. In 1962 he was inspired by Newman to simplify his hard-edged compositions and achieved the circular, pulsating surface of *Bull's eye* (1963, Ottawa, NG of Canada). He influenced Montreal OP art of the 1960s.

Town, Harold Barling born 1924
Canadian abstract painter, printmaker and sculptor, a founder-member of PAINTERS ELEVEN. Colourful, facile and ingenious paintings reminiscent of Kline and Motherwell (*Great divide*, 1966, Toronto, NG of Ontario) earned him his reputation, but his prints and collages are more original.

Towne, Francis 1739/40–1816
British landscape watercolourist. His distinctive style consisted in treating landscape forms in a highly simplified, stylized and almost abstract manner, unusual in the 18th century. He worked in England, Wales and Italy, but his most remarkable watercolours were produced in Switzerland on the way home (*Source of the Arveiron*, London, V&A).

Toyoharu, Utagawa 1737–1814
Japanese UKIYO-E artist, the founder of the Utagawa family of print designers who held an important place in the Japanese print world throughout the 19th century. He trained in Kyoto at the Kano studio, then went to Edo (Tokyo). He was interested in the Western technique of perspective, but unlike other designers, who used it for indoor scenes, Toyoharu preferred it for his landscapes, of which he is one of the earlier masters. An example is the *uki-e* (perspective picture) *New bridge at Fukagawa*.

Toyohiro, Utagawa 1765–1829
Japanese UKIYO-E artist. A native of Edo (Tokyo), Toyohiro was a pupil of Toyoharu and a colleague of Toyokuni I. He is best remembered for having taught Hiroshige. Toyohiro's many hand-painted studies of women in their summer finery are particularly fine, such as the diptych print *Two geishas playing "Stone-scissors-paper"*. These and his Kano-style landscapes are more valued today than the then popular, posturing actor prints of other Utagawa designers.

Toyokuni I, Utagawa 1769–1824
Japanese UKIYO-E artist. He was the first of the four Toyokuni who led the Utagawa family (founded by Toyoharu), leading printmakers in the 19th century. The son of an Edo (Tokyo) doll-maker, he was apprenticed to Toyoharu at an early age. He began by illustrating storybooks but found his *forte* in actor prints and *bijin-ga* (designs of beautiful women). Toyokuni was probably not as good an artist as he was an entrepreneur; he is accused of imitating Shunsho in his actor prints and Utamaro in his *bijin-ga*.

Traini, Francesco active 1321–69
The most important Pisan painter of the 14th century. His style was heavily influenced by the Sienese, especially the Lorenzetti brothers. His one certain work is a polyptych showing *St Dominic and scenes from his life* (1345, Pisa, Museo Civico). The most important work attributed to him is the emotive series of frescos of *The Triumph of Death* on the walls of the Camposanto at Pisa, with its vividly characterized figures and macabre details. The frescos are usually seen as a direct response to the Black Death of 1348, but recently the theory has been revived that they may be by Buffalmalcco and earlier than supposed.

Transitional style
Style of painting and sculpture emerging in north-east France and in the Holy Roman Empire in the 12th century. Transitional art is distinguished from both late Romanesque and early Gothic art by its strongly antique bent and the fluency of its forms. The style is associated with several major monuments and works—with the Klosterneuburg altar made by Nicholas of Verdun (1181, Klosterneuburg, Stiftsmuseum), with the sculpture of the west façade of Laon cathedral and with paintings in the chapter-house of Sigena in northern Spain.

Trecento
Term, literally "300s", used of the 14th century, the "1300s", in Italian art.

Trevisani, Francesco 1656–1746
Italian painter, born in Naples and active in Rome from 1678. He painted cabinet pictures and altarpieces in a colourful style full of echoes of Giordano, marking a reaction against the classicism of Maratta (*Martyrdom of St Andrew*, Rome, S. Andrea delle Fratte). Many French painters frequented his studio in Rome, and he strongly influenced French decorators such as François Lemoyne and Carle Van Loo.

Triptych
Painting consisting of three parts,

panels or canvases, a common form for an altarpiece in the medieval and Renaissance periods. A painting of two parts is termed a **diptych**, one of more than three parts a **polyptych**. A triptych often had its outer sections hinged to the central one so that they could be closed over it, and in this case the reverse sides were often painted.

Tristán, Luis c.1586–1624
Spanish painter, active mainly in Toledo, where from 1603 to 1607 he was a pupil of El Greco. His style was heavily dependent on his master, but Tristán was more soberly naturalistic. In *The Adoration of the shepherds* (1620, Cambridge, Fitzwilliam), for example, the spiritual intensity, physical types and elongated proportions are derived from El Greco, but the figures have a corporeality foreign to him.

Troger, Paul 1698–1762
Austrian painter and engraver, the leading artist of the transition from Baroque to Rococo in central Europe. Born in the south Tyrol, he studied in Italy. After settling in Vienna, he painted innumerable altarpieces and frescos—the latter in a bright palette attuned to the new light-filled coloristic architecture and close to south German Rococo in feeling. His masterpieces are the frescos in the church and library of Altenburg (1732–33). His teaching at the Vienna Academy exercised enormous influence on the next generation of painters, notably Maulbertsch, who was inspired by Troger's vivid oil-sketches.

Trompe l'oeil
French term, meaning "deceive the eye", used to describe the application of illusionistic skill in painting to persuade the spectator that a painted object is a real one. A common example is the depiction of a fly on a painted ledge, as in Petrus Christus' *Portrait of a Carthusian* (c.1445, New York, Metropolitan), but a whole painting may be a *trompe-l'oeil*, as in the still lifes of Harnett.

Troost, Cornelis 1697–1750
Dutch painter, active in Amsterdam. Until 1733 Troost was purely a portraitist, painting official group portraits, such as *The Regents of the Collegium Medicum* (1724, Amsterdam, Rijksmuseum), and informal conversation pieces. Thereafter he struck out to portray (in the Dutch tradition) genre scenes, and (influenced by Gillot and Watteau) scenes from the contemporary stage. He often painted in pastel, notably the five so-called "Nelri" (the initial letters of their titles), pictures of *The feast of Biberius*, showing the progressive effects of drinking (1739–40, The Hague, Mauritshuis). Troost is the most important Dutch painter of the 18th century, and in style and subject matter a figure somewhat comparable to Hogarth, although he lacked Hogarth's biting satire. See vol. 2 p. **244**

Troostwijk, Wouter Johannes van 1782–1810
Dutch painter, mainly of landscape. Influenced by the Dutch 17th-century landscape painters Potter and Adriaen van de Velde, Troostwijk's realistic but highly original vision can be seen in works such as *Raampoortje at Amsterdam* (1809, Amsterdam, Rijksmuseum). Although he died so young, he has a leading place among his contemporaries.

Troy, François de 1645–1730
French portrait painter of the generation of Largillière and Rigaud. Works

such as the portrait of *Charles Mouton* (1690, Paris, Louvre) show a more subdued version of the Flemish Baroque character. He was successful as Director of the Academy and trained his more distinguished son J.-F. Detroy.

Troyon, Constant 1810–65
French landscapist of the BARBIZON school. Troyon first worked at the Sèvres manufactory, and took up landscape painting in the 1830s. He was influenced by the work of Potter and Aelbert Cuyp, seen on a trip to Holland in 1847, and turned to painting animals, often in their natural settings (*Morning*, 1855, Paris, Louvre). In his last years he painted remarkable seascapes. The technical freedom and luminosity of these late works influenced Boudin and Monet.

Trübner, Wilhelm 1851–1917
German painter, an important exponent of 19th-century naturalism in Germany. At the Munich Academy in 1869 he first came into contact with the work of Courbet and became an important member of the Leibl circle. Under Leibl's influence he turned his efforts to balanced composition and naturalistic colour with impressive virtuosity. His contact with Liebermann, when he was an associate member of the Berlin Sezession, further freed his colour and brushwork, and some of his late landscapes have a coloristic radiance that brings them close to Impressionism (*Portal of Stift Neuberg near Heidelberg*, 1913, Mannheim, Städtische Kunsthalle).

Trumbull, John 1756–1843
American painter, celebrated for his depictions of the events of the American War of Independence, in which he had fought. He had two periods with West in London, and one of his most famous works, *The death of General Warren at the Battle of Bunker Hill* (1786, New Haven, Yale University Art Gallery), was painted in West's studio and clearly inspired by his *Death of General Wolfe*. In its forceful movement, however, it also owes something to Copley's *Death of Major Pierson*. Trumbull continued to repeat his popular Revolutionary subjects for the rest of his career, and also painted portraits and some views of Niagara Falls which look forward to the Romantic interests of the next generation of American artists. In 1817 he became President of the American Academy of Fine Arts, but his rule was so conservative and dictatorial that many members resigned in 1825 to found the National Academy of Design. See vol. 3 pp. **58–59**

Tryggvadottir, Nina born 1913
Icelandic painter, living in Paris and London. Since the 1950s she has worked in an ABSTRACT EXPRESSIONIST style characterized by heavy cube forms and bright colours, and has also made collages and designed stained glass.

Tschumi, Otto born 1904
Swiss painter and graphic artist. His first works were inspired by Cubism, which he particularly studied on a visit to Paris in 1925. In the late 1920s and early 1930s he worked as a commercial artist and in 1934 met Klee. He later met Arp and Ernst and became SURREALIST. His graphic work is often satirical, as in his illustrations to novels and poems by Kafka, Melville, Poe and Rimbaud.

Tucker, William born 1935
British sculptor. His coloured abstract sculpture of the early 1960s is usually based on a logical progression. *Anabasis I* (1964, London, Tate), for example, is a

sequence of three knucklebone shapes of different materials interlocking so as to rise from the ground in a diagonal. His concern with visual and structural clarity is also apparent in later works (*Beulah I*, 1971, Tate). This is one of a number made from steel tubing which achieve a kind of curvilinear drawing in space.

Tung Ch'i-Ch'ang see DONG QICHANG

Tung Yüan see DONG YUAN

Tura, Cosimo c.1431–95
Italian painter. He was the founder and, with Cossa and Roberti, the leading painter of the 15th-century school of Ferrara, where he became court painter in 1452. Diverse influences, including Donatello, Pisanello, Mantegna and van der Weyden, resulted in an agitated and intricate style in which brilliant, often harsh colouring and hard, knotted forms create a feeling of great emotional tension. The disturbing quality of his work is increased by the use of bizarre architectural detail, as in the central panel of the Roverella altarpiece (c.1480, London, NG). He painted mainly religious works, his output ranging from small pictures of *The Virgin and Child* (a good example, c.1455, is in Washington, NG) to the huge shutters of a cathedral organ (*The Virgin Annunciate* and *St George and the Princess*, 1469, Ferrara, Cathedral Museum). See vol. 2 p. **121**

Turnbull, William born 1922
British painter and sculptor. He lived in Paris, 1948–50, and early sculpture such as *Mobile stabile* (1949, London, Tate) reflects the influence of the Surrealist work of Giacometti. In the 1950s he made bronze masks and semi-abstract heads and, between 1955 and 1960, hieratic standing *Idols*—primitivistic carvings exploring the textural possibilities of bronze. His sculpture became more impersonal, and he favoured painted steel. He helped organize the 1960 SITUATION exhibitions and his large paintings, much influenced by American abstraction, have usually been based on a single image or colour, sometimes flat and richly textured.

Turner, Joseph Mallord William 1775–1851
British painter, one of the greatest and most original of landscape artists. He began as a painter of conventional topographical views, but in the course of a long and productive career he developed a style of extraordinary imaginative power expressed in a technique—in both oils and watercolour—of unprecedented freedom and subtlety. Very precocious, he exhibited his first watercolour at the Royal Academy in 1790. His watercolours in these early years are close in style to Girtin, whom he met at Dr Monro's and accompanied on sketching trips. Early oil-paintings (the first ones date from 1796) show his interest in Dutch marine painting, and his study of Claude and Wilson helped him to compose works in the grand classical manner. By the turn of the century he was beginning to evolve a personal style, seen, for example, in *The shipwreck* (1805, London, Tate), which has a Romantic sense of drama and movement. In 1802 he had made his first trip abroad, visiting France and Switzerland, and subsequently made several visits to Switzerland and Italy—the Alps and Venice coming to rank with the sea among his favourite subjects. On his travels Turner filled sketchbooks with studies of every aspect of the landscape

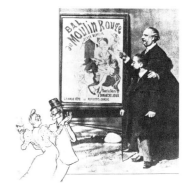
Toulouse-Lautrec: Photograph taken with the Director of the Moulin Rouge (Mansell)

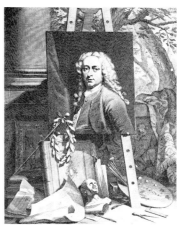
Troost: Engraving by Jacobus Houbracken after a self-portrait (Mansell)

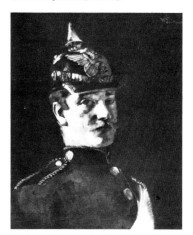
Trübner: *Self-portrait with a helmet*, 1875 Private coll.

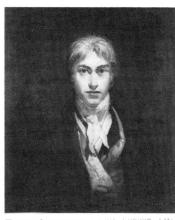
Turner: Self-portrait, c.1798. London, Tate

and people, many of which were executed in brilliant watercolour on pure white paper. The resulting large oil-paintings, such as *The Bay of Baiae, with Apollo and the Sibyl* (1823, Tate), were violently attacked by some critics because of the overwhelming effect of the brilliant colour harmonies, but Turner had several sympathetic patrons (and towards the end of his life a great champion in Ruskin) and was able to develop his increasingly personal vision without constraint. By the last decade of his life, the figurative elements of paintings were almost dissolved in a shimmering haze of light and colour, as in *The Sun of Venice going to sea* (1843, Tate), which was one of Ruskin's favourites. In his later years Turner became increasingly a recluse, and at his death left the huge body of his work which was still in his studio to the nation: the paintings are now mainly in the Tate Gallery, the drawings and watercolours in the British Museum. See vol. 1 pp. *62*, *101*, *156*; vol 3 pp. **72–73**

Tutankhamun 1361–1352 BC
Egyptian Pharaoh, whose tomb near Thebes revealed a vast treasury of NEW KINGDOM funerary art, now mainly in the Egyptian Museum, Cairo. Tutankhamun was one of the last kings of the 18th Dynasty, and probably a brother or son of Akhenaten of Amarna. His tomb, discovered in 1922, was virtually intact. Although the king had re-established the traditional cult of Amun, art in his reign was still heavily influenced by achievements at Amarna in the reign of his predecessor. See vol. 2 pp. **26–27**

Twachtman, John Henry
1853–1902
American landscape painter and etcher. He studied in Europe, and upon his return to America in 1886 painted in the manner of the Barbizon artists. In 1888 his style became clearly Impressionist. His winter landscapes were painted within a narrow colour range, the result often more lyrical than impressionistic (*Winter silence*, Mead Art Gallery, Amherst College).

Twombly, Cy born 1929
American painter, living in Rome since 1957. His large-scale canvases feature white or black grounds covered with random scrawls, repetitive scribbles, drips, patches of flaking colour, fragmentary texts and evocative diagrams (*Untitled*, 1968, New York, MOMA). The sources of this art—simultaneously elegant and crudely spontaneous—include Klee, children's art, graffiti and Surrealist automatism. While indebted to the calligraphic Abstract Expressionists Tomlin and Tobey, he maintains an ironic tone closer to Rauschenberg.

Tworkov, Jack born 1900
American painter, born in Poland. He began by painting landscapes, still lifes and figure paintings in a manner heavily influenced by Cézanne. He worked for the Federal Art Project during the Depression years, met De Kooning (1934) and in 1948–53 they worked in adjacent studios. By the early 1950s he had become notable among the New York ABSTRACT EXPRESSIONISTS. In works such as *Duo I* (1956, New York, Whitney) a grid of slashing, brittle strokes is his principal means of pictorial organization. Since the 1960s he has concentrated more on geometrical designs of pure, solid colours, and during the 1970s the grid became more rigid.

Tytgat, Edgard 1879–1957
Belgian painter, carver and etcher, lithographer and carpet designer. His early work featured Impressionist portraits, landscapes and interiors. He worked as a book illustrator in London (1914–18) and on his return to Belgium painted works, such as *The park at Nivelles* (1922, Liège, Musée des Beaux-Arts), which show his delight in naively painted fairground scenes.

U

Ubac, Raoul born 1911
Belgian artist. In the 1930s he lived in Paris, where he met the Surrealist group. He moved to Carcassonne in 1940 and associated with fellow-Belgians Magritte and the writer Scutenaire. His first paintings were abstract, but after World War II his work became more figurative. He is also a sculptor, well-known for his abstract reliefs on slate (*Red and black earth*, 1973, Paris, Galerie Maeght).

Uccello, Paolo 1396/7–1475
Florentine painter, who combined International Gothic and Renaissance elements to create one of the most attractive and distinctive styles of his generation. Although he lived long, he seems to have painted little, and to his contemporaries he was an eccentric figure. He trained in Ghiberti's workshop, and worked as a mosaicist in Venice, 1425–31, but his first certain surviving work dates from 1436. This, a fresco painting of an equestrian statue of *Sir John Hawkwood* (Florence, Cathedral), announces the preoccupation with perspective which was to run throughout his career. It has two different viewpoints; the horse and rider are seen from eye-level, but the base is seen from below. Vasari and subsequent critics have criticized Uccello's interest in perspective as excessive. He came close to regarding it as an end in itself, but in practice the effects for which he used it were pictorially arresting and appropriate to his subjects, not mere technical exercises. In the magnificent monochrome fresco *The flood* (*c.*1445, Florence, S. Maria Novella), for example, he used double vanishing points and violent recession to intensely dramatic effect. Uccello's best-known works are the three large panels of *The Battle of San Romano* (*c.*1455, Florence, Uffizi; London, NG, and Paris, Louvre), painted for the Medici Palace, and in these his interest in perspective comes out particularly in the foreshortened figures and weapons which recede neatly along the orthogonals. The effect is highly unnaturalistic and, with the simplified geometrical shapes (the horses look like rocking-horses) and brilliant colours, goes to create a splendid fairy-tale picture of a battle rather than a realistic depiction of warfare. The love of decorative display seen here and typical of the International Gothic style is also apparent, combined with virtuoso perspective effects, in two delightful late works, *St George and the dragon* (London, NG), one of the earliest examples of an Italian painting on canvas, and *The night hunt* (Oxford, Ashmolean). Some brilliant perspective drawings also survive. See vol. 2 pp. **106–107**

Uden, Lucas van 1595–1672
Flemish landscape painter, born and mainly active in Antwerp. His landscapes are usually extensive views, showing strong influence from Rubens in their lighting and painterly brushwork as well as in their general conception. At his best his work has great vitality, and his views are often enlivened by figures added by Teniers the Younger (*Wooded landscape with peasants dancing*, Dublin, NG). He was a fine graphic artist.

Uecker, Gunther born 1930
West German artist. He joined Group ZERO in 1961 and became one of its principal members. Like the others, he is interested in the use of light but he is especially known for his works in which nails are stuck into a white ground, in patterns suggesting force fields (*Nail relief*, 1969, Aachen, Neue Galerie).

Ugo da Carpi died 1532
Italian wood engraver, one of the earliest and finest exponents of the chiaroscuro woodcut. He used three and sometimes more superimposed blocks to produce a coloured and shaded print with something of the quality of a wash drawing. There are German examples earlier than Ugo's first dated work in the technique, but they are not so effective. He may have discovered the technique independently, and in 1516 he requested a patent. His best-known woodcuts are of works by Raphael and Parmigianino.

Ugolino di Nerio active 1317–27
Sienese painter. His only signed work is the high altarpiece of S. Croce in Florence. This was dismembered in the 19th century and the fragments are widely dispersed, the majority being in London (NG) and West Berlin (Staatliche Museen). Stylistically it is closely dependent on Duccio.

Uhde, Fritz von 1848–1911
German painter. Influenced by Liebermann and Bastien-Lepage, he spent 1879–80 in Paris and was briefly in Holland (where he studied the Old Masters and work of the Hague school). On Uhde's return to Munich, Liebermann encouraged his use of pure bright colour. His fresh, mildly sentimental pictures, although technically close to Impressionism, reveal a preference for "significant" subject matter, and he is best known for religious scenes in contemporary dress (*Sermon on the Mount*, 1887, Budapest Museum). He also painted genre scenes and fine portraits. In 1892 he was a founder-member of the Munich Sezession. See vol. 3 p. **131**

Ukiyo-e
The dominant movement in Japanese art from the 17th to the 19th century. *Ukiyo-e* means "pictures of the floating world", that is, an art devoted to transient everyday Japanese life, with an emphasis on leisure pursuits. This was the subject chosen by the early printmakers, and the major inspiration of their numerous successors. The taste for such works was bourgeois rather than courtly, though the draughtsmanship and colour sense of the leading exponents reached a new level of refinement. The polychrome print, developed in the mid-18th century from woodcut techniques, inspired many masters, among them Harunobu and Utamaro, whose prints greatly influenced late 19th-century French artists. See vol. 3 pp. 50–51

Underpainting
The preliminary blocking out on the painting surface of the main shapes, lines or tones of a picture that is to be built up in several paint layers. Underpainting is usually in monochrome, sometimes with modelling in white. Conversely, **overpainting** refers to any layer of paint covering a previously dried layer.

Underwood, Leon 1890–1977
British painter, sculptor and printmaker. His work was frequently allegorical and reflected an opposition to 20th-century materialism. It varied according to its subject, from streamlined, dynamic bronzes to static primitivist carvings. Paintings such as *Casement to infinity* (1930, London, Tate) contain accumulations of symbolic objects, and are somewhat Surrealist.

Unit One
Group of avantgarde British painters, sculptors and architects, formed in 1933 on the initiative of Paul Nash in order to increase public awareness of advanced art. In 1934 they published a book of their work with an introduction by Read. Members included Nicholson, Moore and Hepworth. By 1935 the group was breaking up as the aims of abstraction and Surrealism, both encompassed by Unit One, became incompatible.

Usami, Keiji born 1940
Japanese painter. His early works showed the influence of Gorky and of Automatism. In 1965 he began experimenting with cut-outs of human figures in varying relations, and then proceeded to explore the motif with laser beams. *Ghost plan: crack* (1973, Tokyo, Minami Gallery) consists of a photograph in which the silhouettes of various figures are emphasized.

Ushakov, Simon 1626–86
The best-known Russian painter of the 17th century. He was the first to introduce Western details into his icons, a practice decried by traditionalists. Although his historical significance is undoubted, his talent has been overrated. His vigorous woodcuts, especially *The Seven Deadly Sins*, are more successful than his rather sentimental icons (examples in Moscow, Tretyakov Gallery).

Utamaro, Kitagawa 1753–1806
Important Japanese UKIYO-E artist. He joined a studio in Edo (Tokyo) and began his professional career around 1775 with actor prints derived from Shunsho's. He published his first masterpiece, *Mushierabi* (Book of Insects) in 1788, and proceeded to devote himself to illustrating Japanese stories, and producing prints of beautiful women. By 1790, the unique style of the beauties which were his *forte* was influencing everybody in the field. Utamaro was an innovator in the way he pictured women in their surroundings, creating distinctive characters full of vitality, drawn on a relatively grand scale and with bold draughtsmanship. He was fortunate in having as his friend and publisher Tatsuya Juzaburo, a cultured man of the world who watched carefully over his reckless *protégé*. Utamaro lived most of his life in the Yoshiwara Gay Quarters, among some of the most sought-after courtesans of the day. He was volatile and arrogant and in 1804 was imprisoned for allegedly insulting the ancestors of the Shogun in one of his works. The incident broke him and he died two years later. See vol. 3 p. **50**

Utrillo, Maurice 1883–1955
French painter. He was the son of Suzanne Valadon, who, in 1903, encouraged him to take up painting to distract him from drinking and give him a reason to live. He was largely self-taught and painted not only from nature but also frquently after postcards of Montmartre. His finest works belong to his "White" period (*c.*1909–15), in which he depicted deserted Montmartre streets in subtle, milky tones with

touches of rust and richer colours, his paint sometimes thickened with plaster (*Church at St-Hilaire*, c.1911, London, Tate). His output was prolific, but his later work in brighter colours seldom recaptured the melancholy harmonies and compositional solidity which had made him famous. See vol. 3 p. **184**

Valadon, Suzanne 1867–1938

French painter, the mother of Utrillo and a friend of many of the Impressionists. After working as a dishwasher and pursuing a career in the circus she became an artist's model, posing for Puvis de Chavannes and others. She was Renoir's mistress and a life-long friend of Degas; they encouraged her when she took up painting seriously. Her work, much influenced by Degas, has a hard-edged vitality and often bold colouring. She mainly produced figure paintings such as *The blue room* (1923, Paris, Musée National d'Art Moderne).

Valckenborch, Lucas van 1540–97

Netherlandish painter, born in Malines, the most prominent member of a family of landscape and genre painters. In 1566, he fled to Aachen with his brother **Maerten** (1533–1612) to escape Spanish persecution. In 1570 he gained the patronage of Archduke Matthias, whom he accompanied to Linz, and later pursued his career in Frankfurt and Nuremberg. His many versions of *The Tower of Babel* (example, 1568, Munich, Alte Pinakothek) betray a close allegiance to the tradition of Bruegel.

Valdés Leal, Juan de 1622–90

Spanish painter. He was born in Seville, and apart from several years spent at Cordova, where he trained with Castillo, he was active in his native city for all his career, becoming its leading painter after Murillo's death. Like Murillo he mainly painted religious subjects, but his approach was very different. He favoured macabre subject matter, treated with dramatic movement and lighting, nervous brushwork and strident colouring (*Vanitas*, 1660, Hartford, Conn., Wadsworth Atheneum). Most of his work was executed for religious houses in and around Seville, and his masterpiece is the series on *Death and Judgment* (commissioned 1672) in the Hospital of La Caridad, Seville. See vol. 2 p. **209**

Valenciennes, Pierre-Henri de 1750–1819

French landscape painter and art theorist. After studying in Paris, he visited Italy, 1769–77, and evolved a classical, formal manner inspired by Poussin (*Cicero discovering the body of Archimedes*, 1787, Toulouse, Musée des Augustins). His major theoretical book, *Elements of Perspective* (1800), established the principles of Neoclassical landscape. He encouraged direct study from nature but also emphasized the importance of classical studies.

Valentin de Boulogne, Moïse

(called Le Valentin) 1591–1632
French CARAVAGGESQUE painter, all of whose known career was spent in Rome, where he had settled by 1612. The details of his career are largely obscure, and his Christian name is unknown, "Moïse" (the French for Moses) probably being a misunderstanding of the Italian form of "Monsieur". He mainly painted religious scenes, his most important commission being an altarpiece for St Peter's, *The martyrdom of St Processus and St Martinus* (1629, Vatican). His genre scenes, which derive from Manfredi, are generally better known (*Soldiers and Bohemians*, c.1625, Indianapolis Museum of Art).

Vallgren, Ville 1855–1940

Finnish sculptor. He went to Paris in 1877 and first exhibited at the Salon in 1878. His conventionally elegant style of the 1880s was followed by a Symbolist phase when he exhibited with the ROSE+CROIX painters (1892) and was influenced by Rodin. In his small-scale bronzes of the 1890s refined linear rhythms and an organic conception of form combine in an Art Nouveau style. In 1913 he returned to Finland. There is a museum of his work near Helsinki.

Vallotton, Félix 1865–1925

Swiss painter. He studied drawing in Paris in 1882 at the Académie Julian, where he was influenced by Courbet and Manet. In 1891 he showed at the Salon des Indépendants and made his first extremely skilful woodcuts for the *Revue Blanche*. During this period he came under the influence of van Gogh, Toulouse-Lautrec and the Nabis. He exhibited at the first Rose+Croix exhibition in 1892. His work is Realist in its monumentality and straightforward representation, but is distinguished by a strong sense of abstract design and simplification of form (*Summer*, 1892, Zurich, Kunstgewerbemuseum).

Vanderlyn, John 1775–1852

One of the leading American NEO-CLASSICAL painters. He worked for extensive periods in Paris (the only American painter of his generation to do so), and it was there that he painted his first important work, *The death of Jane McCrea* (1804, Hartford, Wadsworth Atheneum), a scene from recent history, the murder of a woman by Indians. The composition derives from ancient relief sculpture and vase-paintings. More sensuous is his best-known work, *Ariadne asleep on Naxos* (1814, Philadelphia, Pennsylvania Academy of Fine Arts), inspired by Giorgione and Titian and the finest piece of nude painting in American art before Eakins. Such splendid works won him a considerable reputation in France, but he had much less success in America, and his later years were embittered and mainly spent painting uninspired portraits.

Vanishing point SEE PERSPECTIVE

Vanitas

Term, from the Latin for vanity, used to describe a type of still life consisting of a collection of objects which symbolize the brevity of human life and the transience of earthly pleasures and achievements. Such paintings were particularly popular in the 16th and 17th centuries, above all in the Netherlands. A skull, a watch, a broken lute, smoking candles and flowers losing their petals were among the common symbols of inevitable decay. Vanitas elements are also found as still-life details in other paintings.

Van Loo family

Family of French painters of Flemish origin. **Jacob** (1614–70), the founder of the line, was a portrait painter who settled in Paris in 1662. His grandson **Jean-Baptiste** (1684–1745) specialized in portraits and history painting. Jean-Baptiste's brother, **Charles-André**,

known as **Carle** (1705–65) was by far the most important of the family. He was one of the most important ROCOCO decorators of his time, and also had a varied output of easel-paintings including many altarpieces for churches in Paris and genre pictures in the manner of Lancret but much larger in scale. His career was very successful, and culminated in his appointments as principal painter to Louis XV in 1762 and Director of the Academy in 1763. Jean-Baptiste's son was **Louis-Michel** (1707–71), who was exclusively a portrait painter, working under the influence of Largillière. From 1736 to 1752 he was court painter to Philip V of Spain.

Vanni, Sam (until 1941 Samuel Besprosvanni) born 1908

Finnish painter, who after World War II turned to abstract and finally concrete art. His compositions are built up around intersecting patterns of dark bands, and frequently include ovals or developments of the oval. He has played an important role as a teacher.

Vantongerloo, Georges 1886–1965

Belgian sculptor and painter, also a designer of architectural projects. After a phase of Neo-Impressionist painting, using block-like strokes with heightened colour, he began to explore structure and universal colour value. In Holland, 1915–19, he met van Doesburg and joined DE STIJL, and between 1917 and 1922 contributed to the journal. His first abstract sculpture in 1917 was an exploration of positive and negative volume, as in *Construction of volume relations* (1921, New York, MOMA). Between 1919 and 1927 he lived at Menton and pursued his investigations of mathematical and algebraic formulae, creating schematic, geometric sculptures of considerable importance to De Stijl achievements. By 1937 curved forms are directly visible in his work. He took an active part in CERCLE ET CARRÉ and in the organization of ABSTRACTION-CRÉATION in Paris. From 1928–29 he made a series of plans and maquettes for airports, bridges and cities. After 1942 he used wire and transparent plastic for his sculpture. See vol. 3 pp. **186–187**

Vanvitelli, Gaspare (Gaspar van Wittel) 1653–1736

Dutch-born topographical painter, who moved to Italy in 1672. He worked mainly in Naples and Rome and had a very successful career with his well composed but rather dry town views. His son was the architect **Luigi** (1700–73), who designed the huge royal palace (begun 1752) at Caserta, near Naples, the swansong of the Italian Baroque.

Vargas, Luis de 1502–68

Spanish painter, born in Seville. He worked in Italy from 1523 until about 1550, when he returned to Spain, bringing with him a style closely dependent on Italian High Renaissance and Mannerist models. Perino del Vaga and Giulio Romano were among his sources. His first dated work is an altarpiece of *The Nativity* with a predella showing *The Epiphany* (1555, Seville Cathedral). The figures are solid, heavy and closely packed, but not without grace. The vision of God in the sky is clearly inspired by the figure of Christ in Michelangelo's *Conversion of St Paul*. Vargas was an influential figure in Seville, and introduced the use of fresco to the city.

Varley, Frederick 1881–1969

English-born Canadian landscape and portrait painter, a founder-member of

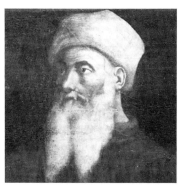

Uccello: Self-portrait from *The founders of Florentine art*, c.1450. Paris, Louvre (Alinari)

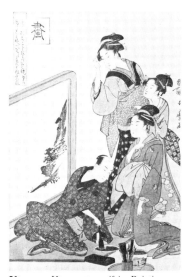

Utamaro: *Utamaro personifying Painting*, 1790–91. London, BM

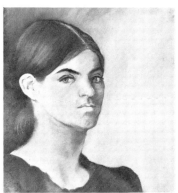

Valadon: Self-portrait, 1883. Paris, Musée National d'Art Moderne

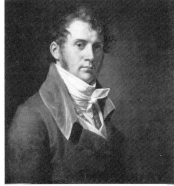

Vanderlyn: Self-portrait, 1800. New York, Metropolitan

the GROUP OF SEVEN. Unlike other members, he prized aesthetic feeling rather than nationalistic expression, and painted orientally-influenced works, such as *Dharana* (1932, Toronto, NG of Ontario).

Varley, John 1778–1843

English landscape painter in watercolour. His style represents a transition from the tinted topographical drawing of the 18th century to the somewhat bolder technique associated with the great names of the English watercolour school. He was an important teacher, Cox, Linnell and Palmer being among his pupils, and wrote two influential books. His brother **Cornelius** (1781–1873) was also a fine watercolourist.

Vasarély, Victor born 1908

French painter born in Hungary, the major pioneer of OP art. After attending a School of Applied Arts in Budapest, he went to Paris in 1930. At first he worked as a graphic designer; between 1933 and 1938 he produced a series of *Harlequins* and *Zebras*, entirely in black and white, reducing the forms to patterns sometimes interlocking with a patterned background. In 1947 he turned to completely abstract work and began to explore optical movement within the canvas. A typical work such as *Timbres II* (1966, Cologne, Wallraf-Richartz Museum) employs trapezoidal shapes of red-orange which appear to advance and recede as the different colours of the background vary in strength; the whole painting pulsates with these waves. Vasarély presented his theories in his *Yellow Manifesto* of 1955, describing his work as the creation of a new art of mechanistic, standardized shapes and colours, replacing traditional easel-painting and creating a new urban folk art. He has produced many prints and has been involved with projects to animate the walls of buildings—for instance at the University of Caracas. His son Yvaral has also experimented with OP art. See vol. 1 pp. 114, 128; vol. 3 p. 244

Vasari, Giorgio 1511–74

Italian painter, architect and art historian, born in Arezzo. He is chiefly remembered for his *Lives of the Most Eminent Painters, Sculptors and Architects*, a seminal work in the development of art criticism and biography. First published in 1550, and with a second, much enlarged edition appearing in 1568, it consolidated the notion of a *rinascita*, a rebirth of the artistic values of ancient Rome, and traced its progression from the innovations of Nicola Pisano and Giotto to the supreme achievements of Michelangelo. This attitude has coloured most subsequent writing on Italian Renaissance art and, despite a rather cavalier approach to some factual detail, Vasari's book is still a fundamental work for scholars of the period. Its lively, anecdotal style has ensured it a permanent wider readership. The geniality which enabled Vasari to gather his material for the *Lives* also earned him numerous commissions as a painter and architect. After completing his training in the workshop of Andrea del Sarto, he moved to Rome and embarked on decorations in the Vatican, then in 1546 proceeded to the histories in the Cancelleria. Its nickname, "the Room of a Hundred Days", referring to the speed of execution, reflects his summary style and his reliance on assistants. Vasari's adulation of Michelangelo is as clear from his painting as from his writing, but his figures seem winsome rather than monumental; indeed their exagger-

ated poses and precious colouring can be classified as Mannerism at its most effete. The suite of decorations in the Sala Grande of the Palazzo Vecchio (begun 1563, Florence) and the adjoining *studiolo* (1570–73) provide the most elaborate examples of these features. He was a better architect than painter, his finest building being the Uffizi, Florence (begun 1560), now the famous art gallery. See vol. 2 p. **166**; vol. 4 p. *117*

Vasnetsov, Victor Mikhailovich 1848–1926

Russian painter. Self-taught, he went to St Petersburg in 1867 and in 1868 he entered the Academy. From 1875 he exhibited his genre pictures of the poor with the WANDERERS (*Moving house*, 1876, Moscow, Tretyakov Gallery). He moved to Moscow in 1878 and was soon painting monumental, realistic historical canvases from Russian epics (*Battlefield after the defeat of Prince Igor*, 1880, Tretyakov Gallery). He was one of the leading spirits in the patron Mamontov's artistic circle and his designs for Mamontov's opera exerted a strong influence on the next generation of artists. His religious work in Vladimir Cathedral in Kiev is also impressive.

Vaughan, Keith 1912–77

British painter. In the early 1940s he was strongly associated with NEO-ROMANTICISM, and made coloured drawings of moonlit houses or night scenes (*Valley landscape*, 1945, London, V&A). Later he concentrated on the male nude in a landscape—in terms of highly simplified forms. By the end of the late 1950s the stylized fragmentations had pushed his work close to abstraction.

Vecchietta (Lorenzo di Pietro) c.1410–80

Italian painter, sculptor, draughtsman and architect, the most influential Sienese artist of the later 15th century. He was a pupil of Sassetta and his subtle and lively style continued the tradition of the Sienese school, but Florentine art also influenced him, especially Domenico Veneziano's strong pictorial structures. These traits are clear in the frescos for the Ospedale alla Scala (1441), in which he collaborated with Domenico di Bartolo. His narrative skills are best seen in his illustrations of Dante's *Divine Comedy* (c.1438–44, London, BM) for Alfonso I of Naples. His style briefly acquired an overwrought expressionism, evident in the frescos of *The Passion* in the Baptistery, Siena, begun in 1450. Later he became increasingly active as a sculptor, especially in bronze, almost certainly encouraged by contact with Donatello, who was in Siena from 1457 to 1459.

Vedder, Elihu 1836–1923

American painter and illustrator. Much of his career was spent in France and Italy. He had mystical leanings, and his best paintings depict haunting private fantasies (*The questioner of the sphinx*, 1863, Boston, MFA).

Vedova, Emilio born 1919

Italian painter, a leading member of the FRONTE NUOVO DELLE ARTI. The earliest influences on his work were those of Rouault and Permeke. He was also greatly impressed by Picasso's *Guernica*, and many of his figurative paintings have an overt political intent. In the late 1940s he worked briefly on Constructivist drawings. In 1950 his abstract paintings became more lyrical and free.

Veduta

Term, from the Italian for view, used to

describe a topographic painting, typically a townscape. Canaletto and his nephew Bellotto practised the genre.

Veen, Otto van 1556–1629

Flemish MANNERIST painter, mainly remembered as the third and most important teacher of Rubens. He was born in Leyden, and before settling in Antwerp in the early 1590s worked in various places, including Rome, where he spent about five years with Federico Zuccaro. His knowledge of Italian art was among the most thorough of any of his contemporaries, and was the basis of his successful career. *The mystic marriage of St Catherine* (1589, Brussels, Musées Royaux des Beaux-Arts), full of echoes of Correggio and Parmigianino, is a typical work, fairly uninspired, but elegant and accomplished. Van Veen was a highly cultivated man, who probably passed on to Rubens some of his love of classical literature as well as of Italian art.

Velazquez (Velásquez), Diego Rodriguez de Silva y 1599–1660

The greatest of Spanish painters. From 1613 to 1618 he trained in his native Seville with Pacheco, whose daughter he married. He was very precocious, and in an early work such as *The Immaculate Conception* (c.1618, London, NG) he had already broken away completely from the rather dry Mannerist style of his master to create a personal kind of naturalism. The figure of the Virgin is modelled very solidly in rich clotted paint and with complete mastery of light and shade. Most of Velazquez's early works were religious scenes or bodegones, to which he brought a new dignity (*An old woman cooking eggs*, 1618, Edinburgh, NG of Scotland), but on a trip to Madrid in 1622 it was his noble and severe portrait of the great poet *Luis de Góngora* (Boston, MFA) that attracted attention. He was recalled to Madrid in the following year by Philip IV's First Minister, the Duke of Olivares, and became court painter. His career at court, principally as a portraitist, was one of unbroken success. Philip had a very high opinion of his personal as well as his professional qualities, and the prestigious court posts with which he was burdened limited his output as a painter. Velazquez's work was always based on acute observation of nature, but his means of expression developed with increasing freedom and subtlety throughout his career, as he used paint to render not what the mind knows to exist but what the eye sees. Thus, in his mature works, the brushwork when viewed at close range seems blurred and at times more abstract than descriptive, but at the correct distance coalesces to render form and atmosphere with astonishing vividness. The great group portrait "*Las Meninas*" (1656, Madrid, Prado), his most complex work, is the most celebrated instance of Velazquez's ability to create a visual world which seems almost palpable in its reality, and in his superb series of equestrian portraits of the 1630s (Prado) he had shown that he had complete mastery of space, form and atmosphere in exterior as well as interior settings. With this growing technical sophistication went a deepening ability to analyse character, and Velazquez always showed total respect for the individuality of his sitters, whether he was portraying Philip IV, the ruler of the world's greatest empire, or the pathetic court dwarfs, of whom he left an unforgettable series of paintings (Prado). Velazquez's greatest single portrait is *Pope Innocent X* (1650, Rome, Galleria Doria-Pamphili), painted on the

second of his two trips to Italy (1629–31, 1649–51), where, responding especially to the great Venetian masters, who helped to loosen his brushwork, he seems to have been much happier than in the stuffy atmosphere of the Spanish court. Apart from portraits and religious and mythological works, which he produced intermittently throughout his career, Velazquez also painted a few very fresh landscapes, some female nudes, of which one survives (London, NG), and one of the greatest of all history paintings, *The surrender of Breda* (1634–35, Prado). It is impossible fully to appreciate Velazquez's genius outside the Prado, and like most Spanish painters he was largely unknown outside his native country until the Napoleonic Wars. In the 19th century, however, his work came as a revelation to progressive artists, notably Manet, who regarded Velazquez as the greatest painter who had ever lived. See vol. 1 pp. *57*, *108*, *110*, *116*; vol. 2 pp. **210–211**; vol. 4 p. *135*

Velde, Bram van born 1895

Dutch painter. His early work was influenced by the naturalistic painting of Breitner. During the 1920s he painted landscapes and flowers in brilliant colours of thinly applied paint. Influenced both by Cubism and Expressionism, he developed a mature style close to American Abstract Expressionism (*Gouache*, 1940, Paris, Jacques Putnam coll.).

Velde, Esaias van de c.1591–1630

Dutch landscape painter, draughtsman and etcher, one of the most important pioneers of naturalism in Dutch landscape. He was born in Amsterdam and worked in Haarlem and, from 1618, The Hague. Some early works reflect the archaic Flemish Mannerist tradition, but he soon turned to a simple naturalistic style, often of great charm. *Landscape with two horsemen* (1614, Enschede, Rijksmuseum Twenthe), for example, is remarkable at this date for its sense of unaffected observation. Such works were a formative influence on several Dutch landscape artists, above all Jan van Goyen, who moved beyond van de Velde in his mastery of atmosphere. See vol. 2 pp. **220–221**

Velde, Henry van de 1863–1957

Belgian painter, designer and architect. He studied in Paris from 1884 to 1885 with Carolus-Duran and in 1889, back in Belgium, he began to paint in a Neo-Impressionist style. In 1893, having discovered the work of William Morris, he became interested in architecture and interior decoration. He began to design houses and galleries (such as the Folkwang Museum at Hagen, 1900–02), furniture and ornaments in an ART NOUVEAU style and introduced the innovations of the architect Rennie Mackintosh to Europe. Between 1901 and 1914 he directed the School of Decorative Arts at Weimar, which in 1919 formed the nucleus of the Bauhaus.

Velde, Willem II van de 1633–1707

The most famous member of a Dutch family of painters, and perhaps the most celebrated name in marine painting. He was the son and pupil of **Willem I** (1611–93) and was also taught by Simon de Vlieger. With his father, he left Amsterdam in 1672 to settle in England under the patronage of Charles II. Their paintings are marked by great accuracy of detail, and to secure this they even made drawings from a boat during naval battles. Whereas Willem I's paintings are somewhat dry, his son's are marked by sensitive observation of atmosphere, and in his finest works by a truly majestic sense of composition (*The cannon shot*, c.1660, Amsterdam, Rijksmuseum). The best collection of the work of father and son is in the National Maritime Museum, Greenwich. Willem II has always been a revered figure among marine painters, and had great influence on the development of seascape painting in England. His brother **Adriaen** (1636–72) was a highly versatile landscape painter, and also painted religious and mythological scenes. Active mainly in Amsterdam, he was known for the quality of his figures and animals, and often added the staffage to the work of van der Heyden, Hobbema, Koninck, Ruisdael, and his teacher Wynants. His most original works are beach scenes which convey a sense of great freshness (*The beach at Scheveningen*, 1658, Kassel, Gemäldegalerie). See vol. 2 p. **223**

Veličković, Vladimir born 1935
Yugoslav painter. Since 1966 he has lived and worked in Paris. His work has often been compared to Francis Bacon's, for both use dislocated, tortured forms to create a disturbed, aggressive mood (*Gibbet no. 3*, 1969, Paris, Musée National d'Art Moderne). One of his recent series has concerned the violence of childbirth.

Vellert, Dirk active 1511–44
Netherlandish painter, engraver and stained-glass designer, who qualified as a master in Antwerp in 1511. He designed and executed many stained-glass windows and carried on a thriving export business. His best-known windows are the monumental series in King's College Chapel, Cambridge. His panels are less distinguished; *The Nativity* (Lille, Musée des Beaux-Arts), with its *putti*, antique ruins and statuary, shows his dependence on Italian motifs. His engravings owe much to Dürer and Lucas van Leyden.

Venezianov, Alexei Gavrilovich 1780–1847
Russian painter. He began his career as a portrait painter, but in 1819 retired from St Petersburg (where he had a post in the civil service) to his country estate at Safonkovo. There he created a new genre—deeply poetic scenes of peasant life, both interiors and landscapes (*Harvesting*, Moscow, Tretyakov Gallery), and introduced a strong element of realism to an essentially classical, idyllic art. He was an influential protagonist of the Russian rural scene, and founded his own school of painting in 1820.

Venne, Adriaen van de 1589–1662
Dutch painter of portraits, landscapes and genre scenes, also a poet. He was born in Delft and worked in Antwerp, Middelburg and The Hague. In Antwerp he came under the influence of "Velvet" Brueghel, as can be seen in his early paintings of village fairs. Later, his palette was restricted to monochromatic greys and browns, and he concentrated on low-life subjects, cripples, beggars and so on (*Beggars' brawl*, 1634, Bergen, Billedgalleri). A zealous Protestant and supporter of the House of Orange, he painted many portraits of the family. There are examples in the Rijksmuseum in Amsterdam.

Verelst, Simon Pietersz. 1644–1721
Dutch flower and portrait painter, the best-known member of a large family of artists. From 1669 he worked in England, where he enjoyed great success, particularly under the patronage of the Duke of Buckingham, who encouraged him to turn to court portraiture.

Vereshchaghin, Vassily Vassilievich 1842–1904
Russian painter. After studies in the St Petersburg Academy (1861–65) he took lessons from Gérôme in Paris. The main subjects of his highly realistic canvases were war and exotic countries. He went twice to Turkestan, where he took part in the war (1869–70) and he also participated and was wounded in the Russo-Turkish War (1877–79). He travelled to India, Palestine, America and Japan. His mercilessly honest depiction of cruelties and atrocities made him a powerful anti-war artist.

Verhaecht, Tobias 1561–1631
Flemish landscape painter, chiefly remembered as the first teacher of Rubens. He travelled in Italy as a young man and painted in a style, similar to Paul Bril's, which left no discernible trace on his pupil (*The punishment of Niobe*, c.1605, Valenciennes, Musée des Beaux-Arts).

Verhulst, Rombout 1624–98
Flemish sculptor, who worked mainly in Holland. He assisted Artus Quellin in the decoration of Amsterdam Town Hall in the 1650s (an enchanting figure of *Venus* is signed by him), and settled in The Hague in 1663, becoming the leading sculptor of monuments commemorating Holland's great men, for which there was then a vogue. His effigies have great nobility of attitude and are as sensitively observed as his portrait busts, with a delicate feeling for texture (Monument of Admiral de Ruyter, 1681, Amsterdam, Nieuwe Kerk).

Verhulst van Bessemeers, Mayeken died 1600
Flemish painter. She was the wife of Coecke van Aelst and mother-in-law of Bruegel, whose sons she is said to have trained (Bruegel died in their infancy). There is great uncertainty about her independent work.

Verkade, Jan 1868–1946
Dutch painter. He trained in Amsterdam and, after a stay in Brussels and Paris, went to Pont-Aven to join Gauguin. After a short association with the Nabis he was converted to Catholicism in 1892 under the influence of Denis, and two years later entered the monastery at Beuron. His former interest in landscape and still life gave way to monumental ambitions in religious art.

Vermeer, Jan 1632–75
Dutch genre painter. Among Dutch artists he is now ranked second only to Rembrandt, but he was almost totally forgotten for two centuries after his death until he was rediscovered by the French critic Thoré. The oblivion into which he fell reflects the obscurity of his life. He is hardly mentioned in contemporary sources, and fewer than 40 paintings are generally attributed to him. The scarcity of dated works makes his development difficult to assess. As far as is known, all his life was spent in his native Delft, where he entered the painters' guild in 1653. The works which are accepted as being his earliest, such as *Christ in the house of Mary and Martha* (c.1654, Edinburgh, NG of Scotland) reflect the influence of the Utrecht Caravaggisti, and *The procuress* (1656, Dresden, Gemäldegalerie) is lively and bright. Soon, however, Vermeer turned to the kind of work with which his name is most closely associated: quiet, small-scale interior scenes, generally showing one or two figures engaged in writing, reading, music-making or everyday tasks. The colour harmonies are of great freshness, subtle yellows and blues predominating, and the figures are self-contained and totally absorbed in their tasks, creating images of perfect serenity, clarity and balance. There are sometimes allegorical overtones. Thus, *A woman weighing pearls* (c.1665, New York, Frick) might be mistaken for a pure genre picture, were it not for the painting of the Last Judgment in the background, coupled with the symbols of vanity—the mirror, the gold and the pearls. Vermeer appears to have worked slowly, and the spellbinding intensity of his work depends not only on the exquisite sensitivity of composition and characterization, but also on his marvellous technique. His paint is applied with unerring sureness, often quite broadly, with small raised points suggesting the fall of light on rough textures and creating an effect of great vibrancy; one critic has described his paint surface as being like "crushed pearls". His relationship with other artists working in Delft (notably de Hoogh) is problematic, but it is generally thought that Fabritius, also an artist of great painterly brilliance, was his master. Apart from his genre scenes, Vermeer also painted a few female portraits, an *Allegory of Faith* (New York, Metropolitan)—he was a Catholic—and an allegory of painting, "*The Artist's Studio*" (Vienna, Kunsthistorisches), and two town views, *A street in Delft* (Amsterdam, Rijksmuseum) and *View of Delft* (The Hague, Mauritshuis). The latter is one of the most remarkable landscapes in the history of art, conveying a sense of physical presence with astonishing immediacy. Vermeer was also a picture dealer, and was probably adversely affected by the financial crisis which followed the French invasion of 1672. At his death, he left his widow and eleven children in poverty. See vol. 1 p. 45; vol. 2 pp. **228–231**

Vermeyen, Jan Cornelisz. 1500–59
Netherlandish painter and engraver, born near Haarlem. From about 1525–30 he worked for the Regent Margaret and, in 1535, accompanied Charles V to Tunis. Tapestry cartoons commemorating this expedition are now in the Kunsthistorisches Museum, Vienna. He was a follower of van Scorel and had an eye for producing expressive portraits of self-important patrons, notably that of *Erard de la Marck* (Amsterdam, Rijksmusem).

Vernet, Claude-Joseph 1714–89
French landscape painter. He spent his formative years in Italy, where he was trained by Panini, and began to paint landscapes in the style of Claude Lorraine (which may have exerted some influence on Vernet's friend, Richard Wilson). After 20 years in Rome he returned in 1753 to Paris for his most important commission, a series of paintings of *The Seaports of France* (1753–62, Paris, Louvre). He also anticipated the Romantics in his dramatic scenes of shipwrecks. His son, **Carle** (1758–1836), specialized in racing pictures and Napoleonic battle-pieces, such as *The morning of Austerlitz* (Versailles), and a strong military flavour also pervaded the work of his grandson, Horace Vernet. See vol. 2 p. **255**

Vernet, Horace 1789–1863
French painter. His meticulous, panoramic canvases swarm with minuscule figures. Horace's smooth, precise finish earned him the contempt of Baudelaire, but also brought him im-

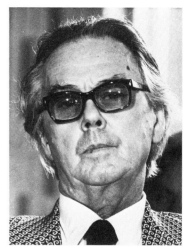

Vasarély: Photograph by Benoit Gysembergh (Camera Press)

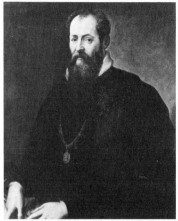

Vasari: Self-portrait, c.1567. Florence, Uffizi (Scala)

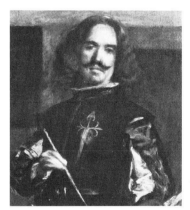

Velazquez: Self-portrait from "*Las Meninas*", 1656. Madrid, Prado (Mansell)

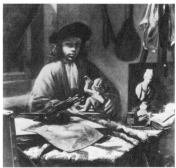

Vermeer: Self-portrait? c.1651. Miami Beach, John and Johanna Bass coll.

mense success in the Salon. In addition to battle scenes, he painted mawkishly sentimental animal studies and pandered to the fashionable taste for oriental subjects. *The Arab tale teller* (1833, London, Wallace Coll.) is a fine example of his clear, narrative approach, although it is significant that the painting predates his visit to Algiers in 1837. He was made Director of the French Academy in Rome, 1828–35.

Veronese, Paulo (Paulo Caliari)
1528–88
Italian painter, born in Verona but working principally within the orbit of Venetian art. He was essentially a great decorator, happiest with scenes of extravagant pomp. At Verona, he absorbed the traditions of pictorial clarity established by Mantegna and the Bellini, while his visit to Mantua in 1552 acquainted him with the illusionistic style of Giulio Romano. He settled in Venice in 1553 and his personal style began to emerge in his first state commission, which he won in the same year, ceiling paintings for the Room of the Council of Ten in the Doge's Palace. Sumptuous colouring, mannered nudes and ingenious perspective effects revealed the influence of Titian and Tintoretto. From 1555 to 1558 Veronese was working on three scenes from the *Book of Esther*, commissioned for S. Sebastiano, Venice, but his finest decorations were produced for Palladio's Villa Maser near Treviso (*c.*1561). Light-hearted in the extreme, these consisted of imaginary landscapes glimpsed through painted archways, and playful *trompe l'oeil* features. Veronese was equally capable of grandeur, however, and his later work at the Doge's Palace (1575–82), with its violent foreshortenings and the superb orchestration of its massing figures, radiates an exuberant majesty. In his religious paintings, Veronese gave priority to visual and anecdotal effects, often secularizing his subjects in the process. Thus, in *The finding of Moses* (*c.*1570, Madrid, Prado) the spectator's eye is drawn to the gorgeous colour harmonies, the rich brocades worn by the well-nourished and emphatically Venetian daughter of Pharaoh, and the anomalous presence of a dwarf-like jester. Similarly, it was the hedonistic trappings of a Renaissance banquet that dominated *The Marriage at Cana* (1562–63, Paris, Louvre) and *The Last Supper* (1573, Venice, Accademia); the latter in particular earning the displeasure of the Inquisition for its portrayal of German soldiers, a buffoon with a parrot, and apostles carving the meat and picking their teeth at the holy event. Accordingly, the picture was renamed *The feast in the house of Levi*, although Veronese's testimony remains a classic defence of artistic licence. His large workshop was continued by his family. See vol. 2 p. **171**

Verrio, Antonio 1630–1707
Italian decorative painter, active in England from 1671. His highly successful career was due to the poverty of native competition in England rather than the quality of his work, which is generally mediocre when measured against that of his best European contemporaries. He worked at Windsor Castle and the palaces of Whitehall and Hampton Court, as well as in country houses such as Burghley and Chatsworth.

Verrocchio, Andrea del (Andrea di Cione) 1435–88
Italian sculptor, painter and metalworker, who had the most important studio in Florence in the second half of the 15th century. He trained as a goldsmith and the value of this background is immediately evident from the exquisite craftsmanship of *The doubting of Thomas* (1465, Florence, Orsanmichele), his first major commission in sculpture. No attempt was made to exploit the dramatic potential of the theme; instead the bronze figures were rendered with a grace of line, a fragile delicacy and, above all, a loving attention to detail. In his youth, Verrocchio may have been a pupil of Donatello and, certainly, the latter's works frequently served as springboards for his own creations, even though their styles were very different. Verrocchio's *David* (*c.*1475, Florence, Bargello), for example, possesses a self-conscious refinement and a buoyancy that was more muted in Donatello's bronze. The unspoken rivalry was apparent once again in Verrocchio's masterpiece, the equestrian statue of *Bartolommeo Colleoni* (1481–90, Venice, Piazza SS. Giovanni e Paolo), which inevitably demands comparison with Donatello's *Gattamelata* statue in Padua. Proud, taut and arrogant, Verrocchio's figure encapsulates present-day conceptions of the ideal Renaissance warrior, with his paradoxical blend of cultural and bellicose qualities. Few paintings can be given to Verrocchio with certainty, but large numbers were produced by his studio. In *The baptism of Christ* (*c.*1472, Florence, Uffizi), Leonardo, Verrocchio's greatest pupil, painted one of the angels. Leonardo took from Verrocchio his superb standards of craftsmanship, and his interest in two contrasting physical types, the gnarled old warrior represented by the Colleoni, and the svelte youth represented by the David. Lorenzo di Credi became Verrocchio's chief painter and Perugino may have been amongst his pupils. See vol. 2 p. **115**

Verspronck, Johannes 1597–1662
Dutch portrait painter, born and active in Haarlem, where he studied with Frans Hals. He was one of the fashionable Dutch portraitists of the mid-17th century and catered for the Protestant bourgeoisie, to whose stolid faces he gave an appealing delicacy. *Young girl in a blue dress* (1641, Amsterdam, Rijksmuseum) is a fine work.

Vertue, George 1684–1756
British engraver and antiquarian. His detailed notebooks are a precious source of information on the British school of art during the period of its rise to independence in the early 18th century.

Vieira da Silva, Maria Elena
born 1908
Naturalized French painter and sculptor, of Portuguese origin. A pupil of Léger and Bourdelle, she first attracted attention in the 1930s with semi-abstract paintings characterized by muted colour and gentle light effects. This has remained her distinctive style (*Overhead railway*, 1955, Düsseldorf, Nordrhein-Westfalen Kunstsammlung).

Vien, Joseph-Marie 1716–1809
French painter of history and genre, a pupil of Natoire. He was in Rome from 1743 to 1750, when the discoveries of antique paintings at Pompeii and Herculaneum were causing great excitement, but his importance as a precursor of Neoclassicism has been exaggerated, not least by himself. *The cupid seller* (1763, Fontainebleau, Château), his best-known work, is based on an antique original, but its rather sickly sentimentality is very far from the high seriousness of his pupil Jacques-Louis David. The Rococo elegance and sly eroticism of *The Greek girl at the bath* (1767, Ponce, Musée) is more characteristic, and *The apotheosis of Winckelmann* (1768, Langres, Musée), which could have been a manifesto of the new movement, is as much Baroque as Neoclassical. His successful career culminated in his appointment as Director of the French Academy in Rome in 1776 and Premier Peintre du Roi in 1789. See vol. 3 p. **56**

Vigarny, Felipe see BIGARNY

Vigée-Lebrun, Elisabeth
1755–1842
French portrait painter. She was taught by her father, the portraitist **Louis Vigée** (1715–67), and also received instruction from Claude-Joseph Vernet and Greuze. Her portraits are elegant, flattering, delicate in touch and charmingly sentimental. She painted more than 20 of Marie-Antoinette (*Marie-Antoinette and her children*, 1787, Versailles). During the Revolution she sought refuge in Italy, and later made a successful career at many European courts before returning to France under Louis XVIII. She was renowned for her wit and charm, and her memoirs (1833–37) provide a fascinating account of the artistic and political events of the age.

Vigeland, Gustav 1869–1943
Norwegian sculptor and wood engraver, the most prolific and famous of Norwegian sculptors. His early work, inspired by study under Rodin in Paris, 1892, was strongly realistic. However, his most famous creation, the monumental series of sculptures in bronze and granite in Frogner Park, Oslo, displayed an increasingly heavy and generalized style. Begun in 1905, the scheme became a lifetime's obsession: it intended to symbolize life and the evolution of man and to unite sculpture with nature. When it was eventually installed in 1944, it was not well received.

Vignon, Claude 1593–1670
French painter and engraver. He travelled in Italy as a young man and absorbed a variety of influences, which were supplemented on his return to France in the 1620s, when he became a picture dealer. This business took him on subsequent trips to Italy. Strong echoes of Caravaggio, Elsheimer, and particularly Rembrandt occur in his eccentric work, which is characterized by a bizarre expressiveness and a richly-textured paint surface (*Croesus receiving tribute from a Lydian peasant*, 1629, Tours, Musée des Beaux-Arts).

Viking art
Art of the Viking people of Scandinavia, whose period of greatest activity lasted from about AD 800 to the mid-11th century. The surviving Viking art for the most part of this period is chiefly wooden sculpture and functional metalwork and jewellery, such as was found in the early 9th-century Oseberg ship burial (Oslo, Bygdøy, Viking Ship Hall). Decorative relief work shows a characteristic mixture of animal motifs and interlace ornament, executed with considerable skill and finely designed. The Viking conversion to Christianity did not radically affect this pagan style, and newly introduced holy figures were enveloped in traditional interlace (as on the memorial stone of the Christian King Harald Bluetooth in the Royal Cemetery, Jellinge, Jutland). Migrating Vikings brought their art to many parts of northern Europe, in particular to their settlements in England and Ireland.

Villard de Honnecourt
active 1st half of 13th century
Frenchman, perhaps an architect, the author of a unique sketchbook (*c.*1220–35, Paris, Bibliothèque Nationale), the only such work to have survived from before the 15th century. It is a miscellany of early 13th-century Gothic groundplans and elevations (notably of Rheims Cathedral), with technical diagrams and figure drawings. Villard showed an acute interest in several arts, and his figure style is linear and fluent, strikingly close to Nicholas of Verdun and to the most classical Gothic sculpture of Rheims.

Villon, Jacques (Gaston Duchamp)
1875–1963
French painter. The brother of Marcel Duchamp and the sculptor Duchamp-Villon, he first studied law and was a magazine draughtsman before becoming a central figure in the SECTION D'OR group. *The table is laid* (1913, New Haven, Yale University), which employs a prismatic variation of Cubism, is typical of his work at this time. Seeking lyrical effects, he later worked in both abstract and representational styles.

Vinckboons, David 1576–1632
Flemish-born landscape painter and print designer, active for most of his career in Amsterdam. He is best known for his panoramic multi-figure genre scenes in the Bruegel tradition (*Kermis*, *c.*1610, Dresden, Gemäldegalerie). In spite of the liveliness of his figures, the most interesting part of his painting is often the landscape. He treats it less schematically than most of his contemporaries and so figures in the transition from Mannerism to naturalism.

Vingt, Les
Group of Belgian SYMBOLIST artists, who banded together in 1884. Their main aim was to bring radical art to Brussels. In the 1880s and 1890s they exhibited works by Gauguin, van Gogh, Seurat, Whistler and Henry van de Velde, as well as work by English artists such as Morris and Beardsley. Les Vingt became the central exhibiting group for Belgian Art Nouveau and showed applied art as well as painting. In 1894 the group changed its name to *La Libre Estétique* (The Free Aesthetic). Its members included Toorop and Ensor.

Vischer family
Family of German sculptors, active in Nuremberg. **Peter the Elder** (*c.*1460–1529), the best-known member, inherited the family shop from his father **Herman the Elder** (died 1488), and ran it with his sons, notably **Herman the Younger** (*c.*1486–1517) and **Peter the Younger** (1487–1528). Their most famous work was the shrine of St Sebald (1488–1519, Nuremberg, St Sebald), a large bronze tabernacle with figures, reliefs and decorative Gothic detail, and some classical and Romanesque motifs. Peter the Elder produced in 1512–13 two lifelike figures for the tomb of the Emperor Maximilian in the Hofkirche, Innsbruck, their designs influenced by Dürer. His sons were more influenced by the art of Italy. See vol. 2 p. **159**

Visser, Carel born 1928
Dutch sculptor and graphic artist. His early works, similar in style to the later Giacometti, were thin awkward pieces welded together with small bits of rusty iron, but *Double-form* (1957, Amsterdam, Stedelijk Museum), a heavy, large-scale piece in iron, fusing a totemic image with elements of Constructivism, is typical of his better-known works.

Vitale da Bologna
documented 1334–61

The most important painter of the Bolognese school in the 14th century. Two signed paintings of *The Virgin and Child*, one in the Vatican, the other, dated *c*.1345, in the Galleria Doria-Bargellini in Bologna, form the foundation for further attributions, which include two fresco cycles at Messarata and Pomposa. His colouring is vivid and his compositions extravagant.

Vittoria, Alessandro 1525–1608
Italian sculptor, active from 1543 in Venice, where he was a pupil of Jacopo Sansovino, and after the latter's death the leading sculptor in the city. He was strongly influenced by the sculpture of Michelangelo and broke from the classicism of Sansovino. There are examples of his monumental work in many Venetian churches, and he was also a medallist and sculptor of small bronzes (*Neptune with a seahorse*, London, V&A), and had a prolific output of portrait busts.

Vivarini family
Family of Venetian painters with a flourishing workshop at Murano. Both **Antonio** (*c*.1419–76/84) and **Bartolommeo** (*c*.1432–99) specialized in carefully composed, highly-finished polyptychs. Antonio painted in a stiff and decorative INTERNATIONAL GOTHIC manner, usually in collaboration with others. He worked with Giovanni d'Alemagna in the Ovetari Chapel of the Eremetani Church, Padua (1448–50), and then with his brother (for example, on the polyptych of *c*.1450 in Bologna, Pinacoteca Nazionale). Bartolommeo's work, influenced by Gentile da Fabriano, is more highly coloured and has a soft density which anticipates Giovanni Bellini's style. **Alvise** (*c*.1445–*c*.1505), Antonio's son, carried on the workshop. He painted religious subjects, often of high quality, influenced by Giovanni Bellini but distinctive, and some simple but perceptive portraits (examples in New York, Brooklyn Museum, and London, NG).

Vivin, Louis 1861–1936
French NAIVE painter. He worked as a postal employee until 1922, when he took up painting full-time. He met the critic Wilhelm Uhde who, in 1928, exhibited Vivin's paintings alongside those of Bombois, Bauchant, Rousseau and Séraphine. *Notre-Dame* (1933, Paris, Musée National d'Art Moderne) is typical of his many urban scenes, with its precise delineation of every brick and paving stone. See vol. 3 p. *141*

Vlaminck, Maurice de 1876–1958
French painter, a leading member of the FAUVES. Eccentric and rebellious, he was a racing cyclist and violinist before taking up painting. Under the impact of the van Gogh retrospective exhibition of 1901, he began to work in vivid colour, eventually using pigments straight from the tube, and in 1905 was branded along with Derain and Matisse as a "wild beast" when they exhibited at the Salon d'Automne. *The bridge at Chatou* (1906, Paris, Musée d'Art Moderne) is typical of his Fauvist period and is more rhythmically structured and more intense in colour and expression than the contemporary work of, for instance, Matisse. Vlaminck was one of the first to admire and collect African tribal art but it had no influence on his work and, despite a brief contact with Cubism, he continued to paint landscape in a style that gradually became less brilliant and more mannered. See vol. 3 p. **143**

Vlieger, Simon de 1600/01–53
Dutch painter, principally of seascapes. Born in Rotterdam, he was active there and in Delft and Amsterdam. Early works reflect the influence of the grey-brown tonality and stormy drama of Porcellis' work, but later seascapes are calmer and more majestic (*Calm sea*, 1649, Vienna, Kunsthistorisches). His spatial construction was much firmer than Porcellis' and in his strength of design as well as his sense of atmosphere he had wide influence.

Vollard, Ambroise 1867–1939
French picture dealer and publisher, a champion of the artistic avantgarde. In 1895 he mounted the first one-man exhibition of Cézanne's work and supported Gauguin financially after 1897. By 1901 he was exhibiting the work of Picasso and became a major dealer in Cubism. He commissioned many contemporary artists to illustrate luxury editions of classical and modern texts, and in 1937 published Picasso's set of 100 etchings, the *Vollard Suite*.

Vordemberge-Gildewart, Friedrich 1899–1963
German painter, who settled in Holland in 1938. He joined the DE STIJL movement in 1924, establishing a close friendship with van Doesburg. In 1925 he was associated with the Abstraction-Création group in Paris. His early works, influenced by Suprematism, consist of contrasting geometric shapes with the addition of montage elements, such as wooden knobs or sections of picture framing (*Composition 19*, 1926, Hanover, Landesgalerie). His later work became more strictly Constructivist.

Vorsterman, Lucas 1595–1675
One of the leading Flemish engravers of the 17th century. From about 1620 to 1622 he was Rubens' most favoured engraver, but a disagreement ended their collaboration, which was not renewed until 1638. Vorsterman also worked for van Dyck for several years, notably on portraits for his *Iconography*. He was a brilliantly versatile technician, capable of capturing the drama of a Rubens painting in deep contrasts of light and shade or the delicacy of a van Dyck drawing in fine sensitive lines.

Vorticism
Short lived British avantgarde movement. The central figure and spokesman was Wyndham Lewis, who was the editor and chief contributor to the magazine *Blast*, which ran for two issues in 1914 and 1915. Lewis was later to define Vorticism as "What I personally did and said at a certain period", but the harsh, mechanistic style of his semi-abstract paintings at this time is apparent in the work of other contributors to *Blast* such as Gaudier-Brzeska, Roberts and Wadsworth. The Vorticist style reflects Cubist and Futurist experiments. The only exhibition was held in London in June 1915. Other artists with stylistic affinities were Nevinson, Epstein and Bomberg. Although as an organized movement it did not survive World War I, it had considerable influence on British modernism in the early 1920s. See vol. 3 pp. 154–155

Vos, Cornelis de 1584–1651
Flemish painter, active mainly in Antwerp. He painted historical, mythological and religious works, but is best known for his portraits, which are attractive, but generally uninspired compared with the work of Rubens and van Dyck. In his speciality of child portraiture, however, de Vos was a match for these two great masters or anyone else. *The artist with his family* (1621, Brussels, Musées Royaux des Beaux-Arts) shows him as a very benign-looking father, and his sympathy with children enabled him to capture their freshness and charm without becoming sentimental or sacrificing any of their individuality. *A young boy* (*c*.1625) and *A young girl* (*c*.1635), both in the Musée Mayer van der Bergh, Antwerp, show him at his exquisitely sensitive best. His brother **Paul** (1596–1678) was a pupil of their brother-in-law Snyders, and painted hunting scenes and still lifes in his manner. Both brothers worked with Rubens, notably for Philip IV's hunting lodge near Madrid, the Torre de la Parada. See vol. 2 pp. **200–201**

Vos, Maerten de 1532–1603
Flemish painter and decorative artist, born in Antwerp, where he was a pupil of Frans Floris. From 1548 to 1558 he was in Rome and Venice, where he worked as Tintoretto's assistant, producing landscapes. He returned to Antwerp, and after Floris' death became the city's leading Romanist painter. Most of his paintings were altarpieces (good examples are in the Musées Royaux des Beaux-Arts, Antwerp), characterized by elongated, mannered figures showing a brisk sense of movement. His rare portraits, by contrast, are striking for their strong directness of presentation (*Gilles Hoffman and his wife*, 1570, Amsterdam, Rijksmuseum).

Vos, Simon de 1603–76
Flemish painter, born and mainly active in Antwerp, where he studied with Cornelis de Vos (probably a relative). He painted sober portraits in the manner of Cornelis (*A lady with a dish of fruit*, Barnard Castle, Bowes Museum) and also religious scenes inspired by Rubens and van Dyck (*The beheading of St Paul*, 1648, Antwerp, Musées Royaux des Beaux-Arts). His best-known and most personal works, however, are his lively and colourful genre scenes (*Gipsy woman telling a young man's fortune*, 1639, Antwerp, Musées Royaux des Beaux-Arts).

Vostell, Wolf born 1932
West German artist, the most important creator of HAPPENINGS in Germany, perhaps in Europe. The main difference between his Happenings and those of, say, Kaprow in America was his interest, not in the definition of "art" but in its content, scope and effect. Already in his *Dé-coll/ages*, arrived at by a process of ripping away layers of images, the accent was mainly on violence. These led to actions performed in public, such as his *TV dé-coll/ages*, in which deliberately badly-tuned televisions would be assaulted in various ways. Possibly his most famous Happening involved a crash between a car and a railway engine.

Vouet, Simon 1590–1649
The most important French painter of the first half of the 17th century. From 1613 to 1627 he worked in Italy (mainly Rome), first adopting a Caravaggesque manner, but then developing an eclectic Baroque style in which the influence of Bolognese classicism played a large part (*The appearance of the Virgin to St Bruno*, 1626?, Naples, S. Martino). In 1627 Vouet was recalled to Paris by Louis XIII and made court painter. French painting was then at a low ebb, and Vouet became enormously successful. Although not a great artist, he was hard working and highly adaptable, and his compromise style suited the taste of the French public

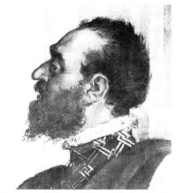
Veronese: Self-portrait from *The feast in the house of Levi*, 1573. Venice, Accademia (Mansell)

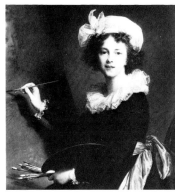
Vigée-Lebrun: Self-portrait, 1790. Florence, Uffizi (Alinari)

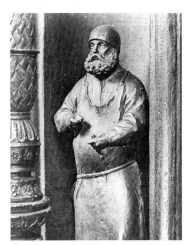
Vischer, Peter the Elder: Self-portrait from the Tomb of S. Sebald, Nuremberg, 1488–1519 (Bildarchiv Foto Marburg)

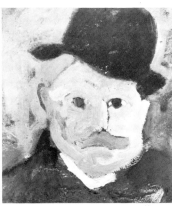
Vlaminck: Portrait by Derain, 1905, Paris, Private coll. (Giraudon)

as a replacement for the Mannerism then current, in a way which the full drama of Caravaggism or the rhetoric of Baroque would not have done. His influence was enormous and many of the leading painters of the next generation trained in his studio, among them Lebrun and Le Sueur. See vol. 2 p. **193**

Vranx, Sebastien 1573–1647
Flemish painter, active mainly in his native Antwerp. He painted landscapes, market scenes and domestic interiors, but is best known for his battle-pieces (*Attack on a convoy*, 1616, Royal coll.). His style marks the transition from Mannerism to naturalism, for, while his compositions are crowded and employ a high viewpoint, individual details are strikingly observed from the life.

Vrel, Jacobus active 1654–62
Dutch genre painter, one of the most enigmatic artists of his generation. The details of his life are completely obscure, but a small group of distinctive paintings, some signed, is given to him. They are of two types: rather bare interior views (*Interior with a woman combing a child's hair*, Detroit Institute of Arts) and street scenes (*Street scene*, Malibu, Getty Museum). In both types he showed an almost naive freshness and charm.

Vroom, Henrick Cornelisz.
1566–1640
Dutch painter born in Haarlem, the first specialist in marine painting. He began as a painter on porcelain. His most characteristic works are sea battles, which he painted with tremendous gusto (*The Battle of Gibraltar*, Amsterdam, Rijksmuseum). He depicted his ships with great detail, but his high viewpoint and bright colouring show that he belongs to the Mannerist rather than the naturalistic tradition. Vroom was also a tapestry designer; his most famous, a set of ten representing *The Defeat of the Spanish Armada*, were executed for the House of Lords in London and destroyed in the fire of 1834. His son, **Cornelis Hendricksz.** (1590/1–1661), active in Haarlem, began as a marine painter, but then turned to landscape.

Vrubel, Mikhail Alexandrovich
1856–1910
The leading Russian Symbolist painter. He studied in St Petersburg, and from 1884 to 1889 lived in Kiev. There he assisted with the restoration of the Church of St Cyril, in preparation for which he visited Venice to study the mosaics in S. Marco. The flat, stylized designs and bright colours of Byzantine art had a considerable influence on his work. In 1889 he moved to Moscow, where he did much work for the wealthy patron Mamontov. *Portrait of the painter's wife* (1898, Moscow, Tretyakov Gallery) is a portrait of Zabela, the singer, the daughter of Mamontov. In 1890 he illustrated Lermontov's poem *The Demon*, and the theme haunted him, as he used the demon as a symbol of his own growing insanity. See vol. 3 p. **156**

Vuillard, Edouard 1868–1940
French INTIMISTE painter. Around 1892 he started painting decorative panels and produced many prints. He was connected with the periodical *La Revue Blanche* and the Nabis. *Mother and sister of the artist* (*c.* 1893, New York, MOMA) typifies his preferred domestic imagery and emphasis on flat pattern: like his friend Bonnard, he was much influenced by Japanese prints. After 1900 he turned to a more naturalistic style. See vol. 3 p. **120**

Vukanović, Beta 1872–1972
German-born Yugoslav painter. She studied in Munich and Paris, where she met and married the Serbian painter **Risto** Vukanović (1873–1918). They opened their own school in Belgrade. From the Impressionism of her early manner she moved to more realistic, Intimiste conceptions. *Young Parisian* (1918, Belgrade, Private coll.), shown at the commemorative exhibition in Belgrade in 1973, is typical of her serenity.

W

Wadsworth, Edward 1889–1949
British painter and printmaker. He was associated with VORTICISM, and his near abstract woodcuts of 1914–15 suggesting the forms of the modern city are among the most radical products of the movement. His large *Dazzle-ships in drydock at Liverpool* (1919, Ottawa, NG of Canada), documents his work as a camouflage artist when the strident geometry of Vorticism was turned to practical use in wartime. In the early 1930s he produced a series of abstracts influenced by the biomorphism of Arp.

Waldmüller, Ferdinand Georg
1793–1865
Austrian still-life, genre, landscape and portrait painter. He studied in Vienna, 1807–11, and worked as a painter in the Baden theatre, then travelled extensively in Italy before becoming Professor of Painting at the Vienna Academy in 1829. His opposition to the rigid programme of the Academy eventually led to his dismissal in 1857. One of the reforms he advocated was that the study of nature should be encouraged, and this is reflected in his own paintings, particularly his landscapes, which are unusually fresh in approach (*Before spring in the Vienna Woods*, 1864, West Berlin, Staatliche Museen). These display a Baroque virtuosity in the use of paint coupled with rich, glowing colour and a use of open-air light which was precocious at this time.

Walker, John born 1939
British painter. An early work such as *Lesson I* (1968, London, Tate) uses gradated sombre colours and a trapezoid-shaped canvas to create a suggestion of perspectival recession and ambiguous, indefinite space. In works of the 1970s, such as *Juggernaut II* (1973–74, Liverpool, Walker Art Gallery), he adopted Matisse's cut-out method, but with layers of coloured canvas.

Walker, Robert *c.* 1605–after 1656
English portrait painter. He was much favoured during the Commonwealth by the leaders of the Parliamentary Party (*Oliver Cromwell*, *c.* 1649, London, NPG). His work often slavishly imitated van Dyck; *John Evelyn* (London, NPG) shows some originality. See vol. 2 p. 207

Walkowitz, Abraham 1880–1965
American painter, associated with the circle of artists who exhibited at Stieglitz's at "291". His modernism stems first from Cézanne and then from Rodin, whose powerful rhythms emerge in the numerous watercolours and drawings of the dancer Isadora Duncan for which he is best known.

Wallis, Alfred 1855–1942
British NAIVE painter. Having probably spent most of his life as a seaman, he taught himself to paint at the age of 70. He was discovered in St Ives, Cornwall, in 1928 by Ben Nicholson and Wood. He used found materials, pieces of wood or cardboard as supports and a limited range of colours—the white, black and green available as ship's paint—and unselfconsciously painted from memory sailing ships and the great days of the Cornish fishing industry (*Voyage to Labrador*, 1935–36?, London, Tate).

Walpole, Horace 1717–97
British man of letters, novelist, amateur architect and connoisseur of painting, the fourth son of the Prime Minister, Sir Robert Walpole. In 1739–41 he toured France and Italy and in 1747 settled at Strawberry Hill, Twickenham, which he made a showpiece of the Gothic revival. In 1762–71 he published the first connected history of art in Britain, *Anecdotes of Painting in England.*

Wanderers
Name given to the Russian artists associated with the Society of Wandering (or Travelling) Exhibitions, founded in 1870 by Kramskoy and others who had resigned from the St Petersburg Academy in protest against academic strictures. The members, who eventually included most of the leading Russian artists of the 1870s and 1880s, among them Perov and Repin, were united by common ethical rather than artistic aims. They wished to justify art by making it socially useful, in particular by depicting the sufferings of the poor and oppressed in an attempt to encourage reforms. Their exhibitions, which travelled from town to town, brought their art to a much wider public than had ever been reached before in Russia. Although it officially lasted until 1923, the once radical society had by then long been under attack from the avantgarde.

Wang Chien see WANG JIAN

Wang Hui 1632–1717
Chinese painter, the pupil both of Wang Jian and Wang Shimin, and the chief landscape painter of the early Qing dynasty. His mastery of a wide range of styles probably stemmed from his familiarity with his second teacher's collection of old masters, and he is even rumoured to have produced perfect copies of Yuan pieces, including the signature. He worked originally in the lower Yangtze region, but in 1691 he was summoned to Peking to supervise the group of artists working on the pictorial record of the Emperor Kangzi's southern progresses. He remained in Peking for some years, working in the Ming scholar tradition and producing fine paintings such as *Landscape* (1677, Paris, Musée Guimet).

Wang Jian 1598–1677
Chinese painter, active in the Taicang region of Jiangsu. Like his friend Wang Shimin, Wang Jian was an important link between the painting of the Ming and Qing periods. Retiring from public life in 1644, he devoted himself to landscape painting, principally to the conscious and explicit imitation of Tang, Song and Yuan masters. With his stress on the importance of a close adherence to authentic antique models, he stands in the line of succession from Dong Qichang, though his taste ran less to the Yuan painters than to the early Song landscapes of Dong Yuan and Juran. Much of his surviving output takes the form of sets of album leaves after named artists, a typical 17th-century format: one such set, dated 1665, is preserved in the National Museum in Stockholm.

Wang Meng *c.* 1301–85
Chinese painter, one of the major painters of the Yuan-Ming transition period and characterized by later critics as one of the "Four Great Masters of the Late Yuan". Wang was a descendant of Zhao Mengfu, and, like him, held office under the Mongols, but he devoted himself largely to the practice of landscape painting, working in the Suzhou region. Though he drew on a wide variety of influences, his own distinguishing feature was a dense brushwork with large numbers of dark strokes forming tortured hills and gnarled pines, such as can be seen in the hanging scroll *Hermitage in the Qingbian mountains* (1366, Shanghai Museum). His reputation declined soon after his death, to be revived in the 16th century by Shen Zhou and Wen Zhengming. See vol. 3 p. **41**

Wang Shimin 1592–1680
Chinese painter, active in the Jiangsu area. A pupil of the great Dong Qichang in the arts of both painting and calligraphy, he carried the mid-Ming LITERATI style into the Qing dynasty. His output consists mainly of landscapes, either of his native lower Yangtze region, or fantastic mountain scenes. He had a great facility for the imitation of Song and Yuan painting, as seen in the six album leaves depicting *Landscapes*, now mounted as a handscroll (Washington, Freer), where each leaf is his interpretation of a different earlier master. As a teacher of Wang Hui and Wu Li, he can be considered the source of the high-Qing "orthodox" school of painting.

Wang Wei *c.* 699–*c.* 761
Chinese LITERATI painter and one of the greatest poets of the Tang dynasty. He reached some of the highest offices of state and was immensely influential in the development of Chinese landscape painting, reputedly pioneering monochrome painting. No authentic work of his hand was still extant in the Northern Song period, though copies may have still contained echoes of his style. Many versions existed at one time of his most important picture, a panorama of his country estate south of the capital, though such copies as remain (for instance that of the Ming dynasty in the Seattle Art Museum) now give very little idea of the work's original appearance. Wang was later elevated into the model of the *literatus* or scholar-painter, in contrast to the so-called professional tradition embodied by Li Sixun.

Wang Yuanqi 1642–1715
Chinese painter. The grandson of Wang Shimin, he continued his forebear's tradition of landscape painting (*Spring morning at Yantan*, 1711, Boston, MFA). He served at the court of the Emperor Kangxi as keeper of the imperial painting and calligraphy collection, and thus had a real influence on the formation of the Palace Collection (now divided between Taiwan and Peking).

Ward, James 1769–1859
English ROMANTIC painter and engraver of animal subjects and landscapes. He began with anecdotal scenes similar to those of his brother-in-law Morland, but turned to much more original paintings of wild animals in richly coloured, dramatic natural settings, which were influenced by Rubens. Works of this kind, such as *Bulls fighting* (*c.* 1804, London, V&A) were much admired by Géricault and Delacroix. His best-known work is the enormous landscape *Gordale Scar, Yorkshire* (1811–15, London, Tate).

Warhol, Andy born 1930
American painter, graphic designer and film-maker, perhaps the best-known POP artist. In the 1950s he worked as an advertising illustrator, and made his début as a painter in 1962, when he exhibited stencilled pictures of multiple dollar bills, Campbell's soup-cans and Coca-Cola bottles (*Green Coca-Cola bottles*, 1962, New York, Whitney). During the 1960s he worked towards a goal of machine-like art devoid of emotional and social comment in a New York studio called "The Factory". Many silk-screen series of celebrities and news events, and also sculptures which duplicate product wrappings, date from this decade (*Brillo Box*, 1964, New York, Peter M. Brant coll.). They reflect his view: "I think it would be terrific if everyone looked alike." In 1966 Warhol announced his retirement as an artist in order to devote himself to producing films, and to his duties as manager of a rock music band and discothèque. He had already won renown for films such as *Sleep* and *Empire*, six hours and eight hours long respectively, showing a man sleeping and the Empire State Building seen continuously from the same viewpoint—"I like boring things." In spite of his films and music he continued to paint, specializing in portraits of celebrities and friends. Applying a heavily-laden brush to the silk-screen stencil, he usually does several versions of each likeness in various colour combinations. His brilliantly dead-pan style of the 1960s both recalled Dada and anticipated Conceptual art, and this, together with his astute management of his impersonal *persona*, makes him an heir both to Duchamp and to Dali. See vol. 1 pp. *123*, *167*; vol. 3 pp. **238–239**, *254*

Wash
Application of diluted watercolour or ink thinned with water, generally brushed on broadly with a loaded brush.

Watercolour
Transparent paint bound with gum arabic and mixed in use with water. It is applied on specially prepared paper or card, usually white, which reflects light up through the paint to give the sparkling luminosity characteristic of the medium. Its popularity grew in the 18th century, when it was used to colour in topographical sketches, and as a medium for fluid, spontaneous and subtly blended painting it was developed to a peak by British landscapists. See vol. 1 pp. 156–157

Watson, Homer Ransford
1858–1936
Canadian painter of Ontario rural life and landscape. He was internationally famous at the peak of his career, but his reputation has since faded. In 1876–77 he visited New York, absorbing the influence of Inness and the Hudson River school. Oscar Wilde dubbed him "the Canadian Constable", a comparison justified by the intense, intimate evocation of familiar landscape (*Before the storm*, 1887, Windsor, Strickland coll.).

Watteau, Jean-Antoine
1684–1721
French painter, one of the greatest of ROCOCO artists. He was born in Valenciennes; the town had recently been ceded to the French, but Watteau's painting was rooted in the Flemish tradition and his early military scenes clearly reflected the influences of Teniers the Younger. In 1702 he moved to Paris, where he worked as a journeyman painter of small, devotional pictures, before becoming a pupil of Gillot, the theatrical

scene-painter. When they quarrelled in 1707 Watteau entered the service of Audran, a highly successful decorative painter. The current taste in this artistic field for capricious and exotic fantasies impregnated Watteau's own style while, even more importantly, Audran's post of concierge at the Palais du Luxembourg allowed him access to Rubens' *Marie de Médicis* cycle. Watteau's adulation of Rubens was crucial, for, along with Giorgione's *Concert Champêtre*, it was Rubens' paintings on the theme of *The Garden of Love* that helped inspire his FÊTES GALANTES. The French Academy invented this category to describe Watteau's invention of a type of painting in which figures in ball-dress or masquerade costume mingled with players from the *Commedia dell'Arte* in an aristocratic dreamland where music, conversation and amorous dalliance held sway. Watteau's figures are exquisitely drawn and coloured, but whereas Rococo artists are generally associated with frivolity, Watteau's scenes are marked by a moving sense of melancholy, born of the knowledge that all sensuous pleasure is transient. "*The Embarkation for Cythera*" (1717, Paris, Louvre) is the most celebrated example of the genre. The explanation for this pervasive melancholy may be that for much of his life Watteau suffered from the consumption which was to cause his premature death. His contemporaries often commented on his irritability and extreme restlessness. In 1719 he came to London, apparently to seek medical advice, but the rigours of an English winter only hastened his end—a particular tragedy as his final work, "*Enseigne de Gersaint*" (Gersaint's signboard, 1721, West Berlin, Charlottenburg), seemed to presage the development of a new, more realistic style. Lancret and Pater were Watteau's principal imitators. See vol. 1 pp. *48*, *109*; vol. 2 pp. **238–239**

Watts, George Frederick
1817–1904
British painter and sculptor. He was one of the last representatives of the tradition which attempted to express the loftiest moral qualities through ideal forms. From 1843 to 1847 he lived in Italy, and Michelangelo and the great Venetian painters, as well as the Elgin Marbles from the Parthenon, were the exemplars for his work. His most characteristic paintings are allegorical (*Hope*, version, 1886, London, Tate). These won him an enormous reputation in the latter part of his career, but they now often seem turgid, and his portraits of great Victorians (he would paint only those whose character he considered suitably elevated) have worn better. His best-known sculpture is *Physical Energy* (1904, London, Kensington Gardens). His home at Compton, Surrey, is now a museum. See vol. 3 p. **83**; vol. 4 p. *49*

Weber, Max 1881–1961
Russian-born American painter, printmaker and sculptor. He emigrated to the USA at the age of ten, and from 1905 to 1909 travelled extensively in Europe, meeting Cézanne, Matisse and Picasso. On his return to America he developed a personal form of Cubism in painting and sculpture (*Figure study*, 1911, Buffalo, Albright-Knox). He exhibited his work at Stieglitz's "291" gallery, and was an important figure in the introduction of up-to-date European trends to American art. From 1917 his work became more representational and increasingly introspective (*The adoration of the moon*, 1944, New York, Whitney).

Weenix, Jan Baptist
1621–before 1663
Dutch painter. He was in Italy, 1642–46, and on his return to Holland painted Italianate landscapes in the manner of Berchem, who may have been his cousin (*Figures in an Italian landscape with ruins*, Detroit Institute of Arts). He also painted hunting-trophy still lifes, and in this he was followed by his very prolific son **Jan** (1642–1719), sixteen of whose paintings are in the Wallace Collection, London. It is often difficult to distinguish between their work.

Weight, Carel born 1908
British painter. He is best known for paintings such as *Lovers interrupted by sprite* (1938, Portsmouth, City Gallery), in which an element of the frightening or bizarre is introduced into an everyday setting. The hallucinatory atmosphere of his work is emphasized by its high-keyed colour; the purply skies and intensified green of his suburban hedgerows combine with a subtly distorted perspective to create a sense of unease even where the imagery is not overtly fantastic.

Weisgerber, Albert 1878–1915
German painter and graphic artist. He studied under Stuck in Munich, and in 1904 began designing posters for the magazine *Jugend*. He spent 1906–07 in Paris, and on his return to Munich the influence of Symbolism and Jugendstil gave way to a more realist approach. After a visit to Italy in 1911 his compositions became more formal, though in the impassioned religious themes of his last years he used Expressionist devices (*David and Goliath*, 1914, Saarbrücken, Saarland-Museum).

Weissenbruch, Hendrik Johannes
1824–1903
Dutch landscape painter in oils and watercolour, a first-generation member of the HAGUE school. His subjects were mostly the Dutch polders, beaches and dunes, and his work, usually painted in subdued colours, is noted for its subtle handling of atmosphere and light effects.

Welfare State
British Performance group, founded in the early 1970s. Their work took the form of street theatre and they considered their work to be in the tradition of popular theatre, circus and music-hall. In 1972 they toured south-west England making HAPPENINGS related to ancient ritual and myth. See vol. 3 p. *243*

Wen Tong c. 1020–79
Chinese painter, the contemporary and close friend of Su Shi. He is also considered a major poet and calligrapher, and had a very distinguished, if stormy, civil service career. Wen's name is most closely associated with the painting of bamboos in monochrome ink (*Study of bamboos*, Taiwan, National Palace Museum), and he was the major proponent of the view that such paintings were the most stringent test of moral worth, the indispensable attribute of the Confucian gentleman. His confident manner, using fine strokes of black ink, which cannot be retouched once laid on the silk, seems to explore the boundaries between the arts of painting and of calligraphy.

Wen Zhengming 1470–1559
Chinese painter. He represents the ideal of the detached scholar who paints in order to commune with nature, and is thus the antithesis of the "professional" artist of the Ming era. He worked in his native city, Suzhou, by this period one of the great artistic and intellectual centres

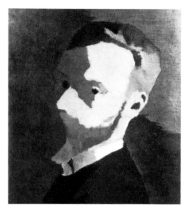
Vuillard: Self-portrait, 1892. Private coll. (Giraudon)

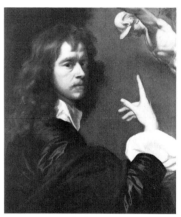
Walker, Robert: Self-portrait, c. 1640–45. Oxford, Ashmolean

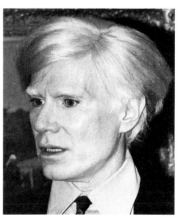
Warhol: Photograph by John Whitman (Camera Press)

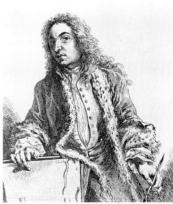
Watteau: Engraving by Boucher (c. 1727) after a self-portrait drawing (Mansell)

of China, studying painting under Shen Zhou. The study of antique masters was of paramount importance in Ming painting, and Wen began by modelling himself on the Yuan painter Zhao Mengfu. The Yuan remained the period in which he felt most at home, and he was largely responsible for the rise in the reputation of Ni Zan's austere, empty landscapes. His paintings of bamboo (such as the monochrome piece in the National Palace Museum, Taiwan) are every bit as forceful as the Song and Yuan originals on which they draw, while his late landscapes have a spaciousness which surpasses their models. The handscroll *The red cliff* (1552, Washington, Freer) illustrates a famous piece by Su Shi, and its empty expanse of water bearing the poet's boat past a confidently depicted cliff is the ideal counterpart to the poem's prolonged meditation on image and reality. Wen had many disciples.

Werefkin, Marianne von
1860–1938
Russian painter. She studied in Repin's St Petersburg studio, and left Russia with Jawlensky in 1896 for Munich. Her *Self-portrait* (1908, Munich, Lenbachhaus) shows an Expressionist style, characterized by bright, clashing colours, which she adopted from the Fauvists via Jawlensky. From 1918 she lived in Italy at Ascona, where the Museo Communale houses some of her work.

Werenskiold, Erik 1855–1938
Norwegian Realist painter, book illustrator and engraver, trained in Oslo, Munich and Paris. With Krohg he was one of the leaders of the national art in Norway in the 1880s. He painted landscapes and psychologically penetrating portraits (*Ibsen*, 1895, Oslo, NG).

Werff, Adriaen van der 1659–1722
Dutch painter. The most celebrated Dutch painter of his age, he was renowned for the porcelain-like finish of his paintings of Arcadian, mythological and religious subjects in the French academic tradition of Lairesse. From 1696 to 1716 he painted half or more of his output for the Elector Palatine Johann Wilhelm, for example the 17 *Scenes from the lives of Christ and the Virgin* (Munich, Alte Pinakothek).

Werkman, Hendrik 1882–1945
Dutch painter and printer. Initially a journalist, he began to make pictures with printing ink in 1923. He used silhouettes and prints of the letters, figures and signs of type-faces, which he built up in multiple layers to produce both figurative and abstract works such as *Composition with the letter X* (1927–28, Amsterdam, Stedelijk).

Wesselmann, Tom born 1931
American painter, one of the leading POP artists. The techniques and imagery of magazine advertisements and billboards are at the heart of his work. His early still lifes and interiors combine real objects and air-brushed representations of Coca-Cola bottles, toasters and so on. He is best known for his *Great American Nude* series, which includes large environmental assemblages such as *Great American nude no. 54* (1962, Aachen, Neue Galerie), in which the flatness of the painted nude contrasts sharply with the three-dimensionality of the bathtub, towel-rack and tiles of the setting. See vol. 1 pp. *154–155*; vol. 3 p. **239**

West, Benjamin 1738–1820
American painter, working principally in England. After training briefly in his native Philadelphia, he left in 1760 to study in Rome, where he absorbed the Neoclassical ideals of Mengs, Winckelmann and Hamilton. Three years later West settled in London, where his studio rapidly became an artistic Mecca for American students abroad, as Matthew Pratt's *The American School* (1765, New York, Metropolitan) records. Early history paintings, such as *Agrippina landing at Brundisium with the ashes of Germanicus* (1768, New Haven, Yale University), betray an uneasy eclecticism, but West made a brilliant innovation with *The death of Wolfe* (1770, Ottawa, NG), where he defied precedent by depicting a specific event from recent history in contemporary costume. At first this was attacked as an affront to the accepted academic canons, but modern-dress history painting was soon taken up by other artists, most brilliantly by Copley. Increasingly West drew away from Neoclassicism, preferring subjects that were to appeal to the Romantics. *Saul and the Witch of Endor* (1777, Hartford, Wadsworth Atheneum) was an essay in the Sublime and a direct inspiration for Allston's treatment of the theme, while the swirling composition of *Death on a pale horse* (1802, Philadelphia, Museum of Art) prefigured the battle scenes of Delacroix. His successful career was marked by a long association with George III and was crowned (1792) with the Presidency of the Royal Academy. His influence was crucial for the American Romantics—Allston, Morse and Trumbull. See vol. 3 p. **58**

Westmacott, Sir Richard
1775–1856
English NEOCLASSICAL sculptor. He trained under his father, also called **Richard** (1747–1808), and from 1793 to 1797 he was in Rome, where he worked in Canova's studio. Back in London he soon became second only to Chantrey as the leading sculptor, and his output, especially of church monuments, was enormous. His style tends to be heavier and clumsier than Chantrey's and his surfaces are rather dead, but his best work has an impressive dignity (Monument to Charles James Fox, 1810–23, London, Westminster Abbey).

Weyden, Rogier van der
1399/1400–1464
Netherlandish painter, one of the greatest and most influential artists of the mid-15th century. Although among early Netherlandish painters he is second in fame only to Jan van Eyck, no signed or documented works survive. On the basis of works mentioned in early sources, however, a convincing oeuvre has been established. It is usually accepted that the Rogelet de la Pâture who was apprenticed to Robert Campin, together with Jacques Daret, in Tournai (1427–35) was Rogier. By 1435 he had settled in Brussels, where he had a workshop until his death, and was official town painter by 1436. Rogier assimilated the style not only of Campin but also of Jan van Eyck, as can be seen in his most famous work, *The Deposition* (Madrid, Prado), which is a fairly early work, certainly done before 1443, the date on a copy, and probably in about 1435. The use of a gold ground, the frieze-like arrangement of the figures and the emotional force recall Campin, but the representational means, which are made to serve the sense of drama, are much more sophisticated than in Campin's work and are derived from van Eyck. The true subject of the painting is the emotions of the participants, and Rogier's subsequent works move in the direction of an increasingly

refined spirituality and heightened poignancy. The altarpiece of *The Last Judgment* (c.1450, Beaune, Hôtel-Dieu) is perhaps his greatest work, noble in conception, rich in imagery, and awesome in power. His final manner is represented by the Columba altarpiece (Munich, Alte Pinakothek); the central panel, representing *The Adoration of the Magi*, is characterized by a serenity and plenitude of space which is new in Rogier's work. Serenity is the keynote also of his portrait style; he painted several half-lengths of fashionable women (examples London, NG, and Washington, NG), which are so similar in manner that the features seem forced into the same mould. Their subtle colouring marvellously complements his sensitivity of line. Rogier's fame and works were widespread in his lifetime and the influence of his style and his inventions continued throughout the century, not only in painting but also in sculpture, in Germany and Spain as well as in the Netherlands, and to some extent in Italy, which he visited in 1450. See vol. 1 p. *90*; vol. 2 pp. **94–95**

Wheatley, Francis 1747–1801
British painter of landscapes and sentimental genre scenes. He is best known for his *Cries of London*, begun in 1792. These, which show milkmaids, flower-sellers and street-vendors in a sweet, appealing guise, have been popular as engravings, decorations on china and, ultimately, table-mats, ever since.

Whistler, James Abbot McNeill
1834–1903
American painter and graphic artist, working principally in England. In 1855 he went to Paris, where he studied under Gleyre and briefly espoused the aims of Courbet's Realist movement. Four years later he settled in London and began to opt for more evocative, Pre-Raphaelite themes. During the early 1860s Whistler also developed an interest in Japanese art, introducing oriental fans and blossoms into his paintings, and, at the same time, became intrigued with the subjectless, pseudo-classical pictures of his friend, Albert Moore. *Symphony in white no. 3* (1867, University of Birmingham, Barber Institute) was a combination of all these qualities. From such subjects Whistler turned his attention to his famous scenes of the Thames, of which *Chelsea: Nocturne in blue and green* (c.1870, London, Tate) is a typically lovely example. In his *Ten o'Clock Lecture* (1885), he analysed his fascination for the subject, explaining how the evening mist invested the riverside with poetry, transforming chimneys into *campanili* and warehouses into palaces of the night. The *Nocturnes* were tangible demonstrations of his creed of aestheticism, which stressed the artist's duty to orchestrate selected elements from nature into a composition that, like music, existed for its own sake, without regard to moral or didactic values. This controversial viewpoint led to the lawsuit with Ruskin, which bankrupted Whistler, but assured him a distinguished place as a precursor of abstract art. Whistler was a dandy with an acerbic wit and a gift for showmanship, as his collected writings, *The Gentle Art of Making Enemies* (1890), clearly illustrate. See vol. 1 p. *150*; vol. 3 pp. **96–97**

Whitely, Brett born 1939
Australian painter, who settled in England in 1961. He first used a painterly style akin to the English St Ives school, and then began to paint fragmented nudes and visceral shapes, often erotic, using a narrow range of pastel shades. A

series of paintings (1964–65) based on the recent Christie murders bypass the horror of the event and exploit a formal, abstract approach to the human figure (*Christie and Kathleen Maloney*, 1964–65, Canberra, NG). Unlike Bacon's grotesque figures, Whitely's have innate bounce and sensuality. His large canvases combine a strong linear element with fluid, expressionist brushwork.

Wildens, Jan 1586–1653
Flemish painter of landscapes and hunting scenes. His masterpiece, the stately *Winter landscape with a hunter* (1624, Dresden, Gemäldegalerie) shows that he was capable of very impressive independent work, but he is best known as a painter of landscape backgrounds for his friend Rubens and other artists.

Wiligelmo
active late 11th/early 12th century
Italian sculptor of the early Romanesque period. His masterpiece is the frieze depicting stories from Genesis on the façade of Modena Cathedral, with its inscription (1099) glorifying the sculptor's work. The figures are squat and vigorous, reflecting the influence of Roman art, but in an original spirit; their heavy stylization lends them monumentality. Wiligelmo's style (imitated by a large workshop) soon became widespread, and effected a popular revival of sculpture in northern Italy.

Wilkie, Sir David 1785–1841
Scottish genre, history and portrait painter. He studied in Edinburgh and in 1805 moved to London, where he achieved great success with his small-scale humorous and anecdotal domestic subjects in the manner of the 17th-century Netherlandish painters such as the Ostade brothers and Teniers the Younger. *Chelsea pensioners reading the Gazette of the Battle of Waterloo* (1822, London, Wellington Museum) was so popular when it was exhibited at the Royal Academy that barriers had to be erected in front of it. In 1825–28 he travelled abroad for reasons of health and, under the influence particularly of Spanish painters such as Murillo and Velazquez, adopted a much broader style and grander subjects, to the regret of many of his contemporaries. He visited the Holy Land in 1840 as research for his religious painting and died at sea on the return journey, inspiring Turner's *Peace: Burial at sea*. See vol. 3 p. **82**

Williams, Frederick born 1927
Australian painter and graphic artist, first known for his etchings based on Goya and Daumier. He studied in London (1951–56). His landscape painting, for which he achieved international recognition, developed from a type of Post-Impressionism to a strong and more tightly concentrated style, in which the representational element nearly vanishes. In paintings such as *Upwey landscape* (1966, Canberra, NG), trees are reduced to dots of paint, hung on a neutral ground.

Willinck, Albert Carel born 1900
Dutch painter. He studied architecture between 1918 and 1920 and then started painting. His early work is abstract and he exhibited with the Novembergruppe in Berlin, but from 1926, when he worked in Le Fauconnier's studio in Paris, he turned to figurative compositions and a form of MAGIC REALISM (*Wilma*, 1932, The Hague, Gemeentemuseum).

Willmann, Michael 1630–1706
With Schönfeld, the most interesting

German painter of the second half of the 17th century. He was born in Königsberg and studied in Amsterdam, absorbing a wide variety of influences from Dutch painting. After travelling and working extensively in central Europe he settled in 1660 at Lubiąż (Leubus) in Poland, where the Collegiate Church has the best collection of his work—12 large oil-paintings in the nave (1661–1700) and a ceiling fresco, *The triumph of Virtue* (1691/2), in the refectory. His style is highly emotional, with a striking use of bold, broken brushwork, well suited to convey intense religious experience. Willmann was also highly esteemed as a painter of portraits, his most famous being *Abbot Rosa* (c.1695) in the Breslau Museum, which also houses two other well-known works—*Landscape with Jacob's dream* (c.1690) and *The kiss of the Virgin* (1682).

Willumsen, Jens Ferdinand
1863–1958
Danish painter, sculptor, engraver, architect and ceramicist. He began as a Naturalist, but was influenced by Gauguin and Symbolism in the early 1880s. *After the tempest* (1905, Oslo, NG) displays a composition of bright, fragmented areas of colour. After a visit to Spain in the 1910s he was deeply affected by El Greco and began to paint in a more expressive manner. His art collection and own works are in the Willumsen Museum, Fredriksund.

Wilson, Richard 1713–82
The outstanding British landscape specialist of the 18th century. Until 1750, when he went to Italy, he probably earned his living chiefly as a painter of portraits—the best are almost up to Hogarth's standard (*Admiral Thomas Smith*, c.1745, Greenwich, National Maritime Museum). In Italy, first in Venice, where he met Zuccarelli, then in Rome, where he discovered the art of Claude and met willing British patrons, he turned wholly to landscape. His Italian period pictures show how skilfully he absorbed the lessons of Claude and Dughet (*Et in Arcadio ego*, 1755, Abbots Worthy, Hampshire, Viscount Enfield coll.). On his return to Britain in 1757 he continued producing Italianate works, but his finest and most original paintings are the ones in which he applied the principles of classical composition to the landscape of England and his native Wales. His masterpiece, *Snowdon from Llyn Nantil* (c.1770, versions, Liverpool, Walker Art Gallery, and Nottingham, Castle Museum), combines nobility and serenity of composition with freshness of observation and a poetic response to the beauty of the mountain scenery. Wilson was a founder-member of the Royal Academy. See vol. 2 p. **255**

Wilton, Joseph 1722–1803
English sculptor. He trained in Flanders and with Pigalle in France, then spent several years in Italy. On his return to England in 1755 he quickly achieved success. He carved the state coach used for coronations and was appointed sculptor to George III. His busts are his best works; his monuments, of which the best-known is that to General Wolfe (1772, London, Westminster Abbey), are often stodgy and clumsy.

Winck, Christian Thomas
1738–97
South German ROCOCO painter. In the 1760s he settled in Munich, and was appointed court painter in 1769. His output consisted mainly of exuberantly anecdotal frescos with landscape settings in Bavarian churches (Starnberg, 1776; Bettbrunn, 1777).

Winckelmann, Johann Joachim
1717–68
German scholar, the key theorist of NEOCLASSICISM, both through his writings and through his friendship with Mengs, who attempted to realize his ideas in paint. In his books *Reflections on the Imitation of Greek Art* (1755), *Observations on the Architecture of the Ancients* (1762) and *History of Ancient Art* (1764), he defined and established the cult of the Greek achievement, proclaiming the classical ideal to be "noble simplicity and calm grandeur".

Winterhalter, Franz Xaver
1805–73
German painter and lithographer, based in Paris for most of his career. He was the most successful court painter of his day, portraying most of Europe's royalty and leading members of the aristocracy. His work is superficial, but has a lavishly glossy romantic charm. He is well represented in the British royal collection.

Wissing, William (Willem) 1656–87
Anglo-Dutch portrait painter. He came to England in 1676 and studied in the studio of Lely. His independent work is heavily indebted to his master, though harsher in colouring, with a certain frenchified extravagance, and a fondness for elaborate still lifes of flowers and foliage. His portraits of William and Mary at Hampton Court are good examples of his style.

Wit, Jakob de 1695–1754
The leading Dutch decorative painter of the 18th century, also an engraver. His most ambitious painting, *Moses selecting the 70 elders* (1737, Amsterdam, Town Hall) is a dismal failure, and he was happier working on a small scale, as in his delicately playful ceiling *Bacchus and Ceres in the clouds* (1751, Heemstede, Huis Boschbeek).

Witkiewicz, Stanislav Ignacy
1885–1939
Polish painter, philosopher and dramatist. Son of a painter and art critic, he studied in Warsaw and spent World War I in Russia. On his return to Poland he founded a group with whom he explored the idea of "pure form", creating shapes which could be variously interpreted. He produced strange, wild compositions (*General confusion*, 1920, Cracow, National Museum), and later began to experiment with painting under the influence of narcotics. His plays are early example of the Theatre of the Absurd.

Witte, Emanuel de 1617–92
Dutch painter, active mainly in Amsterdam. He was very versatile, painting genre, historical and mythological scenes and portraits, but he is best known for his views of church interiors. Sometimes de Witte painted fairly factual views, but more often they are imaginary. His sense of structure and understanding of light were so highly developed, however, that his churches always look like real buildings. He created dramatic vistas and powerful contrasts of light and often conveys an air of mystery which is lacking in the church views of his more sober contemporaries (*Interior of a church*, 1668, Rotterdam, Museum Boymans-van Beuningen).

Witz, Konrad died 1444/6
German-born painter, active in Basel from 1434 and regarded as a member of the Swiss school. His oeuvre is grouped round the signed and dated St Peter altarpiece (1444, Geneva, Museum of Art and History), which contains the celebrated panel of *The miraculous draught of fishes*. The view of Lake Geneva in this is one of the earliest recognizable landscapes in the history of art. The solidity of the figures and details such as the bubbles in the water further show his interest in naturalism and reveal him as the most progressive Swiss artist of his time. See vol. 2 p. **97**

Wölfflin, Heinrich 1864–1945
Swiss art historian and aesthetician. He is one of the most important figures in the development of art history as an academic discipline. His books, including *Classic Art* (1899) and *Principles of Art History* (1915), are mainly concerned with the analysis of style. They established much of the conceptual terminology of art history and are still widely read. See vol. 1 p.110

Wolgemut, Michael 1434–1519
German woodcut designer and painter, born and active in Nuremberg. He began as an assistant to Pleydenwurff and after the latter's death married his widow and took over his large workshop. His paintings are rare and his importance lies mainly in his book illustrations, in particular those for Hartman Schedel's *Weltchronik* (1493). The book was very lavishly illustrated and letterpress and woodcuts were combined in a more effective manner than hitherto. Wolgemut also refined the woodcut technique so that he could achieve effects which previously had been added in paint. Dürer was his pupil.

Wollaston, John active 1736–67
English portrait painter, active in the American colonies. One of the most prolific artists of his time in America, he was particularly successful in New York (1749–53). *Mrs Samuel Gouverneur* (c.1750, Wilmington, Delaware, Winterthur Museum) is typical of his rather clumsy Rococo style.

Wols (Wolfgang Schulze) 1913–51
German-born abstract painter, based in France from 1932. He developed an influential range of biomorphic images in a gently coloured free TACHISTE manner (*Composition*, 1947, New York, MOMA). See vol. 3 pp. **224–225**

Wood, Christopher 1901–30
British painter. From 1926 he was a friend of Nicholson and in the late 1920s their work shared certain characteristics, in particular the application of eccentric lop-sided forms to landscape. While paintings such as *The manicure* (1929, Bradford, City Museum) reflect the impact of contemporary French classicism, in his late works there is a vein of lyric fantasy which anticipates the NEO-ROMANTICISM of the 1940s.

Wood, Grant 1892–1942
American painter, active mainly in his native Iowa. He was largely self-taught and his early paintings were in a picturesque, impressionistic manner. After visiting Munich in 1928, however, he began to depict everyday subjects in a sharp, carefully finished, realistic style. His satirical vision of American provincialism is epitomized in the well-known *American Gothic* (1930, Chicago, Art Institute) and may owe something to the dryness of Northern Renaissance art as well as to the tradition of Neue Sachlichkeit. Wood also painted historical scenes and boldly stylized landscapes which

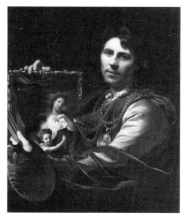
Werff, van der: Self-portrait, 1699. Amsterdam, Rijksmuseum

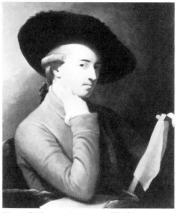
West: Self-portrait, c.1770. Washington, NG, Andrew Mellon coll.

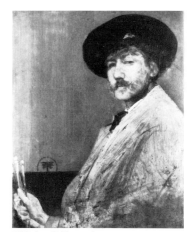
Whistler: *Self-portrait: arrangement in grey*, 1867. Detroit Institute of Arts

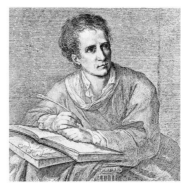
Winckelmann: Portrait engraving by Kauffmann, 1764 (B. T. Batsford Ltd.)

some consider to be his finest works (*Stone City, Iowa*, 1930, Omaha, Joslyn Art Museum). See vol. 1 p. *37*

Woodcut
Method of relief printing, originating in China and used widely in Europe from the 15th century. The design is incised on a block, usually of hardwood, sawn along rather than across the grain, and the "negative" areas of the design, which will take no ink, are then cut away. German and Italian craftsmen of the 16th century raised the technique to a peak of refinement as a medium for original prints and book illustration. Its rough, bold effects were exploited at the end of the 19th century by artists such as Gauguin and Munch, who emphasized the grain and texture of the wood. The art attained a high level in Japan, notably after the invention of polychrome printing by the *ukiyo-e* master Harunobu in the 1760s. See vol. 1 pp. 164–167

Wood engraving
Method of relief printing from a block of hardwood sawn across the grain to give a smooth, hard surface suitable to fine engraving with a burin. As in a woodcut, the incised areas print white, but the effect is closer to that of intaglio metal engraving. After Bewick's development of the medium in the 18th century it became the most popular means of book illustration until the invention of photomechanical processes. See vol. 1 p. 166

Woollaston, Sir Mountford Tosswill born 1910
New Zealand painter, the first to be knighted. Largely self-taught, he based his mature style on Cézanne's principle of overlapping planes transmitted through the broader and more expressionistic manner of Hans Hofmann. His work reflects his emotional responses to a favourite location (*Kumara landscape*, 1962, Auckland City Art Gallery), or to his family and friends.

Woolner, Thomas 1825–92
English sculptor, painter (of animals and landscapes) and poet, the only sculptor member of the original PRE-RAPHAELITE Brotherhood. He produced reliefs and figures of literary and historical characters, and eventually established himself as a portraitist. Because he was unsuccessful early in his career, he emigrated to Australia. On his return to England he devoted himself to medals and portraits, and made his name with his bust of the poet *Tennyson* (1857, Cambridge, Trinity College).

Wootton, John *c.*1682–1764
British sporting painter, the first British sporting artist to attain real distinction. He made his name first with paintings of racehorses at Newmarket and later with hunting scenes. In both he showed his skill at composing groups of figures and horses in wide panoramic landscapes (*Members of the Beaufort hunt*, 1744, London, Tate).

World of Art group
An association founded in 1889 in St Petersburg, by Russian artists hostile both to the realist stance of the older Wanderers group and the prevailing academic school, proposing "art for art's sake" as the only approach for an artist. Benois played an important role in bringing about a reassessment of earlier, Neoclassical Russian art and architecture through the journal *World Art* (1899–1904), in which current European art was also illustrated and discussed. Major artists of the group such as Bakst, Roerich and Vrubel were as active in graphic and stage design as in painting, and became widely known in the West for their sets for the Ballets Russes of Diaghilev.

Wotruba, Fritz born 1907
Austrian sculptor. He was born in Vienna and studied at the School of Fine Arts, 1921–24. In the 1930s he associated with the architect Josef Hoffmann in Vienna and with Maillol in Paris. He lived in exile in Switzerland, 1938–48, before returning to Vienna. Wotruba is the most important modern Austrian sculptor: his semi-abstract work, mainly in stone and bronze, consists mostly of figures and reliefs in an angular and monumental style indebted to primitive art (*Reclining figure*, 1960, New York, Marlborough-Gerson Gallery).

Wouters, Rik 1882–1916
Belgian painter and sculptor. He produced a number of naturalistic busts before taking up painting in 1908, and on a visit to Paris in 1912 he discovered Fauvism. His many exquisite, peaceful domestic interiors and portraits of his wife (*Mme Rik Wouters*, 1912, Paris, Musée National d'Art Moderne) are painted in blushing colours, and are less violent than French Fauvist work. He died in World War I.

Wouwermans, Philips 1619–68
Dutch painter, born and active in Haarlem, where he was a pupil of Frans Hals. His lively touch may owe something to his master, but his subject matter was very different, as he concentrated on horses in landscapes—hunting parties, cavalry skirmishes and so on. Wouwermans was immensely prolific, and died very wealthy. His works were highly prized in the 18th century and he is now perhaps underrated, for however many times he repeated his subjects he kept a sense of freshness. One of the finest collections of his work is in the Dulwich College Picture Gallery, London.

WPA see FEDERAL ART PROJECTS

Wright of Derby, Joseph 1734–97
British painter of portraits, scientific, industrial and literary subjects and landscapes, active mainly in his native Derby. The most remarkable feature of his work is his fascination with light effects. This is seen most strikingly in his tenebrist pictures of scientific demonstrations, such as *An experiment on a bird in an air pump* (*c.*1767, London, Tate). These are among the most original paintings produced in England at this period, and are sensitively characterized as well as powerfully dramatic. His interest in light was directed towards landscape during his stay in Italy, 1773–75, and among the "Sublime" themes he favoured were moonlit grottoes and dramatic volcanic eruptions. He continued to paint similar scenes on his return, imbuing the English landscape with romantic feeling. The best collection of his work is in the Derby Art Gallery. See vol. 1 p. *30*; vol. 2 p. **251**

Wttewael, Joachim 1566–1638
Dutch MANNERIST painter, born and mainly active in Utrecht. He travelled extensively in Italy and France as a young man and developed a Mannerist style of extreme exaggeration. His colours are lividly acidic and he twists limbs and fingers into startling and totally unnecessary contortions, often producing an effect of rather ridiculous whimsical charm. He remained unmoved by the developments happening around him and painted in his unmistakable style until the end (*The Adoration of the shepherds*, Oxford, Ashmolean). The Centraal Museum, Utrecht, has the outstanding collection of his works.

Wu Li 1632–1718
Chinese painter. Like Wang Hui, he was a pupil of Wang Shimin, and the early styles of both painters display strong similarities. An absorption in the study of Song landscape painting led to work of a high technical level, which later gave way to an interest in the more spiritual qualities of the Yuan landscape masters. His landscapes, usually of contorted mountain ranges, show a preoccupation with the quality of light and with pictorial depth which may be evidence of European influence (*Landscape*, 1674, Lugano, Vanolti coll.). Wu, indeed, was in touch with Jesuit missionaries. He became a Catholic priest in 1688, and forsook painting for missionary work.

Wyeth, Andrew born 1917
American figurative painter, the son of the illustrator **Newell Convers Wyeth** (1882–1944). He has spent his entire life painting the landscape and local figures of his native town of Pennsylvania and of a small area of the Maine coastline. He uses watercolour and drybrush and has also revived the technique of egg tempera. His paintings are built up meticulously, predominantly in earth colours, sometimes with patches of brilliant blue. The results are usually nostalgic and highly evocative, often with a strange, eerie quality—empty rooms and unpeopled landscapes contain the unspoken presence of their inhabitants. The intensity of his imagery is created partly by the use of tempera, which gives them a dry, brittle result evoking static electricity. *Christina's world* (1948, New York, MOMA), a portrait of a crippled neighbour, is probably his best-known work. He is one of the most popular contemporary American artists, but his status is controversial. See vol. 3 pp. **226–227**

Wynants, Jan active 1643–84
Dutch landscape painter. He specialized in dunescapes inspired by the sandy countryside around his native Haarlem. He continued to paint them even after he moved to Amsterdam in about 1660 (*Track by a dune with peasants and a horseman*, 1665, London, NG). His realistic approach to the unremarkable details of the landscape probably reflects the influence of Ruisdael, and there is a connection with Wouwermans, who was also from Haarlem and painted splendid dune scenes; it is not clear which artist originated the type.

Wynter, Bryan 1915–75
British painter. He worked in Cornwall, and early paintings such as *Foreshore with gulls* (1949, British Council) apply Cubist stylizations to the local scenery. Later paintings (*Seedtime*, 1958–59, London, Tate), are abstract and yet the dense accumulation of calligraphic signs suggests natural forces.

Wyspiański, Stanisław 1869–1907
Polish painter, illustrator and designer, the leader of the Cracow SEZESSION movement which was founded in 1897. A pupil of Matejko in Cracow, he lived for a time in Paris (1891–94), coming into contact with Gauguin. He grafted Gauguin's linear contours and fierce colour on to the spirit of traditional Polish folk art, as in his designs for stained-glass windows depicting, in harrowing splendour, the kings of Poland in the Wawel Castle in Cracow.

X

Xia Gui active *c.*1180–1230
Chinese painter, a contemporary of Ma Yuan. Xia was active in the Southern Song academy at Jangzhou, and later critics have placed him in the tradition of Li Tang and Fan Kuan. The album leaf entitled *Mountains and clouds* (Peking, Palace Museum), in ink and colour on silk, shows the characteristic willingness amongst artists of this tradition to leave much of the silk pure, the brushwork seeming to melt off into the mist. See vol. 1 p. *158*; vol. 3 p. 40

Xie He active late 5th century
Chinese portrait painter, active at the southern courts of the Southern Song and Qi dynasties at Nanking. He is principally famous as one of the first and certainly the most influential of theorists of Chinese painting. In his time aesthetic and religious speculation, often couched in a deliberately obscure language meant to exclude all but the initiate, was highly fashionable. His own treatise, the *Gu Hua Pin Lu* (Recorded Evaluations of Ancient Paintings), is a critique of 27 named painters, arranged into six classes of achievement, and a theoretical exposition of the six essential elements of good painting. With the exception of Gu Kaizhi, none of the artists discussed has any work surviving even in a copy. It is the six conditions of good painting, still discussed and annotated, on which his importance depends, though the allusiveness of the language makes an accurate translation all but impossible.

Xu Xi died before 975
Chinese painter of flowers and birds (genres which first rose to prominence during his lifetime). He worked at the politically feeble but artistically vital court of the Southern Tang emperor Li Yu in Nanking. His reputation in his field was unparalleled in the Song dynasty, when authentic examples of his work may still have survived. None of the attributed pieces is genuine.

Y

Yamaguchi, Takeo born 1902
Japanese painter, born in Korea. After World War II he painted various abstract and organic forms on monochrome backgrounds. Since 1965 these forms have become unified in such a way that they are indistinguishable from the background. Indeed, works such as *Taku* (1961, New York, MOMA) bear a resemblance to American colour-field painting, though they have their own individuality.

Yamato-e
Japanese painting style, literally "painting of Yamato", which was an ancient name for Japan and for the region which is now the province of Nara. The term *yamato-e* emerged in the Heian period (784–1185), when Chinese styles were prevalent, and the best-known examples are colourful illustrated scrolls on secular subjects (a 12th-century scroll with *The Tale of Genji* is in the Tokugawa Museum, Nagoya). The broad characteristics of the style are the use of bright colours and decorative linear effects.

While the Zen ink-painting styles were dominant, *yamato-e* was largely confined to the decorative arts, but it was revived to some extent by the Tosa school in the 15th century, and became increasingly important as a national expression. See vol. 3 pp. 48–49

Yañez (de la Almedina), Hernando documented 1504–26
Spanish painter, active in Valencia. He is first recorded there in 1506, when he was commissioned jointly with one **Fernando Llanos** to paint the Cosmas and Damian altarpiece (Valencia Cathedral). The two continued to collaborate and had probably both journeyed to Italy in the first years of the 16th century. One of them, generally thought to be the more Leonardesque Yañez, was the Fernando Spagnuolo recorded in 1504 as an assistant of Leonardo on *The Battle of Anghiari* in Florence. They are significant as being among the first Spaniards to have introduced a style dependent on the Italian High Renaissance into Spain. In Valencia, Italian influence remained predominantly Leonardesque well into the 16th century, though increasingly modified by contact with northern and Italian Mannerism.

Yan Hui active 14th century
Chinese painter of Buddhist and Taoist figures. He stands to a certain extent within the tradition of Liang Kai and Muqi, but his art is characterized by such intensity of experience that it takes precedence over strict canons of correct religious representation. None of the small body of work attributed to him is signed, but the pair of hanging scrolls, depicting the Taoist immortals *Hanshan* and *Shide* (Tokyo, National Museum) is usually considered authentic.

Yan Liben died 673
Chinese figure-painter, the most important of the 7th century. Yan painted both secular and Buddhist subjects at the imperial court of the Tang dynasty. Among the very few surviving authentic Tang paintings is his depiction of *Emperor Taizong* (reigned 627–649) *receiving a Tibetan ambassador* (Peking, Palace Museum). The scroll entitled *Portraits of the Emperors* (Boston, MFA) may also be an original, or at least an early copy. Yan used a brush-line of even thickness, and continued to employ the techniques of shading, originally introduced from central Asia, which went out of fashion by the end of the Tang period.

Yeats, Jack Butler 1871–1957
Irish painter, the brother of the poet W. B. Yeats. His early work consisted of illustrations of Irish life in pen and ink, and it was not until 1910 that he painted regularly in oils. He developed a highly personal style in which vivid colours are laid on with a palette knife so that form is almost dissolved in pigment (*Two travellers*, 1942, London, Tate).

Yen Hui see YAN HUI

Yen Li-pen see YAN LIBEN

Yi Chong 1578–1607
Korean painter. He is well-known for his bamboo scenes (in Seoul, Chun Hyong-pil coll., and the National Museum), in which his noble, scholarly character is reflected. He was a member of the Korean royal family, but few facts are known about his life. See vol. 3 p. 43

Yi In-mun 1745–1821
Korean landscape painter, a member of the state Bureau of Painting. His use of

Chinese styles was eclectic: accentuated short lines and axe-cut strokes are combined in harmonious compositions. His paintings are mostly in the National Museum, Seoul. See vol. 3 p. **43**

Yoshitoshi, Tsukioka 1839–92
Japanese UKIYO-E artist, considered the most important print-designer of the Meiji period. A pupil of Kuniyoshi, he was publishing prints of heroes and warriors in bloody combat in his teens. He easily assimilated traditional Japanese styles and the Western influences then flooding into Japan. Yoshitoshi was influential in helping the woodblock print survive the turmoils of the Restoration, when traditional crafts were being discarded as old-fashioned. He is best remembered for his extremely violent, often sadistic prints, reflecting a highly disturbed mental state: he suffered from bouts of insanity and finally killed himself. His series *The 100 Views of the Moon* (begun 1885) showed him at his best, and witnessed the technical perfection woodblock printing reached before photography became supreme.

Yoshiwara, Jiro 1905–72
Japanese painter, most famous as the founder of the GUTAI group in Osaka in 1954. He became a pioneer of abstract painting in Japan in the 1930s, and displayed a delicate sense of colour and awareness of form (*Volcanoes*, 1936, Tokyo, National Museum of Modern Art). His famous *Circle* series belongs to the Gutai period; these bold abstracts are created with a few strokes in the "minimal" tradition of the Zen ink-painters, often leaving areas of canvas bare.

Yuan Dynasty 1271–1368 AD
Important Chinese dynasty, established when the Mongols captured the southern Song capital. The whole of China fell for the first time under alien rule, with the Chinese élite who had ruled under the Song excluded from political power and the native population reduced to an inferior status. Those Chinese scholars forced into seclusion turned increasingly to contemplation, to Buddhism of the Chan (Zen) school and to an art which, despite its concentration on the traditional subject matter of rocks, bamboos and landscape, contained a note either of veiled social criticism or, perhaps more often, of introspective anguish. Some members of the élite, such as Zhao Mengfu, did accept office under the Mongols and produced works of art at their court in Peking, but for later generations the more typical Yuan artist would be Wang Meng or Ni Zan, both eccentrics and recluses. China's incorporation into the Mongol Empire encouraged Islamic and Tibetan influences on decorative arts, but painting remained largely free from foreign influence. See vol. 3 pp. 36–41

Yun Shouping 1633–90
Chinese painter. He refused to seek office under the Qing, attempting to support himself by painting, calligraphy and poetry. An exact contemporary of Wang Hui, he is supposed to have abandoned landscape painting—despairing of ever equalling his friend's achievement. He went on to become the greatest master of the "boneless" technique of flower-painting. Though he died young in poverty, his work later became very popular, and his flower studies were much admired by the Emperor Qianlong. The monochrome album leaf *Flowering pear tree* (Peking, Palace Museum) is a fine example of his restrained style and later imperial taste.

Yusho, Kaiho 1530–1615
Japanese painter of Samurai stock. Having decided to take up painting as a livelihood, he entered the Kano studios in Kyoto and studied under Motonobu and Eitoku. Later he was influenced by the works of the Song Chinese, Liang Kai, and thus became a master both of the colourful Momoyama style and the stark brushwork of Zen-inspired ink-painting. Yusho, untypically for his day, signed most of his screens and sliding door paintings. A splendid example is an opulent six-fold gold screen, *Fishing nets dried on the shore*, in the Imperial Palace collection in Tokyo.

Yvaral (Jean-Pierre Vasarély) born 1934
French painter, a proponent of OP and KINETIC art and a founder-member of GRAV. Like his father, Victor Vasarély, he has devoted himself to visual problems; he has experimented with moiré effects and with "ambiguous structures"—patterns of different shapes which produce effects of continuously varying depth on the plane surface.

Z

Zack, Leon born 1892
Russian painter, stage designer and illustrator, who has lived in Paris since 1923. In the 1950s his work became non-figurative, at first geometric in approach, and later tending towards a freer style. *Painting* (1959, London, Tate), with its strong colours and heavy impasto, demarcated by spider's-web-like lines, is typical of his later abstract work.

Zadkine, Ossip 1890–1967
Russian sculptor, chiefly active in France. He took up the study of art in England (where he had been sent, aged 15, to learn the language) and moved to Paris in 1910. There he formed a deep admiration for Rodin, but CUBISM made an immediate impact on his style. His Cubist experiments maintained an individual, expressive quality (*Mother and child*, 1918, New York, Joseph H. Hirshhorn coll.) and in the 1920s he developed a more curvilinear, opened-out form of figurative work, which evolved gradually into a monumental and dramatic manner. He was in New York during World War II, but returned to Paris, took up teaching, and produced several expressive monuments, notably his best-known work, *The destroyed city* (1953, Rotterdam, Blaak, Schiedamse Dijk). See vol. 1 p. *203*; vol. 3 p. **178**

Zahrtmann, Peder Hendrik Kristian 1843–1917
Danish painter. His best-known paintings are those on the tragic life of the Danish princess Eleonora Christina, Rembrandtesque works focusing on the psychological state of the subject (*Eleonora Christina in Maribo Convent*, 1882, Copenhagen, Statens Museum for Kunst). He also demonstrated a more fanciful imagination in highly-coloured historical genre scenes.

Zao Wou-ki born 1921
Chinese-born painter, living in France since 1948. The main European influences on his work have been Cézanne and Klee. His early figurative works (such as *The Piazza, Venice*, 1951, Paris, Musée National d'Art Moderne) have given way to an entirely abstract manner

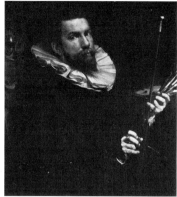

Wttewael: Self-portrait, 1601. Utrecht, Centraal Museum

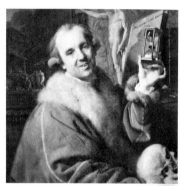

Zoffany: Self-portrait, *c.*1776. Florence, Uffizi (Scala)

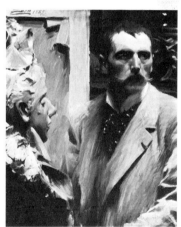

Zorn: Self-portrait, 1889. Florence, Uffizi (Alinari)

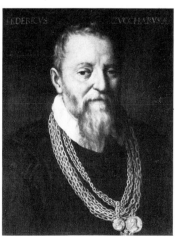

Zuccaro, Federico: Self-portrait. Florence, Uffizi (Mansell)

which is still marked by subtleties of colour and tone and graceful line-drawing, evoking his oriental origins.

Zeitblom, Bartholomaus
1455/60–1520/2

German painter. He had a prosperous and influential workshop in Ulm from about 1482, producing mainly religious works, but also portraits. One of his most important commissions was for the wings of a large altarpiece for the monastery at Blaubeuren, 1494, on which other painters, including Strigel, worked; Netherlandish influence is evident. His style is characterized by tall, elegant figures set in spacious interiors.

Zero, Group
West German group of KINETIC artists, founded in 1957 by Piene and Mack and joined in 1961 by Uecker. Their aims included the direct use of movement and light in art, and the intervention by artists into the environment on a large scale. While their attitude to technology was positive, they stressed the importance of working with, rather than against, nature. Unlike most of the other Kinetic groups of the period, they valued the intrusion of the irrational and the subjective and individual identity.

Zeuxis late 5th/early 4th century BC
Greek painter from Herakleia, active in Athens. None of his work survives, but he is described as one of the most eminent painters of his age. He is said to have taken up and developed the discoveries of his predecessor, Apollodoros, and to have introduced the use of highlights in his pictures, so that even the birds were deceived by the naturalism of his painted grapes. See vol. 2 p. 44

Zhang Xuan
active first half of 8th century

Chinese painter, a major artist at the luxurious and pleasure-loving court of the emperor Xuanzong (reigned 712–56). Zhang's name is associated with paintings of beauties and noble youths in opulent and elegant surroundings. No authentic pieces from his hand survive, but the style in which he worked is represented by extant works of his successor Zhou Fang, and the plain background, graceful figure-grouping and subtle use of colour of *Ladies with maids and fans* (Song dynasty copy, Peking, Palace Museum) are said to retain some of the essence of his refined, courtly art.

Zhao Mengfu 1254–1322
Chinese painter and calligrapher. Despite being a distant relative of the last Song emperor, Zhao took high office with the Mongol Yuan rulers. The major calligrapher of the century, he is also recorded as possessing a full command of all genres of Chinese painting. One of his finest surviving works is the landscape handscroll *Autumn colours on the Qiao and Hua mountains* (1295, Taiwan, National Palace Museum). He was also a master of figure-painting in a style derived from Li Gonglin, but he is best known for his paintings of horses, such as *Eight horses and two grooms crossing a river* (Washington, Freer).

Zhou Fang active c.780–810
Chinese painter, the most influential figure-painter of the late Tang dynasty. Zhou was active in Chang'an, the capital, where he executed Buddhist murals for temples, but is better known for portraits of court ladies. No original work is extant, but both the handscrolls *Ladies playing double-sixes* (Song dynasty copy, Washington, Freer) and *Tuning*

the lute and drinking tea (Song dynasty copy, Kansas City, Nelson Gallery) give a good idea of his elegant style. Figures are arrayed on an empty background in evenly balanced compositions, the physical type depicted being generally well-built in an accurate reflection of late Tang tastes in female beauty.

Zhu Da c.1626–c.1705
Chinese painter. A descendant of the Ming royal house, and a highly eccentric and nonconformist painter, Zhu Da was forced to take to the hills on the Manchu conquest of south China in 1645. To avoid the wearing of the queue, a sign of submission to the new dynasty, he was tonsured as a Buddhist monk in 1648, but around 1660 he became abbot of a Taoist monastery in Jiangzi province, where he lived till his death. As a painter, he had links with the monk-painters of the Song such as Liang Kai and Muqi, his brush technique being based on a heavy load of ink and spontaneous, decisive strokes. His landscapes appear more conventional than his paintings of plants, animals and birds; the latter subjects he seems to have transformed into expressions of political and personal frustration, as for instance in *Water fowl and lotus* (Peking, Palace Museum). Unappreciated in his own lifetime, he was nonetheless popular in Japan, since his work related to Zen Buddhist painting, and has enjoyed great fame since his rediscovery in the late 19th century, both as a predecessor of Chinese nationalism and as a cultural iconoclast pointing new directions in Chinese art.

Zhu Duan
active late 15th/early 16th century

Chinese court painter of the mid-Ming period, working in all the major areas of Chinese painting. It is recorded that he produced landscapes after the Song artists Ma Yuan and Guo Xi, as well as paintings of bamboo, flowers and birds, and figure subjects. Little survives, but there is a famous hanging scroll in ink and colours on paper depicting, in the lightest of brushwork, a *Scholar floating in a boat on an empty lake* (1518, Boston, MFA). With a free use of the bare paper, the effect is of distance and immobility.

Zick, Johann 1702–62 and
Januarius 1730–97
South German fresco-painters of the mid- and late Rococo, father and son. Primarily a painter of church frescos, Johann was discarded in favour of Tiepolo in the Würzburg Residenz but was compensated by a commission for frescos in the Residenz at Bruchsal (1751–54, destroyed but now repainted). His son was also primarily a church painter in Wiblingen, 1778–80; and Rot an der Rot, 1784. In his frescos he attempted to reconcile Baroque illusionism with the severer demands of Neoclassicism. Both also painted Rembrandtesque cabinet pictures.

Ziem, Félix 1821–1911
French painter. His high-keyed seascapes in watercolour and oils are in a style akin to that of late Turner, and he was especially skilled at sunsets and the effect of light on stonework. His favourite subjects were the Bosphorus, Constantinople and, above all, Venice, which he visited every year from 1845 to 1892. *The Grand Canal, Venice* (1849, Nice, Musée Cheret) was the first painting he showed at the Salon.

Zimmermann, Johann Baptist
1680–1758
Bavarian fresco-painter and sculptor in

stucco from Wessobrunn. With his brother, **Dominikus** (1685–1766), he was one of the key figures in the creation of south German ROCOCO, creating frescos and stucco for churches and abbeys in Bavaria and Swabia, but also for the Wittelsbach palaces (including the Amalienburg, 1734–39). With his brother he carried out monumental schemes at Steinhausen (1728–33) and Die Wies (1746–54)—two pilgrimage churches that embody respectively the inauguration and the apogee of south German Rococo.

Zoffany, Johann 1734/5–1810
German-born artist who settled in Britain in 1761. He made his name first as a painter of theatrical pictures, in which the famous actors of the time, above all Garrick, were portrayed in their favourite parts, with their characteristic expressions and gestures faithfully recorded. Zoffany also gave fresh impetus and vigour to the CONVERSATION PIECE, raising the genre to new heights of fashion, his style appealing to the royal family. Extensions of the conversation piece were such elaborate paintings as *The Academicians of the Royal Academy*, 1772, and *The Tribuna of the Uffizi*, painted during the artist's stay in Florence, 1772–76 (both Royal coll.). From 1783 to 1789 Zoffany was in India; he never regained the popularity he had won in the 1760s. See vol. 2 p. **251**

Zoppo, Marco Ruggieri 1432–78
Italian miniaturist and painter of religious subjects. From about 1453 he may have been Squarcione's assistant in Padua, where he was friendly with Mantegna. He worked in Bologna, Ferrara, Venice and the Marches in a mannered and harsh linear style reminiscent of Mantegna and closely related to Cosimo Tura. "*The Cook Madonna*" in Washington (NG) is a signed work.

Zorach, William 1887–1966
Lithuanian-born American sculptor. His early paintings explore Fauvism and Cubism and he became involved with sculpture in 1917, abandoning oils five years later. His initial woodcarvings are angular and related to early Cubism, but his free-standing pieces became increasingly monumental, as in the rounded marble forms of *Mother and child* (1927–30, New York, Metropolitan).

Zorn, Anders 1860–1920
Swedish painter, sculptor and engraver. He studied in Stockholm, but left Sweden for London in the early 1880s, where he became a successful portrait painter in watercolour. He also painted portraits in France and America, having switched to oil-painting around 1888. He was well-known for his society portraits, genre scenes—often with social contrasts—views in his native Dalecarlia and, especially, for paintings and etchings of nude women either indoors or in the Stockholm Archipelago (*In the Skerries*, 1894, Oslo, NG).

Zrzavý, Jan 1890–197?
Czech painter. Unlike many of the leading Czech painters of his generation, he considered Cubism mechanical and a denial of spiritual values in life, and developed a personal poetical style which has been described as a link between Symbolism and the dream world of Surrealism. He painted a wide range of themes—Breton coastal scenes, Czech landscapes, biblical episodes, views of S. Marco, Venice, and figures in mysterious dreamlike settings (*The friends*, 1923, Prague, NG).

Zuccarelli, Francesco 1702–88
Italian landscape and mythology painter. Born in Florence, he studied in Rome and later settled in Venice. Thanks largely to the efforts of Joseph Smith (also Canaletto's patron), his works found a good English market, and in 1752 he went to live in England for 15 very successful years. His views are delicate and artificial and his mythological scenes have charming Rococo detail (*The rape of Europa*, c.1778, Venice, Accademia).

Zuccaro, Taddeo (1529–66) and
Federico (1540/1–1609)
Italian painters, brothers, born near Urbino. Taddeo went to Rome at the age of 14 and developed a smooth and harmonious style, chiefly dependent upon Raphael and Michelangelo. His later, more classical style (*The conversion of St Paul*, c.1558, Rome, S. Marcello al Corso) was popular, and he undertook many decorative commissions in Roman palaces and churches. On his death these were continued by his younger brother and pupil, Federico. Federico, whose style never developed beyond a rather dry Mannerism, travelled to the Netherlands and to England in 1574 and on his return to Italy worked in Rome, Florence and Venice. He was internationally famous during his lifetime and first director of the Academy of St Luke in Rome and an influential art theorist.

Zucchi, Jacopo 1541–90
Florentine late MANNERIST painter. He was a pupil of Vasari, whom he assisted in the painting of the Palazzo Vecchio, Florence. He settled in Rome in 1572, and independently painted frescos of great liveliness in the Palazzo Rucellai and Palazzo di Firenze. The graceful *Cupid and Psyche* (1589, Rome, Galleria Borghese) is typical.

Zuloaga y Zabaleta, Ignacio
1870–1945
Spanish genre, landscape and portrait painter. He drew most of his subject matter from Spanish life and customs. He was trained in Paris, where he knew Degas, Gauguin and Rodin, but his style owes its inspiration to the great masters of Spanish painting—El Greco, Velazquez and Goya.

Zurbarán, Francisco 1598–1664
Spanish painter, active mainly in Seville. Apart from some still lifes and a series of ten paintings on *The Labours of Hercules* (begun 1634, Madrid, Prado) commissioned by Philip IV, he painted almost exclusively religious works. His style combined severe and sombre realism with spiritual intensity and made him an ideal painter for the austere religious orders of Spain and of South America, where many works from his studio were exported. Most characteristically his works depict single figures of saints or monks in prayer or deep meditation. Their draperies are arranged into massively simple folds and they are set against stark backgrounds, standing out with a sense of great physical presence. Often these figures were produced as series (*Carthusian Saints*, Cadiz Museum), but he also produced single pictures, notably of *St Francis* (two fine examples in London, NG). During the 1640s Murillo began to overtake Zurbarán as the most popular painter in Seville. Zurbarán tried to modify his style in the direction of Murillo's, and in doing so lost something of the monumental power of his work. Murillo eventually eclipsed him completely, and in 1658 Zurbarán moved to Madrid, where he died. See vol. 1 p. *146*; vol. 2 p. **209**